Vol. 116 • No. 3 • June 2026

BSSA

Bulletin of the Seismological Society of America

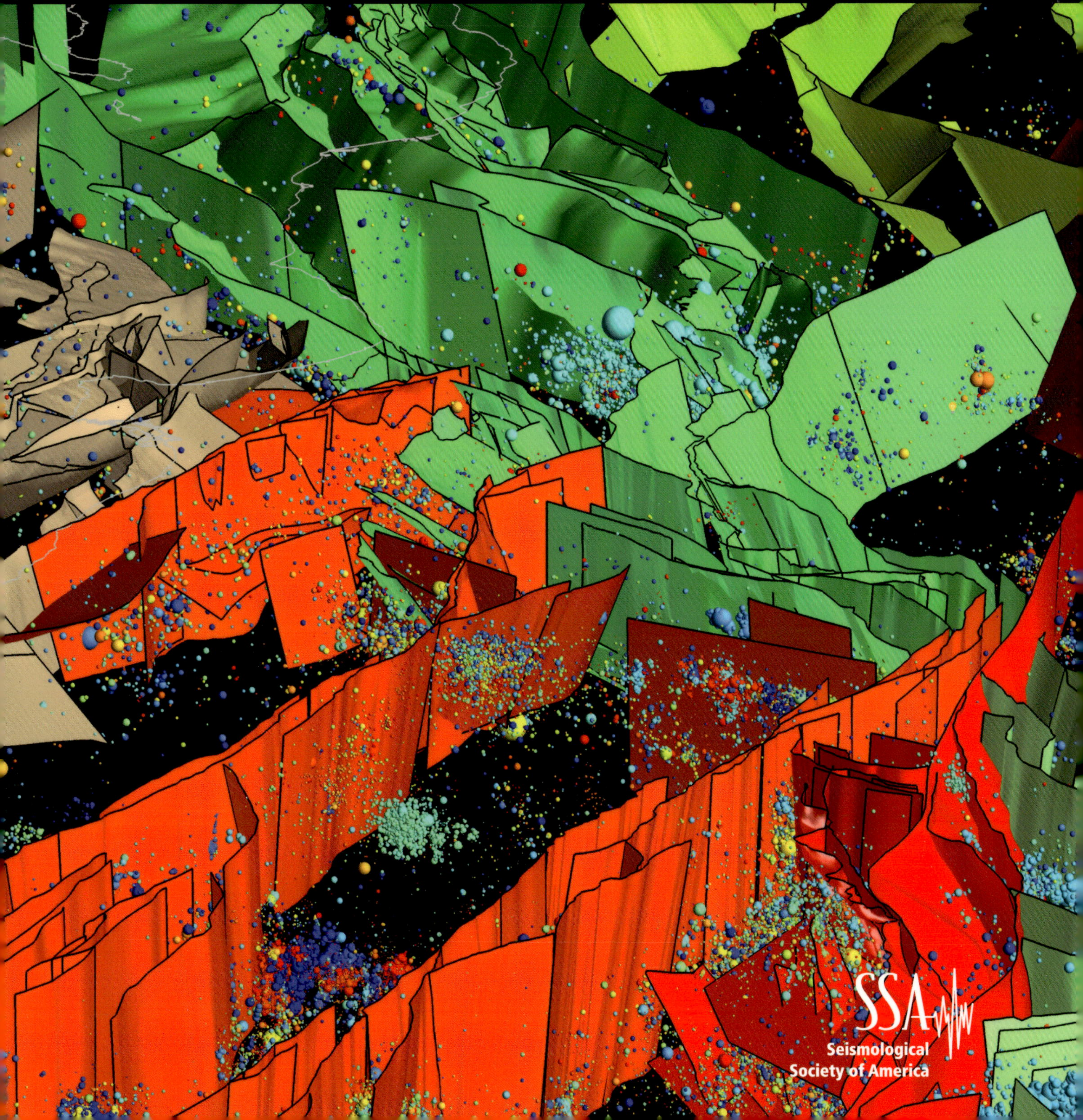

Seismological Society of America

Seismological Society of America

The Seismological Society of America is an international scientific society devoted to the advancement of seismology and the understanding of earthquakes for the benefit of society.

www.seismosoc.org
www.bssaonline.org

BSSA

Bulletin of the Seismological Society of America

Vol. 116 • No. 3 • June 2026

REVIEW ARTICLE

A Fiftieth Year Retrospective on the 1976 M_W 7.5 Motagua Earthquake in Guatemala **839**
Grant Clark, Trenton McEnaney, Jeremy Maurer, Andreas Eckert, Stephen S. Gao, Omar G. Flores, Robin Yani, Tina Niemi, Christoph Grützner, Francisco Gomez, and Jonathan Obrist-Farner

ARTICLES

Calibration of Pressure Sensors for Ocean-Bottom Seismology **860**
Spahr C. Webb, Hatsuki Yamauchi, Theodore A. Koczynski, Walter Masterson, and Peter Liljegren

An Efficient Subspace Detector for Rayleigh Waves, Demonstrated Against Explosions **884**
Joshua D. Carmichael, Jonas A. Kintner, and Richard A. Alfaro-Diaz

Surface-Wave Dispersion Curve Computation and Inversion: A Framework Integrating Quadratic Extrema Interpolation and Randomized Layering with Multiple Initial Models **902**
Lei Pan, Jiannan Wang, and Xiaofei Chen

Toward Operational Earthquake Seismogram Denoising **923**
Nikolaj Dahmen, John Clinton, Men-Andrin Meier, and Luca Scarabello

Quantifying the Impact of Declustering Techniques on Completeness Magnitude Estimation **946**
Massimiliano Guastella, Anna Figlioli, Raffaele Martorana, and Antonino D'Alessandro

ON THE COVER

This perspective 3D view shows a 140 km wide section of mid and upper crustal fault structure in southern California as represented by the Statewide California Earthquake Center's Community Fault Model, published in this BSSA issue ("The Community Fault Model (v. 6.1) for Southern California", Plesch *et al.*). The view is towards the west along the San Andreas Fault Zone (in red, at the right, i.e., northern image margin). Superimposed earthquake hypocenters cover about 40 years of seismic activity along this section of the Pacific-North America plate boundary and are scaled by magnitude (for complete color legends and attributions, see Fig. 1 in Plesch *et al.*). The presented fault model is the latest product of a sustained community research effort to capture detailed 3D sources of seismic hazard in the state.

Image credit: *original composition by the authors of Plesch et al.; see article for content acknowledgements.*

Long-Term *b* Value and Seismic Rate from Earthquake Catalogs with Time-Varying Completeness and Uncertain Magnitudes **963**
Cyrielle Colin, Stéphanie Durand, Thomas Bodin, Marine Laporte, Guillaume Daniel, Pierre Arroucau, and David Marsan

Local Magnitude (M_L) Calibration in the Short-Distance Range—The Case of the Collalto Seismic Network and Surrounding Stations in Northeastern Italy **984**
Enrico Priolo, Maria Adelaide Romano, and Laura Peruzza

Crustal Stress Information Revealed by the Distribution of P and T Axes of Earthquake Focal Mechanisms **1007**
Zhenyue Li and Yongge Wan

Rupture into Slow-Slip Fault Regime During the 2018 M_W 6.9 Island of Hawai'i Earthquake is Followed by Modest Postseismic Slip **1023**
Ingrid A. Johanson, Emily K. Montgomery-Brown, and Michael P. Poland

Constraining the Earthquake Focal Depth Distribution in the Southern Korean Peninsula **1036**
Dong-Hoon Sheen, Ah-Hyun Byun, and Hyeonjun Lee

Ground Motions from Finite Faults with Unknown Geometry **1049**
Charles Bruce Worden, Eric Meyer Thompson, Harriet Zoe Yin, and David Jay Wald

Constraining Rupture-Generator Scaling Using Measured Surface Offsets, Near-Fault Ground Motions, and Rupture Dynamic Simulations **1064**
Camilo I. Pinilla-Ramos and Norman A. Abrahamson

Empirical Modeling of Source Directivity Effects into a Ground-Motion Model for Central Italy **1081**
Leonardo Colavitti, Giovanni Lanzano, Sara Sgobba, and Francesca Pacor

MAILING & SUBSCRIPTION INFORMATION

Subscriptions to the *Bulletin of the Seismological Society of America (BSSA)*: Information regarding institutional subscriptions can be found at www.seismosoc.org/subscriptions. Eligible members of the Seismological Society of America receive online access to *BSSA*. Individuals may apply for membership or determine eligibility by visiting www.seismosoc.org.

Bulletin of the Seismological Society of America (BSSA) is the premier journal of advanced research in earthquake seismology and related disciplines. It first appeared in 1911. Each issue is composed of scientific papers on the various aspects of seismology, including investigation of specific earthquakes, theoretical and observational studies of seismic waves, inverse methods for determining the structure of the Earth or the dynamics of the earthquake source, seismometry, earthquake hazard and risk estimation, seismotectonics, and earthquake engineering. Special issues focus on important earthquakes or rapidly changing topics in seismology.

BSSA (ISSN 0037-1106) is published bimonthly in February, April, June, August, October, and December by the Seismological Society of America, 400 Evelyn Avenue, Suite 201, Albany, CA 94706- 1375. Periodicals postage paid at Berkeley, California and at additional mailing offices.

The Community Fault Model (v. 6.1) for Southern California **1103**
Andreas Plesch, Scott T. Marshall, and John H. Shaw

Stress States on the Eve of Past Earthquakes Inform Earthquake Rupture Through Fault Complexity Along the San Andreas and San Jacinto Faults **1125**
Emery O. Anderson-Merritt, Michele L. Cooke, and Katherine Scharer

Examining the Causes of Regional Differences in California Based on Ground Motions from Small to Moderate Earthquakes **1145**
Camilo I. Pinilla-Ramos, Norman A. Abrahamson, Savvas Marcou, Douglas S. Dreger, Alexandros Savvaidis, Gail M. Atkinson, Behzad Hassani, Chih-Hsuan Sung, and Robert Youngs

A Set of Data-Driven Models to Predict V_{S30} from the Horizontal-to-Vertical Spectral Ratio of Microtremors **1161**
Kushal Sharma Wagle, Joseph P. Vantassel, Adrian Rodriguez-Marek, and Balakumar Anbazhagan

V_{S30} Estimation from Shallow V_S Profiles **1178**
Kenneth S. Hudson

Geospatial Site Amplification Model for California **1199**
Maggie Roberts, Laurie G. Baise, Shiying Nie, James Kaklamanos, and Weiwei Zhan

HVSR- and V_{S30}-Based Adjustment Terms for Geospatial Site Amplification Models for California **1219**
Maggie Roberts, Laurie G. Baise, James Kaklamanos, Weiwei Zhan, Shiying Nie, and Elise Meyer

Geospatial Site Terms for Central and Eastern U.S. Ground-Motion Models Using Physiographic Province and Sediment Thickness **1240**
Elise (Ellie) Meyer, Laurie G. Baise, James Kaklamanos, Shiying Nie, Weiwei Zhan, and Maggie Roberts

A Nonergodic Ground-Motion Model for the San Francisco Bay Area for Small-Magnitude Earthquakes **1264**
Maxime Lacour, Norman Abrahamson, Rie Nakata, Nori Nakata, and Camilo I. Pinilla-Ramos

Characterizing Precariously Balanced Rocks (PBRs) in the Eastern United States for Estimating Maximum Past Earthquake Ground Motions **1280**
Thomas L. Pratt, Mark W. Stirling, Devin McPhillips, and Paula M. Figueiredo

Use of Precariously Balanced Rocks to Constrain Postglacial Earthquake Magnitudes in New England, United States **1311**
Mark W. Stirling and Thomas L. Pratt

The U.S. Geological Survey 2025 Puerto Rico and U.S. Virgin Islands Time-Independent Earthquake Rupture Forecast **1321**
Kevin R. Milner, Alexandra E. Hatem, Richard W. Briggs, Jessica A. Thompson-Jobe, Andrea L. Llenos, Andrew J. Michael, Allison M. Shumway, Edward H. Field, and Kirstie L. Haynie

COMMENTS AND REPLIES

Comment on "The Reduced Detection Rate of Signals That Are Hidden by Earthquakes: Case Studies with Spotlight Detectors That Operate at Seismic Arrays" by Joshua D. Carmichael, Brent G. Delbridge, and Richard Alfaro-Diaz **1352**
Paul G. Richards

Reply to "Comment on 'The Reduced Detection Rate of Signals That Are Hidden by Earthquakes: Case Studies with Spotlight Detectors That Operate at Seismic Arrays,' by Joshua D. Carmichael, Brent G. Delbridge, and Richard Alfaro-Diaz" by Paul G. Richards **1354**
Joshua D. Carmichael, Brent G. Delbridge, and Richard Alfaro-Diaz

ERRATUM

Erratum to An Efficient Subspace Detector for Rayleigh Waves, Demonstrated Against Explosions **1357**
Joshua D. Carmichael, Jonas A. Kintner, and Richard A. Alfaro-Diaz

A Fiftieth Year Retrospective on the 1976 M_w 7.5 Motagua Earthquake in Guatemala

Grant Clark[1], Trenton McEnaney[1], Jeremy Maurer[1], Andreas Eckert[1], Stephen S. Gao[1], Omar G. Flores[2], Robin Yani[3], Tina Niemi[4], Christoph Grützner[5], Francisco Gomez[6], and Jonathan Obrist-Farner*[1]

ABSTRACT

OPEN ACCESS

On 4 February 1976, an $M_w > 7.5$ earthquake ruptured ~240 km of the Motagua fault in Guatemala, causing ~23,000 fatalities. This event provided evidence for the fault's role as a major transform boundary between the North American and Caribbean plates. Field observations, seismological analyses, and postseismic studies helped constrain fundamental aspects of the 1976 earthquake mechanics and the spatial complexity of the rupture. This event opened a window for studies documenting past deformation along this plate boundary across multiple spatial and temporal scales. Five decades of research have established this earthquake as an important event for understanding strike-slip ruptures along major plate boundaries. This review integrates legacy field observations, subsequent analyses, and recent investigations along the North American and Caribbean plate boundary in Guatemala. Our goal is not only to synthesize the details and highlight the importance of the event but also to preserve essential datasets that continue to inform our understanding of plate boundary mechanics, seismic hazard, and the long-term behavior of this major transform fault system.

KEY POINTS

- We review and summarize 50 yr of research on the 1976 $M_w > 7.5$ Motagua earthquake.
- Legacy datasets provide unprecedented documentation of the rupture and effects of the earthquake.
- Poor monitoring and uncertain earthquake recurrence leave Guatemala vulnerable to future large earthquakes.

INTRODUCTION

On 4 February 1976, a devastating $M_w > 7.5$ strike-slip earthquake occurred along the left-lateral Motagua fault in Guatemala. The Motagua fault is part of the Polochic–Motagua fault system and is the primary fault along the North American and Caribbean plate boundary in Guatemala (Lyon-Caen *et al.*, 2006; Fig. 1). The earthquake had both significant societal and scientific impacts.

From a societal point of view, the 1976 Motagua fault earthquake generated a ~240 km surface rupture (Fig. 1b) and resulted in ~23,000 fatalities, >76,000 injuries, and >1.2 million displaced persons. Before the earthquake, no building codes had been implemented for earthquakes (Husid *et al.*, 1976). Most of the adobe structures in the vicinity of the rupture and along its western terminus were completely destroyed (Fig. 2). Several reinforced-concrete structures in Guatemala City also collapsed, resulting in the majority of human casualties. Guatemalan society in general was also affected by the collapse of bridges, roads, and railroad tracks and by extensive landslides and soil liquefaction (Espinosa, 1976). Economic losses reached $1.1 billion (~$6.2 billion adjusted for inflation

1. Department of Earth Sciences and Engineering, Missouri University of Science and Technology, Rolla, Missouri, U.S.A., https://orcid.org/0009-0006-4391-0938 (GC); https://orcid.org/0009-0005-4419-8244 (TM); https://orcid.org/0000-0002-3624-5961 (JM); https://orcid.org/0000-0001-7530-7128 (SSG); https://orcid.org/0000-0002-8734-3895 (JO-F); 2. Centro de Estudios Superiores de Energía y Minas (CESEM), Facultad de Ingeniería, Universidad de San Carlos de Guatemala, Guatemala City, Guatemala, https://orcid.org/0009-0009-2977-1638 (OGF); 3. Instituto Nacional de Sismología, Vulcanología, Meteorología e Hidrología, Guatemala City, Guatemala, https://orcid.org/0000-0002-5321-5377 (RY); 4. Department of Geosciences, University of Missouri-Kansas City, Kansas City, Missouri, U.S.A., https://orcid.org/0000-0002-6837-2594 (TN); 5. Institute for Geological Sciences, Friedrich-Schiller-University Jena, Jena, Germany, https://orcid.org/0000-0003-0777-2751 (CG); 6. Department of Geological Sciences, University of Missouri, Columbia, Missouri, U.S.A., https://orcid.org/0009-0007-0609-7180 (FG)

*Corresponding author: obristj@mst.edu

Cite this article as Clark, G., T. McEnaney, J. Maurer, A. Eckert, S. S. Gao, O. G. Flores, R. Yani, T. Niemi, C. Grützner, F. Gomez, *et al.* (2026). A Fiftieth Year Retrospective on the 1976 M_w 7.5 Motagua Earthquake in Guatemala, *Bull. Seismol. Soc. Am.* **116**, 839–859, doi: 10.1785/0120250268

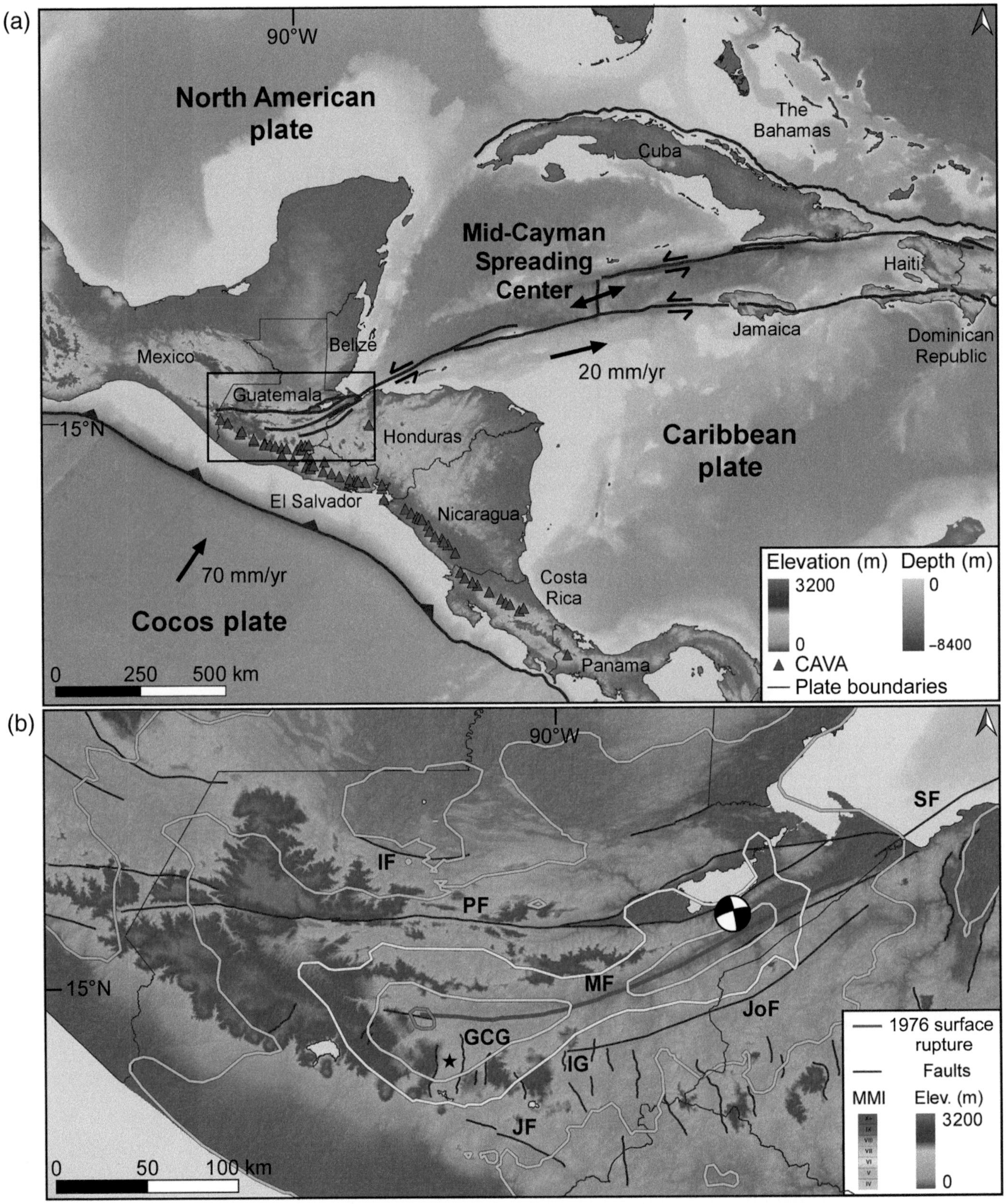

Figure 1. (a) Regional tectonic framework of the North American–Caribbean plate boundary. Red triangles show the location of volcanoes that make up the Central American volcanic arc (CAVA). Black box shows the outline of panel (b). (b) Modified Mercalli intensity (MMI) contours of the 1976 Motagua earthquake (from the U.S. Geological Survey [USGS] catalog; U.S. Geological Survey, 2025) and the rupture trace (red). The focal mechanism solution (FMS) shows the epicenter of the earthquake. Regional faults are shown in black and include the Ixcán fault (IF), Polochic fault (PF), Motagua fault (MF), Jalpatagua fault (JF), Guatemala City graben (GCG), Ipala graben (IG), Jocotán–Chamelecón fault (JOF), and Swan fault (SF; modified from the Global Earthquake Model (GEM) active fault database; Styron and Pagani, 2020). FMSs for the 1976 rupture from Kikuchi and Kanamori (1991). The location of Guatemala City is denoted as a black star. The color version of this figure is available only in the electronic edition.

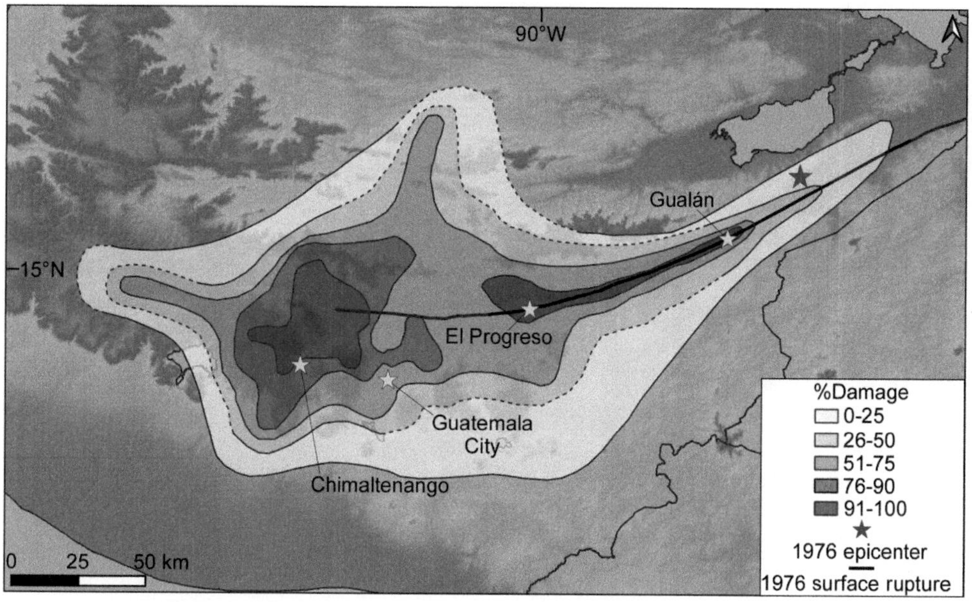

Figure 2. Contour map showing extent of adobe-type structures that collapsed during the 1976 event. Map modified from Espinosa *et al.* (1976). The color version of this figure is available only in the electronic edition.

in 2025), equivalent to ~30% of Guatemala's gross domestic product at the time (Espinosa, 1976).

From a scientific point of view, the 1976 Motagua fault earthquake established several major tectonic facts in Central America. Before 1976, the Motagua fault's activity and regional importance remained poorly documented and understood (Molnar and Sykes, 1969; Muehlberger and Ritchie, 1975; compare with Schwartz, 1976). The earthquake, documented as a classic left-lateral strike-slip faulting event, served as proof that the Motagua fault is a major segment of the transform boundary between the North American and Caribbean plates in Guatemala. Following the event, the U.S. Geological Survey (USGS), in conjunction with the National Observatory (now the Guatemalan Institute for Seismology, Volcanology, Meteorology, and Hydrology), provided extensive documentation of the rupture and damage across the country (Espinosa, 1976; Matumoto and Latham 1976; Plafker *et al.*, 1976; Bucknam *et al.*, 1978; Seed *et al.*, 1981; Harp *et al.*, 1981). This allowed for a comprehensive analysis of one of the longest and largest documented strike-slip ruptures since the 1906 San Andreas earthquake (Plafker, 1976). Furthermore, the event offered a rare well-instrumented (for the time of the earthquake) example of a large intracontinental strike-slip earthquake and allowed seismologists to compare fault mechanics and rupture propagation, contributing to global models of strike-slip fault behavior. Field work validated surface ruptures with an average surface slip of 1.1 m (maximum of 3.4 m) and extensive afterslip and postseismic deformation processes (Bucknam *et al.*, 1978; Lisowski and Thatcher, 1981). Although the earthquake size and the surface rupture length were typical of large strike-slip earthquakes (Wells and Coppersmith, 1994; Thingbaijam *et al.*, 2017), the westward concentration of seismic energy release resulted in noteworthy damage distribution caused by rupture directionality (Fig. 2; Espinosa *et al.*, 1976). Subsequent seismic analysis indicated a complex, multisubevent rupture (Kanamori and Stewart, 1978; Kikuchi and Kanamori, 1982, 1991; Young *et al.*, 1989) and confirmed theoretical stress transfer predictions (Dewey and Julian, 1976; Langer and Bollinger, 1979).

In 2026, 50 yr after the earthquake, the Motagua fault, as part of the Polochic–Motagua fault system, has received limited research attention and compared with other major transform plate boundaries remains poorly monitored and understood. This review synthesizes five decades of research, summarizing the findings and implications of interseismic (including historic earthquake occurrence and the notable absence of a paleoseismic record), coseismic (including surface rupture characteristics, seismological source characteristics, evidence of rupture directivity, and environmental effects and ground-motion indicators), and postseismic (including aftershock, afterslip, and geodetic analyses) observations from the 1976 earthquake. This summary provides a basis for documenting how research on the 1976 Motagua earthquake advanced scientific understanding of the North American and Caribbean plate boundary and continental transform fault behavior in general. In addition, for the first time, we make legacy material available to the scientific community, including the digitization and preservation of analog field material using modern georeferencing techniques (McEnaney and Clark, 2025). It is our hope that these resources will spur continued research into this important event and the plate boundary as a whole.

THE POLOCHIC AND MOTAGUA FAULT SYSTEM

The Polochic–Motagua fault system forms the continental segment of the North American–Caribbean plate boundary in Guatemala, where ~18–20 mm/yr of left-lateral motion is accommodated between the two plates (DeMets *et al.*, 2000). The plate boundary extends from the Mid-Cayman Spreading Center through northern Guatemala to the Cocos–North America–Caribbean diffuse triple junction at the Guatemala City Graben (Fig. 1b; Authemayou *et al.*, 2011; Garnier *et al.*, 2022; Maurer *et al.*, 2025). The boundary transitions from a single-fault strand oceanic transform fault offshore to a more

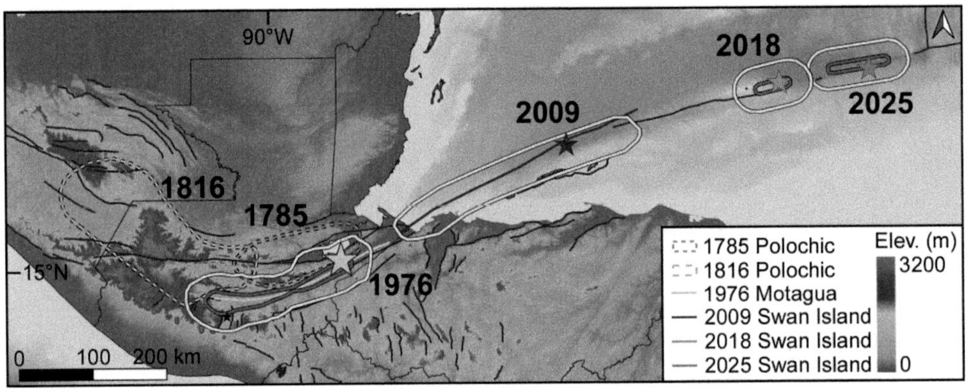

Figure 3. Major earthquakes (magnitude >7) since 1785 on the western segment of the North American–Caribbean plate boundary. Epicenters are shown with colored stars, and ruptured segments are shown in colored lines. Peak ground acceleration (PGA) contours showing 20%*g* (yellow) and 50%*g* (red; from USGS earthquake catalog; U.S. Geological Survey, 2025). The 1785 and 1816 Polochic earthquakes damage areas shown in orange and teal areas, respectively (White, 1984). Faults modified from the GEM active fault database (Styron and Pagani, 2020). The location of Guatemala City is denoted as a black star. The color version of this figure is available only in the electronic edition.

complex system of parallel and secondary strike-slip faults onshore, where deformation is partitioned across multiple structures rather than concentrated along a single trace (Guzmán-Speziale and Molina, 2022).

The oceanic segment of the plate boundary comprises the Mid-Cayman Spreading Center and the Swan fault, also referred to as Swan Islands fault. The Mid-Cayman Spreading Center is a spreading center accommodating 15–17 mm/yr of divergence (Hayman *et al.*, 2011), and the Swan fault extends ~750 km westward from the southern end of the spreading center to Guatemala (Graham *et al.*, 2012). Recent ruptures on the Swan fault include the 2009 M_w 7.3 event (Graham *et al.*, 2012), the 2018 M_w 7.5 event (Cheng and Wang, 2020), and the 2025 M_w 7.6 event (Fig. 3; Kusky *et al.*, 2025). These events are notable because the 2009 and 2018 events were both supershear events and propagated mostly unilaterally from east to west (Bao *et al.*, 2022).

The Swan fault continues onshore as the Polochic–Motagua fault system in Guatemala. The Polochic–Motagua fault system consists of two principal left-lateral strike-slip faults that extend subparallel across Guatemala for ~350 km (Fig. 1b; Plafker *et al.*, 1976; Guzmán-Speziale and Molina, 2022). The Motagua fault traces along the Motagua River valley from the Caribbean coast westward to ~50 km north of Guatemala City (Schwartz *et al.*, 1979), accommodating the majority of plate boundary motion in eastern and central Guatemala (Lyon-Caen *et al.*, 2006; Franco *et al.*, 2012; Ellis *et al.*, 2019; Maurer *et al.*, 2025). The Polochic fault branches off the Motagua fault near the Caribbean coast of Guatemala and is separated from the Motagua fault by the Sierra de las Minas (Fig. 1b). The Polochic fault extends west into Chiapas, Mexico (White, 1984; Authemayou *et al.*, 2012). Both faults exhibit near vertical dips in the upper 15 km of the crust and do not appear to merge at depth (Franco *et al.*, 2009). The seismogenic zone extends to depths of 10–15 km, consistent with Global Positioning System (GPS)-derived locking depths of ~20 km for the Motagua fault and ~5 km for the Polochic fault (Franco *et al.*, 2009; Ellis *et al.*, 2019). Additional structures within the plate boundary zone include the Jocotán-Chamelecón fault system to the south and the Ixcán fault to the north (Fig. 1b), although the contemporary activity and slip rates on these structures remain poorly constrained (Schwartz *et al.*, 1979; Guzmán-Speziale and Molina, 2022). South of the Polochic–Motagua fault system, a series of north–south-trending structures accommodate distributed extension across the western end of the Caribbean plate. These include the Guatemala City graben, the Ipala graben, and the Chiquimula graben in Guatemala, as well as normal fault systems that extend into Honduras (Franco *et al.*, 2009; Rodriguez *et al.*, 2009; Ellis *et al.*, 2019).

Contemporary GPS measurements document the partitioning of plate boundary motion across the fault system (e.g., Franco *et al.*, 2012; Ellis *et al.*, 2019; Maurer *et al.*, 2025). The Motagua fault accommodates ~14.2 ± 1.6 mm/yr of left-lateral motion in eastern Guatemala at its junction with the Swan fault, representing ~80% of the total plate boundary motion (Lyon-Caen *et al.*, 2006; Franco *et al.*, 2012; Ellis *et al.*, 2019). Slip rates on the Motagua fault decrease systematically westward to the Guatemala City graben, with rates falling below 2 mm/yr west of the graben (Ellis *et al.*, 2019). This westward decrease reflects the transfer of motion southward into the extensional zone between the Motagua fault and the Central American volcanic arc (CAVA; Fig. 1a; Rodriguez *et al.*, 2009; Ellis *et al.*, 2019). The Polochic fault accommodates the remaining ~20% of the total plate boundary motion (Franco *et al.*, 2012; Ellis *et al.*, 2019). The partitioning of motion between these two faults represents a significant change from conditions during the Miocene, when the Polochic fault was the dominant structure (Bartole *et al.*, 2019; Obrist-Farner *et al.*, 2020). This transition from Polochic fault dominance to the current Motagua fault-dominated configuration occurred over approximately the past seven million years (Obrist-Farner *et al.*, 2020).

THE 1976 MOTAGUA EARTHQUAKE

Legacy data from the 1976 event

Although the 1976 earthquake was well documented, material related to the earthquake was archived in analog formats,

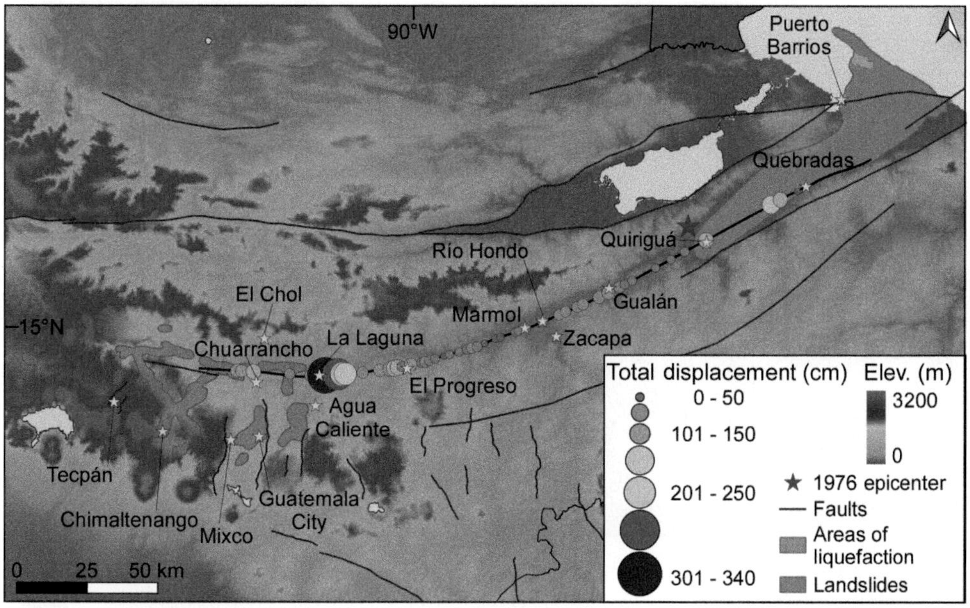

Figure 4. Total displacement measurements taken in April 1976 (Bucknam *et al.*, 1978) along the surface rupture trace. Also shown are landslides (pink regions) and areas of extensive liquefaction (orange region) caused by the 1976 earthquake (Plafker *et al.*, 1976). Faults modified from the GEM active fault database (Styron and Pagani, 2020). White stars show locations of cities and towns discussed in the text. The color version of this figure is available only in the electronic edition.

limiting accessibility to the scientific community. We present digitized rupture measurements from systematic field mapping (Fig. 4), original topographic maps with field annotations during USGS surveys, and a georeferenced collection of 1:10,000 scale aerial photographs spanning the western and central segments of the surface rupture (McEnaney and Clark, 2025). This archive also includes an extensive collection of 35 mm color photographs taken by the USGS team during the expedition (Fig. 5), many of which have not been previously published. We include digitized field notebooks containing detailed observations, measurements, and sketches along with previously published aftershock datasets (Person *et al.*, 1976; Langer and Bollinger, 1979; White and Harlow, 1979) converted to standardized digital formats (McEnaney and Clark, 2025).

Coseismic observations

Surface rupture and field observations. The 1976 Motagua earthquake produced ~240 km of surface rupture along the fault, extending from the lower Motagua Valley in eastern Guatemala to ~50 km north of Guatemala City in the west (Fig. 1b; Plafker *et al.*, 1976). This rupture extended the previously recognized western limit of the fault by 85 km. To the east of the epicenter, the surface trace could not be confirmed because of thick vegetation cover, introducing uncertainty in the precise eastern extent of surface breakage.

Surface displacement along the trace was dominantly left lateral with an average offset of 1.1 m over the entire rupture length (Fig. 4; Plafker *et al.*, 1976). Maximum-horizontal displacement reached 3.40 m ~40 km from the western termination of the earthquake rupture (Fig. 4). Field measurements documented systematic spatial variations in displacement magnitude along the rupture, with regions of above-average slip corresponding to areas of concentrated moment release identified in seismological analyses (Young *et al.*, 1989). Vertical offsets were generally minor relative to horizontal displacement, varying spatially along the rupture (Plafker *et al.*, 1976). Most locations showed vertical components <30% of horizontal offset, with down-to-the-north or down-to-the-south motion depending on local fault geometry. A notable exception occurred along a 10 km segment near the easternmost mapped extent of the surface trace, where vertical displacement was consistently down to the north and locally reached 50% of the sinistral component.

The surface expression of the fault zone exhibited considerable complexity (Fig. 5), with individual fractures reaching lengths of ≤10 m with variable amounts of dilation ≤10 cm. En echelon fractures were oriented at angles ≤35° to the main fault trace, reflecting the distributed nature of deformation within the shallow fault zone. The fault zone width varied from 1 to 9 m, with maximum-observed widths of ~9 m at localities where the fault surface was exposed in highway cuts. Field documentation of these features, including distinctive mole tracks and large lateral offsets, provided detailed characterization of surface rupture morphology (Fig. 5).

Secondary faulting occurred concurrent with the main rupture, with connected faults relatively scarce along most of the rupture length. Notable occurrences included areas near El Progreso, where a subsidiary fault ~1 km long with 20 cm sinistral displacement was oriented roughly parallel to the main fault trace, and near Chuarrancho, where a prominent surface break splayed off the main trace in a northeasterly direction with a sinistral offset of 28 cm (Fig. 4; Plafker *et al.*, 1976). Additional secondary fault systems concentrated primarily south and southwest of the western Motagua fault terminus extended as far as 30 km from the main fault trace but did not connect to the primary rupture at the surface. Individual secondary faults ranged in length from ~100 m to 3.5 km, with strikes commonly between N10°E and N30°E (Plafker *et al.*,

Figure 5. Field photographs showing different characteristics of the surface rupture. (a) Fault trace at La Laguna looking west. (b) Maximum-observed displacement at La Laguna (340 cm) offsetting a stone fence. (c) En echelon cracks along the fault trace near El Chol. (d) A toppled Ceiba tree near Quebradas, with the surface rupture passing directly below it. Person for scale highlighted with red arrow. (e) Offset road and drainage ditch in Hwy CA-10 near Rio Hondo. All locations discussed in the photos are shown in Figure 3. Photos taken by the USGS in 1976. The color version of this figure is available only in the electronic edition.

1976). These secondary structures included reactivated faults and pre-existing features within the Guatemala City graben system, causing substantial damage to houses, roads, and infrastructure in Guatemala City.

Seismological source characterization. Recordings from the World-Wide Standard Seismograph Network provided long-period surface and body waves for source characterization. *P*-wave first-motion data and Love-wave analysis established left-lateral strike-slip faulting along a near-vertical plane with strike varying from N66°E to N98°E, consistent with the Motagua fault geometry at the epicenter (Fig. 1b; Dewey and Julian, 1976; Kanamori and Stewart, 1978).

Source inversion models documented significant spatial and temporal complexity in the rupture process with significant model uncertainties. The earthquake models suggest an asymmetric, segmented, bilateral rupture along the curved Motagua fault system, made of 5–10 subevents, with total seismic moments varying between 2.1 and 3.7×10^{20} N · m (Fig. 6; Kanamori and Stewart, 1978; Kikuchi and Kanamori, 1982; Young *et al.*, 1989). Although the M_w 7.5 magnitude has been persistently used, the range of moment released corresponds to an M_w 7.5–7.7 earthquake.

Surface-wave directivity analysis indicated an asymmetric bilateral faulting pattern with ~70% of moment release propagating westward, optimally modeled with eastern and western segments of 75 and 175 km, respectively (Kanamori and Stewart, 1978). Early analyses using European-only arrays were unable to distinguish bilateral from unilateral rupture (Kikuchi and Kanamori, 1982). Later analyses incorporating 17 stations with better azimuthal coverage established true asymmetric bilateral propagation, though substantial errors indicated significant unresolved complexity (Young *et al.*, 1989).

Rupture velocity estimates range from 2.0 to 3.5 km/s, though this parameter is poorly constrained by teleseismic data. Surface-wave modeling used values of 2.5–3.0 km/s resolving directivity patterns (Kanamori and Stewart, 1978). Body-wave inversions either assumed rupture velocities as input constraints (Kikuchi and Kanamori, 1991) or calculated approximate values from inferred timing and spacing of moment release episodes (Kikuchi and Kanamori, 1982; Young *et al.*, 1989). The inherent nonuniqueness means multiple combinations of rupture velocity, subevent locations, and moment distributions can explain observations equally well (Kikuchi and Kanamori, 1991).

The largest individual moment release subevents varied substantially between studies ($5.3\text{–}9 \times 10^{19}$ N · m) but consistently occurred ~90 km west of the epicenter at ~22–72 s after rupture initiation (Fig. 6b; Kanamori and Stewart, 1978; Kikuchi and Kanamori, 1982; Young *et al.*, 1989), coinciding with maximum surface displacement observations. More than 60% of total moment occurred between 60 and 120 km west of the epicenter, indicating heterogeneous mechanical properties controlled by asperities or varying frictional characteristics.

Dip-slip motion contributed disproportionately to modeled surface-wave amplitudes despite comprising only ~10% percent of total scalar moment (Kikuchi and Kanamori, 1991). Normal faulting near the epicenter (1.5×10^{19} N · m) and reverse faulting at the western terminus (1.1×10^{19} N · m) were identified, with these dip-slip components contributing *P*- and *PP*-wave amplitudes comparable to much larger strike-slip events. The reverse faulting component at the western terminus contrasted with field observations documenting predominantly normal faulting (Plafker *et al.*, 1976; Langer and Bollinger, 1979), highlighting fundamental nonuniqueness in teleseismic inversions.

Average stress-drop estimates were ~30 bars, comparable to worldwide averages for interplate earthquakes (Kanamori and Stewart, 1978). Assuming a seismogenic width of 15 km, seismological analysis indicated average displacement of ~2 m. A discrepancy emerged between this seismologically inferred displacement and the initially measured surface offset averaging 1.1 m (Plafker *et al.*, 1976), possibly reflecting depth-dependent deformation, off-fault deformation, surface layer decoupling, and postseismic creep subsequently documented through field remeasurement campaigns (Bucknam *et al.*, 1978).

Paleoseismic evidence for rupture directivity. Recent analysis of sediment records from six Guatemalan lakes has provided independent evidence for directivity effects during the 1976 earthquake, offering additional constraints on the spatial distribution of ground motion beyond instrumental observations (Fig. 7; Obrist-Farner *et al.*, 2025). Deposits from turbidites triggered by the earthquake were identified in five lakes, with their thickness distribution reflecting the asymmetric nature of shaking during the rupture. Lake Atitlán, located ~40 km southwest of the western rupture terminus, contained the thickest event deposits despite being the most distant from the earthquake epicenter. Lakes positioned closer to the epicenter but perpendicular to the primary rupture propagation path contained substantially thinner deposits. Lake Izabal, located near the epicenter but north of the fault trace, showed no detectable event deposit despite fractures extending to the lake floor that suggest sensitivity to seismic activity (Obrist-Farner *et al.*, 2023). Although factors such as site response, sedimentation rate, and sediment composition can influence the resulting thickness of event deposits, the spatial pattern supports seismological evidence for strong westward directivity (Obrist-Farner *et al.*, 2025), for which >70% of moment release occurred west of the epicenter (Kanamori and Stewart, 1978).

The sediment record also aligns with instrumental observations of asymmetric bilateral rupture (Young *et al.*, 1989) and enhanced ground-motion concentration near the western fault terminus, where the largest individual moment release episodes occurred ~90 km west of the epicenter (Fig. 6; Kikuchi and Kanamori, 1982; Young *et al.*, 1989). The correlation between thick lake deposits at Lake Atitlán, concentrated

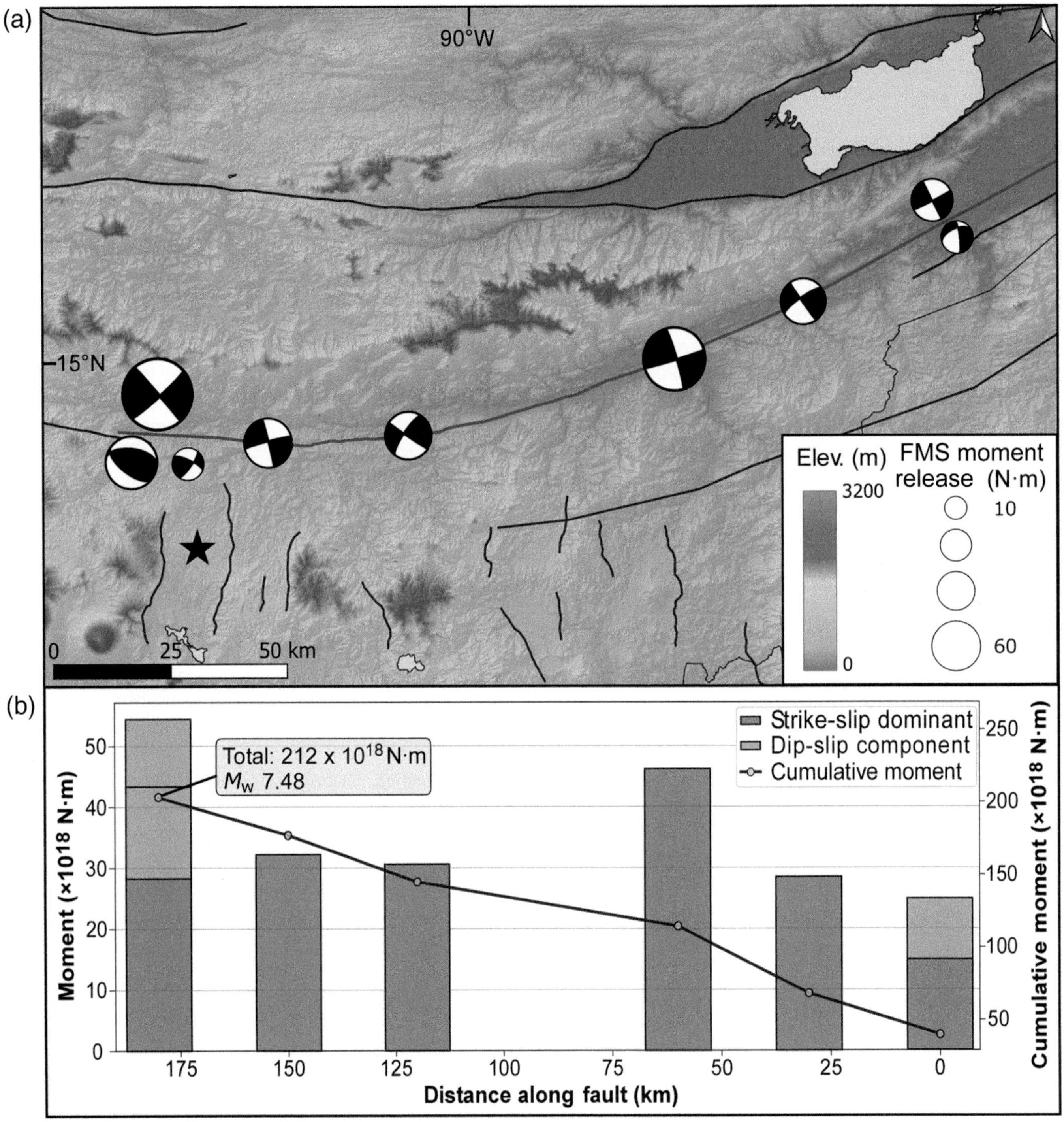

Figure 6. (a) The 1976 Motagua fault surface rupture (red) with the FMS of the modeled subevents from Kikuchi and Kanamori (1991), scaled proportionally to seismic moment. Black lines show major faults from the GEM global active faults database (Styron and Pagani, 2020). The location of Guatemala City is denoted with a black star. (b) Moment estimates for the modeled subevents from Kikuchi and Kanamori (1991). The color version of this figure is available only in the electronic edition.

landslide activity west of Guatemala City (Fig. 4; Harp *et al.*, 1981), and quasi-dynamic rupture modeling results provides evidence that directivity controlled the spatial distribution of strong ground motion (Fig. 7; Obrist-Farner *et al.*, 2025).

Ground failures. Comprehensive landslide mapping using high-altitude U-2 aerial photography provided systematic documentation of earthquake-induced slope failures across the affected region (Harp *et al.*, 1981). The earthquake generated >10,000 landslides across ~16,000 km^2, causing hundreds

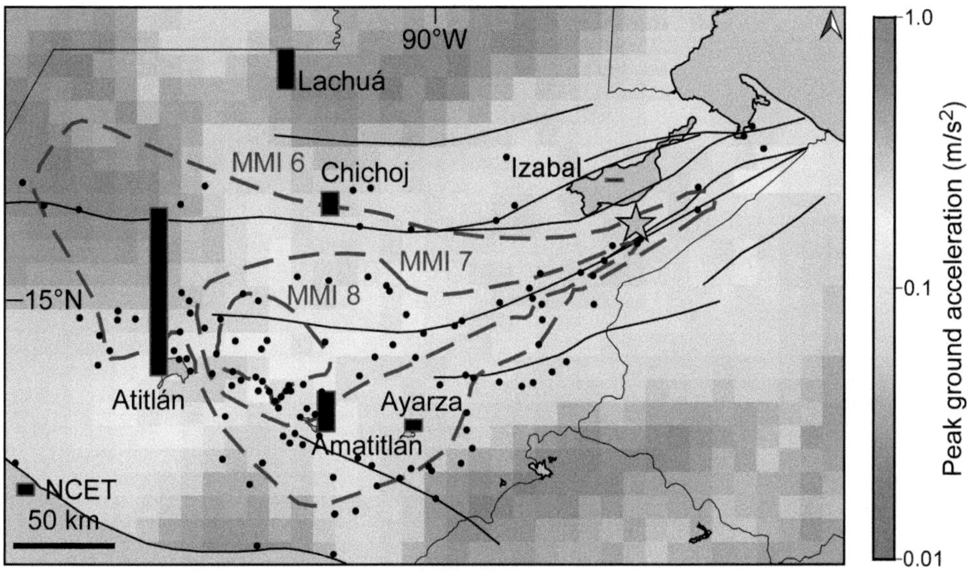

Figure 7. Modeled PGA values from the quasi-dynamic rupture model modified from Obrist-Farner *et al.* (2025). Black bars are normalized cumulative event thickness (NCET) from the studied lakes. Red contours are MMI contours showing areas of damage and black dots are locations with completed MMI questionnaires (Espinosa *et al.*, 1976). NCET at Lake Izabal is zero. The color version of this figure is available only in the electronic edition.

of fatalities and severely disrupting transportation networks (Fig. 4). The predominant types were rock falls and debris slides, most <15,000 m^3 in volume, with 11 events >100,000 m^3. Rock falls typically occurred on slopes steeper than 50° as tensile failures from seismic-wave reflection off canyon walls. Debris slides developed on gentler slopes (30°–50°) in thin, noncohesive soil layers overlying Pleistocene pumice deposits. Approximately 90% of landslides occurred within Pleistocene pumice deposits, which cover only ~20% of the affected region. The highest density of landslides occurred in the highlands west of Guatemala City.

Extensive liquefaction occurred south of Guatemala City near Lake Amatitlán, in the Motagua Valley, along the Atlantic coast of Guatemala and Honduras, near Lake Atitlán to the west of Guatemala City, and along Lake Ilopango in El Salvador (Fig. 4; Plafker *et al.*, 1976). Effects included lateral spreading extending ≤1 km from the main rupture, ground settlement reaching 1 m, and ground cracks >100 cm in width (Caccavale *et al.*, 2019). The affected soils consisted of pumiceous sand layers with relatively low density, making them particularly vulnerable to earthquake-induced liquefaction (Seed *et al.*, 1981).

Postseismic observations

Aftershock sequence. Three seismograph networks documented the aftershock sequence following the 4 February mainshock. A six-station permanent array with vertical seismometers distributed across an area with an approximate diameter of 140 km west of Guatemala City maintained continuous monitoring through 30 June 1976 (Fig. 8a; White and Harlow, 1979). The USGS deployed portable networks in two sequential campaigns, one in the western part of the rupture (eight stations) and one in the eastern part of the rupture with 10 stations (Fig. 8a; Langer *et al.*, 1976; Langer and Bollinger, 1979). An additional temporary deployment of two portable stations operated at six sites between 6 and 10 February, supplemented by a station at Tegucigalpa, Honduras (Matumoto and Latham, 1976).

The permanent network captured secondary faulting south of the western Motagua fault terminus. During the 11 months preceding the earthquake, background seismicity averaged less than one event per day. The mainshock triggered a >50-fold increase in seismicity rates (White and Harlow, 1979). Events were initially timed only for days bracketing nine major aftershocks with body-wave magnitude >4.2 through March 1976. Processing of all events with magnitude >1.5 resumed after 1 April (White and Harlow, 1979). The permanent network catalog provides hypocentral data for 1560 events between 1 February and 30 June 1976 (White and Harlow, 1979). Data demonstrated extensive fracturing between the western Motagua fault and the volcanic chain (Fig. 1), with diffuse seismicity and normal fault mechanisms (White and Harlow, 1979).

A temporary two-station deployment during the first week following the mainshock captured intense initial aftershock activity and revealed patterns of fault activation. Matumoto and Latham (1976) recorded several thousand earthquakes between 6 and 10 February 1976, with adjusted daily counts reaching ≤~5000 events per day at individual sites. The temporal decay of these single-station aftershock rates showed a decline consistent with the classical formulation of Omori's law (Utsu, 1961), although no formal modified Omori-law parameter inversion was performed. Owing to the limited two-station geometry and short recording intervals, only events recorded simultaneously at multiple stations could be reliably located with this subset being composed of 95 aftershocks. These were used to delineate the spatial extent of post-mainshock fault activation, which was defined by a seismically active zone that initially followed the Motagua fault before branching sharply southward ~35 km west of Guatemala City. The highest aftershock activity during the observation period was concentrated along the western extremity of the rupture.

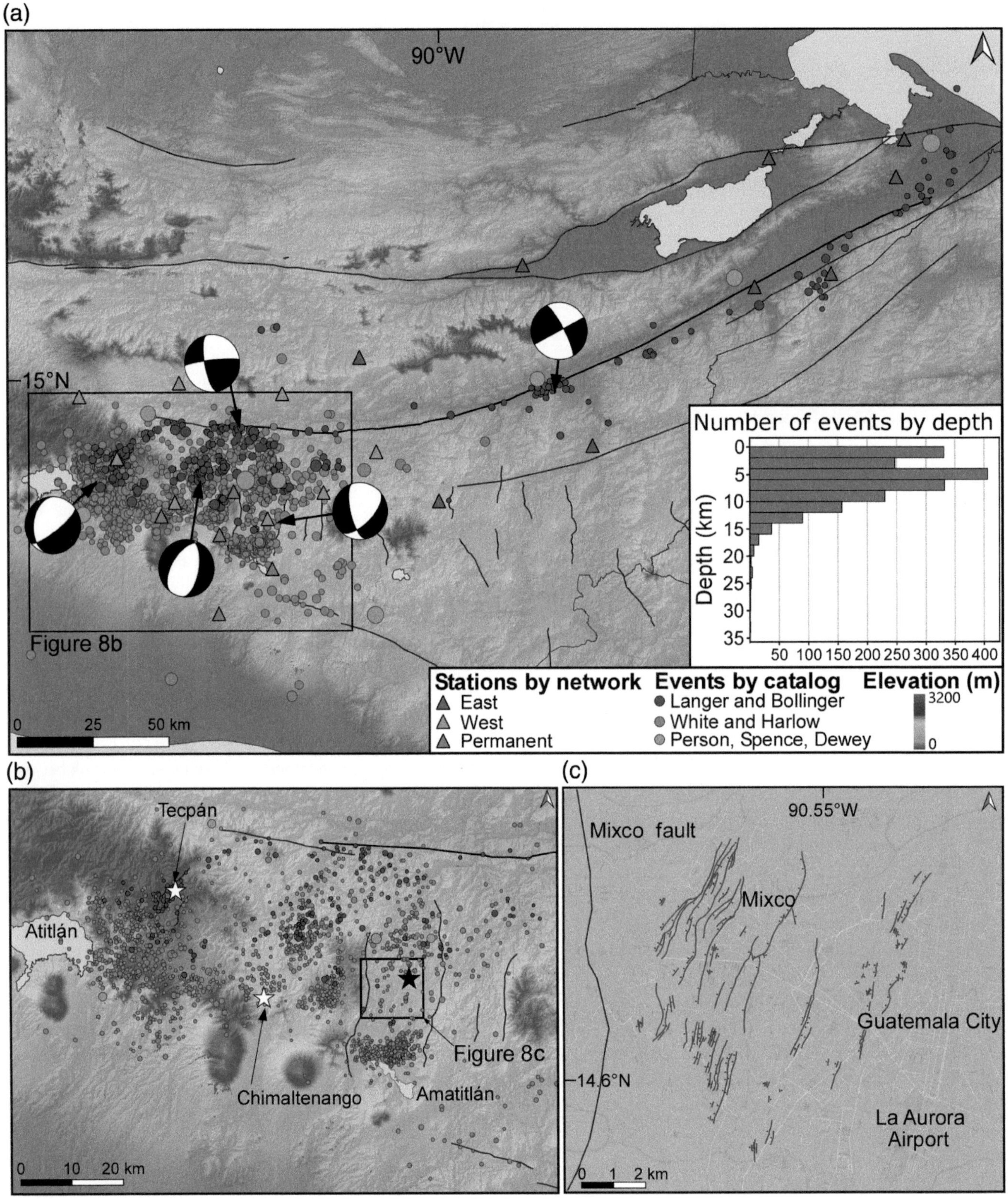

Figure 8. (a) Spatial distribution of aftershocks from the 1976 Motagua earthquake. Teleseismically detected events are shown in blue (Person *et al.*, 1976), events detected by the temporary network are shown in red (Langer and Bollinger, 1979), and events detected by the permanent network stations are shown in green (White and Harlow, 1979). Composite focal mechanisms are displayed for selected aftershocks (Langer and Bollinger, 1979). Faults modified from the GEM Active Fault Database (Styron and Pagani, 2020). Black box shows the outline of panel (b). Inset shows number of events per depth interval using the combined aftershock catalogs. (b) Same as A but focused on the western end of the rupture. Location of Guatemala City denoted as a black star. Black box shows the outline of panel (c). (c) Secondary faulting (red lines) mapped by the USGS in the Guatemala City Graben. The color version of this figure is available only in the electronic edition.

Subsequent USGS portable networks constrained the spatial extent of aftershock activity and documented systematic patterns in epicenter distribution. The western network operated from 9 to 17 February 1976, and the eastern network operated from 18 to 27 February 1976 (Fig. 8; Langer *et al.*, 1976; Langer and Bollinger, 1979). The investigation located 78 hypocenters with magnitude thresholds of ~2.2, later expanded by 178 aftershocks for a combined total of 256 hypocenters (Langer *et al.*, 1976; Langer and Bollinger, 1979). Aftershock epicenters extended ~300 km from the Gulf of Honduras westward to the Guatemalan highlands northeast of Lake Atitlán (Fig. 8a; Langer *et al.*, 1976). At the eastern extent, 12 epicenters were documented southeast of Puerto Barrios, with 8 aftershocks aligned with the inferred Motagua fault extension. Langer *et al.* (1976) interpreted this as the eastern rupture terminus, though these could alternatively represent stress-triggered seismicity on adjacent structures. The seismic moment release from aftershocks was generally uniform along the rupture trace but with notable concentration west of Zacapa corresponding to areas of above-average surface slip (Fig. 4; Langer *et al.*, 1976). Aftershock patterns exhibited systematic 2–3 km southerly offsets, suggesting steep south dip of the fault plane or significant velocity contrasts across the fault zone (Langer *et al.*, 1976).

Aftershocks revealed a linearized pattern extending ~50 km beyond the main fault surface breakage (Fig. 8; Langer and Bollinger, 1979). At the western Motagua fault terminus, epicenters splayed southwest along surface lineaments, with concentration toward the Mixco-Guatemala City region (Langer and Bollinger, 1979). Both networks documented extensive seismicity on secondary faults south of the Motagua fault and west of longitude 90.3° W, with focal depths from near-surface to ~14 km (Langer *et al.*, 1976; Langer and Bollinger, 1979; White and Harlow, 1979). Most aftershocks west of longitude 90.3° W were associated with secondary faulting in the Tecpán, Chimaltenango, Guatemala City, and Agua Caliente regions (Fig. 4; Langer *et al.*, 1976). Matumoto and Latham (1976) inferred a total rupture length of at least 250 km based on the spatial extent of aftershock activity.

Focal mechanism solutions revealed east-northeast–west-southwest left-lateral strike-slip faulting along the Motagua fault and northeast–southwest normal faulting on western terminus splays (Fig. 8a; Langer and Bollinger, 1979). The Mixco fault zone experienced normal dip-slip motion during the mainshock and a large aftershock on 6 February with body-wave magnitude 5.8 (Langer and Bollinger, 1979). The two largest aftershocks, both M_b 5.8, were normal events on the Mixco fault near Guatemala City (Person *et al.*, 1976; Langer and Bollinger, 1979). This secondary normal faulting correlated with theoretical stress patterns at strike-slip fault termini (Langer and Bollinger, 1979).

Afterslip observations. Field measurements documented extensive afterslip along the Motagua fault surface rupture through systematic remeasurement campaigns at eight sites distributed along the fault trace (Bucknam *et al.*, 1978). Three sites within a 50 km segment were regularly revisited over the following 2 yr. The monitoring used direct measurements of offset cultural features, including fence lines, building foundations, and roads, with measurement uncertainties of ~1 cm (Bucknam *et al.*, 1978). No instruments were installed to record afterslip directly. Measurements were made using noninstrumental methods such as visual alignment of offset features, with a standard deviation of ≤1 cm, meaning that smaller amounts of afterslip were near the measurement limit (Bucknam *et al.*, 1978). Initial field surveys in April 1976 established baseline displacements that averaged 1.1 m across the monitored fault section (Bucknam *et al.*, 1978). Subsequent remeasurements revealed continued displacement accumulation, with temporal evolution characterized by both gradual slip and episodic behavior (Bucknam *et al.*, 1978).

The three sites with complete time histories demonstrated the range of afterslip behavior across the monitored section (Fig. 4). At Gualán, displacement increased from 0.93 m four days after the earthquake to 1.06 m by 1745 days, representing 0.13 m of afterslip. At Zacapa, displacement increased from 0.6 m on 8 February 1976 to 0.91 m by 1565 days, representing 0.31 m of afterslip. At Marmol, initial measurements were complicated by temporary concrete repairs installed after the earthquake, but subsequent monitoring documented continued afterslip accumulation to 0.20 m by ~4 yr after the earthquake (Bucknam *et al.*, 1978). The afterslip magnitude at Zacapa represented approximately one-third of the initial coseismic displacement at that location. Episodic behavior was observed at several monitoring sites, including a steplike increase of 1.1 cm recorded during a small aftershock, though this displacement surge did not propagate to another monitoring site positioned 10 km along strike, indicating spatial variability in afterslip coupling and response to seismic triggering. Some short-term temporal variations in afterslip rate suggested possible displacement surges or episodic activity. Temporal correlation between elevated afterslip rates and increased aftershock activity suggested mechanical interaction between continued fault displacement and stress redistribution within the fault zone (Bucknam *et al.*, 1978).

Afterslip time histories demonstrated that displacement was proportional to the logarithm of time since the earthquake, with initial rates of several millimeters per day during the first weeks following the mainshock that decayed progressively over subsequent months (Bucknam *et al.*, 1978). An inverse relationship emerged between total coseismic displacement and subsequent afterslip rate across the monitored sites (Bucknam *et al.*, 1978). Locations that experienced the largest coseismic displacement were associated with the lowest rates of afterslip, and locations with smaller coseismic displacement corresponded to the highest afterslip rates (Bucknam *et al.*, 1978). This spatial pattern extended along the ~50 km monitored section and indicated heterogeneous frictional properties along the fault surface, with areas of high coseismic slip representing zones of more complete stress release during the mainshock and areas of lower coseismic slip accommodating proportionally more postseismic deformation (Bucknam *et al.*, 1978).

By 1980, slip rates at the three comprehensively monitored sites had converged to ~23 mm per year, exceeding not only current estimates for the Motagua fault specifically but also estimates of overall plate boundary motion between the North American and Caribbean plates (Lisowski and Thatcher, 1981; DeMets *et al.*, 2000; Franco *et al.*, 2012; Ellis *et al.*, 2019; Maurer *et al.*, 2025). These anomalously high-postseismic rates indicate that the 1976 earthquake did not completely release accumulated strain, with continued displacement representing the release of residual elastic strain following incomplete coseismic rupture. Understanding the mechanism of this sustained postseismic deformation requires examining the depth and character of the deformation zone. The regular spatial variation in total slip and afterslip along ~50 km of the fault trace suggested that afterslip was not controlled by local near-surface geological factors such as alluvial cover (Bucknam *et al.*, 1978). Studies of afterslip following the 1966 Parkfield earthquake in California indicated a significant component caused by thick alluvium ranging from 0.5 to 3 km in thickness (Scholz *et al.*, 1969), but in Guatemala, the poorly consolidated Quaternary alluvium was estimated to be <100 m thick, too thin to explain the observed afterslip magnitudes and patterns (Bucknam *et al.*, 1978). Instead, the fault-scale spatial coherence of afterslip behavior supported a mechanism involving stable frictional sliding within a mechanically distinct layer several kilometers thick, comparable to the ~4-km-thick layer proposed for the Parkfield segment of the San Andreas fault (Scholz *et al.*, 1969; Bucknam *et al.*, 1978). Within this deeper crustal layer, frictional properties permit continued time-dependent displacement as residual strain from the incomplete mainshock rupture is progressively released through stable sliding rather than seismic failure (Bucknam *et al.*, 1978).

Geodetic observations. A 15-station geodetic network extending 10 km north and 40 km south of the fault, surveyed in 1935 and 1953, was reobserved in 1978 (Lisowski and Thatcher, 1981). The 1978 survey used electronic distance measurement with standard errors of ~10 mm (Lisowski and Thatcher, 1981).

Analysis of 45 common angles revealed systematic horizontal deformation concentrated in the fault-crossing section (Lisowski and Thatcher, 1981). The fault-crossing subsection exhibited accumulated shear strain of 49 ± 5 μstrain with the azimuth of maximum left-lateral shear oriented N54°E ± 4°, closely matching the N65°E strike of the Motagua fault (Lisowski and Thatcher, 1981), consistent with expected displacement gradient for left-lateral slip on the fault.

Dislocation modeling using elastic half-space theory converted observed angle changes into fault-slip estimates (Lisowski and Thatcher, 1981). A uniform-slip model extending from 0 to 15 km depth yielded left-lateral slip of 1.3 ± 0.1 m (Lisowski and Thatcher, 1981). A three-segment model allowing slip to vary with depth indicated 0.8 ± 0.1 m near the surface, increasing to 2.1 ± 0.5 m at 5–15 km depth, with slip below 15 km poorly constrained at 0.8 ± 1.2 m (Lisowski and Thatcher, 1981). The multisegment model provided superior fit and better agreement with the ~2 m of slip inferred from seismic moment calculations (Kanamori and Stewart, 1978), suggesting depth-dependent slip distribution with maximum displacement at seismogenic depths.

KNOWLEDGE GAINED SINCE THE 1976 EARTHQUAKE

Slip rates on the plate boundary and individual fault strands

Slip rates on the main faults of the Polochic–Motagua fault system based on field observations are scarce. Progressive offset of stream terraces at the Rio El Tambor–Rio Motagua confluence near Zacapa documents recurrent left-lateral displacement on the Motagua fault, with the youngest mappable terrace displaying 23.7 m offset and the oldest 58.3 m (Fig. 9; Schwartz *et al.*, 1979). Age constraints based on volcanic tuff and soil development indicate the oldest terrace is younger than 40,000 yr and older than 10,000 yr, yielding late Quaternary slip rates of 1.5–6 mm/yr (Schwartz *et al.*, 1979). Similar geomorphic evidence along the Polochic fault, including offset streams of 35–100 m, suggests comparable Quaternary activity (Schwartz *et al.*, 1979). Schwartz *et al.* (1979) estimated combined the late Quaternary slip rate at 4.5–18 mm/yr for the plate boundary. South-facing scarps along both faults indicate an up-to-the-north vertical component representing up to 5% of lateral slip (Schwartz *et al.*, 1979).

Contemporary GPS-based estimates suggest substantially higher slip rates on the Motagua fault (Franco *et al.*, 2012; Ellis *et al.*, 2019). These studies, however, used relatively simple block models that did not account for distributed deformation, leading to discrepancies between geodetic and geologic slip rates. Recent advances have refined slip-rate estimates and suggest distributed contemporary deformation. Maurer *et al.* (2025) used multiple complementary methods, including strain-rate calculations, 3D elastic dislocation modeling, and 2D finite-element modeling, demonstrating that minor fault segments including the Ixcán fault and Jocotán–Chamelecón fault zone (Fig. 1b) are active and accommodate some proportion of total plate rate. Inclusion of these minor strands and allowing for inelastic bulk crustal strain resolves some discrepancies, with overall lower Motagua fault slip rates (~6 to 8 mm/yr) in closer agreement with geological rates (Maurer *et al.*, 2025). For the Polochic fault, estimated slip rates are slightly higher than the geologic rates (~3 to

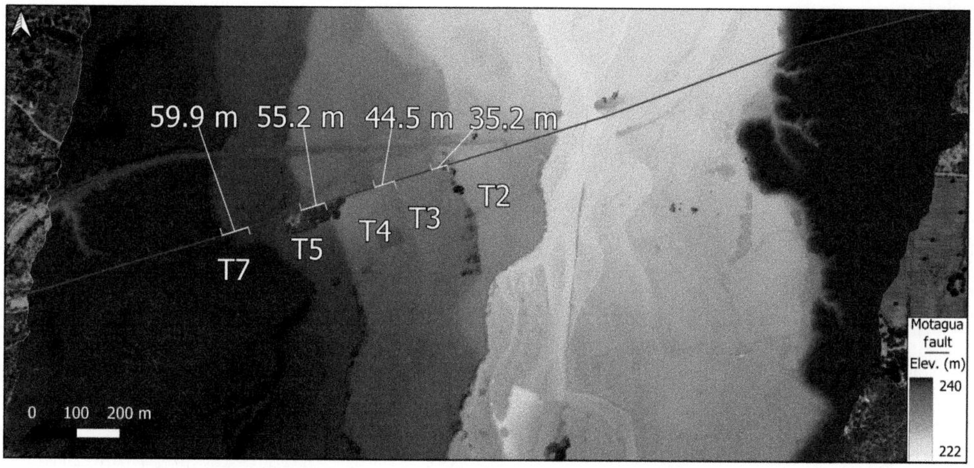

Figure 9. High-resolution drone light detection and ranging (lidar) imagery acquired in 2024 showing the El Tambor River terraces originally documented by Schwartz *et al.* (1979). Terrace surfaces T7, T5, T4, T3, and T2 are labeled following their original classification. Modern agricultural and infrastructural modification between T4–T3 and T3–T2 boundaries resulted in uncertainty in terrace-offset estimates and should be considered when interpreting displacement magnitudes. The color version of this figure is available only in the electronic edition.

7 mm/yr varying along strike), with minor fault segments accommodating 1–3 mm/yr (Maurer *et al.*, 2025).

An extensional zone in the Caribbean plate south of the plate boundary also accommodates distributed deformation between the Motagua fault and the CAVA (Fig. 1a), accommodating 3–5 mm/yr of east–west extension, approximately one-quarter of the total left-lateral plate-boundary motion. Extension is accommodated through normal and oblique-normal faults defining the Guatemala City and Ipala grabens and by dextral motion along the Jalpatagua–Santa Rosa fault system (Fig. 1b; Garnier *et al.*, 2021). These structures define the southern expression of distributed strain transfer from the Polochic–Motagua fault system into the western Caribbean fore-arc (Garnier *et al.*, 2022).

Seismicity on the plate boundary

Permanent seismic network coverage of the Polochic–Motagua fault system has remained sparse since 1976. A six-month deployment of 30 seismic stations in 2005 provided the most comprehensive characterization of microseismicity patterns along the eastern segment of the fault system (Franco *et al.*, 2009). This network recorded 502 local events, with 276 earthquakes precisely located using at least four station observations.

The deployment revealed active seismicity concentrated in the upper 15 km of crust, with the seismogenic zone extending to 10–15 km depth beneath both the Polochic and Motagua faults. This depth range corresponds closely to the ~20 km locking depth derived from GPS models of strain accumulation on the Motagua fault (Lyon-Caen *et al.*, 2006; Franco *et al.*, 2012), confirming the thickness of the mechanically coupled zone. Microseismic activity occurred at comparable rates on both principal faults, distributed along fault traces rather than concentrated in specific segments. Earthquake clusters within north–south-trending grabens south of the Motagua fault exhibited normal faulting on westward-dipping planes, whereas clusters within fold structures north of the Polochic fault showed reverse faulting on south-dipping planes. These focal mechanisms match the GPS-observed transition from dominant east–west strike-slip motion to dominant east–west extension, confirming secondary structures actively participate in accommodating plate boundary deformation.

The comparable microseismic activity on both faults presents an apparent contradiction with geodetic observations. GPS measurements show the Motagua fault accommodates the majority of elastic strike-slip deformation while minimal strain accumulates across the Polochic fault (Franco *et al.*, 2012; Ellis *et al.*, 2019; Maurer *et al.*, 2025). Yet the six-month deployment documented similar earthquake activity rates on both structures. This discrepancy suggests that short-term seismicity patterns may not directly reflect long-term strain accumulation, potentially indicating temporal variations in fault activity, episodic behavior, or substantial aseismic strain release on the Polochic fault.

Regional catalogs confirm seismic activity extends across multiple structures beyond the two principal faults, including the Ixcán, Jocotán–Chamelecón, and other associated fault segments, as well as distributed activity within graben systems (Fig. 10; Guzmán-Speziale and Molina, 2022). This broad distribution further supports geodetic evidence for strain accommodation across a wide plate boundary zone.

Instrumentation limitations influence interpretation of seismicity along the plate boundary. The permanent network maintained since 1976 has poor location control, characterized by high azimuthal gap angles >180° and distances to nearest stations >50 km (González-Negreros and Gaspar-Escribano, 2025). The recent strengthening of the Guatemala National Seismological Network (Yani-Quiyuch *et al.*, 2023) is generating higher-quality data, although completeness magnitude averages around **M** 4.0 for shallow earthquakes along the Polochic–Motagua fault system compared with **M** ≤3.0 in better-monitored areas (Gamboa-Canté *et al.*, 2024). The velocity model has remained unchanged since 1980, potentially contributing to systematic location uncertainties (González-Negreros and Gaspar-Escribano, 2025).

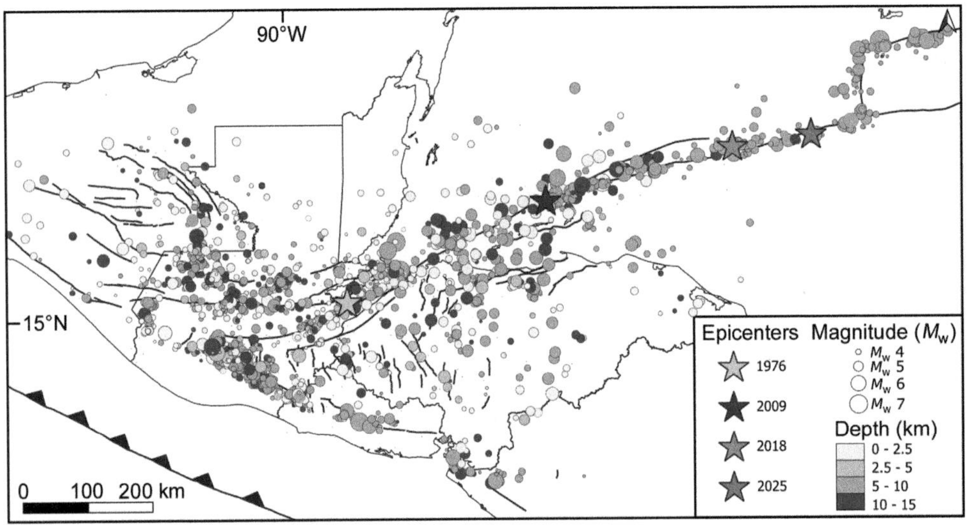

Figure 10. Spatial distribution of upper-crustal (depths ≤15 km) seismic events (magnitude M_w>4) in Central America since 1977. Major rupture epicenters are shown with a star. Events are scaled by magnitude and colored by size. The catalog was compiled from the USGS earthquake catalog (U.S. Geological Survey, 2025) and the catalog provided by Gamboa-Cante *et al.* (2024). All events associated to the subduction zone have been removed. Faults modified from the GEM active fault database (Styron and Pagani, 2020). The color version of this figure is available only in the electronic edition.

Recurrence interval of large earthquakes

Earthquake history of the Polochic–Motagua fault system. Despite its tectonic significance and in contrast to other transform plate boundaries (Fraser *et al.*, 2010; Marco and Klinger 2014; Rockwell *et al.*, 2015; Howarth *et al.*, 2018), there is a notable absence of a thorough and extensive paleoseismic record to document the earthquake history of the Polochic–Motagua fault system. In the centuries preceding the 1976 earthquake, historical records compiled from colonial archives document two seismic periods separated by extended periods of relative inactivity (White, 1984).

The first active period from 1702 to 1822 along the Polochic–Motagua fault system included 18 damaging earthquakes (White, 1984). This period culminated with a rupture of the eastern portion of the Polochic fault in 1785 (magnitude 7.3–7.5, ~175–220 km rupture length) and the western portion in 1816 (magnitude 7.5–7.7, ~240 km rupture length), followed by 5 yr of regional aftershocks through 1821 (Fig. 3; White, 1984). The 1816 event represents the largest earthquake in Guatemala's historical record based on the extent of intensity VII damage (White, 1984). This active period was preceded by a quiescent period extending from ~1560 to 1702, when no damaging earthquakes with magnitudes >6.0 (estimated) were recorded despite reasonably complete historical documentation (White, 1984; Peraldo and Montero, 1999; Peruzza *et al.*, 2021, 2023).

After 1821, the Polochic–Motagua fault system entered a second quiescent period of 123 yr with no damaging earthquakes (estimated magnitude >6.0) documented through instrumental and historical records (White, 1984). The 1945 Quiriguá earthquake on the Motagua fault, near the later epicenter of the 1976 earthquake, marked the beginning of a second active period that culminated with the 1976 Motagua fault rupture (White, 1984).

Beyond colonial and historical documentation of earthquakes (White, 1984; White and Harlow, 1993), lake sediment analysis at Lake Chichój is consistent with irregular seismic activity over 1200 yr (Fig. 7; Brocard *et al.*, 2014, 2016). This record was interpreted to show a distinct cluster of four earthquakes from ~750 to 1000 C.E., moderate activity from ~1000 to 1450 C.E., and a 500 yr quiescence from ~1450 C.E. until the 1976 event. The Lake Chichój record also provides evidence for mixed seismic and aseismic deformation processes along the Polochic fault, with meter-scale creep interpreted during seismically quiescent periods between 1665 and 1976 C.E. (Brocard *et al.*, 2016). Trenches along the Polochic fault provide additional evidence of past seismicity. At least five surface-rupturing earthquakes occurred during the past 17,000 yr, yielding minimum-average recurrence intervals of 3300–4300 yr for large earthquakes (Authemayou *et al.*, 2012).

Additional estimates of recurrence along the Polochic–Motagua fault system are uncertain. When the late Quaternary slip rates (1.5–6.0 mm/yr for the Motagua fault) are combined with the average 1.1 m displacement from the 1976 earthquake, estimated recurrence intervals for large surface-rupturing earthquakes range from 180 to 755 yr (Schwartz *et al.*, 1979). The limited number of trenching investigations, constraining observations to a single location, may not reflect system-wide behavior, particularly given evidence for strain partitioning across multiple parallel fault traces. In addition, age constraints for Quaternary features, such as those investigated by Schwartz *et al.* (1979), remain poor across the wide temporal ranges typical of standard dating methods, contributing to the substantial uncertainty in slip-rate determination. Variation in recurrence estimates for the main faults of the plate boundary, from 180 to 755 yr (geological; Schwartz *et al.*, 1979) to ~160 to 280 yr (Plafker, 1976; White 1984) representing the duration of regional quiescent periods between major transform-fault earthquakes, to 3300–4400 yr (paleoseismic evidence; Authemayou *et al.*, 2012), reflects both methodological uncertainties and complexity in fault system behavior.

Modeling the Polochic–Motagua fault system. Slip deficit rate modeling identifies locked asperities that correspond to historical rupture locations, including the 1976 Motagua, 1816 northern Polochic, and 1785 southern Polochic earthquake zones, providing evidence that current strain accumulation patterns reflect persistent structural controls on rupture behavior (Maurer *et al.*, 2025). The segment that ruptured in 1976 currently exhibits slip deficit rates of 8–10 mm/yr along the eastern Motagua fault, decreasing systematically westward. This spatial pattern of contemporary strain accumulation differs from the 1976 rupture characteristics, for which maximum moment release and surface displacement occurred in the western portions of the rupture despite lower present-day strain accumulation rates in those areas. Modeling suggests that the 1976 earthquake released strain that had accumulated over multiple centuries following the last major Motagua fault rupture, consistent with the extended quiescent period documented in historical records (White, 1984).

Estimates of contemporary Polochic fault slip rates vary substantially among modeling approaches. Whereas earlier geodetic studies indicated slip rates of 3.1–3.3 mm/yr (Ellis *et al.*, 2019), recent elastic slip deficit rate modeling suggests ~6–7 mm/yr (Maurer *et al.*, 2025). However, finite-element modeling that incorporates crustal strain yields intermediate values of 3–4 mm/yr for most of the fault length (Maurer *et al.*, 2025), more consistent with earlier estimates. The higher slip deficit rates may reflect model assumptions about fault locking or elastic behavior that do not fully capture the complexity of strain accommodation across the fault system. These discrepancies highlight remaining uncertainties in quantifying how contemporary strain accumulation is partitioned between the Motagua and Polochic faults and across minor fault segments that collectively contribute 1–3 mm/yr to total plate boundary motion.

Moment deficit rate calculations provide direct estimates of earthquake potential across the entire plate boundary zone. Geodetic models yield moment deficit rates of $0.66–1.3 \times 10^{19}$ N · m/yr for the entire region, depending on assumed elastic crustal thickness and modeling approach, values that exceed estimated moment release rates from historic earthquakes since 1560 ($0.21–0.37 \times 10^{19}$ N · m/yr; White, 1984; Maurer *et al.*, 2025). This discrepancy may be due to an incomplete earthquake catalog or moment release through other means than earthquakes, including postseismic creep and inelastic processes such as folding.

Recurrence time of the 1976 Motagua-style earthquake. Estimating recurrence intervals for earthquakes similar to the 1976 event requires reconciling the mean surface rupture of 1.1 m (Plafker *et al.*, 1976) or 2 m at depth (Kanamori and Stewart, 1978) with spatially variable contemporary slip rates. Using average slip deficit rates of 8–10 mm/yr for the eastern Motagua fault yields recurrence estimates of 110–250 yr for that segment, but the lower rates documented in western portions (~2 to 3 mm/yr) for which maximum 1976 displacement occurred suggest intervals of 300–1000 yr. These calculations assume uniform seismic strain release and do not account for the documented complexity in rupture behavior.

The moment deficit calculations provide an alternative constraint on recurrence timescales. If the 1976 earthquake released ~2.1 to 3.7×10^{20} N · m and contemporary moment accumulation rates on the ruptured segment of the Motagua fault are ~2.16 to 2.25×10^{18} N · m/yr (Maurer *et al.*, 2025), a complete repetition of the 1976 rupture would require ~100 to 170 yr of strain accumulation at current rates. This range is smaller than the 180–755 yr estimates derived from late Quaternary geological slip rates combined with 1976 displacement measurements (Schwartz *et al.*, 1979) and overlaps with the ~160 to 280 yr period between major transform-fault earthquakes on the Polochic–Motagua fault system (Plafker, 1976; White, 1984). Polochic fault slip rates (3–7 mm/yr depending on modeling approach) affect these system-wide estimates because strain partitioning between the parallel fault strands influences how quickly each structure approaches failure.

The concentration of coseismic slip and moment release in the western portions of the 1976 rupture, for which contemporary strain accumulation rates are lower, presents a significant complication. This pattern may indicate that individual fault segments do not rupture uniformly during each earthquake cycle (Dolan *et al.*, 2024). Eastern segments experiencing higher contemporary strain rates may fail through more frequent moderate magnitude events, through different rupture scenarios, or through creep, than the complete fault failure observed in 1976. Alternatively, the eastern segments may be approaching failure conditions faster than the western portions, potentially leading to partial ruptures that differ substantially from the 1976 event in both magnitude and spatial extents.

The limited historical record provides minimal constraint on characteristic Motagua fault rupture behavior. No large Motagua fault earthquakes are documented between 1560 and 1976, representing a single interevent period insufficient to establish typical recurrence patterns (White, 1984). White's historical record could also be incomplete, misattributing events to the subduction zone that could have occurred on the Motagua fault (e.g., Peraldo and Montero, 1999). Nevertheless, whether the 400 yr interval between 1560 and 1976 represents a characteristic recurrence time or an anomalously long period remains unresolved. The presence of locked asperities corresponding to historical rupture zones (Maurer *et al.*, 2025) suggests that contemporary strain accumulation may preferentially load the same fault segments, supporting the possibility of characteristic rupture behavior. However, the temporal switching of major seismic activity between the Motagua and Polochic fault structures over timescales of centuries (White, 1984) indicates that the system does not maintain constant behavior between earthquake cycles. This phenomenon, documented across multiple fault systems globally, potentially reflects how parallel faults within plate boundary zones can trade off slip in time and space to accommodate relative plate motions (Dolan *et al.*, 2024).

LESSONS LEARNED AND IMPLICATIONS FOR FUTURE EARTHQUAKES

The 1976 Motagua earthquake and the past five decades of scientific investigations demonstrate that seismic hazard assessment for the North American–Caribbean plate boundary requires evaluation of the fault system as an integrated whole rather than treatment of individual structures as independent sources. The Motagua and Polochic faults cannot be assessed in isolation from the broader plate boundary extending offshore to the Swan fault and southward into the western Caribbean plate extensional zone.

Hazard models based on contemporary geodetic strain accumulation mischaracterize earthquake probability on parallel fault strands. The current dominance of the Motagua fault in accommodating plate motion (Franco *et al.*, 2012; Ellis *et al.*, 2019; Maurer *et al.*, 2025) does not preclude future large earthquakes on the Polochic fault, which hosted the largest documented historical earthquake despite presently accumulating minimal geodetic strain (White, 1984; Franco *et al.*, 2012). Temporal switching of major seismic activity between these structures over centuries (White, 1984) indicates fault segments can remain quiet while accumulating stress through mechanisms not captured by short-term geodetic monitoring. Probabilistic assessments must assign nonnegligible earthquake probabilities to both principal faults regardless of contemporary strain partitioning.

Stress transfer requires that earthquake scenarios consider cascading effects and mechanical interactions between fault segments. The demonstrated coupling between offshore Swan fault ruptures and the Motagua fault (Graham *et al.*, 2012) indicates that large earthquakes anywhere along the plate boundary alter stress conditions on adjacent structures, similar to other strike-slip plate boundaries (Stein *et al.*, 1997). Hazard assessments based on characteristic earthquake models for individual faults will underestimate the probability of triggered or time-clustered events.

Ground-motion prediction for Guatemala City and other population centers must account for rupture directivity effects rather than relying solely on distance-based attenuation. The concentration of damage in areas along the rupture propagation path (Fig. 7; Espinosa *et al.*, 1976), despite greater epicentral distances (Kanamori and Stewart, 1978; Harp *et al.*, 1981; Young *et al.*, 1989; Obrist-Farner *et al.*, 2025), demonstrates that standard models may substantially underestimate shaking intensity for directivity-favorable locations (e.g., Somerville *et al.* 1997; Spudich and Chiou, 2008). This applies particularly to infrastructure and population centers along the probable rupture direction for potential future events.

Extensive activation of secondary faults during the 1976 earthquake (Plafker *et al.*, 1976; Langer and Bollinger, 1979; White and Harlow, 1979) indicates that seismic hazard extends across a zone tens of kilometers wide. The Guatemala City graben and other extensional structures (Rodriguez *et al.*, 2009; Ellis *et al.*, 2019; Garnier *et al.*, 2022) represent active sources capable of generating damaging earthquakes independently or as triggered events (e.g., the 1917 Guatemala earthquake; Morley, 1918). Urban planning must address hazard from both distant large earthquakes on the Motagua or Polochic faults and proximal moderate earthquakes on secondary structures.

The incomplete paleoseismic record (Authemayou *et al.*, 2012; Brocard *et al.*, 2016) and large uncertainties in recurrence estimates (Schwartz *et al.*, 1979; White, 1984; Maurer *et al.*, 2025) indicate deterministic forecasts remain unreliable. However, the demonstrated capacity of both faults to generate large earthquakes, evidence for fault interaction, and documented temporal clustering (White, 1984) suggest the system concentrates seismic hazard over intervals separated by extended quiescent periods. The sequence of major earthquakes on the Swan fault since 2009 (Fig. 3; Graham *et al.*, 2012; Cheng and Wang, 2020; Calais *et al.*, 2025) combined with the absence of large onshore events since 1976 raises questions about stress accumulation and potential progressive failure, analogous to cascading sequences along the North Anatolian fault (Stein *et al.*, 1997). Comprehensive Coulomb stress analysis across the entire plate boundary is needed to quantify how offshore ruptures and the 1976 event have altered loading conditions and whether current stress conditions favor near-term ruptures on onshore structures.

These considerations require that seismic hazard assessment, building codes, and emergency planning for Guatemala treat the entire plate boundary as an interconnected system. Following the 1976 earthquake, Guatemala implemented improved building codes through standards established by the Guatemalan Association of Structural and Seismic Engineering (AGIES—Normas de Seguridad Estructural Para Guatemala). However, a large proportion of structures remain noncompliant with these recommendations (fig. 2 in Orihuela *et al.*, 2025), leaving substantial portions of the population vulnerable. The patterns of rupture behavior, ground-motion distribution, and secondary fault activation documented in 1976 demonstrate that future large earthquakes will expose significant proportion of Guatemalan society to severe seismic risk. This vulnerability is compounded by rapid population growth and ongoing infrastructure expansion in a developing country, which complicate efforts to implement comprehensive seismic zoning and enforce building standards.

FUTURE RESEARCH NEEDS

Further analysis of the 1976 Motagua earthquake, in combination with contemporary studies of the Polochic–Motagua fault system, will continue to advance our scientific understanding of this plate boundary. Ultimately, better scientific understanding and characterization of seismicity along the Polochic–Motagua fault system will lead to better seismic hazard assessments for the region. We highlight several avenues for scientific research that can be used to improve hazard maps (e.g., Benito *et al.*, 2012; Gamboa-Canté *et al.* 2025) to better characterize risk along this multifault system.

1. Compared with other transform plate boundaries (e.g., San Andreas fault; McPhillips, 2022), the paleoseismic record along the Polochic–Motagua fault system is limited (Authemayou *et al.*, 2012; Brocard *et al.*, 2016). Systematic paleoseismic studies, including on-fault trenching and lacustrine paleoseismic investigations, are required to constrain earthquake recurrence patterns, fault switching behavior, and temporal clustering of seismic activity.
2. Improved quantification of long-term slip rates through geological studies of offset features and dating past earthquakes at more locations throughout the fault system will help characterize the seismic hazard of individual fault strands. Uncertainties remain regarding the activity and slip rates of structures such as the Jocotán–Chamelecón fault zone and the Ixcán fault, which may accommodate portions of plate boundary motion despite limited seismic activity.
3. Expansion of permanent seismic networks and geodetic monitoring capabilities is essential for improving hazard assessment in Guatemala. Improved instrumentation capabilities will help characterize contemporary deformation patterns and strain accumulation across the entire region, increasing the resolution of distributed deformation across multiple fault strands (González-Negreros and Gaspar-Escribano, 2025). Although an early warning system has now been established in Guatemala (e.g., Orihuela *et al.*, 2025) and could provide tens of seconds of advanced notice if a similar 1976 earthquake were to occur (e.g., Orihuela *et al.*, 2023), the lack of high-density instrumentation coverage prevents system efficiency. Current efforts to enhance instrumentation coverage include the Lake Izabal seismic array and the International Continental Scientific Drilling Program Lake Izabal Basin Research Endeavor project (Obrist-Farner *et al.*, 2023).
4. To better understand distributed deformation across the Polochic–Motagua fault system, comprehensive mapping of fault traces and determination of their activity through enhanced seismic monitoring and additional Global Navigation Satellite Systems and Interferometric Synthetic Aperture Radar (InSAR) studies is essential. Current studies lack consistency regarding which structures are active, with disagreement about the role of secondary faults in accommodating plate motion (Guzmán-Speziale and Molina, 2022; Agate *et al.*, 2024; Maurer *et al.*, 2025). The recognition that minor fault segments accommodate slip (Maurer *et al.*, 2025) highlights the need for additional investigations to distinguish active fault strands from inactive structures and quantify their contributions to total strain accommodation. Modern remote sensing techniques, including expanding light detection and ranging (lidar) coverage (currently limited to two locations along the Motagua fault; Fig. 9) and InSAR investigations, can improve fault-trace geometry, confirm uncertain structures, and integrate geomorphic and subsurface observations into unified fault maps.
5. More advanced source modeling for the 1976 event is needed to better resolve the source complexity seen in earlier modeling studies (Kanamori and Stewart, 1978; Kikuchi and Kanamori, 1982, 1991; Young *et al.*, 1989) to understand subevents, moment release, earthquake magnitude, and rupture directivity and how these processes affected ground acceleration and consequent building damage. Additional details on rupture heterogeneity and propagation dynamics through the analysis of digitized waveforms from the 1976 earthquake and the use of modern computational capabilities can help resolve these discrepancies. Waveforms preserved through the Albuquerque Seismological Lab WWSSN Film Chip Preservation Project (Alejandro *et al.*, 2019) provide access to teleseismic records that can be examined using contemporary inversion techniques and higher-resolution analysis methods not available during initial investigations.
6. Provide quantitative constraints for probabilistic seismic hazard assessment across the North American–Caribbean transform system. This is important given that the plate boundary since 1976 has ruptured in a predictive pattern (Fig. 3) similar to observations from the North Anatolian fault (e.g., Stein *et al.*, 1997). Such modeling should evaluate how the sequence of Swan fault ruptures since 2009, combined with the 1976 Motagua earthquake and historical Polochic fault events, has modified loading conditions on all fault segments within the system.
7. Understanding the structural framework that governs fault behavior, rupture dynamics, and the distribution of deformation across the Polochic–Motagua fault system requires comprehensive geological mapping. The most recent nationwide geologic map of Guatemala (Bonis *et al.*, 1970) remains a critical reference but lacks the stratigraphic and structural resolution necessary for comprehensive tectonic and hazard analyses. Subsequent studies have highlighted significant geological complexities, especially along the Motagua valley (Brueckner *et al.*, 2009; Angiboust *et al.*, 2021; Harlow *et al.*, 2025), which can help establish constraints on crustal architecture that controls fault localization and strain partitioning.

CONCLUSION

The 1976 Motagua earthquake established the significance of the Motagua Fault as part of the North American and Caribbean plate boundary. The event exhibited an asymmetric bilateral rupture with strongly westward-directed moment release and substantial spatial variations in slip and destruction. Although surface displacements were significant, seismological inversion models showed higher coseismic slip magnitudes at depth. Beyond the primary rupture, extensive secondary faulting and aftershock activity showcased the complexity of the fault system. Five decades of investigations have illuminated fundamental uncertainties of this plate boundary and its associated hazard. Current recurrence estimates do not allow to quantify how often large earthquake occur, and the fault strands of the plate boundary with high seismic risk are unknown. Understanding this plate boundary requires continued monitoring infrastructure and efforts currently inadequate for a fault system capable of producing large earthquakes of $M_w > 7$. The preservation of legacy data from the 1976 earthquake, in combination with continued scientific investigations and expansion of monitoring capabilities in Guatemala, will provide the foundation for integrated hazard assessment along the North American–Caribbean plate boundary.

DATA AND RESOURCES

All supplemental material, including original topographic maps with field annotations; aerial photographs spanning the western and central segments of the surface rupture; 35 mm color photographs taken by the U.S. Geological Survey (USGS) team during the 1976 expedition; field notebooks containing detailed observations, measurements, and sketches; and previously published aftershock datasets converted to standardized digital formats, are available digitally (McEnaney and Clark, 2025).

DECLARATION OF COMPETING INTERESTS

The authors acknowledge that there are no conflicts of interest recorded.

ACKNOWLEDGMENTS

This work was supported by the U.S. National Science Foundation (NSF) Award EAR-2038179 and EAR-2305799. The authors thank Associate Editor Thomas M. Brocher and Editor-in-Chief Martin Mai for insightful comments that significantly improved the quality of this article.

REFERENCES

Agate, M., F. Caldareri, L. Castillo, A. Garcia, G. Giunta, L. Mixco, J. Requena, C. Rubi Tellez, M. Ruiz, A. Sulli, *et al.* (2024). The pattern of brittle deformation in Central America for an assessment of the seismo-tectonic framework, *J. Maps* **20,** no. 1, 2285479, doi: 10.1080/17445647.2023.2285479.

Alejandro, A. C. B., C. R. Hutt, A. T. Ringler, S. V. Moore, R. E. Anthony, and D. C. Wilson (2019). The Albuquerque Seismological Lab WWSSN film chip preservation project, *Seismol. Res. Lett.* **90,** no. 1, 401–408, doi: 10.1785/0220180275.

Angiboust, S., J. Muñoz-Montecinos, A. Cambeses, T. Raimondo, D. Deldicque, and A. Garcia-Casco (2021). Jolts in the jade factory: A route for subduction fluids and their implications for mantle wedge seismicity, *Earth Sci. Rev.* **220,** 103720, doi: 10.1016/j.earscirev.2021.103720.

Authemayou, C., G. Brocard, C. Brocard, T. Simon-Labric, A. Guttierrez, E. N. Chiquín, and S. Morán (2011). The Caribbean-North America-Cocos Triple Junction and the dynamics of the Polochic-Motagua fault systems: Pull-up and zipper models, *Tectonics* **30,** TC3010, doi: 10.1029/2010TC002814.

Authemayou, C., G. Brocard, C. Teyssier, B. Suski, B. Cosenza, S. Morán-Ical, C. W. González-Véliz, M. A. Aguilar-Hengstenberg, and K. Holliger (2012). Quaternary seismo-tectonic activity of the Polochic fault, Guatemala, *J. Geophys. Res.: Solid Earth* **117,** B07403, doi: 10.1029/2012JB009444.

Bao, H., L. Xu, L. Meng, J. P. Ampuero, and S. Ni (2022). Global frequency of oceanic and continental supershear earthquakes, *Nature Geosci.* **15,** 942–949, doi: 10.1038/s41561-022-01055-5.

Bartole, R., E. Lodolo, J. Obrist-Farner, and D. Morelli (2019). Sedimentary architecture, structural setting, and Late Cenozoic depocentre migration of an asymmetric transtensional basin: Lake Izabal, eastern Guatemala, *Tectonophysics* **750,** 419–433, doi: 10.1016/j.tecto.2018.12.004.

Benito, M. B., C. Lindholm, E. Camacho, Á. Climent, G. Marroquín, E. Molina, W. Rojas, J. J. Escobar, E. Talavera, G. E. Alvarado, and Y. Torres (2012). A new evaluation of seismic hazard for the Central America region, *Bull. Seismol. Soc. Am.* **102,** no. 2, 504–523, doi: 10.1785/0120110015.

Bonis, S., O. Bohnenberger, and G. Dengo (compilers) (1970). Mapa geológico de la República de Guatemala, First Ed.., Instituto Geográfico Nacional, Guatemala City, scale 1:500,000, 4 sheets (in Spanish).

Brocard, G., T. Adatte, O. Magand, H. R. Pfeifer, A. Bettini, F. Arnaud, F. S. Anselmetti, and S. Morán-Icál (2014). The recording of floods and earthquakes in Lake Chichój, Guatemala, during the twentieth century, *J. Paleolimnol.* **52,** 155–169, doi: 10.1007/s10933-014-9784-4.

Brocard, G., F. S. Anselmetti, and C. Teyssier (2016). Guatemala paleoseismicity: From Late Classic Maya collapse to recent fault creep, *Sci. Rep.* **6,** 36976, doi: 10.1038/srep36976.

Brueckner, H. K., H. G. Avé Lallemant, V. B. Sisson, G. E. Harlow, S. R. Hemming, U. Martens, T. Tsujimori, and S. S. Sorensen (2009). Metamorphic reworking of a high-pressure–low-temperature mélange along the Motagua fault, Guatemala: A record of Neocomian and Maastrichtian transpressional tectonics, *Earth Planet. Sci. Lett.* **284,** 228–235, doi: 10.1016/j.epsl.2009.04.032.

Bucknam, R. C., G. Plafker, and R. V. Sharp (1978). Fault movement (afterslip) following the Guatemala earthquake of February 4, 1976, *Geology* **6,** no. 3, 170–173, doi: 10.1130/0091-7613(1978)6<170:FMAFTG>2.0.CO;2.

Caccavale, M., M. Sacchi, E. Spiga, and S. Porfido (2019). The 1976 Guatemala earthquake: ESI scale and probabilistic/deterministic seismic hazard analysis approaches, *Geosciences* **9,** no. 9, 403, doi: 10.3390/geosciences9090403.

Calais, E., B. Delouis, J.-P. Ampuero, H. Bao, F. Courboulex, A. Deschamps, B. de Lépinay, T. Monfret, L. Meng, L. Xu, *et al.* (2025). The 28 January 2020, Mw 7.7, Cayman Trough/Oriente Fault supershear earthquake rupture, *Seismica* **4,** no. 2, doi: 10.26443/seismica.v4i2.1629.

Cheng, C., and D. Wang (2020). Imaging the rupture process of the 10 January 2018 Mw 7.5 Swan Island, Honduras, earthquake, *Earthq. Sci.* **33,** no. 4, 194–200, doi: 10.29382/eqs-2020-0194-03.

DeMets, C., P. E. Jansma, G. S. Mattioli, T. H. Dixon, F. Farina, R. Bilham, E. Calais, and P. Mann (2000). GPS geodetic constraints on Caribbean–North America plate motion, *Geophys. Res. Lett.* **27,** no. 3, 437–440, doi: 10.1029/1999GL005436.

Dewey, J. W., and B. R. Julian (1976). Main event source parameters from teleseismic data, in *The Guatemalan Earthquake of February 4, 1976: A Preliminary Report*, A. F. Espinosa (Editor), *U.S. Geol. Surv. Profess. Pap. 1002*, 14–19, U.S. Geological Survey, Reston, Virginia.

Dolan, J. F., R. J. Van Dissen, E. J. Rhodes, R. Zinke, A. E. Hatem, C. McGuire, R. M. Langridge, and J. R. Grenader (2024). One tune, many tempos: Faults trade off slip in time and space to accommodate relative plate motions, *Earth Planet. Sci. Lett.* **625,** 118484, doi: 10.1016/j.epsl.2023.118484.

Ellis, A., C. DeMets, R. McCaffrey, P. Briole, B. Cosenza Muralles, O. Flores, M. Guzmán-Speziale, D. Hernández, V. Kostoglodov, P. LaFemina, *et al.* (2019). GPS constraints on deformation in northern Central America from 1999 to 2017, part 2: Block rotations and fault slip rates, fault locking and distributed deformation, *Geophys. J. Int.* **218,** no. 2, 729–754, doi: 10.1093/gji/ggz173.

Espinosa, A. F. (Editor) (1976). *The Guatemalan Earthquake of February 4, 1976: A Preliminary Report, U.S. Geol. Surv. Profess. Pap. 1002*, U.S. Geological Survey, Reston, Virginia, 90 pp.

Espinosa, A. F., R. Husid, and A. Quesada(1976). Intensity distribution and source parameters from field observations, in The Guatemalan Earthquake of February 4, 1976, a Preliminary Report, *U.S. Geol. Surv. Profess. Pap. 1002*, 52–66.

Franco, A., C. Lasserre, H. Lyon-Caen, V. Kostoglodov, E. Molina, M. Guzmán-Speziale, D. Monterosso, V. Robles, C. Figueroa, W. Amaya, *et al.* (2012). Fault kinematics in northern Central America and coupling along the subduction interface of the Cocos Plate, from GPS data in Chiapas (Mexico), Guatemala, and El Salvador, *Geophys. J. Int.* **189,** no. 3, 1223–1236, doi: 10.1111/j.1365-246X.2012.05390.x.

Franco, A., E. Molina, H. Lyon-Caen, J. Vergne, T. Monfret, A. Nercessian, S. Cortez, O. Flores, D. Monterosso, and J. Requenna (2009). Seismicity and crustal structure of the Polochic–Motagua fault system area (Guatemala), *Seismol. Res. Lett.* **80,** no. 6, 977–984, doi: 10.1785/gssrl.80.6.977.

Fraser, J., K. Vanneste, and A. Hubert-Ferrari (2010). Recent behavior of the North Anatolian Fault: Insights from an integrated paleoseismological data set, *J. Geophys. Res.: Solid Earth* **115,** B09408, doi: 10.1029/2009JB006982.

Gamboa-Canté, C., M. Arroyo-Solórzano, B. Benito, J. Aguilar, I. G. Arroyo, E. Camacho-Astigarrabia, D. Castro, O. Flores, L. Linkimer, M. G. Marroquín, *et al.* (2024). Seismicity in Central America (1520–2020) and earthquake catalog compilation for seismic hazard assessments, *Bull. Earthq. Eng.* **22,** 7201–7234, doi: 10.1007/s10518-024-02059-9.

Gamboa-Canté, G. A., M. Arroyo-Solórzano, A. Rivas-Medina, and M. B. Benito (2025). Overview of seismic hazard studies in Central America: A comparative analysis of results, *J. South Am. Earth Sci.* **164,** 105630, doi: 10.1016/j.jsames.2025.105630.

Garnier, B., C. DeMets, M. Kaplan, L. Sánchez, D. León, L. Mixco, and A. Staller (2022). Deformation in western Guatemala associated with the NAFCA (North America–Central American Forearc–Caribbean) triple junction: Neotectonic strain localization into the Guatemala City graben, *Tectonics* **41,** no. 2, e2021TC006739, doi: 10.1029/2021TC006739.

Garnier, B., B. Tikoff, O. Flores, B. Jicha, C. DeMets, B. Cosenza-Muralles, D. Hernandez, G. Marroquin, L. Mixco, and W. Hernandez (2021). An integrated structural and GPS study of the Jalpatagua fault, southeastern Guatemala, *Geosphere* **17,** no. 1, 201–225, doi: 10.1130/GES02243.1.

González-Negreros, R., and J. M. Gaspar-Escribano (2025). Analysis of the Guatemalan earthquake catalog, *J. Seismol.* **29,** 565–583, doi: 10.1007/s10950-025-10293-0.

Graham, S. E., C. DeMets, E. Cabral-Cano, V. Kostoglodov, A. Walpersdorf, N. Cotte, M. Brudzinski, R. McCaffrey, and L. Salazar-Tlaczani (2012). GPS constraints on the Mw 7.3 2009 Swan Islands earthquake: Remote triggering and seismic hazard in Honduras, *Geophys. J. Int.* **190,** no. 2, 1329–1338, doi: 10.1111/j.1365-246X.2012.05556.x.

Guzmán-Speziale, M., and E. Molina (2022). Seismicity and seismically active faulting of Guatemala: A review, *J. South Am. Earth Sci.* **115,** 103740, doi: 10.1016/j.jsames.2022.103740.

Harlow, G. E., K. E. Flores, C. Martin, V. B. Sisson, and S. S. Sorensen (2025). Serpentinites of the Guatemala Suture Zone: Varieties, origin, and compositional modification, *Am. J. Sci.* **325,** Art. 4, doi: 10.2475/001c.129404.

Harp, E. L., R. C. Wilson, and G. F. Wieczorek (1981). *Landslides from the February 4, 1976, Guatemala Earthquake, U.S. Geol. Surv. Profess. Pap. 1204-A*, U.S. Geological Survey, Reston, Virginia, 35 pp.

Hayman, N. W., N. R. Grindlay, M. R. Perfit, P. Mann, S. Leroy, and B. Mercier de Lépinay (2011). Oceanic core complex development at the ultraslow spreading Mid-Cayman Spreading Center, *Geochem. Geophys. Geosys.* **12,** Q0AG02, doi: 10.1029/2010GC003240.

Howarth, J. D., U. A. Cochran, R. M. Langridge, K. Clark, S. J. Fitzsimons, K. Berryman, and D. T. Strong (2018). Past large earthquakes on the Alpine fault: Paleoseismological progress and future directions, *New Zeal. J. Geol. Geophys.* **61,** 309–328, doi: 10.1080/00288306.2018.1464658.

Husid, R., A. F. Espinosa, and A. Quesada (1976). Damage and engineering implications, in *The Guatemalan Earthquake of February 4, 1976: A Preliminary Report*, A. F. Espinosa (Editor), *U.S. Geol. Surv. Profess. Pap. 1002*, 67–79, U.S. Geological Survey, Reston, Virginia

Kanamori, H., and G. S. Stewart (1978). Seismological aspects of the Guatemala earthquake of February 4, 1976, *J. Geophys. Res.* **83,** no. B7, 3427–3434, doi: 10.1029/JB083iB07p03427.

Kikuchi, M., and H. Kanamori (1982). Inversion of complex body waves, *Bull. Seismol. Soc. Am.* **72,** no. 2, 491–506, doi: 10.1785/BSSA0720020491.

Kikuchi, M., and H. Kanamori (1991). Inversion of complex body waves—III, *Bull. Seismol. Soc. Am.* **81,** no. 6, 2335–2350, doi: 10.1785/BSSA0810062335.

Kusky, T. M., P. Mann, and J. Meng (2025). The February 8, 2025, Swan Islands (Caribbean Sea) earthquake: Lessons for geohazards on transform plate and microplate boundaries, *J. Earth Sci.* **36,** 852–855, doi: 10.1007/s12583-025-0176-7.

Langer, C. J., and G. A. Bollinger (1979). Secondary faulting near the terminus of a seismogenic strike-slip fault: Aftershocks of the 1976

Guatemala earthquake, *Bull. Seismol. Soc. Am.* **69,** no. 2, 427–444, doi: 10.1785/BSSA0690020427.

Langer, C. J., J. H. Whitcomb, and A. Q. Aburto (1976). Aftershocks from local data, in *The Guatemalan Earthquake of February 4, 1976: A Preliminary Report*, A. F. Espinosa (Editor), *U.S. Geol. Surv. Profess. Pap. 1002*, U.S. Geological Survey, Reston, Virginia, 26–37.

Lisowski, M., and W. Thatcher (1981). Geodetic determination of horizontal deformation associated with the Guatemala earthquake of 4 February 1976, *Bull. Seismol. Soc. Am.* **71,** no. 3, 845–856, doi: 10.1785/BSSA0710030845.

Lyon-Caen, H., E. Barrier, C. Lasserre, A. Franco, I. Arzu, L. Chiquin, M. Chiquin, T. Duquesnoy, O. Flores, O. Galicia, *et al.* (2006). Kinematics of the North American–Caribbean–Cocos plates in Central America from new GPS measurements across the Polochic–Motagua fault system, *Geophys. Res. Lett.* **33,** no. 19, doi: 10.1029/2006GL027694.

Marco, S., and Y. Klinger (2014). Review of on-fault paleoseismic studies along the Dead Sea Fault, in *Dead Sea Transform Fault System: Reviews*, Z. Garfunkel, Z. Ben-Avraham, and E. Kagan (Editors), Vol. 6, Springer, Dordrecht, The Netherlands, 183–205, doi: 10.1007/978-94-017-8872-4_7.

Matumoto, T., and G. V. Latham (1976). Aftershocks of the Guatemalan earthquake of February 4, 1976, *Geophys. Res. Lett.* **3,** no. 10, 599–602, doi: 10.1029/GL003i010p00599.

Maurer, J., A. Eckert, and Q. Sun (2025). Deformation and earthquake potential on the North America–Caribbean–Cocos triple junction in Guatemala, *ESS Open Archive*, 24 July 2025, doi: 10.22541/essoar.175336982.28467707/v1.

McEnaney, T., and G. Clark (2025). 1976 Motagua Earthquake georeferenced database (1.0.0) [Data set], *Zenodo* doi: 10.5281/zenodo.17674716.

McPhillips, D. (2022). Revised earthquake recurrence intervals in California, U.S.A.: New paleoseismic sites and application of event likelihoods, *Seismol. Res. Lett.* **93,** no. 6, 3009–3023, doi: 10.1785/0220220127.

Molnar, P., and L. R. Sykes (1969). Tectonics of the Caribbean and Middle America regions from focal mechanisms and seismicity, *Geol. Soc. Am. Bull.* **80,** no. 9, 1639–1684, doi: 10.1130/0016-7606(1969)80[1639:TOTCAM]2.0.CO;2.

Morley, S. (1918). The Guatemala earthquake of December, 1917 and January, 1918, *The Geograph. Rev.* **6,** 459–469.

Muehlberger, W. R., and A. W. Ritchie (1975). Caribbean–Americas plate boundary in Guatemala and southern Mexico as seen on Skylab IV orbital photography, *Geology* **3,** no. 5, 232–235, doi: 10.1130/0091-7613(1975)3.

Obrist-Farner, J., A. Eckert, P. M. J. Douglas, L. Perez, A. Correa-Metrio, B. L. Konecky, T. Bauersachs, S. Zimmerman, S. Scheidt, M. Brenner, *et al.* (2023). Planning for the Lake Izabal Basin Research Endeavor (LIBRE) continental scientific drilling project in eastern Guatemala, *Sci. Drill.* **32,** 85–95, doi: 10.5194/sd-32-85-2023.

Obrist-Farner, J., A. Eckert, M. Locmelis, J. L. Crowley, B. Mota-Vidaure, E. Lodolo, J. Rosenfeld, and E. Duarte (2020). The role of the Polochic Fault as part of the North American and Caribbean Plate boundary: Insights from the infill of the Lake Izabal Basin, *Basin Res.* **32,** no. 1, 73–92, doi: 10.1111/bre.12431.

Obrist-Farner, J., J. Maurer, D. Gibson, T. McEnaney, A. Eckert, W. F. Kenney, J. Beeson, N. Wattrus, Q. Stangeland, and F. Reyes (2025). Paleoseismic evidence of directivity for the 1976 Mw 7.5 Motagua earthquake, Guatemala, *Geology* **53,** no. 11, 971–976, doi: 10.1130/G53449.1.

Orihuela, B., I. Dallo, J. Clinton, W. Strauch, M. Protti, R. Yani, G. Marroquín, J. Sanchez, F. Vega, M. Marti, *et al.* (2023). Earthquake early warning in Central America: The societal perspective, *Int. J. Disast. Risk Reduc.* **97,** doi: 10.1016/j.ijdrr.2023.103982.

Orihuela, B., A. N. Papadopoulos, J. Clinton, G. Marroquin, M. Protti, W. Strauch, R. Yani-Quiyuch, L. Danciu, and S. Wiemer (2025). Impact assessment of earthquake early warning systems in Central America, *Earthq. Spectra* **41,** no. 4, 3094–3122, doi: 10.1177/87552930251342826.

Peraldo, G., and W. Montero (1999). Sismología histórica de América Central, Instituto Panamericano de Geografía e Historia, México, 346 pp. (in Spanish).

Peruzza, L., E. Esposito, F. E. Rodríguez García, R. A. García Castro, P. Santos, G. Marroquín, L. Mixco, L. Torres Bernhard, R. Torres, D. A. Hernandez, *et al.* (2021). MARCA-GEHN, a prototype macroseismic archive of four Central America countries, *Boll. Geof. Teor. Appl.* **62,** no. s2, 3–196.

Peruzza, L., E. Esposito, F. E. Rodríguez García, and G. Giunta (2023). *A Tool for Archiving and Updating Knowledge About Past Earthquakes in Central America*, IntechOpen, published 15 December 2023, doi: 10.5772/intechopen.1003080.

Person, W. J., W. Spence, and J. W. Dewey (1976). Main event and principal aftershocks from teleseismic data, in *The Guatemalan Earthquake of February 4, 1976: A Preliminary Report*, A. F. Espinosa (Editor), *U.S. Geol. Surv. Profess. Pap. 1002*, 1–13, U.S. Geological Survey, Reston, Virginia.

Plafker, G. (1976). Tectonic aspects of the Guatemala earthquake of 4 February 1976, *Science* **193,** no. 4259, 1201–1208, doi: 10.1126/science.193.4259.1201.

Plafker, G., M. G. Bonilla, and S. B. Bonis (1976). Geologic effects, in *The Guatemalan Earthquake of February 4, 1976: A Preliminary Report*, A. F. Espinosa (Editor), *U.S. Geol. Surv. Profess. Pap. 1002*, U.S. Geological Survey, Reston, Virginia, 38–51.

Rockwell, T. K., T. E. Dawson, J. Young Ben-Horin, and G. Seitz (2015). A 21-event, 4,000-year history of surface ruptures in the Anza seismic gap, San Jacinto Fault, and implications for long-term earthquake production on a major plate boundary fault, *Pure Appl. Geophys.* **172,** 1143–1165, doi: 10.1007/s00024-014-0955-z.

Rodriguez, M., C. DeMets, R. D. Rogers, C. Tenorio, D. Hernandez, P. Hernandez, E. Molina, and A. Correa-Metrio (2009). A GPS and modelling study of deformation in northern Central America, *Geophys. J. Int.* **178,** no. 3, 1733–1754, doi: 10.1111/j.1365-246X.2009.04251.x.

Scholz, C. H., M. Wyss, and S. W. Smith (1969). Seismic and aseismic slip on the San Andreas Fault, *J. Geophys. Res.* **74,** no. 8, 2049–2069, doi: 10.1029/JB074i008p02049.

Schwartz, D. P. (1976). Geology of the Zacapa Quadrangle and vicinity, Guatemala, Central America, *Ph.D. Thesis*, State University of New York, Binghamton, 191 pp.

Schwartz, D. P., L. S. Cluff, and T. W. Donnelly (1979). Quaternary faulting along the Caribbean–North America plate boundary in

Central America, *Tectonophysics* **52,** nos. 1/4, 431–445, doi: 10.1016/0040-1951(79)90258-0.

Seed, H. B., R. G. Ascoli, A. Gomez-Masso, C. K. Chan, and I. Arango (1981). Earthquake-induced liquefaction near Lake Amatitlán, Guatemala, *J. Geotech. Eng. Div.* **107,** no. 4, 501–518, doi: 10.1061/AJGEB6.0001122.

Somerville, P. G., N. F. Smith, R. W. Graves, and N. A. Abrahamson (1997). Modification of empirical strong ground motion attenuation relations to include the amplitude and duration effects of rupture directivity, *Seismol. Res. Lett.* **68,** no. 1, 199–222, doi: 10.1785/gssrl.68.1.199.

Spudich, P., and B. S. J. Chiou (2008). Directivity in NGA earthquake ground motions: Analysis using isochrone theory, *Earthq. Spectra* **24,** 279–298, doi: 10.1193/1.2928225.

Stein, R. S., A. A. Barka, and J. H. Dieterich (1997). Progressive failure on the North Anatolian fault since 1939 by earthquake stress triggering, *Geophys. J. Int.* **128,** no. 3, 594–604, doi: 10.1111/j.1365-246X.1997.tb05321.x.

Styron, R., and M. Pagani (2020). The GEM global active faults database, *Earthq. Spectra* **36,** no. 1 (suppl.), 160–180, doi: 10.1177/8755293020944182.

Thingbaijam, K. K. S., P. Martin Mai, and K. Goda (2017). New empirical earthquake source-scaling laws, *Bull. Seismol. Soc. Am.* **107,** 2225–2246, doi: 10.1785/0120170017.

U.S. Geological Survey (2025). U.S. Geological Survey Earthquake Catalog and ShakeMap Products, peak ground acceleration (PGA) and Modified Mercalli Intensity (MMI) contours for the 4 February 1976 Guatemala, 8 May 2009 Swan Islands, 10 January 2018 Swan Islands, and 12 March 2025 Swan Islands earthquakes, available at https://earthquake.usgs.gov (last accessed November 2025).

Utsu, T. (1961). A statistical study on the occurrence of aftershocks, *Geophys. Mag.* **30,** 521–605.

Wells, D. L., and K. J. Coppersmith. (1994). New empirical relationships among magnitude, rupture length, rupture width, rupture area, and surface displacement, *Bull. Seismol. Soc. Am.* **84,** no. 4, 974–1002, doi: 10.1785/BSSA0840040974.

White, R. A. (1984). Catalog of historic seismicity in the vicinity of the Chixoy–Polochic and Motagua faults, Guatemala, *U.S. Geol. Surv. Open-File Rept. 84-88,* doi: 10.3133/ofr8488.

White, R. A., and D. H. Harlow (1979). Preliminary catalog of aftershocks of the Guatemala earthquake of February 4, 1976, from the area between Guatemala City and Lake Atitlan, *U.S. Geol. Surv. Open-File Rept. 79-864,* doi: 10.3133/ofr79864.

White, R. A., and D. H. Harlow (1993). Destructive upper-crustal earthquakes of Central America since 1900, *Bull. Seismol. Soc. Am.* **83,** no. 4, 1115–1142, doi: 10.1785/BSSA0830041115.

Yani-Quiyuch, R., L. Asturias, and D. Castro (2023). The rupture plane of the February 2022 Mw 6.2 Guatemala, intermediate depth earthquake, *Seismica* **2,** no. 2, doi: 10.26443/seismica.v2i2.691.

Young, C. J., T. Lay, and C. S. Lynnes (1989). Rupture of the 4 February 1976 Guatemalan earthquake, *Bull. Seismol. Soc. Am.* **79,** no. 3, 670–689, doi: 10.1785/BSSA0790030670.

Manuscript received 1 December 2025
Published online 17 February 2026

Calibration of Pressure Sensors for Ocean-Bottom Seismology

Spahr C. Webb*[1], Hatsuki Yamauchi[1], Theodore A. Koczynski[1], Walter Masterson[1], and Peter Liljegren[1]

ABSTRACT

Three types of pressure sensors are used for seismic and oceanographic observations in seafloor instruments: the hydrophone, the differential pressure gauge (DPG), and the high sampling rate absolute pressure gauge (APG). There has not been a good way to accurately calibrate these sensors across the entire frequency range of importance to seismologists (5 mHz to 200 Hz). We constructed a system to introduce time-varying pressure signals into a pressure test chamber to accurately calibrate each sensor at seafloor pressures. The gain decreased by more than 40% and the capacitance of the Hitech HTI-U-90 hydrophone by 25% with depth from 0 to 5000 m effecting the response. The DPG gain increases linearly with log frequency by 3% per decade from 0.1 mHz to about 10 Hz due to the viscoelastic deformation of the o-rings in the overpressure relief valves. The DPG gain changes with temperature and pressure. The time constant for the DPG high-pass capillary leak mechanical filter increases with depth (pressure) and decreases with temperature, increasing from about 100 s at 10 m and 20°C to about 300 s at 5000 m and 2°C. Future work will be required to determine the upper frequency limit of the response of the DPG. Our results show good results to 125 Hz, and suggest the DPG could fully replace hydrophones for many seismic observations at the seafloor. The APG has a simple, stable response ideal for observing large dynamic range signals, but the APG inlet piping acts as a low-pass filter with a corner frequency that may depend on pressure and temperature.

KEY POINTS

- The capacitance of the hydrophone falls by 25%, and the long-period gain decreases by 40% from 0 to 5000 m.
- Differential pressure gauge gain increases 15% from 1 mHz to 10 Hz, and the high-pass corner changes with temperature and pressure.
- Absolute pressure gauges have a stable response, but the inlet tubing acts as a single-pole low-pass filter.

INTRODUCTION

Three types of pressure sensors are used for acoustic and oceanographic observations in fleets of seafloor instruments throughout the world today: the hydrophone, the differential pressure gauge (DPG), and the high sampling rate absolute pressure gauge (APG). The latter two sensors extend the useful range of observations to much lower frequencies than can be obtained with standard hydrophones. The APG sensor, based on the Paroscientific Co. pressure sensor, is known to provide well-calibrated measurements (0.01% of range) of absolute pressure at very low frequency. But here we have extended the frequency range of calibration to frequencies above 50 Hz. At these higher frequencies, the calibration of the sensor was only inferred from the assumed basic principles.

An accurate knowledge of the frequency response of these sensors is essential to obtaining good seismic and acoustic observations, but there has not been a good way to accurately calibrate the response of any of these sensors across the entire frequency range of importance to seismologists. The mechanical and electrical complexity of these sensors suggests the responses inferred from basic principles might not reflect a correct understanding of the operation of these sensors. The long-period response of the DPG is established by the capillary leak mechanical filter within the sensor. The time constant of the filter is determined by the viscosity and compressibility of the silicone oil within the sensor, which both depend on pressure and temperature. Other components, such as the overpressure relief valves and the transducer properties, could lead to resonances and losses affecting the frequency response and gain of the DPG.

Propagation of acoustic signals through piping is a complicated problem with a possible transition in frequency response from a behavior related to the variations in the distensibility

1. Lamont-Doherty Earth Observatory, Columbia University, Palisades, New York, U.S.A., https://orcid.org/0000-0002-7277-174X (SCW); https://orcid.org/0000-0002-8585-9708 (HY); https://orcid.org/0000-0002-1849-9554 (TAK)

*Corresponding author: scw@ldeo.columbia.edu

Cite this article as Webb, S. C., H. Yamauchi, T. A. Koczynski, W. Masterson, and P. Liljegren (2026). Calibration of Pressure Sensors for Ocean-Bottom Seismology, *Bull. Seismol. Soc. Am.* **116**, 860–883, doi: 10.1785/0120250278

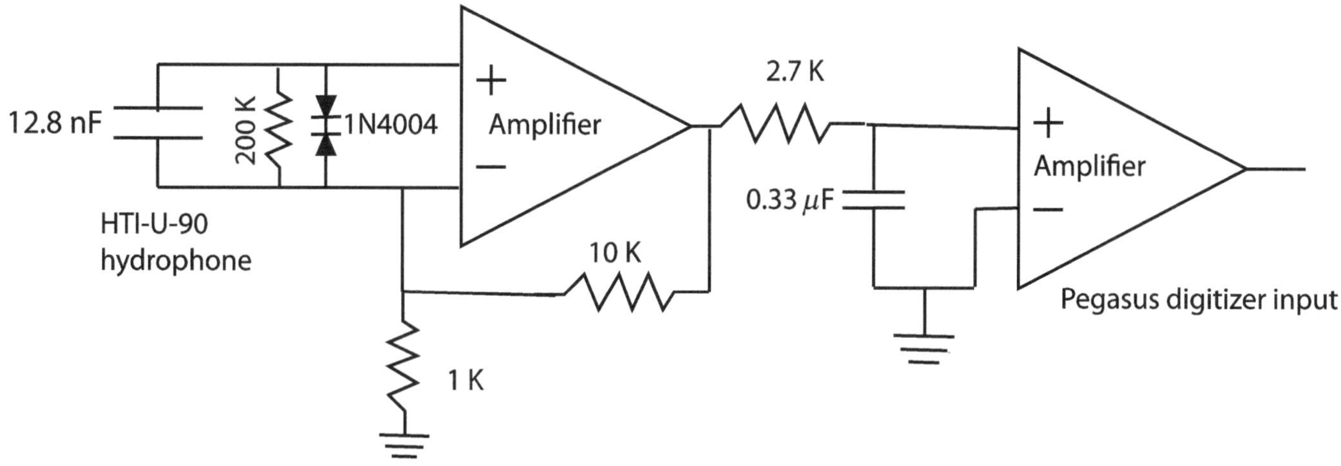

Figure 1. Schematic of the hydrophone circuit. The shunting resistor is the 200 KΩ resistor.

and cross-section of tubing feeding the sensors to a behavior related to fluid viscosity (Lighthill, 1979). This problem is important to understanding both the APG and the DPG responses. The role of the mechanics of the pressure transducer components (particularly the Bourdon tube) in the APG sensor frequency response was unknown, although the manufacturer believes resonances are unlikely below 200 Hz (J. Paros, personal comm., 2017).

The responses of both the DPG and the hydrophone depend on the electronics used to drive the sensors and amplify the response. There has been a history of inaccurate responses for instruments deployed for ocean floor seismology, particularly for the DPG (see discussion in Doran and Laske, 2019). The DPG originally required a complex amplifier system to provide optimum sensitivity for systems limited to 16-bit digitizers (Cox *et al.*, 1984). For the observations shown here, we have used the simplest possible electronics so that the mechanical responses of the sensors could be accurately quantified. With the nearly universal deployment of 24-bit digitizers within ocean-bottom seismometer (OBS) fleets, simple circuits such as those shown later are all that are required to obtain good broadband seismic data from DPG sensors.

To accurately determine the frequency response of these three kinds of pressure sensors, we have constructed a system to introduce time-varying pressure signals into a pressurized test chamber to accurately calibrate each sensor against the others over a range of pressures from 930 m depth to 3732 m depth. By intercomparison of the different sensors, accurate responses of the sensors have been determined over a frequency range from below 5 mHz to above 100 Hz (DPG and hydrophone) or 50 Hz (APG). The consistency of the results allows extrapolation of the responses over pressures ranging from the equivalent of the near surface to full ocean depth (>5000 m) and over temperatures ranging from 0°C to 20°C.

HYDROPHONE

The Hitech HTI-90-U ceramic hydrophone is widely used in OBS fleets worldwide. These are often purchased with a preamplifier system, which includes a passband filter, but for these measurements, we obtained hydrophones without any preamplifier to allow us to determine the electromechanical characteristics of the hydrophone. The hydrophone is a sealed piezoelectric ceramic cylinder filled with air. It produces a voltage that varies with pressure variations. It is always necessary to place a shunting resistor across the outputs of a hydrophone to remove the large signals at low frequency associated with temperature changes (Fig. 1). At low frequencies, the characteristics of the hydrophone should be completely determined by the value of the shunting resistor, the capacitance of the hydrophone, and a single coefficient describing the voltage output associated with a change in pressure. The manufacturer provided specifications for these hydrophones are −198 db rel 1μ Pa/V gain and a hydrophone capacitance of 12.8 nF. We constructed a simple amplifier to provide an adequately large signal to the Nanometrics Pegasus loggers used to digitize the signal. This amplifier has a flat response at frequencies below a corner set by a single-pole antialiasing filter (Fig. 2). The complete response of the hydrophone system should then be determined by the amplifier gain and two poles, a high-pass filter pole (3 dB corner near 62 Hz) set by the capacitance of the hydrophone and the shunting resistor and the single-pole antialiasing filter in the amplifier (3 dB corner near 179 Hz). The hydrophone amplifier was powered by two small batteries, allowing the ground of the hydrophone system to float with respect to the ground for the Pegasus logger. This allowed us to connect the ground of the amplifier board to the negative side of the Pegasus digitizer differential preamplifier and the amplifier output to the positive side (Fig. 1). The Pegasus logger also applies a sharp digital antialiasing filter near the Nyquist frequency. We did not correct for this filter because it was limited to frequencies above those of interest. The Pegasus loggers were programmed to digitize at

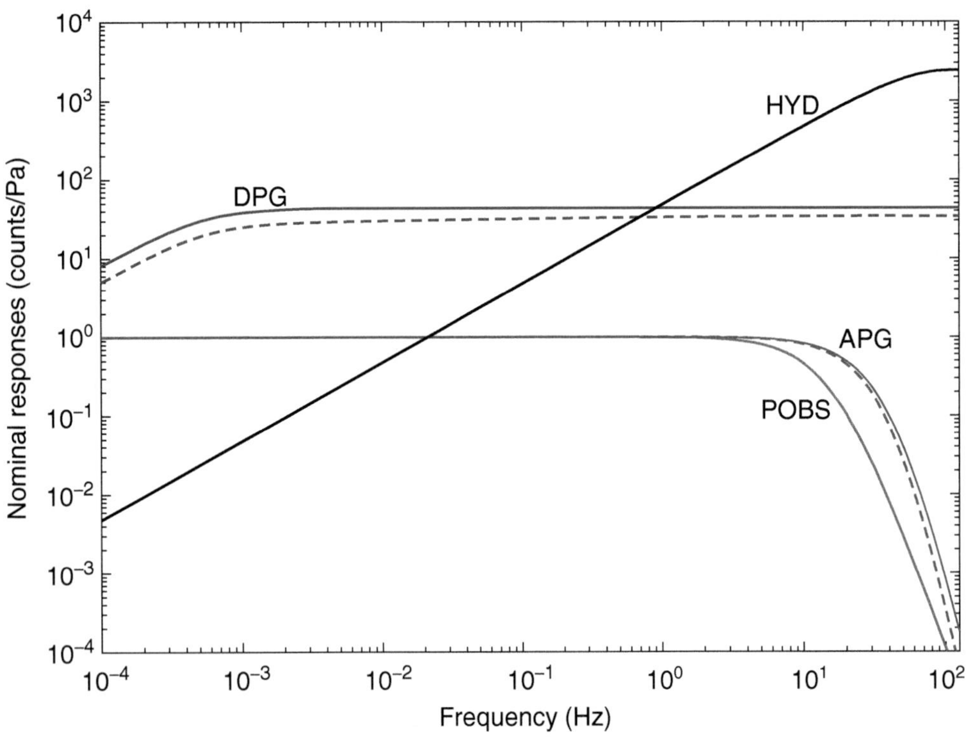

Figure 2. Nominal responses of the hydrophone (black), absolute pressure gauge (APG) without and with inlet response effect (red and red dashed), POBS (magenta), and differential pressure gauge (DPG) without and with valve effect (blue and blue dashed). The Pegasus digitizer antialiasing filter is not included in the responses shown. The color version of this figure is available only in the electronic edition.

250 Hz. The noise floor of the hydrophone system is set by the noise characteristics of the preamplifier system, the size of the shunting resistor, and the gain of the hydrophone. The noise floor of a hydrophone system such as this with an appropriate amplifier is expected to be below typical seafloor noise levels at high frequencies, but signal levels fall toward low frequencies due to the high-pass filter, which limits the usefulness of most hydrophones at frequencies significantly below the microseism peak (0.1 Hz), although large, high-gain hydrophones can produce useful data at periods longer than 100 s period (e.g., Barstow *et al.*, 1989). The noise floor at low frequencies is usually determined by the noise floor of the amplifier.

DPG

The DPG was developed to measure pressure fluctuations at frequencies below those easily accessible with standard hydrophones. DPGs have been widely adapted into the world's OBS fleets. Most groups use DPGs little changed from the mechanical characteristics as described in the original article by Cox *et al.* (1984). The DPG consists of a closed rigid chamber within an enveloping case, both of which are filled with silicon oil of specified viscosity (typically 500 cS). A soft diaphragm on the enveloping case communicates seafloor pressure into the sensor. The difference between the pressure in the interior chamber and the surrounding jacket is measured using a differential pressure sensor installed through the chamber wall. A small tube ("a capillary leak") through the chamber wall allows the pressure to equilibrate between the chamber and the outside despite oil volume changes due to temperature variations (which would change the pressure in the chamber), allowing the differential sensor in the sensor to be very sensitive and of limited dynamic range (typically ±6.9 kPa or ±34 kPa), and so small compared with seafloor pressures. The small diameter of the capillary tube makes it act as a high-pass single-pole filter with a time constant determined by the viscosity and compressibility of the silicone oil flowing through the tube, the diameter and length of the tube, and the volume of the chamber. The tube acts like a resistor, and the volume acts as an equivalent capacitance. The expected response of the DPG is therefore flat in frequency above the corner frequency associated with the capillary leak (Fig. 2).

Overpressure relief valves are installed through the wall of the interior chamber that open when the pressure difference between the interior chamber and outside pressure exceeds some value (typically 21 or 28 kPa) to protect the delicate differential pressure sensors from damage due to rapidly changing pressures during deployment and recovery. It is assumed the valves close tightly while the sensors are on the seafloor. We tested the performance of these valves by driving large sinusoidal pressure signals, while the DPGs were installed within the pressure chamber. Figure 3 shows the valves appearing to open and close tightly near the rated pressures for the valves, although there is clear evidence of hysteresis for opening. The valves appear to close tightly when driven by pressure sinusoids, small compared with the rated opening pressure.

Electronically, the differential pressure sensor in the DPG consists of four piezoresistors in a Wheatstone bridge configuration mounted on a thin diaphragm (Mallon *et al.*, 1990). Additional resistors in series or parallel with some of the piezoresistors act to reduce the sensitivity of the system to temperature and to adjust the gain. The sensor is designed with an operating pressure of only 7 kPa, but has proven to provide useful data in the DPG to at least 60 MPa. A few DPGs have also been constructed using higher range sensors (30 or

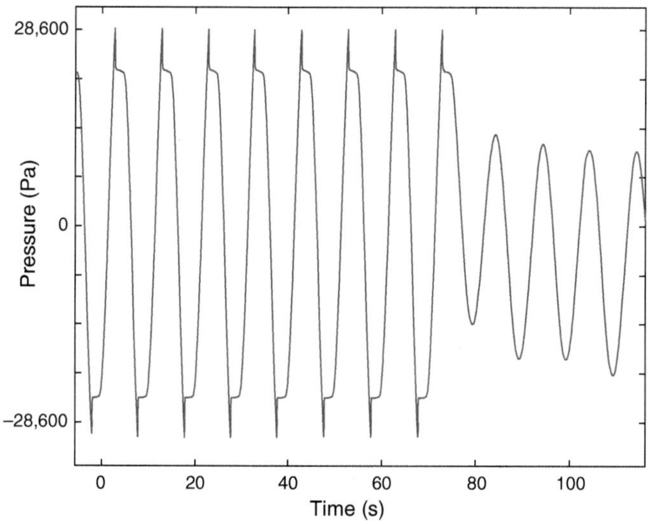

Figure 3. Output of the DPG versus time in seconds during a step decrease in amplitude of an applied sinusoidal pressure signal within the pressure facility, showing the overpressure relief valves opening with obvious hysteresis at pressures exceeding the rated pressure and closing fully when the sine wave is smaller in amplitude. Approximate scale for pressure shown. The color version of this figure is available only in the electronic edition.

90 kPa) with less sensitivity and therefore higher noise levels. DPG noise levels are determined by $1/f$ voltage noise associated with currents in the Wheatstone bridge resistors. Because seafloor pressures are far outside the design range, the gain of these sensors at seafloor pressures is uncertain. The voltage across the bridge varies because the diaphragm is strained by pressure differences across the diaphragm. The sensor typically shows significant offsets even at zero pressure differential. The DPG was developed during an era when only 16-bit digitizers were available. The limited dynamic range of these systems led to the use of amplifier systems for the DPGs, which included a preamplifier stage, then a second AC-coupled amplifier stage (Cox *et al.*, 1984). The electronics used with the DPG sensors have varied over time and between OBS fleets. There has been an unfortunate history of DPG electronics being incorrectly described within OBS fleet documentation. Modern 24-bit digitizers, such as the Pegasus logger, have sufficient dynamic range such that no preamplifier system is needed. Our standard DPG electronics now consists of only a 5 V regulator supplied by a battery. The outputs of the DPG sensor go directly into the differential preamplifier inputs of the Pegasus logger (Fig. 4). The ground of the battery is not connected to the Pegasus ground, such that the DPG system ground floats with respect to the digitizer. This allows the DPG to use the entire dynamic range of the differential pressure sensor.

The expected mechanical frequency response of the DPG systems is described by Cox *et al.* (1984). The manufacturer's specifications for the differential pressure sensor used within

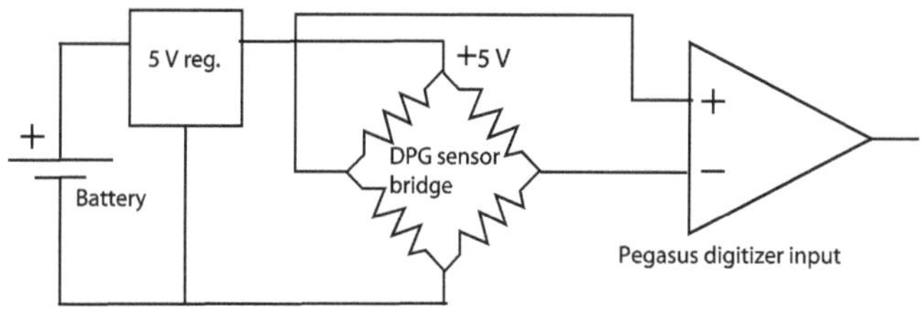

Figure 4. Schematic of the circuit for the DPG used during these tests.

the gauge suggest a factor of three variation is possible in gain between sensors of the same rated pressure range. The effective gain of the system at high frequency depends on sensor gain, but also on losses due to the relative compliances of the sensor, the silicone oil within the chamber, and the compliance of the seals within the overpressure relief valves. The other component of the response is the high-pass filter set by the capillary leak. Cox *et al.* (1984) expected the time constant of this filter to vary strongly with the temperature of the oil, and less strongly with variations in the compressibility of the oil with pressure and temperature. Cox *et al.* (1984), predicted about a factor of two longer time constant for the capillary leak at seafloor temperatures (3°C) compared with room temperature (20°C). There could also be variations in gain due to the compliance of the seals with both temperature and pressure.

The DPG has proven difficult to calibrate in the laboratory. Temperature variations in the laboratory can lead to large pressure changes in the interior chamber because the oil contracts and expands. This can make accurately determining the time constant of the capillary leak difficult. Most efforts to calibrate the DPG have involved installing the sensor within a closed chamber in air at near 1 atm pressure. A problem with calibration at atmospheric pressure is that DPG can have minute air bubbles within the interior chamber (which greatly changes the effective compressibility of the interior oil) or within the capillary tube (which greatly affects the measured capillary leak time constant). To overcome some of these issues, Sasagawa *et al.* (2019) built a system to calibrate the capillary time constant and gain of the DPGs at pressures comparable to seafloor pressures and low temperatures. They observed changes in the time constant with temperature that agreed roughly with the predictions of Cox *et al.* (1984). They also suggested there was a small (5%) dependence of the gain on temperature.

The difficulty in knowing the effective gain of the DPG sensor at seafloor pressure and temperatures led to the development of in situ methods to calibrate the sensor by comparing seafloor records of earthquake arrivals observed by DPGs against data from a colocated broadband seismometer using the expected ratio between pressure and vertical acceleration in long-period Rayleigh waves (Zha and Webb, 2016). Deng *et al.* (2022) have extended this method over a broader frequency range.

The effective frequency response of sound and pressure pulses propagating through compliant narrow tubes was studied by Lighthill (1979). It is not immediately evident that the assumptions that the propagation of pressure variations through the capillary tube in the DPG should be only dependent on viscosity, as described in Cox *et al.* (1984) because the article assumes a fully developed Poiseuille flow through the tube. This requires that sufficient fluid flow through the tubes over long enough times that a complete boundary layer can develop on the walls of the tube. We will show later that this may not be the case for the APG system inlet tube, but to anticipate the results shown here, it appears true for the DPG. The pressure changes due to the tides and resultant fluid flow are likely large enough to ensure a boundary layer flow is always established within the capillary tube. The fluid flow due to sound propagating through the tube at higher frequencies is added to an established flow field and thus well characterized by the Poiseuille flow physics.

The calibration effort described here seeks to examine whether the mechanical characteristics as described in Cox *et al.* (1984) are indeed correct, or whether there are unmodeled characteristics such as resonances of the overpressure relief valves or the capillary tube. We also use observations at the seafloor obtained simultaneously with an APG and a DPG to calibrate the long-period capillary time constant at seafloor pressure and temperatures.

APG

APGs built by Paroscientific Co. have been used for decades for observations of ocean currents, tsunamis, ocean mesoscale eddies, and other oceanographic signals (e.g., Watts *et al.*, 2001) and have recently been used for geodetic purposes (e.g., Ito *et al.*, 2011; Wallace *et al.*, 2016; Chadwick *et al.*, 2022; Woods *et al.*, 2022, 2024). As noted before, the Paroscientific gauge is known to provide well-calibrated pressure data (0.01%) at low frequencies. However, a new method for digitizing ("a new counting method") was required before the sensors could provide sufficient resolution and a high enough sampling rate to be useful for seafloor seismological observations (Webb and Nooner, 2016).

APGs with a 125 Hz sampling rate were installed in many of the OBSs first deployed for the Cascadia Initiative community seismic experiment offshore Oregon and Washington in 2014 (Toomey *et al.*, 2014). This was the first experiment to deploy OBSs in the very shallow water of the continental shelf. The shallow water instruments used large heavy metal covers ("shields") to protect the instruments from damage from trawling, but more importantly, the covers shielded the instruments from ocean floor current, enabling observations that would not otherwise have been possible due to shaking of the seismic sensors by the current (e.g., Webb and Barclay, 2023). APGs were used because it was anticipated that the signal levels from long-period ocean waves would cause the DPG sensors to clip in shallow water, and because the APGs were expected to provide more accurately calibrated long-period responses than could be obtained with the DPGs. The APGs also provided temperature and long-period pressure data that were used for studies of turbidity currents (Johnson *et al.*, 2017) and infragravity waves (e.g., Neale *et al.*, 2015; Smit *et al.*, 2018) and short-period ocean waves (Peureux and Ardhuin, 2016). The Cascadia data have proven crucial to planning experiments that have used APGs for offshore observations of slow-slip events near the trench (e.g., Wallace *et al.*, 2016; Woods *et al.*, 2022) by providing a better understanding of the long-period oceanographic signals that limit observation of vertical uplift associated with slow-slip events or SSEs (e.g., Fredricksen *et al.*, 2019).

A version of the high sampling rate APG has been incorporated into nodes of an underwater communication cable system to be deployed by 2027. The CAM "SMART" cable system will be deployed between Portugal, the Azores, and the Canary Islands.

Noise levels for APGs in the seismic band are typically significantly higher (and above background noise levels) compared with DPG data, which is a limitation for seismic observations, but the advantage of the APG is its large dynamic range (full ocean depth), much larger than any possible oceanographic or seismic signal. This is important for observations in subduction zones in which large nearby seismic events (e.g., Tréhu *et al.*, 2020) can cause standard seismic sensors to clip.

Kubota *et al.* (2021) showed how the ground displacement in the source region of the 2011 Tohoku earthquake could be determined using the dynamic pressure observed by seafloor pressure gauges much more quickly than using observations of the tsunami wave. They estimated ground velocities at the seafloor exceeding 40 cm/s peak to peak and pressure variations associated with the ground displacement exceeding 0.2 MPa peak to peak. Only strong motion seismic sensors or these pressure sensors can observe these signals without clipping.

A recent development that has greatly improved the usefulness of APG data for geodetic (e.g., Woods *et al.*, 2022) and oceanographic observations is the "A-0-A" method to remove long-period drift from APG data (Wilcock *et al.*, 2021), reducing drift to the sub cm/yr level. APGs with A-0-A drift corrections should greatly improve the utility of pressure sensors for long-term observations of ocean currents and seafloor vertical uplift.

PRESSURE FACILITY PRESSURE GAUGE CALIBRATION SYSTEM

We developed a method to introduce controllable, time-varying pressure signals into a pressurized pressure facility vessel to compare the responses of the different sensors across all frequencies of relevance to seismology. We used a "pressure intensifier" to rapidly inject and remove small amounts of fluid from the sealed pressure facility vessel that is pressurized to seafloor pressures, thereby changing the pressure within the pressure facility. The pressure intensifier is a piston that is driven back and forth by hydraulic pressure, controlled by a

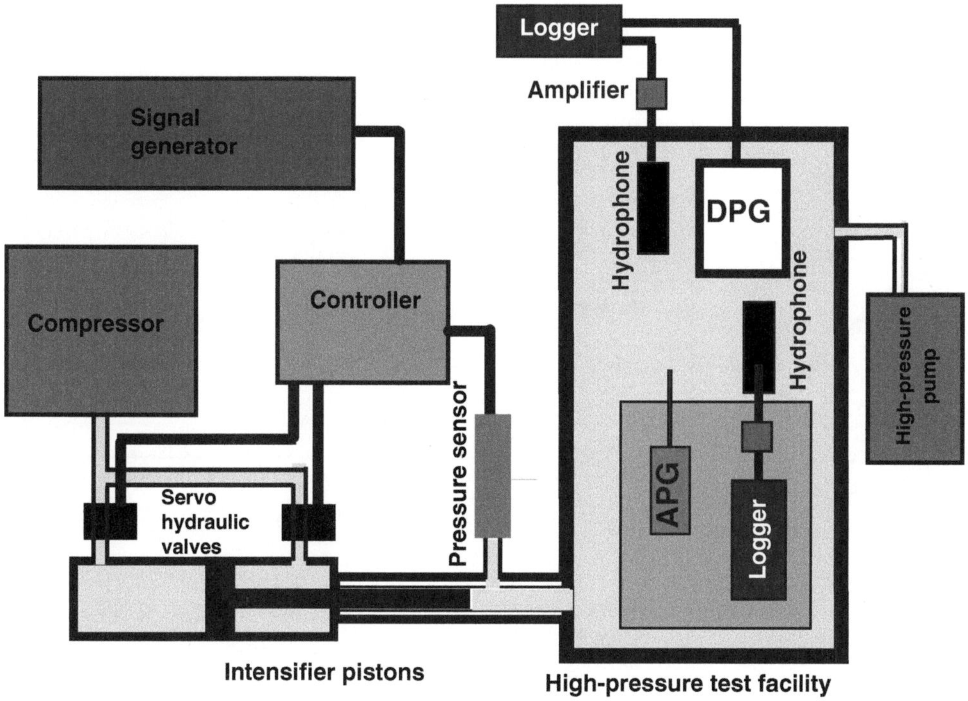

Figure 5. Cartoon of the sensors (DPG, APG, and two hydrophones) within the pressure facility test rig, the pressure intensifier system, and the location of Pegasus loggers. The color version of this figure is available only in the electronic edition.

set of electromechanical valves. The piston drives a much smaller piston to introduce fluid into and out of the pressure vessel to produce time-varying pressure signals. The amplitude of the highest frequency signals for this calibration system is limited by the rate at which fluid can be driven in and out of the pressure vessel and by the speed of the hydraulic valves controlling the intensifier (Fig. 5). The pressure facility is a converted Mark 13 shell with nominal dimensions of about 23 cm ID and 120 cm length. The attainable change in pressure in the facility in the system depends on the stroke volume of the pressure intensifier piston divided by the volume of the pressure facility divided by the adiabatic compressibility of the water/oil mix in the facility.

We first used a digital signal generator that could produce a sine wave that swept through a band of frequencies to control the intensifier hydraulics. During operation, we used a series of sweeps to fill in a broad frequency range. Our analysis of these data showed the digital signal generator produced discrete frequencies, and thus invariably left small "nulls" in the frequency spectrum of the pressure signals. Because frequency transfer functions are essentially ratios of two spectra, the nulls in the spectrum lead to small "tears" in the response function in data from sensors with differing signal-to-noise ratios (SNRs) due to spectral leakage between adjacent frequencies filling in the nulls. We solved this problem by replacing the precise digital signal generator with an analog signal generator. The frequency of this was adjusted using a small motor to slowly turn the dial of the signal generator, allowing sweeps over decadal frequency bands. A switch was repositioned by decades during a series of up and down sweeps in bands from 0.005–0.056 Hz to 5–56 Hz. The switching between decades does produce some small jumps in the transfer function due to broadband spectral bias effects, but otherwise, we have obtained stable, accurate response functions over a broad frequency range.

We installed one Pegasus data logger into a small (21.5 cm OD × 41 cm) pressure case, which was then installed into the pressure test facility chamber. This logger was used to record data from a hydrophone installed externally to this pressure case but within the pressure test vessel. A second system within this same pressure case was used to record the data from an APG also installed within this pressure case. A stainless steel tube through the end cap of the pressure case communicated the pressure in the test facility chamber into the APG. A second Pegasus logger was installed externally to the pressure facility to record the signals from a second hydrophone and from a DPG installed within the pressure chamber (Fig. 5).

In some tests, we installed a different pressure case into the pressure facility that contained a "POBSs" sensor. The POBS system includes two APG sensors sampled at 40 Hz and is equipped with the A-0-A drift removal system. The much more extensive plumbing associated with the POBS system compared with the standard APG system affects the high-frequency response of these APG sensors, as shown later.

The internal Pegasus logging system was an OBS-type Pegasus logger with time maintained using a Seascan Co. temperature-compensated crystal oscillator with a drift rate of order 1 ms/day, whereas the external Pegasus logger used Global Navigation Satellite System-based timing with an absolute time accuracy of 1 μs. The APG logger and POBS instrument each used separate Seascan clocks for timing.

INTERCALIBRATION OF TWO HYDROPHONES

An intercalibration of two Hitech HTI-90-U hydrophones using time-varying pressure signals generated within the closed pressurized pressure facility provides a good illustration of the obtainable accuracy in determining the relative frequency

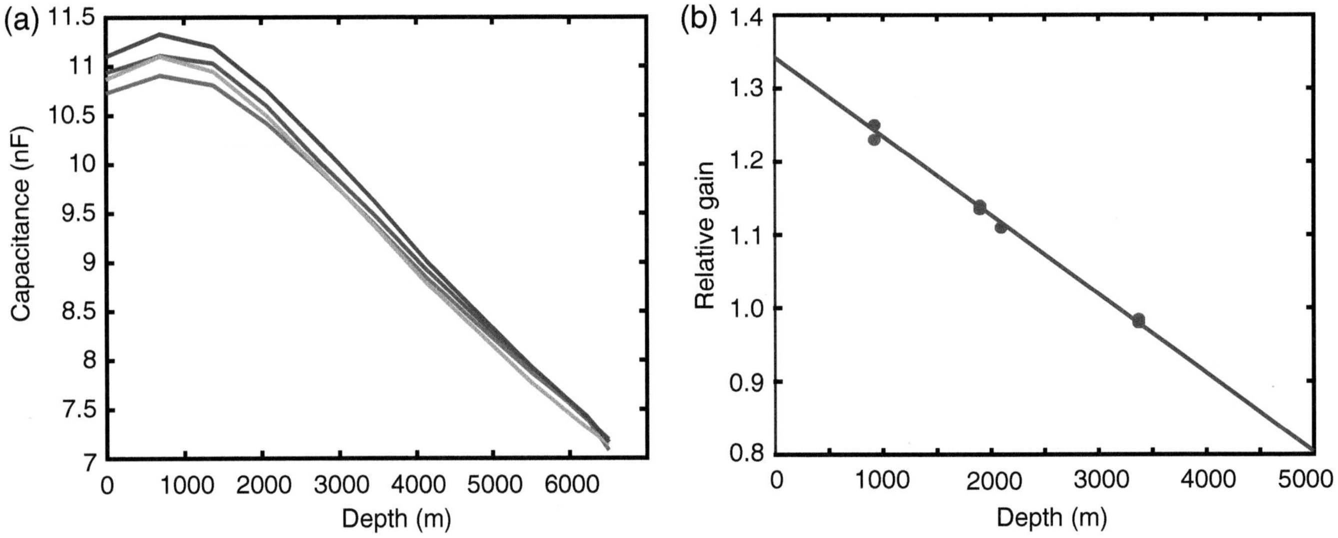

Figure 6. (a) Measured capacitance of five HTI-U-90 hydrophones (shown as different color lines) as a function of pressure, expressed as depth. (b) Gain correction as a function of depth required to fit the measured hydrophone gains to APG determined signal levels at long period for the two hydrophones used during the tests. Data points from the two hydrophones are red and blue circles with a line fit shown. The color version of this figure is available only in the electronic edition.

response of two sensors. The hydrophones were logged after amplification by two separate Nanometrics Pegasus logging systems, one internal and one external to the pressure test facility vessel (Fig. 5). Because component values varied slightly from the nominal values shown in the amplifier schematic shown in Figure 1, the measured values were used in predicting sensor response for each hydrophone. It is always necessary to shunt a hydrophone with a resistor to attenuate large signals associated with changing temperature. The hydrophone acts as a capacitor, such that the response always includes a high-pass single-pole filter that has a corner frequency that depends on the shunting resistor and the capacitance of the hydrophone. Measurements within the pressure facility showed the capacitance of the hydrophones decreases nearly 25% as the pressure increases from 1 atm to the pressure equivalent of 5000 m depth (about 50 MPa, Fig. 6a). The corner frequency of the hydrophone response thus will shift toward higher frequency with increasing depth. Comparisons of the long-period signal level with the APG data (see subsequently) showed the sensitivity (V/Pa) of the hydrophone also fell with increasing pressure by about 40% (Fig. 6b). The gain at long period for hydrophones at frequencies below the filter corner is proportional to the product of the sensitivity and the capacitance thus the total effective gain at long period decreases about 55% as the depth increases from 0 to 5000 m (Fig. 6b). It seems likely that any similarly constructed long-period hydrophone will experience similar changes in the high-pass corner frequency and sensitivity with increasing pressure.

The recorded data from both hydrophone sensors were analyzed using the Welch spectral method. The data were divided into a series of segments. The mean was removed from each segment, and the data were multiplied by either a 4 pi or pi prolate window to minimize broadband spectral leakage (Thomson, 1977). A Fourier transform was then applied to each segment and used to generate spectra and cross-spectra by averaging the results from all the data segments. On some data, a winnowing program automatically deleted a small number of segments with large offsets ("glitches"), mostly associated with stick-slip behavior of the intensifier. The 4pi prolate window provides very high rejection of broadband spectral bias (i.e., leakage between spectral bands) and was critical to obtaining the correct response in parts of the spectrum with rapidly varying energy levels. A pi prolate window was used for some analyses for which a higher frequency resolution was required. For a few data sets, we applied a first difference algorithm to both data sets to reduce the dynamic range of the spectrum to further reduce broadband spectral bias (leakage). This was helpful for data with a large dynamic range. Because the first difference algorithm was applied to both datasets, it should not affect measurements of the relative response.

The relationship of the Fourier transformed sensor output signal $X(f)$ to the Fourier transform of the pressure signal $P(f)$ within the pressure facility is assumed to be related by the complex response function $R(f)$ in the frequency domain with an amplitude in units of Pa/count describing the gain and a complex phase describing the phase shift:

$$P(f) = R(f)X(f). \quad (1)$$

Thus,

$$X(f) = \frac{P(f)}{R(f)} + N(f), \quad (2)$$

in which here we account for the possible noise in the measurements $N(f)$.

We seek to compare measurements of pressure determined by two different sensors to test the estimated response functions:

$$X_1(f) = \frac{P(f)}{R_1(f)} + N_1(f), \tag{3}$$

$$X_2(f) = \frac{P(f)}{R_2(f)} + N_2(f). \tag{4}$$

If we assume that sensor 2 is noise-free, then:

$$X_1(f) = \frac{X_2(f)R_2(f)}{R_1(f)} + N_1(f). \tag{5}$$

We estimate the transfer function $T_{12}(f)$ between X_1 and X_2 by taking the cross product of the two signals in the frequency domain and dividing by the autospectrum of X_2 in which $\langle\rangle$ is the ensemble average of estimates of the spectra.

$$\langle X_2^*(f)X_1(f)\rangle = \frac{R_2(f)}{R_1(f)}\langle X_2^*(f)X_2(f)\rangle + \langle X_2^*(f)N_1(f)\rangle. \tag{6}$$

The second term averages to zero because we assume that the noise in the first sensor is uncorrelated with the second. The transfer function between sensors 1 and 2 is then:

$$T_{12}(f) = \frac{R_2(f)}{R_1(f)} = \frac{\langle X_2^*(f)X_1(f)\rangle}{\langle X_2^*(f)X_2(f)\rangle} = \frac{C_{12}(f)}{S_{22}(f)}, \tag{7}$$

in which C_{12} is the cross spectrum between sensors 1 and 2 and S_{22} is the power or autospectrum of sensor 2. If instead we assume that sensor 1 is noise free rather than sensor 2 we obtain the transfer function:

$$T_{21}(f) = \frac{R_1(f)}{R_2(f)} = \frac{\langle X_1^*(f)X_2(f)\rangle}{\langle X_1^*(f)X_1(f)\rangle}. \tag{8}$$

Providing a second estimate of the ratio of the two response functions:

$$\frac{R_2(f)}{R_1(f)} = \frac{1}{T_{21}(f)} = \frac{S_{11}(f)}{C_{21}(f)}. \tag{9}$$

Both of these estimates of the response are viable; one chooses which one to employ depending on which sensor in the tests is likely to have a better SNR. For this pairing of two hydrophones, the two systems should have identical performance and SNR. We compare both estimates in the figures subsequently. There is bias in the response estimates for signals with less than perfect coherence; the bias is primarily associated with noise in the power spectra, so the two estimates usually have opposite directions of bias for coherences near 1. The difference between the two estimates provides an estimate of the quality of the response estimates.

To better display differences between sensor responses, we normalize each sensor spectrum by dividing the nominal responses expected from theory based on the mechanics and electronics of the sensor $R_{n1}(f)$ and $R_{n2}(f)$:

$$T_{12}^c(f) = \frac{\frac{R_2(f)}{R_{n2}(f)}}{\frac{R_1(f)}{R_{n1}(f)}} = \frac{C_{12}(f)R_{n1}(f)}{S_{22}(f)R_{n2}(f)}, \tag{10}$$

in which now the corrected transfer function $T_{12}^c(f)$ should have an amplitude of 1 and phase of 0° if both nominal responses are correct. Any deviations from an amplitude of one and zero phase imply there are errors in one or both of the two responses. In most cases, we have reasons to believe one or the other sensor is more likely to be correct, at least in some frequency bands. For example, we expect the absolute pressure gauges to provide accurate estimates of pressure at long period. We expect the hydrophone response to be accurate to within a gain factor across most of its frequency band. The differential pressure gauge is assumed to have an uncertain gain and phase at all frequencies.

The coherence squared γ^2 is defined as

$$\gamma^2(f) = \frac{C_{12}^*(f)C_{12}(f)}{[S_{11}(f)S_{22}(f)]}, \tag{11}$$

and is the fraction of the signal energy from sensor 1 that is correlated with sensor 2. If sensor 2 is assumed to be noise-free, it can be shown that the fraction of signal energy in sensor 1 that can be attributed to noise is then

$$1 - \gamma^2(f) = \frac{\langle N_1^*(f)N_1(f)\rangle}{\langle S_1^*(f)S_1(f)\rangle} = \frac{N_{11}(f)}{S_{11}(f)}. \tag{12}$$

A comparison of two (nominally) identical hydrophones provides a good test of our ability to determine the relative response functions between two sensors. We do apply two slightly different nominal response corrections in determining $T_{12}^c(f)$ and $T_{21}^c(f)$ because the responses of the two hydrophones are expected to be slightly different due to small differences in amplifier components from those in the schematic shown in Figure 1. We used the measured values for all the components. The responses have a depth-dependent correction applied to the gain and hydrophone capacitances compared with the manufacturer's specifications, as shown in Figure 6.

The time-varying pressure signals as measured by the two hydrophones (without correcting for the responses) during a series of sweeps are shown in Figure 7a,c. The two time series nearly precisely overlap, and both traces can only be seen in the expanded view in Figure 7c. For these data, the pressure vessel is pressurized to 190 MPa (or 1989 m depth). The variations in amplitude during the sweep series are due to variations in the hydrophone response with frequency, variations in the amplitude of sweeps, and a falling pressure intensifier signal toward

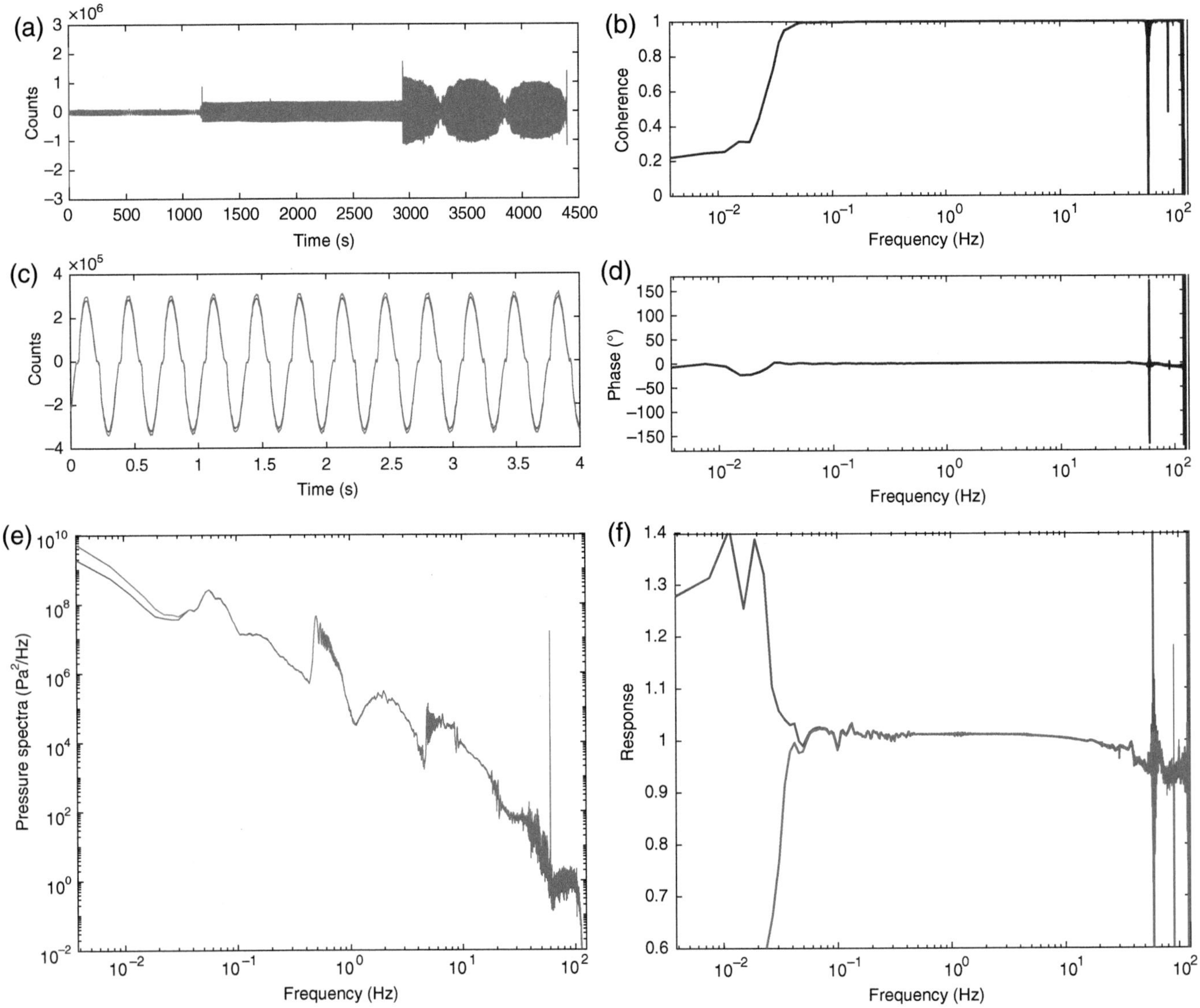

Figure 7. (a) Output signals from two hydrophones during a series of sweeps during a test. The two signals overlap. (c) Same as panel (a), but with an expanded view to show both signals. (e) Spectra of same, (b) coherence squared between the two signals, and (d) phase in degrees between the two signals as a function of frequency. (f) Response function between the two signals, assuming either signal 1 (red curve) or signal 2 (blue curve) is noise-free. Spectral estimates correspond to 250 degrees of freedom. The color version of this figure is available only in the electronic edition.

high frequency because of the finite tubing size into the pressure chamber and the finite speed of the hydraulic valves. A filter with a stop band between 58 and 62 Hz has been applied to the Figure 7a,c data to remove power line noise (60 Hz) in the data from the system with the Pegasus logger and amplifier external to the pressure vessel (Fig. 5). This line is absent in data from the hydrophone system entirely within the pressure facility because the metal tank effectively filters the power line noise. This filter is not applied to the frequency domain measurements (Fig. 7b,d–f).

Figure 7e shows power spectra of these data series after applying the nominal responses for the two sensors (R_{n1} and R_{n2}). The spectra nearly precisely overlap except at frequencies lower than the frequencies of the lowest frequency sweep (Fig. 7e). The abrupt changes in spectral amplitude with frequency are associated with changes in amplitude between sweeps. A large line at 60 Hz is apparent in the one spectrum from the external Pegasus logger, as mentioned earlier. The pressure intensifier system puts out enough signal to calibrate the hydrophones up to frequencies just below the Nyquist frequency of 125 Hz. The sharp drop in spectral level above 100 Hz is associated with the antialiasing filter in the Pegasus digitizer, which has not been corrected for in the spectra shown. Interpreting these data as power spectra allows us to estimate the effective noise floor for the sensors. We do not put formal error estimates on the response functions in this article because it is clear that deviations due to broadband bias effects (spectral leakage) dominate the errors in the response functions rather than random error.

The coherence squared (Fig. 7b) between the two sensors exceeds 0.995 above 0.03 Hz except near 60, 90, and 120 Hz (due to power line noise interference). The pressure intensifier system can provide a sufficient signal to much lower frequencies; the coherence falls toward very low frequencies in Figure 7b because the energy in the signal generator sweeps is mostly limited to frequencies above 0.03 Hz in this particular record. Later figures show coherence between hydrophones and other sensors to frequencies below 0.005 Hz.

The two measured relative response function (T^c_{12} and $1/T^c_{21}$) are shown in Figure 7f. These two response estimates mirror each other around a value near 1 except at high and very low frequencies, showing we have nearly fully accounted for the response of both sensors. To estimate the response functions to an accuracy of 1%, it is necessary to have a coherence squared between the two data sets exceeding 0.99 because any fraction of noise in the estimate of the power spectra leads to a bias error in the response by a similar amount. The relative response functions deviate from 1 at the highest frequencies by up to 5%, likely due to small inaccuracies in the values of components on the amplifier boards.

The phase response between the two hydrophone time series is shown in Figure 7d. It is close to 0° at low frequencies; the small negative deviation in phase toward higher frequencies is likely associated with a small timing error (<0.1 ms) between the two time series. The two hydrophones were recorded by two different Pegasus loggers, one synced to the GNSS timing, the other running on an internal Seascan temperature-compensated quartz crystal clock. Larger differences in timing (up to several milliseconds) are seen in other data runs, consistent with the typical drifts of Seascan clocks over a day or so.

INTERCALIBRATION OF AN APG AND A HYDROPHONE

Intercalibration of the APG and the hydrophones enables the absolute gain of the hydrophones at long periods to be determined as a function of pressure because the APG output is calibrated to a precision of 0.01% of the sensor range by Paroscientific Co. The design of the gauge suggests that any resonances and other frequency dependence should be limited to frequencies well above 1 Hz. The manufacturer states any resonances of the Bourdon tubes within the gauge should occur above 200 Hz (J. Paros, personal comm., 2017).

An infinite response filter (IIR) low-pass filter is used in the APG high-resolution counting scheme (Webb and Nooner, 2016). The low-pass multipole IIR filter corner depends on the operating frequency of the quartz crystal oscillator in the gauge that is measuring the strain in the Bourdon tube used to determine pressure. The corner frequency thus depends on the operating pressure of the gauge and varies by about 15% over the range of the gauge. The calibration signals only cause relatively small changes in the operating pressure, so can we use the mean quartz crystal operating frequency during the measurements to determine the IIR filter response when correcting the APG response.

The frequency response of the hydrophones at low frequencies is expected to depend only on the amplifier response and the single-pole high-pass filter corner set by the capacitance of the hydrophone and the parallel resistor (Fig. 1). Any resonances of these hydrophones are expected to occur at frequencies far above those considered here. The manufacturer provides documentation suggesting a frequency-independent output to at least 2 kHz, other than that determined by the shunting resistor and capacitance of the hydrophone.

To calibrate the hydrophone's absolute gain, we used the relative response of the hydrophone and APG near 1 Hz to determine the gain of the hydrophone. The coherence between the APG and hydrophone is consistently high near 1 Hz in the various pressure runs. Figure 8 shows an example from one set of measurements of our current standard APG compared with a hydrophone. Many runs with the pressure intensifier on the pressure facility were used to construct the results shown in Figure 6b, determining the variation in gain of the hydrophones versus pressure. All runs were done at temperatures between 19°C and 20°C. The capacitance decreases 3% from 21°C to 2°C at atmospheric pressure, but otherwise we did not investigate whether the gain of the hydrophones was temperature dependent. The capacitance for each gauge measured versus depth (Fig. 6a) was used to correct the nominal response of the hydrophones—this is important for getting the relative phase between the APG and hydrophone correct. Figure 6 shows the gain of the two hydrophones versus depth can be fit by the same line after correcting for slightly different capacitance. We use the depth-corrected gains for the hydrophones in the rest of the measurements shown here.

The spectra of the injected pressure signal observed with the APG and with a hydrophone are shown in Figure 8a. The APG spectrum deviates upward from the hydrophone spectrum at frequencies above 20 Hz, due to "counting noise" (see Webb and Nooner, 2016). We were not able to inject a large enough pressure signal into the pressure facility at a short period to overwhelm the counting noise at higher frequencies. At very long period, the noise in the amplifier circuit causes the hydrophone spectrum to deviate upward from the APG spectrum. The coherence squared between the signals observed on the APG and by the hydrophone (Fig. 8b) is otherwise high (above 0.95) from 0.05 to 10 Hz. The averaging in this estimate corresponds to 250 degrees of freedom.

The ratio of the relative corrected response between the hydrophone and APG (Fig. 8c) deviates from 1 above 10 Hz (red curve) unless we include a single-pole filter with a corner frequency near 45 Hz in the response for the APG (blue curve). We believe this filter is due to a mechanical filter set by the tubing and the extensibility of the Bourdon tube, as discussed subsequently. The phase of the response is also consistent with this model of the high-frequency response for the APG. The relative response for this run (after correcting for the nominal

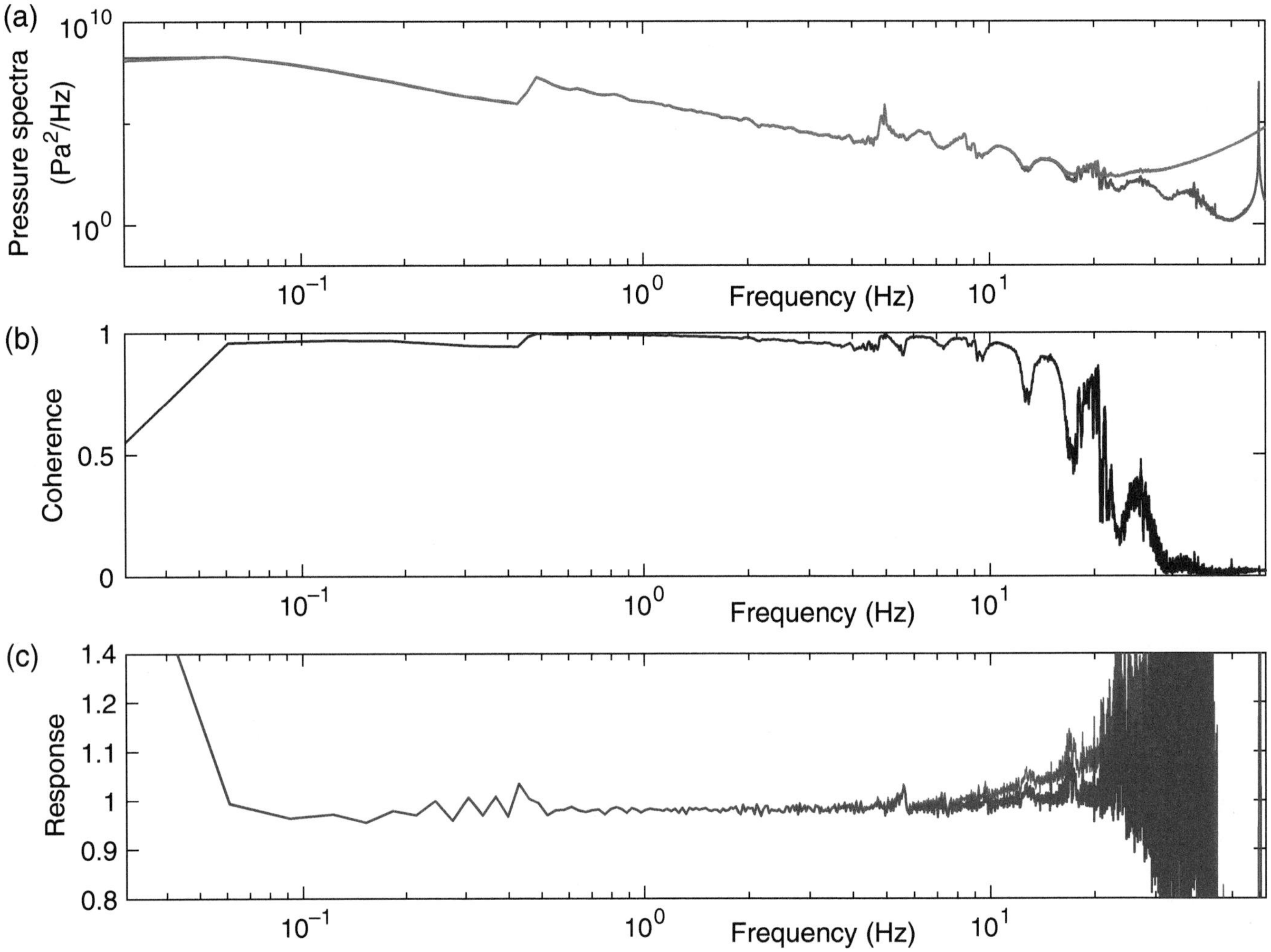

Figure 8. (a) Gain-corrected pressure spectra from a hydrophone (blue curve) and an APG (red curve) during a sweep test. (b) Coherence squared between the two signals. (c) Nominal relative response between the APG and the hydrophone with (blue curve) and without correction (red curve) for the low-pass pole associated with the inlet tubing. The color version of this figure is available only in the electronic edition.

response) estimated for both sensors is equal to 1 to within 1% across most of this band, but deviates by as much as 3% at low frequency and in some bands in which the coherence falls due to limited signal (Fig. 8c). We have used the gain factor curves for the hydrophones shown in Figure 6b, to correct the absolute gain of the hydrophone.

In our current version of the APGs, the pressure signal into the Paroscientific gauge is introduced through the endcap of the pressure case through a stainless steel tube of 1.588 mm internal diameter. Lighthill (1979) describes the propagation of acoustic signals through tubing of varying compliance and dimensions. In the limit in which viscosity is irrelevant, a thin tube terminated by a tube of larger area or a more extensible tube can produce a response that acts like a single-pole low-pass filter even when this section of tubing is compact (short compared with a wavelength). The corner frequency of the low-pass filter is proportional to the length of the narrow section of tubing and to the ratio of the impedances and areas of the two sections. We hypothesize that the Bourdon tube in the Paroscientific sensor acts as a larger (or more extensible) section of tube because it terminates the inlet tube. The corner frequency is expected to depend only on the relative acoustic impedances of the two sections and should thus be mostly independent of temperature and pressure, although the sound speed of the silicon oil changes significantly with pressure and depth (Bradley, 1963). Earlier versions of the APG sensor, including the APGs deployed during the Alaska Amphibious Community Seismic Experiment (Barcheck *et al.*, 2020) and Cascadia Initiative (Toomey *et al.*, 2014) deployments, used smaller diameter polyether ether ketone (PEEK) tubing (0.508 mm internal diameter) for the inlet tubing. The tubing was made larger in our most recent implementation because there was some evidence that high-frequency signals were being attenuated in propagation through the tubing. Our results here show that the tubing does act as a single-pole low-pass filter, limiting the signal level at high frequencies. Viscous effects can also attenuate sound signals in the tubing (Lighthill, 1979). In a newer instrument, the "POBSs" with more extensive tubing, the viscous effects appear to dominate, as shown subsequently.

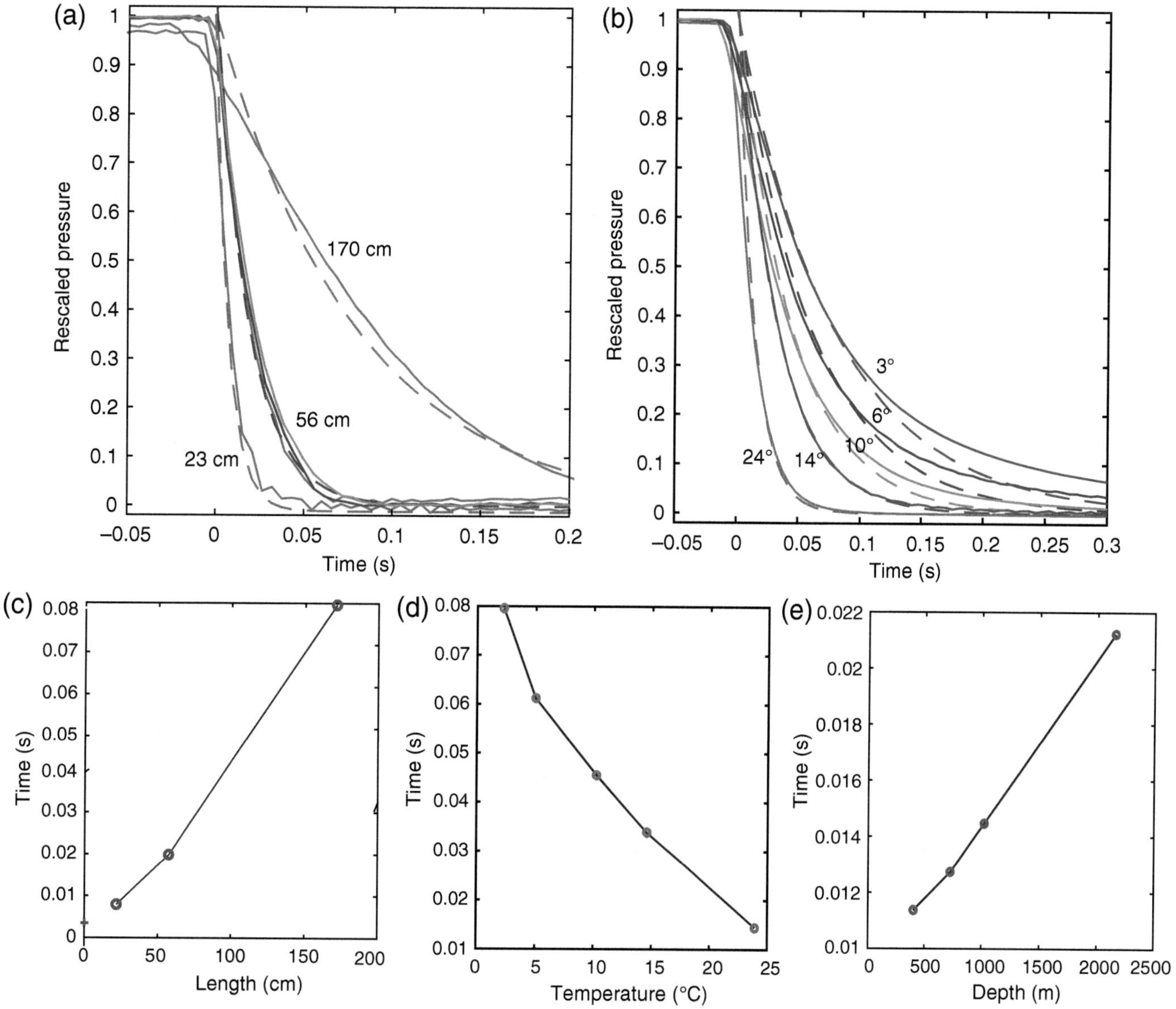

Figure 9. (a) Decay of pressure signal observed by an APG following abrupt release of pressure for three lengths of inlet tubing (solid lines) and exponential fit (dashed lines). The middle set of curves ranges in temperature from 2°C to 25°C, other curves are at about 20°C. (b) Decay of pressure signal observed by a POBS instrument at five temperatures (solid lines) and fits (dashed lines). (c) Plot of time constant versus length of inlet tube in cm (circles). The result for the large inlet tube of our current APG system is shown by the cross symbol. (d) POBs Time constant fits versus temperature. (e) POBS time constant versus pressure in depth. The color version of this figure is available only in the electronic edition.

To further investigate the inlet tubing acting as a low-pass filter, a series of tests was conducted in which the inlet was pressurized to a pressure of 800 kPa using compressed air, with a valve that could be used to abruptly drop the pressure. A different logging system was used that allowed sampling of the APG pressure signal at 180 Hz to better determine the time constant of the system. Measurements with inlet tubing of three different lengths of 0.508 ID PEEK tubing show the exponential time constant of decay increases linearly with the length of the tubing (Fig. 9a,c). The corner frequency of the low-pass filter is related to the time constant τ as $f_c = \frac{1}{2\pi\tau}$. We conducted measurements at multiple temperatures and found no dependence of the time constant on temperature (Fig. 9a). This rules out viscous effects as a control on the corner frequency because the viscosity of the oil used in the tubing is expected to more than double between 21°C and 2°C.

The details of the inlet tubing for APGs have varied some through the several deployments since the first Cascadia Imitative deployments in 2011 (Toomey *et al.*, 2014), but the PEEK tubing length was typically less than 30 cm, suggesting a time constant of less than 0.012 s corresponding to a filter low-pass corner frequency above 13 Hz for the APGs during these deployments (Fig. 9c). This filter thus likely had minor, or no effect on any seismological observations made using this sensor.

We also measured the response of our newer instrument called a “POBS” (pressure OBS), which so far has been used mostly in a series of geodetic experiments offshore of New Zealand tracking slow-slip events on the subduction interface

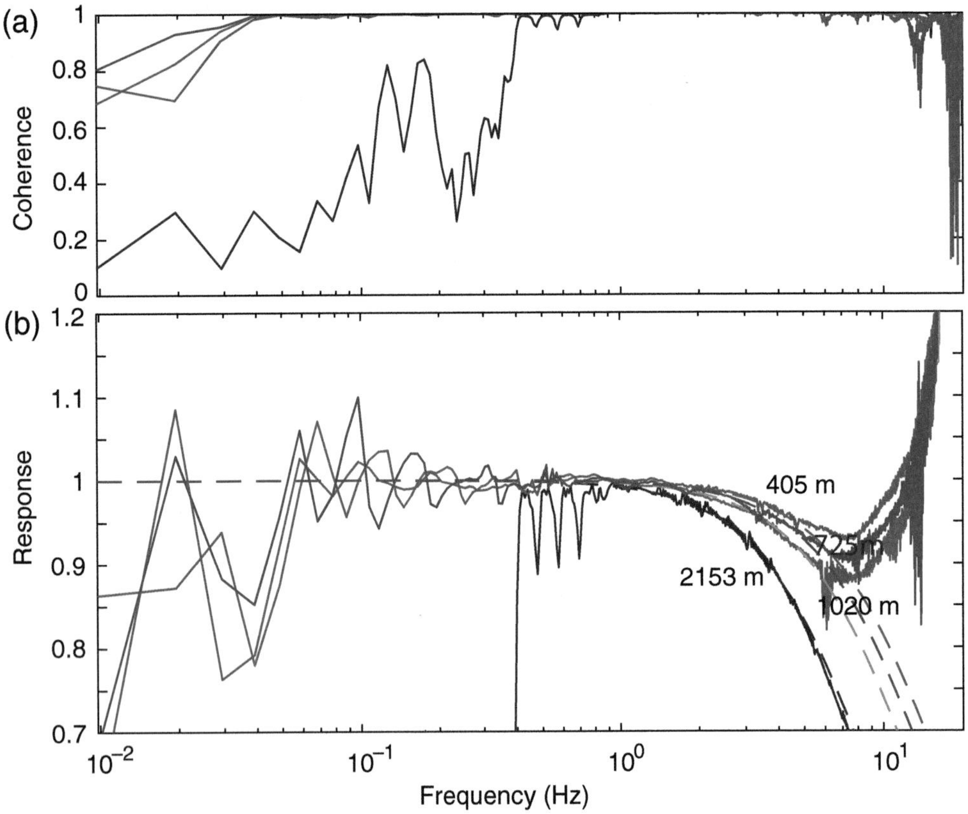

Figure 10. (a) Coherence squared between POBS instrument and the hydrophone at four pressures (405 m: red, 725 m: blue, 1020 m: green, and 2153 m: black), (b) Relative response of POBs instrument to a hydrophone at the four pressures (solid lines). Single-pole filter fit to decay at high frequency with time constants, as shown in Figure 9e (dashed lines). The color version of this figure is available only in the electronic edition.

(Wallace *et al.*, 2016; Woods *et al.*, 2022, 2024). These instruments differ from the standard APG by having a pair of Paroscientific pressure gauges connected together with the inlet plumbing coming through a hydraulic valve implementing a "A-0-A" system for correcting the sensors for drift in absolute gain (e.g., Wilcock *et al.*, 2021). The instrument is built around the Paroscientific Co. instrument called "seismic and ocean sensors or SOS." The POBS sensor has long sections of tubing with an ID of 0.794 mm, and the tubing bifurcates to feed two APG sensors. Unlike measurements on the standard APG system (Fig. 9a), the time constant following a sudden pressure drop depends strongly on temperature, suggesting that in this system, the low-pass filter corner is mostly controlled by viscosity (Fig. 9b,d).

The POBS system has a sampling frequency of 40 Hz, so our frequency-domain measurements are limited to below the Nyquist frequency of 20 Hz. For the POBS response measurement, the POBS pressure case replaced the pressure case with the Pegasus logger originally installed in the pressure facility (Fig. 5). The hydrophone data were only recorded using the externally installed Pegasus logger. A series of measurements of the frequency response of the POBS system against a hydrophone shows the corner frequency of the inlet tubing low-pass filter varies with pressure decreasing from about 14 Hz at 400 m depth to about 7 Hz at 2000 m compared with the 45 Hz observed for our standard APG (Fig. 10). The pressure dependence of the corner frequency (Fig. 9e) is likely a consequence of the pressure dependence of the viscosity of the silicon oil sensor in the sensor tubing (Dow Corning FS-1236 with nominal 300 cs viscosity). The pressure dependence of viscosity for silicon oil tends to be exponential with a coefficient that depends on temperature and the type of oil. Yasutomi *et al.* (1984) suggest an exponential coefficient for the viscosity of silicone oils at 0°C of 30 GPa^{-1} such that the viscosity at a depth of 2000 m (about 20 MPa) will be about a factor of exp(0.6) or 1.8 times larger than the value at 0 m. This value for the coefficient seems to fit the data (Figs. 9e and 10b). We are unable to completely assess whether the apparent filter seen in Figure 10b is well modeled as a single-pole filter. The reason for the deviation at frequencies above 10 Hz is unclear; errors in the correction for the IIR filter gain or hydrophone gain calibration are possibilities, or it could be due to bias associated with lower coherence at higher frequencies (Fig. 10a).

A comparison of the relative responses of the two APGs in the same POBS instrument shows that the responses of the two gauges are extremely similar (Fig. 11c). The coherence squared exceeds 0.99 from the lowest frequency to the Nyquist frequency of 20 Hz. This high coherence (Fig. 11a) is likely partly artificial because the noise in the sensor's logging system may be correlated and thus correlations between sensors recorded by separate logging systems might show less coherence above 5 Hz (in which counting noise becomes important, Webb and Nooner, 2016). The relative response is near 1 across the entire band of the measurements, diverging slightly above 5 Hz. This may be a consequence of slightly different corner frequencies of the antialiasing filters. The similar small divergence in relative phase (Fig. 11b) at short period likely has the same origin.

INTERCALIBRATIONS OF A DPG WITH A HYDROPHONE OR APG

The DPG has been in extensive use in OBS fleets for several decades now. The Novasensor Co. differential sensor within

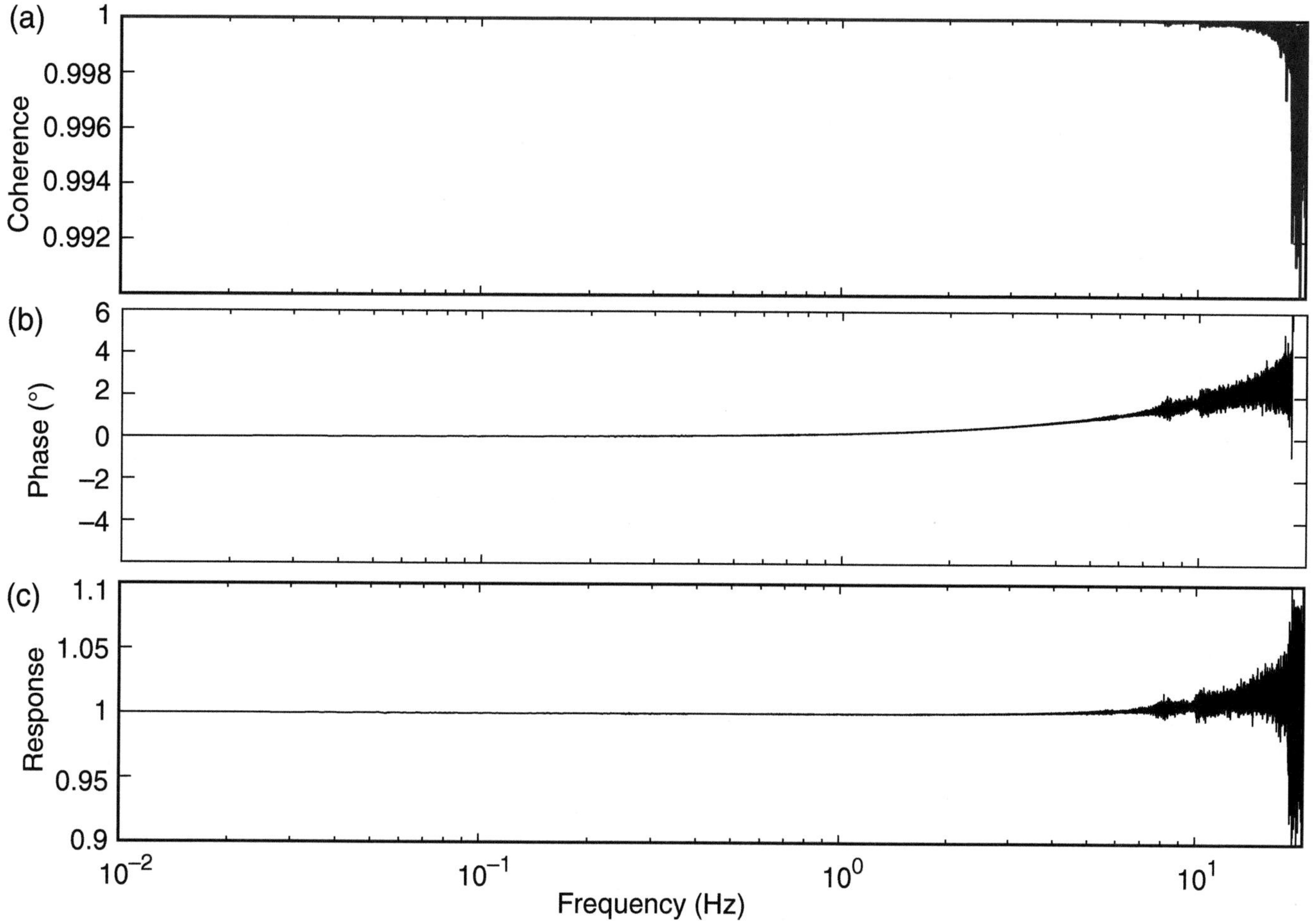

Figure 11. (a) Coherence squared between two pressure sensors within one POBS instrument, (b) relative phase between the two pressure sensors, and (c) relative response between the two pressure sensors. Panels (a) and (b) have the same horizontal axis as (c).

the gauge was expected to have a flat frequency response. Measurements of the relative response of a DPG sensor with a hydrophone (Fig. 12b) or with an APG (Fig. 13b) reveal that the response of the DPG is not constant in frequency, but the gain appears to increase by about 15% from 0.001 to 10 Hz. The rate of increase appears to be roughly constant on a semilogarithmic plot, increasing by about 3% per decade in frequency.

In the next section, we show that the changing gain for the DPG with frequency can be associated with the overpressure relief valves. A small phase retardation (about 2°) at low frequencies is also associated with viscoelastic damping due to the o-rings in these valves (Fig. 12d).

The nominal response curves in Figures 12b and 13b assume the gain of the DPG is equal to the gain of the Novasensor part inside the DPG of 75 mV output for a 7 kPa signal, but the manufacturer states gains from 50 to 150 mV at 7 kPa are all within specification. These relative response curves use the 75 mV value and the Pegasus logger digitization counts/V to correct the response. We conducted measurements at a range of pressures from 930 to 3732 m. The nominal response curves of the DPG with respect to the APG maintain a similar frequency dependence but shift in amplitude with pressure (Fig. 14). The responses show small jogs near 0.5 and 5 Hz associated with changes between sweep ranges of the signal generator due to broadband spectral bias near jumps in signal level. The nominal relative gain between the DPG and APG near 1 Hz increases from about 0.67 to 0.72 as pressure increases from the equivalent of 930–3373 m (depth). The next section shows that the frequency dependence of the gain of the DPG is associated with the overpressure relief valves. We also infer that the absolute gain of the differential pressure sensor within the DPG must increase with pressure (and thus depth).

The DPG/hydrophone relative response data are well constrained up to the Nyquist frequency of 125 Hz, as evident in the high coherence (Fig. 12c), although the coherence falls at long period (below 0.01 Hz) due to a lower SNR for the hydrophone signal. The APG data provide a useful calibration (Fig. 13b) down to about 0.005 Hz, below which the coherence drops quickly (Fig. 13c). At high frequencies, the intensifier cannot provide a sufficiently large signal to exceed the counting noise of the APG, so in most APG runs, the signal generator sweeps were limited to frequencies below 5.6 Hz and the coherence (and hence the usefulness of the response measurements) for the DPG/APG data drops precipitously at higher

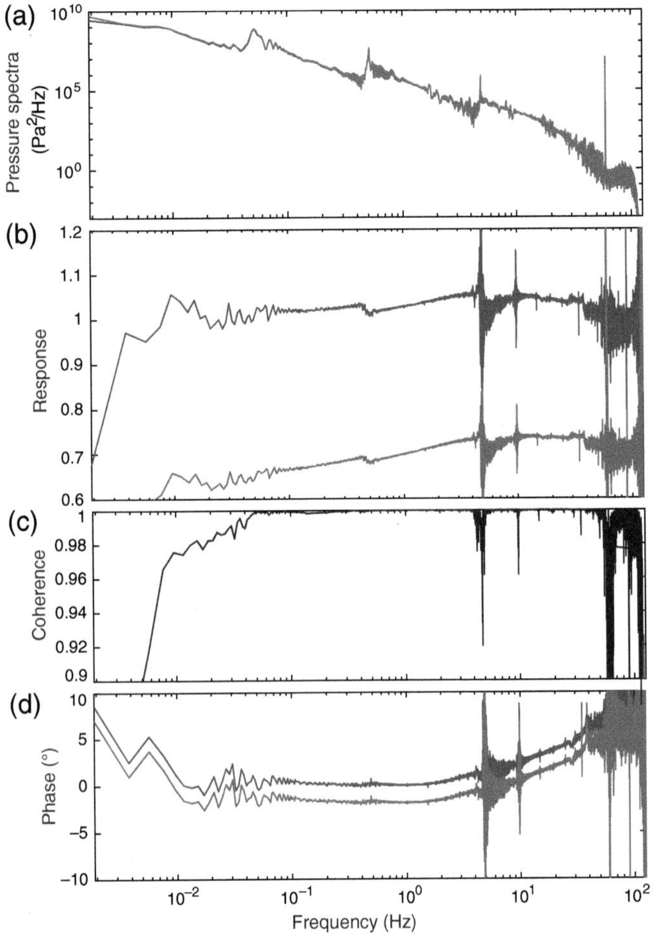

Figure 12. (a) Corrected spectra of DPG (blue) and hydrophone (red line) during a series of sweeps. (b) Relative response between DPG and gain-corrected hydrophone (red line). The red curve shows the response of the DPG uncorrected for o-ring effects; the blue curve includes the correction. Both curves assume a 100 s time constant for the capillary leak.
(c) Coherence between DPG and hydrophone records. (d) Uncorrected (red line) and o-ring effect-corrected phase between DPG and hydrophone (blue line). Panels (a), (b), and (c) have the same horizontal axis as (d). The color version of this figure is available only in the electronic edition.

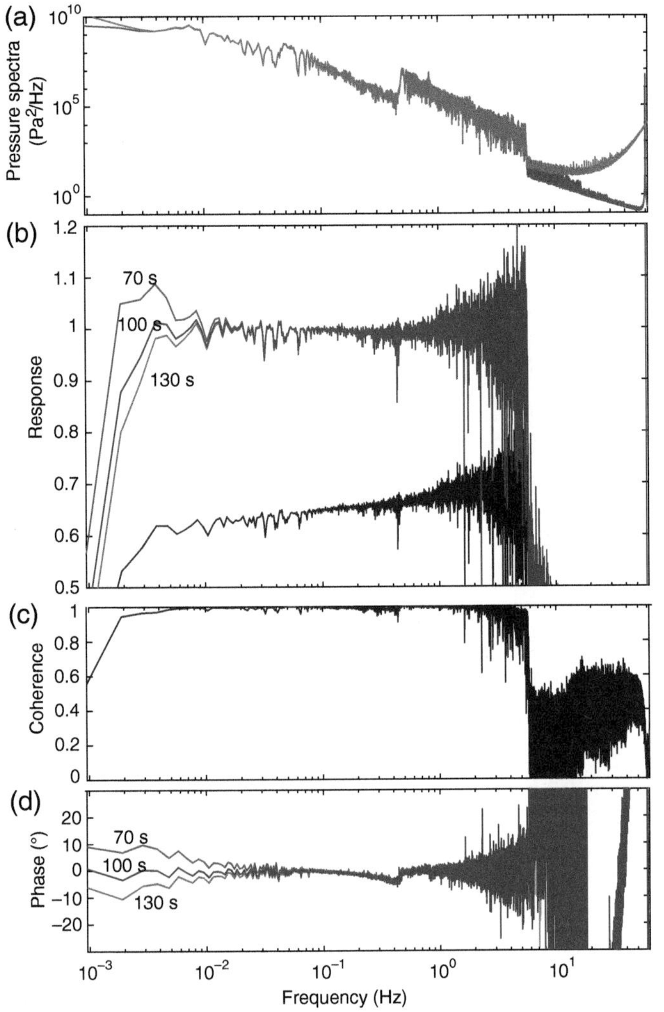

Figure 13. (a) Corrected spectra of DPG (blue line) and APG (red line) during a series of sweeps. (b) Uncorrected for o-ring effect relative response between DPG and APG (black line), assuming a 100 s leak time constant, o-ring, and sensor pressure effect-corrected relative response assuming 100 s (blue line), 70 s (red line), and 130 s (green) leak time constants.
(c) Coherence between the two signals, (d) relative phase assuming 70 s (red line), 100 s (blue line), and 130 s (green line) capillary leak time constant. Panels (a), (b), and (c) have the same horizontal axis as (d). The color version of this figure is available only in the electronic edition.

frequencies (Fig. 13c). The corrected response curve drops above 5 Hz because of bias effects due to the small coherence. There is a small jump in the spectra due to a signal generator sweep change near 0.5 Hz (Fig. 13a) that produces a deviation in the phase of the response (Fig. 13d) near 0.5 Hz due to broadband spectral bias effects.

The relative gain response of the DPG over the hydrophone appears to flatten and may decrease slightly above 10 Hz (Fig. 12b). It is difficult to determine if this decrease toward higher frequency is due to bias from decreasing coherence at high frequency (Fig. 12c), or to errors in the amplifier gain of the hydrophone or to a true small decrease in sensitivity. There are small jumps in the measured relative response near 0.5 and 5 Hz, which can be attributed to broadband spectral bias effects associated with jumps in the spectral level (Fig. 12a). The hydrophone and DPG have very different response curves (Fig. 2) thus broadband spectral bias effects will be different between the two sensors, with the flat DPG response weighting signals roughly uniformly in the spectral domain, whereas the hydrophone bias will be dominated by higher frequencies because the response is proportional to the time derivative of pressure over most of the range. The data show the DPG can provide useful data to at least the Nyquist frequency of 125 Hz, and likely much higher. The DPG has a higher noise floor than the best hydrophone systems at short periods, but the noise floor may be near typical seafloor noise levels except near 5–10 Hz, in which there is a minimum in ambient noise spectral levels in pressure at the seafloor (e.g.,

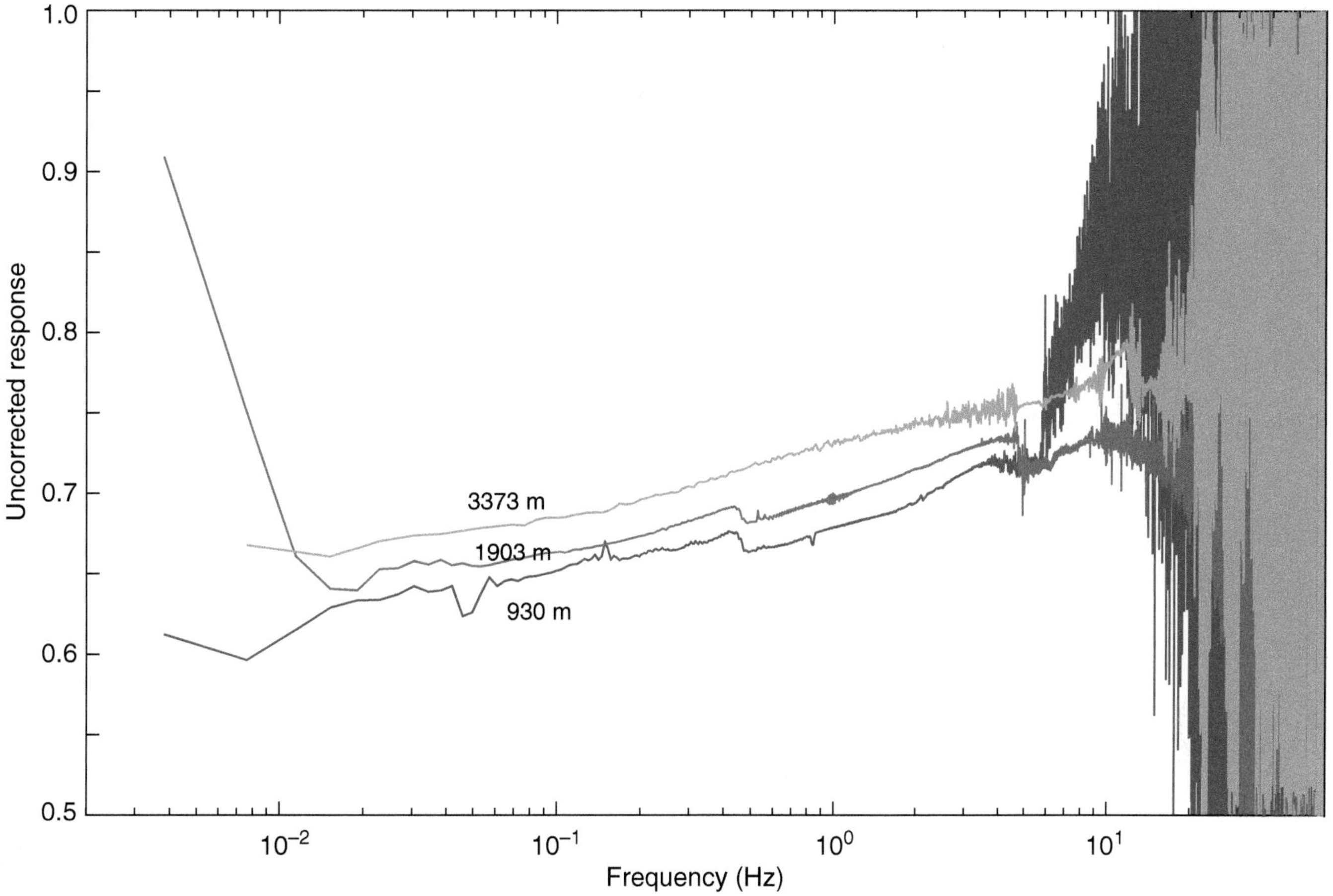

Figure 14. Uncorrected relative response between a DPG and a corrected APG at three pressures, 930 m (blue line), 1903 m (red line), and 3373 m (yellow line). Large divergences below 0.01 Hz and above about 10 Hz are due to low coherence between the signals. The color version of this figure is available only in the electronic edition.

Duennebier *et al.*, 2012). Further work will be required to assess the useful high-frequency limit to DPG data for seafloor seismology. The designers of the Novasensor part suggest the resonant frequency of the silicon wafer diaphragm is above 10 kHz (Mallon *et al.*, 1990). It seems likely the DPG can provide useful data to much higher frequencies than 125 Hz.

EFFECT OF OVERPRESSURE RELIEF VALVE ON DPG RESPONSE

DPGs have been constructed on the same design since roughly 1984 in the machine shop at the Scripps Institution of Oceanography and assembled by engineers at SIO (Steve Constable, personal comm., 2025). Each sensor has two overpressure relief valves that enter either into or out of the reference chamber to prevent damage to the delicate sensor during the rapid changes in pressure experienced during deployment and recovery of the instruments. The overpressure relief valves are Circle Seal Co. 500 series popoff valves with either Viton or Buna-N (Nitrile) o-rings. The DPG used for the tests here has the softer, Buna-N o-rings. All recent DPGs have been constructed using Buna-N o-rings (Jacques Lemire, personal comm., 2025). We include calculations for the Viton rings for completeness. Both kinds of o-ring are compliant, and thus a fraction of the pressure changes external to the reference chamber gets introduced into the chamber, diminishing the pressure difference across the sensor, reducing DPG sensitivity.

The response of these o-rings is viscoelastic; thus, the effective spring constant of the o-rings depends on frequency. The spring constant is expected to vary both with pressure and temperature; both higher pressure and lower temperature are expected to increase the spring constant of the o-ring, reducing the effect of the valve movement on the DPG response. We have used an apparatus developed to measure the anelastic properties of ice (Yamauchi *et al.*, 2024) to measure the magnitude of the spring constant (k [in N/m], Fig. 15a) and loss parameter, or attenuation ($1/Q$, Fig. 15b) as a function of frequency for the two types of o-rings used in the DPG valves at room temperature and 1 atm pressure.

The viscoelastic behavior of a polymer material, such as these o-rings can be described by "master curves," which are a function of frequency. With the master curve method, the spectra of spring constant and attenuation of these o-rings at higher pressure and lower temperatures can be estimated by shifting the measured spectra in frequency by an amount associated with the temperature and pressure using the Williams–Landau–Ferry equation (e.g., Emri, 2005).

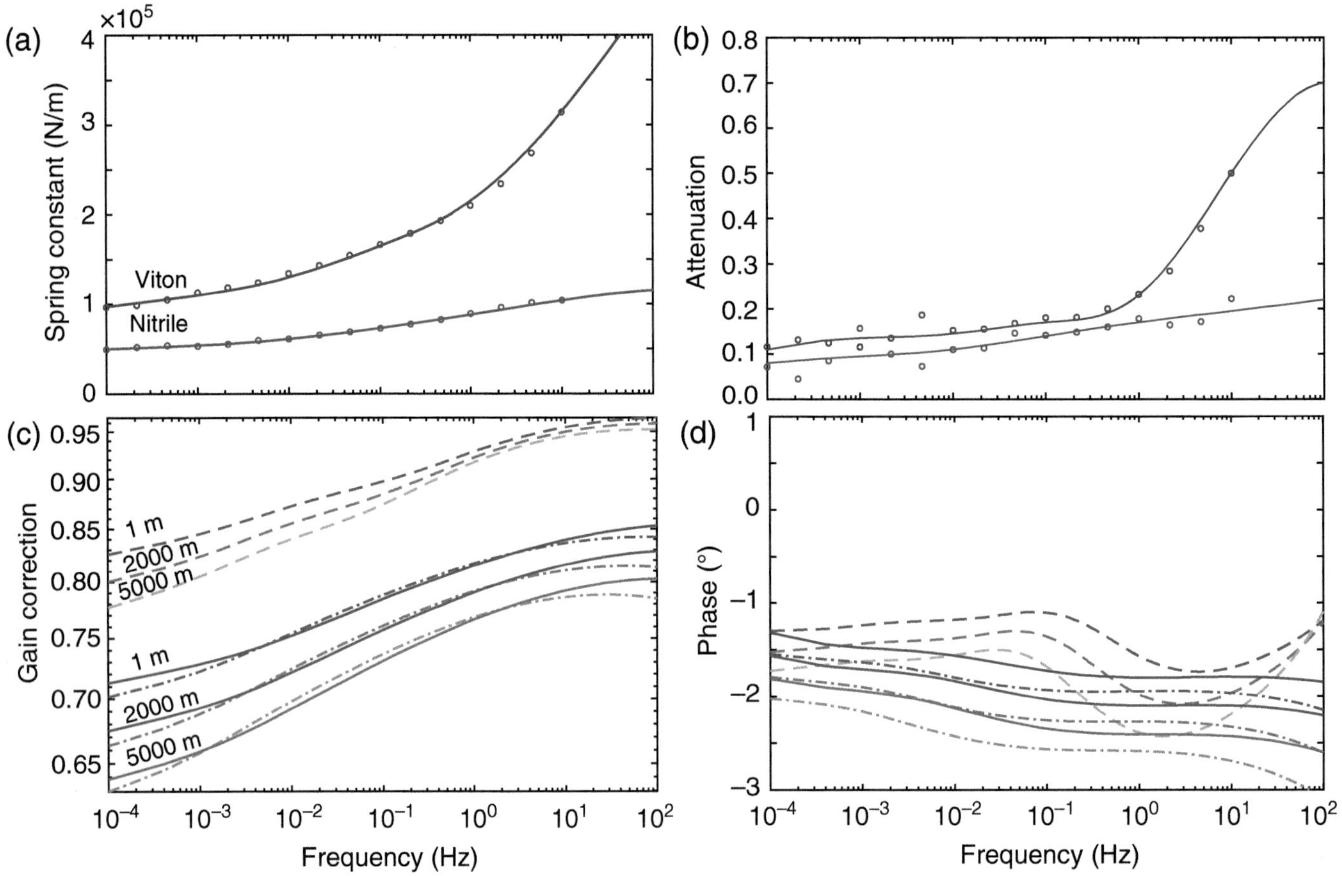

Figure 15. (a) Measured magnitude of the spring constant for compression of the Viton and Nitrile o-rings from overpressure valves (circles) and extrapolated line fits. (b) Measured attenuation ($1/Q$) of the o-rings, (c) predicted gain effect of o-rings on DPG response at 1, 2000, and 5000 m depth at 20°C (Nitrile solid lines) and at 2°C (Nitrile: dashed–dotted lines and Viton: dashed lines), and (d) predicted phase effect of o-rings on DPG response (same line labels as panel c). The color version of this figure is available only in the electronic edition.

To apply the master curve method to our case, we use the results of Fillers and Tschoegl (1977) to estimate the shift factor in frequency for Buna-N (Nitrile) and Viton rings as

$$\alpha(T,H) = \exp(0.08 * (20 - T) + 0.00023 * H), \tag{13}$$

in which T is the temperature in Celsius, and H is the depth in meters. We have extrapolated the data in Figure 15a,b toward higher frequencies by a factor of 5 to allow us to predict the response at lower temperatures and higher pressures. By defining the extrapolated line fits as $k_0(f)$ and $Q_0^{-1}(f)$ as functions of frequency for each type of o-ring (Viton or Nitrile), we can predict the spring constant and attenuation of each o-ring at arbitrary frequency, temperature, and depth as

$$k_c(f,T,H) = k_0(\alpha f), \tag{14}$$

and

$$Q_c^{-1}(f,T,H) = Q_0^{-1}(\alpha f), \tag{15}$$

respectively. The extrapolation has limited accuracy at larger extrapolation, but the errors associated with likely errors in extrapolation are not significant for the final estimates of DPG frequency response, as explained subsequently.

Given an excitation at a single frequency, each popoff valve is expected to be displaced a distance x by the difference in pressure across the valve as

$$x = \frac{(P_e - P_i)A}{k}, \tag{16}$$

in which P_e and P_i are the external and internal pressure, k is the frequency-dependent spring constant, and A is the area of the valve opening. The spring constant is defined as a complex quantity with magnitude and phase determined by the measured loss parameter so

$$k = k_c \exp\left[i \operatorname{atan}\left(\frac{1}{Q_c}\right)\right]. \tag{17}$$

The frequency dependence of the spring constant leads to a gain that depends on frequency. The dissipation in the o-rings leads to a phase lag between the pressure and the displacement of the valve and thus a phase delay in the response.

The change in volume of the internal chamber is $\Delta V = 2Ax$ The 2 arises because there are two valves. If the relative pressure within the internal chamber of volume V is zero when the external pressure is constant, after an external pressure is

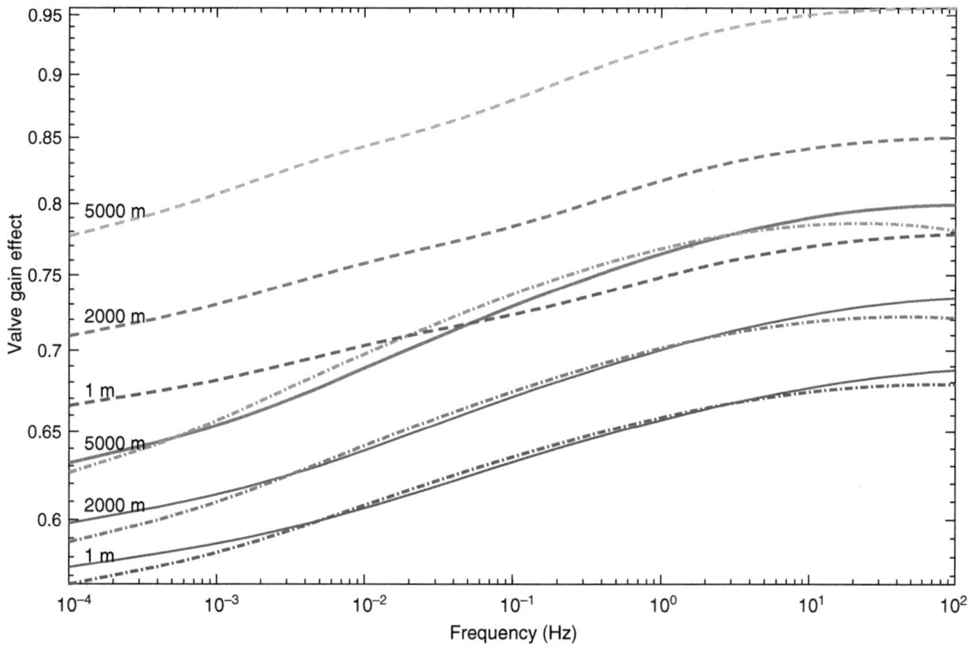

Figure 16. Predicted gain effect, same as Figure 15c, except the figure includes the effect of the pressure-dependent sensor gain. The color version of this figure is available only in the electronic edition.

applied, the displacement of the valve causes the internal pressure to rise to

$$P_i = \frac{2xA}{VC_v} = \frac{2(P_e - P_i)A^2}{VkC_v}, \tag{18}$$

in which C_v is the compressibility of the silicone oil within the reference chamber.

This leads to an expression for the pressure difference across the sensor due to an external pressure P_e of

$$(P_e - P_i) = P_e\left[\frac{1}{1 + \frac{2A^2}{VkC_v}}\right] = P_e G(f). \tag{19}$$

When the spring constant is large, the second term reduces to the difference in pressure across the sensor being equal to the applied pressure. For the components in the DPGs, the predicted gain factor $G(f)$ as a function of frequency, temperature, depth, and type of o-ring in the valves is shown in Figure 15c. The predicted gain increases roughly linearly in log frequency by about 15% from 0.001 to 10 Hz, approximately independently of pressure and depth (and type of o-ring), but with an amplitude offset to the curve that depends on pressure, depth, and type of o-ring. The predicted gain factor is smaller at higher pressures (greater depths), because the effect of decreased compressibility of the oil with depth exceeds the effect of a larger spring constant at higher pressure. The temperature dependence of the gain factor is small; the pressure dependence is dominated by the decrease in compressibility of the silicon oil with depth (see next section). The stiffer Viton rings cause less loss with gain factors closer to one at all depths.

The loss parameter ($1/Q$) is used to predict the phase shift expected due to attenuation (Fig. 15d). The predicted phase shift at long periods lies between −1.5° and −2.5° (increasing with depth). The phase shift is due to a lag between the deformation of the o-rings and the pressure signals due to viscous losses in the o-rings. The phase shift for the two types of o-rings is similar, reflecting similar attenuation at long periods.

The curves in Figure 15c do not allow us to match the amplitude of the relative gain between the DPG and APG observations unless we add a frequency-independent gain factor that increases with depth. Figure 14 shows the uncorrected gain increasing with pressure, whereas the predictions of the o-ring gain factor dependence predict decreasing gain with increasing pressure (Fig. 15c). It is difficult to conceive of a mechanical mechanism that would lead to increasing gain with increasing pressure. We suggest that the increasing gain with increasing pressure observed must be due to a pressure dependence of the gain of the Novasensor differential pressure sensor within the DPG. The increase appears to be linear with depth, requiring the approximate gain correction:

$$G_c = 0.89 + \text{depth}/24{,}940\ \text{m}, \tag{20}$$

on top of the correction for the effect of the o-rings. Figure 16 shows the combined effect of these two gain-correction terms.

The Novasensor is based on four piezoresistors in a Wheatstone bridge configuration mounted on a diaphragm (Mallon *et al.*, 1990). Flexure of the diaphragm causes straining of the piezoresistors, changing their resistance. The piezoresistors are also sensitive to hydrostatic pressure. We measured the resistance of these four resistors as a function of hydrostatic pressure from 0 to 45 MPa and observed a linear change with pressure of 2.75% over this range. The above equation suggests the gain of the sensor increases about 10% from 950 to 3373 m (equivalent hydrostatic pressure). The Novasensor part was designed to operate at pressures near one atmosphere rather than deep-sea pressures. A complex design for the diaphragm was required to prevent breakage of the sensitive sensors (Mallon *et al.*, 1990). The sensors are designed for differential overpressures of just 5 times the rating of the sensor or 35 kPa for the 7 kPa gauge used in most DPGs. We must assume that

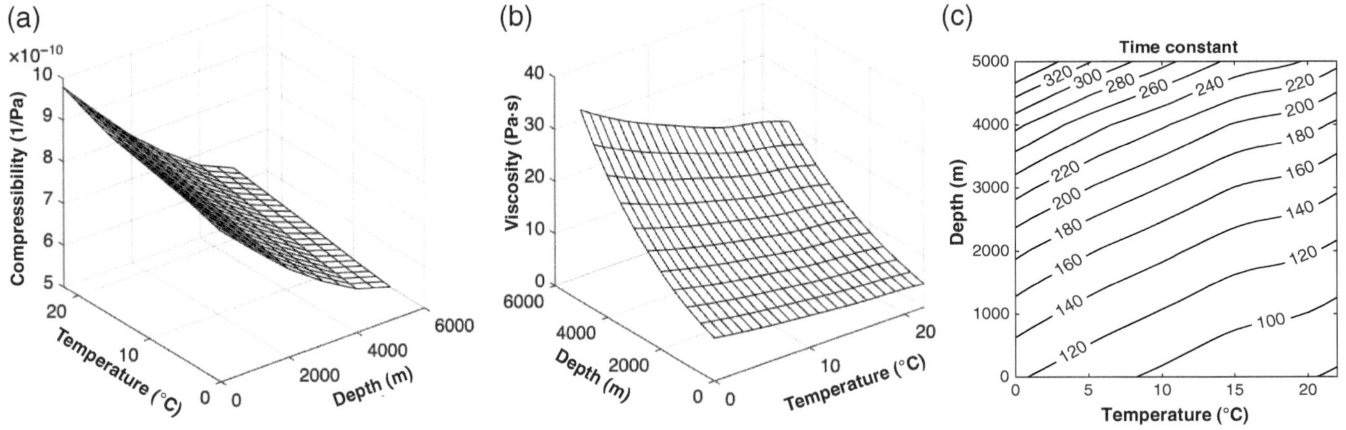

Figure 17. (a) Compressibility of silicone oil versus pressure (depth) and temperature. (b) Silicone oil viscosity versus pressure (depth) and temperature. (c) Predicted time constant (s) for the DPG capillary leak versus temperature and depth.

changes in hydrostatic pressure affect some part of the sensor to produce a slightly higher gain at higher pressure. The higher gain could be due to increasing deformation of the diaphragm with differential pressure exposed to high hydrostatic pressures. The piezoresistors within the sensors are affected by both transverse and longitudinal strains so perhaps the large hydrostatic pressures change the strain direction. The piezoelectric effect is very dependent on the strain orientation (Barlian *et al.*, 2009).

The relative responses of the DPG and HYD (Fig. 12b) or the DPG and the APG (Fig. 13b) are well predicted (within 5%) at all pressures after applying both corrections of the effect of O-ring's compliance and the pressure dependence of sensor gain (Fig. 16). The valve deformation is also predicted to produce about a two-degree phase delay (Fig. 14), which is observed at low frequencies in the measurements (Figs. 12d and 13d) and mostly corrected using the measured attenuation in the o-rings. The phase at frequencies above a few Hertz is not constrained by our measurements because the APG and DPG systems use separate clocks, and so there can be a relative drift of many milliseconds between the timing of the two time series.

DPG CAPILLARY HIGH-PASS FILTER CORNER

The long-period response of the DPG is controlled by a high-pass single-pole mechanical filter established by a small tube in the DPG that allows fluid to leak between the reference chamber and the outside (Cox *et al.*, 1984) to equilibrate the pressure over long timescales. It was apparent to those authors that because the corner frequency depended on the viscosity and compressibility of the silicone oil in the DPG, the corner frequency would decrease between operation at room temperature (20°C) and deep-sea temperatures (2°C).

We use the data in Cox *et al.* (1984) to constrain the compressibility (Fig. 17a). The viscosity of the oil is also pressure dependent. Yasutomi *et al.* (1984) suggest the viscosity of silicone oils increases exponentially with pressure (depth) with a factor equal to about 30 GPa^{-1} (Fig. 17b), which we apply to the data of Cox *et al.* (1984). The capillary leak time constant is proportional to the product of the viscosity times the compressibility times a geometrical factor. We combine the pressure and temperature effects to estimate the expected time constant (and hence corner frequency) for the DPG as a function of pressure and temperature (Fig. 17c).

The geometrical factor in the time constant was estimated by fitting the measured corrected response of the DPG relative to the APG between 0.005 and 0.01 Hz (Fig. 13b). The coherence falls abruptly at lower frequency, and a pi prolate window was used on these data to optimize frequency resolution. The response is best fit with a time constant near 100 s at the pressure (954 m) and temperature (20.6°C) of these data. This value for the time constant also provides the best fit to the phase data (Fig. 13d).

A second constraint on the geometrical factor is obtained by comparing a spectrum of APG data to a spectrum of DPG data, both recorded by the same instrument deployed on the seafloor of the Axial Volcano (1571 m, 3°C) in 2022. To reduce broadband spectral bias (leakage), the spectra of the time derivative of the APG and the DPG data were calculated and compared (Fig. 18), rather than the spectra of the undifferentiated data, as otherwise broadband bias effects from the tides from this fairly short data set dominate. We fit the DPG spectrum to the APG spectrum (Fig. 18a) and the relative phase (Fig. 18c) to determine the best-fitting time constant for the capillary leak. The spectra are fit using the gain dependence described in this article, except the DPG data require a higher gain by a factor of 1.25 for the DPG sensor used in this deployment. As noted earlier, the possible variation in gains for the Novasensor sensors used within DPGs is very large, and a 25% variation is well within specifications. For these data, the best-fitting time constant for the two spectra is about 160–180 s. The phase (Fig. 18c) is fit better by a 200 s time constant, but the low coherence at long period (Fig. 18b) suggests the APG data may be biased. Unfortunately, the duration of the axial seafloor

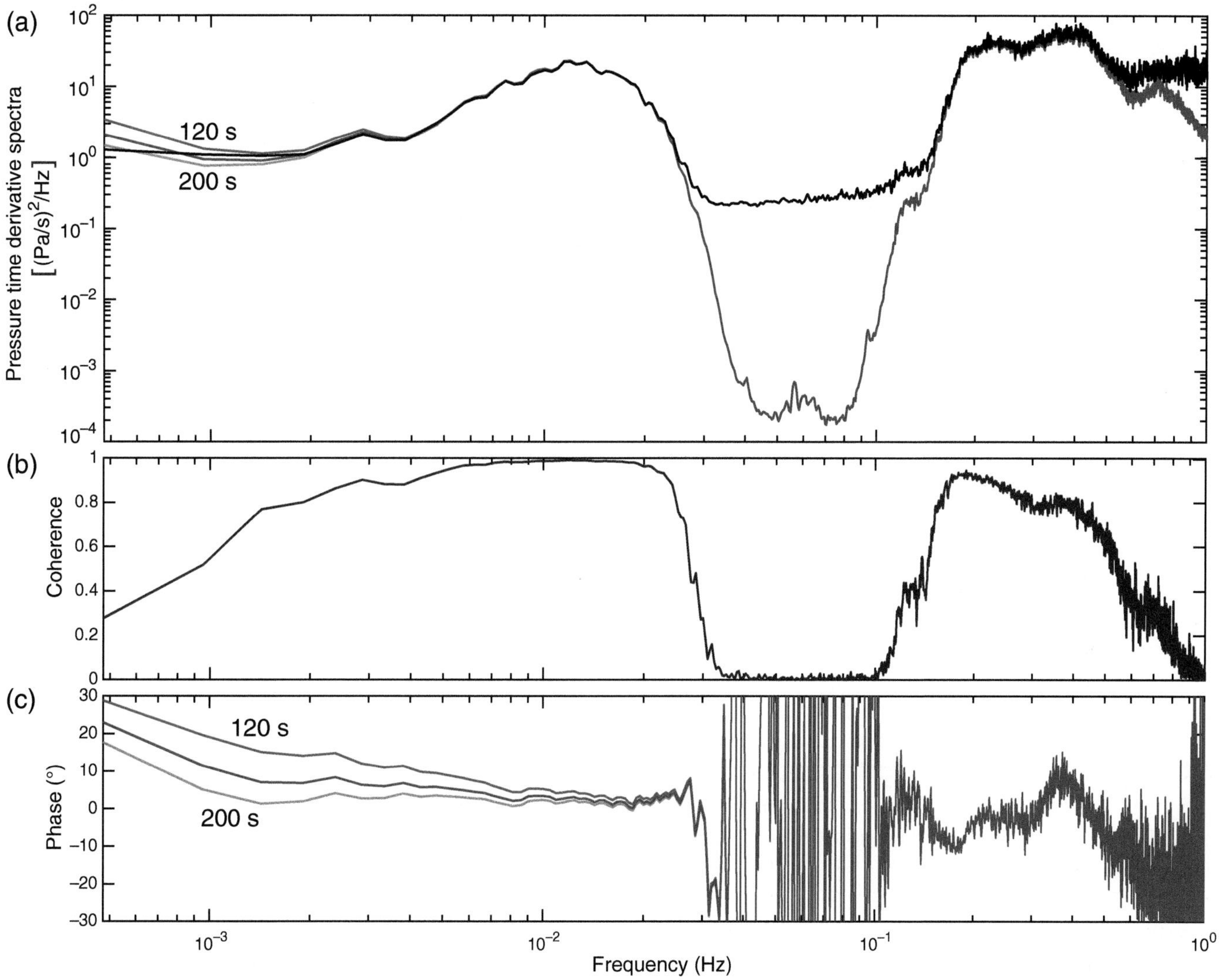

Figure 18. (a) Spectra of the time derivatives of APG (black line) and DPG data from a deployment at the seafloor of an axial volcano. The DPG spectra are corrected assuming a time constant of 120s (red line), 160s (blue line), or 200s (green line). (b) Coherence between the APG and DPG time series. (c) Relative phase between the time series with time constant corrections. Panels (a) and (b) have the same horizontal axis as panel (c). The color version of this figure is available only in the electronic edition.

data is quite short, obtained during an instrument test. A value of 160 s is close to the model shown in Figure 17c.

Sasagawa *et al.* (2019) measured the time constant and gain of a DPG gauge at 1380 m depth within a test facility by changing the pressure in steps by adding weights onto a dead weight tester. They measured a time constant of 138 ± 2 s at 2.5°C and 96 ± 6 s at 22°C. Doran *et al.* (2019) developed a system to drop a DPG sensor a short distant vertically while the instrument was deployed on the seafloor. Four instruments deployed within the San Diego trough showed a wide variation in measured time constants and gains, but the most reliable values appear to be time constants of 160–170 s for a depth of about 1400 m. No temperature value is provided, but Constable *et al.* (2009) suggest a temperature of 4.5°C at the seafloor in the San Diego trough.

The only constraint on the time constant for the DPG at large depths was made by Doran and Laske (2019), who suggested values near 250 s were required to match DPG-derived tidal amplitudes to the predicted tidal amplitudes at seafloor sites near the Hawaiian Islands (depths 4500–5500 m). They determined the gain of the DPGs at shorter periods using the ratio of vertical velocity to pressure in Rayleigh waves following Zha and Webb (2016). Using tidal amplitudes to constrain the corner frequency of the DPGs requires assuming the DPG response is otherwise flat from about 40 s period (peak Rayleigh-wave amplitudes) to the 12.42 hr period of the M2 tide; however, extrapolating Figure 16 suggests the losses due to the o-rings reduce the gain of the DPG at 0.02 mHz compared with the gain at 0.02 Hz by about 18% compared with a flat response. This suggests the time constant for the deep-seafloor DPG data to fit the tidal amplitudes should be about 295 s instead of 250 s. Doran and Laske (2019) note that the time constant for DPGs based on room temperature and one atmosphere measurements in the laboratory was 60 s. Our estimates of the DPG time constant (Fig. 17c) appear to be roughly consistent with these constraints from high-pressure data; however, we note the model is based on predictions for the compressibility and viscosity of silicone oils that may be different from the exact oil used in the DPG and thus of unknown reliability. The capillary leak is based on a syringe needle. The time constant depends on the fourth power of the internal diameter of the needle. It is unknown whether the ID of these parts is the same for all DPGs, some manufactured decades apart. The results earlier suggest some consistency.

CONSTRAINING DPG RESPONSE IN THE FIELD

The large inherent uncertainty in the gain of the Novasensor sensor in any DPG and the large temperature and pressure dependence of the gain of the DPG suggest it may always be necessary to calibrate the DPG sensor on the seafloor for each deployment. For instruments that deploy both APGs and DPGs, the best method to determine the DPG response may be to compare the outputs of the two sensors using long data sets (many days to weeks) to reduce statistical uncertainty. It might be useful to use the APG temperature data to remove the temperature dependence of the DPG at long periods from the data to improve the coherence between the two data sets. We note Yang *et al.* (2021) observed temperature variation effects due to internal waves on DPG data in the 0.002–0.1 mHz band.

Alternatively, for instruments that deploy both hydrophones and DPGs, it may be possible to calibrate the DPGs at short period by comparing data from the two sensors after correcting the hydrophone for the depth-dependent gain and corner frequency.

For deployments of DPGs without APGs or hydrophones, the method of Zha and Webb (2016) using the ratio of pressure to vertical velocity in Rayleigh waves can be applied to determine the gain, but a model for the frequency dependence of the DPG response due to the effect of the o-rings should be included in the response function used in the calculations. The tidal amplitude method of Dornan and Laske (2016) may also be useful, but again, it is important to include a model for the effect of the o-rings. The slope of the o-ring effect varies only modestly with depth and temperature (Fig. 16), so it may be possible to use a single model for that part of the response for all instruments in a deployment.

Poles and zeros representation of the frequency-domain response for the three sensors

A standard way to correct for instrument response is to use a response function expressed as a product of several poles and zeros times a gain. Matlab routines to calculate these responses as a function of depth and temperature can be found in Webb (2025).

The hydrophone response in the frequency domain (Hz) can be modeled by two poles, one for the corner frequency set by the hydrophone capacitance and shunting resistor ($\tau = R_1 C, R_1 \approx 200$ KΩ) and the second by the antialiasing filter in the amplifier ($\beta = R_2 C_2, R_2 \approx 2.7$ KΩ$, C_2 \approx 0.33\ \mu F$). The

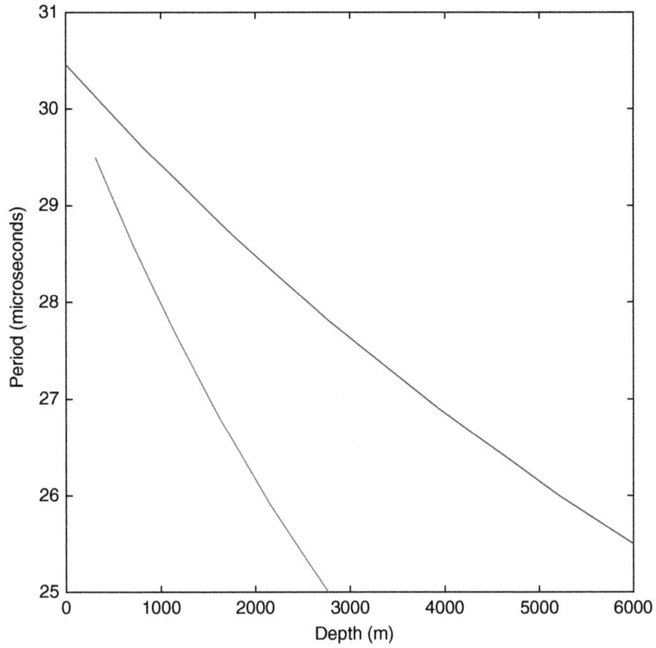

Figure 19. Period of oscillation for the pressure gauge quartz oscillator as a function of depth for two gauges: a 7000 m range gauge (blue curve) and a 4000 m range gauge (red curve). The color version of this figure is available only in the electronic edition.

gain and the capacitance of the hydrophone decrease with depth (see Fig. 6):

$$R_H(f) = \frac{2\pi i f \tau \Gamma \delta}{(1 - 2\pi i f \tau)(1 - i 2\pi f \beta)}, \tag{21}$$

in which the gain Γ matches the manufacturer's specification for gain (−198 db rel 1 μPa/V) and $\delta = 1.342 - 1.075 \times 10^{-4} \times \text{depth}$ which fits the depth-dependent gain from Figure 6b.

The IIR filters in the POBSs and APGs depend on the frequency of the quartz crystal oscillator in the pressure sensor, and, therefore, the corner frequency of the filter changes with the depth of the sensor. Following Webb and Nooner (2016), the IIR filter response in the frequency domain can be modeled as

$$R_{\mathrm{IIR}}(f) = \frac{\alpha}{[1 - (1 - \alpha)\exp(-i2\pi f T)]^p} \approx \frac{1}{[1 - i2\pi f T/\alpha]^p}, \tag{22}$$

in which p is the number of stages in the IIR filter: $p = 5$ for POBS and $p = 8$ for the APG, and $\alpha = 2^{-7}$ for the POBS and the APG. T is the period of the pressure sensor oscillator, which depends on pressure. Figure 19 shows the period of oscillation for two pressure gauges as a function of pressure; one gauge has a range of about 4000 m (41 MPa), and the other about 7000 m depth (69 MPa). Each gauge has a different dependence on pressure; the period of oscillation at a given frequency can be obtained from the coefficients describing the gauge response from Paroscientific Co. The period varies by about 15% over the range of each gauge, which implies the corner frequency of the IIR antialiasing filter

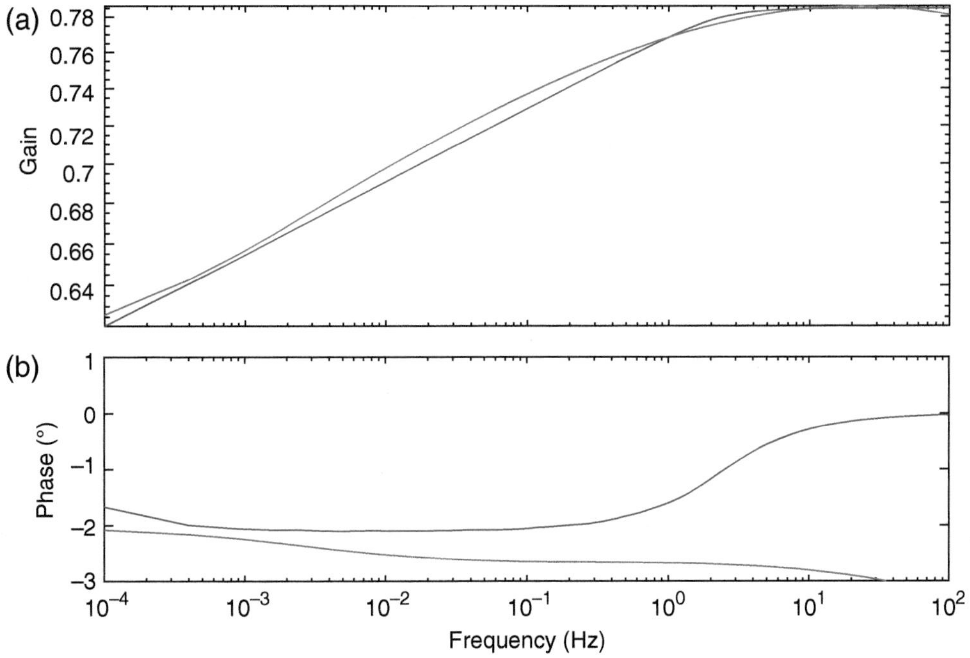

Figure 20. (a) Model of DPG gain response at 2°C and 5000 m for Nitrile o-rings (red) and poles and zeros approximation of the same as described above (blue). (b) Predicted phase (red) and poles and zeros approximation of the same (blue). Panel (a) has the same horizontal axis as panel (b). The color version of this figure is available only in the electronic edition.

will change by the same percentage. An approximation to the IIR filter response with a fixed value for the period T independent of depth may be adequate if the response at high frequency is not important to interpret the seismic data.

The effect of the inlet tube on the APG response can be modeled as an additional pole, as shown subsequently. For the APGs in the current OBSIC fleet, a corner frequency f_c near 13 Hz, is appropriate, while our new standard APG with a larger diameter inlet tube has a higher corner near 45 Hz. For the POBS, the corner frequency will depend on depth and temperature, as shown in Figure 9. At long periods, the APG gain is 1:

$$R_{\mathrm{APG}}(f) = \frac{1}{(1 - if/f_c)[1 - i2\pi f T/\alpha]^p}. \qquad (23)$$

The DPG response requires modeling the viscoelastic response of the o-rings, which causes the gain to increase roughly linearly in log frequency from less than 1 mHz up to a few Hertz in frequency, above which the gain levels off. We can model the DPG response in the frequency-domain $R_{\mathrm{DPG}}(f)$ approximately using a small number of paired poles and zeros that are logarithmically spaced in frequency, with an additional pole to account for the capillary leak:

$$R_{\mathrm{DPG}}(f) = \frac{-2\pi\tau f\Gamma}{(f - i2\pi\tau)} \Pi_{n=1}^{N} \frac{(f - iz_n)}{(f - ip_n)},$$
$$p_n = (f_p)^n/(f_p)^N \gamma,$$
$$z_n = p_n * (1 + \beta). \qquad (24)$$

The τ parameter is the time constant of the capillary leak. We choose the gain parameter Γ to fit the level of the curve following Figure 16. The f_p and γ parameters, together set the frequency of the lowest frequency pole, β sets the slope of the curve in log frequency, and the γ parameter sets the highest frequency pole, which is related to where the curve levels out. In the example in Figure 20, $f_p =$ 4 Hz, $\beta = 0.33$, $\gamma = 1.2$ Hz, $N = 8$, and τ is set very large to fit the response, omitting the effect of the capillary leak. Figure 20 shows the predicted response due to the o-rings at 5000 m depth and 2°C, and the fit to this curve using the poles and zeros of equation (24). The pole and zeros representation also approximates the roughly 2° phase lag at long periods due to losses within the o-rings.

CONCLUSIONS

An intercomparison of data from the three types of pressure sensors used currently for seafloor observations for seismology, the hydrophone, the DPG, and the high-rate APG reveal some discrepancies in the response functions from current standards. The capacitance of the Hitech HTI-90-U hydrophone decreases 25% with pressure from 0 to 5000 m, so that the high-pass corner frequency increases by 25% over the same range. The gain of the hydrophone also decreases with increasing pressure. The combined effect of the gain change and corner frequency change implies the low-frequency gain decreases by about 55% from 0 to 5000 m depth. The response of these hydrophones is simply characterized over a very wide band, from less than 1 mHz to above 125 Hz.

The inlet tubing to the high sampling rate APG acts as a low-pass filter with a corner frequency that depends on the details of the inlet tubing. Most previous observations using APGs from instruments in the OBSIC fleet should have corner frequencies above 13 Hz. More recent instruments with larger tubing have corner frequencies above 45 Hz. These corner frequencies are temperature and pressure-independent. Otherwise, the corrected APG response is flat and well calibrated to at least 30 Hz. The large dynamic range of the APG may make it well-suited for determining ground displacement in earthquake source regions using dynamic pressure (e.g., Kubota *et al.*, 2021) and thereby facilitate tsunami early warning. The POBS instrument, an instrument with dual APGs and extensive plumbing for A-0-A drift correction for the pressure gauges, instead exhibits a much lower corner frequency that is controlled by the viscosity and thus is pressure and temperature-dependent.

The DPG provides useful data to at least 125 Hz, and is likely to be much higher frequency. Further work is required to explore the high-frequency limit. The DPG can perhaps supplant the hydrophone at the seafloor for many short-period seismology applications. The DPG response is affected by losses due to viscoelastic deformation of the o-rings in the overpressure relief valves. The predicted gain increases roughly linearly in log frequency by about 15% from 0.001 to 10 Hz, independent of pressure and depth, but there is an offset in the gain curve that depends on pressure and depth. The gain of the pressure sensor within the DPG also appears to increase with increasing pressure. Both variations are small compared with the expected variability of the gain between DPGs due to the limited accuracy of calibration of the Novasensor part within the DPGs. Methods to calibrate the DPG in situ using either the ratio of amplitude of ground deformation to pressure in Rayleigh waves from earthquakes (Zha and Webb, 2016) and tidal amplitudes (Doran and Laske, 2016) can be used to calibrate the DPG sensors over a wideband if the effect of the increasing gain with increasing pressure due to the o-rings is included in the response. The DPG long-period response is controlled by a high-pass mechanical filter with a time constant that depends on the viscosity and compressibility of silicone oil within the DPG. The time constant increases with pressure and decreases with temperature. The time constant increases from order 60–80 s at 20°C and 1 m depth to order 300 s at 5000 m and 2°C.

DATA AND RESOURCES

The data and software needed to reproduce the figures and calculate responses as a function of temperature and pressure can be found at Zenodo (Webb, 2025). doi: 10.5281/zenodo.17614245.

DECLARATION OF COMPETING INTERESTS

Spahr Webb is partly supported by the Jerome M. Paros/Lamont Research professorship in Observational Sciences at the Lamont Doherty Earth Observatory.

ACKNOWLEDGMENTS

The research was supported by National Science Foundation grants OCE19-33196 and OCE19-24024 and a generous gift from Jerry Paros of the Paroscientific Co. The authors thank an anonymous reviewer and John Collins for constructive and helpful reviews, and the Editor and Associate Editor, Cezar Trifu, for constructive comments helping to improve the article.

REFERENCES

Barcheck, G., G. A. Abers, A. N. Adams, A. Bécel, J. Collins, J. B. Gaherty, P. J. Haeussler, Z. Li, G. Moore, E. Onyango, *et al.* (2020). The Alaska amphibious community seismic experiment, *Bull. Seismol. Soc. Am.* **91,** no. 6, 3054–3063.

Barlian, A. A., W. T. Park, J. R. Mallon, A. J. Rastegar, and B. L. Pruitt (2009). Semiconductor piezoresistance for microsystems, *Proc. IEEE* **97,** no. 3, 513–552.

Barstow, N., G. H. Sutton, and J. A. Carter (1989). Particle motion and pressure relationships of ocean bottom noise: 3900 m depth; 0.003 to 5 Hz, *Geophys. Res. Lett.* **16,** no. 10, 1185–1188.

Bradley, D. L. (1963). Velocity of sound in a Dow Corning 200 fluid as a function of temperature and pressure, *J. Acoust. Soc. Am.* **35,** no. 10, 1565–1567.

Chadwick, W. W., Jr, W. S. D. Wilcock, S. L. Nooner, J. W. Beeson, A. M. Sawyer, and T.-K. Lau (2022). Geodetic monitoring at Axial Seamount since its 2015 eruption reveals a waning magma supply and tightly linked rates of deformation and seismicity, *Geochem. Geophys. Geosyst.* **23,** no. 1, e2021GC010153, doi: 10.1029/2021GC010153.

Constable, S., K. Key, and L. Lewis (2009). Mapping offshore sedimentary structure using electromagnetic methods and terrain effects in marine magnetotelluric data, *Geophys. J. Int.* **176,** no. 2, 431–442.

Cox, C. S., T. K. Deaton, and S. C. Webb (1984). A deep sea differential pressure gauge, *J. Atmos. Ocean. Technol.* **1,** no. 3, 237–246.

Deng, H., C. An, C. Cai, and H. Ren (2022). Theoretical solution and applications of ocean bottom pressure induced by seismic waves at high frequencies, *Geophys. Res. Lett.* **49,** no. 9, e2021GL096952, doi: 10.1029/2021GL096952.

Doran, A. K., and G. Laske (2016). Infragravity waves and horizontal seafloor compliance, *J. Geophys. Res. Solid Earth* **121,** 260–278, doi: 10.1002/2015JB012511.

Doran, A. K., and G. Laske (2019). Seismic structure of marine sediments and upper oceanic crust surrounding Hawaii, *J. Geophys. Res. Solid Earth* **124,** no. 2, 2038–2056, doi: 10.1029/2018JB016548.

Doran, A. K., M. Rapa, G. Laske, J. Babcock, and S. McPeak (2019). Calibration of differential pressure gauges through in situ testing, *Earth Space Sci.* **6,** 2663–2670, doi: 10.1029/2019EA000783.

Duennebier, F. K., R. Lukas, E. M. Nosal, J. Aucan, and R. A. Weller (2012). Wind, waves, and acoustic background levels at station ALOHA, *J. Geophys. Res. Oceans* **117,** no. C3, doi: 10.1029/2011JC007267.

Emri, I. (2005). Rheology of solid polymers, *Rheol. Rev.* **2005,** 49.

Fillers, R. W., and N. W. Tschoegl (1977). The effect of pressure on the mechanical properties of polymers, *Trans. Soc. Rheol.* **21,** no. 1, 51–100.

Fredrickson, E. K., W. S. D. Wilcock, D. A. Schmidt, P. MacCready, E. Roland, A. L. Kurapov, M. A. Zumberge, and G. S. Sasagawa (2019). Optimizing sensor configurations for the detection of slow-slip earthquakes in seafloor pressure records, using the Cascadia subduction zone as a case study, *J. Geophys. Res. Solid Earth* **124,** no. 12, 13,504–13,531.

Ito, Y., T. Tsuji, Y. Osada, M. Kido, D. Inazu, Y. Hayashi, H. Tsushima, R. Hino, and H. Fujimoto (2011). Frontal wedge deformation near the source region of the 2011 Tohoku-Oki earthquake, *Geophys. Res. Lett.* **38,** no. 7, doi: 10.1029/2011GL048355.

Johnson, H. P., J. S. Gomberg, S. L. Hautala, and M. S. Salmi (2017). Sediment gravity flows triggered by remotely generated earthquake waves, *J. Geophys. Res. Solid Earth* **122,** no. 6, 4584–4600.

Kubota, T., T. Saito, H. Tsushima, R. Hino, Y. Ohta, S. Suzuki, and D. Inazu (2021). Extracting near-field seismograms from ocean-bottom pressure gauge inside the focal area: Application to the 2011 M_w 9.1 Tohoku-Oki earthquake, *Geophys. Res. Lett.* **48,** no. 7, e2020GL091664, doi: 10.1029/2020GL091664.

Lighthill, M. J. (1979). *Waves in Fluids*, Cambridge University Press, Cambridge.

Neale, J., N. Harmon, and M. Srokosz (2015). Source regions and reflection of infragravity waves offshore of the US Pacific Northwest, *J. Geophys. Res. Oceans* **120,** no. 9, 6474–6491.

Peureux, C., and F. Ardhuin (2016). Ocean bottom pressure records from the Cascadia array and short surface gravity waves, *J. Geophys. Res. Oceans* **121,** no. 5, 2862–2873.

Mallon, J. R., Jr, F. Pourahmadi, K. Petersen, P. Barth, T. Vermeulen, and J. Bryzek (1990). Low-pressure sensors employing bossed diaphragms and precision etch-stopping, *Sens. Actuators A* **21,** nos. 1/3, 89–95.

Sasagawa, G. S., J. Berger, J. A. Orcutt, and M. A. Zumberge (2019). Development of a differential pressure gauge calibration system, *AGU Fall Meeting Abstracts*, Vol. 2019, S33D-0614.

Smit, P. B., T. T. Janssen, T. H. C. Herbers, T. Taira, and B. A. Romanowicz (2018). Infragravity wave radiation across the shelf break, *J. Geophys. Res. Oceans* **123,** no. 7, 4483–4490.

Thomson, D. J. (1977). Spectrum estimation techniques for characterization and development of WT4 waveguide—I, *Bell Syst. Tech. J.* **56,** no. 9, 1769–1815.

Toomey, D. R., R. M. Allen, A. H. Barclay, S. W. Bell, P. D. Bromirski, R. L. Carlson, X. Chen, J. A. Collins, R. P. Dziak, B. Evers, *et al.* (2014). The Cascadia Initiative: A sea change in seismological studies of subduction zones, *Oceanography* **27,** no. 2, 138–150.

Tréhu, A. M., A. de Moor, J. M. Madrid, M. Sáez, C. D. Chadwell, F. Ortega-Culaciati, J. Ruiz, S. Ruiz, and M. D. Tryon (2020). Post-seismic response of the outer accretionary prism after the 2010 Maule earthquake, Chile, *Geosphere* **16,** no. 1, 13–32.

Wallace, L. M., S. C. Webb, Y. Ito, K. Mochizuki, R. Hino, S. Henrys, S. Y. Schwartz, and A. F. Sheehan (2016). Slow slip near the trench at the Hikurangi subduction zone, New Zealand, *Science* **352,** no. 6286, 701–704.

Watts, D. R., X. Qian, and K. L. Tracey (2001). Mapping abyssal current and pressure fields under the meandering Gulf Stream, *J. Atmos. Ocean. Technol.* **18,** no. 6, 1052–1067.

Webb, S. C. (2025). Data and Software on calibration of seafloor pressure sensors for seismology [Data set], *Zenodo*, doi: 10.5281/zenodo.17614245.

Webb, S. C., and A. H. Barclay (2023). Optimizing ocean bottom seismometers for shallow water using shielding and horizontal pressure gradient data, *J. Geophys. Res. Solid Earth* e2023JB026356, doi: 10.1029/2023JB026356.

Webb, S. C., and S. L. Nooner (2016). High-resolution seafloor absolute pressure gauge measurements using a better counting method, *J. Atmos. Ocean. Technol.* **33,** no. 9, 1859–1874.

Wilcock, W. S., D. A. Manalang, E. K. Fredrickson, M. J. Harrington, G. Cram, J. Tilley, J. Burnett, D. Martin, T. Kobayashi, and J. M. Paros (2021). A thirty-month seafloor test of the A-0-A method for calibrating pressure gauges, *Front. Earth Sci.* **8,** 600671.

Woods, K., L. M. Wallace, C. A. Williams, I. J. Hamling, S. C. Webb, Y. Ito, N. Palmer, R. Hino, S. Suzuki, M. K Savage *et al.* (2024). Spatiotemporal evolution of slow slip events at the offshore Hikurangi subduction zone in 2019 using GNSS, InSAR, and seafloor geodetic data, *J. Geophys. Res. Solid Earth* **129,** no. 8, e2024JB02906, doi: 10.1029/2024JB029068.

Woods, K., S. C. Webb, L. M. Wallace, Y. Ito, C. Collins, N. Palmer, R. Hino, M. K. Savage, D. M. Saffer, and E. E. Davis (2022). Using seafloor geodesy to detect vertical deformation at the Hikurangi subduction zone: Insights from self-calibrating pressure sensors and ocean general circulation models, *J. Geophys. Res. Solid Earth* **127,** no. 12, e2022JB023989, doi: 10.1029/2022JB023989.

Yamauchi, H., C. McCarthy, J. R. Leeman, and B. K. Holtzman (2024). A cryogenic forced oscillation apparatus to measure anelasticity of ice, *Rev. Sci. Instrum.* **95,** no. 7, doi: 10.1063/5.0185885.

Yang, C. F., W. C. Chi, H. van Haren, C. R. Lin, and B. Y. Kuo (2021). Tracking deep-sea internal wave propagation with a differential pressure gauge array, *Sci. Rep.* **11,** no. 1, 23311.

Yasutomi, S., S. Bair, and W. O. Winer (1984). An application of a free volume model to lubricant rheology I—Dependence of viscosity on temperature and pressure, *Mech. Eng.* **105,** no. 12, doi: 10.1115/1.3260907.

Zha, Y., and S. C. Webb (2016). Crustal shear velocity structure in the southern Lau basin constrained by seafloor compliance, *J. Geophys. Res. Solid Earth* **121,** no. 5, 3220–3237.

Manuscript received 4 December 2025
Published online 26 March 2026

An Efficient Subspace Detector for Rayleigh Waves, Demonstrated Against Explosions

Joshua D. Carmichael[*1], Jonas A. Kintner[1], and Richard A. Alfaro-Diaz[1]

ABSTRACT

OPEN ACCESS

We present a new set of Rayleigh-wave detection algorithms (a module) that we derive from two competing, approximate models for elliptically polarized seismic data. This module processes three-component seismograms with sliding windows to output estimates of test statistics and source back azimuths that it can combine from multiple frequency bands. The module automatically adjusts declaration thresholds to maintain a fixed false alarm rate against noise and adapts its sliding window lengths to include a fixed number of waveform cycles per frequency band. We demonstrate these capabilities against real Rayleigh waves that are sourced from airborne explosions in Ukraine. The module shows reliable detection rates against explosions and reasonable estimates of source back azimuths at computational costs akin to those of power detectors. Performance curves show that the detection module exceeds a 0.80 true positive detection rate against a real, ~75 kg Trinitrotoluene yield equivalent source at ranges of 25 km. Back-azimuthal estimates achieve mean errors of ~3° with median absolute deviations of ~10°. Our module thereby demonstrates a capability to automatically detect and directionally locate airborne explosions from three-component seismic data, simultaneously. Plain Language Summary: Rayleigh waves are a type of seismic surface wave that moves each point on the ground in the shape of an ellipse. This article develops and tests a new set of algorithms, or a module, to detect such Rayleigh waves with sensors that record ground motion in the east, north, and vertical directions. Our module operates like the scan feature of traditional car radios, but against seismic data. During its "scan" operation, our module consistently tests a fixed number of waveform cycles for Rayleigh-wave motion and adjusts its sensitivity to falsely trigger fewer than a set number of times per year. Our module also estimates the direction from which the source of this motion came. We test our module against data that we predict from airborne explosion simulations and from real explosions recorded in Ukraine. We thereby detect real events with the energy of about 75 kg of Trinitrotoluene explosive from 25 km away, about 80 out of 100 times. We also correctly estimate the direction back to the source within about 10°. Our article and its supplemental material provide the mathematics, physics, and some data required to understand and use this module.

INTRODUCTION AND ORGANIZATION

Atmospheric and near-surface explosions that are common to battlefield environments produce seismic ground motion that is energetically dominated by Rayleigh waves. The amplitudes of these Rayleigh waves relate explicitly to the integrated peak-overpressure of the explosion-sourced air blast against the ground (Murphy and Shah, 1988; Bonner *et al.*, 2013) and relate implicitly to the explosion's effective yield (Bonner and Russell, 2013). The particle motion of these waves is elliptically polarized within the vertically oriented plane that connects their source and receiver (the sagittal plane) and is typically retrograde in orientation (Fig. 1). This motion differs from that of body waves, which are either linearly polarized along the source to receiver path (P waves), or in planes perpendicular to this path (S waves). It also differs from Love waves, which are surface waves for which linearly polarized motion is confined to directions parallel to Earth's surface. The amplitude, polarization, and azimuthal orientation of Rayleigh waveforms make them particularly useful in forensic efforts to detect explosion signals (Chael, 1997; Britton *et al.*, 2003; Tibuleac and Britton, 2006; Aleqabi *et al.*, 2016; O'Rourke and Baker, 2017), to estimate their back-azimuthal (bearing) angle to a source (Tanis, 1976; Selby, 2001; Baker and Stevens, 2004; Böse *et al.*, 2017; Kintner *et al.*, 2022), and to

1. Los Alamos National Laboratory, Los Alamos, New Mexico, U.S.A., https://orcid.org/0000-0001-5752-5738 (JDC); https://orcid.org/0000-0002-0739-6349 (JAK); https://orcid.org/0000-0001-6723-5996 (RAA)

*Corresponding author: joshuac@lanl.gov

Cite this article as Carmichael, J. D., J. A. Kintner, and R. A. Alfaro-Diaz (2026). An Efficient Subspace Detector for Rayleigh Waves, Demonstrated Against Explosions, *Bull. Seismol. Soc. Am.* **116**, 884–901, doi: 10.1785/0120250209

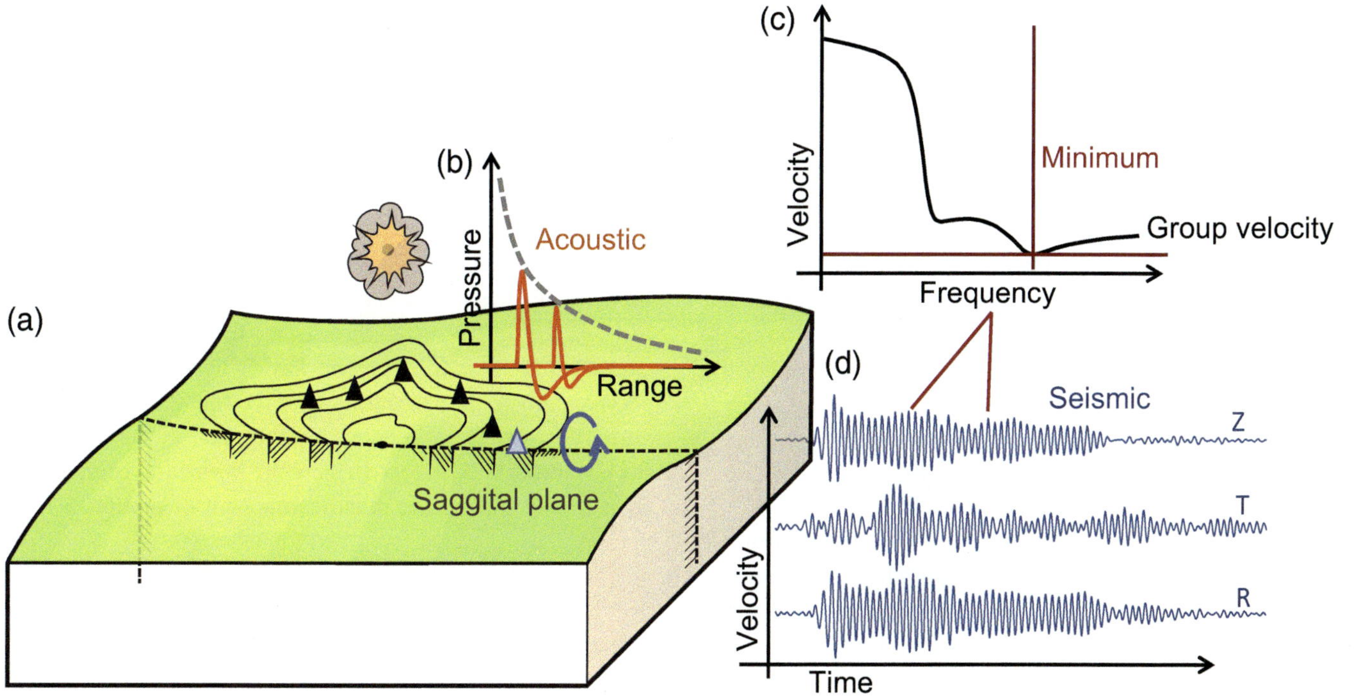

quantify the impact of explosive yield on signal detection rates (Carmichael *et al.*, 2020).

Several confounding factors still challenge monitoring for Rayleigh waveforms. Mechanical processes like scattering and anelastic attenuation in Earth's crust can degrade the amplitude of higher frequency waveforms, or *Rg* signals, (Stevens *et al.*, 2009; Napoli and Russell, 2018). This can limit the reliable observation of explosions with yields of less than several tons to ranges of ~80 km (Schneider *et al.*, 2018). Models of Earth's crust, however, often cannot resolve shallow structural features below such scales (<1°) (Laske *et al.*, 2012). These challenges imply that observers are currently limited in their ability to predict the dominant frequency or detectability of Rayleigh waveforms at local scales in many geographical regions (Gupta and Hartenberger, 1981; Kitov *et al.*, 1997; Kintner *et al.*, 2020). Therefore, small explosions may only produce measurable Rayleigh waveform signals at isolated seismic stations, if any. In these cases, monitoring operations often require back-azimuthal estimates directly from seismograms to assess if they match directions to known explosions, test sites, or conflict zones (Selby, 2001; Baker and Stevens, 2004; Gendzwill, 2007; Costley, 2020; Dando *et al.*, 2023). Improved monitoring of Rayleigh waveform sources at local distances therefore requires at least three scientific capabilities: (1) to detect Rayleigh waveforms sourced by low-magnitude events in noisy environments over multiple frequency bands; (2) to estimate back-azimuthal angles to their sources; and (3) to predict the probability that waves sourced by events of a given size (yield) are reliably detectable. Researchers may further be restricted to using only isolated seismometers.

To provide these capabilities, this study develops and applies a computationally efficient digital signal detector and supporting set of algorithms (a module) to detect and estimate the back azimuth of Rayleigh waveform sources over multiple, overlapping frequency bands. We first provide the equations for the test statistic and our estimates to the source back azimuth for a single frequency band (the Detection in a Single Frequency Band section). Subsections therein then provide related equations for the detector's thresholds (the Practical Detector Thresholds and Bayesian Updates section), its predicted false positive rate (the Practical Detector Thresholds and Bayesian Updates section), and its predicted true positive rate against Rayleigh waveforms in both single and in multiple frequency bands (the From single to multiband detector processing section). The sources of these waveforms include cataloged, airborne explosions that were captured from local distances (< 90 km) by a single seismic station deployed in Ukraine (the Datasets of Near-Surface

Figure 1. (a) Explosive source of Rayleigh waveforms at a significant height of burst (orange and gray symbol) above a site model, in the proximity several seismometers (black and blue triangles). (b) Two snapshots of overpressure signals in air (orange curves) that are sourced by this explosion decay with range (gray, dashed envelope) to produce a ground load (black pressure contours) that drives elliptically polarized, retrograde ground motion (blue, arrowed ellipse). (c) The fundamental-mode dispersion curve for the Rayleigh-wave group velocity (black curve) at the site determines the envelope shape, modulation frequency, and minimum group velocity and frequency (red lines) of later arriving waveforms. (d) Rayleigh waveforms along the vertical (Z), transverse (T), and radial (R) directions at the blue seismometer in (a). Waveform amplitudes depend on the pressure load from (b), and frequency content and envelope shape depend on the dispersion parameters from (c). Sensor components aligned with the sagittal plane (thatched region in (a)) record only radial and vertical motion from Rayleigh waves and transverse motion from Love waves. Waveforms in (d) are sourced by EVID 20220322043246400 (Dando *et al.*, 2023). Physical models produced both the pressure pulses and the dispersion curve; the latter is from a site in Ukraine.

Explosions section). We further use a subset of these waveforms to develop an augmented dataset and quantify the true positive rate of our module versus explosion yield (the Detector Performance Versus Explosion Yield section). Appendix documents the multiband filter bank that our module uses to process those data. The supplemental material (see Section S1, available to this article) develops analytical models for these sources (Section S2) as well as the detector's performance (Sections S3 and S4). Finally, we extend detector operation against synthetic waveforms that we model over a yield grid and then immerse into real background noise to measure the detector's true positive rate against modeled source parameters (Section S5).

RAYLEIGH WAVEFORM DETECTOR

Detection in a single frequency band

We use physical reasoning (Sections S2.1–S2.4) to inform two competing data models of noisy Rayleigh waveforms and thereby derive a test statistic for a digital signal detector at a fixed sample index k. Our competing models represent an $N_S \times 3$ sample of preprocessed, three-component seismic data $[\boldsymbol{x}_N(k)\boldsymbol{x}_E(k)\boldsymbol{x}_Z(k)]$ within a fixed, N_S-sample time window as either composed of only Gaussian noise $[\boldsymbol{n}_N(k)\boldsymbol{n}_E(k)\boldsymbol{n}_Z(k)]$ under a null hypothesis ($\mathcal{H}_0$), or as a Rayleigh waveform $[\boldsymbol{u}_N(k)\boldsymbol{u}_E(k)\boldsymbol{u}_Z(k)]$ added to Gaussian noise under an alternative hypothesis ($\mathcal{H}_1$). The subscripts N, E, and Z refer to the cardinal directions north (N), east (E), and downward (Z) in a right-handed coordinate system. Our data model under $\mathcal{H}_1$ equates the phase-advanced vertical-component Z of this seismogram to a noisy radial-component seismogram, which we represent as a sum of rotated horizontal components N and E. We form a quotient between two approximate probability density functions (PDF or just densities) for these data, which are both parameterized by maximum-likelihood estimates (MLEs) for the unknown noise and waveform model parameters under each hypothesis. One of these MLEs relates to the azimuthal angle of the Rayleigh waveform's source. The quotient itself defines a generalized likelihood ratio (GLR) as our Rayleigh waveform test statistic $s(\boldsymbol{x}_Z)$. We compare this statistic against a threshold η for significance with form a generalized likelihood ratio test (GLRT) (see Kay, 1998). The GRLT determines the decision rule to trigger our Rayleigh-wave detector:

$$s(\boldsymbol{x}_Z) = \left(\frac{N_S - 2}{2}\right) \frac{\mathcal{J}[\boldsymbol{x}_Z(k)]^T \boldsymbol{x}(k)(\boldsymbol{x}^T(k)\boldsymbol{x}(k))^{-1}\boldsymbol{x}^T(k)\mathcal{J}[\boldsymbol{x}_Z(k)]}{\mathcal{J}[\boldsymbol{x}_Z(k)]^T(\boldsymbol{I} - \boldsymbol{x}(k)(\boldsymbol{x}^T(k)\boldsymbol{x}(k))^{-1}\boldsymbol{x}^T(k))\mathcal{J}[\boldsymbol{x}_Z(k)]} \underset{\mathcal{H}_0}{\overset{\mathcal{H}_1}{\gtrless}} \eta. \quad (1)$$

In equation (1), the matrix $\boldsymbol{x}(k) = [\boldsymbol{x}_N(k)\boldsymbol{x}_E(k)]$ stores the horizontal components of motion and $\mathcal{J}[\boldsymbol{x}_Z(k)]$ is the Hilbert-transform (90° phase-advanced) vertical component of motion, in which $\mathcal{J}[\blacksquare]$ is the Hilbert-transform operator of argument $\blacksquare$. The matrix interior to the numerator on the left side of equation (1) projects vectors onto the subspace spanned by $\boldsymbol{X}(k)$. The matrix interior to the denominator on the left side of equation (1) projects vectors onto the subspace that is orthogonal to that spanned by $\boldsymbol{X}(k)$; Sections S3.1–S3.2 in the supplemental material justify this geometric interpretation. The scalar $(N_S - 2)/2$ is the ratio of the degrees-of-freedom (DOF) in the denominator to that in the numerator. Equation (1) collectively indicates that if the threshold exceeds the statistic, the detector declares $\mathcal{H}_0$ is true (absent Rayleigh waveforms); if instead, the test statistic exceeds its threshold, the detector declares that $\mathcal{H}_1$ is true (present Rayleigh waveforms).

We estimate the azimuth $\alpha(k)$ of the source simultaneously with the detection operation through a certain MLE $\hat{\boldsymbol{\theta}}(k) = [\hat{\theta}_1(k),\hat{\theta}_2(k)]^T$ that weights the horizontal components so that they sum to the radial component of motion:

$$\hat{\boldsymbol{\theta}}(k) = (\boldsymbol{X}^T(k)\boldsymbol{X}(k))^{-1}\boldsymbol{X}^T(k)\mathcal{J}[\boldsymbol{x}_Z(k)]. \quad (2)$$

The azimuthal MLE $\hat{\alpha}(k)$ then relates to this parameter vector (equation 2) through:

$$\hat{\alpha}(k) = \arctan 2(\hat{\theta}_2(k),\hat{\theta}_1(k)). \quad (3)$$

In equation (3), $\arctan 2(y,x)$ is the four-quadrant inverse tangent function for arguments y, x. We often estimate the direction back to the source from the sensor (the back azimuth), rather than the azimuth. The back-azimuth estimate is then $\hat{\alpha}(k) + 180°$ when $\hat{\alpha}(k)$ is less than 180° and $\hat{\alpha}(k) - 180°$ when $\hat{\alpha}(k)$ exceeds 180°. Section S3.3 explicitly links these MLEs to the detector. Equation (S28) in the supplemental material provides additional MLEs for the effective number of independent samples that are present in our filtered, noisy data.

The equations that support the Rayleigh waveform detector (equation 1) and azimuthal estimate (equation 3) apply to N_S-sample windows that are centered at a particular index k. To process full seismograms, we extend our algorithm to longer time series with efficient, vectorized operations in a detector "module." This module calls various subroutines to compute the statistic $s(\boldsymbol{x}_Z(k))$ in equation (1) and the azimuth in equation (3) at each point k within a much longer, $L \times 3$ sample seismogram ($L \gg N_S$). These operations reorganize horizontal and vertical components of each seismogram to store pointwise matrix products and their inverses as separate columns in temporary, auxiliary arrays. Our detector algorithm then executes matrix multiplication operations by summing over the rows of these temporary arrays with N_S-sample length sliding windows. Section S3.4 details the techniques that we use build these temporary arrays and speed up our computations.

Practical detector thresholds and Bayesian updates

Our detector processes data contaminated with Gaussian noise during its sliding window operations and consequently outputs a test statistic $s(\boldsymbol{x}_Z)$ that is a random variable. Theory shows that this random variable is a ratio of two, independent sums-of-squares (equation 1, left side) and that it has a central F-distribution when $\mathcal{H}_0$ is true (Kay, 1998; his equation 9.15). We use the cumulative distribution function (CDF) for the F-distribution to estimate the threshold η for our detector in equation (1) and thereby ensure that it maintains an approximately constant false positive probability $\mathrm{Pr}_{\mathrm{FA}}$ against noise (or false alarm rate). The term $\mathrm{Pr}_{\mathrm{FA}}$ is equivalent to the probability that the detector declares $\mathcal{H}_1$ is true, when $\mathcal{H}_0$ is in fact true. We invert this CDF for an estimated detector threshold $\hat{\eta}$ at each point in the processing window:

$$\mathrm{Pr}_{\mathrm{FA}} = 1 - F_{\hat{D}_1,\hat{D}_2}(\hat{\eta}|\mathcal{H}_0). \tag{4}$$

In equation (4), $F_{\hat{D}_1,\hat{D}_2}(\blacksquare|\mathcal{H}_0)$ is the central-F CDF at values $\blacksquare$. Its subscripts $\hat{D}_1$ and $\hat{D}_2$ refer to estimates for the first and second degree-of-freedom parameters (D_1 and D_2), and equate to the effective rank of the matrix $\boldsymbol{X}$ (about 2) and the effective number of statistically independent samples in the N_S-length sliding window, minus 2. Our module computes these initial estimates by binning the test statistic $s(\boldsymbol{x}_Z)$ to form a normalized, empirical density. A subroutine then computes values for $\hat{D}_1$ and $\hat{D}_2$ that minimize a misfit residual between this histogram and a theoretical, central F-density. The module then updates these estimates with an adaptive processing technique that uses Bayesian statistics. Our technique firsts select a coarse time grid with a sample spacing that matches the temporal duration over which the normalized autocorrelation of our test statistic, $s(\boldsymbol{x}_Z)$ is near zero (in which the test statistic decorrelates). It then assigns D_1 and D_2 with prior, modified Beta distributions and uses their densities to sequentially compute their Bayesian estimates from the test statistic. Our algorithm first assigns the support of the modified Beta density for D_1 (the interval in which D_1 is nonzero) so that the misfit between the histogram and a central F-density is entirely due to the uncertainty in our estimate of $\hat{D}_1$; we select the mode (the peak) of this prior density to coincide with $\hat{D}_1$. The module then computes a causal likelihood function from $s(\boldsymbol{x}_Z)$ and the central-F density with a moving four-point window along the coarse grid. The module then uses this likelihood, our prior, and an integration normalization constant to update our estimate for $\hat{D}_1$ as a Bayesian estimate $\hat{D}_{B1}$ at each coarse grid point while holding D_2 fixed at $\hat{D}_2$. Our module repeats completely analogous calculations to compute Bayesian estimates for $\hat{D}_2$ as $\hat{D}_{B2}$ while holding D_1 fixed at $\hat{D}_{B1}$.

Equation (4) uses these Bayesian estimates for $\hat{D}_1$ and $\hat{D}_2$ ($\hat{D}_{B1}$ and $\hat{D}_{B2}$) to invert for $\hat{\eta}$. Our applications typically accept constant false alarm rates that range between $10^{-7} \le \mathrm{Pr}_{\mathrm{FA}} \le 10^{-3}$. An example false alarm rate of $\mathrm{Pr}_{\mathrm{FA}} = 10^{-4}$ predicts fewer than 1 false alarm per year against noise with an $N_S = 20$ s sliding window centered at 1 Hz (see Slinkard *et al.*, 2014; pg. 2774). We empirically found that smaller false alarm rates reduced detection rates on visually apparent Rayleigh waveforms observed within a single octave frequency band centered at about 1 Hz. Higher false alarm rates caused our detector to trigger on spurious waveforms with only partial elliptically polarization between the radial and the phase-shifted vertical components. In each case, these updated estimates for $\hat{\eta}$ produce thresholds that are relatively elevated after a signal declaration against a Rayleigh wave and thereby reduce detector sensitivity over the duration of coarse grid interval. Section S4.1 details the equations that enable these Bayesian estimates.

Detector performance and Bayesian updates

A Rayleigh waveform detector shows good performance if it triggers often on small amplitude Rayleigh waveforms and shows poor performance if it often fails to trigger against larger amplitude waveforms. To measure the performance of our detector at threshold $\hat{\eta}$ (equation 1), we compare its true positive rate (detection probability) against the energy of a Rayleigh waveform in its sliding window. The distribution of the test statistic $s(\boldsymbol{x}_Z)$ defines the detector's detection probability Pr_D. It is equivalent to the rate that the detector declares $\mathcal{H}_1$ is true when $\mathcal{H}_1$ is in fact true (top line of equation 1, right side). Theory predicts that $s(\boldsymbol{x}_Z)$ has a noncentral F-distribution that is parameterized by $\hat{D}_1$,$\hat{D}_2$ (or $\hat{D}_{B1}$,$\hat{D}_{B2}$) and an additional, so-called noncentrality parameter $\lambda = \boldsymbol{\theta}^T[\boldsymbol{u}_{\mathrm{N}}(k)\boldsymbol{u}_{\mathrm{E}}(k)]^T [\boldsymbol{u}_{\mathrm{N}}(k)\boldsymbol{u}_{\mathrm{E}}(k)]\boldsymbol{\theta}/\sigma^2$ (Kay, 1998; his equation 9.15). The detector's Pr_D increases with λ. The approximation $\boldsymbol{u}_R \approx \boldsymbol{X\theta}$ for the radial component of the Rayleigh waveform $\boldsymbol{u}_R$ further demonstrates that λ is proportional to the radial signal-to-noise ratio (SNR), so that $\lambda \approx ||\boldsymbol{u}_R||^2/\sigma^2$. We can then fully parameterize the noncentral F-distribution for $s(\boldsymbol{x}_Z)$ to predict the probability Pr_D that $s(\boldsymbol{x}_Z)$ exceeds its concurrent threshold $\hat{\eta}$:

$$\mathrm{Pr}_D = 1 - F_{\hat{D}_1,\hat{D}_2}(\hat{\eta}|\mathcal{H}_1)| = 1 - F_{\hat{D}_1,\hat{D}_2}(\hat{\eta}|\lambda). \tag{5}$$

In equation (5), $F_{\hat{D}_1,\hat{D}_2}(\blacksquare|\lambda)$ is the noncentral CDF of argument $\blacksquare$ under $\mathcal{H}_1$. The bottom equality in equation (5) shows that the condition that $\mathcal{H}_1$ is true is equivalent to the condition that the data includes a signal, for which $\lambda > 0$. As with equation (4), we update the CDF on the right side of equation (5) to use estimates $\hat{D}_{B1}$,$\hat{D}_{B2}$ after our initial estimates provide $\hat{D}_1$,$\hat{D}_2$.

From single to multiband detector processing

The detector operations that we have documented so far apply to a single set of three-component seismograms preprocessed in single frequency bands that may range in bandwidth from fractions of an octave to several octaves. We now extend these operations to an arbitrary number of data files that we process into multiple, suboctave frequency bands.

To initiate multiband detection against waveform data files, our detector module parses a set of input parameters that facilitate adaptation to our data. Parameters include acceptable ranges of filter parameters, maximum permissible decimation rates, prescribed false alarm rates, and various processing window durations. Given these options, our algorithms first automatically decimate the input data if sample rates significantly exceed the passband of the input filters; such decimation would occur if the input maximum filter cutoff exceeds the Nyquist frequency by a factor of five. We then run all waveform data through standard preprocessing operations that detrend, demean, and end-taper the time series in preparation for filter processing. Next, our algorithms input these data into filter banks that band-pass filter each time series within overlapping, suboctave-width frequency bands (summarized in the Appendix). These banks use Butterworth filters and adapt the order of the filters to maintain a maximum acceptable distortion of the filter amplitude within its passband, and a minimal, acceptable attenuation of the filter amplitude within its stopband; again, these options are set by the input processing parameters. Processing operations then pass each band-pass filtered, three-component seismogram into our detector. A subroutine automatically adjusts the duration of the detector's sliding window N_S so that it overlaps with an input, fixed number of waveform cycles in each band (22.5 cycles, here). This adjustment uses the geometric mean of each suboctave width filter band to estimate the number of cycles. The module then outputs each resultant, band-specific test statistic to equation (4) to compute declaration thresholds. Simple arguments with the OR rule of probability update the single-band false alarm rate constraint $\mathrm{Pr}_{\mathrm{FA}}^{s}$ that we use in equation (4) to a multiband false alarm rate $\mathrm{Pr}_{\mathrm{FA}}^{m}$ constraint according to the number of frequency bands N_{FB} in the filter bank:

$$\mathrm{Pr}_{\mathrm{FA}}^{m} = 1 - (1 - \mathrm{Pr}_{\mathrm{FA}}^{s})^{\frac{1}{N_{\mathrm{FB}}}}. \quad (6)$$

This update increases declaration thresholds relative to those required by single bands because $\mathrm{Pr}_{\mathrm{FA}}^{m} < Pr_{\mathrm{FA}}^{s}$ for any $N_{\mathrm{FB}} > 1$ and $\mathrm{Pr}_{\mathrm{FA}}^{s} < 1$. A subroutine then inputs the resultant threshold estimates, test statistics, and other input parameters, and outputs trigger indexes that mark unique date times of estimated waveform triggers and parameter estimates in each filter band. Equation (6) predicts that a single band alarm rate of $\mathrm{Pr}_{\mathrm{FA}}^{s} = 10^{-4}$ (equation 4) is equivalent to about $\mathrm{Pr}_{\mathrm{FA}}^{m} = 9.1 \times 10^{-6}$ for $N_{\mathrm{FB}} = 11$ bands.

Once our module completes detector processing in individual filter bands, it combines the detector output and enumerates unambiguous event triggers in time. If the detector produces a single-event trigger among multiple frequency bands, this single trigger and its associated signal and noise parameters define the unique detection. If the detector produces multiple triggers that temporally cluster within $\pm N_S$ samples over several frequency bands, the module operates differently. In this case, a subroutine identifies triggers that associate with the maximum waveform SNR estimate among the bands. The trigger defines this date–time as the unique detection and collects the noise and signal parameters associated with that unique detection.

DATASETS OF NEAR-SURFACE EXPLOSIONS

We derived two datasets from an existing event catalog to demonstrate the capabilities of our module against explosion-sourced signals that a single sensor recorded from local distances in a battlefield environment. This demonstration comprises three distinct tests against our two datasets and leverages both the single-band and multiband capabilities of our module. The supplemental material derives synthetic data from physical source models (Sections S2.1–S2.4) to perform more extensive detector testing (Section S5). Those supplemental tests use single frequency bands, multiple frequency bands, initial declaration thresholds, and their Bayesian updates to measure detector performance.

Event catalog

We assembled day-long seismograms sourced by explosions and background seismicity within Ukraine that were cataloged by Dando *et al.* (2023). The authors of that work combined a three-component, broadband seismometer AKBB (50.7012° N, 29.2242° E) sampling at 40 samples per second at the center of a 23-element array to detect, locate, and estimate yields for events located 3–225 km from the array's center (Fig. 2, yellow reverse triangle). This array was historically deployed to record underground nuclear detonations that were equivalent in yield to explosions of several kilotons of Trinitrotoluene (TNT), from regional to teleseismic distances. Dando *et al.* (2023) repurposed this array to catalog ~1330 near-surface explosions with yields that ranged between 1 and 1000 kg over 10 months of recording time. Among this catalog is a single event assigned with an *Rg* phase label that has event identifier (EVID) 20220315095750300 (Fig. 2, leftmost blue circle). We used this event to select additional explosions that had smaller scaled ranges to station AKBB (3.4 $\mathrm{km/kg^{1/3}}$) that we reasoned were also likely to excite *Rg* signals. We then supplemented this dataset with five additional events with overlapping signals in the Dando *et al.* (2023) catalog. Our resulting dataset thereby includes a total of 68 events collected from 47 distinct days spanning from 11 January to 28 July 2022 UTC (Fig. 2, circular markers). Source to receiver distances ranged from 2.8 to 88.2 km, and source yield estimates ranged from 13 to 1400 kg.

Once we collected these 68 events, we tested their seismograms for the presence of Rayleigh waveform motion. This test cut ~60 s waveform segments recorded after their cataloged origin times and input them to a Stockwell transform analysis (Stockwell *et al.*, 1996). Our review adapted this analysis from Meza-Fajardo *et al.* (2015) and computed polarization filters in time–frequency space from the normalized inner product between the radial and the phase-shifted, vertical-component seismograms. We applied these filters to the vertical component Stockwell transforms and then inverse-transformed them into the time domain. We also computed the instantaneous propagation azimuth using the Stockwell transforms of the north, east, and vertical components (Meza-Fajardo *et al.*,

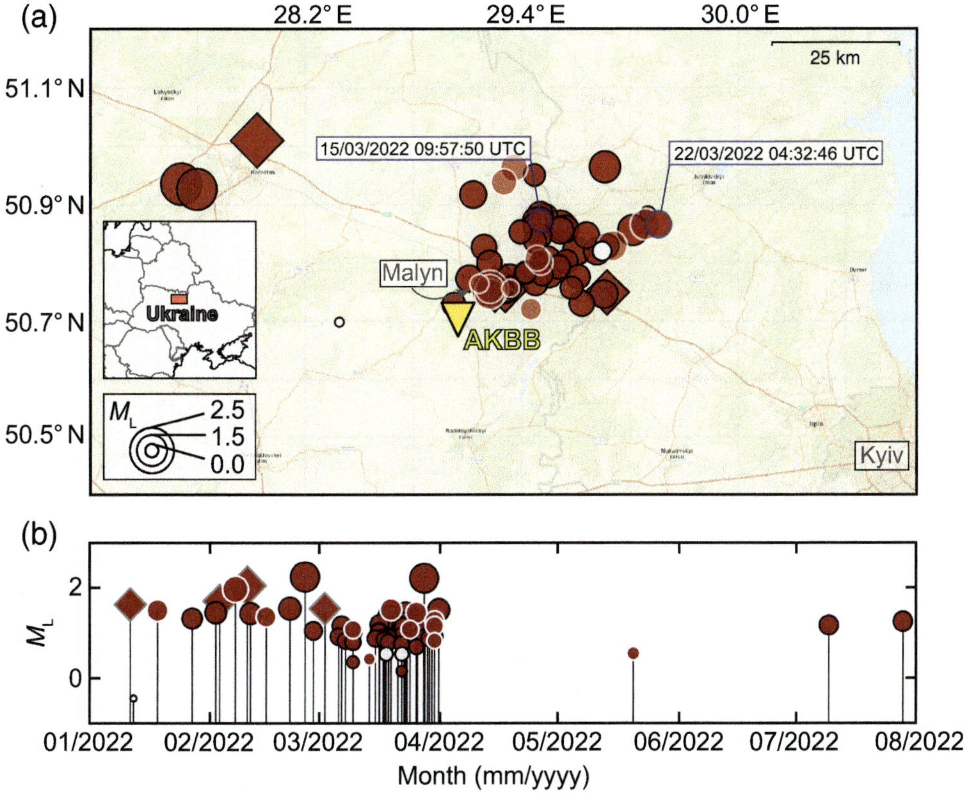

Figure 2. Population of 68 cataloged explosions located in Ukraine within 90 km of station AKBB (a) and plotted as a function of time and maximum magnitude estimate (b) given by Dando *et al.* (2023). Events with blue outlines and indicated origin time show a significant *Rg* signal or consist of signals that are partially superimposed with other events. Marker size increases with the maximum magnitude estimate. Marker outline color indicates whether waveforms sourced by the events include a significant *Rg* signal and form templates (black) or do not (white). The white-filled circles are missed detections from this study. The diamonds are events in which the back-azimuth uncertainty estimate exceeds 45°. The red box marking the inset map of Ukraine shows the size of the detailed study region.

2015, their equations 19–21). Upon correcting the instantaneous azimuth for orientation in the east–west plane, we computed a weighted mean that is based on a wavelet filter to estimate the back azimuth to the source. This operation highlighted any regions of energetic, elliptically polarized retrograde particle motion within each time series, which were often limited to 15 s in duration. The highlighted regions indicate that 58 out of the 68 cataloged events contain significant Rayleigh waveform energy. Processing results for EVID 20220322043246400 (Fig. 2, rightmost blue circle), for example, show remarkably stable polarization and consistent back-azimuthal estimates for waveforms, which are punctuated by early and later arriving signals (Fig. 3b,d). Estimates of the duration of strong polarization match expected arrival times from the cataloged origin time (Fig. 3e, thatched region). A secondary, visual review of the 68 events with a fractional octave filter bank further showed that at least two of the candidate events that contain likely Rayleigh waveforms are mislocated, with apparent *Rg* arrivals preceding cataloged event origin times (e.g., Fig. 4). We conclude that 56 of the 68 events contain marginal-to-likely Rayleigh waveform energy that cannot be rejected as mislocated.

FULL APPLICATION TO REVIEWED CATALOGED DATA

We ran our module against the catalog of 56 reviewed events in full-band, autonomous operation. We preprocessed this full dataset automatically, without any tuning, supervision, or calibration of any kind. This multiband operation autonomously split each data file into 20, 4320 s records of 11 partially overlapping, 0.85 octave-width bands that it truncated between 0.3 and 10.5 Hz and operated at false alarm constraint of $\mathrm{Pr}_{\mathrm{FA}}^{m} = 9.1 \times 10^{-6}$ in each band (which was consistent with a single-band $\mathrm{Pr}_{\mathrm{FA}}^{s} = 10^{-4}$). Each processing operation computed multiple parameter estimates and signal declarations for each three-component time series, over each 0.85 octave width band. We collected declaration times that fell within date bins centered on the expected arrival times of the 56 records of likely Rayleigh waveforms. We selected the width of these bins to match the total duration of each sliding window (about 22.5 s for a band with a 1 Hz center frequency), plus the uncertainty in the propagation time of signals to AKBB, using the CRUST1.0 velocity model (Laske *et al.*, 2012). We considered any declaration counts within these bins to be true positives. This count revealed that our module captured about 95% (53 of 56) of likely *Rg* waveforms in our reviewed dataset when we operated it over 11, 0.85 octave-width frequency bands (Fig. 5a). Our back-azimuthal estimates of known source locations show a mean error from their cataloged value of about 2.7°, an absolute mean error of 11.9°, and a median absolute deviation (MAD) estimate of 9°. About 86% (48 of 56) of the absolute back-azimuthal estimates with signal declarations fell within 20° of their cataloged values, with a maximum error of 70° (Fig. 5b). The total computational time required by our module to split each 24 hr, undecimated three-component record into 20, 4320 s segments, process them in our module, and then organize and write out files on a single core of a 2.9 GHz Intel MacBook Pro laptop (no parallelization) was 84 s.

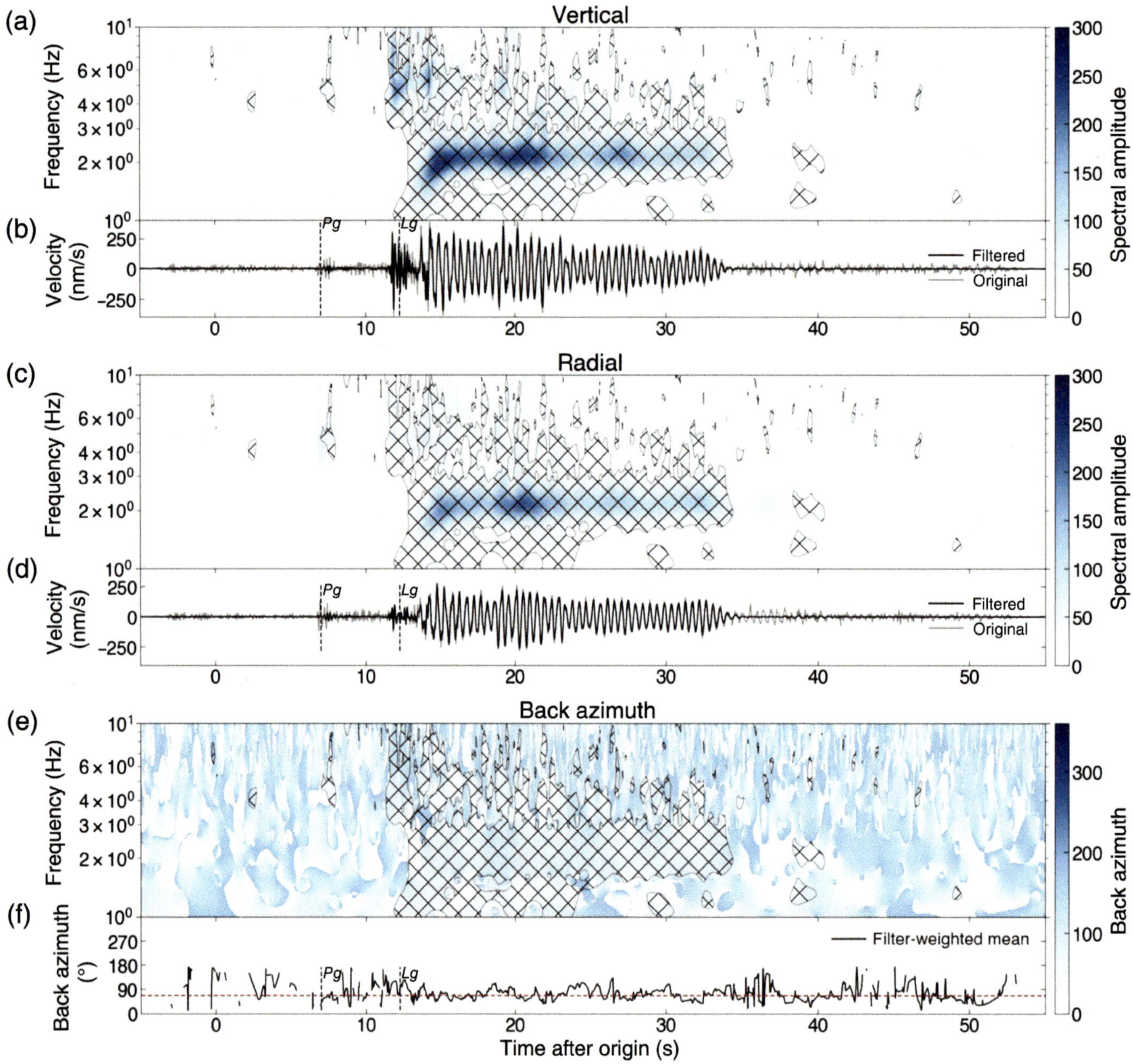

Figure 3. Signals with retrograde-polarized motion that are extracted and applied to EVID 20220322043246400 from Dando *et al.* (2023). Vertical- (a) and radial (c)-component spectrograms are filtered in time–frequency space to show polarized retrograde motion (hatched). Vertical (b) and radial (d)-component velocity waveforms correspond to the spectrograms in (a,c). The original waveform (gray) superimposes with the filtered, retrograde polarized surface (black). The dashed vertical lines indicate the predicted body wave *Pg* (6.1 km/s) and *Lg* (3.5 km/s) arrivals from the Dando *et al.* (2023) location. (e) The instantaneous back azimuth calculated for each time–frequency value with the (hatched) polarization filter overlay. (f) A filter-weighted mean of the hatched azimuthal values compared with the source-to-station azimuth of EVID 20220322043246400 (red, horizontal line).

Once this bulk processing was completed, we reviewed each declaration. We now consider four specific examples here. These examples test if our module triggers against partially overlapping signals (example 1), if it falsely triggers against earthquake signals that lack Rayleigh waveform energy (example 2), determines the cause of the three false negatives (example 3), and explains a possible cause of any azimuthal errors exceeding 45° (example 4).

Example 1: Detection of multiple, overlapping *Rg* signals

We queried our module output on 25 March 2022 after our catalog review had shown that Dando *et al.* (2023) logged multiple, closely timed events soon after 22:00:00 (UTC) on that day with distance ranges of 16–33 km from AKBB.

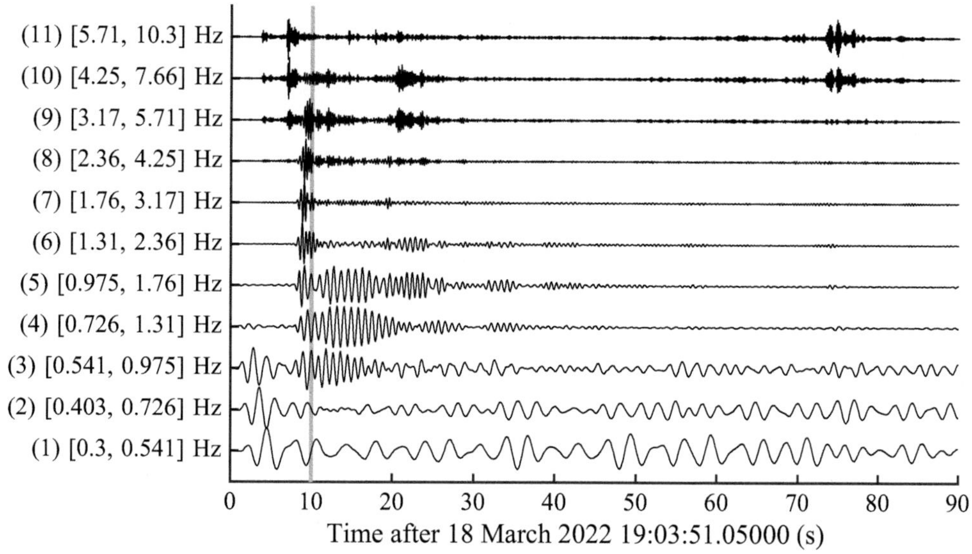

Figure 4. Output of a 0.85 octave-width filter bank that processes 90 s duration vertical-component waveforms at AKBB sourced by a cataloged event that has likely been mislocated (EVID 20220318190401300). The orange vertical line near 10 s shows the cataloged origin time. The three neighboring frequency bands indexed by (3), (4), and (5) show visually evident *Rg* motion. Text labels along the vertical axis indicate the corner frequencies of each filter. The color version of this figure is available only in the electronic edition.

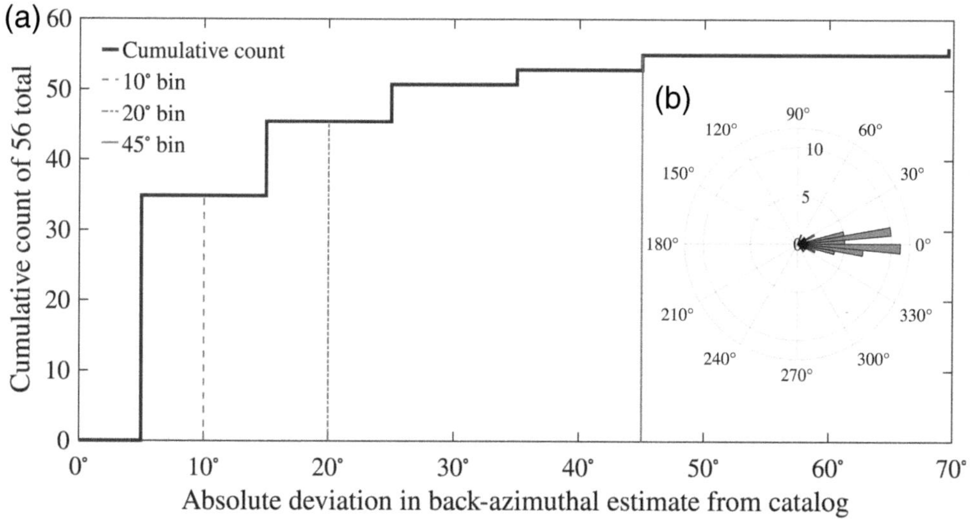

Figure 5. (a) Cumulative true positive count for the module. True positives indicate cataloged events with template labels (vertical axis), compared against the absolute difference between the back-azimuthal estimate and the back azimuth with the cataloged event (horizontal axis). The plot shows that the detector triggered against 53 of 56 template events, and that it estimated back azimuths for 66% of declared events within 10° of cataloged locations, and that it estimated back azimuths for 86% of declared events within 20° of cataloged locations. (b) A polar histogram of back-azimuthal errors (not cardinal angle) shows a 2.7°-mean distribution and a maximum, absolute back-azimuthal error of about 70°. Azimuthal errors that exceed 45° (solid, vertical line) in (a) are all sourced by events with yields exceeding 2250 kg. The color version of this figure is available only in the electronic edition.

This query indicated that the module output peak SNR test statistics in the 1.31–2.36 Hz band within time bins centered at four of five cataloged events, with two cataloged events producing time bins that significantly overlapped (Fig. 6a). This also indicates that the module returned true positives for all five events. The Bayesian declaration thresholds were remarkably stable and showed little change over the 4320 s processing window (Fig. 6b, c). Back-azimuthal estimates output by our detector also provide an excellent match to back azimuths that we compute from cataloged event locations over this processing window and differ from cataloged values by less than 3.17° (Fig. 6f). Additional review suggests that the prior, lower band (0.975–1.76 Hz) also contains signals that are visually consistent with our interpretation of well-developed *Rg* waveforms.

Module output collected from data sourced on 22 March 2022 similarly shows multiple trigger times and well-resolved back-azimuthal directions (plots omitted). In detail, output files showed that the 1.31–2.36 Hz band contained multiple, distinct clusters of apparent *Rg* signals that we timed with events that the Dando *et al.* (2023) catalog lists with distinct EVIDs. Declaration times output by our module match the cataloged times for these additional events within the duration of our sliding window, and our back-azimuthal estimates generally agree with their locations. Back-azimuthal estimates for the earliest arrivals agree within 2° of the cataloged location; outliers include an event with a median back-azimuthal estimate of $\hat{\alpha} = 78°$ that arrives after 04:39:32 (UTC), which provides only a fair match to the back azimuth from the Dando *et al.* (2023) location solution (within 17°). The significant overlap of multiple preceding

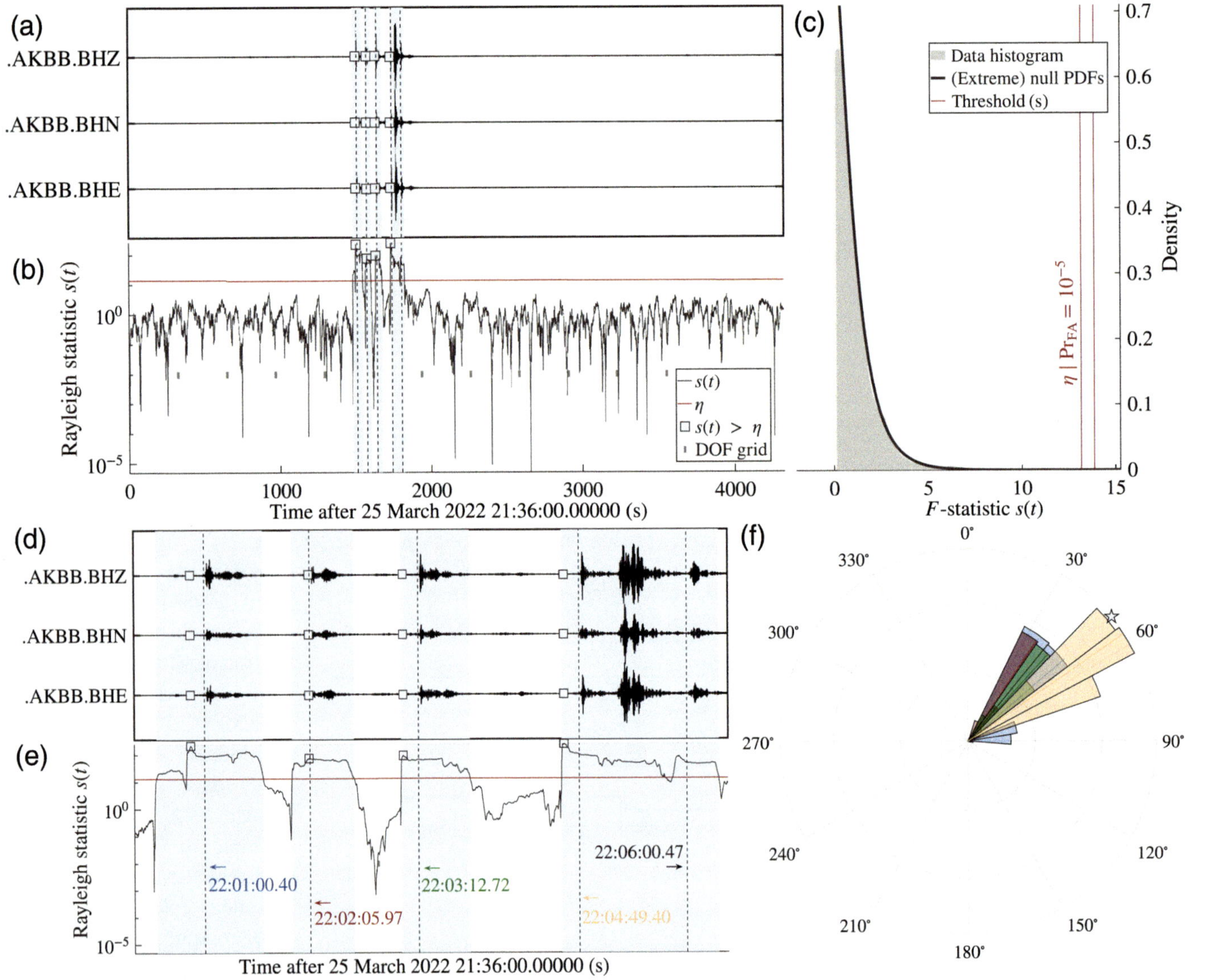

Figure 6. Rayleigh waveform detector summary against 4320 s of data recorded after 25 March 2023 21:36:00 (UTC) at station AKBB. (a) Seismograms that include explosion-sourced velocity seismograms in the 1.31–2.36 Hz band. Squares mark declared elliptically polarized waveforms, and sky-blue regions indicate their duration. Vertical, black dashes mark expected arrival times of cataloged events. (b) The test statistic (black; log-scale) compared with a threshold (red) for event declaration. Thresholds update over an algorithmically determined coarse time grid (gray tick marks). (c) The empirical density (gray histogram) formed by binning the test statistic in (b). The predicted densities (black) correspond to the minimum and maximum thresholds (red) for a multiband false alarm rate of 9.1×10^{-6}. (d) Truncated waveforms that trigger the detector, limited to a 365 s duration window. (e) The test statistic for (d). Colored text marks cataloged event times; two fall within the last declaration window. (f) Polar histograms of the algorithm's back-azimuth estimates against the four declared events, separated by color to associate with the text in (e). A star shows the mean, cataloged back azimuths. The absolute maximum back-azimuthal error between cataloged and algorithm estimates is less than 3.17°. Unmarked concentric circles show radial bin widths (about 467 counts). PDF, probability density function and DOF, degree of freedom.

waveforms likely perturbs the polarization of the later-arriving surface waves and contributes to this error. We collectively conclude that our module reliably triggers against both isolated and overlapping *Rg* signals and shows a fair to good capability to localize their source back azimuths.

Example 2: Detection during a likely earthquake

We next queried module output after 21 March 2022 04:48:00 (UTC) to assess if our detector was susceptible to false alarms against background seismicity. These data captured both *Rg* signals from the same azimuthal direction, and an apparent, regionally distant earthquake that produced little or no Rayleigh-wave energy in the same band (Fig. 7a,b). The earlier declaration indicates a true positive against a cataloged event located 30 km from AKBB (EVID 20220321050533800) with a peak SNR test statistic over 0.97–1.76 Hz. This test statistic remained unelevated over the time duration of the (larger) earthquake signal (Fig. 7a). Instead, the test statistic during the earthquake is consistent with values that we computed against background noise (Fig. 7b). The module's back-

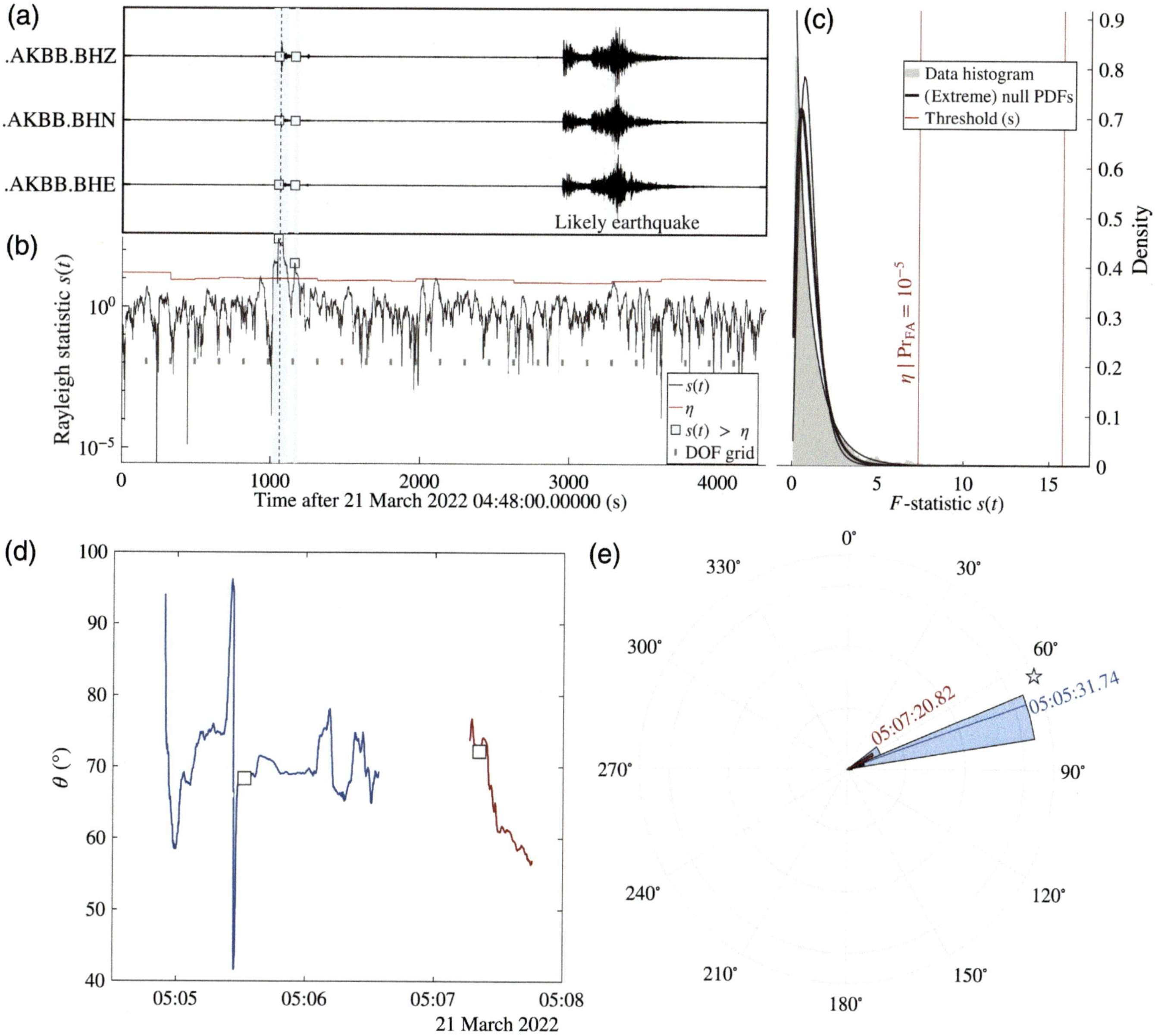

azimuth estimate over the duration of the *Rg*waveforms (Fig. 7d, blue) also match the back azimuth of the cataloged location within 5.4° (Fig. 7e). We note that the earthquake signal may change the test statistic's distribution and lead to a heavier-than-expected tail in its histogram, which may have significantly elevated the detector's declaration thresholds (Fig. 7c). From this example, we suggest that our module does not output false alarms against high-SNR signals that are not elliptically polarized.

Figure 7. Rayleigh waveform detector summary against 4320 s of velocity domain waveform data recorded after 21 March 2023 04:48:00 (UTC) at station AKBB, in frequency band 0.97–1.76 Hz. Data show the detector's insensitivity to waveforms that are not elliptically polarized. (a) Seismograms in the same format as those shown in Figure 6a. The "likely earthquake" text labels an event with about 1000 s duration and substantial signal-to-noise ratio (SNR). The vertical dashes show the expected arrival time for EVID 20220321050557200. (b) A test statistic in the same format as that shown in Figure 6b. It is unelevated during a likely earthquake. Manual review of this event shows little or no elliptically polarized motion. (c) Same as Figure 6c, but binned over the test statistic in (b). (d) A time series for the back-azimuthal estimate over the sky-blue regions in (a,b), separated by color. (e) Polar histograms for (d), with declaration times marked in text. The star marks the cataloged back azimuth for EVID 20220321050557200. The mean azimuth matches both declared event azimuths within 5.4°. Unmarked concentric circles show radial bin widths (about 850 counts).

Example 3: False negatives (missed detections)

Our module missed a total of three cataloged events with origin times of 12 January 2022 08:46:46 (UTC), 18 March 2022 19:04:01 (UTC), and 22 March 2022 04:36:50 (UTC). Filter bank processing against waveform data centered at the first cataloged time (12 January 2022 08:46:46 (UTC)) shows an absence of any significantly energetic signal and likely suggests

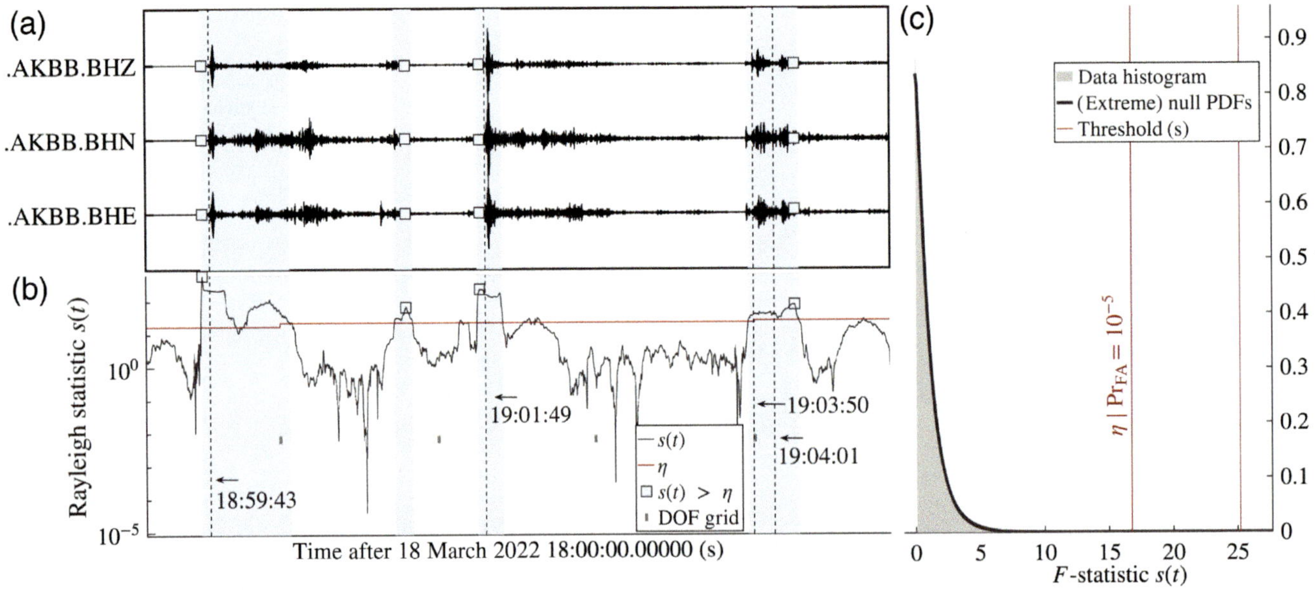

Figure 8. (a–c) Like Figure 6a,c,d, but data include seismograms that record a missed detection (false negative) for EVID 20220318190401300. The vertical dashes marked expected arrival times, and text marks cataloged times. The time 19:04:01 marks the catalog time (UTC) of a missed detection.

that this cataloged event is better labeled as a false alarm. Analogous processing against the second cataloged time (18 March 2022 19:04:01 (UTC)) showed an evident *Rg* signal at the expected arrival time from its cataloged location about 22 km away. We reprocessed seismograms that contained this cataloged time and determined that the detector's declaration thresholds were relatively elevated at the expected arrival time for its Rayleigh waveform signal. This signal was both preceded and followed by other waveforms, one of which did trigger our detector (Fig. 8). The module apparently missed the last of these three events (22 March 2022 04:36:50 (UTC)) because the module's triggering algorithm had not "turned off" from a prior declaration (plot omitted). The signal therefore went explicitly undeclared, even though the test statistic exceeded its concurrent threshold.

Example 4: Large back-azimuthal errors

Four of our 56 back-azimuthal estimates produced particularly large errors that exceeded 45° (marked in Fig. 2). The cataloged yields for these sources also each exceeded 2250 kg and were therefore significantly larger than the geometric mean of 730 kg for the 56-event population. We queried the module output for these events and determined that the center frequency of the band that produced these back-azimuthal estimates was also greater than we would have manually selected to process, given the relative absence of body waves in lower bands. Module output from data sourced by EVID 20220203105331500, for example, shows an azimuthal estimate of 187° (a 50° error from the 237° back azimuth in the catalog) in the frequency band 0.97–1.77 Hz, which provided the maximum waveform SNR among the 11 bands. We reran our detector against these data in the lower 0.40–0.73 Hz band and output a significantly distinct azimuthal estimate of 233°. This estimate shows an excellent agreement with the 237° cataloged back azimuth (a 4° error). The three other events show qualitatively similar improvements with data filtered in lower bands. We conclude that the criteria that use the frequency band that provides the peak SNR and back-azimuthal estimates can, at times, produce poorer azimuthal estimates. We expect this to occur more often for larger explosions that might excite lower frequency Rayleigh-wave modes (like the first minimum in Fig. 1c) that are buried in noise for smaller explosions.

DETECTOR PERFORMANCE VERSUS EXPLOSION YIELD

Our 53 event declarations provide too sparse of data to measure the true positive rate of our module against source yield. We therefore constructed a semiempirical, augmented dataset to supplement our catalog data and better bound our module's true positive detection rate, while controlling for *Rg* waveform variability. To build this dataset, we first selected the *Rg*-labeled waveform that was sourced by EVID 20220315095750300 as a "template" from which to build this dataset. Magnitude estimates ($M_L = 0.9$) for this cataloged event associate with an explosive yield equivalent of $W = 410$ kg using an empirical relationship for Novaya Zemlya, and $W = 33$ kg using a local magnitude relationship derived from United Kingdom data (see Dando *et al.*, 2023). We assigned a yield to our template event using the larger of these two distinct estimates (410 kg). We then confirmed that our module triggered against the waveforms sourced by this event in autonomous operation (Fig. 9). This latter test confirmed that the module declared

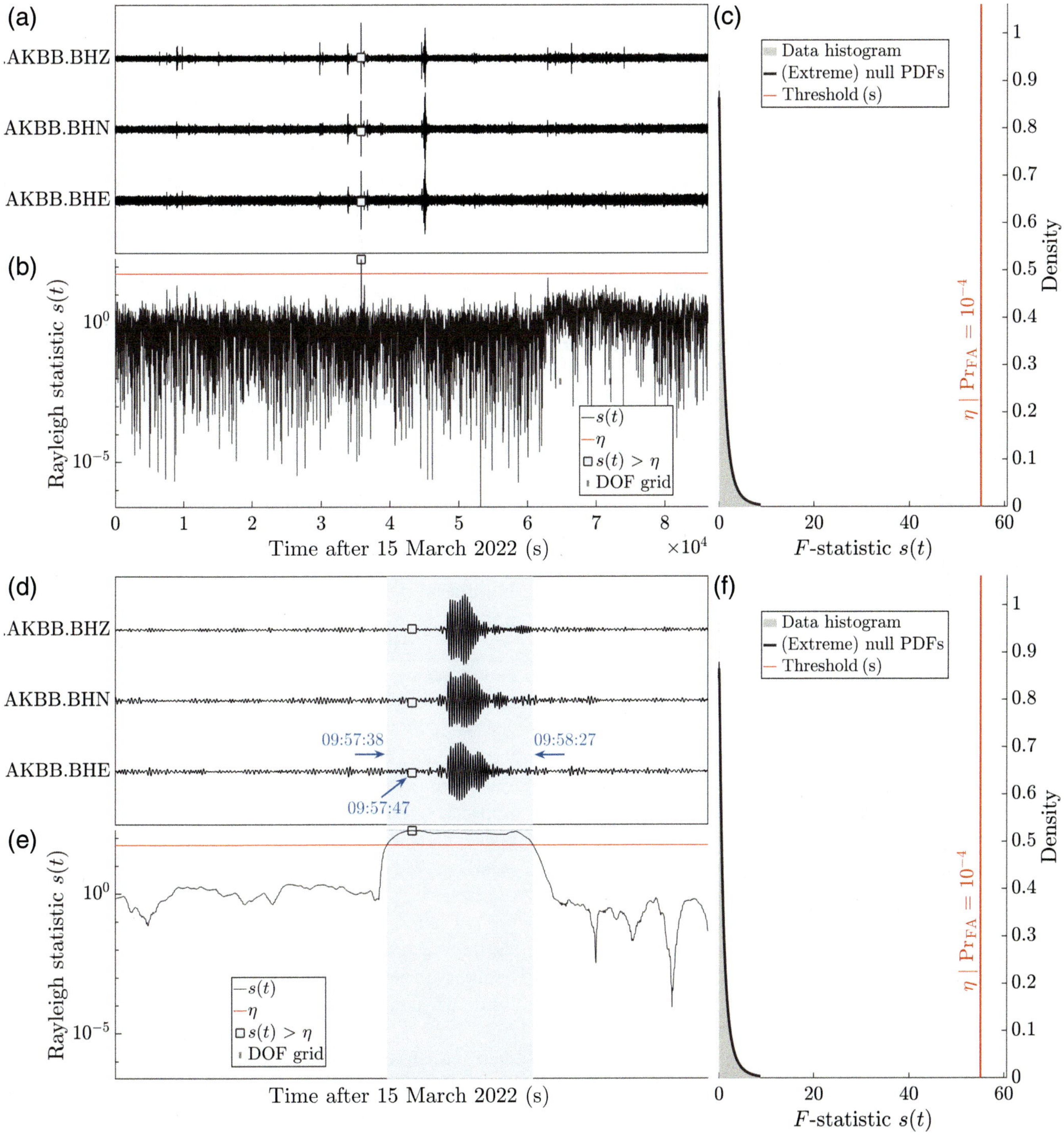

Figure 9. Like Figure 6a–c, but data include 24 hr, three-component seismograms recorded by AKBB after 15 March 2022 00:00:00 (UTC). (a) A full day of three-component seismograms filtered to 0.75–1.37 Hz. The squares mark a single trigger against elliptically polarized motion, and no triggers against an unpolarized, high-SNR waveform that appears about 12.5 hr after the record start time. (b) The log-scale (vertical axis) test statistic (black) superimposed with thresholds for event detection (red) that are consistent with a single-band false alarm rate of 10^{-4}. The times that the algorithm updates thresholds are imperceptible. (c) A histogram (gray) for the test statistic in (b), superimposed with predicted, theoretical density (black) for a central-*F* statistic with 2.0 and 15.0 degrees-of-freedom, as well as thresholds for detection (red line). (d) A truncated view of the output from the Rayleigh-wave detector that is shown in (b) and focused around *Rg* arrivals from EVID 20220315095750300. Text marks the start and end times of when the test statistic exceeds its threshold, and its peak (a square). (e) The duration (blue shading) over which the filtered waveform exceeds its coincident declaration threshold (red line). (f) Identical to (c).

a true positive against this event, and that it output median back-azimuthal estimates of $\hat{\alpha} = 31°$ (equation 3) that fairly matched the 40° that we computed from the location data of Dando *et al.* (2023). Next, we built an amplitude grid to scale the template waveforms and thereby mimic signals sourced by smaller explosions. To relate these amplitudes to yield, we combined the magnitude-to-yield relationship for Novaya Zemlya with the amplitude-to-magnitude relationship that is summarized elsewhere (Carmichael, Delbridge, and Alfaro-Diaz, 2025, their equation B2). We required that the relative body-wave magnitude of each synthetic source be within −1.25 to −0.2 magnitude units of the template; we did not scale the template waveforms up in amplitude because they were already detectable. Our resulting, scaled waveforms thereby represented signals sourced by explosions with a fixed location that sampled a range of yields that were unavailable in the natural data. We then injected (added) the seismograms back into our entire population of 47, 24-hr periods, once every 24 min. We also randomized the order in which we injected the scaled waveforms into the data. This randomization prevented signals of the same amplitude from superimposing with noise recorded at the same time of day, across multiple days. This schedule started 20 or more minutes after the start of the day and ended 20 or more minutes before the end of each day. It thereby allowed 58 full-duration templates to randomly sample daily background noise environments per yield bin.

Single-band detector operation against the augmented dataset

Once we assembled our augmented dataset, we processed the resulting compound seismograms with our module. We performed the same preprocessing operations that we used in our automated run against the day-long seismograms that captured EVID 20220315095750300 and operated our detector at a 10^{-4} false alarm rate against seismograms that we filtered over the same 0.85 octave-width 0.75–1.37 Hz frequency band. Our module thereby processed seismograms in 24-hr batches and automatically updated declaration thresholds and data parameters multiple times per day. This job collectively outputs a set of summary event files that either include signal declarations against scaled templates at known injection times or that missed them (generated false negatives). We counted the number of true positive event declarations within sliding-window-width date bins centered at these injection times and averaged our results over source yield. These resulting averages empirically measured the expected true positive detection rate of our Rayleigh-wave module versus explosive mass. A centered, moving average of these samples along our yield grid then provided a performance curve that predicted our module's detection rates against augmented explosion size (Fig. 10). Critical points along this curve include yield-detection rate pairs (0 kg, 0.025), (132 kg, 0.8), and (185 kg, 0.95). The first point measures our modules' declaration rate against date bins that record background seismicity and estimates that our detector falsely triggers about 2.5% of the time; such background seismicity is unlikely to include pure noise, and our visual review suggests that these triggers may be declarations against low amplitude, elliptically polarized signals (e.g., the later detection in Fig. 7). The second point shows that our module regularly triggers (80% of the time) against explosions that have 32% of the yield value of EVID 20220315095750300. The third point shows that our module reliably triggers (95% of the time) against explosions that have 45% of the yield value of the same explosion The module's mean estimate for the back azimuths to these sources show errors of about 10° and very low MAD values (1°). These back-azimuthal estimates show no apparent dependence on yield (plots omitted here). The "sediment" magnitude-to-yield relationship that Dando *et al.* (2023) provide from United Kingdom data would significantly reduce the critical yield values required to achieve a particular detection rate. We therefore interpret the detection rates of our module in a relative rather than an absolute sense, as interpreted in Dando *et al.* (2023).

Multiband detector operation against the augmented dataset

We next consider the multiband operation of our module against another (new) realization of the same augmented data set that we built from a template sourced by EVID 20220315095750300. This module used its filter bank to process the data in 11 overlapping, 0.85 octave-width frequency bands that were limited between 0.3 and 10.3 Hz (detailed in Appendix). The module therefore, used $N_{\mathrm{FB}} = 11$ bands to update declaration thresholds in each band. These additional bands required a reduction from the prior false alarm constraint of $\Pr_{\mathrm{FA}}^{s} = 10^{-4}$ in a single band to $\Pr_{\mathrm{FA}}^{m} = 9.1 \times 10^{-6}$ in each of the 11 bands (equation 6). This constraint likely overestimated the thresholds because about half of the $N_{\mathrm{FB}} = 11$ filter-bank's frequency bands have significant overlap with neighboring bands so that the effective number of independent bands is likely fewer than 11. Our module also adjusted the duration of the sliding window in each band to match the 22.5 cycles per ~1 Hz that we used in our prior tests.

This test processed our augmented seismograms in 24-hr batches, as before. We repeated our postprocessing binning operations against the module output and produced new performance curves against our data. A comparison between realizations of the single- and multiband performance curves (Fig. 11) shows a significantly improved detection rate against smaller yield explosions and against low amplitude, elliptically polarized background seismicity. Specific cases show that explosions with estimated yields of only 18% of the template's original explosive size produce *Rg* waveforms that regularly trigger our module (a 0.80 detection rate). This provides a 39% reduction in the size of explosions that are required to trigger our detector, compared with those required from single

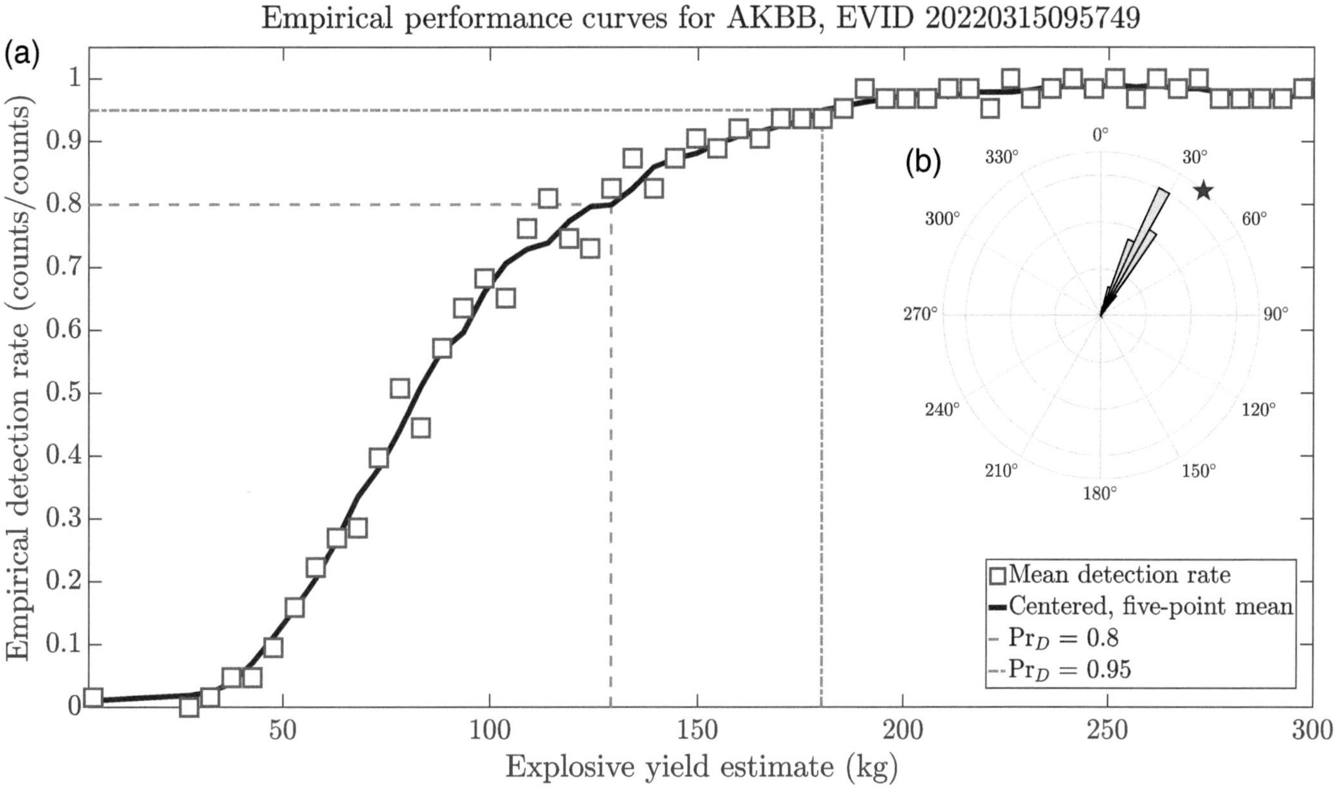

Figure 10. One realization of performance curves for the single-band (0.75–1.37 Hz) operation of the module against 47, 24-hr duration datasets recorded at station AKBB. Input data includes waveforms sourced by EVID 20220315095750300, which were scaled to mimic explosions of smaller yield and then added back into the data, once per 24 min. (a) Scattered squares mark the mean detection rate of our module (vertical axis) against the pseudoyield of the explosion source (horizontal axis). The dark curve displays the five-point, centered average of observed detection rates. The dashed lines collectively show that our module should detect signals from explosions 80% of the time if they exceed 132 kg in yield, and 95% of the time if they exceed 185 kg in yield, at a 25 km range. (b) A polar histogram that quantifies the distribution of source back azimuths that our module outputs (blue bars), compared against the source back azimuth cataloged by Dando *et al.* (2023) (red star). Concentric circles mark radial bin widths (unnumbered). Data show a mean back-azimuthal error of about ~8°–13° relative to the cataloged location. The color version of this figure is available only in the electronic edition.

band processing (73 kg versus 119 kg). Explosions that reliably trigger our detector (that meet or exceed a 0.95 detection rate) show a less marked reduction in yield (145 kg versus 175 kg) because the performance curves flatten at larger yields. Back-azimuthal estimates for these source locations agree and show similar mean errors (11°), and a low MAD (1°) (Fig. 11). We report no apparent dependence on back-azimuthal error with explosion yield. We conclude that our multiband module processing increases true positive detection rates relative to single-band module operation and outputs almost identical back-azimuthal estimates.

CONCLUSIONS AND FUTURE WORK

Explosions and shallow earthquakes generate Rayleigh waveform energy that is observed as elliptically polarized particle motion confined near Earth's surface. Numerous monitoring applications require a capability to passively and predictively detect such noisy Rayleigh seismograms, estimate the azimuth back to their sources, process data with an efficiency that competes with that of energy detector algorithms, and all without required tuning or observer supervision. This contribution derives, mathematically justifies, and empirically demonstrates a Rayleigh waveform detector module that achieves each of these goals. In detail, our module processes input data in sliding windows to compute and (optionally) fuse test statistics across multiple, suboctave-width frequency bands. This module adapts the duration of its sliding windows to trigger against a consistent number of Rayleigh waveform cycles per frequency band and updates its declaration thresholds to achieve fixed false alarm rates. It outputs estimates for back-azimuthal angles to sources continuously, and in parallel with these routine detection operations. We demonstrate these capabilities with several tests against real seismograms that record cataloged explosions in Ukraine. We report five significant outcomes of these experiments:

1. The module's detection rates against real, explosion-sourced waveforms capture about 95% of cataloged events that produce significant Rayleigh waveform energy, which we cross validate with Stockwell transforms.
2. Absolute mean errors in our back-azimuthal estimates to real explosion sources do not exceed 12°, mean errors do

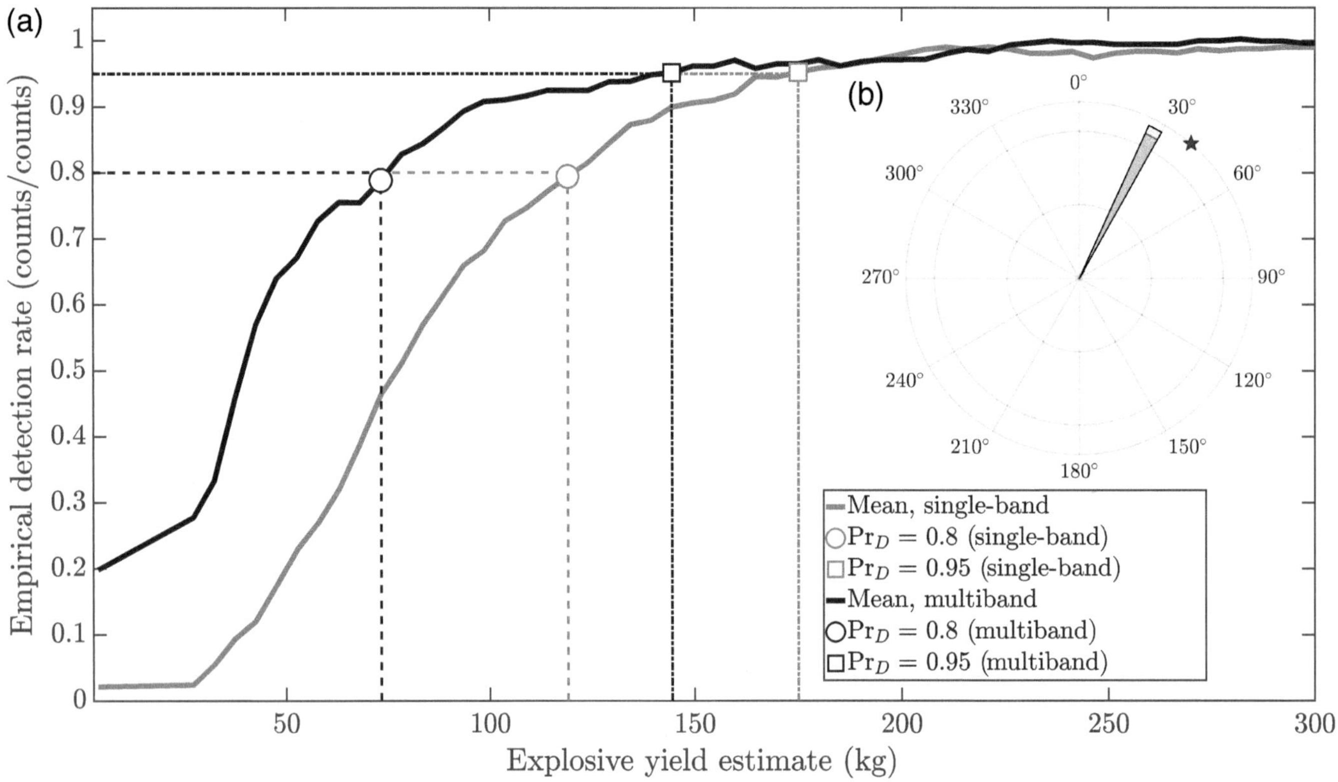

Figure 11. (a) Comparison between performance curves that use single-band (gray) and multiband (black) operation, in the format of Figure 10. These realizations show that the multiband detector triggers against explosions ~50 kg smaller in yield than does the single-band detector, for the same 0.80 detection rate. It triggers against explosions ~30 kg smaller in yield than does the single-band detector, for the same 0.95 detection rate. (b) The back-azimuthal location of the single-band (light bar) versus the multiband detector (darker bar) shows a similar ~10° error relative to the cataloged source location (red star). Concentric circles mark radial bin widths (unnumbered). The color version of this figure is available only in the electronic edition.

not exceed 3°, and MADs of these back-azimuthal estimates do not exceed 10°, when we refer to the cataloged locations as ground truth. We observed the largest estimates in back-azimuthal errors (exceeding 45°) to be sourced by larger yield events; we suggest that lower frequency modes in these *Rg* seismograms may improve back-azimuthal estimates.

3. The module shows significant success at detecting and estimating the back azimuth to explosion sources from Rayleigh waveform signals that temporally overlap with other signals. Such an overlap led to a false negative (missed detection) in one instance.
4. The module achieves reliable (>95% of the time) detection rates against Rayleigh waveforms sourced by (augmented) airborne explosions that exceed 185 kg in yield, at ranges of 25 km, in a single, suboctave frequency band.
5. Autonomous, multiband processing improves Rayleigh waveform detection sensitivity. The module regularly triggers (80% of the time) against explosions that are ~40% smaller than required to trigger our module with single-band processing. In one example, this reduced the yield of regularly detectable explosions from ~120 kg to ~75 kg, at a range of 25 km.

Our intended future work includes three goals. First, we will assess the transportability of our detector in environments that may include significant Love-wave generation. We have initiated such tests against more recent explosions that include battlefield environments in Ukraine (near Lviv), Russia (the Toropets event), against industrial explosions in the United States (Tennessee and Pennsylvania state), and against experimental explosions with cataloged ground-truth locations and measured yields (e.g., Viens *et al.*, 2025). Second, we will use crustal models to predict the propagation-dependent width of *Rg* waveform envelopes (e.g., Fig. S1, available in the supplemental material to this article) along with our azimuthal estimates to help constrain source locations. We intend to integrate such detection-to-location methods into more routine, near-real-time event processing. Third, we will exercise this detector in the ongoing set of dynamic network experiments (Berg *et al.*, 2025). These experiments can help develop more efficient pipelines by inputting waveform amplitudes from our module directly into algorithms designed to estimate the yield from observed *Rg* waveforms and crustal models.

DATA AND RESOURCES

The authors generated all module algorithms and subroutines with MATLAB v.2024b (https://www.mathworks.com/products/new_

products/release2024b.html), which was last accessed July 2025. We generated all figures with MATLAB v.2024b and Python3 (https://www.python.org/downloads/, last accessed May 2025). The authors accessed all waveform data from Earthscope (formerly the Incorporated Research Institutions for Seismology, or IRIS) using Python3 and ObsPy. The signal detection tools that the authors used to assemble detections remain available to any reader from the corresponding author (joshuac@lanl.gov). The authors did not use any Artificial Intelligence (AI) technology to write, review, or organize any text, figures, or the code that is included in our algorithms. The supplemental material stores a 68-element catalog of events that locate within a fixed scaled range of station AKBB, in spreadsheet file format. Other supplemental materials include JSON format files output by our module on year-(day of year) 2022-081. The Microsoft Word document in the supplemental material compartmentalizes our model for physical source parameters (Section S2), probabilistic models for the detector (Section S3), its Bayesian implementation (Section S4), and three tests against semiempirical datasets (Section S5). Text includes high-level commands for physical models and several subroutine algorithms. Snippets of code that enable efficient computations for the detector module appear on pages 65–70 of Carmichael (2023).

DECLARATION OF COMPETING INTERESTS

The authors acknowledge that there are no conflicts of interest recorded.

ACKNOWLEDGMENTS

Input from two anonymous reviewers, David Harris, and the editorial staff at the *Bulletin of the Seismological Society of America* helped significantly shorten and improved the readability of this article. Discussions with Scott Koermer and Chris G. Carr of Los Alamos National Laboratory improved the supplemental material. Research presented in this article was partially supported by the Laboratory Directed Research and Development program of Los Alamos National Laboratory under project number 20220188DR and project number 20250853ECR. Remaining Low-Yield Nuclear Monitoring (LYNM) research was funded by the National Nuclear Security Administration, Defense Nuclear Nonproliferation Research and Development (NNSA DNN R&D). The authors acknowledge important interdisciplinary collaboration with scientists and engineers from Mission Test and Support Services (MSTS), Pacific Northwest National Laboratory (PNNL), and Sandia National Laboratories (SNL). Los Alamos National Laboratory is supported by the U.S. Department of Energy National Nuclear Security Administration under Contract Number DE-AC52-06NA25396. This article has been authored with number LA-UR-25-24421 (Carmichael, Kintner, *et al.*, 2025) by Triad National Security under Contract with the U.S. Department of Energy, Office of Defense Nuclear Nonproliferation Research and Development. The authors did not use AI to respond to any reviewer comments.

REFERENCES

Aleqabi, G. I., M. E. Wysession, and H. A. Ghalib (2016). Characterization of seismic sources from military operations in urban terrain (MOUT): Examples from Baghdad, *Bull. Seismol. Soc. Am.* **106,** no. 1, 23–41.

Baker, G. E., and J. L. Stevens (2004). Backazimuth estimation reliability using surface wave polarization, *Geophys. Res. Lett.* **31,** no. 9, doi: 10.1029/2004GL019510.

Berg, E. M., J. D. Carmichael, C. J. Young, S. J. Eras, and K. M. Hodgkinson (2025). The dynamic networks experiments: Virtual experiments to quantify gains in nuclear explosion monitoring: EM Berg *et al.*, *Pure Appl. Geophys.* 182**,** 4959–4976.

Bonner, J., and D. R. Russell (2013). M_{Rg}: A magnitude scale for 1 s Rayleigh waves at local distances with focus on yield estimation, *Bull. Seismol. Soc. Am.* **103,** no. 5, 2898–2905.

Bonner, J. L., D. R. Russell, and R. E. Reinke (2013). Modeling surface waves from aboveground and underground explosions in alluvium and limestone, *Bull. Seismol. Soc. Am.* **103,** no. 6, 2953–2970.

Böse, M., J. F. Clinton, S. Ceylan, F. Euchner, M. van Driel, A. Khan, D. Giardini, P. Lognonne, and W. B. Banerdt (2017). A probabilistic framework for single-station location of seismicity on Earth and Mars, *Phys. Earth Planet. In.* **262,** 48–65.

Britton, J. M., D. Harris, I. M. Tibuleac, and J. L. Bonner (2003). Detection of mining explosions for a southern Asia seismic database, *Proc. of the 25th Seismic Research Review-Nuclear Explosion Monitoring: Building the Knowledge Base*, 211–219.

Carmichael, J. D. (2023). A waveform detection tutorial: A (very) short course [Slides], *LA-UR-23-23408*, Los Alamos National Laboratory (LANL), Los Alamos New Mexico, doi: 10.2172/1968196.

Carmichael, J. D., B. G. Delbridge, and R. Alfaro-Diaz (2025). The reduced detection rate of signals that are hidden by earthquakes: Case studies with spotlight detectors that operate at seismic arrays, *Bull. Seismol. Soc. Am.* **115,** no. 4, 1449–1465.

Carmichael, J. D., J. A. Kintner, R. A. Alfaro-Diaz, and S. C. Koermer (2025). An efficient subspace detector for Rayleigh waves, demonstrated against explosions, *No. LA-UR-25-24421*, Los Alamos National Laboratory (LANL), Los Alamos, New Mexico.

Carmichael, J., R. Nemzek, N. Symons, and M. Begnaud (2020). A method to fuse multiphysics waveforms and improve predictive explosion detection: Theory, experiment and performance, *Geophys. J. Int.* **222,** no. 2, 1195–1212.

Chael, E. P. (1997). An automated Rayleigh-wave detection algorithm, *Bull. Seismol. Soc. Am.* **87,** no. 1, 157–163.

Costley, R. D. (2020). Battlefield acoustics in the First World War: Artillery location, *Acoust. Today* **16,** 31–39.

Dando, B. D., B. P. Goertz-Allmann, Q. Brissaud, A. Köhler, J. Schweitzer, T. Kværna, and A. Liashchuk (2023). Identifying attacks in the Russia–Ukraine conflict using seismic array data, *Nature* **621,** no. 7980, 767–772.

Gendzwill, D. (2007). Locating cannons by sound ranging in World War I, *The Leading Edge* **26,** no. 1, 27–29.

Gupta, I. N., and R. A. Hartenberger (1981). Seismic phases and scaling associated with small high-explosive surface shots, *Bull. Seismol. Soc. Am.* **71,** no. 6, 1731–1741.

Kay, S. M. (1998). *Fundamentals of Statistical Signal Processing: Volume II Detection Theory*, Prentice-Hall, New Jersey.

Kintner, J. A., K. M. Cleveland, R. Modrak, and A. Dunham (2022). Rayleigh wave propagation in the Bighorn Mountains region, Wyoming, *Bull. Seismol. Soc. Am.* **112,** no. 1, 153–170.

Kintner, J. A., K. Michael Cleveland, C. J. Ammon, and A. Nyblade (2020). Testing a local-distance Rg/Sg discriminant using observations from the Bighorn region, Wyoming, *Bull. Seismol. Soc. Am.* **110,** no. 2, 727–741.

Kitov, I. O., J. R. Murphy, O. P. Kusnetsov, B. W. Barker, and N. I. Nedoshivin (1997). An analysis of seismic and acoustic signals

measured from a series of atmospheric and near-surface explosions, *Bull. Seismol. Soc. Am.* **87,** no. 6, 1553–1562.
Laske, G., G. Masters, Z. Ma, and M. E. Pasyanos (2012). CRUST1. 0: An updated global model of Earth's crust, *Geophys. Res. Abstract*, Vol. 14, 743 pp.
Meza-Fajardo, K. C., A. S. Papageorgiou, and J. F. Semblat (2015). Identification and extraction of surface waves from three-component seismograms based on the normalized inner product, *Bull. Seismol. Soc. Am.* **105,** no. 1, 210–229.
Murphy, J. R., and H. K. Shah (1988). An analysis of the effects of site geology on the characteristics of near-field Rayleigh waves, *Bull. Seismol. Soc. Am.* **78,** no. 1, 64–82.
Napoli, V. J., and D. R. Russell (2018). Transmission and reflection of fundamental-mode *Rg* signals from atmospheric and underground explosions, *Bull. Seismol. Soc. Am.* **108,** no. 6, 3590–3597.
O'Rourke, C. T., and G. E. Baker (2017). A spectrogram-based method of *Rg* detection for explosion monitoring, *Bull. Seismol. Soc. Am.* **107,** no. 1, 34–42.
Schneider, F. M., F. Fuchs, P. Kolínský, E. Caffagni, S. Serafin, M. Dorninger, G. Bokelmann and , and AlpArray Working Group (2018). Seismo-acoustic signals of the Baumgarten (Austria) gas explosion detected by the AlpArray seismic network, *Earth Planet. Sci. Lett.* **502,** 104–114.
Selby, N. D. (2001). Association of Rayleigh waves using backazimuth measurements: Application to test ban verification, *Bull. Seismol. Soc. Am.* **91,** no. 3, 580–593.
Slinkard, M., D. Schaff, N. Mikhailova, S. Heck, C. Young, and P. G. Richards (2014). Multistation validation of waveform correlation techniques as applied to broad regional monitoring, *Bull. Seismol. Soc. Am.* **104,** no. 6, 2768–2781.
Stevens, J. L., H. Xu, and G. E. Baker (2009). An upper bound on *Rg* to Lg scattering using modal energy conservation, *Bull. Seismol. Soc. Am.* **99,** no. 2A, 906–913.
Stockwell, R. G., L. Mansinha, and R. P. Lowe (1996). Localization of the complex spectrum: The S transform, *IEEE Trans. Signal Process.* **44,** no. 4, 998–1001.
Strang, G., and T. Nguyen (1996). *Wavelets and Filter Banks*, SIAM, Philadelphia, Pennsylvania.
Tanis, F. J. (1976). Study of a seismic mortar location technique, *No. ERIM1068006F.*
Tibuleac, I. M., and J. M. Britton (2006). An automated short-period surface-wave detection algorithm, *Bull. Seismol. Soc. Am.* **96,** no. 1, 334–343.
Viens, L., B. G. Delbridge, J. M. McLaughlin, L. Luong, T. Ta, S. Bilek, and D. Cadol (2025). Rapid and temporary deployment of fiber-optic arrays to measure surface chemical explosion series with distributed acoustic sensing, *Seismol. Res. Lett.* **96,** 3280–3294.

APPENDIX

Suboctave filter bank that supports the Rayleigh-wave detector

Filter banks are a series of related filters that decompose a digital signal into (often narrowband) components (Strang and Nguyen, 1996). Here, we consider a filter bank populated with suboctave-width band-pass Butterworth filters that have special properties. These properties relate the low and high corner frequencies within each band to each other, and to the corner frequencies of adjacent bands. This appendix provides the relevant equations and leverages resources published by the Stanford Center for Computer Research in Computer and Music that detail suboctave filter bank processing.

TABLE A1
Example Summary of Suboctave Filter Bank Frequency Bands that Our Module Uses to Process Seismic Data Collected at Station AKBB

Band	Frequency f_L–f_H (Hz)	Order
1	0.30–0.54	4
2	0.40–0.73	4
3	0.54–0.975	4
4	0.73–1.30	4
5	0.975–1.76	4
6	1.31–2.36	4
7	1.76–3.17	4
8	2.36–4.25	4
9	3.17–5.71	4
10	4.25–7.66	4
11	5.71–10.3	5

Each filter band represents a Butterworth filter that is 0.85 octaves in width, has less than 3 dB distortion in its pass band, at least −37.6 dB of attenuation in its stopband, and has a transition band steepness of 0.85.

Within analysis band k of a filter bank, we write the lower frequency corner as $f_L(k)$ and the upper frequency corner as $f_H(k)$. We suppose this analysis band has a width of n_{oct} octaves (often, $n_{\mathrm{oct}} < 1$). The upper and lower corner then relate through a pair of equations:

$$f_H(k) = 2^{n_{\mathrm{oct}}} f_L(k) f_L(k+1) = \sqrt{f_L(k) f_H(k)} = (2^{n_{\mathrm{oct}}/2}) f_L(k). \tag{A1}$$

The first line in equation (A1) shows that band k has a width $\mathrm{BW} = f_H(k) - f_L(k) = f_L(k)(2^{n_{\mathrm{oct}}} - 1)$ Hz. The second line shows that consecutive bands overlap by $\Delta f = f_H(k) - f_L(k+1) = (2^{n_{\mathrm{oct}}/2})(2^{n_{\mathrm{oct}}/2} - 1) f_L(k)$ Hz. The algorithms in our detector module restrict processing to bands bounded between minimum and maximum frequencies $f_{\min}$ and $f_{\max}$, which the user may optionally define. We select an example minimum frequency of $f_{\min} = 0.30$ Hz and a maximum frequency of $f_{\max} = 10.50$ Hz, which generally cannot exceed the Nyquist frequency of the seismometer digitizer. The bounds that we select include the expected frequency of minimum group velocity of a Rayleigh wave, using geological site models in Ukraine. We then set $f_L(1) = f_{\min}$ and iteratively calculate the lower and upper limit of each element in the filter bank from equation (A1). The algorithm terminates when then high pass filter at the next iteration exceeds $f_{\max}$ (when $f_H(k+1) > f_{\max}$). We also adjust the order of each filter within this bank. In detail, our algorithms compute the lowest order of a digital Butterworth filter for which

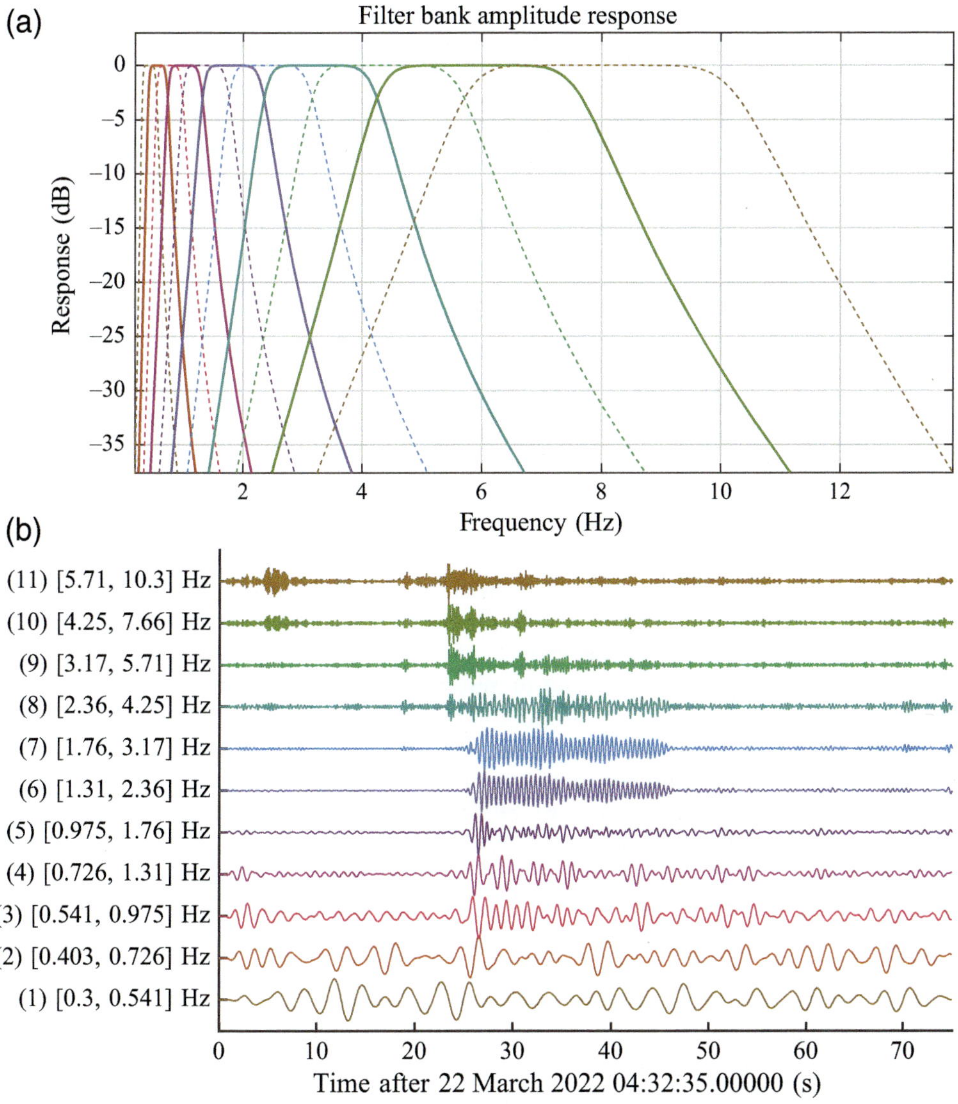

Figure A1. (a) Magnitude of the frequency response (units: dB) for 11 filters within a 0.85 octave-width filter bank that our Rayleigh-wave detector module implements. The solid versus dashed lines separate curves for display purposes only. The frequency axis extends beyond the last corner frequency of the last band to show the attenuation of the frequency response. (b) The filter bank output of a vertical-component seismogram, acquired from station AKBB. Data capture about 80 s of ground motion after 22 March 2022 04:32:35 (UTC). The text on the vertical axis displays the associated filter bank corner frequencies.

the passband ripple does not exceed a certain power (−3 dB), and for which the stopband attenuation is at least a certain power (−37.6 dB). We similarly require a transition band steepness of 0.85 dB to match the default values that are present in some commercial audio processing software. These constraints prevent processed seismograms from being heavily distorted in one band versus another and generally produce fourth and fifth-order filters (in this example). Table A1 includes a list of 11 adjacent frequency bands our algorithm truncated between 0.30 Hz and less than 10.55 Hz. Figure A1 shows their associated frequency response curves with a set of 80 s vertical-component seismograms that we collected from station AKBB after 22 March 2022 04:32:35 (UTC). Bands six and seven show evident, long-duration Rayleigh waveforms with nearly monochromatic energy content that is concentrated between about 27 and 47 s after the start time of the record.

Manuscript received 25 August 2025
Published online 11 March 2026

Surface-Wave Dispersion Curve Computation and Inversion: A Framework Integrating Quadratic Extrema Interpolation and Randomized Layering with Multiple Initial Models

Lei Pan[1,2,3], Jiannan Wang[1,2,3], and Xiaofei Chen*[1,2,3]

ABSTRACT

OPEN ACCESS

Surface-wave dispersion curve computation is a fundamental tool for seismic wavefield simulation and subsurface characterization. However, models containing low-velocity layers (LVLs) present persistent challenges due to the "mode-kissing" phenomenon, in which adjacent dispersion curve branches converge closely, leading to missed critical roots in conventional root-finding methods and compromising inversion completeness. To address this, we propose a quadratic extrema interpolation method that strategically augments sampling points at mode-kissing zones, thereby resolving previously undetected roots while maintaining computational efficiency by focusing on function morphology rather than conducting additional forward simulations. Comparative analyses against the widely used Computer Programs in Seismology package demonstrate that the proposed method significantly reduces root-omission rates and achieves substantial speed improvements in computing dispersion curves. For inversion, we adopt a wavelength-constrained layering scheme that adapts to the depth-dependent resolution of surface-wave data, combined with depth-zoned empirical relationships; this design balances geophysical plausibility and computational efficiency, whereas statistical aggregation of results from multiple initial models addresses inversion nonuniqueness. Validation through numerical simulations (near-surface and crustal LVL models) and real data applications (Mirandola site and USArray) confirms the method's robustness: it accurately resolves LVLs and key structural features, with results consistent with independent measurements and existing models, providing a reliable tool for subsurface characterization in engineering and geological studies. To facilitate the adoption and application of this workflow, an open-source program *QEDispInv*, encompassing both forward computation and inversion of dispersion curves, has been developed and released in conjunction with this work.

KEY POINTS

- Quadratic extrema interpolation reduces root omission efficiently in dispersion curve computation.
- Wavelength-constrained layering and multimodel statistics are integrated to mitigate nonuniqueness.
- We validate with numerical and field data, releasing the open-source tool QEDispInv for adoption.

Supplemental Material

INTRODUCTION

The estimation of shear-wave (*S*-wave) velocities is widely recognized as a powerful tool for revealing the detailed structure of

1. Guangdong Provincial Key Laboratory of Geophysical High-resolution Imaging Technology, Southern University of Science and Technology, Shenzhen, China, https://orcid.org/0000-0003-1471-5501 (LP); https://orcid.org/0000-0002-0612-6371 (JW); https://orcid.org/0000-0002-0950-8121 (XC); 2. Shenzhen Key Laboratory of Deep Offshore Oil and Gas Exploration Technology, Southern University of Science and Technology, Shenzhen, China; 3. Department of the Earth and Space Sciences, Southern University of Science and Technology, Shenzhen, China

*Corresponding author: chenxf@sustech.edu.cn

Cite this article as Pan, L., J. Wang, and X. Chen (2026). Surface-Wave Dispersion Curve Computation and Inversion: A Framework Integrating Quadratic Extrema Interpolation and Randomized Layering with Multiple Initial Models, *Bull. Seismol. Soc. Am.* **116**, 902–922, doi: 10.1785/0120250207

the Earth across a vast depth range, from a few meters to several hundred kilometers (Park *et al.*, 1998; Yang *et al.*, 2008; Shen, Ritzwoller, and Schulte-Pelkum, 2013; Xia, 2014). In near-surface studies, accurate *S*-wave velocity determination facilitates the detection of shallow geological anomalies, such as low-velocity layers or subsurface discontinuities, which is critical for engineering site investigation, geohazard assessment, and groundwater exploration (Karagoz *et al.*, 2015; Yang *et al.*, 2018; Ji *et al.*, 2021). For deeper investigations, reliable *S*-wave velocity structures are essential for addressing large-scale geoscientific problems, including crustal and uppermost mantle characterization, tectonic activity analysis, and lithospheric evolution research (Lin *et al.*, 2008; Yao and Van Der Hilst, 2009; Guo *et al.*, 2015; Wu *et al.*, 2020; Chen *et al.*, 2022).

The workflow of *S*-wave velocity estimation consists of four core steps: the acquisition of seismic surface-wave data, the imaging of dispersion energy, the forward computation of theoretical dispersion curves (forward modeling), and the inversion of dispersion curves (inversion). Forward modeling calculates theoretical dispersion curves—relationships between wave velocity and frequency—for a given subsurface model, providing the theoretical basis for linking subsurface structure to observed wave behavior. Inversion, by contrast, translates observed dispersion features into *S*-wave velocity profiles, realizing the practical value of geophysical data; both steps are equally critical for ensuring reliable results.

Forward modeling of dispersion curves has seen significant advancements since Thomson (1950) and Haskell (1953) established matrix-based solutions for layered media. Subsequent developments, including delta matrix formulations (Dunkin, 1965), generalized reflection/transmission coefficients (Kennett, 1983; Luco and Apsel, 1983), and stabilized propagator algorithms (Chen, 1993; Hisada, 1994), have addressed numerical instabilities. However, models containing low-velocity layers (LVLs) remain challenging: conventional root-finding methods often fail to capture critical phase velocities at modal convergence zones ("mode-kissing") (Liu *et al.*, 2009; Gao *et al.*, 2016), leading to missed roots and compromised inversion completeness. Although specialized approaches like secular function families (He *et al.*, 2006) and frequency-adaptive verification (Wu and Chen, 2022) mitigate detection failures, they incur prohibitive computational costs—an issue for modern probabilistic inversion frameworks requiring $>10^6$ forward evaluations (Bodin *et al.*, 2012; Sambridge, 2014). Building on adaptive sampling strategies (Pan and Chen, 2025) and recent advances in mode distribution estimation (Fan *et al.*, 2007; Pan *et al.*, 2022), this study introduces innovative hierarchical sampling refinement to balance solution completeness and computational efficiency.

Dispersion curve inversion aims to find the optimal 1D *S*-wave velocity profile by minimizing misfit between observed and theoretical curves (Song *et al.*, 2008; Hobiger *et al.*, 2013; Poormirzaee and Fister Jr, 2021), but it is inherently nonlinear, with multiple local extrema, strong nonuniqueness, and sensitivity to parameter settings (Dal Moro and Pipan, 2007; Pan, Chen, *et al.*, 2019). To address these challenges, researchers define reasonable parameter search spaces (e.g., dynamically adjusted ranges via two-stage strategies, Yang *et al.*, 2023) and simplify frameworks by treating *P*-wave velocities and densities as known (via empirical relationships with *S*-wave velocities), focusing inversion on *S*-wave velocities and layer thicknesses.

A variety of optimization algorithms have been applied to dispersion inversion. Bionic algorithms (e.g., genetic algorithms) explore broad model spaces but are sensitive to initial settings (Lomax and Snieder, 1995; Lu and Zhang, 2006; Song *et al.*, 2012; Qin *et al.*, 2020); probabilistic methods (e.g., Markov Chain Monte Carlo) handle nonuniqueness but are computationally expensive (Sambridge, 1999a,b; Bodin *et al.*, 2012; Shen, Ritzwoller, Schulte-Pelkum, *et al.*, 2013); gradient-based algorithms (e.g., conjugate gradient, quasi-Newton) are efficient but prone to local minima (Pasyanos *et al.*, 2001; Gofer *et al.*, 2017; Pan, Chen, *et al.*, 2019; Yin *et al.*, 2020); and neural networks (Yang *et al.*, 2022, 2023) bypass iteration but require large datasets.

Beyond the inversion of picked dispersion curves, advanced techniques have been developed to exploit more information from seismic surface-wave data. One major direction is surface-wave waveform inversion. Although this approach, in its classic full-waveform inversion form, theoretically offers the highest resolution by fitting the entire seismogram, it is notoriously challenging due to high nonlinearity and a strong dependence on the initial model (Foti *et al.*, 2014). To mitigate this challenge, various strategies have been proposed (e.g., Bozdağ *et al.*, 2011; Dou and Ajo-Franklin, 2014; Pérez Solano *et al.*, 2014; Wu *et al.*, 2014; Groos *et al.*, 2017; Pan *et al.*, 2018; Pan, Gao, and Bohlen, 2019; Li *et al.*, 2019; Liu *et al.*, 2019). The other major direction is dispersion spectrum inversion (e.g., Ryden and Park, 2006; Maraschini *et al.*, 2010; Zhang and Alkhalifah, 2019; Liu *et al.*, 2023), which directly inverts the 2D dispersion energy image. This bypasses the often subjective and challenging step of manually picking dispersion curves and is particularly useful for complex wavefields where modes are faint or interfere. Although these advanced methods offer powerful alternatives, the classic approach of inverting picked dispersion curves remains prevalent due to its computational efficiency, robustness against amplitude inaccuracies, and intuitive physical basis. Therefore, improving the accuracy and efficiency of the forward modeling and inversion steps within this established framework, as we propose here, continues to be a critical area of research with broad practical applications.

This study focuses on advancing *S*-wave velocity estimation by integrating optimized forward modeling and gradient-based inversion. By enhancing forward computation to improve the accuracy and efficiency of theoretical dispersion curves, and addressing the limitations of gradient-based inversion through geophysically constrained initial models and dynamic search space adjustments, we aim to provide a robust framework for S-wave velocity estimation across both near-surface and deeper depth ranges, supporting diverse geoscientific and engineering applications.

METHOD

Forward computation

Root-searching scheme. The computation of surface-wave dispersion curves relies fundamentally on accurately solving the dispersion equation $D(c,f) = 0$ across a range of frequencies f to determine phase velocities c for each mode. Our approach adopts the adaptive root-searching scheme (Algorithm 1, Pan and Chen, 2025) for its efficiency and stability in layered media. This scheme strategically determines phase-velocity sampling points to minimize expensive evaluations of the dispersion function $D(c,f)$, which is computed here using the delta matrix method (Dunkin, 1965). Central to the algorithm is the estimator $N(c)$ (Fan *et al.*, 2007), which predicts the number of roots (modes) at a given frequency based on layer properties and thicknesses:

$$N(c) = 2f\Re\left\{\sum_{i=1}^{N-1}(s_i + r_i)h_i\right\},$$
$$r_i = (1 - c^2/\alpha_i^2)^{1/2}, s_i = (1 - c^2/\beta_i^2)^{1/2}, \qquad (1)$$

in which h_i is the thickness, α_i and β_i are the P- and S-wave velocities in the ith layer. Initial coarse sampling points c_j are derived by solving $N(c) = j\varepsilon$ ($j = 0,1,2,\ldots$) across the permissible phase velocity range $[c_{\min},c_{\max}]$, in which ε ($\varepsilon \le 1$) controls sampling density. These intervals are subsequently refined M times via iterative halving to ensure adequate coverage between potential roots. The bisection method (Burden and Faires, 2016) is then applied within each refined interval bracketed by a sign change in $D(c,f)$ to precisely locate roots corresponding to dispersion curve modes.

However, a significant limitation of this approach arises in models containing LVLs, in which the phenomenon of "mode-kissing" occurs. At these points, adjacent dispersion curve branches converge closely, causing their corresponding roots in $D(c,f)$ to approach within a minimal phase-velocity separation. The standard sampling strategy, while efficient for well-separated roots, can fail to place a sampling point between such kissing roots. This leads to missed root identification, manifesting as gaps in the computed dispersion curves in which modes are absent. The dispersion function profile at such frequencies clearly illustrates this challenge: adjacent roots lie very close together, yet no sampling point exists between them to trigger the bisection search. Consequently, critical modes remain undetected, compromising the completeness of the computed dispersion curves for subsequent inversion.

This inherent limitation of Algorithm 1 in handling mode-kissing scenarios necessitates the development of novel methodologies (presented in subsequent sections) to ensure robust and complete dispersion curve computation for complex layered media, particularly those involving LVLs. The efficiency of the root-searching scheme remains foundational, but its susceptibility to root omission at kissing points underscores the requirement for advanced solutions to achieve reliable forward modeling in practical applications like large-scale Bayesian surface-wave inversion.

TABLE 1
Parameters for Model 1

No.	Depth (km)	Density (g/cm^3)	V_S (km/s)	V_P (km/s)
1	0.00	1.78	0.18	1.50
2	0.01	1.85	0.35	1.70
3	0.02	1.80	0.25	1.60
4	0.04	1.93	0.60	1.90

Enhanced root search via quadratic extrema interpolation. The computation of dispersion curves in layered media containing LVLs presents a persistent challenge: the "mode-kissing" phenomenon in which adjacent roots of the dispersion function $D(c,f)$ converge within minimal phase-velocity separation. To elucidate the distribution pattern of the dispersion function, a four-layer model incorporating an LVL was utilized. The parameters of the model are detailed in Table 1. Under the original root-searching scheme (Algorithm 1, Pan and Chen, 2025), sampling points are determined using the estimator $N(c)$ (Fan *et al.*, 2007) and refined via interval halving as shown in Figure 1b. However, if the initial sampling density is insufficient, particularly when roots are separated by less than the sampling increment, no sample point may exist between the kissing roots. This results in a sign-change interval being overlooked during bisection, leading to missed roots and gaps in the dispersion curves. As demonstrated in Figure 1a, such omissions manifest as discontinuities in dispersion curves (red block), compromising solution integrity for subsequent inversion processes. The underlying mechanism is revealed in Figure 1c, where the dispersion function at 19.7 Hz shows two roots near 0.267 km/s separated by less than the sampling increment δc, with no intermediate sample point (black vertical lines) to trigger bisection root-finding. This sampling gap directly causes the missing roots observed in the dispersion curve profile.

To address this fundamental limitation while maintaining computational efficiency, we introduce a quadratic extrema interpolation method that strategically augments sampling at kissing points. Unlike model degradation approaches (Pan and Chen, 2025), our technique operates directly on the dispersion function's local morphology without auxiliary model computations. For any interval in which consecutive samples c_j, c_{j+1}, and c_{j+2}, we evaluate the function at three points. These values enable the construction of a quadratic approximation $Q(c) = ac^2 + bc + d$ via least-squares minimization. This fitting process is applied iteratively in a "sliding window" fashion

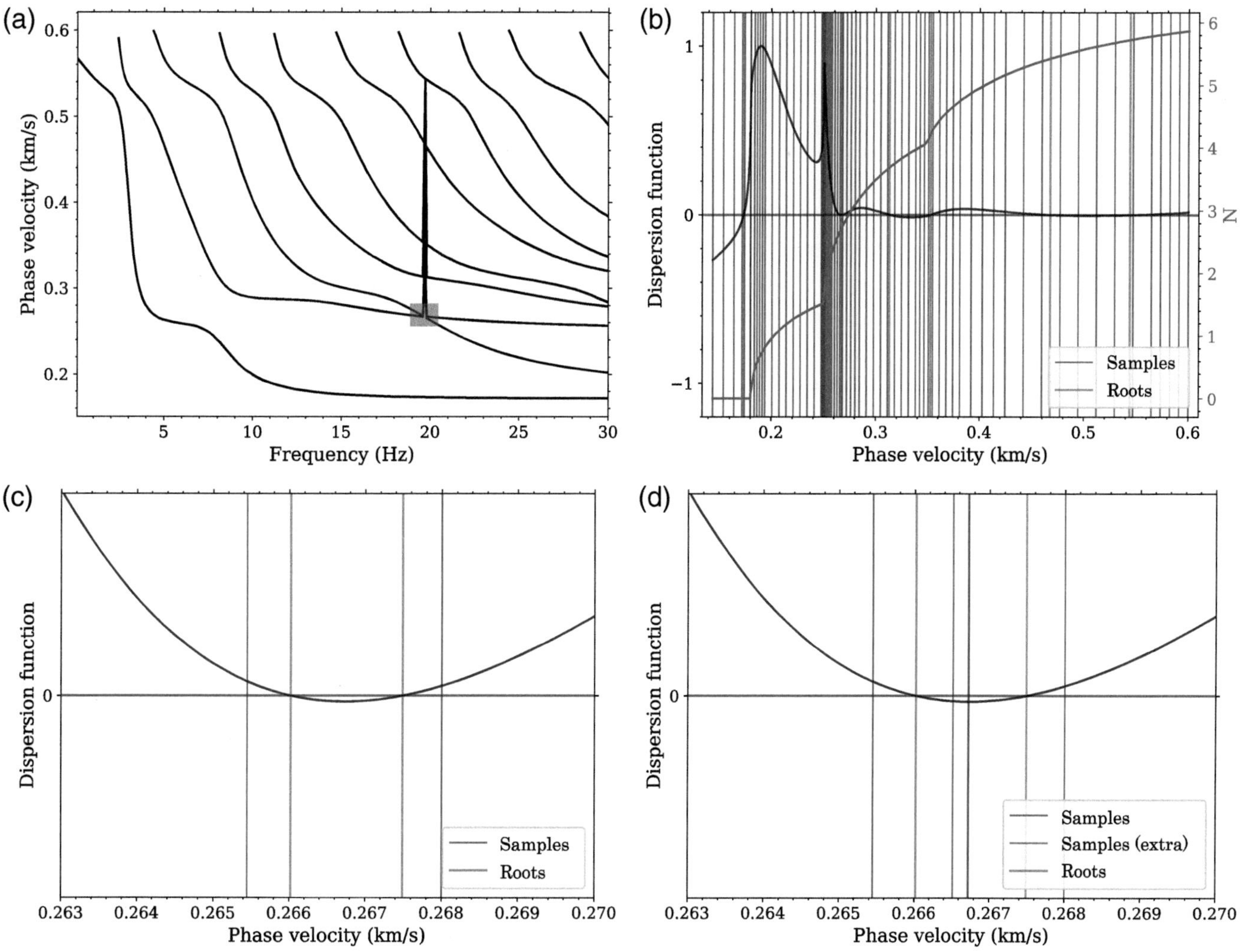

Figure 1. Comparative analysis of sampling augmentation and resolution of mode-kissing root omissions (a) Dispersion curves computed via standard root-searching scheme showing mode discontinuity (red block) at kissing point. (b) Phase-velocity sampling framework: Dispersion function $D(c)$ (black curve) with original samplings (black vertical lines) and root-count estimation $N(c)$ (blue curve, equation 1) at 19.7 Hz frequency. (c) Zoomed dispersion function profile in the omission region (compare with panel a red block) showing kissing roots within sampling gap. (d) Enhanced sampling via quadratic extrema interpolation: Supplementary phase-velocity probes (blue vertical lines) resolving previously undetected kissing roots. The color version of this figure is available only in the electronic edition.

across all consecutive triplets of sampling points to ensure the entire phase-velocity range is examined for potential extrema. The vertex of this parabola, located at the extremum point $c_{\text{ext}} = -b/(2a)$, provides a mathematically optimal location for supplementary sampling. The point will be added to the samples if it is between c_j and c_{j+2}. As conceptually illustrated in our schematic analysis, this extremum corresponds to the inflection region between kissing roots. The new sample c_{ext} (blue vertical lines in Fig. 2a) is inserted between the original sampling points (black vertical lines), creating a refined interval for bisection root-finding. This strategic placement bridges the critical gap where kissing roots would otherwise evade detection. Iterative quadratic extrema refinement progressively enhances sampling resolution. As visualized in Figure 2b, the second-cycle interpolation generates a supplementary phase-velocity probe (blue vertical line) using prior sampling coordinates, strategically targeting regions vulnerable to kissing-point root omissions. Note that this conceptual diagram illustrates the methodological workflow; the phase-velocity samples depicted serve exclusively as procedural exemplars for visual clarification and do not represent actual computational results. The supplementary phase-velocity samples from iterative quadratic extrema detection are revealed in Figure 1d.

The implementation workflow proceeds as follows: (1) execute the baseline root-searching scheme to establish initial phase-velocity samples; (2) apply quadratic interpolation iteratively within critical intervals to compute extremum-based supplementary samples; (3) re-execute bisection root-finding using the augmented sample set. This hierarchical refinement is demonstrated in Figures 1 and 2, in which the supplementary samples (blue vertical lines) resolve previously undetected

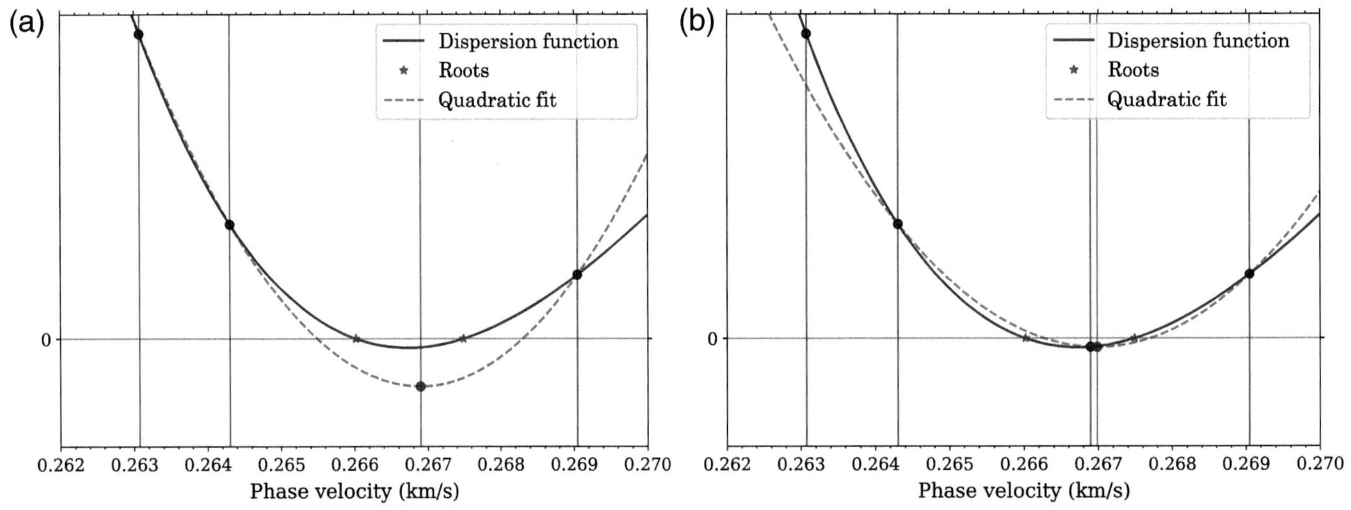

Figure 2. Iterative quadratic extrema detection for dispersion function refinement. (a) Initial and (b) secondary refinement cycles demonstrating targeted sampling augmentation. The black curve indicates dispersion function $D(c)$. The blue curve indicates quadratic fit to three consecutive evaluation points. The red asterisks indicate identified roots of $D(c) = 0$. The black vertical lines indicate original phase-velocity samples from root-searching scheme. The blue vertical lines indicate supplementary samples derived from extrema of quadratic fits, strategically placed to resolve root omissions near kissing points. The color version of this figure is available only in the electronic edition.

roots. Compared with model degradation strategies requiring additional forward simulations, our approach maintains computational efficiency by adding only function evaluations at extremum points. The method's robustness stems from its foundation in function morphology rather than layer-specific heuristics, ensuring applicability across diverse velocity structures. This approach's reliance on the function's true morphology necessitates a careful choice of the forward solver. We deliberately use the unnormalized Delta matrix method (Dunkin, 1965) for this reason. Although normalization is often used to avoid numerical overflow, it can distort the secular function and introduce noncontinuous derivatives, which are detrimental to our parabolic fitting procedure. In our tests, the unnormalized Dunkin method proved to be numerically stable across a wide-frequency range, whereas alternative unnormalized methods, like that of Buchen and Ben-Hador (1996), were prone to overflow at high frequencies.

Comparison with CPS. To rigorously evaluate the efficacy of our dispersion curve computations, we conducted systematic comparisons against results generated by the widely adopted Computer Programs in Seismology (CPS) package (Herrmann, 2013). Within CPS's framework, the *sdisp96* module employs the parameter FACR to govern its root-search algorithm. This critical parameter establishes a trade-off between computational efficiency and solution completeness: lower FACR values accelerate computation but risk omitting higher order modes, while elevated FACR values improve mode detection at the expense of significantly increasing runtime. For representative benchmarking, we adopted the CPS default configuration (FACR = 5.0) consistent with common practice.

To quantitatively evaluate the computational efficiency of the proposed dispersion curve algorithm, we generated an ensemble of 1000 randomized six-layer models with uniform layer thicknesses. The underlying half-space was assigned a fixed shear-wave velocity of 0.5 km/s, while the overlying five layers had V_S values sampled uniformly from the range 0.1–0.5 km/s, establishing systematic velocity inversions. Compressional-wave velocities V_P were derived through the empirical relation $V_P = 1.732 \times V_S$, consistent with Poisson solid approximations. Densities ρ were calculated using the Gardner *et al.* (1974) formulation $\rho = 0.31 \times (V_P \times 1000)^{0.25} (g/\mathrm{cm}^3)$.

The parametric distributions governing these randomized velocity structures are comprehensively tabulated in Table 2. For each model, full-mode Rayleigh-wave dispersion curves were computed across the frequency spectrum 1–100 Hz using 1000 linearly spaced frequency points. The computations were executed on a dedicated scientific computing platform (Intel Core i7-7700 K, 32 GB RAM) under identical environmental conditions to eliminate hardware-induced performance variance. Our choice of comparison mode was guided by the demands of practical inversion scenarios. In a typical inversion workflow, the forward model is required to calculate phase velocities at a discrete, and often irregular, set of frequencies to compute the misfit. For instance, shallow structure analysis often uses linear sampling in frequency, whereas deeper studies may use a mix of period and frequency sampling. A flexible forward solver must therefore be efficient in this "on-demand" mode, without relying on the continuity of a full, regularly sampled curve. It is important to note that for this benchmark, both our method and the CPS package were tasked with computing dispersion curves at 1000 linearly spaced frequency points. This required running CPS in its "frequency-list" mode, in which each frequency is treated as an independent searching

TABLE 2
Layer-Wise Parameter Ranges for Random Velocity Models

No.	Depth (km)	V_S (min) (km/s)	V_S (max) (km/s)
1	0.000	0.1	0.5
2	0.008	0.1	0.5
3	0.016	0.1	0.5
4	0.024	0.1	0.5
5	0.032	0.1	0.5
6	0.040	0.5	0.5

problem. We chose this mode because it is more analogous to practical inversion workflows, which require forward modeling at discrete, often irregularly spaced, frequency points. This differs from CPS's highly optimized default mode, in which it leverages continuity between adjacent periods to accelerate calculations. Our choice ensures a direct and relevant comparison of the root-finding performance for the intended application. Computational efficiency was quantified by total execution time per model and total number of missing roots. In root omission statistics, multiple missing roots occurring at a single frequency are counted as a single omission event.

The comparative benchmark analysis in Figure 3 highlights performance variations between the proposed methodology and the established CPS framework under specialized testing conditions. As quantified in panel (a), CPS demonstrates reduced solution completeness across the 1000-model ensemble, with root omissions occurring in 874 realizations (87.4% of cases) and maximum omissions reaching 54 roots per simulation. These observations reflect adaptation challenges in CPS's sampling strategy when resolving mode-kissing phenomena within complex velocity layer configurations. As indicated by the dashed vertical lines in Figure 3a, our proposed method achieves omission-free performance significantly earlier in the random model ensemble than CPS, demonstrating a more robust performance across a wider range of velocity structures.

In stark contrast, the novel quadratic extrema interpolation algorithm reduces both occurrence rate and maximum omission severity by an order of magnitude: merely 101 simulations (10.1%) exhibited root omissions, with the worst-case scenario capped at four missing roots. This dramatic improvement is attributed to the adaptive sampling mechanism that strategically augments phase-velocity probes near kissing points. The velocity model exhibiting maximum CPS omissions (54 roots) is detailed in panel (b), featuring a challenging low-velocity layer sequence. The exact parameters for this model are provided in the supplemental material, available to this article, to ensure reproducibility. Diagnostic dispersion curve comparisons for this high-difficulty model appear in panels (c) and (d). The CPS implementation (panel d) shows extensive mode discontinuities across multiple frequency bands, particularly after 40 Hz, in which kissing-point root omissions manifest as broken dispersion branches. Conversely, the proposed methodology (panel c) generates complete, physically consistent dispersion surfaces across all frequencies, demonstrating its robust handling of complex velocity transitions. This dramatic improvement is attributed to the adaptive sampling mechanism that strategically augments phase-velocity probes near kissing points. To provide a more direct and detailed comparison, we have added two magnified views of the mode-kissing zones in panels (e) and (f). In these panels, the computed dispersion points from our method (dark blue circles) and CPS (red dots) are plotted together. It is now visually evident that in these critical zones, where two dispersion branches converge very closely in phase velocity, the CPS method's sampling interval is too coarse to place a point between the two roots. Without a sample point separating them, the sign change in the dispersion function is not detected, leading to the simultaneous omission of both roots. In stark contrast, our quadratic extrema interpolation method adaptively adds new sample points in the most critical location, ensuring both modes are robustly resolved.

Building upon the analysis of root omission robustness, we now evaluate the computational efficiency of the proposed methodology against the established CPS framework. This comparison leverages the same ensemble of 1000 randomized six-layer models described earlier, with dispersion curves computed across 1–100 Hz at 1000 linearly spaced frequency points. For full-mode dispersion curves, CPS required a total processing time of 1 hr 17 min 35 s. In contrast, the proposed algorithm completed identical calculations in just 6 min 09 s, representing a 12.6 × acceleration. This efficiency gain is attributed to adaptive sampling strategies.

In practical scenarios especially for traditional surface-wave applications in which surface-wave inversion typically relies solely on fundamental-mode dispersion data, the efficiency advantage becomes even more pronounced. CPS expended 19 min 43 s to compute fundamental-mode curves across the test ensemble, whereas the proposed method achieved the same geophysical constraints in merely 1 min 08 s, yielding a 17.4 × speed enhancement. Such dramatic reductions in runtime underscore the methodology's suitability for computationally intensive tasks, such as transdimensional Bayesian inversions requiring millions of forward model evaluations, in which time savings directly translate to feasible high-resolution uncertainty quantification.

The computational efficiency breakthrough is driven by intelligent phase-velocity sampling through quadratic extrema interpolation. This method strategically augments sampling points at critical mode-kissing zones by detecting local extrema through iterative quadratic fitting. The approach eliminates unnecessary dispersion function evaluations in regions of low root density while ensuring complete root detection in which adjacent dispersion branches converge.

Inversion

Building upon the efficient forward modeling framework established in the Numerical Inversion Example section, we

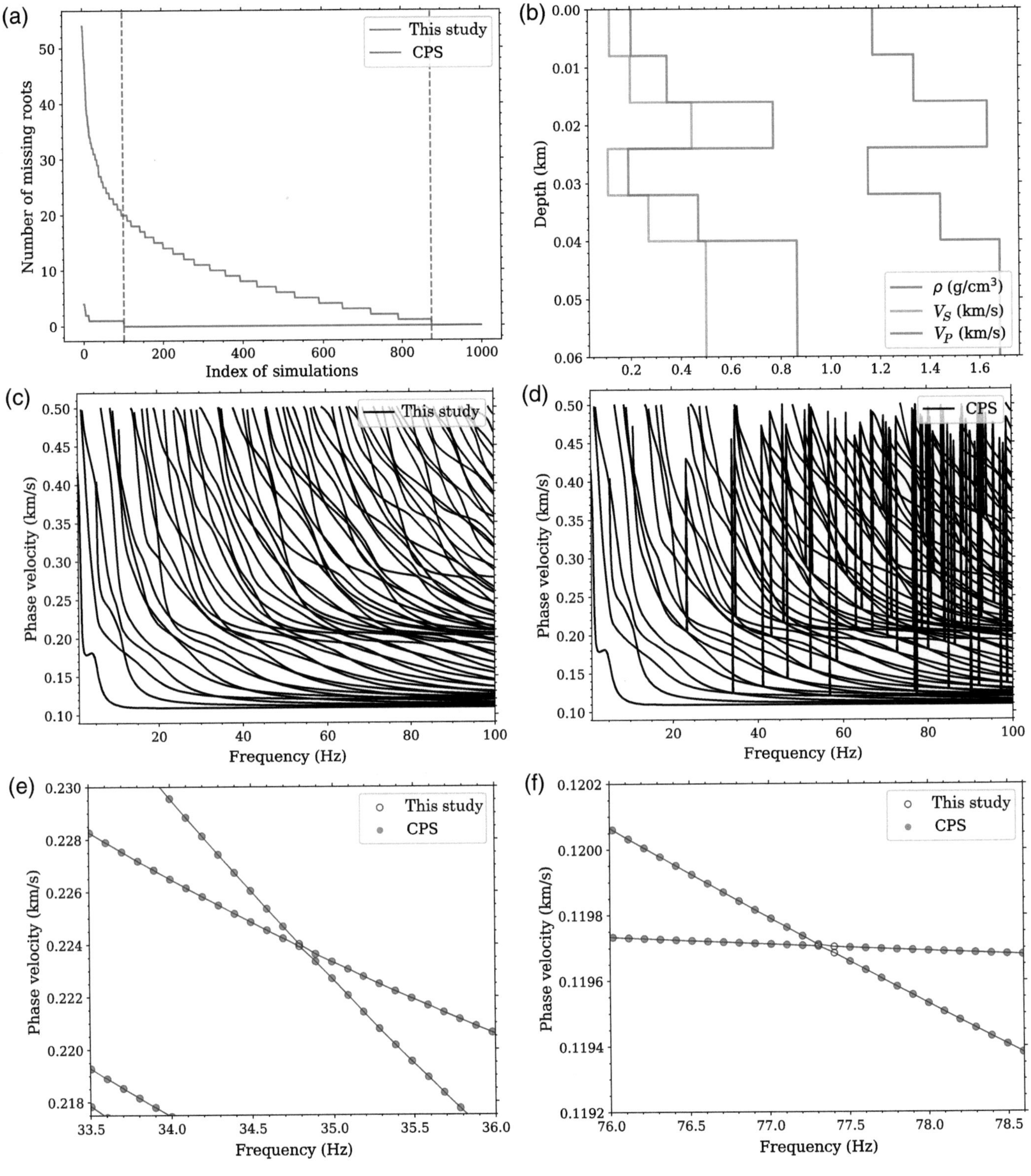

Figure 3. Comprehensive analysis of root-omission patterns in dispersion curve computation. (a) Comparative root omission frequency: proposed method (red) versus Computer Programs in Seismology (CPS) (blue). The dashed vertical lines mark simulation indices in which root omissions cease. (b) Velocity model exhibiting peak root-omission count for CPS (the parameters for this model are listed in the supplemental material). Comparative dispersion curves for this model computed via (c) our methodology and (d) CPS implementation. (e,f) Magnified views of two mode-kissing zones from panel (d), directly comparing the results of our method (dark blue circles), which successfully resolve the roots, against the results from CPS (red dots), which exhibit root omission. The color version of this figure is available only in the electronic edition.

implement a gradient-based optimization approach using the L-BFGS-B algorithm (limited-memory Broyden–Fletcher–Goldfarb–Shanno with boundary constraints, Zhu *et al.*, 1997) to solve the surface-wave dispersion inversion problem. This quasi-Newton optimization technique provides an optimal balance between computational efficiency and convergence stability for large-scale parameter estimation problems.

The parameterization strategy focuses exclusively on V_S as the primary inversion parameter, acknowledging its dominant control on surface-wave dispersion characteristics. This targeted approach reduces solution nonuniqueness while maintaining geophysical interpretability. V_P and ρ are determined through empirical relationships, ensuring petrophysical consistency throughout the model space. To account for varying geological conditions at different depth scales, we have developed a depth-dependent framework for these relationships (e.g., for shallow geotechnical studies versus deep crustal structures), the details of which are provided in the supplemental material. This empirical coupling significantly reduces the dimensionality of the inverse problem while maintaining geophysical plausibility.

The objective function minimizes the L2-norm misfit between observed and calculated multimodal Rayleigh-wave phase velocities:

$$\Phi(\mathbf{V_S}) = \frac{1}{M}\sum_{m=1}^{M} w_m \frac{1}{N_m}\sum_{i=1}^{N_m}[c_{\text{calc}}(\mathbf{V_S},f_i) - c_{\text{obs}}(f_i)]^2 + \lambda\left\|\mathbf{L}\Delta(\mathbf{V_S} - \mathbf{V_S}^{\text{ref}})\right\|_2^2, \quad (2)$$

in which M is the number of modes used for inversion and w_m is the weight factor according to the mode m. Within the data misfit term, $c_{\text{obs}}(f_i)$ and $c_{\text{calc}}(\mathbf{V_S},f_i)$ denote observed and calculated phase velocities at frequency f_i, respectively, across N_m frequency points at mode m. The differential regularization component introduces three specialized variables to enforce geologically plausible solutions. The finite-difference operator **L**, mathematically expressed as a sparse matrix with [1,−1] diagonals, implements vertical smoothness constraints by computing velocity gradients between adjacent layers. Its action on the perturbation vector generates velocity derivatives that penalize oscillatory transitions lacking physical justification. The trade-off parameter λ dynamically balances these competing objectives: higher values emphasize model smoothness during early iterations when velocity uncertainties are pronounced, while reduced weighting prioritizes data fit as solutions approach convergence. Although the regularization parameter λ can be mathematically derived through established techniques like L-curve analysis, its ultimate determination remains inherently interpretive within geophysical inversion workflows. This interpretive dimension arises from the critical need to harmonize algorithmic outputs with geological plausibility of the resulting velocity model and consistency with regional subsurface constraints.

Layering definition based on wavelength constraints. Surface-wave dispersion inversion relies heavily on a well-constrained model parameterization to balance resolution capabilities with the nonuniqueness of the inverse problem. The approach presented herein is designed to reflect the depth-dependent resolution of surface-wave data—higher at shallow depths and decreasing with depth—while introducing controlled randomness to explore plausible subsurface configurations. This parameterization strategy is tailored to generate layered earth models that respect the physical constraints of surface-wave propagation, particularly the relationship between wavelength and subsurface sensitivity, building on the foundational logic of systematic layering linked to wavelength characteristics as discussed by Cox and Teague (2016).

The layering scheme begins with defining the shallowest interfaces using the minimum resolved wavelength ($\lambda_{\min}$) from the experimental dispersion curves of the fundamental mode, as shallow depths are most reliably resolved by surface waves. The first interface (d_1) is defined as $d_1 = (\lambda_{\min}/2) \times a$, in which a is a scaling factor constrained to the range $0 < a \le 1$. This flexibility in d_1 allows for fine adjustments to capture subtle near-surface variations, acknowledging that surface-wave data are most sensitive to shallow stratigraphy; this choice aligns with the observation that $\lambda_{\min}$-related depths (e.g., $\lambda_{\min}/2$) are critical for anchoring shallow velocity constraints.

For layers below d_2, layer thicknesses are generated using a multiplicative factor (b), in which each layer's b_i is randomly selected within a user-defined range ($b_{\min} < b < b_{\max}$) with $b_{\min} > 1$. This means the thickness of each deeper layer is determined by multiplying the thickness of the immediately overlying layer by a unique b value drawn from the specified range, ensuring controlled variability in how thicknesses increase with depth. This design is motivated by the diminishing resolution of surface waves at greater depths because deeper structures are less well constrained by surface-wave data. Unlike fixed thicknesses, this approach produces depth-dependent layer dimensions that naturally adapt to the reduced sensitivity of surface waves to deep subsurface features, echoing the idea of systematic layering adjustments.

The layering process terminates when the maximum depth of the deepest layer exceeds $\lambda_{\max}/2$, in which $\lambda_{\max}$ is the maximum resolved wavelength from the dispersion curves of the fundamental mode. This termination criterion is rooted in the understanding that surface-wave dispersion data provide limited constraint beyond depths of approximately $\lambda_{\max}/2$, making deeper layers less reliable and unnecessary for fitting the experimental data.

To account for the inherent uncertainty in subsurface stratigraphy, the actual velocity interfaces within the model are randomized within the bounds of the predefined layer depth ranges. For example, the interface between the first and second layers is randomly positioned between 0 and d_1, introducing plausible variability while remaining within the physically

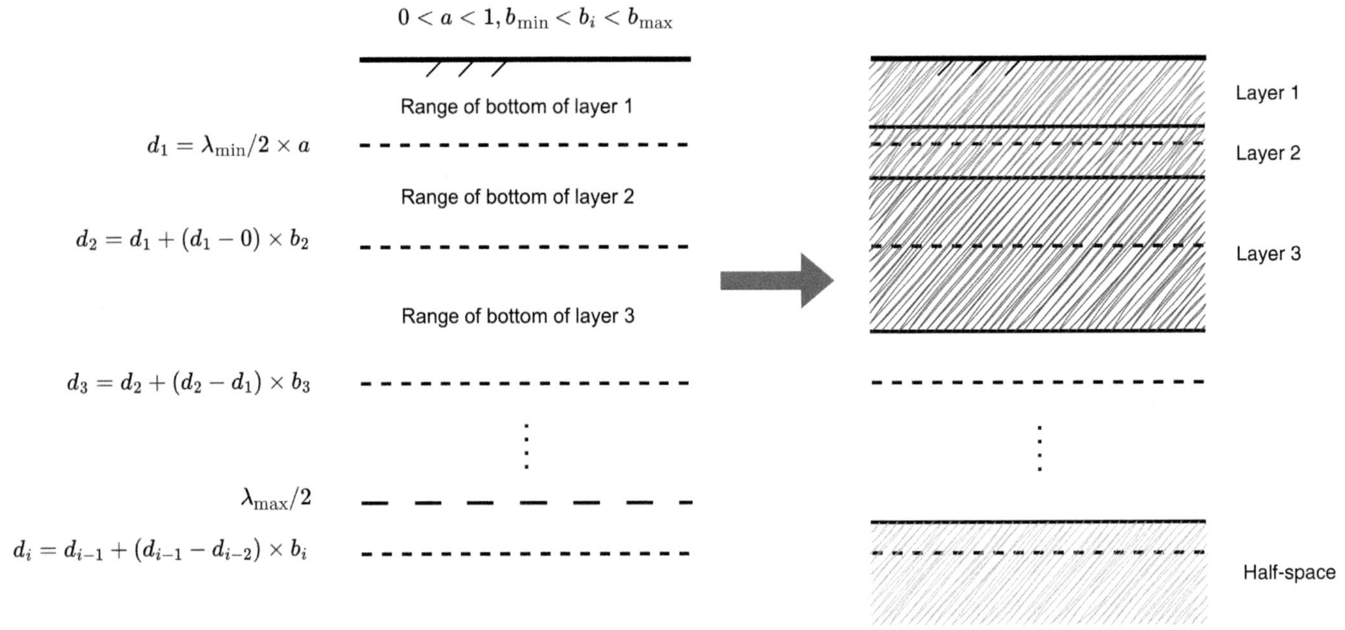

Figure 4. Schematic illustration of the layering definition process for surface-wave inversion. The color version of this figure is available only in the electronic edition.

meaningful bounds set by $\lambda_{\min}$. This randomization ensures that the parameterization explores a range of potential subsurface configurations, mitigating the risk of over-reliance on a single deterministic layering scheme and addressing the nonuniqueness of the inverse problem. Figure 4 shows the workflow for defining subsurface layers for the inversion.

Notably, the minimum and maximum resolved wavelengths ($\lambda_{\min}$ and $\lambda_{\max}$) are both derived from the experimental dispersion curves of the fundamental mode. This choice is guided by two key considerations. First, fundamental-mode dispersion curves are generally easier to extract from field data and tend to yield higher-quality results, which aligns with the practical emphasis on reliable data utilization in surface-wave inversion. Second, even when higher-mode dispersion curves can be extracted, they typically correspond to higher frequencies, which primarily enhance constraints on shallow subsurface structures—a feature that aligns with the inherent strength of surface-wave methods in resolving near-surface features, as noted in related discussions of depth-dependent resolution. The introduction of the scaling factor a in the definition of the first interface d_1 explicitly incorporates this focus on shallow resolution: by allowing fine adjustments to d_1 within a physically meaningful range ($0 < a \leq 1$), it enables the model to better capture the subtle near-surface variations that both fundamental-mode data and higher-frequency components (including those from higher modes) are well suited to resolve.

In summary, this parameterization strategy balances physical constraints (via wavelength-dependent depth bounds) with controlled randomness (via scaling factors and interface randomization), generating layered models that are both geophysically plausible and adaptable to the resolution limits of surface-wave data. By explicitly linking layer dimensions to the wavelength content of the dispersion data and incorporating variability in interface positions, the approach supports robust inversion by encompassing a range of realistic subsurface scenarios.

Inversion workflow. The inversion workflow outlined here focuses on optimizing and aggregating results from a controlled ensemble of initial models, with an emphasis on statistical robustness to address inversion nonuniqueness.

A predefined number of initial models (denoted as N) is generated, in which each model adheres to the layering rules established in the preceding section. This ensures consistency in the structural framework of all initial models while introducing variability through randomization of parameters (e.g., the scaling factor a and multiplicative factor b) within their respective bounds. The use of N models, typically set to a sufficiently large value (e.g., 100–500), is intended to broadly sample the plausible range of subsurface configurations permitted by the layering constraints, thereby mitigating bias from any single starting point.

To set the initial shear-wave velocity (V_S) for these N models, we leverage the relationship between surface-wave phase velocity and subsurface V_S, following the approach outlined in Fang *et al.* (2015). As a rule of thumb, the fundamental-mode Rayleigh-wave phase velocity is most sensitive to V_S at depths approximately 1/3 of its corresponding wavelength. For a uniform half-space Poisson solid, the phase velocity c of Rayleigh waves relates to V_S as $c = 0.92V_S$. Guided by this relationship, we derive the initial V_S at depths of 1/3 of each wavelength from the extracted fundamental-mode dispersion curve: $V_S \approx 1.1c$, in which c is the measured phase velocity at the corresponding

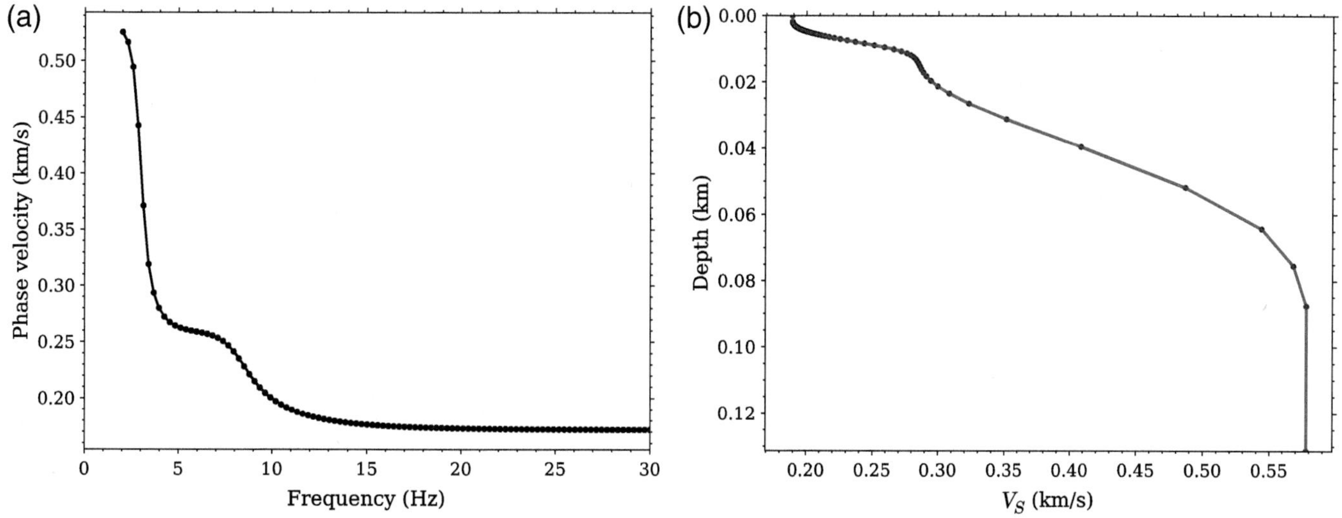

Figure 5. (a) Fundamental-mode theoretical dispersion curves of model 1. The black dots represent key data points on the dispersion curve. (b) Initial shear-wave velocity derived from phase velocity values. The black dots in this figure correspond to the positions of the black dots in (a) after converting the frequency–phase velocity data to depth–shear-wave velocity data. The red line shows the initial shear-wave velocity model obtained by linearly interpolating the black dots, which is processed to avoid abrupt velocity jumps. The color version of this figure is available only in the electronic edition.

wavelength. These discrete values are then subjected to a smoothing operation to avoid abrupt velocity jumps (such as artificial LVL or high-velocity layer) before being interpolated across the layers defined by our layering scheme to form a complete initial V_S model. This process and its key results are visually demonstrated in the accompanying Figure 5. Specifically, Figure 5a shows the theoretical fundamental-mode dispersion curve of model 1, with black dots marking the critical data points of frequency and phase velocity that serve as the basis for subsequent calculations. Figure 5b presents the initial V_S model derived from the phase velocity values.

Each of these N initial models is inverted using the L-BFGS-B algorithm, a bound-constrained quasi-Newton method well suited for gradient-based refinement of layered earth parameters. As a gradient-dependent algorithm, L-BFGS-B requires the calculation of sensitivity kernels (i.e., gradients), which are recomputed at each iteration to guide the model update. The inversion process for each model terminates when one of two conditions is met: a maximum number of iterations (e.g., 100) is reached, or the fractional reduction in the objective function between steps falls below a predefined relative tolerance (e.g., 10^{-5}). The sensitivity kernels describe how changes in subsurface parameters affect the theoretical dispersion curve. Following the approach outlined in Pan, Chen, *et al.* (2019), sensitivity kernels for compression-wave velocity (V_P), shear-wave velocity (V_S), and mass density (ρ) are first computed individually. These kernels quantify the partial derivatives of phase velocity (c) with respect to each parameter ($\partial c/\partial V_P$, $\partial c/\partial V_S$, $\partial c/\partial \rho$), capturing how small perturbations in V_P, V_S, or ρ propagate to changes in the dispersion curve. Figure 6 shows the sensitivity kernels of V_S, V_P, and ρ for model 1, visualizing the depth-dependent sensitivity of phase velocity to each parameter, with V_S exhibiting the strongest sensitivity in shallow to mid-depths, consistent with the focus on V_S adjustment in inversion.

To align with the inversion framework, in which only V_S is adjusted (with V_P and ρ derived from empirical relationships with V_S), the total sensitivity of c to V_S (dc/dV_S) is obtained using the derivative chain rules. Specifically, because $V_P = f(V_S)$ and $\rho = g(V_S)$ via depth-zoned empirical relationships, their derivatives with respect to V_S (dV_P/dV_S and $d\rho/dV_S$) are combined with the individual sensitivity kernels: $dc/dV_S = (\partial c/\partial V_S) + (\partial c/\partial V_P)(dV_P/dV_S) + (\partial c/\partial \rho)(d\rho/dV_S)$. This aggregated gradient ensures the L-BFGS-B algorithm efficiently updates V_S by accounting for both its direct impact on c and its indirect influence through V_P and ρ.

Following the completion of all N inversions, statistical analysis is performed on the set of acceptable models (those with misfit values deemed reasonable for the study) to derive a final representative model. This analysis focuses on two key metrics: the median V_S and the 10th/90th percentiles (P_{10}/P_{90}) at each depth. The median V_S is used to define the central trend of the inverted results, providing a robust estimate of the most probable velocity at each depth. The P_{10} and P_{90} percentiles quantify the spread of the inverted models, capturing the range of plausible velocities consistent with the experimental data and reflecting epistemic uncertainty. Corresponding median, P_{10}, and P_{90} values for V_P and ρ are then derived using the depth-zoned empirical relationships applied to the statistical results of V_S.

This workflow leverages the structured variability of N initial models to explore the solution space, uses the L-BFGS-B algorithm for efficient optimization, integrates empirical relationships for complementary parameters, and employs median and percentile statistics to distill a final model that balances central tendency with uncertainty. By anchoring the process

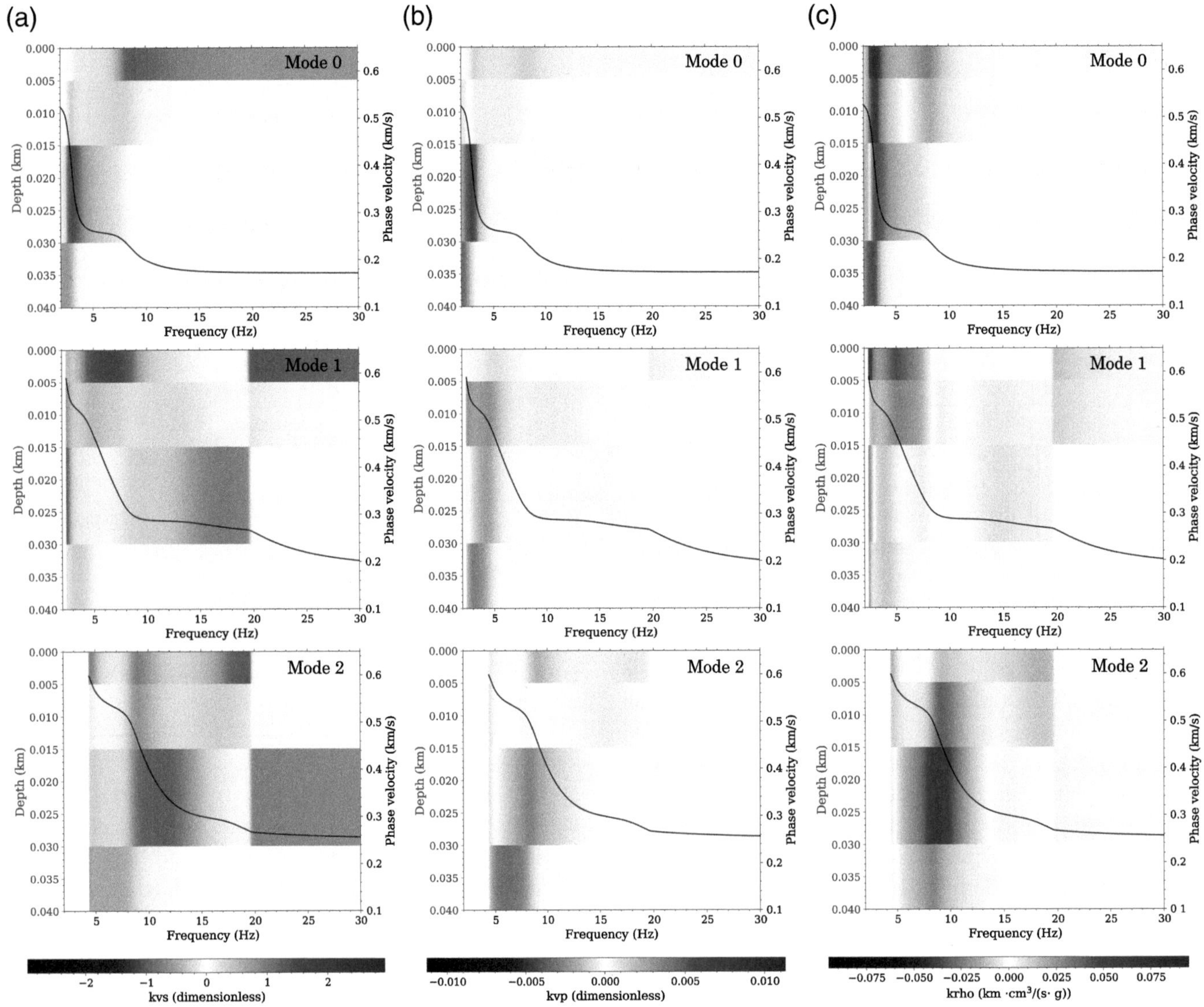

Figure 6. Sensitivity kernels of (a) V_S, (b) V_P, and (c) ρ for model 1. Each row displays results for a distinct mode, with columns corresponding to the sensitivity kernels of V_S (first column), V_P (second column), and ρ (third column). The black curve in each subplot represents the dispersion curve of the respective mode. The color version of this figure is available only in the electronic edition.

in predefined layering rules and statistical aggregation, it produces results that are both consistent with the constraints of surface-wave data and reflective of inversion nonuniqueness.

NUMERICAL INVERSION EXAMPLE

Near-surface model

A five-layer theoretical earth model as described in Yang *et al.* (2024) was adopted in this numerical simulation to generate test data, ensuring consistency with the model settings used in their research. The specific parameters of this model are shown in Table 3. To obtain simulated Rayleigh-wave data, the CPS program (developed by Herrmann, 2013) was utilized to generate multimodal synthetic seismograms based on the above earth model, following the same approach as Yang *et al.* (2024). In the simulation of data acquisition, 64 seismometers were deployed to record vertical seismic signals from an active source, with a minimum source offset of 10 m and a spatial interval of 2 m between seismometers. Subsequently, the frequency–Bessel (F-J) transform method (Wang *et al.*,

TABLE 3
Parameter Values of the Five-Layer Theoretical Model (Converted from Table 1 in Yang *et al.*, 2024)

No.	Depth (km)	Density (g/cm^3)	V_S (km/s)	V_P (km/s)
1	0.000	1.900	0.400	0.700
2	0.002	1.700	0.200	0.300
3	0.006	1.800	0.300	0.500
4	0.011	2.000	0.500	0.900
5	0.016	2.100	0.650	1.100

2019; Li *et al.*, 2021) was applied to process the recorded Rayleigh-wave data for dispersion energy imaging, which is known for its ability to effectively reveal higher-mode dispersion information. Finally, multimode dispersion curves were extracted by manually selecting local energy extremes from the dispersion energy image, providing the key input data for subsequent inversion analyses. The entire data generation and processing workflow, along with key intermediate results, is visually illustrated in Figure 7.

Inversions are performed using the L-BFGS-B algorithm, with layer thicknesses fixed and only V_S adjusted to minimize the misfit between theoretical and experimental dispersion curves. Layering parameters are set to $a = 0.5$, $b_{\min} = 1.0$, and $b_{\max} = 1.5$ to define the structural framework of initial models. Initial shear-wave velocity (V_S) is estimated based on the fundamental-mode dispersion curve, ensuring consistency with the sensitivity characteristics of surface waves. A total of 100 initial models are generated under these settings to sample the plausible solution space.

The inversion results are visualized in Figure 8. Figure 8a demonstrates that the theoretical dispersion curves of all 100 inverted models (black curves) align closely with the target experimental dispersion curve (red dots), indicating a high-quality fit between the inverted solutions and the input data. In Figure 9a, the theoretical dispersion curves of the inverted models are plotted with transparency scaled by their final objective function values. The high density of opaque black curves confirms that most of the initial models converged to solutions with a low misfit, reflecting a robust fitting performance. Figure 8b reveals that the inverted models (captured by the yellow 2D histogram) generally reproduce the characteristics of the target model (red line). Notably, the LVL between 2 and 6 m is accurately resolved, with the distribution of inverted V_S values tightly clustering around the target velocity range in this depth interval. For deeper regions, although absolute velocity values exhibit slight scatter, the overall velocity trend of the inverted models aligns well with the target model. It is important to emphasize that the final result is represented by the median V_S (blue line) derived from the 2D histogram of inverted models, which, due to the layering strategy, does not present as a strictly layered profile. However, in the shallow depth range (in which constraints from surface-wave data are stronger), the layered features of the target model are effectively recovered, as evidenced by the close agreement between the median curve and the target model within these depths.

To further evaluate the performance of our proposed inversion framework, particularly the advantage of our randomized, wavelength-constrained layering, we conducted an additional comparative experiment. For this test, we utilized a more traditional inversion approach based on the open-source program *DisbaTomo*. This approach also employs the L-BFGS-B algorithm and a multiple initial model strategy to mitigate the risk of converging to local minima. The crucial difference, however,

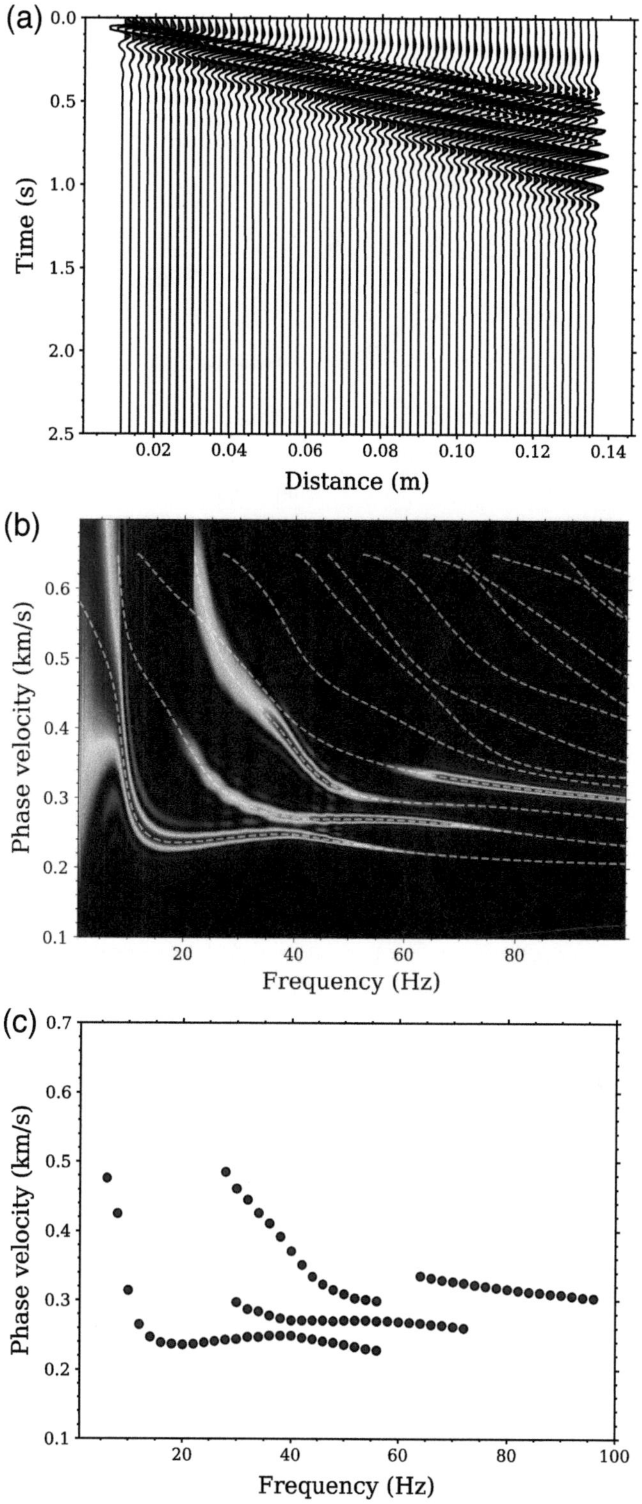

Figure 7. Extracted Rayleigh-wave dispersion curves from numerical simulation data: (a) simulated theoretical Rayleigh-wave records generated based on the five-layer model; (b) dispersion energy spectrum imaged using the frequency–Bessel (F–J) transform method; and (c) multimode dispersion curves manually picked along local energy extremes from the dispersion spectrum, serving as key input for subsequent inversion analysis. The color version of this figure is available only in the electronic edition.

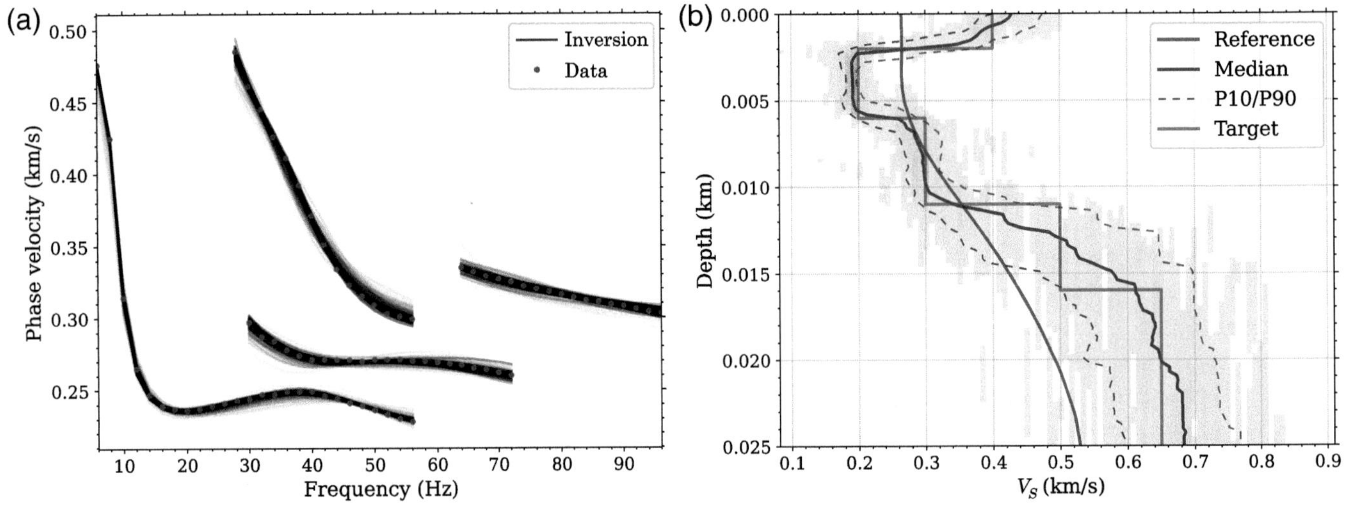

Figure 8. Inversion results and model comparison for the target near-surface model. (a) Comparison of theoretical dispersion curves from 100 inverted models with the picked dispersion curves used for inversion. The red dots represent the picked dispersion curves; black curves denote theoretical dispersion curves of inverted models, with transparency inversely proportional to objective function values (higher values correspond to greater transparency). (b) Comparison of inverted models with the target model. The gray lines indicate reference models; the red line represents the target model; the yellow 2D histogram shows the distribution of inverted models. The blue line denotes the depth-dependent median V_S of the histogram, and black dashed lines represent the corresponding P_{10} and P_{90} bounds. The color version of this figure is available only in the electronic edition.

is that it relies on a fixed layering scheme, in which all initial models share the same predefined layer boundaries.

We performed two tests with this fixed-layering method, with the results shown in Figure 9. In the first test, we created an idealized scenario in which the fixed-layer parameterization was set to be identical to the layering of the true target model. As expected, the inversion performed exceptionally well, with the theoretical dispersion curves fitting the data accurately (Fig. 9a) and the inverted velocity models showing very little difference from the target model (Fig. 9b). This demonstrates that a fixed-layering approach is effective if, and only if, the true subsurface structure is known a priori—a condition never met in real-world applications.

In the second, more realistic test, we defined a fixed-layering structure that was inconsistent with the true target model. Although the inversion still achieves a good data fit for the dispersion curves (Fig. 9c), the resulting velocity profile (Fig. 9d) highlights a key drawback of this approach. Although the profile is effectively an averaged representation of the true model, the velocity steps are forced to occur at the predefined, fixed-layer boundaries. This creates the misleading impression of sharp interfaces at arbitrary depths, which are merely artifacts of the chosen parameterization. This artifact is particularly evident in the 12–17 m depth range of Figure 10d, in which the inverted velocity step does not correspond to a true geological boundary but is simply an average of the true velocities in that region, presented as a sharp change.

This comparison highlights a significant risk of fixed layering strategies: they can produce velocity profiles with sharp boundaries that appear geologically plausible but are, in fact, artifacts of the predefined parameterization. An analyst might incorrectly interpret these artificial steps as real subsurface interfaces. In contrast, our proposed method, with its randomized and adaptive layering, exhibits more desirable behavior. Where data constraints are strong, the statistical aggregation of results can accurately resolve true discontinuities. Conversely, where constraints are weak (as is common at greater depths for both methods), our process naturally yields a smoother velocity profile. This smoothing is a more honest representation of the model uncertainty and the data's limited resolving power, effectively avoiding the creation of such phantom interfaces. Although other strategies exist, such as including layer thickness as a free parameter in the inversion, they typically double the number of parameters, significantly increasing the complexity and nonuniqueness of the inverse problem.

Crustal LVL and uppermost mantle model

The second test model is derived from an example within the software DisbaTomo, the source for which is available in Data and Resources. This model features a crustal LVL. Crustal LVLs like that in this test model are widely observed in global geological surveys, including tectonically active regions (Zhang *et al.*, 2020, 2023), rift zones (Guo *et al.*, 2022), and stable cratons (Marzen *et al.*, 2019). They form through key geological processes: partial melting reduces shear-wave velocity via low-rigidity molten phases; fluid saturation of fractures or pores lowers rock stiffness; compositional layers (e.g., clay-rich sediments) have inherently low velocities; and elevated temperatures (near magmatic intrusions) reduce rock rigidity.

The data used for inversion consist of theoretical dispersion curves calculated from this model; these curves are then subjected to frequency-band constraints that mimic

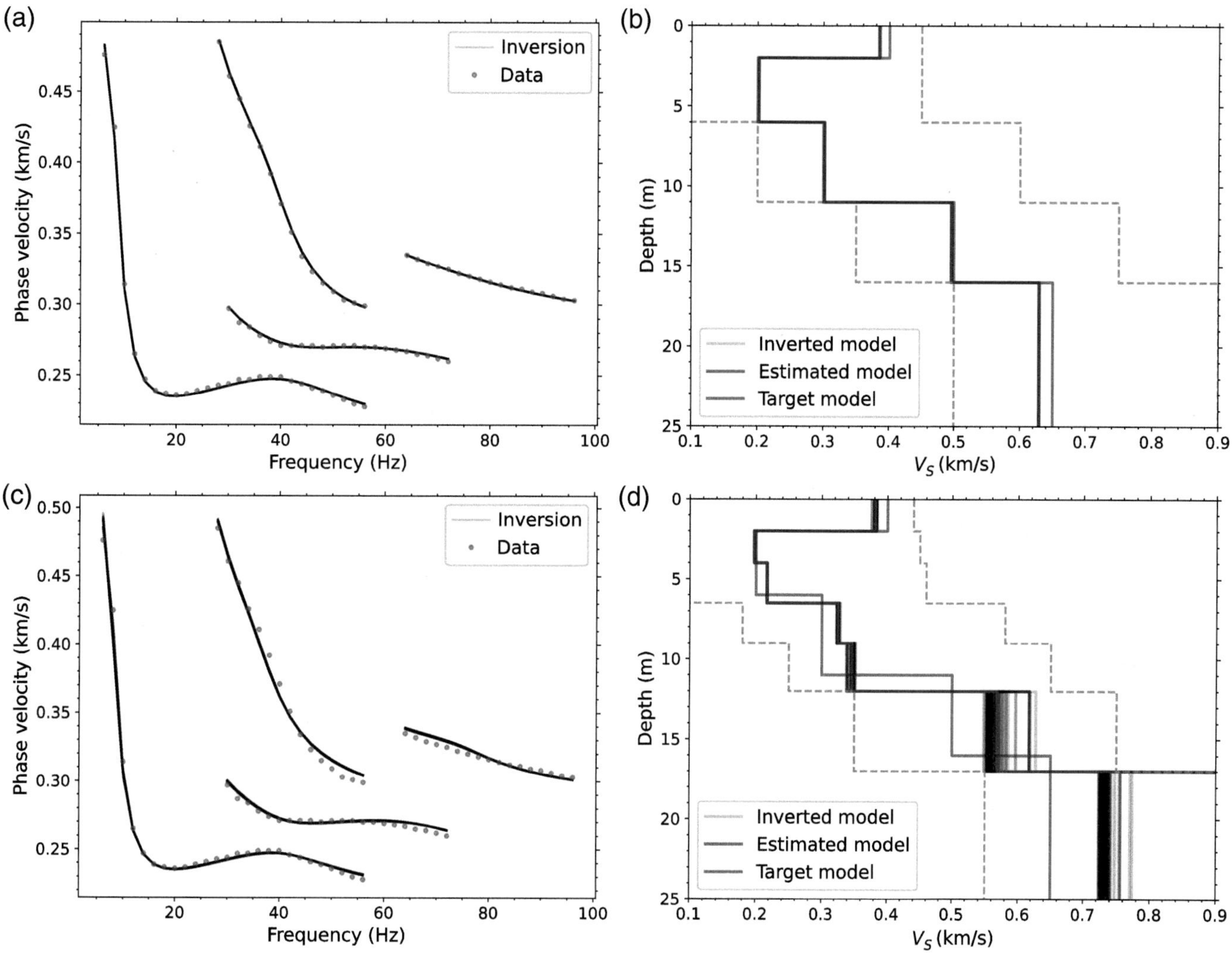

Figure 9. Comparative inversion results using a fixed-layering scheme. (a,b) The results when the model's layering is identical to the true target model. (c,d) The results when the model's layering is inconsistent with the target model. In panels (a) and (c), comparison of the data fit is shown. The black curves are the theoretical dispersion curves corresponding to the final inverted models, and the red dots are the input dispersion data. In panels (b) and (d), comparison of the inverted velocity models with the target model is shown. The gray-solid lines are the final inverted models from each run; the red line is the weighted average of all inverted models; the blue line is the true target model; and the gray-dashed lines indicate the parameter search bounds. The color version of this figure is available only in the electronic edition.

the extractable dispersion ranges commonly encountered in routine processing of real-world data. In addition, noise is introduced into the theoretical dispersion curves. To reflect real-world scenarios, in which higher-mode dispersion curves typically exhibit poorer signal-to-noise ratios, greater noise magnitudes are applied specifically to higher mode curves. This setup ensures the test model more closely approximates practical inversion conditions, accounting for both frequency limitations and mode-dependent noise characteristics of field data.

Layering parameters are configured as $a = 0.8$, $b_{min} = 1.0$, and $b_{max} = 1.5$ to establish the structural framework for initial models. A total of 100 initial models are generated under these constraints to adequately sample the plausible solution space. The results visualized in Figure 10 confirm the reliability of the inversion outcomes. Specifically, the theoretical dispersion curves corresponding to the inverted models show a close fit with the input data, indicating effective alignment between the inverted solutions and the observed information. In terms of the subsurface velocity structure, the inverted models successfully capture the key features of the target model, most notably, the crustal LVL is well resolved, and the velocity variation trend in the deep part is consistent with the target model. As previous studies (Chen *et al.*, 2022; Li *et al.*, 2025) have pointed out, the low-frequency segment of the fundamental-mode dispersion curve primarily constrains the structure of the uppermost mantle, whereas the introduced higher-mode dispersion curves enhance the constraint on the crustal structure. This is evident in the figure through the accurate recovery of the crustal LVL, which benefits from the strengthened constraint of higher-mode dispersion curves on crustal features.

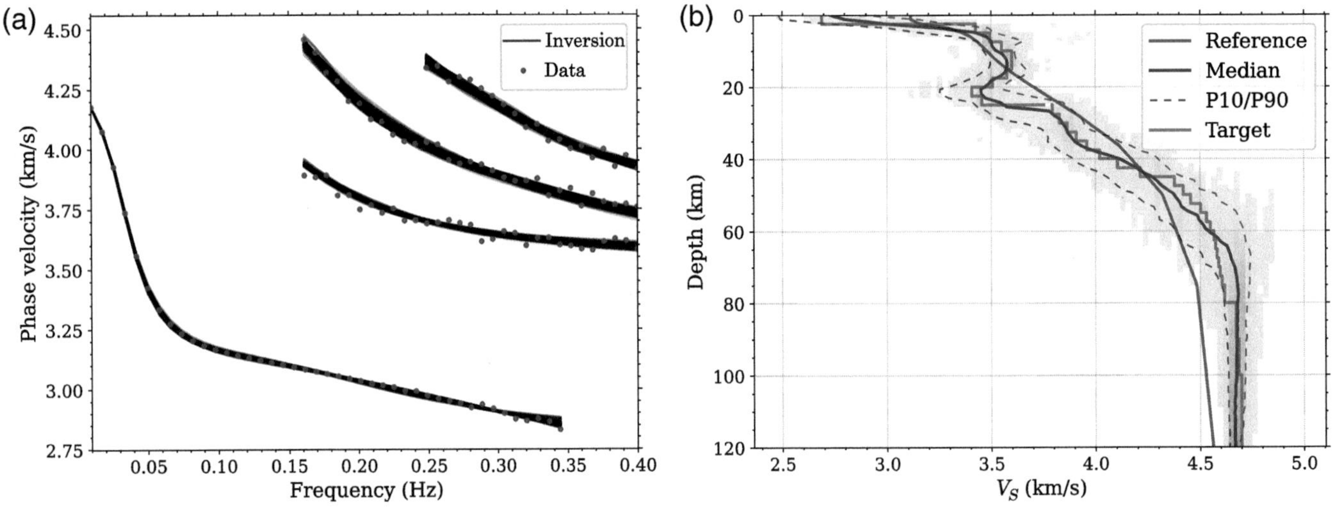

Figure 10. Inversion results and model comparison for the target crustal low-velocity layer (LVL) and uppermost mantle model. (a) Comparison of theoretical dispersion curves from 100 inverted models with the picked dispersion curves used for inversion. (b) Comparison of inverted models with the target model. The color version of this figure is available only in the electronic edition.

REAL DATA INVERSION EXAMPLE

Field data application at the Mirandola site

The field dispersion curve data used in this study were derived from the Mirandola site in Italy, with the original seismic survey conducted under the InterPACIFIC project (Garofalo *et al.*, 2016a,b) and the dispersion curves extracted by Yang *et al.* (2023). Specifically, the data include both active and passive Rayleigh-wave dispersion curves.

Because the inversion focuses on the shallow subsurface (<40 m), empirical relationships for the shallow subsurface are adopted for converting V_P and ρ from V_S. The Mirandola site is located in the Po River Plain, in which the test site is characterized primarily by alluvial sediments, featuring alternating sequences of silty clay layers and sandy soil layers typical of alluvial plains. For the V_S-to-V_P conversion, a value of 4 for V_P/V_S is used, considering that the subsurface is dominated by silty clay and sandy soil layers. The empirical V_S–ρ relationship is derived through quadratic regression analysis applied to characteristic lithological ρ–V_S value pairs. The structural framework of initial models is defined using layering parameters set to $a = 0.8$, $b_{\min} = 1.0$, and $b_{\max} = 1.5$. Initial shear-wave velocity (V_S) values are estimated from the fundamental-mode dispersion curve. To ensure comprehensive sampling of the feasible solution space, 100 initial models are generated under these parametric constraints.

Figure 11a illustrates the fitting performance between the dispersion curves derived from the inverted model and the observed data, with an overall reasonable agreement. However, slight discrepancies are observed in the high-frequency ranges: specifically, for the fundamental-mode dispersion curve at frequencies above 15 Hz and for the first-mode dispersion curve at frequencies above 50 Hz. Such deviations can be attributed to two potential factors. First, for shallow subsurface conditions, high-frequency components of dispersion curves are particularly sensitive to medium attenuation (Q factor), and the incomplete consideration of attenuation effects in the inversion process may lead to suboptimal fitting in these frequency ranges. Second, the conversion relationship between shear-wave velocity (V_S) and compression-wave velocity (V_P) becomes more complex in shallow layers, in which geological heterogeneities are often prominent; thus, the empirical relationship adopted in the inversion may introduce minor biases that are more evident at high frequencies. These factors reflect the inherent complexity of surface-wave inversion in capturing high-frequency details.

To validate the reliability of the inverted shear-wave velocity (V_S) model, a comparative analysis was performed against results obtained from three well-established invasive methods (Garofalo *et al.*, 2016b): crosshole (XH), downhole (DH), and seismic dilatometer test (SDMT). The XH method calculates seismic wave velocities by measuring the travel time of S waves or P waves between a source and receivers positioned at the same depth in separate boreholes, with its reliability rooted in local measurements along short travel paths. The DH method, in contrast, deploys receivers within a borehole while activating the source at the ground surface, enabling velocity estimation through analysis of wave propagation from the surface to subsurface receivers. The SDMT, as an invasive technique integrated with in situ penetration, provides V_S profiles by leveraging seismic signals acquired during the advancement of a dilatometer, and has been shown to yield results consistent with other invasive methods in previous studies.

Figure 11b reveals that the inverted V_S model exhibits a comparable trend in the overall velocity structure to the results from the three invasive methods. A distinct interface, clearly identified by XH, DH, and SDMT at approximately 7.5 m, was captured in the inverted model at a slightly deeper position of around 10 m. Notably, the second interface at 25 m in the

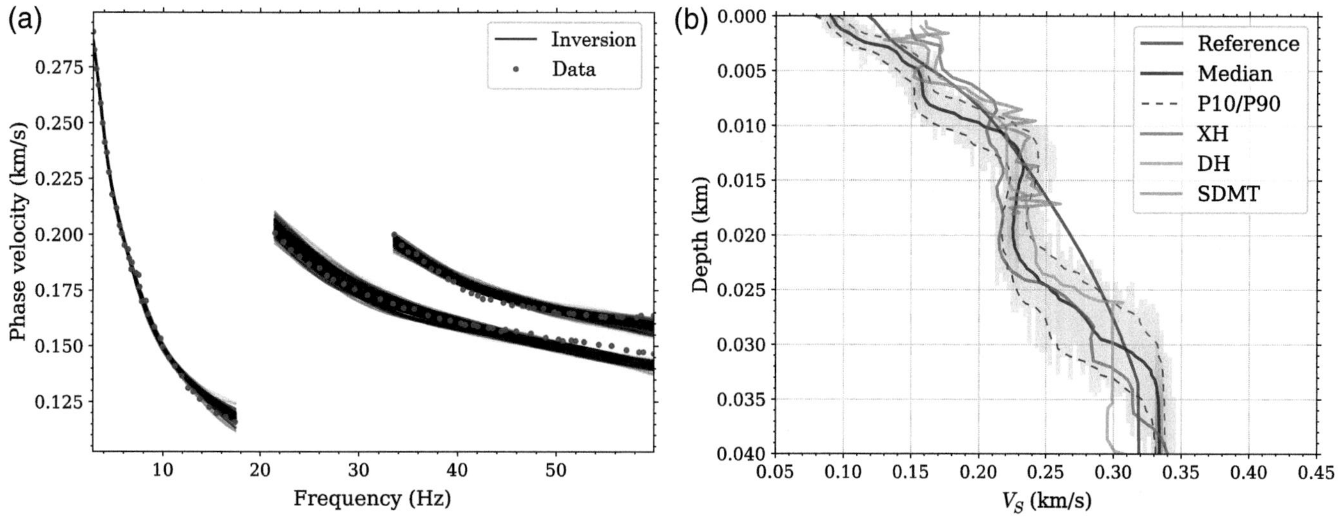

Figure 11. Inversion results and model comparison for field data application at the Mirandola site. (a) Comparison of theoretical dispersion curves from 100 inverted models with the picked dispersion curves used for inversion. (b) Comparison of inverted models with models from other methods. The brown line represents the V_S model obtained by the crosshole (XH) method, the pink line denotes the V_S model from the downhole (DH) method, and the cyan line shows the V_S model derived from the seismic dilatometer test (SDMT). The color version of this figure is available only in the electronic edition.

inverted model shows good agreement with the positions derived from XH and DH measurements, mirroring the ability of invasive methods to effectively detect key subsurface features as observed in the InterPACIFIC project.

The differences between the V_S model derived from surface-wave dispersion curves and those obtained by XH, DH, and SDMT methods can be primarily attributed to the discrepancy in the volume of material sampled by each method. Invasive methods such as XH, DH, and SDMT provide measurements that are representative only of the soil column immediately around the boreholes, reflecting highly localized subsurface conditions. In contrast, surface-wave methods, as a noninvasive approach, sample a much larger and more comprehensive volume of the subsurface underlying the measurement array. For a subsurface with vertical and lateral heterogeneity—a common feature in natural geological settings—this fundamental difference in the "sampling" volume of the subsurface material can naturally lead to variations in the derived V_S profiles. Such differences are a result of the distinct spatial scales at which each method operates rather than an indication of inaccuracy in either set of results.

USArray data

For the second real-world data application, we utilize the vertical-component data recorded by 93 stations of the USArray Transportable Array located in the eastern United States (as shown in Fig. 12a), with the data collection period spanning from 1 June to 1 December 2011. It is worth noting that these are the same stations as those used in the first application described in Wu *et al.* (2020). In the data processing stage, we first segment the continuous records into daily-length segments. Then, we remove the instrument response from each of these daily segments to ensure the authenticity and reliability of the subsequent analysis. Subsequently, to mitigate the impacts of inhomogeneous distribution of ambient seismic field sources, earthquake events, and instrumental irregularities, we perform preprocessing steps, including temporal normalization and spectral whitening, on the raw ambient seismic noise data prior to computing cross correlations (Bensen *et al.*, 2007). After that, we compute the cross-correlation functions (CCFs) for each day between all possible pairs of stations and stack these daily CCFs. Finally, we calculate the dispersion spectrum in the frequency-phase velocity (*f-c*) domain using the frequency–Bessel (F–J) transform method, which is presented in Figure 12b. Based on this dispersion spectrum, multimode dispersion curves are manually extracted by identifying local energy extremes, as shown in Figure 12c, and these curves serve as critical input data for subsequent inversion analyses.

Given that the inversion targets the velocity structure of the crust and the uppermost mantle, the empirical relationships for converting V_P to V_S and ρ to V_S are adopted from Brocher (2005) described by the previous section. For model layering, the parameters are specified as $a = 0.8$, $b_{\min} = 1.0$, and $b_{\max} = 1.5$. Initial shear-wave velocity (V_S) values are estimated from the fundamental-mode dispersion curve. A total of 100 initial models are generated based on these settings to sufficiently explore the plausible solution space.

Figure 13 illustrates the inversion results and comparative analysis for the target region. Figure 13a demonstrates a close fit between the theoretical dispersion curves of the inverted models and the actual field data, confirming that the inversion has effectively captured the seismic wave propagation characteristics reflected in the observed data. Figure 13b presents the inverted velocity structure, with key features validated through comparison with the results from Shen and Ritzwoller (2016).

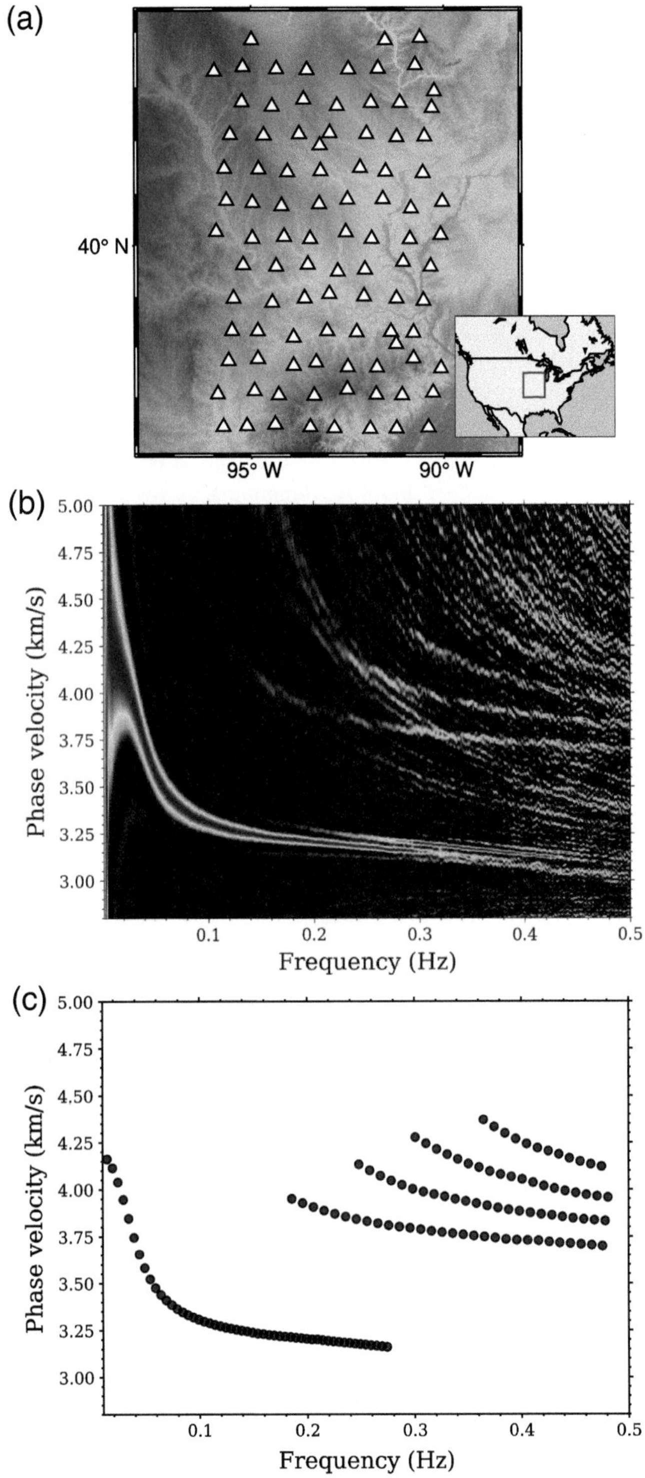

Figure 12. Observation station distribution and dispersion curves for seismic inversion in North America. (a) Distribution of observation stations (white triangles) across the study region in North America. The bottom-right inset marks the geographical location of the study region within North America (outlined by the red line). (b) Dispersion spectrum in the frequency-phase velocity (*f-c*) domain, derived from cross-correlation functions (CCFs) using the frequency–Bessel (F–J) transform method. (c) Multimode dispersion curves manually extracted by identifying local energy extremes in the dispersion spectrum. The color version of this figure is available only in the electronic edition.

To verify the reliability of our inversion, we interpolated a 1D shear-wave velocity profile for the study area from Shen's 3D shear-wave velocity structure of North America, then compared it with our inverted model. Overall, the two models show consistent main velocity variation trends: both accurately identify the Moho discontinuity at a similar depth, which serves as a critical marker of crust–mantle boundary and confirms the robustness of both inversion frameworks in resolving fundamental structural interfaces. However, several notable differences exist: first, Shen's model exhibits lower velocities in the sedimentary layer, which may be related to its specific parameterization of the top sedimentary layer (defined by thickness and linear velocity increase with depth), potentially emphasizing the low-velocity characteristics of shallow sediments; second, our model reveals a distinct interface at approximately 17 km depth within the middle crust, a feature not clearly resolved in Shen's model—a discrepancy that could stem from differences in inversion resolution because our approach may have stronger sensitivity to middle crustal structures; third, there are differences in velocity values in the uppermost mantle: Shen's model shows relatively higher velocities in this region, whereas our model presents a slightly lower velocity range. These observed differences may arise from a combination of factors related to model parameterization, inversion strategies, and data constraints. Shen and Ritzwoller (2016) adopted a Bayesian Monte Carlo algorithm with a layered parameterization that emphasizes smooth velocity variations: the model was divided into three main layers (sedimentary layer, crystalline crust, and uppermost mantle), with cubic B-splines regulating vertical smoothness and a total of 13 free parameters per location. In addition, the crustal velocity was constrained to increase monotonically with depth. This setup is designed to prioritize overall structural smoothness and stability, which may lead to a more generalized representation of subsurface features, and thus, the interface in the middle crust may not be as prominently displayed in their results. In contrast, our inversion framework, with its distinct parameter settings and layering strategy, may preserve more detailed structural information, thereby identifying additional interfaces.

Another key factor is the difference in data used for inversion. Our inversion incorporates multimode dispersion curves, whereas Shen's work relies primarily on fundamental-mode dispersion curves. Previous studies have shown that higher-mode dispersion curves can enhance the constraint on crustal structures, which may contribute to our model's ability to resolve finer crustal features. Meanwhile, variations in data input (such as the frequency range of seismic data) and prior constraints could also lead to differences in velocity characteristics in the uppermost mantle. It should be noted that both approaches have their own rationality and applicability, and the differences in results reflect the characteristics of different inversion strategies and data constraints.

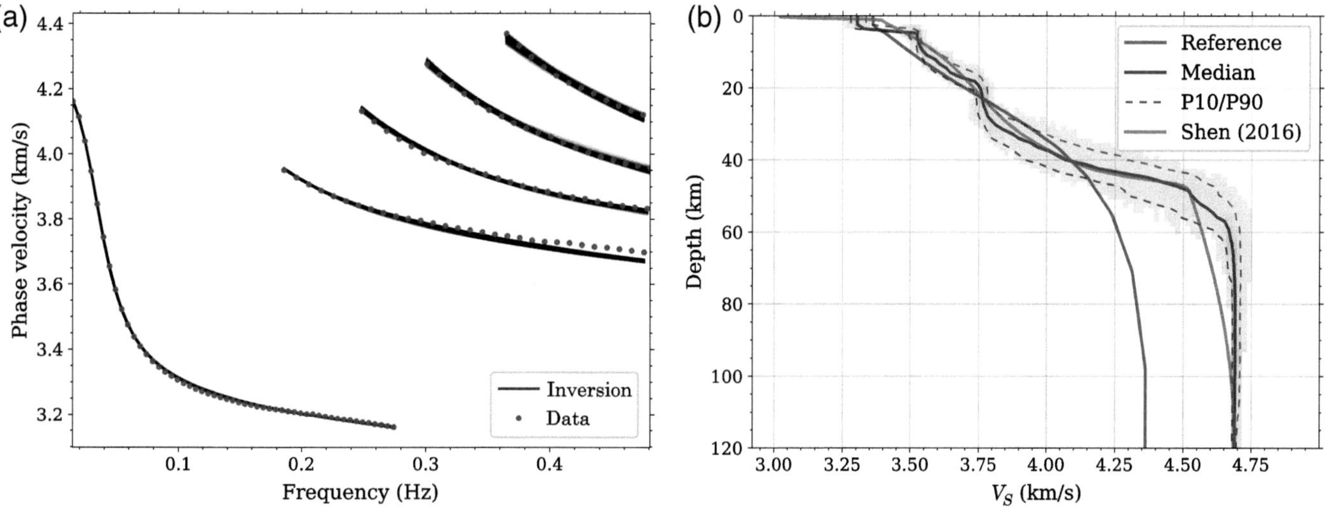

Figure 13. Inversion results and model comparison for real-data application from USArray data. (a) Comparison between theoretical dispersion curves of 100 inverted models (gray curves) and the picked dispersion curves (red dots) used for inversion. (b) Comparison between inverted models (represented by the 2D histogram of velocity distributions and median curve) and the model from Shen and Ritzwoller (2016) (red line). The color version of this figure is available only in the electronic edition.

CONCLUSION

This study presents a comprehensive framework for robust computation and inversion of surface-wave dispersion curves, with a focus on addressing key challenges in complex layered media containing LVLs. The core innovation lies in the development of a quadratic extrema interpolation method, which strategically augments sampling points at "mode-kissing" zones in which adjacent dispersion curve branches converge. This approach effectively resolves the root-omission issue of conventional root-searching schemes, ensuring the completeness of computed dispersion curves—a critical improvement for subsequent inversion accuracy.

Comparative analyses against the widely used CPS framework validate the superiority of the proposed method. In tests on 1000 randomized six-layer models, the new method reduces root-omission rates from 87.4% (CPS) to 10.1% while achieving a 12.6 × speedup in full-mode dispersion curve computation. For fundamental-mode calculations, the efficiency advantage is even more pronounced (17.4 × acceleration), making it highly suitable for large-scale Bayesian inversion workflows that require massive forward model evaluations.

The inversion framework further enhances practical applicability by integrating wavelength-constrained layering definition and depth-zoned empirical relationships for deriving V_P and density from V_S. This design balances geophysical plausibility with computational efficiency: the layering scheme adapts to the depth-dependent resolution of surface-wave data, whereas empirical relationships (calibrated for shallow, middle, and deep layers) reduce inversion dimensionality without compromising accuracy. Statistical aggregation of results from multiple initial models effectively addresses inversion nonuniqueness, ensuring robust velocity structure recovery.

Validation through numerical simulations and real-world data applications confirms the method's reliability. In near-surface models, it accurately resolves LVLs and reproduces target velocity trends; in crustal and uppermost mantle models, it successfully identifies key structural features such as crustal LVLs. Field data tests at the Mirandola site and with USArray data further demonstrate consistency with independent measurements (e.g., crosshole, downhole) and existing crustal models, verifying its potential for practical geophysical exploration.

Overall, this study advances surface-wave analysis by bridging the gap between computational efficiency and solution completeness in complex media. The proposed methods provide a robust tool for subsurface characterization, with broad applications in near-surface engineering, crustal structure investigation, and lithospheric studies. Future work will focus on integrating attenuation effects and expanding to 3D inversion to handle lateral heterogeneity.

DATA AND RESOURCES

The figures in this study were plotted using the matplotlib (https://www.matplotlib.org) library. The Mirandola site data were obtained from the study by Yang *et al.* (2023). The cross-correlation functions of the USArray and the frequency–Bessel (F–J) transform program were sourced from the open-source repository CC-FJpy (https://github.com/ColinLii/CC-FJpy). The crustal low-velocity layer (LVL) and uppermost mantle model, along with related data, were retrieved from DisbaTomo (https://github.com/pan3rock/DisbaTomo). The code implemented in this study is available at https://github.com/pan3rock/QEDispInv. All websites were last accessed in February 2026. The supplemental material for this article includes specific model parameters for the velocity structure shown in Figure 3b. It also provides a detailed technical description of the depth-based empirical relationships used to estimate *P*-wave velocity (V_P) and density (ρ) from *S*-wave velocity (V_S) across the shallow subsurface, the middle layer, and the deep crustal layer.

DECLARATION OF COMPETING INTERESTS

The authors acknowledge that there are no conflicts of interest recorded.

ACKNOWLEDGMENTS

The authors are grateful to Editor-in-Chief P. Martin Mai, Associate Editor Shengji Wei, and two anonymous reviewers for their constructive feedback, which has greatly improved the quality of this article. This work was supported by the National Science and Technology Major Project of China (Number 2024ZD1001101), the National Key Research and Development Program of China (Number 2024YFC3012905-5), the Major Program of the National Natural Science Foundation of China (Number 42494863-06), and the Key Program of the National Natural Science Foundation of China (Number 42430102). Support was also provided by the Shenzhen Key Laboratory of Deep Offshore Oil and Gas Exploration Technology (Grant Number ZDSYS20190902093007855) and the Guangdong Provincial Key Laboratory of Geophysical High-resolution Imaging Technology (Number 2022B1212010002).

REFERENCES

Bensen, G., M. Ritzwoller, M. Barmin, A. L. Levshin, F. Lin, M. Moschetti, N. Shapiro, and Y. Yang (2007). Processing seismic ambient noise data to obtain reliable broad-band surface wave dispersion measurements, *Geophys. J. Int.* **169,** no. 3, 1239–1260.

Bodin, T., M. Sambridge, H. Tkalčić, P. Arroucau, K. Gallagher, and N. Rawlinson (2012). Transdimensional inversion of receiver functions and surface wave dispersion, *J. Geophys. Res.* **117,** no B2.

Bozdağ, E., J. Trampert, and J. Tromp (2011). Misfit functions for full waveform inversion based on instantaneous phase and envelope measurements, *Geophys. J. Int.* **185,** no. 2, 845–870.

Brocher, T. M. (2005). Empirical relations between elastic wavespeeds and density in the earth's crust, *Bull. Seismol. Soc. Am.* **95,** no. 6, 2081–2092.

Buchen, P., and R. Ben-Hador (1996). Free-mode surface-wave computations, *Geophys. J. Int.* **124,** no. 3, 869–887.

Burden, R. L., and J. D. Faires (2016). *Numerical Analysis*, Tenth Ed., Cengage Learning. See Section 2.1 for the bisection method.

Chen, J., L. Pan, Z. Li, and X. Chen (2022). Continental reworking in the eastern South China block and its adjacent areas revealed by F-J multimodal ambient noise tomography, *J. Geophys. Res.* **127,** no. 11, e2022JB024776 , doi: 10.1029/2022JB024776.

Chen, X. (1993). A systematic and efficient method of computing normal modes for multilayered half-space, *Geophys. J. Int.* **115,** no. 2, 391–409.

Cox, B. R., and D. P. Teague (2016). Layering ratios: A systematic approach to the inversion of surface wave data in the absence of a priori information, *Geophys. J. Int.* **207,** no. 1, 422–438.

Dal Moro, G., and M. Pipan (2007). Joint inversion of surface wave dispersion curves and reflection travel times via multi-objective evolutionary algorithms, *J. Appl. Geophys.* **61,** no. 1, 56–81.

Dou, S., and J. B. Ajo-Franklin (2014). Full-wavefield inversion of surface waves for mapping embedded low-velocity zones in permafrost, *Geophysics* **79,** no. 6, EN107–EN124.

Dunkin, J. W. (1965). Computation of modal solutions in layered, elastic media at high frequencies, *Bull. Seismol. Soc. Am.* **55,** no. 2, 335–358.

Fan, Y., X. Chen, X. Liu, J. Liu, and X. Chen (2007). Approximate decomposition of the dispersion equation at high frequencies and the number of multimodes for Rayleigh waves, *Chin. J. Geophys.* **50,** no. 1, 222–230.

Fang, H., H. Yao, H. Zhang, Y.-C. Huang, and R. D. van der Hilst (2015). Direct inversion of surface wave dispersion for three-dimensional shallow crustal structure based on ray tracing: Methodology and application, *Geophys. J. Int.* **201,** no. 3, 1251–1263.

Foti, S., C. G. Lai, G. J. Rix, and C. Strobbia (2014). *Surface wave Methods for Near-Surface Site Characterization*, CRC Press.

Gao, L., J. Xia, Y. Pan, and Y. Xu (2016). Reason and condition for mode kissing in MASW method, *Pure Appl. Geophys.* **173,** 1627–1638.

Gardner, G., L. Gardner, and A. Gregory (1974). Formation velocity and density—The diagnostic basics for stratigraphic traps, *Geophysics* **39,** no. 6, 770–780.

Garofalo, F., S. Foti, F. Hollender, P.-Y. Bard, C. Cornou, B. R. Cox, M. Ohrnberger, D. Sicilia, M. Asten, G. Di Giulio, *et al.* (2016a). Interpacific project: Comparison of invasive and non-invasive methods for seismic site characterization. Part I: Intra-comparison of surface wave methods, *Soil Dynam. Earthq. Eng.* **82,** 222–240.

Garofalo, F., S. Foti, F. Hollender, P.-Y. Bard, C. Cornou, B. R. Cox, M. Ohrnberger, D. Sicilia, M. Asten, G. Di Giulio, *et al.* (2016b). Interpacific project: Comparison of invasive and non-invasive methods for seismic site characterization. Part II: Inter-comparison between surface-wave and borehole methods, *Soil Dynam. Earthq. Eng.* **82,** 241–254.

Gofer, E., R. Bachrach, and S. Marco (2017). Anisotropic surface-wave characterization of granular media, *Geophysics* **82,** no. 6, MR191–MR200.

Groos, L., M. Schäfer, T. Forbriger, and T. Bohlen (2017). Application of a complete workflow for 2d elastic full-waveform inversion to recorded shallow-seismic Rayleigh waves, *Geophysics* **82,** no. 2, R109–R117.

Guo, P., S. C. Singh, V. A. Vaddineni, I. Grevemeyer, and E. Saygin (2022). Lower oceanic crust formed by in situ melt crystallization revealed by seismic layering, *Nature Geosci.* **15,** no. 7, 591–596.

Guo, Z., Y. J. Chen, J. Ning, Y. Feng, S. P. Grand, F. Niu, H. Kawakatsu, S. Tanaka, M. Obayashi, and J. Ni (2015). High resolution 3-d crustal structure beneath NE China from joint inversion of ambient noise and receiver functions using NECESSArray data, *Earth Planet. Sci. Lett.* **416,** 1–11.

Haskell, N. A. (1953). The dispersion of surface waves on multilayered media, *Bull. Seismol. Soc. Am.* **43,** no. 1, 17–34.

He, Y., W. Chen, and X. Chen (2006). Normal modes computation by generalized reflection-transmission coefficients method in planar layered half space, *Chin. J. Geophys.* **49,** no. 4, 965–973.

Herrmann, R. B. (2013). Computer programs in seismology: An evolving tool for instruction and research, *Seismol. Res. Lett.* **84,** no. 6, 1081–1088.

Hisada, Y. (1994). An efficient method for computing green's functions for a layered half-space with sources and receivers at close depths, *Bull. Seismol. Soc. Am.* **84,** no. 5, 1456–1472.

Hobiger, M., C. Cornou, M. Wathelet, G. D. Giulio, B. Knapmeyer-Endrun, F. Renalier, P.-Y. Bard, A. Savvaidis, S. Hailemikael, B. N. Le, *et al.* (2013). Ground structure imaging by inversions of Rayleigh wave ellipticity: Sensitivity analysis and application to European strong-motion sites, *Geophys. J. Int.* **192,** no. 1, 207–229.

Ji, Z., B. Wang, W. Yang, W. Wang, J. Su, B. Wei, H. Wang, and T. Hu (2021). Observation of higher-mode surface waves from an active source in the Hutubi basin, Xinjiang, China, *Bull. Seismol. Soc. Am.* **111,** no. 3, 1181–1198.

Karagoz, O., K. Chimoto, S. Citak, O. Ozel, H. Yamanaka, and K. Hatayama (2015). Estimation of shallow S-wave velocity structure and site response characteristics by microtremor array measurements in Tekirdag region, NW turkey, *Earth Planets Space* **67,** no. 1, 176.

Kennett, B. (1983). *Seismic Wave Propagation in Stratified Media*, Cambridge University Press, New York.

Li, H., J. Chen, Z. Li, X. Chen, H. Cai, X. Feng, G. Zhang, and Z. Jin (2025). Mid-crustal low-velocity zones beneath southeastern coastal china revealed by multimodal ambient noise tomography: Insights into mesozoic magmatic activities, *Tectonophysics* **898,** 230636.

Li, J., S. Hanafy, Z. Liu, and G. T. Schuster (2019). Wave-equation dispersion inversion of love waves, *Geophysics* **84,** no. 5, R693–R705.

Li, Z., J. Zhou, G. Wu, J. Wang, G. Zhang, S. Dong, L. Pan, Z. Yang, L. Gao, Q. Ma, *et al.* (2021). Cc-fjpy: A python package for extracting overtone surface-wave dispersion from seismic ambient-noise cross correlation, *Seismol. Res. Lett.* **92,** no. 5, 3179–3186.

Lin, F.-C., M. P. Moschetti, and M. H. Ritzwoller (2008). Surface wave tomography of the western United States from ambient seismic noise: Rayleigh and love wave phase velocity maps, *Geophys. J. Int.* **173,** no. 1, 281–298.

Liu, Q., X. Chen, L. Gao, Z. Yu, and J. Chen (2023). Direct image dissimilarity inversion of ambient noise multimodal dispersion spectrograms, *Bull. Seismol. Soc. Am.* **113,** no. 5, 1960–1981.

Liu, X., Y. Fan, and X. Chen (2009). Research on the cross of the dispersion curves of Rayleigh waves and multi-modes coupling phenomenon, *Chin. J. Geophys.* **52,** no. 5, 994–1002.

Liu, Z., J. Li, S. M. Hanafy, and G. Schuster (2019). 3d wave-equation dispersion inversion of Rayleigh waves, *Geophysics* **84,** no. 5, R673–R691.

Lomax, A., and R. Snieder (1995). The contrast in upper mantle shear-wave velocity between the east European platform and tectonic Europe obtained with genetic algorithm inversion of Rayleigh-wave group dispersion, *Geophys. J. Int.* **123,** no. 1, 169–182.

Lu, L., and B. Zhang (2006). Inversion of Rayleigh waves using a genetic algorithm in the presence of a low-velocity layer, *Acoust. Phys.* **52,** no. 6, 701–712.

Luco, J. E., and R. J. Apsel (1983). On the green's functions for a layered half-space. Part I, *Bull. Seismol. Soc. Am.* **73,** no. 4, 909–929.

Maraschini, M., F. Ernst, S. Foti, and L. V. Socco (2010). A new misfit function for multimodal inversion of surface waves, *Geophysics* **75,** no. 4, G31–G43.

Marzen, R. E., D. J. Shillington, D. Lizarralde, and S. H. Harder (2019). Constraints on Appalachian orogenesis and continental rifting in the southeastern United States from wide-angle seismic data, *J. Geophys. Res.* **124,** no. 7, 6625–6652.

Pan, L., and X. Chen (2025). Efficient computation of dispersion curves in low-velocity-layered half-spaces, *Bull. Seismol. Soc. Am.* **115,** no. 4, 1381–1391.

Pan, L., X. Chen, J. Wang, Z. Yang, and D. Zhang (2019). Sensitivity analysis of dispersion curves of Rayleigh waves with fundamental and higher modes, *Geophys. J. Int.* **216,** no. 2, 1276–1303.

Pan, L., S. Yuan, and X. Chen (2022). Modified generalized R/T coefficient method for surface-wave dispersion-curve calculation in elastic and viscoelastic media, *Bull. Seismol. Soc. Am.* **112,** no. 5, 2280–2296.

Pan, Y., L. Gao, and T. Bohlen (2018). Time-domain full-waveform inversion of Rayleigh and Love waves in presence of free-surface topography, *J. Appl. Geophys.* **152,** 77–85.

Pan, Y., L. Gao, and T. Bohlen (2019). High-resolution characterization of near-surface structures by surface-wave inversions: From dispersion curve to full waveform, *Surv. Geophys.* **40,** no. 2, 167–195.

Park, C. B., R. D. Miller, and J. Xia (1998). Imaging dispersion curves of surface waves on multi-channel record, *SEG Technical Program Expanded Abstracts 1998*, Society of Exploration Geophysicists, 1377–1380.

Pasyanos, M. E., W. R. Walter, and S. E. Hazler (2001). A surface wave dispersion study of the Middle East and North Africa for monitoring the comprehensive nuclear-test-ban treaty, *Pure Appl. Geophys.* **158,** no. 8, 1445–1474.

Pérez Solano, C., D. Donno, and H. Chauris (2014). Alternative waveform inversion for surface wave analysis in 2-d media, *Geophys. J. Int.* **198,** no. 3, 1359–1372.

Poormirzaee, R., and I. Fister Jr (2021). Model-based inversion of Rayleigh wave dispersion curves via linear and nonlinear methods, *Pure Appl. Geophys.* **178,** no. 2, 341–358.

Qin, T., Y. Zhao, S. Hu, C. An, W. Bi, S. Ge, L. Capineri, and T. Bohlen (2020). An interactive integrated interpretation of GPR and Rayleigh wave data based on the genetic algorithm, *Surv. Geophys.* **41,** no. 3, 549–574.

Ryden, N., and C. B. Park (2006). Fast simulated annealing inversion of surface waves on pavement using phase-velocity spectra, *Geophysics* **71,** no. 4, R49–R58.

Sambridge, M. (1999a). Geophysical inversion with a neighbourhood algorithm—I. Searching a parameter space, *Geophys. J. Int.* **138,** no. 2, 479–494.

Sambridge, M. (1999b). Geophysical inversion with a neighbourhood algorithm—II. Appraising the ensemble, *Geophys. J. Int.* **138,** no. 3, 727–746.

Sambridge, M. (2014). A parallel tempering algorithm for probabilistic sampling and multimodal optimization, *Geophys. J. Int.* **196,** no. 1, 357–374.

Shen, W., and M. H. Ritzwoller (2016). Crustal and uppermost mantle structure beneath the United States, *J. Geophys. Res.* **121,** no. 6, 4306–4342.

Shen, W., M. H. Ritzwoller, and V. Schulte-Pelkum (2013). A 3-D model of the crust and uppermost mantle beneath the central and western us by joint inversion of receiver functions and surface wave dispersion, *J. Geophys. Res.* **118,** no. 1, 262–276.

Shen, W., M. H. Ritzwoller, V. Schulte-Pelkum, and F.-C. Lin (2013). Joint inversion of surface wave dispersion and receiver functions: A Bayesian Monte-Carlo approach, *Geophys. J. Int.* **192,** no. 2, 807–836.

Song, X., H. Gu, X. Zhang, and J. Liu (2008). Pattern search algorithms for nonlinear inversion of high-frequency Rayleigh-wave dispersion curves, *Comput. Geosci.* **34,** no. 6, 611–624.

Song, X., L. Tang, X. Lv, H. Fang, and H. Gu (2012). Application of particle swarm optimization to interpret Rayleigh wave dispersion curves, *J. Appl. Geophys.* **84,** 1–13.

Thomson, W. T. (1950). Transmission of elastic waves through a stratified solid medium, *J. Appl. Phys.* **21,** no. 2, 89–93.

Wang, J., G. Wu, and X. Chen (2019). Frequency-bessel transform method for effective imaging of higher-mode Rayleigh dispersion curves from ambient seismic noise data, *J. Geophys. Res.* **124,** no. 4, 3708–3723.

Wu, B., and X. Chen (2022). A versatile solver of the normal modes for horizontal stratified complicated models, *Seismol. Res. Lett.* **93,** no. 3, 1852–1867.

Wu, G.-X., L. Pan, J.-N. Wang, and X. Chen (2020). Shear velocity inversion using multimodal dispersion curves from ambient seismic noise data of USArray transportable array, *J. Geophys. Res.* **125,** no. 1, e2019JB018213 , doi: 10.1029/2019JB018213.

Wu, R.-S., J. Luo, and B. Wu (2014). Seismic envelope inversion and modulation signal model, *Geophysics* **79,** no. 3, WA13–WA24.

Xia, J. (2014). Estimation of near-surface shear-wave velocities and quality factors using multichannel analysis of surface-wave methods, *J. Appl. Geophys.* **103,** 140–151.

Yang, J., H. Zhu, W. Wang, Y. Zhao, and H. Zhang (2018). Isotropic elastic reverse time migration using the phase-and amplitude-corrected vector p-and s-wavefields, *Geophysics* **83,** no. 6, S489–S503.

Yang, X.-H., P. Han, Z. Yang, and X. Chen (2023). Two-stage broad learning inversion framework for shear-wave velocity estimation, *Geophysics* **88,** no. 1, WA219–WA237.

Yang, X.-H., P. Han, Z. Yang, M. Miao, Y.-C. Sun, and X. Chen (2022). Broad learning framework for search space design in Rayleigh wave inversion, *IEEE Trans. Geosci. Remote Sens.* **60,** 1–17.

Yang, X.-H., Y. Zhou, P. Han, X. Feng, and X. Chen (2024). Near-surface Rayleigh wave dispersion curve inversion algorithms: A comprehensive comparison, *Surv. Geophys.* **45,** no. 3, 773–818.

Yang, Y., M. H. Ritzwoller, F.-C. Lin, M. Moschetti, and N. M. Shapiro (2008). Structure of the crust and uppermost mantle beneath the western United States revealed by ambient noise and earthquake tomography, *J. Geophys. Res.* **113,** no. B12, doi: 10.1029/2008JB005833.

Yao, H., and R. D. Van Der Hilst (2009). Analysis of ambient noise energy distribution and phase velocity bias in ambient noise tomography, with application to SE Tibet, *Geophys. J. Int.* **179,** no. 2, 1113–1132.

Yin, X., H. Xu, B. Mi, X. Hao, P. Wang, and K. Zhang (2020). Joint inversion of Rayleigh and love wave dispersion curves for improving the accuracy of near-surface s-wave velocities, *J. Appl. Geophys.* **176,** 103939.

Zhang, Z., J. Feng, and H. Yao (2023). 3-d azimuthal anisotropy structure reveals different deformation modes of the crust and upper mantle in the southeastern Tibetan plateau, *Front. Earth Sci.* **11,** 1095609.

Zhang, Z., H. Yao, and Y. Yang (2020). Shear wave velocity structure of the crust and upper mantle in southeastern Tibet and its geodynamic implications, *Sci. China Earth Sci.* **63,** no. 9, 1278–1293.

Zhang, Z.-D., and T. Alkhalifah (2019). Wave-equation Rayleigh-wave dispersion inversion using fundamental and higher modes, *Geophysics* **84,** no. 4, EN57–EN65.

Zhu, C., R. H. Byrd, P. Lu, and J. Nocedal (1997). Algorithm 778: L-BFGS-B: Fortran subroutines for large-scale bound-constrained optimization, *ACM Trans. Math. Softw.* **23,** no. 4, 550–560.

Manuscript received 22 August 2025
Published online 19 February 2026

Toward Operational Earthquake Seismogram Denoising

Nikolaj Dahmen*[1], John Clinton[2], Men-Andrin Meier[1], and Luca Scarabello[1]

ABSTRACT

OPEN ACCESS

Earthquake catalogs are built from continuous seismic recordings through a series of steps, including signal detection, phase arrival picking, arrival association, event localization, and amplitude-based magnitude determination. Although each step can be automated, ever-present noise in the waveforms often limits reliable processing to larger events or quieter stations or necessitates manual data review to ensure high-quality results. In this study, we introduce Earthquake Seismogram Denoiser (EQS-denoiser), a deep learning–based denoising model trained on earthquake and noise signals recorded in Switzerland and preprocessed to refine label quality. Our objective is to improve automated analysis of continuous seismic waveform streams across the full network, enhancing earthquake monitoring and characterization. We demonstrate its performance in three key tasks essential for catalog curation: (1) signal detection, in comparison with deep learning pickers; (2) signal denoising, against conventional digital filters; and (3) phase arrival picking using denoised data versus raw data. In all cases, the denoiser outperforms baseline methods, particularly under low signal-to-noise ratio conditions. We integrate EQS-denoiser into an end-to-end earthquake monitoring framework to maximize detections and optimally recover signals from continuous data. Furthermore, we assess how existing phase pickers can best leverage denoised data to improve identification of arrival times and estimate associated timing uncertainty using test-time augmentation. We demonstrate through a case study of a small alpine sequence how EQS-denoiser significantly advances the generation of seismicity catalogs compared with both a deep learning picker–based catalog and the manually reviewed Swiss catalog. In automated processing, denoising enables more reliable signal detection, a greater number of phase picks with fewer false picks, more accurate automated peak amplitude estimation for magnitude determination, and enhanced waveforms for other types of data analysis. This results in a deeper seismicity catalog that, after relative relocation, achieves location quality comparable to the manual-reviewed catalog while extending to lower-magnitude earthquakes.

KEY POINTS

- We present a denoising model integrated into an end-to-end pipeline to build deeper seismicity catalogs.
- The denoising model outperforms deep learning pickers in signal detection and improves phase picking.
- Denoised data yield better signal characterization, amplitude measurements, and magnitude estimates.

Supplemental Material

INTRODUCTION

Earthquake monitoring relies on continuous, high-quality seismic recordings (seismograms) to detect and characterize seismicity across the entire magnitude range. However, ambient noise—from natural sources such as wind or ocean waves and anthropogenic activity such as traffic or industrial operation—can obscure low-amplitude earthquake signals, limiting the performance of automated procedures. Deep learning tools have been a game changer in earthquake monitoring because they can learn complex, nonlinear relationships in seismic data that conventional methods struggle to capture, enabling, for example, the detection of earthquake signals and the identification of phase arrivals amid high levels of

1. Institute of Geophysics, ETH Zurich, Zurich, Switzerland, https://orcid.org/0000-0002-9114-6747 (ND); https://orcid.org/0000-0002-2949-8602 (M-AM); https://orcid.org/0000-0002-5197-6076 (LS); 2. Swiss Seismological Service, ETH Zurich, Zurich, Switzerland, https://orcid.org/0000-0001-8626-2703 (JC)

*Corresponding author: nikolaj.dahmen@eaps.ethz.ch

Cite this article as Dahmen, N., J. Clinton, M.-A. Meier, and L. Scarabello (2026). Toward Operational Earthquake Seismogram Denoising, *Bull. Seismol. Soc. Am.* **116**, 923–945, doi: 10.1785/0120250198 background noise (e.g., Ross *et al.*, 2018; Zhu and Beroza, 2019; Mousavi *et al.*, 2020; Mousavi and Beroza, 2022).

In this study, we propose and evaluate a deep learning denoising approach and its integration into the seismic network monitoring pipeline to enhance the observation of weak event signals that otherwise might remain unobserved, consequently extending the completeness of seismicity catalogs on the low magnitude end. We anticipate that the denoised data will not only improve signal detection and phase picking, but the cleaned waveforms will also enable better earthquake characterization.

We use the UNet deep learning architecture, originally developed for medical image segmentation (Ronneberger *et al.*, 2015) and later applied to decompose audio time-series data using time–frequency representation (e.g., Jansson *et al.*, 2017), as well as to denoise seismic data with DeepDenoiser (Zhu *et al.*, 2019). Similar to segmentation models, DeepDenoiser predicts a time–frequency mask that separates the seismic signal into event and noise components. With MarsQuakeNet, Dahmen *et al.* (2022, 2024) extended the UNet denoising model to three components and applied it to the NASA InSight dataset for the detection and denoising of teleseismic marsquake and meteorite impact signals, leading to a deeper seismicity catalog with enhanced characterization and location. To a large extent, we follow the MarsQuakeNet architecture and training procedure.

In addition to similar denoising methods operating in the time–frequency domain (e.g. Tibi *et al.*, 2021; Heuel and Friederich, 2022; Quinones and Tibi, 2024), several models have been proposed that work directly in time domain to output denoised time series (e.g., Yin *et al.*, 2022; Trappolini *et al.*, 2024). Without labeled training data, unsupervised approaches employ autoencoder-based architectures that learn compact latent representations of seismic recordings, capture essential features such as event signals, and reconstruct the waveform from these representations while suppressing uncorrelated noise (Vincent *et al.*, 2008). These methods can also include thresholding strategies to attenuate residual noise components (e.g., Saad *et al.*, 2022).

Denoising was tested in a case study on the Long Beach Array in which earthquakes were located through backprojection imaging (Yang *et al.*, 2022) and phase detection examples were shown on continuous data from single stations (e.g., Yin *et al.*, 2022; Trappolini *et al.*, 2024). However, relatively little attention has been paid to how denoising approaches can be practically integrated into standard seismic monitoring workflows and how they impact seismicity catalogs. We adopt and adjust MarsQuakeNet for local seismic data and investigate how denoised data can improve earthquake catalogs in combination with existing phase pickers, association, and location algorithms.

We train and test the denoising model on seismic data recorded in Switzerland, where the Swiss Seismological Service (SED), in collaboration with partner institutions, operates a dense seismic network to monitor seismicity within the country and its border regions (Diehl *et al.*, 2025). SED curates the seismicity catalog using highly sensitive broadband and short-period seismometers, as well as strong-motion accelerometers. Various signal detectors and pickers are in use, although all waveform data are ultimately manually reviewed and picked to ensure high-quality picks and reliable magnitudes (Diehl *et al.*, 2025). SED catalogs ~500–2000 earthquakes each year, with magnitudes ranging from below 0 to beyond 4 (FDSN webservice, 2025).

The network includes different types of seismic monitoring sensors that are deployed in widely varying environments, from quiet vaults to noisy urban settings, requiring complex, station-specific adjustments and detection thresholds for automated monitoring. As a result, sensor recording at many of the noisy sites are effectively excluded from, or rarely used for, automated monitoring. In light of this limitation, deep learning–based denoising holds great potential to adapt to diverse noise conditions and support network-wide monitoring by improving and automating signal detection, phase picking, and peak amplitude estimation for magnitude determination.

The objectives of this study are to implement the denoising approach and assess its impact on automated monitoring and seismicity catalogs. We focus on improving the characterization of small earthquakes, which are typically only detectable at stations near the epicenter and are not well captured by current procedures. To achieve this, we introduce the deep learning denoising model, termed Earthquake Seismogram Denoiser (EQS-denoiser), to use all recordings despite varying and high noise levels. EQS-denoiser is designed not as a standalone approach but to be integrated within existing national monitoring system, with specific training on near epicenter recordings. We do not include more distant earthquake recordings from larger earthquakes because these cases are typically well characterized by the current monitoring procedures of the Swiss network.

The main contributions of this study are:

- The preparation of a dedicated training dataset for denoising with event data precleaning to improve the denoising label waveforms
- Training of the denoising model and implementation in processing pipelines from signal detection, continuous data denoising, and phase picking with pick timing uncertainty to the final seismicity catalog
- Demonstration of the advantages and limitations of the denoising model on signal detection, signal denoising, and phase picking and its impact on final seismicity catalogs in comparison with another deep learning phase picker and a high-quality manually picked catalog

In the following, we describe the denoising model and its training process, along with the data selection, preprocessing,

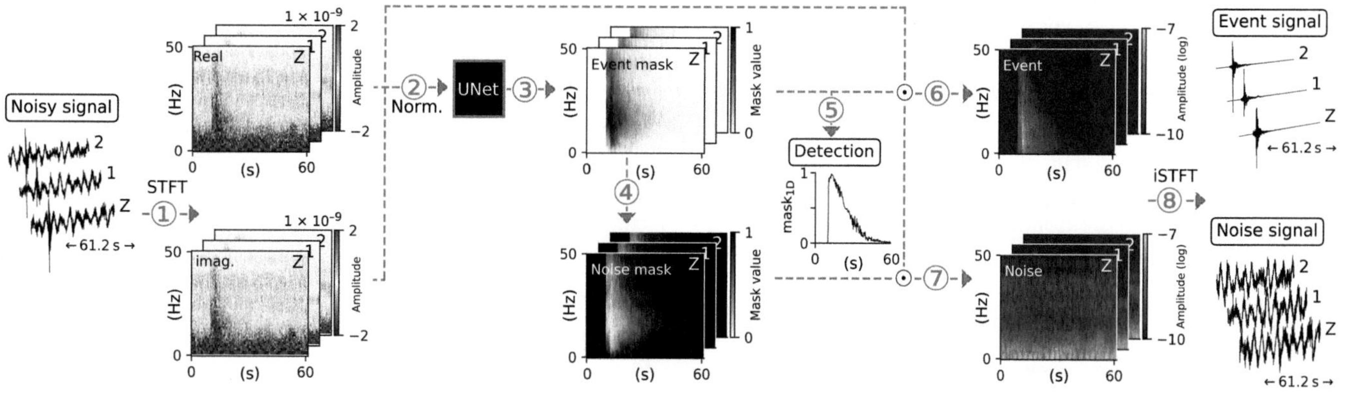

and augmentation. Then we focus on deriving robust phase picks with meaningful timing uncertainty from denoised data. We evaluate the performance of the denoising model for the signal detection and denoising tasks, as well as the impact of denoised data on phase picking. We propose a procedure to apply EQS-denoiser to continuous data and combine individual denoised time windows to capture event signals in an optimal way. Finally, we test the impact of the denoising approach on seismicity catalogs through a case study of a dense sequence, comparing the results with catalogs derived from a deep learning phase picker and the SED catalog.

Figure 1. Overview of the denoising method. (1) The recorded three-component velocity time series are transformed from time domain to time–frequency domain (short time Fourier transform [STFT]). (2) The normalized STFT coefficients ($m/s/\sqrt{Hz}$) serve as the input for the denoising model, (3) which outputs event masks, and (4) corresponding noise masks are derived from these (Noise mask $= \mathbf{1}_n -$ Event mask). (5) We obtain a 1D mask time series, mask_{1D}, used for detection by extracting the maximum values of the event masks along the frequency axes and averaging them across the three components. For detected signals, we separate the STFT coefficients with (6) event and (7) noise masks into event and noise components through elementwise multiplication (represented by magnitude spectrogram, in $\log_{10}(m/s/\sqrt{Hz})$, and (8) that can be backtransformed to time domain using the inverse STFT (iSTFT). The color version of this figure is available only in the electronic edition.

METHOD AND DATASET

We build a dataset by combining real, well-recorded earthquake with noise signals to simulate noisy earthquake recordings and then train a denoising model to recover the original earthquake signals.

Denoising approach

Figure 1 shows the denoising approach, generally following Dahmen *et al.* (2022) and Zhu *et al.* (2019): (1) we transform preprocessed, three-component velocity waveforms into a time–frequency representation using the short-time Fourier transform (STFT). We compute the STFT of 61.2 s long, 100 samples per second waveforms with 48 samples per window and 24 samples of overlap, thereby slightly favoring time over frequency resolution. These STFT parameters result in dimensions of 256 time bins and 64 frequency bins, which is convenient for the following processing within the model. (2) We apply a robust normalization to the real and imaginary components of the STFT coefficients, which serve as the model input. The model is based on the UNet architecture (Ronneberger *et al.*, 2015), consisting of convolutional layers with Rectified Linear Unit (ReLU)-activations and (max-) pooling operations within a contractive path for hierarchical feature extraction and (transposed) convolutional layers and ReLU-activation along the expansive path to restore high-resolution dense output maps (see Table S1, available in the supplemental material to this article). (3) The model outputs are a set of three single-component segmentation masks with values between 0 and 1, which identify the share of event energy per time–frequency bin and (4) allow us to derive noise masks. (5) To use the model for event signal detection, we compress the event masks into a mask time series mask_{1D} that allows for convenient collection of detections above a selected threshold. For each timestep, we average the maximum mask values across all three components. Although we usually observe event signals across a wide frequency range, taking the maximum value also allows for the detection of narrow-banded signals. (6) For detected signals, we separate the event signal by element-wise multiplication of the event mask with the STFT coefficients. (7) Similarly, we isolate the noise signal. (8) Finally, we obtain denoised waveforms and noise waveforms by computing the inverse STFT.

Data selection

To build the training dataset, we use real event and noise data. We create the event dataset by considering all earthquakes listed in the SED catalog between 2009 and August 2024 (FDSN webservice, 2025) and select the associated waveforms from available networks (see Data and Resources) that meet the following criteria: (1) the waveform has a *P* pick included in the manually revised location, (2) the epicentral distance of the recording is ≤30 km, (3) the waveforms are sampled at ≥100 samples per second, (4) three-component recordings are available, (5) the event signal reaches a minimum time- and frequency-domain signal-to-noise ratio (SNR) as detailed in the Data Processing section, and (6) the preprocessing as also described in the next section was successful.

Starting with nearly 16,000 events cataloged in that time period with >200,000 associated waveforms with *P* picks, we initially excluded about half of the recordings because of the epicentral distance criteria. The majority (>75%) of the remaining waveforms are excluded because of the SNR criteria, leaving a total of 28,793 event waveforms, which we collect as 180-s-long time series with the *P* pick aligned at 60 s (see Fig. S1). The event signals originate from 383 stations with—on average 75 earthquake seismograms each. However, variations are large, and stations with low background noise and nearby seismicity are overrepresented. The related event magnitudes are distributed from **M** − 1 to nearly **M** 5, peaking around **M** 1, and are recorded relatively uniformly in 4–30 km epicentral distance, with fewer recordings below 4 km. Records from recent years are more frequent because of the densification of the Swiss network.

Furthermore, we build a separate noise dataset by randomly selecting waveforms from stations used for phase picking by SED from 2022 to mid-2024. We exclude periods containing events in the SED catalog with a 1 hr buffer to avoid including potentially uncataloged fore- or aftershocks while retaining teleseismic earthquake signals as part of the noise dataset. We collect data equally throughout different seasons and equally from broadband and short-period seismometers, as well as accelerometers, corresponding to HH, HG, and EH channels for the CH network. We add a small number of more exotic channels related to other types of instruments, higher sampling rates, or other network operators (EL?, HN?, FH?, DH?, where "?" is a wildcard character representing the component) to expose the model to different noise conditions.

To make the model more robust against transient noise signals, we collect additional waveforms that contain large spikes, identified by a high short-term average (STA)/long-term average (LTA) ratio, and add them to the dataset.

In total, we collect ~360,000 three-component noise signals (80 s each) from 451 sensors with 798 records each on average. Of these, 10% are specifically selected because they contain impulsive signals, and the remaining signals are randomly sampled (Fig. S2).

Then we split event and noise datasets by the last digit of their day-of-year (DOY): recordings on DOY ending on XX0, XX1-2, and XX3-9 are assigned to the test, validation, and training dataset (10%/20%/70%).

Data preprocessing

With 300 stations across Switzerland, the seismic network monitored by the SED is very dense (Diehl *et al.*, 2025). But given relatively low event magnitudes, seismogram SNRs are typically low across the full time–frequency signal, and the time windows also include pre- and postevent noise. Any background noise contained in the event data will map back into the training data and ultimately into the denoised signal. We perform extensive preprocessing of the event signals as a form of pretraining label cleaning to reduce this effect (Fig. 2):

First (step 1, in Fig. 2a), we apply a prefiltering step and deconvolve the raw recordings to physical units, converting them to velocity for each sensor type. This ensures that the frequency spectra are relatively flat, providing inputs of similar magnitude for the denoising model.

Second (step 2), we apply a signal-specific band-pass filter, deriving and applying a separate passband for each waveform to capture the frequency range where the signal is best recorded. To do so, we compute spectra of the event signal and the pre-event noise and identify the frequency band where the spectral amplitude of the event signal exceeds that of the pre-event noise spectra by a factor of 10 across a broad frequency range (Fig. 2b,c). This step typically removes the long-period noise and high-frequency noise near the Nyquist frequency. We discard recordings whose spectral amplitude does not exceed the pre-event spectral amplitude by at least a factor of 10 across a board frequency range or whose time-domain SNR, after signal-specific band-pass filtering, is <10 dB.

Third (step 3), we taper the end of the event signal to remove background noise following the event signal, ensuring that the event signal amplitudes smoothly decay to zero. To achieve this, we compute spectral envelopes, perform a linear fit on their logarithmic coda decay, and suppress the coda amplitudes accordingly (Fig. 2d). Because the coda is not the primary focus of our analysis, we do not employ more sophisticated frequency-dependent coda decay models.

Fourth (step 4), we zero out the pre-event noise up to the first zero-crossing before the *P* pick and apply an amplitude taper to this segment to smooth the onset and minimize the introduction of high-frequency artifacts. Furthermore, we downsample the data to 100 samples per second.

Although these precleaning steps may slightly alter the waveform properties, for training, it is sufficient that the waveforms remain realistic rather than perfectly accurate. The procedure ensures that parts of the signal unrelated to the actual event, such as long period or high-frequency noise, as well as pre- and postevent, are not labeled as event energy. This automated processing produces cleaner signals, but it requires a relatively high SNR and a *P* pick. Failures occur only in some cases when aftershocks or strong transient noise signals corrupt the fit of the coda; such cases are excluded from the training data. The processing was confirmed by visual review of the event dataset.

Data augmentation

We combine event and noise signals in various randomly selected event and noise pairs and trim them to 61.2 s waveforms while maintaining the main event signal in the selected time window. We perform extensive data augmentation to improve the robustness and generalization of the model by

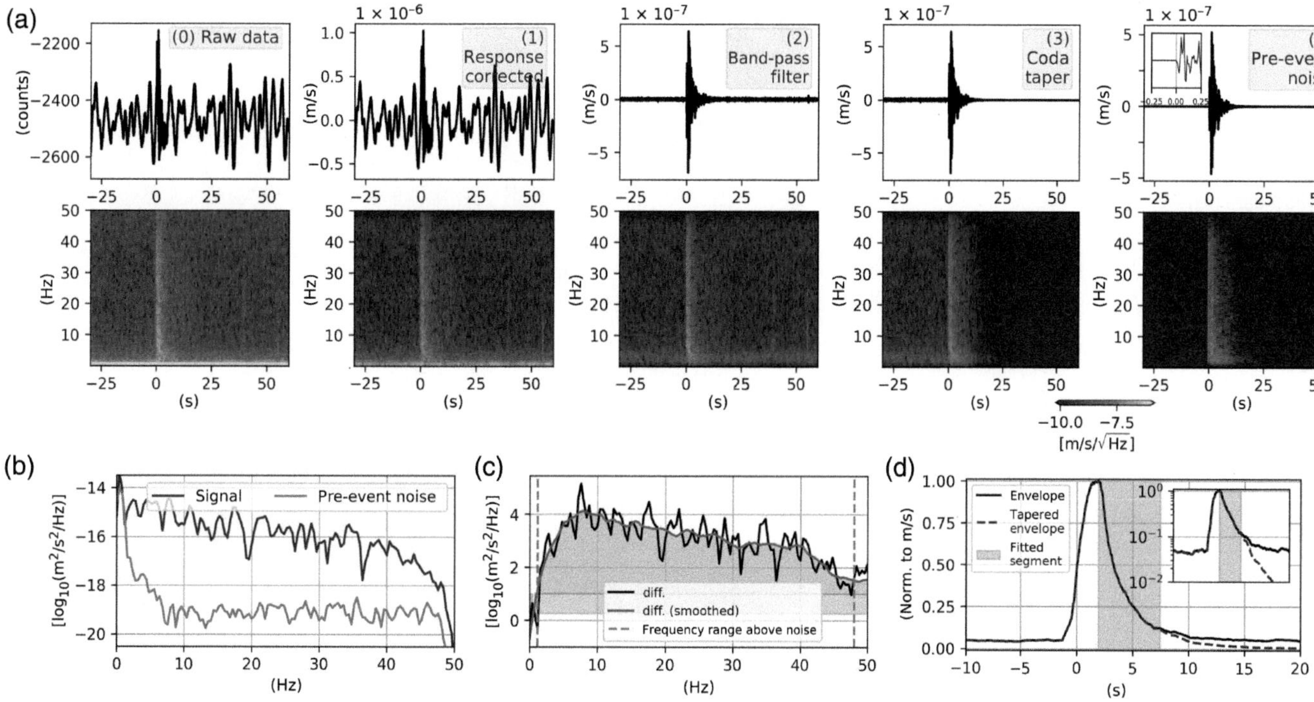

Figure 2. Preprocessing of training data labels from raw signals to cleaned event signals. (a) Starting with the raw data, (0) we apply a prefilter and deconvolve the instrument response to obtain velocity waveforms (1); next, we apply a band-pass filter (2) with signal-specific cutoff frequencies as determined in (b,c); we add a taper to the coda to reduce the postevent amplitudes to zero (3), as designed in (d); and (4) finally, we set the pre-event noise to 0 at the first zero-crossing before the *P* pick with a taper to reduce discontinuities (inset shows zoom on first arrival) and downsample the data to 100 Hz. The signal-specific cutoff frequencies of the band-pass filter are selected by (b) comparing the event and pre-event noise spectra and by (c) identifying the frequency range in which the event is above the noise spectral signal by a factor of 10 (or 1 on $\log_{10}$ scale). To suppress the postevent noise amplitudes, (d) we compute envelopes from the absolute amplitude values smoothed with boxcar, obtain a linear fit on the log values (shown in inset), and reduce the waveform amplitudes to follow this fit. The color version of this figure is available only in the electronic edition.

(1) varying the SNR by up or down-scaling the amplitudes of the event signal; (2) randomly shifting the event signal within the time window; (3) flipping polarities and (horizontally) rotating the waveforms; (4) including a second, weaker event before or after the main event; (5) subselecting different parts of the longer noise waveform; and (6) including a share of only-noise waveforms. The share of only-noise signals has a larger influence on the detection abilities of the model and will be evaluated during the model performance test. In addition, we add samples in which all three components are identical, representing one of the original components, to enable the model to handle one-component data at inference.

During each epoch of the model training and validation, we randomly recombine 1,011,500 event and noise signals on the fly. Because the number of available event and noise signals in our dataset is smaller, we reuse signals multiple times. In this step, we select event signals recorded on stations that are underrepresented in the dataset slightly more frequently to balance the dataset (Fig. S1). During the full model training of 30 epochs, the model encounters >30 million unique event–noise combinations.

Model training

During model training, we minimize the difference between the predicted and true event masks (Fig. 1) using the binary cross-entropy loss with an Adam optimizer (Kingma, 2014), both standard choices for this kind of task. We start with an initial learning rate of 1×10^{-4}, which controls the step size during optimization, and reduce it by a factor of 10 when the validation loss plateaus. We terminate the training process when the validation loss stops decreasing significantly for several epochs and restore the best model weights (Fig. S3).

PHASE PICKING AND TIMING UNCERTAINTIES ON DENOISED DATA

The determination of automated *P* and *S* onset times has been greatly improved using deep learning phase pickers. Here, we evaluate how denoising may further improve this task. We use EQTransformer (EQT) (Mousavi *et al.*, 2020) implemented in SeisBench (Woollam *et al.*, 2022) because it can be easily applied to determine both *P* and *S* picks without optimizing picking parameters as required with conventional pickers.

An ideal denoising model should completely remove the background noise, leaving only the event signals as nonzero amplitudes. We find that for the phase picking task, reintroducing small amounts of noise as a form of water level can improve the process. This is because phase pickers typically require the presence of background noise to perform well.

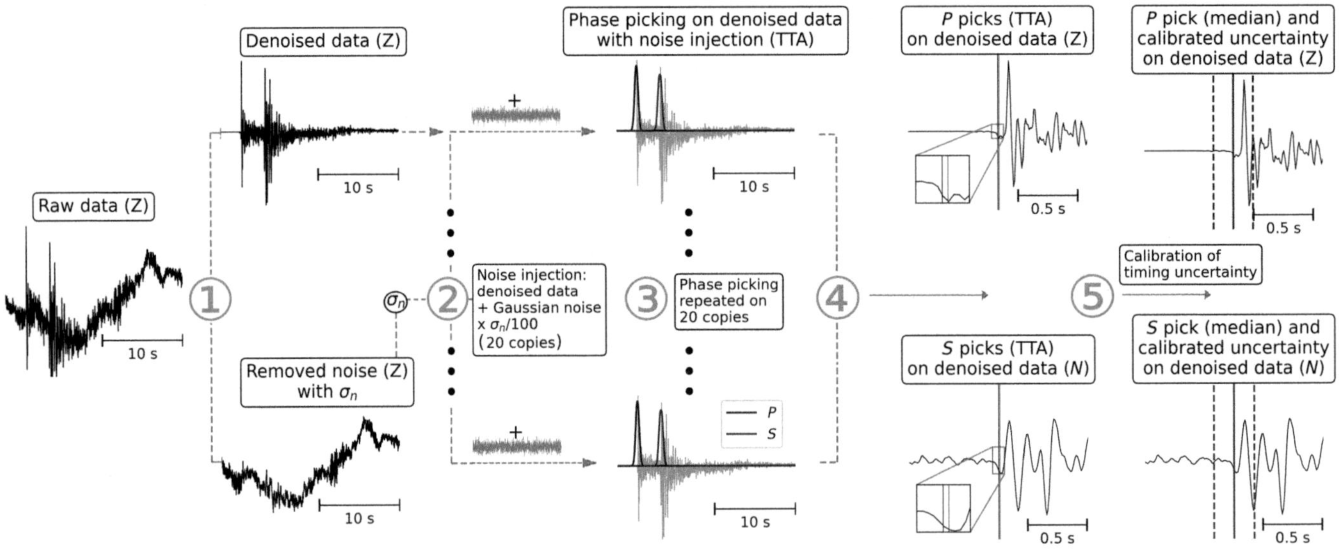

Figure 3. Phase picking and uncertainty estimation using test-time augmentation (TTA) with noise injection. (1) Raw data are separated into event (denoised data) and noise signals (removed noise) with standard deviation σ_n. (2) Gaussian noise scaled by $\sigma_n/100$ is added to 20 copies of the denoised data. (3) Phase picks are obtained with EQTransformer (EQT) on each copy, and individual TTA phase picks are collected as peaks of the model confidence. (4) Final phase picks are obtained as the median value of individual phase picks, weighted by their respective model confidence peak values; the inset shows a zoom into the partly overlapping TTA phase picks. (5) Uncertainties are adjusted through calibration. The color version of this figure is available only in the electronic edition.

For example, deep learning pickers are trained on data with background noise, and conventional pickers often compute ratios (e.g., STA/LTA) that cannot handle waveforms with amplitudes equal to 0. In addition, our denoising model strongly suppresses the background noise—typically by~40 dB—but leaves weak noise signals and some discontinuities across the 61.2 s prediction windows. Even small noise remnants can impair phase picking as deep learning pickers typically consume normalized-amplitude data and do not take their absolute values into account. Similarly, conventional pickers such as STA/LTA rely on amplitude ratios and are sensitive to small noise remnants (Fig. S4). These issues are less important and can be managed when denoising event-triggered data but become critical when applied to continuous data. Adding a small amount of Gaussian noise to the denoised waveform masks low-amplitude noise remnants, thereby reducing false triggers without compromising the picking performance. In addition, by repeating phase picking on multiple variations of the same denoised waveform with injected noise, we can estimate aleatoric uncertainties based on the variability of the resulting picks, corresponding to the approach known as test-time augmentation (TTA) (Wang *et al.*, 2019).

Figure 3 summarizes the procedure: (1) the raw data are decomposed into a denoised event and noise signal. (2) Then we reintroduce some Gaussian noise to copies of the denoised signal. To estimate the amount of noise to cover up weak noise remnants, we couple the water level to the noise level of the original recordings: we compute the standard deviation of the (removed) noise waveforms σ_n and generate different Gaussian noise time series with amplitude scaled by $\sigma_n/100$, which are then added to copies of the denoised event signal. (3) We then perform the phase picking on 20 variations of the denoised data efficiently in batches and collect individual *P* and *S* picks as the peak values of the model confidence time series for *P* and *S*. We accept phase picks if at least 25% of the cases include model confidence peaks with values above a threshold of 0.5 at nearby timesteps (<1 s). (4) We determine the final pick as the median value of the picks and the initial uncertainty as the standard deviation of the peak times. We weight the calculation of median and standard deviation by the corresponding model confidence peak value to incorporate the information given by the model confidence of each peak. (5) The initial pick timing uncertainty is calibrated later on using the test dataset. By linking the amplitude of the added Gaussian noise to the removed noise, we can estimate phase picking uncertainties that also reflect the denoising process.

We calibrate the pick timing uncertainties using the method introduced by Kuleshov *et al.* (2018) and adapted by Armstrong *et al.* (2023) for seismic phase pick timing to produce 90% confidence intervals that contain the true pick in 90% of the cases while remaining as narrow as possible. As described in the next section, we use a subset of the test dataset with manual phase picks that we assume are ground truth (T_{true}), repick phases on denoised data with EQT ($T_{\mathrm{processed}}$), and estimate the initial timing uncertainty Δt_i. We compare the initial uncertainty estimates (Δt_i) with the picking residuals $r_{P/S} = T_{P/S,\mathrm{processed}} - T_{P/S,\mathrm{true}}$ and then calibrate the uncertainties to confidence intervals (Δt_c) that statistically cover the observed pick residuals. Specifically, we adjust the timing uncertainties until the empirical coverage—the proportion of picks within a predicted interval—matches the nominal coverage (the target confidence level of 90%) by performing a monotonic mapping using isotonic regression (Kuleshov *et al.*, 2018). As a result, the normalized error $\frac{|r|}{\Delta t_c}$ should be <1 in 90% of the cases.

In addition to providing a measure of timing uncertainty, TTA improves the consistency of deep learning–based phase pickers, which are known to produce inconsistent results with small variations in input data (Park *et al.*, 2023).

PERFORMANCE EVALUATION

We assess the model quantitatively on the test dataset by addressing several key questions related to its denoising performance. These include: How accurately can the model distinguish between event and noise signals? How effectively does the model denoise event signals? Does it introduce distortions, phase shifts, or alter peak amplitude measurements? What effect does denoising have on phase picking tasks, especially in terms of phase picking accuracy? To answer these questions, we prepare a test dataset by corrupting clean event signals with noise signals (of varying intensity), as shown in Figure 4, producing a controlled set of noisy event signals. We then apply denoising to restore the original waveforms and compare them to the clean event signals.

We benchmark the signal detection against EQT (Mousavi *et al.*, 2020) as available through SeisBench (Woollam *et al.*, 2022) using the model trained on the Swiss ETHZ dataset. We compare the denoising performance against a 1–30 Hz band-pass filters as typically applied in processing of local seismic data in Switzerland. Furthermore, we evaluate the effect of denoised data on phase picking with EQT compared with the same approach on raw data. We follow the procedure and metrics as documented in Dahmen *et al.* (2024) and other related studies (Tibi *et al.*, 2022; Yin *et al.*, 2022). We also use these metrics to compare different instances of the denoising model trained on variations of the datasets because loss values are not directly comparable when the underlying data change.

Figure 5 summarizes each element in the performance test. Each of the 6 metrics is computed for 10,000 event and noise signal combinations at 11 different SNR levels (in increments of 2 dB). At each SNR value, the median value and distribution are provided. The SNR shown here is computed from the standard deviation of the main event signal, using a 10 s window, and the background noise before combining them. The SNR spans a wide range, from event waveforms that are visually indistinguishable from the background noise to those with very clear signals (see examples in Fig. S5).

Signal detection

We evaluate the ability of EQS-denoiser to detect signals by predicting whether a given waveform contains an event signal. For this task, we use the mask time series mask_{1D} (Fig. 1) derived from the predicted event masks. We select a conservative detection threshold of 0.33 after testing several candidate values (Fig. S6). For comparison, we apply EQT on the same set of waveforms, collecting event detections when the model confidence for *P* or *S* arrivals exceeds a threshold of 0.5 (selected from several tested thresholds; see Fig. S7). Note that the two thresholds are algorithm-specific and therefore not directly comparable.

At each SNR level, we count how often an event signal is correctly detected (true positives) and how often the model failed to detect the event signal (false negative) in the noisy event waveforms. To estimate false positives, we run also the detection on 10,000 noise waveforms alone. Because these do not include event signals, the predictions are independent of the SNR. In this test, we include an equal share of samples with and without event signals; however, when applied to continuous data, the model encounters mainly noise waveforms, making false positives more frequent. To address this, we set a rather conservative threshold for EQS-denoiser.

We quantify the detections using precision (the proportion of true positive among all positive detections) and recall (the proportion of true positives among all actual positives). We also report their harmonic mean, the F1 score.

The test (Fig. 5a) demonstrates that EQS-denoiser achieves higher precision and recall than EQT, in nearly the entire SNR range. In particular, EQS-denoiser delivers higher precision, related to a significantly lower number of false positive detections. We repeat the same test using only impulsive noise signals—in these cases, we find that EQS-denoiser outperforms EQT even more clearly owing to much fewer false-positive detections. These results are based on our selected detection threshold, which could be further optimized, though any choice ultimately involves a trade-off between false positives and false negatives. In addition to EQT, we have also tested PhaseNet (Zhu and Beroza, 2019) trained on Swiss data and implemented in SeisBench (Woollam *et al.*, 2022), but EQT provides slightly better performance both with denoised and raw data in our test case.

Waveform retrieval

Next we investigate the overall quality of the denoised waveforms by computing the waveform similarity of denoised and noise-free event waveforms using the zero-lag cross correlation (Fig. 5b). As a benchmark, we repeat the same test with a 1–30 Hz causal (and acausal) band-pass filter, which is typically used in manual review and phase picking by SED.

Both denoised and filtered waveforms show much higher cross-correlation values than those computed from the raw data across the full SNR range. Because the causal filter introduces a phase shift, the cross-correlation values are generally lower than the case with the acausal filter. We find that denoising is comparable to an acausal filter at very high and low SNR values but produces more reliable waveforms between ~−13 and −4 dB.

Note that we always compute the cross correlation over the main event signal window regardless of whether the signal is

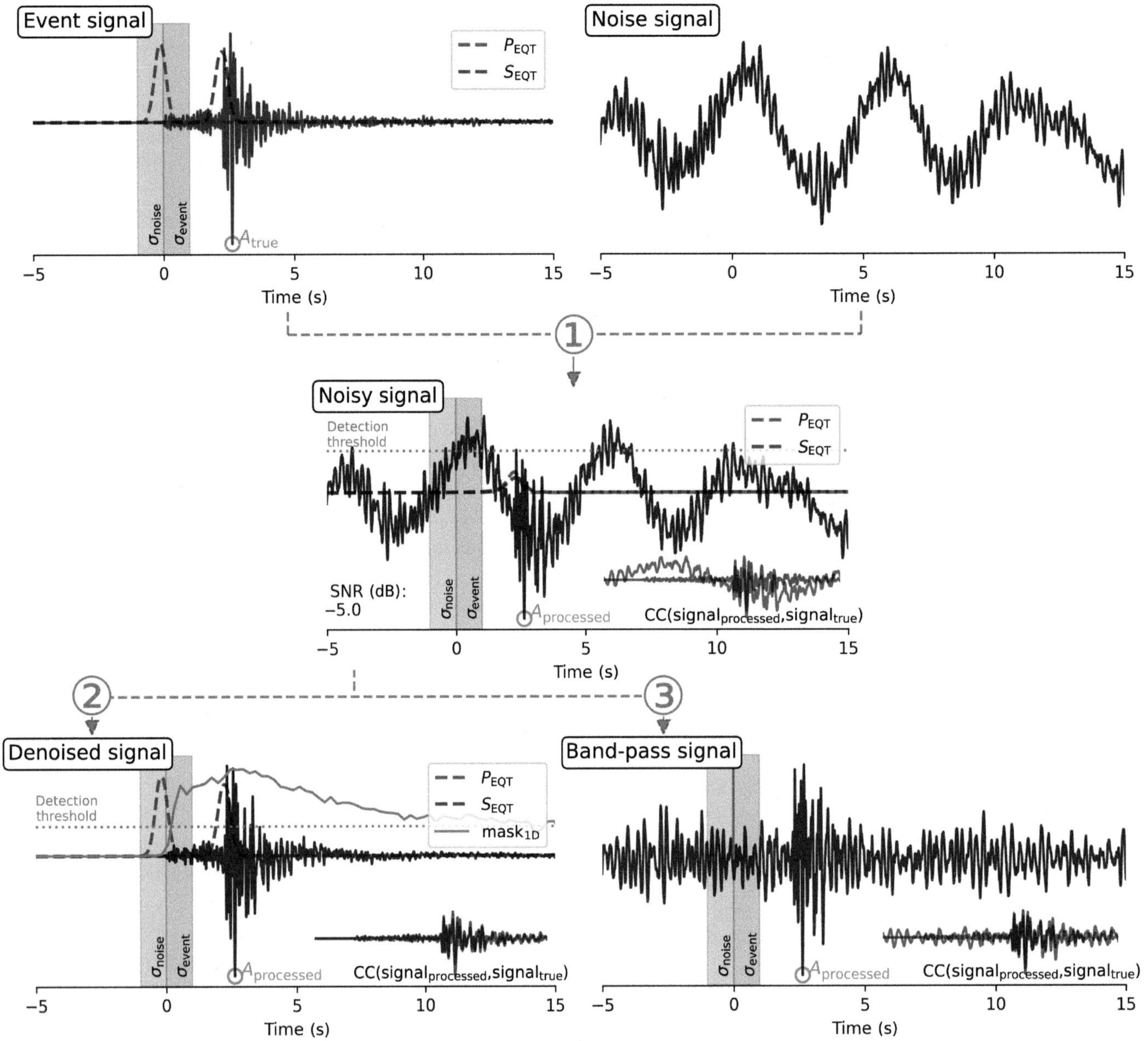

Figure 4. Denoising performance test: dataset construction and performance metrics. (1) We construct noisy event signals by combining event and noise signal with given signal-to-noise ratio (SNR) and remove the noise with (2) Earthquake Seismogram Denoiser (EQS-denoiser) or (3) a 1–30 Hz band-pass filter. Annotations indicate metrics that are evaluated in performance tests, including the detection (P_{EQT}, S_{EQT}, or $mask_{1D}$ compared with a detection threshold), P and S pick residuals ($T_{processed} - T_{true}$), the SNR estimated from the ratio of standard deviation of waveforms before and after fixed P arrival ($SNR_{pre} = \frac{\sigma_{event}}{\sigma_{noise}}$), the peak amplitude ratio ($\frac{A_{processed}}{A_{true}}$), and the waveform similarity compared with the clean event signal (cross correlation, CC(signal$_{processed}$,signal$_{true}$)). The phase picks on noisy and denoised signals are compared with picks on the clean event signal to obtain pick residuals; peak amplitudes and cross correlation are relative to clean event signal. The color version of this figure is available only in the electronic edition.

distinguishable from the background noise or not. This means that on raw and band-pass-filtered data, we always capture the event signal. However, for denoised waveforms, cross-correlation values are averaging cases in which meaningful waveforms were retrieved and cases in which no event signal was detected and the resulting waveform is close to zero. Using the detection threshold of the EQS-denoiser, we can identify the subset of cases in which meaningful waveforms were obtained. For these, we find that clear event signals can be retrieved even down to very low SNRs, though only for a decreasing share of the test cases.

In addition to the quality of the full waveform, we monitor how the peak amplitudes are affected by denoising. We plot the ratio of peak amplitudes of the denoised waveforms and noise-free waveforms and similarly for raw and band-pass-filtered data (Fig. 5c). In each case, the logarithms of the peak

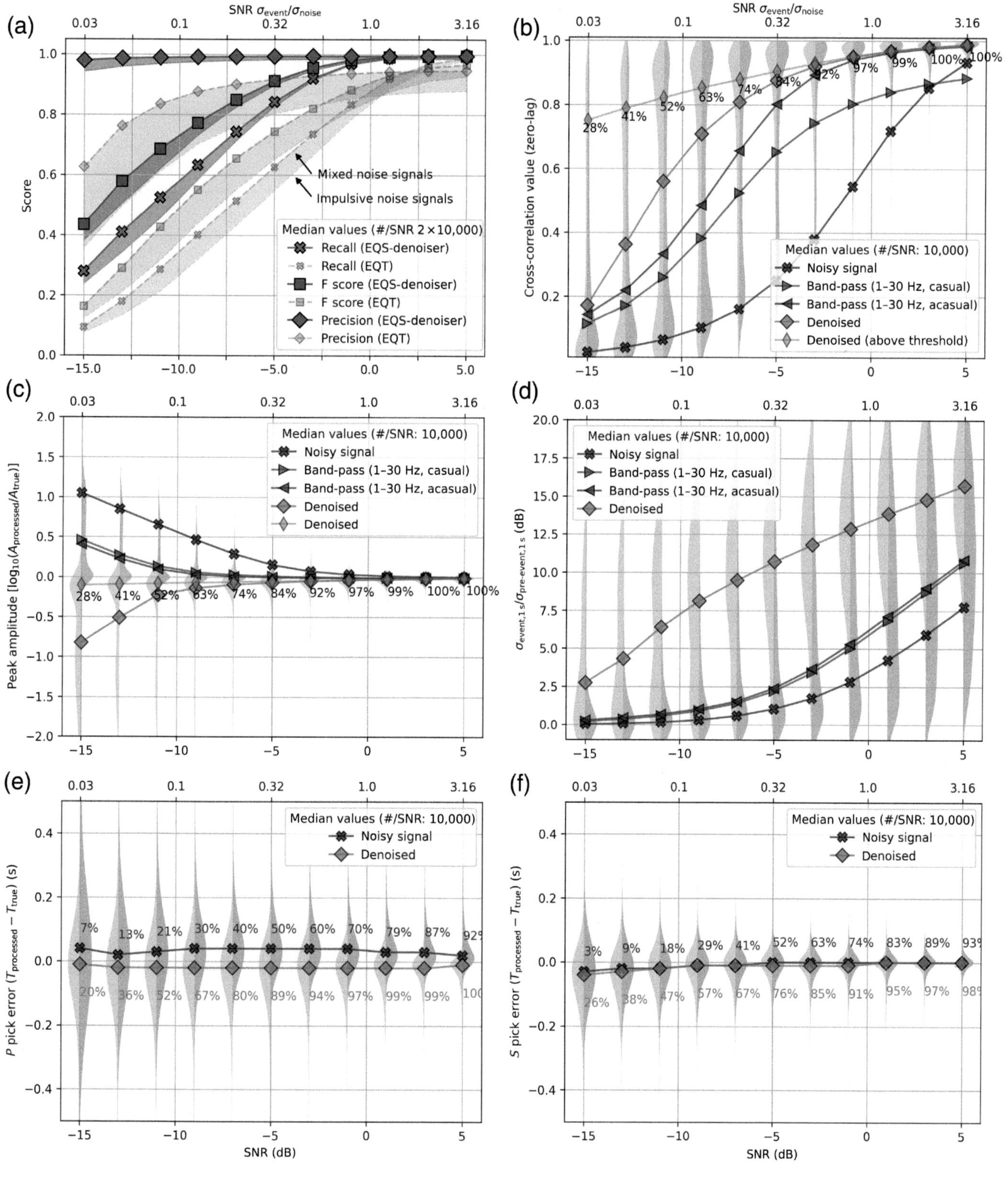

Figure 5. Denoising performance test results. Panels show median values and distribution of values across 10,000 event and noise signal combination at each SNR step: (a) signal detection metrics of EQS and EQT, (b) waveform similarity, (c) peak amplitude ratio, and (d) SNR (signal onset versus pre-event) of denoised, 1–30 Hz band-pass and raw data. (b) and (c) also show the quantities computed for the subset of waveforms detected, corresponding to the recall in (a). (e) *P* and (f) *S* pick residuals on denoised and raw data relative to pick on noise-free data. For the detection test in (a) 10,000 noise signals were additionally processed. Differences between using randomly selected noise (mixed noise) or noise with impulsive signals for phase picking are indicated. Shaded areas in (b–d) show the distribution for denoised and band-pass-filtered data and in (e,f) for denoised and noisy data. The color version of this figure is available only in the electronic edition.

amplitude ratios are close to 0 at high SNRs, which implies correct peak amplitude retrieval. Moving to lower SNRs, the denoised data tend to underestimate the peak amplitude. This is strongly driven by averaging cases with and without detected event signals; considering only cases with detected event signals, we still observe an underestimation of the peak amplitudes by ~20% at the lowest SNR. These absolute errors are much smaller than those observed in the band pass and raw data, in which peak amplitudes are overestimated by +180% or +1000% at the lowest SNR, respectively. In these cases, the measured peak amplitudes of raw and band-pass data simply correspond to the background noise amplitude. Because magnitudes typically scale with the logarithm of the peak amplitude, we can directly estimate the expected median magnitude errors at the lowest SNR to be ~−0.1, +0.45, and +1.05 magnitude units for denoised, band-pass, and noisy data, respectively.

The SNR of recorded event signals is typically estimated compared with its pre-event noise level. We compute SNR_{pre} using the standard deviation of the first second of the waveform after event start and compare it with the first second before event start to monitor the clarity of the signal onset (Figs. 4 and 5d). We deliberately do not include a buffer between the two windows to retain sensitivity to any acausal energy. The denoising significantly improves this quantity nearly across the full SNR range by >5 dB compared with band-pass data, implying that signal onsets are clearer. When considering the full event waveform instead of only the onset, we obtain improvements of 10–15 dB compared with band-pass data. Furthermore, EQS suppresses pre-event noise by ~40 dB across the test dataset, as measured by the ratio of the standard deviation of the pre-event noise before and after denoising (e.g., see Fig. S5).

Phase picking

Following the same approach as described in the previous section, we estimate the phase picking errors using EQT on denoised and raw data for *P* and *S* (Fig. 5e,f) compared with phase picking on noise-free data (Fig. 4). In this test, we do not use the TTA approach with repeated predictions to have a fair comparison, yet we again superimpose a white noise time series with low amplitudes on the denoised data before phase picking.

We observe that *P* picks are consistently early on denoised data. This effect is likely associated to acausal energy remnants introduced by the denoising process operating and averaging over a time–frequency bins, effectively smearing out signal onsets. In contrast, picking on the raw data tends to produce delayed picks. The absolute value of the *P* residuals from denoised data is smaller than those from the raw data across the full SNR range. *S* residuals are similar for both raw and denoised data. The main benefit of denoised data is the much higher share of waveforms that can be picked with comparable quality (percentages in Fig. 5e,f), corresponding to a much higher share of picked waveforms at very low to intermediate SNRs. Consequently, the picking statistics on denoised data include more low-quality waveforms, which in turn likely increases the median picking residuals. Phase picking with TTA tends to further improve the results by slightly increasing the share of picked waveforms.

In addition, we evaluate the performance of EQT on 1–30 Hz causal band-pass-filtered data, though we observe slightly better picking performance with raw data. The filter tends to increase the *P* pick and *S* pick residuals, though it allows for more *S* picks (Fig. S8).

Alternative tested model instances

We test several model instances trained on variations of the training dataset. In particular, we evaluate the influence of the share of noise-only waveforms for signal detection and denoising by training the same model on smaller datasets in which 10%, 30%, 50%, 70%, or 90% of the samples include event signals. We observe that as the share of noise-only samples increases, the precision of the earthquake signal detection improves, whereas both the recall and the waveform similarity of the denoised data decrease slightly (Fig. S9). In this sense, the construction of the training dataset introduces an implicit detection threshold that must be taken into account, not only for the denoising model but likely also for other types of models. For continuous data denoising, we prioritize high precision to minimize false positives, and we therefore use the model trained on equal share of event and noise signals. If denoising is applied only to triggered data, training with a higher share of event signals might be preferred.

Calibrating picking timing uncertainties

We calibrate the pick timing uncertainties on the manual picks using the subset of automatic picks that also have manual SED picks, similar to Figure 5e,f. The timing uncertainties initially derived from the standard deviation of the TTA picks (Fig. 3) correlate with the picking residuals but generally underestimate the picking errors. The calibration procedure (Fig. S10) results in calibration factors for *P* and *S*, which increase the confidence intervals to capture the uncertainty introduced by denoising and phase picking. In the test dataset, the calibrated 90% confidence intervals contain 90% of picks for *P* and *S*, respectively. Note that we add one sample to the standard deviation value to avoid uncertainties equal to zero and allow proper scaling, and we also consider the bias in phase picking, which is visible in form of a nonzero picking residual median.

During inference, we make repeated phase picks for each waveform, collect individual pick times, calculate the standard deviation, and apply the calibration factors for *P* and *S* to obtain statistically meaningful timing uncertainties.

APPLICATION OF DENOISING TO CONTINUOUS DATA

As demonstrated by the signal detection test, the denoising model outperforms commonly used phase pickers trained on Swiss data, suggesting that there is a real benefit to applying the denoising model to continuous data instead of only triggered data. Phase picking models are commonly applied to short time windows of continuous data, and to ensure that signals that extend across adjacent time windows are not missed, overlapping time windows are used. The predictions of overlapping results are then averaged or combined in a separate step.

In a similar fashion, we apply the denoising model to continuous data. However, averaging overlapping waveforms does not make sense in this case. Similarly, merging fixed parts of waveforms (e.g., the inner 50%) from overlapping time windows may introduce discontinuities within the event signal, making this approach also unsuitable.

Instead, we introduce a scheme based on overlapping time windows with a selection criterion that identifies, for each event signal, the waveform across parallel solutions in which the signal is best captured. In the following, we distinguish the waveforms of the full time window (61.2 s long) and the event signals as (typically) shorter subsegments of a time windows.

As shown in Figure 6a, we divide the continuous data in 50% overlapping windows corresponding to two series of non-overlapping windows with 50% shifted start times—named (Fig. 6b) even and (Fig. 6c) odd series. For each series, we compute the STFT coefficient, predict event masks, and derive the detection functions $mask_{1D}$. We make detections if $mask_{1D}$ is greater than the selected detection threshold and find the approximate start and end of the event signal. We assign a detection score to each individual detection, which corresponds to the sum of the $mask_{1D}$ values from the start to the end of each detection. This detection score is usually high if the event signal is well contained within a time window, and it is lower if the signals extend across several time windows or are cutoff. Consequently, the score allows us to pick the window in which the event signal is best recorded. If an event signal was only detected in one of the two $mask_{1D}$ series, we proceed with the related window; otherwise, we use the time window with the highest detection score. As an additional step, we repeat the prediction of event masks while aligning the event signal start within the time window (Fig. 6d). In most cases, this alignment leads to the highest detection score. The motivation for this step is illustrated by the first event signal (around STFT bin 400), in which the coda is truncated in the even series and its onset is partially cut in the odd series. In the new prediction, the full event signal is fully retrieved. In cases involving weak event signals or multiple closely spaced event signals, the original time windows may yield higher scores. In such instances, we use the original time windows.

As a result of this procedure, we obtain a detection list with the approximate signal start and end times, as well as the time window in which each event signal is best recorded. For each event signal, we select the waveform from the preferred time window. In case of dense seismicity, time windows containing event signals may still overlap, and we trim the 61.2-s-long waveforms to match the start and end of each event signal with several seconds buffer. In case the trimmed waveforms are still overlapping, we trim the coda of the earlier event signal in favor of maintaining the *P* and *S* arrivals of the later event signal. In the end, we keep only the part of the waveform containing detected event signals and discard the rest of the continuous data. Although this approach may omit weaker event signals that fall below our detection threshold, these faint signals are typically not well retrieved (Fig. 5). Furthermore, this reduces storage demands and significantly speeds up downstream tasks such as phase picking because only relevant segments of the full continuous waveform need to be processed. Figure 6 also includes cases that illustrate how this procedure improves upon nonoverlapping solutions, which may miss or only partially recover event signals located near the edges of time window (e.g., event signal around time bin 5000).

CATALOG COMPARISON: CASE STUDY OF EARTHQUAKE SEQUENCE

We demonstrate how EQS-denoiser can enhance seismicity catalogs through a case study of a relatively dense, low-magnitude seismic sequence. We compare results from the manually curated SED catalog against automatic catalogs created using the EQT picker applied with both raw and denoised data. Lists of phase picks are obtained using EQT on denoised data and raw data, hereafter referred to as the EQS-denoiser and EQT catalog. Next we employ SeisComP for the event association, location, and magnitude determination (Helmholtz Centre Potsdam, 2008). We adopt the same pipeline as used in the SED automatic detection and manual characterization workflow to evaluate not only the improvement in detection but also the impact on the catalog of introducing denoised data in a fully automated manner.

Bourg-Saint-Pierre/Mont Dolent Sequence 2025

As a case study, we select a 24 hr period between 7 and 8 February 2025, during which SED cataloged 33 events with magnitudes ranging from **M** 0.4 to 2.3 west of Bourg-Saint-Pierre, a border region between Switzerland, France, and Italy. Events in this sequence were first identified in early 2025, and none of the events from this location and sequence are included in the training dataset. We use the 24 active stations within ~30 km of the sequence, operated by institutions in Switzerland, France, and Italy (see Data and Resources). This set of stations includes various instrument types operating across a wide range of noise conditions, from quiet vaults to noisy urban settings. At the time, the SED catalog includes two additional earthquakes located over 175 km outside the study area, and one event situated ~50 km from the sequence; these events were processed using stations not part of our subset.

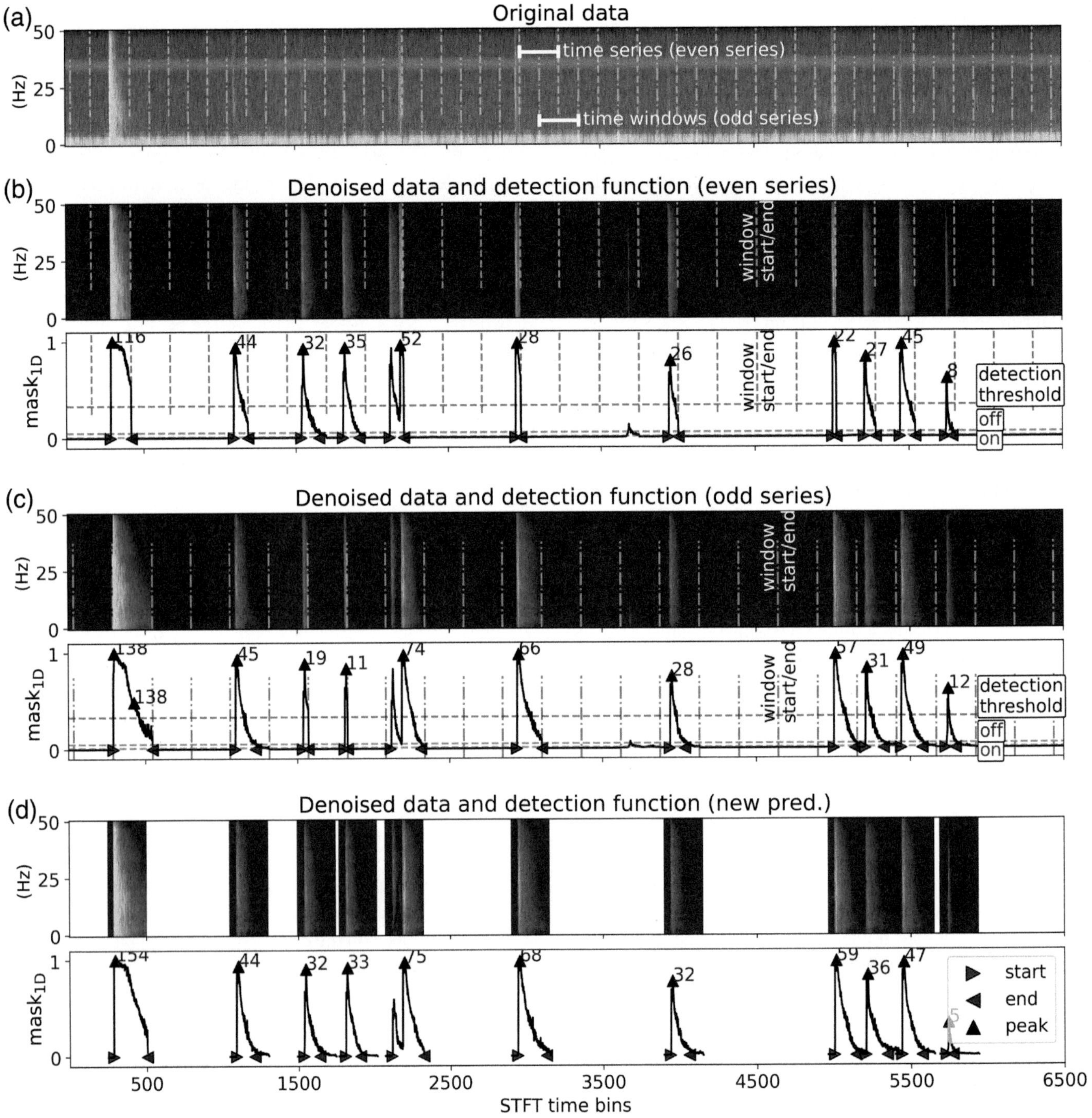

Figure 6. Continuous data denoising. (a) The original signal (recorded at 8D.RAW1.HHZ) is divided into 61.2 s time windows with 50% overlapping, yielding (b) even series and (c) odd series with time windows offset by 31.1 s. Shown for each series are denoised data spectrograms and detection function $mask_{1D}$, in which vertical lines (odd series are indicated by dashed–dotted lines; even series are indicated by dashed lines) indicate the start and end of individual time windows. Detected events above our selected threshold are annotated with approximately start ($mask_{1D}$ exceeds on threshold) and end ($mask_{1D}$ drops below off threshold) and detection score. Additionally shown are (d) the denoised data and detection function computed from time windows with detections aligned within window. For overlapping detections, the denoised waveform associated with the highest score across three parallel solutions is selected. The total data length are ~26 min; spectrograms show log amplitude range from 10^{-10} (blue) to 10^{-7} (yellow) m/s/$\sqrt{\text{Hz}}$. The color version of this figure is available only in the electronic edition.

Workflow

We apply EQS-denoiser on the continuous data as previously described and present representative 24 hr data examples in Figures 7–9, demonstrating the performance across diverse noise conditions: (1) a broadband seismometer at a relatively quiet location (CH.MFERR.HHZ) that is closest to the

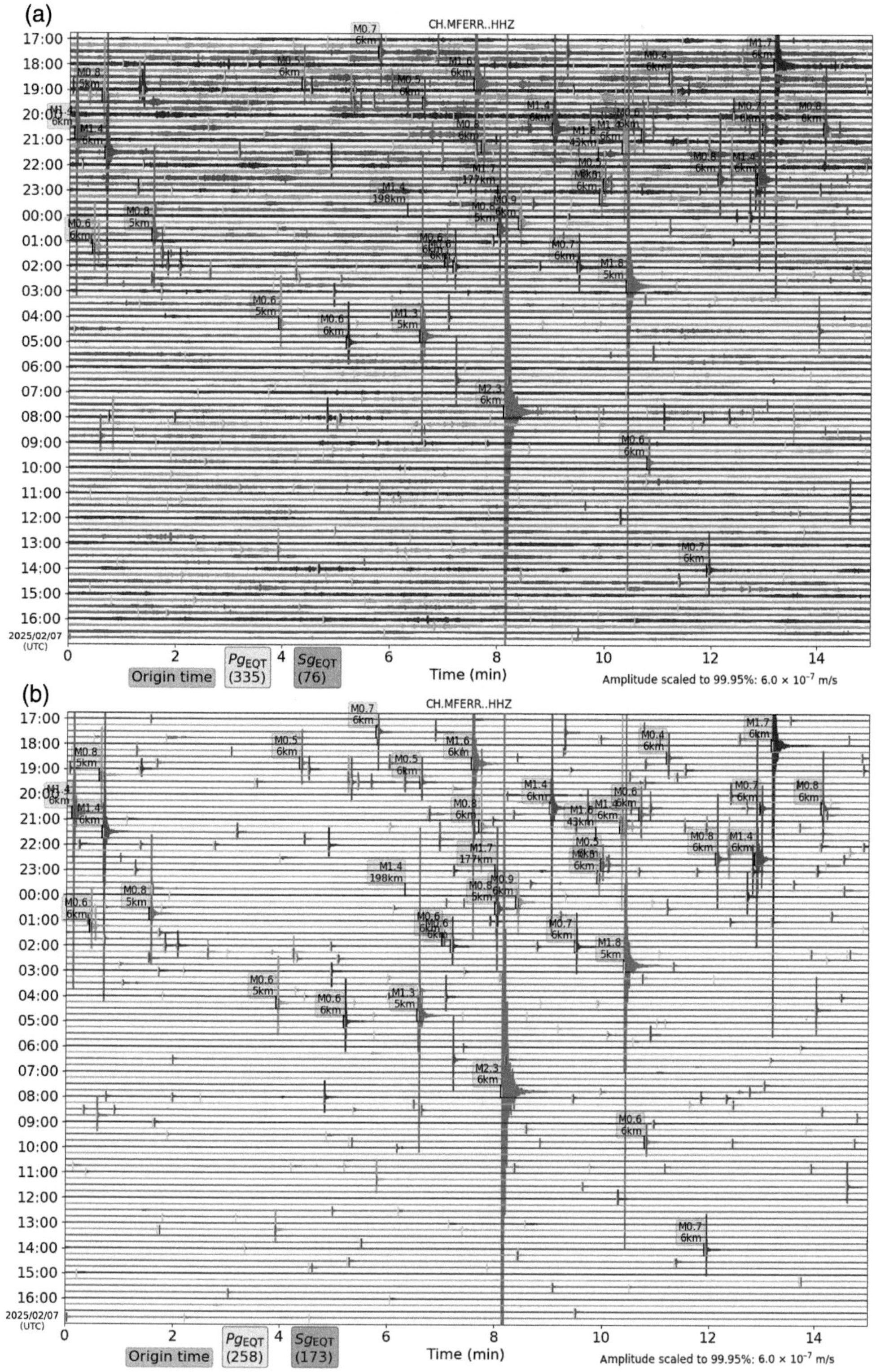

Figure 7. Helicorder plot of a 24-hr recording from broadband seismometer closest to sequence (CH.MFERR.HHZ). (a) Band-pass data with EQT picks (on raw data) and (b) denoised data with EQT picks (on denoised data). Earthquakes in Swiss Seismological Service (SED) catalog are added with origin time, magnitude, and epicentral distance; origin time (black), *Pg* (gold) and *Sg* picks (red) are annotated as vertical lines. Total number of *Pg* and *Sg* picks are indicated at bottom of each subplot. The color version of this figure is available only in the electronic edition.

sequence, (2) a strong-motion seismometer located near a dam with variable background noise (CH.SEMOS.HGZ), and (3) a broadband seismometer deployed on the slopes of Mont Blanc with various impulsive noise signals related to anthropogenic activity (GU.BLANC.HHZ). We annotate the phase picks obtained by EQT on the denoised data and the origin time of events in the SED catalog with epicentral distance and magnitude. For comparison, we show the original data with a 1–45 Hz band-pass filter with EQT picks made on raw data. Visually, denoising yields significantly clearer waveforms compared with the conventional band-pass filter, especially at stations with high background noise levels. Notably, the EQS-denoiser maintains robust denoising performance even under challenging noise conditions and effectively handles impulsive noise signals. In contrast, EQT frequently misidentifies various impulsive noise signals contained in the raw data as arrivals, as most clearly observed at GU.BLANC. Cataloged events within the target distance range of up to 30 km are clearly detected in the denoised data, along with additional uncataloged event signals.

We process the picks collected from denoised and raw data separately using the SeisComP pipeline. This includes phase association and initial location estimation via the *scanloc* module, event relocation using the *screloc* module with the *NonLinLoc* locator for probabilistic hypocenter estimation in a 3D velocity model (Diehl *et al.*, 2021), and amplitude and magnitude estimation

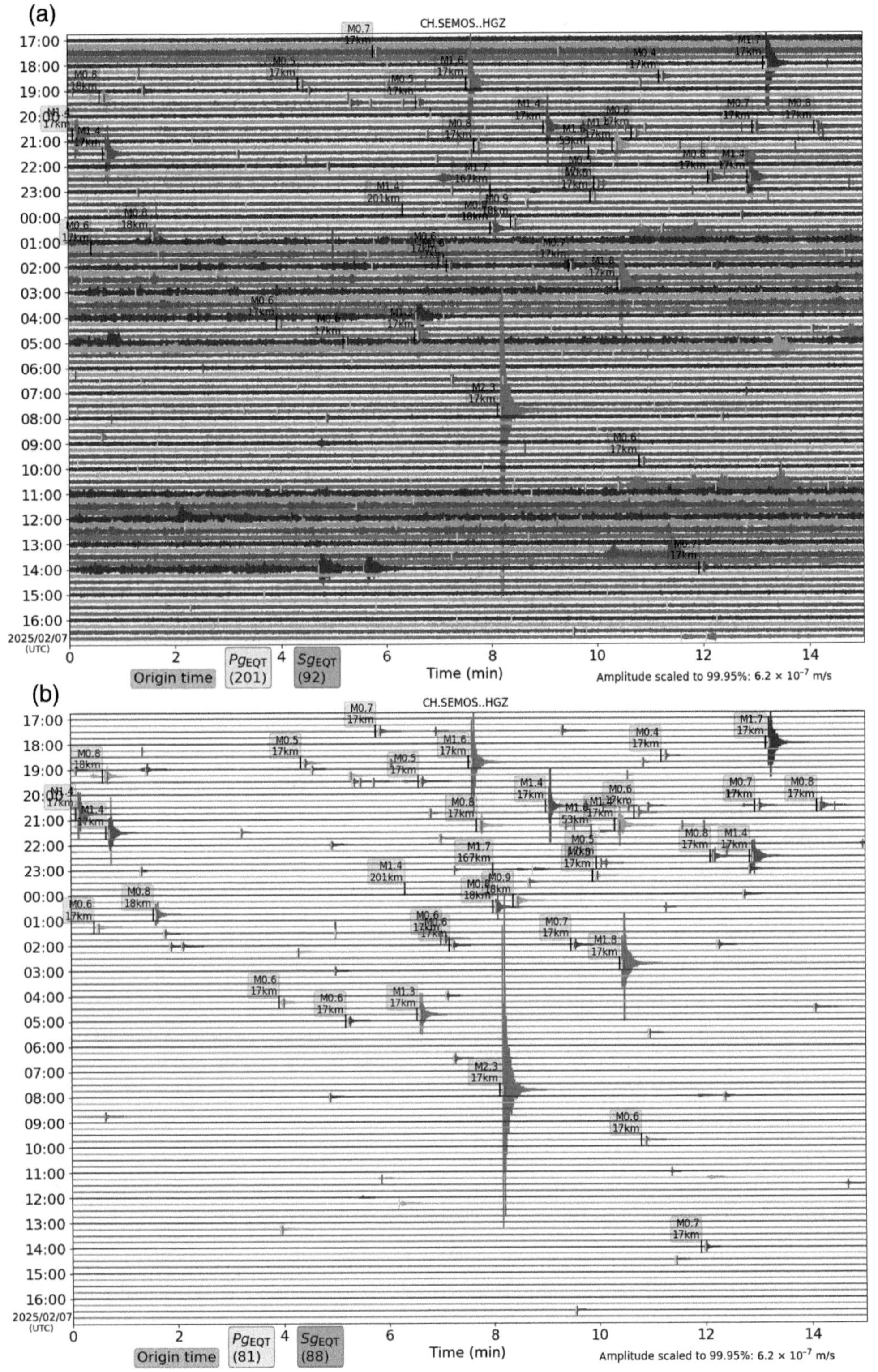

Figure 8. Caption follows Figure 7 for short-period seismometer (CH.SEMOS.HGZ). The color version of this figure is available only in the electronic edition.

using the Swiss local magnitude M_{Lhc} (Diehl *et al.*, 2025). For these processing steps, we largely adopt the same parameter settings used in the routine processing by SED.

Figure 10 shows examples of (panel a) an **M** 0.5 event contained in the SED catalog (panel b) and an **M** 0.1 event newly identified. For each event, we compare the band-pass-filtered data with the denoised data in time and frequency domains. EQT picks on raw and denoised data are shown, as well as manual SED picks when available. EQT also picks several arrivals related to the weaker event on the raw data, though we note six associated picks are required to catalog the event. High SNR arrivals are picked equally on raw and denoised data. As expected from the performance test (Fig. 5), the denoised data provide more picks at low SNRs. We also notice cases in which EQT picks on denoised data are early, most clearly on CH.MFERR despite relatively clear arrivals.

The denoised peak amplitudes are slightly underestimated compared with the original data, and as the noise contamination increases, the differences become larger. The spectra of raw and denoised data match well when the SNR is high (e.g., CH.MFERR, CH.SALAN), apart from noise at long periods and at high frequencies (as contained in the pre-event noise). In low SNR cases, the spectra only overlap within a narrow frequency range at which the event signal is strongest, and the largest discrepancies are observed at frequencies at which the raw event signal matches the pre-event noise. Despite this, the denoised spectra retain the overall spectra of the original signal, with amplitude reductions consistent with the removal of the background noise (pre-event noise).

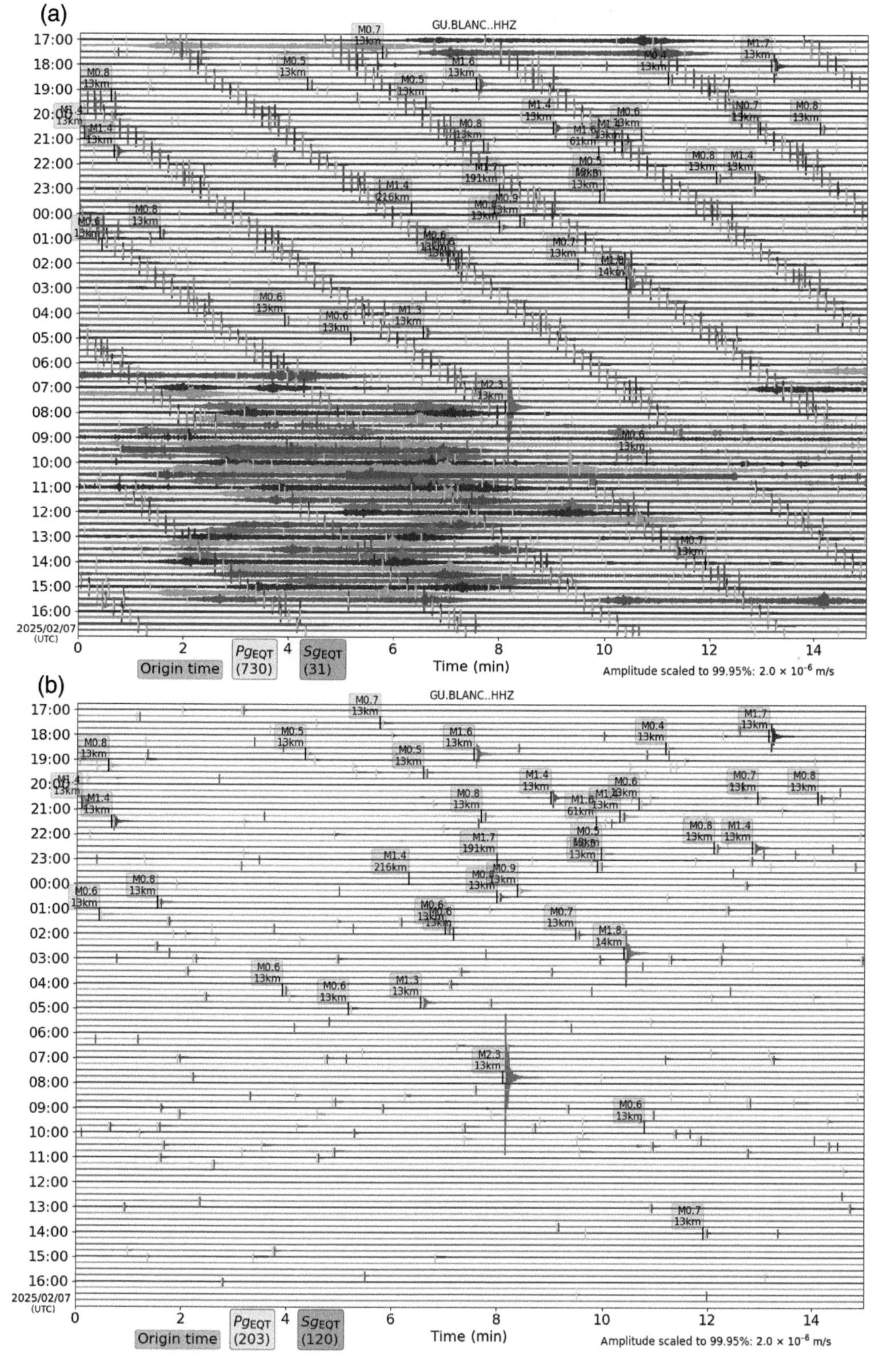

Figure 9. Caption follows Figure 7 for broadband seismometer (GU.BLANC.HHZ). The color version of this figure is available only in the electronic edition.

Results

Locations. We summarize the EQS-denoiser, EQT, and SED catalogs in Table 1 and on the map in Figure 11, which also shows the station set used in the case study. The EQT catalog contains 8855 phase picks compared with 3365 in the EQS-denoiser catalog. This large difference comes mainly from the number of *P* picks, whereas the number of *S* picks is more similar. After phase association, 10% of the EQT picks are associated into events, as are 46% of the EQS-denoiser picks. Visual inspection of the data and picks (Figs. 7–9), as well as the results of the association step, indicates that the high share of *P* picks in the EQT catalog is related to false triggers on impulsive noise signals. The final catalogs for this 24 hr period exhibit 94, 55, and 34 (excluding the 2 events outside of the study area) events for EQS-denoiser, EQT, and SED catalogs, respectively. A manual review of the newly identified events confirms that these are all true events. The locations of EQS-denoiser and EQT catalogs show a wider spread compared with SED locations; in particular, we observe a higher number of events only contained in the EQS-denoiser catalog on the western side of the sequence. In general, the location constraints in east–west direction might be lower considering the distribution of (high-quality) stations. The EQT locations generally show the widest distribution, with more events mislocated to the east of the sequence (compared with the SED location). In many of these cases, EQS-denoiser locations are closer to the sequence than EQT locations. In addition, the EQT catalog contains several events that are located far outside of the region. These observations are also visible in the location quality summarized in Figure 12a: the median root mean square (RMS) residuals between observed and modeled arrivals are generally lower for EQS-denoiser events compared with EQT events, though

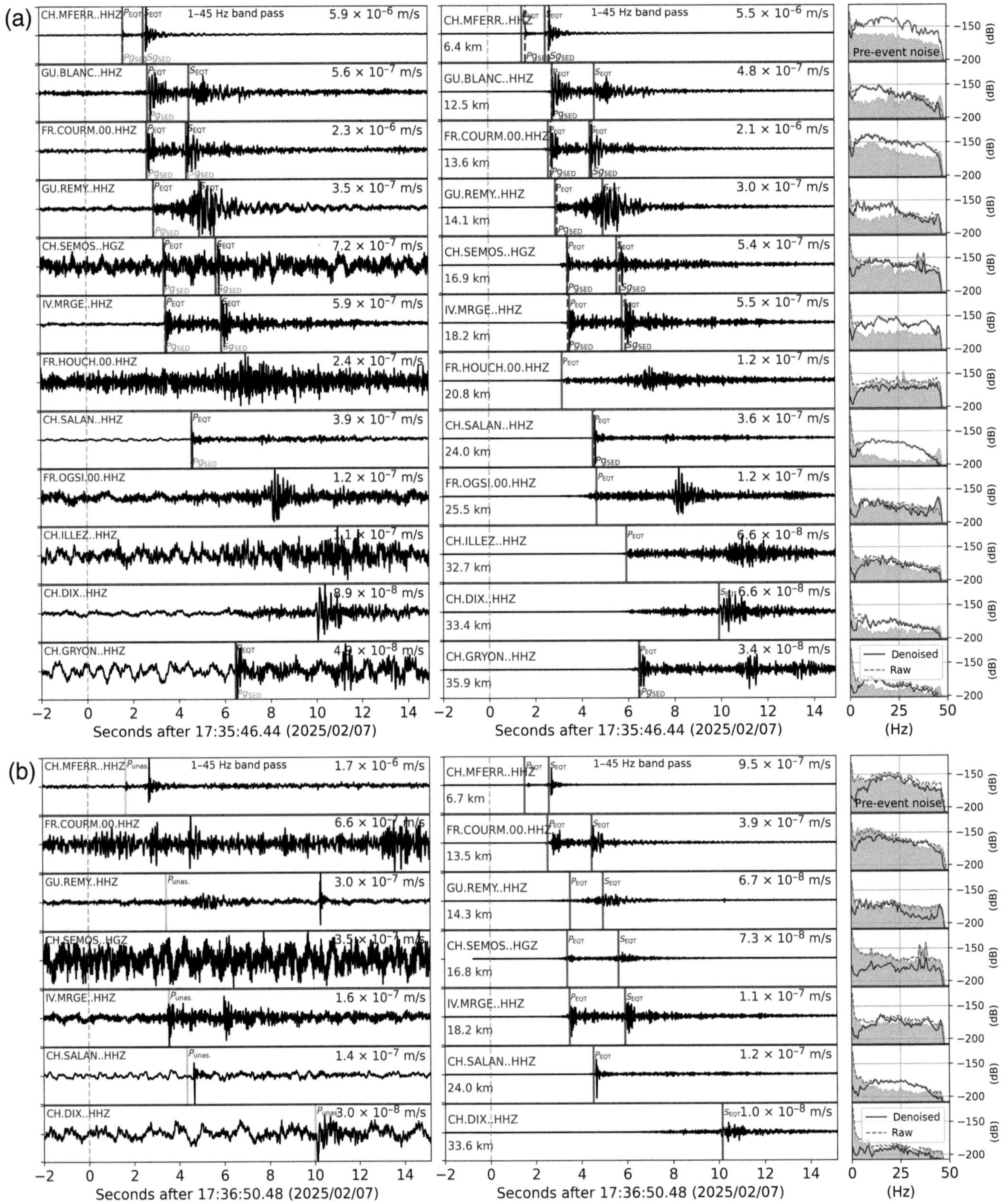

Figure 10. Event waveform examples. (a) **M** 0.5 event at 17:35:46 2025/02/07 shown with (left) original and (middle) denoised data with EQT annotations and manual SED picks (if available). Waveforms are band-pass filtered for plotting only. (Right) Velocity spectra of original (raw data, green-dashed) and denoised event data (red), and pre-event noise (raw data, gray-shaded). (b) **M** 0.1 event at 17:36:50 2025/02/07 only available in EQS-denoiser catalog; includes unassociated EQT picks on raw data. Spectra are computed using Welch's power spectral density estimate with a window length of 256 samples and 128-sample overlap over event time window. The color version of this figure is available only in the electronic edition.

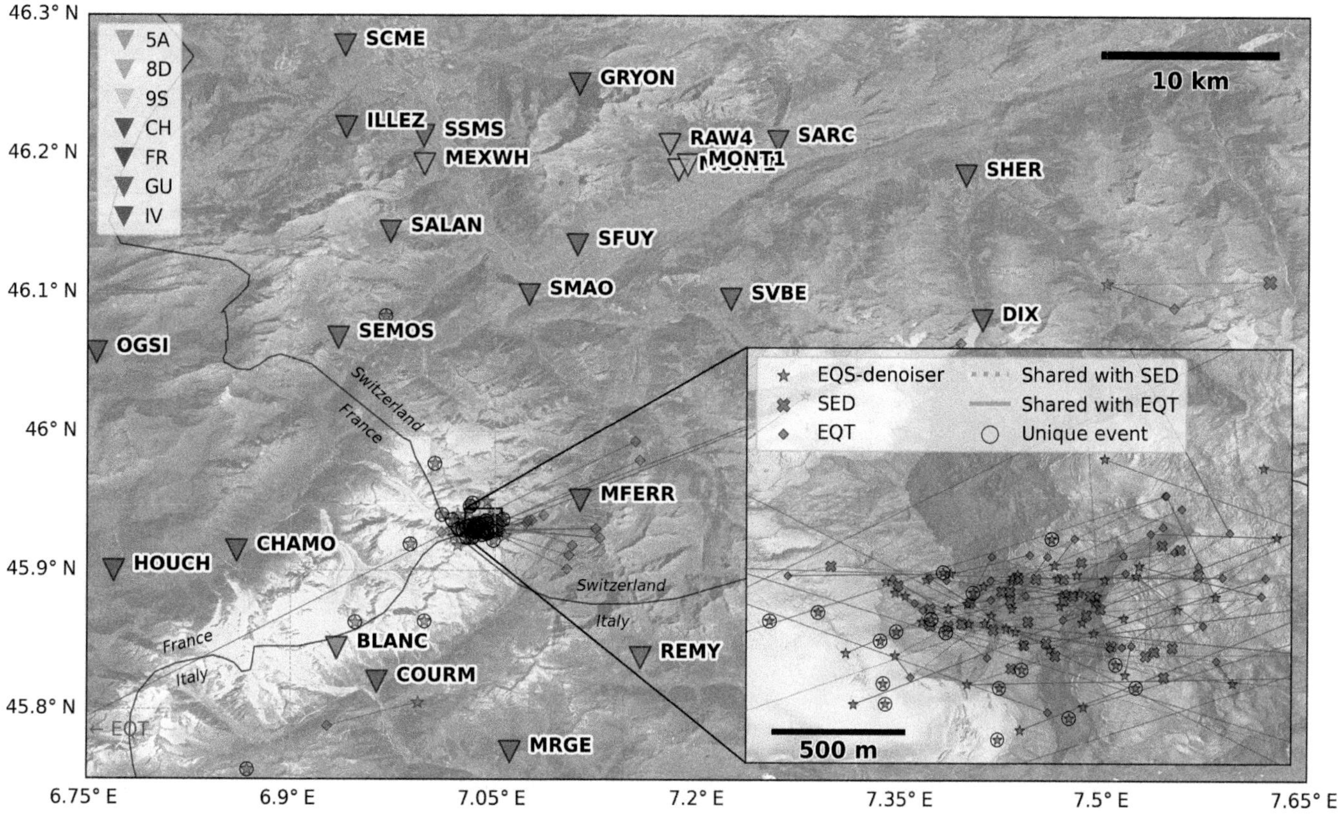

both automated catalogs have higher RMS values than the SED catalog with manual picks. This observation remains even when considering only the subset of events in the SED catalog. Notably, both automated catalogs, specifically the EQS-denoiser catalog, include more phase picks than the SED catalog. As a result, they also include more uncertain picks from low-SNR recordings, which can increase the RMS residuals.

To further benchmark our denoising model, we repeat our case study using DeepDenoiser (Zhu and Beroza, 2019), available through SeisBench (Woollam *et al.*, 2022). The recordings processed with DeepDenoiser contain various strong noise signals and artifacts (Fig. S11). These residual noise signals produce numerous false-positive picks, leading to a high number of events, the vast majority of which are false positives (Fig. S12).

In addition, we test EQT on band-pass-filtered data to see if this might serve as a stronger baseline compared with EQT on raw data. A catalog derived for the same case study includes more picks and also more events. However, several of these additional events were false events and mislocated events caused by the contamination of additional false-positive picks on impulsive noise signals. Overall, EQT applied on raw data led to the more reliable

Figure 11. Map view comparison of event locations in EQS-denoiser, EQT, and SED catalogs and stations used in case study. Shared events in EQS-denoiser or EQT catalog that are also contained in SED catalog are joined with red-dotted line; events in EQS-denoiser catalog that are also shared with EQT catalog are joined by a blue line. Catalog-unique events are marked with open circles. One EQT event and two SED events (near Basel/France, Glarus/CH) lie farther outside of shown area. Note that the SED catalog uses all available stations, explaining the discrepancy in the location of the event at around 7.6° E (Zinal/CH). The color version of this figure is available only in the electronic edition.

TABLE 1
Comparison of Earthquake Seismogram Denoiser (EQS-denoiser), EQTransformer (EQT), and Swiss Seismological Service (SED) Catalogs, With Picking and Location Statistics; Root Mean Square (RMS) Residual of Observed and Modeled Arrivals

Category/Metric	EQS-Denoiser	EQT	SED
Data/picker	Denoised data/EQT	Raw data/EQT	Filtered data/manual
Number picks (share *P* picks)	3365 (61%)	8855 (89%)	470 (67%)
Associated picks (share)	1539 (46%)	820 (10%)	470
Number events	94	55	34 (+2 outside of region)
Average number picks/event	16.37	15.7	13.8
Median RMS residual/event	0.157 s	0.194 s	0.068 s

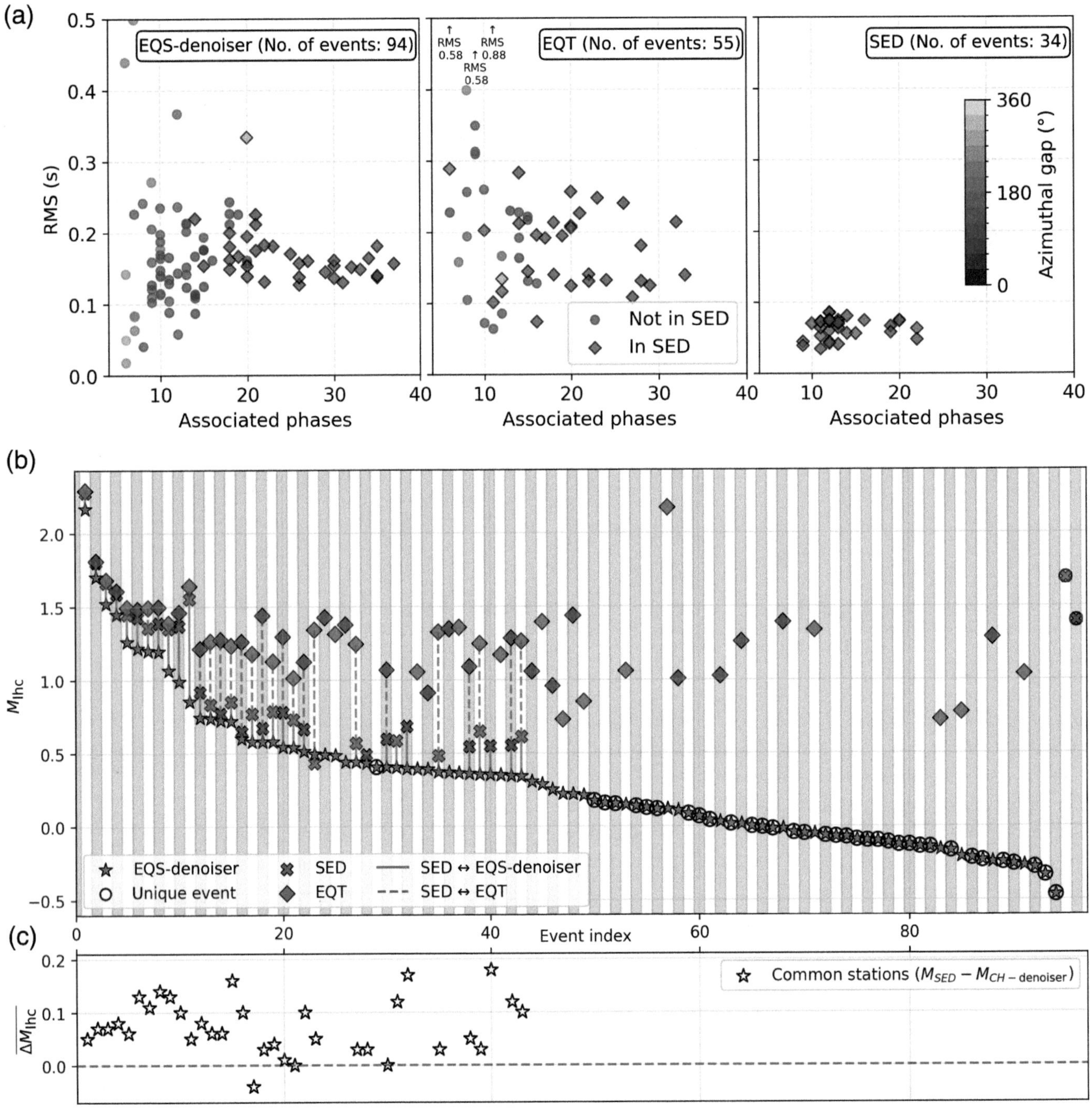

Figure 12. Comparison of EQS-denoiser, EQT, and SED catalogs. (a) Location quality visualized by root mean square (RMS) arrival-time residuals, number of associated phases, and azimuthal gap for each event. Three EQT events are outside of shown range. (b) Comparison of magnitudes across catalogs (if available) and (c) average station–magnitude difference considering only common subset of stations used for magnitude calculation in SED and EQS-denoiser catalog. (b) and (c) are sorted by the magnitudes estimated from denoised data. Note that magnitudes differ also because of differences in locations and different data preprocessing in SED catalog (magnitude-dependent band pass). The two events unique to the SED catalog are outside of the study region. The color version of this figure is available only in the electronic edition.

results. All catalogs derived for the case study are summarized and compared in Table S2.

Magnitudes. The Swiss local magnitude M_{Lhc} is derived from the peak displacement amplitude on a simulated Wood–Anderson seismometer and incorporates corrections for station amplification and geometric-based attenuation. In addition, in the SED manual review, the practice is to apply a magnitude-dependent band-pass filter for smaller events. All waveforms out to a magnitude-dependent distance, including those without picks, are then preselected using an SNR threshold and undergo a manual review to exclude noise-contaminated recordings, which makes this step time consuming.

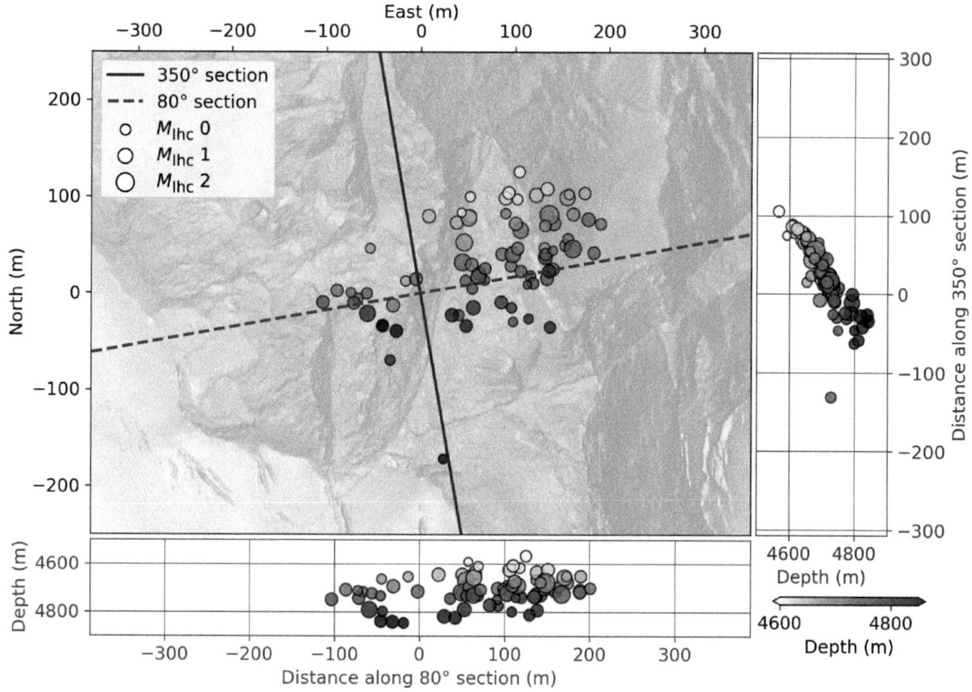

Figure 13. High-resolution EQS-denoiser catalog. Shown is a subset of 84 relocated events using the double-difference relative relocation method (Scarabello, 2021). The panels on the side and bottom show cross sections along the profiles indicated on map. Figure shows a zoom-in on the main structure; note that not all events are visible in every panel. The color version of this figure is available only in the electronic edition.

Here, we compute M_{Lhc} values for the EQS-denoiser and EQT catalogs using the denoised data and the original data, respectively, using each record with a P pick within the set of 24 stations. Unlike what is done for the SED catalog, we skip the SNR threshold and manual review. The event magnitude is computed as the median of the station magnitudes. Figure 12b compares the event magnitudes for the three catalogs; note that these are derived from partly different station subsets. For larger events, the magnitude estimates are relatively consistent across the three catalogs. The denoised magnitudes tend to be slightly lower than those from SED; EQT magnitudes are higher. This trend becomes more significant moving to lower magnitudes, in which magnitudes based on original data (EQT) show a clear tendency to be overestimated. The SED catalog contains magnitudes down to M_{Lhc} 0.4–0.5. Events unique to the EQS-denoiser and EQT catalogs have denoised magnitudes mostly in the M_{Lhc} 0–0.5 range, and we see EQS-denoiser extending the catalog to even lower magnitudes (M_{Lhc} − 0.5 to 0). For weak events shared by both automated catalogs, we observe large differences in magnitudes, which is explained by the noise contamination in the original data. Notably, we do not apply an SNR threshold for the EQT catalog because almost none of the waveforms associated with weak events would meet the criteria. In practice, magnitudes would not be reported in these cases using original data.

In (Fig. 12c), we compare common station magnitudes shared between the SED and EQS-denoiser catalog. On average, the EQS-denoiser station magnitudes are ~0.1 magnitude units lower than those in the SED catalog. Taking into account our tests (Fig. 5), we attribute this discrepancy to both noise contamination in the original data and the tendency of the denoising process to underestimate peak amplitudes.

High-resolution EQSs. The EQS-denoiser catalog extends the SED catalog by nearly a factor of 3 toward the low magnitudes. However, compared with the SED catalog with manual picks, the quality of the locations are generally lower. We show that using the double-difference relative relocation method (Waldhauser and Ellsworth, 2000), we can significantly improve the quality of the catalog. We use the SeisComP module *scrtdd* (Scarabello, 2021) to relocate the events and present the resulting EQS-denoiser catalog in Figure 13. This approach, with the extension provided in *scrtdd*, jointly refines relative and absolute hypocenters by minimizing both differential travel-time residuals at common stations between pairs of earthquakes and absolute travel-time residuals. The *scrtdd* module is already implemented in a near-real-time automated pipeline at the SED. Of the 94 detected events, 84 are found to have relative relocations; the remaining 10 were isolated events that cannot be relocated with the double-difference technique because they have no neighboring events. Compared with the original locations (Fig. 11), the relocation procedure focuses the events on a much smaller structure. The events illuminate an ~200–300-m-wide and deep structure that exhibits a southward dip. When repeating the double-difference relocation with the SED catalog, we observe a similar structure but only obtain similar fine-scale features when using the full multi-month dataset because the relocation improves with the number of events and phases. Although we do not discuss the tectonic context of this sequence in detail, this case study demonstrates the ability of EQS-denoiser to extend seismicity catalogs not only in terms of event counts but also by contributing high-quality solutions comparable with manual curated catalogs.

DISCUSSION

We have demonstrated that deep learning denoising, in this case the EQS-denoiser documented in this article, can significantly improve automated monitoring (in combination with existing methods) and can extend even high-quality manually curated earthquake catalogs, as well as catalogs obtained using widely used deep learning phase pickers. EQS-denoiser provides more reliable event signal detections compared with EQT, as indicated in our test by a higher F1 score (Fig. 5a) and observed in the case study (Table 1) by the much higher share of associated phase picks. Denoising greatly improves the quality of the waveforms, is on par with (acausal) band-pass filter at high SNRs, and outperforms standard filters at intermediate SNRs (Fig. 5b). Because denoising models always output a waveform, we add the detection criteria to identify the cases where meaningful waveforms are retrieved and discard the remaining noise waveforms. This also reduces the processing cost of downstream applications.

The model performance is critically dependent on the preprocessing of the raw event signals, which removes noise contamination as far as possible, to improve the label event waveforms in training. As a consequence and compared with DeepDenoiser, EQS-denoiser leaves substantially fewer noise remnants, which significantly improves downstream tasks as observed in the case study (Figs. S11 and S12). We make similar observations when applying both denoising models on data recorded outside of Switzerland, as shown in Figure S13. Because both models use similar UNet architecture, we attributed the better performance of EQS-denoiser primarily to our training data preprocessing strategy (Fig. 2) and the application scheme used for continuous data (Fig. 6).

Nevertheless, we encountered several issues when applying phase pickers to denoised data caused by small noise remnants and discontinuities between time windows (Fig. S4), which we solved by applying a detection threshold and by reintroducing small amounts of Gaussian noise as a form of water level during picking. When event signal preprocessing of the training data is omitted and event signals still contain background noise, these issues might be less severe for sensors with stationary noise conditions. However, this likely comes at the expense of reduced denoising quality.

In addition to stabilizing the picking performance, reintroducing noise to the denoised data in form of TTA during phase picking enables the estimation of timing uncertainties, covering both the denoising and picking process. Note that EQT includes a function for estimating epistemic uncertainties via test-time dropout; our approach estimates aleatoric uncertainty and can be applied to other deep learning or conventional phase pickers without built-in uncertainty estimation. Although the quality of the phase picks still largely depends on the picking model, we find that denoising improves the process by extending the number of picks at low SNRs, while simultaneously maintaining or slightly improving quality (Fig. 5e,f, Table 1). However, compared with manual SED phase picks, EQS-denoiser automated phase picks still resulted in higher RMS event residuals, indicating room for improvement through the use of a dedicated picker tailored for denoised data. Similarly, our tests indicate that the EQT phase picks on raw data do not reach the quality of manual picks, which is also evident in their high event RMS residual (Table 1).

Magnitude estimation typically requires manual review to exclude noisy stations from the analysis, even if ad hoc magnitude-dependent high-frequency filters are applied. This can be automated by including SNR thresholds, although this does not exclude impulsive noise signals contained in the event window and does not work when the event signals are very weak. With denoised data, the magnitude estimation can be automated, though the effect on the magnitudes needs to be considered: our test show that the denoising model tends to underestimate the peak amplitudes by ~−20% or 0.1 $\log_{10}$ units at low SNRs, whereas raw or band-pass filtered amplitudes are overestimated by ~+170% or +1000%, respectively (Fig. 5c). This is also reflected in our case study, in which denoised magnitudes are ~0.1 units lower than SED values (Fig. 12c), but raw-data magnitudes are highly overestimated.

Our case study outlines the processing workflow from the raw data to a final EQS-denoiser catalog and highlights the benefit of denoised data in terms of event quality and quantity. We leveraged the established SeisComP infrastructure but did not exhaustively explore parameters in the association or location procedure, which could be further fine-tuned to adjust the level of desired quality level of the automated solutions, for example, by increasing or decreasing the number of phase picks required for a solution. Because denoising improves the waveform similarity (Fig. 5b; Dahmen *et al.*, 2024), we expect it can also improve other processing approaches such as template matching. For example, this could facilitate a better review of unassociated picks observed only at the station closest to the sequence (Fig. 7).

Our training dataset included overlapping event waveforms, suggesting that the model should also perform effectively on dense seismic sequences with short interevent times. Future work will evaluate its performance on such dense sequences beyond the Swiss dataset (e.g., 2016–2017 central Italy sequence, Michele *et al.*, 2020) and determine whether retraining or fine-tuning is required. We expect the model to generalize to other earthquake datasets with similar epicentral distances and magnitude distributions, provided that preprocessing, instrumentation, and tectonic settings are comparable to those in our study.

We note that EQS-denoiser is not designed for teleseismic signals. In fact, a small fraction of such signals may be contained in our dataset labeled as noise. Effective denoising of teleseismic signals would require a separate training dataset and longer time windows (e.g., Dahmen *et al.*, 2022).

We trained a single model using data from 400 stations in the Swiss and partner networks, covering various sensor types and found that its denoising performance is comparable to that of models trained on individual stations. That said, signal detection could be improved with station-specific models, which may be more robust against impulsive noise signals at particularly noisy stations and reduce false positives. However, station-specific models substantially increase training demands and processing complexity, so we proceed with a single model.

EQS-denoiser is designed to operate on three-component data, but our tests indicate that it can also be applied to single-component data by repeating the data across three input channels of the model, as was done during training for a small subset (Fig. S14).

The denoising model leverages time–frequency decomposition to separate recorded signals by their frequency content and concentrate event features into spatially coherent time–frequency features, making them easier to process with convolutional kernels. This facilitates the identification of time-varying frequency ranges in which the signal is preserved, but remaining frequency bands, such as those dominated by long-period noise, are selectively suppressed. In addition, noise signals sharing the same frequency band as the event signal occurring before, during, or after the event signal are largely suppressed. The masking approach downscales the amplitudes of existing signals rather than generating signals, which reduces the risk of introducing spurious signals. Drawbacks of the masking approach are that the model cannot compensate for signals lost because of destructive interference of event and noise signals, yet this remains a limitation for all approaches because denoising is fundamentally an ill-posed problem. In addition, the STFT binning—or any other type of time–frequency representation—means that the model operates on discrete time–frequency bins, which can smooth peak amplitudes and smear sharp signals like phase onsets, potentially introducing acausal energy. In contrast, time-domain models (e.g., Yin *et al.*, 2022; Trappolini *et al.*, 2024) offer optimal time resolution but also must operate on high-resolution input and face challenges in capturing long-range temporal information, requiring additional trade-offs to be considered. Both approaches have been extensively evaluated and discussed in the audio source separation community (e.g., Stoller *et al.*, 2018; Stöter *et al.*, 2019; Rouard *et al.*, 2023) in which each indicates advantages depending on the evaluation metric. A fair comparison of both types of approaches, trained and benchmarked on the same dataset, would enable a more detailed evaluation of their impacts on seismic signal denoising and help determine which approach is better suited for specific downstream task. For this purpose, the dataset used in this study will be available (see Data and Resources).

CONCLUSION AND OUTLOOK

We have demonstrated the potential of EQS-denoiser to streamline and enhance the entire earthquake monitoring workflow, from denoising raw continuous data to signal detection and phase picking, to magnitude determination, and the generation of a deeper seismicity catalog. Importantly, EQS-denoiser and the denoised data are compatible with an end-to-end processing framework such as SeisComP (Helmholtz Centre Potsdam, 2008). By effectively denoising recordings, including those from noisy stations, and feeding them directly into automated phase picking and magnitude determination workflows, EQS-denoiser not only reduces the need for manual review but also produces more detailed and accurate catalogs compared with standard automated methods. This is reflected in a higher share of associated phase picks, improved event location quality, and more reliable magnitude estimates. Moreover, denoised data generally improve detailed waveform analysis beyond the scope of this study (e.g., Dahmen *et al.*, 2024). The full integration of EQS-denoiser into the SeisComP platform will extend these improvements across the Swiss network and can be readily adopted by other monitoring networks. As demonstrated in this study, we anticipate that denoised waveforms will refine seismicity catalogs and enhance the observation of ongoing seismic processes, particularly by identifying weaker signals that may otherwise remain undetected, while reducing the manual workload.

DATA AND RESOURCES

We used seismic waveform data from the permanent Swiss Seismological Service (SED) network (CH: Swiss Seismological Service [SED] at ETH Zurich, 1983) and from temporary SED deployments (8D: SED at ETH Zurich, 2005; 8R: SED at ETH Zurich, 2018a; 9S: SED at ETH Zurich, 2012; G2: SED at ETH Zurich, 2006; S: SED at ETH Zurich, 2008; XY: SED at ETH Zurich, 2018b; YZ: SED at ETH Zurich, 2024). Additional data were provided by the CERN seismic network (C4: CERN, 2016); the Matterhorn Cryosphere Observatory (1I: University of Innsbruck, WSL/SLF Davos, 2015); the AlpArray Seismic Network (Z3: AlpArray Seismic Network, 2015); industrial partners of the SED in Switzerland (5A: SED at ETH Zurich, 2021); and partner networks in Italy (GU: University of Genoa, 1967; OX: Istituto Nazionale di Oceanografia e di Geofisica Sperimentale (OGS), 2016; IV: Istituto Nazionale di Geofisica e Vulcanologia [INGV], 2005), France (8C: Helmstetter *et al.*, 2020; FR: Epos-France, 1995), RA: RESIF, 1995), Germany (BW: Department of Earth and Environmental Sciences, Geophysical Observatory, University of Munchen, 2001; GR: Federal Institute for Geosciences and Natural Resources, 1976; LE: Erdbebendienst Südwest Baden-Württemberg and Rheinland-Pfalz, 2009), Austria (OE: Zentralanstalt für Meterologie und Geodynamik [ZAMG], 1987), and others (MN: MedNet Project Partner Institutions, 1990). Waveform data from the SED permanent network and most collaborating networks in the greater Alpine region are openly accessible via the European Integrated Data Archive (EIDA) at http://www.orfeus-eu.org/data/eida. Data acquired by temporary networks for Ph.D. projects or industry collaborations remain restricted or embargoed. The SED earthquake catalog for the period used in this study can be accessed through the FDSN webservice (FDSN webservice, 2025). The preprocessed event and noise dataset used for model training, validation, and testing, as well as benchmarking, is available for the publicly accessible networks at doi: 10.5281/zenodo.17865808 (Dahmen, 2025a). The trained model and the example code that demonstrate its use are available at doi: 10.5281/zenodo.17935347 (Dahmen, 2025b). All websites were last accessed in December 2025. The supplemental material for this article includes an overview of the dataset, denoising model architecture and training process, tests on detection thresholds and model variations, calibration of the pick timing uncertainty, and data examples.

DECLARATION OF COMPETING INTERESTS

The authors acknowledge that there are no conflicts of interest recorded.

ACKNOWLEDGMENTS

The authors are grateful to Silvia Castellaro, the editorial board, reviewer Rigobert Tibi, and two anonymous reviewers for their thorough evaluation of this article and for providing constructive feedback that greatly improved this study. The authors thank Tobias Diehl for discussions on the relocation method and the tectonics of the case study area. This work was partially supported by the TRANSFORM^2 project. TRANSFORM^2 is funded by the European Union under Project Number 101188365 within the HORIZON-INFRA-2024-DEV-01-01 call.

REFERENCES

AlpArray Seismic Network (2015). AlpArray Seismic Network (AASN) temporary component, doi: 10.12686/alparray/z3_2015.

Armstrong, A. D., Z. Claerhout, B. Baker, and K. D. Koper (2023). A deep-learning phase picker with calibrated Bayesian-derived uncertainties for earthquakes in the Yellowstone volcanic region, *Bull. Seismol. Soc. Am.* **113,** no. 6, 2323–2344.

CERN (2016). CERN Seismic Network, doi: 10.12686/sed/networks/c4.

Dahmen, N. (2025a). Dataset: Earthquake Seismogram Denoiser (eqs- denoiser), doi: 10.5281/zenodo.17865808.

Dahmen, N. (2025b). niko-d/EarthquakeSeismogramDenoiser: v1.0.0, doi: 10.5281/zenodo.17935347.

Dahmen, N., J. Clinton, S. Stähler, M.-A. Meier, S. Ceylan, F. Euchner, D. Kim, A. Horleston, C. Durán, G. Zenhäusern, *et al.* (2024). Revisiting Martian seismicity with deep learning-based denoising, *Geophys. J. Int.* **239,** no. 1, 434–454.

Dahmen, N. L., J. F. Clinton, M.-A. Meier, S. C. Stähler, S. Ceylan, D. Kim, A. E. Stott, and D. Giardini (2022). MarsQuakeNet: A more complete marsquake catalog obtained by deep learning techniques, *J. Geophys. Res.* **127,** no. 11, e2022JE007503.

Department of Earth and Environmental Sciences, Geophysical Observatory, University of Munchen (2001). BayernNetz, doi: 10.7914/SN/BW.

Diehl, T., C. Cauzzi, J. Clinton, T. Kraft, P. Kästli, F. Massin, F. Lanza, V. Simon, F. Grigoli, M. Hobiger, *et al.* (2025). Earthquakes in Switzerland and surrounding regions during 2019 and 2020, *Swiss J. Geosci.* **118,** 15.

Diehl, T., E. Kissling, M. Herwegh, and S. M. Schmid (2021). Improving absolute hypocenter accuracy with 3D Pg and Sg body-wave inversion procedures and application to earthquakes in the Central Alps region, *J. Geophys. Res.* **126,** no. 12, e2021JB022155.

Epos-France (1995). Epos-France Broad-band network (RLBP), doi: 10.15778/RESIF.FR.

Erdbebendienst Südwest Baden-Württemberg and Rheinland-Pfalz (2009). Erdbebendienst Südwest, doi: 10.7914/SN/LE.

FDSN webservice (2025). EIDA FDSNWS event query service, available at http://eida.ethz.ch/fdsnws/event/1/query?starttime=2009-01-01T00:00:00&endtime=2024-08-31T23:59:59&minmagnitude=-1&minlongitude=5.6&maxlongitude=11.1&minlatitude=45.4&maxlatitude=48.3&eventtype=earthquake&format=text&nodata=404.&Accessed:&2025-07-24 (last accessed December 2025).

Federal Institute for Geosciences and Natural Resources (1976). German Regional Seismic Network (GRSN), doi: 10.25928/MBX6-HR74.

Helmholtz Centre Potsdam (2008). The SeisComP seismological software package, *GFZ Data Services*, doi: 10.5880/GFZ.2.4.2020.003.

Helmstetter, A., P. Guéguen, and , and RESIF (2020). Seismic network 8C: Monitoring swarms in the Mont-Blanc and Vallorcine area (RESIF - SISMOB), doi: 10.15778/RESIF.8C2019.

Heuel, J., and W. Friederich (2022). Suppression of wind turbine noise from seismological data using nonlinear thresholding and denoising autoencoder, *J. Seismol.* **26,** no. 5, 913–934.

Istituto Nazionale di Geofisica e Vulcanologia (INGV) (2005). Rete Sismica Nazionale (RSN), doi: 10.13127/SD/FBBBTDTD6Q.

Istituto Nazionale di Oceanografia e di Geofisica Sperimentale - OGS (2016). North-east Italy Seismic Network, doi: 10.7914/SN/OX.

Jansson, A., E. Humphrey, N. Montecchio, R. Bittner, A. Kumar, and T. Weyde (2017). Singing voice separation with deep u-net convolutional networks, available at https://openaccess.city.ac.uk/id/eprint/19289/ (last accessed December 2025).

Kingma, D. P. (2014). Adam: A method for stochastic optimization, arXiv preprint arXiv:1412.6980, doi: 10.48550/arXiv.1412.6980.

Kuleshov, V., N. Fenner, and S. Ermon (2018). Accurate uncertainties for deep learning using calibrated regression, *International Conference on Machine Learning*, PMLR, 2796–2804.

MedNet Project Partner Institutions (1990). Mediterranean very broadband seismographic network (MedNet) [Data Set], doi: 10.13127/sd/fbbbtdtd6q.

Michele, M., L. Chiaraluce, R. Di Stefano, and F. Waldhauser (2020). Fine-scale structure of the 2016–2017 Central Italy seismic sequence from data recorded at the Italian National Network, *J. Geophys. Res.* **125,** no. 4, e2019JB018440, doi: 10.1029/2019JB018440.

Mousavi, S. M., and G. C. Beroza (2022). Deep-learning seismology, *Science* **377,** no. 6607, eabm4470, doi: 10.1126/science.abm4470.

Mousavi, S. M., W. L. Ellsworth, W. Zhu, L. Y. Chuang, and G. C. Beroza (2020). Earthquake transformer–an attentive deep-learning model for simultaneous earthquake detection and phase picking, *Nat. Commun.* **11,** no. 1, 3952.

Park, Y., G. C. Beroza, and W. L. Ellsworth (2023). A mitigation strategy for the prediction inconsistency of neural phase pickers, *Bull. Seismol. Soc. Am.* **94,** no. 3, 1603–1612.

Quinones, L., and R. Tibi (2024). Denoising seismic waveforms using a wavelet-transform-based machine-learning method, *Bull. Seismol. Soc. Am.* **114,** no. 4, 1777–1788.

RESIF (1995). RESIF-RAP French Accelerometric Network, doi: 10.15778/RESIF.RA.

Ronneberger, O., P. Fischer, and T. Brox (2015). U-net: Convolutional networks for biomedical image segmentation, *International Conference on Medical Image Computing and Computer-Assisted Intervention*, Springer, pp. 234–241.

Ross, Z. E., M.-A. Meier, E. Hauksson, and T. H. Heaton (2018). Generalized seismic phase detection with deep learning, *Bull. Seismol. Soc. Am.* **108,** no. 5A, 2894–2901.

Rouard, S., F. Massa, and A. Défossez (2023). Hybrid transformers for music source separation, *ICASSP 2023-2023 IEEE International Conference on Acoustics, Speech and Signal Processing (ICASSP)*, IEEE, pp. 1–5.

Saad, O. M., Y. Chen, A. Savvaidis, W. Chen, F. Zhang, and Y. Chen (2022). Unsupervised deep learning for single-channel earthquake data denoising and its applications in event detection and fully automatic location, *IEEE Trans. Geosci. Remote Sens.* **60,** 1–10.

Scarabello, L. (2021). Swiss-seismological-service/scrtdd: v1. 6.1 (v1. 6.1), *Zenodo*, doi: 10.5281/zenodo.15088933.

SED at ETH Zurich (2005). Temporary deployments in Switzerland associated with aftershocks and other seismic sequences, doi: 10.12686/sed/networks/8d.

SED at ETH Zurich (2006). GEOBEST baseline seismic monitoring networks for deep geothermal energy projects in Switzerland, doi: 10.12686/sed/networks/g2.

SED at ETH Zurich (2008). Seismology at school program, ETH Zurich, doi: 10.12686/sed/networks/s.

SED at ETH Zurich (2012). Temporary deployments in Switzerland associated with landslides, doi: 10.12686/sed/networks/xp.

SED at ETH Zurich (2018a). Bedretto underground laboratory for geosciences and geoenergies (BULGG) seismic network, Switzerland, doi: 10.12686/sed/networks/8r.

SED at ETH Zurich (2018b). Stations deployed for Risk Model Switzerland, doi: 10.12686/sed/networks/xy.

SED at ETH Zurich (2021). Temporary deployments operated by industry partners of the Swiss Seismological Service, typically associated with geothermal monitoring projects, doi: 10.12686/sed/networks/xy.

SED at ETH Zurich (2024). Gotthard highway tunnel baseline seismic monitoring network, Switzerland, doi: 10.12686/sed/networks/yz.

Stoller, D., S. Ewert, and S. Dixon (2018). Wave-u-net: A multi-scale neural network for end-to-end audio source separation, arXiv preprint arXiv:1806.03185, doi: 10.48550/arXiv.1806.03185.

Stöter, F.-R., S. Uhlich, A. Liutkus, and Y. Mitsufuji (2019). Open-unmix-a reference implementation for music source separation, *J. Open Source Software* **4,** no. 41, 1667.

Swiss Seismological Service (SED) at ETH Zurich (1983). National Seismic Networks of Switzerland, doi: 10.12686/sed/networks/ch.

Tibi, R., P. Hammond, R. Brogan, C. J. Young, and K. Koper (2021). Deep learning denoising applied to regional distance seismic data in Utah, *Bull. Seismol. Soc. Am.* **111,** no. 2, 775–790.

Tibi, R., C. J. Young, and R. W. Porritt (2022). Comparative study of the performance of seismic waveform denoising methods using local and near-regional data, *Bull. Seismol. Soc. Am.* **113,** 548–561.

Trappolini, D., L. Laurenti, G. Poggiali, E. Tinti, F. Galasso, A. Michelini, and C. Marone (2024). Cold diffusion model for seismic denoising, *J. Geophys. Res.* **1,** no. 2, e2024JH000179, doi: 10.1029/2024JH000179.

University of Genoa (1967). Regional seismic network of North Western Italy, doi: 10.7914/SN/GU.

University of Innsbruck, WSL/SLF Davos (2015). Matterhorn cryosphere observatory, Switzerland, doi: 10.12686/sed/networks/1I.

Vincent, P., H. Larochelle, Y. Bengio, and P.-A. Manzagol (2008). Extracting and composing robust features with denoising autoencoders, *Proceedings of the 25th International Conf. on Machine Learning*, pp. 1096–1103.

Waldhauser, F., and W. L. Ellsworth (2000). A double-difference earthquake location algorithm: Method and application to the northern Hayward fault, California, *Bull. Seismol. Soc. Am.* **90,** no. 6, 1353–1368.

Wang, G., W. Li, M. Aertsen, J. Deprest, S. Ourselin, and T. Vercauteren (2019). Aleatoric uncertainty estimation with test-time augmentation for medical image segmentation with convolutional neural networks, *Neurocomputing* **338,** 34–45.

Woollam, J., J. Münchmeyer, F. Tilmann, A. Rietbrock, D. Lange, T. Bornstein, T. Diehl, C. Giunchi, F. Haslinger, D. Jozinović, *et al.* (2022). SeisBench—A toolbox for machine learning in seismology, *Bull. Seismol. Soc. Am.* **93,** no. 3, 1695–1709.

Yang, L., X. Liu, W. Zhu, L. Zhao, and G. C. Beroza (2022). Toward improved urban earthquake monitoring through deep-learning-based noise suppression, *Sci. Adv.* **8,** no. 15, eabl3564, doi: 10.1126/sciadv.abl3564.

Yin, J., M. A. Denolle, and B. He (2022). A multitask encoder–decoder to separate earthquake and ambient noise signal in seismograms, *Geophys. J. Int.* **231,** no. 3, 1806–1822.

Zentralanstalt für Meterologie und Geodynamik (ZAMG) (1987). Austrian Seismic Network, doi: 10.7914/SN/OE.

Zhu, W., and G. C. Beroza (2019). Phasenet: A deep-neural-network-based seismic arrival-time picking method, *Geophys. J. Int.* **216,** no. 1, 261–273.

Zhu, W., S. M. Mousavi, and G. C. Beroza (2019). Seismic signal denoising and decomposition using deep neural networks, *IEEE Trans. Geosci. Remote Sens.* **57,** no. 11, 9476–9488.

Manuscript received 11 August 2025
Published online 15 January 2026

Quantifying the Impact of Declustering Techniques on Completeness Magnitude Estimation

Massimiliano Guastella*[1,2], Anna Figlioli[2], Raffaele Martorana[3,4], and Antonino D'Alessandro[4]

ABSTRACT

Seismicity analysis and earthquake hazard assessment require catalogs of independent events and accurate estimates of completeness. The magnitude of completeness (M_c) defines the threshold below which earthquakes are likely to be missed; declustering, used to remove dependent events, can substantially alter M_c by reshaping the lower tail of the frequency–magnitude distribution. Because such changes propagate to the Gutenberg–Richter *b*-value, method choices may bias downstream analyses. Using a regional instrumental catalog from southern Italy, we try to quantify how widely used declustering approaches affect catalog-based estimates of M_c. We apply three declustering families: fixed window (Gardner and Knopoff original formulation, including Gruenthal and Uhrhammer windows), linked window (Reasenberg, three parameter configurations), and nearest neighbor. Then we estimate M_c with five catalog-based methods: maximum curvature, goodness-of-fit test, median-based analysis of segment slope, entire magnitude range, and magnitude of completeness by *b*-value stability. Comparing across declustered and observed catalogs, we evaluate how declustering event removal modifies the frequency–magnitude distribution and in turn the sensitivity of catalog-based M_c methods to these modifications. Resampling is used to assess precision and stability, the results remain essentially unchanged even with small bootstrap sizes, indicating the need but large numbers of resamples are unnecessary. Overall, the analysis highlights that declustering choice and completeness estimation are critical decisions and should be reported jointly when deriving the *b*-value for seismic hazard applications.

OPEN ACCESS

KEY POINTS

- Declustering alters the shape of the frequency–magnitude distribution.
- Completeness estimates sensitivity to the choice of declustering technique.
- Bootstrap resampling identifies over- and underestimation in standalone M_c estimates.

INTRODUCTION

Earthquake catalogs are important datasets to understand seismicity, earthquake physics, and earthquake hazard (Huang *et al.*, 1994; Liu *et al.*, 1996; Xu and Gao, 2014). Catalogs provide valuable information about the occurrence, location, and magnitude of earthquakes over a specific time period. The standard probabilistic seismic hazard analysis (PSHA) framework treats earthquake occurrence as a stationary Poisson process, implying that the probability of a future event is independent of the history of previous events within the same source zone (Cornell, 1968). Earthquake declustering is the process of removing dependent events from a seismic catalog so that only independent events remain. A not declustered catalog can bias frequency–magnitude statistics and hazard estimates by inflating event counts in clustered periods or regions. Consequently, best practices in seismic analysis recommend carefully choosing the declustering procedure and exploring multiple methods to estimating hazard parameters (Luen and Stark, 2012; Taroni and Akinci, 2021). At present, many algorithms are available for declustering

1. Dipartimento d'Ingegneria Civile ed Ambientale, Università Sapienza, Rome, Italy, https://orcid.org/0009-0006-9841-6275 (MG); 2. Dipartimento di Scienze della Terra e del Mare, Università degli studi di Palermo, Palermo, Italy, https://orcid.org/0000-0002-5101-6788 (AF); 3. Sezione di Milano, Istituto Nazionale di Geofisica e Vulcanologia, Milan, Italy, https://orcid.org/0000-0002-4421-9501 (RM); 4. Osservatorio Nazionale dei Terremoti, Istituto Nazionale di Geofisica e Vulcanologia, Rome, Italy, https://orcid.org/0000-0002-0074-3125 (AD)

*Corresponding author: massimiliano.guastella@uniroma1.it

Cite this article as Guastella, M., A. Figlioli, R. Martorana, and A. D'Alessandro (2026). Quantifying the Impact of Declustering Techniques on Completeness Magnitude Estimation, *Bull. Seismol. Soc. Am.* **116**, 946–962, doi: 10.1785/0120250144 earthquake catalogs. These approaches range from longstanding simple window-based methods to newer statistically adaptive formulations, each embedding different assumptions about spatiotemporal triggering and parameterization. Consequently, declustered outcomes are method dependent, and no single procedure is universally preferred as shown in many studies (Amini, 2014; Azak *et al.*, 2018; Taroni and Akinci, 2021; Juellyan *et al.*, 2023; Perry and Bendick, 2024).

Another core aspect of hazard analysis is the completeness magnitude (M_c). This threshold magnitude represents the lower limit of earthquake magnitudes that can be reliably detected and recorded by the seismic network. Any earthquake with a magnitude below this threshold may either go unnoticed or be underrepresented in the catalog (Rydelek and Sacks, 1989). Accurate estimation of completeness allows researchers to obtain reliable statistical analysis and interpretation of earthquake patterns and behavior (Mignan and Woessner, 2012). However, it is widely recognized that earthquake catalogs are inherently incomplete, meaning that they do not capture the full extent of seismic activity in a given area. This incompleteness stems from various factors, including instrumental limitations, network coverage, data processing techniques, and the influence of natural phenomena on earthquake detection. Furthermore, the occurrence of large-magnitude earthquakes may lead to a decreased number of detected earthquakes in the immediate aftermath. This can often be attributed to the "blind time" immediately after a large seismic event, when seismic networks miss smaller successive events because of the saturation of seismic sensors and the general high level of seismic noise (Kagan, 2004; Helmstetter *et al.*, 2006). This blind time produces an increase in the completeness of the catalog because of the loss of data during a seismic sequence. In addition, the spatial distribution of seismic monitoring networks contributes to catalog incompleteness. Uneven network coverage, particularly in remote or inaccessible regions, can lead to gaps in earthquake detection and reporting. Sparse monitoring stations in certain areas result in reduced seismic data availability, leading to incomplete catalogs for these regions (Schorlemmer *et al.*, 2010; Abd el-aal, 2012; Mignan and Chouliaras, 2014; Gonzalez, 2017; D'Alessando *et al.*, 2021).

Data processing techniques also play an important role in catalog completeness. Signal processing algorithms and filtering methods applied to raw seismic data can introduce biases and affect the detection and identification of earthquakes, particularly in case of small-magnitude events. Under these circumstances, the selection of appropriate processing parameters is crucial to optimize event detection and minimize data loss. Furthermore, natural phenomena can have an impact on a catalog's completeness. High levels of background noise from environmental factors, such as oceanic waves, cultural noise, or anthropogenic activities, can also mask or obscure seismic signals. In a wide range of magnitudes within seismogenic zones, the distribution of earthquake sizes can typically be effectively represented through a power law relationship (Abercrombie, 1995).

There are primarily two approaches to estimating the completeness magnitude: (1) catalog-based methods, which rely solely on catalog data, and (2) waveform-based methods. These latter methods have been exemplified in studies by Sereno and Bratt (1989) and Gomberg (1991). Waveform-based methods that require estimating the signal-to-noise ratio for numerous events at many stations are time-consuming and cannot generally be performed as part of a particular seismicity study (Wiemer and Wyss, 2000). In the vast majority of instances, methods relying on catalogs ascertain the M_c-value by identifying the threshold beneath which the cumulative frequency–magnitude distribution (FMD) diverges from the Gutenberg–Richter (G-R) law (Gutenberg and Richter, 1944). The G-R law, shown in equation (1), models the relationship between earthquakes magnitudes and their frequencies in a given area. It states that the logarithm of the number of earthquakes with magnitude greater than or equal to a given value decreases linearly with that magnitude. This relationship is quantified by a characteristic parameter known as the *b*-value, which represents the relative frequency of small to large earthquakes (Ishimoto and Iida, 1939; Gutenberg and Richter, 1944). Mathematically, it can be expressed as

$$\log(N) = a - b(M - M_{\min}), \quad (1)$$

in which N represents earthquakes with a magnitude greater than or equal to a specific magnitude (M_w), a and b are the parameters of the G-R law, and M_{min} represents the lower magnitude cutoff used to fit the relation. The *a*-value, or "b-value intercept," reflects the seismicity rate at a specific magnitude. A higher *a*-value suggests a higher level of seismic activity, and a lower value indicates relatively fewer earthquakes. The *b*-value, or slope parameter, is a core parameter for hazard analysis. It characterizes the relative distribution of earthquake magnitudes: a high *b*-value indicates a larger proportion of small earthquakes, a lower *b*-value indicates a larger proportion of large earthquakes (Schorlemmer *et al.*, 2005). In most catalog-based methods, M_c is inferred from the expected behavior of seismicity by fitting a G-R model to the observed FMD (Mignan and Woessner, 2012). In the context of the G-R law, the magnitude at which the lower end of the observed FMD departs from the G-R model is taken as an estimate of M_c (Zuniga and Wyss, 1995).

The observed catalog shows a gradual curvature. This kind of model has been explained by different formulations of the detection function, including the cumulative normal distribution, also called the error function (ERF) (Ringdal, 1975; Ogata and Katsura, 1993; Ogata and Katsura, 2006). The ERF model uses the parameters μ and σ to describe this gradual curvature. Here, μ represents the mean detection threshold magnitude, indicating the central point of the detection function, whereas

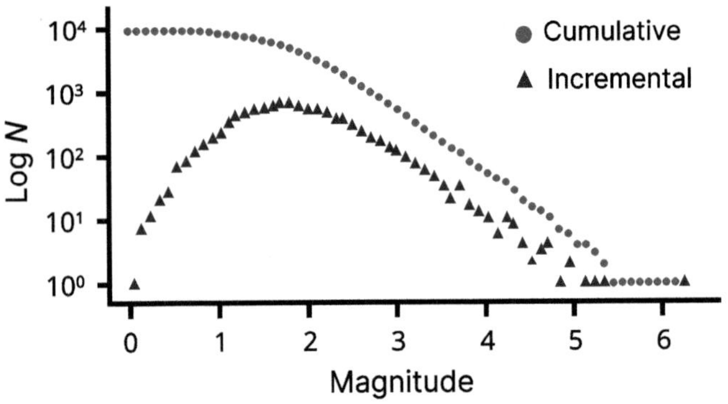

Figure 1. Synthetic gradually curved frequency–magnitude distribution (FMD) based on the error function (ERF) model (Ringdal 1975; Ogata and Katsura, 2006), with parameters $\mu = 2.0$ and $\sigma = 0.5$. The color version of this figure is available only in the electronic edition.

σ represents the standard deviation, indicating the spread or variability of the detection probabilities around this mean (Fig. 1). In the context of this model, the incremental FMD is characterized by a gradual curvature below the completeness magnitude and indicates that smaller earthquakes are less likely to be detected compared with larger ones. Understanding the FMD shape and how declustering alters it are essential aspects to obtain reliable and meaningful results. Declustering acts by filtering events as well as the completeness magnitude, although on a different basis. The balance between necessities of the study and sample size should be always pursued. It is also suggested a visual inspection of the curvature to help evaluate the performance of different M_c and avoid relying exclusively on numeric results (Mignan and Woessner, 2012). In this study, we aim to quantify the sensitivity of catalog-based estimates of M_c by comparing results obtained from the observed catalog with declustered catalogs generated using different algorithms.

MATERIALS AND METHODS

The seismic catalog (Fig. 2), provided by Istituto Nazionale di Geofisica e Vulcanologia (INGV), covers a range of 18 yr from 2005 to 2022. It comprises a comprehensive record of 26.300 earthquakes that occurred within this timeframe. The catalog encompasses a wide range of magnitudes, starting from 0.1 and reaching a maximum magnitude of 5.8. Geographically, it captures seismic activity in the region of Sicily, Italy, with coverage extending from longitude 11.6420 E to 16.4700 E and latitude 35.0020 N to 39.6957 N. Figure 3 depicts a heatmap showcasing the distribution of earthquakes frequencies for the observed catalog, classified in 0.5 yr interval and 0.1 magnitude increments. The highest concentration of event lies between 1.8 and 2.6;counts decrease rapidly for $M \geq 3.5$ and $M \leq 1.0$. We used three widely adopted algorithms that rely on different assumptions. The first declustering algorithm used is the Gardner and Knopoff window approach, extended with the Gruenthal and Uhrhammer variants (Gardner and Knopoff, 1974; Uhrhammer, 1986; Van Stiphout *et al.*, 2012). The Reasenberg linked-window method (Reasenberg, 1985) with the three parameters configuration reported by Van Stiphout *et al.* (2012). Finally, we applied the nearest-neighbor approach to make comparisons with more recent algorithms (Zaliapin and Ben-Zion, 2020). A total of eight catalogs were produced, including the observed not declustered catalog, and they were analyzed using five catalog-based methods to estimate the magnitude of completeness: maximum curvature (MAXC) (Wyss *et al.*, 1999, Wiemer and Wyss, 2000), goodness-of-fit test (GFT) (Wiemer and Wyss, 2000), median-based analysis of segment slope (MBASS) (Amorese, 2007), entire magnitude range (EMR) (Woessner and Wiemer, 2005), and magnitude of completeness by b-value stability (Cao and Gao, 2002). This analytical design enables a direct assessment of the sensitivity of M_c to the different decluster settings used. Method-specific uncertainties were quantified via bootstrap resampling using 500, 1000, 2000, and 3000 replicates for each catalog–method combination. A simulation analysis was conducted using synthetically generated catalogs to delve into the differences between the results obtained from M_c estimates in the observed catalog. Because of the gradually curved shape of the studied FMD, synthetic catalogs were based on the ERF model parameters. Magnitude of completeness computational calculations were performed using the statistical software R based on Mignan and Woessner (2012) and Amorese (2007). In addition, simulation analysis was conducted using the rseismNet R package. The declustering operations, for which the python software were used, were carried out using the OpenQuake Engine package by the Global Earthquake Modeling Foundation. (Silva *et al.*, 2014).

Declustering algorithms

Declustering a seismic catalog typically yields two products: a copy of the original catalog in which each event is classified according to the chosen algorithm and a subcatalog containing only events considered independent. Although these algorithms act on different decision rules, they both filter events in a way that can interact with M_c. In this study, we applied the fixed-window Gardner and Knopoff declustering algorithm with the variant space–time windows of Gruenthal and Uhrhammer (Gardner and Knopoff, 1974; Uhrhammer, 1986; Van Stiphout *et al.*, 2012). To extend the comparison beyond fixed windows, we also used the linked-window Reasenberg algorithm (Reasenberg, 1985) with three parameter configurations described in practice following Van Stiphout *et al.* (2012) and the newer emerging nearest-neighbor approach, which identifies clusters via a proximity metric in space–time–magnitude (Zaliapin and Ben-Zion, 2020). This allowed us to explore method-parameter-dependent variability of declustering outcomes on the Sicilian catalog.

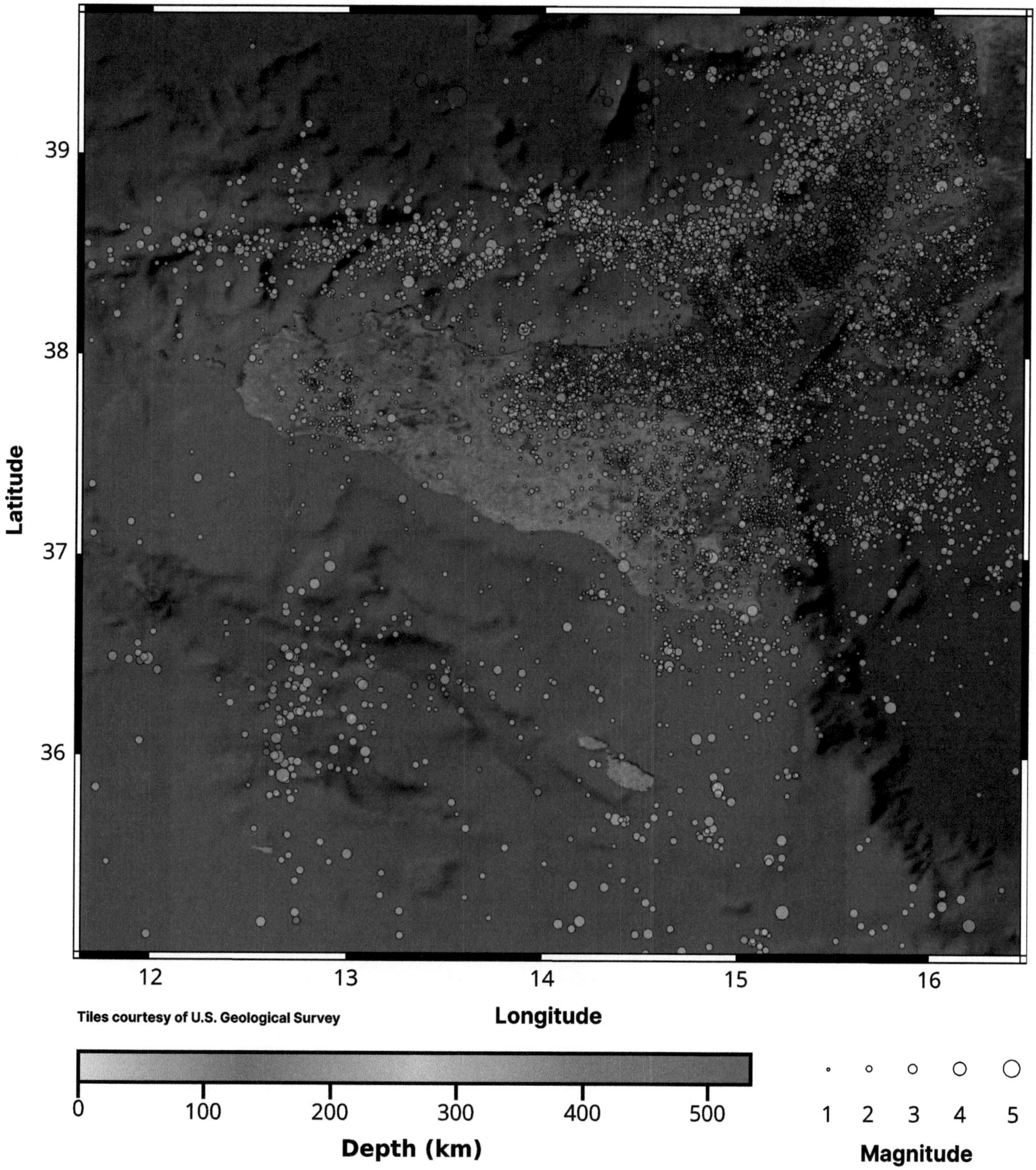

Figure 2. Events spatial distribution of the analyzed seismic catalog (2005–2022). The color version of this figure is available only in the electronic edition.

Gardner and Knopoff approach

One of the earliest and still widely used approaches is the Gardner and Knopoff algorithm (Gardner and Knopoff, 1974). It belongs to the family of windowing techniques that separate dependent from independent events by applying magnitude-dependent fixed windows in time and space. In practice, for each earthquake, a temporal window and a spatial radius are defined as functions of its magnitude, and any event occurring within the bounds set by a larger event is classified as a dependent and removed from the background. Different space–time windows have been proposed in the literature, each

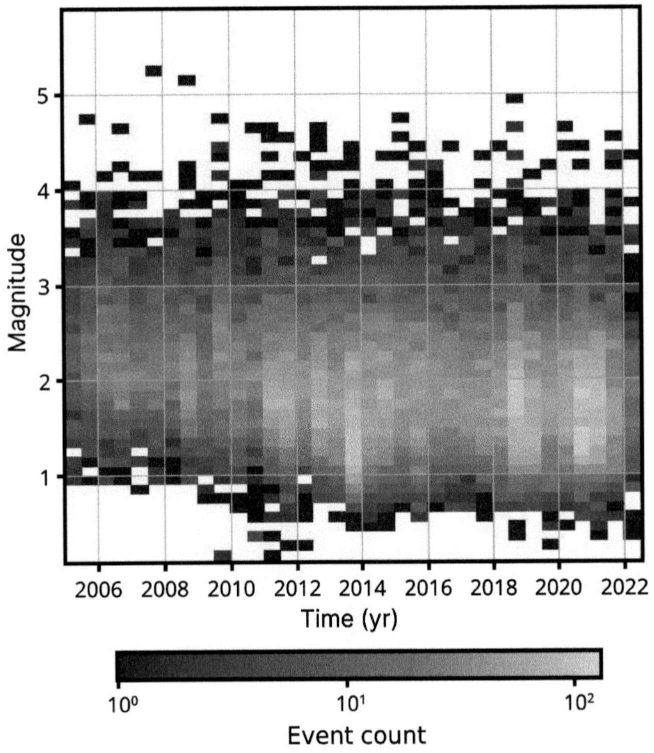

Figure 3. Observed seismic event density over time (year and magnitude bin size, respectively, are equal to 0.5 and 0.1). The color version of this figure is available only in the electronic edition.

empirically calibrated on specific regional seismicity. The original coefficients by Gardner and Knopoff are calibrated on southern California seismicity (Gardner and Knopoff, 1974), whereas the alternative parameter sets proposed by Gruenthal and by Uhrhammer are based on regional catalogs of Central Europe and northern–central California, respectively (Uhrhammer, 1986; Van Stiphout *et al.*, 2012). As shown in equations (2)–(4), each windowing formulation defines magnitude-dependent thresholds that govern how closely spaced events are considered dependent:

$$\text{Distance (Gardner and Knopoff)} = 10^{0.1238M+0.983}(\text{km})$$
$$\text{Time (Gardner and Knopoff)} = 10^{0.5409M-0.547}(\text{days}), \quad (2)$$

$$\text{Distance (Gruenthal)} = e^{1.77+(0.037+1.02M)^2}(\text{km})$$
$$\text{Time (Gruenthal)} = 10^{2.8+0.024M}(\text{days}), \quad (3)$$

$$\text{Distance (Uhrhammer)} = e^{-1.024+0.804M}(\text{km})$$
$$\text{Time (Uhrhammer)} = e^{-2.87+1.235M}(\text{days}). \quad (4)$$

Because of maximum magnitude observed in the original catalog does not reach the magnitude threshold set by the authors, the Gardner and Knopoff and Gruenthal time window definitions for $M \geq 6.5$ are not reported as not needed. This declustering algorithm consists of an iterative process that involves the following steps:

1. The earthquakes are sorted in descending order according to magnitude and initially considered as potential mainshocks.
2. The iteration starts, and each event is evaluated individually to determine if it meets the criteria to be classified as a mainshock, foreshock, or aftershock.
3. The first event corresponds to the maximum magnitude value in the catalog, meaning that it is a mainshock.
4. When a mainshock is detected, the time–space window is applied both forward and backward. At this point, an assessment is made to determine if other events fall within the spatial temporal distance defined by the window. If an earthquake satisfies the distance criterion and falls within the time window of a larger event, it is labeled as an aftershock or foreshock.
5. The process resumes from the last labeled mainshock event, repeating the procedure until all events in the series have been classified.

Reasenberg approach

Reasenberg implements a linked-window method in which each event opens a time–space interaction window, and any subsequent event that falls within is linked and in turn opens its own window so that clusters grow transitively (Reasenberg, 1985). The temporal parameters ($\tau_{\min}$,$\tau_{\max}$) delimit the admissible bounds of the prospective look-ahead time τ. For a target detection probability p_1, τ is calculated as shown in equation (5),

$$\tau = -\ln(1-p_1)t10^{-\frac{2}{3}(\Delta M-1)}, \quad (5)$$

in which $\Delta M = M_{max} - x_{meff}$ is the magnitude contrast between the current largest event and the membership threshold in magnitude x_{meff} and t is a timescale constant. The value from equation (5) is then truncated to $[\tau_{\min},\tau_{\max}]$. The interaction distance follows the spatial criterion well summarized in Molchan and Dmitrieva (1992) and shown in equation (6),

$$\log_{10} d(\text{km}) = 0.4M_0 - 1.943 + k, \quad (6)$$

in which d is the maximum separation for linkage, M_0 is the magnitude of the reference event, and $k \in \{0,1\}$ switches between using the distance to the last linked event ($k = 0$) or to the largest event currently in the cluster ($k = 1$). In addition, x_k controls how strongly the effective lower magnitude cutoff is raised during an active sequence via $x_{\text{eff}} = x_{meff} + x_k M_{\max}$; a larger x_k means a higher cutoff, and therefore fewer small events are linked. Finally, r_{fact} is the scale factor that sets the spatial neighborhood (Kanamori and Anderson, 1975); a larger r_{fact}

TABLE 1
Parameter Configuration Used for the Reasenberg Declustering Algorithm, Including Standard Values and Parameter Ranges Described by Van Stiphout *et al.* (2012)

Parameter	Standard	Min	Max
τ_{min} (days)	1	0.5	2.5
τ_{max} (days)	10	3	15
p	0.95	0.9	0.99
x_k	0.5	0	1
x_{meff}	1.5	1.6	1.8
r_{fact}	10	5	20

widens the spatial window, allowing more permissive linking, whereas smaller values tighten it, leading to a more conservative linking. Even though the parameter choices often follow the standard setting (Van Stiphout *et al.*, 2012), we decided to also use the minimum and maximum configurations (Schorlemmer and Gerstenberger, 2007) summarized in Table 1:

1. The earthquakes are sorted in chronological order and initially left unassigned as potential cluster seeds.
2. Starting from the first unassigned event, define its interaction zone by a look-ahead time window and a magnitude-dependent spatial distance threshold.
3. Scan forward in time and link any subsequent event that falls within both the temporal and spatial criteria to the current cluster; each linked event opens its own interaction zone and can link further events.
4. When no additional links are found, close the cluster, designate the largest-magnitude member as the mainshock, and label earlier members as foreshocks and later members as aftershocks.
5. Mark all cluster members as assigned and continue from the next unassigned event until the entire catalog is processed; obtain the declustered catalog by retaining mainshocks only.

Nearest-neighbor approach

The nearest-neighbor approach constructs a directed tree by assigning to each earthquake j a single nearest predecessor $i < j$ within a joint space–time–magnitude proximity (Zaliapin and Ben-Zion, 2013a,b; Zaliapin and Ben-Zion, 2020). The core quantity is the proximity between two events (equation 7), which combines interevent time, spatial separation, and a magnitude weighting consistent with Gutenberg–Richter statistics:

$$\eta_{ij} = t_{ij} r_{ij}^{d} \, 10^{-wm_i}, \tag{7}$$

in which $t_{ij} = t_j - t_i$ is the interevent time; r_{ij} is the epicentral distance between the events; m_i is the magnitude of the potential parent i; w, and d control, respectively, the magnitude weighting and the spatial scaling. Following the declustering recommendations of Zaliapin and Ben-Zion (2020), we work with epicenters only and set $w = 0$ and $d = 1.5$.

Each event is linked to its nearest-neighbor in this proximity,

$$i^*(j) = \arg\min_{i<j} \eta_{ij}, \tag{8}$$

and the link strength is summarized by

$$\xi_j = \log_{10}(\eta_{i^*(j)j}). \tag{9}$$

A data-driven cutoff on ξ_j (equivalently, $\xi_j \le \log_{10}\eta_0$), estimated from the empirical typically bimodal distribution of ξ_j, separates clustered from background links:

$$\text{Link}(j) = \begin{cases} \text{Clustered} & \text{if } \xi_j \le \log_{10}\eta_0, \\ \text{Background} & \text{if } \xi_j > \log_{10}\eta_0. \end{cases} \tag{10}$$

1. For each earthquake, compute its proximity to every earlier earthquake, assign as parent the earlier event with the smallest proximity, and record the base-10 logarithm of that minimum proximity as the link strength.
2. Using a data-driven cutoff derived from the empirical distribution of link strengths, classify each parent–child link as either clustered or background and retain only the clustered links.
3. From the retained links, identify connected groups (families); within each family, designate the largest-magnitude event as the mainshock, label events that occur before it as foreshocks, and label those that occur after it as aftershocks.
4. Apply random thinning based on the normalized score with a single global threshold; the retained events form the declustered catalog.

CATALOG-BASED METHODS TO ESTIMATE THE COMPLETENESS MAGNITUDE

MAXC

The MAXC technique (Wyss *et al.*, 1999; Wiemer and Wyss, 2000) is a catalog-based method used to estimate the magnitude of completeness in earthquake catalogs. It operates by calculating the maximum value of the first derivative of the frequency–magnitude curve. In practical terms, this method identifies the magnitude that corresponds to the mode of the noncumulative FMD. By identifying the magnitude associated with the highest frequency of events in the FMD, it aims to capture a significant point of deviation from the linear cumulative part of the Gutenberg–Richter law.

GFT

The GFT method, developed by Wiemer and Wyss (2000), is a parametric method used to assess quantitatively the differences

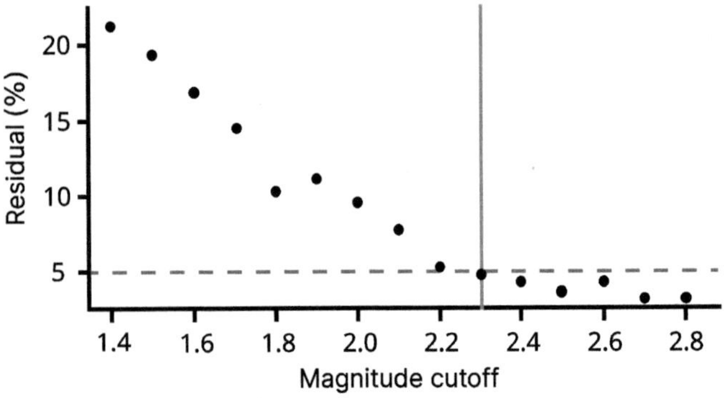

Figure 4. Goodness-of-fit test (GFT) method: residual are plot as a function of magnitude cutoff interval. The completeness is identified (vertical line) as the first value that achieve the confidence level (dashed horizontal line). The color version of this figure is available only in the electronic edition.

between the observed and synthetic distributions, providing a measure of how well the G-R law fits the input data. The procedure begins by selecting a magnitude cutoff range, which represents the potential magnitude of completeness values. The G-R law is then applied to calculate the theoretical distribution of earthquake magnitudes using maximum-likelihood estimation of the parameters a and b from the observed data. The next step involves comparing the observed cumulative number of events (Bi) in each M_{co} with the predicted cumulative number of events (Si) from the theoretical distribution. The absolute difference R between Bi and Si is calculated for each magnitude cutoff using the equation (11):

$$R(a,b,M_{co}) = 100 - \left(\frac{\sum_{M_{co}}^{M_{max}} |B_i - S_i|}{\sum_i B_i} 100 \right). \quad (11)$$

By evaluating R at different magnitude thresholds, the test identifies the M_c-value that satisfies the desired confidence level. If the observed and theoretical distributions exhibit large differences, indicating a poor fit, a higher M_c-value will be selected. Conversely, if the observed and theoretical distributions align well, the M_c-value will be lower.

The completeness magnitude is defined as the first magnitude cutoff at which the residual falls below the horizontal line corresponding to the desired confidence level (e.g., 95% fit) as presented in Figure 4. If the desired confidence level cannot be achieved, 90% may be used as a compromise. If even the 90 confidence level cannot be reached, the MAXC estimate is used instead.

MBASS

Amorese (2007) introduced the MBASS method as a nonparametric technique for estimating the magnitude of completeness in earthquake catalogs. It is based on the change-point detection principles to identify multiple discontinuities in the incremental FMD, with the primary discontinuity corresponding to completeness. The MBASS method builds on the multiple change-point procedure developed by Lanzante (1996), which has demonstrated success in climate data analysis by employing resistant, solid, and nonparametric approach. In the context of earthquake catalog, the MBASS algorithm follows an iterative process to estimate M_c. Initially, the FMD is divided into segments, defined by magnitude cutoffs. For each segment, the slope is calculated and then iteratively tested for change points, representing potential M_c-values. The null hypothesis states that the frequencies are equal. The acceptance or rejection of the null hypothesis of no change at the identified change point is based on the Wilcoxon–Mann–Whitney test (Wilcoxon, 1945), a widely used nonparametric statistical test. The significance level for evaluating the statistical significance of each change point is typically chosen in advance. In this study, a significance level of 5 has been chosen. The change-point test is iteratively applied to the magnitude series as long as the statistical significance of each new change point remains below the specified significance level. Each iteration generates a list of $N + 1$ change points, and prior to applying the change-point test in subsequent iterations, the magnitude series is adjusted by subtracting the median of each segment slope from the corresponding points. The final M_c estimate is determined based on the identified change points, typically using the magnitude associated with the best test statistic as the M_c-value which corresponds to the main discontinuity. Figure 5 depicts the identification of the main discontinuity obtained through 3000 bootstrap sample for the observed catalog. Other discontinuities may correspond to upper-magnitude breakpoints (Wesnousky, 1994). The MBASS procedure cannot be applied to cumulative FMD data because, in common with many other statistical procedures, the Wilcoxon–Mann–Whitney test requires independence within groups (Hollander and Wolfe, 1973).

EMR

The EMR method (Woessner and Wiemer, 2005) offers a parametric approach to estimating the completeness magnitude using a two-part model that combines the Gutenberg–Richter law and a cumulative normal distribution function. This method accounts for both the complete and incomplete parts of the magnitude–frequency distribution. In the EMR model, the first component of the model incorporates the G-R law and represents the part of the earthquake catalog in which earthquake detection is assumed to be reliable and complete, capturing the entirety of seismic activity above the completeness. The second component of the model incorporates a cumulative normal distribution function, denoted as q, which characterizes the detection capability of the seismic network. This component addresses the incomplete part in the catalog, modeling the incremental frequency magnitude below M_c, acknowledging that some events might not be

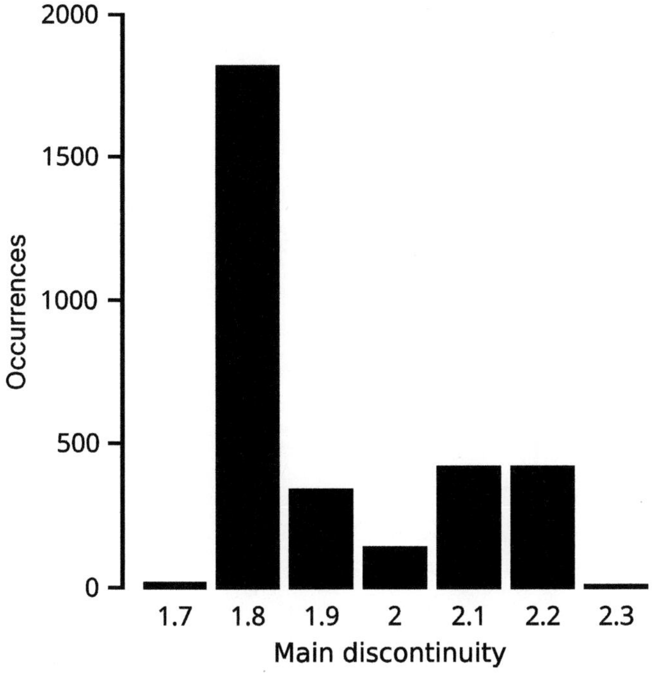

Figure 5. Median-based analysis of the segment slope method (MBASS) method—occurrences of the magnitude cutoff (M_{co}) identified as the main discontinuity obtained for the observed catalog through 3000 bootstrap samples.

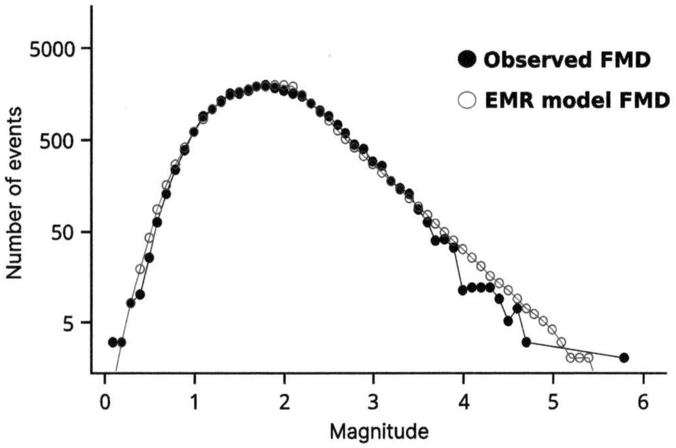

Figure 6. Observed and predicted incremental FMD. The parameters of the EMR model were obtained through maximum-likelihood (b = 0.93, μ = 1.06, σ = 0.33). The color version of this figure is available only in the electronic edition.

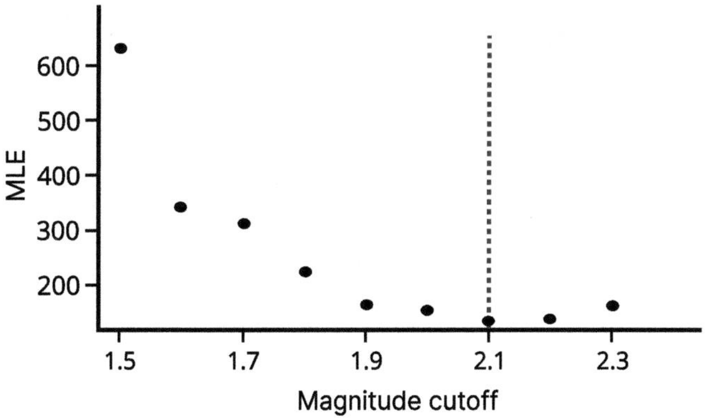

Figure 7. EMR method: maximum-likelihood estimate (MLE) of the completeness magnitude M_c. The EMR fit statistic is evaluated over candidate magnitude cutoffs; it decreases to a distinct minimum at 2.1 (dashed vertical line), so it is selected as the M_c because it provides the best fit (lowest-misfit). The color version of this figure is available only in the electronic edition.

detected. Figure 6 shows the reconstruction of the FMD model performed by the EMR method. The choice of the normal cumulative distribution function is based on visual inspection and modeling of a variety of catalogs, as well as comparisons to other possible functions, but is not based on physical reasoning. Thus, cases exist for which the choice of another function might be more appropriate. However, synthetic tests endorse that estimates of M_c can be correct even if this assumption is violated (Woessner and Wiemer, 2005). The probability of detecting an earthquake with magnitude M_w, given a specific detectability level determined by the parameters μ and σ, can be quantified by the following function:

$$q(M|\mu,\sigma) = \frac{1}{\sigma\sqrt{2\pi}}\int_{-\infty}^{M_c} \exp\left(-\frac{(M-\mu)^2}{2\sigma^2}\right) dM \quad \text{for } M < M_c, \tag{12}$$

$$q(M|\mu,\sigma) = 1 \quad \text{for } M \geq M_c. \tag{13}$$

The parameter μ represents the magnitude at which 50% of the earthquakes are detected. The parameter σ represents the standard deviation, reflecting the width of the magnitude range over which partial detection occurs. A larger σ corresponds to a wider range of magnitudes over which the detection capability gradually changes. By explicitly incorporating M_c into the equations (12) and (13), as proposed by the authors, the EMR method enables completeness estimation through the minimization of maximum-likelihood function (Fig. 7). This statistical technique aims to identify the values of the parameters (μ and σ) that maximize the likelihood of observing the seismicity data.

Magnitude of completeness by *b*-value stability

The magnitude of completeness by b-value stability (MBS), initially proposed by Cao and Gao (2002) and further developed by Woessner and Wiemer (2005), offers an approach to estimate the completeness magnitude based on the stability of the b-value with respect to the cutoff magnitude (M_{co}). The MBS method operates under the assumption that the b-value estimates exhibit an increasing trend for M_{co}-values lower than

M_c and remain constant for M_{co}-values greater than or equal to M_c. Deviations from this trend indicate inaccurate b-value estimates when M_{co} is below M_c. Because M_{co} approaches M_c, the b-value converges to its true value and plateaus, reflecting the stable seismicity characteristics. In the original formulation, M_c was arbitrarily defined as the magnitude at which the change in b-value between successive magnitude bin is <0.03. However, Woessner and Wiemer identified the instability of this criterion due to variations in the frequency of events within individual magnitude bins. To address this instability and introduce an objective measure, they proposed using the b-value uncertainty (δb) as the criterion. The b-value uncertainty, originally introduced by Shi and Bolt (1982), is computed as depicted in equation (14):

$$\delta b = 2.3b^2 \sqrt{\frac{\sum_{i=1}^{N}(M_i - \overline{M})^2}{N(N-1)}}. \quad (14)$$

As displayed in equation (14) b represents the estimated b-value, $\overline{M}$ is the mean magnitude, N denotes the number of events, and Mi represents individual cutoff magnitudes. This formulation stabilizes the MBS method numerically. According to the MBS method, M_c is defined as the first magnitude increment at which the absolute difference between the average b-value (bave) and the individual b-value (b) is less than or equal to the b-value uncertainty (δb). The bave is calculated by averaging the b-values of successive cutoff magnitudes within a half magnitude range ($dM = 0.5$) using a bin size of 0.1 (Mignan and Woessner, 2012). The MBS method aims to identify M_c by monitoring the changes in the b-value as M_{co} increases (Fig. 8). When completeness is reached, the b-value exhibits a decline for smaller magnitudes, indicating a shift in earthquake occurrence patterns. Compared with other techniques, the MBS method tends to yield higher M_c-values, as evidenced in the findings presented by Woessner and Wiemer (2005) along with the greater uncertainty.

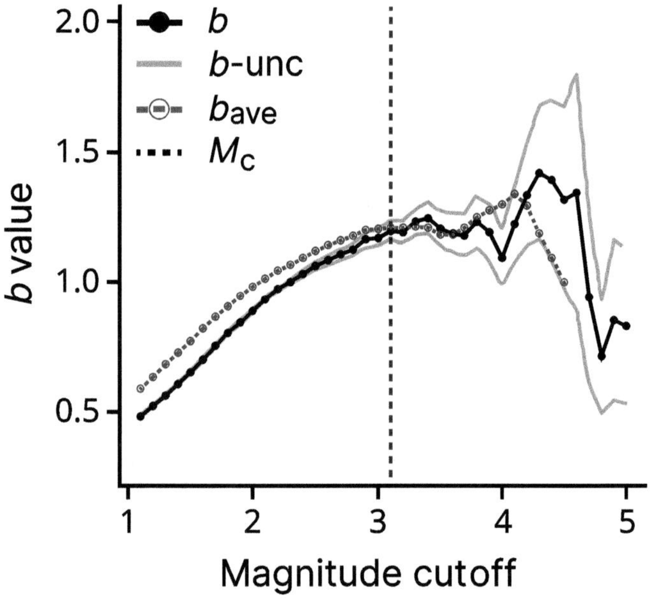

Figure 8. Magnitude of completeness by b-value stability (MBS) method: b-value estimate as a function of minimum magnitude cutoff (M_{co}) with the relate uncertainty. The black circles are used for individual b-values, yellow bands for the uncertainty, and red circles for the b-value average trend. A vertical line marks as M_c (vertical dashed line) the first magnitude increment at which the condition $\Delta b \leq \delta b$ is met. The color version of this figure is available only in the electronic edition.

Evaluating bias in M_c estimation methods for curved datasets

To further investigate the bias of magnitude of completeness estimation methods in case of curved datasets, synthetic catalogs were generated on the ERF model assumptions (Ringdal, 1975; Ogata and Katsura, 2006) for different parameter sets and the M_c estimation was computed. The parameters were varied systematically to span a broad range of potential real-word scenarios, covering integer μ-values from 1 to 3, whereas σ-values ranging from 0.1 to 3.0 with the increments being in steps of 0.1. To ensure the simulations accurately reflected the logarithmic relationship between earthquake magnitude and frequency as mandated by the Gutenberg–Richter law, the b-value was set to 1. To assess the sensitivity of the Gutenberg–Richter slope β to the completeness threshold, we first estimated M_c and quantified its uncertainty via bootstrap resampling. We then took the bootstrap mean of M_c as a baseline and defined a sequence of increasingly conservative thresholds by adding multiples of the M_c standard deviation. For each threshold, β was re-estimated by maximum likelihood using only events above that cutoff (Aki, 1965; Mignan, 2019a). The results across the two models (and both catalog sizes) show that the methods differ in performance depending on the underlying FMD shape, and visual inspection can assist in evaluating the reasonability of a method (Mignan and Woessner, 2012; Mignan and Chen, 2016).

Given the extensive set of simulation, we focus on reporting two representative parameter sets. The first uses the EMR detection parameters for our dataset ($\mu = 1.06$, $\sigma = 0.33$); the second adopts a curved-FMD configuration ($\mu = 2.0$, $\sigma = 0.5$) that better reflects the observed catalog (Fig. 9, panels a–d). Through such analysis, it becomes apparent whether certain techniques are better suited for particular types of seismic activities or specific regions and how the complexities of real-world data impact M_c accuracy (Mignan, 2012). The simulation test was primarily focused on MAXC, GFT, and MBASS. The exclusion of the EMR method from this analysis stems from its fundamental assumption of a normal distribution for the incomplete segment of the dataset, which directly corresponds to the simulated parameters (μ, σ). On the contrary, a comparison between EMR model and a synthetic catalog built on different μ and σ may provide insight on the performance of

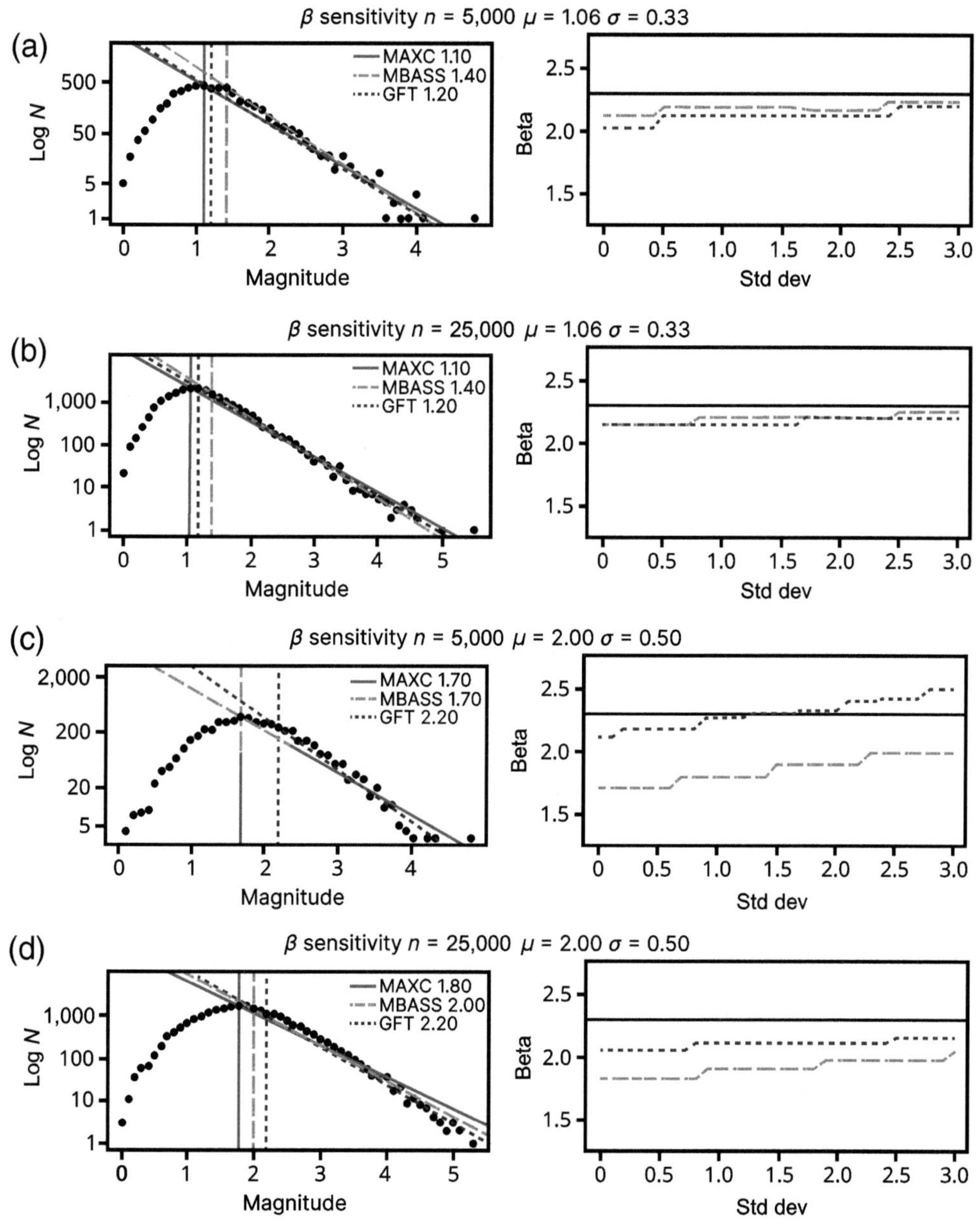

Figure 9. Curved-FMD simulations based on the bulk FMD model of Ringdal (1975). Panels (a,b) use $\mu = 1.06$, $\sigma = 0.33$, and panels (c,d) use $\mu = 2.0$, $\sigma = 0.50$, each with N = 5,000 and 25,000 events. Left panels: FMDs with completeness estimates M_c with maximum curvature (MAXC) (solid red), MBASS (dotted–dashed cyan), GFT (dashed purple). Right panels: sensitivity of the GR slope β to M_c. The horizontal black line indicates the theoretical value β_{true} used in the simulations, and the cyan and purple curves show β estimated with M_c set to the MBASS and GFT completeness estimates, perturbed by k standard deviations above their bootstrap mean (x-axis label "Std dev" gives k). In all cases, β is the GR slope ($\beta = b \ln 10$) estimated by maximum likelihood for $M \geq M_c$. The color version of this figure is available only in the electronic edition.

the method. In addition, the MBS method was not considered owing to its notable lack of stability. It has been observed that the MBASS and GFT methods might underestimate or overestimate M_c, particularly on certain magnitude samples. To mitigate this issue, it is advised to use bootstrapping techniques (Efron, 1979; Haukoos and Lewis, 2005).

The technique is useful for analyzing data sets in which prior information is sparse, distributional assumptions are unclear, and further data may be difficult to acquire (Henderson, 2005). Adopting a cautious stance involves using the mean plus one to three standard deviations, enhancing the reliability of M_c estimation in the context of curved FMDs (Mignan and Woessner, 2012).

RESULTS AND DISCUSSION

Bootstrap results (3000 resamples) are presented in Figure 10, which summarizes the FMDs for the observed catalog and for all declustered catalogs considered. For each panel, the incremental FMD is shown together with the bootstrap-based magnitude of completeness estimates obtained with all methods adopted in this work (MAXC, MBASS, EMR, GFT, and MBS), reported as color-coded vertical bars. The numerical M_c-values and related uncertainties are reported, in method order, in Tables 2–6.

The completeness magnitude estimated using the MAXC method remains <2.0 for the observed catalog and for all declustered catalogs, with the exception of the one generated using the nearest-neighbor algorithm (Table 2). The Reasenberg and Uhrhammer declustered catalogs, which retain the largest proportion of events, reproduce the observed catalog's completeness around 1.8–1.9. Catalogs declustered with the Gardner–Knopoff and Gruenthal windows show a slight increase in M_c, although values remain <2.0 despite substantial differences in event counts. Notably, the nearest-neighbor catalog yields a higher M_c of 2.1, despite retaining a similar number of events as Gardner–Knopoff windows and far more than Gruenthal windows. Because MAXC identifies the mode of the incremental FMD, this outcome suggests that nearest neighbor preferentially removes earthquakes <2.1, thereby shifting the modal bin to higher magnitudes because of its distinct declustering approach.

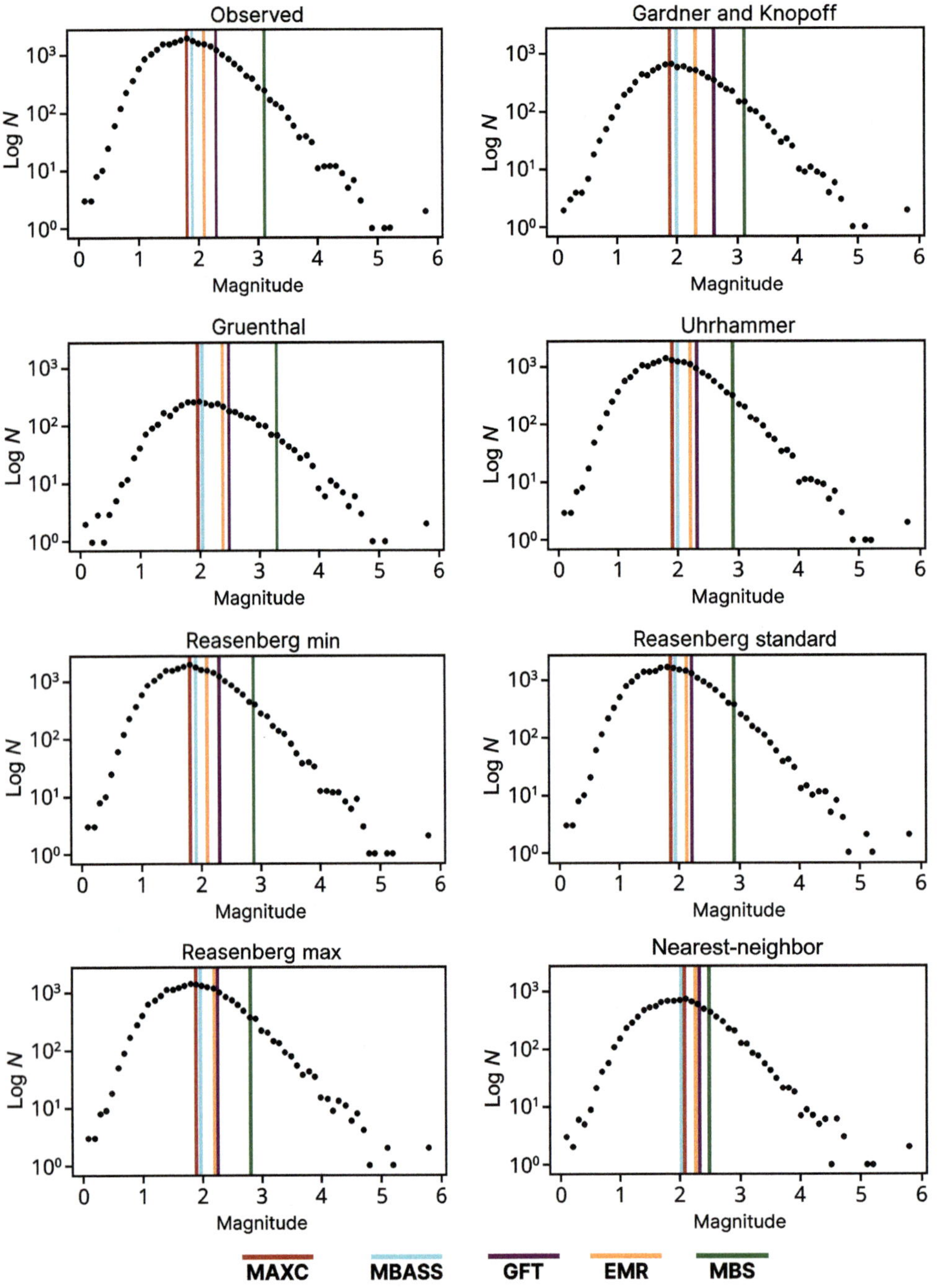

Figure 10. Incremental FMDs for the observed catalog and for all declustered catalogs considered. Color vertical bars indicate the bootstrap-based (3000 resamples) completeness estimates obtained with the catalog-based methods employed: MAXC (red), MBASS (cyan), GFT (purple), EMR (orange), and MBS (green).

The MBASS method defines completeness as the first statistically significant break in the slope of the incremental FMD. The similarity in the results between the MBASS and MAXC methods necessitates cautious interpretation (Tables 2 and 3), particularly in light of MAXC's tendency to underestimate M_c in gradually curved FMD (Mignan 2012). Because it consists of an iterative procedure, it has shown a higher uncertainty. It is worth to note that the MBASS results for the nearest-neighbor declustered catalog show roughly half the uncertainty compared with other declustering algorithms. Single-run MBASS tend to be more variable: estimates reach ~2.1 for Reasenberg and Gardner and Knopoff and reach the peak at 2.3 for Gruenthal. After bootstrap resampling, the observed catalog and those declustered with the Reasenberg, Uhrhammer, and Gardner–Knopoff algorithms show similar results ($M_c < 2.0$). Compared with the MAXC method, the MBASS method showed less sensitivity to the declustering. The Gruenthal and nearest-neighbor methods align, with both catalogs giving slightly higher M_c estimates about 2.0–2.1, even though Gruenthal declustered catalog has <50% of events.

The EMR method M_c results are higher than those of both the MAXC and MBASS methods as illustrated in Table 4. The observed catalog and those declustered with the Reasenberg and Uhrhammer approaches return M_c-values between 2.1 and 2.2. In contrast, the Gardner–Knopoff and nearest-neighbor algorithms achieve 2.3, and the Gruenthal catalog reaches 2.4. Contrary to the results of the MAXC method, it is observed a similarity between Gardner–Knopoff and nearest-neighbor methods despite significant differences in event count. This suggests that EMR is less influenced by which magnitudes are removed than by the total number of events. Single-run and bootstrap estimates coincide across all catalogs, indicating a stable performance. Although the EMR method models the incomplete part of the FMD, the observed discrepancies between synthetic and real catalogs underscore limitations in its effectiveness for defining detection thresholds. The authors recommend caution in its use because of its limited reliability and theoretical foundation (Mignan and Woessner, 2012).

The GFT and MBS methods produced the most conservative estimates of M_c obtained in this study, along with

TABLE 2
Completeness Magnitude (M_c) Estimates and *b*-Values (with Standard Deviations $M_{c_{sd}}$, b_{sd}) for Each Catalog Using the Maximum Curvature (MAXC) Method

Catalog	nboot	M_c	$M_{c_{sd}}$	b	b_{sd}	Events
Observed	Single-run	1.80	—	0.880	—	26,300
Observed	500	1.85	0.022	0.876	0.032	26,300
Observed	3,000	1.85	0.022	0.876	0.033	26,300
Gruenthal	Single-run	1.90	—	0.590	—	4,226
Gruenthal	500	1.96	0.110	0.626	0.039	4,226
Gruenthal	3,000	1.96	0.115	0.626	0.041	4,226
Gardner and Knopoff	Single-run	1.80	—	0.730	—	9,498
Gardner and Knopoff	500	1.90	0.094	0.733	0.024	9,498
Gardner and Knopoff	3,000	1.91	0.099	0.731	0.026	9,498
Nearest neighbor	Single-run	2.10	—	0.840	—	10,188
Nearest neighbor	500	2.09	0.092	0.868	0.053	10,188
Nearest neighbor	3,000	2.10	0.084	0.871	0.051	10,188
Uhrhammer	Single-run	1.80	—	0.850	—	18,847
Uhrhammer	500	1.85	0.020	0.849	0.020	18,847
Uhrhammer	3,000	1.85	0.022	0.849	0.020	18,847
Reasenberg max	Single-run	1.80	—	0.840	—	19,945
Reasenberg max	500	1.85	0.021	0.842	0.021	19,945
Reasenberg max	3,000	1.85	0.025	0.841	0.022	19,945
Reasenberg standard	Single-run	1.80	—	0.870	—	22,981
Reasenberg standard	500	1.85	0.023	0.863	0.032	22,981
Reasenberg standard	3,000	1.85	0.020	0.865	0.028	22,981
Reasenberg min	Single-run	1.80	—	0.880	—	25,316
Reasenberg min	500	1.84	0.024	0.873	0.036	25,316
Reasenberg min	3,000	1.84	0.026	0.873	0.038	25,316

Results are shown for single-run and bootstrap replicates (500 and 3000).

TABLE 3
Completeness Magnitude (M_c) Estimates and *b*-Values (with Standard Deviations $M_{c_{sd}}$, b_{sd}) for Each Catalog Using the Median-Based Analysis of the Segment Slope Method (MBASS) Method

Catalog	nboot	M_c	$M_{c_{sd}}$	b	b_{sd}	Events
Observed	Single-run	1.80	—	0.800	—	26,300
Observed	500	1.89	0.137	0.841	0.060	26,300
Observed	3,000	1.90	0.143	0.845	0.063	26,300
Gruenthal	Single-run	2.30	—	0.730	—	4,226
Gruenthal	500	2.02	0.188	0.652	0.061	4,226
Gruenthal	3,000	2.01	0.187	0.648	0.060	4,226
Gardner and Knopoff	Single-run	2.10	—	0.790	—	9,498
Gardner and Knopoff	500	1.97	0.152	0.747	0.061	9,498
Gardner and Knopoff	3,000	1.96	0.150	0.745	0.061	9,498
Uhrhammer	Single-run	1.80	—	0.770	—	18,847
Uhrhammer	500	1.95	0.154	0.847	0.071	18,847
Uhrhammer	3,000	1.96	0.155	0.848	0.071	18,847
Nearest neighbor	Single-run	2.10	—	0.900	—	10,188
Nearest neighbor	500	2.06	0.088	0.882	0.048	10,188
Nearest neighbor	3,000	2.06	0.090	0.881	0.049	10,188
Reasenberg max	Single-run	2.10	—	0.900	—	19,945
Reasenberg max	500	1.92	0.143	0.824	0.063	19,945
Reasenberg max	3,000	1.92	0.142	0.825	0.062	19,945
Reasenberg standard	Single-run	1.80	—	0.790	—	22,981
Reasenberg standard	500	1.92	0.146	0.843	0.065	22,981
Reasenberg standard	3,000	1.92	0.144	0.845	0.064	22,981
Reasenberg min	Single-run	1.80	—	0.800	—	25,316
Reasenberg min	500	1.90	0.144	0.843	0.064	25,316
Reasenberg min	3,000	1.89	0.141	0.841	0.063	25,316

Results are shown for single-run and bootstrap replicates (500 and 3000).

TABLE 4

Completeness Magnitude (M_c) Estimates and b-Values (with Standard Deviations $M_{c_{sd}}$, b_{sd}) for Each Catalog Using the Entire Magnitude Range (EMR) Method

Catalog	nboot	M_c	$M_{c_{sd}}$	b	b_{sd}	Events
Observed	Single-run	2.10	—	0.930	—	26,300
Observed	500	2.12	0.044	0.941	0.020	26,300
Observed	3,000	2.13	0.044	0.943	0.021	26,300
Gruenthal	Single-run	2.40	—	0.760	—	4,226
Gruenthal	500	2.35	0.069	0.749	0.025	4,226
Gruenthal	3,000	2.36	0.069	0.750	0.026	4,226
Gardner and Knopoff	Single-run	2.30	—	0.860	—	9,498
Gardner and Knopoff	500	2.30	0.037	0.869	0.020	9,498
Gardner and Knopoff	3,000	2.30	0.037	0.868	0.020	9,498
Nearest neighbor	Single-run	2.30	—	0.980	—	10,188
Nearest neighbor	500	2.29	0.042	0.979	0.024	10,188
Nearest neighbor	3000	2.30	0.038	0.980	0.022	10,188
Uhrhammer	Single-run	2.20	—	0.950	—	18,847
Uhrhammer	500	2.19	0.025	0.950	0.015	18,847
Uhrhammer	3,000	2.19	0.026	0.950	0.015	18,847
Reasenberg max	Single-run	2.20	—	0.930	—	19,945
Reasenberg max	500	2.18	0.039	0.931	0.018	19,945
Reasenberg max	3,000	2.18	0.036	0.932	0.017	19,945
Reasenberg standard	Single-run	2.10	—	0.920	—	22,981
Reasenberg standard	500	2.16	0.050	0.944	0.021	22,981
Reasenberg standard	3,000	2.15	0.050	0.943	0.022	22,981
Reasenberg min	Single-run	2.10	—	0.930	—	25,316
Reasenberg min	500	2.14	0.048	0.948	0.023	25,316
Reasenberg min	3,000	2.14	0.048	0.947	0.023	25,316

Results are shown for Single-Run and bootstrap replicates (500 and 3000).

high uncertainty values (Tables 5 and 6). The GFT results range between 2.2 and 2.7, the second highest M_c estimations of the entire study. In both single-run and bootstrap computations, the catalogs declustered with the Reasenberg, Uhrhammer, and nearest-neighbor approaches match the observed catalog M_c of 2.3. Cases of under- or overestimation arise only in two fixed-window approaches used. For the catalog declustered with the Gardner and Knopoff algorithm, the single GFT run yields 2.7, but the bootstrap stabilizes the estimate around 2.5. Same bootstrap results are achieved for the Gruenthal declustered catalog, but resampling raises the single run M_c initial estimation of 2.3. The application of the GFT provides valuable insights into the alignment of the observed seismic data with the expected statistical distribution according to the Gutenberg–Richter law. This alignment or lack thereof can help understanding the representativeness of our catalog in capturing the range of seismic activities. As a matter of fact, it is also used as indirect assessment of upgrades in the seismic network. Despite the well-known limit of selecting the first M_{co} that achieves the test statistic, the results offer a good compromise between managing undersampling and being conservative. It appears reasonable to consider slightly higher value of the M_{co} that demonstrate improved performance in statistical testing as completeness.

The MBS method gives the most conservative completeness and shows the widest separation across declustering choices (Table 6). Initially, the computation failed to identify the completeness for the observed catalog: the range of potential values adopted from (Mignan and Woessner, 2012) was centered around the value of MAXC (1.8 for the observed catalog), resulting in a maximum and minimum value of M_{co} of 1.1 and 3.0, respectively. After expanding the range of potential completeness values from 20 to 40, MBS immediately identified M_c above 3.0, confirming the initial suspicion and demonstrating that caution should be exercised in defining the values of M_{co} to be tested when applying this methodology. When the number of events is slightly reduced, as in the catalogs declustered with the Uhrhammer and Reasenberg algorithms, the MBS recorded lower results. In contrast, the catalogs declustered with Gardner and Knopoff and Gruenthal windows, which are more aggressive, yield higher M_c estimates. The nearest-neighbor catalog is a special case. Although its number of events is comparable to the Gardner and Knopoff declustered catalog, the single run overestimates M_c at 2.6, and the bootstrap stabilizes at just <2.5, making it distinctly lower than all other catalogs.

The Gutenberg–Richter b-value varies systematically with declustering aggressiveness and the fraction of events retained.

TABLE 5
Completeness Magnitude (M_c) Estimates and b-Values (with Standard Deviations $M_{c_{sd}}$, b_{sd}) for Each Catalog Using the Goodness-of-Fit Test (GFT) Method

Catalog	nboot	M_c	$M_{c_{sd}}$	b	b_{sd}	Events
Observed	Single-run	2.30	—	0.990	—	26,300
Observed	500	2.34	0.123	1.015	0.042	26,300
Observed	3,000	2.35	0.127	1.017	0.042	26,300
Gruenthal	Single-run	2.30	—	0.730	—	4,226
Gruenthal	500	2.52	0.276	0.808	0.092	4,226
Gruenthal	3,000	2.53	0.271	0.811	0.091	4,226
Gardner and Knopoff	Single-run	2.70	—	0.970	—	9,498
Gardner and Knopoff	500	2.54	0.249	0.942	0.082	9,498
Gardner and Knopoff	3,000	2.56	0.250	0.946	0.082	9,498
Nearest neighbor	Single-run	2.30	—	0.980	—	10,188
Nearest neighbor	500	2.34	0.080	0.994	0.033	10,188
Nearest neighbor	3,000	2.34	0.084	0.995	0.034	10,188
Uhrhammer	Single-run	2.30	—	0.970	—	18,847
Uhrhammer	500	2.28	0.102	0.976	0.033	18,847
Uhrhammer	3,000	2.28	0.106	0.978	0.033	18,847
Reasenberg max	Single-run	2.20	—	0.930	—	19,945
Reasenberg max	500	2.23	0.060	0.947	0.020	19,945
Reasenberg max	3,000	2.24	0.065	0.947	0.021	19,945
Reasenberg standard	Single-run	2.20	—	0.950	—	22,981
Reasenberg standard	500	2.24	0.060	0.972	0.021	22,981
Reasenberg standard	3,000	2.24	0.064	0.971	0.023	22,981
Reasenberg min	Single-run	2.30	—	1.000	—	25,316
Reasenberg min	500	2.29	0.094	1.000	0.031	25,316
Reasenberg min	3,000	2.29	0.105	1.003	0.035	25,316

Results are shown for single-run and bootstrap replicates (500 and 3000).

Fixed-window methods (Gruenthal and Gardner and Knopoff), which retain roughly 15%–35% of the events, yield the strongest depressions in b-value (typically in range 0.10–0.25). For example, relative to the observed catalog, under MAXC, an initial b-value equal to 0.88 drops to 0.73 with Gardner and Knopoff and to 0.62 with Gruenthal; with EMR, the b-value decreases from 0.94 to 0.75. Milder fixed-windowing (Uhrhammer), retaining ~70%, preserves b-value close to the observed catalog. The Reasenberg (all configuration, between 75% and 95% retained) b-value results mimic the observed catalog, indicating minimal distortion of the magnitude–frequency slope. The nearest-neighbor approach (40% retained) shows M_c method–dependent behavior: small increases under EMR and MBASS and small decreases for MAXC and GFT but and a more marked drop under MBS (0.17). Because b governs the relative weight of larger magnitudes, even modest shifts are consequential for long-return-period hazard (Marzocchi and Taroni, 2014; Teng and Baker, 2019; Taroni and Akinci, 2021).

CONCLUSIONS

Catalog-based methods offer a simple instrumental approach to compute M_c estimations. They are time-saving and easy to implement; the computation involves only the magnitude vector to infer the completeness from the expected behavior of seismicity (Mignan and Woessner, 2012). Given the observed catalog, starting with a simpler method such as MAXC for an initial estimation of M_c could be practical, especially when the FMD shows a gradual curve (Mignan and Woessner, 2012). This method provides a baseline understanding of seismic completeness, setting the stage for more detailed analyses. The MAXC technique offers several advantages that make it time-saving and easy to handle. First, it relies on simple mathematical assumptions, specifically the calculation of derivatives. This makes it computationally efficient and relatively straightforward to implement. Second, even though MAXC tends to underestimate systematically M_c in case of gradual curved shape FMD (Mignan and Woessner, 2012), it is widely used as starting point to define the range of the potential completeness magnitudes for other methods.

The use of resampling techniques has proven to be highly effective. By resampling the catalog data, it was possible to assess the stability and uncertainty of completeness estimates. Even with a minimum bootstrap value, the completeness results remained stable. Different methods offer varied analytical perspective of M_c, emphasizing that no single approach is universally applicable. Therefore, choosing the appropriate methodology must be contingent on the intended purpose of the study, ensuring that the assessment of M_c aligns with the context and the unique geological features of the region under investigation.

TABLE 6

Completeness Magnitude (M_c) Estimates and *b*-Values (with Standard Deviations $M_{c_{sd}}$, b_{sd}) for Each Catalog Using the Magnitude of Completeness by the *b*-Value Stability (MBS) Method

Catalog	nboot	M_c	$M_{c_{sd}}$	b	b_{sd}	Events
Observed	Single-run	3.10	—	1.19	—	26,300
Observed	500	3.06	0.152	1.201	0.057	26,300
Observed	3,000	3.05	0.165	1.201	0.067	26,300
Gruenthal	Single-run	3.40	—	1.04	—	4,226
Gruenthal	500	3.27	0.312	1.073	0.253	4,226
Gruenthal	3,000	3.29	0.313	1.084	0.299	4,226
Gardner and Knopoff	Single-run	3.10	—	1.08	—	9,498
Gardner and Knopoff	500	3.15	0.258	1.136	0.187	9,498
Gardner and Knopoff	3,000	3.15	0.278	1.140	0.281	9,498
Nearest neighbor	Single-run	2.60	—	1.06	—	10,188
Nearest neighbor	500	2.47	0.276	1.022	0.106	10,188
Nearest neighbor	3,000	2.48	0.274	1.024	0.104	10,188
Uhrhammer	Single-run	2.90	—	1.11	—	18,847
Uhrhammer	500	2.92	0.185	1.128	0.055	18,847
Uhrhammer	3,000	2.94	0.191	1.134	0.062	18,847
Reasenberg max	Single-run	2.90	—	1.07	—	19,945
Reasenberg max	500	2.85	0.297	1.088	0.126	19,945
Reasenberg max	3,000	2.84	0.264	1.082	0.088	19,945
Reasenberg standard	Single-run	2.90	—	1.10	—	22,981
Reasenberg standard	500	2.94	0.257	1.131	0.082	22,981
Reasenberg standard	3,000	2.94	0.262	1.129	0.085	22,981
Reasenberg min	Single-run	2.90	—	1.14	—	25,316
Reasenberg min	500	2.94	0.177	1.156	0.050	25,316
Reasenberg min	3,000	2.94	0.179	1.160	0.057	25,316

Results are shown for single-run and bootstrap replicates (500 and 3000).

The range of M_c-values obtained from different techniques may not always overlap. Such discrepancies arise because these methods do not necessarily adhere to a uniform definition of M_c (Mignan and Woessner, 2012). In summing up the findings of the study, it is crucial to acknowledge that even when a particular technique yields a low uncertainty estimate for the magnitude of completeness, it does not inherently affirm the reliability of the estimation itself. Rather, it suggests that the estimated output is robust within the context of the dataset analyzed. Declustering may have a direct impact on M_c estimation: more aggressive algorithms tend to remove proportionally more small events and can shift M_c upward, which in turn depresses the Gutenberg–Richter *b*-value (Mizrahi *et al.*, 2021; Taroni and Akinci, 2021; Pavlenko and Zavyalov, 2022; Bi *et al.*, 2024).

Lowering the number of events did not always produce more conservative M_c estimates, suggesting the influence of the shape of the FMD and the assumptions of the method used. Using the Gardner and Knopoff declustering algorithm, the MBS completeness results differ markedly from that obtained with nearest-neighbor declustered catalog, which removed a similar number of events yet yield a clearly lower estimate. This contrast shows that changes are driven more by "where" and "how" events are removed than by how many. Declustering often removes earthquakes from high-productivity, high-sensitivity subregions. Considering the entire catalog, these areas contribute many small events that depress the apparent completeness and mask the higher completeness of less sensitive regions. Although waveform overlap after mainshocks briefly suppresses detection of small events, the spatial heterogeneity persists much longer. A successive step may be based on grid M_c method, including the Bayesian approach described by Mignan *et al.* (2011), to quantify it.

DATA AND RESOURCES

The earthquake catalog used in this study was obtained from the Italian National Institute of Geophysics and Volcanology (Istituto Nazionale di Geofisica e Vulcanologia, INGV) through the ISIDe database (ISIDe Working Group, INGV, doi: 10.13127/ISIDe).

DECLARATION OF COMPETING INTERESTS

The authors acknowledge that there are no conflicts of interest recorded.

ACKNOWLEDGMENTS

The authors thank the two anonymous reviewers for their thoughtful and constructive feedback. Their insights guided the revisions and helped the authors refine the presentation and interpretation of the work. The authors believe these changes have enhanced the article's clarity and coherence.

REFERENCES

Abd el-aal, A. E. (2012). Very broadband seismic background noise analysis of permanent good vaulted seismic stations, *J. Seismol.* **17,** doi: 10.1007/s10950-012-9308-5.

Abercrombie, R. E. (1995). Earthquake source scaling relationships from -1 to 5 ML using seismograms recorded at 2.5 km depth, *J. Geophys. Res. Solid Earth* **100,** no. B12, 24,015–24,036.

Aki, K. (1965). Maximum likelihood estimate of b in the formula log N=a-bM and its confidence limits, *Bull. Earthq. Res. Inst. Univ. Tokyo* **43,** 237.

Amini, H. (2014). Comparing Reasenberg and Gruenthal Declustering Methods for North of Iran, *Proc. of the Second European Conf. on Earthquake Engineering and Seismology (2ECEES)*, Istanbul, Türkiye, 25–29 August 2014.

Amorese, D. (2007). Applying a change-point detection method on frequency-magnitude distributions, *Bull. Seismol. Soc. Am.* **97,** no. 5, 1742–1749, doi: 10.1785/0120060181.

Azak, T., D. Kalafat, K. Şeşetyan, and M. B. Demircioğlu (2018). Effects of seismic declustering on seismic hazard assessment: A sensitivity study using the Turkish earthquake catalogue, *Bull. Earthq. Eng.* **16,** no. 8, 3339–3366, doi: 10.1007/s10518-017-0174-y.

Bi, J., C. Song, and F. Cao (2024). Declustering characteristics of the North China Plain seismic belt and its effect on probabilistic seismic hazard analysis, *Sci. Rep.* **14,** no. 1, 22,170, doi: 10.1038/s41598-024-73815-9.

Cao, A. M., and S. S. Gao (2002). Temporal variations of seismic b-values beneath northeastern japan island arc, *Geophys. Res. Lett.* **29,** 48-1.

Cornell, C. A. (1968). Engineering seismic risk analysis, *Bull. Seismol. Soc. Am.* **58,** no. 5, 1583–1606, doi: 10.1785/BSSA0580051583.

D'Alessando, A., L. Greco, S. Scudero, and V. Lauciani (2021). Spectral characterization and spatiotemporal variability of the background seismic noise in Italy, *Earth Space Sci.* **8,** doi: 10.1029/2020EA001579.

Efron, B. (1979). Bootstrap methods: Another look at the jackknife, *Ann. Stat.* **7,** no. 1, 1–26, doi: 10.1214/aos/1176344552.

Gardner, J. K., and L. Knopoff (1974). Is the sequence of earthquakes in southern California, with aftershocks removed, Poissonian? *Bull. Seismol. Soc. Am.* **64,** 1363–1367.

Gomberg, J. (1991). Seismicity and detection/location threshold in the southern Great Basin seismic network, *J. Geophys. Res. Solid Earth* **96,** no. B10, 16,401–16,414.

Gonzalez, A. (2017). The Spanish National Earthquake catalogue: Evolution, precision and completeness, *J. Seismol.* **21,** no. 3, 435–471, doi: 10.1007/s10950-016-9610-8.

Gutenberg, B., and C. F. Richter (1944). Frequency of earthquakes in California, *Bull. Seismol. Soc. Am.* **34,** no. 4, 185–188, doi: 10.1785/BSSA0340040185.

Haukoos, J. S., and R. J. Lewis (2005). Advanced statistics: Bootstrapping confidence intervals for statistics with "difficult" distributions, *Acad. Emerg. Med.* **12,** no. 4, 360–365, doi: 10.1197/j.aem.2004.11.018.

Helmstetter, A., Y. Y. Kagan, and D. D. Jackson (2006). Comparison of short-term and time-independent earthquake forecast models for southern California, *Bull. Seismol. Soc. Am.* **96,** no. 1, 90–106.

Henderson, A. R. (2005). The bootstrap: A technique for data-driven statistics, *Clin. Chim. Acta* **359,** nos. 1/2, 1–26, doi: 10.1016/j.cccn.2005.04.002.

Hollander, M., and D. A. Wolfe (1973). *Nonparametric Statistical Methods*, John Wiley & Sons, New York.

Huang, W. Q., W. X. Li, and X. F. Cao (1994). Completeness analysis of earthquake catalogs in China Main Land II, *Acta Seismol. Sin.* **7,** no. 4, 529–538.

Ishimoto, M., and K. Iida (1939). Observations of earthquakes registered with the microseismograph constructed recently, *Bull. Earthq. Res. Inst.* **17,** 443–478.

Juellyan, J., B. Setiawan, M. Hasan, H. Yunita, M. Sungkar, and T. Saidi (2023). Comparing Gardner-Knopoff, Gruenthal, and Uhrhammer earthquake declustering methods in Aceh, Indonesia, *IOP Conf. Ser.* **1245,** 012010.

Kagan, Y. Y. (2004). Short-term properties of earthquake catalogs and models of earthquake source, *Bull. Seismol. Soc. Am.* **94,** no. 4, 1207–1228, doi: 10.1785/012003098.

Kanamori, H., and D. L. Anderson (1975). Theoretical basis of some empirical relations in seismology, *Bull. Seismol. Soc. Am.* **65,** no. 5, 1073–1095.

Lanzante, J. R. (1996). Resistant, robust and non-parametric techniques for the analysis of climate data, *Int. J. Climatol.* **16,** 1197–1226.

Liu, J., Q. F. Chen, and Y. Chen (1996). Completeness analysis of the seismic catalog in North China region, *Earthquake* **16,** no. 1, 59–67.

Luen, B., and P. B. Stark (2012). Poisson tests of declustered catalogues, *Geophys. J. Int.* **189,** no. 1, 691–700.

Marzocchi, W., and M. Taroni (2014). Some thoughts on declustering in probabilistic seismic-hazard analysis, *Bull. Seismol. Soc. Am.* **104,** no. 4, 1838–1845, doi: 10.1785/0120130300.

Mignan, A. (2012). Functional shape of the earthquake frequency-magnitude distribution and completeness magnitude, *J. Geophys. Res. Solid Earth* **117,** no. B8, doi: 10.1029/2012JB009347.

Mignan, A. (2019a). rseismNet: Earthquake frequency–magnitude distribution and network statistics, GitHub Repository, available at https://github.com/amignan/rseismNet (last accessed November 2025).

Mignan, A., and C. C. Chen (2016). The spatial scale of detected seismicity, *Pure Appl. Geophys.* **173,** 117–124, doi: 10.1007/s00024-015-1133-7.

Mignan, A., and G. Chouliaras (2014). Fifty years of seismic network performance in Greece (1964–2013), *Seismol. Res. Lett.* **85,** 657–667, doi: 10.1785/0220130209.

Mignan, A., and J. Woessner (2012). Estimating the magnitude of completeness for earthquake catalogs, *Commun. Online Resour. Stat. Seism. Anal.*, 1–45, doi: 10.5078/corssa-00180805.

Mignan, A., M. Werner, S. Wiemer, C. Chen, and Y. Wu (2011). Bayesian estimation of the spatially varying completeness magnitude of earthquake catalogs, *Bull. Seismol. Soc. Am.* **101,** 1371–1385, doi: 10.1785/0120100223.

Mizrahi, L., S. Nandan, and S. Wiemer (2021). The effect of declustering on the size distribution of mainshocks, *Seismol. Res. Lett.* **92,** no. 4, 2333–2342, doi: 10.1785/0220200231.

Molchan, G. M., and O. E. Dmitrieva (1992). Aftershock identification: Methods and new approaches, *Geophys. J. Int.* **109,** no. 3, 501–516.

Ogata, Y., and K. Katsura (1993). Analysis of temporal and spatial heterogeneity of magnitude frequency distribution inferred from earthquake catalogues, *Geophys. J. Int.* **113,** 727–738.

Ogata, Y., and K. Katsura (2006). Immediate and updated forecasting of aftershock hazard, *Geophys. Res. Lett.* **33,** L10305 , doi: 10.1029/2006GL025888.
Pavlenko, V. A., and A. D. Zavyalov (2022). Comparative analysis of the methods for estimating the magnitude of completeness of earthquake catalogs, *Izv. Phys. Solid Earth* **58,** 89–105.
Perry, M., and R. Bendick (2024). A comparative analysis of five commonly implemented declustering algorithms, *J. Seismol.* **28,** no. 3, 829–842, doi: 10.1007/s10950-024-10221-8.
Reasenberg, P. A. (1985). Second-order moment of central California seismicity, 1969–1982, *J. Geophys. Res. Solid Earth* **90,** no. B7, 5479–5495.
Ringdal, F. (1975). On the estimation of seismic detection thresholds, *Bull. Seismol. Soc. Am.* **65,** 1631–1642.
Rydelek, P. A., and I. S. Sacks (1989). Testing the completeness of earthquake catalogs and the hypothesis of self-similarity, *Nature* **337,** 251–253.
Schorlemmer, D., and M. C. Gerstenberger (2007). RELM testing center, *Seismol. Res. Lett.* **78,** no. 1, 30–36, doi: 10.1785/gssrl.78.1.30.
Schorlemmer, D., F. Mele, and W. Marzocchi (2010). A completeness analysis of the National Seismic Network of Italy, *J. Geophys. Res. Solid Earth* **115,** no. B4, doi: 10.1029/2008JB006097.
Schorlemmer, D., S. Wiemer, and M. Wyss (2005). Variations in earthquake-size distribution across different stress regimes, *Nature* **437,** 539–542, doi: 10.1038/nature04094.
Sereno, T. J., Jr., and S. R. Bratt (1989). Seismic detection capability at NORESS and implications for the detection threshold of a hypothetical network in the Soviet Union, *J. Geophys. Res. Solid Earth* **94,** no. B8, 10,397–10,414.
Shi, Y., and B. A. Bolt (1982). The standard error of the magnitude frequency b-value, *Bull. Seism. Soc. Am.* **72,** 1677–1687.
Silva, V., H. Crowley, M. Pagani, D. Monelli, and R. Pinho (2014). Development of the OpenQuake engine, the Global Earthquake Model's open-source software, *Nat. Hazards* **72,** 1409–1427, doi: 10.1007/s11069-013-0618-x.
Taroni, M., and A. Akinci (2021). Good practices in PSHA: Declustering, b-value estimation, foreshocks and aftershocks inclusion, *Geophys. J. Int.* **224,** no. 2, 1174–1187, doi: 10.1093/gji/ggaa462.
Teng, G., and J. W. Baker (2019). Seismicity declustering and hazard analysis of the Oklahoma–Kansas region, *Bull. Seismol. Soc. Am.* **109,** no. 6, 2356–2366.
Uhrhammer, R. (1986). Characteristics of Northern and Central California seismicity, *Earthq. Notes* **57,** no. 1, 21.
Van Stiphout, T., J. Zhuang, and D. Marsan (2012). Seismicity declustering, *Commun. Online Resour. Stat. Seismicity Anal.*, doi: 10.5078/corssa52382934.
Wesnousky, S. G. (1994). The Gutenberg-Richter or characteristic earthquake distribution, which is it? *Bull. Seismol. Soc. Am.* **84,** 1940–1958.
Wiemer, S., and M. Wyss (2000). Minimum magnitude of completeness in earthquake catalogs: Examples from Alaska, the Western United States, and Japan, *Bull. Seismol. Soc. Am.* **90,** no. 4, 859–869.
Wilcoxon, F. (1945). Individual comparisons by ranking methods, *Biometrics Bull.* **1,** 80–83.
Woessner, J., and S. Wiemer (2005). Assessing the quality of earthquake catalogues: Estimating the magnitude of completeness and its uncertainty, *Bull. Seismol. Soc. Am.* **95,** no. 2, 684–698.
Wyss, M., A. Hasegawa, S. Wiemer, and N. Umino (1999). Quantitative mapping of precursory seismic quiescence before the 1989, M7.1 off-Sanriku earthquake, Japan, *Ann. Geophys.* **42,** doi: 10.4401/ag-3765.
Xu, W., and M. Gao (2014). Statistical analysis of the completeness of earthquake catalogs in China mainland, *Chin. J. Geophys.* **57,** no. 9, 2802–2812.
Zaliapin, I., and Y. Ben-Zion (2013a). Earthquake clusters in southern California I: Identification and stability, *J. Geophys. Res. Solid Earth* **118,** no. 6, 2847–2864, doi: 10.1002/jgrb.50179.
Zaliapin, I., and Y. Ben-Zion (2013b). Earthquake clusters in southern California II: Classification and relation to physical properties of the crust, *J. Geophys. Res. Solid Earth* **118,** no. 6, 2865–2877, doi: 10.1002/jgrb.50178.
Zaliapin, I., and Y. Ben-Zion (2020). Earthquake declustering using the nearest-neighbor approach in space-time-magnitude domain, *J. Geophys. Res. Solid Earth* **125,** no. 4, e2018JB017120, doi: 10.1029/2018JB017120.
Zuniga, F. R., and M. Wyss (1995). Inadvertent changes in magnitude reported in earthquake catalogs: Their evaluation through b-value estimates, *Bull. Seismol. Soc. Am.* **85,** 1858–1866.

Manuscript received 6 June 2025
Published online 23 February 2026

Long-Term b Value and Seismic Rate from Earthquake Catalogs with Time-Varying Completeness and Uncertain Magnitudes

Cyrielle Colin*[1], Stéphanie Durand[1], Thomas Bodin[2], Marine Laporte[1,2], Guillaume Daniel[3], Pierre Arroucau[3], and David Marsan[4]

ABSTRACT

Seismic hazard assessment relies on the statistical analysis of seismic catalogs. In this context, a robust estimation of the long-term *b* value and seismic rate is required. This assumes that the Magnitude-Frequency Distribution parameters are considered constant over the entire period of the catalog, providing a single set of values for both historical and instrumental records. However a major challenge arises from the differences in size, quality, and completeness between these records. In addition, magnitude uncertainties are often neglected, leading to biased parameter estimates. We propose an approach to jointly estimate the long-term *b* value and seismic rate while explicitly accounting for magnitude uncertainties and temporal variations of completeness through a detection function. The inversion is performed using a Bayesian framework providing a full probabilistic solution, from which posterior distributions, parameter uncertainties and trade-offs can be derived. After illustrating the benefits of the method on synthetic catalogs, we apply it to the seismic catalog of the Alps. We jointly invert for one *b* value and one seismic rate while allowing separate detection functions for the historical and instrumental periods, each with its own level of uncertainty. Our results demonstrate that accounting for both magnitude uncertainties and time-varying detectability leads to improved estimates of seismic parameters. The resulting probabilistic framework provides reliable inputs for probabilistic seismic hazard assessment.

KEY POINTS

- The b value and seismic rate are estimated in a Bayesian framework accounting for magnitude uncertainties.
- The b value, seismic rate, and detection functions are jointly estimated from the full earthquake catalog.
- A fully probabilistic framework for probabilistic seismic hazard assessment is developed, including parameter uncertainties and trade-offs.

INTRODUCTION

The Gutenberg–Richter (GR) law remains the most used empirical relationship to model earthquake recurrence in Probabilistic Seismic Hazard Assessment (PSHA) (Baker, 2008; Stucchi *et al.*, 2011; Grünthal *et al.*, 2018; Martin *et al.*, 2018; Drouet *et al.*, 2020; Danciu *et al.*, 2021; Kumar *et al.*, 2025). It describes the distribution of earthquake magnitudes within a region and a time frame. In Gutenberg and Richter (1944), the formulation of this law reads:

$$\log_{10} N(m) = a - bm, \tag{1}$$

in which $N(m)$ is the total number of events with magnitudes greater than m.

The b value controls the slope of this relation: the larger the b value, the higher the number of small-magnitude events with respect to the number of large-magnitude ones. The b value is commonly close to 1, but has been shown to vary both in time and space for specific regions and time periods (Wiemer and Wyss, 1997; Cao and Gao, 2002; Beauval and Scotti, 2003; Ogata and Katsura, 2006; Gui *et al.*, 2020; Morales-Yáñez *et al.*, 2022). The activity parameter, the a value, corresponds

1. Université Claude Bernard Lyon 1, LGL-TPE, ENS de Lyon, UJM Saint-Etienne, CNRS, Villeurbanne, France, https://orcid.org/0009-0000-5930-0188 (CC); https://orcid.org/0000-0002-2415-6793 (SD); https://orcid.org/0000-0001-8978-0661 (ML); 2. Instituto de Ciencias del Mar (ICM) - CSIC, Barcelona, Spain, https://orcid.org/0000-0002-7393-6112 (TB); 3. Electricité de France (EDF)-DT-TEGG, Aix-en-Provence, France, https://orcid.org/0000-0002-1018-411X (GD); https://orcid.org/0000-0003-4142-227X (PA); 4. Université de Savoie Mont Blanc, Chambéry, France

*Corresponding author: cyrielle.colin@univ-lyon1.fr

Cite this article as Colin, C., S. Durand, T. Bodin, M. Laporte, G. Daniel, P. Arroucau, and D. Marsan (2026). Long-Term *b* Value and Seismic Rate from Earthquake Catalogs with Time-Varying Completeness and Uncertain Magnitudes, *Bull. Seismol. Soc. Am.* **116**, 963–983, doi: 10.1785/0120250240 to the logarithm of the number of events with magnitude M higher or equal to zero, that is, $a = \log_{10}(N_{M\geq 0})$. The a value can also be related to the seismic rate λ, defined as the expected number of events with magnitude higher than or equal to 0 per unit time because $N(M \geq 0) = \lambda \Delta T$, in which ΔT is the considered time period. However, in PSHA the a value is generally defined per unit of time, as an annual rate of exceedance $a_{\mathrm{annual}} = \log_{10}(\lambda)$.

Estimating the b value, the a value, their associated uncertainties, and covariances is crucial for seismic hazard studies (e.g., Taroni and Akinci, 2021). Several methods have been recently developed to study temporal variations of b value (Van der Elst, 2021; Laporte *et al.*, 2025) and a value (Van der Elst and Page, 2023) due to rapid changes in seismicity related to the seismic cycle. In PSHA, however, the goal is to estimate long-term b and a values. A resulting well-known challenge is that PSHA relies on seismic catalogs that combine both historical and instrumental data, with large variations in magnitude uncertainties and detection. Figure 1 illustrates the challenges raised by long-term catalogs. In Figure 1a, we present the historical catalog of France that spans over more than 1500 yr, providing valuable information about rare, large-magnitude earthquakes, but suffers from low detectability (i.e., the ability to detect small events) due to the absence of modern instrumentation. In contrast, the instrumental catalog of France shown in Figure 1a, covers 50 yr only but includes many smaller events (high detectability) thanks to the progressive deployment of seismic networks. This contrast in detectability between historical and instrumental catalogs is also visible on their respective histograms, shown in Figure 1b. The instrumental catalog contains more small earthquakes because of higher detectability. In addition, on top of the temporal variation of detectability, the uncertainties associated with magnitude estimates are substantially different between historical (typically greater than 0.5) and instrumental datasets (between 0.2 and 0.5), as the methods for estimating magnitudes differ significantly. Therefore, to maximize the level of information for PSHA, it is essential to integrate both temporal changes in detectability and in magnitude uncertainties (Rhoades, 1996; Beauval and Scotti, 2004).

To efficiently estimate the parameters of the GR law, it is necessary to account for detectability and catalog incompleteness. Indeed, the GR law is only valid under the assumption that all events are detected. Therefore, classical methods truncate catalogs and only keep magnitudes greater than or equal to a completeness magnitude M_c for estimating b (Aki, 1965; Utsu, 1966). Under this condition, Aki (1965) and Utsu (1966) show that the b value can be calculated using a Maximum-Likelihood Estimation (MLE) following:

$$\beta = \frac{1}{\overline{m} - M_c}, \tag{2}$$

in which $\beta = b \times ln(10)$, and $\overline{m}$ is the mean of the magnitudes greater than M_c, the completeness magnitude. As a result, the estimation of the parameters of the GR law strongly depends on the choice of M_c. A wrong M_c leads to biased parameters. If M_c is chosen too low, the Magnitude-Frequency Distribution (MFD) is no longer well approximated by an exponential over the full range of magnitudes, and if M_c is too high, the number of events is reduced, which affects the accuracy of the b value and the resulting a value estimates.

An additional complexity comes from the fact that M_c can vary in time and space, and also depends on the tectonic context. Some studies account for varying completeness levels for the estimation of both the b value and the a value (Molchan *et al.*, 1970; Weichert, 1980; Kijko and Sellevoll, 1989, 1992; Kijko and Smit, 2012; Dutfoy, 2020, 2025). The approach by Weichert (1980) has gained popularity for seismic hazard studies due to its ability to incorporate temporally varying M_c. In parallel, numerous methods have been developed over the last half-century to estimate the magnitude of completeness (Stepp, 1972; Tinti and Mulargia, 1985b; Wiemer and Wyss, 2000; Woessner and Wiemer, 2005; Amorèse, 2007; Mignan *et al.*, 2011; Hakimhashemi and Grünthal, 2012). This continues to be an important field of research, as shown by more recent studies (Lombardi, 2021; Godano and Petrillo, 2023; Godano *et al.*, 2024). However, the determination of M_c remains challenging, and no unique solution has yet emerged (Kijko and Smit, 2017).

To avoid the problem of truncating catalogs above M_c and discarding small events, some methods propose to modulate the GR law with a detection function or to use a minimum magnitude difference (Ringdal, 1975, 1986; Von Seggern and Blandford, 1976; Habermann, 1983; Veneziano and Van Dyck, 1987; Ringdal and Kævrna, 1992; Ogata and Katsura, 1993; Woessner and Wiemer, 2005; Daniel *et al.*, 2008; Kijko and Smit, 2017; Van der Elst, 2021; Van der Elst and Page, 2023; Lippiello and Petrillo, 2024; Laporte *et al.*, 2025). The detection function corresponds to the probability of detecting a seismic event of a given magnitude, which allows us to model the gradual transition from incompleteness to completeness. In this way, instead of setting an arbitrary threshold on magnitudes, all events in the catalog can be used for the inference process. As with the completeness magnitude, the detection function can vary over time and in space, that can be accounted for (see e.g., Laporte *et al.*, 2025, for an application that includes temporal variations in detectability).

Methods to estimate GR law parameters also need to take magnitude uncertainties into account (Kijko and Sellevoll, 1992; Kijko *et al.*, 2016). Indeed, it has been shown that parameters a and b may be slightly overestimated when neglecting magnitude uncertainties (Tinti and Mulargia, 1985a; Rhoades, 1996; Rhoades and Dowrick, 2000). As suggested in Marzocchi and Sandri (2003), this effect is particularly strong for regions of moderate seismicity, in which data are sparse, and uncertainties play a significant role. In addition, for catalogs covering a long period (historical and instrumental), such as those used

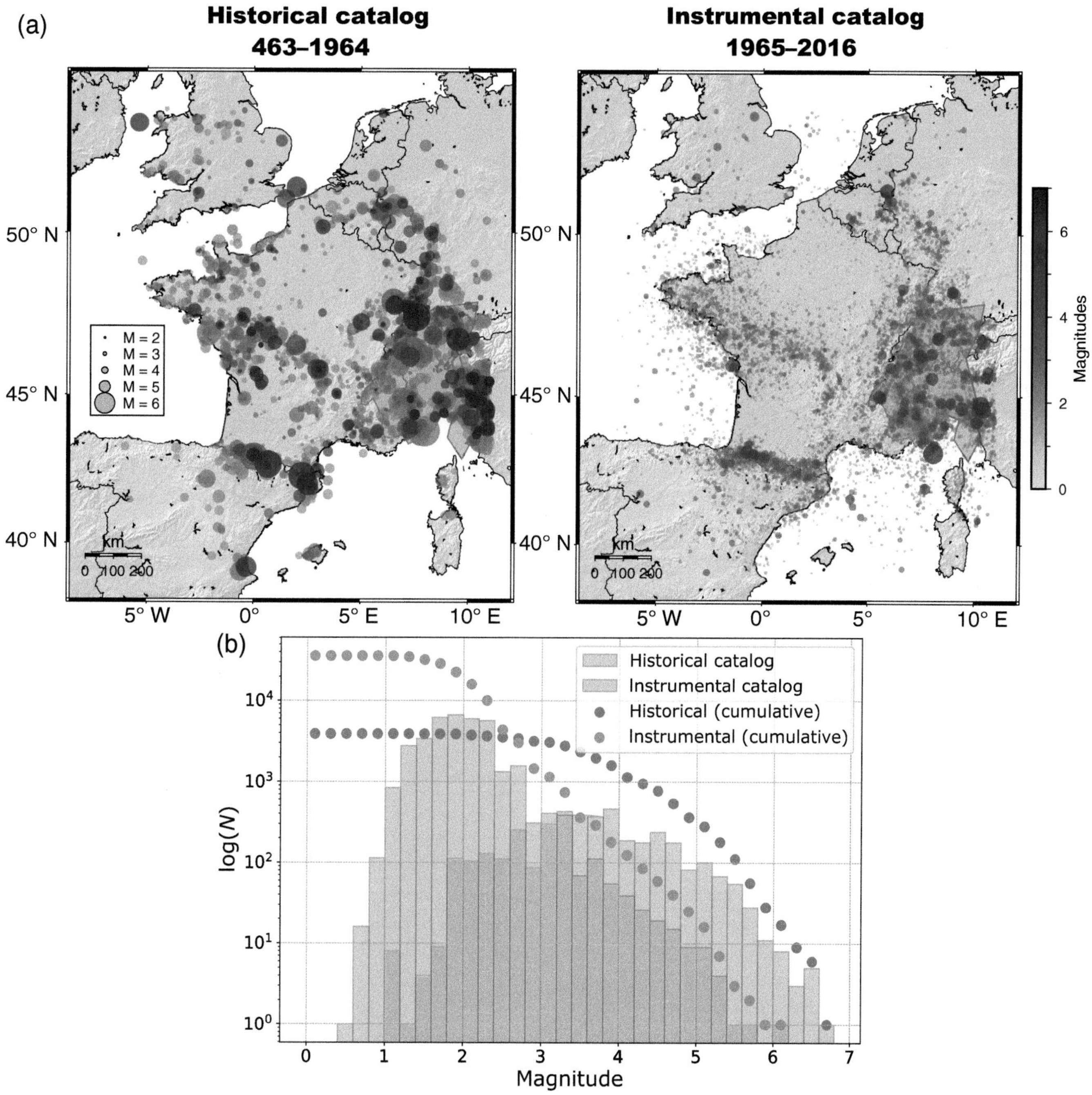

Figure 1. Historical and instrumental catalogs of metropolitan France spanning the time period from 463 to 2016. (a) The earthquake catalog is divided in two subcatalogs, the historical catalog from 463 to 1964 and the instrumental catalog from 1965 to 2016. The orange zone corresponds to the Alpine domain considered in this study. (b) Magnitude-Frequency Distribution (MFD), cumulative (colored circles) or not (colored histograms), from the historical (purple) and instrumental (orange) catalogs of metropolitan France (Drouet *et al.*, 2020). The color version of this figure is available only in the electronic edition.

in PSHA studies, uncertainties can be inhomogeneous through time. Although having a certain degree of standardization and being relatively accurate, uncertainties from the instrumental part may come from various sources, such as seismic noise, the number of recording stations, homogenization during magnitude scale conversion (e.g., M_w M_l, M_0, Baumont *et al.*, 2018; Manchuel *et al.*, 2018; Traversa *et al.*, 2018) or unknown focal mechanism (Daniel, 2014). In contrast, historical magnitudes are inverted for or converted from macroseismic intensities based on testimonies of earthquake consequences on people and buildings (Beauval and Scotti, 2004; Manchuel *et al.*, 2018). Their uncertainties are therefore larger and more difficult to quantify. Generally, Gaussian or uniform distributions are used to model uncertainties, depending on the type of magnitude (historical or instrumental) (Tinti and Mulargia, 1985a; Kijko *et al.*, 2016). For example, Beauval and Scotti (2004) used a Gaussian distribution for instrumental uncertainties and a uniform distribution for historical uncertainties.

Current approaches for estimating the b value and the a value are mainly frequentist, in which the solution is a set of parameters that maximizes a likelihood function. These optimization methods are based on partial derivatives to explore the parameter space locally, and they do not account for the nonuniqueness of the solution (Aki, 1965; Weichert, 1980). Another limitation of frequentist methods is that the parameters are often not estimated jointly; that is, one first estimates the b value and then derives its optimal a value counterpart. These two parameters are, however, strongly correlated, and this process can lead to bias in their estimation. On the contrary, Bayesian methods offer a more flexible framework by allowing parameters to be inferred simultaneously. They enable the quantification and propagation of uncertainties, and provide a complete posterior distribution of the solution (with covariances between model parameters) rather than a single point estimate. Numerical methods exist to explore and approximate the posterior distributions, such as Markov chain Monte Carlo (McMC) algorithms (Metropolis *et al.*, 1953; Hastings, 1970; Sambridge *et al.*, 2006; Gallagher *et al.*, 2009).

To address all these challenges, we propose a new method in which a detection function is used to model the loss of detectability for small earthquakes and in which magnitude uncertainties are explicitly accounted for. This allows us to use the full catalog to estimate our parameters, with no truncation. The a and b values are jointly estimated together with the parameters of the detection function. In the following sections, we first present the theory behind the method. We then present results obtained for a synthetic catalog and compare these results with those obtained with frequentist approaches such as Aki (1965) and Dutfoy (2020). We also compare these results with the recent b-positive and a-positive methods (Van der Elst, 2021; Van der Elst and Page, 2023). Our synthetic tests demonstrate the importance of incorporating magnitude uncertainties in the likelihood as well as time variations of the detection function. Finally, we apply this algorithm to the French catalog for the Alps, accounting for both time-varying detection and magnitude uncertainties.

METHODS

Here, we present the Bayesian framework used to characterize the parameters of the GR law. We first present the likelihood function for observed magnitudes, and then the Poisson likelihood for the number of detected events. Then, these two likelihood functions are combined to jointly estimate the b value, the seismic rate λ, and the parameters of the detection function. We finally generalize this approach to catalogs using a time-varying detection function.

Magnitude-frequency distibution

Modeling incompleteness with a detection function.

The dataset is an earthquake catalog with N observed events of magnitudes m_i ($i = 1,\ldots,N$):

$$\mathbf{m} = [m_1,m_2,\ldots,m_N]. \tag{3}$$

It is accepted that the distribution of magnitudes follows an exponential law for which the exponent is β, directly related to the b value ($\beta = b \times \ln(10)$). However, this is only valid above a completeness magnitude M_c due to detection issues, as illustrated in Figure 1b. Therefore, for $m_i \geq M_c$, the probability to observe m_i knowing β is given by the following likelihood distribution:

$$P_{\mathrm{GR}}(m_i|\beta) = \beta e^{-\beta(m_i - M_c)}. \tag{4}$$

This is the classical expression involved in the b value estimation methods that requires a truncation of the catalog above the completeness magnitude M_c. In this study, we instead model the entire MFD of detected earthquakes, even below this completeness threshold. For this purpose, we modulate the exponential GR law (Fig. 2a) with a detection function, denoted $q(m)$ (Fig. 2b). The likelihood becomes

$$P_{\mathrm{GR}}(m_i|\beta,\mu,\sigma) = \frac{1}{K} q(m_i) e^{-\beta m_i}, \tag{5}$$

and is illustrated in Figure 2c. K is a normalization constant used to normalize the probability distribution such that its integral is set equal to 1 for magnitudes above $m_{\min}$ (i.e., minimum magnitude of the dataset):

$$K = \int_{m_{\min}}^{\infty} q(m) e^{-\beta m} dm, \tag{6}$$

K is represented by the pink shaded area in Figure 2c. Assuming that the amplitude of seismic noise follows a Gaussian distribution, the probability to detect an event of magnitude m can be described by an error function, characterized by two parameters μ and σ:

$$q(m) = \frac{1}{2} + \frac{1}{2} \mathrm{erf}\left(\frac{m - \mu}{\sqrt{2}\sigma}\right), \tag{7}$$

(Ringdal, 1975; Ogata and Katsura, 1993; Daniel *et al.*, 2008). This detection function (shown in Fig. 2b) implies that earthquakes with magnitude m equal to μ have a 50% probability of being detected. This probability grows to 84% when $m = \mu + \sigma$. This 84% threshold can be considered as the equivalent of a completeness magnitude (Daniel *et al.*, 2008). In the case of an error function, equation (6) can be solved with a closed-form solution:

$$K = \frac{1}{\beta} q(m_{\min}) e^{-\beta m_{\min}} + e^{\frac{\sigma^2 \beta^2}{2} - \beta\mu} [1 - q(m_{\min} + \sigma^2 \beta)]. \tag{8}$$

Considering that earthquake magnitudes are independent of each other, the likelihood of observing the entire dataset given β, μ, σ, denoted $P(\mathbf{m}|\beta,\mu,\sigma)$, is the product of individual probabilities (equation 5), as in Ogata and Katsura (1993):

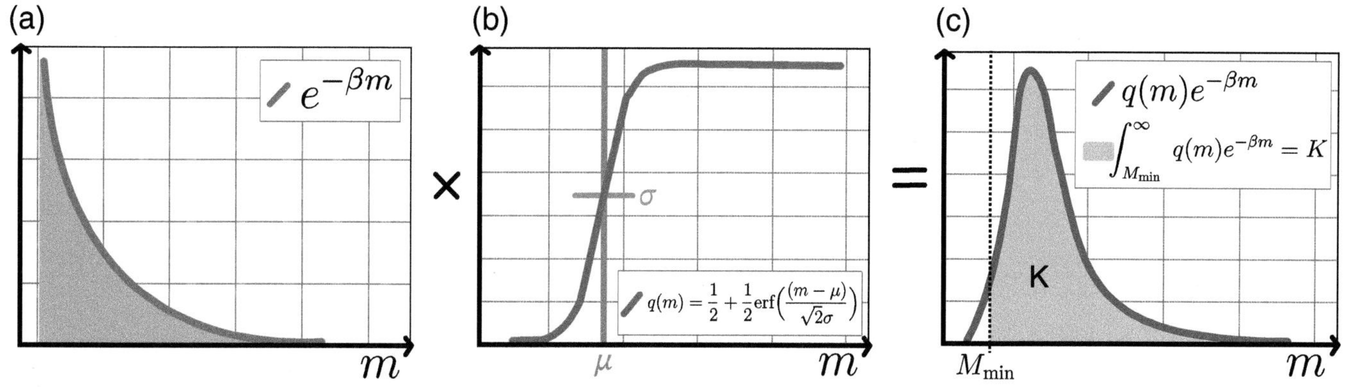

Figure 2. (a) Probability of occurrence: Gutenberg–Richter law modeled by an exponential law with the exponent β. (b) Probability of detection: detection function $q(m)$, here defined as an error function (see equation 7) characterized by two parameters μ and σ (Ogata and Katsura, 1993). (c) Probability of observation: product of the exponential law (a) with the detection function (b), as in equation (9). K, the normalizing constant, corresponds to the area beneath the curve from $M_{\min}$ to ∞ (pink-shaded area). The color version of this figure is available only in the electronic edition.

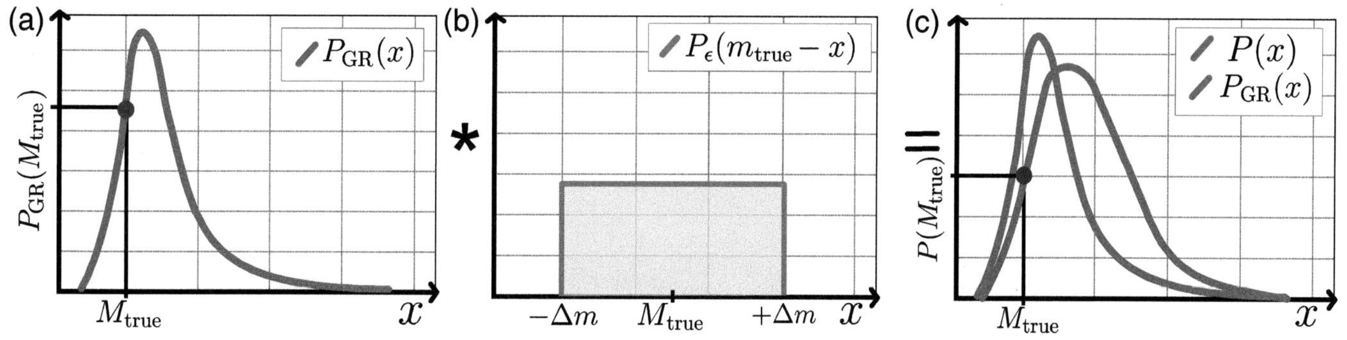

Figure 3. (a) P_{GR}, the Gutenberg–Richter law modulated by a detection function. (b) Distribution of magnitude errors P_ϵ, here chosen to be a uniform law. (c) $P(x)$ the convolution between P_{GR} and P_ϵ giving the distribution of observed magnitudes when accounting for their uncertainties (purple curve). The color version of this figure is available only in the electronic edition.

$$P(\mathbf{m}|\beta,\mu,\sigma) = \prod_i^N P_{\mathrm{GR}}(m_i|\beta,\mu,\sigma) = \left(\frac{1}{K}\right)^N e^{-\beta N \overline{m}} \prod_i^N q(m_i), \tag{9}$$

in which $\overline{m}$ is the mean magnitude,

$$\overline{m} = \frac{1}{N}\sum_{i=1}^{N} m_i. \tag{10}$$

Equation (9) is equivalent to what is developed in Ogata and Katsura (1993).

Accounting for magnitude uncertainties. Now, let us take into account the uncertainties associated with each observed magnitude m_i, which can be written as the sum of two random variables:

$$m_i = m_{\mathrm{true}} + \epsilon, \tag{11}$$

in which m_{true}, the true magnitude, follows the GR distribution P_{GR} (Fig. 3a) as given in equation (5) and the error on the magnitude ϵ follows a distribution P_ϵ. The distribution of the sum of two random and independent variables can be computed by convolving their individual distributions. Therefore:

$$P(m_i) = \int_{-\infty}^{+\infty} P_{\mathrm{GR}}(x)P_\epsilon(m_i - x)dx. \tag{12}$$

Equation (12) is valid for any P_ϵ. For instance, for magnitude errors following a normal distribution $\mathcal{N}$, characterized by a variance Δm^2, the likelihood of observing a given magnitude is

$$P(m_i|\beta,\mu,\sigma) = \int_{-\infty}^{+\infty} \frac{1}{K} q(x)e^{-\beta x}\mathcal{N}(x|m_i,\Delta m^2)dx. \tag{13}$$

However, in this study, we will detail the case where the magnitude errors follow a uniform distribution $\mathcal{U}$ in the range $[-\Delta m_i; +\Delta m_i]$, as shown in Figure 3b. In this case, we can rewrite the likelihood of observing a given magnitude as

$$P(m_i|\beta,\mu,\sigma) = \int_{-\infty}^{+\infty} \frac{1}{K} q(x) e^{-\beta x} \mathcal{U}_{-\Delta m_i}^{+\Delta m_i}(m_i - x) dx$$
$$= \frac{1}{2K\Delta m_i} \int_{m_i^{\text{inf}}}^{m_i^{\text{sup}}} q(x) e^{-\beta x} dx, \quad (14)$$

with,

$$m_i^{\text{inf}} = m_i - \Delta m_i m_i^{\text{sup}} = m_i + \Delta m_i, \quad (15)$$

This integral can be solved in a closed-form solution (Fig. 3c):

$$P(m_i|\beta,\mu,\sigma) = \frac{1}{2\beta K \Delta m_i} (\mathrm{e}^{-\beta \mathrm{m}_i^{\text{inf}}} \mathrm{q}(\mathrm{m}_i^{\text{inf}}) - \mathrm{e}^{-\beta \mathrm{m}_i^{\text{sup}}} \mathrm{q}(\mathrm{m}_i^{\text{sup}})$$
$$+ e^{\frac{\sigma^2\beta^2}{2} - \beta\mu} [q(m_i^{\text{sup}} + \sigma^2\beta) - q(m_i^{\text{inf}} + \sigma^2\beta)]). \quad (16)$$

Again, considering that the magnitudes are independent, the likelihood of observing the whole dataset, $P(\mathbf{m}|\beta,\mu,\sigma)$, is given by the product of all individual likelihoods (equation 16):

$$P(\mathbf{m}|\beta,\mu,\sigma) = \prod_i^N P(m_i|\beta,\mu,\sigma), \quad (17)$$

which gives

$$P(\mathbf{m}|\beta,\mu,\sigma) = \left(\frac{1}{2\beta K}\right)^N \prod_{i=1}^N \frac{1}{\Delta m_i} \left(e^{-\beta m_i^{\text{inf}}} q(m_i^{\text{inf}}) - e^{-\beta m_i^{\text{sup}}} q(m_i^{\text{sup}}) \right.$$
$$\left. + e^{\frac{\sigma^2\beta^2}{2} - \beta\mu} \left[q(m_i^{\text{sup}} + \sigma^2\beta) - q(m_i^{\text{inf}} + \sigma^2\beta) \right] \right). \quad (18)$$

Seismic rate. The a value in the GR law corresponds to the logarithm of the expected number of events with magnitude greater than zero. It is also linked to the seismic rate λ as

$$a = \log_{10}(\lambda \Delta T) = \log_{10}(N_{M \geq 0}), \quad (19)$$

in which λ is the number of events with magnitude greater than zero per unit time, and ΔT, the time range of the catalog. With this definition, a is proportional to the logarithm of the number of events with magnitude greater than or equal to zero. Given the seismic rate λ, the probability of having N events in a time interval ΔT is given by a Poisson law:

$$P(N|\lambda) = \frac{(\lambda \Delta T)^N e^{-\lambda \Delta T}}{N!}. \quad (20)$$

Note that this approach is different from the point process of Ogata and Katsura (1993). In their study, the seismic rate is not part of the likelihood, while here the seismic rate is treated as an independent random variable.

In our case, not all events are detected because of network detectability issues. The true seismic rate λ is thus different from the observed seismic rate, denoted $\tilde{\lambda}$. This is illustrated in Figure 4. The ratio $\tilde{\lambda}/\lambda$ is given by the following ratio of integrals (see Fig. 4):

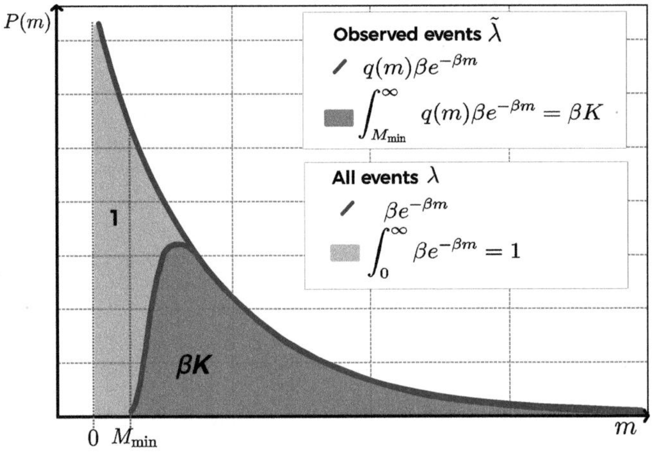

Figure 4. Distributions of observed events (pink curve) and all events, including non-detected ones (gray curve). $\tilde{\lambda}$ is proportional to the pink-shaded area and λ to the gray-shaded area. The color version of this figure is available only in the electronic edition.

$$\frac{\tilde{\lambda}}{\lambda} = \frac{\int_{m_{\min}}^{\infty} q(m)\beta e^{-\beta m} \mathrm{d}m}{\int_0^{\infty} \beta e^{-\beta m} \mathrm{d}m} = \beta K, \quad (21)$$

with K given in equation (6). Graphically, equation (21) can be seen as taking the ratio between the pink and gray-shaded areas presented in Figure 4. Finally, for a given observed catalog, the likelihood of observing N events in a period of time ΔT is thus:

$$P(N|\beta,\lambda,\mu,\sigma) = \frac{(\tilde{\lambda}\Delta T)^N}{N!} e^{-\tilde{\lambda}\Delta T} = \frac{(\beta K \lambda \Delta T)^N}{N!} e^{-\beta K \lambda \Delta T}. \quad (22)$$

Note that $P(N|\beta,\lambda,\mu,\sigma)$ also depends on the detection function parameterized with μ and σ through the normalization constant K. For example, because μ increases, fewer events will be detected, and the observed number of events N will be reduced.

Joint likelihood for magnitudes and number of events

In this work, we will consider time scales larger than the seismic cycle, which allows us to assume a constant b value and seismic rate. We also assume that earthquake magnitudes and their times of occurrence are independent (Kagan, 2002; Helmstetter *et al.*, 2006). This means that the size of an earthquake (magnitude) does not influence the timing of subsequent events. Although the assumption of independence is widely applied, it is worth noting that in certain cases, such as aftershock sequences or induced seismicity, this assumption does not hold. In these cases, time-dependent models (like the Epidemic-Type Aftershock Sequences, or ETAS, model) that account for dependencies between occurrence time and magnitude should be used. Otherwise, the catalog should be preliminarily declustered (Ogata, 1988, 1999; Zhuang *et al.*, 2002). However, for many tectonic regions and long-term seismic hazard assessment, the assumption of independence between earthquake magnitudes and times remains a reasonable and practical simplification. With this assumption, the joint probability of magnitudes and occurrences can be written as

$$\mathcal{P}(\mathbf{m},N|\beta,\mu,\sigma,\lambda) = P(\mathbf{m}|\beta,\mu,\sigma) \times P(N|\beta,\lambda,\mu,\sigma). \tag{23}$$

Thus, the full likelihood distribution can then be computed by multiplying equations (18) and (22). Conveniently, some terms cancel out, and some constants that do not depend on our unknown parameters β,λ,μ,σ, can be removed ($\frac{\Delta T}{2N!}$). This leads to the following formula for the joint likelihood for observed magnitudes $\mathbf{m}$ and number of events N knowing β,λ,μ,σ:

$$\mathcal{P}(\mathbf{m},N|\beta,\lambda,\mu,\sigma) \sim \prod_{i=1}^{N} \frac{1}{\Delta m_i}\Bigg(-e^{-\beta m_i^{\text{sup}}} q(m_i^{\text{sup}}) + e^{-\beta m_i^{\text{inf}}} q(m_i^{\text{sup}}) + e^{\frac{\sigma^2\beta^2}{2}-\beta\mu}\Big[q(m_i^{\text{sup}}+\sigma^2\beta) - q(m_i^{\text{inf}}+\sigma^2\beta)\Big]\Bigg) \times \lambda^N e^{-\beta K\lambda\Delta T}, \tag{24}$$

It is important to recall that equation (24) holds for an error detection function and uniform magnitude uncertainties. These choices might not be appropriate for every application. We thus develop in the Appendix all the equations to get the joint likelihood, equation (24), for Gaussian magnitude uncertainties and another detection function.

Combining different periods with different detectability

Equation (24) is only valid for a catalog in which the detectability does not vary with time. One way to account for the temporal variations of the detection function (i.e., temporal changes in μ and σ) is to split the catalog into smaller subcatalogs as illustrated in Figure 5. In this study, the times of change will be fixed. The parameters β and λ will be treated as constant over time, which is a common assumption in PSHA studies, for example, Baker (2008) and Drouet *et al.* (2020). For J periods, we therefore invert for one single pair of β and λ values, and J detection functions characterized by μ_j,σ_j, with $j \in [1,J]$. The ensemble of model parameters Ω to be estimated can then be written as

$$\Omega = [\beta,\lambda,\mu_1,\sigma_1,\ldots,\mu_J,\sigma_J], \tag{25}$$

and the entire set of observed data as

$$\overline{\mathbf{m}} = [\mathbf{m}_1,\mathbf{m}_2,\ldots,\mathbf{m}_J],\mathbf{N} = [N_1,N_2,\ldots,N_J], \tag{26}$$

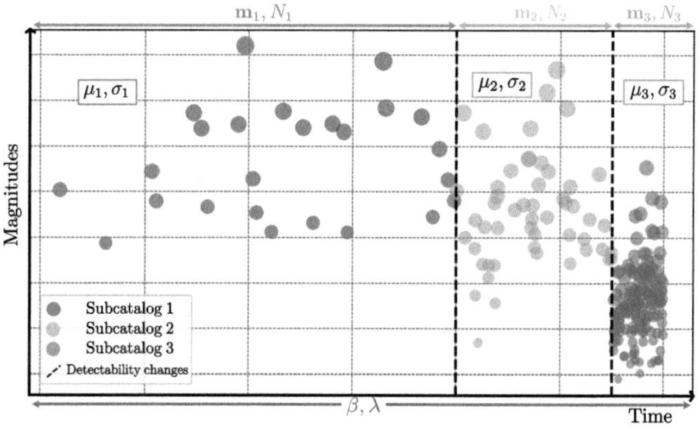

Figure 5. Example of a catalog with two changes of the detection function (vertical dashed lines). Each subcatalog ($\mathbf{m}_1$, $\mathbf{m}_2$, $\mathbf{m}_3$) is characterized by a different detection function (μ_1, σ_1, μ_2, σ_2, μ_3, σ_3), and β and λ remain constant for the whole period of time, an assumption only valid when considering time scales larger than the seismic cycle. The color version of this figure is available only in the electronic edition.

in which $\mathbf{m}_j$ is a subcatalog for period j, which contains N_j events. The magnitudes and number of events in each subcatalog being independent, the likelihood for the entire catalog can be written by taking the product of likelihoods in each period (see equation 24):

$$\mathcal{P}(\overline{\mathbf{m}},\mathbf{N}|\Omega) = \prod_{j=1}^{J} \mathcal{P}(\mathbf{m}_j,N_j|\beta,\lambda,\mu_j,\sigma_j). \tag{27}$$

Inversion using a Bayesian framework

Equation (27) could be used to estimate model parameters Ω that maximize the likelihood (Aki, 1965; Utsu, 1966; Weichert, 1980). However, here, we adopt a Bayesian framework that provides a full posterior distribution of solutions $\mathcal{P}$ which includes parameter trade-offs and uncertainties. According to Bayes' theorem, $\mathcal{P}(\Omega|\overline{\mathbf{m}},\mathbf{N})$ is proportional to the product between the prior distribution and the likelihood function $\mathcal{P}(\overline{\mathbf{m}},\mathbf{N}|\Omega)$.

$$\mathcal{P}(\Omega|\overline{\mathbf{m}},\mathbf{N}) \propto \mathcal{P}(\Omega)\mathcal{P}(\overline{\mathbf{m}},\mathbf{N}|\Omega). \tag{28}$$

In this work, we assign independent prior distributions to the parameters. Although the data may reveal correlations between these parameters, our prior knowledge about each is treated as independent. This assumption greatly simplifies the Bayesian inference process. For each parameter, we adopt a uniform prior distribution over a fixed range, based on realistic values derived from the literature. These bounds should be tailored to the specific seismotectonic context and the detectability of earthquakes over the period covered by the catalog. The range of b values can be wide; it can be extended or truncated depending on the context. In the literature, b values between

0.7 and 1.3 are commonly observed in intraplate regions. Larger variations of b values are observed in the context of geothermal or volcanic activity. In such cases, the b value may exceed 2.0 (Farrell *et al.*, 2009; Rodríguez-Pérez *et al.*, 2021). In a tectonic context, such as the San Andreas zone, the b value can be less than 0.5 (Wiemer and Wyss, 1997; Wyss *et al.*, 2004). Similarly, for the activity parameter (i.e., a value), regions like subduction zones have high a values due to the large seismic activity, but metropolitan France is an intraplate region and the seismic activity is low to moderate. The choice of the prior for μ must be adjusted and guided by the level of detectability of the seismic network and the approximated variations of completeness over the studied time; a reasonable prior range for μ is between 0.5 and 6.5. The prior distribution on σ can be set between 0.01 and 1.0. As we will see in the following sections, the solution is never clipped by the bounds of the prior. This uninformative prior makes the solution independent on the choice of the bounds.

The posterior distribution (equation 28) is approximated using an McMC algorithm following the Metropolis–Hastings scheme (Metropolis *et al.*, 1953; Hastings, 1970). This method generates a large set of models Ω distributed according to the posterior distribution. At each step, a new set of model parameters is proposed by perturbing the current one, and accepted or rejected based on the posterior probability ratio. A normal distribution is typically used for proposing models, with its variance tuned to achieve an acceptance rate of about 40%. After a burn-in phase (50,000 iterations), the chain converges, and samples are drawn from the stationary distribution $\mathcal{P}(\Omega|\overline{\mathbf{m}})$. For all tests and applications, we run the McMC for at least 300,000 iterations to fully explore the parameter space. The posterior mean is then approximated by averaging the sampled models. For details about the McMC algorithm, we refer the reader to Gallagher *et al.* (2009) and Sambridge and Gallagher (2021).

APPLICATION TO SYNTHETIC CATALOG WITH MAGNITUDES UNCERTAINTIES

Catalog with a constant detection function

Let us consider a catalog with a constant detection function over the whole time period, implying that the parameters μ and σ are constants. We build a synthetic catalog of 1000 independent magnitudes that are randomly drawn from a Gutenberg–Richter law characterized by a b value of 1.0 and modulated by an error detection function defined by $\mu = 3.0$ and $\sigma = 0.5$ (see Fig. 6k). To mimic magnitude errors, we perturb each independent magnitude m_i with a random error drawn from a uniform law over the interval $[m_i - \Delta m, m_i + \Delta m]$. Occurrence times follow a Poisson law characterized by a seismic rate $\lambda = 2500$, equivalent to $a = \log_{10}(\lambda \Delta T) = 5.70$, with ΔT the duration of the catalog.

To estimate the set of parameters (b,a,μ,σ), we sample the posterior distribution using an McMC approach with 500,000 iterations. This ensemble of models is used to approximate the 4D posterior density function $\mathcal{P}(\Omega|\overline{\mathbf{m}},\mathbf{N})$. To visualize this 4D probabilistic solution, 1D marginal distributions are plotted in Figure 6a–d and 2D mariginal distributions are plotted in Figure 6e–j. The 1D marginal distributions on each parameter can be characterized by their mean and standard deviation. The mean ± 1 standard deviation is shown with dotted lines in Figure 6a–d. The 2D marginals are useful to show the trade-offs and correlations between pairs of parameters. Figure 6 shows that the McMC recovers well the values of the four parameters. We can use the average values for each parameter to build the predicted MFD (blue line, Fig. 6k) and compare it with the synthetic catalog. This method permits the use of all 1000 earthquakes with their associated uncertainties to estimate the a and b parameters, with no need to truncate the dataset above a completeness threshold as usually done (Aki, 1965; Weichert, 1980).

Comparison with the standard Aki's approach

We now compare our method with the maximum likelihood approach of Aki (1965), which only uses events with magnitude above a predetermined completeness threshold. We reuse the synthetic catalog presented in the previous section (with errors added to the magnitudes). Aki's method does not account for magnitude uncertainties. For a fair comparison, we therefore first run our method by assuming there are no errors on the observed magnitudes, by setting $\Delta m = 0$ in the likelihood (see Fig. 7). For Aki's method (see equation 2), we invert for b for a range of completeness magnitudes M_c and then use the inferred b to estimate $a = \log_{10}(N) + bM_c$ (colored dots Fig. 7). Figure 7 summarizes the results. The results from Aki's method show two effects. When the catalog is cut at a magnitude lower than M_c, the estimate is incorrect as the loss of detection is not modeled and b is underestimated (and so is a). When the catalog is truncated at a magnitude larger than M_c, the results still fluctuate significantly due to the introduction of an error to the magnitude values. Noting that an overestimated completeness threshold also leads to overestimated b values (Lolli *et al.*, 2014). Moreover, the uncertainties in the estimated b value increase when truncating at a magnitude larger than M_c due to the reduced number of magnitudes used in the MLE (Kijko and Smit, 2012).

These values are compared with the 2D marginal distributions obtained with our method by setting $\Delta m = 0$ in the likelihood (blue-shaded area in Fig. 7). Note that both the blue 2D density and the posterior mean (blue dot) or Aki's results are far from real values (red cross). This is because magnitude uncertainties have been neglected.

We then run our method, including the correct level of magnitude uncertainties in the likelihood, $\Delta m = 0.5$ for our catalog (see Fig. 7). The obtained 2D posterior distribution is plotted in green in Figure 7. This posterior distribution

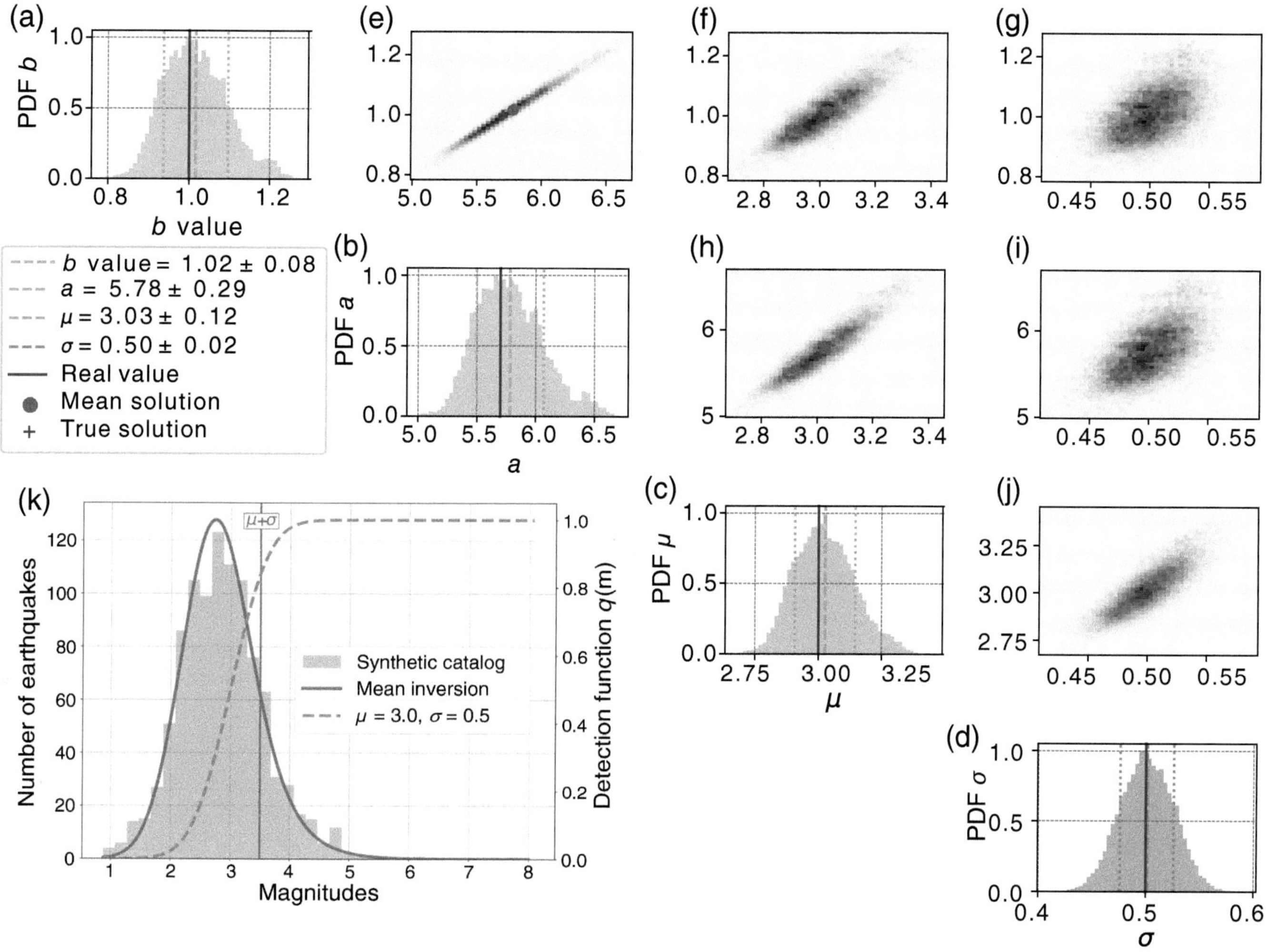

Figure 6. 1D (a–d) and 2D (e–j) marginal posterior distributions obtained after the Markov chain Monte Carlo (McMC) exploration. The four 1D marginal distributions for each parameter are plotted in panels (a–d). The red lines in panels a–d correspond to the true values used to generate the synthetic catalog. Mean (dashed lines) and standard deviation (dotted lines) are also shown. The 2D marginal distributions panels (e–j) are shown for each couple of parameters on off-diagonal panels. The red crosses correspond to the true values and the blue dots indicate the mean. (k) Magnitude distribution of the synthetic catalog with 1000 events (b = 1.0, a = 5.70, μ = 3.0, σ = 0.5, and Δm = 0.5) (brown histogram) and the detection function (orange-dashed curve). The blue line represents the MFD predicted with the mean estimated parameters (b,a,μ,σ). PDF, probability density function. The color version of this figure is available only in the electronic edition.

now includes the real value (red cross), and the posterior mean (green dot) is now closer to the real value. The offset between the blue and green distributions in Figure 7 shows the bias on b and a generated by neglecting magnitude uncertainties.

Importance of taking magnitude uncertainties into account

Figure 8 highlights the bias on each parameter b,a,μ,σ that arises when ignoring magnitude uncertainties. In Figure 8, we use the same synthetic catalog as in the Catalog with a constant detection function section. The 1D marginal distributions for each parameter b, a, μ, and σ obtained with our inversion, including magnitude uncertainties (or not) in the likelihood, are shown in Figure 8a–d, with green and blue histograms, respectively. When the magnitude uncertainties are not accounted for (likelihood equation 9), we observe a systematic offset relative to the true values in the posterior distributions (blue distributions in Fig. 8). This bias disappears when magnitude uncertainties are included in the likelihood (see equation 18). This effect is illustrated by the green distributions in Figure 8. Neglecting uncertainties leads to overestimated b, a, μ, σ. These systematic errors are in agreement with Rhoades and Dowrick (2000). Because the Gutenberg–Richter law is an exponential law, the effect of perturbing the magnitudes with a uniform law is not symmetric. It tends to increase the number of small magnitudes compared with large magnitudes. This is a possible reason for the observed overestimation illustrated in Figure 8.

Finally, we have, so far, assumed that the level of uncertainty is known, which in reality is difficult to assess. We thus performed some tests to investigate the impact of wrong Δm on our results. It reveals that making a moderate error (±10% of

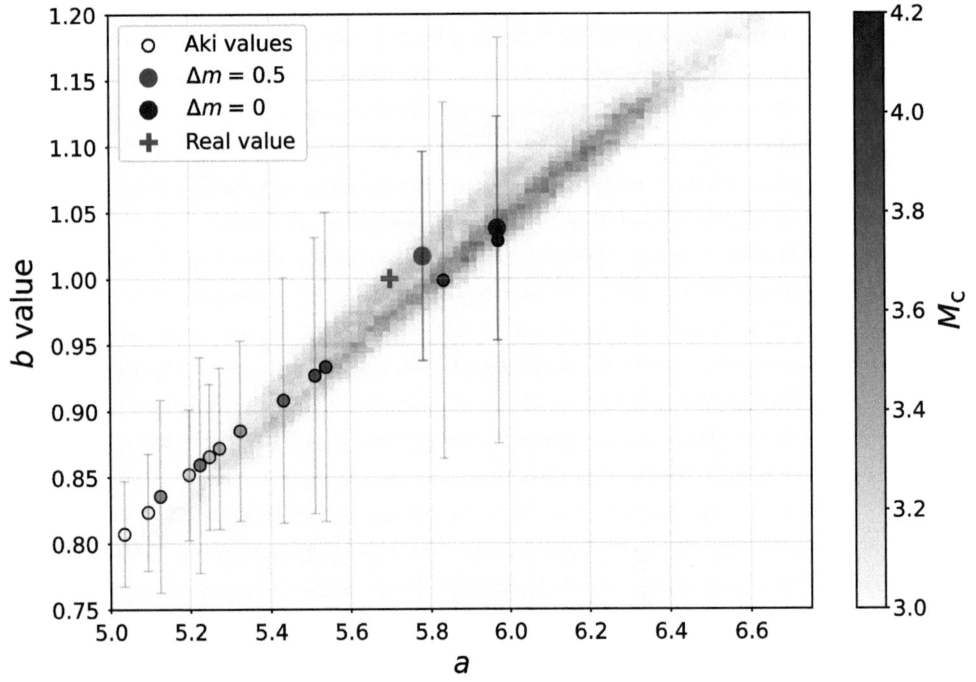

Figure 7. Comparison between our method and Aki's method. The synthetic catalog has been generated for $b = 1.0$ and $a = 5.70$, and includes magnitude errors drawn from a uniform distribution with $\Delta m = 0.5$, and a detection function characterized by $\mu = 3.0$ and $\sigma = 0.5$. The green-shaded 2D distribution represents the posterior distribution obtained when magnitude uncertainties are accounted for in the likelihood, the green point stands for the posterior mean. The blue shaded 2D distribution represents the posterior distribution obtained when magnitude uncertainties are ignored in the likelihood, the blue point stands for the posterior mean. Maximum-Likelihood Estimate (MLE) estimated from Aki's method (without accounting for uncertainties) are shown for various M_c with their 1σ uncertainties. The color version of this figure is available only in the electronic edition.

error) on Δm does not affect the b and a values, but it seems to have a greater impact on the detection functions' parameters.

Time-varying detectability

We finally test our method on a new synthetic catalog in which earthquake detection varies over time. We construct a synthetic catalog in which the seismic rate λ and the b value remain constant through time (as commonly assumed in PSHA), and only detectability changes between the subperiods. This synthetic catalog spans a fictive period between 1960 and 2016 with $b = 1.0$, $a = 4.47$ and is divided into two periods. To be consistent with the definition of a in PSHA and other studies, hereafter, the a value will be the number of events per unit of time, that is, an annual rate of exceedance $a_{\text{annual}} = \log_{10}(\frac{N}{\Delta T}) = \log_{10}(\lambda)$. The detection function for the first subcatalog (1960–2000) is defined by $\mu_1 = 4.0$ and $\sigma_1 = 0.5$, whereas the detection function for the second subcatalog (2000–2016) is characterized by $\mu_2 = 3.0$ and $\sigma_2 = 0.3$. Differences in detection are visible in Figure 9a: in the first subcatalog (red points), small earthquakes are less frequently detected due to lower network performance (which is equivalent to high values of the μ and σ parameters of the detection function); in the second subcatalog (green points), small earthquakes are more effectively detected, leading to twice as many recorded events, despite a shorter observation period. We draw magnitude uncertainties in uniform laws with $\Delta m_1 = 0.5$ for the first and $\Delta m_2 = 0.3$ for the second subcatalog. This configuration mimics a realistic combination of a historical and an instrumental catalog.

We apply our method and present the results in Figure 9b and Table 1. The blue dot in Figure 9b shows the posterior mean for b and a with their 1σ error bar, and Table 1 summarizes the posterior means for each estimated parameter $(b, a, \mu_1, \sigma_1, \mu_2, \sigma_2)$. The resulting mean values are consistent with the true values of the synthetic catalog.

We compare our results with those obtained using the method described in Dutfoy (2020). This author generalizes the MLE approach of Weichert (1980), used in PSHA, to estimate the parameters of the GR law while accounting for detectability changes. It requires defining magnitude bins that are described by a completeness period (Stepp, 1972; Tinti and Mulargia, 1985b) and a completeness magnitude. Note that this method does not account for magnitude uncertainties. We apply this generalized Weichert's method for four different values of M_c (two for each subcatalog), distinct from the theoretical value $(\mu + \sigma)$. The results (shown in Fig. 9b) present the maximum-likelihood solution for b and a with their 1σ uncertainty ellipse. They show that when M_c is misestimated, the inversion fails to retrieve the synthetic catalog's a and b parameters. This discrepancy is particularly significant when M_c for the second subcatalog (in green) is incorrect because this catalog contributes more events to the inversion.

We also compare our results (Fig. 9c) with the recently developed b-positive and a-positive methods of Van der Elst (2021) and Van der Elst and Page (2023) in Figure 9c. These approaches are typically applied over moving time-windows to investigate temporal variations of the b and a values. In our context, however, we aim to derive time-independent parameters by combining historical and instrumental catalogs. For consistency, we therefore apply the b positive and a positive approaches over a single time window spanning the entire catalog duration. The b-positive approach relies on

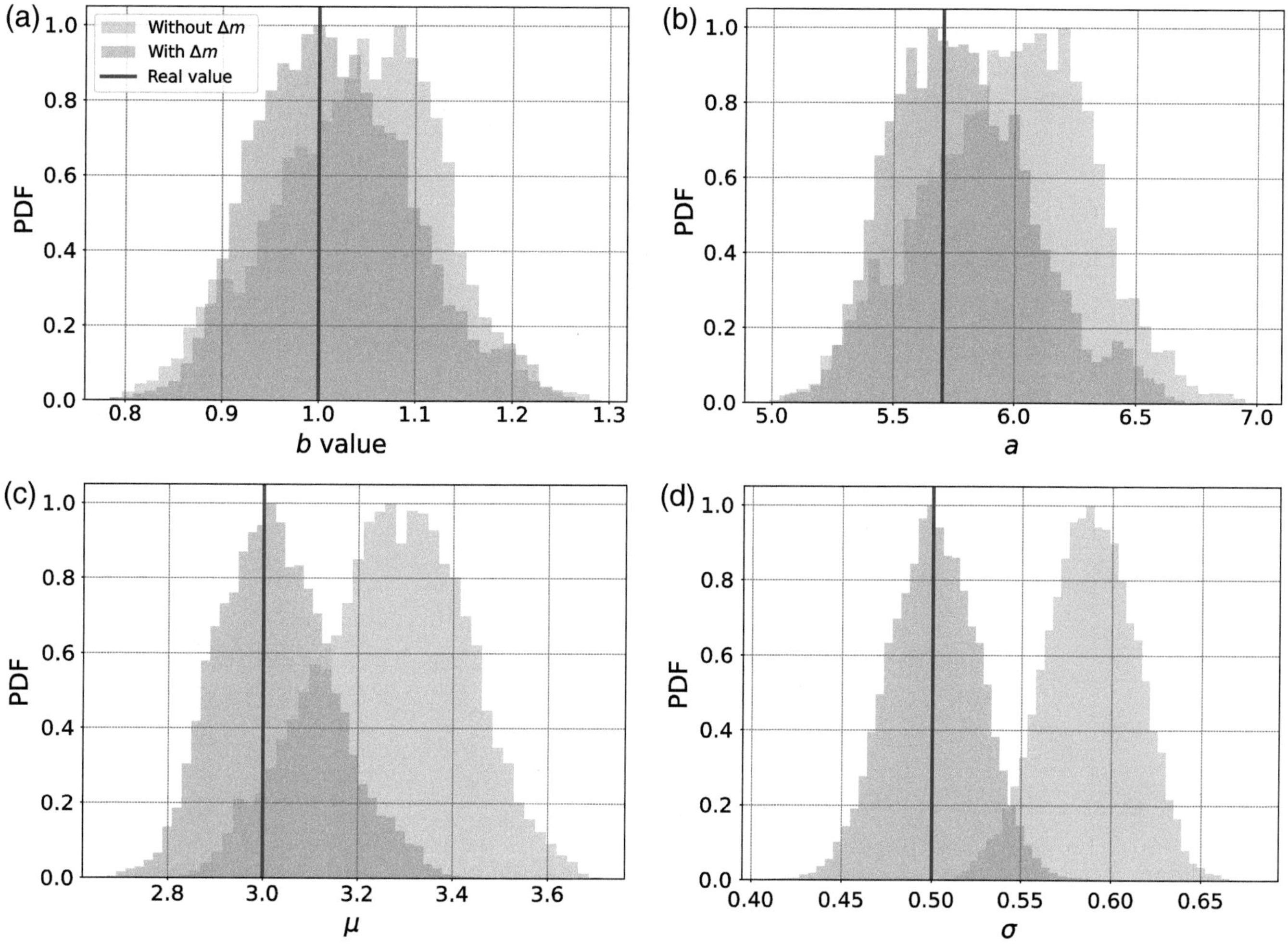

Figure 8. Effects of taking into account magnitude uncertainties on b, a, μ, and σ posterior distributions (panels a–d respectively). Histograms shows the 1D marginal distributions for each parameter, obtained after performing two inversions, with (green histogram) and without (blue histogram) accounting for uncertainties. The red vertical lines are the true values used to generate the synthetic catalog. The color version of this figure is available only in the electronic edition.

constructing a catalog of magnitude differences between consecutive events, which is also expected to follow an exponential law. Small-magnitude differences must be truncated below a chosen threshold, which is also used in the a-positive approach, Van der Elst and Page (2023). The a-positive approach uses pairs of earthquakes to measure interevent times to the next larger earthquake to define the seismic rate. We refer the reader to Van der Elst (2021) and Van der Elst and Page (2023) for details. Contrary to our Bayesian approach, note here that the two b positive and a positive procedures are carried out consecutively and separately, which prevents estimating correlations between a and b value estimates. Uncertainties for these methods are estimated using a bootstrap procedure: starting from the synthetic catalog, we generate 100 resampled versions by randomly drawing magnitudes and occurrence times with replacement, and the variability of the resulting estimates provides the confidence intervals. We show the results for five different δM_c values (Fig. 9c). The values of δM_c were determined by inspecting the magnitude-difference distribution and identifying the point in which it deviates from the expected Gutenberg–Richter law; the onset of this curvature marks the minimum δM_c. Our δM_c are larger than what is suggested in b positive, but this is required to jointly apply b positive and a positive methods. The resulting GR parameters vary significantly with the chosen threshold δM_c. In Figure 9c, we show the results for a δM_c range that gives the b and a estimates closest to the true values. Similarly to the classical approach of maximum likelihood over truncated catalogs Aki (1965), when δM_c is too low, the estimates are biased as the catalog is incomplete and does not follow an exponential law. Conversely, setting δM_c too high ensures completeness but discards many events, which reduces the precision of the estimates. In particular, when the number of events in the catalog becomes too small, the estimation of both a and b becomes unstable. In this case also, open intervals, which are the periods following an earthquake for which no larger event has been recorded until the end of the dataset, become more frequent (Van der Elst and Page, 2023). Although such intervals are included in the seismic rate estimate, they bias the results if they are too numerous. In our

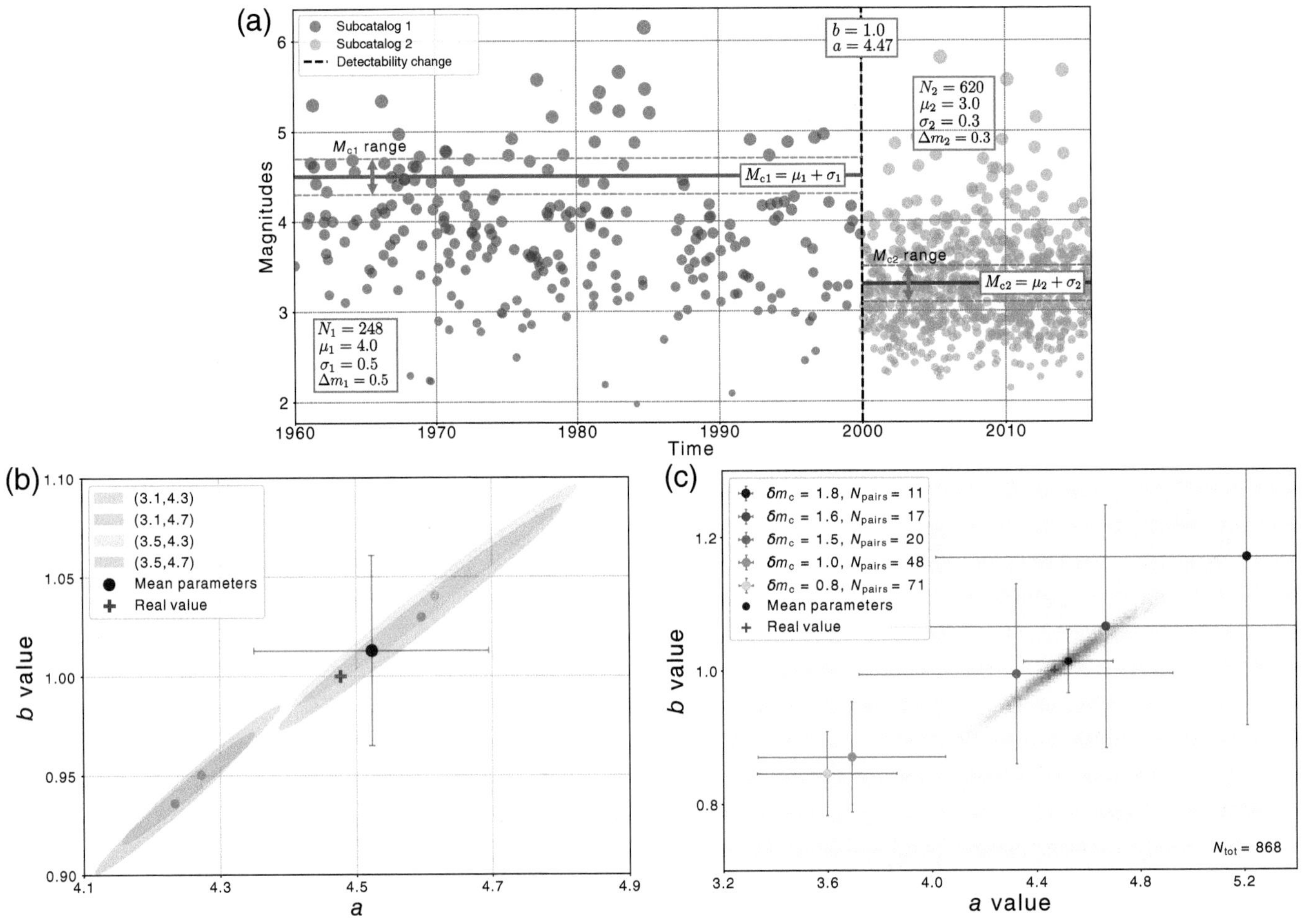

analysis, the fraction of open intervals varies between 8% and 35%, and becomes too high (above 25%) for $\delta M_c = 1.6$ and 1.8. These tests thus show the sensitivity of these approaches (Van der Elst, 2021; Van der Elst and Page, 2023) to parameters that must be defined at the outset, which can be difficult to constrain for real catalogs. In contrast, our Bayesian approach includes a prior distribution, avoiding the need to fix any values. Our approach also jointly infers the b and a values and completeness, while taking into account magnitude uncertainties and providing a probabilistic estimate of the detection functions temporal changes between historical and instrumental periods. Moreover, our framework provides covariances between parameters and thus is well-suited for PSHA.

Figure 9. Comparison of the results obtained with our approach and those from the MLE method (Weichert, 1980; Dutfoy, 2020) using a synthetic catalog with two periods of detectability. (a) Magnitudes over time for our synthetic catalog. The red magnitudes correspond to the subset with lower detectability (see μ_1, σ_1), green ones to the subset with higher detectability (see μ_2, σ_2). The parameters $b = 1.0$ and the $a = 4.47$ remain constant throughout the entire catalog period. Horizontal lines are the estimated true value of completeness magnitude, and dashed lines correspond to the M_c tested for the MLE (Weichert, 1980; Dutfoy, 2020). (b) Results of the inversions. Comparison of the b and a values obtained with our method (blue dot and 1σ uncertainty) against those from several inversions using the MLE method (Weichert, 1980; Dutfoy, 2020) for different completeness magnitudes (M_{c1},M_{c2}) for the two subcatalogs. $M_{c1} = 4.3$ or 4.7, $M_{c2} = 3.1$ or 3.5. (c) Comparison of the b and a values obtained with our method (shown as a gridded posterior density function) with the b positive and a positive methods' results. The latter provides MLEs (dots) for five different δm_c, with a $M_{min} = 0$ and above a $M_{ref} = 0$ (Van der Elst, 2021; Van der Elst and Page, 2023). N_{pairs} indicates the number of pairs retained for the inversion, that is, magnitude differences above δm_c (see the total number of events in the bottom right corner). Uncertainties are estimated with bootstrap by generating 100 resampled versions of the synthetic catalog by randomly drawing magnitudes and occurrence times with replacement. The color version of this figure is available only in the electronic edition.

APPLICATION TO A REAL EARTHQUAKE CATALOG IN THE FRENCH ALPS

Data

We now study the seismicity of the Alpine region (orange-shaded zone in Fig. 1), which is characterized by moderate seismicity. The importance of this region for seismic hazard studies relies on the proximity of populated areas and the presence of electric infrastructures such as nuclear power plants or water dams. As the Alpine region is spread over several countries,

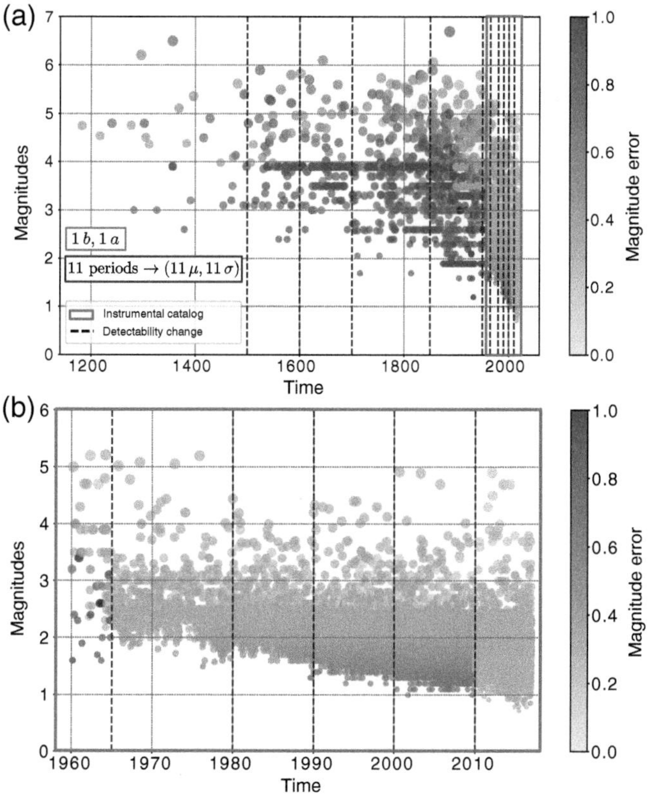

Figure 10. Alpine catalog (a) with zoom on the Alpine instrumental catalog (1965–2016) for visibility (b). The color bar shows the magnitude uncertainties. The dashed lines correspond to our fixed detectability changes. The color version of this figure is available only in the electronic edition.

the contribution of all countries is needed to build seismic catalogs (Stucchi *et al.*, 2013; Cara *et al.*, 2015) and to produce reliable PSHA across Europe (Danciu *et al.*, 2021). For the real application, we use the Alpine subset of the French catalog built for updating the seismic hazard map of France and described in Drouet *et al.* (2020). The catalog is shown in Figure 10. It is composed of a historical part and an instrumental part. It is a combination of several catalogs: FCAT-17 (Cara *et al.*, 2015; Senfaute *et al.*, 2015; Baumont *et al.*, 2018; Manchuel *et al.*, 2018; Traversa *et al.*, 2018), SHARE European Earthquake Catalogue (SHEEC) (Stucchi *et al.*, 2013; Woessner *et al.*, 2015) and LDG (Laboratoire de Détection et de Géophysique). In addition, this catalog has been declustered to remove all aftershock sequences and swarms (Gardner and Knopoff, 1974; Burkhard and Grünthal, 2009; Drouet *et al.*, 2020).

All magnitudes in our composite catalog are homogenized to moment magnitude M_w, which allows for reliable event comparisons. The uncertainties of the historical catalog are based on the quality of the macroseismic data and the reliability of depth estimation for the historical events (Manchuel *et al.*, 2018; Traversa *et al.*, 2018). For the events of the instrumental part, a generic uncertainty value of 0.2 magnitude units is used. It represents the typical uncertainty associated with the magnitude conversion equations between M_L and M_w (Martin *et al.*, 2018). Magnitude errors are represented in color in Figure 10, and as expected, they are higher for the historical part of the catalog (before 1965) than for the instrumental part in Figure 10b.

The goal of this application is to estimate a single b and a for the entire time period, while accounting for temporal variations in detectability and magnitude uncertainties. This assumption of a stationary b value is motivated by the need to provide a stationary earthquake MFD to PSHA studies.

For this study, we can assume that the detection varies only temporally and not spatially. Unlike Laporte *et al.* (2025), we are not inverting for temporal discontinuities; instead, we arbitrarily define the detection changes based on the literature and our knowledge of the seismic network modifications since 1960 (Drouet *et al.*, 2020; Dutfoy, 2020). We set detection changes every 100 yr for the historical catalog and every 10 yr for the instrumental catalog. This results in eleven temporal subcatalogs shown in Figure 10a,b by the black dashed lines.

TABLE 1
Summary of the Real and Mean Posterior Values and Their 1σ Uncertainties Obtained With Our Method for Each Parameter for a Synthetic Catalog Including Two Periods of Detectability Shown in Figure 9a

Parameter	Real Value	Mean ± Std
b	1.0	1.01 ± 0.05
a	4.47	4.52 ± 0.17
μ_1	4.0	3.98 ± 0.06
σ_1	0.50	0.50 ± 0.03
μ_2	3.0	2.98 ± 0.05
σ_2	0.30	0.27 ± 0.02

Results

We apply our method and use the prior distributions of parameters as described in the method section. We obtain a multidimensional a posteriori distribution for b, a, and the eleven μ and σ values corresponding to each subperiod. Table 2 summarizes the mean of the posterior distribution. The posterior marginal distributions for b and a are shown in Figure 11a,b. The estimated b value is 1.14 ± 0.01 for the whole catalog, and the a value is 7.30 ± 0.02 ($\log_{10}$ of the number of events). Generally, in PSHA, the a value is expressed as an annual rate of exceedance and must be normalized by the surface area of the region to allow meaningful comparisons. The a value is then written as: $a_{\text{surface}} = a - \log_{10}(S) - \log_{10}(\Delta T) = \log_{10}(\frac{N}{S\Delta T})$, in which S is the surface area of the region, and ΔT is the time period. Using this definition, we obtain $a_{\text{surface}} = 5.31$ for a region of 10^6 km^2. This value is consistent with expectations for a region such as the Alps, and comparable to the a_{surface} of 5.10 reported by Drouet *et al.* (2020).

As can be seen in Table 2, for the subcatalogs corresponding to the historical part (subcatalogs 1–5), μ and σ are high

TABLE 2
Posterior Mean for GR Parameters *b* and *a* Values, and Detection Function Parameters μ and σ, Obtained With Our Approach Applied on the French Alpine Catalog

GR Parameters	***b***	***a***		
	1.14 ± 0.01	7.30 ± 0.02		
Detection Functions				
Catalog	**Time Period**	**Number of Events**	μ	σ
Subcatalog 1	1182–1500	31	5.54 ± 0.16	0.79 ± 0.06
Subcatalog 2	1500–1599	63	4.40 ± 0.10	0.54 ± 0.05
Subcatalog 3	1600–1699	125	3.90 ± 0.06	0.35 ± 0.04
Subcatalog 4	1700–1849	350	3.82 ± 0.04	0.47 ± 0.02
Subcatalog 5	1850–1949	866	3.35 ± 0.03	0.44 ± 0.01
Subcatalog 6	1950–1964	168	3.23 ± 0.05	0.42 ± 0.03
Subcatalog 7	1965–1979	1003	2.20 ± 0.01	0.16 ± 0.01
Subcatalog 8	1980–1989	1385	1.97 ± 0.008	0.09 ± 0.006
Subcatalog 9	1990–1999	2630	1.72 ± 0.005	0.05 ± 0.006
Subcatalog 10	2000–2009	3659	1.58 ± 0.006	0.05 ± 0.008
Subcatalog 11	2010–2016	3806	1.41 ± 0.008	0.16 ± 0.005

(greater than 3.30 and 0.45, respectively), reflecting the fact that earthquakes are poorly detected and documented. For the instrumental part of the catalog, corresponding to the subcatalogs 6 to 11, μ and σ gradually decrease over time, indicating the improvement in detection capabilities from the 1960s onward and the expansion of the seismological network. Figure 11c illustrates this variation of detectability by showing the detection functions obtained for each subcatalog using their respective posterior mean μ and σ values (Table 2). Between the periods 2000–2009 and 2010–2016, the catalogs have not been produced by the same agencies. This may explain the change in σ between the two periods.

The advantage of our approach is to provide probabilistic solutions. Therefore on top of the posterior mean for each parameter, we also have access to their uncertainties. These are illustrated in Figure 11 on panels d, e, f, and g. In Figure 11d, we plot an ensemble of 1000 sampled detection functions, randomly drawn from the posterior ensemble, as a density plot for three different subcatalogs (1, 5, and 11). Density plots in Figure 11d are wider for older subcatalogs, which reflects a larger level of uncertainty in the detection function parameters, due to a lower number of events and larger magnitude uncertainties in old subcatalogs. We show a similar plot for the MFD for the same three subcatalogs (Fig. 11e–g). For this, we display 1000 accepted models (b, a, μ, σ) as a density plot. Again, old subcatalogs with fewer events and larger magnitude uncertainties yield a broader posterior distribution. This trend is particularly pronounced for historical subcatalogs with sparse data (Fig. 11e). On the other hand, most recent subcatalogs contain many events (Fig. 11f, g), and the parameters are better estimated, with lower uncertainties. In this case, the ensemble of sampled MFD models is narrower and closely follows the catalog histogram.

Nevertheless, several studies showed that b and a values estimated from declustered catalogs are affected by the declustering methods (Marzocchi and Taroni, 2014; Mizrahi *et al.*, 2021; Field *et al.*, 2022). As modern PSHA studies (e.g., Gerstenberger *et al.*, 2024) use full catalog (i.e., non-declustered catalogs), we also performed the inversion using the complete French Alps catalog. We obtained a mean posterior b value of 1.34 and a value of 7.93. Both parameters are noticeably higher than those estimated from the declustered catalog (b = 1.14 and a = 7.30). A higher a value is expected as this estimate now includes the aftershock seismicity on top of the background seismicity. A higher b value may indicate an effect of the declustering algorithm.

DISCUSSION AND PERSPECTIVES

PSHA relies on the estimation of the long-term b and a values (and their variances and covariances), assumed to remain constant over the period of the catalog, which is longer than the seismic cycle. Because seismic catalogs typically span long time periods and combine historical and instrumental data, it is crucial to properly integrate these two complementary but different sources. Classically, GR parameter estimation is performed by applying the maximum-likelihood approach (Aki, 1965; Utsu, 1966; Weichert, 1980; Dutfoy, 2020). These methods strongly depend on how well the completeness magnitude is estimated and how it changes over time (Woessner and Wiemer, 2005; Hakimhashemi and Grünthal, 2012). In this study, we propose a method for the joint estimation of the GR law parameters that includes temporal changes in completeness and magnitude uncertainties. For this purpose, we explicitly modulate the GR law with a detection function as in Ringdal (1986), Ogata and Katsura (1993), and Daniel *et al.* (2008), which allows us to use the entire earthquake catalog, including events below the completeness threshold. In this study, we have used an error function as a detection function, but for other purposes, other types of detection functions can be used (see Appendix for alternative likelihood function with the Gumbel detection function, equation A1).

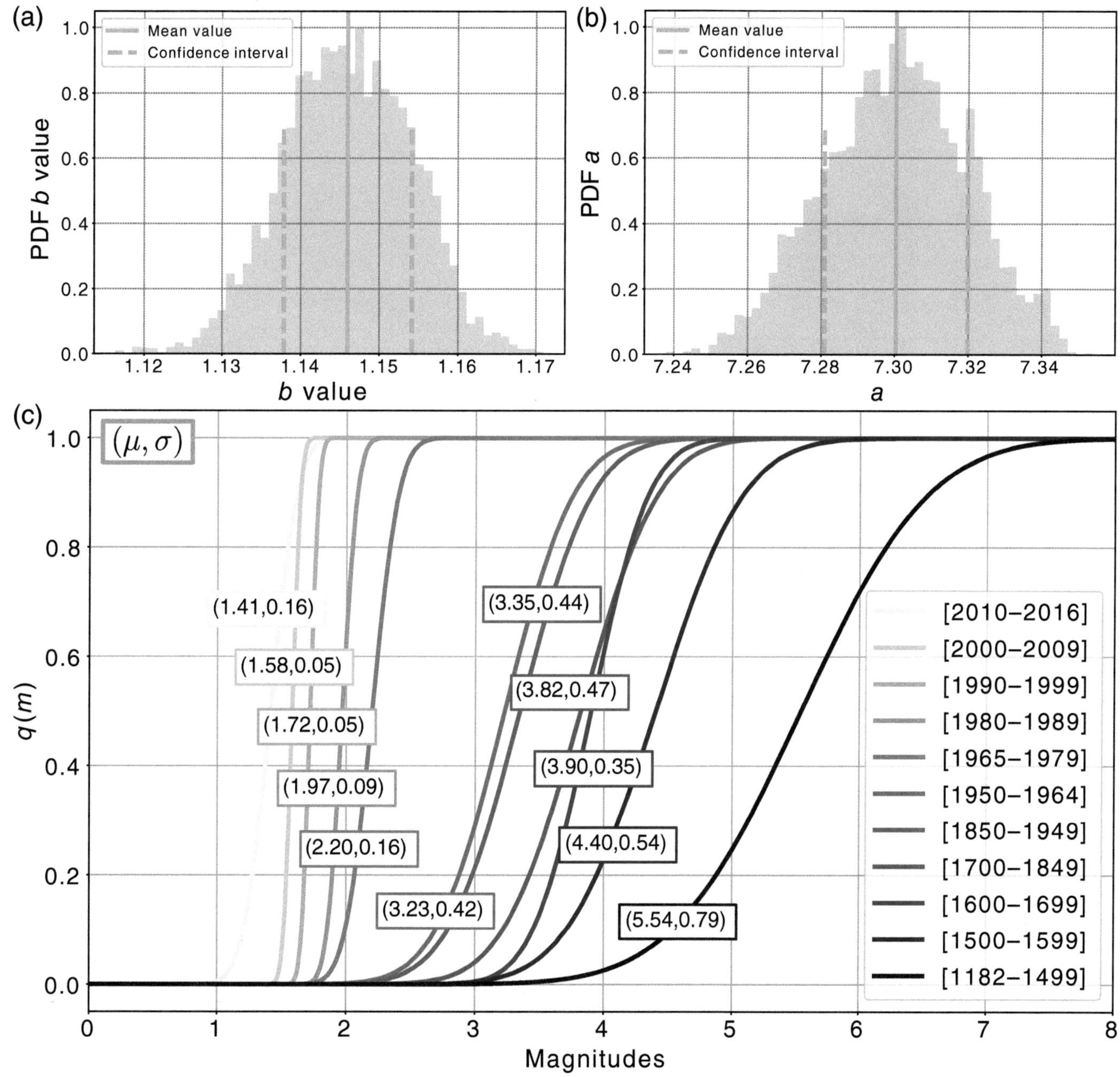

Figure 11. Results of the application of our method on the French catalog for the Alpine region. (a) Marginal posterior distribution for the b value. (b) Marginal posterior distribution for the a value. (c) Detection functions obtained for the posterior mean parameters of the eleven subcatalogs. The variation over time is represented with the color scale. (d) 1000 sampled detection functions (randomly chosen within the posterior ensemble) displayed as a density plot for subcatalogs 1, 5, and 11. (e–g) 1000 accepted MFD models (randomly chosen within the posterior ensemble) for subcatalogs 1, 5, and 11, respectively. The color version of this figure is available only in the electronic edition. *(Continued)*

Comparing the outcomes derived from traditional approaches (Aki, 1965; Weichert, 1980; Dutfoy, 2020; Van der Elst, 2021; Van der Elst and Page, 2023) with those obtained using our method reveals that these methods work under certain conditions including the choice of arbitrary parameters accounting for catalog incompleteness and they do not allow to take into account the magnitude uncertainties (Figs. 7 and 9). Instead, our approach naturally accounts for temporal fluctuations in detectability and magnitude uncertainties without strong a priori assumptions, outperforming existing methods and better suits PSHA purposes that require robust a and b values estimates using historical and instrumental catalog.

When applied to a real dataset, our method can quantify detectability changes in the French Alps area over time. By discretizing the period into successive time windows, we demonstrate the progressive improvement of the earthquake

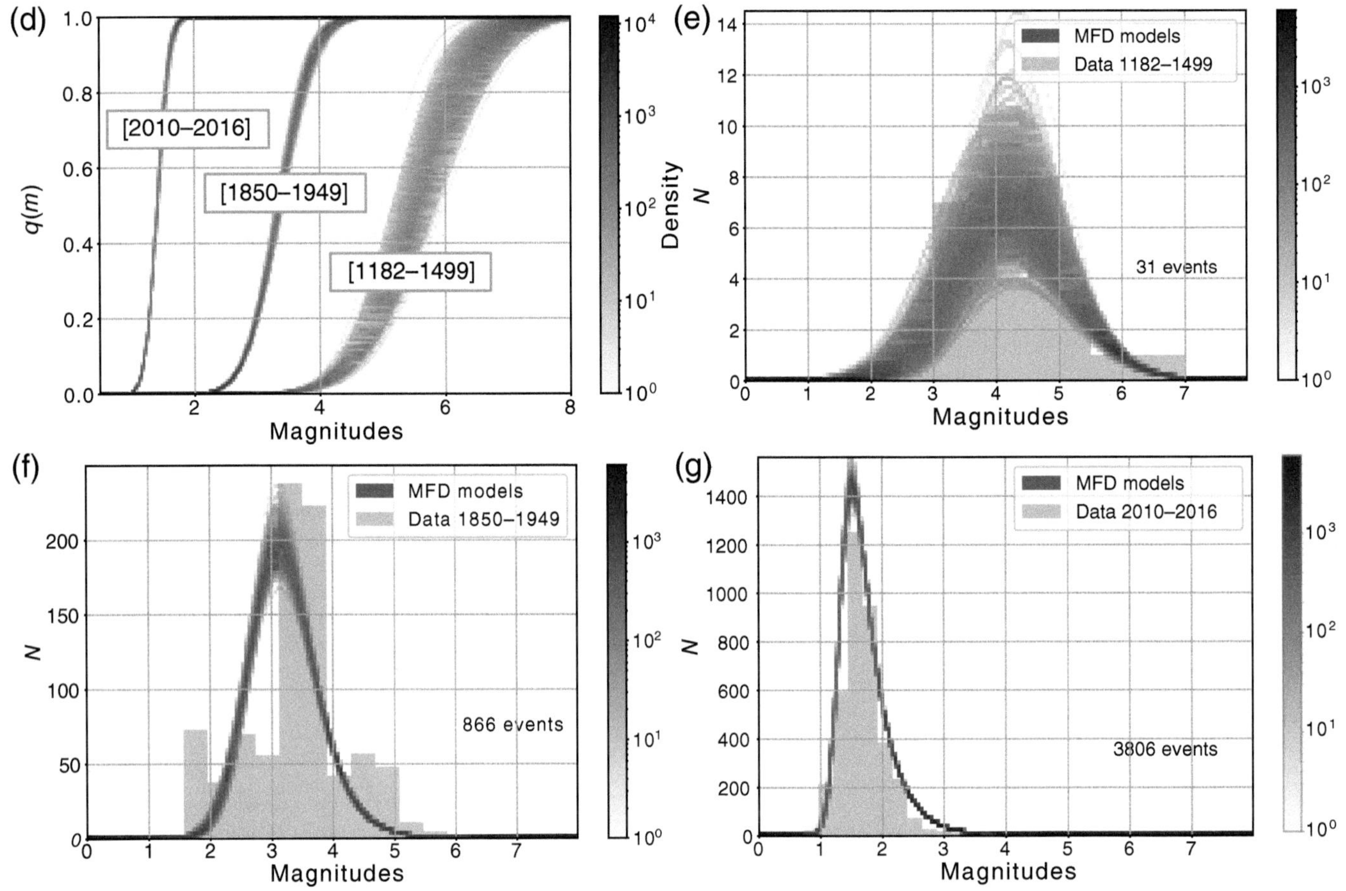

Figure 11. Continued

archiving effort in France over the time period of the catalog (i.e., 463–2016).

Accounting for magnitude uncertainties in the estimation of GR parameters helps reduce potential biases (Tinti and Mulargia, 1985a; Rhoades, 1996). Properly accounting for magnitude uncertainties is especially important in regions of moderate seismicity and when combining catalogs with varying error levels, such as historical and instrumental data (Marzocchi and Sandri, 2003). Several methods have been proposed to address this issue (Tinti and Mulargia, 1985a; Kijko *et al.*, 2016). In our approach, we incorporate these uncertainties by convolving the GR law with the distribution of errors. In this study, we have assumed a uniform distribution for the magnitude uncertainties, but we provide in equation (12) the general expression and appendices with alternative likelihood functions considering other magnitude error distributions (Gaussian, equations A13–A16). Unlike methods such as Aki (1965) or Weichert (1980), Dutfoy (2020), Van der Elst (2021), and Van der Elst and Page (2023), which ignore magnitude errors, our method successfully estimates the GR parameters while explicitly including this key source of uncertainty (Figs. 7 and 8). It also distinguishes between the uncertainty levels of historical and instrumental data, ensuring more realistic modeling.

For PSHA studies, it is generally assumed that magnitudes and occurrence times are independent (Kagan, 2002; Helmstetter *et al.*, 2006). This assumption holds over the large timescales typically used in PSHA and is reinforced by the use of declustered catalogs. In such catalogs, only background seismicity is retained, whereas aftershock sequences, in which magnitudes and times are not independent, are removed. This independence allows us to have two likelihoods, one for magnitudes and one for the number of events. We have, however, tested our method on a synthetic ETAS-type catalog. It reveals the ability to capture the true b value and the full seismic rate, including the aftershock seismicity. We will continue to explore this in future work. Moreover, we choose to model the detection function as an error function and to represent magnitude uncertainties using a uniform distribution. These are practical and conservative choices: the error function captures a smooth detection transition, while the uniform distribution reflects limited knowledge about historical magnitude errors. As shown in Figure 11e, estimating GR parameters for the historical catalog remains challenging due to the limited data, but our assumptions provide a robust and unbiased framework.

From a Bayesian perspective, this framework provides a full probabilistic characterization of the parameters, rather than relying on a single value that maximizes a likelihood function (Keller *et al.*, 2014; Viallet *et al.*, 2019). This is particularly useful for properly propagating epistemic uncertainties in PSHA. In addition, the ability to include a much larger number of earthquakes without truncating the catalog in the estimation process offers the opportunity to improve constraints on the estimated parameters.

In this study, the completeness periods were fixed in advance, which introduces a strong a priori assumption. We plan for future developments to jointly invert for the duration of these completeness periods along with the detection functions and seismicity parameters, using a transdimensional approach as in the b Bayesian method proposed by Laporte *et al.* (2025). This would further reduce model assumptions and improve robustness. Another further refinement of the method could be to account for the spatial inhomogeneity of earthquake detection capability. This would account for the time and space variations of the MFD. Spatial variations of the b value or the seismic rate are currently a topic of active research (Montuori *et al.*, 2016; Taroni *et al.*, 2021). Our current method requires a proper definition of a spatial zone with a homogeneous b value. However, as done for the inversion of seismic velocities in tomography (e.g., Bodin and Sambridge, 2009) or for spatial variations of b values (Morales-Yáñez *et al.*, 2022), the method can be extended to jointly invert for spatially varying b and a values, as well as region-specific detection functions. Such improvements would make the method optimal for PSHA applications, in which spatial heterogeneities and data limitations must be carefully accounted for. In addition, the flexibility of this probabilistic framework is also expected to provide a solid foundation for incorporating diverse sources of uncertainty coherently, thereby contributing to more reliable and transparent seismic hazard models.

DATA AND RESOURCES

The software described in the article is available at GitHub: https://github.com/cyriellecolin/long_term_b_a_values_colin_2025 (last accessed January 2026). The data used are those of the French catalog Manchuel *et al.* (2018) and Drouet *et al.* (2020).

DECLARATION OF COMPETING INTERESTS

The authors acknowledge that there are no conflicts of interest recorded.

ACKNOWLEDGMENTS

This work was funded in the framework of the SIGMA3 2024–2028 project (Electricité de France [EDF], French Atomic and Alternative Energies Commission [CEA], České energetické závody [Czech Energy Company, CEZ] Group, Pacific Gas and Electric Company [PG&E], VTT, swissnuclear, Central Research Institute of [the] Electric Power Industry [CRIEPI], Stuk, uniper, Vattenfall). The research leading to these results has received funding from the Spanish Ministry of Science and Innovation, ATR2023-143517/AEI/10.13039/. The authors also acknowledge funding through the Grant CEX2024-001494-S funded by AEI 10.13039/501100011033. This project has received funding from the European Union's Horizon Europe research and innovation programme under the Marie Skłodowska-Curie grant agreement number 101204132. The authors thank the Editor, the Associate Editor, the anonymous reviewer, and M. Taroni for their thorough revision and relevant comments, which have helped us clarify and strengthen some aspects of this article.

REFERENCES

Aki, K. (1965). Maximum likelihood estimate of b in the formula log N= a-bM and its confidence limits, *Bull. Earthq. Res. Inst. Tokyo Univ.* **43,** 237–239.

Amorèse, D. (2007). Applying a change-point detection method on frequency-magnitude distributions, *Bull. Seismol. Soc. Am.* **97,** no. 5, 1742–1749.

Baker, J. W. (2008). An introduction to probabilistic seismic hazard analysis (PSHA), *White paper, version* **1,** no. 3.

Baumont, D., K. Manchuel, P. Traversa, C. Durouchoux, E. Nayman, and G. Ameri (2018). Intensity predictive attenuation models calibrated in M_w for metropolitan France, *Bull. Earthq. Eng.* **16,** 2285–2310.

Beauval, C., and O. Scotti (2003). Mapping b-values in France using two different magnitude ranges: Possible non power-law behavior, *Geophys. Res. Lett.* **30,** no. 17.

Beauval, C., and O. Scotti (2004). Quantifying sensitivities of PSHA for France to earthquake catalog uncertainties, truncation of ground-motion variability, and magnitude limits, *Bull. Seismol. Soc. Am.* **94,** no. 5, 1579–1594.

Bodin, T., and M. Sambridge (2009). Seismic tomography with the reversible jump algorithm, *Geophys. J. Int.* **178,** no. 3, 1411–1436.

Burkhard, M., and G. Grünthal (2009). Seismic source zone characterization for the seismic hazard assessment project PEGASOS by the Expert Group 2 (EG1b), *Swiss J. Geosci.* **102,** 149–188.

Cao, A., and S. S. Gao (2002). Temporal variation of seismic b-values beneath northeastern Japan island arc, *Geophys. Res. Lett.* **29,** no. 9, 48–1.

Cara, M., Y. Cansi, A. Schlupp, P. Arroucau, N. Béthoux, E. Beucler, S. Bruno, M. Calvet, S. Chevrot, A. Deboissy, *et al.* (2015). SI-Hex: a new catalogue of instrumental seismicity for metropolitan France, *Bull. Soc. Géol. France* **186,** no. 1, 3–19.

Danciu, L., S. Nandan, C. G. Reyes, R. Basili, G. Weatherill, C. Beauval, A. Rovida, S. Vilanova, K. Sesetyan, P.-Y. Bard, *et al.* (2021). The 2020 update of the European Seismic Hazard Model-ESHM20: model overview, *EFEHR Tech. Rept.*, **1.**

Daniel, G. (2014). Bias in magnitude for earthquakes with unknown focal mechanism. *Geophys. Prospect.* **62**, 848–861.

Daniel, G., D. Marsan, and M. Bouchon (2008). Earthquake triggering in southern Iceland following the June 2000 M_s 6.6 doublet, *J. Geophys. Res. Solid Earth* **113,** no. B5.

Davison, A. C. (2003). *Statistical Models*, Vol. 11, Cambridge University Press.

Drouet, S., G. Ameri, K. Le Dortz, R. Secanell, and G. Senfaute (2020). A probabilistic seismic hazard map for the metropolitan France, *Bull. Earthq. Eng.* **18,** no. 5, 1865–1898.

Dutfoy, A. (2020). Estimation of the Gutenberg–Richter earthquake recurrence parameters for unequal observation periods and imprecise magnitudes, *Pure Appl. Geophys.* **177,** no. 10, 4597–4606.

Dutfoy, A. (2025). Bayesian estimation of the Gutenberg–Richter parameters: Essentially exact posterior distributions-Application to the Alps domain, France, *Pure Appl. Geophys.*, 1–16.

Farrell, J., S. Husen, and R. B. Smith (2009). Earthquake swarm and b-value characterization of the Yellowstone volcano-tectonic system, *J. Volcanol. Geotherm. Res.* **188,** nos. 1/3, 260–276.

Field, E. H., K. R. Milner, and N. Luco (2022). The seismic hazard implications of declustering and Poisson assumptions inferred from a fully time-dependent model, *Bull. Seismol. Soc. Am.* **112,** no. 1, 527–537.

Gallagher, K., K. Charvin, S. Nielsen, M. Sambridge, and J. Stephenson (2009). Markov chain Monte Carlo (mcmc) sampling methods to determine optimal models, model resolution and model choice for Earth Science problems, *Mar. Pet. Geol.* **26,** no. 4, 525–535.

Gardner, J., and L. Knopoff (1974). Is the sequence of earthquakes in Southern California, with aftershocks removed, Poissonian? *Bull. Seismol. Soc. Am.* **64,** no. 5, 1363–1367.

Gerstenberger, M. C., S. Bora, B. A. Bradley, C. DiCaprio, A. Kaiser, E. F. Manea, A. Nicol, C. Rollins, M. W. Stirling, K. K. Thingbaijam, *et al.* (2024). The 2022 Aotearoa New Zealand national seismic hazard model: Process, overview, and results, *Bull. Seismol. Soc. Am.* **114,** no. 1, 7–36.

Godano, C., and G. Petrillo (2023). Estimating the completeness magnitude mc and the b-values in a snap, *Earth Space Sci.* **10,** no. 2, e2022EA002540 .

Godano, C., G. Petrillo, and E. Lippiello (2024). Evaluating the incompleteness magnitude using an unbiased estimate of the b-value, *Geophys. J. Int.* **236,** no. 2, 994–1001.

Grünthal, G., D. Stromeyer, C. Bosse, F. Cotton, and D. Bindi (2018). The probabilistic seismic hazard assessment of Germany-version 2016, considering the range of epistemic uncertainties and aleatory variability, *Bull. Earthq. Eng.* **16,** 4339–4395.

Gui, Z., Y. Bai, Z. Wang, D. Dong, S. Wu, and T. Li (2020). Spatiotemporal Seismotectonic Implications for the Izu–Bonin–Mariana subduction zone from b-values, *Seismol. Res. Lett.* **91,** no. 3, 1679–1693.

Gutenberg, B., and C. F. Richter (1944). Frequency of earthquakes in California, *Bull. Seismol. Soc. Am.* **34,** no. 4, 185–188.

Habermann, R. E. (1983). Teleseismic detection in the Aleutian Island arc, *J. Geophys. Res. Solid Earth* **88,** no. B6, 5056–5064.

Hainzl, S. (2016). Apparent triggering function of aftershocks resulting from rate-dependent incompleteness of earthquake catalogs, *J. Geophys. Res. Solid Earth* **121,** no. 9, 6499–6509.

Hakimhashemi, A. H., and G. Grünthal (2012). A statistical method for estimating catalog completeness applicable to long-term nonstationary seismicity data, *Bull. Seismol. Soc. Am.* **102,** no. 6, 2530–2546.

Hastings, W. K. (1970). Monte Carlo sampling methods using Markov chains and their applications, *Biometrika* 57, no. 1, 97–109.

Helmstetter, A., Y. Y. Kagan, and D. D. Jackson (2006). Comparison of short-term and time-independent earthquake forecast models for southern California, *Bull. Seismol. Soc. Am.* **96,** no. 1, 90–106.

Kagan, Y. Y. (2002). Seismic moment distribution revisited: I. Statistical results, *Geophys. J. Int.* **148,** no. 3, 520–541.

Keller, M., A. Pasanisi, M. Marcilhac, T. Yalamas, R. Secanell, and G. Senfaute (2014). A Bayesian methodology applied to the estimation of earthquake recurrence parameters for seismic hazard assessment, *Qual. Reliab. Eng. Int.* **30,** no. 7, 921–933.

Kijko, A., and M. A. Sellevoll (1989). Estimation of earthquake hazard parameters from incomplete data files, Part I. utilization of extreme and complete catalogs with different threshold magnitudes,*Bull. Seismol. Soc. Am.* **79,** no. 3, 645–654.

Kijko, A., and M. A. Sellevoll (1992). Estimation of earthquake hazard parameters from incomplete data files, Part II. Incorporation of magnitude heterogeneity, *Bull. Seismol. Soc. Am.* **82,** no. 1, 120–134.

Kijko, A., and A. Smit (2012). Extension of the Aki-BUtsu b-value estimator for incomplete catalogs, *Bull. Seismol. Soc. Am.* **102,** no. 3, 1283–1287.

Kijko, A., and A. Smit (2017). Estimation of the frequency–magnitude Gutenberg–Richter b-value without making assumptions on levels of completeness, *Seismol. Res. Lett.* **88,** no. 2A, 311–318.

Kijko, A., A. Smit, and M. A. Sellevoll (2016). Estimation of earthquake hazard parameters from incomplete data files. Part III. Incorporation of uncertainty of earthquake-occurrence model, *Bull. Seismol. Soc. Am.* **106,** no. 3, 1210–1222.

Kumar, R., R. Yadav, H. Mittal, A. Saini, and O. Mishra (2025). Estimation of earthquake recurrence parameters for the Himalayan seismic belt: A comprehensive analysis, *Nat. Hazards*, 1–39.

Laporte, M., S. Durand, T. Bodin, B. Gardonio, and D. Marsan (2025). b-Bayesian: The full probabilistic estimate of b-value temporal variations for non-truncated catalogs, *J. Geophys. Res. Solid Earth* **130,** no. 3, e2024JB029973 .

Lippiello, E., and G. Petrillo (2024). b-more-incomplete and b-more-positive: Insights on a robust estimator of magnitude distribution, *J. Geophys. Res. Solid Earth* **129,** no. 2, e2023JB027849 .

Lolli, B., P. Gasperini, and G. Vannucci (2014). Empirical conversion between teleseismic magnitudes (m_b and M_s) and moment magnitude (M_w) at the Global, Euro-Mediterranean and Italian scale, *Geophys. J. Int.* **199,** no. 2, 805–828.

Lombardi, A. (2021). A normalized distance test for co-determining the completeness magnitude and b-value of earthquake catalogs, *J. Geophys. Res. Solid Earth* **126,** no. 3, e2020JB021242 .

Manchuel, K., P. Traversa, D. Baumont, M. Cara, E. Nayman, and C. Durouchoux (2018). The French seismic catalogue (FCAT-17), *Bull. Earthquake Eng.* **16,** 2227–2251.

Marsan, D., and Z. E. Ross (2021). Inverse migration of seismicity quiescence during the 2019 Ridgecrest sequence, *J. Geophys. Res. Solid Earth* **126,** no. 3, e2020JB020329 .

Martin, C., G. Ameri, D. Baumont, D. Carbon, G. Senfaute, J.-M. Thiry, E. Faccioli, and J. Savy (2018). Probabilistic seismic hazard assessment for south-eastern France, *Bull. Earthq. Eng.* **16,** no. 6, 2477–2511.

Marzocchi, W., and L. Sandri (2003). A review and new insights on the estimation of the b-value and its uncertainty, *Ann. Geophys.* **46,** no. 6.

Marzocchi, W., and M. Taroni (2014). Some thoughts on declustering in probabilistic seismic-hazard analysis, *Bull. Seismol. Soc. Am.* **104,** no. 4, 1838–1845.

Metropolis, N., A. W. Rosenbluth, M. N. Rosenbluth, A. H. Teller, and E. Teller (1953). Equation of state calculations by fast computing machines, *J. Chem. Phys.* **21,** no. 6, 1087–1092.

Mignan, A., M. Werner, S. Wiemer, C.-C. Chen, and Y.-M. Wu (2011). Bayesian estimation of the spatially varying completeness magnitude of earthquake catalogs, *Bull. Seismol. Soc. Am.* **101,** no. 3, 1371–1385.

Mizrahi, L., S. Nandan, and S. Wiemer (2021). The effect of declustering on the size distribution of mainshocks, *Bull. Seismol. Soc. Am.* **92,** no. 4, 2333–2342.

Molchan, G., V. Keilis-Borok, and G. Vilkovich (1970). Seismicity and principal seismic effects. *Geophys. J. Int.* **21,** no. 3, 323–335.

Montuori, C., M. Murru, and G. Falcone (2016). Spatial variation of the b-value observed for the periods preceding and following the 24 August 2016, Amatrice earthquake (ml 6.0)(Central Italy), *Ann. Geophys.*, doi: 10.4401/ag-7273.

Morales-Yáñez, C., L. Bustamante, R. Benavente, C. Sippl, and M. Moreno (2022). B-value variations in the Central Chile seismic gap assessed by a Bayesian transdimensional approach, *Sci. Rep.* **12,** no. 1, 21710.

Ogata, Y. (1988). Statistical models for earthquake occurrences and residual analysis for point processes, *J. Am. Stat. Assoc.* **83,** no. 401, 9–27.

Ogata, Y. (1999). Seismicity analysis through point-process modeling: A review, in *Seismicity Patterns, Their Statistical Significance and Physical Meaning*, M. Wyss, K. Shimazaki, and A. Ito (Editors), Pageoph Topical Volumes, Birkhäuser, Basel, 471–507.

Ogata, Y., and K. Katsura (1993). Analysis of temporal and spatial heterogeneity of magnitude frequency distribution inferred from earthquake catalogues, *Geophys. J. Int.* **113,** no. 3, 727–738.

Ogata, Y., and K. Katsura (2006). Immediate and updated forecasting of aftershock hazard. *Geophys. Res. Lett.* **33,** no. 10.

Rhoades, D. (1996). Estimation of the Gutenberg-Richter relation allowing for individual earthquake magnitude uncertainties, *Tectonophysics* **258,** nos. 1/4, 71–83.

Rhoades, D. A., and D. J. Dowrick (2000). Effects of magnitude uncertainties on seismic hazard estimates, *Proc. of the 12th World Conf. on Earthquake Engineering*, Auckland, New Zealand, 30 January–4 February.

Ringdal, F. (1975). On the estimation of seismic detection thresholds, *Bull. Seismol. Soc. Am.* **65,** no. 6, 1631–1642.

Ringdal, F. (1986). Study of magnitudes, seismicity, and earthquake detectability using a global network, *Bull. Seismol. Soc. Am.* **76,** no. 6, 1641–1659.

Ringdal, F., and T. Kværna (1992). Continuous seismic threshold monitoring, *Geophys. J. Int.* **111,** no. 3, 505–514.

Rodríguez-Pérez, Q., M. Monterrubio-Velasco, F. R. Zúñiga, C. M. Valdés-González, and R. Arámbula-Mendoza (2021). Spatial and temporal b-value characterization at Popocatépetl volcano, Central Mexico, *J. Volcanol. Geotherm. Res.* **417,** 107320.

Sambridge, M., and K. Gallagher (2021). Inverse theory, Monte Carlo method, *Encyclopedia of Solid Earth Geophysics*, Springer, Cham, Switzerland, 821–827.

Sambridge, M., K. Gallagher, A. Jackson, and P. Rickwood (2006). Trans-dimensional inverse problems, model comparison and the evidence, *Geophys. J. Int.* **167,** no. 2, 528–542.

Senfaute, G., A. Pecker, P. Labbé, J. Sidaner, C. Berge-Thierry, J. Rzepka, and P. Contri (2015). Contribution of the sigma research program to analyses of uncertainties in seismic hazard assessment, *9ieme Colloque National*, AFPS, France, 30 November 2015–02 December 2025.

Sornette, D. (2006). *Critical Phenomena in Natural Sciences: Chaos, Fractals, Self-Organization and Disorder: Concepts and Tools*, Springer, Berlin, Heidelberg.

Stepp, J. (1972). Analysis of completeness of the earthquake sample in the Puget Sound area and its effect on statistical estimates of earthquake hazard, in *Proc. of the 1st Int. Conf. on Microzonazion*, Seattle, Vol. 2, pp. 897–910.

Stucchi, M., C. Meletti, V. Montaldo, H. Crowley, G. M. Calvi, and E. Boschi (2011). Seismic hazard assessment (2003–2009) for the Italian building code, *Bull. Seismol. Soc. Am.* **101,** no. 4, 1885–1911.

Stucchi, M., A. Rovida, A. A. Gomez Capera, P. Alexandre, T. Camelbeeck, M. B. Demircioglu, P. Gasperini, V. Kouskouna, R. M. Musson, M. Radulian, *et al.* (2013). The SHARE European earthquake catalogue (SHEEC) 1000–1899, *J. Seismolog.* **17,** 523–544.

Taroni, M., and A. Akinci (2021). Good practices in PSHA: declustering, b-value estimation, foreshocks and aftershocks inclusion; a case study in Italy, *Geophys. J. Int.* **224,** no. 2, 1174–1187.

Taroni, M., J. Zhuang, and W. Marzocchi (2021). High-definition mapping of the Gutenberg–Richter b-value and its relevance: A case study in Italy, *Bull. Seismol. Soc. Am.* **92,** no. 6, 3778–3784.

Tinti, S., and F. Mulargia (1985a). Effects of magnitude uncertainties on estimating the parameters in the Gutenberg-Richter frequency-magnitude law, *Bull. Seismol. Soc. Am.* **75,** no. 6, 1681–1697.

Tinti, S., and F. Mulargia (1985b). An improved method for the analysis of the completeness of a seismic catalogue, *Lettere al Nuovo Cimento (1971-1985)* **42,** 21–27.

Traversa, P., D. Baumont, K. Manchuel, E. Nayman, and C. Durouchoux (2018). Exploration tree approach to estimate historical earthquakes M_w and depth, test cases from the French past seismicity, *Bull. Earthq. Eng.* **16,** no. 6, 2169–2193.

Utsu, T. (1966). A statistical significance test of the difference in b-value between two earthquake groups, *J. Phys. Earth* **14,** no. 2, 37–40.

Van der Elst, N. J. (2021). B-positive: A robust estimator of aftershock magnitude distribution in transiently incomplete catalogs, *J. Geophys. Res. Solid Earth* **126,** no. 2, e2020JB021027 .

Van der Elst, N. J., and M. T. Page (2023). a-positive: A robust estimator of the earthquake rate in incomplete or saturated catalogs, *J. Geophys. Res. Solid Earth* **128,** no. 10, e2023JB027089 .

Veneziano, D., and J. Van Dyck (1987). Statistical analysis of earthquake catalogs for seismic hazard, in *Stochastic Approaches in Earthquake Engineering: US-Japan Joint Seminar, May 6–7, 1987*, Springer, Boca Raton, Florida, pp. 385–427.

Viallet, E., N. Humbert, and P. Mottier (2019). Updating a probabilistic seismic hazard assessment with instrumental and historical observations based on a Bayesian inference, *Nucl. Eng. Des.* **350,** 98–106.

Von Seggern, D., and R. Blandford (1976). Seismic threshold determination, *Bull. Seismol. Soc. Am.* **66,** no. 3, 753–788.

Weichert, D. H. (1980). Estimation of the earthquake recurrence parameters for unequal observation periods for different magnitudes, *Bull. Seismol. Soc. Am.* **70,** no. 4, 1337–1346.

Wiemer, S., and M. Wyss (1997). Mapping the frequency-magnitude distribution in asperities: An improved technique to calculate recurrence times? *J. Geophys. Res. Solid Earth* **102,** no. B7, 15,115–15,128.

Wiemer, S., and M. Wyss (2000). Minimum magnitude of completeness in earthquake catalogs: Examples from Alaska, the western United States, and Japan. *Bull. Seismol. Soc. Am.* **90,** no. 4, 859–869.

Woessner, J., and S. Wiemer (2005). Assessing the quality of earthquake catalogues: Estimating the magnitude of completeness and its uncertainty, *Bull. Seismol. Soc. Am.* **95,** no. 2, 684–698.

Woessner, J., D. Laurentiu, D. Giardini, H. Crowley, F. Cotton, G. Grünthal, G. Valensise, R. Arvidsson, R. Basili, M. B. Demircioglu, *et al.* (2015). The 2013 European seismic hazard model: key components and results, *Bull. Earthq. Eng.* **13,** 3553–3596.

Wyss, M., C. G. Sammis, R. M. Nadeau, and S. Wiemer (2004). Fractal dimension and b-value on creeping and locked patches of the San Andreas fault near Parkfield, California, *Bull. Seismol. Soc. Am.* **94,** no. 2, 410–421.

Zhuang, J., Y. Ogata, and D. Vere-Jones (2002). Stochastic declustering of space-time earthquake occurrences, *J. Am. Stat. Assoc.* **97,** no. 458, 369–380.

APPENDIX

This appendix summarizes the main equations of the study and provides in addition alternative likelihood functions considering another detection function and another magnitude error distribution. The error function model relies on the hypothesis that the amplitude of seismic noise is lognormally distributed. This model has been found to be a good model in a variety of cases (Ogata and Katsura, 1993; Woessner and Wiemer, 2005; Daniel *et al.*, 2008). However, a different detection function can be proposed when considering that the seismic noise is continuous and saturates the detection. This kind of consideration is relevant during aftershock sequences. In that case, it can be shown that the probability that an earthquake of magnitude m is detected (see e.g., Davison, 2003; Sornette, 2006; Hainzl, 2016; Marsan and Ross, 2021) takes the form of a Gumbel function:

$$q(m) = \exp\left(-\exp\left(-\frac{m-\mu}{\sigma}\right)\right). \tag{A1}$$

In this appendix, we first provide the equations for magnitude uncertainties following a uniform law and then for Gaussian magnitude uncertainties. In both cases, we develop the equations for an error detection function and for a Gumbel detection function.

Magnitude uncertainties following a uniform law

We start from equation (14) used in the case of uniform uncertainties in which we will include different detection functions $q(m)$:

$$P(m_i|\beta,\mu,\sigma) = \int_{-\infty}^{+\infty} \frac{1}{K} q(x) e^{-\beta x} \mathcal{U}_{-\Delta m_i}^{+\Delta m_i}(m_i - x)dx. \tag{A2}$$

Error detection function. We first consider an error detection function:

$$q(m) = \frac{1}{2} + \frac{1}{2}\mathrm{erf}\left(\frac{m-\mu}{\sqrt{2}\sigma}\right). \tag{A3}$$

This yields for a given magnitude m_i,

$$P(m_i|\beta,\mu,\sigma) = \frac{1}{2\beta K \Delta m_i}\Bigg(e^{-\beta m_i^{\mathrm{inf}}} q(m_i^{\mathrm{inf}}) - e^{-\beta m_i^{\mathrm{sup}}} q(m_i^{\mathrm{sup}}) + e^{\frac{\sigma^2\beta^2}{2}-\beta\mu}[q(m_i^{\mathrm{sup}} + \sigma^2\beta) - q(m_i^{\mathrm{inf}} + \sigma^2\beta)]\Bigg), \tag{A4}$$

with,

$$m_i^{\mathrm{inf}} = m_i - \Delta m_i m_i^{\mathrm{sup}} = m_i + \Delta m_i. \tag{A5}$$

For a catalog $\mathbf{m}$, assuming the events are independent,

$$P(\mathbf{m}|\beta,\mu,\sigma) = \left(\frac{1}{2\beta K}\right)^N \prod_{i=1}^{N} \frac{1}{\Delta m_i} e^{-\beta m_i^{\mathrm{inf}}} q(m_i^{\mathrm{inf}}) - e^{-\beta m_i^{\mathrm{sup}}} q(m_i^{\mathrm{sup}}) + e^{\frac{\sigma^2\beta^2}{2}-\beta\mu}[q(m_i^{\mathrm{sup}} + \sigma^2\beta) - q(m_i^{\mathrm{inf}} + \sigma^2\beta)]). \tag{A6}$$

Combined with the likelihood of the seismic rate we get the final likelihood:

$$\mathcal{P}(\mathbf{m},N|\beta,\lambda,\mu,\sigma) \sim \prod_{i=1}^{N} \frac{1}{\Delta m_i}\Bigg(-e^{-\beta m_i^{\mathrm{sup}}} q(m_i^{\mathrm{sup}}) + e^{-\beta m_i^{\mathrm{inf}}} q(m_i^{\mathrm{sup}}) + e^{\frac{\sigma^2\beta^2}{2}-\beta\mu}\Big[q(m_i^{\mathrm{sup}} + \sigma^2\beta) - q(m_i^{\mathrm{inf}} + \sigma^2\beta)\Big]\Bigg) \times \lambda^N e^{-\beta K \lambda \Delta T}. \tag{A7}$$

Equations (A3)–(A7) are the same as equations (7), (16), (15), (18), and (24), respectively, of the main text.

Gumbel detection function. Let us now consider a Gumbel detection function:

$$q(m) = \exp\left(-\exp\left(-\frac{m-\mu}{\sigma}\right)\right). \tag{A8}$$

For a given magnitude m_i,

$$P(m_i|\beta,\mu,\sigma) = \frac{1}{2K\Delta m_i}\Bigg(\sigma e^{-\beta\mu}\Gamma(\beta\sigma)\Bigg\{\Gamma_i\Big(\beta\sigma, e^{-\frac{m_i inf - \mu}{\sigma}}\Big) - \Gamma_i\Big(\beta\sigma, e^{-\frac{m_i sup - \mu}{\sigma}}\Big)\Bigg\}\Bigg), \tag{A9}$$

in which $\Gamma_i(a,x)$ is the incomplete gamma function $\Gamma_i(a,x) = \frac{1}{\Gamma(a)}\int_0^x t^{a-1}e^{-t}dt$ and with,

$$m_i^{\mathrm{inf}} = m_i - \Delta m_i m_i^{\mathrm{sup}} = m_i + \Delta m_i. \tag{A10}$$

For a catalog $\mathbf{m}$, this yields

$$P(\mathbf{m}|\beta,\mu,\sigma) = \left(\frac{\sigma\Gamma(\beta\sigma)}{2K}\right)^N e^{-N\beta\mu}\prod_{i=1}^{N}\frac{1}{\Delta m_i}\left(\Gamma_i\left(\beta\sigma,e^{-\frac{m_i\,\inf-\mu}{\sigma}}\right)\right.$$
$$\left.-\Gamma_i\left(\beta\sigma,e^{-\frac{m_i\,\sup-\mu}{\sigma}}\right)\right), \quad \text{(A11)}$$

and including the seismic rate we get

$$\mathcal{P}(\mathbf{m},N|\beta,\lambda,\mu,\sigma)$$
$$\sim\prod_{i=1}^{N}\frac{1}{\Delta m_i}\left(\Gamma_i\left(\beta\sigma,e^{-\frac{m_i\,\inf-\mu}{\sigma}}\right)-\Gamma_i\left(\beta\sigma,e^{-\frac{m_i\,\sup-\mu}{\sigma}}\right)\right)$$
$$\times[\sigma\lambda\beta\Gamma(\beta\sigma)]^N e^{-\beta(N\mu-K\lambda\Delta T)}. \quad \text{(A12)}$$

Equations (A8)–(A12) are the same as equations (7), (16), (15), (18), and (24), respectively, of the main text but for the Gumbel detection function.

Magnitude uncertainties following a Gaussian law

Let us now consider Gaussian magnitude uncertainties as in equation (13) of the study:

$$P(m_i|\beta,\mu,\sigma) = \int_{-\infty}^{+\infty}\frac{1}{K}q(x)e^{-\beta x}\mathcal{N}(x|m_i,\Delta m_i^2)dx$$
$$= \int_{-\infty}^{+\infty}\frac{1}{K\Delta m_i\sqrt{2\pi}}q(x)e^{-\beta x}e^{-\frac{1}{2}\left(\frac{m_i-x}{\Delta m_i}\right)^2}dx. \quad \text{(A13)}$$

Compared with the case of the uniform law, there is no closed-form for this integral that must be numerically integrated.

Error detection function. In the case of an error detection function (equations 7 and A3), this yields for a given magnitude m_i,

$$P(m_i|\beta,\mu,\sigma) = \frac{1}{K\Delta m_i\sqrt{2\pi}}$$
$$\int_{-\infty}^{+\infty}\left(\frac{1}{2}+\frac{1}{2}\mathrm{erf}\left(\frac{x-\mu}{\sqrt{2}\sigma}\right)\right)e^{-\beta x}e^{-\frac{1}{2}\left(\frac{m_i-x}{\Delta m_i}\right)^2}dx, \quad \text{(A14)}$$

and for a catalog $\mathbf{m}$,

$$P(\mathbf{m}|\beta,\mu,\sigma_e) = \left(\frac{1}{K\sqrt{2\pi}}\right)^N\prod_{i=1}^{N}\frac{1}{\Delta m_i}$$
$$\left[\int_{-\infty}^{+\infty}\left(\frac{1}{2}+\frac{1}{2}\mathrm{erf}\left(\frac{x-\mu}{\sqrt{2}\sigma}\right)\right)e^{-\beta x}e^{-\frac{1}{2}\left(\frac{m_i-x}{\Delta m_i}\right)^2}dx\right]. \quad \text{(A15)}$$

Combined with the likelihood of the seismic rate we get the final likelihood:

$$\mathcal{P}(\mathbf{m},N|\beta,\lambda,\mu,\sigma)$$
$$\sim\prod_{i=1}^{N}\frac{1}{\Delta m_i}\left[\int_{-\infty}^{+\infty}\left(\frac{1}{2}+\frac{1}{2}\mathrm{erf}\left(\frac{x-\mu}{\sqrt{2}\sigma}\right)\right)e^{-\beta x}e^{-\frac{1}{2}\left(\frac{m_i-x}{\Delta m_i}\right)^2}dx\right]$$
$$\times(\beta\lambda)^N e^{-\beta K\lambda\Delta T}. \quad \text{(A16)}$$

Gumbel detection function. In the case of a Gumbel detection function (equation A8), this brings for a given magnitude m_i,

$$P(m_i|\beta,\mu,\sigma) = \frac{1}{K\Delta m_i\sqrt{2\pi}}$$
$$\int_{-\infty}^{+\infty}\left(\exp\left(-\exp\left(-\frac{m-\mu}{\sigma}\right)\right)\right)e^{-\beta x}e^{-\frac{1}{2}\left(\frac{m_i-x}{\Delta m_i}\right)^2}dx, \quad \text{(A17)}$$

and for a catalog $\mathbf{m}$,

$$P(\mathbf{m}|\beta,\mu,\sigma) = \left(\frac{1}{K\sqrt{2\pi}}\right)^N\prod_{i=1}^{N}\frac{1}{\Delta m_i}$$
$$\left[\int_{-\infty}^{+\infty}\left(\exp\left(-\exp\left(-\frac{m-\mu}{\sigma}\right)\right)\right)e^{-\beta x}e^{-\frac{1}{2}\left(\frac{m_i-x}{\Delta m_i}\right)^2}dx\right]. \quad \text{(A18)}$$

Combined with the likelihood of the seismic rate we get the final likelihood:

$$\mathcal{P}(\mathbf{m},N|\beta,\lambda,\mu,\sigma)$$
$$\sim\prod_{i=1}^{N}\frac{1}{\Delta m_i}\left[\int_{-\infty}^{+\infty}\left(\exp\left(-\exp\left(-\frac{m-\mu}{\sigma}\right)\right)\right)e^{-\beta x}e^{-\frac{1}{2}\left(\frac{m_i-x}{\Delta m_i}\right)^2}dx\right]$$
$$\times(\beta\lambda)^N e^{-\beta K\lambda\Delta T}. \quad \text{(A19)}$$

Manuscript received 2 October 2025
Published online 19 February 2026

Local Magnitude (M_L) Calibration in the Short-Distance Range—The Case of the Collalto Seismic Network and Surrounding Stations in Northeastern Italy

Enrico Priolo*[1], Maria Adelaide Romano[1], and Laura Peruzza[1]

ABSTRACT

OPEN ACCESS

We calibrate local magnitude equations for northeastern Italy, centered on the Collalto seismic network, using the International Association of Seismology and Physics of the Earth's Interior (IASPEI) parametric formulation and a modified approach from Chovanová and Kristek (2018). Our goal is to develop an M_L distance correction well constrained at short distances, adhering to the Richter definition. Using digital data from 2012 to 2023, we find initial parameters similar to those obtained by Bragato and Tento (2005) on an independent dataset. These values differ significantly from the literature, but their physical meaning is questionable. We then introduce an additional procedural step to reduce the bias likely caused by data oversampling in the 10–40 km range. The resulting equations are $M_L^H = \mathrm{Log}A_H - (-1.545\mathrm{Log}(R/100) + 0.001357(R-100) - 3 + S_i^H)$ and $M_L^V = \mathrm{Log}A_V + 0.238 - (-1.555\mathrm{Log}(R/100) + 0.000995(R-100) - 3 + S_i^V)$ for the horizontal and vertical components, respectively; the S_i represent static corrections for each station and instrumentation configuration. Our new scale is valid for distances 7–200 km and magnitudes from −0.8 to 5.8. It aligns pretty well with the Hutton and Boore (1987) equation from 15 to 160 km, despite the different coefficients; below 50 km distance, where it is best constrained, it generally provides higher values than the other Italian laws and laws tuned for the shortest distances. Average residuals reveal a ± 0.1 perturbation between 40 and 170 km, closely matching a pattern found by Bragato and Tento as well. Our findings highlight the critical impact of distance oversampling and confirm a regional perturbation of wave propagation that affects the Wood–Anderson amplitudes. Our scale aligns linearly with independently calculated M_w and shows to be reliable for the investigated magnitude range across the whole regional area. Thus, it is usable by both local and regional networks in all of northeastern Italy.

KEY POINTS

- Using 2012–2023 data, we calibrate an M_L scale for NE Italy for distances 7–200 km and magnitudes −0.8 to 5.8.
- The new M_L equations address oversampling bias, regional attenuation, and station-specific corrections.
- Consistent with Richter's definition, the new scale performs reliably for dense local and regional networks.

Supplemental Material

INTRODUCTION

The steady increase in industrial activities that exploit the Earth's underground resources has led to the proliferation of dedicated seismic monitoring networks. These networks detect and locate weak earthquakes and microquakes, typically within a range of a few kilometers to a few tens of kilometers. "Industry-oriented" networks are more local and denser than those used for regional or national monitoring of natural seismicity. They are often deployed in populated areas, as industrial activities frequently occur there (e.g., enhanced geothermal projects near cities such as Pohang in South Korea, Strasbourg in France, or Basel in Switzerland). To date, several protocols and

1. National Institute of Oceanography and Applied Geophysics – OGS, Trieste, Italy, https://orcid.org/0000-0002-4392-6781 (EP); https://orcid.org/0000-0002-7191-0496 (MAR); https://orcid.org/0000-0001-7781-5775 (LP)

*Corresponding author: epriolo@ogs.it

Cite this article as Priolo, E., M. A. Romano, and L. Peruzza (2026). Local Magnitude (M_L) Calibration in the Short-Distance Range—The Case of the Collalto Seismic Network and Surrounding Stations in Northeastern Italy, *Bull. Seismol. Soc. Am.* **116**, 984–1006, doi: 10.1785/0120250059 regulations have been developed to provide guidelines for designing such monitoring networks and using data obtained from monitoring subsurface phenomena to prevent potentially dangerous earthquakes (e.g., Majer *et al.*, 2012; MiSE-UNMIG, 2014; Maury *et al.*, 2023). All these protocols require real-time seismic monitoring and quasi-real-time determination of seismological parameters.

Standard processing of seismic data acquired through dense networks allows for the estimation of event time, location, and magnitude. Additional parameters, such as corner frequency, seismic moment, and stress drop, can also be estimated depending on data quality. Magnitude and distance to industrial activities form the basis for protocols aimed at mitigating and managing induced seismicity, such as the well-known "traffic light system" (Bommer *et al.*, 2006; Majer *et al.*, 2012). Therefore, the accuracy of magnitude estimation at short distances (i.e., less than 10–15 km from a seismic station) is critically important, not only for scientific purposes but also for implementing effective management protocols.

The concept of the local magnitude scale (M_L) was introduced in the original study by Richter (1935), who established an empirical law valid for southern California that has been used worldwide for decades to measure the size of earthquakes at distances between 20 and 600 km. This formula defines M_L as a function of the maximum trace amplitude A_{max}, measured in millimeters and recorded by a Wood–Anderson standard torsion seismometer, corrected for a distance-dependent term, and it is usually known in the following form:

$$M_L = \text{Log}A_{max} - \text{Log}A_0(D), \quad (1)$$

in which D is the epicentral distance of the recording station.

Richter (1958) defines the term $-\text{Log}A_0(D)$—today we call it the attenuation term—in tabular form in such a way that $M_L = 3$ if the recorded maximum amplitude is 1 mm for an earthquake at a distance of 100 km. The determination of the term $-\text{Log}A_0(D)$ with such a convention is called magnitude calibration.

In the 1980s, Bakun and Joyner (1984) calibrated the M_L formula for central California, and Hutton and Boore (1987) re-evaluated it for southern California using much larger datasets. These studies were later adopted by the International Association of Seismology and Physics of the Earth's Interior (IASPEI) into the general log-linear formulation used worldwide

$$M_L = \text{Log}A - (n\text{Log}R + KR + C + S), \quad (2)$$

in which A is the Wood–Anderson horizontal displacement amplitude measured in nm, R is the hypocentral distance in km, n and K are coefficients normally related to geometrical spreading and intrinsic attenuation, respectively, C is a constant used to calibrate the formula to a reference value, and S is the station correction (Bormann, 2012).

Although many studies have been conducted to calibrate local magnitude at the regional or national level, very few studies have addressed the problem of estimating local magnitude at short distances (i.e., less than about 15 km), which is required for dense, industry-oriented networks.

For some events induced by hydraulic fracturing at the Preese Hall well near Blackpool, United Kingdom, Butcher *et al.* (2017) showed that the local magnitude calculated by the local monitoring network at short hypocentral distances was significantly higher than the magnitude estimated by the UK National Seismic Network stations, which were located at distances between 80 and 110 km. The authors attributed this discrepancy to the influence of sedimentary layers at the local scale that increase the amplitudes. Therefore, they recalculated the coefficients of the formula used at the national level (Ottenmöller and Sargeant, 2013) and defined a new formula that can be used locally for hypocentral distances in the 5–20 km range.

Luckett *et al.* (2019) added a new exponential term to the classical formula based on the observation that the single-station M_L calculated at stations less than 10 km away is up to one unit higher than the M_L calculated at the most distant stations; in this way, they reduced the scatter due to the unexpectedly high values at short hypocentral distances and allowed the use of a single formula for all distances. They applied this correction to datasets from the United Kingdom, Norway, and the 2016 Amatrice, Italy, seismic sequence and demonstrated the effectiveness of this approach for different areas. Remarkably, they acknowledge that the form of this additional term was chosen "simply because it describes the observed data," whereas "the underlying physical reason is not clearly understood."

In this work, we calibrate the local magnitude equation for the area monitored by the Collalto seismic network. This network has been operational since 2012 and monitors natural and potentially induced seismicity in the vicinity of the Collalto underground gas storage facility (Priolo *et al.*, 2015) in northeastern Italy (Fig. 1). We employ the general parametric formula for the magnitude proposed by IASPEI (Bormann *et al.*, 2012) and determine the best constants for our study area using a modification of the approach proposed by Chovanová and Kristek (2018) for Slovakia.

We deliberately adopt the standard IASPEI M_L formulation without introducing additional empirical distance-dependent correction terms (e.g., Luckett *et al.*, 2019) or resorting to a nonparametric formulation (e.g., Bragato and Tento, 2005; Lolli *et al.*, 2015), to preserve consistency with the internationally accepted definition of local magnitude and to ensure direct comparability with the practices adopted by the majority of authoritative seismic monitoring networks.

We use all the available digital data for the decade 2012–2023 from the Collalto seismic network, and from some stations of the northeast Italy (NEI) regional network managed by the National Institute of Oceanography and Applied Geophysics

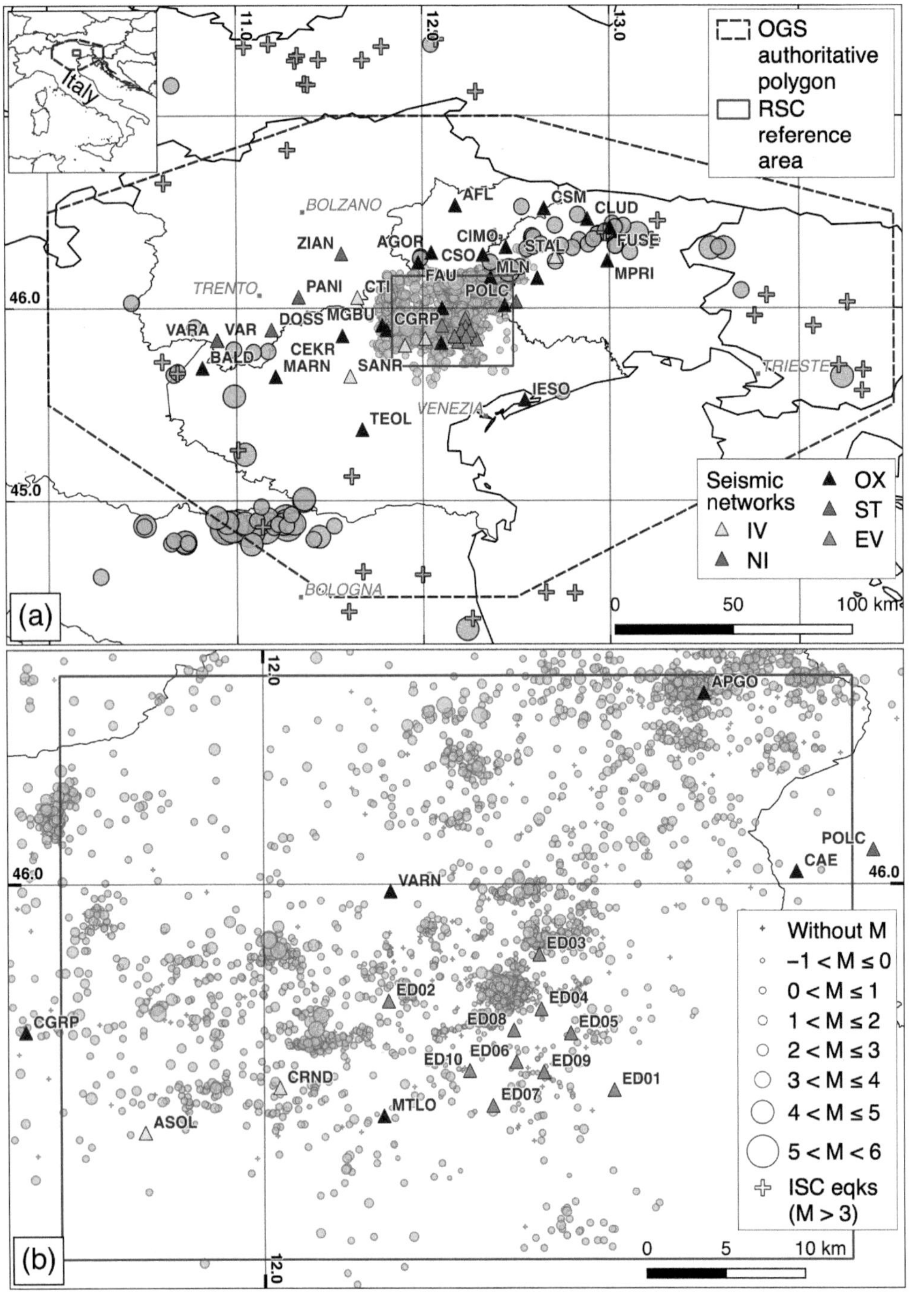

Figure 1. Map of the study area with the earthquakes and stations used. The inset in the upper left corner shows the location map of the study area within Italy. Panels (a) and (b) show the stations locations and two different groups of earthquakes from the entire earthquake dataset: regional earthquakes (gray symbols, panel a; circles and crosses represent the National Institute of Oceanography and Applied Geophysics [OGS] or National Institute of Geophysics and Volcanology [INGV], and International Seismological Centre [ISC] locations, respectively) and local earthquakes (green circles, panel b). The red rectangle in both panels (a) and (b) represents the reference area monitored by the Collalto network (Priolo *et al.*, 2015), and the polygon with the black dashed line encloses the authoritative seismic monitoring area of the OGS. The size of the earthquake symbols is proportional to the local magnitude as it appears in the original catalogs (see also the legend). The seismic stations (triangles) are colored according to the seismic network to which they belong to (see also the International Federation of Digital Seismograph Networks [FDSN] codes in the legend on the left): EV, Collalto Seismic Network; IV, Italian National Seismic Network; NI, northeast Italy Broadband Network; OX, northeast Italy Seismic Network; and ST, Trentino Seismic Network. The color version of this figure is available only in the electronic edition.

(OGS), with a maximum distance of about 250 km between earthquakes and stations; the earthquake catalog covers the magnitude range from M_L − 0.8 to 5.8, and provides adequate distance/azimuth coverage for most of the stations. We compute Wood–Anderson amplitudes from the entire dataset of available full waveforms, and apply ad hoc developed pre- and postprocessing techniques to select the right signals and obtain reliable amplitudes even for noisy signals. Furthermore, some procedures are used to reduce erroneous amplitude values, inadequate azimuthal coverage, insufficient range coverage, and to test the statistical robustness of the results.

MAGNITUDE CALIBRATION: METHOD

The IASPEI Working Group on Magnitude Measurement recommends the following standard formula for calculating M_L for crustal earthquakes in regions with similar attenuation characteristics to southern California (Bormann, 2012):

$$M_L = \mathrm{Log}A + 1.11\mathrm{Log}R + 0.00189R - 2.09, \tag{3}$$

in which R is the hypocentral distance instead of the epicentral distance of the original Richter (1935) formula, and A, measured in nm, accounts for the correct Wood–Anderson seismograph response, that is, a static magnification of 2080 instead of 2800 and a damping factor of 0.7 instead of 0.8 (Uhrhammer and Collins, 1990). Thus, for $A = 10^6/2080$ nm and R = 100 km, equation (3) results in $M_L = 3$ (Havskov and Ottenmöller, 2010).

Note also that equation (3) can be expressed equivalently by explicitly specifying the reference distance at which the magnitude is calibrated, that is,

$$M_L = \mathrm{Log}A_{WA} + 1.11\mathrm{Log}(R/100) + 0.00189(R - 100) + 3.0, \quad (4)$$

in which A_{WA} accounts for the change of amplitude unit from nm to mm, 100 represents the reference hypocentral distance in km for which the maximum horizontal displacement of an original Wood–Anderson seismograph of 1 mm would be associated with an $M_L = 3$. Equation (4) is the form given by Hutton and Boore (1987), who also suggest using a shorter reference distance of 17 km to calculate the magnitude of earthquakes detected by local networks; at a hypocentral distance $R = 17$ km, an earthquake of magnitude $M_L = 2$ would result in $A = 1$ mm.

Equations (3) and (4) apply only to regions with attenuation characteristics similar to those of southern California, and they remain the standard practice for M_L computation in most seismological observatories worldwide. In regions with different attenuation properties, IASPEI guidelines leave the choice of the functional form of the equation and the constraints imposed on the fitted empirical parameters entirely open. Nevertheless, most authors have calibrated M_L using the general log-linear formulation given in equation (2). It is beyond the scope of this article to provide a detailed review of all the investigations conducted to calibrate M_L for different areas; instead, for the targets we are more interested in (i.e., short distances/small earthquakes, and northeastern Italy), we address:

- the works of Butcher *et al.* (2017) and Luckett *et al.* (2019), already mentioned in the introduction, because they extend M_L estimation to short distances; and
- the calibrations proposed for Italy by Spallarossa *et al.* (2002), Bragato and Tento (2005), Bobbio *et al.* (2009), and Di Bona (2016) for northwestern, northeastern, and southern Italy, respectively; and by Lolli *et al.* (2015) and Di Bona (2016) for the entire Italian territory.

To calibrate the local magnitude, that is, to perform a linear regression of equation (2), we initially adopt the method proposed by Chovanová and Kristek (2018)—a data-driven procedure organized in three consecutive steps—and implement it in a MATLAB code. After several sensitivity tests and validation of the inversion procedure using synthetic datasets, we add a fourth statistically driven step, aimed at reducing the bias caused by oversampled distances on the inversion results. The formalism of the method is as follows.

Let j and i be the indices from 1 to N_E and N_S for the earthquakes and the stations, respectively. Substituting the amplitude and distance data into equation (2) we obtain an overdetermined linear system of the form:

$$\mathrm{Log}A_{ji} = M_{Lj} + n\mathrm{Log}R_{ji} + KR_{ji} + S_i + C; j = 1,\ldots N_E; i = 1,\ldots N_S. \quad (5)$$

Because not all the stations record the same event, we indicate with N the total number of the available waveform amplitudes, that is, the Wood–Anderson simulated peak amplitudes. Because the magnitude of the jth event and the constant C are coupled, we cannot determine them separately. We then define

$$M_j = M_{Lj} + C, \quad (6)$$

and introduce it into the system (5), which gives us

$$\mathrm{Log}A_{ji} = M_j + n\mathrm{Log}R_{ji} + KR_{ji} + S_i; j = 1,\ldots N_E; i = 1,\ldots N_S. \quad (7)$$

We also impose the condition that the station coefficients (i.e., the static correction) give an average value of zero,

$$S_1 + S_2 + \ldots + S_{Ns} = 0. \quad (8)$$

The coefficient C and the station coefficients S_i will be solved in the final calibration step.

The linear system given by equations (7) and (8) is solved with the MATLAB operator "\", which provides the least-square solution that minimizes the residuals in the two-norm using a QR factorization (decomposition into an orthogonal matrix Q and an upper triangular matrix R).

The first step of the solution procedure aims to remove the outliers from the global linear system. Equations (7) and (8) are solved for the unknown parameters n, K, and S_i, and the residuals r_{ji} are calculated as

$$r_{ji} = \mathrm{Log}A_{ji} - (M_j + n\mathrm{Log}R_{ji} + KR_{ji} + S_i); j = 1,\ldots N_E; i = 1,\ldots N_S. \quad (9)$$

Outliers are defined as the data outside a quantity proportional to the interquartile range of the residuals (IQR). This step consists of an iterative process in which equation (9) is solved, IQR is estimated, outliers are removed from the dataset, and the linear system is updated with the remaining data for a new iteration step. Iteration stops when all outliers are removed from the dataset.

In the second step, a solution is found that minimizes the unbiased sample standard deviation of the residuals σ, which is defined as

$$\sigma = \mathrm{sqrt}((\Sigma r_{ij}^2)/(N - (N_E + N_S + 1))). \quad (10)$$

In this case, the best solution to the following equation:

$$\mathrm{Log}A_{ji} - n\mathrm{Log}R_{ji} - K\,R_{ji} = M_j + S_i, \quad (11)$$

is found through a local grid search in the space of parameters n and K, in a neighborhood of the final solution of the previous step. In practice, given n and K, taken in the selected grid interval, we get residuals for calculating equation (10) by estimating M_j and S_i from equation (11) using regression analysis. The grid search can be repeated by changing the grid resolution to an acceptable value. The second step was applied iteratively (three iterations on average), starting from a coarser grid and refining it until the minimum was clearly identified. Given the simplicity of the misfit function and the limited dimensionality of the parameter space, this approach proposed by Chovanová and Kristek (2018) proved sufficiently accurate and robust, and no evidence of aliasing effects related to periodic noise was observed in the inversion results.

The third step determines the constant C and then the static station coefficients S_i. Assuming that $\overline{n}$ and $\overline{K}$ are the best solutions for n and K found after the previous step, the constant C is estimated as follows:

$$\overline{C} = -M_0 + \mathrm{Log}A_0 - \overline{n}\mathrm{Log}R_0 - \overline{K}R_0, \tag{12}$$

in which M_0 is the reference magnitude for which at a source–station distance R_0 a reference Wood–Anderson peak amplitude A_0 is found. Finally, the static station coefficients are calculated as follows:

$$S_i = \mathrm{Log}A_{ji} - (\overline{n}\mathrm{Log}R_{ji} + \overline{K} + R_{ji} + \overline{C}) - M_j, \tag{13}$$

together with condition (8).

We add a fourth, final, statistically driven step, aimed at reducing the bias of oversampled distances on the inversion results. To this end, we extract by random selection on the original data N_D subsets of amplitude/distance/station, with a more uniform distance distribution, and invert them. Then, the overall parameters n, K, and S_i are calculated as the mean of the individual parameters found for the N_D subsets.

We have verified the MATLAB code implementing the method of Chovanová and Kristek (2018) by some synthetic tests. We create synthetic amplitude datasets with the same distance and magnitude distributions of our original data (see subsequently in the text), using the parametric magnitude law developed by Di Bona (2016; see his equation 13) for Italy, namely:

$$M_L = \mathrm{Log}A + 1.667\mathrm{Log}(R/100) + 0.001736(R-100) + 3, \tag{14}$$

as a reference for the calculation of WA synthetic amplitudes.

The first dataset contains the WA amplitudes calculated exactly by equation (14) from the original magnitudes. In the second and third datasets, the WA amplitudes are calculated after a perturbation is applied to the magnitudes, assuming a normal or a uniform distribution of the perturbation. Different datasets are created for the latter types to account for the different perturbation values (e.g., 0.3, 0.5 magnitude units). The results of the inversion show that the parameters n and K are accurately determined for the first dataset, whereas the accuracy of n and K coefficients decreases when the WA amplitude (or, equivalently, the reference magnitude) is increasingly perturbed. Further details are given in Text S1 of the supplemental material, available with this article.

STUDY AREA AND DATA

The area in which we have a statistically meaningful number of low-magnitude and short-distance earthquake recordings is in northeastern Italy, at the border between the southern Alpine front and the northern Veneto plain (Fig. 1, red rectangle).

From a tectonic point of view, this area is characterized by a west-southwest–east-northeast (WSW-ENE)-trending, south-southeast (S-SE) verging fold-and-thrust system, partly hidden under Quaternary sediments (Picotti *et al.*, 2022), and is undergoing an active shortening of ~1 mm/yr in north-west–southeast (NW-SE) direction in response to the convergence between the Adria and Eurasia plates, as revealed by Global Positioning System (GPS) velocities (Anderlini *et al.*, 2020). The Parametric Catalog of Italian Earthquakes (CPTI15 v4.0; Rovida *et al.*, 2020, 2022) reports three main events in the study area: the Asolo earthquake (M_w 6.4) in 1695 in the southwestern corner, and two events in the Alpago-Cansiglio in the northeastern corner, one in 1873 with M_w 6.3 and one in 1936 with M_w 6.1. On the other hand, the seismic activity of the last fifty years, monitored at the regional scale by OGS, is quite moderate; the instrumental record shows only two dozen events with $M_L > 3.0$ and a single event with $M_L = 4.0$ occurred more than 40 yr ago (namely on 14 October 1980, see Sugan *et al.*, 2024; and Data and Resources).

In this area, OGS was commissioned by Edison Stoccaggio S.p.A. in 2010 to set up a dense local network for high-resolution seismicity monitoring around the "Collalto Stoccaggio" underground gas storage concession (Priolo *et al.*, 2015). The Collalto seismic network (RSC) began operating in 2011 and has been fully operational since 1 January 2012. It consists of ten seismic stations (orange triangles in Fig. 1, station codes ED01-ED10) and one permanent geodetic station at the ED06 site. The RSC is equipped with broadband seismometers, mostly deployed in boreholes at depths ranging from 5 to 155 m. Five stations are also equipped with accelerometers deployed at the ground surface. Real-time data acquisition, alerting, and automatic location of events are performed by the BRTT Antelope system. Signals are sampled at 200 Hz for the broadbands and 100 Hz for the accelerometers, then are transmitted to the OGS acquisition center, processed, and archived permanently in miniSEED format (Incorporated Research Institutions for Seismology [IRIS], 2012). Routine locations are performed using both Hypo71 (Lee and Lahr, 1975) and Hypoellipse (Lahr, 1999) codes. The first program provides locations consistent with those of the regional NEI seismic network managed by OGS, and the second provides more refined locations for studies of the seismicity and seismotectonics at the local scale. The local magnitude M_L indicated in the RSC catalogs so far is estimated using the parametric attenuation law obtained by Bragato and Tento (2005) for northeastern Italy, and corrections to remove the static residuals of the stations derived empirically. The magnitude of completeness of the RSC network ranges from about 0.0 in the central part of the area up to 1.0 in the remaining parts. More details can be found in Priolo *et al.* (2015) and Romano *et al.* (2019).

The monitoring purposes of the local RSC network are enhanced by the real-time exchange of signals from some surrounding stations, which contribute to the automatic detection of events, discrimination between true/false events and local/regional/teleseismic events, automatic and manual relocation, and postprocessing. In particular, since 1977, the OGS has been managing the NEI regional seismic network (Priolo *et al.*, 2005; Bragato *et al.*, 2021); it alerts local civil protection authorities to regional events above the perception threshold (about $M_L > 2.5$) and publishes preliminary earthquake locations in quasi-real time on a dedicated website and on major social media, and revised bulletins later. The NEI network currently comprises 43 stations with a station spacing of about 15–40 km. The OGS also shares the signals of some stations in real time with the Italian nationwide seismic monitoring systems of the National Institute of Geophysics and Volcanology (INGV) (Rete Sismica Nazionale [RSN]; Michelini *et al.*, 2016), other regional data providers, and, at the international level, with the authorities of neighboring countries such as Slovenia and Austria.

For this study, we use data from the RSC network and some stations of the other networks, selected to extend the range of observations outside the core area, beyond the reference distance of 100 km, as local magnitude is by definition calibrated on observations at a distance of 100 km; we can thus provide the best constraints in a wider range of magnitude and distance applicable to northeastern Italy (Fig. 1).

Even if our analysis refers to the last twelve years, it is also worth remembering that the OGS network in NEI has crossed nearly all the technological changes in the seismological devices of the last 50 yr. Some articles have recalibrated the formulas used for magnitude assessment (see Moratto *et al.*, 2017; Sandron *et al.*, 2018, and references therein), and investigated the time–space variation of the magnitude of completeness (e.g., Gentili *et al.*, 2011; Peresan and Gentili, 2018). Nevertheless, a truly uniform measure of magnitude all over the decades is only partially reached.

The colored triangles in Figure 1 are the stations used to calibrate M_L in this study. The basic information on these stations is given in Table 1. Further information is in Text S2 and Table S2.

The earthquake data set used for M_L calibration at short distances is for the time period from 1 January 2012 to 31 March 2023, and consists of two groups as follows:

1. The entire RSC catalog in the previously quoted reference time frame (Fig. 1b); it contains 3491 earthquakes located by Hypoellipse and a custom velocity model estimated by Romano *et al.* (2019) in the reference area of the Collalto network (red rectangle in Fig. 1). For studying the impact of parsing the earthquake dataset on a priori rules, such as those based on location quality, the RSC catalog is subdivided in two separate data subsets. A first subset, containing the best-constrained hypocentral solutions (BC subset), has been built according to the following criteria (from Husen and Hardebeck, 2010): gap ≤ 180°; at least eight arrival times with at least one phase read at an epicentral distance less than or equal the hypocentral depth and one *S*-phase read at an epicentral distance less than or equal 1.4 times the hypocentral depth. The BC subset contains 1535 hypocentral solutions. The second subset contains all the remaining 1956 events.
2. A complementary list of 125 earthquakes selected from those recorded by the regional NEI network in the same period and located mainly (though not exclusively) far from the Collalto network, at distances of up to about 200 km (Fig. 1a). The minimum threshold in magnitude increases from 3 to 4, depending on the distance from the reference area. For this list of events, the hypocentral solutions are provided by different agencies, that is, OGS (mainly when epicenters fall within its authoritative polygon that covers Friuli Venezia Giulia, Veneto, and partially the Trento Province), INGV, and ISC (ISC epicenters shown by gray crosses in Fig. 1). No information about the contributing stations (i.e., arrival times) is easily accessible for this earthquake list.

The inclusion of events with larger magnitude and distances than the "core" dataset (e.g., $M_L > 5$ of the Emilia sequence) makes the calibration more robust and extends its range of validity. We are aware that the earthquake list used in this study is not uniform in terms of completeness, quality of hypocentral solutions, algorithm, and velocity model used for location, and estimation of the initial magnitude. A sensitivity analysis we performed on the effects of location error on the M_L estimates (see Text S3) shows that the geometric uncertainty has a negligible impact at large station–earthquake distances, of the order of 10^{-2} magnitude units for 1 km of mislocation at 100 km distance. The bias remains acceptable, up to about 10 km event–station distance, at about M_L 0.15 for 1 km of mislocation at 10 km distance. This location uncertainty component depends on the distance corrections, but always increases exponentially at very short distances ($R < 5$ km). In our case study, such very short distances are not represented in the dataset.

The data processing to calculate the Wood–Anderson peaks is as follows. For each earthquake, the raw waveforms from all available stations are extracted as a 240 s window with 40 s of pre-event signal before the event origin time t_0. In a preprocessing step, the signals are checked for possible fragmentation: small gaps are interpolated (SAC command *merge gap interp*),

TABLE 1
Overview of the Station Sites

Station Code	Net Code	Location	Longitude E (°)	Latitude N (°)	Elevation (m)	First Installation Date (yyyy/mm/dd)	Channel
AFL	OX	Alpe Faloria	12.1755	46.5283	2235	1995/01/01	SH, EH, HN
AGOR	OX	Agordo	12.0472	46.2829	631	2007/01/06	HH, HN
APGO	OX	Alpago	12.3630	46.1516	598	2017/04/15	EH, HN
ASOL	IV	Asolo	11.9023	45.8003	181	2011/01/17	HN
BALD	OX	Monte Baldo	10.8187	45.6830	1911	2007/11/08	HH, HN
CAE	OX	Caneva	12.4378	46.0089	870	1995/01/01	SH, HH, HN
CEKR	OX	Cima Ekar (Asiago)	11.5685	45.8492	1365	2019/04/01	EH, HN
CGRP	OX	Cima Grappa	11.8047	45.8806	1757	2005/04/21*	HH, HN
CIMO	OX	Cimolais	12.4448	46.3116	710	2005/04/21	HH, HN
CLUD	OX	Cludinicco	12.8814	46.4569	635	2011/02/15	HH, HN
CRND	IV	Cornuda	12.0131	45.8361	159	2011/11/04	HN
CSM	OX	Casera Mimoias	12.6515	46.5125	1635	1995/01/01	SH, HH, HN
CSO	OX	Casso	12.3228	46.2724	1060	1995/01/01	SH, EH, HN
CTI	IV	Castel Tesino	11.6497	46.0482	1180	2003/03/01	EH, HH
DOSS	ST	Dosso del Sommo	11.1884	45.8808	1660	2011/12/11	HH, HN
ED01	EV	Susegana Santa Lucia	12.2892	45.8346	54	2011/12/03	HH, EH, HN
ED02	EV	Farra di Soligo	12.1031	45.9057	205	2011/12/03	HH, HN
ED03	EV	Corbanese	12.2278	45.9429	235	2011/12/03	HH
ED04	EV	Santa Maria di Feletto	12.2295	45.8994	182	2011/12/03	HH
ED05	EV	San Michele di Feletto	12.2538	45.8801	110	2011/12/03	HH, HN
ED06	EV	Collalto Campo 6	12.2085	45.8570	174	2011/12/03	HH, HN
ED07	EV	Nervesa della Battaglia	12.1894	45.8222	167	2011/12/03	HH, HN
ED08	EV	Collalto Cucco	12.2065	45.8825	194	2011/12/15	HH, HN
ED09	EV	Susegana Castello	12.2315	45.8488	105	2011/12/03	HH
ED10	EV	Santa Croce del Montello	12.1702	45.8500	144	2011/12/03	HH
FAU	OX	Forcella Aurine	11.9753	46.2322	1430	1995/01/01*	SH
FUSE	OX	Fusea	13.0011	46.4142	520	2007/12/13	HH, HN
IESO	OX	Iesolo	12.5464	45.5178	0	2001/04/01	SH, EH, HN
MARN	OX	Marana	11.2099	45.6378	785	2009/11/24	HH, HN
MGBU	OX	Monte Grappa	11.7813	45.9041	1517	2022/05/01	HH, HN
MLN	OX	Malnisio	12.6154	46.1495	814	1995/11/02	SH, HH, HN
MPRI	OX	Monte Prat	12.9872	46.2400	762	1995/01/01	SH, EH, HH, HN
MTLO	OX	Montello	12.0991	45.8136	350	1995/01/01	SH, HH, HN
PANI	ST	Panarotta	11.3349	46.0508	1985	2008/01/01	EH, HN
POLC	NI	Polcenigo	12.5005	46.0266	150	2007/12/13	HH, HN
SANR	IV	Sandrigo	11.6099	45.6400	51	2012/01/23	HN
STAL	IV	Staligial	12.7104	46.2601	625	2010/05/25	HH, HN
TEOL	IV	Teolo	11.6740	45.3617	370	2002/03/06	SH, HH
VARA	ST	Varagna	10.8965	45.8260	1735	2012/11/19	EH
VARN	OX	Varnada	12.1048	45.9933	1265	2006/11/16	SH, HH, HN
ZIAN	ST	Ziano di Fiemme	11.5632	46.2764	1154	2012/11/19	EH

In the channel field, sensor types are defined according to the International Federation of Digital Seismograph Network (FDSN) channel convention (see Data and Resources).
*Cessation of operation.

whereas the signal is discarded if large gaps are found (usually the gaps are similar for all three components). A procedure was then implemented to calculate the Wood–Anderson (WA) maximum values from all available waveforms for all considered events. In the first step, the corresponding instrument correction is applied for each waveform, and the WA waveform is simulated (SAC command *transfer from polezero ... to ...*).

For simulating the WA response and restricting the larger band of the modern digital seismometers to that of the WA, the suggestions by Havskov and Ottenmöller (2010) and the IASPEI magnitude recommendations (Bormann *et al.*, 2012) are followed. We distinguish between weak events, for which the corner frequency lies within the plateau of the WA spectral response, and moderate events, which have relevant content of low frequencies. After a sensitivity analysis, we set the magnitude threshold of M_L 3.5 to apply different processing filters. In practice, we apply within the same SAC command the WA simulation—a phaseless band-pass filter applied to the displacement in the band 1.25–20 Hz—and a band-pass cosine taper to improve the signal-to-noise ratio (SNR), which depends on the earthquake magnitude. The cosine tapers are 0.625–1.25 Hz and 20–40 Hz for $M_L < 3.5$, and 0.01–0.1 Hz and 20–40 Hz for $M_L \geq 3.5$. Text S4 shows some examples of the impact of the band-pass filter.

The maximum Wood–Anderson zero-to-peak amplitudes for all three components are measured in a precalculated time window that includes the approximate theoretical arrival times of the most energetic phases. Only signals for which the signal-to-noise ratio (SNR, defined as the ratio between the maximum WA amplitudes in the signal and noise windows) is above a certain threshold provide WA peaks to be further processed, whereas the others are discarded. Because the origin time t_0 of the event in the extracted waveforms is at 40 s, we define the noise window for the calculation of the SNR as [5, 35] s from the beginning of the waveform. The signal window is set to $[t_0 + t_P, t_0 + t_P + 3 * (t_R - t_P)]$ s, in which t_P and t_R are the theoretical travel times for the P and Rayleigh waves, respectively, and $t_0 = 40$ s. The SNR thresholds for retaining the WA peak calculations are set to 1.53 and 2.5, respectively, for the waveforms with a measured P-wave arrival time (according to the location details given in the RSC catalog), and for all other waveforms. These two thresholds were determined empirically after several tests during which we also checked that the dominant period of the signals is smaller than the dominant period of the noise, a condition for ensuring accurate signal amplitude measurements. They have been demonstrated to be effective for removing most of the spurious amplitudes. Some examples of the results of this step are shown in Figure 2.

A further cleaning of the dataset is performed manually to remove spurious peaks not caused by earthquakes, as identified by anomalies in the Log(A) versus distance diagram, or by inconsistencies between WA waveforms' amplitudes derived from simultaneous recordings by colocated seismometers and accelerometers. We point out that this last step is possible because we identify each station configuration with great care, as described subsequently. Finally, data with very large residuals after the iterations of the first step of the inversion are also identified, checked, and eventually removed.

In real networks, even if the monitoring site coordinates remain the same, the technical characteristics of stations change over time. Sometimes these changes are not limited to the mechanical/electronic devices, but affect the deployment of sensors (e.g., depth or sensor coupling to the ground). In addition, some stations often have more than one sensor, for example, a seismometer and an accelerometer. Because we want to use all available data coming from different instruments and installations, these changes cannot obviously be mixed; thus, we have: (1) carefully traced the different instrument configurations, and (2) identified the time periods in which a given station maintains the same configuration. To distinguish the records, we append a letter to the original station code, so that the different configurations of the "same" station can be identified (see Text S2 for more details). These new station codes are used in the regression process. In this way, for each uniform station configuration, an independent station correction S_i is obtained from equation (2).

To our knowledge, no previous study has ever explored the consequences of such changes in the station correction parametrization; nonetheless, we acknowledge that detailed "station books", that is, the record of all the changes in station configuration, are not always available. We consider these records fully reliable for the RSC stations (network code EV), and for some NEI stations (network code OX). This approach offers several advantages, such as the possibility to evaluate the amplitude consistency between different configurations, the possibility to detect erroneous instrumental response functions used for instrument correction, and the retention of different configurations (e.g., a change in sensor depth) without affecting the overall regression. Conversely, the disadvantage is that a comprehensive, time-dependent station characterization has to be entered for the computation of magnitudes. All these aspects will be commented on later in the Discussion section.

The result of the processing described earlier is a huge table of three-component peak amplitudes with accompanying SNR values, station names, hypocentral distances, and some ancillary information about the related earthquakes. These data are used in the calibration procedure.

Figure 3 shows the distribution of the entire WA amplitude dataset in relation to (1) the source-receiver hypocentral distance, and (2) the magnitude values provided by the authoritative agency. The dataset consists of 36,225 station records with WA peak amplitudes; note that WA amplitudes may not be available for all three components. The hypocentral distances range from 2.8 to 295 km, with a median value of 24.5 km. The 5th–95th percentiles are 10.5–143.5 km. There are about 1200 observations for distances below 10 km. The magnitude values range from −0.8 to 5.8, with a median value of 0.95 and 5th–95th percentiles of 0.05–3.75. Note that the magnitude–frequency distribution does not follow a usual G-R pattern as completeness varies spatially.

RESULTS

The first step of the regression begins with a data set consisting of 34,805 and 28,038 WA peak amplitudes for the horizontal and vertical components, respectively. Following the Richter specification for the individual processing of the two horizontal components, and taking into account that the magnitudes of the two horizontal components have the same attenuation term, we calculate

$$\mathrm{LogWA}_H = 0.5(\mathrm{LogWA}_X + \mathrm{LogWA}_Y), \qquad (15)$$

and use WA_H for the inversion. If only one horizontal component is available, that value is used. The threshold for removing outliers was set to 1.8 times the interquartile range (IQR) for both components. After 19 and 15 iterations, respectively,

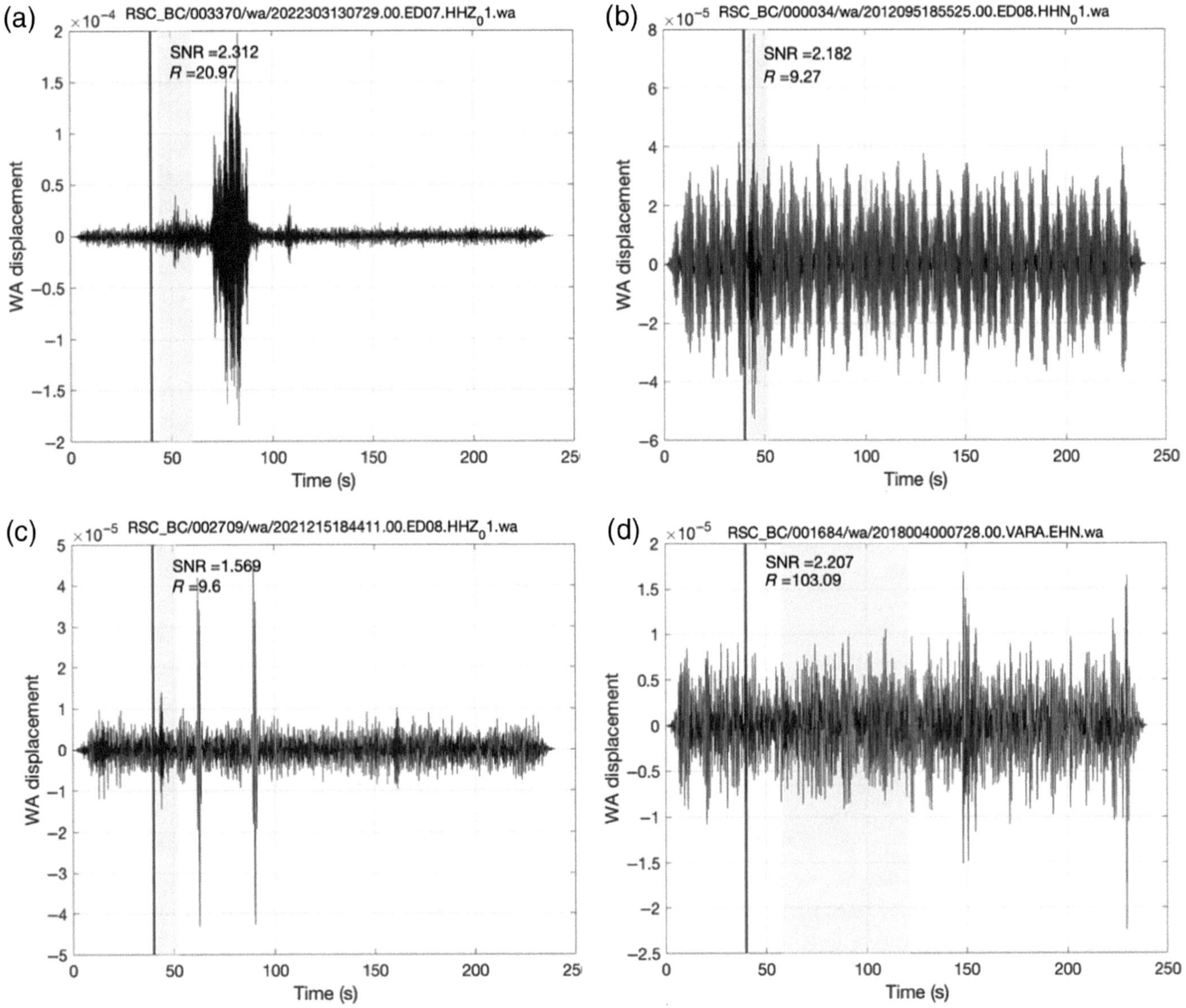

Figure 2. Examples of simulated Wood–Anderson recordings. The red line represents the origin time t0 (40 s after the start of the waveform), the reddish shadow shows the time window of theoretical arrivals of the most energetic phases, based on station–hypocenter distance and a simplified constant velocity model; the estimated signal-to-noise ratio (SNR) values and the hypocentral station–event distance R are listed in the upper left part of each frame. (a) A small event at about 21 km distance from the station, followed soon after by another stronger event. The SNR is about 2.3, and the peak amplitude is correctly identified. (b) Small event, embedded in a strong periodic component of ambient noise, with a manual P-phase arrival-time pick. The WA peak is clearly recognizable. The SNR is 2.18. (c) Small event with P-wave time pick embedded in ambient noise and with two other pronounced signals shortly after the theoretical arrival window. The waveform of the event is only faintly recognizable. The SNR is about 1.57. (d) Small event at about 100 km distance, embedded in the ambient noise, with no pick. The waveform of the event is not clearly recognizable. The SNR is about 2.2. This example represents the case of a doubtful event with the highest SNR value in the group of events without manual picks; the peak amplitude was discarded. The color version of this figure is available only in the electronic edition.

for the horizontal and vertical components, 3,006 and 2,592 outliers are removed, resulting in an input dataset for step 2 with 31,799 and 25,446 amplitudes belonging to 3,405 and 3,302 earthquakes. Figure 4 shows a summary plot of the dataset at the first and the last iteration. The figure also shows that the threshold for the outliers has changed (i.e., decreased) with the iterations. For example, for the horizontal component, it starts at 0.4644 for the first iteration and ends at 0.3525 for the last iteration. The parameters n and K obtained at the end of the first step are $(n,K)_H = (-2.262, 0.004265)$ and $(n,K)_V = (-2.346, 0.004476)$.

The grid search of the second step is performed with ranges/grid increments of -2.220 to $-2.206/2.0 \times 10^{-4}$ and 0.0041–$0.00422/3.0 \times 10^{-6}$ for the horizontal component. The final (i.e., best) values found for the two components are: $(n,K)_H = (-2.212, 0.004168)$ and $(n,K)_V = (-2.346, 0.004475)$.

The coefficients n and K determined so far differ from those proposed for California or the entire Italian territory.

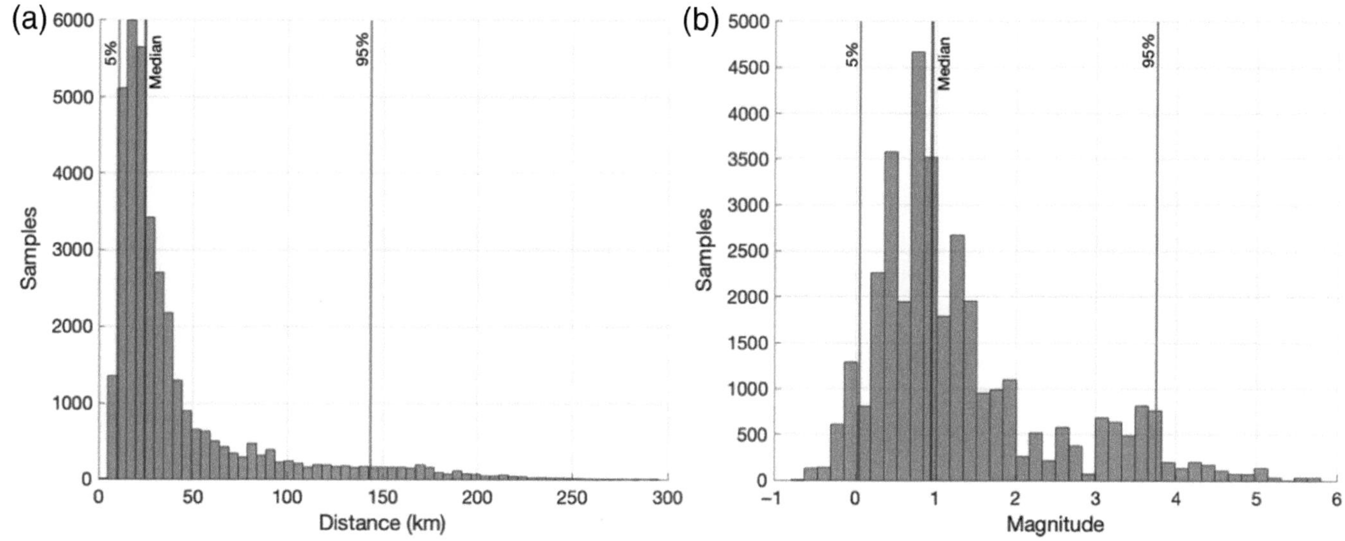

Figure 3. WA amplitude data set: (a) hypocentral distance distribution; (b) earthquake magnitude distribution. Each panel also shows the median value and the 5th and 95th percentiles of the distribution. The color version of this figure is available only in the electronic edition.

Specifically, our values for n are significantly lower—typically ranges are between −1.1 and −1.8—and the sign of K is reversed. In contrast, our coefficients closely align with those determined by Bragato and Tento (2005) for the horizontal component, which are $n = -2.23$ and $K = 0.0039$. Their 2005 study covered a similar geographic region but used a completely different dataset: earthquakes from 1995 to 2002, primarily located in Friuli and Slovenia; our analysis uses events from 2012 to 2023, mostly located in the Veneto and Friuli regions. In addition, the two studies rely on different groups of recording stations and instrumentation. Bragato and Tento performed a nonparametric inversion to determine the attenuation term $-\mathrm{Log}(A_0)$ and showed that it exhibits a complex behavior that the parametric inversion could not reproduce.

In the present study, after having verified the codes with synthetic datasets, as described in the Magnitude Calibration: Method section, we also performed an inversion using the best-constrained locations of the Collalto network only (BC dataset; see the Study Area and Data section), which consists of 17,510 observations, predominantly within distances below 80 km. The n and K coefficients we obtained from this test (namely $(n,K)_H = (-3.055,0.0143)$) indicate an even more pronounced divergence from common values. We thus hypothesize that the drift toward anomalous n and K coefficients, although it could be affected by wave propagation properties through the upper crust, may be strongly influenced by the nonuniform distribution of data points across distance ranges. As clearly illustrated in Figure 3, the number of amplitudes at 10–40 km distance is ten to twenty times greater than the ones at distances >60 km. Figure 5 clearly shows how the parameters n and K influence the theoretical curve of the $-\mathrm{Log}A_0(R)$ term, in two distinct distance ranges; n primarily dominates in the 0–70 km range (Fig. 5a), whereas K becomes dominant at distances beyond approximately 100 km, causing the curve to bend (upward for concordant sign of n and K, downward if reverse, Fig. 5b). We stress that Figure 5 is intended solely for illustrative purposes to show the results of a sensitivity analysis; the curve labeled as "Global Inversion" represents our intermediate result of the global inversion, which is physically implausible.

Thus, as previously mentioned, we introduce a fourth, statistically driven step to reduce the bias caused by the oversampling of distances in the inversion results. By a Monte Carlo-based subsampling approach, we create several datasets with a more uniform distance distribution by randomly selecting amplitudes from the original dataset and performing separate inversions on each selection. Specifically, we parse the distances into 60 linear bins in the range of 0–300 km and form 30 different datasets by random sampling, imposing an upper threshold of 200 samples per bin. Figure 6 provides an example of one such subset.

For the 30 datasets with random search of a more uniform distance distribution, we obtain 30 (n, K) solutions, for both the horizontal and vertical components; we then calculate their mean and standard deviation, which turn out to be

$$(\overline{n},\overline{K})_H = (-1.545 \pm 0.072635,0.001357 \pm 0.000249), \quad (16)$$

$$(\overline{n},\overline{K})_V = (-1.555 \pm 0.075095,0.000995 \pm 0.000266). \quad (17)$$

By imposing $M_L = 3$ for a Wood–Anderson peak amplitude of 1 mm at a distance of 100 km, we obtain the final equations for the horizontal component, which can be written as

$$M_L^H = \mathrm{Log}A_H - (-1.545\mathrm{Log}(R/100) + 0.001357(R-100) - 3 + Si), \quad (18a)$$

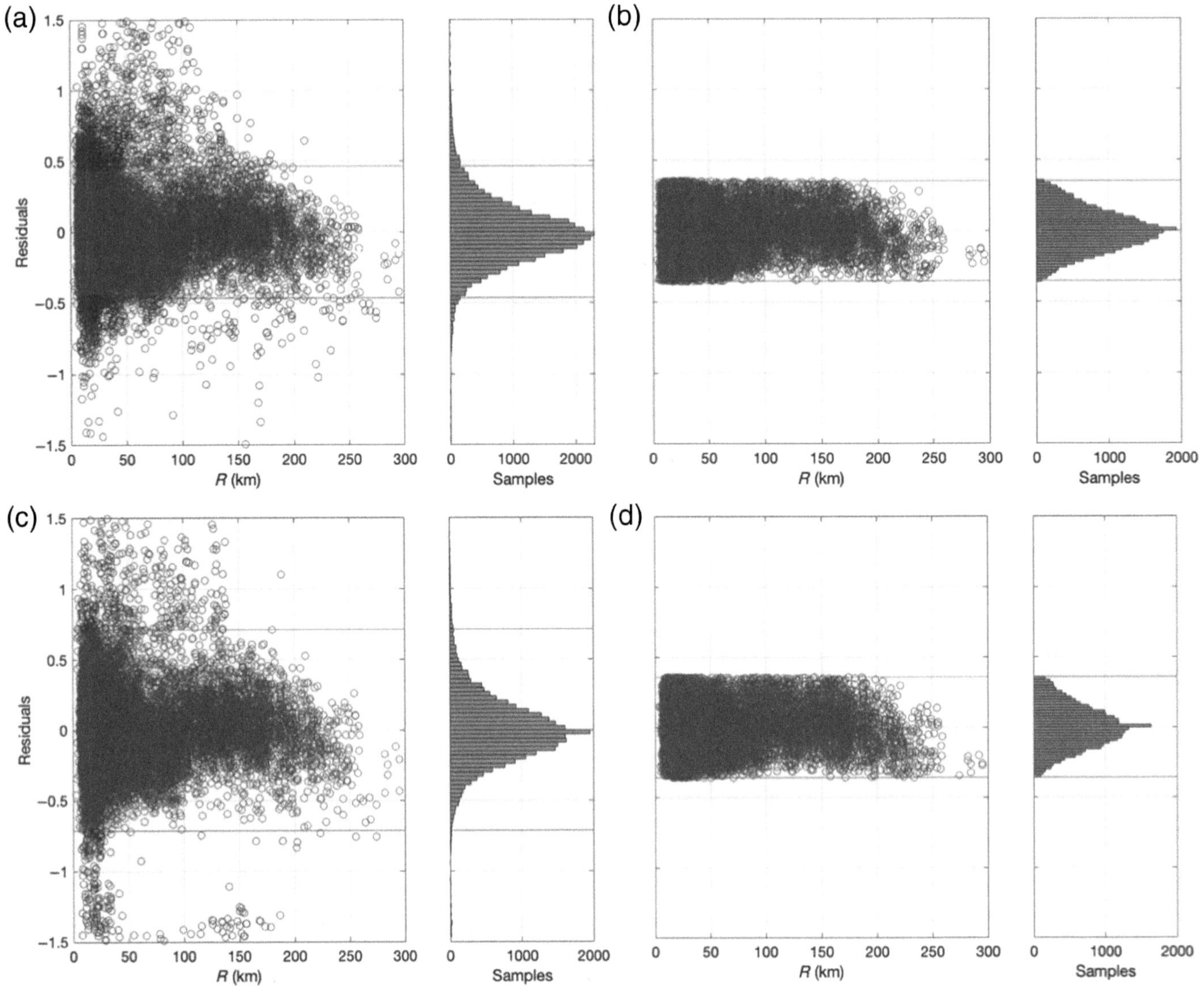

or, alternatively,

$$M_{\mathrm{L}}^{H} = \mathrm{Log}A_{H} - (-1.545\mathrm{Log}R + 0.001357R - 0.0457 + Si), \tag{18b}$$

in which A_H represents the horizontal Wood–Anderson amplitude expressed in mm, R is the hypocentral distance in km, and S_i represents the static station coefficient used for calculating the station–M_{L} for the ith station. Table 2 and Figure 7 show the static station coefficients S_i obtained at the end of the calibration for the latest station configuration (the complete list of coefficients is given in Table S2).

For the vertical component, the coefficient C is calculated differently because it is incorrect to normalize the equations for both components by imposing the same condition, given that the peak amplitudes on the vertical components tend to be smaller than those on the horizontal components. Considering that the attenuation properties (n, K coefficients) obtained for the global and decimated inversions are almost identical for the vertical and horizontal components, we verify that the

Figure 4. Distribution of station magnitude residuals as a function of distance. (a,b) and (c,d) refer to the horizontal and vertical components, respectively. On the left (a, c), the distribution of residuals for the entire data set at the first iteration; on the right (b, d) at the last iteration (i.e., when all outliers have been removed) for the refined data set. The circles represent the residuals, with those that lie within the predefined limits in blue and the outliers in red; the horizontal red lines represent the limits that are set at 1.8 of the interquartile range (IQR) of the residual distribution at the current iteration. The color version of this figure is available only in the electronic edition.

amplitude ratio H/V has an almost constant value with distance, and then estimate it to be 1.73 (see details in Text S5). Thus, the vertical-component equations need an additional correction term equal to $\mathrm{Log}(H/V) = 0.238$, resulting in

$$M_{\mathrm{L}}^{V} = \mathrm{Log}A_{V} + 0.238 - \left(-1.555\mathrm{Log}\left(\frac{R}{100}\right) + 0.000995(R - 100) - 3 + Si\right), \tag{19a}$$

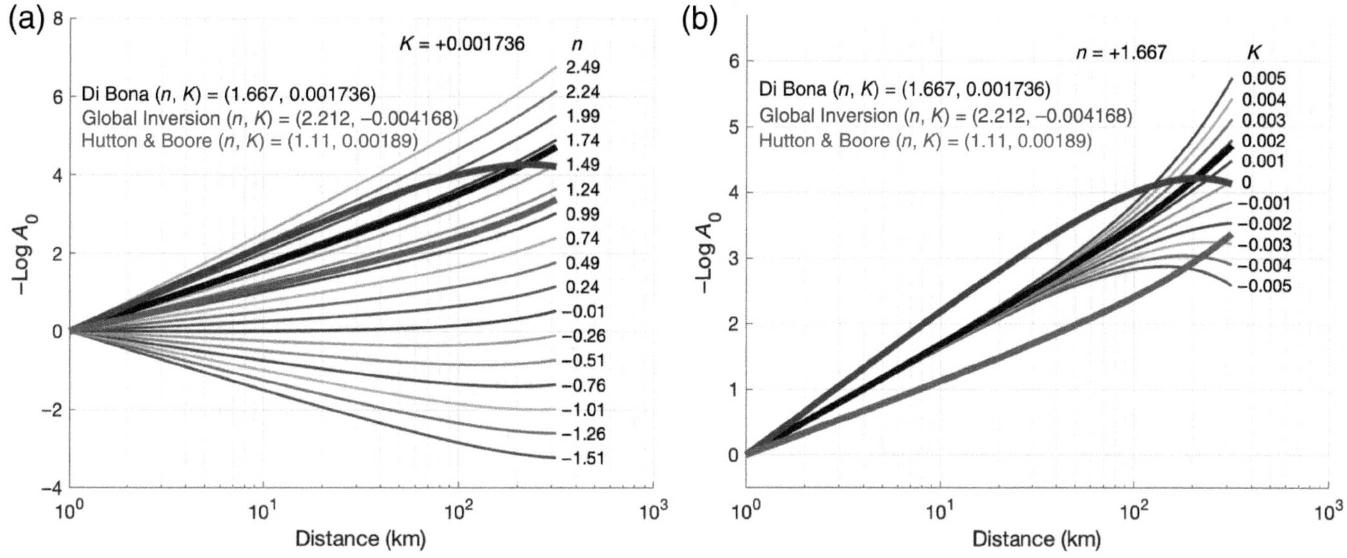

Figure 5. Sensitivity analysis of the n and K parameters. The panels represent the theoretical shape of the term minus $\text{Log}A_0(R)$. (a) Varying n for fixed $K = +0.001736$; (b) varying K for fixed $n = +1.667$. The numbers to the right of each curve indicate the value of the varying parameter (n for panel a and K for panel b). The fixed reference values used in the two panels are the coefficients of the magnitude law by Di Bona (2016). The thick lines in both panels represent the magnitude laws by Di Bona (2016) in blue, Hutton and Boore (1987) in magenta, and the value obtained in this study for global inversion of the entire dataset in red. The color version of this figure is available only in the electronic edition.

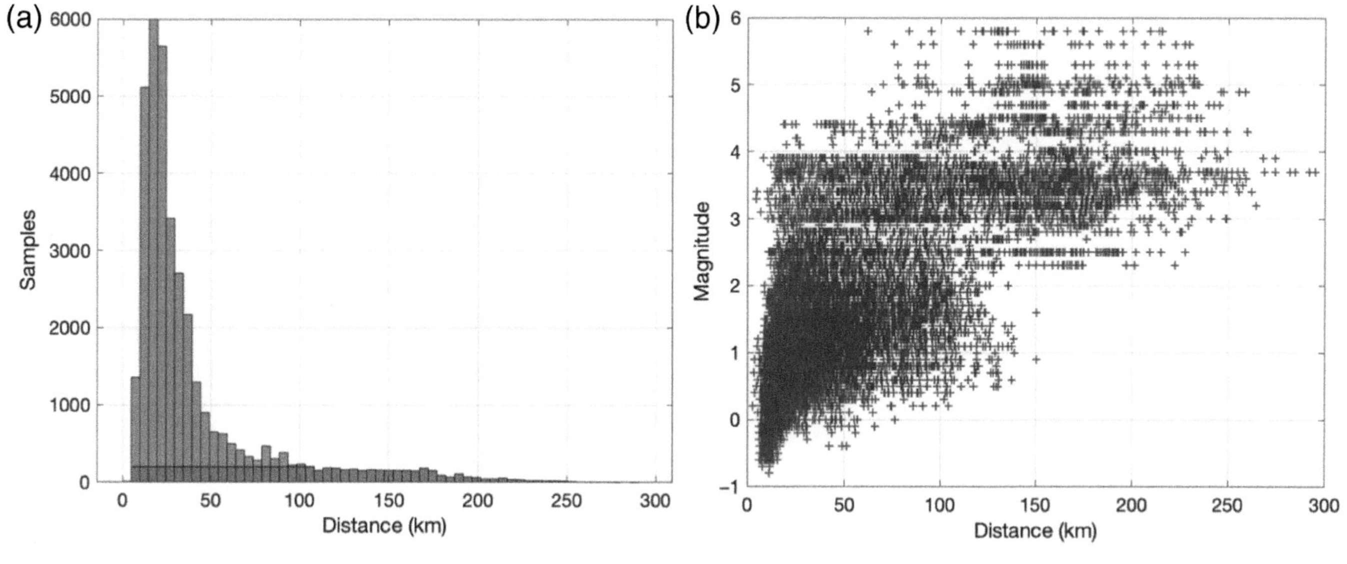

Figure 6. Example of a decimated subset versus the original dataset over distance. (a) Sample histogram versus distance of the original dataset (blue) and the decimated subset (brown). (b) Original magnitude versus distance of the initial dataset (blue crosses) and a decimated subset (red). The color version of this figure is available only in the electronic edition.

or, alternatively,

$$M_L^V = \text{Log}A_V - (-1.555\text{Log}R + 0.000995R + (0.0105 - 0.238) + Si). \quad (19b)$$

The first thing one can note in Figure 7 is that static station coefficients are within ±0.6, with most between ±0.4, a range which is in agreement with Bormann (2012). Another observation is that there is generally good agreement between configurations consisting of a seismometer and accelerometer deployed close to each other (e.g., BALD and BALD_z, CGRP and

TABLE 2
Static Station Coefficients for the Latest, Current Station Configuration; Two Codes in Case of Double Sensor

Station Code	Net-Code	Current Code	Sensor Type	Simplified Site Geology	S_i Horizontal Previous	S_i Horizontal New	S_i Vertical New
AFL	OX	AFL_b	Seism.	Dolostones, shallow water carbonatic platform, Upper Triassic	n.a.	−0.301	−0.2404
AGOR	OX	AGOR_b	Seism.	Bioclastic limestones, Upper Permian	−0.133	−0.199	−0.193
		AGOR_y	Acc.			−0.142	−0.131
APGO	OX	APGO_b	Seism.	Fluvioglacial and alluvial sediments of the mountains	n.a.	+0.477	+0.553
ASOL	IV	ASOL	Acc.	n.a.	n.a.	−0.264	−0.339
BALD	OX	BALD	Seism.	Micritic limestones, basins deposits, Jurassic–Cretaceous	+0.62	+0.464	+0.227
		BALD_z	Acc.			+0.441	+0.237
CAE	OX	CAE_c	Seism.	Micritic limestones, basins deposits, Jurassic–Cretaceous	+0.10	−0.198	−0.261
		CAE_z	Acc			−0.134	−0.250
CEKR	OX	CEKR_a	Seism.	n.a.	n.a.	−0.286	−0.193
CGRP	OX	CGRP	Seism.	Micritic limestones, basins deposits, Jurassic–Cretaceous	n.a.	−0.008	−0.161
		CGRP_x	Acc.			−0.024	−0.101
CIMO	OX	CIMO_b	Seism.	Dolostones, shallow water carbonatic platform, Upper Triassic	−0.24	−0.507	−0.323
		CIMO_y	Acc.			n.a.	n.a.
CLUD	OX	CLUD	Seism.	Massive dolostones and dolomitic limestones, Lower-Medium Triassic	−0.32	−0.468	−0.080
		CLUD_z	Acc.			−0.491	−0.127
CRND	IV	CRND	Acc.	n.a.	n.a.	−0.514	−0.677
CSM	OX	CSM_d	Seism.	Fluvioglacial and alluvial sediments of the mountains	−0.1	−0.225	−0.160
		CSM_z	Acc.			−0.115	−0.110
CSO	OX	CSO_d	Seism.	Fluvioglacial and alluvial sediments of the mountains	−0.3	−0.451	−0.310
		CSO_z	Acc.			n.a.	n.a.
CTI	IV	CTI_c	Seism.	n.a.	n.a.	+0.112	−0.007
DOSS	ST	DOSS	Seism.	Micritic limestones, basins deposits, Jurassic–Cretaceous	+0.08	+0.055	+0.052
		DOSS_z	Acc.			n.a.	n.a.
ED01	EV	ED01_f	Seism.	Fluvioglacial and alluvial sediments of the alluvial plain, Quaternary	+0.13	−0.033	−0.106
		ED01_x	Acc.			−0.044	−0.134
ED02	EV	ED02_f	Seism.*	Polygenic and heterometric conglomerates, marls, and siltstones, Plio-Quaternary	−0.04	−0.165	+0.218
ED03	EV	ED03_g	Seism.*	Polygenic and heterometric conglomerates, marls, and siltstones, Plio-Quaternary	+0.17	−0.124	+0.392
ED04	EV	ED04_d	Seism.*	Polygenic and heterometric conglomerates, marls, and siltstones, Plio-Quaternary	+0.32	+0.120	+0.407
ED05	EV	ED05_d	Seism.*	Polygenic and heterometric conglomerates, marls, and siltstones, Plio-Quaternary	+0.29	+0.020	+0.033
		ED05_z	Acc.			+0.161	+0.134
ED06	EV	ED06_h	Seism.*	Polygenic and heterometric conglomerates, marls, and siltstones, Plio-Quaternary	+0.33	+0.229	+0.038
		ED06_s	Acc.			+0.240	+0.044
ED07	EV	ED07_e	Seism.*	Polygenic and heterometric conglomerates, marls, and siltstones, Plio-Quaternary	+0.29	+0.118	−0.021
		ED07_s	Acc.			+0.303	+0.038
ED08	EV	ED08_g	Seism.*	Polygenic and heterometric conglomerates, marls, and siltstones, Plio-Quaternary	+0.17	+0.023	+0.414
		ED08_x	Acc.			+0.204	+0.090
ED09	EV	ED09_g	Seism.*	Polygenic and heterometric conglomerates, marls, and siltstones, Plio-Quaternary	+0.23	−0.056	−0.068

(continued)

TABLE 2 (*Continued*)

Station Code	Net-Code	Current Code	Sensor Type	Simplified Site Geology	S_i Horizontal Previous	S_i Horizontal New	S_i Vertical New
ED10	EV	ED10_f	Seism.*	Polygenic and heterometric conglomerates, marls, and siltstones, Plio-Quaternary	+0.23	−0.081	+0.272
FAU	OX	FAU	Seism.	Basement, paragneiss, and schists, pre-Paleozoic	−0.16	−0.187	−0.120
FUSE	OX	FUSE	Seism.	Massive dolostones and dolomitic limestones, lower-medium Triassic	−0.24	−0.286	−0.184
		FUSE_z	Acc.			−0.270	−0.179
IESO	OX	IESO_c	Seism.	Fluvioglacial and alluvial sediments of the alluvial plain, Quaternary	+0.64	+0.485	+0.386
		IESO_z	Acc.			n.a.	n.a.
MARN	OX	MARN	Seism.	Volcanic rocks (basalts, ignimbrites) Oligocene	+0.29	+0.276	+0.189
		MARN_z	Acc.			+0.201	+0.153
MGBU	OX	MGBU	Seism.	n.a.	n.a.	−0.149	−0.085
		MGBU_z	Acc.			n.a.	n.a.
MLN	OX	MLN_b	Seism.	Micritic limestones, basins deposits, Jurassic–Cretaceous	−0.19	−0.369	−0.244
		MLN_z	Acc.			−0.279	−0.125
MPRI	OX	MPRI_c	Seism.	Micritic limestones, basins deposits, Jurassic–Cretaceous	+0.21	−0.194	−0.244
		MPRI_z	Acc.			−0.142	−0.143
MTLO	OX	MTLO_d	Seism.	Sandstone-shale alternation (Flysch), Paleocene–Eocene	+0.58	+0.338	+0.073
		MTLO_x	Acc.			+0.331	+0.109
PANI	ST	PANI_b	Seism.	Basement, paragneiss, and schists, pre-Paleozoic	−0.15	−0.146	−0.122
		PANI_z	Acc.			n.a.	n.a.
POLC	NI	POLC	Seism.	n.a.	+0.38	+0.129	+0.050
		POLC_z	Acc.			n.a.	n.a.
SANR	IV	SANR	Acc.	n.a.	n.a.	−0.167	−0.397
STAL	IV	STAL_a	Seism.	n.a.	n.a.	−0.011	−0.075
		STAL_z	Acc.			n.a.	n.a.
TEOL	IV	TEOL_d	Seism.	Sandstone-shale alternation (Flysch), Paleocene–Eocene	+0.58	+0.423	+0.342
VARA	ST	VARA	Seism.	Micritic limestones, basins deposits, Jurassic–Cretaceous	n.a.	+0.453	+0.360
VARN	OX	VARN_e	Seism.	Micritic limestones, basins deposits, Jurassic–Cretaceous	+0.24	+0.098	−0.164
		VARN_x	Acc.			+0.107	−0.168
ZIAN	ST	ZIAN_a	Seism.	Volcanic rocks (basalts, ignimbrites), Oligocene	+0.16	−0.117	+0.058

The simplified site geology information is taken from Klin *et al.* (2021). Previous static station coefficients are the ones used for magnitude calculation in the Collalto network catalog (Priolo *et al.*, 2015). The complete list of instrument configurations and static station coefficients for the period considered in this study is listed in Table S2.
*Borehole Deployment.

CGRP_x, MTLO_d and MTLO_x, and VARN_e and VARN_x, as well as others). For the stations of the Collalto network (code ED##), we note, in Table 2 and Table S2, that the corrections estimated for the seismometers deployed in boreholes are lower than those of the corresponding accelerometer, if available. Unfortunately, some stations of this network have had a troubled life, with malfunctions of borehole sensors that have been replaced temporarily by surface sensors. This is the case for stations ED01, ED02, ED04, and ED05, where we can see a marked variability of values related mainly to the depth at which the sensor is deployed. For example: for ED01_d, ED01_e, and ED01_f which have the sensor at −153, −34, and 0 m, respectively, we have values of −0.336, −0.202, and −0.033; for ED04_b and ED04_c, which are installed at surface, we have values of approximately +0.4, whereas for ED04_a and ED04_d, which are at 27 m of depth, we have values of approximately +0.12. These observations are consistent with the expectation of more ground-motion amplification near or at the ground surface: the smaller the value of S_i, the lower the amplification at the station. It is also worth noting that values of S_i approaching zero do not necessarily correspond to "neutral," that is, nonamplifying, sites; this is the result of the 0-sum condition of equation (8), due to the station group used for calibration. Figure S4 shows the spatial distribution of the latest S_is. However, any interpretation of its physical meaning needs additional investigation and data that are out of the scope of this work.

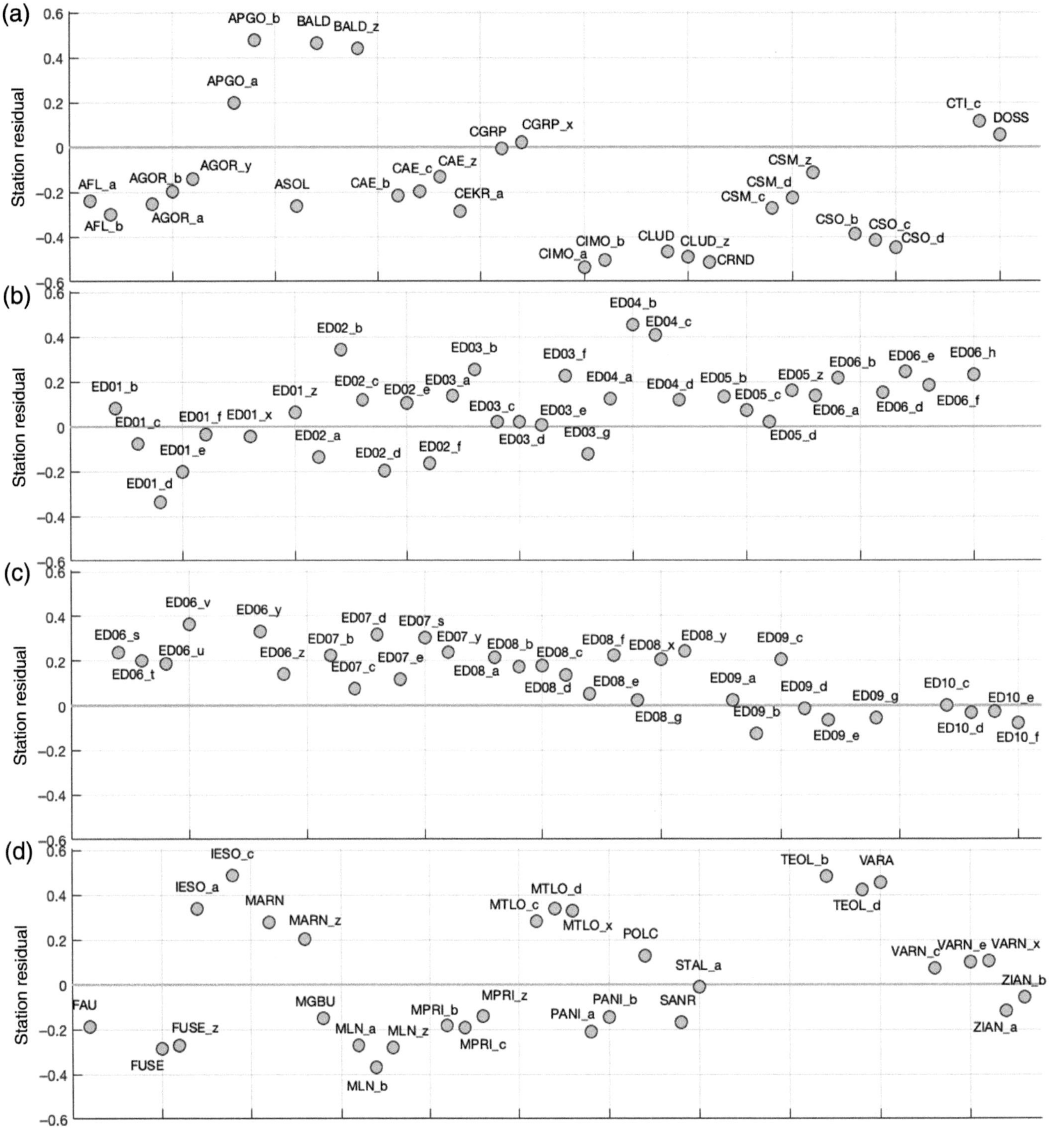

DISCUSSION

In the following, the results are discussed only for the horizontal component.

Figure 8 shows the newly obtained M_Ls compared with the previously available magnitudes. In Figure 8a, the single-station M_L values are plotted versus station distances; events with $2 < M_L < 3$ at distances greater than 100 km are less represented because they are not present in the RSC catalog, and the events that we used from other catalogs are all of M_L 3.0 or larger. Figure 8b compares the single-station M_L values

Figure 7. Static station coefficients calculated in this study for the horizontal component (S_i in equation 5), grouped alphabetically in four panels. Each station can have different configurations, as indicated by a supplementary letter after the station code (e.g., CODE_a). Seismometers have subsequent configurations labeled by ascending letters, starting with _a; accelerometers with descending letters, starting with _z. The complete list of station configurations is given in Table S2. The color version of this figure is available only in the electronic edition.

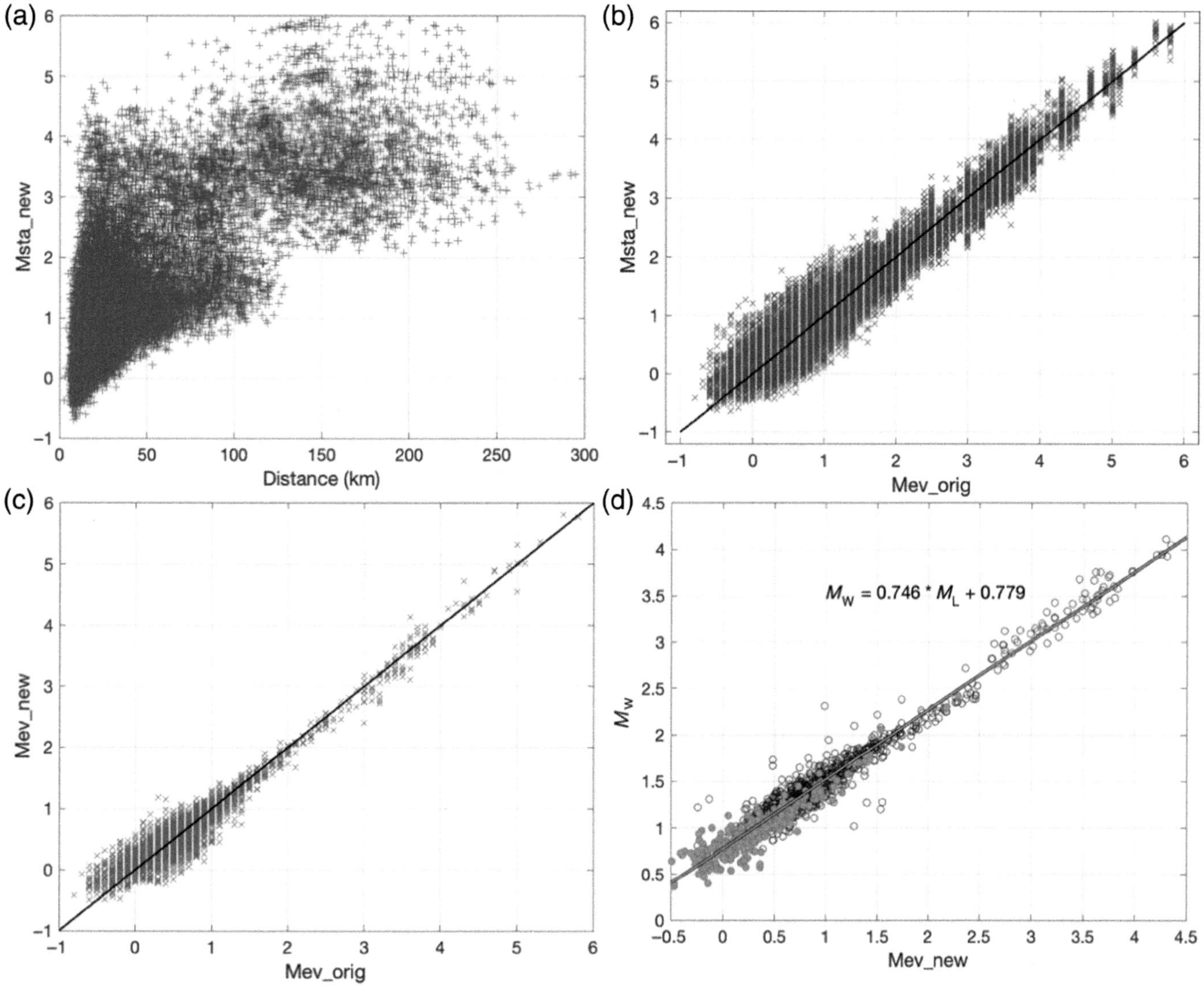

Figure 8. Magnitude comparison plots for the horizontal component (equation 18). (a) Single-station M_L values versus station distances. (b) Single-station M_L values obtained in this study versus the original event–M_Ls. The black line represents the 1:1 identity. (c) Event–M_L values obtained in this study against the original event–M_L. (d) Moment-magnitude M_ws available for the study area versus event–M_L values obtained in this study; in blue and orange, the values by Tarchini *et al.* (2025) and by Peruzza *et al.* (2022), respectively. The dark, solid line and the equation above it indicate the linear best fit to the data obtained by orthogonal regression. The color version of this figure is available only in the electronic edition.

obtained in this study with the original event–M_L values; the data are well aligned on the diagonal, with a global variability that tends to decrease with magnitude, along with the sample size. This trend is further supported by Figure 8c, which plots the event–M_L values obtained in this study against the original event–M_L values from the dataset. Here, it is clear that the tendency to estimate smaller M_L values becomes more pronounced for events below M_L 2. Finally, Figure 8d illustrates the relationship between the moment magnitude M_w and the new M_L values, both of which are available for some events in the study area. The M_w values are taken from Tarchini *et al.* (2025) for the wide area of NEI, and by Peruzza *et al.* (2022) for a small-magnitude but highly productive seismic sequence that occurred in 2021 near the center of the Collalto network. Note that the available M_w values of Tarchini *et al.* (2025) were calculated uniformly up to a maximum M_w 4.3, and the analyzed time window does not include the main events of the 2012 Emilia sequence. Compared to these two studies, the linear M_w–M_L relationship now obtained by orthogonal regression (OR) (Castellaro and Bormann, 2007) is slightly steeper, but data are less dispersed and feature a more pronounced linear trend in the whole magnitude range. We remind that the OR method is appropriate if the ratio between the errors of the two variables lies between 0.7 and 1.8, a condition that is satisfied by our dataset.

Figure 9 shows the distribution of the station–M_L residuals (single-station M_L minus mean event-M_L) versus hypocentral distance. We use a logarithmic and linear distance scales in panels a and b, respectively because the M_L calibration law

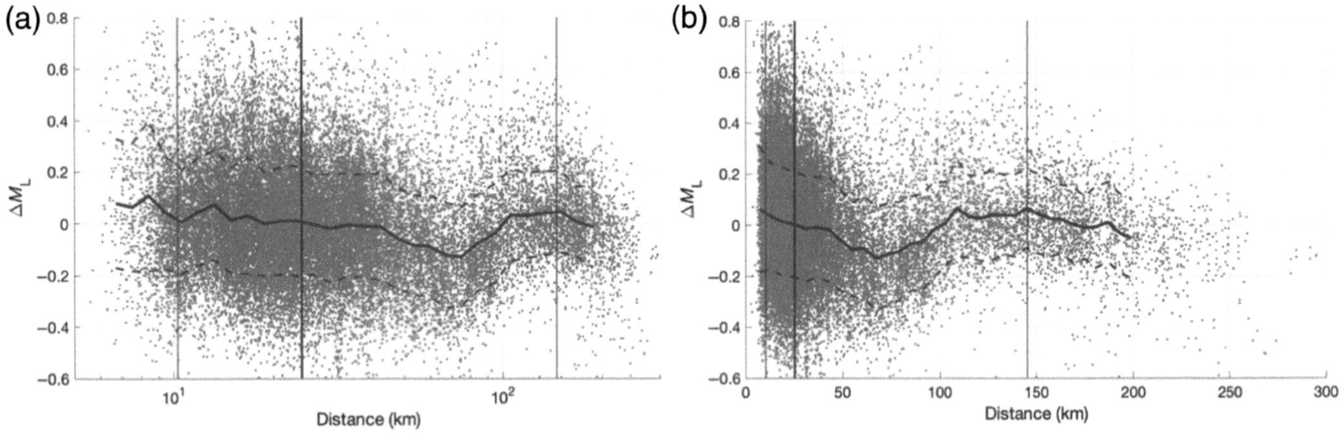

Figure 9. Single-station M_L residuals versus distance for the horizontal component. Panels (a) and (b) show the same data but using logarithmic and linear distance scales, respectively. The thick solid and thin red dashed lines along the distance represent the mean and the mean plus/minus the first standard deviation of the single-station M_L residuals. They are calculated for the logarithmic and linear scale from bins of 0.05 and 6 km, respectively, and represented for the 1st–99th percentile range, that is, 7–205 km. The vertical red lines represent the confidence limit of the 5th percentile, median, and 95th percentile of the distance dataset. The color version of this figure is available only in the electronic edition.

depends on the distance with both the logarithmic terms, which is more sensitive to the short distances, and a linear term that becomes more important at large distances (see also Fig. 5). The average of the residuals is generally around zero, but a clear fluctuation starts at about 40 km, with a negative kink between 40 and 100 km—the minimum being −0.1 at about 65 km—and a positive kink with residual average of about 0.04–0.06 from 100 till about 170 km distance. Slightly positive average residuals, though with small fluctuations, are present in the very short distance range, with values decreasing from about 0.08 at 6–7 km to zero at about 20 km. The standard deviation σ of the residuals is on average of 0.17–0.18. Thus, 0.35 corresponds to 2σ, that is, a confidence value of about 95% that can be taken as a measure of the intraevent variability of the M_Ls estimated by equations (18).

From Figure 9, we can also derive other key elements to assess the validity of the M_L calibration law established in this study. The median hypocentral distance represented is approximately 24.5 km; the minimum and maximum distances are 2.8 and 295 km, respectively. The 5th–95th percentiles range of the distance distribution is 10.5–143.5 km, and the 1st–99th percentile range is 7–205 km (not shown in Fig. 9). Similar values apply to the vertical component.

Based on these results, our equations are valid for distances up to approximately 200 km and magnitudes up to 5.8.

In Figure 10, we compare the M_L equation derived in this study for the horizontal component (equations 18, with $S_i = 0$) with several other equations that are commonly used or relevant to our study. Figure 10a shows the theoretical M_L values calculated by varying the distance for a constant amplitude of 1 mm, and Figure 10b shows the difference between the various equations and that of this study to better visualize the differences in the calibration curves.

Seven equations are compared with the one obtained in this study. These equations are, in order:

- the parametric equation by Bragato and Tento (2005), denoted as BT2005nk, developed for northeastern Italy;
- the nonparametric stepwise law from the same study, denoted as BT2005step;
- the parametric equation (13) by Di Bona (2016), denoted as DB2016, developed for the entire Italian territory;
- the parametric equation by Spallarossa *et al.* (2002), denoted as SBAC2002, calibrated for northwestern Italy;
- the parametric equation by Hutton and Boore (1987), denoted as HB1987, developed for southern California;
- the parametric equation by Butcher *et al.* (2017), denoted as BEtAl2017, which was specifically developed for near-event receivers in the area of New Ollerton town (England) and holds for distances $R \leq 17$ km;
- the parametric equation by Luckett *et al.* (2019), denoted as LEtAl2019, which extended the IASPEI M_L equation (Bormann, 2012) to short distances by incorporating an exponential term, using data from the United Kingdom, central Italy, and Norway.

It should be noted, however, that the equations developed for the Italian territory are used sporadically, and do not represent the common practise for the bulletins published by the various agencies: the INGV national seismic network calculates M_L with the equation HB1987 (Di Maro *et al.*, 2022); the regional networks managed by the University of Genova for northwestern Italy, and by OGS for the northeastern Italy, have adopted duration magnitude since a long time (Bindi *et al.*, 2005; Bragato *et al.*, 2021). The only systematic application of the BT2005nk is done by the Collalto network.

The first notable feature is that, within the validity distance range of this study, the M_L values estimated by equations (18) are, on average, consistent with those derived from the other

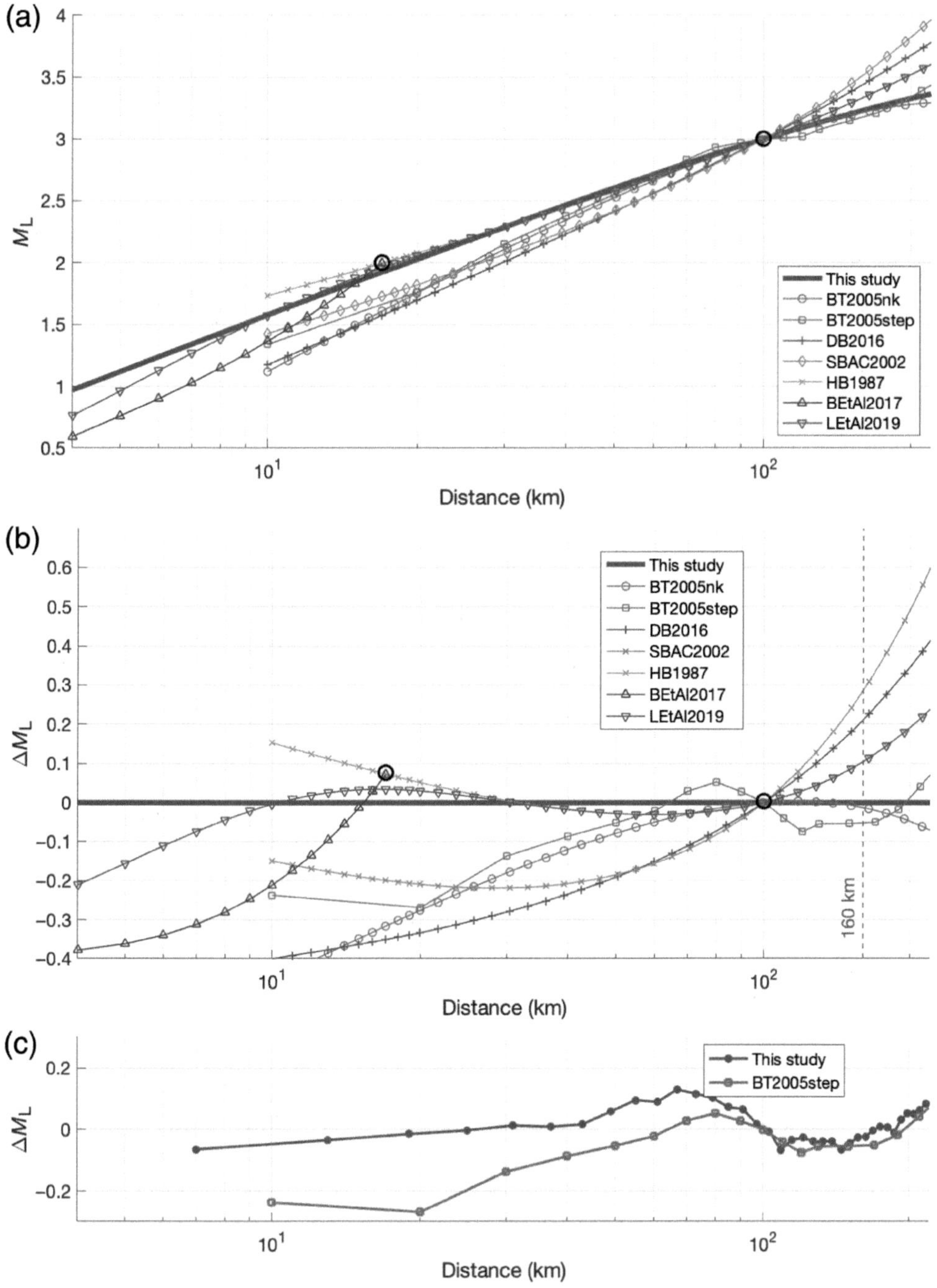

Figure 10. Comparison of the M_L calibration equation of this study with other formulas, labeled as in the main text. (a) M_L corresponding to an amplitude of 1 mm at different distances. (b) Differences between the M_L of this study and the M_Ls of various formulas. (c) Comparison between the average M_L residuals of this study (plotted with the opposite sign from Fig. 9) and the difference between the nonparametric law by Bragato and Tento (2005) and the M_L of this study. The two small black circles in (a) and (b) indicate the calibration points at $R = 100$ km and $M_L = 3$ (original reference set by Richter) and at $R = 17$ km and $M_L = 2$, introduced by Hutton and Boore (1987). For further details, see the text. The color version of this figure is available only in the electronic edition.

equations. Specifically, the maximum variation does not exceed 0.3 for distances of 25–160 km, which is a commonly accepted reference value for the uncertainty in M_L estimation. For distances greater than 160 km, the differences in the calculated M_Ls become more pronounced, in part due to the inversion of the sign of the coefficient K in our equation. The most significant discrepancies at these distances are observed only with the equations by Spallarossa *et al.* (2002) and Di Bona (2016). In contrast, the agreement remains rather strong with the equations by Hutton and Boore (1987) and Luckett *et al.* (2019)—note that these two laws coincide for approximately $R > 30$ km— as well as with those by Bragato and Tento (2005) for $R > 40$ km. In the short-distance range ($R <$ 15 km), the M_L values from this study differ by at most approximately −0.15 and −0.35 from the two laws specifically developed for short distances—those by Luckett *et al.* (2019) and Butcher *et al.* (2017) (see Fig. 10a,b).

The comparison with the laws by Bragato and Tento (2005) requires a more detailed discussion. These authors calibrated M_L for an area slightly larger than the one of this study, incorporating several earthquakes to the east, from Slovenia and Croatia, using a different inversion scheme and a dataset entirely independent from the one used in this study. Their records are from the period 1995–2002 (ours from 2012 to 2023) and a smaller number of stations than in our study (25 stations in total, compared to the 41 stations used here). Twelve stations were common to both studies, but, at the time of the study by Bragato and Tento (2005), most were equipped with short-period sensors, instead of broadband sensors and accelerometers. Their study is focused on the regional distances represented by the NEI seismic network, rather than on the short-distance range of the RSC network, and represents a more limited interval of magnitude (0.5–5.2 in Bragato and Tento, 2005, −0.8 to 5.8 in this study).

The n and K coefficients obtained from the initial, global inversion of our new dataset (namely −2.212 and 0.004168 for the horizontal component) are very similar to those of Bragato's parametric curve (−2.23 and 0.0039), including the nonphysical, reverse sign for the K coefficient. Conversely, the final parametric curve obtained from the decimated subsets has remarkably different coefficients (i.e., −1.545 and 0.001357), and is physically more reliable as K approaches zero.

The obtained residuals closely match the deviation of the nonparametric M_L curve of Bragato and Tento (2005) from our law, showing a bump approximately between 40 and 100 km followed by a trough (Fig. 10c). This perturbation of WA amplitudes was attributed to the presence of the Moho discontinuity, the depth of which in northern Italy ranges from 25 to 35 km south of the Alpine chain (Finetti, 2005). We emphasize that the use of a log-linear parametric formulation is essential for identifying a general trend; by quantifying distance-dependent perturbations through the behavior of the residuals, a systematic (i.e., nonrandom) structure may indicate the presence of an underlying physical cause, the nature of which must be investigated independently.

We also note additional advantages of using a parametric law rather than a nonparametric one: a parametric law provides a simple, continuous, and differentiable function of distance, requires only a few coefficients, and avoids possible artificial discontinuities associated with tabular interpolation. Both our parametric law and the nonparametric law of Bragato and Tento exhibit a slight downward bending (Fig. 10a). Despite differences in datasets and inversion formalisms, this consistency suggests that the observed downward bending may reflect a regional feature that should be accounted for in the M_L calibration law. In our approach, the K term is left unconstrained to allow the inversion to best fit the observed dataset, and the resulting solution is well constrained over short-to-intermediate distances (≤200 km). Imposing a hard physical constraint on K (i.e., $K \leq 0$) would alter the n coefficient and degrade the fit in the distance range most relevant for regional M_L calibration, which is inconsistent with the observations. We therefore consider the unconstrained-K approach more suitable for obtaining a globally optimal fit within the applicable distance range. We also find no compelling need to adopt a more complex formulation for the short-distance range. Although Luckett *et al.* (2019) observed that applying the standard equation leads to increased residuals at distances shorter than approximately 15 km, necessitating an additional empirical correction term, our results show that the residuals of the newly calibrated, IASPEI-like equation remain small (mean < 0.1 below 15 km; see Fig. 9a) and do not exhibit any abrupt increase down to 7 km, which we set as the minimum distance validity limit. Furthermore, our calibration curve compares very well with that proposed by Luckett *et al.* (2019) down to 7 km (Fig. 10a,b).

Subsequent studies have provided a more comprehensive understanding of the perturbation of WA amplitudes. Bragato *et al.* (2011) observed that in the Po Plain PGA is systematically enhanced at distances between 70 and 200 km. The authors confirm that this amplification is caused by the reflection of seismic waves at the Moho discontinuity, noting that this effect is "…maximized at hypocentral distances between 90 and 160 km, where the PGA increases by a factor larger than 2.4." Sugan and Vuan (2014) analyze the role of postcritically reflected S waves and multiples from the Moho discontinuity in influencing the ground motion for medium to large earthquakes in northeastern Italy. They demonstrate that high-amplitude *SmSM* phases (Moho reflections and multiples) can be identified within the Po Plain and at the boundaries between the Po Plain and the Alpine chain—thus also affecting northeastern Italy. These phases are observed at epicentral distances greater than 80 km, within a period range of 0.25–3 s, and a group velocity approximately between 2.6 and 3.2 km/s. It is noteworthy that this period partly overlaps with that of the Wood–Anderson seismometer. Di Bona (2016) also points out that his law is suitable for calculating M_L for the entire Italian territory, but "… The only exception is represented by short-distance estimates in northeastern Italy, where increasingly negative residuals for decreasing distances are observed". It is also worth noting that Luckett *et al.* (2019), analyzing the New Ollerton dataset, demonstrated a decrease in local seismic velocities and changes in amplitudes at short distances for very shallow events, thus highlighting variations in the properties of the very shallow crust. We emphasize that our study considers crustal earthquakes with focal depths of at least 4–5 km, corresponding to the upper part of the seismogenic layer in our study area. Detecting similar variations, if present, in a large dataset such as ours would be relevant but would also require a more subtle and demanding analysis, which is beyond the scope of the present work.

We conclude that the pattern of magnitude residuals shown in Figure 10c, independently obtained by Bragato and Tento in 2005, and now by this study, has a physical explanation in the crustal/Moho propagation characteristics.

Another topic worth briefly discussing is the reference distance chosen for the calibration. The original definition was developed for Southern California. In regions with significantly different wave attenuation within the first 100 km, Hutton and Boore (1987) recommend scaling at a 17 km hypocentral distance. This recommendation was adopted by Baumbach *et al.* (2003) for NW Turkey and by Langston *et al.* (1998) for Tanzania. A shift to a shorter reference distance for M_L calibration is indeed justified by the increasing availability of earthquake data at distances less than 100 km, due to the growing number of measurement stations. However, we emphasize that the value of 17 km is tied to the equation of Hutton and Boore (1987) because it corresponds to a Wood–Anderson amplitude of 10 mm at 17 km for an M_L 3 earthquake, or, equivalently, to an amplitude of 1 mm at 17 km for an M_L 2.0 earthquake. If the M_L law changes, the distance at which M_L

decreases by 1 unit below its value at 100 km is no longer 17 km. For example, for the M_L laws shown in Figure 10a, this distance would be approximately 27 km for the law of Spallarossa *et al.* (2002), about 30 km for the law of Di Bona (2016; his equation 13), and roughly 19 km for the law of this study. This can be clearly seen in the M_L law by Butcher *et al.* (2017), which was developed for very near events ($R < 5$ km), was anchored at 17 km, and cannot be applied to larger distances.

Last but not least, the static station coefficients calculated in this study are reported for each documented change in station configuration and are therefore dependent on time and deployment. From Table 2 and Figure S4, we can also observe a reasonably good coherence between the site geology and the static station coefficient: the lower the coefficient, the harder the site or the deeper the sensor deployment. Site geology was taken from Klin *et al.* (2021), in which the site amplification conditions are evaluated by various methods, also in the spectral domain. A thorough investigation of the correlation with the results of that study, as well as of the physical origin of the station corrections (e.g., local geology, very short path effects, site amplification, and their relationship with site response parameters), would require a dedicated, station-focused analysis and potentially additional datasets. Such an analysis is beyond the scope of the present work and will be addressed in a separate, future study.

CONCLUSIONS

We calibrate a local magnitude scale for the area of northeastern Italy, centered around the Collalto seismic network, using the parametric formulation recommended by IASPEI (Bormann *et al.*, 2012) and adopting a modification of the data-driven approach proposed by Chovanová and Kristek (2018). The main aim of the study is to develop an M_L calibration law that is well constrained at short distances for small earthquakes, does not drift for regional distances and moderate earthquakes, and remains consistent with the original Richter definition, using 100 km as the reference distance.

The WA amplitude dataset is derived from digital waveform data collected at 41 stations, between January 2012 and March 2023, referring to more than 3600 earthquakes with magnitudes ranging from −0.8 to 5.8. It includes nearly 35,000 observations for the horizontal component and about 28,000 observations for the vertical component, covering distances between 4 and 295 km.

The parameter values obtained in this study from the simultaneous inversion of the entire dataset are very similar to those reported by Bragato and Tento (2005), who used a different inversion scheme and an independent dataset, although the physical validity of the result is questionable. This similarity suggests that the coefficients may, at least in part, reflect intrinsic characteristics of the study area, as also noted by Di Bona (2016). Nonetheless, we hypothesize that other factors may also influence the inversion results.

We argue that the anomalous coefficient values likely arise from the uneven distribution of data points across distance ranges. To reduce the bias from oversampling, we apply a Monte Carlo-based subsampling approach, generating multiple datasets with more uniform distance distributions by randomly selecting points from the original dataset and performing separate inversions. The final solution, given by equations (18) and (19) for the horizontal and vertical components, expresses amplitudes in millimeters and includes static station coefficients that vary over time with station configuration. These equations are valid for distances of 7–200 km and magnitudes of −0.8 to 5.8. The static station coefficients are consistent with expectations (Bormann, 2012), remaining within ±0.6, and show reasonably good coherence with site geology and deployment modality.

The M_L equation derived here is, on average, consistent with other equations commonly used or relevant to our study area; in particular, it is close to the formula proposed by Hutton and Boore (1987) in the distance range 15–160 km, with M_L differences lower than 0.1. It is worth noting, however, that in the short-distance range ($R < 15$ km), which is the primary focus of this study, the curves by Luckett *et al.* (2019) and Butcher *et al.* (2017) provide lower values than ours, whereas that by Hutton and Boore (1987) overestimates the magnitude compared with ours. For distances below 25 km, the formulas (both parametric and nonparametric) of Bragato and Tento (2005), which were developed for the same area, also yield magnitude values that are at least 0.2 lower than ours. At distances of about 50–200 km, the average M_L residuals of our parametric law confirm the perturbation of WA amplitudes for which systematic (i.e., nonrandom) structure is attributed to the presence of the Moho discontinuity.

Finally, in the magnitude range −0.5 to 4.3, our M_L law exhibits a strong linear relationship with the available M_w values, and is less affected by the systematic drift that appears at low magnitudes when compared with other laws. This suggests that our new law provides a more accurate estimate of earthquake energy across the entire range analyzed.

Our new calibration scale provides reliable M_L estimates in northeastern Italy, even at short distances, while maintaining coherence with the standard IASPEI formula. It is also suitable for consistent application, accommodating observations from both dense local networks and regional networks. Thus, it is suitable for local magnitude estimation in the whole area of northeastern Italy.

DATA AND RESOURCES

The earthquake catalog used in this study is available upon request to the authors. The complete catalog of the northeast Italy (NEI) network by the National Institute of Oceanography and Applied Geophysics (OGS) can be found at https://terremoti.ogs.it/ (last accessed March 2025). Continuous waveform data of NEI (OGS) and RSN (INGV) networks are available at European Integrated Data Archive (EIDA): https://eida.ingv.it/it/ (last accessed February 2025). Information and data on the Collalto seismic network (RSC) can be found at http://rete-collalto.crs.inogs.it (last accessed February 2025). Seismic data of the RSC are acquired and processed using the BRTT Antelope system at http://www.brtt.com/ (last accessed March 2025), supplemented by some procedures and functions developed by OGS staff. The unique identifiers (e.g., channel convention) for data sources exchanged and archived in formats and services defined by the International Federation of Digital Seismograph Networks are described at http://docs.fdsn.org/projects/source-identifiers/en/v1.0/ (last accessed February 2025). The poles and zeros file (.paz) for simulating the Wood–Anderson response is provided by the EarthScope Data Services (DS) at the following link: https://ds.iris.edu/pipermail/sac-help/2013-March/001430.html (last accessed March 2025). The following software systems were used: Seismic Analysis Code (SAC) (Version 102.0, 2020; Goldstein *et al.*, 2003 and Helffrich *et al.*, 2013) available at http://ds.iris.edu/ds/nodes/dmc/software/downloads/sac/ (last accessed March 2025); GNU Awk (gawk) version 4.2.0 (Free Software Foundation), with its GNU implementation GAWK at: www.gnu.org/software/gawk (last accessed August 2021); and MATLAB, versions R2018b and 2019b, Natick, Massachusetts: The MathWorks Inc. at https://www.mathworks.com/products/matlab.html (last accessed November 2025), Hypo71 at https://pubs.usgs.gov/publication/ofr72224 (last accessed March 2025), and HYPOELLIPSE https://pubs.usgs.gov/of/1999/ofr-99-0023/ (last accessed March 2025). The MATLAB code was used to implement the whole method of magnitude calibration as proposed by Chovanová and Kristek (2018), the additional step to reduce the bias caused by data oversampling along distance, and all Figures from 2 to 10. Maps of Figure 1 have been created using the free and open-source QGIS. This article is accompanied by supplemental material. The supplemental material for this article contains five text sections. Text S1 describes the synthetic tests performed to verify the MATLAB code used in our study, which implements the method of Chovanová and Kristek (2018). Text S2 summarizes the instrumental settings of the stations, the station subcodes associated with each configuration, and the static station correction coefficients obtained after magnitude calibration. Text S3 presents a sensitivity analysis of the effect of an incorrect hypocentral location on M_L estimation. Text S4 details the sensitivity analysis of the impact of the band-pass filter on large earthquakes. Text S5 reports the amplitude ratio estimated between the horizontal and vertical components.

DECLARATION OF COMPETING INTERESTS

The authors acknowledge that there are no conflicts of interest recorded.

ACKNOWLEDGMENTS

This study was carried out within the RETURN Extended Partnership and received funding from the European Union Next-GenerationEU (National Recovery and Resilience Plan—NRRP, Mission 4, Component 2, Investment 1.3—D. D. 1243 2 August 2022, PE0000005). This study has used data acquired by the seismic networks managed by the National Institute of Oceanography and Geophysics (OGS), the National Institute of Geophysics and Volcanology (INGV), and the Geological Survey of the Provincia Autonoma di Trento. The regional networks of OGS are managed and supported within agreements with the Civil Protection of the Regione Autonoma Friuli Venezia Giulia and Regione Veneto; the network of Collalto is managed by OGS within an agreement with Edison Stoccaggio S.p.a, a society of EDF group recently acquired by Snam through its subsidiary Stogit Adriatica S.p.a. The authors thank the technical staff of the Centro Ricerche Sismologiche (CRS-OGS) for the management of these networks and the data acquired by them.

The authors are grateful to the Editor and the four reviewers, in particular Reviewer 2 (anonymous) and 3 (Paolo Gasperini), for their constructive and thorough comments, which greatly improved this article. The authors also thank Luca Moratto of OGS for the M_w data of the Refrontolo seismic sequence of 2021, which are represented in Figure 8.

REFERENCES

Anderlini, L., E. Serpelloni, C. Tolomei, P. M. De Martini, G. Pezzo, A. Gualandi, and G. Spada (2020). New insights into active tectonics and seismogenic potential of the Italian Southern Alps from vertical geodetic velocities, *Solid Earth* **11,** 1681–1698, doi: 10.5194/se-11-1681-2020.

Bakun, W. H., and W. B. Joyner (1984). The ML scale in central California, *Bull. Seismol. Soc. Am.* **74,** 1827–1843, doi: 10.1785/BSSA0740051827.

Baumbach, M., D. Bindi, H. Grosser, C. Milkereit, S. Parolai, R. Wang, S. Karakisa, S. Zünbül, and J. Zschau (2003). Calibration of an ML scale in northwestern Turkey from 1999 Izmit aftershocks, *Bull. Seismol. Soc. Am.* **93,** 2289–2295, doi: 10.1785/0120020157.

Bindi, D., D. Spallarossa, C. Eva, and M. Cattaneo (2005). Local and duration magnitudes in northwestern Italy, and seismic moment versus magnitude relationships, *Bull. Seismol. Soc. Am.* **95,** 592–604, doi: 10.1785/0120040099.

Bobbio, A., M. Vassallo, and G. Festa (2009). A local magnitude scale for southern Italy, *Bull. Seismol. Soc. Am.* **99,** 2461–2470, doi: 10.1785/0120080364.

Bommer, J. J., S. Oates, J. M. Cepeda, C. Lindholm, J. Bird, R. Torres, G. Marroquín, and J. Rivas (2006). Control of hazard due to seismicity induced by a hot fractured rock geothermal project, *Eng. Geol.* **83,** 287–306, doi: 10.1016/j.enggeo.2005.11.002.

Bormann, P. (Editor) (2012). *New Manual of Seismological Observatory Practice (NMSOP-2)*, IASPEI, GFZ German Research Centre for Geosciences, Potsdam.

Bormann, P., J. Dewey, and , and the IASPEI/CoSOI Working Group on Magnitude Measurement (2012). The new IASPEI standards for determining magnitudes from digital data and their relation to classical magnitudes, Information Sheet 3.3, in *New Manual of Seismological Observatory Practice (NMSOP-2)*, P. Bormann (Editor), IASPEI, GFZ German Research Centre for Geosciences, Potsdam, 44 pp.

Bragato, P. L., and A. Tento (2005). Local magnitude in northeastern Italy, *Bull. Seismol. Soc. Am.* **95,** no. 2, 579–591, doi: 10.1785/0120040100.

Bragato, P. L., P. Comelli, A. Saraò, D. Zuliani, L. Moratto, V. Poggi, G. Rossi, C. Scaini, M. Sugan, C. Barnaba, *et al.* (2021). The OGS-northeastern Italy seismic and deformation network: Current status and outlook, *Seismol. Res. Lett.* **93,** no. 3, 1704–1716, doi: 10.1785/0220200372.

Bragato, P.L., M. Sugan, P. Augliera, M. Massa, A. Vuan, and A. Saraò (2011). Moho reflection effects in the Po plain (northern Italy) observed from instrumental and intensity data, *Bull. Seismol. Soc. Am.* **101,** no. 5, 2142–2152, doi: 10.1785/0120100257.

Butcher, A., R. Luckett, J. Verdon, M. Kendall, B. Baptie, and J. Wookey (2017). Local magnitude discrepancies for near-event receivers: Implications for the UK traffic-light scheme, *Bull. Seismol. Soc. Am.* **107,** no. 2, 532–541, doi: 10.1785/0120160225.

Castellaro, S., and P. Bormann (2007). Performance of different regression procedures on the magnitude conversion problem, *Bull. Seismol. Soc. Am.* **97,** no. 4, 1167–1175, doi: 10.1785/0120060102.

Chovanová, Z., and J. Kristek (2018). A local magnitude scale for Slovakia, Central Europe, *Bull. Seismol. Soc. Am.* **108,** no. 5A, 2756–2763, doi: 10.1785/0120180059.

Di Bona, M. (2016). A local magnitude scale for crustal earthquakes in Italy, *Bull. Seismol. Soc. Am.* **106,** 242–258, doi: 10.1785/0120150155.

Di Maro, R., L. Arcoraci, P. Battelli, M. Berardi, C. Castellano, B. Castello, D. Latorre, A. Marchetti, L. Margheriti, F. Mele, *et al.* (2022). Bollettino Sismico Italiano 2015, *Quad. Geofis.* **176,** 1–52, doi: 10.13127/qdg/176.

Finetti, I. R. (2005). Crustal tectono-stratigraphic sections across the western and eastern Alps from ECORS-CROP and Transalp seismic data, in *CROP Project: Deep Seismic Exploration of the Central Mediterranean and Italy*, Vol. 7, Elsevier Science and Technology, Amsterdam, The Netherlands, 109–117.

Gentili, S., M. Sugan, L. Peruzza, and D. Schorlemmer (2011). Probabilistic completeness assessment of the past 30 years of seismic monitoring in northeastern Italy, *Phys. Earth Planet. In.* **186,** 81–96, doi: 10.1016/j.pepi.2011.03.005.

Goldstein, P., D. Dodge, and M. Firpo (2003). SAC2000: Signal processing and analysis tools for seismologists and engineers, Incorporated Research Institutions for Seismology (IRIS).

Havskov, J., and L. Ottenmöller (2010). *Routine Data Processing in Earthquake Seismology*, Springer, 347 pp., doi: 10.1007/978-90-481-8697-6.

Helffrich, G., J. Wookey, and I. Bastow (2013). *The Seismic Analysis Code. A Primer and User's Guide*, Cambridge University Press, doi: 10.1017/CBO9781139547260.

Husen, S., and J. L. Hardebeck (2010). Earthquake location accuracy, *Community Online Resource for Statistical Seismicity Analysis*, doi: 10.5078/corssa-55815573.

Hutton, L., and D. M. Boore (1987). The ML scale in southern California, *Bull. Seismol. Soc. Am.* **77,** 2074–2094, doi: 10.1785/BSSA0770062074.

Incorporated Research Institutions for Seismology (IRIS) (2012). SEED reference manual: Standard for the exchange of earthquake data, Incorporated Research Institutions for Seismology – IRIS, available at https://www.fdsn.org/pdf/SEEDManual_V2.4.pdf (last accessed March 2025).

Klin, P., G. Laurenzano, C. Barnaba, E. Priolo, and S. Parolai (2021). Site amplification at permanent stations in northeastern Italy, *Bull. Seismol. Soc. Am.* **111,** 1885–1904, doi: 10.1785/0120200361.

Lahr, J. (1999). HYPOELLIPSE: A computer program for determining local earthquake hypocentral parameters, magnitude, and first-motion pattern, *U.S. Geol. Surv. Open-File Rept. 99-23*, available at http://pubs.usgs.gov/of/1999/ofr-99-0023 (last accessed March 2025).

Langston, C. A., R. Brazier, A. A. Nyblade, and T. J. Owens (1998). Local magnitude scale and seismicity rate for Tanzania, East Africa, *Bull. Seismol. Soc. Am.* **88,** no. 3, 712–721, doi: 10.1785/BSSA0880030712.

Lee, W. H. K., and J. C. Lahr (1975). HYP071 (Revised): A computer pro- gram for determining hypocenter, magnitude and first-motion pattern of local earthquakes, *U.S. Geol. Surv. Open-File Rept. 75-311*, doi: 10.3133/ofr75311.

Lolli, B., P. Gasperini, and F. Mele (2015), Recalibration of the distance correction term for local magnitude (ML) computations in Italy, *Seismol. Res. Lett.* **86,** 1383–1391, doi: 10.1785/0220150020.

Luckett, R., L. Ottemöller, A. Butcher, and B. Baptie (2019). Extending local magnitude M_L to short distances, *Geophys. J. Int.* **216,** no. 2, 1145–1156, doi: 10.1093/gji/ggy484.

Majer, E., J. Nelson, A. Robertson-Tait, J. Savy, and I. Wong (2012). Protocol for addressing induced seismicity associated with enhanced geothermal systems, *DOE/EE-0662*, U.S. Department of Energy.

Maury, J., M. Peter-Borie, P. Dominique, F. De Santis, E. Klein, and I. Contrucci (2023). Guide de bonnes pratiques pour la maìtrise de la sismicité induite par les opérations de géothermie profonde, BRGM Éditions, available at https://www.ecologie.gouv.fr/sites/default/files/documents/Guide-geothermie.pdf (last accessed September 2024).

Michelini, A., L. Margheriti, M. Cattaneo, G. Cecere, G. D'Anna, A. Delladio, M. Moretti, S. Pintore, A. Amato, A. Basili, *et al.* (2016). The Italian National Seismic Network and the earthquake and tsunami monitoring and surveillance systems, *Adv. Geosci.* **43,** 31–38, doi: 10.5194/adgeo-43-31-2016.

MiSE-UNMIG (2014). Guidelines for monitoring seismicity, ground deformation and pore pressure in subsurface industrial activities, Ministero per lo Sviluppo Economico (MiSE)—Ufficio nazionale minerario per gli idrocarburi e le georisorse (UNMIG), available at https://unmig.mase.gov.it/geomonitoraggi/linee-guida-per-i-monitoraggi/ (last accessed March 2025).

Moratto, L., A. Saraò, and E. Priolo (2017). Moment magnitude (Mw) estimation of weak seismicity in Northeastern Italy, *Seismol. Res. Lett.* **88,** 1455–1464, doi: 10.1785/0220170063.

Ottenmöller, L., and S. Sargeant (2013). A local magnitude scale ML for the United Kingdom, *Bull. Seismol. Soc. Am.* **103,** 2884–2893, doi: 10.1785/0120130085.

Peresan, A., and S. Gentili (2018). Seismic clusters analysis in northeastern Italy by the nearest-neighbor approach, *Phys. Earth Planet. In.* **274,** 87–104, doi: 10.1016/j.pepi.2017.11.007.

Peruzza, L., M. A. Romano, M. Guidarelli, L. Moratto, M. Garbin, and E. Priolo (2022). An unusually productive microearthquake sequence brings new insights to the buried active thrust system of Montello (southeastern Alps, northern Italy), *Front. Earth Sci.* **10,** doi: 10.3389/feart.2022.1044296.

Picotti, V., M. A. Romano, A. Ponza, F. L. Guido, and L. Peruzza (2022). The Montello thrust and the active mountain front of the eastern southern Alps (northeast Italy), *Tectonics* **41,** doi: 10.1029/2022TC007522.

Priolo, E., C. Barnaba, P. Bernardi, G. Bernardis, P. L. Bragato, G. Bressan, M. Candido, E. Cazzador, P. Di Bartolomeo, G. Durì, *et al.* (2005). Seismic monitoring in northeastern Italy: A ten-year experience, *Seismol. Res. Lett.* **76,** no. 4, 446–454, doi: 10.1785/gssrl.76.4.446.

Priolo, E., M. Romanelli, M. P. Plasencia Linares, M. Garbin, L. Peruzza, M. A. Romano, P. Marotta, P. Bernardi, L. Moratto, D. Zuliani, *et al.* (2015). Seismic monitoring of an underground natural gas storage facility: The Collalto Seismic Network, *Seismol. Res. Lett.* **86,** 109–123, doi: 10.1785/0220140087.

Richter, C. F. (1935). An instrumental earthquake magnitude scale, *Bull. Seismol. Soc. Am.* **25,** 1–32.

Richter, C. F. (1958). *Elementary Seismology*, W. H. Freeman, San Francisco, California, 578 pp.

Romano, M. A., L. Peruzza, M. Garbin, E. Priolo, and V. Picotti (2019). Microseismic portrait of the Montello thrust (southeastern Alps, Italy) from a dense, high-quality seismic network, *Seismol. Res. Lett.* **90,** 1502–1517, doi: 10.1785/0220180387.

Rovida, A., M. Locati, R. Camassi, B. Lolli, and P. Gasperini (2020). The Italian earthquake catalogue CPTI15, *Bull. Earthq. Eng.* **18,** no. 7, 2953–2984, doi: 10.1007/s10518-020-00818-y.

Rovida, A., M. Locati, R. Camassi, B. Lolli, P. Gasperini, and A. Antonucci (2022). Catalogo Parametrico dei Terremoti Italiani (CPTI15), versione 4.0 [Data set], *Istituto Nazionale di Geofisica e Vulcanologia (INGV)*, doi: 10.13127/cpti/cpti15.4.

Sandron, D., A. Rebez, and D. Slejko (2018). Calibration of the duration magnitude for the north-eastern Italy seismometric network (OX) on the basis of the revised local magnitudes of the Trieste station, *Bull. Geofis. Teor. Appl.* **59,** no. 3, 249–266, doi: 10.4430/bgta0237.

Spallarossa, D., D. Bindi, P. Augliera, and M. Cattaneo (2002). An ML scale in northwestern Italy, *Bull. Seismol. Soc. Am.* **92,** 2205–2216, doi: 10.1785/0120010201.

Sugan, M., and A. Vuan (2014). On the ability of Moho reflections to affect the ground motion in northeastern Italy: A case study of the 2012 Emilia seismic sequence, *Bull. Earthq. Eng.* **12,** 2179–2194, doi: 10.1007/s10518-013-9564-y.

Sugan, M., A. Saraò, A. Magrin, A. Snidarcig, G. Bressan, G. Renner, M. A. Romano, M. Guidarelli, M. Santulin, P. Di Bartolomeo, *et al.* (2024). Focal mechanisms of the southeastern Alps and surroundings (2.0) [Data set], *Zenodo*, doi: 10.5281/zenodo.10853582.

Tarchini, G., L. Moratto, and A. Saraò (2025). A comprehensive moment magnitude catalog for the northeastern Italy region, *Seismol. Res. Lett.* **96,** no. 4, 2714–2723, doi: 10.1785/0220240303.

Uhrhammer, R. A., and E. R. Collins (1990). Synthesis of Wood–Anderson seismograms from broadband digital records, *Bull. Seismol. Soc. Am.* **80,** 702–716.

Manuscript received 21 March 2025
Published online 12 March 2026

Crustal Stress Information Revealed by the Distribution of P and T Axes of Earthquake Focal Mechanisms

Zhenyue Li[1] and Yongge Wan*[1]

ABSTRACT

OPEN ACCESS

Earthquake focal mechanisms provide essential constraints on the stress state of the Earth's crust. Conventional stress tensor inversion relies on fitting slip directions on multiple faults, but because double-couple focal mechanisms can also be represented by the orientations of P and T axes, such inversions effectively fit the spatial distribution of these axes. This study examines whether the distribution patterns of P and T axes alone can directly constrain the crustal stress tensor. We perform modeling experiments that simulate fault instability and slip under a range of stress states and fault failure criteria. The results show that systematic changes in stress conditions produce distinct and predictable transitions in P and T axes distributions. The geometric centers of clustered axes correspond to the orientations of the principal stress axes. A clustered P axis distribution combined with a circular T axis pattern indicates comparable magnitudes of σ_2 and σ_3, whereas a clustered T axis distribution with a circular P axis pattern does not require and to be similar in magnitude. Randomly intermingled P and T axes distributions do not occur in the simulations, indicating that such patterns observed in real data likely reflect stress heterogeneity or inaccuracies in focal mechanism solutions. These conclusions are validated using real fault-slip data and earthquake focal mechanisms. The results provide a practical framework for diagnosing stress heterogeneity, evaluating data quality, and anticipating the reliability of stress inversion outcomes.

KEY POINTS

- Whether the P and T axes distribution of focal mechanisms reflects crustal stress remains unclear.
- The distribution patterns of P and T axes are indicative of the stress orientation and shape ratio.
- Applying P and T axes analysis to field data enables robust assessment of stress inversion results.

INTRODUCTION

Pre-existing faults in the Earth's crust progressively accumulate stress as a result of continuous tectonic plate motion. When the accumulated stress exceeds the fault strength, the fault ruptures and releases elastic energy in the form of an earthquake. Faults with diverse orientations are distributed throughout the crust. The likelihood of fault activation and the associated slip behavior are controlled by the prevailing stress field in the crust. Therefore, earthquake focal mechanisms provide important constraints on the tectonic stress near the source region.

In an effort to reconstruct the background stresses that drive fault slip, researchers have developed various strategies for stress inversion using either fault-slip data (e.g., Angelier, 1984; Michael, 1984) or focal mechanisms (e.g., Gephart and Forsyth, 1984; Michael, 1987; Hardebeck and Michael, 2006; Vavryčuk, 2014; Martínez-Garzón *et al.*, 2016; Wan *et al.*, 2016; Li *et al.*, 2020; Beaucé *et al.*, 2022). These strategies are widely used in geodynamic studies (e.g., Delvaux and Barth, 2010; Sheng and Meng, 2020; Nouri *et al.*, 2023). The fundamental principle of stress inversion from fault-slip data and from earthquake focal mechanism data is essentially the same because it involves determining a stress tensor that best fits the observed fault-slip directions. In essence, the inversion defines a mapping from fault parameters (strike, dip, and slip) to the stress tensor. Although the procedure may at first appear unrelated to the P, B, and T axes

1. Institute of Disaster Prevention, Sanhe, China, https://orcid.org/0009-0009-1931-154X (ZL)

*Corresponding author: wanyg217217@vip.sina.com.cn

Cite this article as Li, Z., and Y. Wan (2026). Crustal Stress Information Revealed by the Distribution of P and T Axes of Earthquake Focal Mechanisms, *Bull. Seismol. Soc. Am.* **116**, 1007–1022, doi: 10.1785/0120250275 of focal mechanisms, the fault geometry can be equivalently represented by the orientations of the P and T axes, with the B axis uniquely determined by their mutual orthogonality. Using these orientations as input thus reformulates the inversion as estimating the stress tensor directly from the P and T axes.

From a physical perspective, understanding the principle of inferring stress using the orientations of the P and T axes requires first transforming the double-couple focal mechanism into a description of moment tensor. The moment tensor expresses how tectonic stress is released on a specific fault, essentially representing the released stress tensor. The P, B, and T axes are the three principal stress axes of the moment tensor. Tectonic stress is released in various forms across different faults, and the inversion of the stress driving these fault activities is achieved by fitting the forms of tectonic stress release on various faults. Therefore, it is certain that the distribution of P and T axes of focal mechanisms is intricately linked to the driving forces that activate fault movements.

Recognizing this intrinsic relationship allows a preliminary estimation of the stress characteristics, such as the orientations of the principal stress axes, and an evaluation of whether the focal mechanism data are consistent with a homogeneous stress model, based on the distribution patterns of the P and T axes before stress inversion. Such an evaluation provides a valuable complement to conventional stress inversion analyses. Current stress inversion approaches (Gephart and Forsyth, 1984; Michael, 1987; Vavryčuk, 2014) generally assume that the focal mechanisms within a study area represent a homogeneous stress field. However, this assumption may not always hold in practical applications. The boundaries of study regions are often defined arbitrarily, which may encompass areas influenced by different stress regimes. Even in regions governed by a relatively uniform stress field, small earthquakes can still be affected by local stress perturbations. Moreover, focal mechanism solutions may carry considerable uncertainties because their reliability depends on well-constrained velocity models, adequate station coverage, and high-quality waveform data. These requirements are seldom satisfied for small events, leading to substantial discrepancies between the observed and the actual faulting mechanisms. If a dataset contains a large number of focal mechanisms that do not belong to the same stress regime, the inferred stress may fail to represent the true stress conditions.

In conventional approaches, this issue is typically assessed by comparing the misfit between the observed and theoretical slip directions of individual faults after stress inversion (Li, Wan, *et al.*, 2023). However, the selected fault plane in each focal mechanism may be incorrect (Vavryčuk, 2014; Martínez-Garzón *et al.*, 2016), and there is no clear consensus on the threshold of deviation that indicates data inconsistency. Consequently, this problem is often overlooked in practical applications. Understanding the theoretical relationship between stress and the expected distributions of the P and T axes allows for an assessment of the internal consistency of focal mechanism data before stress inversion. Substantial deviations of the P and T axes from any plausible stress-controlled pattern indicate that the dataset may not reflect a homogeneous stress field, thereby calling the reliability of the inversion results into question.

The aforementioned analysis highlights the importance of understanding the theoretical distribution patterns of P and T axes from focal mechanisms under varying stress states to successfully invert for stress. Building on this premise, this study aims to reveal the tectonic stress information encoded in these different P and T distribution patterns. Given the complex relationship between the stress tensor and the P/T axes, we address this problem using synthetic experiments. In the following sections, we first introduce the principles guiding the synthetic experiments. We then examine the distribution patterns of P and T axes generated under different experimental conditions and interpret the associated stress information. Finally, we test the applicability of the conclusions obtained from the synthetic experiments using several sets of fault slip and focal mechanism data.

SYNTHETIC EXPERIMENTS

Earthquake focal mechanisms simulation

This section is organized into three parts to clarify the design principles of the synthetic experiments for simulating focal mechanisms. The first part describes how a stress tensor is constructed from the stress parameters inverted from fault-slip data. The second part defines the mechanical conditions under which a fault becomes unstable and ruptures under the applied stress. The third part introduces the resulting fault-slip modes driven by the imposed stress and details the procedures used to generate focal mechanisms from these slip motions.

Expression of the stress tensor

The inversion of stress from fault-slip data is based on the assumption that faults slip in the direction of the maximum shear stress acting on their plane (Wallace, 1951; Bott, 1959). Because fault slip cannot capture the isotropic component of the stress tensor, and the data provide only the direction of slip rather than the magnitude of the shear stress along that direction, the inversion yields a stress tensor that preserves the shape but not the absolute magnitude of the true stress—namely, a normalized stress tensor (Michael, 1987; Vavryčuk, 2014). This tensor is characterized by four independent parameters: three describing the orientations of the principal stresses, and one defining the stress shape, which is expressed as

$$R = \frac{\sigma_1 - \sigma_2}{\sigma_1 - \sigma_3}, \tag{1}$$

in which σ_1, σ_2, and σ_3 represent the magnitudes of the maximum, intermediate, and minimum principal compressive stresses, respectively, with R ranging from 0 to 1.

Following our previous study (Li, Wan, *et al.*, 2023), we define the magnitudes of the three principal stresses as $\sigma_1 = 1 + R$, $\sigma_2 = 1 - 2R$, and $\sigma_3 = -2 + R$ (with compression taken as positive and tension as negative). Under this formulation, the normalized stress tensor can be expressed in terms of four parameters, as follows:

$$\sigma = \begin{bmatrix} \boldsymbol{l} \\ \boldsymbol{m} \\ \boldsymbol{k} \end{bmatrix}^T \begin{bmatrix} 1+R & & \\ & 1-2R & \\ & & -2+R \end{bmatrix} \begin{bmatrix} \boldsymbol{l} \\ \boldsymbol{m} \\ \boldsymbol{k} \end{bmatrix}, \quad (2)$$

in which

$$\boldsymbol{l} = [\cos\delta\cos\varphi, \cos\delta\sin\varphi, \sin\delta], \quad (3)$$

$$\boldsymbol{m} = [\sin\varphi\sin\lambda + \cos\varphi\sin\delta\cos\lambda, \\ -\cos\varphi\sin\lambda + \sin\varphi\sin\delta\cos\lambda, -\cos\delta\cos\lambda], \quad (4)$$

$$\boldsymbol{k} = [-\sin\varphi\cos\lambda + \cos\varphi\sin\delta\sin\lambda, \\ \cos\varphi\cos\lambda + \sin\varphi\sin\delta\sin\lambda, -\cos\delta\sin\lambda]. \quad (5)$$

In the aforementioned equations, $\boldsymbol{l}$, $\boldsymbol{m}$, and $\boldsymbol{k}$ denote the directions of the σ_1, σ_2 and σ_3 axes, respectively. The symbols φ and δ represent the azimuth and plunge of the σ_1 axis, whereas λ defines the orientation of the σ_3 axis. Specifically, λ is the angle between the σ_3 axis and the strike of the plane for which the normal is parallel to the σ_1 axis.

Fault failure criteria

The Mohr–Coulomb failure criterion (Beeler *et al.*, 2000) provides the condition for fault destabilization, which is expressed as

$$\tau \geq \mu(\sigma - P) + C. \quad (6)$$

In the formula, σ and τ represent the normal and shear stresses, respectively, acting on the fault. The variable μ denotes the friction coefficient, P is the pore pressure, and C represents the rock cohesion. Earthquakes occur on faults that satisfy this criterion (Vavryčuk, 2014; Beaucé *et al.*, 2022).

In the $\sigma - \tau$ coordinate system, equation (6) corresponds to the area above a straight line. The intercepts of the failure line with the σ- and τ axes are determined by the pore pressure and rock cohesion, respectively. However, this criterion cannot be directly applied to evaluate fault activation in the synthetic experiments, because the stresses are normalized, and both pore pressure and cohesion must be normalized accordingly. Geometrically, the Mohr–Coulomb failure criterion describes the relative position of the failure line with respect to the Mohr circle. Fault instability (Vavryčuk *et al.*, 2013; Vavryčuk, 2014) is defined based on the normalized distance from the projection of a fault on the Mohr circle to the critical failure line, which is tangential to the circle at a single point (Fig. 1). Faults with the same instability lie along the same failure line. Consequently, fault instability can serve as an alternative representation of the position of the failure line, naturally incorporating the effects of pore pressure and cohesion through the same normalization applied to the stress. Reformulated in terms of instability, the Mohr–Coulomb criterion indicates that a fault becomes unstable and rupture occurs when its instability exceeds the critical value corresponding to the failure line. Conversely, faults with instability below this threshold remain stable.

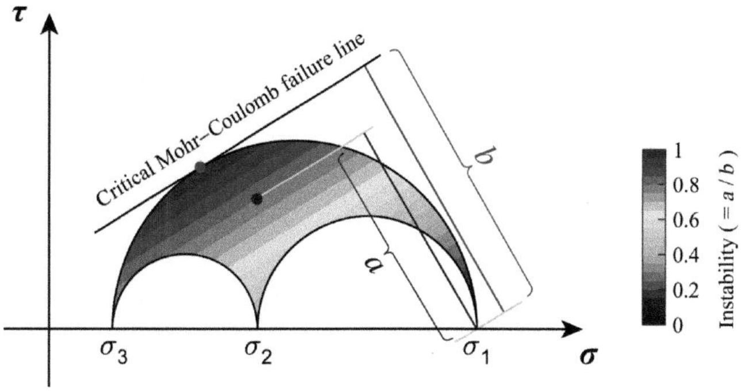

Figure 1. Schematic diagram illustrating the definition of the fault instability. The blue point in the diagram represents an arbitrary fault, whereas the red point corresponds to the most unstable faults. The instability (*I*) is defined as the ratio of the length of the blue line segment to that of the red line segment. The colors within the Mohr circle indicate the variation of fault instability. The color version of this figure is available only in the electronic edition.

The exact value of critical instability in geological environments remains unknown, requiring estimation through synthetic experiments. As indicated in equation (6), reducing cohesion and increasing pore pressure shift the failure line to the right in the $\sigma - \tau$ coordinate system, which corresponds to a decrease in critical instability. Accordingly, the failure line defined by the minimum cohesion and the maximum pore pressure provides a lower bound on the critical instability. Because natural earthquakes typically occur along pre-existing fractures, cohesion can be assumed to reach a minimum value of 0. Furthermore, pore pressure cannot exceed the magnitude of the minimum principal stress because any excess would induce fractures perpendicular to the minimum principal stress direction. Therefore, assuming a cohesion of 0 and pore pressure equal to the magnitude of the minimum principal stress, and using an average friction coefficient of 0.6 within the crust (Byerlee, 1978; Jia *et al.*, 2018; Lei *et al.*, 2020), we estimate the lower bound of critical instability to be approximately 0.7. In this study, focal mechanisms are simulated for critical instability values of 0.7, 0.8, 0.9, and 0.95 to examine the spatial variations of P, B, and T axes associated with different critical instability levels.

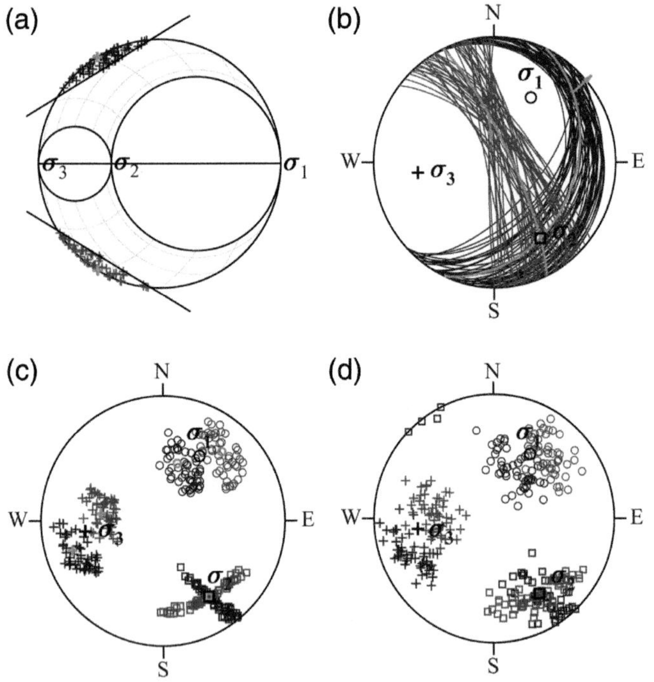

Figure 2. An example of a synthesized earthquake focal mechanism, with the azimuth and dip of the σ_1 axis set to 30° and 40°, respectively, the azimuth of the σ_3 axis set to −97°, and a stress shape ratio of 0.7. (a) Mohr diagram showing faults that satisfy the failure criterion, with blue and red symbols distinguishing faults on either side of the σ_1 axis in the upper and lower semicircles, respectively. Green crosses mark the two most unstable faults. (b) Faults that satisfy the failure criterion. Green arrows indicate slip directions of the most unstable faults. (c) P (circles), B (squares), and T (crosses) axes of the focal mechanisms without noise. (d) P, B, and T axes of focal mechanisms with random noise of 15° to the normal and slip directions of the synthetic earthquake faults. Black circles, squares, and crosses in panels (b–d) mark the orientations of the three principal stress axes projected in a lower hemisphere equal-area projection. The color version of this figure is available only in the electronic edition.

Synthetic focal mechanisms

The process for synthesizing earthquake focal mechanisms is as follows.

1. Construct the stress tensor based on the given stress directions and shape ratio.
2. Randomly generate a sufficient number of faults with various orientations, calculate their instability, and select a specified number of faults from the group with instability exceeding the critical threshold to serve as the simulated seismic fault planes.
3. Calculate the theoretical slip direction (shear stress direction) for the selected fault planes. Then, based on the relationships among source parameters in the double-couple source model, the parameters of the other nodal plane and the P, B, and T axes can be derived (Stein and Wysession, 2003).
4. If necessary, introduce perturbations into the simulated earthquake focal mechanisms, following the approach of Vavryčuk (2014), to simulate noisy observations.

Figure 2 shows an example of synthesizing earthquake focal mechanisms, for which the stress orientations and the shape ratio are chosen arbitrarily. The friction is set at 0.6, and the critical instability is 0.93. Figure 2a depicts faults within the Mohr circle that satisfy the Mohr–Coulomb failure criterion, whereas Figure 2b shows the spatial orientations of these faults relative to the principal stress axes. Figure 2c shows the distribution of the P, B, and T axes of the focal mechanisms because these faults rupture under the applied stress, exhibiting a two-butterfly pattern for the P and T axes (Vavryčuk, 2011) and an X-shaped distribution for the B axes. After introducing random angular perturbations of 15° to the normal and slip directions of the synthetic earthquake faults, Figure 2d displays the resulting distributions. Compared with Figure 2c, these patterns become less distinct and increasingly cluster around the principal stress axes.

In this example, the critical instability is set to a relatively high value, resulting in synthetic fault clusters that are more concentrated near the two most unstable faults. The P, B, and T axes of the synthetic focal mechanisms are correspondingly clustered around the three principal stress axes (Fig. 2c,d), and their distribution provides a clear indication of the orientations of these principal stress axes. However, when only a single fault cluster is present, the P and T axes exhibit only one butterfly wing of the expected pattern, and the geometric centers of their distributions deviate slightly from the σ_1 and σ_3 axes (consistent with Vavryčuk, 2011, 2014). If these geometric centers are used to estimate the principal stress axes, the resulting deviations do not introduce significant errors. The relationship between the distribution of the P, B, and T axes and the principal stress orientations under other experimental conditions will be systematically investigated in the following section.

Experimental results

The orientation of stress and faults is relative. Once the stress state and failure criterion are defined, the relative orientations of faults that satisfy the failure criterion with respect to the principal stress axes remain constant, even if the orientations of the principal stresses are changed. This indicates that the choice of principal stress orientations does not influence the experimental results, allowing them to be assigned arbitrarily. In this study, we adopt the stress orientation used in the experiment described in the Synthetic focal mechanisms section. With the friction coefficient fixed at 0.6, the shape ratio and the critical instability coefficient become the primary factors controlling the results. This section explores various combinations of these two parameters. For each case, 500 synthetic faults are generated, and no noise is introduced.

Spatial orientation of the faults

Figure 3 shows the distribution of fault normals, with two colors used to differentiate faults located on either side of the σ_1 axis. It is clear that the distribution pattern of the fault normals

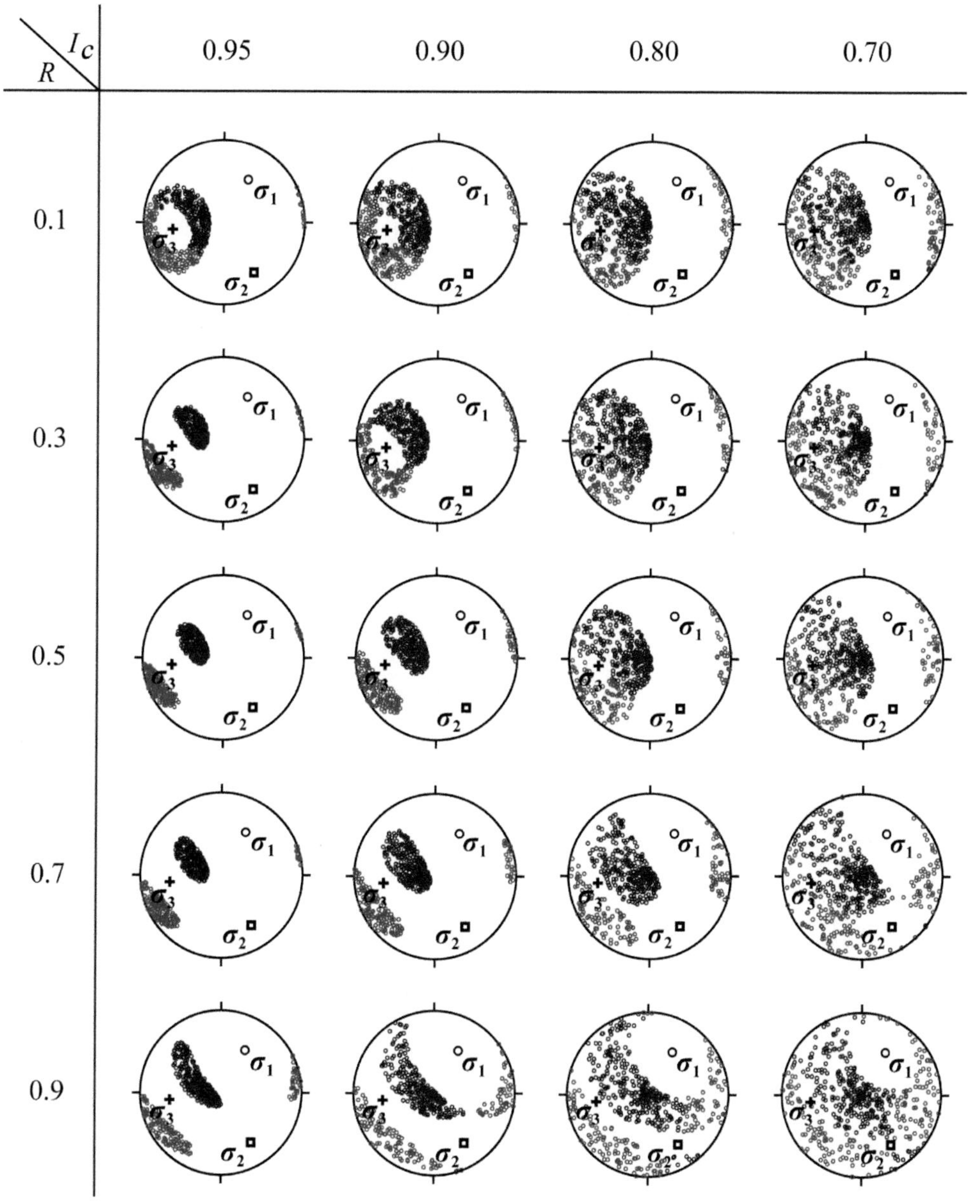

Figure 3. Distribution of fault normals in synthetic experiments with varying R values and critical instability coefficients (I_c). Each subplot represents an equal-area stereographic projection of the lower hemisphere, showing the orientations of fault normals and principal stress orientations under different experimental conditions. Blue and red circles indicate faults located on either side of the σ_1 axis. The color version of this figure is available only in the electronic edition.

is closely linked to both the shape ratio and the critical instability. Based on the normalization method for the three principal stresses ($\sigma_1 = 1 + R$, $\sigma_2 = 1 - 2R$, and $\sigma_3 = -2 + R$) and the definition of the R value as given in equation (1), when $R = 0$, σ_2 equals σ_1. Under this condition, the compressive stress is uniformly distributed in all directions within the plane formed by the intermediate and maximum compressive stress axes and is equal to σ_1. The orientations of these two axes within the plane are indistinguishable and have no fixed direction. As a result, as R approaches 0, the normals of the synthetic faults are distributed around the σ_3 axis. As R increases from 0 to 0.5, σ_2 is positive, causing the intermediate stress to be compressive, with compressive stress gradually decreasing to 0. From 0.5 to 1, σ_2 turns negative, resulting in tensile intermediate stress, with tensile stress on this axis gradually increasing. At $R = 1$, σ_2 equals σ_3. In the plane formed by the intermediate and minimum compressive stress axes, tensile stress in all directions becomes equal to σ_3. The orientations of the intermediate and minimum compressive stress axes within this plane are indistinguishable and have no fixed direction. Therefore, as R approaches 1, the normals of the synthetic faults are oriented around the σ_1 axis. From the perspective of the Mohr circle, a decrease in the critical instability coefficient corresponds to an expanding area where the failure line intersects the Mohr circle. Faults within this intersected region satisfy the failure criterion. As a result, when the critical instability coefficient decreases, the diversity of faults that meet the failure criterion increases. In the experiments with the same R value shown in Figure 3, a lower critical instability coefficient leads to a broader distribution of fault orientations.

Spatial orientation of the P and T axes

Figure 4 illustrates the distributions of the P and T axes under various experimental conditions, demonstrating that their spatial patterns are jointly controlled by the R value and the critical instability coefficient. When $R = 0$, the maximum and intermediate compressive stress axes do not have fixed orientations within the plane they define, resulting in a circular distribution of the P axes around this plane. In this case, if the orientation of the σ_3 axis can be statistically constrained from the distribution of the T axes, the stress orientations inferred

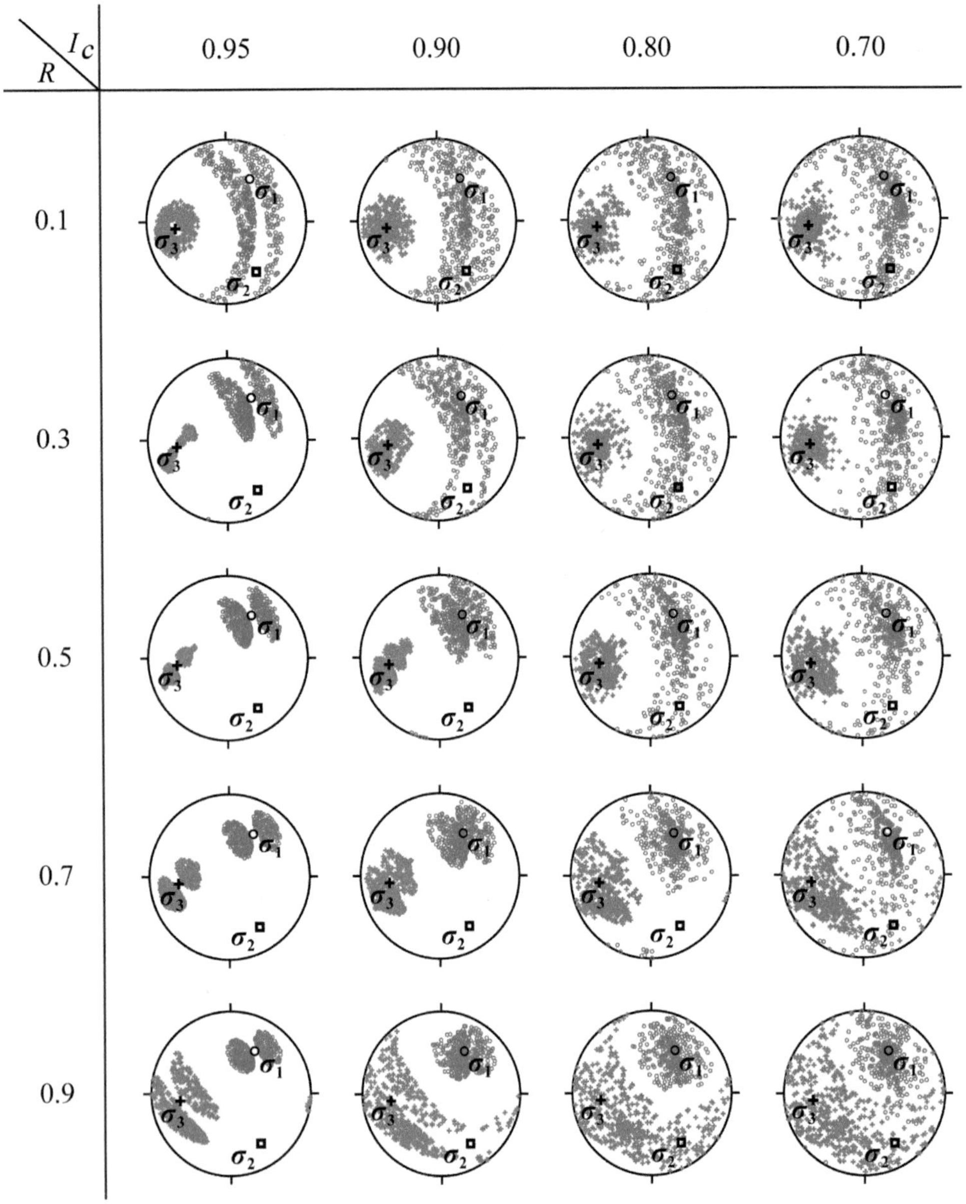

Figure 4. Distributions of P (red circles) and T (blue crosses) axes from synthetic focal mechanisms obtained under different R values and critical instability conditions. The plots are shown in an equal-area projection of the lower hemisphere. The color version of this figure is available only in the electronic edition.

from the P and T axes distributions will remain reliable. Similarly, when $R = 1$, the intermediate and minimum compressive stress axes do not have fixed orientations within their plane, resulting in a circular distribution of the T axes around this plane. If the orientation of the σ_1 axis can be statistically constrained from the P axes distribution, the inferred stress orientations will be reliable. When $R = 0.1$, which is close to its minimum value, the difference between the maximum and intermediate principal stress axes becomes relatively small. In this case, if the orientation of the σ_3 axis is accurately determined, the inferred stress orientation can be regarded as reliable. Similarly, when $R = 0.9$, accurately determining the orientation of the σ_1 axis ensures the reliability of the inferred stress orientation. Consistent with these expectations, Figure 4 shows that for $R = 0.1$, the T axes cluster around the σ_3 axis, whereas for $R = 0.9$, the P axes cluster around the σ_1 axis.

When the critical instability is set to 0.95, the P and T axes in the experiments exhibit the highest degree of concentration. As the critical instability decreases, fault diversity increases, resulting in a progressively broader distribution of the P and T axes. This gradual expansion of the distribution range makes it increasingly difficult to statistically constrain the orientations of the principal stress axes. An interesting phenomenon observed in the experiments is that the P axes exhibit a circular distribution when R ranges from 0.1 to 0.7. As the critical instability decreases, this circular pattern of the P axes extends over a wider range of R values. In contrast, the T axes display a circular distribution only under higher R values and when the critical instability exceeds 0.9. These results indicate that a circular distribution of the P axes does not necessarily correspond to a lower R value, whereas a circular distribution of the T axes is associated with a higher R value. This represents the only definitive information about stress magnitudes that can be inferred from the distributions of the P and T axes.

Analysis of the experimental results reveals that the P and T axes do not always cluster around the principal stress axes simultaneously. In some cases, one set of axes may form a distinct cluster near a principal stress axis, whereas the other does not. In other cases, both sets may exhibit clustering, or neither does, as observed in the experiment for which both R and I_c are 0.7. More importantly, whenever either the P or T axes form a clustered distribution, the clusters consistently align with their corresponding principal stress axes.

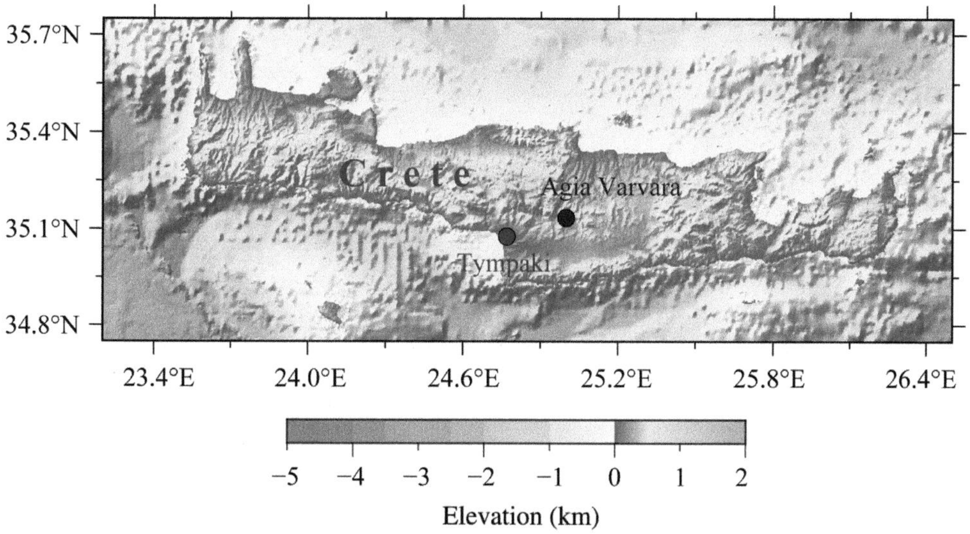

Figure 5. Map showing the locations of Agia Varvara (AVB) and Tympaki (TYM) in Crete, Greece. The color version of this figure is available only in the electronic edition.

In real geophysical applications, the stress shape ratio and the critical instability level are generally unknown, making it difficult to anticipate the dispersion of the P and T axes. Synthetic experiments show that when either the P or T axes form a concentrated cluster, they reliably capture the orientations of the principal stresses, ensuring robust statistical estimates. Because the P and T axes become more dispersed, statistical estimates of the principal stress orientations naturally exhibit larger deviations. Nevertheless, even when the P or T axes are dispersed, the distribution remains consistent with a uniform stress model, and a heterogeneous stress field is not required to explain the observation. This raises the question of whether, in real data, it is possible to distinguish dispersion of the P and T axes caused by low-critical instability from that resulting from stress heterogeneity.

As shown in Figure 4, the dispersion of the P and T axes associated with low-critical instability exhibits a systematic pattern: as the critical instability decreases, the P or T axes gradually transition toward a circular distribution, and regular intersections appear only when the critical instability reaches its minimum, as in the case for which both R and I_c are 0.7. In contrast, a heterogeneous stress field generally produces a more random dispersion of P/T axes, which clearly differs from the patterns associated with low-critical instability. Moreover, significant uncertainties in the observational data can also produce a seemingly random dispersion of P and T axes. Consequently, if observational data exhibit a random intersecting pattern of the P and T axes, this indicates inconsistency with a uniform stress model. In such cases, it is essential to carefully assess both the reliability of the focal mechanism solutions and the spatial homogeneity of the stress field within the study area.

CASE STUDIES

Fault-slip data and earthquake focal mechanisms are two primary datasets used for crustal stress inversion. Field-measured slickensides provide parameters such as fault strike, dip, and slip angle, allowing direct comparison with focal mechanisms. A key difference is that fault-slip data specify a single fault plane, whereas focal mechanisms involve two possible fault planes, making stress inversion based on fault-slip data generally more straightforward. In this study, both datasets are used to evaluate the applicability of the synthetic experiment results to observational data. Two fault-slip datasets from Crete, Greece, are analyzed, together with focal mechanism datasets from deep-focus earthquakes in the Tonga subduction zone and from earthquakes near Yangbi County, Yunnan Province, China. These datasets have also been widely analyzed in previous studies (e.g., Michael, 1984; Angelier, 1990; Vavryčuk, 2004, 2014; Li, Li, *et al.*, 2023; Li, Wan, *et al.*, 2023).

In each case study, stress inversion is performed on the respective dataset, followed by an evaluation of whether the inferred stress orientations and shape ratio align with the observed distribution patterns of the P and T axes, in accordance with the relationships established from the synthetic experiments.

Fault-slip data from Crete

We employed two sets of fault-slip data measured in the Agia Varvara (AVB) and Tympaki (TYM) areas of Crete, Greece, consisting of 33 and 38 slickenside measurements, respectively, as documented by Angelier (1990). The geographic locations of these two sites within Crete are shown in Figure 5.

AVB dataset

The 33 slickensides from the AVB region are shown in Figure 6a, and the spatial distribution of the P, B, and T axes derived from these fault-slip data is presented in Figure 6b. We applied the Michael (1984) linearization method to invert the regional stress. Figure 6c shows the optimal stress orientation along with its uncertainty range, whereas Figure 6d presents the optimal stress shape ratio and its uncertainty. The optimal stress tensor was obtained from the entire dataset, and its uncertainty was evaluated by performing 500 inversions, each using a randomly selected 80% subset of the data.

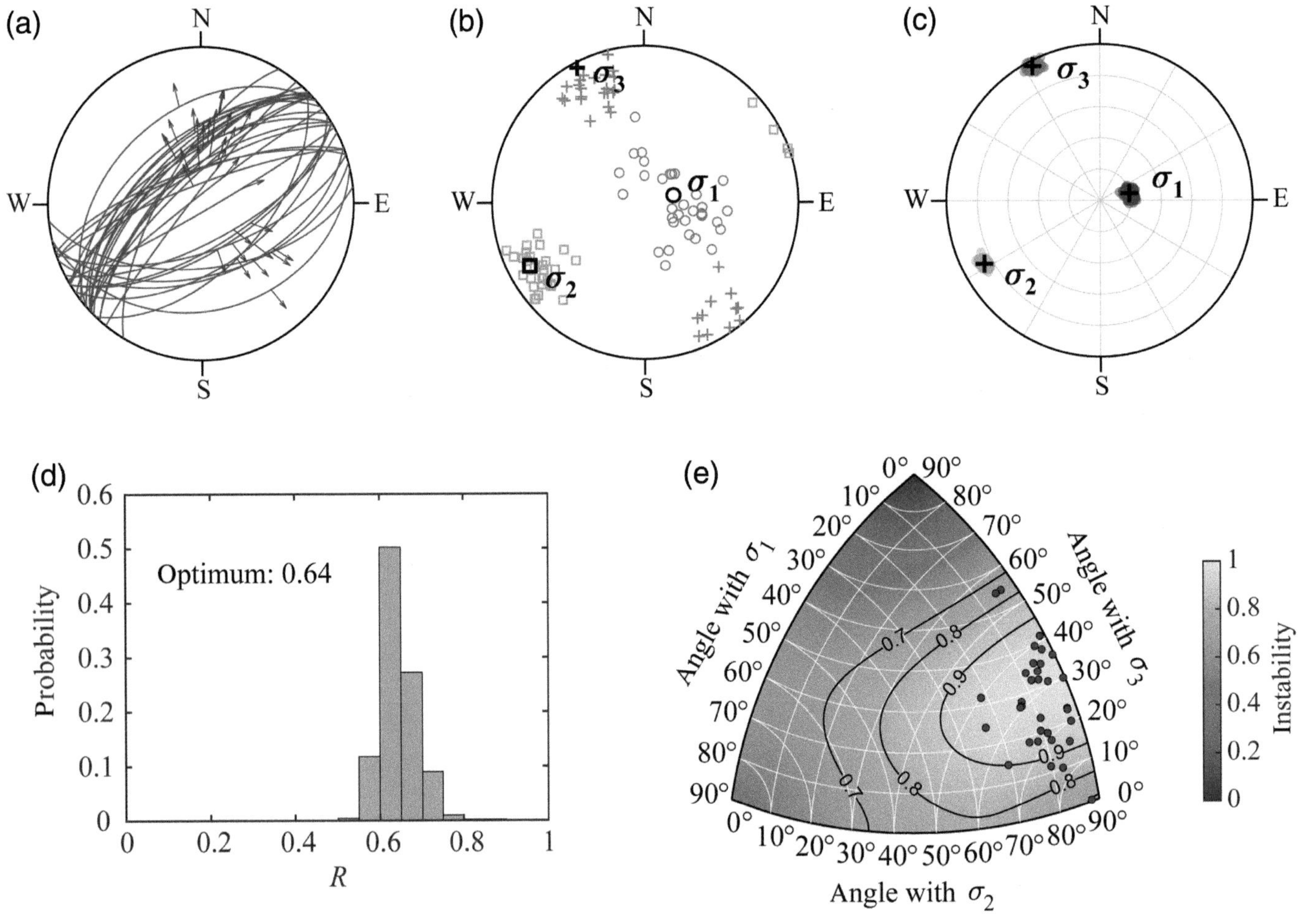

Figure 6. Stress inversion results for the AVB region. (a) Fault-slip data, red arrows indicate slip directions. (b) Distribution of P (red circles), B (green squares), and T (blue crosses) axes derived from the fault-slip data, along with the optimal orientations of the three principal stress axes. (c) Optimal stress orientations (black crosses) and their uncertainty ranges. (d) Optimal stress shape ratio and its uncertainty. (e) Distribution of fault instability under the optimal stress tensor in the principal stress axes coordinate system, with red dots representing the fault projections. The vertices at the top, left, and right of the spherical triangle correspond to the projection points of the σ_1, σ_2, and σ_3 axes, respectively. The white arcs represent spatial directions that are equiangular to the principal stress axes, whereas the black curves, labeled with numbers, indicate instability contours. The gradient colors in the figure correspond to the instability of faults with normals oriented in various spatial directions (for more details, see Li, Wan, *et al.*, 2023). The color version of this figure is available only in the electronic edition.

The inversion results indicate that uncertainties in both the stress orientations and the stress shape ratio are small, suggesting that the derived stress is reliable. When plotted alongside the optimal stress orientation, the P, B, and T axes are closely clustered around σ_1, σ_2, and σ_3, respectively (Fig. 6b), providing a clear basis for inferring the orientations of the principal stresses.

Figure 6e shows the distribution of fault instability under the optimal stress tensor, plotted in the coordinate system of the principal stress axes. Most of the faults measured from slickensides exhibit instability values exceeding 0.9. When compared with the results of the synthetic experiments conducted with a critical instability of 0.9 and shape ratios of 0.5 and 0.7, the observed data from the AVB region show good agreement with the synthetic predictions (Fig. 4). This consistency explains the clustering patterns observed in both the fault orientations (Fig. 6a) and the P, B, and T axes (Fig. 6b).

TYM dataset

The same procedure was applied to the TYM dataset, and the results are presented in Figure 7. As shown in Figure 7c,d, the σ_1 axis exhibits very small orientation uncertainty, whereas slightly larger uncertainties are observed for the σ_2 and σ_3 axes. The R value is close to 1, with only minor variation. The relatively greater uncertainties of the σ_2 and σ_3 axes arise from the nature of the stress state, for which a high R value reduces the distinguishability between these two principal stress orientations within their defining plane. Under such conditions, once the σ_1 axis orientation is well constrained, the overall stress orientation can be regarded as accurate. Hence, the stress inversion results are both precise and reliable.

The P, B, and T axes form distributions that encircle the principal stress axes, with the B and T axes showing broader dispersion than the P axes (Fig. 7b). This wider spread also

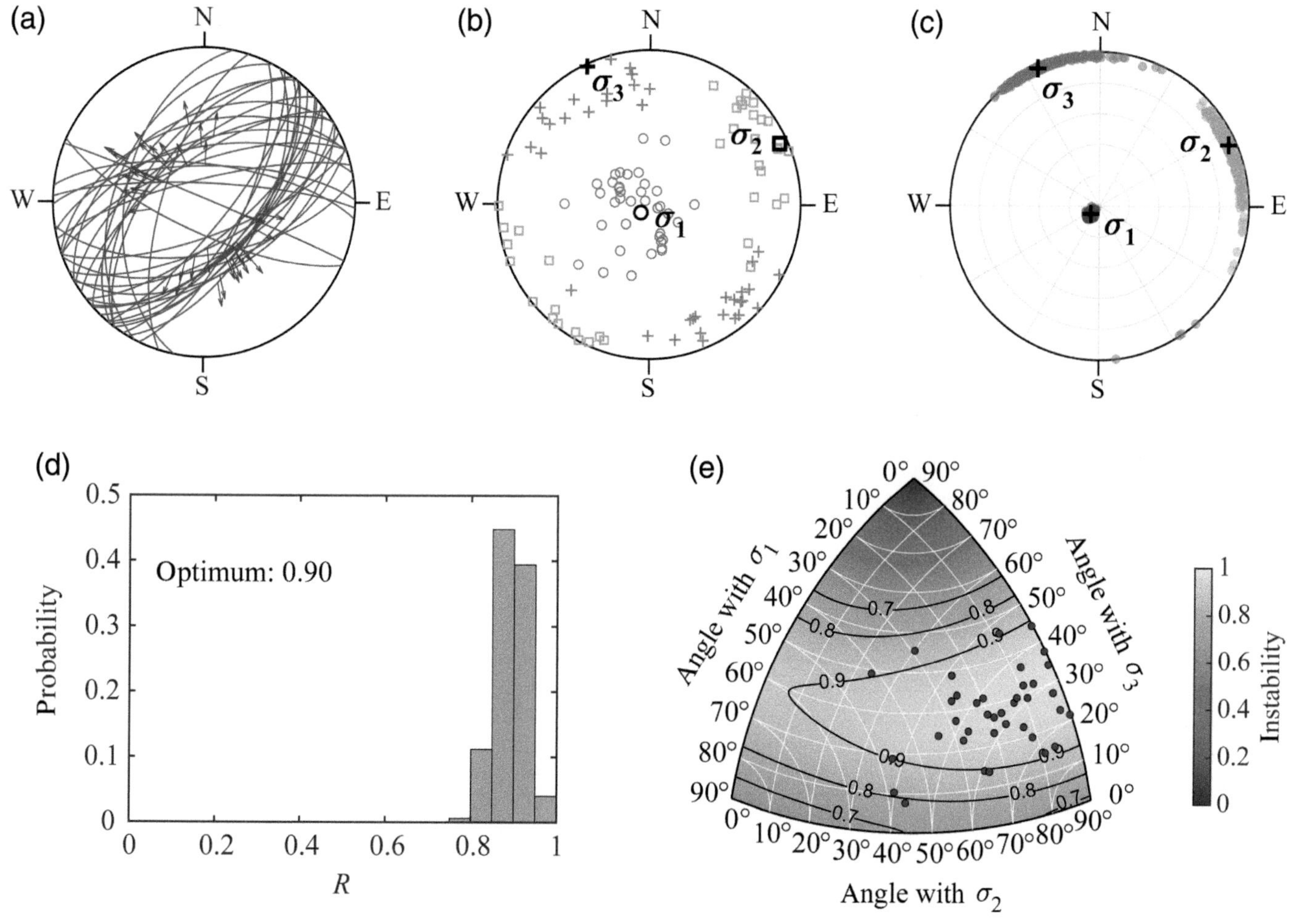

Figure 7. Stress inversion results for the TYM region. Description of the panels follows the format of Figure 6. The color version of this figure is available only in the electronic edition.

reflects the stress characteristics associated with an R value close to 1. The geometric centers of the B and T axes distributions approximately correspond to the positions of the σ_2 and σ_3 axes, respectively. Most importantly, the distribution of the P axes closely matches the orientation of the σ_1 axis, confirming that the P, B, and T axes derived from the fault-slip data in this region can reliably indicate the orientations of the principal stresses. Figure 7e shows that the instability values of most faults exceed 0.9. Comparing this result with the synthetic cases in Figure 4, in which $R = 0.9$, and the critical instability is set to 0.9 and 0.95, and noting that the distribution of the T axes does not exhibit a circular pattern, it can be inferred that the critical instability in this region falls within the range of 0.9–0.95. Owing to this high-critical instability, the faults are predominantly clustered into two groups on either side of the σ_1 axis, as illustrated in Figure 7a.

Focal mechanisms from the deep Tonga subduction zone

The Tonga subduction zone has experienced numerous earthquakes, and focal mechanism solutions for moderate-to-large events are available from institutions such as the Global Centroid Moment Tensor (Global CMT) project and the U.S. Geological Survey. Previous studies (e.g., Vavryčuk, 2004) have shown that the stress field in the southern segment of the subduction zone (19.5°–27° S) at depths of 500–700 km is generally homogeneous. Therefore, focal mechanism data from this region are particularly well-suited for validating our synthetic results. Focal mechanism data were obtained from the Global CMT catalog (Dziewonski *et al.*, 1981; Ekström *et al.*, 2012; see Data and Resources) for earthquakes occurring between 1 January 1976, and 31 December 2020. The spatial distribution of these events is shown in Figure 8a. Gray circles mark earthquakes with focal depths greater than 100 km, whereas red circles highlight events occurring at depths of 500–700 km with magnitudes of $M_w > 5.5$ in the southern segment of the subducting slab. A total of 403 such events are shown in red, and these data are used for the present analysis.

Figure 8b,d presents the stress inversion results for the southern deep segment of the subducting slab. The stress tensor was inverted from focal mechanism data using the iterative approach proposed by Vavryčuk (2014). The procedure begins by randomly selecting one of the two nodal planes from each

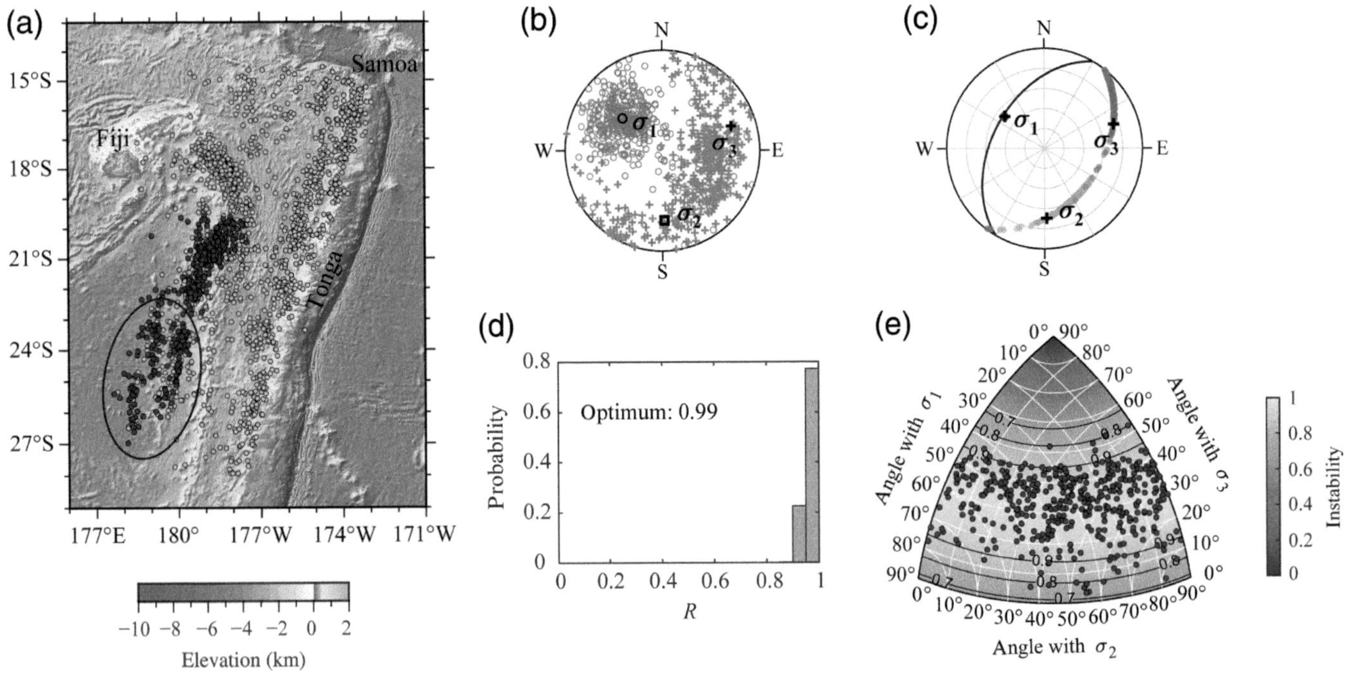

Figure 8. Stress inversion results for the southern deep region of the Tonga subduction zone. (a) Distribution of earthquake epicenters. Gray circles represent earthquakes deeper than 100 km. Red circles highlight events at depths of 500–700 km with moment magnitude (M_w) greater than 5.5, located in the southern part of the slab. The two nearly parallel segments within the ellipse exhibit substantial internal stress differences. (b) Distributions of the P (red circles) and T (blue crosses) axes of focal mechanisms together with the principal stress orientations. (c–e) Subfigure descriptions follow the format of Figure 6. In Figure 8c, the blue arc indicates the geometry of the southern segment at depths of 500–700 km. The color version of this figure is available only in the electronic edition.

focal mechanism to estimate an initial stress tensor. During each iteration, the nodal plane exhibiting higher instability for each event is identified based on the current stress tensor, and the tensor is subsequently updated using these selected planes. The uncertainty of the inverted stress tensor is assessed by adding a random perturbation of 10° to the normal and slip directions of any nodal plane of the focal mechanisms, followed by inverting the perturbed focal mechanisms. This process is repeated 500 times to evaluate the uncertainty range of the inverted stress. The results show that the uncertainty in the orientation of the σ_1 axis is very small, whereas the uncertainties in the orientations of the σ_2 and σ_3 axes are significantly larger within the plane perpendicular to the σ_1 axis (Fig. 8c). This is attributed to the stress R value being approximately 1.

In Figure 8c, the blue arc outlines the morphology of the southern segment of the subducting slab, following Vavryčuk (2004). The σ_1 axis is aligned with the slab, and the shape ratio is close to 1. This suggests that, at the greatest depths of the subduction zone, the slab is hindered by the lower mantle material. Such resistance causes the maximum compressive stress to align with the subduction direction (Vavryčuk, 2004; Bonnardot *et al.*, 2009; Hrubcová *et al.*, 2024), whereas the compressive stresses within the plane perpendicular to this axis remain nearly uniform. In terms of deviatoric stress, the region exhibits a uniaxial compressional regime, with the principal compressive stress axis parallel to the subduction direction and nearly isotropic tensile stresses within the perpendicular plane. These findings provide a coherent reconstruction of the regional geodynamic processes and reinforce the reliability of the stress inversion results.

The P axes are clustered around the σ_1 axis, whereas the T axes form a circular pattern near the plane defined by the σ_2 and σ_3 axes (Fig. 8b). According to the conclusions drawn from the synthetic experiments, the clustering of the P axes indicates the orientation of the σ_1 axis, whereas the circular distribution of the T axes suggests that the R value is close to 1. These observations are consistent with the stress inversion results. For this case, stress inversion is not strictly necessary because the distributions of the P and T axes alone suffice to infer the orientations of the principal stresses and the stress shape ratio. Figure 8e illustrates the distribution of instability for the fault planes selected from each focal mechanism, corresponding to the optimal stress tensor. Most faults exhibit instability values greater than 0.8, with a pronounced concentration above 0.9. When comparing Figure 8b,e with the synthetic results in Figure 4, in which $R = 0.9$ and I_c values are set to 0.8 and 0.9, the present observations closely resemble those for $I_c = 0.8$.

A few T axes appear within regions predominantly occupied by P axes, and conversely, some P axes occur within areas mainly dominated by T axes (Fig. 8b). Because such crossover patterns do not occur in the synthetic experiments, this sparse intermingling likely reflects local stress perturbations rather

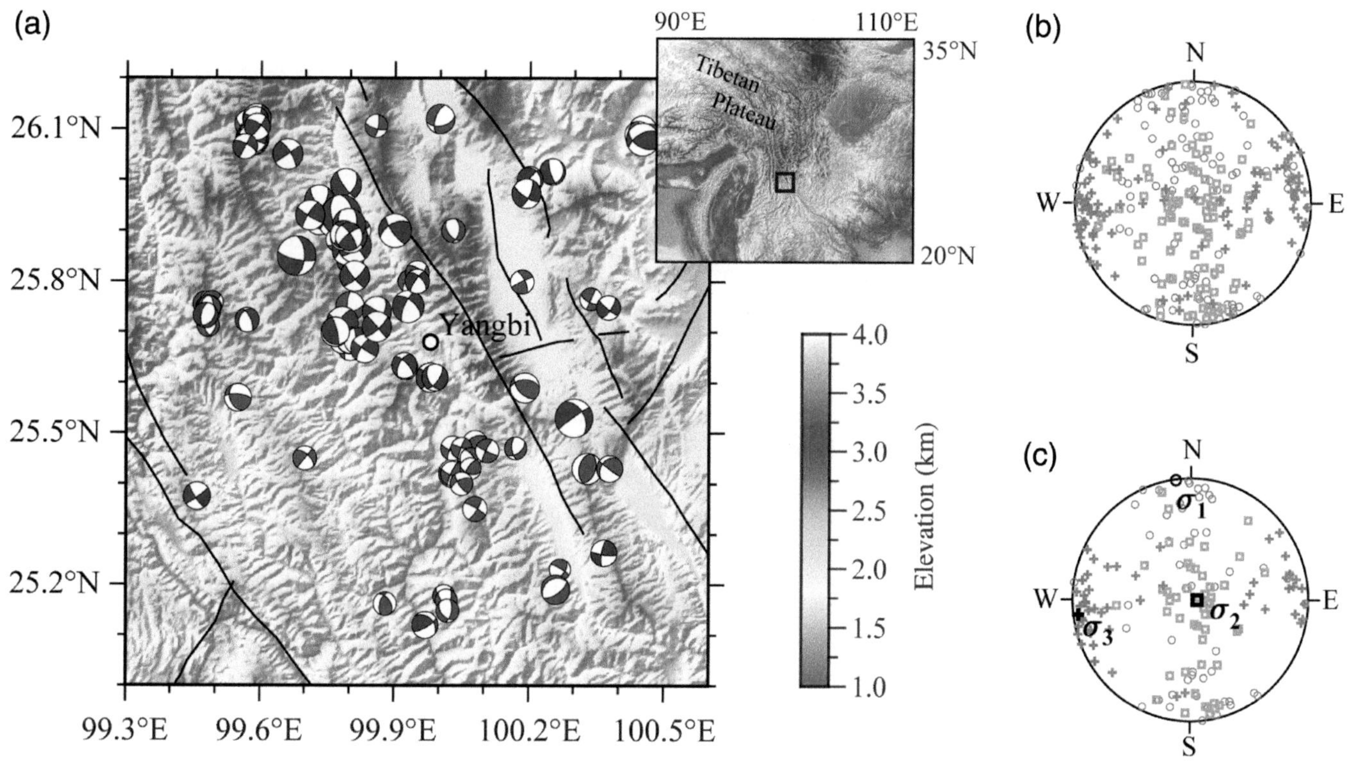

Figure 9. Focal mechanisms near the Yangbi earthquake. (a) Epicentral distribution of the events, with the inset in the top right corner showing the geographic location of the study area. Blue focal mechanism plots are from the catalog of Sheng *et al.* (2022). Red focal mechanism plots are from the catalog of Xu *et al.* (2020) and represent events with moment magnitudes ≥3.5, with focal mechanisms determined using data from over eight stations. Focal mechanism plot size is proportional to earthquake magnitude. (b) P (Red circles), B (green rectangles), and T (blue crosses) axes for all focal mechanisms. (c) P, B, and T axes for the filtered focal mechanisms, together with the stress orientations derived from these data. The color version of this figure is available only in the electronic edition.

than the regional stress field. Hrubcová *et al.* (2024) conducted a detailed stress field investigation of the same region and demonstrated that the two nearly parallel seismic segments marked by ellipses in Figure 8a host distinct stress regimes. In the eastern segment, the stress orientation is consistent with the overall down-dip compression of the subducting slab. In contrast, the western segment corresponds to a flattened and stagnated slab in the mantle transition zone, where deformation, fragmentation, and rheological heterogeneity generate a complex internal stress field. Because earthquakes within the stagnated slab represent only a small fraction of the entire catalog, using all events together still produces a stress field that primarily reflects the subduction-related background stress. The mixed P/T distributions reflect the heterogeneous stress within the stagnated slab. This case demonstrates that assessing the P and T patterns before stress inversion provides a valuable diagnostic for identifying distinct stress regimes.

Focal mechanisms near Yangbi County, Yunnan Province, China

In real geological settings, stress heterogeneity and uncertainties in focal mechanism determinations, particularly for small earthquakes, may obscure the theoretical P and T patterns shown in Figure 4. When this occurs, the stress cannot be inferred directly from these distributions. To illustrate this limitation, we analyze seismic activity near Yangbi County in Yunnan Province, China. In May 2021, a sequence of earthquakes struck this region, culminating in an M_s 6.4 mainshock. The sequence followed a typical foreshock–mainshock–aftershock evolution (Yang *et al.*, 2022) and has since attracted considerable research attention (e.g., Gong *et al.*, 2022; Zhu *et al.*, 2022; Li, Li, *et al.*, 2023).

We investigate the stress state in the vicinity of the Yangbi epicenter using available focal mechanism data. The dataset is compiled from two regional focal mechanism catalogs for Yunnan, published by Xu *et al.* (2020) and Sheng *et al.* (2022). We selected events located within a 1° × 1° area centered on the Yangbi mainshock (99.95° E, 25.62° N) and ensured that no duplicate events were retained. For earthquakes appearing in both catalogs, the focal mechanisms are generally consistent, therefore, we adopted the solutions from Sheng *et al.* (2022). In total, 99 events were collected, spanning the period from September 1972 to September 2017 and covering moment magnitudes from M_w 3.0 to 5.8. The spatial distribution of these events is shown in Figure 9a.

After collecting the focal mechanism data near the Yangbi earthquake, we attempt to infer the orientations of the principal stresses by examining the distribution patterns of the P, B, and T axes. However, when plotting all P, B, and T axes together (Fig. 9b), the three axes appear irregularly distributed across the projected equatorial circle. This irregular pattern, which contrasts with the distributions observed in the synthetic experiments, prevents the identification of the principal stress directions. According to our findings, the observed irregular distribution of P and T axes reflects either stress heterogeneity or inaccuracies in certain focal mechanisms. We infer that most earthquakes were governed by the regional background stress, whereas the remaining events likely represent noise unrelated to this stress system. Such noise can obscure the true P and T patterns associated with tectonic events, making it essential to identify and remove these events.

Noise can arise from stress heterogeneity or inaccuracies in focal mechanism determinations, and appropriate criteria can be applied to filter such events. Smaller earthquakes, due to their limited fault dimensions, are more strongly influenced by local stress variations. Accurately resolving their focal mechanisms also requires a more detailed velocity model than that typically used for larger events, as using a coarse model can introduce substantial errors. In addition, the Xu *et al.* (2020) catalog indicates the number of stations involved in each inversion, and events constrained by too few stations may contain significant inaccuracies. Considering these factors, we excluded events with $M_w < 3.5$ and those from the Xu *et al.* (2020) catalog derived from fewer than eight stations, while ensuring that the remaining dataset was sufficiently large to represent the P and T distributions. The resulting distribution for the remaining 51 events is shown in Figure 9c. With potential noise events removed, the P and T axes become clearly distinguishable, better reflecting the underlying tectonic stress.

The T axes form an east–west cluster with nearly horizontal inclinations, whereas the P and B axes display circular distributions around a north–south-oriented plane with a dip close to 90°. Within the range of $R \leq 0.5$ in Figure 4, the synthetic distributions of the P and T axes generated for different critical instability values are broadly consistent with those observed here. These characteristics indicate that the σ_3 axis is oriented approximately east–west with a nearly horizontal inclination. However, the orientations of σ_1 and σ_2, as well as the associated shape ratio, cannot be resolved solely from the distributions of the P and T axes. To further constrain the stress field, we performed a stress inversion using the filtered focal mechanisms (Fig. 10) and plotted the resulting stress orientations together with the P, B, and T axes in Figure 9c. The inferred orientation of the σ_3 axis is fully consistent with the estimate derived from the T axes distribution.

Comparison between Figure 9b and c reveals that, although we successfully eliminated most noise events that could interfere with our direct estimation of stress information, some tectonic events that conform to the stress model were inadvertently excluded. Specifically, these excluded events feature T axes close to the σ_3 axis, with the P and B axes aligned near the plane formed by the σ_1 and σ_2 axes. It is crucial to critically assess whether these excluded events should be classified as noise within the context of the background stress. This validation is carried out by comparing the stress inversion results obtained from the filtered and unfiltered datasets, as shown in Figures 10 and 11, respectively.

A comparison of the two figures indicates that the stress inversion results obtained before and after data filtering are highly consistent. This suggests that the dataset is dominated by tectonic events, with only a few noise events insufficient to obscure the stress signals associated with these tectonic events. The consistency of the stress results before and after filtering highlights the value of comparing fault instability and slip misfit distributions across the datasets. After filtering, the proportion of faults with instability values below 0.8 decreased, as expected, because stable faults should not be activated unless associated with noise events. Simultaneously, the fraction of data exhibiting smaller slip misfits increased, whereas that of larger misfits decreased. These improvements in both fault instability and slip directions provide strong evidence that most of the excluded events were indeed noise.

This case also indicates that examining the overlap of the P and T axes is a valuable approach for assessing stress homogeneity and data quality before stress inversion, consistent with previous findings (Hrubcová and Vavryčuk, 2023; Hrubcová *et al.*, 2025).

DISCUSSION

In studies of crustal tectonic stress, it is often of interest to determine whether the orientations of the principal stress axes can be inferred directly from the spatial clustering of the P, B, and T axes derived from focal mechanisms (McKenzie, 1969; Célérier, 2010). Here, we evaluate the validity and limitations of this approach through a series of systematic synthetic experiments and case analyses. The four case studies were deliberately selected for their representativeness and to encompass the different distribution patterns identified in the synthetic experiments. In terms of the clustering characteristics of the P, B, and T axes, the AVB case represents a pattern in which all three axes are clustered around their respective principal stress directions. The TYM case shows one relatively clustered axis, whereas the other two are moderately dispersed. The Tonga case features clustered P axes, with the other two forming circular distributions. In addition, the Yangbi case exhibits an apparent deviation from the theoretical distributions. However, after excluding potentially noisy events, the observed pattern approaches the theoretical configuration characterized by clustering of the T axes and a circular distribution of the P and B axes.

Both the synthetic experiments and the case studies show that, under a homogeneous stress field, focal mechanisms can exhibit various patterns: both P and T axes clustered, one axis clustered whereas the other is dispersed, or both axes nonclustered. This indicates that a dispersed distribution of the

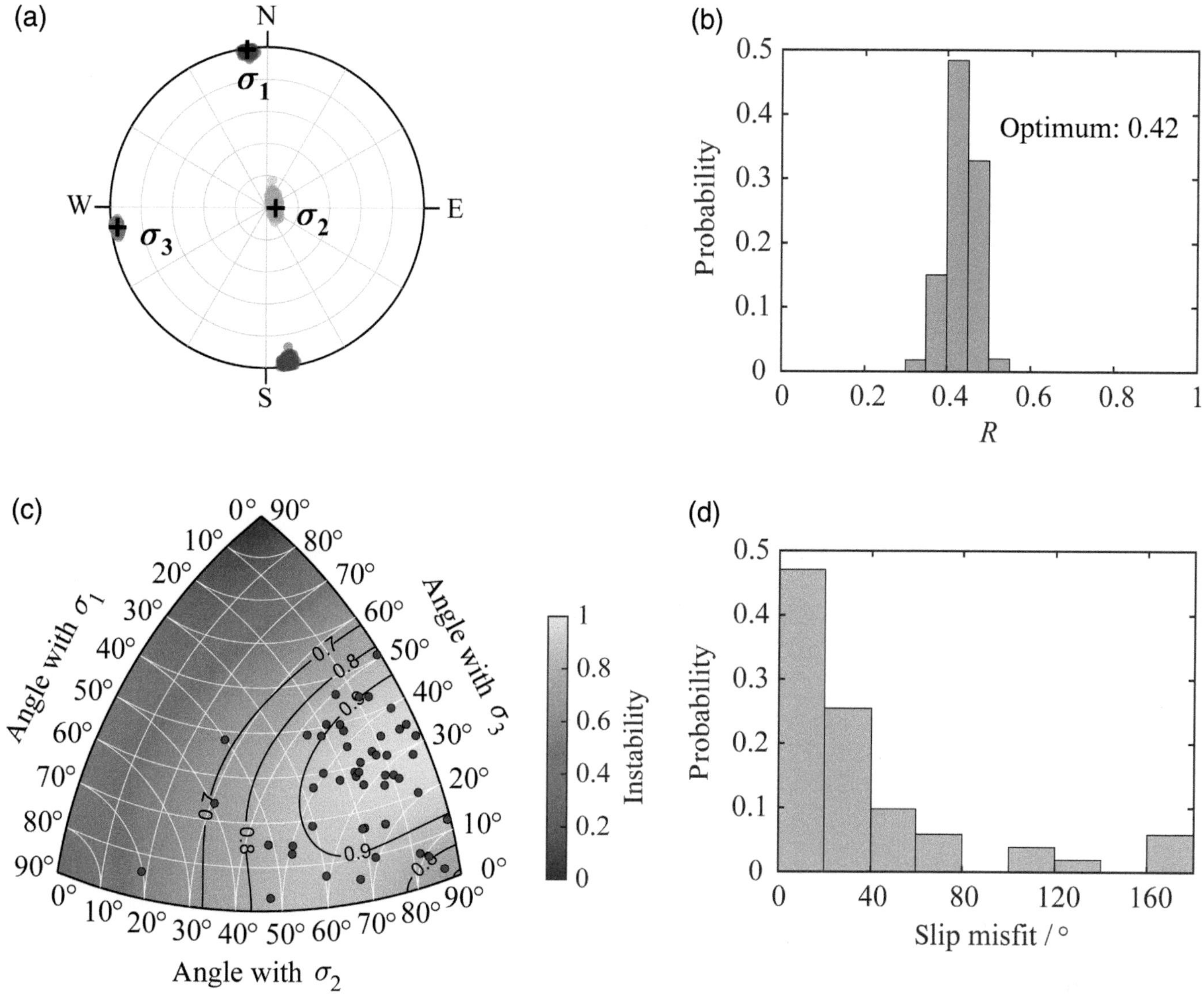

Figure 10. Stress inversion results for the filtered focal mechanisms. (a) Principal stress orientations and their associated uncertainties. (b) Stress shape ratio and its uncertainty. (c) Distribution of fault instability. (d) Statistics of the misfit between observed and modeled fault slip. The color version of this figure is available only in the electronic edition.

P or T axes can still follow a homogeneous stress model. Therefore, in practical applications, dispersion of either P or T axes should not be taken as evidence of stress heterogeneity, whereas an irregular intermingling of the two axes generally indicates a heterogeneous stress field or low data quality.

Because the dispersion of P/T axes stems from the intrinsic geometric variability of faults (Fig. 3), a wide spatial distribution of fault orientations likewise does not indicate stress heterogeneity or poor data quality. The two fault-slip datasets from the Crete region illustrate this point: both AVB and TYM reflect well-constrained regional stress states, yet TYM exhibits a broader range of fault orientations due to its higher stress shape ratio and slightly lower critical instability coefficient, rather than heterogeneous stress or data issues. The low misfit between observed and predicted slip directions (fig. 6 of Li, Wan, *et al.*, 2023) further supports this conclusion.

Whether estimating stress from the distribution of P and T axes or conducting conventional stress inversion, both approaches require a sufficient quantity and diversity of observations because limited sampling cannot effectively constrain the stress tensor (Hardebeck and Hauksson, 2001; Martínez-Garzón *et al.*, 2016). In practice, however, the diversity of available observations is inherently governed by the unknown stress state and fault failure conditions, making it difficult to assess whether the collected dataset adequately reflects the true variability (e.g., the two sets of fault-slip data from the Crete region). Under such circumstances, the discrepancy between the inverted and actual stress fields remains uncertain. Nevertheless, the stress information inferred from the P and T distributions shows good agreement with that derived from conventional inversion methods.

Under a prescribed stress state, two conjugate fault sets are symmetrically oriented about the axis, have identical failure potential, and slip may occur on either set if present in the

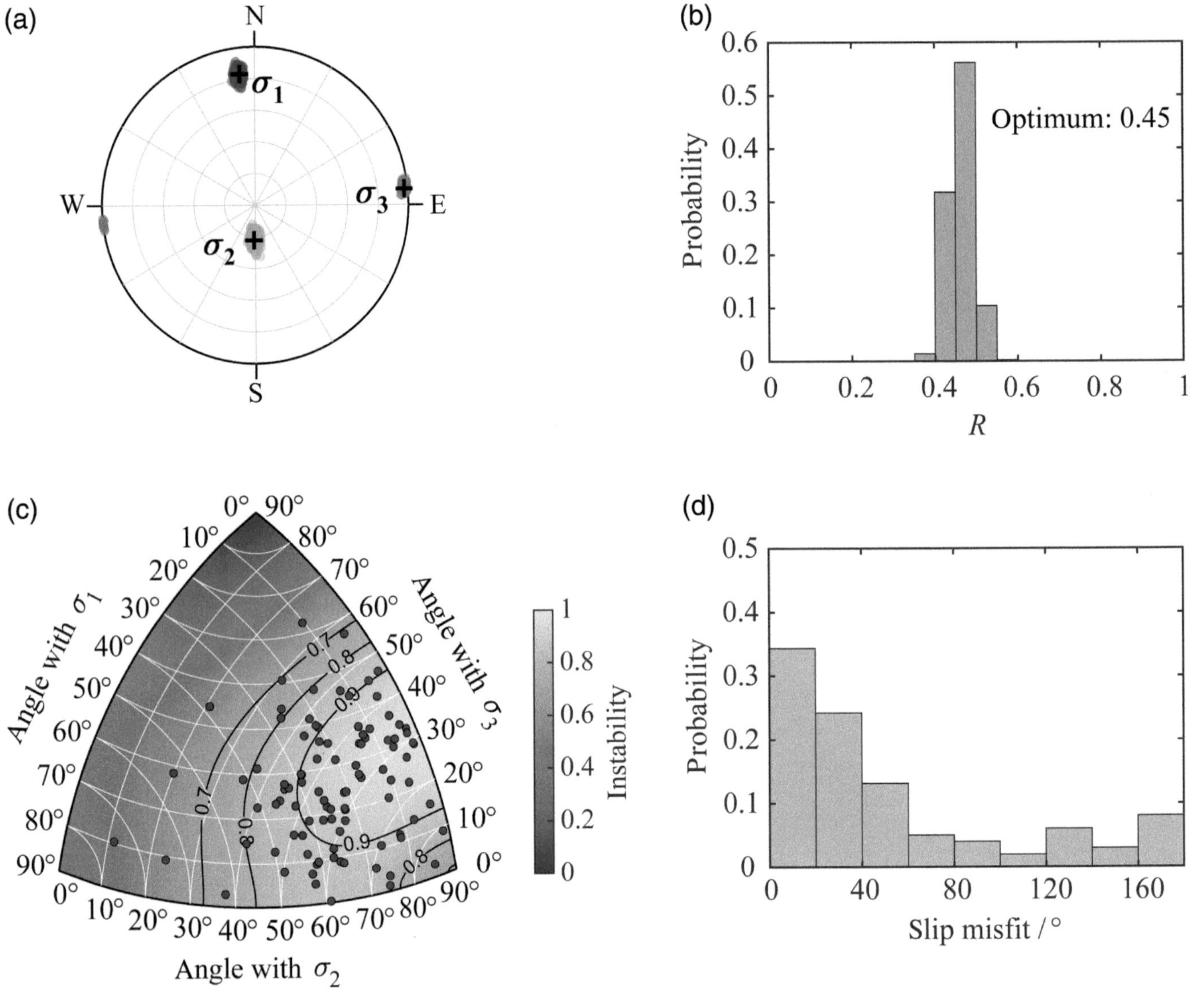

Figure 11. Stress inversion results for all focal mechanisms. Description of the panels follows the format of Figure 10. The color version of this figure is available only in the electronic edition.

subsurface. In our synthetic experiments, both fault sets are modeled simultaneously, resulting in two groups of P and T axes symmetrically distributed with respect to the principal stress axes. However, based on the P/T distributions alone, the observed clustering does not uniquely indicate whether two conjugate fault sets are active or only a single one. When both fault sets are active, the principal stress orientations can be inferred without bias. If only one fault set is active, the P and T axes are confined to one side of the principal stress axes, and the geometric center of their distribution shows a slight offset from the true stress orientations. Nevertheless, because the clustering remains coherent, the estimated principal stress orientations remain close to the true values (Figs. 2c and 4). In cases for which both fault sets are present but slip is dominated by one of them, the deviation of the cluster center from the principal stress axes is even smaller.

Current stress inversion practices typically derive the regional stress field directly from fault slip or focal mechanism data, without prior assessment of stress homogeneity or data quality. Consequently, the reliability and stability of the inversion results are often difficult to evaluate in advance. This study clarifies the relationship between the distributions of the P and T axes and both stress orientation and shape ratio, providing a valuable complement to conventional inversion methods. We recommend that, before performing stress inversion, researchers first evaluate whether the observed P and T distributions conform to theoretical patterns (Fig. 4). A significant number of marked deviations may indicate stress heterogeneity or insufficient data quality within the study region. In such cases, adjusting the spatial extent of the study area or excluding potential noise events can help mitigate these effects and enhance the reliability of the subsequent stress inversion results.

CONCLUSION

We conducted systematic synthetic experiments to simulate fault-slip behavior, represented by focal mechanisms, under a range of stress states and failure criteria within the crust. The study aimed to assess whether the spatial distributions of the P and T axes can directly reveal information about the tectonic stress without performing a formal stress inversion. The results demonstrate that these distributions inherently encode both the orientation and shape ratio of the stress tensor, a conclusion further supported by real-world observations. The main findings of this study are summarized as follows.

1. The distribution patterns of the P and T axes exhibit systematic variations with changes in the stress shape ratio and failure criterion. For experiments with the same critical instability, as the stress shape ratio increases from 0 to 1, the P axes gradually transition from forming a circular distribution near the plane perpendicular to the σ_3 axis to clustering around the σ_1 axis. Conversely, the T axes evolve from clustering around the σ_3 axis to forming a circular distribution near the plane perpendicular to the σ_1 axis. Under conditions of a constant shape ratio, decreasing the critical instability leads to broader distributions of the P and T axes, owing to the increasing diversity of faults that satisfy the failure criterion.
2. The clustered distribution of either the P or T axes clearly indicates the orientation of the corresponding principal stress axis. The clustering of these two axes is mutually independent, and whichever axis exhibits clustering, the geometric center of the cluster reliably identifies the direction of its associated principal stress axis.
3. The simulated P and T axes can display dispersed or circular distributions even under a homogeneous stress. This indicates that, in real datasets, the observation of a nonclustered distribution of P or T axes does not necessarily reflect a heterogeneous stress field.
4. A circular distribution of the T axes develops only under high stress shape ratios, whereas a circular distribution of the P axes can arise across a much broader range of ratios. This implies that a circular T pattern is diagnostic of a relatively high shape ratio, whereas a circular P pattern provides no meaningful constraint on it. Accordingly, only the T axes offer direct insight into the shape ratio encoded in the combined P and T distributions.
5. Under a homogeneous stress field, the P and T axes overlap only when the critical instability coefficient reaches its minimum, and their combined distribution follows a systematic pattern. In practical applications, an irregular intermingling of P and T axes indicates either a heterogeneous stress field or significant noise within the data. Hence, the distribution characteristics of the P and T axes can be used to qualitatively assess stress homogeneity and data quality before performing stress inversion.

DATA AND RESOURCES

No new data were generated or analyzed for this study, as existing data were used instead. Fault-slip data for the Agia Varvara (AVB) and Tympaki (TYM) regions are documented in the published article by Angelier (1990). Focal mechanism data for the Tonga subduction zone are available from the Global Centroid Moment Tensor (Global CMT) Project database (www.globalcmt.org; last accessed July 2025). Focal mechanisms for the area near Yangbi County, China, are obtained from the published articles of Xu *et al.* (2020) and Sheng *et al.* (2022). These data can be obtained by contacting the corresponding authors of the respective publications.

DECLARATION OF COMPETING INTERESTS

The authors acknowledge that there are no conflicts of interest recorded.

ACKNOWLEDGMENTS

The authors thank Associate Editor Václav Vavryčuk and the two anonymous reviewers for their careful evaluation and constructive comments, which have substantially improved the clarity and quality of this article. The authors also gratefully acknowledge financial support from the National Natural Science Foundation of China (Grant Number 42174074).

REFERENCES

Angelier, J. (1984). Tectonic analysis of fault slip data sets, *J. Geophys. Res.* **89,** no. B7, 5835–5848, doi: 10.1029/JB089iB07p05835.

Angelier, J. (1990). Inversion of field data in fault tectonics to obtain the regional stress-III. A new rapid direct inversion method by analytical means, *Geophys. J. Int.* **103,** no. 2, 363–376, doi: 10.1111/j.1365-246X.1990.tb01777.x.

Beaucé, E., R. D. Van Der Hilst, and M. Campillo (2022). An iterative linear method with variable shear stress magnitudes for estimating the stress tensor from earthquake focal mechanism data: Method and examples, *Geophys. J. Int.* **112,** no. 3, 1224–1239, doi: 10.1785/0120210319.

Beeler, N. M., R. W. Simpson, S. H. Hickman, and D. A. Lockner (2000). Pore fluid pressure, apparent friction, and Coulomb failure, *J. Geophys. Res.: Solid Earth* **105,** no. B11, 25,533–25,542, doi: 10.1029/2000JB900119.

Bonnardot, M.-A., M. Régnier, C. Christova, E. Ruellan, and E. Tric (2009). Seismological evidence for a slab detachment in the Tonga subduction zone, *Tectonophysics* **464,** nos. 1/4, 84–99, doi: 10.1016/j.tecto.2008.10.011.

Bott, M. H. P. (1959). The mechanics of oblique slip faulting, *Geol. Mag.* **96,** no. 2, 109–117, doi: 10.1017/S0016756800059987.

Byerlee, J. (1978). Friction of rocks, *Pure Appl. Geophys.* **116,** 615–626, doi: 10.1007/BF00876528.

Célérier, B. (2010). Remarks on the relationship between the tectonic regime, the rake of the slip vectors, the dip of the nodal planes, and the plunges of the P, B, and T axes of earthquake focal mechanisms, *Tectonophysics* **482,** nos. 1/4, 42–49, doi: 10.1016/j.tecto.2009.03.006.

Delvaux, D., and A. Barth (2010). African stress pattern from formal inversion of focal mechanism data, *Tectonophysics* **482,** 105–128, doi: 10.1016/j.tecto.2009.05.009.

Dziewonski, A. M., T. A. Chou, and J. H. Woodhouse (1981). Determination of earthquake source parameters from waveform data for studies of global and regional seismicity, *J. Geophys. Res.* **86,** no. B4, 2825–2852, doi: 10.1029/JB086iB04p02825.

Ekström, G., M. Nettles, and A. M. Dziewoński (2012). The global CMT project 2004–2010: Centroid-moment tensors for 13,017 earthquakes, *Phys. Earth Planet. In.* **200–201,** 1–9, doi: 10.1016/j.pepi.2012.04.002.

Gephart, J. W., and D. W. Forsyth (1984). An improved method for determining the regional stress tensor using earthquake focal mechanism data: Application to the San Fernando Earthquake Sequence, *J. Geophys. Res.* **89,** no. B11, 9305, doi: 10.1029/JB089iB11p09305.

Gong, W., L. Ye, Y. Qiu, T. Lay, and H. Kanamori (2022). Rupture directivity of the 2021 M_W6.0 Yangbi, Yunnan earthquake, *J. Geophys. Res.: Solid Earth* **127,** e2022JB024321, doi: 10.1029/2022JB024321.

Hardebeck, J. L., and E. Hauksson (2001). Crustal stress field in southern California and its implications for fault mechanics, *J. Geophys. Res.* **106,** no. B10, 21,859–21,882, doi: 10.1029/2001JB000292.

Hardebeck, J. L., and A. J. Michael (2006). Damped regional-scale stress inversions: Methodology and examples for southern California and the Coalinga aftershock sequence, *J. Geophys. Res.: Solid Earth* **111,** no. B3, doi: 10.1029/2005JB004144.

Hrubcová, P., and V. Vavryčuk (2023). Tectonic stress changes related to plate spreading prior to the 2021 Fagradalsfjall eruption in SW Iceland, *Tectonophysics* **851,** 229761, doi: 10.1016/j.tecto.2023.229761.

Hrubcová, P., G. Rastjoo, and V. Vavryčuk (2024). Stress variations in southern Tonga slab derived from deep-focus earthquakes, *J. Geophys. Res.: Solid Earth* **129,** e2023JB028039, doi: 10.1029/2023JB028039.

Hrubcová, P., V. Vavryčuk, T. Fischer, and J. Doubravová (2025). Stress variations and non-shear earthquakes before the 2021 Iceland eruption trace magmatic fluid flow, *Commun. Earth Environ.* **6,** 575, doi: 10.1038/s43247-025-02533-5.

Jia, S. Q., D. W. Eaton, and R. C. Wong (2018). Stress inversion of shear-tensile focal mechanisms with application to hydraulic fracture monitoring, *Geophys. J. Int.* **215,** no. 1, 546–563, doi: 10.1093/gji/ggy290.

Lei, X., J. Su, and Z. Wang (2020). Growing seismicity in the Sichuan Basin and its association with industrial activities, *Sci. China Earth Sci.* **63,** no. 11, 1633–1660, doi: 10.1007/s11430-020-9646-x.

Li, Z., J. Li, H. Yao, and B. Wang (2023). Stress analysis for the seismogenic mechanism of the Yangbi M_S 6.4 earthquake sequence in May 2021, *Chin. J. Geophys.* **66,** no. 4, 1448–1459, doi: 10.6038/cjg2022Q0035.

Li, Z., Y. Wan, X. Hu, F. Yang, and R. Yan (2020). A genetic algorithm for stress tensor inversion and its application to the northeast margin of the Tibetan Plateau, *Chin. J. Geophys.* **63,** no. 2, 562–572, doi: 10.6038/cjg2020N0047.

Li, Z., Y. Wan, R. Liu, X. Guo, and S. Sheng (2023). Fault stability analysis and its application in stress inversion quality assessment, *Environ. Earth Sci.* **82,** no. 2, 609, doi: 10.1007/s12665-023-11304-4.

Martínez-Garzón, P., Y. Ben-Zion, N. Abolfathian, G. Kwiatek, and M. Bohnhoff (2016). A refined methodology for stress inversions of earthquake focal mechanisms, *J. Geophys. Res.: Solid Earth* **121,** no. 12, 8666–8687, doi: 10.1002/2016JB013493.

McKenzie, D. P. (1969). The relation between fault plane solutions for earthquakes and the directions of the principal stresses, *Bull. Seismol. Soc. Am.* **59,** no. 2, 591–601, doi: 10.1785/BSSA0590020591.

Michael, A. J. (1984). Determination of stress from slip data: Faults and folds, *J. Geophys. Res.* **89,** no. B13, 11,517–11,526, doi: 10.1029/JB089iB13p11517.

Michael, A. J. (1987). Use of focal mechanisms to determine stress: A control study, *J. Geophys. Res.* **92,** no. B1, 357–368, doi:10.1029/JB092iB01p00357.

Nouri, A., B. Rahimi, V. Vavryčuk, and F. Ghaemi (2023). Spatially varying crustal stress along the Zagros seismic belt inferred from earthquake focal mechanisms, *Tectonophysics* **846,** 229653, doi: 10.1016/j.tecto.2022.229653.

Sheng, S., and L. Meng (2020). Stress field variation during the 2019 Ridgecrest earthquake sequence, *Geophys. Res. Lett.* **47,** no. 10, e2020GL087722, doi: 10.1029/2020GL087722.

Sheng, S., X. Hu, X. Wang, Y. Wan, H. Li, Z. Li, X. Tian, X. Wang, and S. Zhang (2022). Study on the crustal stress field of Yunnan and its adjacent areas, *Chin. J. Geophys.* **65,** no. 9, 3252–3267, doi: 10.6038/cjg2022P0536.

Stein, S., and M. Wysession (2003). *An Introduction to Seismology, Earthquakes, and Earth Structure*, Blackwell Publishing, Malden, Massachusetts, 228 pp.

Vavryčuk, V. (2004). Inversion for anisotropy from non-double-couple components of moment tensors, *J. Geophys. Res.* **109,** no. B2, doi: 10.1029/2003JB002926.

Vavryčuk, V. (2011). Principal earthquakes: Theory and observations from the 2008 West Bohemia swarm, *Earth Planet. Sci. Lett.* **305,** nos. 3/4, 290–296, doi: 10.1016/j.epsl.2011.03.002.

Vavryčuk, V. (2014). Iterative joint inversion for stress and fault orientations from focal mechanisms, *Geophys. J. Int.* **199,** no. 1, 69–77, doi: 10.1093/gji/ggu224.

Vavryčuk, V., F. Bouchaala, and T. Fischer (2013). High-resolution fault image from accurate locations and focal mechanisms of the 2008 swarm earthquakes in West Bohemia, Czech Republic, *Tectonophysics* **590,** 189–195, doi: 10.1016/j.tecto.2013.01.025.

Wallace, R. E. (1951). Geometry of shearing stress and relation to faulting, *J. Geol.* **59,** no. 2, 118–130, doi: 10.1086/625831.

Wan, Y., S. Sheng, J. Huang, X. Li, and X. Chen (2016). The grid search algorithm of tectonic stress tensor based on focal mechanism data and its application in the boundary zone of China, Vietnam and Laos, *J. Earth Sci.* **27,** no. 5, 777–785, doi: 10.1007/s12583-015-0649-1.

Xu, Y., K. D. Koper, R. Burlacu, R. B. Herrmann, and D. N. Li (2020). A new uniform moment tensor catalog for Yunnan, China, from January 2000 through December 2014, *Seismol. Res. Lett.* **91,** no. 2A, 891–900, doi: 10.1785/0220190242.

Yang, T., B. Li, L. Fang, Y. Su, Y. Zhong, J. Yang, M. Qin, and Y. Xu (2022). Relocation of the foreshocks and aftershocks of the 2021 M_S 6.4 Yangbi earthquake sequence, Yunnan, China, *J. Earth Sci.* **33,** 892–900, doi: 10.1007/s12583-021-1527-7.

Zhu, G., H. Yang, Y. J. Tan, M. Jin, X. Li, and W. Yang (2022). The cascading foreshock sequence of the M_S 6.4 Yangbi earthquake in Yunnan, China, *Earth Planet. Sci. Lett.* **591,** 117594, doi: 10.1016/j.epsl.2022.117594.

Manuscript received 3 December 2025
Published online 23 March 2026

Rupture into Slow-Slip Fault Regime During the 2018 M_w 6.9 Island of Hawai'i Earthquake is Followed by Modest Postseismic Slip

Ingrid A. Johanson*[1], Emily K. Montgomery-Brown[2], and Michael P. Poland[2]

ABSTRACT

On 4 May 2018, a M_w 6.9 earthquake occurred on the south flank of Kīlauea, in the midst of an historic event that included a voluminous eruption from Kīlauea's lower East Rift zone and caldera collapse at its summit. The earthquake was a consequence of both short- and long-term stress buildup due to magmatic activity associated with the eruption and steady flank motion, respectively, and it revealed features of Kīlauea's décollement fault that can inform understanding of future earthquake activity. We used geodetic data to determine the distributions of slip during the coseismic and postseismic periods and compared these with areas of known fault slip during past earthquakes and slow-slip events (SSEs). The 2018 earthquake ruptured into an area of the décollement fault that was active during quasi-regular SSEs that occurred in the two decades prior to 2018 but that have not been observed since. The coseismic slip model indicates that the amount of motion on the décollement fault was several times greater than what typically occurred during SSEs, suggesting that it may take decades for the fault to rebuild stress to the point at which SSEs will occur again. Postseismic afterslip also occurred in an area of the fault known to experience slow slip; however, unlike at other creeping faults, postseismic afterslip was rapid, being largely over within 2–3 days. The rapid nature and small magnitude of the postseismic afterslip may be due to the lack of a viscoelastic relaxation component, which is possibly a result of the shallow dip of the décollement fault not transferring stress efficiently into the lower crust.

KEY POINTS

- The 2018 earthquake included rupture into an established area of slow slip on Kīlauea's décollement fault.
- Slow-slip events have ceased on this portion of the fault, and it is estimated that it will take nearly six decades to regain the stress released in the earthquake.
- Postseismic afterslip was modest, and no evidence of viscoelastic relaxation was observed.

Supplemental Material

INTRODUCTION

Interactions between magmatic and tectonic processes are perhaps nowhere better demonstrated than on large basaltic volcanoes, in which strong feedback between magmatic intrusions and slip on faults related to unstable flanks is relatively common (e.g., Froger *et al.*, 2015; Poland *et al.*, 2017; Mattia *et al.*, 2020). This is especially true at Kīlauea, Hawai'i, where magmatic activity in the volcano's East Rift zone can drive, and be driven by, seaward motion of the volcano's south flank (e.g., Cayol *et al.*, 2000; Brooks *et al.*, 2008; Montgomery-Brown *et al.*, 2015; Kundu *et al.*, 2020). Flank motion at Kīlauea occurs due to slip along a shallowly dipping (~5°) décollement fault via a combination of steady sliding, episodic slow-slip events (SSEs), and occasional strong earthquakes (Denlinger and Morgan, 2014). The occurrence of different types of slip behavior on the décollement and its relation to magmatic intrusions and hazardous earthquakes is ambiguous; however, seismic and eruptive activity in 2018 provides an opportunity for a detailed exploration of these questions.

The 4 May 2018, M_w 6.9 earthquake on the south flank of Kīlauea occurred at 12:32 p.m. Hawaii Standard Time (HST), just one day after the opening of the first fissure of the 2018 lower East Rift zone eruption. The eruption was initiated by an intrusion that began in the middle East Rift Zone on 30 April

1. U.S. Geological Survey, Hawaiian Volcano Observatory, Hilo, Hawai'i, U.S.A., https://orcid.org/0000-0002-6049-2225 (IAJ); 2. U.S. Geological Survey, Cascades Volcano Observatory, Vancouver, Washington, U.S.A., https://orcid.org/0000-0001-6787-2055 (EKM-B); https://orcid.org/0000-0001-5240-6123 (MPP)

*Corresponding author: ijohanson@usgs.gov

Cite this article as Johanson, I. A., E. K. Montgomery-Brown, and M. P. Poland (2026). Rupture into Slow-Slip Fault Regime During the 2018 M_w 6.9 Island of Hawai'i Earthquake is Followed by Modest Postseismic Slip, *Bull. Seismol. Soc. Am.* **116**, 1023–1035, doi: 10.1785/0120240222 and propagated 20 km downrift in just 24 hours. Magma reached the surface at about 05:00 p.m. HST on 3 May, with the first of 24 eruptive fissures forming in and around the Leilani Estates subdivision (Neal *et al.*, 2019; Patrick *et al.*, 2020; Anderson *et al.*, 2024).

The 2018 earthquake likely occurred as a result of the East Rift Zone opening in response to dike intrusion (Chen *et al.*, 2019; Kundu *et al.*, 2020). Strong south flank earthquakes often follow East Rift Zone intrusions (e.g., Poland *et al.*, 2008) due to stress transfer to the south flank (Cayol *et al.*, 2000; Brooks *et al.*, 2008). The earthquake occurred in the midst of increased rates of earthquakes on Kīlauea's south flank, although the majority of these events were spread throughout the flank crust rather than either on the décollement fault or in the plane of the dike intrusion (Neal *et al.*, 2019). The 2018 earthquake was also preceded by two foreshocks (M_L 5.7 and 4.4) in the hours before the mainshock, as well as a M_L 5.1 event the day before. The M_w 6.9 earthquake was felt broadly across the island; fortunately, no injuries or major damage were reported. In the first hour following the earthquake, there was a distinct migration of aftershocks to the southwest, after which diffuse aftershocks continued for months.

The timing of the earthquake roughly coincided with an increase in the rate of magma withdrawal from the summit, suggesting an opening of the conduit that connected the summit and East Rift zone (Anderson *et al.*, 2019). That increased magma flux through the East Rift zone would follow the earthquake is not surprising, given the strong evidence of feedback between décollement slip and rift zone opening (Cayol *et al.*, 2000; Brooks *et al.*, 2008; Montgomery-Brown *et al.*, 2010; Kundu *et al.*, 2020). In the three months following the earthquake, over 1 km^3 of lava erupted from lower East Rift Zone vents, destroying hundreds of structures in one of the most impactful eruptions on the Island of Hawai'i during the past 200 yr (Neal *et al.*, 2019; Dietterich *et al.*, 2021).

The M_w 6.9 south flank earthquake is notable for its relation to both past flank earthquakes and quasi-periodic SSEs, as well as its lack of a long-lasting postseismic transient. The epicenter of the 2018 earthquake was similar to that of the 1975 M_w 7.7 Kalapana earthquake, as well as several earlier south flank earthquakes (Nettles and Ekström, 2004; Klein *et al.*, 2001; Liu *et al.*, 2018). These earthquakes are attributed to a shallowly dipping décollement fault that underlies Kīlauea's south flank at a depth of ~6 km at the shoreline (Morgan *et al.*, 2003). The décollement is interpreted to be the interface between the volcanic pile and the underlying oceanic crust. As such, it dips slightly (5°-10°) inland as the weight of the island bends the crust downward (Zucca and Hill, 1980; Denlinger and Morgan, 2014).

In addition to producing large earthquakes, the décollement fault also creeps steadily (Owen *et al.*, 2000) and moves during regular SSEs (Cervelli *et al.*, 2002; Brooks *et al.*, 2006; Montgomery-Brown *et al.*, 2015). The 2018 earthquake ruptured south from its epicenter (Kehoe *et al.*, 2019) through a locked portion of the fault and into the region that produces SSEs (Lin *et al.*, 2020). Since the 2018 earthquake, no SSEs have occurred on the south flank; the last such event was in October 2015.

The relative magnitude of the postseismic transient was modest; however, as this study shows, the time over which postseismic motion occurred was remarkably brief—only 2–3 days. Although the 2018 earthquake occurred adjacent to parts of the fault that creep interseismically and within a region that produces SSEs, there was little shallow afterslip.

Kīlauea hosts a dense network of geodetic instrumentation, including over 70 continuous Global Navigation Satellite System (GNSS) stations and numerous campaign GNSS sites that provided comprehensive spatial and temporal coverage of surface deformation before, during, and after the 2018 M_w 6.9 South Flank earthquake. We modeled these data to determine the co- and postseismic slip distributions on the décollement and examined the slip pattern in the context of past slip behavior.

COSEISMIC DATA REDUCTION AND MODELING

At the beginning of the 2018 eruption, 67 continuous GNSS stations were operating on the Island of Hawai'i, to which we added data from four GNSS stations operating on other Hawaiian islands (Fig. 1). Forty-five of these stations are owned and operated by the U.S. Geological Survey (USGS) Hawaiian Volcano Observatory (HVO), and an additional 24 are operated by the Pacific Geodetic Facility at the University of Hawai'i at Mānoa (PGF). The Jet Propulsion Lab (JPL) operates two continuous GNSS stations: on Mauna Kea (MKEA) and at Kokee Park on Kaua'i (KOKB). On the morning of 1 May, five campaign Global Positioning System (GPS) stations were set up on benchmarks along the middle East Rift Zone (77FL, 931_, HEIH, KALR, and PUL2). With the progression of the intrusion further downrift, two telemetered, rapid-response stations (ERZ1 and ERZ2) were installed on 2 May, and campaign occupations of two additional benchmarks in the lower East Rift Zone began (NANT and MOAN). On the day of the earthquake, the station coverage thus included nine sites in addition to the existing GNSS network (Fig. 1).

Immediately after the earthquake, on 5 May, three additional campaign sites were deployed on Kīlauea's south flank (LAER, PULU, and 69FL). UNAVCO Inc. (now EarthScope Consortium) provided 11 campaign GPS setups, which arrived about one week after the earthquake. Six of these were deployed to Kīlauea's south flank (DELT, PEPE, MOLE, PMOO, PILI, and NALI), whereas the remaining five were deployed around Kīlauea's summit.

As a result of these deployments, 89 coseismic GNSS vectors were determined for stations throughout the Hawaiian Islands; however, the available data span different time periods and were collected with different temporal sampling, requiring a variety of approaches to obtain a robust coseismic offset. In addition to the heterogeneous equipment setups, the

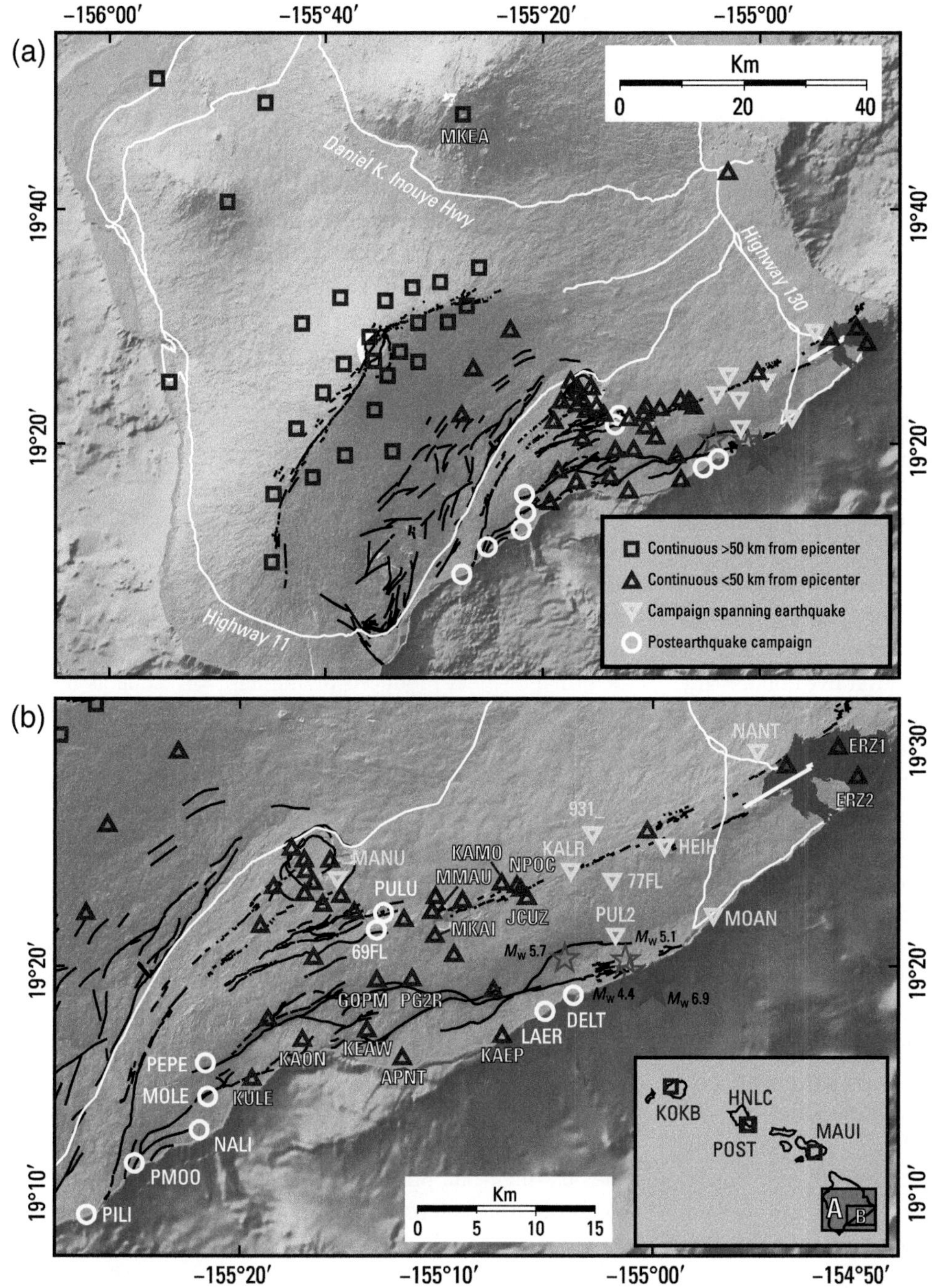

Figure 1. Location map of Global Navigation Satellite System (GNSS) stations on the Island of Hawai'i used in this study. The symbol types correspond with how the data were analyzed and are described in the text. The red filled star shows the epicenter location of the 2018 earthquake, and the outlined stars are the locations of significant foreshocks. The red filled polygon in the lower East Rift zone is the area that was eventually covered by lava during the 2018 eruption, and the white thick line is the location of eruptive fissures. The white thin lines are major roads, and black lines are mapped fault and fissure traces from the U.S. Geological Survey Quaternary Fault and Fold database. The inset map shows the extents of boxes A and B, as well as the locations of four off-island GNSS stations used in the analysis. Station names are included for those mentioned in the text. The color version of this figure is available only in the electronic edition.

earthquake occurred amidst a major volcanic event. This means that care must be taken to separate the coseismic and postseismic displacements from the large deformation signals associated with summit deflation, middle East Rift Zone contraction, and a growing intrusion in the lower East Rift Zone (Neal *et al.*, 2019). We focused our analysis on horizontal displacements because the shallow dip of the décollement fault results in vertical deformation that is less varied and lower in magnitude by comparison, although the earthquake was large enough to result in up to 35 cm of vertical offset at some sites. All sites on Kīlauea's south flank showed coseismic subsidence, which is consistent with offshore décollement slip (e.g., Brooks *et al.*, 2008; Montgomery-Brown *et al.*, 2010).

Daily positions were calculated as described in Ellis *et al.* (2025) and in a similar manner to Murray and Svarc (2017) using 15-s samples processed with the GIPSY/OASIS package published by JPL. These were then rotated into the 2014 International Terrestrial Reference Frame (ITRF14, Altamimi *et al.*, 2017). GNSS stations more than 50 km from the earthquake epicenter (blue squares in Fig. 1) were not strongly affected by volcanic deformation, and so we obtained coseismic offsets from daily positions using Est_noise (Langbein, 2004). Est_noise is a computer program that estimates the strength and exponent of power law noise in geodetic time series, together with time-dependent parameters such as interseismic rate or postseismic decay. It also estimates the uncertainties of these time-dependent parameters in the presence of power law noise. We used Est_noise to fit a model consisting of a displacement rate and an earthquake offset to daily positions 60 days before until 60 days after the earthquake (Fig. S1, available in the supplemental material to this article).

To isolate coseismic motions from volcanic and postseismic displacements for stations within 50 km of the epicenter, we used subdaily, epoch-by-epoch processing. In this way, the change in position during just the few minutes around the earthquake could be extracted. Subdaily coseismic offsets were further separated into two categories based on sampling frequency. High-sample-rate (1 Hz) data were available from most continuous GNSS stations (blue triangles in Fig. 1); however, the seven campaign deployments, as well as one non-telemetered station (MANU), had only low-rate data (15- or 30-s sampling, yellow triangles in Fig. 1).

Epoch-by-epoch processing was accomplished using the software program Track, which is part of the GAMIT/GLOBK package (Herring *et al.*, 2018). Track calculates relative position changes between rover stations and a reference. We created a network of station pairs using Delaunay triangulation and ran separate instances of track on each station pair (Grapenthin *et al.*, 2014). Coseismic offsets for each station pair were then extracted by subtracting the average position from five minutes before the earthquake origin time at 22:32:54 UTC from the average position over five minutes after the passage of surface waves (Fig. S1). The time at which surface waves are likely to have passed was estimated by calculating the epicentral distance to the farthest station in the pair, dividing by a wavespeed of 2 km/s, and then adding a 1-min buffer. A slow wavespeed was deliberately chosen to avoid cutting the time too close.

To transform the set of coseismic offset pairs from track into single-station offsets, we performed a network adjustment. Because no reasonable set of stations was stationary enough to hold fixed for this purpose, we instead minimized the misfit between the epoch-by-epoch offsets and those derived from daily time series for the 33 stations greater than 50 km from the epicenter. The daily positions were themselves referenced to ITRF14 before offsets were calculated. As such, this process approximated transforming the high-rate offsets into the ITRF14 reference frame as well.

Coseismic offsets for stations at low data rates were obtained in the same manner but with a sampling of 30 s (Fig. S1). Because of the lower sampling rate, a longer pre- and post-earthquake time span needed to be averaged for robust station positions (15 min before and 17 min after the earthquake origin time). In this case, it is not possible to fully avoid surface waves, and so we attempted to include enough time that we can average through them. Although there was not a strong difference between the results using 1 Hz epoch-by-epoch solutions and those using 30-s data, we nonetheless prefer the higher-rate solutions where available.

Campaign sites that were set up after the earthquake required yet another approach for obtaining the coseismic offset (white circles in Fig. 1). At locations where postseismic deformation was detectable, coseismic displacements were much larger, allowing us to ignore postseismic displacements in stations that do not easily allow that motion to be distinguished. The south flank campaign sites deployed after the earthquake were all previously included in HVO's annual campaign measurements, so whereas none of these stations had data spanning the earthquake, all had annual measurements going back several years, most recently in July 2017. We were therefore able to estimate coseismic offsets at these stations by extrapolating their "interseismic" velocity as measured after 2013 to the time of the earthquake (Fig. S1). Although this interseismic period includes an SSE in 2015, SSE offsets at continuous stations are on the order of 2–3 cm, which is only about 10% of the total station motion during this time period. Station LAER was first surveyed in 2017 after the original benchmark, LAEP, was destroyed; therefore, LAEP was used to define the pre-earthquake velocity.

The nine campaign sites installed after the earthquake recorded coseismic offsets that are noisier than offsets determined from the continuous stations (Fig. 2). Some of this could be attributed to contamination by postseismic displacements; however, these sites could also have been affected by the strong deformation field produced by the East Rift Zone as magma moved from its middle to its lower sections. Nonetheless, the coseismic offsets estimated here are consistent with the continuous and high-rate offsets. Furthermore, uncertainties propagated through the extrapolation described earlier are among the highest in the coseismic dataset (Table S1), and therefore, the offsets are downweighted appropriately in the subsequent inversion.

We constructed a preferred set of coseismic displacements (Table S1) by combining results from the various methods. The offsets from daily solutions were chosen for all stations greater than 50 km from the earthquake epicenter. Among stations closer than 50 km from the epicenter, the preferred vectors were those from 1 Hz high-rate processing. If no 1 Hz data were available for a station, then the preferred vector was from the 30 s high-rate processing. Finally, stations deployed after the earthquake had preferred displacements based on extrapolated pre-earthquake velocities.

Coseismic displacements were inverted for distributed dip-slip on a rectangular dislocation in an elastic half-space to determine the slip distribution using the general functional form:

$$\begin{bmatrix} \mathbf{WG} \\ \beta\nabla^2 \end{bmatrix}^{-1} \begin{bmatrix} \mathbf{W}\vec{\mathbf{d}} \\ \mathbf{0} \end{bmatrix} = \vec{\mathbf{m}}, \quad (1)$$

in which $\mathbf{G}$ is the matrix of Green's function determined using Okada's equations for surface motion due to slip on a buried dislocation (Okada, 1985; Beauducel, 2021), $\mathbf{W}$ is a weighting matrix based on the data variance from Est_noise, $\vec{\mathbf{d}}$ is the data vector, $\vec{\mathbf{m}}$ is the vector of model elements, that is, dip-slip on the discretized fault plane, which was divided into 2×2 km elements, and $\beta\nabla^2$ represents Laplacian smoothing with

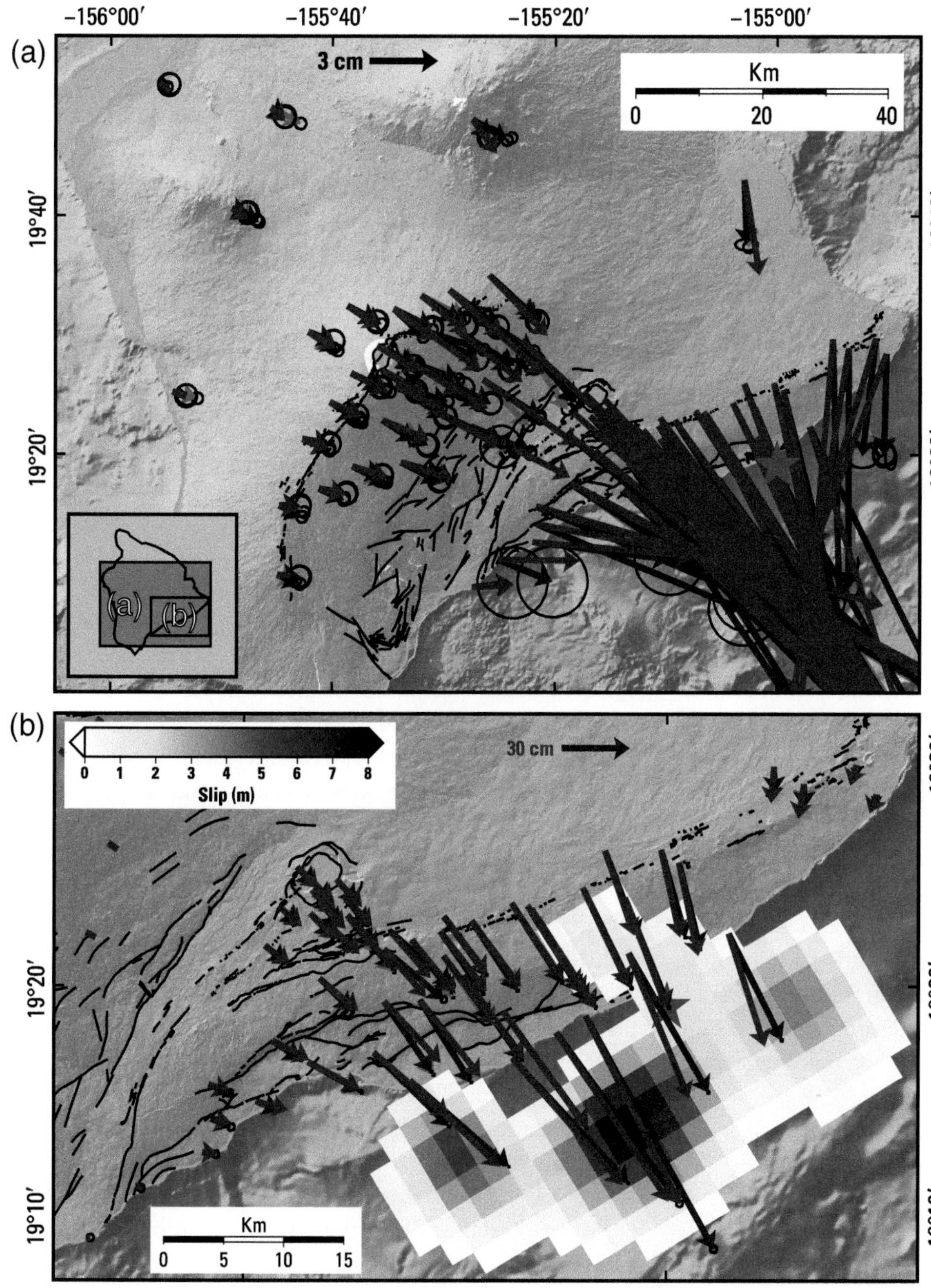

Figure 2. Preferred coseismic displacement vectors (black vectors) with two-sigma error ellipses and model fits (blue vectors) for the 2018 earthquake. (a) Data and model fits for island-wide stations; note reduced displacement scale relative to panel (b). (b) Zoom of strongly deforming area on Kīlauea's south flank, with coseismic displacement vectors (black), model fits (blue), and coseismic slip model. Model elements with zero slip are not plotted. The red star is the 2018 earthquake epicenter. The color version of this figure is available only in the electronic edition.

relative weight β, determined by examining the trade-off between model roughness and data fit (Hansen, 1992). Smoothing the model in this way allows us to ensure the model roughness does not exceed the resolution suggested by a series of checkerboard tests (Fig. S3). In addition, a positivity constraint was applied by performing the inversion using Matlab's constrained linear least-squares function, lsqlin, such that only thrust-directed dip-slip was allowed.

The depth and shallow dip of the décollement fault make its geometry difficult to determine uniquely from geodetic data. We therefore followed previous studies (e.g. Owen *et al.*, 2000; Montgomery-Brown *et al.*, 2015) by fixing the model dip to 5° (also consistent with other modeling results; Lay *et al.*, 2018; Liu *et al.*, 2018; Kundu *et al.*, 2020). We further chose a model depth such that the seaward edge is 5.25 km below the surface, which places the projection of the earthquake epicenter at ~7.5 km depth. This is deeper than the hypocenter location of 5.8 km but in line with seismic reflection surveys that find the décollement at this depth range (Hills *et al.*, 2002). We then performed a series of inversions using the model procedure described earlier, holding the dip and depth of the décollement fault fixed but varying the strike. We determined that the best-fitting fault strike is 239°, a value similar to that of Lay et al. (2018), who found that a fault strike of 235° best explained the radiation pattern of Love waves, and the same as that of Kundu *et al.* (2020) based on a model of coseismic continuous GNSS data. The moment magnitude determined from modeling our preferred coseismic displacement field is M_w 7.1 (Fig. 2), which is higher than the seismically derived USGS moment magnitude of M_w 6.9 and lower than the value of M_w 7.2 determined by Bai *et al.* (2018), also using geodetic data. Our displacement field is dominated by offsets determined within minutes of the earthquake, such that there should be little contamination from postseismic slip.

POSTSEISMIC DATA REDUCTION AND MODELING

Postseismic displacements were challenging to determine for two reasons. First, significant rift contraction and summit deflation were occurring simultaneously with the postseismic period. Second, where postseismic displacements could be clearly observed, they were small and did not continue past 2–3 days (Fig. S5). This meant that it was only possible to discern postseismic displacements at stations closest to the zone of afterslip, and those displacements had a high degree of uncertainty. It was also not possible to discern postseismic displacements at campaign stations that were set out after the earthquake. Even if a site was occupied within 24 hr of the earthquake, a large proportion of the postseismic signal was missed.

Furthermore, a small amount of misfit between coseismic offsets determined using the high-rate data and daily positions suggests the possibility of an additional component of postseismic motion that did not last more than 24 hr (Table S3). The size of the one-day postseismic offsets was about the same as their uncertainties, and they could be due to errors in the time series fitting or unmodeled volcanic deformation. Nonetheless, their directions are coherent in a way that suggests they could be due to décollement slip (Fig. S4). We do not include these, however, in the primary postseismic deformation field because of the high uncertainty in their origin.

Our first goal was to remove motions associated with the passage of the intrusion from the time series—displacements that had the appearance of an exponential function at stations close to the East Rift Zone. We did this by fitting a step function and subsequent exponential decay beginning at the time of the intrusion (30 April, 2018) using the program Est_noise (Langbein, 2004). For this work, we used the following functional form to describe exponential decay:

$$d = A(1 - e^{-\tau/t}), \tag{2}$$

in which d is the displacement due to the exponential process, A is the amplitude (final displacement), t is the time since the beginning of the decay process, and τ is the decay time constant. We used six stations close to the East Rift Zone (MKAI, KAMO, MMAU, NPOC, JCUZ, and GOPM) to define τ in equation (2), with a result for the intrusion of $\tau_{in} = 3.3$ days. This means that 95% of the exponential decay process was completed within 10 days (Fig. S5).

We then used six stations near the earthquake rupture plane (APNT, KAEP, KAON, KEAW, KULE, and PG2R) to define the decay time constant for the earthquake postseismic process (τ_{eq}), also using equation (2). In some cases, only the north component, which contained the largest signal, was useful for constraining τ_{eq}. The postseismic signal was fit with a decay time constant of 16 hr, meaning that postseismic slip was 95% complete within 2 days and 99% complete within 3.5 days (Fig. S5).

With the two decay parameters fixed, we then used Est_noise to estimate their relative presence in a wider set of stations (Fig. 3). Postseismic motion (or its absence) could be reasonably resolved from stations on Kīlauea's south flank, near the East Rift Zone, and for three stations on the south flank of Mauna Loa. Stations near Kīlauea's summit and lower East Rift Zone eruption site, however, experienced too much local deformation to adequately resolve a postseismic signal. Given the short time over which postseismic deformation evolved and the small amplitude of the signal, there is significant uncertainty in the exact pattern, but the clustering of postseismic deformation in the southwest part of Kīlauea matches the progression of aftershocks to the southwest through the first day after the earthquake.

Postseismic slip was estimated using an identical inversion setup as that for coseismic slip (equation 1) but using a fault plane shifted to the southwest to better capture the more southwestern centroid of the postseismic motion (Fig. 3). The total amount of resolved slip is relatively small, with an equivalent moment magnitude of M_w 6.5. The majority of the slip occurred southwest of the coseismic rupture, with a small amount of overlap with the coseismic slip plane. This matches the southwestward progression of aftershocks during the day following the earthquake, as well as first impressions based on the fact that postseismic motions were primarily visible in southwestern flank GNSS stations.

DISCUSSION

Relation to past earthquakes

The epicenter of the 2018 earthquake is in a similar location to that of the 1975 M_w 7.7 Kalapana earthquake (Nettles and Ekström, 2004; Liu *et al.*, 2018; Fig. 4); however, the distribution of coseismic slip is quite different. In particular, the 1975 earthquake involved slip on the décollement surface directly under the on-shore portion of the south flank and adjacent to the East Rift Zone, whereas the majority of slip in the 2018 earthquake involved the off-shore portion of the fault. Although geodetic data spanning the 1975 earthquake are not as comprehensive as those from 2018, they are sufficiently robust to model the slip distribution, which is also supported by the distribution of aftershocks (Klein *et al.*, 2001; Owen and Bürgmann, 2006). The 2018 epicenter is also similar to those of earthquakes in 1989, 1908, and 1890 (Klein *et al.*, 2001), which suggests that this part of the fault has consistently been a location of stress concentration (Kundu *et al.*, 2020).

As illustrated best by Interferometric Synthetic Aperture Radar (InSAR), the greatest strain concentration on the south flank due to dike intrusion in the days just before the 2018 earthquake was also very close to the location of the eventual epicenter (Fig. 4). Rift dilation events, for example the 2007 Father's Day intrusion/eruption and 2011 Kamoamoa eruption, have commonly been accompanied or immediately followed by moderate to large flank earthquakes (Poland *et al.*,

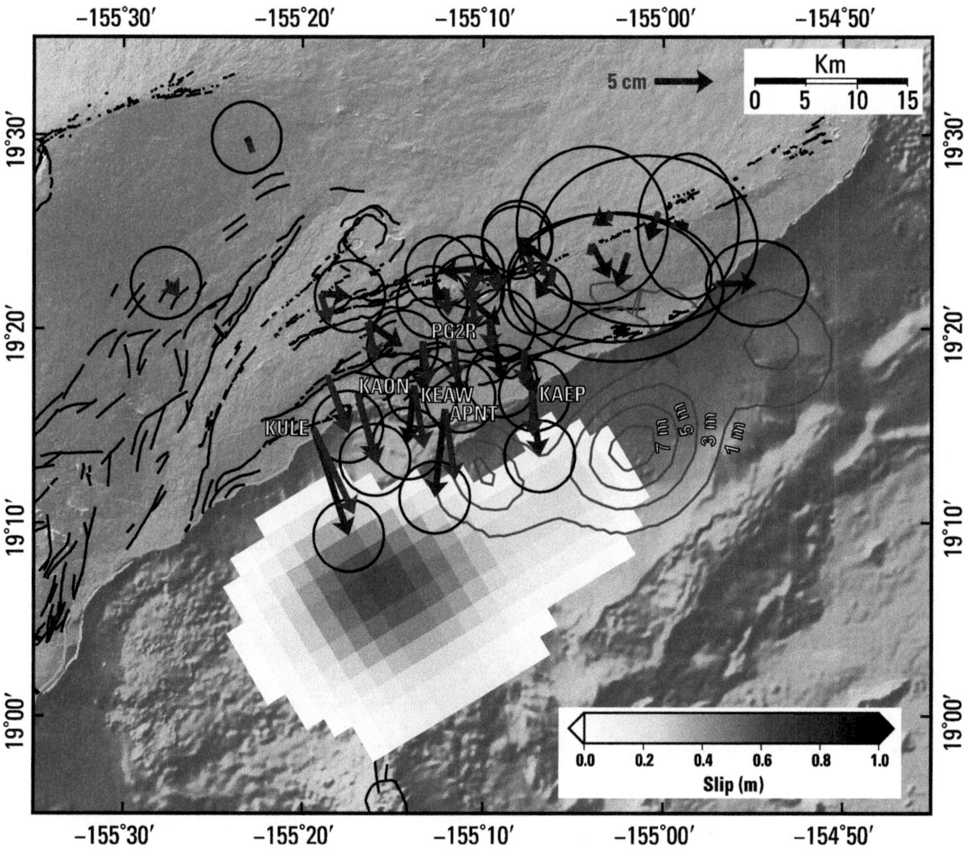

Figure 3. Postseismic data (black vectors) with one-sigma error ellipses and model fits (blue vectors) with modeled postseismic afterslip. Model elements with zero slip are not plotted. The red star is the 2018 earthquake epicenter. Contours of slip from the coseismic slip model are shown in red. The color version of this figure is available only in the electronic edition.

2008; Montgomery-Brown *et al.*, 2015) and SSEs (Brooks *et al.*, 2008), and the association between rift opening and décollement earthquakes and slip is well established by stress modeling (Cayol *et al.*, 2000; Brooks *et al.*, 2008; Kundu *et al.*, 2020). That the short-time-scale stress changes would encourage an epicenter location that has repeated over decades suggests that the stresses experienced in the first four days of the intrusion have repeated through the decades. Specifically, that he features of the rift that caused a concentration of stress at the earthquake epicenter location are persistent and regularly cause such a concentration (Kundu *et al.*, 2020).

An examination of 1 Hz GNSS time series shows that the first station to move following earthquake initiation was JOKA, which is near the East Rift Zone and inland from the epicenter (Fig. 5, Animation S1). Stations to the south, such as KAEP and APNT, began to move some seconds later, with a delay that is longer than can be explained by surface-wave travel times. This matches well with the results of seismic backprojection that shows the earthquake first ruptured inland toward the rift before moving offshore and proceeding southwestward (Kehoe *et al.*, 2019). The strip of landward rupture occurred on the décollement beneath the area where InSAR showed a concentration of surface strain related to rift expansion, and raises the possibility that the intrusion-related strain influenced both the epicentral location and the initial seconds of rupture. This is consistent with models of increased Coulomb stress at the earthquake location caused by the intrusion (Kundu *et al.*, 2020).

In addition to encouraging slip at the earthquake epicenter, Chen *et al.* (2019) showed that by the time of the 2018 earthquake, uprift portions of the East Rift Zone were undergoing contraction, such that thrust motion on the décollement fault near those areas would be discouraged (Fig. 4). In particular, on-shore portions of the décollement close to the rift zone were discouraged from slipping. This is consistent with our modeling, which found no slip in on-shore areas adjacent to the East Rift Zone (Figs. 2 and 4). A repeat of the 1975 earthquake's rupture distribution, which was primarily on-shore (Klein *et al.*, 2001), was therefore discouraged, perhaps explaining why, after rupturing landward, the earthquake did not continue to slip the on-shore fault portions.

Relation to SSEs

In addition to generating large earthquakes, Kīlauea's south flank décollement fault also creeps interseismically at rates of up to 28 cm/yr (Owen *et al.*, 2000; Sinnett, 2014) and experiences quasi-periodic SSEs (Brooks *et al.*, 2006). Between 2003 and 2015, SSEs on the south flank occurred about every 2.44 ± 0.15 yr (Montgomery-Brown *et al.*, 2015). This includes events in January 2005, June 2007, February 2010, May 2012, and October 2015. The next SSE in that sequence was projected to occur between February and August 2018; however, no SSE occurred before the 2018 M_w 6.9 earthquake, and no SSE has been observed since.

The sizes and locations of early SSEs could be separated into two patches with different repeat times (Brooks *et al.*, 2006; Foster *et al.*, 2013). Montgomery-Brown *et al.* (2015) found that since 2003, the SSEs had a fairly stable size and location, with the interesting exception that the 2012 SSE included more slip to the southwest than previous events (Fig. 6). The 2012

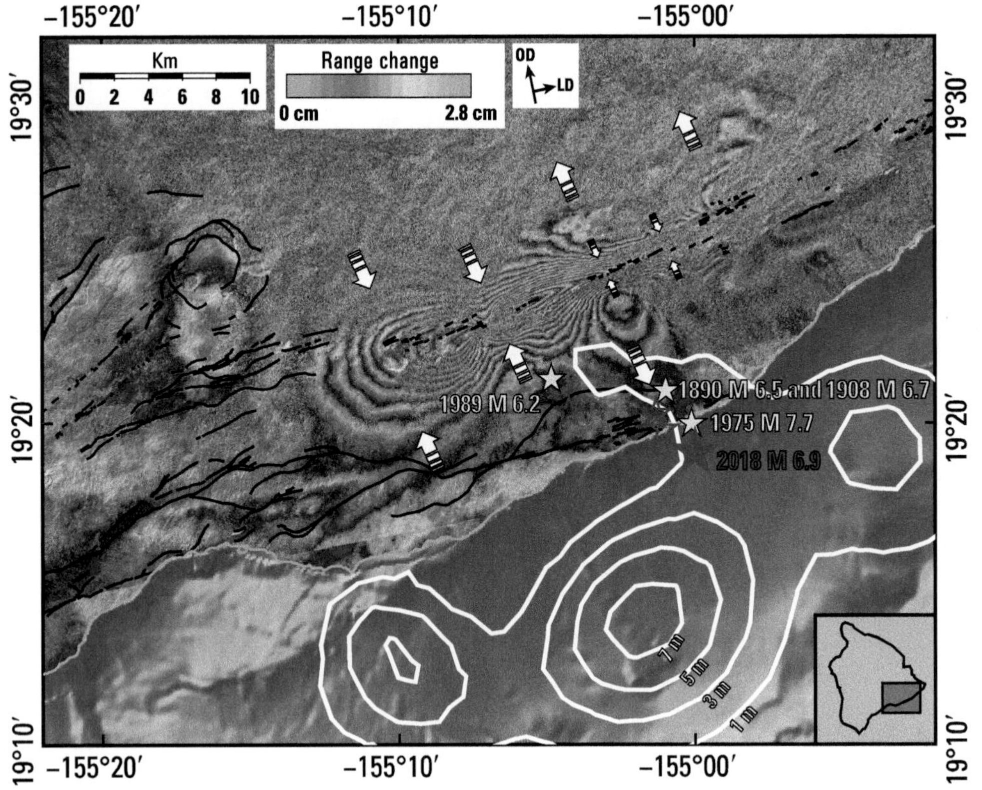

Figure 4. Pre-earthquake interferogram from ascending track 124 of the European Space Agency's Sentinel-1A satellite spanning 20 April 2018 to 2 May 2018, covering the time period of the initial East Rift Zone dike intrusion but not the 4 May 2018 earthquake. Each color band represents an additional 2.8 cm of change in distance between the ground and the satellite (range change). The Sentinel-1A satellite looks at the ground with an average angle of 36°. The broad white arrows show an interpreted and generalized sense of motion toward and away from Kīlauea's East Rift Zone, represented by the interferogram. The white contours are slip from the 2018 coseismic model of this study. The red-filled star is the 2018 epicenter, and the outlined red stars are significant foreshocks as shown in Figure 1. The yellow stars are the epicenters of significant, nearby historic earthquakes. The 1890 and 1908 epicenter locations are as given by Klein *et al.* (2001). LD, look direction; and OD, orbit direction. Inset map at lower right shows extent of figure relative to the Island of Hawai'i. The color version of this figure is available only in the electronic edition.

event is also the largest of the identified SSEs, with an equivalent moment magnitude of M_w 6.1, whereas the average since 2003 is M_w 5.7. The 2015 event was only slightly smaller than that of 2012, at M_w 6.0.

The SSEs produced a characteristic cluster of seismicity near Poliokeawe Pali (Fig. 6). This cluster was consistently active together with the SSEs since they were first identified in 1998. The Poliokeawe cluster has also been active as far back as 1974, before continuous GNSS could confirm SSE occurrence, suggesting that SSEs were nonetheless happening during that time (Montgomery-Brown *et al.*, 2015). The 2012 SSE produced seismicity in a second cluster near Kūkalauʻula Pali, southwest of the Poliokeawe cluster (Fig. 6). This is the only event that produced a clear clustering in this second area, which corresponds with the southwest extension of slip during the 2012 SSE.

Both the coseismic and postseismic slip regions of the 2018 earthquake overlap with areas of the fault that have slipped in SSEs (Lin *et al.*, 2020). The location of peak coseismic slip corresponds to the northernmost location of slow slip, while the southern extent of coseismic slip matches the southern extent of slow slip in all events except 2012. This suggests that the fault properties that define the slip patches for SSEs also influence the extent of slip in a seismogenic event.

Although the 2018 rupture may not have had the energy to continue to the south, it did load the fault enough to produce modest postseismic afterslip, which overlaps with the southwestern extension of slow slip in 2012. The spatial coincidence between the postseismic slip and the 2012 SSE indicates that the extent and location of postseismic slip were influenced by pre-existing fault properties that allow slow slip, rather than only the redistribution of stress from coseismic slip in this earthquake.

The aftershocks of the 2018 earthquake include distinct clustering near the Poliokeawe and Kūkalauʻula clusters (Fig. 6). Although the overall pattern of aftershocks delineates the down-dip extension of the coseismic rupture, the concentration of aftershocks in the two established SSE clusters is consistent with activation of the same patches that produce the SSEs.

A close association between slow slip and seismogenic slip has been observed in other locations, notably on the San Andreas fault near Parkfield, California, and on the Longitudinal Valley fault in Taiwan (Murray and Segall, 2005; Tang *et al.*, 2023). It has been proposed that the probability of a large earthquake will increase during an SSE because slow slip loads the seismogenic portion of the fault (Segall and Bradley, 2012; Obara and Kato, 2016). In the case of the 2018 Kīlauea earthquake, the expected SSE had not yet occurred, but the fault was primed to produce one.

Lin *et al.* (2020) showed that a set of reasonable fault properties could produce coseismic slip that penetrates the slow-slip region, and that the differences in effective stress on the coseismic and slow-slip patches could be key for controlling the

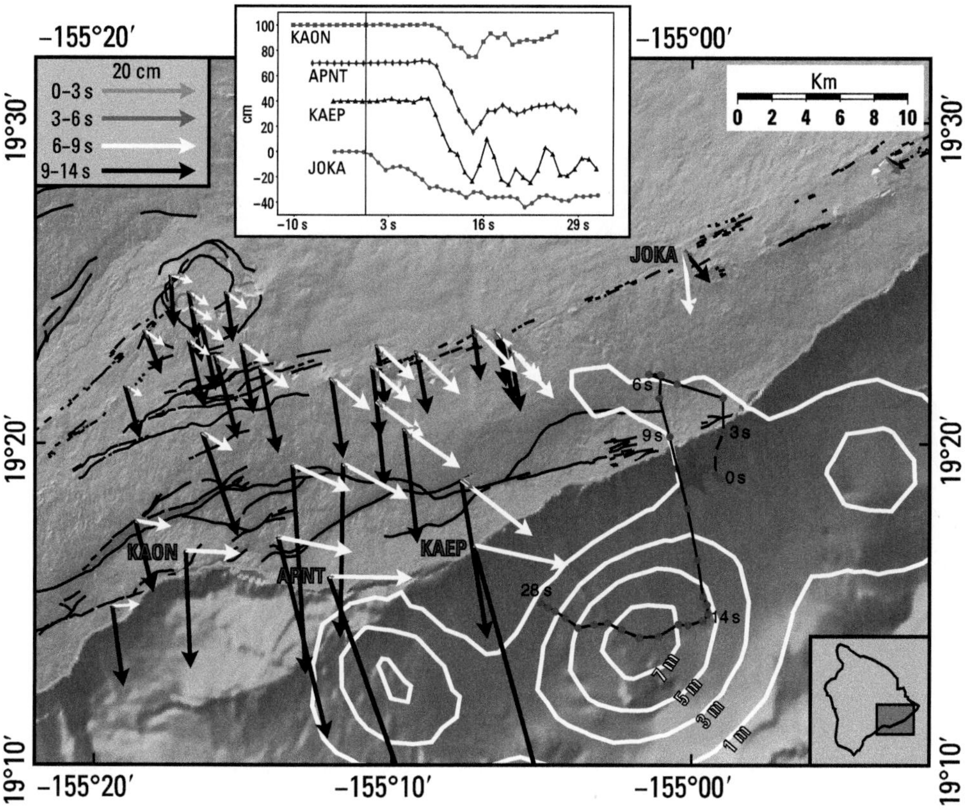

Figure 5. Displacement vectors for several time periods within the first 15 s of the 2018 earthquake rupture. High-rate Global Positioning System (GPS) time series were shifted by a surface-wave travel time of 3 km/s before displacement vectors were calculated, such that all vectors should be corrected for epicentral distance. The inset graph shows the north–south displacements for four stations. Each time series in the inset spans from 22:32:54 to 22:33:30 UTC clock time, but is shifted by the surface-wave travel time, such that 0 s is the time when the first large motions should arrive at each station. The red dots are the centers of energy release determined by Kehoe *et al.* (2019) using seismic backprojection and with a time sampling of 1 s. Centroids corresponding with the windowing of the GPS vectors have the number of seconds postrupture printed beside them. The white contours are slip from the 2018 coseismic model of this study. Inset map at lower right shows extent of figure relative to the Island of Hawai'i. The color version of this figure is available only in the electronic edition.

extent of this penetration. It is possible that being close in time to the occurrence of a repeating SSE meant that the stress differences between the two patches were somewhat lessened and (as shown by Lin *et al.*, 2020) allowed the earthquake to grow larger than it might have otherwise.

Nonetheless, more energy was released from the SSE slip patches during the earthquake than happens during a typical SSE. The geodetically modeled coseismic moment release from the parts of the fault that overlap with the 2015 SSE is 1.96×10^{19} N · m. With an average SSE moment release of 8.43×10^{17} N · m, it would take roughly 23 SSEs to equal the amount of energy release in the slow-slipping parts of the 2018 earthquake. If we assume that the rate of SSEs after 2003 (2.44 ± 0.15 yr/SSE) reflected the fault loading rate, it will take 56 yr ± 3 yr (based on the repeat time and uncertainty given by Montgomery-Brown *et al.*, 2015) to reload the slow-slip patches to the point where they will once again produce SSEs. Given that loading from the volcanic system is highly variable, there is likely more epistemic uncertainty in the estimate than stated above; nevertheless, it appears likely that decades may pass before SSE behavior is again observed on Kīlauea's south flank.

Postseismic observations

The most striking characteristics of the postseismic period for the 2018 earthquake are the rapid nature of the transient and the localized nature of the motion, whereas the magnitude of the postseismic slip is uncommon only when compared with other creeping faults. The afterslip was 99% complete within 3.5 days, and its location on the fault plane was along strike with (southwest of) the coseismic rupture, as opposed to up- or down-dip.

The short duration of the postseismic transient is uncommon for an earthquake of this size. Other M ∼ 7 earthquakes, such as the 2019 M_w 7.1 Ridgecrest earthquake, produced clear postseismic transients spanning months to years (Ward *et al.*, 2022). Months-long postseismic transients are typically due to relaxation of the lower crust or upper mantle in response to stress changes from the earthquake (e.g., Pollitz *et al.*, 2000), although they are sometimes also attributed to long-lasting fault afterslip, as was the case with the M_w 6.0 Parkfield, California, earthquake (Freed, 2007). Other examples of long-lasting afterslip on thrust faults include the M_w 7.8 Pedernales earthquake in Ecuador, which displayed afterslip lasting up to 60 days (Rolandone *et al.*, 2018), and the 2012 M_w 7.6 Nicoya earthquake in Costa Rica, which displayed afterslip lasting at least 70 days (Malservisi *et al.*, 2015). Within 2–3 days after the 2018 Kīlauea earthquake, however, GNSS station time series only showed motion that is consistent with the ongoing volcanic activity (Fig. S5).

The rapid decay of the postseismic transient following the 2018 earthquake suggests that viscoelastic relaxation was not part of the postseismic deformation, and the motion can be attributed entirely to rapid afterslip. One factor influencing the lack of viscoelastic relaxation associated with the 2018 earthquake is the very shallow dip of Kīlauea's décollement fault.

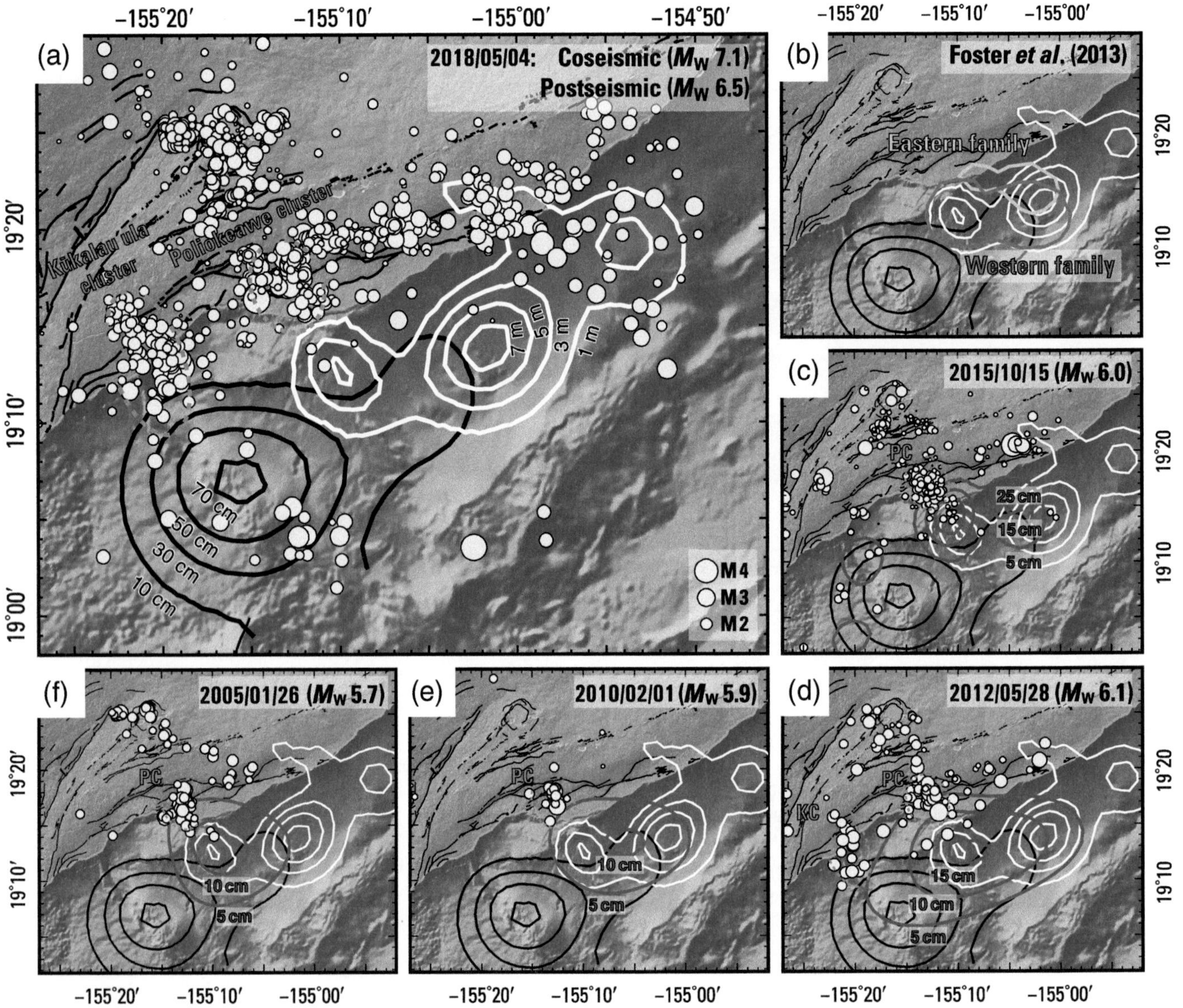

Although the earthquake was large, the rupture was wholly contained within the brittle portion of the crust and did not extend into the mobile lower crust. This is evidenced by the lack of postseismic slip down-dip of the coseismic rupture; all postseismic motion occurred along-strike with the coseismic (Fig. 6). The pre-earthquake contraction above where the East Rift Zone and the décollement intersect, which acted to discourage thrust motion on this part of the fault, also may have shielded the down-dip extension of the décollement fault from coseismic stress changes (Fig. 4).

With a geodetic postseismic moment magnitude of M_w 6.5 versus the coseismic magnitude of M_w 7.1, afterslip comprises 13% of the total moment. Although not unusually small for earthquakes in general, this is smaller than that seen from earthquakes that are similarly close to creeping or slow-slipping fault segments, such as the San Andreas fault near Parkfield. The 2004 M_w 6.0 Parkfield earthquake provides a useful contrast: it occurred adjacent to slow-slipping portions of the San Andreas fault and generated more postseismic slip than coseismic, lasting for months following the event (Johanson *et al.*, 2006). The viscoelastic contribution to the postseismic deformation at Parkfield was small and difficult to distinguish from deep afterslip but nonetheless contributed to the overall deformation field (Bruhat *et al.*, 2011). Although relaxation processes are a response to stress, they also change the stress field themselves, such that afterslip can respond to

Figure 6. (a) Association between coseismic (white contours) and postseismic (black contours) slip for the 2018 M_w 6.9 earthquake from this study and aftershock distribution. (b) Comparison of the extent of slip during the 2018 earthquake with the locations of slow-slip event (SSE) families determined by Foster *et al.* (2013). The magenta and yellow lines outline the location of repeating SSEs observed between 1997 and 2013. (c–f) Comparison of slip during the 2018 earthquake with slip determined for SSEs by Montgomery-Brown *et al.* (2015). The dates of the SSEs are given in the upper right corner, and each is plotted with three days of seismicity. The locations of seismic clusters mentioned in the text are shown with green dashed lines and the label: KC, Kūkalau'ula cluster; and PC, Poliokeawe cluster. The color version of this figure is available only in the electronic edition.

viscoelastic relaxation stresses in addition to coseismic stresses (Johnson *et al.*, 2009; Fukuda and Johnson, 2021). As such, one possibility for why the postseismic afterslip in the 2018 earthquake was proportionally smaller and quicker than for the 2004 Parkfield earthquake is that, without a viscoelastic relaxation process reloading the fault, there was no ongoing driving force to continue afterslip.

CONCLUSIONS

The 2018 M_w 6.9 Kīlauea south flank earthquake was a product of several competing processes, including long-term stress accumulation, short-term stress transfer due to a major magmatic event, and fault behavior that included segments that are locked, creeping, and that slip quasi-periodically. It occurred within and adjacent to slow-slipping portions of Kīlauea's décollement fault but did not have the magnitude of afterslip that is associated with earthquakes on creeping faults. The earthquake ruptured into an area that has produced regular SSEs since 1998, and possibly as far back as 1974, putting a stop to their occurrence and potentially delaying the next SSE by several decades. The absence of a protracted postseismic deformation signal may be due to the lack of a viscoelastic response, which would have directly created longer time span deformation and might have reloaded slow-slipping fault regions, thus driving longer-term afterslip.

DATA AND RESOURCES

Continuous Global Navigation Satellite System (GNSS) data used in this study are available from the Earthscope Consortium archive (https://www.unavco.org/data). Campaign data collected during the 2018 earthquake and eruption are available from Johanson *et al.* (2019). Additional pre-event campaign GNSS data used in this study are available from Johanson and Miklius (2026). Daily positions were calculated using the GIPSY/OASIS software package (https://gipsy-oasis.jpl.nasa.gov), and high-rate positions were calculated using Track, which is part of the GAMIT/GLOBK software package (http://www-gpsg.mit.edu/gg/). GNSS time series modeling was accomplished using Est_noise (https://www.usgs.gov/node/279390) and functions in NumPy (https://numpy.org) and ObsPy (https://obspy.org). Model computations were performed using Matlab (https://mathworks.com), with Green's function computations performed using Okada85 by Beauducel (2021). Large portions of the figures were created using the Generic Mapping Tools (https://www.generic-mapping-tools.org) and fault traces were obtained from the U.S. Geological Survey (USGS) Quaternary fault and fold database (U.S. Geological Survey and University of California, Berkeley, 2006). All websites were last accessed in August 2025. The supplemental material for this article includes three files with the preferred coseismic displacement field and the postseismic displacement field (Tables S1 and S2) and with an additional one-day component of motion of unknown origin (Table S3). It also includes two files with coseismic and postseismic slip model results (Tables S4 and S5). Five supplemental figures are also included. Figure S1 illustrates the results of multiple approaches for obtaining coseismic displacements. Figure S2 shows the residuals to the coseismic model. Figure S3 is the results of a checkerboard test for both the coseismic and postseismic models. Figure S4 is a plot of the one-day vectors included in Table S3. Finally, Figure S5 shows examples of time-series modeling for selected stations. The supplemental material also includes an animation of high-rate Global Positioning System results showing the accumulation of coseismic displacement within the first 30 s of earthquake rupture.

DECLARATION OF COMPETING INTERESTS

The authors acknowledge that there are no conflicts of interest recorded.

ACKNOWLEDGMENTS

This article benefited from the contributions of our reviewers, Kyle Anderson, Francisco Delgado, and an anonymous reviewer. The authors are grateful to all Hawaiian Volcano Observatory personnel and volunteers who were involved in collecting geodetic data during the 2018 earthquake and eruption, especially Asta Miklius and Sarah Conway. Data collection and archival were made possible by project support from UNAVCO Inc. (now Earthscope Consortium).
Any use of trade, firm, or product names is for descriptive purposes only and does not imply endorsement by the U.S. Government.

REFERENCES

Altamimi, Z., L. Métivier, P. Rebischung, H. Rouby, and X. Collilieux (2017). ITRF2014 plate motion model, *Geophys. J. Int.* **209,** no. 3, 1906–1912.

Anderson, K. R., I. A. Johanson, M. R. Patrick, G. Mengyang, P. Segall, M. P. Poland, E. K. Montgomery-Brown, and A. Miklius (2019). Magma reservoir failure and the onset of caldera collapse at Kīlauea volcano in 2018, *Science* **366,** no. 6470, eaaz1822, doi: 10.1126/science.aaz1822.

Anderson, K. R., T. Shea, K. J. Lynn, E. K. Montgomery-Brown, D. A. Swanson, M. R. Patrick, B. R. Shiro, and C. A. Neal (2024). The 2018 eruption of Kīlauea: Insights, puzzles, and opportunities for volcano science, *Annu. Rev. Earth Planet. Sci.* **52,** 21–59.

Bai, Y., L. Ye, Y. Yamazaki, T. Lay, and K. F. Cheung (2018). The 4 May 2018 M_w 6.9 Hawaii island earthquake and implications for tsunami hazards, *Geophys. Res. Lett.* **45,** 11,040–11,049.

Beauducel, F. (2021). Okada: Surface deformation due to a finite rectangular source, *MATLAB Central File Exchange*, available at https://www.mathworks.com/matlabcentral/fileexchange/25982-okada-surface-deformation-due-to-a-finite-rectangular-source (last accessed September 2021).

Brooks, B. A., J. Foster, D. Sandwell, C. J. Wolfe, P. Okubo, M. Poland, and D. Myer (2008). Magmatically triggered slow slip at Kilauea volcano, Hawaii, *Science* **321,** no. 589, 1177.

Brooks, B. A., J. H. Foster, M. Bevis, L. N. Frazer, C. J. Wolfe, and M. Behn (2006). Periodic slow earthquakes on the flank of Kilauea volcano, Hawaii, *Earth Planet. Sci. Lett.* **246,** nos. 3/4, 207–216.

Bruhat, L., S. Barbot, and J. Avouac (2011). Evidence for postseismic deformation of the lower crust following the 2004 M_w 6.0 Parkfield earthquake, *J. Geophys. Res.* **116,** B08401, doi: 10.1029/2010JB008073.

Cayol, V., J. H. Dieterich, A. T. Okamura, and A. Miklius (2000). High magma storage rates before the 1983 eruption of Kilauea, Hawaii, *Science* **288,** no. 5475, 2343–2346.

Cervelli, P., P. Segall, K. Johnson, M. Lisowski, and A. Miklius (2002). A. Sudden aseismic fault slip on the south flank of Kilauea volcano, *Nature* **415,** 1014–1018.

Chen, K., J. D. Smith, J. P. Avouac, Z. Liu, Y. T. Song, and A. Gualandi (2019). Triggering of the M_w 7.2 Hawaii earthquake of 4 May 2018 by a Dike intrusion, *Geophys. Res. Lett.* **46,** 2503–2510.

Denlinger, R. P., and J. K. Morgan (2014). Instability of Hawaiian volcanoes, in *Characteristics of Hawaiian Volcanoes*, M. P. Poland, C. M. Landowski, and T. J. Takahashi (Editors), U.S. Geological Survey Professional Paper 1801, 149–176.

Dietterich, H. R., A. K. Diefenbach, S. A. Soule, M. H. Zoeller, M. P. Patrick, J. J. Major, and P. R. Lundgren (2021), Lava effusion rate evolution and erupted volume during the 2018 Kīlauea lower East Rift zone eruption, *Bull. Volcanol.* **83,** no. 4, 25.

Ellis, A. P., I. A. Johanson, and M. P. Poland (2025). Deformation of Mauna Loa before, during, and after its 2022 eruption, *Bull. Volcanol.* **87,** no. 1, 8.

Foster, J. H., A. R. Lowry, and B. A. Brooks (2013). Fault frictional parameters and material properties revealed by slow slip events at Kilauea volcano, Hawaiʻi, *Geophys. Res. Lett.* **40,** no. 23, 6059–6063.

Freed, A. M. (2007). Afterslip (and only afterslip) following the 2004 Parkfield, California, earthquake, *Geophys. Res. Lett.* **34,** L06312, doi: 10.1029/2006GL029155.

Froger, J.-L., V. Famin, V. Cayol, A. Augier, L. Michon, and J.-F. Lenat (2015). Time-dependent displacements during and after the April 2007 eruption of Piton de la Fournaise, revealed by interferometric data, *J. Volcanol. Geotherm. Res.* **296,** 55–68.

Fukuda, J., and K. M. Johnson (2021). Bayesian inversion for a stress-driven model of afterslip and viscoelastic relaxation: Method and application to postseismic deformation following the 2011 M_W 9.0 Tohoku-Oki earthquake, *J. Geophys. Res.* **126,** no. 5, e2020JB021620, doi: 10.1029/2020JB021620.

Grapenthin, R., I. A. Johanson, and R. M. Allen (2014). Operational real-time GPS-enhanced earthquake early warning, *J. Geophys. Res.* **119,** 7944–7965.

Hansen, P. (1992). Analysis of discrete ill-posed problems by means of the l-curve, *SIAM Rev.* **34,** no. 4, 561–580.

Herring, T. A., R. W. King, M. A. Floyd, and S. C. McClusky (2018). GAMIT Reference Manual Release 10.7, available at http://geoweb.mit.edu/gg/docs.php (last accessed August 2025).

Hills, D., J. Morgan, G. Moore, and S. Leslie (2002). Structural variability along the submarine south flank of Kilauea volcano, Hawaiʻi, from a multichannel seismic reflection survey, in *Hawaiian Volcanoes: Deep Underwater Perspectives*, E. Takahashi, P. W. Lipman, M. O. Garcia, J. Naka, and S. Aramaki (Editors), Vol. 128, Geophysical Monograph Series, American Geophysical Union, Washington, D.C., 105–124.

Johanson, I. A., and A. Miklius (2026) Campaign GNSS data from 2013-2017 for Kīlauea's southeastern flank, *U.S. Geol. Surv. Data Release*, doi: 10.5066/P147WXSZ.

Johanson, I. A., S. Conway, and A. Miklius (2019). Kilauea Volcano 2018, *GAGE Facility, GPS/GNSS Observations Dataset*, doi: 10.7283/2PRD-G763.

Johanson, I. A., E. J. Fielding, F. Rolandone, and R. Bürgmann (2006). Coseismic and postseismic slip of the 2004 Parkfield earthquake from space-geodetic data, *Bull. Seismol. Soc. Am.* **96,** 269–282, doi: 10.1785/0120050818.

Johnson, K. M., R. Bürgmann, and J. T. Freymueller (2009). Coupled afterslip and viscoelastic flow following the 2002 Denali fault, Alaska earthquake, *Geophys. J. Int.* **176,** no. 3, 670–682.

Kehoe, H. L., E. D. Kiser, and P. G. Okubo (2019). The rupture process of the 2018 M_w 6.9 Hawaiʻi earthquake as imaged by a genetic algorithm-based back-projection technique, *Geophys. Res. Lett.* **46,** 2467–2474.

Klein, F. W., A. D. Frankel, C. S. Mueller, R. L. Wesson, and P. G. Okubo (2001). Seismic hazard in Hawaii: High rate of large earthquakes and probabilistic ground-motion maps, *Bull. Seismol. Soc. Am.* **91,** no. 3, 479–498.

Kundu, B., R. K. Yadav, R. Bürgmann, K. Wang, D. Panda, and V. K. Gahalaut (2020). Triggering relationships between magmatic and faulting processes in the May 2018 eruptive sequence at Kīlauea volcano, Hawaii, *Geophys. J. Int.* **222,** no. 1, 461–473.

Langbein, J. (2004). Noise in two-color electronic distance meter measurements revisited. *J. Geophys. Res.* **109,** B04406, doi: 10.1029/2003JB002819.

Lay, T., L. Ye, H. Kanamori, and K. Satake (2018). Constraining the dip of shallow, shallowly dipping thrust events using long-period love wave radiation patterns: Applications to the 25 October 2010 Mentawai, Indonesia, and 4 May 2018 Hawaii Island earthquakes, *Geophys. Res. Lett.* **45,** 10,342–10,349.

Lin, J. T., K. S. Aslam, A. M. Thomas, and D. Melgar (2020). Overlapping regions of coseismic and transient slow slip on the Hawaiian décollement, *Earth Planet. Sci. Lett.* **544,** 116353.

Liu, C., T. Lay, and X. Xiong (2018). Rupture in the 4 May 2018 M_W 6.9 earthquake seaward of the Kilauea East Rift Zone fissure eruption in Hawaii, *Geophys. Res. Lett.* **45,** no. 18, 9508–9515.

Malservisi, R., S. Y. Schwartz, N. Voss, M. Protti, V. Gonzalez, T. H. Dixon, Y. Jiang, A. V. Newman, J. Richardson, J. I. Walter, *et al.* (2015). Multiscale postseismic behavior on a megathrust: The 2012 Nicoya earthquake, Costa Rica, *Geochem. Geophys. Geosys.* **16,** 1848–1864.

Mattia, M., V. Bruno, E. Montgomery-Brown, D. Patanè, G. Barberi, and M. Coltelli (2020). Combined seismic and geodetic analysis before, during, and after the 2018 Mount Etna eruption, *Geochem. Geophys. Geosys.* **21,** no. 9, e2020GC009218, doi: 10.1029/2020GC009218.

Montgomery-Brown, E. K., D. K. Sinnett, M. P. Poland, P. Segall, T. Orr, H. Zebker, and A. Miklius (2010). Geodetic evidence for en echelon dike emplacement and concurrent slow slip during the June 2007 intrusion and eruption at Kīlauea volcano, Hawaii, *J. Geophys. Res.* 115, B07405, doi: 10.1029/2009JB006658.

Montgomery-Brown, E. K., M. P. Poland, and A. Miklius (2015). Delicate balance of magmatic-tectonic interaction at Kīlauea Volcano, Hawaiʻi, revealed from slow slip events, in *Hawaiian Volcanoes From Source to Surface*, R. J. Carey, V. Cayol, M. P. Poland, and D. Weis (Editors), Vol. 208, American Geophysical Union, Geophysical Monograph, Washington, D.C., 269–288.

Morgan, J. K., G. F. Moore, and D. A. Clague (2003). Slope failure and volcanic spreading along the submarine south flank of Kilauea volcano, Hawaii, *J. Geophys. Res.* **108,** 2415, doi: 10.1029/2003JB002411.

Murray, J. R., and P. Segall (2005). Spatiotemporal evolution of a transient slip event on the San Andreas fault near Parkfield, California, *J. Geophys. Res.* **110,** B09407, doi: 10.1029/2005JB003651.

Murray, J. R., and J. Svarc (2017). Global positioning system data collection, processing, and analysis conducted by the U.S. Geological survey earthquake hazards program, *Seismol. Res. Lett.* **88,** no. 3, 916–925.

Neal, C. A., S. R. Brantley, L. Antolik, J. Babb, M. Burgess, K. Calles, M. Cappos, J. C. Chang, S. Conway, L. Desmither, *et al.* (2019). The 2018 rift eruption and summit collapse of Kīlauea volcano, *Science* **363,** no. 6425, 367–374.

Nettles, M., and G. Ekström (2004). Long-period source characteristics of the 1975 Kalapana, Hawaii, earthquake, *Bull. Seismol. Soc. Am.* **94,** no. 2, 422–429.

Obara, K., and A. Kato (2016). Connecting slow earthquakes to huge earthquakes, *Science* **353,** no. 6296, 253–257.

Okada, Y. (1985) Surface deformation due to shear and tensile faults in a half-space, *Bull. Seismol. Soc. Am.* **75,** no. 4, 1135–1154.

Owen, S, P. Segall, M. Lisowski, A. Miklius, P. Denlinger, and M. Sako (2000). Rapid deformation of Kilauea volcano: Global Positioning System measurements between 1990 and 1996, *J. Geophys. Res.* **105,** 18,983–18,993.

Owen, S. E., and R. Bürgmann (2006). An increment of volcano collapse: Kinematics of the 1975 Kalapana, Hawaii, earthquake, *J. Volcanol. Geotherm. Res.* **150,** 163–185.

Patrick, M. R., B. F. Houghton, K. R. Anderson, M. P. Poland, E. Montgomery-Brown, I. Johanson, W. Thelen, and T. Elias (2020). The cascading origin of the 2018 Kīlauea eruption and implications for future forecasting, *Nat. Commun.* **11,** 5646.

Poland, M. P., A. Miklius, T. Orr, A. J. Sutton, C. R. Thornber, and D. Wilson (2008). New episodes of volcanism at Kilauea volcano, Hawaii, *Eos Trans. AGU* **89,** no. 5, 37–38.

Poland, M. P., A. Peltier, A. Bonforte, and G. Puglisi (2017). The spectrum of persistent volcanic flank instability: A review and proposed framework based on Kīlauea, Piton de la Fournaise, and Etna, *J. Volcanol. Geotherm. Res.* **339,** 63–80.

Pollitz, F. F., G. Peltzer, and R. Bürgmann (2000). Mobility of continental mantle: Evidence from postseismic geodetic observations following the 1992 Landers earthquake, *J. Geophys. Res.* **105,** 8035–8054.

Rolandone, F., J. M. Nocquet, P. A. Mothes, P. Jarrin, M. Vallée, N. Cubas, S. Hernandez, M. Plain, S. Vaca, and Y. Font (2018). Areas prone to slow slip events impede earthquake rupture propagation and promote afterslip, *Sci. Adv.* **4,** eaao6596, doi: 10.1126/sciadv.aao6596.

Segall, P., and A. M. Bradley (2012). Slow-slip evolves into megathrust earthquakes in 2D numerical simulations, *Geophys. Res. Lett.* **39,** no. 18, doi: 10.1029/2012GL052811.

Sinnett, D. K. (2014), Short- and long-term deformation of Kilauea and Mauna Loa volcanoes, Hawaii, *Doctoral Dissertation*, Stanford University, 187 pp.

Tang, C.-H., Y. N. Lin, H. Tung, Y. Wang, S.-J. Lee, Y.-J. Hsu, J. B. H. Shyu, Y.-T. Kuo, and H.-Y. Chen (2023). Nearby fault interaction within the double-vergence suture in eastern Taiwan during the 2022 Chihshang earthquake sequence, *Commun. Earth Environ.* **4,** 333.

U.S. Geological Survey (USGS) and University of California, Berkeley (2006). Quaternary fault and fold database for the United States, available at https://www.usgs.gov/natural-hazards/earthquake-hazards/faults (last accessed August 2025).

Ward, L. A., K. A. Guns, B. R. Smith-Konter, X. Xu, Y. Bock, and D. T. Sandwell (2022). Vertical postseismic deformation of the 2019 Ridgecrest earthquake sequence, *J. Geophys. Res.* **127,** e2021JB023331, doi: 10.1029/2021JB023331.

Zucca, J. J., and D. P. Hill (1980). Crustal structure of the southeast flank of Kilauea volcano, Hawaii, from seismic refraction measurements, *Bull. Seismol. Soc. Am.* **70,** no. 4, 1149–1159.

Manuscript received 6 September 2024
Published online 3 February 2026

Constraining the Earthquake Focal Depth Distribution in the Southern Korean Peninsula

Dong-Hoon Sheen*[1,2], Ah-Hyun Byun[3], and Hyeonjun Lee[2]

ABSTRACT

The accurate determination of earthquake focal depth is critical for understanding regional seismic processes, characterizing seismogenic behavior, and assessing seismic hazard. However, precise focal depth determination remains a significant challenge owing to theoretical limitations, sparse station geometry, uncertainties in velocity models, and errors in arrival-time picking. This study evaluated the uncertainty of earthquake focal depths in the southern Korean Peninsula using seismic station geometry and investigated regional seismogenic characteristics. We selected 304 earthquakes with magnitudes between 2.0 and 4.9 recorded from 2018 to 2022, for which *P*- and *S*-wave arrivals were manually picked from dense seismic stations. To quantify uncertainty, we conducted Monte Carlo simulations using synthetic datasets generated with multiple velocity models, random sampling of station locations, and varied initial focal depths. Gradient boosting analysis identified the minimum distance to a station and the number of near-epicentral *P* and *S* arrivals as the dominant factors reducing focal depth errors. We propose geometry-based criteria that allow approximately 95% of local crustal events to be located with focal depth errors within 5 km and epicentral errors within 2 km: (1) at least seven stations within 100 km, including two within 50 km and one within 10 km of the epicenter; (2) at least one *S* wave within 50 km; and (3) primary and secondary azimuthal gaps less than 160° and 220°, respectively. These criteria are region-specific, and further validation is required for application elsewhere. Applying these constraints revealed a bimodal focal depth distribution in the southern Korean Peninsula, with primary concentrations at 5–12 and 12–22 km. Shallow earthquakes occur widely across the southern Korean Peninsula, whereas deeper events are preferentially located near the boundaries of the Okcheon fold belt and in the Gyeongsang basin. Our findings also highlight the need for caution when interpreting offshore focal depths, which may be biased by insufficient station geometry.

KEY POINTS

- Accurately determining focal depths of earthquakes is challenging in regions with sparse station geometry.
- We propose geometry-based criteria for locating crustal events with focal depth errors within 5 km.
- A bimodal focal depth distribution was found in the Southern Korean Peninsula, at 5–12 and 12–22 km.

Supplemental Material

INTRODUCTION

The hypocenter of an earthquake, particularly its focal depth, is a fundamental parameter for understanding regional seismic processes (Husen *et al.*, 1999; Kato and Seno, 2003; Jung *et al.*, 2022). Among hypocentral parameters, focal depth is particularly critical for characterizing regional seismogenic behavior and assessing its seismic hazard (Iio and Kobayashi, 2002; Jackson, 2002; Allen *et al.*, 2004; Ma and Atkinson, 2006; Jiang and Lapusta, 2016; Dong *et al.*, 2018).

Despite its importance, focal depth remains the most poorly constrained component of earthquake location. Routine travel-time inversion methods often struggle to determine depth uniquely because of fundamental and practical limitations, including uneven station geometry, uncertainties in crustal velocity models, and arrival-time picking errors (Jackson, 1980; Kissling *et al.*, 1994; Rowe and Thurber, 1995; Shearer, 1997; Engdahl *et al.*, 1998; Hauksson and Shearer, 2005; Husen *et al.*, 2010; Eisner and Bourne, 2014). One fundamental requirement for resolving depth is the presence of stations at close range. Gomberg *et al.* (1990) noted that a correctly

1. Department of Geological and Environmental Sciences, Chonnam National University, Gwangju, Republic of Korea, https://orcid.org/0000-0002-3271-0344 (D-HS); 2. Research Institute for Geological Environment and Geohazard, Chonnam National University, Gwangju, Republic of Korea; 3. Earthquake and Volcano Bureau, Korea Meteorological Administration, Seoul, Republic of Korea

*Corresponding author: dhsheen@jnu.ac.kr

Cite this article as Sheen, D.-H., A.-H. Byun, and H. Lee (2026). Constraining the Earthquake Focal Depth Distribution in the Southern Korean Peninsula, *Bull. Seismol. Soc. Am.* **116**, 1036–1048, doi: 10.1785/0120250211

timed S wave at a station within approximately 1.4 times the focal depth distance from the epicenter provides a strong constraint on focal depth. When nearby stations are absent, particularly above or close to the hypocenter, solutions become highly nonunique, and in practice, catalog depths are often fixed to default values (e.g., 10 km) rather than being independently constrained. These challenges are amplified in regions with unfavorable network geometry. Offshore or near-margin earthquakes, constrained only by one-sided and distant stations, are particularly prone to biased focal depths.

Because earthquake location is a nonlinear inverse problem, iterative solvers can be sensitive to initial assumptions, occasionally converging to spurious solutions if the starting depth or velocity model is poorly chosen (Pavlis, 1986; Klein, 2002). Furthermore, the formal uncertainties reported by standard location algorithms often underestimate the true errors because they rely on linear assumptions that do not hold for depth determination (Boyd and Snoke, 1984). Therefore, Tarantola (1986) advocated probabilistic global optimization methods to address the possibility of multiple solutions in such nonlinear problems. Collectively, these issues demonstrate that conventional travel-time inversion is often inadequate for resolving focal depths reliably. This can lead to substantial uncertainties in estimated focal depths, which must be carefully considered during data interpretation and regional seismic analyses to ensure that inferred depth patterns reflect genuine seismogenic behavior rather than artifacts of the earthquake location process. To address this issue, we adopted a Monte Carlo simulation-based approach to characterize the expected range of depth uncertainties under realistic observational and modeling conditions.

Although focal depth remains the most poorly constrained component of an earthquake hypocenter, efforts to quantify and classify location accuracy have primarily focused on estimating the epicentral location. Bondár *et al.* (2004) proposed empirical criteria for evaluating epicenter accuracy based on seismic network geometry and introduced the concept of ground-truth (GT) events. Analyzing a global dataset of calibration events, including nuclear explosions and well-constrained earthquakes, they demonstrated that dense, evenly distributed station coverage is essential for accurate epicentral estimation. They further defined geometry-dependent GT criteria, indicating that local network solutions require at least ten stations (all within 250 km), one station within 30 km, and specified azimuthal gap constraints to achieve ~5 km epicentral accuracy at 95% confidence. Bondár and McLaughlin (2009) further refined the GT criteria with a significantly larger dataset, introducing a network quality metric and demonstrating through extensive Monte Carlo simulations that network geometry is a reliable predictor of location accuracy. In particular, they showed that having at least one seismic station within ~10 km of the epicenter and maintaining a secondary azimuthal gap of ≤160° significantly improves confidence in event locations. These studies underscore the importance of defining objective location quality metrics, which can inform future efforts to assess and constrain focal depth uncertainty.

Applying analogous GT criteria to focal depth is far more challenging. The focal depths of tectonic earthquakes are often poorly constrained by available data, making them unsuitable for direct GT classification. Unlike epicentral positions, which can be independently verified by dense networks or close-in observations, absolute focal depths rarely have external validation except in special cases (e.g., quarry blasts or deep borehole seismic experiments). Consequently, there is no widely adopted "GT" scale for depth in routine catalogs, and depth uncertainties are often underreported or ignored. Thus, alternative approaches that specifically address hypocentral depth reliability are necessary.

The southern Korean Peninsula presents a seismotectonic setting where low-to-moderate intraplate seismicity is monitored by a seismic network with a density comparable with those in more seismically active regions such as Japan and Taiwan. Despite this favorable monitoring capability, accurate determination of focal depths remains challenging owing to the inherent trade-offs between network geometry and location uncertainties. This study leveraged both network geometry and Monte Carlo simulation to evaluate the uncertainty of focal depths in this region. Local crustal events are defined as earthquakes within the continental crust of the southern Korean Peninsula, located using stations within ~100 km of the epicenter, including near-offshore cases. We defined geometry-based criteria to identify events with potentially reliable depth constraints and validated these criteria through extensive probabilistic location analyses that incorporated realistic conditions of picking errors and velocity model uncertainties. Our approach specifically tested whether the geometry-based selection criteria can ensure focal depth uncertainty within ±5 km at approximately 95% confidence. For a small number of selected events, we validated the inferred focal depths using depth phases. Using events that met these criteria, we investigated the focal depth distribution of local crustal earthquakes in the southern Korean Peninsula, thereby providing more robust insights into the regional seismogenic behavior.

DATA

We selected 304 earthquakes with local magnitudes of 2.0–4.9 from the Korea Meteorological Administration earthquake catalog for 2018–2022, in which P waves were identifiable at a minimum of four stations located within 100 km of the epicenter (Fig. 1a). The seismic phases were manually picked from waveforms recorded at 368 seismic stations (Fig. 1b).

The locations were determined using a 1D velocity model (Kim *et al.*, 2011) and the HYPOINVERSE software (Klein, 2002) using the default settings, except that the initial depth was set to 10 km. Figure 2 presents summary statistics characterizing the observation geometry and phase arrival distributions

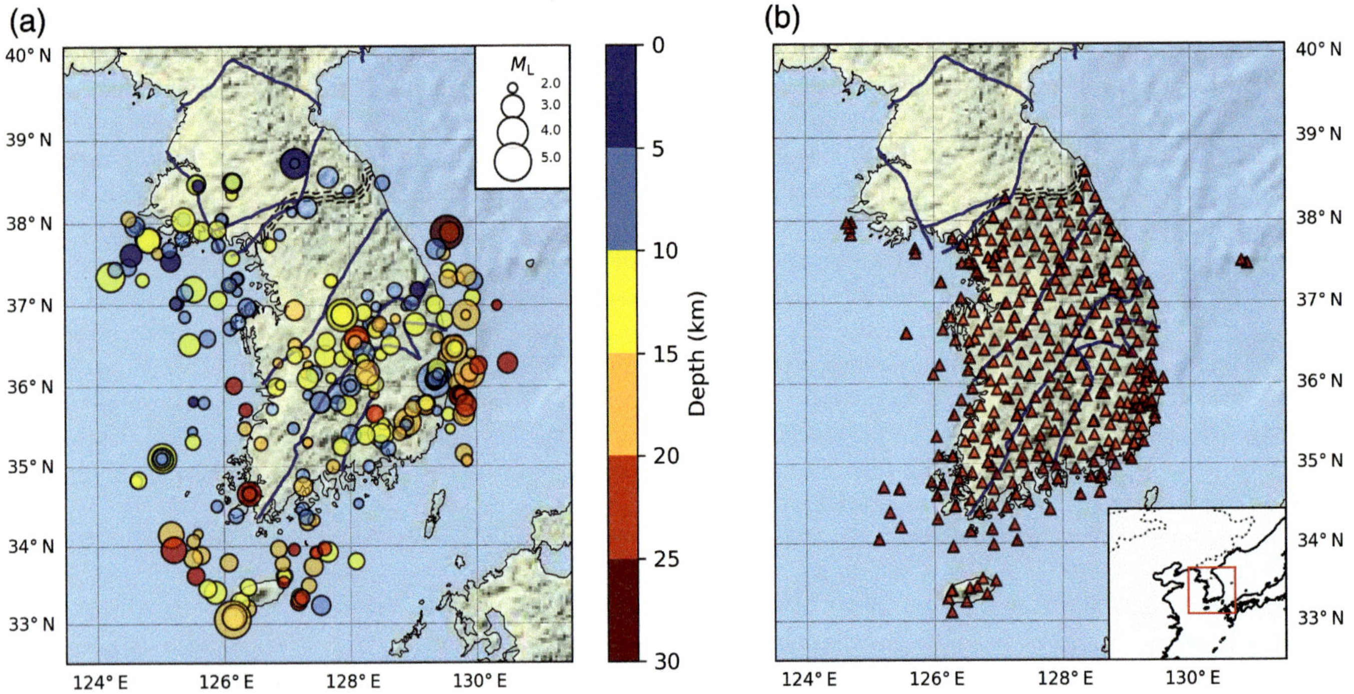

Figure 1. Maps showing the distribution of (a) earthquakes from 2018 to 2022 in the Korean Peninsula and (b) seismic stations used in this study. The blue solid lines indicate tectonic boundaries. The inset in panel (b) shows the location of the study area (red box) in Northeast Asia.

for event locations. An average of 31 stations were used per event, with a mean nearest-station distance of 23 km. Most events were of small magnitude (M_L 2.0–3.0), and over 70% had at least one station within 30 km. The number of *P*- and *S*-wave arrivals within 50 and 100 km varied substantially across events, with certain events having more than 20 arrivals even at close distances. A wide range of azimuthal coverage, as quantified by primary and secondary gap angles (the largest and second-largest azimuthal separations between adjacent stations, respectively), was observed across the dataset; although certain events had relatively good angular coverage (i.e., small gap angles), others exhibited large azimuthal gaps exceeding 180°, indicating poor station coverage in certain directions.

Despite these overall favorable observational conditions, for 20 earthquakes (7% of the total), the hypocenter determination process either failed to converge or required fixing the focal depth to obtain a solution. Gomberg *et al.* (1990) suggested that correctly timed *S* phases at stations located within approximately 1.4 times the focal depth from the epicenter provide strong constraints on focal depth determination. A total of 163 events met this criterion, with focal depths ranging from 4 to 24 km. A number of these depths exceed the typical maximum seismogenic depth of 15–20 km (Scholz, 1998). However, the depth extent of the seismogenic zone can vary locally. Accordingly, it is essential to critically assess whether the determined focal depths represent genuine seismogenic behavior or result from artifacts introduced during the earthquake location process.

METHODS

Monte Carlo simulations using synthetic data

Bondár *et al.* (2004) and Bondár and McLaughlin (2009) proposed criteria for accurate epicentral location that are largely based on datasets with events for which epicenters are well constrained. However, the focal depths of tectonic earthquakes are often poorly constrained, making them less suitable for developing depth-sensitive GT criteria. Because our dataset largely consists of events with significant uncertainty in focal depth, and formal error estimates from linearized inversion may not adequately represent true depth uncertainties (Boyd and Snoke, 1984), we employed extensive Monte Carlo simulations using synthetic data to develop and evaluate depth-constraint criteria.

Although most earthquake location programs provide uncertainty estimates for the determined hypocenter, these estimates cannot always be regarded as true statistical errors (Boyd and Snoke, 1984). As an alternative to covariance-based uncertainty estimation, a Monte Carlo approach can be employed, in which random perturbations are added to arrival times and velocity models (Bondár and McLaughlin, 2009; Lomax *et al.*, 2009). Although each solution is still obtained through nonlinear inversion, repeating the location process with perturbed inputs allows for the construction of empirical distributions of hypocentral parameters. These distributions provide a more realistic representation of the statistical uncertainty of the solution because they inherently incorporate complex error sources and bypass the restrictive assumptions of linearized models.

Using the local crustal velocity model of Kim *et al.* (2011), *P*- and *S*-wave travel times were computed for an arbitrary

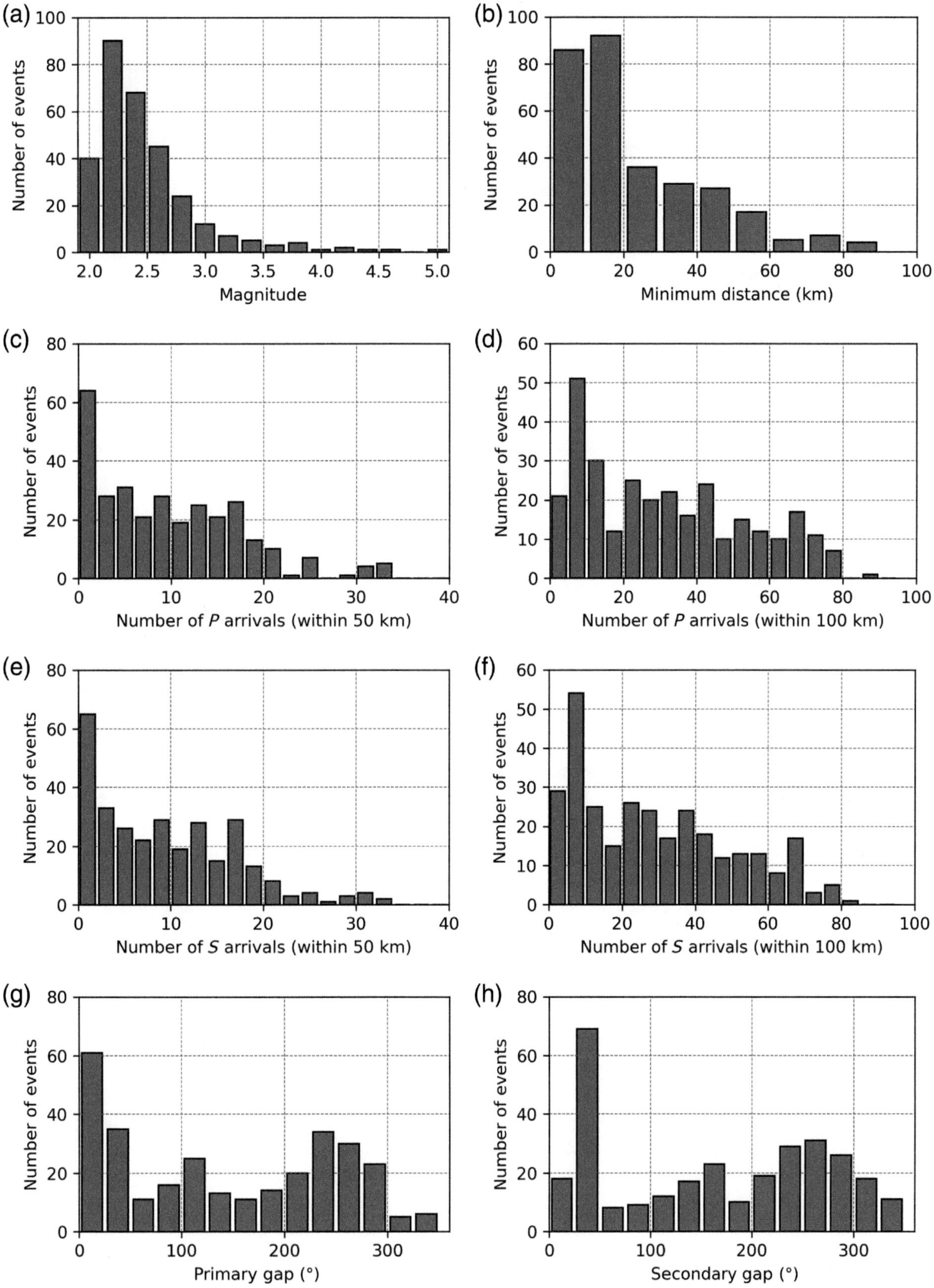

Figure 2. Summary of event characteristics and station geometry metrics for earthquake location. (a) Magnitude distribution of events. (b) Histogram of the minimum distance from each event to the nearest station. (c,d) Number of *P*-wave arrivals within 50 and 100 km from the epicenter. (e,f) Number of *S*-wave arrivals within 50 and 100 km from the epicenter. (g,h) Distribution of primary and secondary azimuthal gap angles for all events.

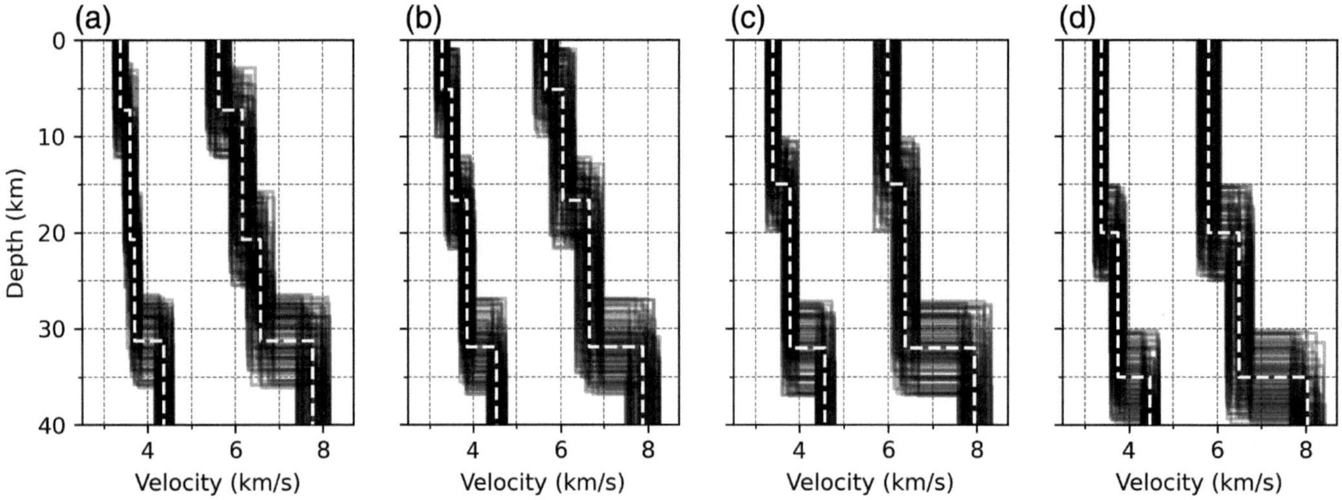

Figure 3. 1D velocity models used for locating earthquake hypocenters. (a) Kim *et al.* (2011), (b) Chang and Baag (2006), (c) Kim and Kim (1983), and (d) Kennett and Engdahl (1991). The white dashed lines represent the original models, and the thin solid lines represent the perturbed velocity models.

seismic network within a 150 km aperture consisting of 1680 seismic stations. The epicenter was assumed to be located at the center of the seismic network, and focal depths ranged from 5 to 25 km in 1 km increments. For each trial, ten seismic stations were randomly selected to determine the hypocenter, and the estimated and true focal depths were compared. This process was repeated 100,000 times for each focal depth, both with and without random noise (±2 s) added to the travel times to assess the effect of observational uncertainty. Consequently, 4.2 million sets of travel times were generated. Earthquake hypocenters were located using the HYPOINVERSE program (Klein, 2002) for three 1D local velocity models, to account for epistemic uncertainty in the crustal structure: those developed by Kim *et al.* (2011), Chang and Baag (2006), and Kim and Kim (1983) (Fig. S1, available in the supplemental material to this article). Because this study sought to establish criteria for accurately determining the focal depth of local earthquakes using a dense network, hypocenters were determined using only travel times from stations within 100 km of the epicenter.

In this simulation, the choice of ten stations within 100 km reflects a conservative configuration for local earthquake location, based on the assumption that such station density is necessary to achieve high-accuracy focal depth determination. This criterion is more stringent than the GT5 guideline (Bondár *et al.*, 2004), which requires at least ten stations within 250 km for epicentral accuracy. Following Bondár and McLaughlin (2009), who recommended excluding stations beyond the crossover distance to improve location reliability, we adopted a 100 km threshold to ensure more robust depth resolution—particularly feasible in the densely instrumented southern Korean Peninsula.

To assess the relative importance of input features influencing focal depth uncertainty, we employed a gradient boosting method, which is a widely used ensemble method capable of capturing nonlinear relationships. Before model training, all input features were normalized to ensure comparability across variables with different units and scales. The dataset was then randomly divided into training and test subsets using an 80:20 split. Gradient boosting was applied with 100 estimators, a learning rate of 0.1, and a maximum tree depth of 3. Cross-validation was not performed because the aim was to evaluate feature relevance rather than optimize predictive performance.

Monte Carlo simulations using local crustal earthquakes

Four 1D velocity models, three developed for the Korean Peninsula (Kim *et al.*, 2011; Kim and Kim, 1983; Chang and Baag, 2006) and one representing the global average (Kennett and Engdahl, 1991), were selected as base models for the Monte Carlo earthquake location simulations of the observed local earthquakes. To account for potential deviations from the true crustal velocities, each model was perturbed by modifying layer velocities by ±5% and allowing layer depths to vary within 5 km (Fig. 3). For each base model, 100 perturbed variants were generated and subsequently employed in the hypocenter determinations.

For each earthquake shown in Figure 1a, 500 sets of *P*- and *S*-wave arrival times were generated using the bootstrap method. Arrival times were randomly resampled with replacement. To reflect picking and potential velocity model uncertainties, we added Gaussian noise to the resampled arrival times with standard deviations of 0.2 s for *P* waves and 0.5 s for *S* waves. These values were deliberately chosen to be larger than the standard deviations of the arrival-time residuals obtained from event locations in the Data section (0.11 and 0.19 s for *P* and *S* waves, respectively).

Hypocenter determination using linearized inversion is inherently sensitive to the choice of initial hypocentral parameters because of the nonlinear relationship between observed

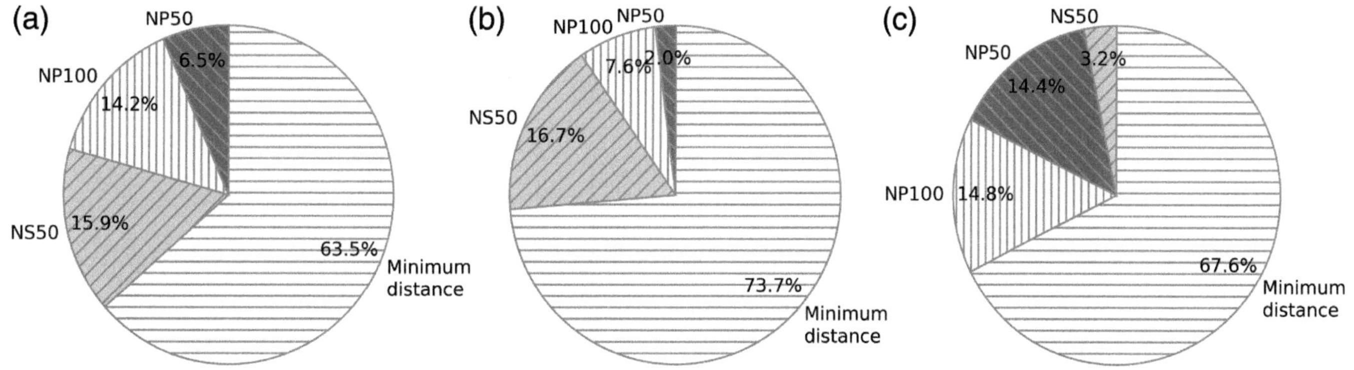

Figure 4. Pie charts showing the relative importance of features representing the station geometry around an event in reducing focal depth error, as determined by the gradient boosting method. (a), (b), and (c) are based on location results using travel times with random noise, calculated with the velocity models of Kim *et al.* (2011), Chang and Baag (2006), and Kim and Kim (1983), respectively. NP and NS indicate the number of *P* and *S* arrivals, respectively, and the following number denotes the epicentral distance. See the main text for detailed label definitions.

travel times and both the hypocentral parameters and the velocity model. This sensitivity can result in convergence to local minima rather than the global optimum (Pavlis, 1986; Klein, 2002). Tarantola (1986) described this as an inherent property of nonlinear inverse problems and advocated probabilistic approaches to address the occurrence of multiple solutions and the dependence on initial parameters. Therefore, in this study, seven predefined initial focal depths ranging from 5 to 20 km were used for earthquake location to mitigate potential biases associated with the choice of initial focal depth.

For each earthquake, hypocenter determination was performed using all combinations of 100 perturbed velocity models, 500 bootstrapped sets of *P*- and *S*-wave arrival times, and the seven initial focal depths with the HYPOINVERSE program (Klein, 2002). Because bootstrap resampling allows duplication, the number of unique observations may be reduced, and azimuthal gaps increased.

RESULTS

Criteria derived from synthetic simulations

Various metrics were evaluated to develop depth-constraint criteria, including minimum distance to the nearest station, the number of *P* and S arrivals as a function of epicentral distance, the primary and secondary azimuthal gaps, and the network quality metric of Bondár and McLaughlin (2009). The gradient boosting method identified the minimum distance to a station (Min. dist.) as the most important metric in reducing focal depth error while highlighting the number of *S* arrivals within a distance of 50 km (NS50), *P* arrivals within 100 km (NP100), and *P* arrivals within 50 km (NP50) as other significant contributing factors (Fig. 4). These four most dominant features collectively explained approximately 98.6%–99.7% of the total feature importance, depending on the velocity model. Azimuthal gaps and the network quality metric were substantially less important than other features in constraining focal depth, each contributing <1% to the total feature importance. The patterns observed in the gradient boosting analysis are consistent with the error distributions shown in Figure S2, in which focal depth errors systematically decrease when key geometric criteria, such as proximity to stations and dense *P*- and *S*-wave observations, are met. The strong influence of nearest-station distance on focal depth determination can be attributed to its role in expanding the takeoff-angle span, which provides a more accurate geometric constraint on depth resolution. In contrast, primary and secondary azimuthal gaps exert a more pronounced influence on epicentral errors than on depth uncertainties.

Based on the results of the simulations, depth-constraint criteria were developed to select events with well-constrained focal depths. Figure 5 shows the cumulative distribution of mislocations obtained from the simulations. Even when the velocity model used to generate travel times is the same as that used for hypocenter determination and no noise is added, insufficient arrival times or poor station distribution can lead to errors not only in determining the focal depth, but also the epicenter location. When a different velocity model is used, and random noise is added to the travel times, difficulties in accurately determining both the focal depth and epicenter location often increase.

We defined the decision threshold for reliable location as achieving focal depth and epicentral errors within ±5 and ±2 km, respectively, in at least 95% of simulations. Throughout this study, focal depth errors were reported as absolute values. This criterion was evaluated using cumulative distribution functions derived from Monte Carlo simulations. As shown in Figure 5, solid lines represent the subset of events that meet the 95% depth and epicentral error thresholds under all tested scenarios, provided the station distribution meets the following criteria:

1. at least seven stations within 100 km, including two within 50 km and one within 10 km of the epicenter;
2. at least one *S*-wave arrival within 50 km; and

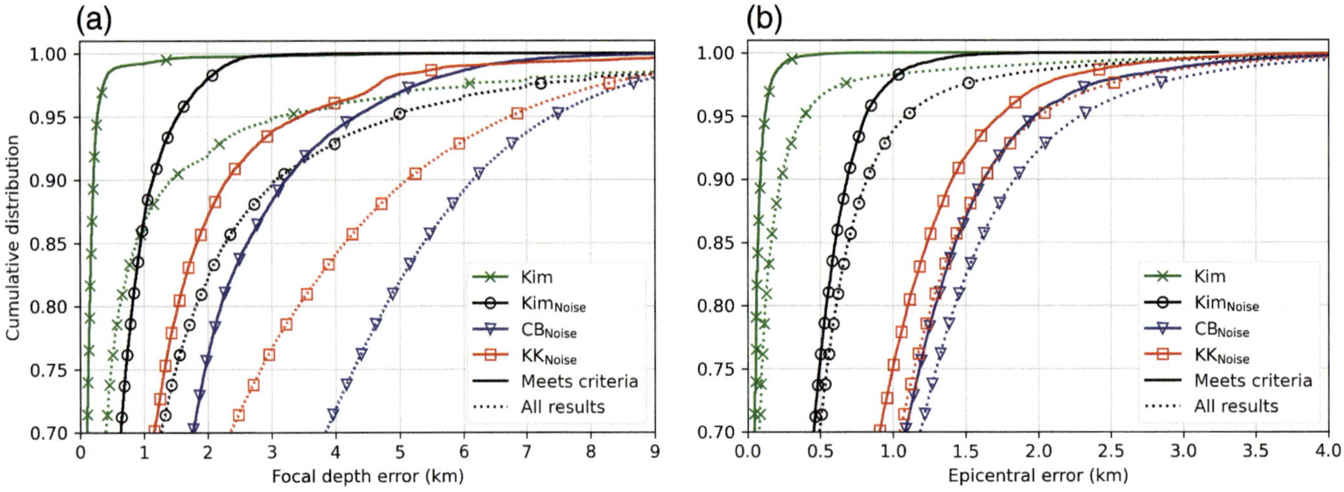

Figure 5. Cumulative distribution of (a) focal depth errors and (b) epicentral errors from synthetic Monte Carlo simulations using three velocity models: Kim *et al.* (2011), Chang and Baag (2006), and Kim and Kim (1983), denoted as Kim, CB, and KK, respectively. The solid lines represent location results for events satisfying the criteria established in this study, and all location results are shown with dotted lines.

3. primary and secondary azimuthal gaps less than 160° and 220°, respectively.

To assess the statistical reliability of the earlier criteria, we performed a secondary bootstrap analysis. From the initial simulation results, we extracted only those samples that satisfied the proposed geometric criteria. This filtered dataset was then resampled 10,000 times to compute the 95% confidence intervals (CIs) for the error distributions under the constrained conditions. The resulting CIs quantify the robustness of location errors when our quality control thresholds are applied in practice. As shown in Table 1, the proposed geometric criteria consistently yield reliable location estimates, with 95% of focal depth and epicentral errors constrained within 5 and 2 km, respectively, even under realistic levels of arrival-time uncertainty.

Origin-time residuals across the Monte Carlo simulations indicate that the proposed criteria do not produce trends as clear as those observed for focal depth or epicentral distance errors. A trade-off between shallower inferred depths and earlier origin times is apparent when hypocenters are determined within the same velocity layer as the true focal depth; however, this coupling stalls when events are mislocated into a layer with different velocities.

Validation with local earthquake data

To evaluate the practical applicability of the criteria derived from synthetic tests, we applied them to observed local earthquake data. Figure 6 compares focal depths estimated from Monte Carlo simulations with those obtained from the original inputs of the local crustal earthquakes (Fig. 1a). Each symbol represents the average of 500 focal depths determined by bootstrapping the original phase arrival times into 500 randomized sets for a given velocity model and initial focal depth. Random perturbations in travel times, bootstrap resampling allows duplication, and velocity models can lead to nonconvergent solutions. The proportion of nonconvergence was 6.2% for events meeting the proposed criteria and 32.0% for those that did not, indicating that our criteria substantially improve convergence reliability. This difference may reflect that events

TABLE 1

Bootstrap-Based 95% Confidence Intervals (CIs) for the 95th Percentile of Focal Depth and Epicentral Errors Obtained From Synthetic Monte Carlo Simulations Under Three Local Velocity Models and With/Without Arrival-Time Noise

		Focal Depth Error (km)		Epicentral Error (km)	
Velocity Model	**Noise**	**95th Percentile**	**95% CI**	**95th Percentile**	**95% CI**
Kim *et al.* (2011)	No	0.28	0.27–0.28	0.12	0.12–0.13
Kim *et al.* (2011)	Yes	1.53	1.50–1.57	0.81	0.80–0.82
Chang and Baag (2006)	No	2.43	2.37–2.48	1.64	1.62–1.67
Chang and Baag (2006)	Yes	4.32	4.22–4.42	1.98	1.94–2.01
Kim and Kim (1983)	No	2.52	2.43–2.64	1.35	1.33–1.37
Kim and Kim (1983)	Yes	3.46	3.33–3.57	1.74	1.70–1.77

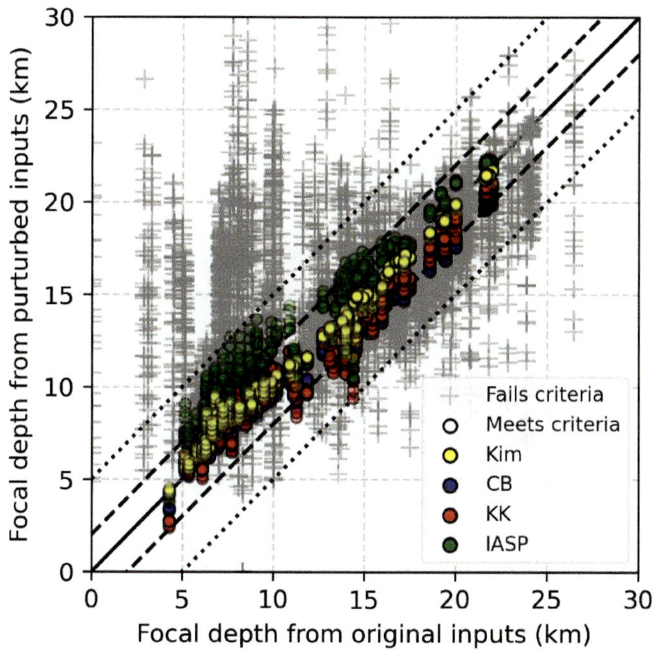

Figure 6. Comparison of focal depths estimated from the original inputs (Fig. 1) and Monte Carlo simulations. A solid line marks the 1:1 relationship, with dashed and dotted lines showing deviations of ±2 and ±5 km, respectively. The circles and crosses represent the results that meet the criteria (92 events) and those that fail (212 events), respectively. Kim, CB, and KK, and IASP refer to results obtained from perturbed velocity models based on those of Kim *et al.* (2011), Chang and Baag (2006), Kim and Kim (1983), and Kennett and Engdahl (1991), respectively, which are shown in Figure 5.

failing the criteria often had larger location uncertainties in the original catalog, making them inherently more difficult to constrain. Only converged solutions are shown in the figure.

Meeting the proposed criteria allows for the determination of the focal depth with an accuracy of 5 km (mean absolute error: 1.4 ± 1.0 km), even in the presence of significant uncertainty regarding the velocity structure, arrival times, and initial depth. Conversely, the focal depths of events that do not meet the criteria show significant variation (3.4 ± 3.7 km). Focal depths are consistent within ±2 km across different velocity models, except for those derived from perturbed versions of the IASP91 velocity model of Kennett and Engdahl (1991). This may show a trade-off between focal depth and velocity (Dietz and Ellsworth, 1990).

DISCUSSION

The depth distribution of earthquakes within the continental crust is governed by several factors, including temperature, strain rate, lithology, and the ambient stress state on faults. Although intraplate regions are characterized by extremely low strain rates, large earthquakes, a phenomenon attributed to transient perturbations in local stress or fault strength that release elastic energy from a prestressed lithosphere (Calais *et al.*, 2016), can still occur. In this regard, the distribution of focal depths has been considered a proxy for the long-term thermomechanical properties of the crust (Hauksson and Meier, 2019), and the thickness of the seismogenic layer is closely linked to crustal strength (Ito, 1999).

Of the 304 analyzed local earthquakes (Fig. 1a), 92 satisfied the proposed criteria; among these, six were near-offshore events, and the remainder were onshore. To obtain a more robust characterization of focal depth distribution in the southern Korean Peninsula, we analyzed focal depths using a normalized histogram and Gaussian kernel density estimate (Fig. 7a). The estimate was weighted by the inverse of the bootstrap standard deviation for each event, giving higher weights to better-constrained depths. Bandwidth was selected using Scott's rule, which adapts the smoothing parameter based on data variance and sample size. For each of the 92 events that met the proposed criteria, the standard deviation of the focal depths obtained from Monte Carlo simulations was used as the weighting factor, reducing the influence of events with higher uncertainty. Earthquakes occurring in the southern Korean Peninsula exhibit a bimodal focal depth distribution, with primary concentrations at peaks of 9.4 and 14.8 km. This bimodal pattern remains robust even when excluding geometric criteria, and persists when the criteria are slightly relaxed or tightened (Tables S1 and S2, Figs. S3 and S4). Focal depth histograms generated under varying criteria consistently reveal distinct bimodal focal depth distributions. In addition, a similar bimodal pattern is observed when considering all 304 events from Figure 1a without applying the criteria. Among these, most offshore events that do not satisfy the criteria are located at depths >15 km, and their focal depths may require further validation using moment tensor inversion or depth-phase analysis.

The observed bimodal distribution of focal depths in this study aligns with findings from several stable continental regions (SCRs) globally. Similar bimodal patterns have been documented in the North Alpine foreland basin in Europe, the Al Kalabsha region in Egypt, and the Kachchh basin in India, where seismicity is concentrated in the upper- and lower-thirds of the crust, separated by an aseismic mid-crustal layer (Klose and Seeber, 2007). This distribution is often interpreted as reflecting rheological layering, with brittle strength peaks in the upper and lower crust bounded by a ductile middle crust (Brace and Kohlstedt, 1980; Deverchère *et al.*, 2001). Variations in the depth and strength of bimodality across SCRs are attributed to differences in thermal gradients, crustal composition, fluid presence, and inherited structural boundaries.

Across the southern Korean Peninsula, earthquakes primarily occur at depths of 5–12 km. Events deeper than 12 km are also found in many areas, excluding the Gyeonggi Massif. Notably, several deeper earthquakes (approaching 20 km) occur near the boundaries of the Okcheon fold belt and within the Gyeongsang basin (Fig. 7b,c).

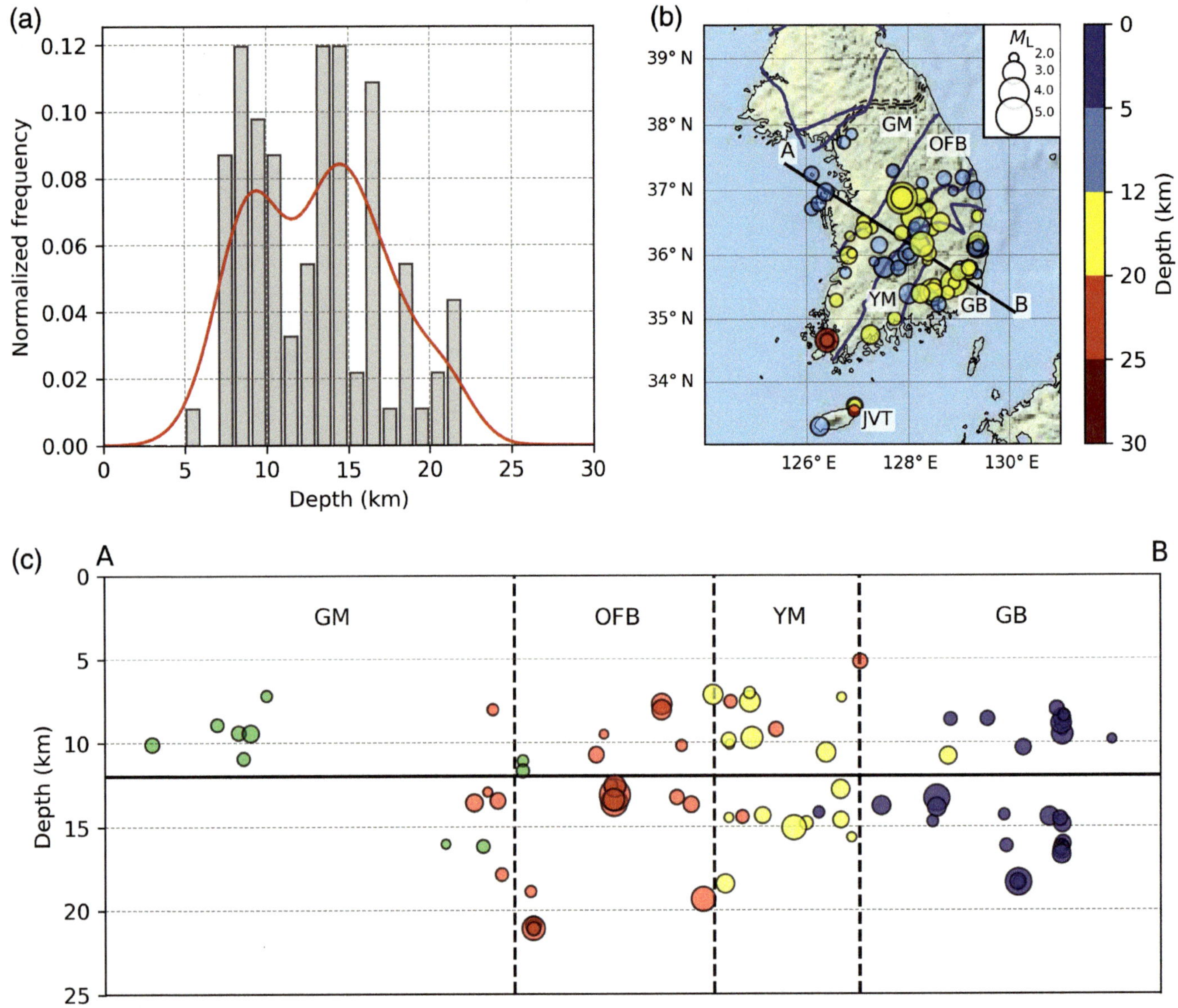

Figure 7. (a) Focal depth histogram for the 92 earthquakes that met the proposed criteria in this study. The red solid line shows a Gaussian kernel density estimate of the depths, with weights based on the Monte Carlo-estimated uncertainties. (b) Map showing the epicentral locations of the same events, with colors representing focal depths, highlighting spatial patterns in depth distribution. The A–B transect line marks the profile used in panel (c). The solid blue lines indicate tectonic boundaries. (c) Depth distribution of the events projected onto the A–B transect. The circle color indicates the tectonic unit, size corresponds to earthquake magnitude. The vertical dashed lines mark tectonic boundaries, and the horizontal solid line denotes 12 km depth. GB, Gyeongsang basin; GM, Gyeonggi Massif; JVT, Jeju volcanic terrain; OFB, Okcheon fold belt; and YM, Yeongnam Massif.

Han *et al.* (2023) also reported that the focal depths of earthquakes in the peninsula are confined at depths of 3–20 km and exhibit a bimodal distribution, with peaks at approximately 7.5 and 13.5 km. They further noted that earthquakes in the Yeongnam and Gyeonggi massifs are relatively shallow (<10 km), whereas those in the Okcheon fold belt occur at intermediate depths (10–16 km). Although their event selection did not involve the rigorous criteria proposed in this study, their findings agree with ours, suggesting that the observed trends are robust despite potential depth-related uncertainties.

As shown in Figure 7b, deep crustal earthquakes (>20 km) are located in the southwestern Korean Peninsula and offshore the eastern side of Jeju volcanic island. Five events in the southwest are part of the 2020 Haenam earthquake sequence, which consisted of 74 earthquakes that occurred over two weeks from 26 April to 8 May 2020 (Hong *et al.*, 2020; Sheen, 2021). Their focal depths are estimated to lie between 20 and 21 km, with standard deviations of approximately 2.6 km. Although these depths slightly exceed the typical maximum seismogenic depth of 15–20 km (Scholz, 1998), the occurrence of this sequence has been interpreted as being associated with the relatively low temperature (~205°C) in the source region (Hong *et al.*, 2020). In thermally elevated regions, the lower boundary of the maximum seismogenic depth is relatively shallow. In contrast, in cooler

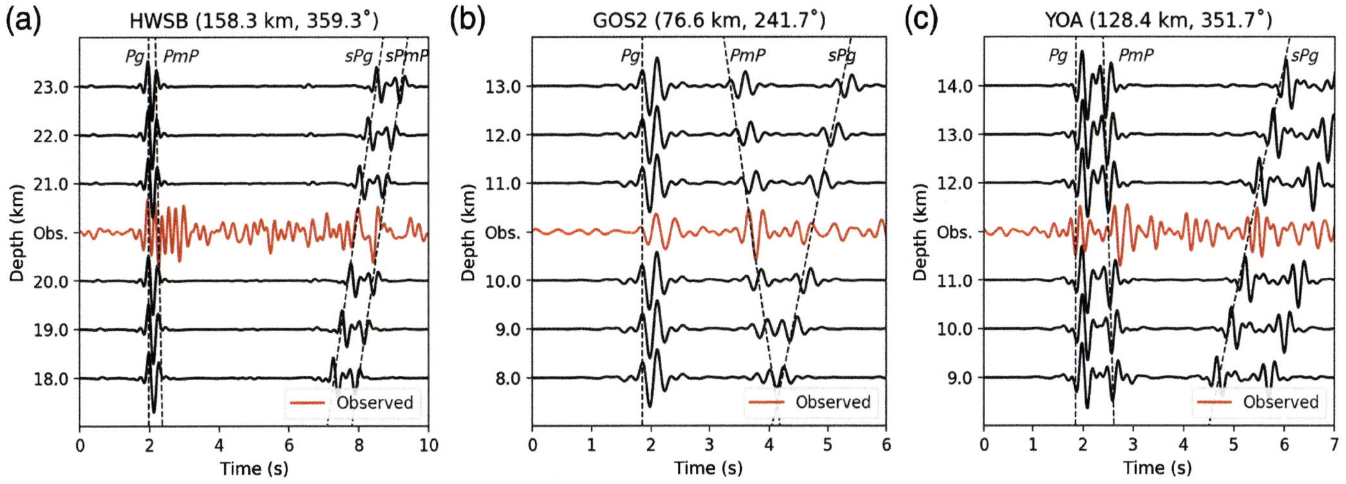

Figure 8. Comparison between the observed waveforms (red) and synthetic seismograms (black) showing reference phases (*Pg* and *PmP*) and their corresponding depth phases (*sPg* and *sPmP*). (a) Deeper offshore Jeju event, (b) and (c) two nearby shallow events. The station code is indicated at the top of each panel, with epicentral distance and azimuth given in parentheses.

regions, the lower boundary extends deeper, reaching depths of 25–30 km (Brace and Byerlee, 1970; Sibson, 1982; Wong and Chapman, 1990; Tanaka, 2004; Zuza and Cao, 2020).

The focal depth of one event in the eastern offshore region of Jeju Island is estimated at 21.3 ± 3.5 km, whereas two nearby events, located approximately 9 km away, have focal depths of 13.2 ± 4.7 km and 12.9 ± 3.9 km. In addition, one event in the western part of Jeju is located at a depth of 11.2 ± 3.6 km. To further constrain these estimates, depth phases such as *sPg* and *sPmP*, together with their corresponding reference phases (*Pg* and *PmP*), were examined, as they provide useful constraints in regions with sparse seismic network coverage (Ma and Atkinson, 2006; Yuan *et al.*, 2020). Complications from water multiples or crustal reverberations in depth-phase identification are negligible in our study area, where offshore earthquakes occur at water depths of less than 1 km and thick sedimentary basins are absent. We note that depth phases are particularly sensitive to focal depth but relatively robust to moderate velocity model variations (Ma, 2010), offering an independent validation check for the bootstrap-derived depths. Therefore, synthetic seismograms were generated following the method of Zhu and Rivera (2002), using the 1D velocity model of Kim *et al.* (2011), and were compared with the observed waveforms. As shown in Figure 8, the observed seismograms for the eastern offshore Jeju events match well with synthetics corresponding to focal depths of ~21 km for the deeper event and ~11 km for the two shallower events. This agreement indicates that the focal depth of the deep offshore earthquake near Jeju Island is robustly constrained and satisfies the criteria proposed in this study, thereby supporting the reliability and applicability of our approach for constraining focal depths.

Geophysical observations suggest that the southeastern Korean margin is characterized by continental rifting, magma underplating, a thin lithosphere, and pronounced upper-mantle upwelling (Cho *et al.*, 2004; Lee *et al.*, 2022). However, offshore events in this region were located at depths greater than 20 km (Fig. 1a) and are inconsistent with these geophysical interpretations that imply the existence of a seismogenic zone restricted to shallower crustal depths in this region. Monte Carlo simulations also locate these events at depths of 18–22 km.

Figure 9a shows a focal depth histogram derived from Monte Carlo simulations for the 2019 M_L 4.1 event occurring offshore the southeastern Korean margin, which does not meet the proposed criteria and is absent from Figure 7b. This event failed the nearest-station and azimuthal gap thresholds, with its closest station located ~30 km away and primary and secondary azimuthal gaps of 248° and 258°, respectively. The cataloged depth of this event is 21 km, which lies within the uncertainty bounds of the simulation estimate (18.1 ± 5.7 km) derived from the successfully converged solutions used to construct the histogram in Figure 9a. However, the depth phase of this event indicates a focal depth of approximately 11 km, which is significantly shallower than that inferred from travel-time inversion (Fig. 9b). This estimate is consistent with the focal depth derived from the moment tensor solution of Song *et al.* (2022), which is approximately 9 km. Therefore, the cataloged depths of many offshore earthquakes, as determined from travel-time inversion, should be regarded with caution because they may be biased by insufficient station geometry and thus seismologically unreliable.

CONCLUSIONS

The accurate determination of earthquake focal depth is paramount for understanding the seismogenic behavior and seismic hazard of a region. This study successfully developed and evaluated objective depth-constraint criteria for the southern Korean Peninsula using extensive Monte Carlo simulations with

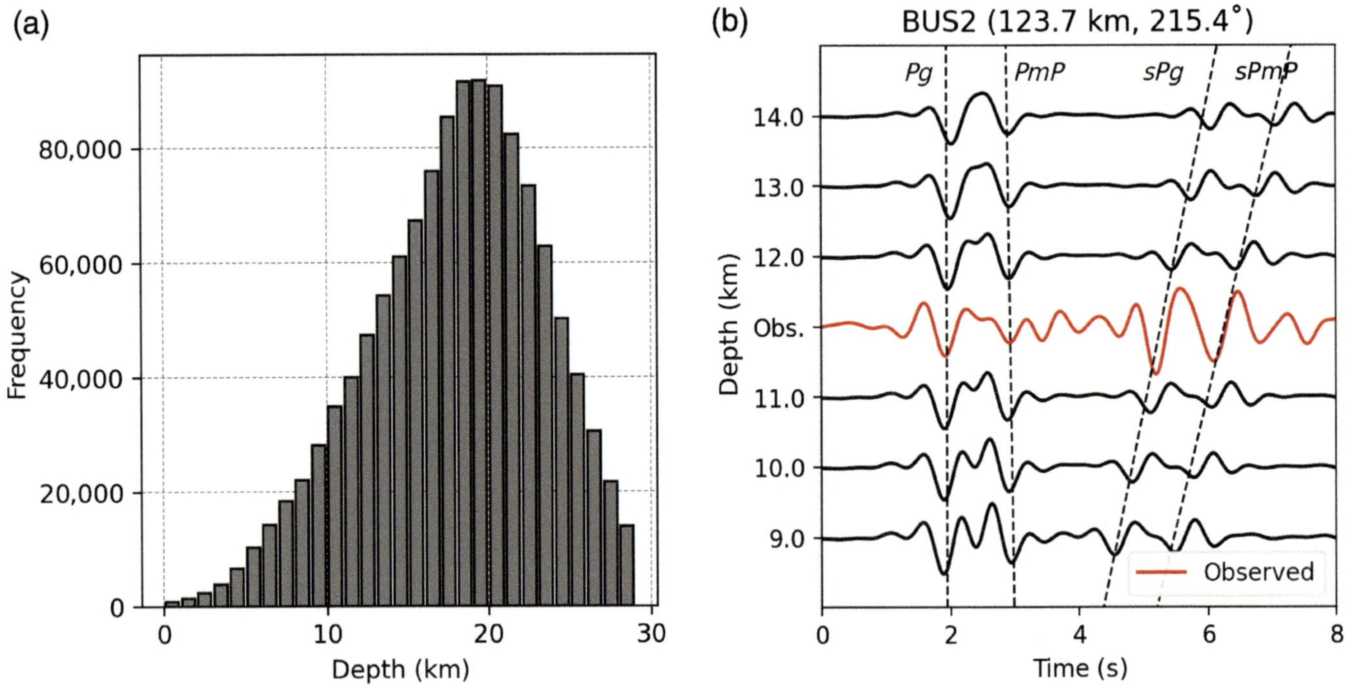

Figure 9. (a) Focal depth histogram for the 2019 M_L 4.1 offshore southeastern Korean margin event, obtained from Monte Carlo simulations. (b) Comparison between the observed waveforms (red) with synthetic seismograms (black) showing reference phases (*Pg* and *PmP*) and their corresponding depth phases (*sPg* and *sPmP*). The station code is indicated at the top with epicentral distance and azimuth given in parentheses.

synthetic and observed data. A key finding is that nearest-station distance is the dominant control on focal depth reliability, whereas azimuthal coverage exerts a comparatively minor influence on focal depth resolution. We infer that shorter epicentral distances broaden the range of takeoff angles sampled by the network, thereby stabilizing focal depth estimates. Based on these results, we proposed a practical geometry-based criterion: (1) at least seven stations within 100 km, including two within 50 km and one within 10 km of the epicenter; (2) at least one *S* phase within 50 km; and (3) primary and secondary azimuthal gaps smaller than 160° and 220°, respectively. This set of criteria enables approximately 95% of crustal events to be located with focal depth and epicentral errors within 5 and 2 km, respectively. Practically, this favors network densification that secures nearby *P* and *S* phase observations. These criteria significantly enhance the reliability of focal depth determination, allowing most crustal events to be located with high accuracy even amidst uncertainties in velocity models and arrival times.

We emphasize that these findings are specific to intraplate crustal earthquakes in the southern Korean Peninsula, where dense seismic networks and regional 1D velocity models enable reliable focal depth determination. Although the results demonstrate robust internal consistency and reliable performance across different velocity models and focal depths within the crust, extrapolation to other tectonic environments, such as subduction zones or offshore regions with sparse station coverage, should be approached with caution. The proposed criteria were developed for local crustal earthquakes and may not be suitable for deep-focus, regional, or teleseismic events. A broader application would require further validation in alternative geological contexts and with 3D structural models.

Based on events meeting these rigorous criteria, our analysis provides a robust characterization of the focal depth distribution in the southern Korean Peninsula. We revealed a distinct bimodal distribution of earthquake depths, with concentrations at 5–12 and 12–22 km, which spatially correlate with different tectonic units: shallower events are widespread across the region, whereas deeper events are concentrated near tectonic boundaries, particularly where the Okcheon fold belt contacts adjacent tectonic units and within the Gyeongsang basin. These findings are largely consistent with those of previous studies, reinforcing the observed trends.

Although the occurrence of several deeper crustal earthquakes, such as the Haenam sequence, aligns with specific thermal conditions in their source regions, our study also underscores the critical need for caution regarding the cataloged depths of many offshore earthquakes. These depths, often derived from routine travel-time inversions, can be unreliable owing to inadequate station geometry and may contradict estimates from other methods, such as depth phase analysis and moment tensor solutions. This research significantly contributes to a more reliable understanding of the seismogenic characteristics of the southern Korean Peninsula by providing a refined methodology for accurate focal depth determination.

DATA AND RESOURCES

The earthquake catalog and seismic waveforms can be obtained from https://necis.kma.go.kr (last accessed August 2025). The catalog for earthquakes that meet the proposed criteria is available at https://github.com/dhsheen/KR_GTevents (last accessed November 2025). The supplemental material includes additional tables and figures that support the main analysis. Figure S1 presents a comparison of 1D velocity models considered in this study. Figure S2 shows how errors vary with each metric, highlighting azimuthal gaps control on epicenters, whereas focal depth resolution is chiefly constrained by nearby arrivals. Figure S3 shows the focal depth distribution for all earthquakes considered in the study without applying the geometric criteria, whereas Figure 7 in the main text shows the distribution for only the 92 events that satisfy the criteria. Table S1 summarizes the peak depths, peak widths, and interpeak separation of the bimodal focal depth distribution in the southern Korean Peninsula, comparing results with and without the proposed geometric criteria. Table S2 and Figure S4 present sensitivity tests that explore how varying the geometric criteria (i.e., slightly tightening or relaxing thresholds) affects the resulting focal depth distributions, demonstrating that the bimodality persists under these variants.

DECLARATION OF COMPETING INTERESTS

The authors acknowledge that the research was conducted in the absence of any commercial or financial relationships that could be construed as a potential conflict of interest.

ACKNOWLEDGMENTS

The authors would like to express their sincere gratitude to the two anonymous reviewers, the Editor, and the YoungHee Kim Associate Editor for their constructive comments and insightful suggestions, which greatly helped improve the quality and completeness of this article. This work was supported by the Korea Meteorological Administration (KMA) Research and Development Program under Grant Number KMI2022-01010. A. H. Byun was supported by the Development of earthquake information production technology (KMA2022-02121).

REFERENCES

Allen, T. I., G. Gibson, A. Brown, and J. P. Cull (2004). Depth variation of seismic source scaling relations: implications for earthquake hazard in southeastern Australia, *Tectonophysics* **390,** 5–24.

Bondár, I., and K. L. McLaughlin (2009). A new ground truth data set for seismic studies, *Seismol. Res. Lett.* **80,** 465–472.

Bondár, I., S. C. Myers, E. R. Engdahl, and E. A. Bergman (2004). Epicenter accuracy based on seismic network criteria, *Geophys. J. Int.* **156,** 483–496.

Boyd, T. M., and J. A. Snoke (1984). Error estimates in some commonly used earthquake location programs, *Seismol. Res. Lett.* **55,** 3–6.

Brace, W. F., and J. D. Byerlee (1970). California earthquakes: Why only shallow focus? *Science* **168,** 1573–1575.

Brace, W. F., and D. L. Kohlstedt (1980). Limits on lithospheric stress imposed by laboratory experiments, *J. Geophys. Res.* **85,** 6248–6252.

Calais, E., T. Camelbeeck, S. Stein, M. Liu, and T. J. Craig (2016). A new paradigm for large earthquakes in stable continental plate interiors, *Geophys. Res. Lett.* **43,** 10,621–10,637.

Chang, S.-J., and C.-E. Baag (2006). Crustal structure in southern Korea from joint analysis of regional broadband waveforms and travel times, *Bull. Seismol. Soc. Am.* **96,** 856–870.

Cho, H. M., H. J. Kim, H. T. Jou, J. K. Hong, and C.-E. Baag (2004). Transition from rifted continental to oceanic crust at the southeastern Korean margin in the East Sea (Japan Sea), *Geophys. Res. Lett.* **31,** L07606, doi: 10.1029/2003GL019107.

Deverchère, J., C. Petit, N. Gileva, N. Radziminovitch, V. Melnikova, and V. San'Kov (2001). Depth distribution of earthquakes in the Baikal rift system and its implications for the rheology of the lithosphere, *Geophys. J. Int.* **146,** 714–730.

Dietz, L. D., and W. L. Ellsworth (1990). The October 17, 1989, Loma Prieta, California Earthquake and its aftershocks: Geometry of the sequence from high-resolution locations, *Geophys. Res. Lett.* **17,** 1417–1420.

Dong, Y., S. Ni, D. A. Yuen, and Z. Li (2018). Crustal rheology from focal depths in the North China Basin, *Earth Planet. Sci. Lett.* **497,** 123–138.

Eisner, L., and S. J. Bourne (2014). Precision of earthquake hypocenter locations in the UK and implications for induced seismicity studies, *Geophys. J. Int.* **199,** 1941–1955.

Engdahl, E. R., R. D. van der Hilst, and R. Buland (1998). Global teleseismic earthquake relocation with improved travel times and procedures for depth determination, *Bull. Seismol. Soc. Am.* **88,** 722–743.

Gomberg, J., K. M. Shedlock, and S. W. Roecker (1990). The effect of S-wave arrival times on the accuracy of hypocenter estimation, *Bull. Seismol. Soc. Am.* **80,** 1605–1628.

Han, J., K. J. Seo, S. Kim, D.-H. Sheen, D. Lee, and A.-H. Byun (2023). Research catalog of inland seismicity in the Southern Korean Peninsula from 2012 to 2021 using deep learning techniques, *Seismol. Res. Lett.* **95,** 952–968.

Hauksson, E., and M.-A. Meier (2019). Applying depth distribution of seismicity to determine thermos-mechanical properties of the seismogenic curst in the Southern California: comparing lithotectonic blocks, *Pure Appl. Geophys.* **176,** 1061–1081.

Hauksson, E., and P. M. Shearer (2005). Southern California hypocenter relocations with waveform cross-correlation, part 1: Results using the double-difference method, *Bull. Seismol. Soc. Am.* **95,** 896–903.

Hong, T.-K., S. Park, J. Lee, D. Chung, and W. Kim (2020). One-off deep crustal earthquake swarm in a stable intracontinental region of the southwestern Korean Peninsula, *Phys. Earth Planet. In.* **308,** 106582.

Husen, S., L. Jeanne, and J. L. Hardebeck (2010). Theme IV-Understanding seismicity, catalogs and their problems, earthquake location accuracy, *Community Online Resource for Statistical Seismicity Analysis*, 35 pp., doi: 10.5078/corssa-55815573.

Husen, S., E. Kissling, E. Flueh, and G. Asch (1999). Accurate hypocentre determination in the seismogenic zone of the subducting Nazca plate in northern Chile using a combined on-/offshore network, *Geophys. J. Int.* **138,** 168–701.

Iio, Y., and Y. Kobayashi (2002). Is the plastic flow uniformly distributed below the seismogenic region? *Earth Planets Space* **54,** 1085–1090.

Ito, K. (1999). Seismogenic layer, reflective lower crust, surface heat flow and large inland earthquakes, *Tectonophysics* **306,** 423–433.

Jackson, J. (1980). Errors in focal depth determination and the depth of seismicity in Iran and Turkey, *Geophys. J. Int.* **61,** 285–301.

Jackson, J. (2002). Strength of the continental lithosphere: Time to abandon the jelly sandwich? *GSA Today* **12,** no. 9, 4–10.

Jiang, J., and N. Lapusta (2016). Deeper penetration of large earthquakes on seismically quiescent faults, *Science* **352,** no. 6291, 1293–1297.

Jung, Y., J-U. Woo, and J. Rhie (2022). Enhanced hypocenter determination of the 2017 Pohang earthquake sequence, South Korea, using a 3-D velocity model, *Geosci. J.* **26,** 499–511.

Kato, N., and T. Seno (2003). Hypocenter depths of large interplate earthquakes and their relation to seismic coupling, *Earth Planet. Sci. Lett.* **210,** 53–63.

Kennett, B. L. N., and E. R. Engdahl (1991). Travel times for global earthquake location and phase association, *Geophys. J. Int.* **105,** 429–465.

Kim, S. J., and S. G. Kim (1983). A study on the crustal structure of South Korea by using seismic waves, *J. Korean Inst. Mining Geol.* **16,** 51–61 (in Korean with English abstract)

Kim, S., J. Rhie, and G. Kim (2011). Forward waveform modelling procedure for 1-D crustal velocity structure and its application to the southern Korean Peninsula, *Geophys. J. Int.* **185,** 453–468.

Kissling, E., W. L. Ellsworth, D. Eberhart-Phillips, and U. Kradolfer (1994). Initial reference models in local earthquake tomography, *J. Geophys. Res.* **99,** 19,635–19,646.

Klein, F. W. (2002). User's guide to HYPOINVERSE-2000, a Fortran program to solve for earthquake locations and magnitudes, *U.S. Geol. Surv. Open-File Rept. 00-224,* 121 pp.

Klose, C. D., and L. Seeber (2007). Shallow seismicity in stable continental regions, *Seismol. Res. Lett.* **78,** 554–564.

Lee, S., A. Saxena, J.-H. Song, J. Rhie, and E. Choi (2022). Contributions from lithospheric and upper-mantle heterogeneities to upper crustal seismicity in the Korean Peninsula, *Geophys. J. Int.* **229,** 1175–1192.

Lomax, A., A. Michelini, and A. Curtis (2009). Earthquake location, direct, global-search methods, in *Encyclopedia of Complexity and Systems Science*, R. Meyers (Editor), Springer, 2449–2473.

Ma, S. (2010). Focal depth determination for moderate and small earthquakes by modeling regional depth phases sPg, sPmP, and sPn, *Bull. Seismol. Soc. Am.* **100,** 1073–1088.

Ma, S., and G. M. Atkinson (2006). Focal depths for small to moderate earthquakes (mN ≥ 2.8) in western Quebec, southern Ontario, and northern New York, *Bull. Seismol. Soc. Am.* **96,** 609–623.

Pavlis, G. L. (1986). Appraising earthquake hypocenter location errors: A complete, practical approach for single-event locations, *Bull. Seismol. Soc. Am.* **76,** 1699–1717.

Rowe, C. A., and C. H. Thurber (1995). Ray tracing calculations and seismic event location using a three-dimensional model., *Bull. Seismol. Soc. Am.* **85,** 735–740.

Scholz, C. H. (1998). Earthquakes and friction laws, *Nature* **391,** 37–42.

Shearer, P. M. (1997). Improving local earthquake locations using waveform cross correlation: Application to the Whittier Narrows, California, earthquake sequence, *J. Geophys. Res.* **102,** no. B4, 8269–8283.

Sheen, D.-H. (2021). Analysis of the 2020 Haenam, Korea, earthquake sequence, *Geosci. J.* **25,** 33–42.

Sibson, R. H. (1982). Fault zone models, heat flow, and the depth distribution of earthquakes in the continental crust of the United States, *Bull. Seismol. Soc. Am.* **72,** 151–163.

Song, J.-H., S. Kim, J. Rhie, and D. Park (2022). Moment tensor solutions for earthquakes in the southern Korean peninsula using three-dimensional seismic waveform simulations, *Front. Earth Sci.*, doi: 10.3389/feart.2022.945022.

Tanaka, A. (2004). Crustal thermal structure and its relationship to seismogenic layer in and around Japan, *Earth Planets Space* **56,** 1195–1199.

Tarantola, A. (1986). A strategy for nonlinear elastic inversion of seismic reflection data, *Geophysics* **51,** 1893–1903.

Wong, I. G., and D. S. Chapman (1990). Deep intraplate earthquakes in the western United States and their relationship to lithospheric temperatures, *Bull. Seismol. Soc. Am.* **80,** 589–599.

Yuan, J., H. Kao, and J. Yu (2020). Depth-scanning algorithm: Accurate, automatic, and efficient determination of focal depths for local and regional earthquakes, *J. Geophys. Res.* **125,** e2020JB019430, doi: 10.1029/2020JB019430.

Zhu, L., and L. A. Rivera (2002). A note on the dynamic and static displacements from a point source in multilayered media, *Geophys. J. Int.* **148,** 619–627.

Zuza, A. V., and W. Cao (2020). Seismogenic thickness of California: Implications for thermal structure and seismic hazard, *Tectonophysics* **782–783,** 228426.

Manuscript received 27 August 2025
Published online 13 February 2026

Ground Motions from Finite Faults with Unknown Geometry

Charles Bruce Worden*[1], Eric Meyer Thompson[2], Harriet Zoe Yin[2], and David Jay Wald[2]

ABSTRACT

Earthquake emergency response and loss modeling require accurate models of ground-motion intensity metrics (IMs), such as those produced by ShakeMap. In the critical minutes and hours after an earthquake, however, knowledge of the earthquake source geometry limits the accuracy of these models, especially in areas where seismic instrumentation is insufficient to constrain the shaking intensity pattern. Previous attempts to overcome this limitation have centered on computing the mean distance metrics from a suite of assumed source geometries. That approach is inadequate with modern ground-motion models (GMMs) because they typically include terms for the hanging wall effect, depth to top of rupture, and other nonlinear terms. Such approaches also propagate the distance uncertainty through the GMMs and may not properly allocate the additional uncertainty into the between- and within-event components. Here we present Finite-Fault SIMulation with Mixed Effects Regression (FFSIMMER), a method to address these limitations by computing IM distributions from a suite of rupture realizations that fully accounts for all geometry-related GMM terms and allows for the separation of the between- and within-event components of the total uncertainty. The accuracy of this method is limited by the available constraints on the source parameters. To address this, FFSIMMER can incorporate constraints based on knowledge of the source, such as the approximate strike and dip based on knowledge of the plate tectonics and focal mechanism of the earthquake. We demonstrate the improvement in accuracy that can be achieved with the 2025 M 7.7 Mandalay, Burma (Myanmar), earthquake by incorporating constraints on the range of plausible source parameters.

OPEN ACCESS

KEY POINTS

- After an earthquake, a lack of knowledge about source geometry limits the accuracy of ground-motion models.
- We address this by modeling ground motions from rupture realizations that align with available information.
- Emergency response efforts benefit from the improved shaking estimates immediately following earthquakes.

INTRODUCTION

U.S. Geological Survey (USGS) earthquake response protocols, including the generation of near real-time earthquake information products such as ShakeMap (Wald *et al.*, 2022), require accurate estimation of ground-motion intensity metrics (IMs) well before a finite-fault model is available (usually hours to a day after the event). IMs for a particular earthquake or magnitude are primarily controlled by the distance to the earthquake rupture surface, so any estimate that is based on distance metrics derived from a point source will have limited accuracy. Directly substituting point-source distances for rupture-surface distances will additionally yield underpredicted IMs because the point-source distance is always larger than the analogous source distance. Prior work to address this issue has focused on adjusting the source-to-site distances used as input to ground-motion models (GMMs).

Electric Power Research Institute, Inc. (EPRI) (2004), for instance, computed distance and uncertainty correction factors for four GMM formulations for the central and eastern United States. The factors sought to provide corrections to epicentral distance that would produce the median IMs at a site for a range of rupture geometries. Harmsen (2008) discussed the computation of average distances for arbitrarily oriented line sources at the surface. Chiou and Youngs (2008) simulated 101 rupture realizations for each point source in the Next Generation Attenuation (NGA) database, and they took the

1. Synergetics Inc., Geologic Hazards Science Center, Golden, Colorado, U.S.A., https://orcid.org/0000-0003-1181-685X (CBW); 2. U.S. Geological Survey, Geologic Hazards Science Center, Golden, Colorado, U.S.A., https://orcid.org/0000-0002-6943-4806 (EMT); https://orcid.org/0000-0002-0670-6579 (HZY); https://orcid.org/0000-0002-1454-4514 (DJW)

*Corresponding author: cbworden@contractor.usgs.gov

Cite this article as Worden, C. B., E. M. Thompson, H. Z. Yin, and D. J. Wald (2026). Ground Motions from Finite Faults with Unknown Geometry, *Bull. Seismol. Soc. Am.* **116**, 1049–1063, doi: 10.1785/0120250179 median values for various parameters, including rupture distance (R_{RUP}), Joyner–Boore distance (R_{JB}; Joyner and Boore, 1981), fault width, and depth to top of rupture (Z_{TOR}). In another approach, Scherbaum *et al.* (2004) used simulations of ruptures to develop conversion factors from point source to rupture distances. Later, Thompson and Worden (2018) developed a method that modeled the mean finite-fault distance by systematically integrating over a range of rupture parameters (strike, dip, area, and position of the fault plane relative to the hypocenter). The process also produced uncertainty of the distance variable that could be propagated through the GMM to account for the additional uncertainty in the IMs that results from the approximation of the distances.

GMMs generally take the form

$$\mathrm{IM}_{ij} = \mu_{\mathrm{IM},ij} + \delta B_{\mathrm{IM},i} + \delta W_{\mathrm{IM},ij}, \quad (1)$$

in which $\mu_{\mathrm{IM},ij}$ is the mean of IM_{ij} and is evaluated with a vector of predictor variables (e.g., magnitude) for the *i*th event and *j*th site. The standard deviation of IM_{ij} is $\sigma_{\mathrm{IM},ij}$, which is decomposed into $\delta B_{\mathrm{IM},i}$ and $\delta W_{\mathrm{IM},ij}$, which are the zero-mean between-event random effect and the remaining within-event residual, respectively. The standard deviation of $\delta B_{\mathrm{IM},i}$ and $\delta W_{\mathrm{IM},ij}$ are τ_{IM} and ϕ_{IM}, respectively. Many IMs are lognormally distributed, in which case the IM is defined with a logarithmic transform (e.g., the natural log of peak ground acceleration [PGA]). A substantial limitation of the approaches discussed previously is that they make the basic assumption that an unbiased IM can be obtained from a GMM by substituting the mean of an uncertain random variable into the GMM for which the GMM was developed, assuming that the variable is known precisely. This approach is only accurate for linear functions, and modern GMMs are highly nonlinear (e.g., Bozorgnia *et al.*, 2014). Thus, simply adjusting the rupture distance supplied to GMMs is insufficient. Recently, Stallone *et al.* (2024) introduced a method that simulates IM uncertainty due to uncertain source parameters with a Monte Carlo approach, but this deviates from the ShakeMap framework in that it does not condition the IM distributions on observed IMs.

We present a new framework for modeling IM distributions in the absence of a known rupture surface. Our goal is to condition the IM distributions to be consistent with as much information as possible regarding the earthquake's size and geometry. We stochastically simulate sets of possible rupture planes, computing the IMs for each rupture realization and working with the distribution of IMs rather than the distribution of distances. This approach is analogous to the event-based approach to probabilistic seismic hazard analysis in OpenQuake (Pagani *et al.*, 2014) and avoids any assumptions on the linearity of the GMMs with respect to distance and estimates the contribution of the uncertainty into the within- and between-event standard deviations. We call this new approach Finite-Fault SIMulation with Mixed Effects Regression (FFSIMMER). By default, the distribution of rupture orientation parameters (e.g., strike and dip) is extremely broad because few constraints are reasonable in an automated system. Therefore, we then describe how the rupture orientation parameter distributions can be constrained during the response to an earthquake to achieve more accurate IM estimates.

METHODOLOGY

We seek to find the mean and standard deviation of the IMs from a suite of possible ruptures that are consistent with an earthquake's magnitude, depth, source mechanism (if available), and tectonic setting (active, stable, or subduction). This diverges from prior approaches that have sought to find distance adjustments that may be used as inputs to the GMMs. We represent each possible rupture as a single rupture plane, which we will refer to as a rupture plane realization. Because we produce the IMs for each rupture plane realization via GMM estimates, we fully account for GMM terms that require knowledge of the rupture, such as hanging wall and depth to top of rupture terms.

Rupture plane realizations

We use a simple approach to generate suites of rupture plane realizations. Figure 1 illustrates the parameters that define the geometry of a rupture plane. For each realization, we make several assumptions to construct rupture planes consistent with the earthquake origin, tectonic environment, and mechanism (if available). These assumptions include a magnitude–area scaling relationship (Table 1), minimum and maximum fault dip, and an initial aspect ratio for the fault.

We drew realizations of the rupture plane strike from a uniform distribution from zero to 360°, and the dip (δ_i) from a uniform distribution with limits based on the tectonic region and mechanism given in Table 1. For active crustal regions (ACRs), we inspected the range of dip angles by mechanism in the Next Generation Attenuation West version 2 (NGA-West2) database (Ancheta *et al.*, 2013, 2014) and selected approximate representative ranges, as summarized in Table 1. For stable continental regions (SCRs), we used the range in dips for each mechanism reported in the Central and Eastern United States Seismic Source Characterization (CEUS-SSC) (2012) project report. Following Mai *et al.* (2005), we select the along-strike fractional position of the hypocenter (dy) from a truncated normal distribution with a mean of 0.5 and standard deviation 0.23 along the fault length from 0 to L (Fig. 1).

For ACRs with a known earthquake mechanism, we use the Hanks and Bakun (2008) magnitude–area scaling relationship. When the earthquake mechanism is unknown for ACRs, we use Wells and Coppersmith (1994). For SCRs, we use the Somerville (2014) magnitude–area scaling relationship. For shallow crustal earthquakes in subduction zones, we use the same relationship as ACRs. For interface and slab subduction events, we use Thingbaijam *et al.* (2017) when the mechanism

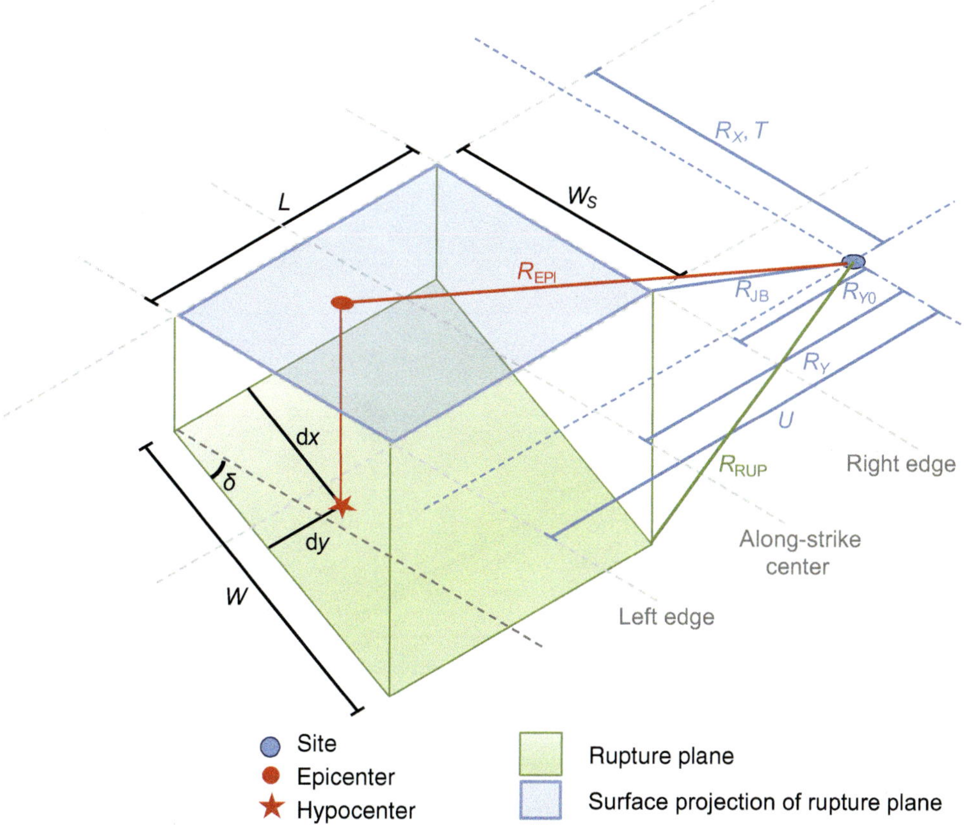

Figure 1. Illustration of geometry parameters for a single-segment rupture plane, showing the hypocenter, epicenter, and a site location. L is the along-strike rupture length, W is the down-dip rupture width, δ is the dip, W_S is the surface projection of the fault width, dx is the fractional strike-normal position of the hypocenter on the rupture plane, and dy is the fractional strike-parallel position of the hypocenter on the rupture plane; R_{JB}, R_{EPI}, and R_{RUP} are the Joyner–Boore, epicentral, and closest distance to rupture, respectively. R_X and T are the strike-normal site coordinate; R_Y, U, and R_{Y0} are strike-parallel coordinates with different definitions of the origin. Refer to Ancheta *et al.* (2013) and Spudich and Chiou (2015) for additional details of these distance definitions.

is known and Strasser *et al.* (2010) when the mechanism is unknown. Table 1 summarizes these assumptions. Using the selected scaling relation from Table 1, we compute the rupture area mean (μ_A). We note that the scaling relations also provide a standard deviation (σ_A) from the earthquake magnitude, assuming that the rupture area is distributed as $\log_{10}(A) \sim \mathcal{N}(\mu_A, \sigma_A^2)$. However, we do not select from this distribution and only use the mean to be consistent with the practices of the USGS National Seismic Hazard Model (NSHM) project (refer to table 13 in Field *et al.*, 2014). For the ith rupture plane realization (RP_i), we calculate the rupture length (L_i) and width (W_i) from the rupture area realization (A_i) and an assumed initial aspect ratio (length/width). We compute the initial aspect ratio with the equations developed by Huang *et al.* (2024), which are based on event magnitude and fault dip. For events below a cutoff magnitude (which depends on the fault dip), the aspect ratio is constant (~1.3). For larger events, the aspect ratio increases linearly with magnitude (equations 2 and 3 in Huang *et al.*, 2024). Here, we use the term "initial" because the aspect ratio can be modified subsequently based on seismogenic zone constraints.

Because the hypocentral depth (Z_H) is at times poorly constrained (Yeck *et al.*, 2025), we draw realizations ($Z_{H,i}$) from a normal distribution with mean Z_H and standard deviation 10 km with the constraint that it is not less than zero nor greater than the maximum seismogenic depth (SZ_{MAX}). We selected the standard deviation of Z_H based on consultation with the USGS National Earthquake Information Center (NEIC; P. Earle, written comm., 2024).

The maximum depth of the seismogenic zone additionally constrains W_i. First, we check whether the height of the rupture plane exceeds the seismogenic zone thickness. If it does, we adjust W_i to fill the seismogenic zone and then recompute L_i from A_i and the updated W_i. We assume the seismogenic depth range is 0–20 km for ACRs based on the hypocentral depth range in the NGA-West2 database (Ancheta *et al.*, 2014) and 0–15 km for SCRs based on the CEUS-SSC (2012) report (Table 1). To ensure the depth to the bottom of the rupture realization does not exceed SZ_{MAX}, we compute the minimum allowable down-dip distance

$$dx_{\mathrm{MIN}} = \max\left(0, W_i - \frac{SZ_{\mathrm{MAX}} - Z_{H,i}}{\sin(\delta_i)}\right). \quad (2)$$

Similarly, to ensure the depth to the top of the rupture realization ($Z_{\mathrm{TOR},i}$) is not less than the minimum seismogenic depth (SZ_{MIN}), we compute the maximum allowable down-dip distance

$$dx_{\mathrm{MAX}} = \min\left(W_i, W_i - \frac{W_i \sin(\delta_i) - Z_{H,i}}{\sin(\delta_i)}\right). \quad (3)$$

We then generate realizations of the down-dip coordinate (dx_i) from a Weibull distribution based on Mai *et al.* (2005). They showed that the distribution of dx (from a fractional

TABLE 1
Rupture Plane Assumptions That Vary by Tectonic Region and Mechanism

Tectonic Region	Subregion	Mech.	M-A Reference	Seis. Range (km)	Dip (deg) U(*a*, *b*)
ACR		All	Wells and Coppersmith (1994)	0–20	U(35, 90)
		N	Hanks and Bakun (2008)	0–20	U(40, 60)
		R	Hanks and Bakun (2008)	0–20	U(35, 50)
		SS	Hanks and Bakun (2008)	0–20	U(75, 90)
SCR		All	Somerville (2014)	0–15	U(35. 90)
		N	Somerville (2014)	0–15	U(40, 60)
		R	Somerville (2014)	0–15	U(35, 50)
		SS	Somerville (2014)	0–15	U(75, 90)
Sub	Crustal	All	Wells and Coppersmith (1994)	0–20	U(35, 90)
		N	Hanks and Bakun (2008)	0–20	U(40, 60)
		R	Hanks and Bakun (2008)	0–20	U(35, 50)
		SS	Hanks and Bakun (2008)	0–20	U(75, 90)
	Interface	R	Thingbaijam *et al.* (2017)	0–55	U(35, 50)
	Slab	All	Strasser *et al.* (2010)	0–Inf	U(35, 90)
		N	Thingbaijam *et al.* (2017)	0–Inf	U(40, 60)
		R	Thingbaijam *et al.* (2017)	0–Inf	U(35, 50)
		SS	Thingbaijam *et al.* (2017)	0–Inf	U(75, 90)

ACR, active crustal region; M-A, magnitude–area relationship; Mech., source mechanism; N, normal faulting; R, reverse faulting; SCR, stable continental region; Seis. range, seismogenic zone depth range; SS, strike-slip faulting; Sub, subduction region; U(*a*, *b*), uniformly distributed from *a* to *b*.

parameter of zero to one) follows a Weibull distribution with a scale parameter of 0.612 and a shape parameter of 3.353.

Ground-motion IM realizations

For each rupture plane realization RP_i, we calculate distance metrics to site j, including R_{RUP} (the rupture distance, i.e., the closest distance to the fault), R_{JB} (the Joyner–Boore distance, i.e., the distance to the surface projection of the fault plane; Joyner and Boore, 1981), the strike-normal distances (R_X, T), and the strike-parallel distances (R_Y, U, R_{Y0}; Spudich and Chiou, 2015). Along with Z_{TOR}, we use these parameters to evaluate the $\mu_{IM,ij}$. GMM inputs that are not defined relative to the source create an additional complication. This includes the time-averaged shear-wave velocity to 30 m depth (V_{S30}) and basin depth parameters such as the depth to the 1 km/s shear-wave velocity horizon ($Z_{1.0}$). There are two different ways in which we handle the site terms: (1) using reference V_{S30} and $Z_{1.0}$ values in evaluating the site and basin terms, and (2) using site-specific estimates of V_{S30} and $Z_{1.0}$. The first option is more efficient because it simplifies the problem to one dimension: the event-specific GMM is constructed from the simulated rupture planes, and the distributions in the grid are conditioned only on epicentral distance. This 1D representation of the GMM is then applied to the 2D grid of sites via interpolation and subsequent application of site amplification terms. The downside of this approach is that site-specific effects must be accounted for with a subsequent step, after the distributional parameters of the IM are estimated. In contrast, the second option simulates the IM distribution for each site in the 2D grid and so it is more computationally expensive. The benefit of this approach is that the estimated site-specific parameters are used in the calculation of the IMs for each site prior to reducing the results into distributional parameters.

This process is repeated for multiple realizations (subscript i, count n) of the rupture and multiple sites (subscript j, count m). We then compute the mean and standard deviation of the $\mu_{IM,ij}$ realizations at each site, $\langle \mu_{IM,i} \rangle_j$ and $\sigma_{\mu,j}$, respectively. Figure 2 illustrates this process for the PGA IM and a generic **M** 7.0 earthquake with a 10 km hypocentral depth. The figure includes 50 $\mu_{IM,ij}$ realizations (colored lines), $\langle \mu_{IM,i} \rangle_j$ (black line), and the $\langle \mu_{IM,i} \rangle_j \pm \Delta\sigma_{\mu,j}$ region (shaded area). These realizations demonstrate that the additional uncertainty due to the unknown rupture geometry is heteroscedastic.

For a given IM, we define the residual due to the uncertainty in the rupture geometry as $R_{\mu,ij} = \mu_{IM,ij} - \langle \mu_{IM,i} \rangle_j$ and apply mixed-effects regression to estimate the between- and within-event terms

$$R_{\mu,ij} = \delta B_{\mu,i} + \delta W_{\mu,ij}, \quad (4)$$

in which $\delta B_{\mu,i}$ is the zero-mean between-event residual term with standard deviation τ_μ, $\delta W_{\mu,ij}$ is the zero-mean within-event residual term with standard deviation ϕ_μ, and total residual variance is $\sigma_\mu^2 = \phi_\mu^2 + \tau_\mu^2$.

It turns out that it is more convenient to apply the law of total variance to estimate τ_μ and ϕ_μ, which is given by

$$\mathrm{Var}(Y) = E[\mathrm{Var}(Y|X)] + \mathrm{Var}(E[Y|X]), \quad (5)$$

in which $\mathrm{Var}(Y)$ is the total variance of the random variable Y, that is, the residuals $R_{\mu,ij}$, $E[\mathrm{Var}(Y|X)]$ is the expected value of the variance of Y given the random variable X, and $\mathrm{Var}(E[Y|X])$

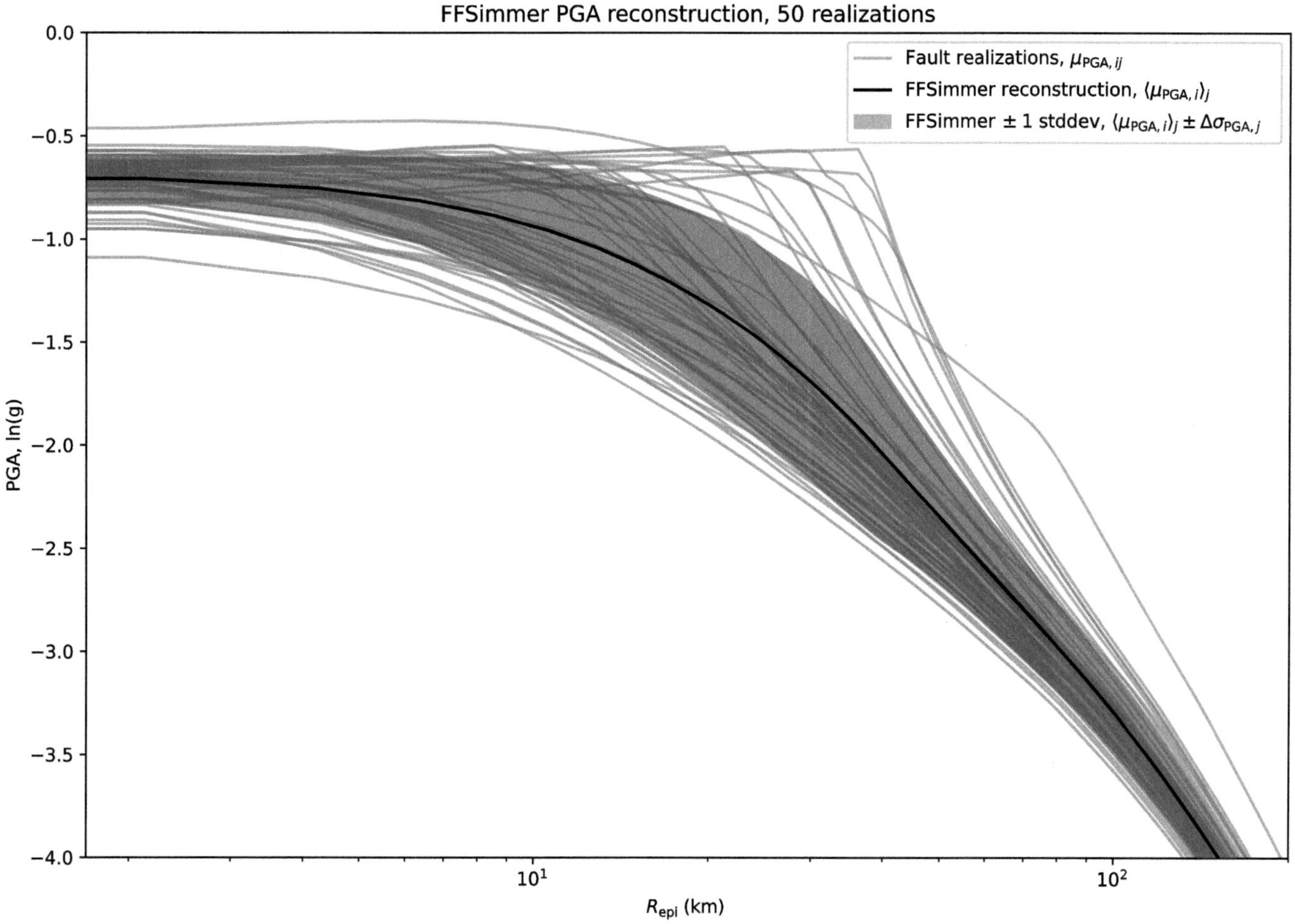

Figure 2. A set of peak ground acceleration (PGA) realizations ($\mu_{IM,ij}$) as a function of epicentral distance ("R_{epi}") from 50 faults for an **M** 7.0 earthquake at 10 km depth. The black line is the mean of the realizations ($\langle\mu_{IM,i}\rangle_j$). The magenta band shows the mean plus or minus 1 standard deviation ("stddev"; $\Delta\sigma_{\mu,ij}$, see derivation in the Ground-motion IM realizations section). "FFSimmer" refers to the method described in this article. FFSimmer, Finite-Fault SIMulation with Mixed Effects Regression. The color version of this figure is available only in the electronic edition.

is the variance of the expected value of Y given X. In this context, X is the different rupture plane realizations (i.e., RP_i), and so $\mathrm{Var}(E[Y|X])$ (i.e., the group variance) is that part of the total variance that is explained by the between-event variance (i.e., τ_μ^2). $E[\mathrm{Var}(Y|X)]$ is the residual variance, or that part of the total variance that is unexplained by the grouping, that is, ϕ_μ^2.

The mean of the $R_{\mu,ij}$ residuals across all locations j is $\langle R_{\mu,j}\rangle_i$ and the mean of $R_{\mu,ij}$ across all realizations i and locations j is $\langle R_{\mu,ij}\rangle$. Thus, the total variance of the GMM predicted mean (equation 5) can be restated as

$$\sigma_\mu^2 = \mathrm{Var}(R_{\mu,ij}) = E[\mathrm{Var}(R_{\mu,ij}|\mathrm{RP}_i)] + \mathrm{Var}(E[R_{\mu,ij}|\mathrm{RP}_i]), \quad (6)$$

which can be evaluated as

$$\sigma_\mu^2 = \frac{1}{n}\sum_{i=1}^{n}\frac{1}{m}\sum_{j=1}^{m}(R_{\mu,ij} - \langle R_{\mu,j}\rangle_i)^2 + \frac{1}{n}\sum_{i=1}^{n}(\langle R_{\mu,j}\rangle_i - \langle R_{\mu,ij}\rangle)^2, \quad (7)$$

and includes two terms:

$$\phi_\mu^2 = \frac{1}{n}\sum_{i=1}^{n}\frac{1}{m}\sum_{j=1}^{m}(R_{\mu,ij} - \langle R_{\mu,j}\rangle_i)^2, \quad (8)$$

$$\tau_\mu^2 = \frac{1}{n}\sum_{i=1}^{n}(\langle R_{\mu,j}\rangle_i - \langle R_{\mu,ij}\rangle)^2. \quad (9)$$

We define the variance of the IM at each site, $\mathrm{Var}(R_{\mu,j}|\mathrm{RP}_i)$, across all realizations as $\sigma_{\mu,j}^2$. The site variance can then be decomposed into its group (between-event) and residual (within-event) variances:

$$\Delta\tau_{\mu,j}^2 = \frac{\tau_\mu^2}{\sigma_\mu^2}\sigma_{\mu,j}^2, \quad (10)$$

$$\Delta\phi_{\mu,j}^2 = \frac{\phi_\mu^2}{\sigma_\mu^2}\sigma_{\mu,j}^2, \quad (11)$$

$$\Delta\sigma_{\mu,j}^2 = \Delta\phi_{\mu,j}^2 + \Delta\tau_{\mu,j}^2, \quad (12)$$

in which $\Delta\tau_{\mu,j}^2$ is the additional between-event variance at each site and $\Delta\phi_{\mu,j}^2$ is the additional within-event variance at each site due to the rupture plane uncertainty. Although the decomposition is an approximation, it allows us to accommodate variance in the IMs as a function of site due to the ensemble of rupture plane realizations. These terms are added to the between- and within-event variances of the GMM(s) to produce a total between- and within-event standard deviation of the ground motion for each site:

$$\tau^*_{\mathrm{IM},j} = \sqrt{\tau^2_{\mathrm{IM},j} + \Delta\tau^2_{\mu,j}}, \tag{13}$$

and

$$\phi^*_{\mathrm{IM},j} = \sqrt{\phi^2_{\mathrm{IM},j} + \Delta\phi^2_{\mu,j}}, \tag{14}$$

in which $\tau_{\mathrm{IM},j}$ is the between-event standard deviation of the GMM, $\phi_{\mathrm{IM},j}$ is the within-event standard deviation of the GMM, and $\tau^*_{\mathrm{IM},j}$ and $\phi^*_{\mathrm{IM},j}$ are the total between- and within-event standard deviation at each point. Thus, the final within- and between-event variances are heteroscedastic even if the GMM uncertainties themselves are homoscedastic.

Finally, the total standard deviation of the process, including the unknown rupture model is

$$\sigma^*_{\mathrm{IM},j} = \sqrt{(\tau^*_{\mathrm{IM},j})^2 + (\phi^*_{\mathrm{IM},j})^2}. \tag{15}$$

RESULTS

We begin by comparing the FFSIMMER method to prior methods to account for unknown rupture geometry. Then, we assess the performance of the alternative methods. Finally, we demonstrate how the default distribution parameters of FFSIMMER can be constrained when additional information can be inferred about the earthquake.

Comparison of alternative methods

We compare estimates of the mean PGA for a point source (i.e., substituting epicentral distance for R_{JB} and hypocentral distance for R_{RUP}), the EPRI (2004) distance adjustments, the Thompson and Worden (2018), hereafter "PS2FF," distance adjustments, and FFSIMMER assuming 10 km deep generic earthquakes with magnitudes 5, 6.5, and 8 (Fig. 3). Figure 3a,c,e is for a GMM (Boore *et al.*, 2014) that uses R_{JB}, and Figure 3b,d,f is for a GMM (Abrahamson *et al.*, 2014) that uses R_{RUP} as the primary distance metric (Fig. 3).

Figure 3 indicates that FFSIMMER PGA tends to be higher than the corresponding point source at medium to long distances (>20 km), whereas that's not always the case at short distances. For **M** 5 and 6.5, the EPRI and PS2FF methods tend to overestimate the near-source PGA due to limitations in the approaches for the R_{RUP}-based GMM (Fig. 3b,d,f). At **M** 8, the larger PGAs from FFSIMMER at short distances are likely because the rupture realizations nearly always reach the surface due to the large size of the rupture planes. Figure 4 uses the same rupture assumptions and GMMs as Figure 3 but changes the IM to be the 1.0 s spectral acceleration [SA(1.0)], and it exhibits similar trends as PGA.

Performance assessment

To evaluate the performance of FFSIMMER, we compared its results and those of other methods to the IMs from a set of earthquakes in the NGA-West 2 data set (Ancheta *et al.*, 2014). To focus the performance metrics on data sensitive to the rupture geometry, we select events with a magnitude of at least 6.0 and with at least 20 records. From that subset, we kept only the events that have a finite-fault model in the ShakeMap Atlas (Marano *et al.*, 2023). These criteria yield 30 events and a total of 4291 records. We then computed IM residuals with five methods: assuming a point source, assuming a known finite fault, using the EPRI distance corrections to a point source, using the PS2FF distance corrections to a point source, and using FFSIMMER. We calculated residuals for PGA, peak ground velocity (PGV), and SA at 21 periods from 0.01 to 10.0 s based on the spectral periods used by the USGS's NSHM project (Petersen *et al.*, 2024). The GMM is an equally weighted combination of four NGA-West2 models: Abrahamson *et al.* (2014), Boore *et al.* (2014), Campbell and Bozorgnia (2014), and Chiou and Youngs (2014). Once the residuals were computed for each method and each IM, we applied a mixed-effects regression to determine the intercept (bias), group variance (i.e., the between-event variance), and residual variance (i.e., the within-event variance). The results are shown in Figure 5.

From Figure 5a, we can see that the finite fault provides the lowest overall bias, which could be expected given that rupture geometry exerts a strong influence on the IMs. Therefore, we use the finite-fault results as the baseline against which we compare the other methods. In other words, we cannot expect the approximations of the rupture geometry to perform better than the finite-fault results. The point-source method significantly underpredicts the IMs by about 0.35 natural log units on average, or about 42%. The EPRI and PS2FF approaches improve on the point-source approach with an underprediction of about 0.2 units, or about 22%, relative to the finite-fault results. FFSIMMER, on the other hand, predicts more accurate PGA, PGV, and the higher-frequency SAs, underpredicting by about 0.1 units, or around 10%.

Figure 5b shows the group variance. This is equivalent to the between-event variance of GMMs. The finite fault produces the greatest group variance because each event is better fit than with the other models. In other words, for a fixed total variance, a better-fitting model will have more variance assigned to the model (group) variance and less to the residual variance. The other models perform similarly to one another. This result is reasonable considering that they are only approximations based upon on-average statistics. Figure 5c shows the residual variance of the models and metrics—the equivalent of the within-event variance of GMMs. Here the finite-fault model produces the lowest residual variance, whereas the EPRI,

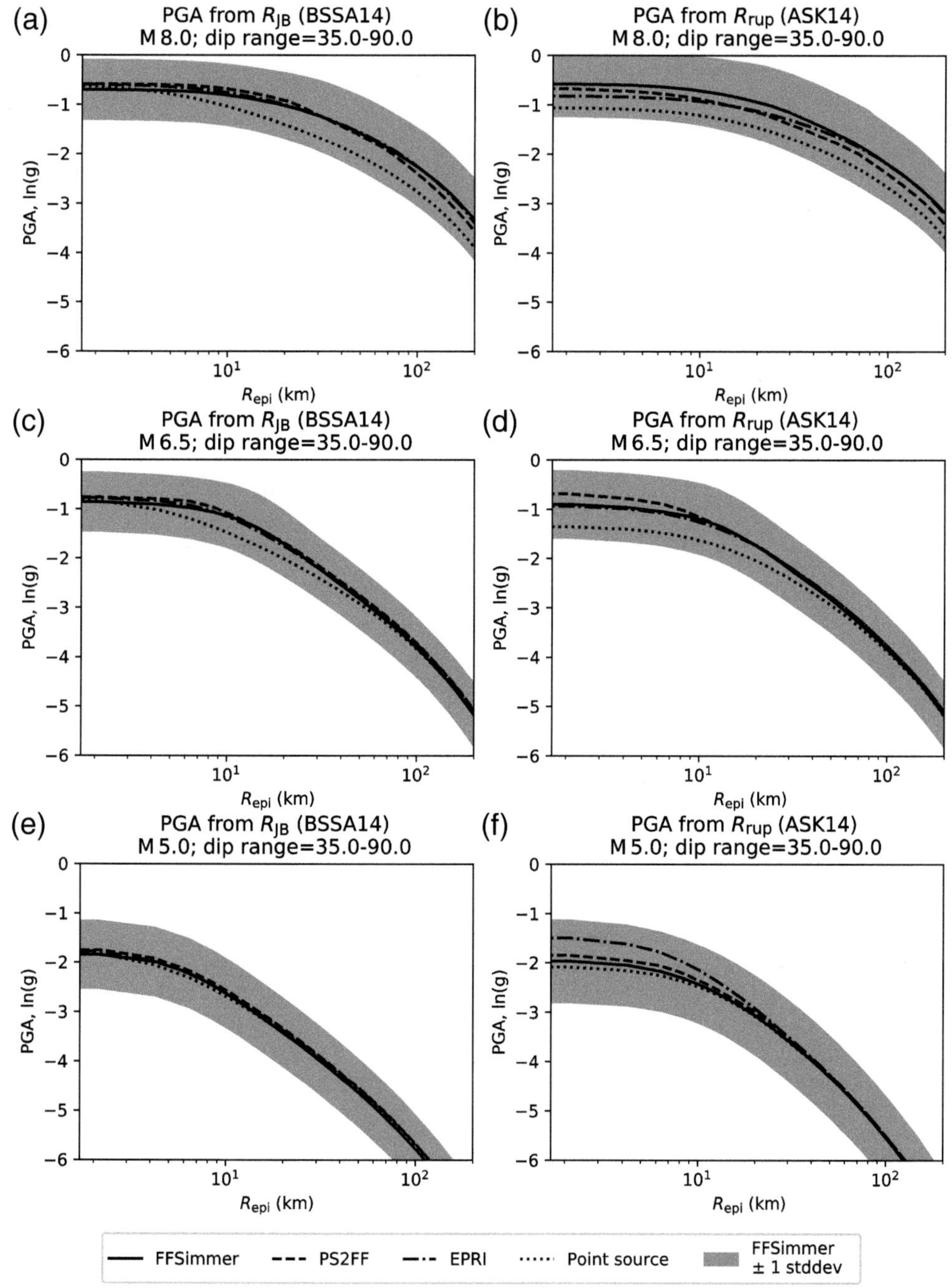

Figure 3. Mean predicted PGA as a function of epicentral distance ("R_{epi}") for magnitudes (a,b) 8, (c.d) 6.5, and (e, f) 5 and hypocentral depth of 10 km, derived from (a,c,e) a ground-motion model (GMM; Boore *et al.*, 2014, "BSSA14") that uses Joyner–Boore distance (Joyner and Boore, 1981, R_{JB}), and (b,d,f) a GMM (Abrahamson *et al.*, 2014, "ASK14") that uses closest distance to rupture (R_{RUP}). Results are shown for a point source, the distance formulations of EPRI (2004) and Thompson and Worden (2018, "PS2FF"), and FFSIMMER (the method described herein). The shaded bands show the FFSIMMER mean PGA plus and minus one standard deviation ("stddev"; $\sigma^*_{PGA,j}$). EPRI, Electric Power Research Institute.

PS2FF, and FFSIMMER show a smaller improvement over the point source. Again, this can be reasonably anticipated by the improvement in the overall fit suggested by Figure 5a.

FFSIMMER is not appreciably different from the EPRI and PS2FF models in terms of group or residual variance. This result suggests that although FFSIMMER provides a better on-average bias than the EPRI, PS2FF, or point-source methods, it is not uniformly better across events. Indeed, Figures 6 and 7 show the individual bias results of 8 of the 30 events (we chose the events with the most data). In some cases, FFSIMMER is consistent with the finite fault, but in other situations it is greater or less than the finite-fault bias. It is, however, on average, a better predictor of IMs than the point source or the EPRI or PS2FF methods, as shown by Figure 5a.

Constraints on source geometry

The primary application for FFSIMMER is in the first minutes to hours after an earthquake when few data are available to constrain the source beyond its initial location. However, in some cases, enough is known about the tectonic region, and enough preliminary data are available, to provide constraints on the early representation of the source. This can be especially valuable for large (**M** 7+) events for which the fault length plays a primary role in the spatial distribution of IMs. Others have developed workflows to identify causative fault planes in near-real time (e.g., Evans *et al.*, 2020; Böse *et al.*, 2024); however, these approaches typically rely on early instrumental data availability. Here, we explore simple modifications to the FFSIMMER assumptions that can be applied on an ad hoc basis to improve IM estimates for **M** 7+ events in which we are confident enough to further constrain the rupture geometry. We use the recent **M** 7.7 Mandalay, Burma (Myanmar), earthquake to illustrate this workflow.

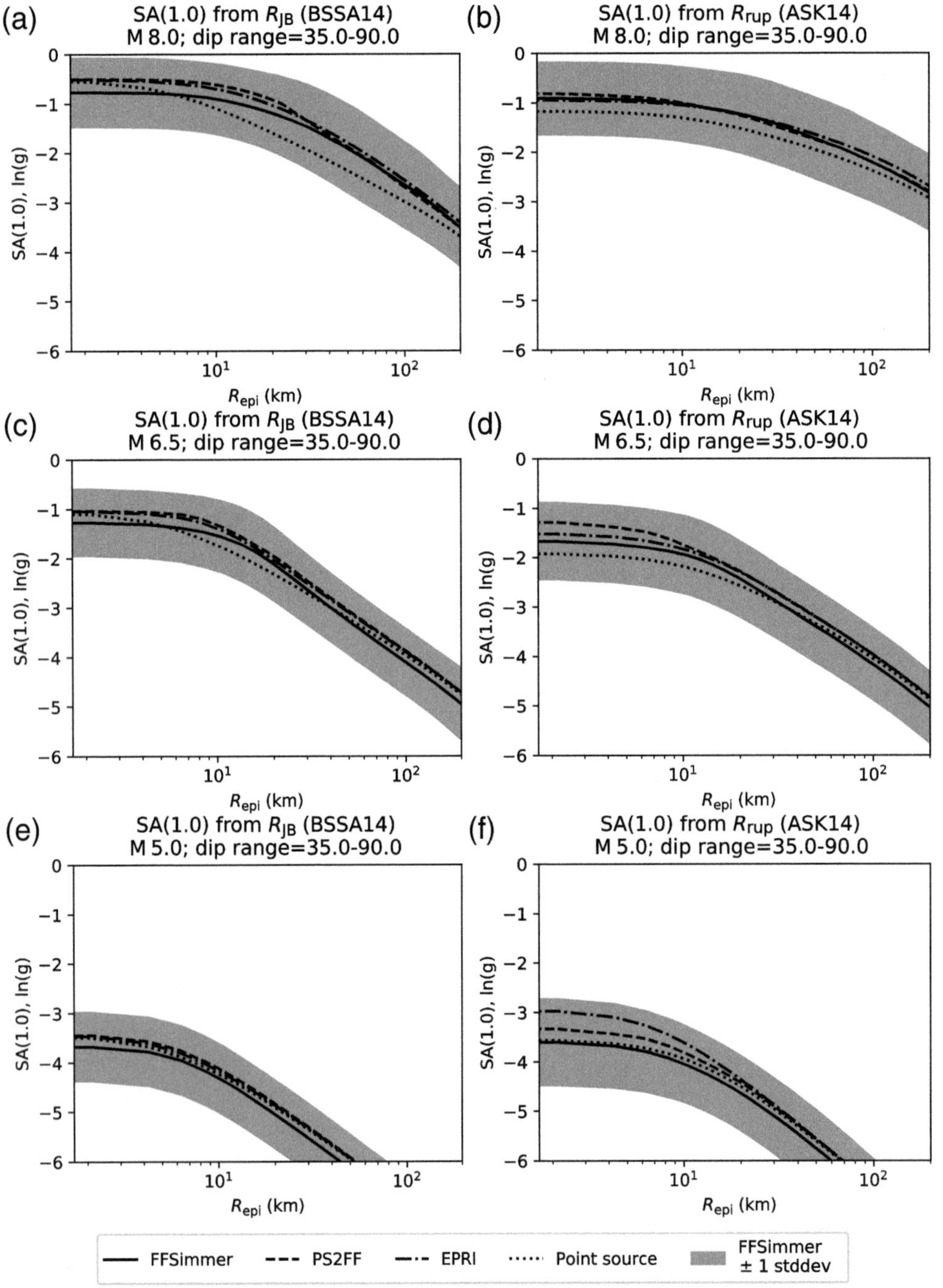

Figure 4. 1.0 s spectral acceleration [SA(1.0)] as a function of epicentral distance ("R_{epi}") from earthquakes of magnitude (a,b) 8, (c,d) 6.5, and (e,f) 5 and a hypocentral depth of 10 km, derived from (a,c,e) a GMM (Boore *et al.*, 2014, "BSSA14") that uses Joyner–Boore distance (Joyner and Boore, 1981, R_{RUP}), and (b,d,f) a GMM (Abrahamson *et al.*, 2014, "ASK14") that uses closest distance to rupture (R_{RUP}). Results are shown for a point source, the distance formulations of EPRI (2004) and Thompson and Worden (2018, "PS2FF"), and FFSIMMER (the method described herein). The shaded bands show the FFSIMMER mean SA(1.0) plus and minus one standard deviation ("stddev"; $\sigma^*_{SA(1.0),j}$).

For this event, the hypocenter coincided with the well-documented hazardous strike-slip Sagaing fault (Johnson *et al.*, 2023) with a north–south orientation (Fig. 8a). The early NEIC centroid moment tensor (CMT; USGS, 2017) solution (Fig. 8a) is consistent with the interpretation of rupture of the north–south, near-vertical fault. The north–south CMT nodal plane has a strike of 1° and a dip of 82°, which we use to constrain the FFSIMMER source representation. We selected the north–south nodal plane based on and its consistency with the geometry of the Sagaing fault. We place no constraints on the fractional along-strike distance (dy) because no evidence was available at the time shortly after the earthquake to indicate a preferred directionality of the rupture plane from the hypocenter. It later became clear that the rupture extended primarily to the south of the hypocenter.

For this event, we compare four distinct source representations to illustrate the improvements that the FFSIMMER algorithm can provide relative to a point source and the full finite fault (Fig. 8). To focus the comparisons on the sensitivity to the source representation, we exclude observation data (i.e., the IMs are not conditioned upon instrumental recordings or "Did You Feel It?" data). The "true point-source" result (Fig. 8b) directly substitutes point-source distances for rupture-surface distances into the GMMs. The "FFSIMMER unconstrained" source (Fig. 8c) employs the algorithm described in this article with the default assumptions in Table 1. Figure 8c also shows the up-dip traces of the corresponding 50 rupture plane realizations, with strike and dip ranges of 0°–360° and 75°–90°, respectively (Table 1). This FFSIMMER unconstrained source is the same as was used in the initial ShakeMap for this event that was produced about 23 min after the origin. The "FFSIMMER constrained" source (Fig. 8e) also generates rupture realizations for computing the IMs; however, the strike

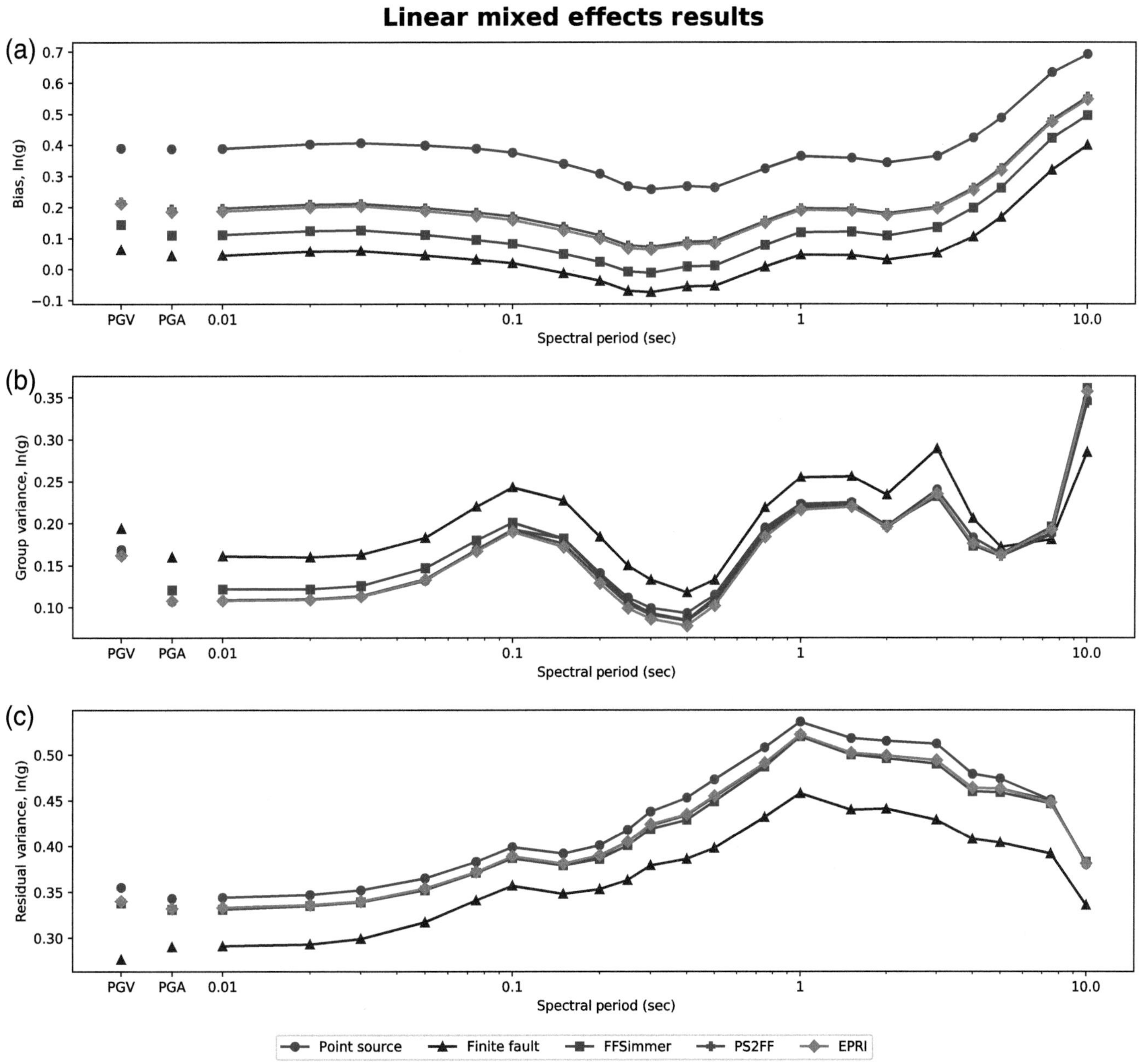

Figure 5. Results of the mixed-effects regression on 30 events for the specified ground-motion metrics: (a) intercept (bias), (b) group variance, and (c) residual variance. PGV is the peak ground velocity. The units for PGV values plotted are ln(cm/s), not ln(g) as indicated. Results are shown for five alternative earthquake source representations: a point source, the distance formulations of EPRI (2004), the distance formations of Thompson and Worden (2018, "PS2FF"), FFSIMMER (the method described in this article), and directly computing distances from a finite fault. The color version of this figure is available only in the electronic edition.

and dip are set to 1° and 82°, respectively. The "final fault geometry" source (Fig. 8f) uses the most recent source representation. The rupture geometry used by ShakeMap evolves with time; the first version was based on teleseismic waveform inversion and was included about 3 hr after the origin. This was refined with time, and the most recent version is based on a detailed fault trace determined several days after the event origin using satellite observations of the surface rupture (Reitman *et al.*, 2025). Although the main goal of FFSIMMER is to produce more realistic shaking distributions rapidly following an earthquake, this approach can be used to understand how these changes to shaking distribution can affect downstream impact estimates from the Prompt Assessment of Global Earthquakes for Response (PAGER) model (Wald *et al.*, 2010). To illustrate the sensitivity of impact estimates to the source representation, Figure 8d shows estimated fatalities for each source representation. Impact estimates have implications for emergency response, particularly in a large and damaging event like the recent Burma (Myanmar) earthquake.

DISCUSSION

The FFSIMMER software allows the user to compute IMs and their uncertainties in three ways: (1) a set of individual points

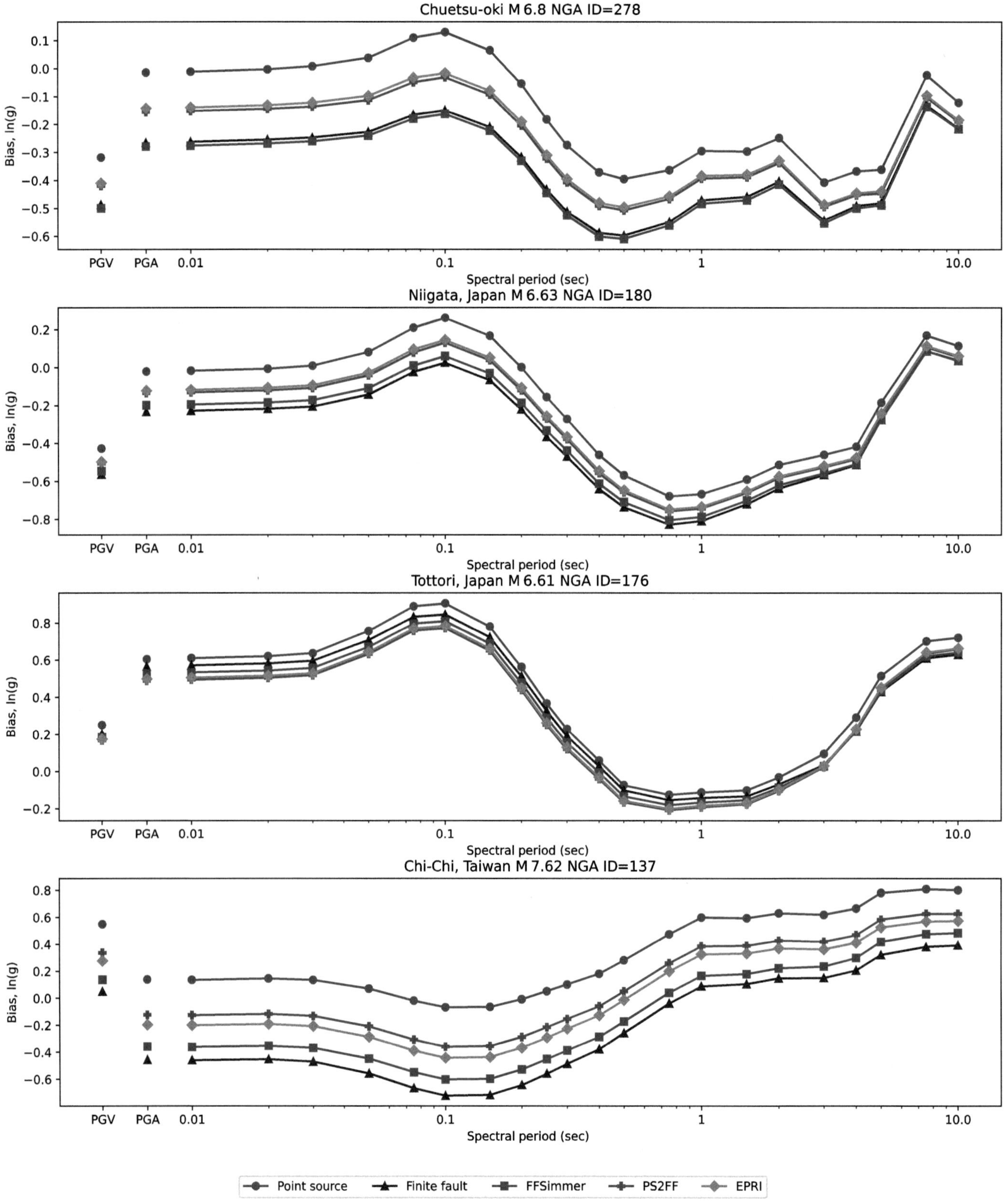

Figure 6. Mean residual bias for four example events used in the analysis using five alternative earthquake source representations: a point source, the distance formulations of EPRI (2004), the distance formations of Thompson and Worden (2018, "PS2FF"), FFSIMMER (the method described in this article), and directly computing distances from a finite fault. The units for PGV values plotted are ln(cm/s), not ln(g) as indicated. NGA, Next Generation Attenuation. The color version of this figure is available only in the electronic edition.

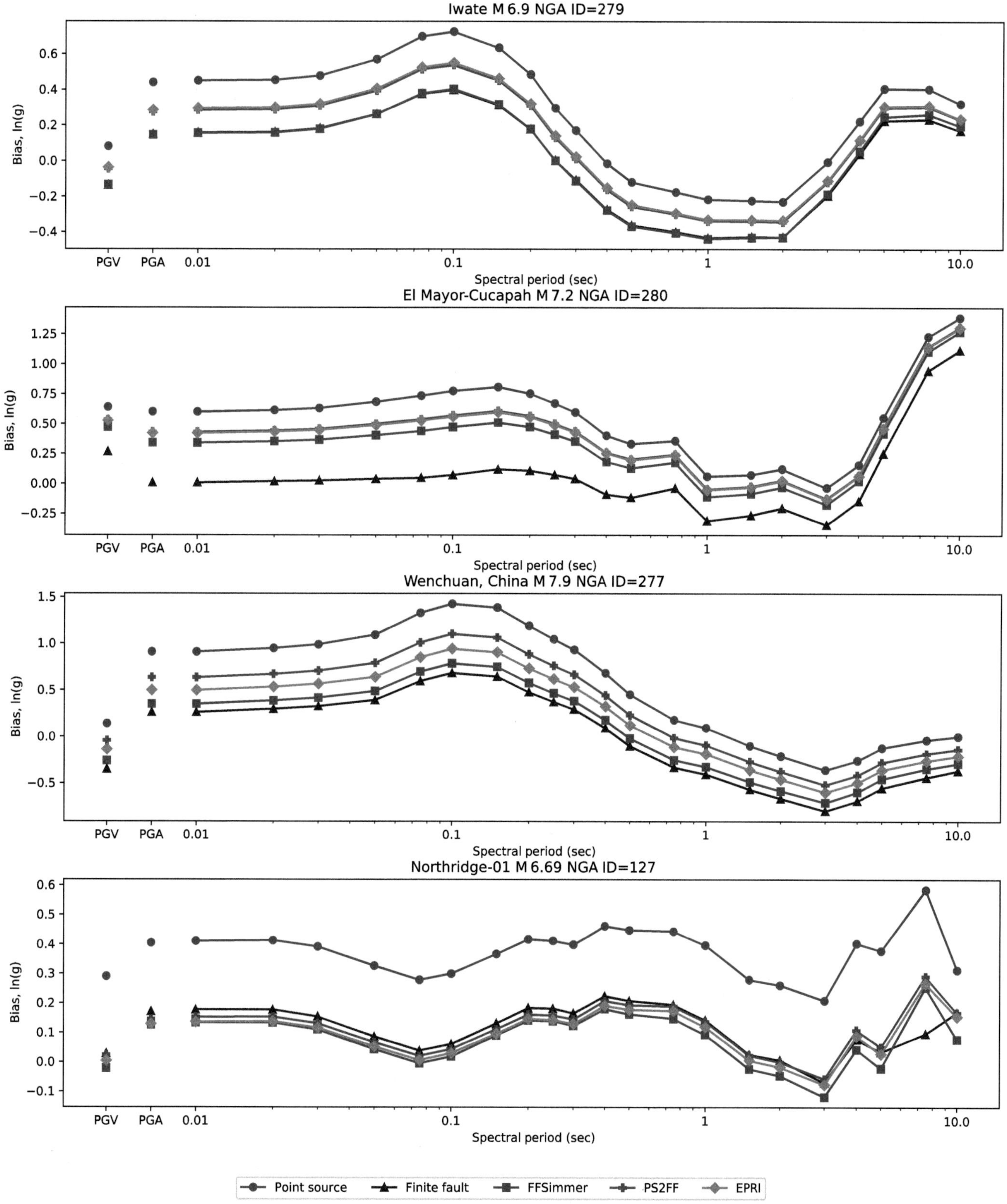

Figure 7. Mean residual bias for four example events used in the analysis using five alternative earthquake source representations: a point source, the distance formulations of EPRI (2004), the distance formations of Thompson and Worden (2018, "PS2FF"), FFSIMMER (the method described in this article), and directly computing distances from a finite fault. The units for PGV values plotted are ln(cm/s), not ln(g) as indicated. The color version of this figure is available only in the electronic edition.

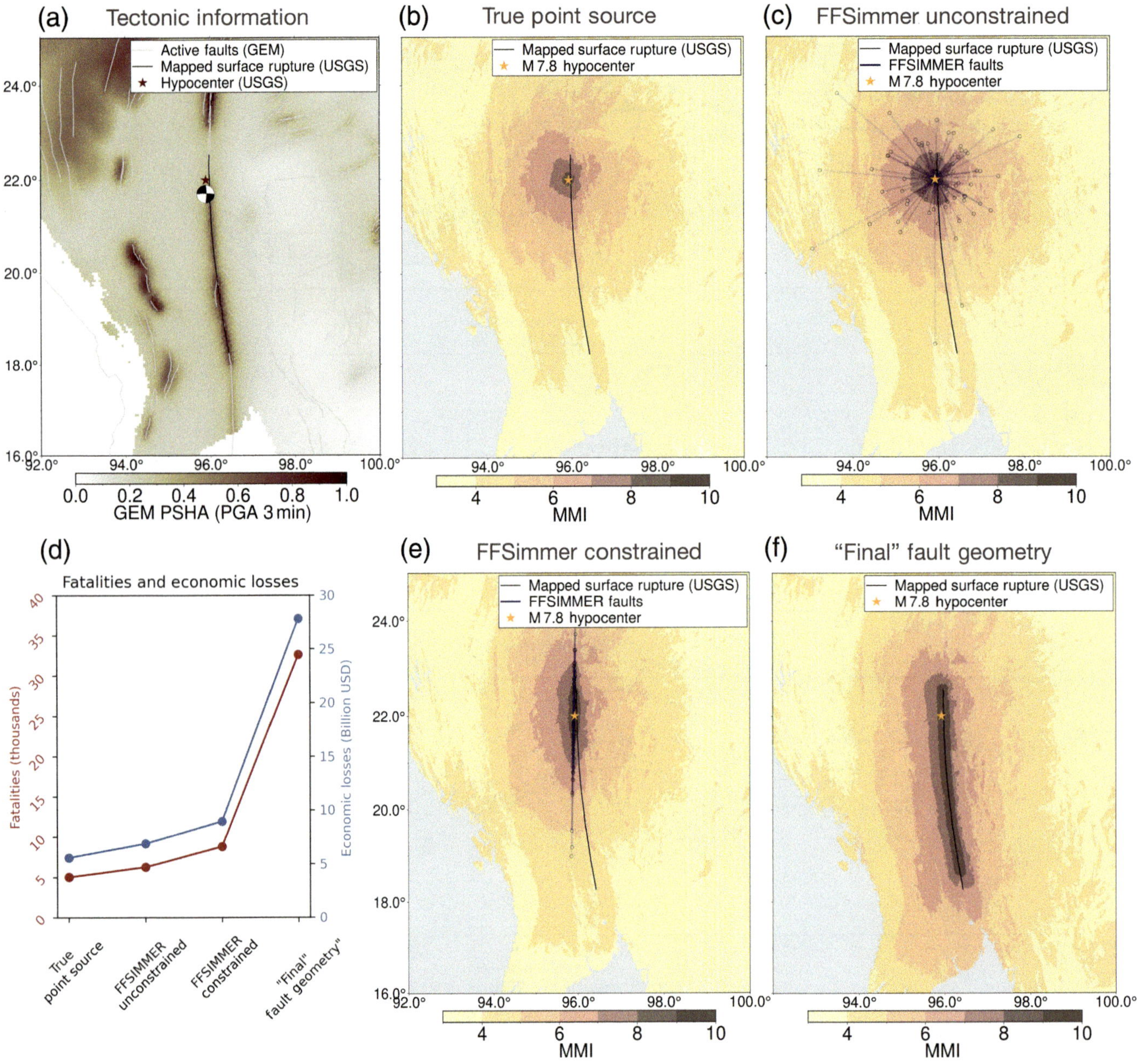

Figure 8. (a) Overview of the tectonic setting, with population count per square kilometer (LandScan; Lebakula *et al.*, 2024) shown as a base layer, active faults in thin black lines (Global Earthquake Model; Styron and Pagani, 2020), the mapped surface rupture as a thick-red line (U.S. Geological Survey [USGS]), and the hypocenter and centroid moment tensor solution locations; (b,c,e,f) four possible iterations of the ShakeMap, each with a different representation of the source and the resulting shaking and loss estimates plotted in terms of modified Mercalli intensity (MMI); and (d) a comparison of Prompt Assessment of Global Earthquakes for Response (PAGER)-estimated fatalities associated with each ShakeMap iteration. Legend in panel (b) applies to panels (b,c,e,f).

at arbitrary locations relative to the modeled faults, (2) a grid of points assuming that the distribution of IMs about the epicenter is isotropic, and (3) a grid of points assuming the distribution of IMs about the epicenter is anisotropic. USGS ShakeMaps use gridded points to construct maps of IMs, and so option (2) is appropriate until further constraints, or a finite-fault model, become available. This is because the relative orientation of the ruptures to epicentral distance is arbitrary, we lack information to constrain it further, and it is computationally less expensive. We provide a mechanism for users to constrain the range of dips, depths, and other geometric parameters in situations in which additional knowledge of the fault geometry is available. In these cases, option (3) is appropriate. This situation arises when the tectonic environment, a moment tensor solution, or other early context provides constraints on the rupture strike and dip.

One limitation of FFSIMMER is that we represent each rupture realization with single plane, which may not be appropriate for longer ruptures on multisegment faults. Another limitation is that the FFSIMMER method requires 1 or

2 min more computation time than the point source, PS2FF, or EPRI methods. FFSIMMER requires the computation of IMs for each of the fault realizations, computation of summary statistics, and then interpolation. The point source, PS2FF, and EPRI methods only require a single IM evaluation at a single array of distances: the point source at each prediction location, PS2FF at mean distances provided by a table lookup against the point-source distances, and EPRI at distances that provide the median IMs using specific formulas for rupture and JB distances. However, we have been able to optimize FFSIMMER for ShakeMap using the OpenQuake HazardLib GMMs (Pagani *et al.*, 2014) to minimize the effect of the extra computations, so that the runtime differences of just one or two minutes are small enough that we can use FFSIMMER in near-real-time applications.

An advantage of FFSIMMER is that the additional variances of the within- and between-event uncertainties of the GMMs are computed directly and may simply be added to the GMM variances. The additional uncertainty of the PS2FF method is in terms of rupture surface distances, so it must be propagated through the GMM by means of the partial derivative of the GMM with respect to distance. This partial derivative may have to be computed numerically, especially in cases of multiple weighted GMMs. The EPRI method provides formulas for the additional uncertainty, but these were developed for a limited set of pre-2003 GMMs.

The unconstrained FFSIMMER source, when compared to the true point source, provides a broader footprint of shaking with higher intensities near the source, increasing shaking and loss estimates (Fig. 8). In the case of the Burma (Myanmar) event, constraining the strike and dip distributions in FFSIMMER elongates the high-intensity shaking footprint along strike (Fig. 8e), which increases estimated fatalities (Fig. 8d). Satellite observations of this event indicate that the rupture length was ~460 km (Reitman *et al.*, 2025), which far exceeded the expected rupture length (141 km) from the Wells and Coppersmith (1994) scaling relationship. More specifically, 460 km is about at the 99th percentile level, whereas the mean rupture length of the FFSIMMER realizations was about 170 km in both cases. This unusually long and shallow rupture accounted for most of the later increases in shaking and loss estimates (Fig. 8d). This illustrates that the accuracy of FFSIMMER is constrained by the ability of magnitude scaling relationships to predict the rupture size, and thus FFSIMMER can only provide limited improvements for outlier events such as this. Nonetheless, the distribution of rupture lengths used in FFSIMMER captures the range of rupture lengths expected empirically from scaling relations and did increase the loss estimates relative to the true point source and the FFSIMMER unconstrained approach. We note that the approach of constraining the rupture plane realizations has the potential for the greatest improvements over the typical FFSIMMER unconstrained approach and over a true point source for large strike-slip earthquakes because the shaking in this geometry is most sensitive to the geometry of the selected rupture plane. Currently, constraints on the FFSIMMER source can be implemented only with expert input. For example, specifying strike and dip values or constraints on the rupture direction still requires manual intervention. Future work can explore how these criteria can be standardized and how the process of applying FFSIMMER source constraints can be automated.

SUMMARY

We have described a new method for estimating IMs when a finite fault is unavailable. Our method, called "FFSIMMER," assumes a random assortment of finite faults consistent with the earthquake's origin, magnitude, tectonic regime, and moment tensor (if available). For each fault realization we compute a set of IMs, making full use of GMM terms such as distance to rupture, hanging wall or footwall, and depth to top of rupture. We are then able to compute a mean IM across the realizations for each site across all the fault realizations and the residuals versus the mean. This is in contrast to previous methods that developed models for mean finite-fault distances instead of IMs directly. We can then determine the group and residual variance of using the law of total variance. These are additional variances that may be added to the GMMs between- and within-event variances, respectively. We illustrate how the accuracy of FFSIMMER can be improved through event-specific geometry constraints using the **M** 7.7 Mandalay, Burma (Myanmar), earthquake provides.

We tested the FFSIMMER approach against 30 **M** 6+ NGA-West2 (Ancheta *et al.*, 2014) events that had at least 20 seismic stations, and a finite fault defined in the ShakeMap Atlas (Marano *et al.*, 2023). Although the results varied from event to event, on aggregate the FFSIMMER approach produced results that are more consistent with the finite source than the other methods we tested against. Although the FFSIMMER method requires considerably more computation than either the PS2FF or EPRI, which require only table lookups or fixed formulas, respectively, our implementation in Python runs fast enough for use in near-real-time products like ShakeMap.

DATA AND RESOURCES

The Next Generation Attenuation (NGA) flatfile was obtained from https://peer.berkeley.edu/research/databases/databases (last accessed July 2025). The code that implements Finite-Fault SIMulation with Mixed Effects Regression (FFSIMMER) is available at Worden *et al.* (2018).

DECLARATION OF COMPETING INTERESTS

The authors acknowledge that there are no conflicts of interest recorded.

ACKNOWLEDGMENTS

This article was improved by reviews by Grace Parker, Graeme Weatherill, an anonymous reviewer, and Sanjay Singh Bora, associate editor.

Any use of trade, firm, or product names is for descriptive purposes only and does not imply endorsement by the U.S. Government.

REFERENCES

Abrahamson, N. A., W. J. Silva, and R. Kamai (2014). Summary of the ASK14 ground motion relation for active crustal regions, *Earthq. Spectra* **30,** no. 3, 1025–1055, doi: 10.1193/070913EQS198M.

Ancheta, T. D., R. B. Darragh, J. P. Stewart, E. Seyhan, W. J. Silva, B. S.-J. Chiou, K. E. Wooddell, R. W. Graves, A. R. Kottke, *et al.* (2013). PEER NGA-West2 database, *PEER Rept. No. 2013/03*, Pacific Earthquake Engineering Research Center, University of California, Berkeley, California, 134 pp.

Ancheta, T. D., R. B. Darragh, J. P. Stewart, E. Seyhan, W. J. Silva, B. S.-J. Chiou, K. E. Wooddell, R. W. Graves, A. R. Kottke, D. M. Boore, *et al.* (2014). NGA-West2 database, *Earthq. Spectra* **30,** no. 3, 989–1005, doi: 10.1193/070913EQS197M.

Boore, D. M., J. P. Stewart, E. Seyhan, and G. M. Atkinson (2014). NGA-West2 equations for predicting PGA, PGV, and 5% damped PSA for shallow crustal earthquakes, *Earthq. Spectra* **30,** no. 3, 1057–1085, doi: 10.1193/070113EQS184M.

Böse, M., S. Ceylan, J. Andrews, F. Massin, J. Clinton, J. K. Saunders, O. Tatar, and M. Türkoğlu (2024). Rapid finite-fault models for the 2023 Mw 7.8 Kahramanmaraş, Türkiye, earthquake sequence, *Seismol. Res. Lett.* **95,** no. 5, 2761–2778, doi: 10.1785/0220230426.

Bozorgnia, Y., N. A. Abrahamson, L. A. Atik, T. D. Ancheta, G. M. Atkinson, J. W. Baker, A. Baltay, D. M. Boore, K. W. Campbell, B. S. J. Chiou, *et al.* (2014). NGA-West2 research project, *Earthq. Spectra* **30,** no. 3, 973–987, doi: 10.1193/072113EQS209M.

Campbell, K. W., and Y. Bozorgnia (2014). NGA-West2 ground motion model for the average horizontal components of PGA, PGV, and 5% damped linear acceleration response spectra, *Earthq. Spectra* **30,** no. 3, 1087–1115, doi: 10.1193/062913EQS175M.

Central and Eastern United States-Seismic Source Characterization (CEUS-SSC) (2012). Central and Eastern United States seismic source characterization for nuclear facilities, EPRI, U.S. DOE, and U.S. NRC, Palo Alto, California, 3176 pp.

Chiou, B.-J., and R. R. Youngs (2008). NGA model for average horizontal component of peak ground motion and response spectra, *PEER Rept. 2008-09*, Pacific Earthquake Engineering Research Center, University of California, Berkeley, California, 293 pp.

Chiou, B. S. J., and R. R. Youngs (2014). Update of the Chiou and Youngs NGA model for the average horizontal component of peak ground motion and response spectra, *Earthq. Spectra* **30,** no. 3, 1117–1153, doi: 10.1193/072813EQS219M.

Electric Power Research Institute, Inc. (EPRI) (2004). CEUS ground motion project final report, *EPRI Rept. No. 1009684*, Palo Alto, California, 336 pp.

Evans, W. S., A. Plesch, J. H. Shaw, N. L. Pillai, E. Yu, M. Meier, and E. Hauksson (2020). A statistical method for associating earthquakes with their source faults in Southern California, *Bull. Seismol. Soc. Am.* **110,** no. 1, 213–225, doi: 10.1785/0120190115.

Field, E. H., R. J. Arrowsmith, G. P. Biasi, P. Bird, T. E. Dawson, K. R. Felzer, D. D. Jackson, K. M. Johnson, T. H. Jordan, C. Madden, *et al.* (2014). Uniform California Earthquake Rupture Forecast, Version 3 (UCERF3)—The Time-Independent Model, *Bull. Seismol. Soc. Am.* **104,** no. 3, 1122–1180, doi: 10.1785/0120130164.

Hanks, T. C., and W. H. Bakun (2008). M-log A observations for recent large earthquakes, *Bull. Seismol. Soc. Am.* **98,** no. 1, 490–494, doi: 10.1785/0120070174.

Harmsen, S. (2008). Appendix C. Distance to a fault with random strike, in *Documentation for the 2008 Update of the United States National Seismic Hazard Maps*, M. D. Petersen, A. D. Frankel, S. C. Harmsen, C. S. Mueller, K. M. Haller, R. L. Wheeler, R. L. Wesson, Y. Zeng, O. S. Boyd, and D. M. Perkins, *et al.* (Editors), *U.S. Geol. Surv. Open-File Rept. 2008-1128*, 61 pp., doi: 10.3133/ofr20081128.

Huang, J.-Y., N. A. Abrahamson, C.-H. Sung, and S.-H. Chao (2024). New empirical source-scaling laws for crustal earthquakes incorporating fault dip and seismogenic-thickness effects, *Seismol. Res. Lett.* **95,** no. 4, 2352–2367, doi: 10.1785/0220240034.

Johnson, K., M. Villani, K. Bayliss, C. Brooks, S. Chandrasekhar, T. Chartier, Y.-S. Chen, J. Garcia-Pelaez, R. Gee, R. Styron, *et al.* (2023). Global Seismic Hazard Map (Version v2023.1.0) [Dataset], *Zenodo*, doi: 10.5281/ZENODO.8409647.

Joyner, W. B., and D. M. Boore (1981). Peak horizontal acceleration and velocity from strong-motion records including records from the 1979 Imperial Valley, California, earthquake, *Bull. Seismol. Soc. Am.* **71,** no. 6, 2011–2038, doi: 10.1785/BSSA0710062011.

Lebakula, V., J. Epting, J. Moehl, C. Stipek, A. Reith, B. Reynolds, D. Adams, J. Kaufman, J. Gonzales, S. Basford, *et al.* (2024). LandScan silver edition [Data set], Oak Ridge National Laboratory, doi: 10.48690/1531770.

Mai, P. M., P. Spudich, and J. Boatwright (2005). Hypocenter locations in finite-source rupture models, *Bull. Seismol. Soc. Am.* **95,** no. 3, 965–980, doi: 10.1785/0120040111.

Marano, K. D., M. Hearne, K. S. Jaiswal, E. M. Thompson, C. B. Worden, and D. J. Wald (2023). ShakeMap Atlas 4.0 and AtlasCat: An archive of the recent and the historical earthquake ShakeMaps, and impacts for global hazard analyses and loss model calibration, *Seismol. Res. Lett.* **95,** no. 2A, 879–899, doi: 10.1785/0220220324.

Pagani, M., D. Monelli, G. Weatherill, L. Danciu, H. Crowley, V. Silva, P. Henshaw, L Butler, M. Nastasi, L. Panzeri, *et al.* (2014). OpenQuake engine: An open hazard (and risk) software for the global earthquake model, *Seismol. Res. Lett.* **85,** no. 3, 692–702, doi: 10.1785/0220130087.

Petersen, M. D., A. M. Shumway, P. M. Powers, N. Field, M. P. Moschetti, K. Jaiswal, K. R. Milner, S. Rezaeian, A. D. Frankel, A. L. Llenos, *et al.* (2024). The 2023 U.S. 50-State National Seismic Hazard Model: Overview and implications, *Earthq. Spectra* **40,** no. 1, 5–88, doi: 10.1177/87552930231215428.

Reitman, N. G., Y. Wang, Y.-T. Kuo, C. Hanagan, A. E. Hatem, C. B. DuRoss, W. D. Barnhart, H. Z. Yin, R. W. Briggs, J. A. Thompson Jobe, *et al.* (2025). Remote surface rupture observations for the M7.7 2025 Mandalay, Burma (Myanmar) Earthquake, *U.S. Geol. Surv. Data Release*, doi: 10.5066/P1RYMWCK.

Scherbaum, F., J. Schmedes, and F. Cotton (2004). On the conversion of source-to-site distance measures for extended earthquake source models, *Bull. Seismol. Soc. Am.* **94,** no. 3, 1053–1069, doi: 10.1785/0120030055.

Somerville, P. (2014). Scaling relations between seismic moment and rupture area of earthquakes in stable continental regions, *PEER Rept. 2014/14*, Pacific Earthquake Engineering Research Center, Berkeley, California, 22 pp.

Spudich, P. A., and B. Chiou (2015). Strike-parallel and strike-normal coordinate system around geometrically complicated rupture traces: Use by NGA-West2 and further improvements, *U.S. Geol. Surv. Open-File Rept. 2015-1028*, 20 pp., doi: 10.3133/ofr20151028.

Stallone, A., J. Selva, L. Cordrie, L. Faenza, A. Michelini, and V. Lauciani (2024). ProbShakemap v1.0: A Python toolbox propagating source uncertainty to ground motion prediction for urgent computing applications, *Comput. Geosci.* **195,** 105748, doi: 10.1016/j.cageo.2024.105748.

Strasser, F. O., M. C. Arango, and J. J. Bommer (2010). Scaling of the source dimensions of interface and intraslab subduction-zone earthquakes with moment magnitude, *Seismol. Res. Lett.* **81,** no. 6, 941–950, doi: 10.1785/gssrl.81.6.941.

Styron, R., and M. Pagani (2020). The GEM global active faults database, *Earthq. Spectra* **36,** no. 1_suppl, 160–180, doi: 10.1177/8755293020944182.

Thingbaijam, K. K. S., P. M. Mai, and K. Goda (2017). New empirical earthquake source-scaling laws. *Bull. Seismol. Soc. Am.* **107,** no. 5, 2225–2246, doi: 10.1785/0120170017.

Thompson, E. M., and C. B. Worden (2018). Estimating rupture distances without a rupture, *Bull. Seismol. Soc. Am.* **108,** no. 1, 371–379, doi: 10.1785/0120170174.

U.S. Geological Survey (USGS) (2017). Advanced National Seismic System (ANSS) comprehensive catalog of earthquake events and products, *U.S. Geol. Surv. Earthquake Hazards Program*, doi: 10.5066/F7MS3QZH.

Wald, D. J., K. S. Jaiswal, K. D. Marano, D. B. Bausch, and M. G. Hearne (2010). PAGER - Rapid assessment of an earthquake's impact, *U.S. Geol. Surv. Fact Sheet 2010-3036*, 4 pp., doi: 10.3133/fs20103036.

Wald, D. J., C. B. Worden, E. M. Thompson, and M. Hearne (2022). ShakeMap operations, policies, and procedures, *Earthq. Spectra* **38,** no. 1, 756–777, doi: 10.1177/87552930211030298.

Wells, D. L., and K. J. Coppersmith (1994). New empirical relationships among magnitude, rupture length, rupture width, rupture area, and surface displacement, *Bull. Seismol. Soc. Am.* **84,** no. 4, 974–1002, doi: 10.1785/BSSA0840040974.

Worden, C. B., M. Hearne, and E. M. Thompson (2018). ShakeMap v4 Software, *U.S. Geol. Surv. Soft. Release*, doi: 10.5066/P97FHE0I.

Yeck, W. L., B. Herrmann, J. Patton, W. Barnhart, and H. Benz (2025). Estimating earthquake source depth using teleseismic broadband waveform modeling at the USGS National Earthquake Information Center, *Seismol. Res. Lett.* **96,** no. 6, 3643–3655, doi: 10.1785/0220240372.

Manuscript received 29 July 2025
Published online 23 February 2026

Constraining Rupture-Generator Scaling Using Measured Surface Offsets, Near-Fault Ground Motions, and Rupture Dynamic Simulations

Camilo I. Pinilla-Ramos*[1] and Norman A. Abrahamson[2]

ABSTRACT

This study shows evidence based on observations of near-fault ground motions and surface offset that regions with larger-than-average surface offset exhibit weaker ground motions at frequencies >0.5 Hz. This negative correlation of surface offset and high-frequency ground motion is inconsistent with current scaling in kinematic rupture generators. Using rupture dynamic simulations with a linear slip-weakening rheology model combined with observed data enables us to define an input parameter space that is consistent with the observations. Given the multiparameter nature of rupture dynamics, we focus on two parameters: static stress drop and the slip-weakening distance. Under this framework, the observed scaling can be explained if the static stress drop is positively correlated with the slip-weakening distance. We explore the implications of our findings for kinematic source modeling constrained by our rupture-dynamic simulations. We conclude that the ratio between the time of positive acceleration and the total rise time (TRT) is negatively correlated with the TRT, which contrasts with the current assumption of keeping this percentage fixed. Moreover, this study shows that regions with larger-than-average static stress drops tend to radiate weaker high-frequency energy and stronger low-frequency energy.

KEY POINTS

- Sites located near regions of larger-than-average surface offset exhibit weaker high-frequency ground motions.
- Regions with larger static stress drop lead to weaker high-frequency and stronger low-frequency energy radiation.
- The ratio between the time of positive acceleration over the total rise time is negatively correlated in source-time functionss.

Supplemental Material

INTRODUCTION

Currently, efforts are underway to complement empirical ground-motion models (GMMs) with 3D regional-scale physics-based simulations in seismic hazard analysis (SHA; Graves *et al.*, 2011; Rodgers *et al.*, 2019; McCallen, Petersson, *et al.*, 2021; McCallen, Petrone, *et al.*, 2021). The description of the source and the 3D velocity structure needs to be adequately constrained to provide accurate and realistic ground motions for use in SHA. The source characterization used in traditional seismic hazard applications based on GMMs describes the large-scale properties of the source, such as rupture geometry (length, width, dip, and depth), magnitude, and style of faulting. For numerical simulations, additional parameters governing the spatiotemporal evolution of the rupture are also required. Defining the scaling for these additional parameters is a foundational step for any effort to constrain the earthquake source model for either kinematic or dynamic rupture models. The evolution of the physical processes underlying seismic ruptures modulates the slip velocity at different length scales within the source volume, which is manifested at the surface after wave propagation as the frequency-dependent amplitude of the ground motion.

Kinematic rupture generators approximate the complex physics of faulting underlying rupture dynamics using simplified rules that enable an efficient prescription of rupture evolution. One simplified rule used in most kinematic rupture generators is the assumption that the slip velocity at all frequencies increases proportionally with the total slip and thus with magnitude (e.g., Graves and Pitarka, 2010; Song and Somerville, 2010; Irikura

1. GFZ, Helmholtz-Zentrum für Geoforschung, Potsdam, Germany, https://orcid.org/0000-0002-4034-6618 (CIP-R); 2. Department of Civil Engineering, University of California, Berkeley, Berkeley, California, U.S.A., https://orcid.org/0000-0001-7900-6023 (NAA)

*Corresponding author: cpinilla@gfz.de

Cite this article as Pinilla-Ramos, C. I., and N. A. Abrahamson (2026). Constraining Rupture-Generator Scaling Using Measured Surface Offsets, Near-Fault Ground Motions, and Rupture Dynamic Simulations, *Bull. Seismol. Soc. Am.* **116**, 1064–1080, doi: 10.1785/0120250197 and Miyake, 2011), including local increments of slip velocity in subfaults with larger than average slip. This assumption works well for sources with rupture dimensions or slip within the worldwide average, as shown by the validation of the Statewide California Earthquake Center (SCEC) broadband platform (Dreger *et al.*, 2015), but it does not work well for scenarios with above-average or below-average slip for a given magnitude (i.e., deviations from an average static stress drop). To show the scaling of the ground motion with static stress drop in kinematic source models based on this assumption, we generate a set of simulated ground motions using the Graves and Pitarka (GP) rupture generator (Graves and Pitarka, 2010, 2015, 2016) with a 1D velocity structure for different average slips keeping the same rupture area, that is, representing scenarios with different static stress drops. To focus on the physics-based aspects of the simulations, we remove the stochastic module of the SCEC broadband platform (Maechling *et al.*, 2014) and extend the physics-based scheme to 10 Hz. A summary of this numerical implementation is provided in the Kinematic modeling section in the supplemental material available to this article and is similar to that of Artale Harris *et al.* (2025).

Using the assumption that the slip velocity is proportional to the total slip, the effect of above-average or below-average static stress drops on the simulated ground motion is evaluated by doubling or halving the median slip for an earthquake with a moment magnitude (M_w) of 7 while keeping the rupture area equal to the median area for M_w 7. The scenarios with half and double the slip correspond to moment magnitudes of M_w 6.8 and 7.2, respectively. The ratios of the Fourier amplitude spectra (FAS) of the simulated ground motion for the two scaled slip cases are shown in Figure 1. The FAS ratios range from 1.5 to 2 across the whole frequency range of 0.1–10 Hz.

In contrast to the strong scaling observed in simulations using the GP rupture generator, the recorded ground-motion data, a representation of the observations, exhibit a different scaling. Using the Next Generation Attenuation West (NGA-W) datasets (Power *et al.*, 2008; Ancheta *et al.*, 2014; Buckreis *et al.*, 2025), it has been observed a weaker correlation at low frequencies and a negative correlation at high frequencies between the event terms and a proxy for static stress drop given by $\Delta M_w = (M_w - 4) - \log_{10}(A)$, in which A is the estimated rupture area and M_w is the earthquake moment magnitude. The NGA-W projects provide the most extensive ground-motion dataset for crustal active regions, and after new releases, the number of available recordings and earthquakes has increased significantly. Using the data from the NGA-W project (Power *et al.*, 2008; green-dotted curve, Fig. 1), the scaling at high frequencies remains constant when the static stress drop is increased. With the inclusion of more earthquakes in the NGA-W2 and NGA-W3 datasets (orange and blue curves), a negative scaling is observed at high frequencies: the ground-motion amplitude decreases as the static stress drop increases. The scaling shown from the NGA-W and NGA-W2 projects is based on spectral acceleration

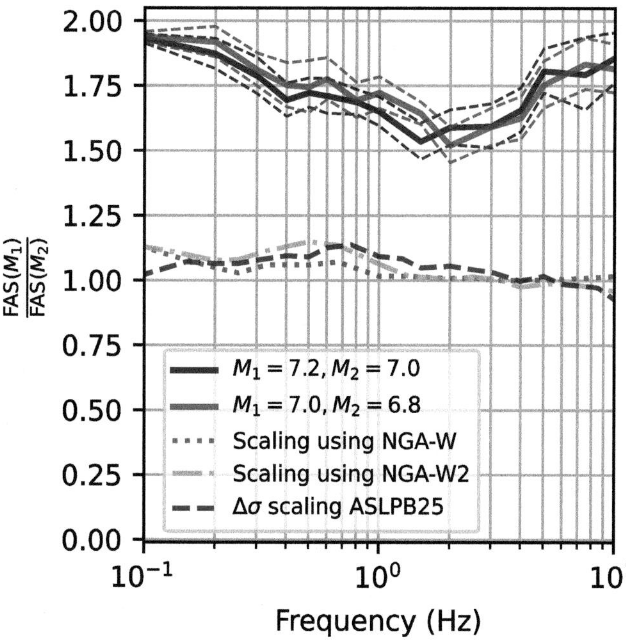

Figure 1. Comparison between the ground-motion scaling in the Graves and Pitarka (GP) rupture generator and the scaling from empirical ground-motion models (GMMs). For the GP rupture generator, we keep the same area of an M_w 7 earthquake and Double and halve the slip, implying a 0.2 magnitude step. The solid red and black lines are the scaling from the GP rupture generator comparing two different pairs of magnitudes. The dashed lines are ± 1 standard deviation. The dotted green line and the dashed orange line are the scaling from the Next Generation Attenuation West (NGA-W) and NGA-W2 datasets using spectral acceleration. The blue line represents the scaling based on the NGA-W3 dataset and Fourier amplitude spectra (FAS). The color version of this figure is available only in the electronic edition.

and for the NGA-W3 project on FAS. In particular, using the newest dataset from NGA-W3 project, Abrahamson *et al.* (2025; denoted as ASLPB25 GMM) found a negative scaling of the event terms with respect to ΔM for frequencies >3 Hz (Fig. 1) and weak positive scaling for frequencies of 0.2–3 Hz.

The discrepancy between the static-stress-drop scaling from kinematic simulations and the observations represented by the empirical datasets may arise from limitations either in the empirical data or from simplifications in the rupture generator that do not capture the correct physical behavior for static stress-drop scaling. These discrepancies serve as the basis for this study, which has two main objectives. The first objective is to identify additional observational data to evaluate the proper scaling of the radiated energy at different length scales (frequencies), expressed at the surface as ground motions, with slip along the rupture. The second objective is to determine a physical explanation for the found scaling of the radiated energy with static stress drop and at the same time be consistent with the observations. The findings of our study have important implications for both rheology models in rupture dynamics and the formulation of source-time functions (STFs) in kinematic source modeling. We propose scaling relationships between the key parameters needed to describe kinematically constrained rupture evolutions. This insight can be leveraged to create more accurate rupture generators for kinematic source modeling.

CONCEPTUAL DISCUSSION ON DIFFERENCES BETWEEN FAULT SLIP AND SLIP VELOCITY

Before beginning the observational and numerical analyses, it is important to emphasize the distinction between the source of total slip and the radiated energy, the latter manifested as ground motion after wave propagation. The average total slip scales with the dimensions of the rupture (Wells and Coppersmith, 1994; Leonard, 2010). The wider the rupture, the longer it can propagate without being affected by the geometrical limits on the rupture dimension and the geometrical complexities of faults that bring back information to initiate the stopping phase (Day, 1982a,b) or healing when the slip has extended for a sufficiently long time window. This slip scaling has a physical limit in the transition from crack-like to pulse-like rupture propagation. The latter occurs when a ruptured patch stops slipping while the rupture continues to propagate (Ampuero and Ben-Zion, 2008). In this case, slip stops being dependent on magnitude and are mainly constrained by the seismogenic width (Scholz, 1994). When the rupture propagates as a crack, the slip scales with magnitude and width (Shaw and Scholz, 2001; Shaw and Wesnousky, 2008; Scholz, 2019). Because of the wide seismogenic width, megathrust subduction earthquakes are extreme examples of this scaling. When the interlocking width reaches 150–200 km, ruptures can exhibit slips of several tens of meters, as in the Maule earthquake (2010 M_w 8.8, maximum slip around 20 m; Delouis *et al.*, 2010; Hayes *et al.*, 2013; Yue *et al.*, 2014) and the Tohoku earthquake (2011 M_w 9.12, maximum slip around 60–80 m; Ito *et al.*, 2011; Silverii *et al.*, 2014; Yamazaki *et al.*, 2018). In summary, at a given static stress drop, the total slip depends mainly on the overall geometrical constraints and complexities and the size of the seismic rupture.

Most energy radiation occurs during the dynamic-stress-drop process, in which slip acceleration becomes positive (Dunham, 2007), and it occurs in a narrow region known as the process zone (Ida, 1972; Palmer *et al.*, 1973). Kinematically, and as sketched in Figure 2, this temporal region is represented in rupture generators by the time window between the beginning of the shear dislocation and when the maximum-slip velocity occurs βT. The interaction of the process zone with heterogeneities that the rupture undergoes governs how the accumulated strain energy is radiated as elastic waves (Papageorgiou and Aki, 1983; Bernard and Madariaga, 1984; Rice *et al.*, 1994; Ben-Zion and Morrissey, 1995). By causality, how this process develops depends more on the local rate and state parameters of the rupture tip and process zone than on the overall geometry of the fault. The local rate and state parameters of the rupture tip and process zone include the slip velocity, slip, time of contact, rupture velocity, released energy of the rupture, surface energy flux, environmental conditions, damage, and breakage evolution in the volume surrounding the fault, among several other physical processes (e.g., Dieterich, 1979a,b; Ruina, 1983; Lyakhovsky *et al.*, 2016; Abdelmeguid *et al.*, 2024). Therefore, there is a clear difference in the origin of energy radiation at low and high frequencies, as well as in total slip. High frequencies are mostly radiated during spatiotemporal variations in the dynamic stress drop caused by local changes in the rupture velocity (Bernard and Madariaga, 1984; Rice *et al.*, 1994). In contrast, low frequencies and total slip develop throughout the duration of the rupture's growth, without encountering constraints that trigger the stopping phase. These concepts should be considered or incorporated when performing kinematic source modeling.

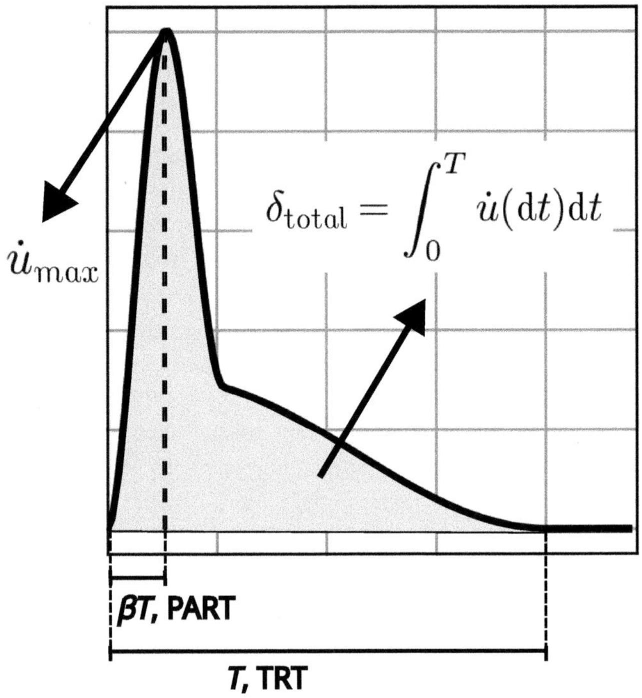

Figure 2. Conceptual sketch of the main parameters to be defined in a source time function (STF) for kinematic source modeling. These main parameters are total rise time (TRT), positive acceleration rise time (PART), maximum slip velocity ($\dot{u}_{max}$), and total slip δ_{total}.

LIMITATIONS OF THE EMPIRICAL RESULTS

The empirical evaluation of ground-motion scaling with static stress drop depends on estimates of the rupture area and on interpretations of the physical meaning of the event terms. The weak scaling of static stress drop observed in empirical data for large-magnitude earthquakes may be due to errors in the rupture areas and/or to the limited number of such events in the empirical dataset.

The event terms are estimated using a mixed-effects regression (Abrahamson and Youngs, 1992). The ground motion

$Y_{es}(f)$ at frequency f recorded on site s from earthquake e can be decomposed as follows:

$$\ln(Y_{es}(f)) = \mathrm{GMM}_{\mathrm{med}}(M_{\mathrm{w}}, D_{es}, V_{S30}, f) + \delta B_e(f) + \delta P_e(f)R + \delta W_{es}(f), \quad (1)$$

in which D_{es} is a distance metric between earthquake e and station s, $\delta B_e(f)$ is the event term, $\delta P_e(f)$ is an event-specific path term that captures between-event attenuation deviations from the backbone statistical model, $\delta W_{es}(f)$ is the remaining within-event residual, and $\mathrm{GMM}_{\mathrm{med}}(M_{\mathrm{w}}, D_{es}, V_{S30}, f)$ is the median prediction of ground-motion amplitude conditioned on the set of predictors. Here, $\delta B_e(f)$ is usually interpreted as an average source effect, but it can include part of the regional wave propagation patterns depending on the velocity structures each earthquake was propagated through and the sampling of ray paths for a given earthquake. Whereas the inclusion of $\delta P_e(f)$ aims to remove wave propagation effects with distance, still $\delta B_e(f)$ maps regional-scale amplification patterns manifested in wave propagation (e.g., Pinilla-Ramos *et al.*, 2026).

The rupture areas in the empirical datasets are derived from the dimensions of finite ruptures inferred from finite-fault inversions, which, as shown in the next section, introduce substantial uncertainties into the analysis. These rupture-area estimates, despite being noisy statistical predictors, identify instances of earthquakes of the same magnitude but with larger or smaller rupture areas than the worldwide average, being a proxy for static stress drop. Therefore, if the predictors are too noisy, the statistical analysis will identify a scaling between them, but the resulting estimate will be weaker.

OBSERVATIONAL MODEL TO ASSESS THE RELATIONSHIP BETWEEN SLIP AND SLIP VELOCITY

Can we use slip fields from finite-fault inversions as a reliable statistical predictor?

In principle, a finite-fault inversion of large-magnitude earthquakes allows for the identification of the spatial distribution of total slip within a seismic rupture. The wave field adopted for full moment tensor inversions tends to be based on waveforms that have been low-pass filtered or observed at teleseismic distances because if high frequencies are included in the analysis, the inversion can exhibit strong biases caused by poorly constrained velocity structures used for computing the Green's functions (Doody *et al.*, 2024). A common approach for finite-fault inversions is to include a joint inversion scheme in the moment tensor, along with waveforms at teleseismic and regional distances, and to enhance it with geodetic data from Global Positioning System or Interferometric Synthetic Aperture Radar techniques (Hayes, 2017). For example, following this approach, several studies have conducted joint finite-fault inversions of the 1999 Chi-Chi earthquake (Ma *et al.*, 2000, 2001; Chi *et al.*, 2001; Johnson *et al.*, 2001; Wu *et al.*, 2001; Zeng and Chen, 2001; Zhang *et al.*, 2004; Hayes, 2017). The different finite-fault inversions of the Chi-Chi earthquake from these studies are shown in Figure 3, which are extracted from the SRCMOD database (Mai and Thingbaijam, 2014). Because of the nonuniqueness of solutions from this approach, these studies exhibit significantly different spatial distributions of the slip field and total amplitudes. If surface offset or geodetic deformations are included in the joint inversion, the resulting slip-field distribution shares similarities. For instance, the northernmost region of the rupture (right-upper corner of the ruptures in Fig. 3) exhibits a patch of large slip in several inversions because the surface offset was especially large around this location.

Another example is the 2023 Pazarcik earthquake, which is one of the best-recorded earthquakes in terms of near-fault recordings. Several studies have conducted inversions for the slip for this earthquake (e.g., Barbot *et al.*, 2023; Delouis *et al.*, 2023; Gabriel *et al.*, 2023; Chen and Zhou, 2024). There are significant differences between the inverted slip distributions, suggesting that the actual spatial slip distribution of the rupture is not well constrained by the inversion process.

Slip based on surface offset

As shown earlier, estimating the slip distribution of the rupture from finite-fault inversions is challenging. Given the large uncertainties in the subsurface slip distribution estimated by the finite-fault inversions, an alternative is to use the surface offset instead of the slip at depth. Using the surface offset avoids the uncertainties caused by wave propagation in finite-fault inversions from poorly constrained Green's functions. Surface offsets have their own set of uncertainties caused by instrumental and measurement errors. In fact, Sarmiento *et al.* (2024) concluded that an uncertainty of 11%–17% is necessary to capture these measurement errors. Additional surface slip may also result from tectonic relaxation occurring hours or days after the mainshock, but before the measurements were conducted, leading to overestimates of coseismic slip. The relaxation after postseismic slip is a tectonic process that may add surface offset variations of 10–20 cm in the first two weeks after the mainshock of large-magnitude crustal earthquakes (e.g., the Wenchuan earthquake, Shao *et al.*, 2011), representing an additional 10% of uncertainties in the measured values. These uncertainties are far smaller than the slip uncertainties from finite-fault inversions, as shown in Figure 3, making the former a better statistical predictor.

The surface offset can differ from the slip at depth; however, it is directly related to the dynamic features that locally drive the rupture at depth. We treat spatial variations in surface offset as a proxy for the underlying slip profile at depth, assuming that these offsets reflect corresponding local changes in the average static stress drop. This is consistent with simplified physical models. For instance, in a homogeneous half-space and a rupture with a constant static stress drop, the surface offset can be estimated as the integral over all subfaults that,

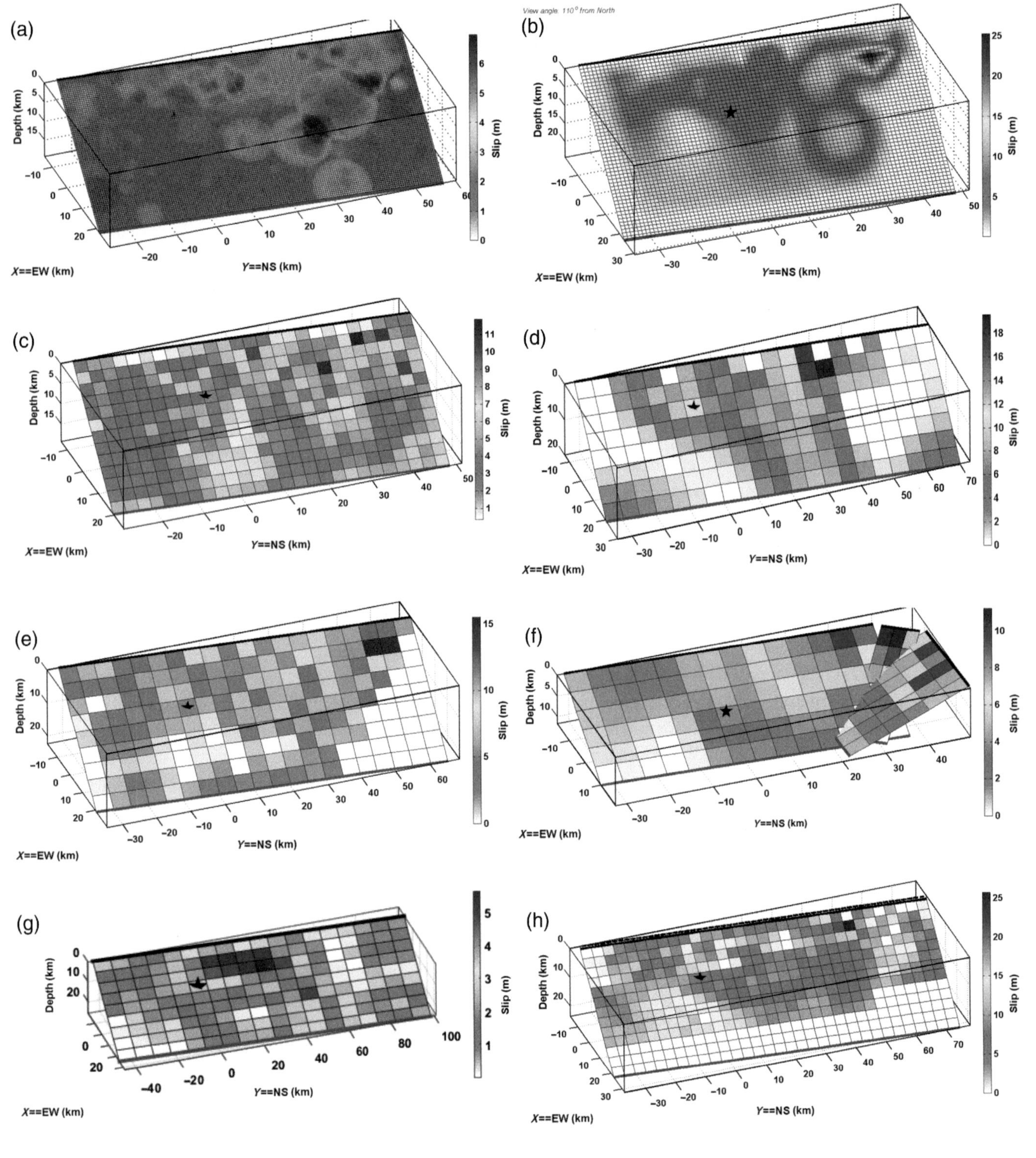

Figure 3. Different finite-fault inversions for the Chi-Chi earthquake using the SRCMOD database (Mai and Thingbaijam, 2014). We used the figures generated by the website of this project. (a) Zeng and Chen (2001). (b) Wu *et al.* (2001). (c) Zhang *et al.* (2004). (d) Ma *et al.* (2001). (e) Ma *et al.* (2000). (f) Johnson *et al.* (2001). (g) Hayes (2017). (h) Chi *et al.* (2001). The color version of this figure is available only in the electronic edition.

through their Green's functions, contribute to the slip at a given location, in this case, at the surface. Under this framework, the total surface deformation at a location $\vec{x}$, $s(\vec{x})$, perpendicular to the fault strike can be written for a strike-slip mechanism as (e.g., Segall, 2010, his equation 4.25)

$$s(x) = \frac{\Delta\sigma}{\mu}\left[\frac{x}{|x|}\sqrt{W^2 + x^2} - x\right], \qquad (2)$$

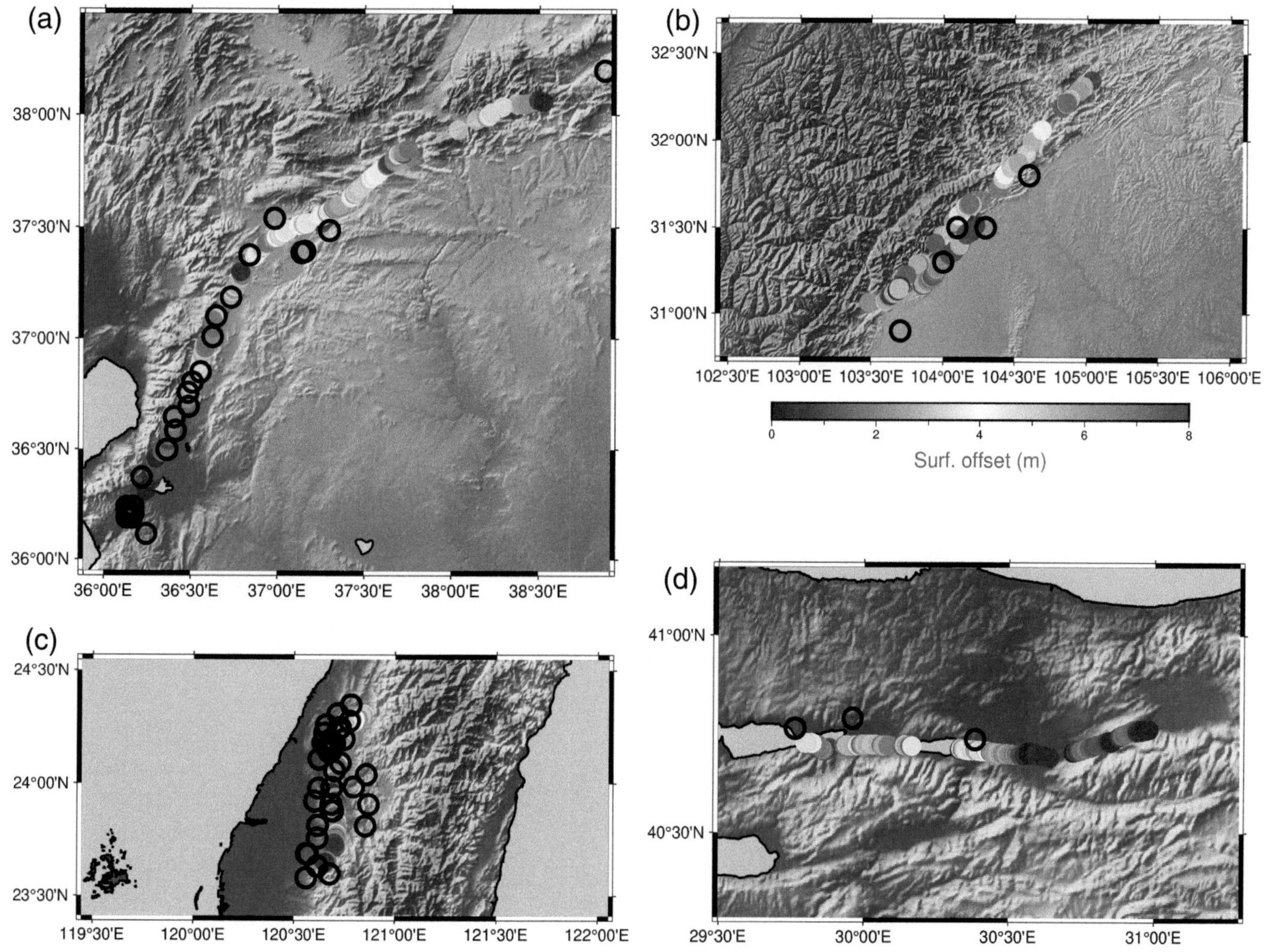

Figure 4. Maps showing the location of the stations (black circles) and the surface offset measurements. (a) Pazarcik. (b) Wenchuan. (c) Chi-Chi. (d) Kocaeli. The scale of the color map is shorter than the maximum surface offset (from Chi-Chi, >20 m) to enhance visibility. See more details of the Chi-Chi profile in Figure 5. The color version of this figure is available only in the electronic edition.

in which $\Delta\sigma$, μ, and W are the static stress drop, shear modulus, and rupture width, respectively. Although this equation represents a highly simplified Earth model, if we replace the elementary Green's functions with those appropriate for a heterogeneous medium, the solution remains primarily governed by the static-stress-drop distribution at depth. Therefore, if a fault segment shows a larger-than-average surface offset, the static stress drop and slip at depth will likely exhibit the same pattern.

Dataset

We analyze four large historical earthquakes with near-fault ground-motion recordings and surface-rupture measurements: the 1999 M_w 7.67 Chi-Chi, Taiwan; 1999 M_w 7.48 Kocaeli, Türkiye; 2008 M_w 7.9 Wenchuan, China; and 2023 M_w 7.75 Pazarcik, Türkiye, earthquakes . The spatial distributions of the surface offset measurements and selected nearby seismic stations used in our analysis are shown in Figure 4. The Chi-Chi and Pazarcik earthquakes are relatively well recorded near the fault, which allows limiting the stations for the analysis to be within 10 km of the rupture. The Kocaeli and Wenchuan earthquakes have sparser spatial sampling of ground motions in the near-fault region, prompting us to extend the radius of the selected stations to 15 km from the rupture. A summary of these ruptures obtained from the geometry of finite-fault analyses of the NGA-West3 project (Buckreis *et al.*, 2025) is listed in Table 1. Both Turkish earthquakes have strike-slip mechanisms, with a fault width between 20 and 25 km. The Chi-Chi and Wenchuan earthquakes have oblique-reverse mechanisms with fault widths of 37 and 45 km, respectively.

The surface offset data are from Sarmiento *et al.* (2024) for the Chi-Chi, Wenchuan, and Kocaeli earthquakes and from DuRoss *et al.* (2024) for the Pazarcik earthquake. Histograms of the surface offset data for each event are displayed in Figure S1, which shows that the Pazarcik and Wenchuan surface offset distributions are narrower, with the smallest standard deviation. In contrast, the Chi-Chi and Kocaeli surface offset distributions are closer to uniform over the central range of

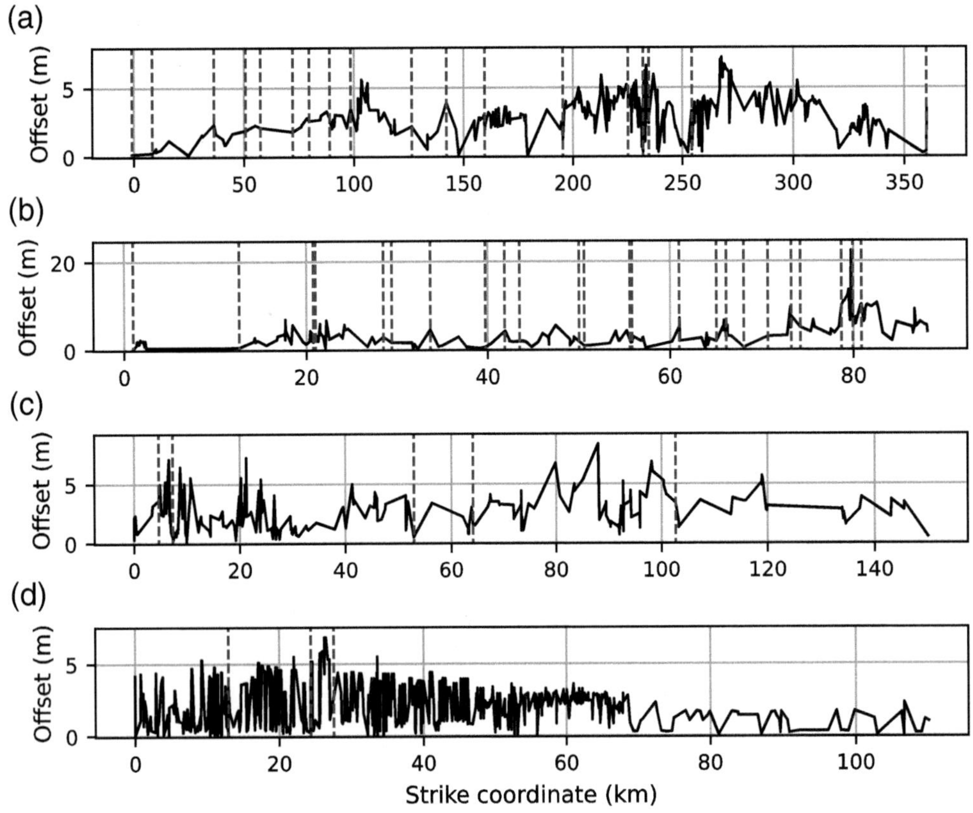

Figure 5. Profiles of the surface offset along the strike coordinate. The zero coordinate corresponds to the southernmost point of each rupture, except for the Kocaeli earthquake, which represents the westernmost point. The vertical dashed red lines represent the location of the stations along the rupture that are used in our analysis. (a) Pazarcik. (b) Chi-Chi. (c) Wenchuan. (d) Kocaeli. The axes are scaled according to the length and largest surface offset of each earthquake. The color version of this figure is available only in the electronic edition.

displacements. The surface offset along the strike is shown in Figure 5. The Pazarcik and Wenchuan earthquakes developed a symmetric offset distribution along the strike. In contrast, the largest offsets for the Kocaeli and Chi-Chi earthquakes are biased toward one side of the rupture. For the Chi-Chi earthquake, the northern section of the rupture exhibits larger offsets, consistent with some of the finite-fault inversions, and the Kocaeli earthquake exhibits the largest offsets in the western half of the rupture.

Relationship between surface offset and ground motion

To evaluate the relation between variability of the local slip and the local ground motion, we compute the correlation coefficient of the residuals for surface offset and ground motions near the surface rupture location. For the surface offset, we compute the within-event residuals using the LA23 fault displacement model (Lavrentiadis and Abrahamson, 2023). For the ground motion, we compute the within-event residuals of the effective amplitude spectrum (EAS, Kottke *et al.*, 2021) given in the NGA-W3 project flatfile (Buckreis *et al.*, 2025) relative to the Bayless and Abrahamson (2019) GMM. The EAS is a standard FAS smoothing for the two horizontal components to characterize ground-motion amplitude.

We select seismic stations with the shortest distance to the rupture (R_{RUP}) within 10–15 km to represent the near-fault ground motion. The 10 or 15 km limit depends on the earthquake, as described in the Dataset section. We select the surface offset within-event residuals along the surface rupture that are within $1.1 \times R_{RUP}$ of the station. We compute the mean of the surface offset residuals within this distance range for each station. The mean surface offset residuals are provided in the .csv file of the supplemental material.

We use the within-event residuals to remove average event-specific effects from the surface offset and EAS data. Using the

TABLE 1
Parameters That Characterize the Analyzed Earthquakes

Earthquake	M_w	Median Slip (m)	Standard Deviation Slip (LN Units)	L (km)	W (km)	Dip (°)	Rake (°)
Pazarcik	7.75	3.20	0.69	360	25	70	−4
Chi-Chi	7.62	3.28	0.82	88	37	33	55
Wenchuan	7.9	2.60	0.68	150	45	50	138
Kocaeli	7.51	2.20	1.02	138	20	80	180

L and W are the rupture length and width, respectively. M_w was adopted based on reported values from the Next Generation Attenuation West3 (NGA-W3) dataset (Buckreis *et al.*, 2025).

within-event residuals, the analysis will show the relation between the along-strike variations in the surface slip and the along-strike variations of the EAS. The within-event residuals normalized by the within-event standard deviation are denoted ϵ.

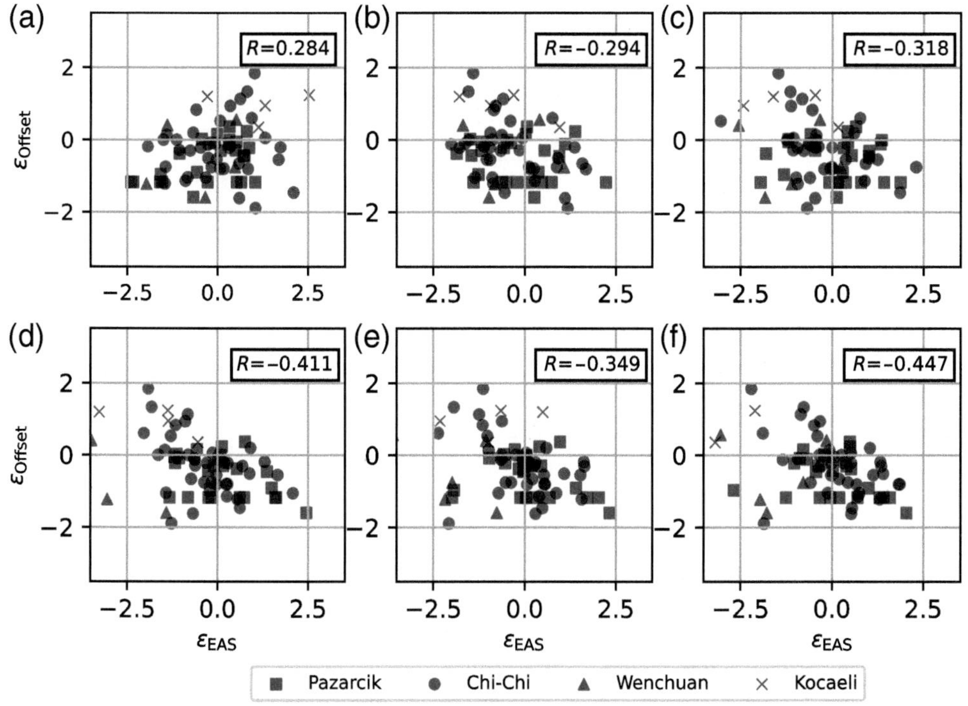

Figure 6. Comparison of the epsilons (number of standard deviations) from within-event residuals of surface offset and Fourier amplitude. (a) 0.25, (b) 0.5, (c) 1.0, (d) 3.0, (e) 5.0, and (f) 10.0 Hz. The R in the upper-right part of each plot is the correlation coefficient.

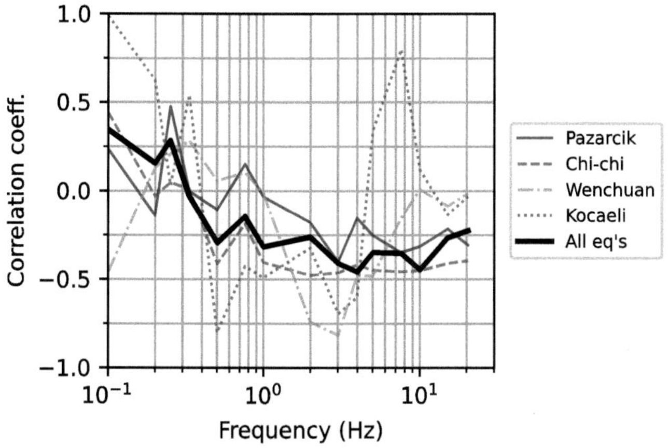

Figure 7. Correlation coefficient between surface offset and Fourier amplitude as a function of frequency. The lighter lines represent each event separately, and the thick black line represents the whole combined dataset's scaling. It is important to highlight that the Kocaeli and Wenchuan earthquakes have only five recordings, which can increase the uncertainty in the correlation-coefficient estimation. The color version of this figure is available only in the electronic edition.

The relation between the within-event epsilons of the surface offset (ϵ_{Disp}) and the within-event epsilons of the EAS (ϵ_{EAS}) at different frequencies are shown in Figure 6. At low frequencies (0.25 Hz), the slope is positive, indicating a positive correlation coefficient, whereas at higher frequencies, the slope is negative, indicating a negative correlation coefficient. The correlation coefficient between surface offset and the EAS is shown as a function of frequency in Figure 7. At frequencies above 1 Hz, there is a negative correlation ranging from −0.25 to −0.5. Below 1 Hz, the negative correlation weakens, and below 0.3 Hz, the correlation becomes positive. The negative scaling above 1 Hz is consistent with the results from the evaluation of the event terms with area residuals described previously.

PHYSICAL MODEL TO EXPLAIN THE OBSERVED CORRELATION

The empirical data indicate that regions with above-average slip radiate below-average energy at high frequencies (short-length scales), leading to below-average ground motions in this frequency range. Based on the Kostrov-like STFs (Fig. 2), we can explain this behavior in a kinematic scheme by delaying the time at which the STF reaches the peak in the stage with positive acceleration and at the same time increasing the area under the slip velocity after the STF phase with positive acceleration. This will reduce high-frequency radiation and simultaneously increase total slip, consistent with the observations.

To conduct this analysis, we perform a set of rupture-dynamic simulations to explore constraints in the parameter space consistent with the observed scaling between surface offset and Fourier amplitude. Recognizing that the physics behind rupture dynamics is a complex, multivariable process, we adopt a linear slip-weakening rheology model (Ida, 1972; Palmer *et al.*, 1973) and focus on variations in two parameters: the initial shear stress (which controls the static stress drop) and the slip-weakening distance D_c. The slip-weakening distance results spontaneously in rate- and state-dependent rheology models (e.g., rate- and state-dependent friction; Cocco and Bizzarri, 2002; Bizzarri and Cocco, 2003). In contrast, we prescribe in our analysis D_c using a linear slip-weakening model to assess its impact on the evolution of the source time function. Here, D_c modulates the compactness of the energy during the dynamic stress drop stage and the high-frequency radiation. We keep the peak and dynamic shear-stress resistance constant, and we vary combinations of D_c and $\Delta\sigma$, allowing us to understand the impact of these two parameters on the radiated energy and total slip.

Numerical modeling

For the simulations, we use the code FaultMod, based on the Galerkin discontinuous finite-element method, which uses linear and piecewise basis functions (Barall, 2009). We adopt a vertical strike-slip fault of length 60 km and width 15 km, consistent with the area of an M_w 6.95 earthquake (Leonard, 2010), embedded in a volume of 100 km length, 60 km width, and 30 km depth, representing a half-space. The elastic material properties are homogeneous and isotropic: shear-wave velocity 3248 m/s, compressional-wave velocity 5626 m/s, and density 2670 $\mathrm{kg/cm^3}$. We adopt a unilateral rupture by inducing the nucleation at a location 5 km from one of the along-strike boundaries and at the center of the down-dip width (7.5 km depth). We use a similar setup as the SCEC Benchmark problem TPV5 (Harris *et al.*, 2018). The nucleation is induced by a small overstress of the shear stress locally by 0.44% of the peak resistance in a radius of 5 km (similar to Day *et al.*, 2005). The D_c varies from 0.2 to 1.8 m, and the static and dynamic friction coefficients are kept fixed for all simulations: 0.677 and 0.525, respectively, consistent with the resistance parameterization of the Benchmark validation TPV5. The initial normal stress is 120 MPa, and we vary the initial shear stress to obtain static stress drops ranging from 3 to 13 MPa.

The geometry of the fault and the distribution of the receivers are shown in Figure 8. We adopt tetrahedral elements in the mesh with a size of 50 m, and after 10 elements surrounding the fault, the mesh undergoes three coarsenings. This enables capture of the elastodynamic interaction between fault elements by focusing the mesh's spatial sampling near the fault. This mesh enables sampling six points per wavelength, thereby achieving numerical accuracy up to 10 Hz (Petersson and Sjögreen, 2023). Another important element to constrain in the linear slip-weakening model is the spatial sampling of the process zone length. We follow the recommendations of Day *et al.* (2005) to determine the number of elements required to adequately sample the process zone in space. Because there is no analytical solution to estimate the spatial manifestation of the process zone for mode II rupture propagation, we then conduct a numerical test to assess whether we are properly sampling the length of the process zone in cases of small D_c, which is included in the supplemental material. This numerical test (see Fig. S2) shows that halving the element size (to 25 m) yields the same spatiotemporal description of the slip velocity, indicating that we can properly sample the process zone using elements of 50 m. The set of ($\Delta\sigma$,D_c) pairs used in the analysis is listed in Table 2.

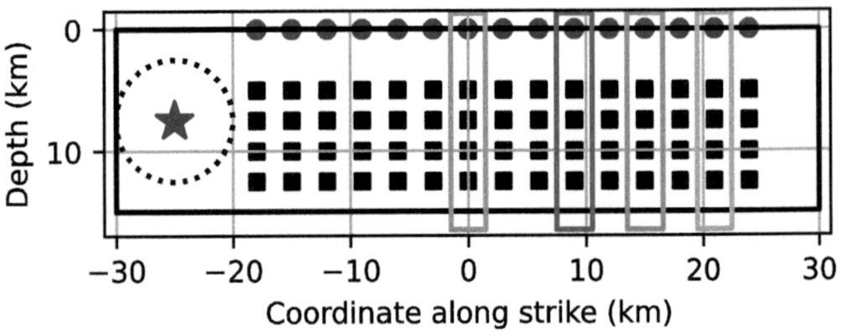

Figure 8. Geometry of the fault adopted. The red star represents the location of the hypocenter, and the black squares denote the receivers in the rupture below the surface. The green circles denote the receivers at the surface are. The dotted circle denote the nucleation region. The colored rectangles represent examples of four different samples of ($\Delta\sigma$, D_c) pairs as part of the sampling conducted. The color version of this figure is available only in the electronic edition.

The evolution of slip velocity at a subfault within the rupture is shown in Figure 9a for four different pairs of $\Delta\sigma$ and D_c. D_c modulates the width and slope of the initial phase of the STF, being the stage of dynamic-stress-drop development, which controls the high-frequency radiation in Kostrov-like STFs. Sharper or more impulsive rise-time evolution increases high-frequency radiation. The increase in the stress drop plays a key role in increasing the slip velocity after the end of the dynamic-stress-drop phase. This can be observed in the local rupture evolution shown in Figure 9a between the cases of static stress drop ranging from 5 to 11 MPa, allowing for a direct comparison of the STFs' phases.

The frequency content of the four STFs is shown in Figure 9b. The Fourier spectra were smoothed by convolving them with a Hanning window of 27 points after resampling the frequencies with 300 samples equally spaced in log(*f*) from 0.006 to 15 Hz. The Fourier amplitudes at low frequencies increase with static stress drop. Increasing D_c impacts how

TABLE 2
Pairs of ($\Delta\sigma$, D_c) Use the Analysis and Its Nucleation Length in Kilometers

	Static Stress Drop $\Delta\sigma$ (MPa)					
D_c (m)	**3**	**5**	**7**	**9**	**11**	**13**
0.2	OK	OK	NR	NR	NR	NR
0.4	OK	OK	OK	OK	OK	NR
0.8	NN	OK	OK	OK	OK	OK
1.2	NN	OK	OK	OK	OK	OK
1.4	NN	NN	OK	OK	OK	OK
1.6	NN	NN	OK	OK	OK	OK
1.8	NN	NN	OK	OK	OK	OK

NN means simulations in which a nucleation radius >5 km is needed for the nucleation, given the current simulation's setup. NR means instances in which the ($\Delta\sigma$, D_c) pair with the adopted mesh does not have enough resolution to solve the process zone. OK corresponds to ($\Delta\sigma$, D_c) pairs that properly nucleate.

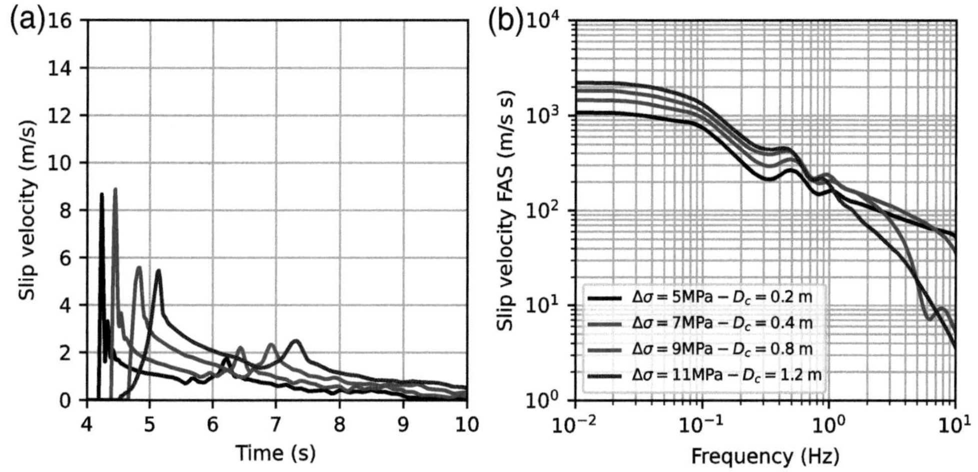

Figure 9. (a) Slip velocity evolution as a function of time at strike coordinate −9 km and at the center of the rupture down-dip (7.5 km depth). (b) Comparison of the STFs in the Fourier domain at the same location. Four different combinations of D_c and static stress drop are displayed as described in the key. The color version of this figure is available only in the electronic edition.

subfaults radiate energy at high frequencies, represented by a decay of the Fourier spectrum at lower frequencies for larger D_c values. The combined effects of increasing static stress drop and D_c lead to a conceptual model that is consistent with the observed correlation. At larger static stress drops, the Fourier amplitudes are larger at low frequencies, being consistent with the classical rupture models developed in the 70s (e.g., Brune, 1970; Madariaga, 1976; Boatwright, 1981). If, at the same time, we increase D_c and $\Delta\sigma$, Fourier spectra with higher static stress drop fall below the spectra with lower static stress drop at high frequencies, generating a negative scaling of the high-frequency Fourier amplitudes for scenarios with larger slip for the same magnitude. This analysis shows that if $\Delta\sigma$ and D_c are positively correlated, they can explain the observed scaling between Fourier amplitude and surface offset under the framework adopted in the simulations.

Analysis of the simulations

Given our simulations' setup, we have 29 $(\Delta\sigma,D_c)$ pairs that provide simulations that properly nucleate with a nucleation radius of 5 km and have a spatial discretization to sample the process zone properly, given our mesh. Each simulation uses a constant D_c and $\Delta\sigma$ over the rupture, but in earthquakes, D_c and $\Delta\sigma$ spatially vary. We assume that the surface offset and the near-fault ground motion are controlled by the local values of D_c and $\Delta\sigma$ at depth. To approximate the effect of variability in D_c and $\Delta\sigma$ over the rupture plane, we randomly draw waveforms for each receiver location from the 29 waveforms associated with the D_c–$\Delta\sigma$ pairs at this position. By sampling from the 29 simulations independently at each receiver, we generate many stochastic realizations of the rupture, each representing a possible distribution of D_c and $\Delta\sigma$ along the fault while preserving the physics captured in the original deterministic runs. As a result, we obtain different realizations of the set of ground motions and surface slips at the 14 receivers located beyond the strike coordinate at −18 km. Ground motions were obtained from receivers located 1 km perpendicular to the fault trace, being a representation of the near-fault ground motions. This approach allows us to assess how local variations in the dynamic parameters controlling surface offset and near-fault ground motion can be evaluated without rerunning the full forward model for every heterogeneous configuration. In addition, the sampling conducted assumes that the $\Delta\sigma$ and D_c are spatially uncorrelated along strike, which ignores the spatial correlations found in evaluations of ruptures (e.g., Mai and Beroza, 2002); however, this assumption is consistent with the approach used for the observational analysis, which also does not account for spatial correlations in the observations along strike. Because we are not conditioning any spatial sampling in the rupture, we can treat the sampling with any characteristic length scale in which the radiated wavefield is governed by the local dynamics represented by a given $(\Delta\sigma,D_c)$ pair.

To seek a parameter space consistent with the observations, we generate 30,000 stochastic rupture realizations varying $(\Delta\sigma,D_c)$ at each receiver, as described earlier, and compute the correlation between the within-event residuals of the surface offset and those of the Fourier amplitudes at different frequencies. We then select the set of $(\Delta\sigma,D_c)$ pairs that has the closest correlation to the target observed correlation (smoothed R in Fig. 7) based on ordinary least-squares metrics. We repeat this process 100 times, resulting in 100 sets of 14 $(\Delta\sigma,D_c)$ pairs that best approximate the correlation obtained from the observations. The correlation coefficients as a function of frequency are shown in Figure 10a as gray curves. The mean of the 100 curves, shown by the bold-blue curve, is similar to the smoothed target observational correlation (yellow curve), indicating that we can identify a parameter space that is consistent with the observations.

The 100 samples of combinations of 14 $(\Delta\sigma,D_c)$ pairs that can approximate the observed correlation are shown in Figure 10b. There is a trend between $\Delta\sigma$ and D_c, indicating that regions with larger static stress drop require larger D_c to converge to the target correlation, consistent with the aforementioned conceptual analysis. This trend has a correlation coefficient R of 0.70 between $\ln(D_c)$ and $\ln(\Delta\sigma)$. The relationship between $\Delta\sigma$ and D_c is consistent with our initial conceptual analysis.

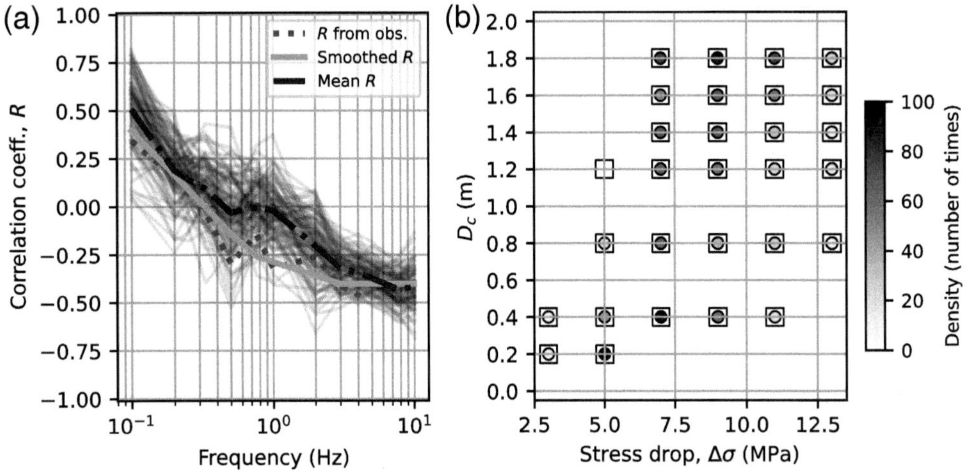

Figure 10. (a) Correlation coefficients obtained from the simulations by comparing the scaling of the STF between surface offset and ground-motion amplitude as a function of frequency. Gray curves are the R-curve for one rupture sample. The blue curve represents the mean of the gray curves. The red and yellow curves represent the observed correlation and its smoothed version, respectively. (b) Scatter plot of D_c as a function of static stress drop ($\Delta\sigma$) for each solution. The color map shows the number of times a (D_c,$\Delta\sigma$) pair is repeated when combining all 100 best samplings that explain the observed scaling. The color version of this figure is available only in the electronic edition.

IMPACT ON KINEMATICALLY CONSTRAINED STFS

Features of the GP rupture generator

The strong static-stress-drop scaling in the GP rupture generator is driven by the current STF parameterization. The shape of the Liu STF (Liu *et al.*, 2006) adopted by the GP rupture generator is shown in Figure 2. The time for which the slip acceleration is positive is fixed at 13% of the total rise time (TRT; $\beta = 0.13$ in Fig. 2), independent of magnitude, rupture dimensions, area, or total slip. The total area under the STF represents the local total slip, and its mean over the rupture area scales with magnitude (Wells and Coppersmith, 1994; Leonard, 2010; Thingbaijam *et al.*, 2017). The rise time also scales with magnitude (Graves and Pitarka, 2010, 2016), as reflected in the duration of the shear dislocation, which is modulated by the rupture geometry, and captured by the corner frequency and its direct dependency on magnitude (e.g., Hanks and Thatcher, 1972). The combined effect of scaling the rise time and total slip with magnitude yields a constant peak slip velocity independent of magnitude, which is the target sought by the authors of the GP rupture generator (A. Pitarka, personal comm., 2025).

The GP rupture generator modifies the relationships used to determine the rise time of shallow subfaults: the TRT at depths shallower than 5 km (and deeper than 18 km) is doubled. This scheme implies that, on average, the time of positive acceleration of the local shear dislocation (positive acceleration rise time, PART in Fig. 2) for the shallow part of the rupture is twice as long as at depth. The consequence is that at least the radiated high-frequency energy is weakened in the first 5 km, and the high-frequency ground motion will be generated from subfaults deeper than 5 km. For the intermediate- to low-frequency radiation, understanding the rupture as a Haskell rupture function with a symmetric STF would suggest that not only the high-frequency but also the intermediate- to low-frequency radiation would come from the STFs with steeper positive acceleration, corresponding to subfaults deeper than 5 km. The latter would imply that the intermediate- to low-frequency radiation would arise from the overall rupture time function and its convolution with the stage of positive acceleration of the local STF. Therefore, STFs from the GP rupture generator in subfaults deeper than 5 km would also be consistent with the STFs shown in Figure 9, not only for high frequencies but also for intermediate-to-low-frequencies. Moreover, the adoption of this shallow region of weak radiation is consistent with rate- and state-dependent friction models. A wide range of geologic materials, as fault gauges, exhibit velocity-strengthening mechanisms under tectonic stress and temperature usually found at depths shallower than 3 km (e.g., Scholz, 1998), thereby reducing the radiated energy. However, we acknowledge that this is an active area of research in our field.

Scaling relationships for TRT, PART, and $\dot{u}_{max}$ as a function of δ_{total}

To reconcile the differences between the static-stress-drop scaling from the rupture generators and the scaling from the observations, the relationships used to set the time window during which slip acceleration is positive and the peak slip velocity need to be adjusted. Therefore, the last stage of our analysis focuses on the implications of our findings on constraining kinematic source modeling. We translate the physical relationships between $\Delta\sigma$ and D_c into kinematic constraints for STFs. The main components to constrain in STFs are depicted in Figure 2. In addition to the total slip (δ_{total}) and the peak slip velocity ($\dot{u}_{max}$), we need to define the TRT and the duration of PART, the phase in which the slip acceleration is positive. We define the ratio between PART and TRT as β. To compute PART and TRT, we adopt a methodology similar to that used to estimate duration from acceleration waveforms, such as the parameter D_{5-95} (the time between the 5% and 95% of the normalized Arias intensity; Pinilla-Ramos *et al.*, 2023), but here we use 1% rather than 5% and the velocity waveforms. First, we

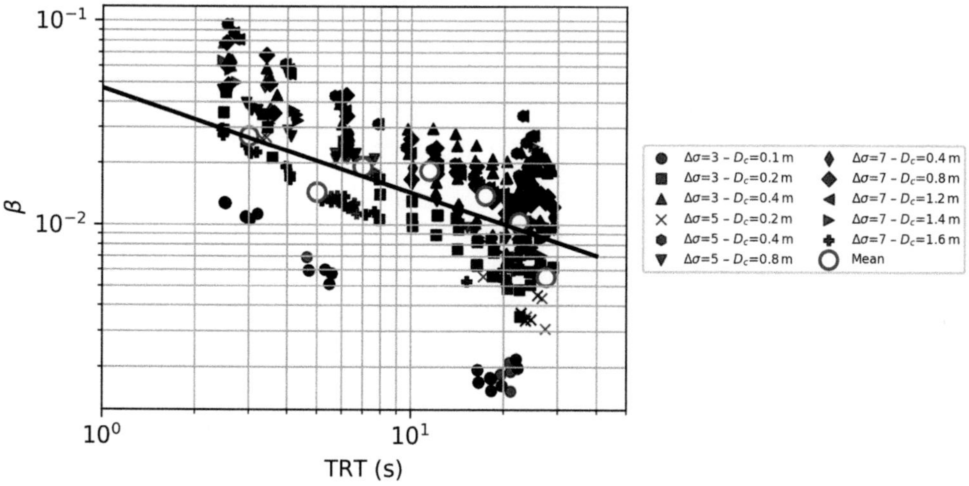

Figure 11. Scatter plot of the ratio β between the PART over the TRT as a function of TRT. The white dots are the mean for the binned data, and the black line is a linear model. For visibility purposes, a subset of the $(D_c, \Delta\sigma)$ pairs is displayed. The color version of this figure is available only in the electronic edition.

convert the waveforms to energy by squaring them, and then we estimate the beginning of the STF, T_0 as the time at which 1% of the total accumulated energy is reached. PART is computed as the time between T_0 and when the STF reaches its maximum value, βT. TRT is computed as the time elapsed from T_0 to the point at which the total accumulated energy reaches 95%. TRT and β values from a subset of STFs from the rupture dynamic simulations that best approximated the observational scaling are shown in Figure 11 using subfaults located between 5 and 10 km depth. Longer shear dislocations have proportionally shorter phases of positive acceleration. This negative correlation between these two parameters should be incorporated into kinematic source models.

The relationship between the kinematic parameters (δ_{total}, $\dot{u}_{\max}$, TRT, and PART) and the dynamic parameters ($\Delta\sigma$ and D_c) is depicted in the correlogram in Figure 12a using subfaults at depths ranging from 5 to 10 km. δ_{total} is uncorrelated with $\dot{u}_{\max}$, and $\dot{u}_{\max}$ is negatively correlated with PART and TRT. TRT and, in particular, PART, are positively correlated with δ_{total}, which is consistent with larger static stress drop generating longer phases of positive acceleration, and is consistent with the findings of Schmedes *et al.* (2010). Moreover, whereas Schmedes *et al.* (2010) found a weak correlation between $\dot{u}_{\max}$ and δ_{total}, our analysis shows no correlation. A key implication of these relationships is that PART scales with TRT, but at the same time, the ratio between them β shrinks for longer shear dislocations.

The correlation coefficient between $\Delta\sigma$ and D_c is strong (0.7 when both parameters are in the log-space), in contrast to the results of Petukhin *et al.* (2025), who found an almost null correlation between these parameters (−0.09). This difference arises because adding the observational constraint that surface offset and Fourier amplitudes are positively correlated requires also a positive correlation between $\Delta\sigma$ and D_c to explain the observations. The largest correlation is between $\ln(\delta_{\text{total}})$ and $\ln(D_c)$ ($R = 0.92$), which implies that several parameters with positive correlation with δ_{total} contribute to its scaling, not just D_c. Another key result is the anticorrelation between $\ln(\dot{u}_{\max})$ and $\ln(\Delta\sigma)$. The observational constraints on the input parameters imply that a subfault with larger static stress drop requires a larger D_c to accommodate the rupture process, and increasing D_c decreases $\dot{u}_{\max}$. This relationship implies that regions with larger static stress drops, and therefore larger slip, radiate stronger low to intermediate frequencies and weaker high frequencies.

Implementation for kinematic source modeling

Defining all the kinematic parameters as a function of slip (and therefore magnitude) is a common approach in rupture generators for kinematic source modeling (e.g., Graves and Pitarka, 2010, 2016). This is an understandable step because one of the main input parameters to generate a rupture is the moment magnitude. Thus, we can build scaling relationships between the three main components needed to constrain kinematic source modeling ($\dot{u}_{\max}$, TRT, and PART) conditioned on δ_{total}. Following the same approach as the GP rupture generator, we begin constraining TRT for each subfault in the rupture by defining a reference TRT (TRT_{ref}) and a reference δ_{total} ($\delta_{\text{total-ref}}$) for a given magnitude scaling and potentially a fault geometry. Then, using the relationships between these parameters, we can express TRT as a function of δ_{total},

$$\text{TRT} = \text{TRT}_{\text{ref}} \left(\frac{\delta_{\text{total}}}{\delta_{\text{total-ref}}} \right)^{b_1}, \tag{3}$$

in which δ_{total} is the local total slip at a given subfault and b_1 is the scaling coefficient, shown in Figure 12b. The PART can be constrained similarly,

$$\text{PART} = \text{PART}_{\text{ref}} \left(\frac{\delta_{\text{total}}}{\delta_{\text{total-ref}}} \right)^{b_2}. \tag{4}$$

The $\dot{u}_{\max}$ has the strongest correlation with the PART, so $\dot{u}_{\max}$ can be expressed as

$$\dot{u}_{\max} = \dot{u}_{\max\text{-ref}} \left(\frac{\text{PART}}{\text{PART}_{\text{ref}}} \right)^{b_3}. \tag{5}$$

The coefficients b_i are shown in Figure 12b. We emphasize that our analysis is built over a rupture consistent with the

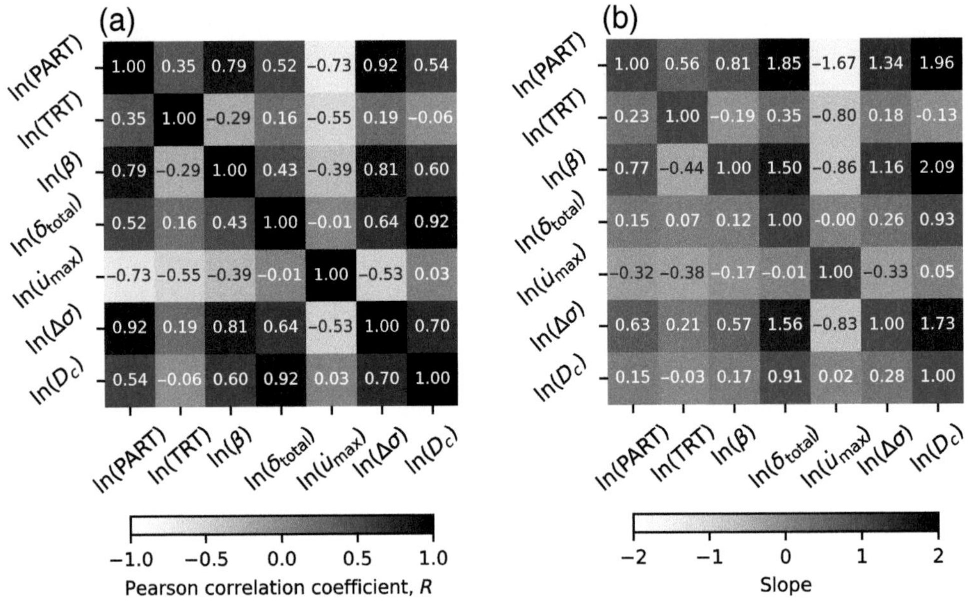

Figure 12. (a) Correlation coefficient between ln(PART), ln(TRT), ln(β), ln(δ_{total}), ln($\dot{u}_{max}$), ln($\Delta\sigma$), and ln(D_c) (see definition in Fig. 2). (b) Linear scaling (slope, b) in the log scale of the kinematic parameters needed to constrain STFs: $\ln(Y) = b\ln(X) + a$. The vertical axis represents the dependent parameter (Y) as a function of the independent parameter (X) on the horizontal axis.

geometry of an M_w 6.95 strike-slip earthquake (mode II rupture propagation) with a fixed geometry for all realizations. The slopes shown in Figure 12b may change for other rupture geometries.

An example of the scaling developed in this study is shown in Figure 13 for three different STFs: a central case with a total slip of 4 m and then Doubling and halving the slip, a reference TRT of 3 s, PART of 4% of the reference TRT, and a mean $\dot{u}_{max}$ of 8.0 m/s. After the stage of positive acceleration, we adopt a functional form as a power decay with time to describe the stage of negative acceleration, $f(t) = c(\mathrm{TRT} - t)^n$. As shown previously, the STF with half of the total slip exhibits a sharper stage of positive acceleration, resulting in a more impulsive response and illuminating higher frequencies. In contrast, the STF that doubles the total slip has a gentler slope and weaker high-frequency radiation.

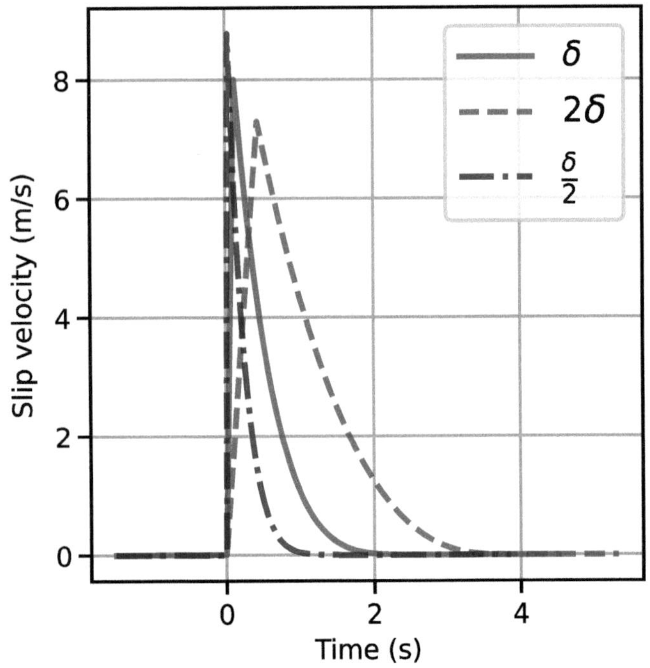

Figure 13. Example showing the obtained scaling of STFs by implementing the results of this study by doubling and halving the slip in a subfault. The total slip is the integral below the curve. The phase of positive acceleration ends at PART. Then, for this example, a power decay was adopted to model the stage of negative acceleration. The color version of this figure is available only in the electronic edition.

POSSIBLE PHYSICAL MECHANISMS FOR THE OBSERVED CORRELATION

This study shows that the radiation of high-frequency energy is negatively correlated with surface offset. As discussed previously, surface offset can serve as a proxy for the slip distribution at depth and represents the local static stress drop within a rupture. The Fourier amplitude recorded at the surface is the manifestation of the slip velocity in nearby regions of the rupture when the wavefield is observed in the near field. Therefore, we can state that the high-frequency part of the STF scales negatively with static stress drop (or slip). Conversely, the low-frequency radiation scales with static stress drop, as expected. In this section, we discuss potential physical mechanisms that can account for this behavior.

The numerical modeling suggests that we need to increase D_c (at fixed stress resistance) and therefore the fracture energy, to explain the observations in response to higher static stress drops. Our findings are consistent with those of Guatteri and Spudich (2000), who held the static-stress-drop constant and varied the dynamic stress drop, finding a negative correlation between the strength excess and the weakening slip distance. In our analysis, we keep an approach that varies the initial shear stress and modulates the fracture energy with D_c.

At least three mechanisms modulate the cohesive or process zone length (the spatial manifestation of D_c). The cohesive or process zone is the response of materials with finite shear resistance to the stress singularity at the crack tip. Barenblatt (1962) introduced this concept for engineering materials, and it was subsequently implemented in seismological applications using a linear slip-weakening mechanism (Ida, 1972; Palmer *et al.*, 1973). This model represents the region where the material has reached its peak stress limit and begins to exhibit nonlinear behavior and/or plastic or inelastic flow. Larger static stress drops lead to larger intensity factors driving the rupture, which may require a longer process zone behind the crack tip to accommodate the increment in shear stress on materials with finite resistance (chapter 8.5, Freund, 1990). On the other hand, increasing static stress drop increases rupture velocity (Andrews, 1976, 1985; Dunham, 2007). Faster ruptures lead to a contraction of the process zone by a phenomenon referred to as "Lorentz" contraction based on the framework of special relativity theory (Freund, 1990; Day *et al.*, 2005; Fineberg and Svetlizky, 2014). The third element is the increase in material resistance caused by shearing under faster strain rates. This phenomenon has been explored in engineering materials, showing a strong increase in material resistance when the rupture velocity exceeds 50% of the terminal rupture velocity (Rosakis and Zehnder, 1985, and references therein). This last phenomenon can be captured by augmenting the fracture-energy balance with a slip-velocity-dependent (or rupture-velocity) term. The first and third mechanisms lead to an expansion of the process zone or an increase in fracture energy, and the second leads to a contraction. Our analysis suggests that increasing the static stress drop requires a larger D_c to match the observed scaling. Therefore, the two mechanisms leading to an expansion of the process zone and an increase in the fracture energy when increasing static stress drop govern the physical behavior over the mechanism that contracts the process zone in earthquakes. We may speculate that this is because the rupture velocity may fluctuate around a fixed value (~70%–80% of the local shear-wave velocity). Within this range of fluctuations, the process zone contraction may be of second order compared with the other two physical mechanisms that modulate the process zone length. We are not referring to the manifestation of supershear in this analysis, which may introduce additional complexities to mode II rupture propagation. To the authors' knowledge, there are no analytical solutions for the contraction of the process zone during mode II rupture propagation in the supershear regime, which is an unexplored region. The contraction in sub-Rayleigh rupture propagation tends to a cohesive zone of zero length for mode II when the rupture velocity approximates the maximum terminal rupture velocity (91% of the local shear-wave velocity, which is the Rayleigh-wave velocity). Therefore, this is an active area of research in this field.

CONCLUSIONS

Our observational analysis shows that the variability of high-frequency ground motion along the strike is negatively correlated with surface offset. Currently used kinematic rupture generators are unable to model the negative correlation obtained from the observations.

A positive correlation between static stress drop and the slip-weakening distance D_c may be an alternative to capture the negative correlation in rupture dynamics simulations. Increasing D_c decreases the frequency at which the FAS decays, diminishing the high-frequency radiation. At the same time, increasing static stress drop leads to increased low-frequency radiation, consistent with classical source models of the 70s. This implies that if static stress drop and D_c are positively correlated, they can explain the observed scaling.

Using the domain of D_c and $\Delta\sigma$ pairs that lead to correlations consistent with the observations, we proposed a set of relationships to constrain STFs in kinematic source modeling. We find a negative linear relationship between ln(PART/TRT) and ln(TRT), with PART being the time window with positive acceleration and TRT the total duration of STFs. This implies that the phase of positive acceleration in the STF proportionally shrinks relative to TRT as TRT increases. Current STF parameterizations keep a fixed percentage of TRT as the stage of positive slip acceleration (Tinti *et al.*, 2005; Liu *et al.*, 2006; Graves and Pitarka, 2010). Our relationships can be used to develop new STF scaling for kinematic rupture generators consistent with the correlations from the observational framework between surface slip and the Fourier amplitudes of near-fault ground motions.

Incorporating this approach into kinematic rupture generators will lead to significant changes in the simulation results: regions with larger-than-average within-event total slip (and therefore larger local static stress drop) radiate energy with stronger low-frequency content and weaker high-frequency content. The opposite occurs for regions with smaller-than-average within-event total slip.

DATA AND RESOURCES

The ground-motion amplitude at different frequencies comes from Buckreis *et al.* (2025). The surface offset data come from Sarmiento *et al.* (2024) for the Chi-Chi, Kocaeli, and Wenchuan earthquakes and from DuRoss *et al.* (2024) for the Pazarcik earthquake. This study has supplemental material, which includes a thorough description of the kinematic simulations, for which results are used in the introduction; a numerical test to assess mesh resolution for small D_c values; and two additional figures. In addition, the mean surface offset residuals are provided in the .csv file of the supplemental material.

DECLARATION OF COMPETING INTERESTS

The authors acknowledge that there are no conflicts of interest recorded.

ACKNOWLEDGMENTS

Chih-Hsuan (Karen) Sung preprocessed the data for the relationship between stress drop and between-event terms from the Abrahamson *et al.* (2025; denotes as ASLPB25) ground-motion model (GMM).

Grigorios Lavrentiadis provided deep discussions about field survey measurements of surface offset. The authors acknowledge the Texas Advanced Computing Center (TACC) at The University of Texas at Austin for providing computational resources that have contributed to the research results reported within this article.

REFERENCES

Abdelmeguid, M., M. S. Mia, and A. Elbanna (2024). On the interplay between distributed bulk plasticity and local fault slip in evolving fault zone complexity, *Geophys. Res. Lett.* **51,** no. 14, e2023GL108060, doi: 10.1029/2023GL108060.

Abrahamson, N., C.-H. Sung, G. Lavrentiadis, C. Pinilla-Ramos, and J. Bayless (2025). Ergodic Ground-motion model for Fourier amplitude for crustal earthquakes in the Western United States, *Technical Rept. CalTrans*, Copy can be requested through Caltrans (R&D).

Abrahamson, N., and R. Youngs (1992). A stable algorithm for regression analyses using the random effects model, *Bull. Seismol. Soc. Am.* **82,** no. 1, 505–510.

Ampuero, J.-P., and Y. Ben-Zion (2008). Cracks, pulses and macroscopic asymmetry of dynamic rupture on a bimaterial interface with velocity-weakening friction, *Geophys. J. Int.* **173,** no. 2, 674–692.

Ancheta, T., R. Darragh, J. Stewart, E. Seyhan, W. Silva, B. Chiou, K. Wooddell, R. Graves, A. Kottke, D. M. Boore, *et al.* (2014). NGA-West2 database, *Earthq. Spectra* **30,** no. 3, 989–1005.

Andrews, D. J. (1976). Rupture velocity of plane strain shear cracks, *J. Geophys. Res.: Solid Earth* **81,** no. 32, 5679–5687.

Andrews, D. J. (1985). Dynamic plane-strain shear rupture with a slip-weakening friction law calculated by a boundary integral method, *Bull. Seismol. Soc. Am.* **75,** no. 1, 1–21.

Artale Harris, P., A. Pitarka, A. Akinci, and A. Cuius (2025). Broadband near-fault ground-motion simulations using a modified f-k Method in Central Italy, *Bull. Seismol. Soc. Am.* doi: 10.1785/0120250165.

Barall, M. (2009). A grid-doubling finite-element technique for calculating dynamic three-dimensional spontaneous rupture on an earthquake fault, *Geophys. J. Int.* **178,** no. 2, 845–859.

Barbot, S. D., H. Luo, T. Wang, Y. Hamiel, O. Piatibratova, M. T. Javed, C. Braitenberg, and G. Gurbuz (2023). Slip distribution of the February 6, 2023 Mw 7.8 and Mw 7.6, Kahramanmaraş, Turkey earthquake sequence in the East Anatolian Fault Zone, *Seismica* **2,** no. 3, doi: 10.26443/seismica.v2i3.502.

Barenblatt, G. (1962). The mathematical theory of equilibrium cracks in Brittle fracture, *Adv. Appl. Mech.* **7,** no. 7, 55–129.

Bayless, J., and N. A. Abrahamson (2019). Summary of the BA18 ground-motion model for Fourier amplitude spectra for crustal earthquakes in California, *Bull. Seismol. Soc. Am.* **109,** no. 5, 2088–2105.

Ben-Zion, Y., and J. Morrissey (1995). A simple re-derivation of logarithmic disordering of a dynamic planar crack due to small random heterogeneities, *J. Mech. Phys. Solids* **43,** no. 9, 1363–1368.

Bernard, P., and R. Madariaga (1984). High-frequency seismic radiation from a buried circular fault, *Geophys. J. Int.* **78,** no. 1, 1–17.

Bizzarri, A., and M. Cocco (2003). Slip-weakening behavior during the propagation of dynamic ruptures obeying rate- and state-dependent friction laws, *J. Geophys. Res.: Solid Earth* **108,** no. B8, doi: 10.1029/2002JB002198.

Boatwright, J. (1981). Quasi-dynamic models of simple earthquakes: Application to an aftershock of the 1975 Oroville, California, earthquake, *Bull. Seismol. Soc. Am.* **71,** no. 1, 69–94.

Brune, J. (1970). Tectonic stress and the spectra of seismic shear waves from earthquakes, *J. Geophys. Res.: Solid Earth* **75,** no. 26, 4997–5009.

Buckreis, T., J. Stewart, and Y. Bozorgnia (2025). Data Resources for NGA-West3 Project, *Technical Rept.*, Natural Hazards Risk & Resiliency Research Center B. John Garrick Institute for the Risk Sciences - University of California, Los Angeles, California.

Chen, J., and Y. Zhou (2024). Coseismic slip distribution of the 2023 earthquake doublet in Turkey and Syria from joint inversion of Sentinel-1 and Sentinel-2 data: An iterative modelling method for mapping large earthquake deformation, *Geophys. J. Int.* **237,** no. 1, 636–648.

Chi, W.-C., D. Dreger, and A. Kaverina (2001). Finite-source modeling of the 1999 Taiwan (Chi-Chi) earthquake derived from a dense strong-motion network, *Bull. Seismol. Soc. Am.* **91,** no. 5, 1144–1157.

Cocco, M., and A. Bizzarri (2002). On the slip-weakening behavior of rate- and state dependent constitutive laws, *Geophys. Res. Lett.* **29,** no. 11, 11-1–11-4.

Day, S. (1982a). Three-dimensional finite difference simulation of fault dynamics: Rectangular faults with fixed rupture velocity, *Bull. Seismol. Soc. Am.* **72,** no. 3, 705–727.

Day, S. (1982b). Three-dimensional simulation of spontaneous rupture: The effect of nonuniform prestress, *Bull. Seismol. Soc. Am.* **72,** no. 6A, 1881–1902.

Day, S., L. Dalguer, N. Lapusta, and Y. Liu (2005). Comparison of finite difference and boundary integral solutions to three-dimensional spontaneous rupture, *J. Geophys. Res.: Solid Earth* **110,** doi: 10.1029/2005JB003813.

Delouis, B., J.-M. Nocquet, and M. Vallée (2010). Slip distribution of the February 27, 2010 Mw = 8.8 Maule Earthquake, central Chile, from static and high-rate GPS, InSAR, and broadband teleseismic data, *Geophys. Res. Lett.* **37,** no. 17, doi: 10.1029/2010GL043899.

Delouis, B., M. van den Ende, and J. Ampuero (2023). Kinematic rupture model of the 6 February 2023 Mw 7.8 Türkiye earthquake from a large set of near-source strong-motion records combined with GNSS offsets reveals intermittent supershear rupture, *Bull. Seismol. Soc. Am.* **114,** no. 2, 726–740.

Dieterich, J. H. (1979a). Modeling of rock friction: 1. Experimental results and constitutive equations, *J. Geophys. Res.: Solid Earth* **84,** no. B5, 2161–2168.

Dieterich, J. H. (1979b). Modeling of rock friction: 2. Simulation of preseismic slip, *J. Geophys. Res.: Solid Earth* **84,** 2169–2175.

Doody, C., A. Rodgers, A. Chiang, M. Afanasiev, C. Boehm, L. Krischer, and N. Simmons (2024). Improved earthquake source parameters with 3D wavespeed models in California and Nevada, *Seismol. Res. Lett.* **96,** no. 1, 499–509.

Dreger, D., G. Beroza, S. Day, C. Goulet, T. Jordan, and P. Spudich (2015). Validation of the SCEC broadband platform V14.3 simulation methods using pseudo spectral acceleration data, *Seismol. Res. Lett.* **86,** no. 1, 39–47.

Dunham, E. M. (2007). Conditions governing the occurrence of supershear ruptures under slip-weakening friction, *J. Geophys. Res.: Solid Earth* **112,** no. B7, doi: 10.1029/2006JB004717.

DuRoss, C., N. Reitman, A. Hatem, H. Mason, G. Lavrentiadis, D. Asimaki, C. Milliner, M. Karakaş, and B. Seçen (2024). Are field observations of surface rupture useful? An example from the 2023 Mw 7.8 Pazarcık, Turkey (Türkiye), earthquake, *Seismol. Res. Lett.* **96,** no. 2A, 848–867.

Fineberg, J., and I. Svetlizky (2014). Classical shear cracks drive the onset of dry frictional motion, *Nature* **509,** no. 4799, 205–208.

Freund, L. B. (1990). *Dynamic Fracture Mechanics*, Cambridge University Press, Cambridge, United Kingdom.

Gabriel, A., T. Ulrich, M. Marchandon, J. Biemiller, and J. Rekoske (2023). 3D dynamic rupture modeling of the 6 February 2023, Kahramanmaraş, Turkey Mw 7.8 and 7.7 earthquake doublet using early observations, *Seism. Record* **3,** no. 4, 342–356.

Graves, R., T. Jordan, S. Callaghan, E. Deelman, E. Field, G. Juve, C. Kesselman, P. Maechling, G. Mehta, K. Milner, *et al.* (2011). CyberShake: A physics-based seismic hazard model for Southern California, *Pure Appl. Geophys.* **168,** no. 3, 1420–9136.

Graves, R., and A. Pitarka (2010). Broadband ground-motion simulation using a hybrid approach, *Bull. Seismol. Soc. Am.* **100,** no. 5A, 2095–2123.

Graves, R., and A. Pitarka (2015). Refinements to the Graves and Pitarka (2010) broadband ground-motion simulation method, *Seismol. Res. Lett.* **86,** no. 1, 2136–2153.

Graves, R., and A. Pitarka (2016). Kinematic ground-motion simulations on rough faults including effects of 3D stochastic velocity perturbations, *Bull. Seismol. Soc. Am.* **106,** no. 5, 2136–2153.

Guatteri, M., and P. Spudich (2000). What can strong-motion data tell us about slip-weakening fault-friction laws? *Bull. Seismol. Soc. Am.* **90,** no. 1, 98–116.

Hanks, T., and W. Thatcher (1972). A graphical representation of seismic source parameters, *J. Geophys. Res.: Solid Earth* **77,** no. 23, 4393–4405.

Harris, R. A., M. Barall, B. Aagaard, S. Ma, D. Roten, K. Olsen, B. Duan, D. Liu, B. Luo, K. Bai, *et al.* (2018). A suite of exercises for verifying dynamic earthquake rupture codes, *Seismol. Res. Lett.* **89,** no. 3, 1146–1162.

Hayes, G. P. (2017). The finite, kinematic rupture properties of great-sized earthquakes since 1990, *Earth Planet. Sci. Lett.* **468,** 94–100.

Hayes, G. P., E. Bergman, K. L. Johnson, H. M. Benz, L. Brown, and A. S. Meltzer (2013). Seismotectonic framework of the 2010 February 27 Mw 8.8 Maule, Chile earthquake sequence, *Geophys. J. Int.* **195,** no. 2, 1034–1051.

Ida, Y. (1972). Cohesive force across the tip of a longitudinal-shear crack and Griffith's specific surface energy, *J. Geophys. Res.: Solid Earth* **77,** no. 20, 3796–3805.

Irikura, K., and H. Miyake (2011). Recipe for predicting strong ground motion from crustal earthquake scenarios, *Pure Appl. Geophys.* **168,** no. 1, 85–104.

Ito, T., K. Ozawa, T. Watanabe, and T. Sagiya (2011). Slip distribution of the 2011 off the Pacific coast of Tohoku earthquake inferred from geodetic data, *Geophys. J. Int.* **63,** no. 7, doi: 10.5047/eps.2011.06.023.

Johnson, K. M., Y.-J. Hsu, P. Segall, and S.-B. Yu (2001). Fault geometry and slip distribution of the 1999 Chi-Chi, Taiwan Earthquake imaged from inversion of GPS data, *Geophys. Res. Lett.* **28,** no. 11, 2285–2288.

Kottke, A., N. Abrahamson, D. Boore, Y. Bozorgnia, C. Goulet, J. Hollenback, T. Kishida, O.-J. Ktenidou, E. Rathje, W. Silva, *et al.* (2021). Selection of random vibration theory procedures for the NGA-East project and ground-motion modeling, *Earthq. Spectra* **37,** no. 1_suppl, 1420–1439.

Lavrentiadis, G., and N. Abrahamson (2023). Fault-displacement models for aggregate and principal displacements, *Earthq. Spectra* **41,** no. 4, doi: 10.1177/87552930231201531.

Leonard, M. (2010). Earthquake fault scaling: Self-consistent relating of rupture length, width, average displacement, and moment release, *Bull. Seismol. Soc. Am.* **100,** no. 5, 1971–1988.

Liu, P., R. Archuleta, and S. Hartzell (2006). Prediction of broadband ground-motion time histories: Hybrid low/high-frequency method with correlated random source parameters, *Bull. Seismol. Soc. Am.* **96,** 2118–2130.

Lyakhovsky, V., Y. Ben-Zion, A. Ilchev, and A. Mendecki (2016). Dynamic rupture in a damage-breakage rheology model, *Geophys. J. Int.* **206,** no. 2, 1126–1143.

Ma, K.-F., J. Mori, S.-J. Lee, and S. B. Yu (2001). Spatial and temporal distribution of slip for the 1999 Chi-Chi, Taiwan, earthquake, *Bull. Seismol. Soc. Am.* **91,** no. 5, 1069–1087.

Ma, K.-F., T.-R. A. Song, S.-J. Lee, and H.-I. Wu (2000). Spatial slip distribution of the September 20, 1999, Chi-Chi, Taiwan, Earthquake (MW7.6)—Inverted from teleseismic data, *Geophys. Res. Lett.* **27,** no. 20, 3417–3420.

Madariaga, R. (1976). Dynamics of an expanding circular fault, *Bull. Seismol. Soc. Am.* **66,** no. 3, 639–666.

Maechling, P., F. Silva, S. Callaghan, and T. Jordan (2014). SCEC broadband platform: System architecture and software implementation, *Seismol. Res. Lett.* **86,** no. 1, 27–38.

Mai, P., and G. Beroza (2002). A spatial random field model to characterize complexity in earthquake slip, *J. Geophys. Res.: Solid Earth* **107,** no. B11, ESE 10-1–ESE 10-21.

Mai, P. M., and K. K. S. Thingbaijam (2014). SRCMOD: An online database of finite-fault rupture models, *Seismol. Res. Lett.* **85,** no. 6, 1348–1357.

McCallen, D., A. Petersson, A. Rodgers, A. Pitarka, M. Miah, F. Petrone, B. Sjogreen, N. Abrahamson, and H. Tang (2021). EQSIM—A multidisciplinary framework for fault-to-structure earthquake simulations on exascale computers part I: Computational models and workflow, *Earthq. Spectra* **37,** no. 2, 707–735.

McCallen, D., F. Petrone, M. Miah, A. Pitarka, A. Rodgers, and N. Abrahamson (2021). EQSIM—A multidisciplinary framework for fault-to- structure earthquake simulations on exascale computers, part II: Regional simulations of building response, *Earthq. Spectra* **37,** no. 2, 736–761.

Palmer, A., J. Rice, and R. Hill (1973). The growth of slip surfaces in the progressive failure of over-consolidated clay, *Proc. Math. Phys. Sci.* **332,** no. 1591, 527–548.

Papageorgiou, A. S., and K. Aki (1983, 06). A specific barrier model for the quantitative description of inhomogeneous faulting and the prediction of strong ground motion. I. Description of the model, *Bull. Seismol. Soc. Am.* **73,** no. 3, 693–722.

Petersson, N., and B. Sjögreen (2023). User's guide to SW4, version 3.0, *Lawrence Livermore National Laboratory LLNL-SM-741439.*

Petukhin, A., P. Galvez, P. Somerville, J. Ampuero, M. Mai, A. Pitarka, K. Yoshida, and K. Irikura (2025). Insights into slip-rate time functions, rupture parameter correlations, and ground motions from validated multicycle earthquake ruptures, *Bull. Seismol. Soc. Am.* **115,** no. 4, 1591–1610.

Pinilla-Ramos, C., N. Abrahamson, R. Kayen, V. Phung, and P. Castellanos-Nash (2023). Ground-motion model for significant duration constrained by seismological simulations, *Bull. Seismol. Soc. Am.* **114,** no. 2, 1015–1032.

Pinilla-Ramos, C. I., N. A. Abrahamson, S. Marcou, D. S. Dreger, A. Savvaidis, G. M. Atkinson, B. Hassani, C. Sung, and R. Youngs (2026). Examining the causes of regional differences in California based on ground motions from small-to-moderate earthquakes, *Seismol. Res. Lett.* Accepted for publication.

Power, M., B. Chiou, N. Abrahamson, Y. Bozorgnia, T. Shantz, and C. Roblee (2008). An overview of the NGA project, *Earthq. Spectra* **24,** no. 1, 3–21.

Rice, J. R., Y. Ben-Zion, and K.-S. Klm (1994). Three-dimensional perturbation solution for a dynamic planar crack moving unsteadily in a model elastic solid, *J. Mech. Phys. Solids* **42,** no. 5, 813–843.

Rodgers, A. J., N. Anders Petersson, A. Pitarka, D. B. McCallen, B. Sjogreen, and N. Abrahamson (2019). Broadband (0–5 Hz) fully deterministic 3d ground-motion simulations of a magnitude 7.0 Hayward Fault earthquake: Comparison with empirical ground-motion models and 3D path and site effects from source normalized intensities, *Seismol. Res. Lett.* **90,** no. 3, 1268–1284.

Rosakis, A., and A. Zehnder (1985). On the dynamic fracture of structural metals, *Int. J. Fract.* **27,** no. 3, 1573–2673.

Ruina, A. (1983). Slip instability and state variable friction laws, *J. Geophys. Res.: Solid Earth* **88,** no. B12, 10,359–10,370.

Sarmiento, A., D. Madugo, Y. Bozorgnia, A. Shen, S. Mazzoni, G. Lavrentiadis, T. Dawson, C. Madugo, A. Kottke, S. Thompson, *et al.* (2024). Flatfiles and related digital products for the fault displacement hazard initiative database, doi: 10.1177/87552930241262766.

Schmedes, J., R. J. Archuleta, and D. Lavallée (2010). Correlation of earthquake source parameters inferred from dynamic rupture simulations, *J. Geophys. Res.: Solid Earth* **115,** no. B3, doi: 10.1029/2009JB006689.

Scholz, C. (1994). Reply to comments on "A reappraisal of large earthquake scaling" by C. Scholz, *Bull. Seismol. Soc. Am.* **84,** no. 5, 1677–1678.

Scholz, C. (1998). Earthquakes and friction laws, *Nature* **391,** no. 6662, 37–42.

Scholz, C. (2019). *The Mechanics of Earthquakes and Faulting*, Third Ed., Cambridge University Press, Cambridge, United Kingdom.

Segall, P. (2010). *Earthquake and Volcano Deformation*,C. Book (Editor), Princeton University Press, Princeton, New Jersey.

Shao, Z., R. Wang, Y. Wu, and L. Zhang (2011). Rapid afterslip and short-term viscoelastic relaxation following the 2008 M_w 7.9 Wenchuan earthquake, *Earthq Sci.* **24,** no. 2, 163–175.

Shaw, B. E., and C. H. Scholz (2001). Slip-length scaling in large earthquakes: Observations and theory and implications for earthquake physics, *Geophys. Res. Lett.* **28,** no. 15, 2995–2998.

Shaw, B. E., and S. G. Wesnousky (2008). Slip-length scaling in large earthquakes: The role of deep-penetrating slip below the seismogenic layer, *Bull. Seismol. Soc. Am.* **98,** no. 4, 1633–1641.

Silverii, F., D. Cheloni, N. D'Agostino, G. Selvaggi, and E. Boschi (2014). Post-seismic slip of the 2011 Tohoku-Oki earthquake from GPS observations: Implications for depth-dependent properties of subduction megathrusts, *Geophys. J. Int.* **198,** no. 1, 580–596.

Song, S. G., and P. Somerville (2010). Physics-based earthquake source characterization and modeling with geostatistics, *Bull. Seismol. Soc. Am.* **100,** no. 2, 482–496.

Thingbaijam, K., M. Martin, and K. Goda (2017). New empirical earthquake source-scaling laws, *Bull. Seismol. Soc. Am.* **107,** no. 5, 2225–2246.

Tinti, E., E. Fukuyama, A. Piatanesi, and M. Cocco (2005). A kinematic source-time function compatible with earthquake dynamics, *Bull. Seismol. Soc. Am.* **95,** no. 4, 1211–1223.

Wells, D., and K. Coppersmith (1994). New empirical relationships among magnitude, rupture length, rupture width, rupture area, and surface displacement, *Bull. Seismol. Soc. Am.* **84,** no. 4, 974–1002.

Wu, C., M. Takeo, and S. Ide (2001). Source process of the Chi-Chi earthquake: A joint inversion of strong motion data and global positioning system data with a multifault model, *Bull. Seismol. Soc. Am.* **91,** no. 5, 1128–1143.

Yamazaki, Y., K. F. Cheung, and T. Lay (2018). A self-consistent fault slip model for the 2011 Tohoku earthquake and tsunami, *J. Geophys.: Res. Solid Earth* **123,** no. 2, 1435–1458.

Yue, H., T. Lay, L. Rivera, C. An, C. Vigny, X. Tong, and J. C. Báez Soto (2014). Localized fault slip to the trench in the 2010 Maule, Chile M = 8.8 earthquake from joint inversion of high-rate GPS, teleseismic body waves, InSAR, campaign GPS, and tsunami observations, *J. Geophys. Res.: Solid Earth* **119,** no. 10, 7786–7804.

Zeng, Y., and C.-H. Chen (2001). Fault rupture process of the 20 September 1999 Chi-Chi, Taiwan, earthquake, *Bull. Seismol. Soc. Am.* **91,** no. 5, 1088–1098.

Zhang, W., T. Iwata, K. Irikura, A. Pitarka, and H. Sekiguchi (2004). Dynamic rupture process of the 1999 Chi-Chi, Taiwan, earthquake, *Geophys. Res. Lett.* **31,** no. 10, doi: 10.1029/2004GL019827.

Manuscript received 7 August 2025
Published online 5 March 2026

Empirical Modeling of Source Directivity Effects into a Ground-Motion Model for Central Italy

Leonardo Colavitti*[1], Giovanni Lanzano[2], Sara Sgobba[2], and Francesca Pacor[2]

ABSTRACT

Assessing the spatial variability of seismic shaking in the epicentral area of an earthquake is one of the major challenges to be addressed in seismic hazard estimates. Among the main contributions to the ground-motion variability, source directivity plays a predominant role, inducing spectral amplifications in the direction of rupture propagations, even for small- to moderate-magnitude earthquakes. The scope of this work is to provide an empirical predictive model that can be used to modulate the ground-motion amplitudes, according to the expected source directivity effects. The proposed directivity corrective term is built for acceleration spectral ordinates, parameterizing the azimuthal trend of the leftover residuals of a fully nonergodic regional model, after removing the systematic effects of source, site, and propagation. Our study is focused on the area of Central Italy, which is dominated by a complex system of normal faults that has generated several seismic sequences in the past 30 yr. The residual analysis is carried out using the recordings of 456 events in magnitude ranging from 3.2 to 6.5, showing that about one-third of the examined earthquakes exhibit a clear ground-motion azimuthal pattern. The directivity correction model is based on three empirical relations, which describe (1) azimuthal variations modeled via a theoretical directivity factor, (2) spectral variation of directivity amplitude using a first-order Gaussian function, and (3) the correlation between moment magnitude and the period of maximum directivity effect. We demonstrated that the introduction of a source directivity correction, applied to a real-case scenario, has a considerable impact and may result in a 20% reduction of aleatory variability with respect to the uncorrected nonergodic model. This model offers an empirically based and physically consistent framework for capturing spatial variations in ground shaking, thereby improving the reliability of seismic hazard evaluations and informing risk mitigation strategies.

KEY POINTS

- Source directivity is crucial for ground-motion variability of moderate earthquakes in Central Italy.
- We propose an empirical model capturing azimuthal variations in ground motion caused by source directivity.
- Directivity correction in a real-case scenario reduces aleatory variability and is useful for hazard analysis.

Supplemental Material

INTRODUCTION

Source directivity is one of the main contributors to the ground-motion variability in the epicentral area. It reflects the complexity of the rupture process and produces anisotropic shaking caused by the propagation of the rupture front. This phenomenon leads to seismic ground motions that differ significantly from expected ground-motion amplitudes, often resulting in amplified shaking in the direction of rupture propagation, when the rupture velocity approaches the *S*-wave velocity (Chen, 2017).

The directivity effect has been well recognized since the works of Benioff (1955) and Kasashara (1960) in recordings of large earthquakes ($M_w > 7$) in California and in Alaska, respectively, and it has been theoretically described in the work of Ben-Menahem (1961). However, in the 1970s, a description of source directivity was provided (Aki, 1968; Trifunac and Brune, 1970;

1. Department of Earth, Environmental and Life Sciences, University of Genoa, Genoa, Italy, https://orcid.org/0000-0002-9364-7676 (LC); 2. Istituto Nazionale di Geofisica e Vulcanologia, Milan, Italy, https://orcid.org/0000-0001-7947-4281 (GL); https://orcid.org/0000-0002-5669-8650 (SS); https://orcid.org/0000-0001-5745-0414 (FP)

*Corresponding author: leonardo.colavitti@edu.unige.it

Cite this article as Colavitti, L., G. Lanzano, S. Sgobba, and F. Pacor (2026). Empirical Modeling of Source Directivity Effects into a Ground-Motion Model for Central Italy, *Bull. Seismol. Soc. Am.* **116**, 1081–1102, doi: 10.1785/0120250200

Boore and Joyner, 1978), especially at low frequencies and for large events (e.g., Parkfield 28 June 1966). Quantitative approaches have successfully emerged in later years (Boatwright, 2007). From the 1980s onward, the study of source directivity has been considered not only as a purely scientific application but also as a key parameter for seismic hazard assessment. In fact, directivity entered for the first time into the ground-motion models (GMMs) with the work of Campbell (1987), and Douglas *et al.* (1988) demonstrated that directivity depends furthermore on the frequency and involves a frequency shift of the radiated spectra—in other words, a Doppler effect. Later Somerville *et al.* (1997) first considered the directivity as a function depending on few source parameters and frequency. In the following years, the existence and quantification of the directivity effect for small-magnitudes earthquakes became a matter of debate in the scientific community, as highlighted by various recent literature (Tan and Helmberger, 2010; Courboulex *et al.*, 2013; Chen *et al.*, 2014; Pacor, Gallovič, *et al.*, 2016; Colavitti, Lanzano, Sgobba, Pacor, and Gallovič, 2022; Calderoni *et al.*, 2023). Over the past 20 yr, because of the development of broadband seismic networks, we are able to observe and detect directivity not only for earthquakes with large (e.g., 1992 M_w 7.3 Landers earthquake, e.g., Velasco *et al.*, 1994) but also with moderate (López-Comino *et al.*, 2012; Wen *et al.*, 2015) and small magnitudes (Yamada *et al.*, 2005; Tomic *et al.*, 2009; Chen *et al.*, 2010). Some efforts to incorporate source directivity effects into GMMs were also carried out in the framework of the Next Generation Attenuation (NGA)-West2 project (Spudich and Chiou, 2008; Chiou and Spudich, 2013; Spudich *et al.*, 2014), but researchers concluded that none of the existing models has a functional form that smoothly transitions between large- and small-magnitude events. In the past 20 yr, some works attempted to take into account the effects of pulse-like ground motions (e.g., Bray and Rodriguez-Marek, 2004; Baker and Cornell, 2008) as a possible parameterization of directivity. Baker (2007) proposed a technique for identifying large velocity pulses in ground motion records, which are generally stronger in the direction orthogonal to the strike of the fault. Recent works by Ross *et al.* (2020) and Weatherill and Lilienkamp (2024) have adopted machine learning approaches to capture the directivity in probabilistic seismic hazard assessment (PSHA) models. Gentile and Galasso (2020) observed that some works have proposed modifications to the conventional PSHA framework to model the pulse-occurrence probability, the pulse period distribution, and the spectral amplification induced by forward-directivity effects (Chioccarelli and Iervolino, 2010; Shahi and Baker, 2011; Spudich *et al.*, 2013). More recently, Bayless *et al.* (2024) proposed an empirical directivity correction factor that can be applied to traditional GMMs to be implemented in PSHA. Indeed, there is a growing interest in incorporating directivity effects into GMMs for PSHA, and several researchers have started to propose explicit models to account for directivity within the hazard framework (Weatherill and Lilienkamp, 2024; Lilienkamp and Weatherill, 2025).

The present study aims to provide an empirical correction equation to adjust the predictions of a fully nonergodic GMM for acceleration response spectra, taking into account directivity effects through few input parameters. In this regard, previous investigations by several authors (Baltay *et al.*, 2017; Kotha *et al.*, 2019; Huang *et al.*, 2023) have observed a clear azimuthal pattern in the leftover aleatory variability, which can be attributed to nonsystematic source effects, such as directivity effects and radiation pattern.

The current research extends the work of Colavitti, Lanzano, Sgobba, Pacor, and Gallovič (2022), who studied the directivity phenomenon on the basis of residuals of a GMM for the Fourier amplitude spectra (FAS), considering a recording dataset of earthquakes occurred in Central Italy, where the seismotectonic context is dominated by normal-fault earthquakes. This study highlights that directivity can explain the spatial variability of ground motion also of small- to moderate-magnitude events because the directivity correction was observed for a range of magnitude between 3.2 and 5.5. The magnitude validity of the model is also extended to larger magnitudes using the data from a global dataset of strong events (Sgobba, Felicetta, *et al.*, 2021). This is relevant, given that most of previous research traditionally has focused on directivity of large earthquakes; however, this work aims at providing an efficient broadband correction term for low to strong earthquakes.

This article is organized as follows: the Dataset and Regional Setting section introduces the data and the station configuration; the Method section summarizes the methodological framework; and the Identification of Directive Events section defines the criteria adopted to identify events with directivity, with an explicit comparison with the previous study of Colavitti, Lanzano, Sgobba, Pacor, and Gallovič (2022). The Spectral Parameterization of Directivity Effects section constitutes the core of the present study and discusses the spectral parameterization of directivity effects, addressing spectral normalization through Gaussian fitting, the modeling of the bandwidth of directivity effects, and the magnitude scaling of the peak period. Finally, the Application of the Directivity Correction Model on Ground-Motion Prediction section presents the application of the proposed directivity correction model to ground-motion prediction, focusing on real-case scenarios from the calibration dataset related to events from the 2016–2017 Central Italy seismic sequence.

DATASET AND REGIONAL SETTING

The dataset used in this study consists of high-quality acceleration and velocity waveforms of events that occurred in Central Italy in the time period from 2009 to 2018 (Spallarossa *et al.*, 2023) and includes the major seismic sequences of the region in recent years. Following the occurrence of the 2009 L'Aquila and the 2016 Amatrice–Visso–Norcia sequence, the number of seismic stations significantly increased, and several seismological studies were conducted on this study area, some of them focused on source directivity using different techniques (Pischiutta *et al.*, 2016; Spagnuolo *et al.*, 2016; Calderoni *et al.*, 2017, 2023; Convertito *et al.*, 2017; Wang *et al.*, 2019; Colavitti, Lanzano, Sgobba, Pacor, and Gallovič, 2022). As shown by various works (e.g., Boncio *et al.*, 2000; Roberts and Michetti, 2004; Di Luccio *et al.*, 2010; Buttinelli *et al.*, 2018), the study area is complex both from tectonic and geological points of view, and in general, almost the whole seismicity significant for the seismic hazard assessment (Faure Walker *et al.*, 2021) is triggered by normal faults.

The dataset encompasses >35,000 seismic recordings from 456 events (considering earthquakes recorded by at least 6 stations) and 460 stations (Fig. 1a,b) for which we computed the horizontal components of the spectral acceleration (SA) ordinates, logarithmically equispaced in the period interval from 0.04 to 2 s, for a reference damping ratio of 5%. The waveforms were automatically processed, selecting spectral amplitudes with signal-to-noise ratios (SNRs) >3. Details of the processing scheme are described by Pacor, Spallarossa, *et al.* (2016) and Castro *et al.* (2022). The recording stations belong to two main permanent networks and several temporary stations. The main networks are (1) Rete Accelerometrica Nazionale (DPC, 1972) managed by the Italian Civil Protection Department and (2) Rete Sismica Nazionale operated by Istituto Nazionale di Geofisica e Vulcanologia (INGV Seismological Data Centre, 2006). In addition, some events have been recorded by some temporary networks, which were installed to monitor the seismic sequences after the major events in the area of study since 2009. As shown in Figure 1c, the dataset is sampled in distance (R) and magnitude (M_w) ranges corresponding to 10–100 km and 3.2–6.5, respectively.

As described by Sgobba, Felicetta, *et al.* (2021), we use a mixed definition of magnitude because our objective is to define an M_w, moment magnitude-based model, a metric widely used in ground-motion prediction equations because it is not affected by saturation at high magnitudes. For strong earthquakes ($M_w \geq$ 4.0), we used M_w estimates obtained from specific studies on Regional Centroid Moment Tensor (Pondrelli *et al.*, 2010) available in the ITalian ACcelerometric Archive (ITACA) database (Felicetta *et al.*, 2023). For weaker earthquakes, the local magnitude (M_L) was considered, computed following the calibration by Di Bona (2016). In these cases, the differences between M_L and M_w are much smaller, and M_L estimates are approximated to those of M_w. The distance metric is the Joyner–Boore distance for events with $M_w > 5.5$ and epicentral distance for the smaller-magnitude earthquakes.

The recordings distribution is strongly characterized by small-magnitude events, with 70% of the recordings with a magnitude less than 4 and 12 events with $M_w > 5$. Regarding the distance distribution, there is a non-negligible amount of near-source recordings, even if the bulk data are included in the distance range between 20 and 120 km. The average depth of the considered events is ~10 km, typical of the seismicity in the Central Italy region (Chiarabba *et al.*, 2009; Michele *et al.*, 2020).

METHOD

The method to identify the directivity events in the present study is outlined in the following steps: (1) calibration of the nonergodic ground-motion model for the investigated area; (2) azimuthal modeling of the aleatory residuals of the GMM and identification of the directive events; (3) comparison of the results obtained in this study with those obtained using the same method in a work by Colavitti, Lanzano, Sgobba, Pacor, and Gallovič (2022) with reference to FAS; (4) spectral normalization and parameterization of directivity effects via Gaussian fit; and (5) empirical modeling of the relation between the M_w and the vibration period in which the maximum effects of directivity are observed. The first three steps are in this section, and the latter two steps are tackled in the Identification of Directive Events and Spectral Parameterization of Directivity Effects sections.

Reference nonergodic GMM

The methodology starts from the calibration of a fully nonergodic GMM by identifying the systematic contributions of variability of event, source, site, and path (e.g., Al-Atik *et al.*, 2010, and several following studies). The reference GMM is calibrated for the geometric mean of horizontal components of 69 ordinates of the 5% SA in the period from 0.04 to 2 s, available in the flatfile by Spallarossa *et al.* (2023).

The calibration model is a modified version of the one used by Sgobba, Lanzano, and Pacor (2021) for the Central Italy and presents the following functional form:

$$\log_{10} Y = a + F_M(M) + F_R(M,R) + \delta B_e + \delta S2S_s + \delta L2L_{\text{source}} + \delta P2P_p + \delta W_0, \quad (1)$$

in which Y is the aforementioned intensity measures; a, $F_M(M)$, $F_R(M,R)$ are the fixed effects; δB_e, $\delta S2S_s$, $\delta L2L_{\text{source}}$, and $\delta P2P_p$ represents the zero-mean Gaussian-distributed random effects. The detailed description of each feature is provided in Appendix and follows the same calibration scheme used for other GMMs, developed in the same context for Central Apennines by Sgobba, Lanzano, and Pacor (2021) and Sgobba *et al.* (2024) and Colavitti, Lanzano, Sgobba, Pacor, and Gallovič (2022); the model coefficients and standard deviations of this study are provided in Table T1 of ESupp2, available to this article.

The need for nonergodic model calibration is required to better isolate the remaining aleatory terms, thus removing all of the other systematic effects not related to source directivity from total residuals. The calibration is performed via a mixed-effect regression (Bates *et al.*, 2015), allowing the estimation of the coefficients with fixed terms and of the different repeatable random terms, including the leftover aleatory

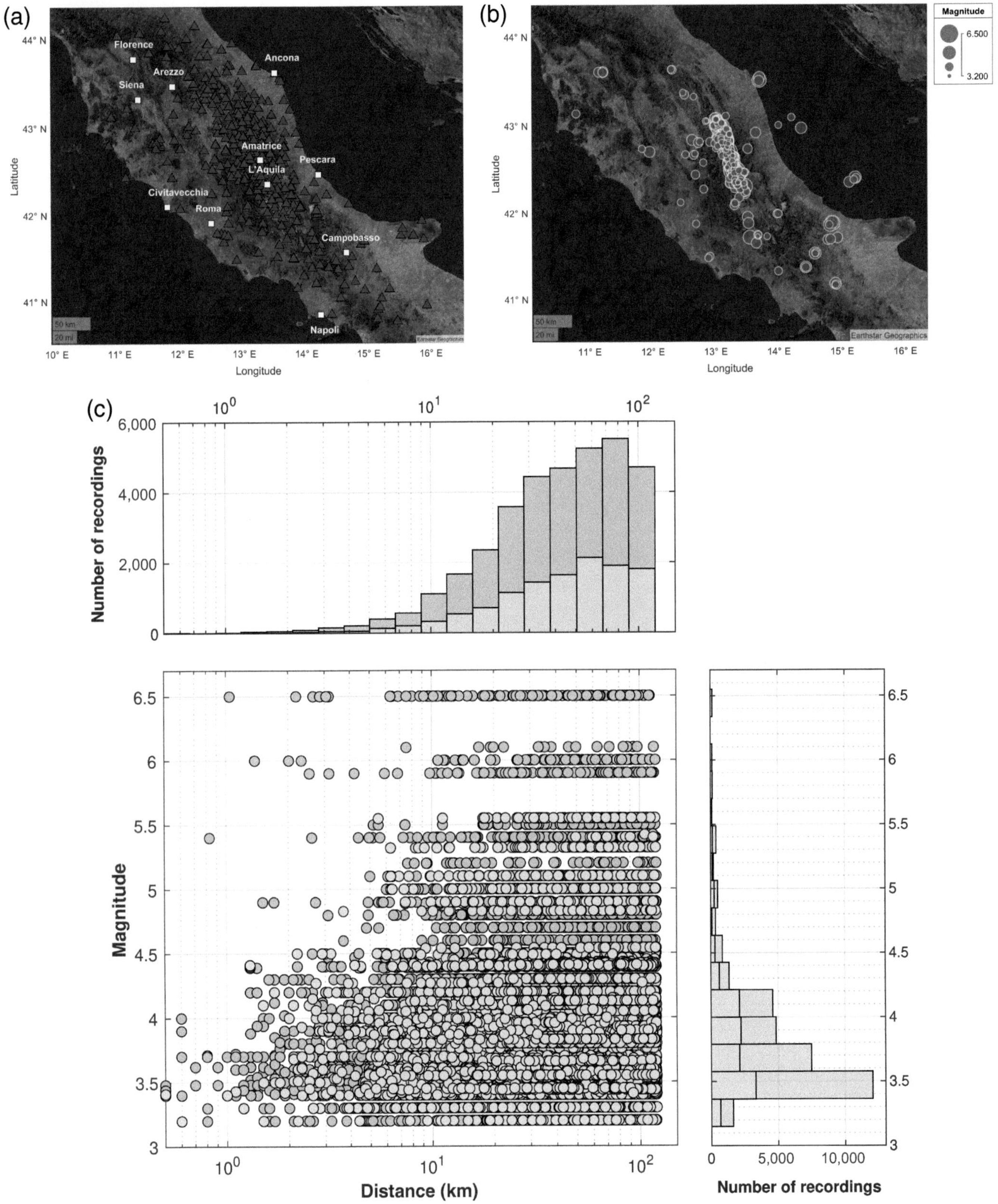

Figure 1. Map of the stations (a) and earthquakes (b) used for the analysis of directivity effects (more details for the selection in the Method section). (c) Magnitude–distance scatter plot. Gray shows all the events considered for the analysis, and yellow shows the directive events identified in this work. The color version of this figure is available only in the electronic edition.

Event: 161030115817, M 4, No. of records = 147

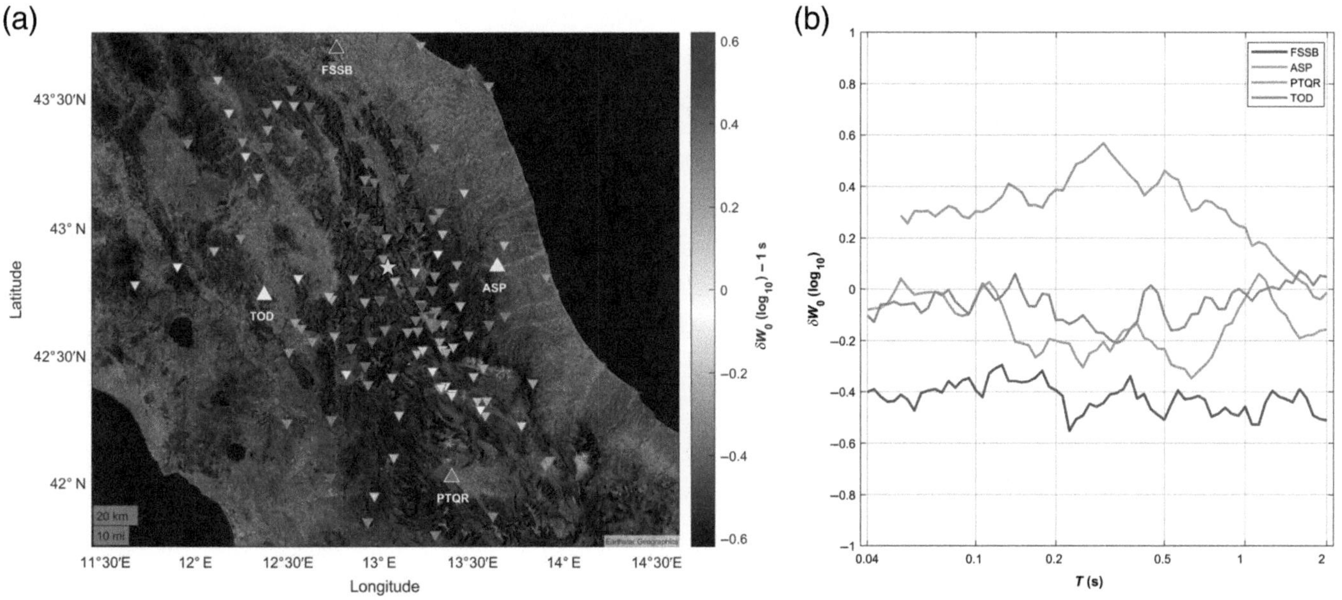

variability, denoted by δW_0 in equation (1) and that reflects the part of variability that is still not modeled.

Azimuthal modeling of the aleatory residuals

For each event of the dataset, we analyze the spatial distribution of the aleatory residuals, as shown in Figure 2 for SA at $T = 1$ s of an example earthquake with M_w 4.0 that occurred on 30 October 2016 at 11:58:17 UTC during the 2016 Norcia seismic sequence in Central Italy.

Here, δW_0 values are positive (red triangles) in the southeast direction from the epicenter (marked by the yellow star) with amplitude values of 0.6 log10 units at the station PTQR, indicating an amplification with respect to the reference GMM median prediction. Conversely, a de-amplification (negative δW_0, blue triangles) is observed in the area at northwest with respect to the epicenter, like for the station FSSB, which has values from −0.3 to −0.55 $\log_{10}$ units. The stations TOD and ASP, respectively, located west and east of the epicenter have almost null residuals (average values of −0.10 and −0.15 $\log_{10}$ units over the analyzed periods), indicating that they are azimuthally located in a neutral position. In these cases, we observe an azimuthal variation of δW_0 values similar to the study of Colavitti, Lanzano, Sgobba, Pacor, and Gallovič (2022), with a trend represented by a periodic function with periodicity 2π and a maximum amplification angle around 171° (see Fig. 3), coherent with the nodal planes solutions from the time domain moment tensor (Scognamiglio *et al.*, 2009) available from the seismological service of INGV (strike 338° and 171°). We assume that these effects are related to directivity, associated with a unilateral rupture propagation.

Azimuthal contributions related to radiation pattern are expected to be lower to affect low frequencies (<0.5 Hz; Castro *et al.*, 2006; Kotha *et al.*, 2019) and to amplify perpendicular to the fault strike (Haskell, 1963). Assuming as a working hypothesis that the rupture is unilateral, and based on these findings, we modeled the aleatory residuals as

$$\delta W_0 = \delta D2D(\theta) + \delta W_{\mathrm{nodir}}, \tag{2}$$

in which $\delta D2D(\theta)$ represents a function that fits the residual for each event with respect to the source-to-site azimuth θ (measured clockwise from north to the direction connecting the source and the recording site). Here, $\delta W_{\mathrm{nodir}}$ represents the remaining residuals cleared by the azimuthal effect. The δW_0 in equation (2) can be fitted by the equation

$$\delta D2D(\theta) = \log_{10} C_d^n(\theta) - \langle \log_{10} C_d^n(\theta) \rangle, \tag{3}$$

in which C_d is the directivity factor (Hirasawa and Stauder, 1965; Ruiz *et al.*, 2011; Pacor, Gallovič, *et al.*, 2016) that models the shift of the apparent corner frequency f_a, as the product of the corner frequency f_c and the function $C_d(\theta)$. The spectral amplitudes scale proportionally with respect to C_d^n, in which n is the value of the exponent controlling the type of the source model ($n = 2$ for omega-squared, $n = 1$ for the model with two corner frequencies) and $\langle\,\rangle$ denotes azimuthal averaging. In the ground-motion modeling, n represents the "strength" of the directivity because larger n values correspond to higher directivity effects.

Figure 2. (a) Spatial distribution of the δW_0 residuals at spectral acceleration (SA) at $T = 1$ s for an M_w 4.0 event that occurred on 30 October 2016 at 11:58:17. The yellow star is the epicenter, and reverse triangles represent the recording stations. The blue and red colors indicate negative and positive δW_0 (under- and overestimation). (b) Amplitude values of the stations PTQR (orange), FSSB (blue), TOD (green), and ASP (light blue). The color version of this figure is available only in the electronic edition.

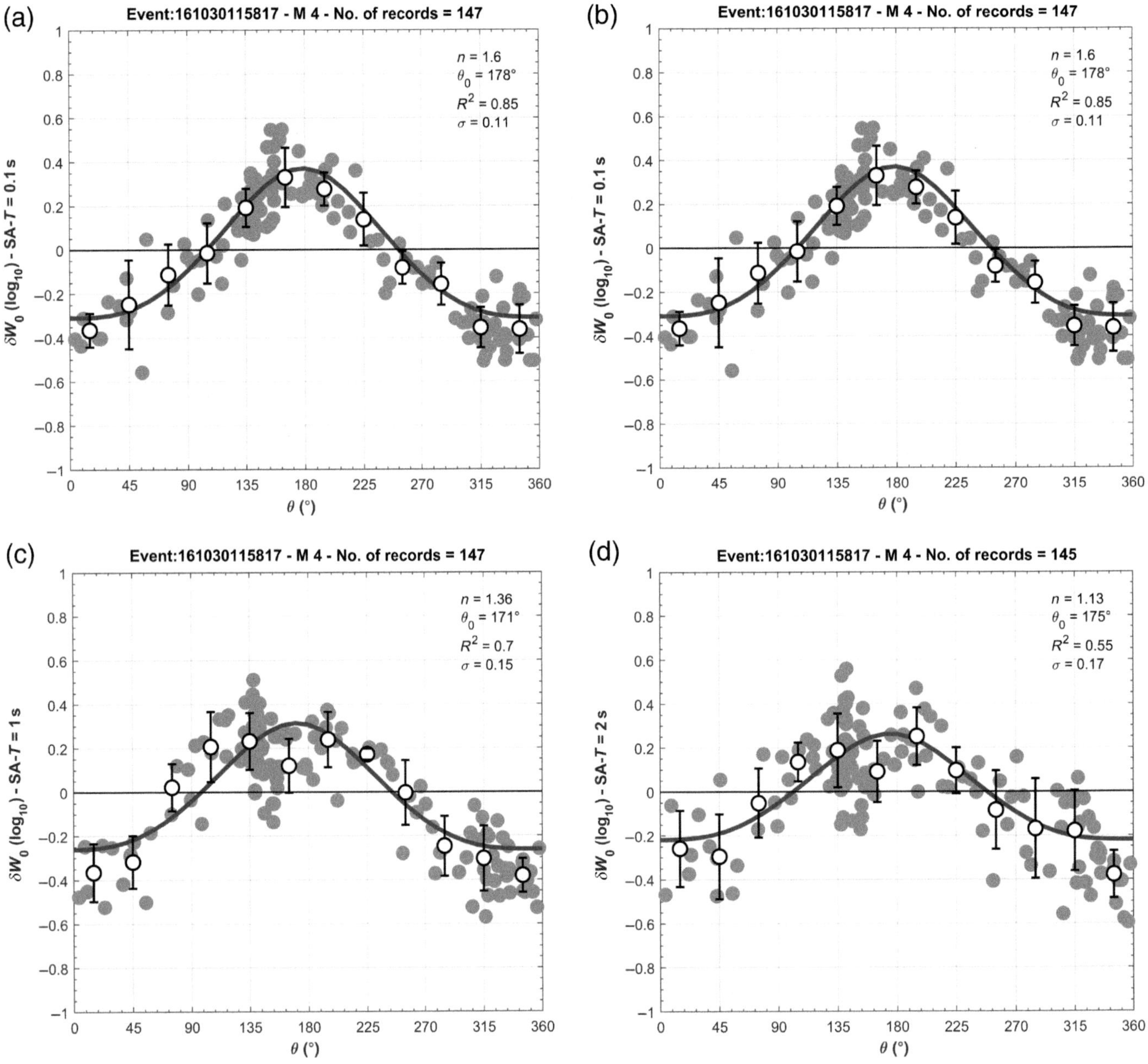

Figure 3. Azimuthal variation of the aleatory residuals for an M_w 4.0 event occurred at 11:58:17 on 30 October 2016 at (a) $T = 0.1$ s, (b) $T = 0.2$ s, (c) $T = 1$ s, and (d) $T = 2$ s. The red line shows the fitting model. The color version of this figure is available only in the electronic edition.

We adopt the formulation of Convertito *et al.* (2013) for the directivity factor C_d, which can be written as follows:

$$C_d = \sqrt{\frac{k^2}{[1 - (\frac{v_r}{c})\cos(\theta - \theta_0)]^2} + \frac{(1 - k)^2}{[1 + (\frac{v_r}{c})\cos(\theta - \theta_0)]^2}}, \quad (4)$$

in which $\frac{v_r}{c} = \alpha$ is the Mach number, the ratio between rupture velocity and *S*-wave velocity; θ_0 is the azimuth of the rupture direction; and parameter k, which spans from 0 to 1, indicates the relative portion of the rupture length along the rupture direction θ_0. We fit the aleatory residuals with the latter function, in which the fitting variables are the angle of rupture direction θ_0, the ratio k, the Mach number α, and the exponent n. However, because of the strong trade-off among the directivity parameters related to the C_d formulation (see Pacor, Gallovič, *et al.*, 2016), several strategies can be adopted to constrain the inversion efficiently (see Fig. S1).

Although a more appropriate option would be an event-by-event calibration, we took advantage of the results by Colavitti, Lanzano, Sgobba, Pacor, and Gallovič (2022) on FAS ordinates, which tested alternative combinations in which α and k were either fixed to literature values or jointly estimated through a nonlinear optimization approach (Marquardt, 1963). The authors then assumed constant values for k and α as in Colavitti, Lanzano, Sgobba, Pacor, and Gallovič (2022) by fixing $k = 0.85$ and $\alpha = 0.50$ and estimating the parameters n and θ_0 from the results of model fitting. These values were selected as a compromise between the trends emerging from the inversion tests and physically consistent ranges reported in the literature (Convertito *et al.*, 2017; Ren *et al.*, 2017). This choice ensured a stable and reasonable fit for the majority of the events and allows the model to adequately reproduce the azimuthal dependence of the aleatory residuals.

Figure 3 shows the azimuthal variations of the aleatory residuals δW_0 for the same event of Figure 2 at different vibrating periods, corresponding to 0.1, 0.2, 1, and 2 s and the fitting curve, where we also report the fitting parameters R^2 and σ. As we can observe, the direction of rupture propagation θ_0 remains almost constant as the period changes, attending on the typical values of the strike of the main faults of the Central Apennines (Herrmann *et al.*, 2011; Calderoni *et al.*, 2015; Tinti *et al.*, 2016), as well as the associated model variability σ, which is quite low (in the range 0.11–0.17 $\log_{10}$ units) and pretty constant. The value of n is maximized for periods T equal to 0.2 s and then gradually decrease for higher periods (n = 1.1 for $T = 2$ s). The same trend occurs if we analyze the determination coefficient R^2, which is the measure of goodness of fit between the observed and modeled data. In this particular event, R^2 reaches values close to 0.9 at $T = 0.2$ s and is >0.50 at all vibration periods.

IDENTIFICATION OF DIRECTIVE EVENTS

The criteria adopted for the identification of directive events still follow the approach of Colavitti, Lanzano, Sgobba, Pacor, and Gallovič (2022) and rely on two conditions:

1. The coefficient of determination R^2 must be >0.50 for ≥10% of the intensity measures considered.
2. The standard deviation of the values of the angle of rupture propagation θ_0, computed for each vibration period, must be <20°.

It should also be noted that in the C_d fitting, the azimuth is computed assuming a point-source approximation for the causative fault. This simplification is considered valid in this study because the dataset is largely composed of small-magnitude events. As a result, we classify 175 of 456 events, resulting in ~38% of the total number of earthquakes. Figure 1c shows the magnitude–distance distribution of the records of the directive events with yellow dots: the recordings are >12,000 with magnitudes between 3.2 and 5.6. The largest events (M_w 6.0 and 6.5) in the dataset were excluded from the directivity analysis not because they are not earthquakes with directivity but because such effects should be observed at periods longer than 2 s, not well sampled by our dataset. In addition, for these events, the point-source approximation in azimuth computation may be an oversimplification. In the previous study, Colavitti, Lanzano, Sgobba, Pacor, and Gallovič (2022) identified 162 of 456 events (35%), applying the same criteria to the results of the FAS model. The list of events and some additional metadata are available in Colavitti, Lanzano, Sgobba, and Pacor, 2022. If we consider only the directive events for both the studies on SA and FAS, 136 earthquakes are common and therefore constitute ~30% of the total number of analyzed events.

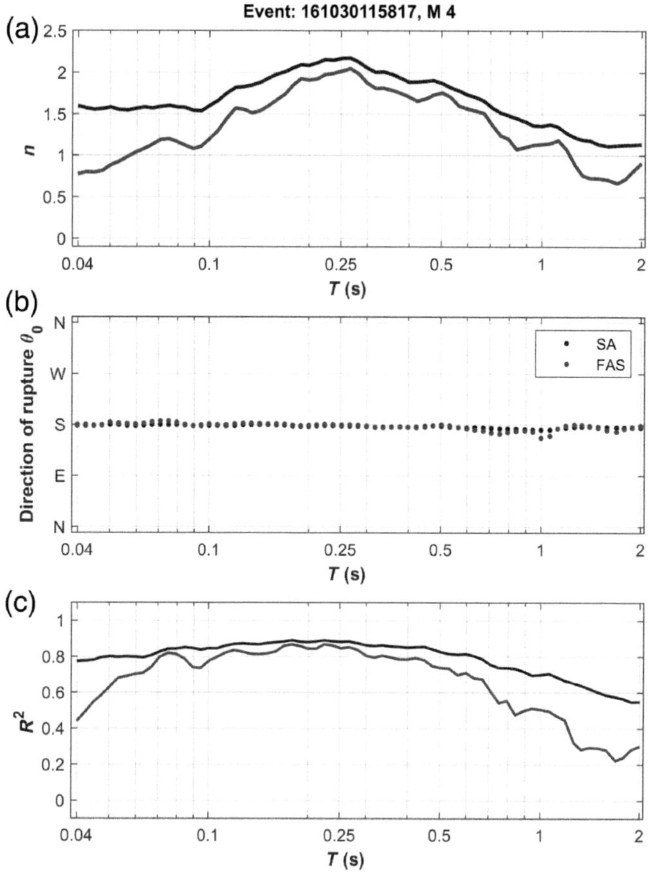

Figure 4. Directivity amplitude n (a), direction of rupture propagation θ_0 (b), and coefficient of determination R^2 of azimuthal fitting (c) versus period for the same event as in Figure 2. The blue curve represents the fitting results for the SA model (this study), and the red curve shows the Fourier amplitude spectra (FAS) results by Colavitti, Lanzano, Sgobba, Pacor, and Gallovič (2022). The color version of this figure is available only in the electronic edition.

Comparison with FAS studies

Figure 4 shows the spectral trend of the regression parameters (n, θ_0, and R^2) for an event with remarkable directivity, in which the blue curve represents the fitting results for the SA model (this study) and the red curve shows the FAS model as computed in the previous study by Colavitti, Lanzano, Sgobba, Pacor, and Gallovič (2022).

The value of n, which is proportional with the intensity of the directivity phenomenon, has a bell spectral shape (Fig. 4, top panel) because there is generally a period when directivity maximizes and n assumes its maximum value. (See the Taxonomy of the directivity parameters section.) From the middle panel of Figure 4, we can see that the angle of rupture direction θ_0 is quite

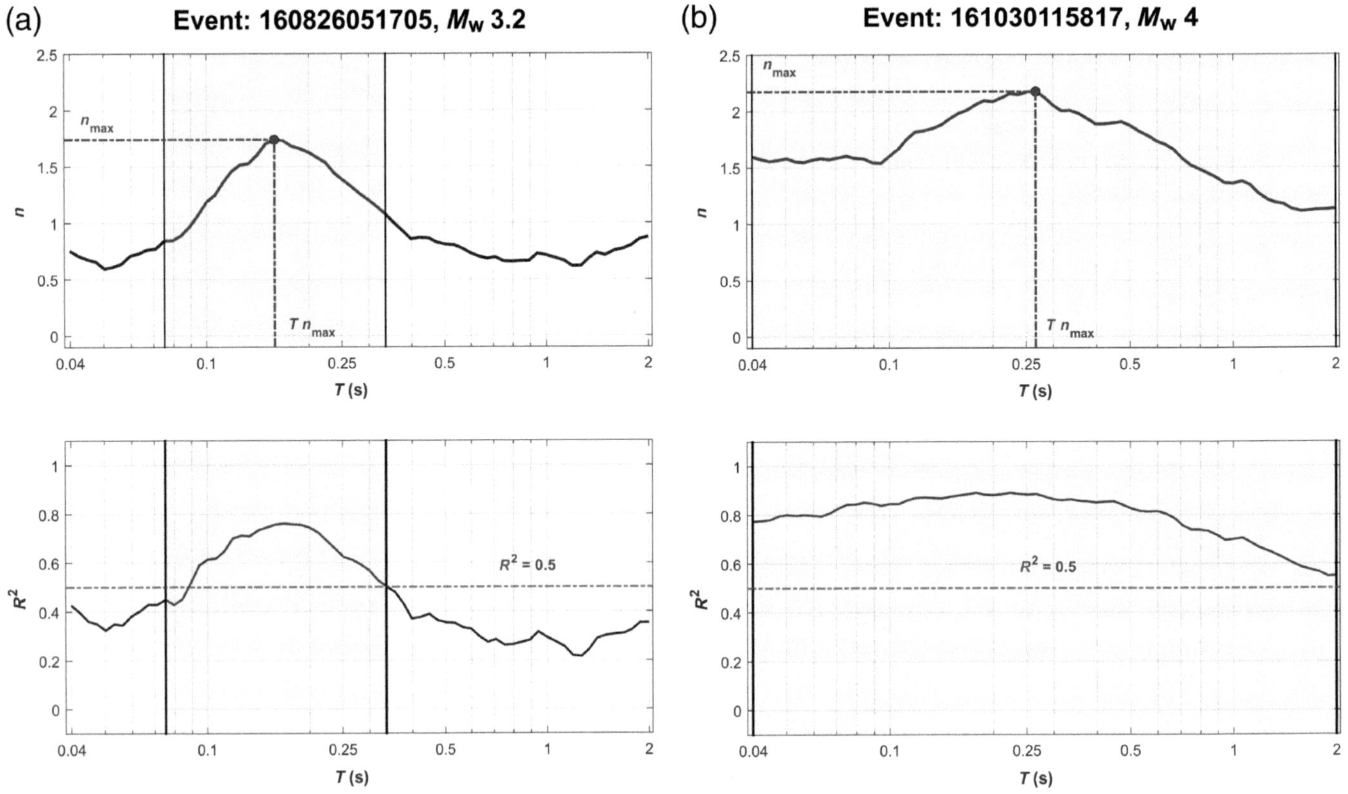

Figure 5. Directivity amplitude n (top) and coefficient of determination R^2 (bottom) versus period for (a) M_w 4.0 30/10/2016 11:58:17 and (b) M_w 3.2 26/08/2016 05:17:05. The blue curve represents the fitting results for the SA model, and the red circle shows the coordinate of Tn_{max} (on x axis) and n_{max} (along the y axis). The horizontal dashed red line delimits the band with the $R^2 = 0.5$, corresponding to the yellow shadow interval, which represents the directivity band ΔT. The color version of this figure is available only in the electronic edition.

constant along the south direction and matches for SA and FAS models, as also observed by Colavitti, Lanzano, Sgobba, Pacor, and Gallovič (2022) and Wang *et al.* (2019).

By comparing the trends of the SA and FAS curves, we can observe that the values of n obtained from SA analysis are consistently higher than those obtained from the regressions in FAS (see Fig. S2). This suggests that the effects of directivity on ground motion are more evident in the SA amplitudes. The analysis of Colavitti, Lanzano, Sgobba, Pacor, and Gallovič (2022) on the regression results for FAS revealed a direct correlation between n and R^2 because the coefficient of determination increases with the value of n. SA analysis (Fig. S2a) shows that the n values are systematically higher than the corresponding in FAS (Fig. S2b). Moreover, the frequency distribution of the directive events in SA is wider, especially toward higher frequencies, for example, between 5 and 25 Hz (corresponding to short periods, between 0.04 and 0.2 s). Our results seem in line with the Van Houtte *et al.* (2015) considerations, explaining that the directivity effects for the spectral ordinates are evident in a range of periods wider than around the pulse period. Figure S3 provides the comparison between SA and FAS directivity bands for other magnitude classes, reaching similar conclusions.

Taxonomy of the directivity parameters

Figure 5 shows the spectral curves of n and R^2 for two directive events (M_w 4.0, 30 October 2016, 11:58:17 UTC and M_w 3.2, 26 August 2016, 05:17:05 UTC) with different characteristics. The yellow shading interval identifies the period range in which the R^2 values are persistently >0.5, as shown in bottom panels of Figure 5. The event on the left side (Fig. 5a) shows directivity-related amplification in a narrow band (0.075–0.35 s), peaked around 0.15 s. The earthquake on the right (Fig. 5b) has a broader directivity band, with a peak at 0.25 s, and n values on average are higher than the event in Figure 5a.

To account for these differences and support the parameterization of directivity, we introduce a set of modeling parameters that describe the basic characteristics observed in Figure 5. We can define the following:

- n_{max}, the amplitude peak at which the maximum directivity is observed
- Tn_{max}, the period corresponding to the maximum directivity
- ΔT, the directivity band (i.e., the yellow-shaded areas in Fig. 5), representing the range of consecutive periods in which the value of R^2 is persistently >0.50

SPECTRAL PARAMETERIZATION OF DIRECTIVITY EFFECTS

Before proceeding to the spectral parameterization, we perform some additional checks: (1) a careful visual inspection to verify the continuity of the directivity bandwidth, excluding events that exhibit multiple noncontinuous bands; (2) removal of events with frequency of n_{max} ($fn_{max} = 1/Tn_{max}$) lower than the corner frequency f_c estimated by Morasca *et al.* (2023), based on the result of a nonparametric generalized inversion technique and the assumption of an omega-square source model (see Fig. S4); and (3) exclusion of events for which fn_{max} approaches the upper limit of frequency range considered in the analysis, that is, the events with $fn_{max} > 20$ Hz because modeling the spectral peak close to the upper limit of the range could be challenging. As a result, the number of considered events used for parameterization drops to 139. For the main features of these events and the parameters useful for the parameterization, please refer to the Table T2.

As a first exploratory step, we divided the dataset of directive events on the basis of the value of Tn_{max}, identifying the curves that fell within five period intervals, ensuring that each range included a sufficient number of curves to be able to perform a statistical analysis of the results. The ranges considered are 0.04–0.10 s (28 events), 0.10–0.18 s (35 events), 0.18–0.27 s (25 events), 0.27–0.57 s (22 events), and 0.57–2.00 s (20 events). Because in each subgroup there are directive events with different values of n_{max}, to examine the shape of the $n(T)$ curves, we normalized each curve with respect to the value of n_{max} and calculated, period by period, the median of the normalized curves. The median n/n_{max} curves for each range are shown in Figure 6. The averaged curves have similar shapes with only a shift of the period of peak. Considering the shape similarity of the curves with respect to period, it is reasonable to parameterize directivity not only by normalizing the $n(T)$ curve by its maximum value n_{max} but also the period T with respect to the period at which the maximum occurs Tn_{max}.

As a second exploratory step, we made a further subdivision of the normalized curves in each range based on the value of n_{max}. In particular, following Colavitti, Lanzano, Sgobba, Pacor, and Gallovič (2022), we identified events with (1) weak directivity ($n_{max} < 0.8$), (2) moderate directivity ($0.8 \le n_{max} < 1.3$), (3) strong directivity ($1.3 \le n_{max} \le 1.8$), and (4) super strong directivity ($n_{max} \ge 1.8$). For each of these subgroups, we calculated the median normalized curve and (see Figs. S5 and S6) for each period range with different colors.

It is clear that the normalized curves of earthquakes exhibiting super-strong directivity have a distinct shape that is much broader than those of the other earthquakes, the latter being more bandlimited. This suggests that there is a correlation between the strength of the directivity (i.e., the value of n_{max}) and the directivity bandwidth. This behavior is consistent with kinematic fractal source models: Herrero and Bernard (1994) and Ruiz *et al.* (2011) showed that k^{-2} type sources produce directivity effects that remain coherent across a large frequency band and at all azimuths, agreeing with our conclusion. This evidence is also supported by work by Colavitti, Lanzano, Sgobba, Pacor, and Gallovič (2022), which demonstrated that there is a

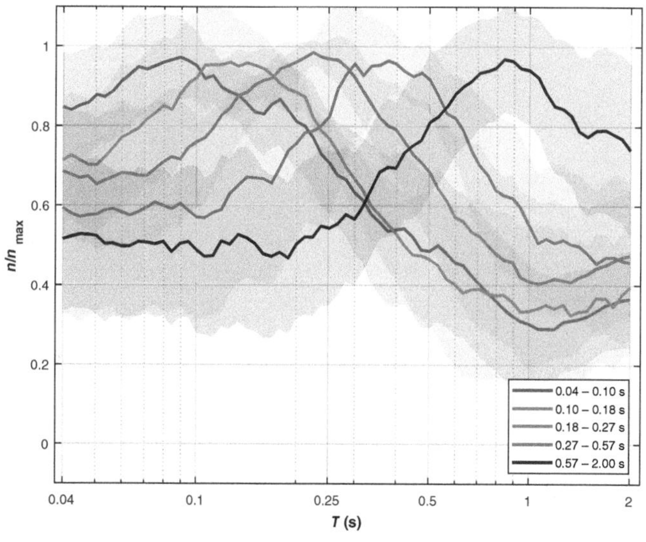

Figure 6. $\frac{n}{n_{max}}$ as a function of period. The curves represent the median of normalized curves for each period range in which the Tn_{max} is included. The shaded areas represent the standard deviation with respect to the median curve. The color version of this figure is available only in the electronic edition.

positive correlation between ΔT and n_{max}, that is, events with a wider directivity band are also those with the highest n_{max} values (see figs. 11 and 15 of Colavitti, Lanzano, Sgobba, Pacor, and Gallovič, 2022).

Spectral normalization via Gaussian fit

According to the final considerations of the previous section, we normalized the spectral amplitudes of n with respect to n_{max} and the period T with respect to Tn_{max}. Figure 7 shows the curves $\frac{n}{n_{max}}$ versus $\log_{10}\frac{T}{Tn_{max}}$ for each directive earthquake of the 139 selected events (in gray). As we can observe, all the normalized curves have a peak at the coordinates with $[\log_{10}\frac{T}{Tn_{max}}, \frac{n}{n_{max}}] = [0,1]$ by construction.

The dashed blue line in Figure 7 represents the median values of the normalized curves. The observed curves are more densely sampled at intermediate periods, when more observations are available. For this reason, the median is more scattered along the tails, where data are sparse. Based on the shape of median normalized curve, we decide to fit the empirical trend with a Gaussian curve of order 1, which is defined as follows:

$$f(x) = a_1 * \exp\left[-\left(\frac{x - b_1}{c_1}\right)^2\right], \tag{5}$$

in which $f(x)$ represents the function to parameterize with respect to x parameter, a_1 is the amplitude, b_1 the median value of the distribution along x, and c_1 is a coefficient that controls the shape of the Gaussian (standard deviation of the distribution). The idea of modeling directivity through the parameterization with the

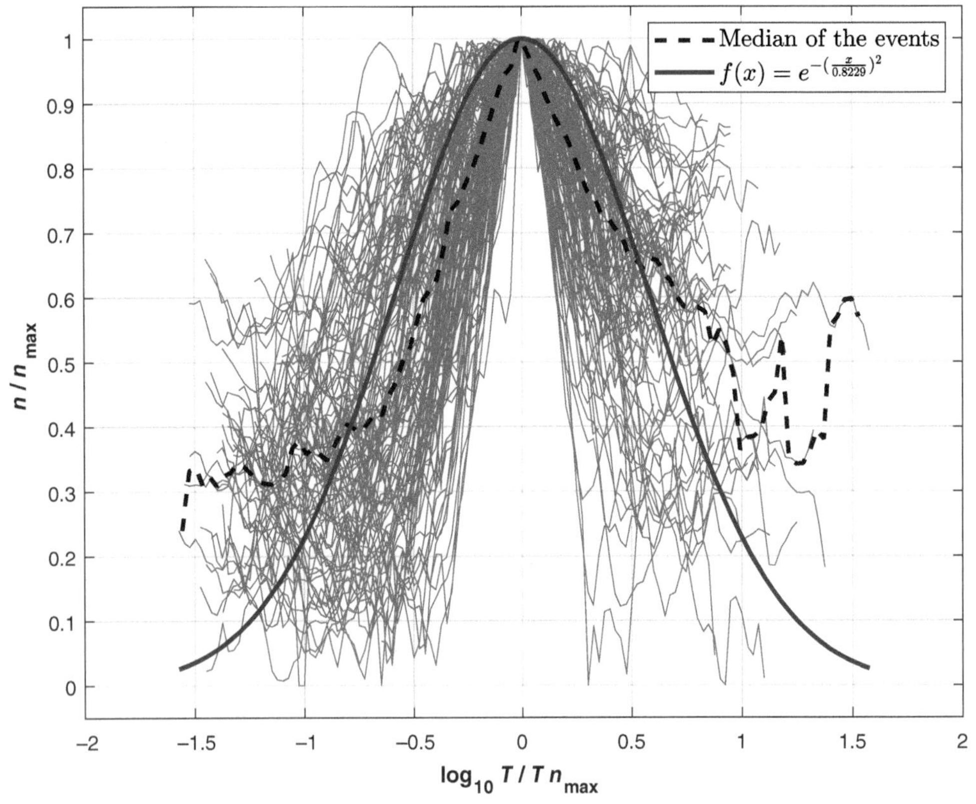

Figure 7. Normalized curves $\frac{n}{n_{max}}$ versus $\log_{10} \frac{T}{Tn_{max}}$. Each curve represents a directive earthquake. The median of normalized curves is represented as a dashed blue line, and the solid red line represents the best fitting using a first-order Gaussian curve. The color version of this figure is available only in the electronic edition.

Gaussian function of the period has also been adopted by Spudich *et al.* (2013) and Bayless *et al.* (2024).

Considering our problem in which a_1 has maximum amplitude equal to 1, $f(x) = \frac{n}{n_{max}}$ and $x = \log_{10} \frac{T}{Tn_{max}}$, equation (5) becomes

$$\frac{n}{n_{max}} = \exp\left[-\left(\frac{\log_{10}(\frac{T}{Tn_{max}}) - b_1}{c_1}\right)^2\right]. \quad (6)$$

The solid red line in Figure 7 shows the fit according to the first-order Gaussian constraining the model with $\frac{n}{n_{max}} = 1$ and $\log_{10} \frac{T}{Tn_{max}} = 0$. In this way, c_1 is equal to 0.8229, which is the value obtained for the median curve considering all the events. This value is representative of the entire dataset of events with directivity, without considering the difference related to the width of the directivity band, which could affect the estimates of c_1. To account for these features, the directivity band ΔT is introduced as a model parameter in the Gaussian curve fitting in the next section.

Modeling the bandwidth of the directivity effects

To model c_1 as a continuous function of n_{max}, we subdivided the dataset of directive events based on the value of n_{max}. Specifically, we created subsets of curves starting from the minimum n_{max}, that is, $n_{max,1} = 0.6$, and used a fixed selection interval of $\Delta n = 0.3$.

The first subset ($i = 1$) includes curves with n_{max} values in the range $n_{max,1} < n_{max} < n_{max,2}$ in which $n_{max,2} = n_{max,1} + \Delta n = 0.9$. We repeated the selection by increasing the value of $n_{max,1}$ by half of the selection interval, that is, $\Delta n/2 = 0.15$, so that each new subset ($i = 2$) partially overlapped with the previous one (e.g., for the second interval $n_{max,1} = 0.75$ and $n_{max,2} = 1.05$). We thus proceeded up to the interval that contained the curve with highest value of n_{max} in the dataset and we finally obtained 21 subsets (i = 1, 2, ...21). Figure 8 shows an example of this procedure considering two generic consecutive intervals ($i = 7$ and $i + 1 = 8$): the empirical values of n_{max} are arranged in ascending order, and the overlapped selected intervals are represented.

In particular, the bounds of the seventh window are shown with a dashed-dotted line (n_{max} range 1.27–1.48), eighth window with a black dashed line (n_{max} range 1.37–1.58). The overlap interval between these two consecutive selections (n_{max} between 1.37 and 1.48) is represented by a screened pink area. The number of events grows fairly linearly with n_{max} in the range between 1 and 1.75, guaranteeing roughly the same number of samples for each interval. On the contrary, the variation changes its rate on the tails, resulting in intervals sampled from a smaller number of data. For each subset, we performed the Gaussian fit and estimated the value of c_1 (equation 6); later, we assigned it to the mean value of the n_{max} selection interval. According to Figure 8b, the values of c_1 increase with n_{max} as expected, suggesting a linear fitting of the empirical data. (The blue and orange points are the corresponding points computed for the sampling case for Fig. 8a.) In the Figure S7, we can see the values of c_1 obtained from the regression with the associated variability, which increases in the tails; this is partly due to the smaller number of data used for the regressions in that ranges of n_{max}.

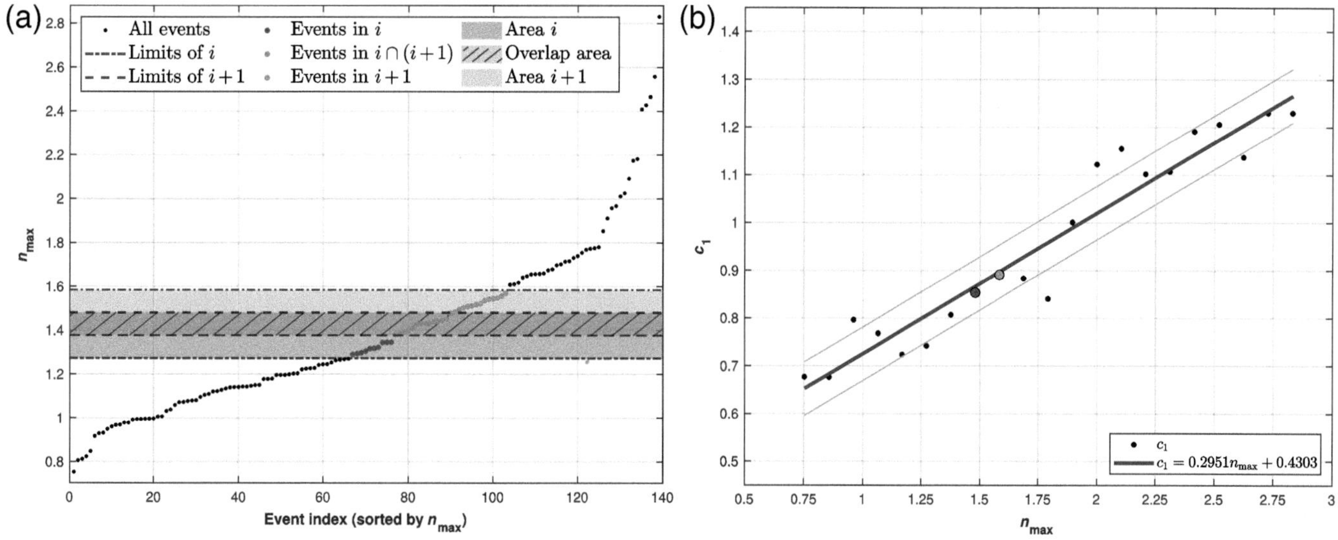

Figure 8. (a) Ordinal number of directive events (dots) ordered by increasing value of n_{max}. We highlight the case in which $i = 7$ and $i + 1 = 8$. Limits of ith interval in dashed-dotted lines; limits of $(i + 1)$th with a dashed black line. The blue dots are events in the ith window range, and the orange dots are events in the $(i + 1)$th window range. The pink points belong to both intervals. (b) Empirical relation between c_1, coefficient of the Gaussian fitting curve and n_{max}. The blue and orange points represent the c_1 value at ith and $(i + 1)$th intervals. The solid red line shows the best fit, and the standard deviation interval is represented with thin gray lines. The color version of this figure is available only in the electronic edition.

The linear model interpolating the observed data points is

$$c_1 = 0.2951 n_{max} + 0.4303;$$
$$\sigma = 0.0553, \tag{7}$$

and is shown in Figure 8b as a continuous red line. The determination coefficient is $R^2 = 0.92$.

Magnitude scaling of peak period

According to Colavitti, Lanzano, Sgobba, Pacor, and Gallovič (2022), there is a relationship between the frequency at which the maximum directivity occurs and the magnitude of the event: in particular, it is observed in the analysis of FAS that as the magnitude increases, the peak frequency decreases. We transferred this observation to the analysis in SA, looking for a positive direct relationship between magnitude and Tn_{max}. This trend was also observed in the analysis of pulse-like waveforms of strong earthquakes: the logarithm of the pulse period Tp is linearly correlated with the magnitude of the event, and several empirical equations are available in the literature to describe this dependence (Somerville, 2003; Baker, 2007; Spudich *et al.*, 2013; Bayless *et al.*, 2024, among the others). As an example, Sgobba, Felicetta, *et al.* (2021) proposed an empirical relationship Tp–M_w by collecting the recordings with pulses in the velocity time histories in the near-source strong-motion, version 2.0 (NESS2.0) database, which includes global events with $M_w > 5.5$. This classification was obtained through an identification algorithm similar to the one proposed by Shahi and Baker (2011).

In our case study, the modeling of the empirical relationship would be very limited to small magnitudes because the dataset of directive events is valid for a range from 3.2 to 5.2. We propose to extend the validity of the predicted model to larger-magnitude events by including the pulse periods provided by Sgobba, Felicetta, *et al.* (2021), specifically those associated with normal faulting (Table 1).

Considering that pulse occurrence are related to forward directivity effects, we assume that the period when directivity is maximized Tn_{max} is physically comparable to the pulse period Tp observed in NESS2.0 recordings. Figure 9a shows the empirical data we were considering for calibration, taking into account that the pulse period of the NESS2.0 events is obtained as the average of the periods of the individual pulse recordings.

In other words, we assume that for the larger-magnitudes events, the period Tp corresponds to Tn_{max}, treating the pulse observed in the time domain as a corresponding peak of the spectral amplitudes in the frequency domain. This equivalence implies that the high-frequency amplification of small earthquakes scales with magnitude, turning into a low-frequency pulse for strong earthquakes. This assumption is in line with several studies on pulse-like effects (e.g., Somerville, 2003; Chioccarelli and Iervolino, 2010), which observed amplifications of the spectral ordinates corresponding to the pulse period. Similar to existing empirical relations, we adopted a linear fit with $\log_{10}(Tn_{max})$. The fitting equation is

$$\log_{10}(Tn_{max}) = 0.3858 M_w - 2.189, \tag{8}$$

with a determination coefficient R^2 equal to 0.6029.

In Figure 9b, the model calibrated in this study is compared with existing T_p–M_w empirical relations. The results are in line with the available equations predictions by Sgobba, Lanzano,

TABLE 1
Summary of the Parameters of the Normal-Fault Events in Near-Source Strong-Motion, Version 2.0 – NESS2.0 (Sgobba, Felicetta, *et al.*, 2021) with Pulse Records ($M_w > 5.2$)

Event	Date (UTC) (yyyy/mm/dd hh:mm:ss)	Magnitude	Nrecs	*Tp* (s)	Std. Dev.
Irpinia (Italy)	1980/11/23 18:34:53	6.9	2	2.7545	1.4998
Kalamata (Greece)	1986/09/13 17:24:34	5.9	1	1.8970	–
Aigio (Greece)	1995/06/15 00:15:47	6.5	1	0.8330	–
Umbria–Marche (Italy)	1997/09/26 00:33:11	5.7	1	1.4	–
Umbria–Marche (Italy)	1997/09/26 09:40:24	6.0	2	1.0850	0.2376
L'Aquila (Italy)	2009/04/06 01:32:40	6.1	4	1.2968	0.4453
L'Aquila (Italy)	2009/04/07 17:47:37	5.5	5	0.8008	0.3430
Kumamoto (Japan)	2016/04/15 16:25:06	7.0	14	4.7285	3.0264
Amatrice (Italy)	2016/08/24 01:36:32	6.0	4	1.3422	0.7045
Ussita (Italy)	2016/10/26 19:18:06	5.9	4	1.1847	0.1395
Norcia (Italy)	2016/10/30 06:40:18	6.5	7	2.5060	1.7953
Capitignano (Italy)	2017/01/18 10:14:12	5.5	3	0.5833	0.0950

Nrecs indicates the number of records used for the event calibration; *Tp* is the peak period of the directivity effect; Std. Dev. represents the associated standard deviation.

and Pacor (2021); Baker (2007); and Somerville (2003) for soil, although these relations are extrapolated for earthquakes of lower magnitude. Major differences are observed by Spudich *et al.* (2013) and Somerville (2003) for rock, for which the predicted period T at low magnitudes is lower than that obtained from the model calibrated for Central Italy.

APPLICATION OF THE DIRECTIVITY CORRECTION MODEL ON GROUND-MOTION PREDICTION

In this section, we quantify the impact of the GMM correction for the effect of source directivity on spectral amplitudes predicted without directivity. We incorporate the directivity effect into the nonergodic empirical model in equation (1), which is consistent with the calibration dataset. Note that this procedure is extended to events with magnitudes >5.2, supported by the results from equation (8).

The steps to calculate the median prediction of the GMM corrected for directivity effects are as follows:

- Step 1: Fix the input parameters, that is, the moment magnitude M_w of the event and the "power" of directivity, represented by the parameter n_{max}. (The empirical range spans from 0 to 2.85.) All input parameters of the reference GMM must also be fixed, even if they are not directly relevant for predicting the directivity effect according to the model proposed in this work. In particular, for the reference GMM, the epicentral distance and parameters related to random effects correction must also be defined.
- Step 2: Estimate the value of Tn_{max} by equation (8) and the value of c_1 by equation (7).

  Given $x(T,M_w) = \log_{10} \frac{T}{Tn_{max}(M_w)}$, the spectral variation of parameter n can be obtained from equation (6) as

$$n(T,M_w,n_{max}) = n_{max} * \exp\left[-\left(\frac{\log_{10}(\frac{T}{Tn_{max}})}{c_1(n_{max})}\right)^2\right]. \quad (9)$$

- Step 3: Calculate the azimuthal variation of the amplitude of the motion using the directivity coefficient C_d, in which the angle of maximum directivity θ_0, the parameters $k = 0.85$, and Mach number $\alpha = \frac{v_r}{c} = 0.50$ are fixed. As a rough preliminary estimate, θ_0 can generally be obtained from studies of the geological structures in the area, identifying directions parallel to the most likely strikes of the ruptures. The polarity of the directivity cannot be determined a priori because we had no evidence of a prevailing orientation (see Colavitti, Lanzano, Sgobba, Pacor, and Gallovič, 2022). Other works (e.g., Calderoni *et al.*, 2023), on the contrary, observed preferential polarity toward the southeast. The amplitude in the generic direction θ is then modulated period by period by the parameter n, obtained from equation (9), as

$$\delta D2D(\theta,T,M_w,n_{max}) = \log_{10} C_d^n(T,M_w,n_{max})(\theta) - \langle \log_{10} C_d^n(\theta) \rangle. \quad (10)$$

- Step 4: The final directivity corrected prediction Y_{corr} is obtained as

$$\log_{10} Y_{corr}(\theta,T,M_w,n_{max},R_{JB}) = \log_{10} Y(M_w,R_{JB}) + \delta D2D(\theta,T,M_w,n_{max}), \quad (11)$$

in which $\log_{10} Y_{corr}$ is the median prediction without directivity correction (see equation 1) and R_{JB} represents the Joyner-Boore distance.

Figure 10 shows examples of median SA predictions for a scenario at an R_{JB} of 5 km and the angle of maximum directivity $\theta_0 = 0°$ by varying the other input parameters, that is, M_w (Fig. 10a), θ (Fig. 10b), and n_{max} (Fig. 10c). In this example, random-effects corrections of the reference GMM are set to zero.

Figure 10a shows the SA predicted scenarios with and without source directivity correction using 4 M_w classes, equal to

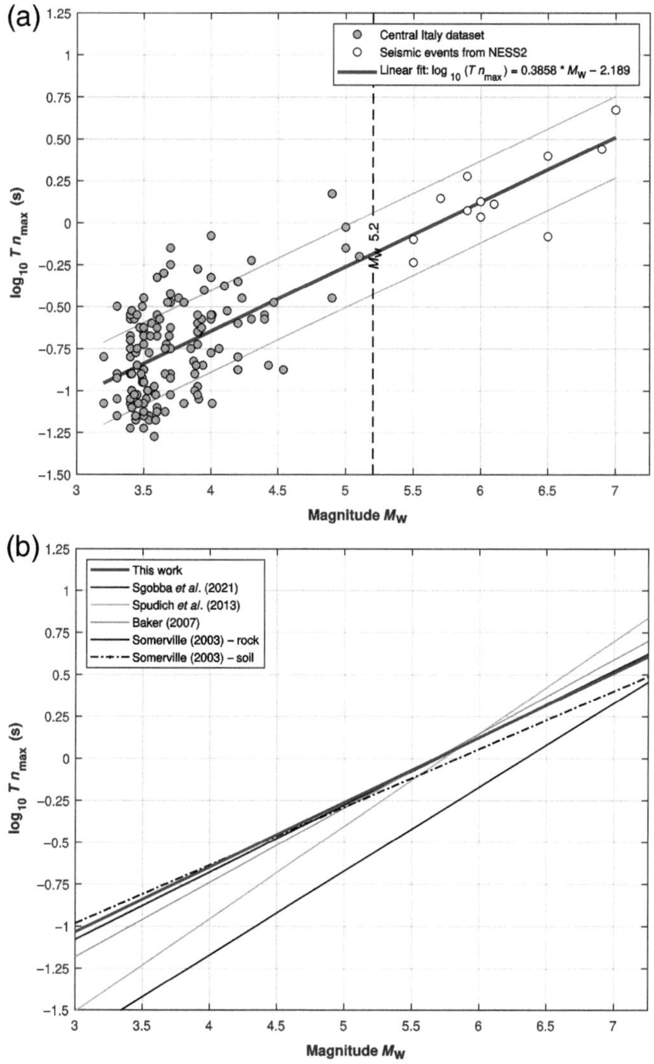

Figure 9. (a) Moment magnitude M_w versus $\log_{10}(Tn_{max})$: empirical data from this study (gray circles) and NESS2 (Table 1; white circles). The red line represents the linear fit (equation 8). (b) Empirical models M_w–$\log_{10}(Tn_{max})$ compared with the model in equation (6). The color version of this figure is available only in the electronic edition.

3.5 (blue), 4.5 (red), 5.5 (violet), and 6.5 (turquoise). In this hypothesis, we keep the value of $n_{max} = 1$ and $\theta = \theta_0$. First, we observe that the general trends of the predictions including directivity effects reproduce the shift of the peak period toward higher values as magnitude increases, as also observed in previous investigations by Bayless and Abrahamson (2019) and Sgobba, Felicetta, *et al.* (2021). Then, for all curves with different magnitudes, source directivity produces an increase at all periods compared with the predictions without directivity. The proposed procedure provides a broader spectral correction method, different from the application of band-limited methods (e.g., Chioccarelli and Iervolino, 2010; Shahi and Baker, 2011). In these latter studies, the correction is applied within a narrow range around the pulse period and is generally valid for medium- to large-magnitude earthquakes. Figure 10b shows the comparison of predicted spectra with directivity correction at different azimuths (0°, 45°, 90°, 135°, and 180°) versus the SA amplitudes without directivity (dashed black lines). In our convention, $\theta = 0°$ represents an observer in directive position with respect to the epicenter, $\theta = 180°$ an antidirective position and $\theta = 90°$ the neutral position. As expected, the predictions for the model without directivity corrections is close to those obtained for $\theta = 90°$. The discrepancies are related to the full nonergodic model, which includes both directive and nondirective events in the calibration dataset. For the considered azimuth, we observed a variation of SAs amplitudes that includes directivity corrections, showing the most significant increases for the observer in the directive position (around +50% at $T = 0.35$ s), the largest decreases for those in the antidirective position (−33% at the same period). In the neutral position ($\theta = 90°$), the empirical predictions with and without directivity are similar with a reduction in the corrected SA amplitudes of 17%. It should be noted that because the C_d function is not symmetrical with respect to zero, the percentages of increase and decrease in the directivity and antidirectivity positions are not equal.

Figure 10c shows that the different impact of the value of n_{max}, considering five values from 0 to 2.5 with a step of 0.5. In this case, we still consider an earthquake with M_w equal to 5.5 and an angle of maximum directivity of 0°. The case with $n_{max} = 0$ corresponds to the case without directivity and coincides with the nonergodic GMM without correction. Because we have been able to see experimentally in the construction of the parameterization, as the value of n_{max} increases, the values of the spectral ordinates also increase. Always referring to the peak of the acceleration response spectra ($T = 0.35$ s), the increase between $n_{max} = 0$ (no directivity) and $n_{max} = 2.5$ (very strong directivity) is up to +230% i.e. that is more than three times the prediction without directivity.

Real-case scenarios: Events in the calibration dataset

As a final consistency check, we applied the model with directivity correction to the events in the dataset with evidence of directivity to assess the reliability of our proposed directivity model. Figure 11 shows this application for the M_w 4 event of 30 October 2016 at 11:58:17 UTC, which we have already analyzed in Figures 2–4. This event was recognized as directivity across the entire period range with $n_{max} = 2.1$ at $Tn_{max} = 0.27$ s and directivity angle of 171° to the north.

The case study includes three cases, relevant for directivity analysis:

- Stations PTQR in Figure 11a and ACC in Figure 12a, in forward directivity position (the rupture propagates toward the site)
- Stations TOD in Figure 11b and ASP in Figure 12b, in neutral position
- Stations FSSB in Figure 11c and NCR in Figure 12c, in backward directivity position (the rupture propagates away from the site)

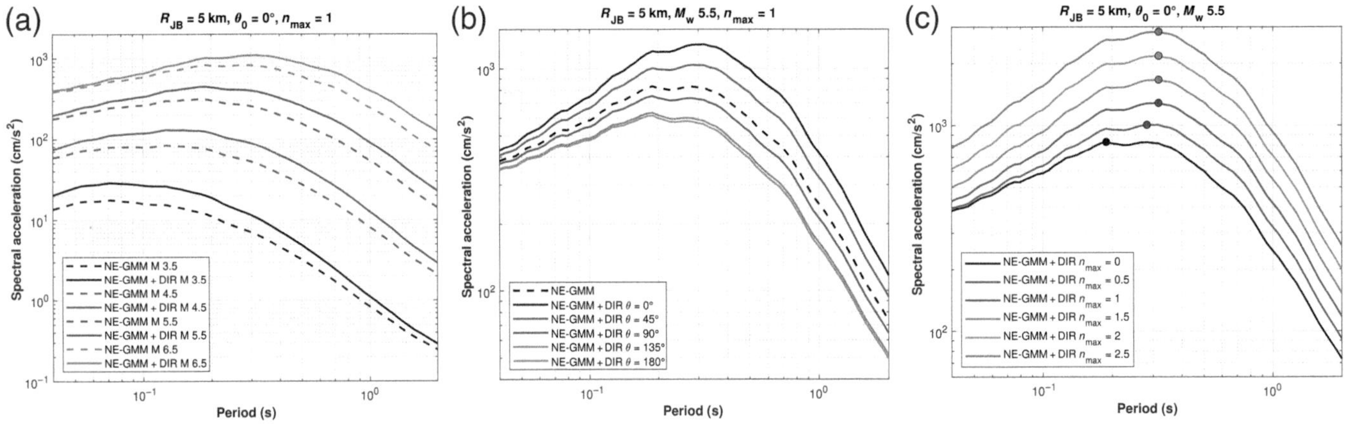

Figure 10. Ground-motion model (GMM) predictions with and without directivity correction. (a) M_w; (b) angle of maximum directivity θ_0; and (c) n_{max}, in which circles mark the Tn_{max} for each curve. The color version of this figure is available only in the electronic edition.

In the forward directivity cases (Figs. 11a and 12a), the correction factor caused by the directivity source enhances the spectral amplitudes and significantly improves the agreement between predicted and observed spectra. The corrected model (solid red line) closely follows the observed spectrum, remaining well within the confidence interval (shaded gray area), which represents the standard deviation of the nonergodic model (see the Standard deviation assessment section).

The impact of the directivity correction for stations in the neutral position cases (Figs. 11b and 12b: TOD and ASP stations, respectively) is negligible, as expected, because these stations are less affected by directivity effects. Nevertheless, the corrected predictions still lie within the expected uncertainty bounds and provide a robust fit between model and observed spectrum.

Finally, in the cases with backward directivity (Figs. 11c and 12c), the prediction without the directivity correction tends to overestimate the observed ground motion, whereas the application of our model yields a much better match with respect to the observed spectrum. Overall, this improvement is systematic and consistent across the events analyzed in the Central Italy dataset. For further examples demonstrating the model's performance, refer to Fig. S8 (Amatrice aftershock), Fig. S9 (Norcia aftershock), and Fig. S10 (Capitignano mainshock).

Standard deviation assessment

In Figure 13, we show the aleatory standard deviations σ_0 of the nonergodic GMM with and without correction for the directivity effects as a function of the investigated period for the calibration dataset (solid lines). In particular, the blue lines represent the σ_0 of δW_0 residuals in equation (1), and the red line is the aleatory standard deviation of $\delta W_{\mathrm{nodir}}$ in equation (2). The application of the directivity model consistently reduces the σ_0 across all periods with an average reduction of ~13%, with maximum reduction at $T = 0.2$ s of 20% and minimum reduction of 9% for the longest period (T = 2.0 s).

In addition, we computed the σ_0 considering only the recording of the directive events, as defined by the criteria described in the Identification of Directive Events section 4 (see the dashed lines in Fig. 13). As expected, the aleatory variability of the directive events is generally higher than that computed for all events, reflecting the strong spatial anisotropy of seismic motion; these events are also those for which the directivity correction is expected to have the largest impact on the aleatory standard deviation. The reduction of σ_0 is stronger, with an average reduction of ~20% across all periods.

CONCLUSIONS

In this study, we developed a fully data-driven model to parameterize the directivity effects into a GMM for Central Italy. The model is based on a dataset of 456 normal fault earthquakes with magnitudes from 3.2 to 6.5 recorded between 2009 and 2018. Adopting the approach of Colavitti, Lanzano, Sgobba, Pacor, and Gallovič (2022), we isolated directivity as part of the aleatory residual component of a nonergodic GMM after systematically removing source, path, and site contributions through GMM calibration. Different from Colavitti, Lanzano, Sgobba, Pacor, and Gallovič, (2022), our analysis was carried out in terms of SA, with the ultimate goal of predicting directivity effects for hazard applications. Similar to the previous investigation, we found that ~30% of the events exhibit clear directivity signatures, and almost all of the directive events were recognized in both the FAS and SA analyses, confirming the robustness and repeatability of the approach followed.

Our results show that the effect is more apparent in SA with respect to FAS analyses, with broader frequency bands and higher peak values, possibly because of differences between SA and FAS (see Tothong *et al.*, 2007; Douglas and Boore, 2011).

The proposed directivity parameterization requires the definition of three input parameters, namely, the M_w of the event, the maximum amplitude of the directivity parameter n_{max}, and

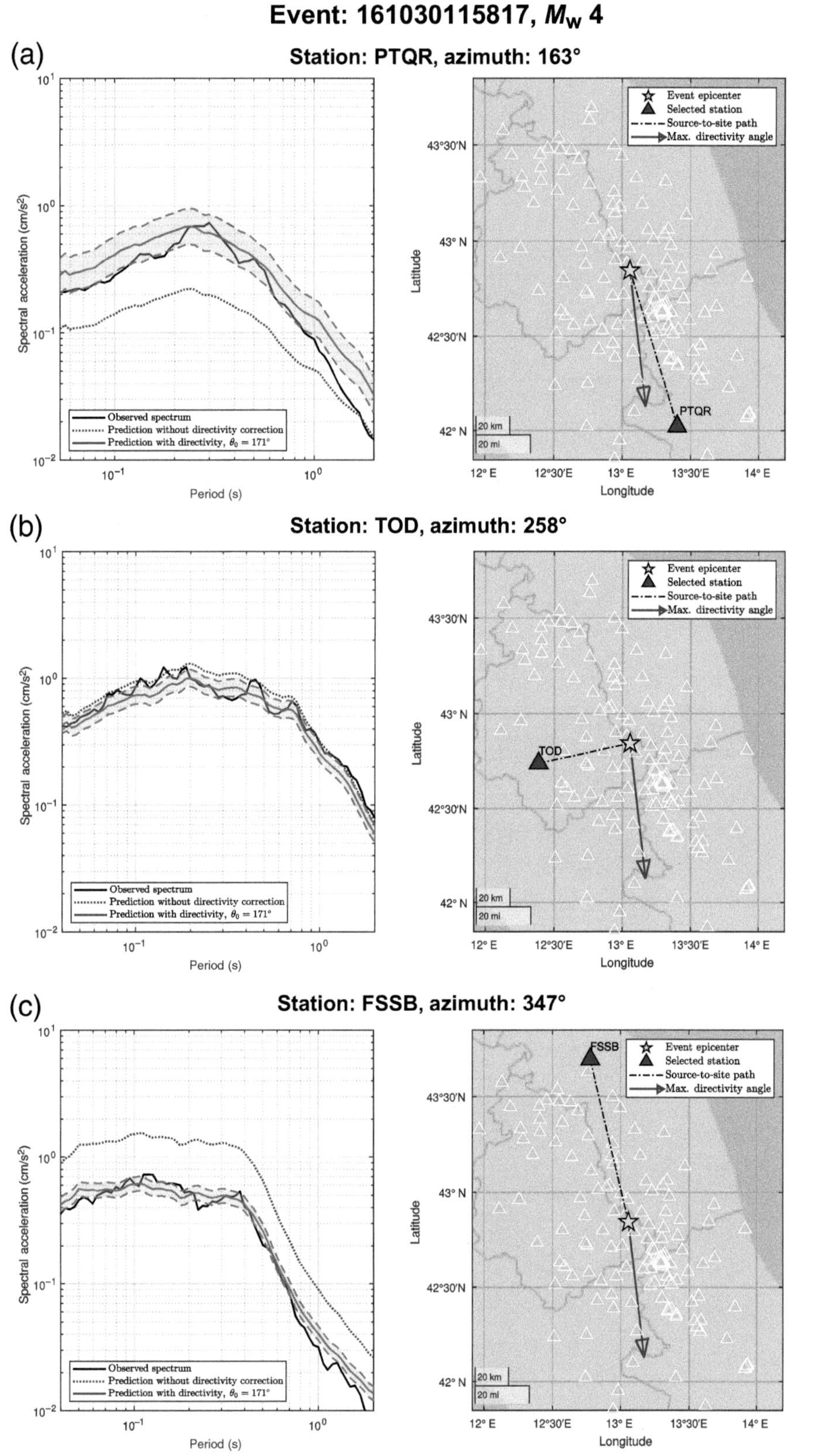

Figure 11. Observed and predicted spectra for the M_w 4 event of 30 October 2016 at 11:58:17 UTC. For each panel, we have two subplots: on the left, the comparison between observed spectra (black solid line), predicted spectra with and without directivity correction (solid red line and dashed line, respectively), is shown. The gray band between the two dashed gray lines represents the uncertainty associated with the spectrum predicted using the directivity correction. On the right, the map with the epicenter and the selected station. (a) PTQR (forward directivity), (b) TOD (neutral position), and (c) FSSB (backward directivity). The red arrow indicates the directivity angle (171°) corresponding to n_{max}. The color version of this figure is available only in the electronic edition.

the angle of maximum directivity θ_0. The corrective model consists of three empirical relationships to be used in this sequence:

1. A linear relationship between $\log_{10}(Tn_{max})$ (spectral period corresponding to n_{max}) and M_w. The validity of the empirical equation is extended to higher magnitudes using pulse-like periods T_p of global normal faulting earthquakes, included in the NESS2.0 database (Sgobba, Felicetta, *et al.*, 2021)
2. A standardized Gaussian distribution for the $\log_{10} \frac{T}{Tn_{max}}$ as a function of $\frac{n}{n_{max}}$, in which n_{max}. The empirical relation depends only on a shape factor c_1 (standard deviation of normal distribution, which controls the width of directivity period band), which is linearly dependent on n_{max}, confirming that the directivity bandwidth scales with directivity strength.
3. A function to describe, for each spectral period, how the directivity effects vary with azimuth. For this purpose, we have adapted the directivity function C_d introduced by Boatwright (2007) and formulated by Convertito *et al.* (2013), similar to other studies developed in California using the empirical Green's function approach (Hirakawa *et al.*, 2023; Parker *et al.*, 2025).

To simplify the use of this relation, we have constrained some parameters to fixed values ($k = 0.85$ and Mach number $\alpha = 0.50$), leaving the

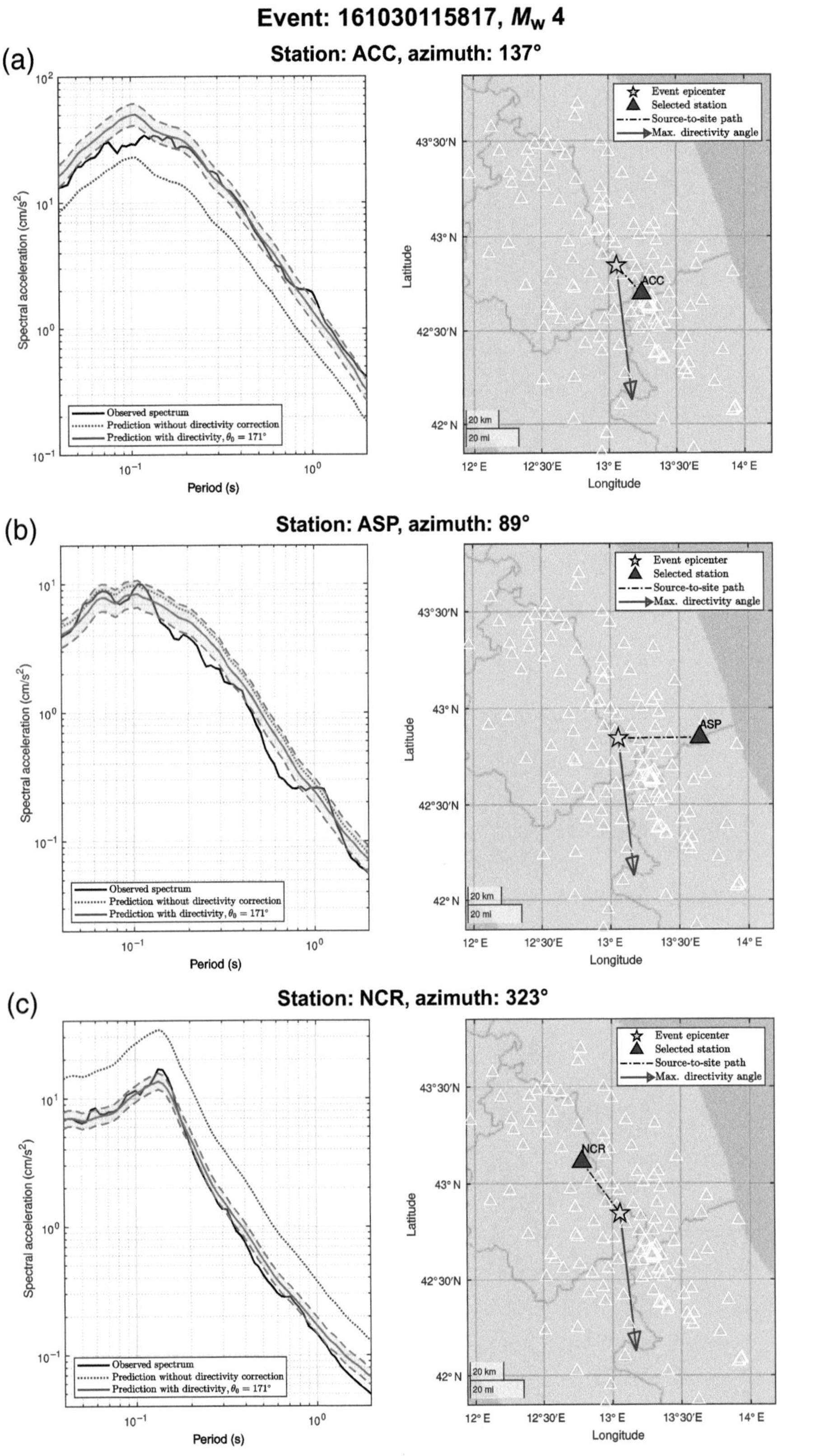

Figure 12. Observed and predicted spectra for the M_w 4 event of 30 October 2016 at 11:58:17 UTC. For each panel, we have two subplots: on the left, a comparison between observed spectra (solid black line), predicted spectra with and without directivity correction (solid red line and dashed line, respectively) is shown. The gray band between the two gray-dashed lines represents the uncertainty associated with the spectrum predicted using the directivity correction. On the right is shown the map with the epicenter and the selected station. (a) ACC (forward directivity), (b) ASP (neutral position), and (c) NCR (backward directivity). The red arrow indicates the directivity angle (171°) corresponding to n_{max}. The color version of this figure is available only in the electronic edition.

angle of maximum directivity θ_{max} and spectral amplitude n as free variables. The first empirical equation (relation between $\log_{10}(Tn_{max})$ and M_w) represents an original contribution of this work compared with previous studies and seems to confirm that there is a scalability of the directivity effects from strong to weak earthquakes, affecting frequency ranges that shift continuously towards higher frequencies.

Our findings are consistent with previous investigations (Somerville, 2003; Baker, 2007; Spudich *et al.*, 2013; Sgobba, Felicetta, *et al.*, 2021), reinforcing the idea of the robustness of our data-driven parameterization. With particular regard to the potential impact on the ground motion, the proposed model allows us to generate shaking field that vary with azimuth, in agreement with the direction of rupture propagation. The model prediction can lead to an increase of spectral amplitudes up to three times the prediction without directivity correction. We also observed that the introduction of this directivity corrective term within the nonergodic GMM for Central Italy has a considerable impact also on the associated variability, leading to a reduction of the aleatory standard deviation of the GMM ranging from 20% to 13% along the analyzed periods.

Future developments in properly predicting directivity will cover different aspects, such as:

1. Extend this approach to a larger and spatially wider dataset in Italy (e.g., ITACAext 2.0 by Lanzano

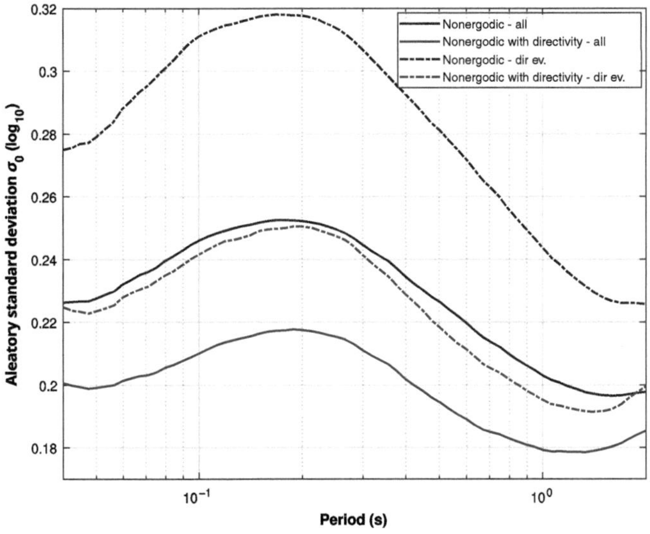

Figure 13. Aleatory standard deviations σ_0 (in $\log_{10}$ units) as a function of period for the nonergodic GMM with (red curves, standard deviation of δW_{nodir}) and without application of the directivity corrective model (blue curves standard deviation of δW_0). The solid lines represent the aleatory standard deviations for all the events; dashed lines represent the σ_0 computed only on the recordings of the directive events. The color version of this figure is available only in the electronic edition.

et al., 2025), including the recordings of the major sequences in the past 60 yr, also caused by focal mechanisms different from normal.

2. Extend the range of periods to values greater than 2 s (potentially ≤10 s), to better capture the spectral characteristics of high-magnitude earthquakes (including also events outside Italy), for which periods of maximum directivity are expected to be shifted to longer periods. This spectral extension will also allow verification of the assumed compatibility between Tn_{max} and the pulse period T_p.
3. Introduce the geometry of the fault because a point-like representation of the source (epicenter coordinates) has still been considered to compute the event-to-site azimuths in these analyses with a dataset mainly composed of small- to medium-magnitude earthquakes.

The model is thus currently designed to reconstruct shaking fields of past earthquakes and predict scenarios, imposing the values of θ_0 and n_{max}. Although empirical statistics for n_{max} and for the occurrence rate of directive events (~30% in this dataset) are available, they have not yet been analyzed with the specific goal of deriving probability distribution functions suitable for PSHA. Extending the framework to include a probabilistic description of these quantities and enabling its integration within a fully probabilistic seismic hazard workflow represent important directions for future developments.

DATA AND RESOURCES

Analyses were performed using MATLAB software (https://www.mathworks.com, MathWorks, 2023). For the nodal planes analyzed for the event in Figure 2 in this article, we refer to the seismological service of Istituto Nazionale di Geofisica e Vulcanologia (https://terremoti.ingv.it/en/event/8881771; Scognamiglio *et al.*, 2009). The characteristics of all events used in the reference ground-motion model (GMM), which is calibrated for the geometric mean of the horizontal components of 69 spectral acceleration ordinates at 5% damping in the period 0.01–2 s are available in the flatfile by Spallarossa *et al.* (2023). A detailed description of each feature of the GMM adopted in this study is provided in Appendix. All websites were last accessed in July 2025. The supplemental material for this article includes ESuppl with Figure S1, which represents several strategies adopted to constrain the inversion; Figures S2 and S3, which presents a direct comparison with the Fourier amplitude spectra model developed by Colavitti, Lanzano, Sgobba, Pacor, and Gallovič (2022); Figure S4, which provides details of the quality control for the analyzed events; Figures S5 and S6, which further explore the concept of directivity parameterization; Figure S7, which investigates the standard deviation of the Gaussian distribution; and Figures S8–S10, which show comparisons between observed and predicted spectra for events with significant directivity. Table T1 of ESupp2 provides the model coefficients and standard deviations, and the random effects of the model are available upon request by contacting the authors. Finally, a table summarizing the main characteristics of the directivity events analyzed in this study is available in Table T2 of ESupp3.

DECLARATION OF COMPETING INTERESTS

The authors acknowledge that there are no conflicts of interest recorded.

ACKNOWLEDGMENTS

The authors are very grateful to Daniele Spallarossa (University of Genoa, Department of Earth, Environment and Life Sciences) for the continuous encouragement and for making the dataset used in this work available and to František Gallovič (University of Prague, Czech Republic) for the fruitful discussion about this work. This research was supported in the frame of two activities: the Work Package 3—Scenario and Ground-Motion Models of the Seismic Hazard Centre (Centro di Pericolosità Sismica) of Istituto Nazionale di Geofisica e Vulcanologia and SECURE project (Regional-scale earthquake ground-motion predictions through physics-based and empirical approaches: A case study Central Italy, https://progetti.ingv.it/en/secure, last accessed July 2025), part of Pianeta Dinamico (Working Earth), Geosciences for the Understanding of the Dynamics of the Earth and the Consequent Natural Risks (CUP code D53J19000170001), funded by the Italian Ministry of University and Research (MIUR), within Work Package 2.1 - Kinematic and dynamic earthquake rupture modeling. The authors also thank Associate Editor Ricardo Taborda, Deputy Editor-in-Chief Junghyun Park, Managing Editor Katie Pegram, and the reviewers Jeff Bayless and Evan Hirakawa for their constructive comments and valuable suggestions, which significantly improved the quality of the article.

REFERENCES

Aki, K. (1968). Seismic displacements near a fault, *J. Geophys. Res.* **73,** 5359–5376.

Al-Atik, L., N. A. Abrahamson, J. J. Bommer, F. Scherbaum, F. Cotton, and N. Kuehn (2010). The variability of ground-motion prediction models and its components, *Seismol. Res. Lett.* **81,** no. 5, 794–801, doi: 10.1785/gssrl.81.5.794.

Baker, J. W. (2007). Quantitative classification of near-fault ground motions using wavelet analysis, *Bull. Seismol. Soc. Am.* **97,** 1486–1501, doi: 10.1785/0120060255.

Baker, J. W., and C. A. Cornell (2008). Vector-valued intensity measures for pulse-like near-fault ground motions, *Eng. Struct.* **30,** 1048–1057, doi: 10.1016/j.engstruct.2007.07.009.

Baltay, A., T. C. Hanks, and N. A. Abrahamson (2017). Uncertainty, variability, and earthquake physics in ground-motion prediction equations, *Bull. Seismol. Soc. Am.* **107,** no. 4, 1754–1772, doi: 10.1785/0120160164.

Bates, D., B. Mächler, B. Bolker, and S. Walker (2015). Fitting linear mixed-effects models using Ime4, *J. Stat. Software* **67,** no. 1, 1–48, doi: 10.18637/jss.v067.i01.

Bayless, J., and N. A. Abrahamson (2019). Summary of the BA18 ground-motion model for Fourier amplitude spectra for crustal earthquakes in California, *Bull. Seismol. Soc. Am.* **109,** no. 5, 2088–2105, doi: 10.1785/0120190077.

Bayless, J., N. A. Abrahamson, and P. G. Somerville (2024). A rupture directivity adjustment model and its application in seismic hazard, *Earthq. Spectra* **41,** 753–781, doi: 10.1177/87552930241290632.

Benioff, H. (1955). *Earthquakes in Kern County California During 1952,* Department of natural resources, Division of Mines 171, 199–204.

Ben-Menahem, A. (1961). Radiation of seismic surface-waves from finite moving sources, *Ph.D. Thesis,* California Institute of Technology.

Boatwright, J. (2007). The persistence of directivity in small earthquakes, *Bull. Seismol. Soc. Am.* **97,** 1850–1861, doi: 10.1785/0120050228.

Boncio, P., F. Brozzetti, and G. Lavecchia (2000). Architecture and seismotectonics of a regional low-angle normal fault zone in central Italy, *Tectonics* **19,** no. 6, 1038–1055, doi: 10.1029/2000TC900023.

Boore, D., and W. Joyner (1978). The influence of rupture incoherence on seismic directivity, *Bull. Seismol. Soc. Am.* **68,** no. 2, 283–300.

Bray, J. D., and A. Rodriguez-Marek (2004). Characterization of forward-directivity ground motions in the near fault region, *Soil Dynam. Earthq. Eng.* **24,** 815–828, doi: 10.1016/j.soildyn.2004.05.001.

Buttinelli, M., G. Pezzo, L. Valoroso, P. De Gori, and C. Chiarabba (2018). Tectonics inversions, fault segmentation, and triggering mechanisms in the central Apennines normal fault system: Insights from high-resolution velocity models, *Tectonics* **37,** doi: 10.1029/2018TC005053.

Calderoni, G., R. Di Giovambattista, and G. Ventura (2023). A reliable procedure to estimate the rupture propagation directions from source directivity: The 2016-2018 Central Italy seismic sequence, *Seismol. Res. Lett.* **94,** 1912–1924, doi: 10.1785/0220220318.

Calderoni, G., A. Rovelli, Y. Ben-Zion, and R. Di Giovambattista (2015). Along-strike rupture directivity of earthquakes of the 2009 L'Aquila, Central Italy, seismic sequence, *Geophys. J. Int.* **205,** 399–415, doi: 10.1093/gji/ggv275.

Calderoni, G., A. Rovelli, and R. Di Giovambattista (2017). Rupture directivity of the strongest 2016-2017 central Italy earthquakes, *J. Geophys. Res.* **122,** doi: 10.1002/2017JB014118.

Campbell, K. W. (1987). Predicting strong ground motion in Utah in evaluation of regional and urban earthquake hazard, *U.S. Geol. Surv. Open-File Rept. 87-585,* **2,** L1–L90.

Castro, R. R., G. Franceschina, F. Pacor, D. Bindi, and L. Luzi (2006). Analysis of the frequency dependence of the S-wave radiation pattern from local earthquakes in Central Italy, *Bull. Seismol. Soc. Am.* **96,** no. 2, 415–426, doi: 10.1785/0120050066.

Castro, R. R., D. Spallarossa, F. Pacor, L. Colavitti, G. Lanzano, C. Vidales-Basurto, and S. Sgobba (2022). Temporal Variation of the Spectral Decay Parameter Kappa Detected before and after the 2016 Main Earthquakes of Central Italy, *Bull. Seismol. Soc. Am.* **112,** no. 6, 3037–3045, doi: 10.1785/0120220107.

Chen, Y. S. (2017). Incorporating rupture directivity effects into probabilistic seismic hazard analysis, *Ph.D. Thesis,* Earthquake Engineering and Engineering Seismology, Scuola Universitaria Superiore IUSS Pavia.

Chen, P., T. H. Jordan, and L. Zhao (2010). Resolving fault plane ambiguity for small earthquakes, *Geophys. J. Int.* **181,** 493–501, doi: 10.1111/j.1365-246X.2010.04515.x.

Chen, Y., J. Letort, F. Cotton, and S. Drouet (2014). High-frequency directivity effects: Evidence from analysis of the Les Saintes records, *J. Seismol.* **18,** 457–466, doi: 10.1007/s10950-014-9419-2.

Chiarabba, C., A. Amato, M. Anselmi, P. Baccheschi, I. Bianchi, M. Cattaneo, G. Cecere, L. Chiaraluce, M. G. Ciaccio, P. De Gori, *et al.* (2009). The 2009 L'Aquila (central Italy) M_w 6.3 earthquake: Main shock and aftershocks, *Geophys. Res. Lett.* **36,** no. 18, doi: 10.1029/2009GL039627.

Chiarabba, C., M. Buttinelli, M. Cattaneo, and P. De Gori (2020). Large earthquakes driven by fluid overpressure: The Apennines normal faulting system case, *Tectonics* **39,** e2019TC006014, doi: 10.1029/2019TC006014.

Chioccarelli, E., and I. Iervolino (2010). Near-source seismic demand and pulse-like records: A discussion for L'Aquila earthquake, *Earthq. Eng. Struct. Dynam.* **39,** 1039–1062, doi: 10.1002/eqe.987.

Chiou, B. S. J., and P. Spudich (2013). The Chiou and Spudich directivity predictor DPP, in *Chapter 6 of PEER Report No. 2013/09,* P. Spudich (Editor), Pacific Earthquake Engineering Research Center, Berkeley, California.

Colavitti, L., G. Lanzano, S. Sgobba, and F. Pacor (2022). CI-FAS_Directivity: List of earthquakes with evidence of directivity in Central Italy [Data set], *Istituto Nazionale di Geofisica e Vulcanologia (INGV),* doi: 10.13127/ci_dataset/CI-FAS_directivity.

Colavitti, L., G. Lanzano, S. Sgobba, F. Pacor, and F. Gallovič (2022). Empirical evidence of frequency-dependent directivity effects from small-to-moderate normal fault earthquakes in Central Italy, *J. Geophys. Res. Solid Earth* **127,** e2021JB023498, doi: 10.1029/2021JB023498.

Convertito, V., F. Catalli, and A. Emolo (2013). Combining stress transfer and source directivity: The case of the 2012 Emilia seismic sequence, *Sci. Rep.* **3,** 3114, doi: 10.1038/srep03114.

Convertito, V., R. De Matteis, and A. Pino (2017). Evidence for static and dynamic triggering of seismicity following the 24 August 2016 $M_w = 6.0$, Amatrice (Central Italy) earthquake, *Pure Appl. Geophys.* **174,** 3663–3672, doi: 10.1007/s00024-017-1559-1.

Courboulex, F., A. Dujardin, M. Vallée, B. Delouis, C. Sira, A. Deschamps, L. Honoré, and F. Thouvenot (2013). High-frequency directivity effect for an M_w 4.1 earthquake, widely felt by the population in southeastern France, *Bull. Seismol. Soc. Am.* **103,** no. 6, 3347–3353, doi: 10.1785/0120130073.

Di Bona, M. (2016). A local magnitude scale for crustal earthquakes in Italy, *Bull. Seismol. Soc. Am.* **106,** no. 1, 242–258, doi: 10.1785/0120150155.

Di Bucci, D., M. Buttinelli, C. D'Ambrogi, D. Scrocca and , and RETRACE-3D Working Group (2021). RETRACE-3D project: A multidisciplinary collaboration to build a crustal model for the 2016-2018 Central Italy seismic sequence, *Boll. Geof. Teor. Appl.* **62,** 1–18, doi: 10.4430/bgta0343.

Di Luccio, D., G. Ventura, R. Di Giovambattista, A. Piscini, and F. R. Cinti (2010). Normal faults and thrusts reactivated by deep fluids: The 6 April 2009 M_w 6.3 L'Aquila earthquake, central Italy, *J. Geophys. Res.* **115,** B06315, doi: 10.1029/2009JB007190.

Douglas, J., and D. M. Boore (2011). High-frequency filtering of strong-motion records, *Bull. Earthq. Eng.* **9,** 395–409, doi: 10.1007/s10518-010-9208-4.

Douglas, A., J. A. Hudson, and R. G. Pearce (1988). Directivity and the Doppler effect, *Bull. Seismol. Soc. Am.* **78,** 1376–1372.

DPC (1972). Italian strong motion network [Data set], Presidency of Council of Ministers—Civil Protection Department, *International Federation of Digital Seismograph Networks*, doi: 10.7914/SN/IT.

Faure Walker, J., P. Boncio, B. Pace, G. Roberts, L. Benedetti, O. Scotti, F. Visini, and L. Peruzza (2021). Fault2SHA Central Apennines database and structuring active fault data for seismic hazard assessment, *Sci. Data* **87,** no. 8, doi: 10.1038/s41597-021-00868-0.

Felicetta, C., E. Russo, M. D'Amico, S. Sgobba, G. Lanzano, C. Mascandola, F. Pacor, and L. Luzi (2023). Italian Accelerometric Archive v4.0 - Istituto Nazionale di Geofisica e Vulcanologia, Dipartimento della Protezione Civile Nazionale, doi: 10.13127/itaca.4.0 (in Italian).

Gentile, R., and C. Galasso (2020). Accounting for directivity-induced pulse-like ground motions in building portfolio loss assessment, *Bull. Earthq. Eng.*, doi: 10.1007/s10518-020-00950-9.

Haskell, N. A. (1963). Radiation pattern of Rayleigh waves from a fault of arbitrary dip and direction of motion in a homogeneous medium, *Bull. Seismol. Soc. Am.* **53,** no. 3, 619–642.

Herrero, A., and P. Bernard (1994). A kinematic self-similar rupture process for earthquakes, *Bull. Seismol. Soc. Am.* **84,** no. 4, 1216–1228, doi: 10.1785/BSSA0840041216.

Herrmann, R. B., L. Malagnini, and I. Munafò (2011). Regional moment tensors of the 2009 L'Aquila earthquake sequence, *Bull. Seismol. Soc. Am.* **101,** no. 3, 975–993, doi: 10.1785/0120090278.

Hirakawa, E., G. A. Parker, A. Baltay, and T. Hanks (2023). Rupture directivity of the 25 October 2022 M_w Alum Rock earthquake, *The Seism. Rec.* **3,** no. 2, 144–155, doi: 10.1785/0320230013.

Hirasawa, T., and W. Stauder (1965). On the seismic body waves from a finite moving source, *Bull. Seismol. Soc. Am.* **55,** no. 2, 237–262.

Huang, J. Y., C. H. Sung, S. H. Chao, and N. A. Abrahamson (2023). Including radiation pattern effects in ground-motion models for Taiwan, *Bull. Seismol. Am.* **113,** no. 3, 1248–1268, doi: 10.1785/0120220167.

INGV Seismological Data Centre (2006). Rete Sismica Nazionale (RSN), Istituto Nazionale di Geofisica e Vulcanologia (INGV), Italy, doi: 10.13127/SD/X0FXnH7QfY (in Italian).

Kasashara, K. (1960). An attempt to detect azimuth effect on spectral structures of seismic waves (the Alaskan earthquakes of April 7, 1958), *Bull. Earthq. Res. Inst.* **38,** 207–218.

Kotha, S. R., F. Cotton, and D. Bindi (2019). Empirical models of shear-wave radiation pattern derived from large datasets of ground-shaking observations, *Sci. Rep.* **9,** no. 981, doi: 10.1038/s41598-018-37524-4.

Lanzano, G., L. Vitrano, D. Bindi, C. Felicetta, S. Sgobba, L. Luzi, and F. Pacor (2025). ITACAext2.0: A high-quality parametric table of strong-to-weak motion recordings for Seismological and Engineering Research in Italy, *Seismol. Res. Lett.* **XX,** 1–22, doi: 10.1785/0220240309.

Lilienkamp, H., and G. Weatherill (2025). Efficient incorporation of rupture directivity into probabilistic seismic hazard using a deep learning-based approach, *Earthq. Spectra* **41,** no. 3, 2487–2513, doi: 10.1177/87552930251340668.

López-Comino, J. Á., F. D. L. Mancilla, J. Morales, and D. Stich (2012). Rupture directivity of the 2011, M_w 5.2 Lorca earthquake (Spain), *Geophys. Res. Lett.* **39,** no. 3, L03301, doi: 10.1029/2011GL050498.

Marquardt, D. (1963). An algorithm for least-squares estimation of nonlinear parameters, *SIAM J. Appl. Math.* **11,** no. 2, 431–441, doi: 10.1137/0111030.

MathWorks (2023). MATLAB, version 9.15, R2023b, Natick, Massachusetts, The MathWorks Inc., available at https://www.mathworks.com (last accessed July 2025).

Michele, M., L. Chiaraluce, R. Di Stefano, and F. Waldhauser (2020). Fine-scale structure of the 2016-2017 Central Italy seismic sequence from data recorded at the Italian National Network, *J. Geophys. Res. Solid Earth* **125,** no. 4, e2019JB018440, doi: 10.1029/2019JB018440.

Morasca, P., M. D'Amico, S. Sgobba, G. Lanzano, L. Colavitti, F. Pacor, and D. Spallarossa (2023). Empirical correlations between a FAS non-ergodic ground motion model and a GIT derived model for Central Italy, *Geophys. J. Int.* **233,** no. 1, 51–68, doi: 10.1093/gji/ggac445.

Pacor, F., F. Gallovič, R. Puglia, L. Luzi, and M. D'Amico (2016). Diminishing high-frequency directivity due to a source effects: Empirical evidence from small earthquakes in the Abruzzo region, Italy, *J. Geophys. Res. Solid Earth* **43,** 5000–5008, doi: 10.1002/2016GL068546.

Pacor, F., D. Spallarossa, A. Oth, L. Luzi, R. Puglia, L. Cantore, A. Mercuri, and D. Bindi (2016). Spectral models for ground motion prediction in the L'Aquila region (central Italy): Evidence for stress-drop dependence on magnitude and depth, *Geophys. J. Int.* **204,** 697–718, doi: 10.1093/gji/ggv448.

Parker, G. A., A. Baltay, and E. T. Hirakawa (2025). An empirical Green's function approach for isolating directivity effects in earthquake ground-motion amplitudes, *Bull. Seismol. Soc. Am.* **115,** no. 5, 2336–2354, doi: 10.1785/0120240264.

Pischiutta, M., A. Akinci, L. Malagnini, and A. Herrero (2016). Characteristics of the strong ground motion from the 24th August 2016 Amatrice earthquake, *Ann. Geophys.* **59,** doi: 10.4401/ag-7219.

Pondrelli, S., S. Salimbeni, A. Morelli, G. Ekström, M. Olivieri, and E. Boschi (2010). Seismic moment tensors of the April 2009, L'Aquila (Central Italy), earthquake sequence, *Geophys. J. Int.* **180,** no. 1, 238–242, doi: 10.1111/j.1365-246X.2009.04418.x.

Ren, Y., H. Wang, and R. Wen (2017). Imprint of rupture directivity from ground motions of the 24 August 2016 M_w 6.2 Central Italy earthquake, *Tectonics* **36,** 3178–3191, doi: 10.1002/2017TC004673.

Roberts, G. P., and A. M. Michetti (2004). Spatial and temporal variations in growth rates along active normal fault systems: An example from the Lazio - Abruzzo Apennines, central Italy, *J. Struct. Geol.* **26,** 339–376, doi: 10.1016/S0191-8141(03)00103-2.

Ross, Z. E., D. T. Trugman, K. Azizzadenesheli, and A. Anandkumar (2020). Directivity modes of earthquake populations with unsupervised learning, *J. Geophys. Res: Solid Earth* **125,** e2019JB018299, doi: 10.1029/2019JB018299.

Ruiz, J. A., D. Baumont, P. Bernard, and C. Berge-Thierry (2011). Modelling directivity of strong ground motion with a fractal, k^{-2}, kinematic source model, *Geophys. J. Int.* **186,** no. 1, 226–244, doi: 10.1111/j.1365-246X.2011.05000.x.

Scognamiglio, L., E. Tinti, and A. Michelini (2009). Real-time determination of seismic moment tensor for the Italian region, *Bull. Seismol. Soc. Am.* **99,** no. 4, 2223–2242, doi: 10.1785/0120080104.

Sgobba, S., C. Felicetta, T. Bortolotti, A. Menafoglio, G. Lanzano, and F. Pacor (2024). A geostatistical modelling of empirical amplification functions and related site proxies for shaking scenarios in Central Italy, *Soil Dynam. Earthq. Eng.* **179,** 108496, doi: 10.1016/j.soildyn.2024.108496.

Sgobba, S., C. Felicetta, G. Lanzano, F. Ramadan, M. D'Amico, and F. Pacor (2021). NESS2.0: An updated version of the worldwide dataset for calibrating and adjusting ground-motion models in near source, *Bull. Seismol. Soc. Am.* **111,** no. 5, 2358–2378, doi: 10.1785/0120210080.

Sgobba, S., G. Lanzano, L. Colavitti, P. Morasca, M. C. D'Amico, and D. Spallarossa (2023). Physics-based parameterization of a FAS nonergodic ground motion model for Central Italy, *Bull. Earthq. Eng.* **21,** 4111–4137, doi: 10.1007/s10518-023-01691-1.

Sgobba, S., G. Lanzano, and F. Pacor (2021). Empirical nonergodic shaking scenarios based on spatial correlation models: An application to central Italy, *Earthq. Eng. Struct. Dynamics* **50,** no. 1, 60–80, doi: 10.1002/eqe.3362.

Shahi, S. K., and J. W. Baker (2011). An empirically calibrated framework for including the effects of near-fault directivity in probabilistic seismic hazard analysis, *Bull. Seismol. Soc. Am.* **101,** no. 2, 742–755, doi: 10.1785/0120100090.

Somerville, P. G. (2003). Magnitude scaling of the near fault rupture directivity pulse, *Phys. Earth Planet.* **137,** 201–212, doi: 10.1016/S0031-9201(03)00015-3.

Somerville, P. G., N. F. Smith, R. W. Graves, and N. A. Abrahamson (1997). Modification of empirical strong ground motion attenuation relations to include the amplitude and duration effects of rupture directivity, *Seismol. Res. Lett.* **68,** no. 1, 199–222, doi: 10.1785/gssrl.68.1.199.

Spagnuolo, E., A. Cirella, and A. Akinci (2016). Investigating the effectiveness of rupture directivity during the August 24, 2016 M_w 6.0 central Italy earthquake, *Ann. Geophys.* **59,** doi: 10.4401/ag-7213.

Spallarossa, D., L. Colavitti, G. Lanzano, S. Sgobba, F. Pacor, and C. Felicetta (2023). CI-SA Flatfile: Parametric table of the 5% Acceleration response spectra ordinates and associated metadata for the shallow active crustal events in Central Italy (2009-2018) – Data set, *Istituto Nazionale di Geofisica e Vulcanologia (INGV)*, doi: 10.13127/CI_dataset/CI-SA_flatfile.

Spudich, P., and B. Chiou (2008). Directivity in NGA earthquake ground motions; analysis using isochrone theory, *Earthq. Spectra* **24,** 279–298, doi: 10.1193/1.2928225.

Spudich, P., J. R. Bayless, J. Baker, B. S. J. Chiou, B. Rowshandel, S. K. Shahi, and P. Somerville (2013). Final report of the NGA-West2 directivity working group, *Pacific Earthquake Engineering Research Center Rept. 2013/02*, University of California, Berkeley.

Spudich, P., B. Rowshandel, S. K. Shahi, J. W. Baker, and B. S. J. Chiou (2014). Comparison of NGA- West2 directivity models, *Earthq. Spectra* **30,** 1199–1221, doi: 10.1193/080313EQS222M.

Tan, Y., and D. Helmberger (2010). Rupture directivity characteristics of the 2003 Big Bear sequence, *Bull. Seismol. Soc. Am.* **100,** no. 3, 1089–1106, doi: 10.1785/0120090074.

Tinti, E., L. Scognamiglio, A. Michelini, and M. Cocco (2016). Slip heterogeneity and directivity of the M_L 6.0. Amatrice earthquake estimated with rapid finite-fault inversion, *Geophys. Res. Lett.* **43,** 10,745–10,752, doi: 10.1002/2016GL071263.

Tomic, J., R. E. Abercrombie, and A. Do Nascimento (2009). Source parameters and rupture velocity of small $M \leq 2.2$ reservoir induced earthquakes, *Geophys. J. Int.* **179,** 1013–1023, doi: 10.1111/j.1365-246X.2009.04233.x.

Tothong, P., A. C. Cornell, and W. Baker (2007). Explicit directivity-pulse inclusion in probabilistic seismic hazard analysis, *Earthq. Spectra* **23,** no. 4, 867–891.

Trifunac, M. D., and J. N. Brune (1970). Complexity of energy release during the Imperial Valley, California, earthquake of 1940, *Bull. Seismol. Soc. Am.* **60,** 137–160.

Van Houtte, C., T. Larkin, and C. Holden (2015). The counter-intuitive relationship between earthquake response spectra and Fourier amplitude spectra, *Proceedings of the New Zealand Society for Earthquake Engineering Annual Conference*, Rotorua, New Zealand, New Zealand Society for Earthquake Engineering.

Velasco, A., C. J. Ammon, and T. Lay (1994). Empirical Green function deconvolution of broadband surface waves: Rupture directivity of the 1992 Landers, California (M_w 7.3) earthquake, *Bull. Seismol. Soc. Am.* **84,** no. 3, 735–750, doi: 10.1785/BSSA0840030735.

Wang, H., Y. Ren, R. Wen, and P. Xu (2019). Breakdown of earthquake self-similar scaling and source rupture directivity in the 2016-2017 central Italy seismic sequence, *J. Geophys. Res.: Solid Earth* **124,** 3898–3917, doi: 10.1029/2018JB016543.

Weatherill, G., and H. Lilienkamp (2024). Capturing directivity in probabilistic seismic hazard analysis for New Zealand: Challenges, implications, and a machine learning approach for implementation, *Bull. Seismol. Soc. Am.* **114,** 373–398, doi: 10.1785/0120230161.

Wen, R. Z., H. W. Wang, and Y. Ren (2015). Rupture directivity from strong-motion recordings of the 2013 Lushan aftershocks, *Bull. Seismol. Soc. Am.* **105,** no. 6, 3068–3082, doi: 10.1785/0120150100.

Yamada, T., J. J. Mori, S. Ide, H. Kawakata, Y. Ilio, and H. Ogasawara (2005). Radiation efficiency and apparent stress of small earthquakes in a South African gold mine, *J. Geophys. Res.* **110,** B01305, doi: 10.1029/2004JB003221.

APPENDIX

Nonergodic ground-motion model for spectral acceleration

The model used in this study is a modified version of the one used by Sgobba, Lanzano, and Pacor (2021); Sgobba *et al.* (2024); for the Central Italy, which has the functional form

$$\log_{10} Y = a + F_M(M) + F_R(M,R) + \delta B_e + \delta S2S_s + \delta L2L_{\text{source}} + \delta P2P_p + \delta W_0, \quad \text{(A1)}$$

in which Y is the aforementioned intensity measures; a, $F_M(M)$, $F_R(M,R)$ are the fixed effects; and δB_e, $\delta S2S_{\text{ref},s}$, $\delta L2L_{\text{source}}$, and $\delta P2P_p$ represent the zero-mean Gaussian-distributed random effects.

Fixed effects. With reference to equation (A1):

- a represents the offset
- F_M is the scaling with magnitude in which

$$F_M(M) = b_1(M_w - M_h) \quad \text{for } M \le M_h$$
$$F_M(M) = b_2(M_w - M_h) \quad \text{otherwise}, \quad \text{(A2)}$$

  b_1 and b_2 are coefficients obtained from linear least-square regression, with M_h hinge magnitude fixed at 5.0.
- $F_R(M,R)$ represents the scaling with distance

$$F_R(M,R) = [c_1(M_w - M_{\text{ref}}) + c_2] \log_{10} \frac{\sqrt{R^2 + h^2}}{R_{\text{ref}}} + c_3(\sqrt{R^2 + h^2} - R_{\text{ref}}), \quad \text{(A3)}$$

  in which $F_R(M,R)$ is divided into a contribution due to the geometrical spreading computed by nonlinear regression (c_1 represent the magnitude-dependent term; c_2 the magnitude-independent term) and the anelastic attenuation (c_3 regionally dependent term); M_{ref} is the reference magnitude obtained from a preliminary nonlinear regression; R_{ref} is the reference distance at 1 km; and h is the pseudodepth equal to 6 km. R is the Joyner–Boore distance for events with magnitudes >5.5, for which the geometry of the fault was defined. For lower-magnitude events, the Joyner–Boore distance is assumed to be equal to the epicentral distance because the small area of the rupture surface makes the event equivalent to a point-like source. The site effect is not modeled in the fixed-term functional, but the median prediction is scaled with respect to the average ground motion of six reference sites, identified in the study by Morasca *et al.* (2023), namely, stations LSS, MNF, SLO, SNO, SDM, and NRN, all belonging to the seismic network of the DPC (DPC, 1972), with station code IT.

Random effects. The random effects introduced into the model are characterized by a normal distribution with zero mean and associated standard deviation. Specifically,

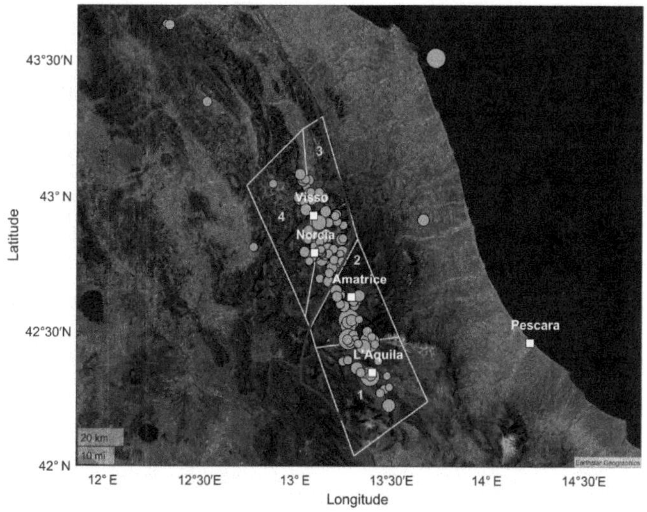

Figure A1. Polygons (yellow lines) for the source regionalization used to determine the $\delta L2L_{\text{source}}$ term according to the RETRACE-3D geological model (Di Bucci *et al.*, 2021). Clusters are numbered from south to north and are (1) Lazio-Abruzzo, (2) Laga Foredeep, (3) Sibillini, and (4) Umbria–Marche. The red line shows the Sibillini thrust. The gray dots show the location of the directive earthquakes for which size is proportional to the event magnitude. The color version of this figure is available only in the electronic edition.

- δB_e is the between-event term with associated standard deviation τ and represents the median error of each event with respect to the prediction of the ergodic GMM.
- $\delta S2S_s$ is the site-to-site term with associated standard deviation ϕ_{S2S}, defining the systematic bias of ground motions recorded at each station.
- $\delta L2L_{\text{source}}$ is the source term with associated standard deviation τ_{L2L}, which describes the systematic bias of the source regions. This term is estimated through a clustering approach that is based on geological considerations, different from what was published by Sgobba, Lanzano, and Pacor (2021). In this study, we group the earthquakes considering the boundaries defined by the main fault structures that have been identified in the geological model for Central Italy, called *RETRACE3D*–Central Italy earthquakes integrated crustal model (Di Bucci *et al.*, 2021).

Following these constraints and some considerations regarding the segmentation of fault systems derived from intense pre-existing crustal heterogeneities (Chiarabba *et al.*, 2020), the events are aggregated in four polygons, identifying the following clusters: (1) cluster number 1(Lazio-Abruzzo), (2) cluster number 2 (Laga Foredeep), (3) cluster number 3 (Sibillini), and (4) cluster number 4 (Umbria–Marche). In the rest of the area, we considered a background seismicity with a mean value of the location term equal to zero. A map of the clusters applied in this study is shown in Figure A1.

Here, $\delta P2P_p$ is the path term with associated standard deviation ϕ_{P2P}, which represents the systematic deviation along each source-to-site path (from each identified source region to the sites) and is related to anisotropy in the properties of the crustal propagation medium. The path terms are estimated by dividing the whole region into squared cells spaced every 0.2° that allow to capture the spatial distribution of the attenuation behavior (cell-specific attenuation), as defined by Sgobba *et al.* (2023).

The standard deviations of the different random effects can be combined to obtain the total variability σ_{tot}, as

$$\sigma_{tot} = \sqrt{\tau^2 + \phi^2_{S2S} + \tau^2_{L2L} + \phi^2_{P2P} + \sigma_0}, \qquad (A4)$$

in which σ_0 is the standard deviation of the leftover residuals δW_0. Further details on GMM calibration are available in work by Sgobba, Lanzano, and Pacor (2021), Sgobba *et al.* (2023). The model coefficients and related standard deviations of this work are provided in Table T1 of ESupp2. The random effects of the model are available upon request.

Manuscript received 11 August 2025
Published online 5 March 2026

The Community Fault Model (v. 6.1) for Southern California

Andreas Plesch*[1], Scott T. Marshall[2], and John H. Shaw[1]

ABSTRACT

We present a new version of the Statewide California Earthquake Center (SCEC) Community Fault Model (CFM 6.1) for southern California that describes more than 400 active faults that accommodate relative motions across the Pacific-North American plate boundary. CFM 6.1 is a substantially enhanced representation of the southern California fault system, with systematically updated and improved fault surfaces using detailed fault traces, precisely relocated earthquake and machine learning-enabled hypocenter catalogs (Ross, Trugman, *et al.*, 2019), and new focal mechanism solutions (Lin *et al.*, 2007; Hauksson *et al.*, 2012 + updates; Yang *et al.*, 2012), among other datasets. Several of the new fault representations, such as for the 2019 Ridgecrest, California (M 6.4 and 7.1) events, were developed using an objective, constraint-based interpolation method (Riesner *et al.*, 2017). This resulted in reproducible fault representations that are more precise and often more segmented and interconnected than in previous model versions. The CFM 6.1 was peer reviewed and includes preferred representations for each fault system, along with alternative fault representations for which significant differences in subsurface structure have been proposed. Based on the earthquake-to-fault association method of Evans *et al.* (2020), the fault representations in CFM 6.1 show a 5.8% increased association with regional seismicity compared to CFM 5.2, with 89.7% of M 3 and larger events most likely associated with a CFM 6.1 fault. The faults also show a much higher degree of interconnectivity than in previous model versions, which will have implications for the assessment of potential earthquake ruptures involving multiple, distinct faults. The model is documented and distributed through a new website with a map and 3D views to facilitate broad usage with a wide range of applications in seismology, tectonic geodesy, computational modeling, and probabilistic and deterministic seismic hazard assessment.

KEY POINTS

- New Community Fault Model (CFM) is a substantially improved and community reviewed 3D model of active faults in Southern California.
- The >400 model faults associate with 89.7% of **M** 3+ catalog events, a strong increase over earlier models.
- The new CFM is openly available for use in earthquake research and can improve seismic hazard assessments.

INTRODUCTION

Digital, 3D representations of active fault systems have become widely used to simulate dynamic rupture propagation (e.g., Oglesby, 2005; Duan and Oglesby, 2007; Douilly *et al.*, 2020; Lozos and Harris, 2020), model wave propagation and strong ground motions (e.g., Olsen and Archuleta, 1996; Graves *et al.*, 1998; Olsen *et al.*, 2009; Lozos *et al.*, 2025), interpret observed geodetic ground surface displacements (e.g., Meade and Hager, 2005; Fialko, 2006; Gonzalez-Ortega *et al.*, 2014; Evans *et al.*, 2015), predict fault-slip rates (e.g., Marshall *et al.*, 2013, 2017; Dorsett *et al.*, 2019; Devine *et al.*, 2022; Elston *et al.*, 2024) and assess regional earthquake hazards (e.g., Graves *et al.*, 2011; Field *et al.*, 2017). The Statewide California Earthquake Center (SCEC) Community Fault Model (CFM; Plesch *et al.*, 2007) was the first comprehensive and widely used regional compilation of 3D fault representations, and since its inception, models have been developed in other seismically active regions throughout the world (e.g., Hubbard *et al.*, 2012; Seebeck *et al.*, 2022, 2024). The CFM described in Plesch *et al.* (2007) consisted of 164 faults, with the emphasis on the San Andreas system and other major faults. The model has evolved to include increased geometric complexity and additional

1. Department of Earth and Planetary Sciences, Harvard University, Cambridge, Massachusetts, U.S.A., https://orcid.org/0000-0002-3355-9199 (AP); https://orcid.org/0000-0002-3971-3812 (JHS); 2. Department of Geological and Environmental Sciences, Appalachian State University, Boone, North Carolina, U.S.A., https://orcid.org/0000-0001-8879-6514 (STM)

*Corresponding author: plesch@fas.harvard.edu

Cite this article as Plesch, A., S. T. Marshall, and J. H. Shaw (2026). The Community Fault Model (v. 6.1) for Southern California, *Bull. Seismol. Soc. Am.* **116**, 1103–1124, doi: 10.1785/0120250247

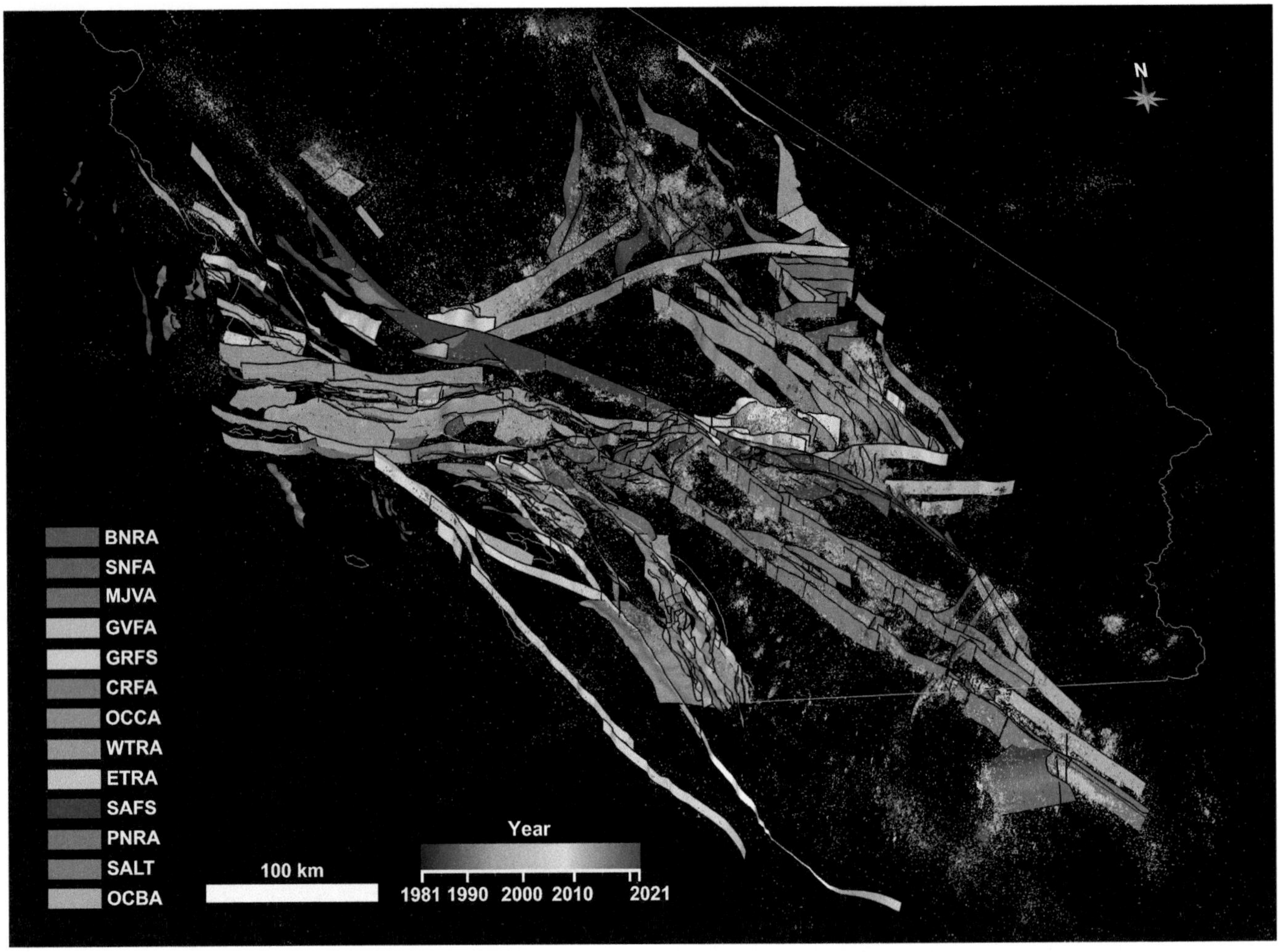

Figure 1. Perspective view of the Community Fault Model (CFM) 6.1. Faults are bounded at depth by the local seismogenic thickness (after Nazareth, 2004) and appear as bands. Small dots represent relocated hypocenters (after Hauksson et al., 2012), which are colored according to their time of occurrence. Fault color corresponds to fault area (letter A in legend), which is the top level in the CFM's hierarchical naming system. BNRA, Basin and Range; CRFA, Coast Ranges; ETRA, Eastern Transverse Ranges; GRFS, Garlock fault system; GVFA, Great Valley; MJVA, Mohave; OCBA, Offshore Continental Borderland; OCCA, Offshore Central California; PNRA, Peninsular Ranges; SAFS, San Andreas fault system; SALT, Salton Sea; SNFA, Sierra Nevada; and WTRA, Western Transverse Ranges. The color version of this figure is available only in the electronic edition.

faults, including blind sources and splays that link other major structures. Specifically, the model has evolved through several iterations since the first comprehensive peer-reviewed model was released (Plesch *et al.*, 2007). These updates include major new fault additions and refinements, and improvements to the naming and metadata structure in CFM versions 4 and 5 (Plesch and Shaw, 2010; Nicholson *et al.*, 2011, 2014, 2020; Plesch *et al.*, 2018). With this, the inventory of faults has grown to 445 fault objects in CFM 6.1 (Fig. 1). CFM 6.1 also serves as the southern California portion of CFM 7.0, which expands geographic scope to all of California. The ability to resolve the detailed structure of these faults has improved with enhancements to seismic catalogs, including advances in relative-relocation methods (Lin *et al.*, 2007; Hauksson *et al.*, 2012 + updates), machine learning-enabled detection of events to low-magnitude thresholds (Ross, Trugman, *et al.*, 2019), and enhanced focal mechanism catalogs (Yang *et al.*, 2012; Cheng *et al.*, 2023). In addition, numerous local studies of faults based on field, structural, and seismological methods have improved our understanding of the 3D geometry of southern California faults (e.g., Hubbard *et al.*, 2014; Hughes *et al.*, 2018; Jänecke *et al.*, 2018; Wolfe *et al.*, 2019, 2022; Plesch *et al.*, 2020; Don *et al.*, 2022). CFM 6.1 integrates these new and refined representations into a comprehensive model that more capably defines the spatial distribution of active faulting and seismicity in the southern California plate margin.

To organize the model, we use a four-part hierarchical naming system that, in descending order, includes Fault Area, Fault Zone, Fault Section, and Fault Name. Where possible, these designations are aligned with those used in the U.S. Geological Survey (USGS) Quaternary Fault and Fold (Qfault) database (U.S. Geological Survey and California Geological Survey, 2025). This ensures that users can properly relate fault information from the CFM and Qfault database, such as geometry and slip rate, respectively. We provide additional information as metadata that describes the fault type, area-weighted average fault strike and dip, total surface area, as well as the primary references and data resources used to develop the fault representation. The model and metadata are accessible through the CFM Explorer, a website (see Data and Resources) with robust search and download capabilities, and map and 3D visualization tools. The complete model archive (Marshall *et al.*, 2023) is available via a doi hosted at Zenodo.org as a component of CFM 7.0 (see Data and Resources).

ACTIVE FAULTING IN SOUTHERN CALIFORNIA

Southern California contains a large, complex, and distributed network of faults that accommodate relative motion between the Pacific and North American plates (Fig. 2). The San Andreas fault (SAF) represents the primary plate-boundary structure, accommodating roughly two-thirds of the relative plate motion (e.g., Weldon and Humphreys, 1986; Loveless and Meade, 2011; McGill *et al.*, 2015; Devine *et al.*, 2022). In the south, slip on the Imperial fault and Brawley seismic zone is transferred to the SAF, forming the Salton trough (SALT; Rockwell and Sylvester, 1979). The SAF extends northwestward across the Peninsular, Transverse, and Coast Ranges. A series of other right-lateral strike-slip faults to the west of the SAF accommodate lesser amounts of relative plate motion across the Inner California Borderlands and Peninsular Ranges, including (but not limited to) the Santa Cruz-Catalina ridge, San Clemente, Rose Canyon-Newport Inglewood, Elsinore, and San Jacinto faults (e.g., Bohannon and Geist, 1998; Legg *et al.*, 2015). Right-lateral strike-slip faulting also occurs in the Eastern California shear zone (ECSZ), which extends from the Mojave block into the Southern Sierra Nevada region (Dokka and Travis, 1990; Savage *et al.*, 1990). Faults in the ECSZ generated the 1992 **M** 7.3 Landers and 1999 **M** 7.1 Hector Mine earthquakes (Savage *et al.*, 1990; Hauksson *et al.*, 1993; Pollitz *et al.*, 2001). The Garlock fault, which accommodates left-lateral motion, bounds the ECSZ to the south and, to the north, defines the southern limit of Basin and Range extension (Smith, 1962, 1975; Smith and Ketner, 1970; Burchfiel and Davis, 1972; Astiz and Allen, 1983; McGill *et al.*, 2015). The 2019 **M** 6.4 and 7.1 Ridgecrest, California (Ross, Idini, *et al.*, 2019; Plesch *et al.*, 2020) earthquake sequence occurred on a set of left- and right-lateral strike-slip faults that accommodate overall right-lateral shear which extends north of the Garlock fault into the southern Basin and Range province.

The so-called "big bend" (a large restraining bend) in the SAF drives approximately north–south shortening throughout many regions of southern California (Donnellan *et al.*, 1993; Argus *et al.*, 2005; Marshall *et al.*, 2009, 2013; Devine *et al.*, 2022). This includes the Transverse Ranges, which are characterized by active thrust and oblique-reverse faulting on generally east–west-oriented structures that drive folding, uplift, and mountain building (Huftile and Yeats, 1995, 1996; Marshall *et al.*, 2008; Hubbard *et al.*, 2014). In the Western Transverse Ranges, these faults extend south into the Santa Barbara Channel, Ventura, and Los Angeles basins, where many of the active structures are blind (Schneider *et al.*, 1996; Shaw and Suppe, 1996; Shaw and Shearer, 1999). These faults produced the 1971 **M** 6.6 San Fernando, 1987 **M** 5.9 Whittier Narrows, and 1994 **M** 6.7 Northridge earthquakes (Dolan *et al.*, 1995; Huftile and Yeats, 1996; Hauksson, 2000; Shaw *et al.*, 2002). Active faulting in the Western Transverse Ranges extends eastward to the San Bernardino Mountains and farther east into the Eastern Transverse Ranges. In the Peninsular Ranges and Inner California Borderlands, active deformation occurs on right-lateral strike-slip systems, with additional northwest–southeast-trending thrust and reverse faults that accommodate modest amounts of shortening (Crouch and Suppe, 1993; Rivero *et al.*, 2000; Grant *et al.*, 2002; Rivero and Shaw, 2011). Many of these structures reactivate Miocene-aged extensional detachments (Crouch and Suppe, 1993; Rivero *et al.*, 2000; Rivero and Shaw, 2011) that formed during rifting of the California continental lithosphere as microplates were captured by the Pacific plate and moved northwestward relative to the North American plate (Kamerling and Luyendyk, 1985; Luyendyk *et al.*, 1985; Hornafius *et al.*, 1986; Nicholson *et al.*, 1994). These faults generated the 1986 **M** 5.3 Oceanside earthquake sequence (Hauksson and Jones, 1988; Rivero *et al.*, 2000), and the regional system extends northward into Santa Monica Bay and the Los Angeles basin (Grant *et al.*, 1999; Shaw and Shearer, 1999). North of the big bend in the SAF shortening is accommodated in the southern Coast Ranges. In the eastern margin of the southern Coast Ranges, blind-thrust faults extend into the foothills of the San Joaquin Valley and produced the 1983 **M** 6.5 Coalinga and 1985 **M** 6.1 Kettleman Hills earthquakes (Stein and Ekström, 1992; Guzofski *et al.*, 2007). In the western portion of the southern Coast Ranges, active faulting extends offshore and includes a series of generally northwest–southeast-striking thrust, reverse, and right-lateral strike-slip faults. One of these blind-thrust faults generated the 2003 **M** 6.5 San Simeon earthquake (McLaren *et al.*, 2008).

In aggregate, the active southern California system includes all major fault types (right- and left-lateral strike-slip, reverse, normal, and many oblique-slip faults), and represents a complex, interconnected network that poses a significant earthquake hazard. CFM 6.1 seeks to represent the geometric complexity of these faults to facilitate a wide range of earthquake science with emphasis on regional hazard assessment, including geodynamic fault systems modeling, dynamic rupture and earthquake simulations, strong ground motion forecasting, and probabilistic hazard assessments.

3D FAULT MODELING: DATA SETS AND METHODS

We generally follow the data preparation and fault construction methods described in Plesch *et al.* (2007). These involve georeferencing datasets in a 3D computer-aided design

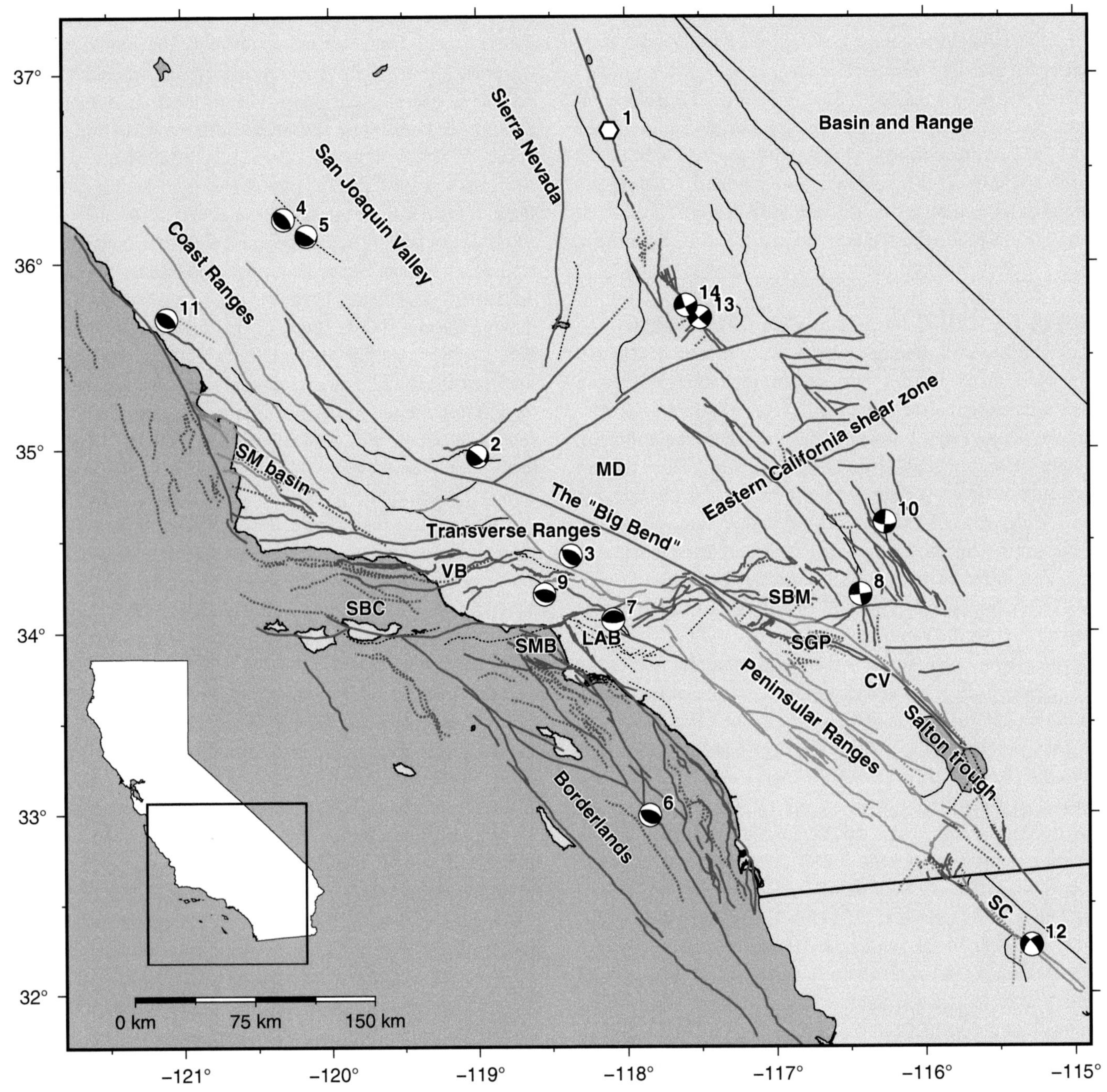

Figure 2. Map view of CFM fault traces with traces updated in CFM 4, 5, and 6 highlighted in gold, red, and blue, respectively. Upper tiplines of blind faults are indicated with dashed lines. Geographic features discussed in the text are labeled. Abbreviations are as follows: CV, Coachella Valley; LAB, Los Angeles basin; MD, Mojave Desert; SBC, Santa Barbara Channel; SBM, San Bernardino Mountains; SC, Sierra Cucapah; SGP, San Gorgonio Pass; SM basin, Santa Maria basin; SMB, Santa Monica Bay; and VB, Ventura basin. Historic focal mechanisms or epicenters include: (1) 1872 M 7.4 Owens Valley (shown with a hexagon), (2) 1952 **M** 7.5 Kern County, (3) 1971 **M** 6.6 San Fernando, (4) 1983 **M** 6.7 Coalinga, (5) 1985 **M** 6.1 Kettleman Hills, (6) 1986 **M** 5.5 Oceanside, (7) 1987 **M** 5.9 Whittier-Narrows, (8) 1992 **M** 7.3 Landers, (9) 1994 **M** 6.7 Northridge, (10) 1999 **M** 7.1 Hector Mine, (11) 2003 **M** 6.5 San Simeon, (12) 2010 **M** 7.2 El Mayor-Cucapah, (13) 2019 **M** 6.4 Ridgecrest, (14) 2019 **M** 7.1 Ridgecrest. An inset map of California shows the map location and extent. The color version of this figure is available only in the electronic edition.

application and using interpolation and extrapolation methods to develop complete, geologically viable fault representations. In addition, where applicable, we employ an objective and fully reproducible workflow (Riesner *et al.*, 2017) to develop fault surfaces based on uncertainty-weighted interpolation constraints from fault traces, seismicity, nodal plane orientations, and fault smoothness. These objective methods are best suited to faults that have produced a significant number of earthquakes, including large earthquakes and their aftershock sequences, such as the 2019 **M** 6.4 and 7.1 Ridgecrest events (Plesch *et al.*, 2020).

Because no single data source is sufficient to fully define southern California faults in 3D, fault representations in the

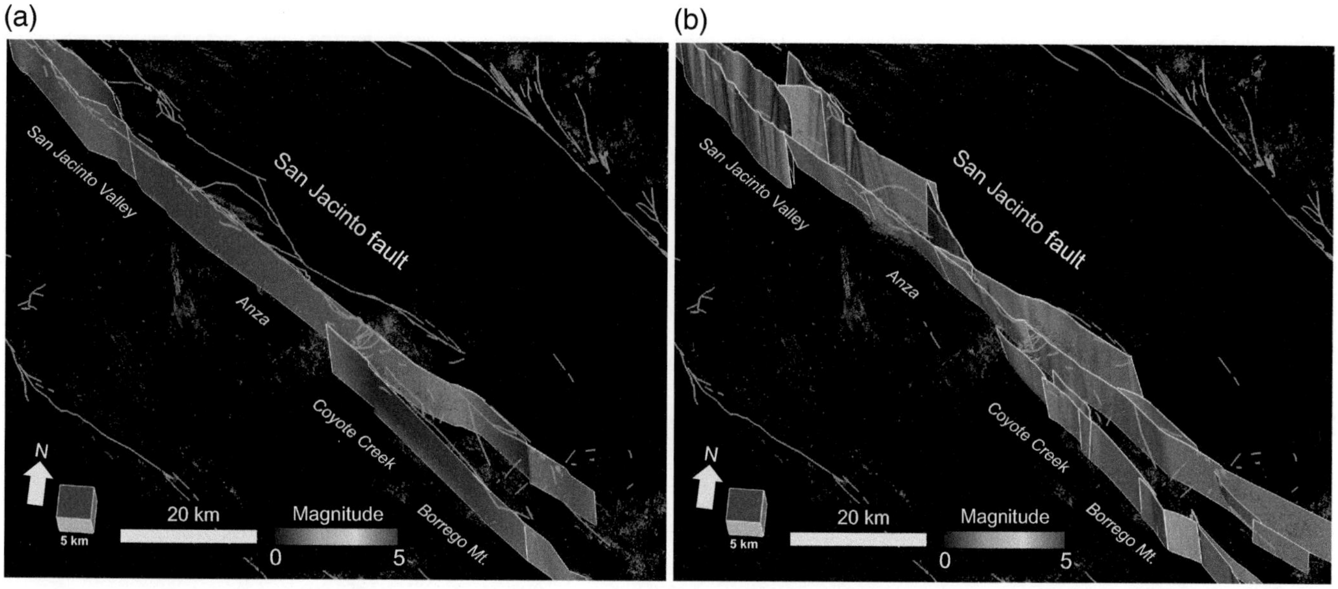

Figure 3. A portion of the CFM San Jacinto fault representation. (a) CFM version 3, (Plesch *et al.*, 2007) includes 10 fault sections along the full fault; (b) CFM 6.1 includes 28 sections based on refinement of the surfaces using relocated hypocenters (colored points; after Hauksson *et al.*, 2012) and Qfault fault traces (green). The color version of this figure is available only in the electronic edition.

CFM are based on many different types of constraints, including surface traces (e.g., USGS QFaults), earthquake focal mechanisms and hypocentral distributions (Lin *et al.*, 2007; Hauksson *et al.*, 2012; Ross, Trugman, *et al.*, 2019), well penetrations (Tsutsumi *et al.*, 2001; Hubbard *et al.*, 2014), seismic reflection profiles (Shaw and Shearer, 1999; Oskin *et al.*, 2000; Wolfe *et al.*, 2019, 2022), and geologic cross sections (see descriptions subsequently). In the development of CFM 6.1, we integrate modern, state-of-the-art datasets and other constraints that help refine fault geometries, including precisely relocated earthquake and machine-learning-enabled hypocenter catalogs, and focal mechanism solutions (Lin *et al.*, 2007; Hauksson *et al.*, 2012; Yang *et al.*, 2012; Ross, Trugman, *et al.*, 2019). In addition, we use detailed fault traces from the USGS Quaternary Fault and Fold database (Qfaults; U.S. Geological Survey and California Geological Survey, 2025), as well as local studies of individual fault systems. We place particular emphasis on the degree of segmentation of fault systems and the manner in which faults interact with adjacent structures. As such, CFM 6.1 contains more highly segmented and complex representations of many faults (Fig. 3), as well as new fault segments that link larger fault systems. We describe many of these refinements in more detail subsequently. They will likely impact the tendency of ruptures in dynamic models to arrest or pass through geometric asperities (Diao *et al.*, 2024; Huang *et al.*, 2025) and thus influence the tendency of ruptures to extend across multiple fault segments or fault systems.

In some cases, faults that are defined in the shallow crust intersect one another when projected to depth. This is particularly common in areas where both shallowly dipping thrust faults and steeply dipping strike-slip faults are present. There are several ways in which these fault systems may interact (e.g., Rivero *et al.*, 2000). In developing the CFM, we seek to define the appropriate, kinematically viable configuration when adequate data are available to do so. However, in cases where we lack this information, we represent faults as mutually interpenetrating to ensure that potential earthquake source locations and fault areas are effectively represented.

MODEL PEER EVALUATION

CFM 6.1 comprises preferred representations of the more than 400 known active faults that are deemed capable of generating moderate-to-large earthquakes. For many faults, particularly where we lack detailed subsurface information, the model database includes one or more alternative representations. Most often, major alternative representations are distinguished by the difference in dip angle or degree of segmentation of the fault, as well as the manner in which they interact with other, adjacent fault systems. Notable alternative fault representations exist for bends or stepovers (including differences in dip angle) in the San Andreas (Fig. 4) and other strike-slip faults, as well as for major thrust and reverse faults in the Transverse Ranges. Whereas the CFM database maintains these alternative representations, CFM 6.1 contains a "preferred" model defined by the set of faults that are ranked to be most realistic based on a process of expert peer evaluation.

As part of the evaluation for CFM 6, alternative representations in CFM 5.3 for 23 major faults were considered by a group of 29 SCEC investigators spanning the disciplines of geology, seismology, and geophysics. This CFM peer-review process involved scientists visualizing major alternative fault representations using a specially developed web-based survey

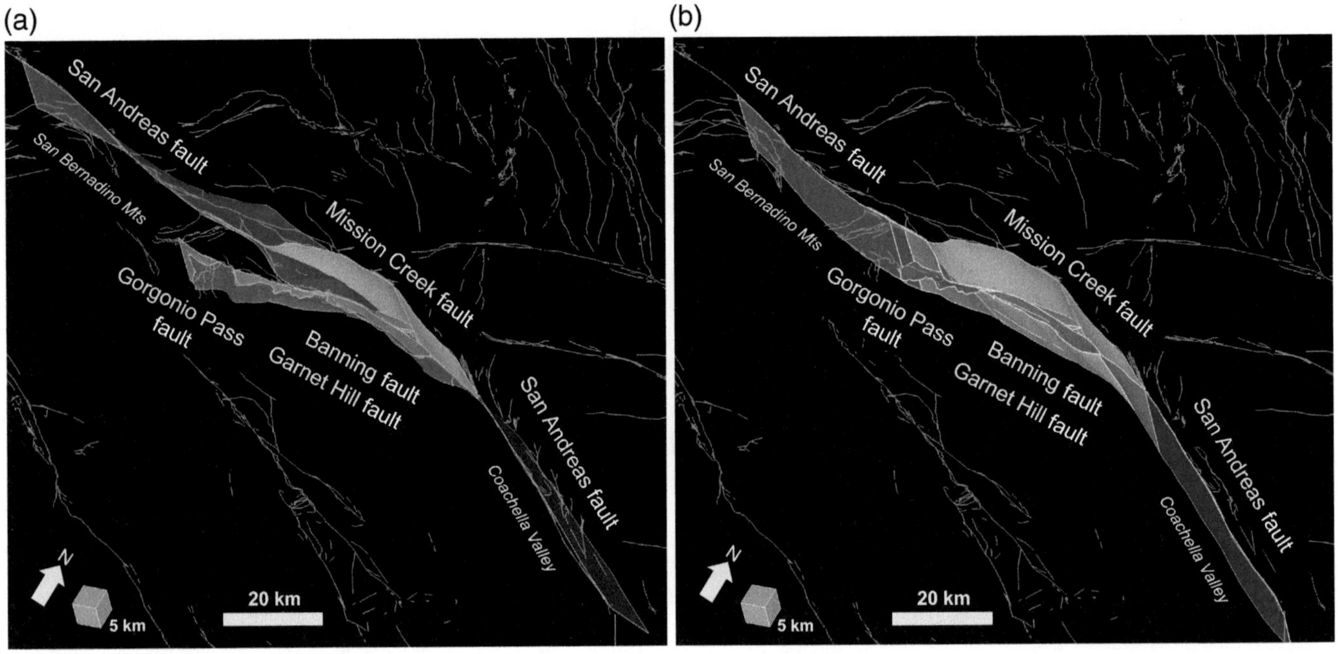

Figure 4. Oblique view of two alternative fault models in the San Gorgonio Pass region. (a) The San Andreas fault zone (SAFZ) after Fuis *et al.* (2012), Carena *et al.* (2004), and Yule and Sieh, (2003); and (b) SAFZ after Seeber and Armbruster (1995), Rasmussen and Reeder (1986), and Nicholson *et al.* (2012). The color version of this figure is available only in the electronic edition.

tool. Each reviewed fault group had a unique survey page with images of the fault alternatives, a brief description of the basis for these representations, and links to the web-based CFM Explorer 3D interface, allowing users to interact with the faults and visualize how the surfaces relate to seismicity. Participants ranked the fault groups and were encouraged to provide comments on ways that the model representations might be further improved. Once the review period was complete, the evaluation tool provided reviewer response information to the development team. The fault representations receiving the highest overall ranking by the reviewers were incorporated into the "preferred model" in CFM 6.1. As a result, 14 out of the 23 faults evaluated had a new representation designated as the preferred model in CFM 6.1 (highlighted in Fig. 5).

MODEL UPDATES BY REGION

The CFM 6.1 model area spans a broad range of geomorphic and tectonic regions, reflecting the diversity of faulting styles across the North-American-Pacific plate boundary. These regions shape the top tier of the model hierarchy, which comprises nine fault groups: Great Valley, Basin and Range, Garlock, Mojave, Eastern Transverse Ranges, Peninsular Ranges, Offshore Continental Borderland, Western Transverse Ranges, and SAF. Here, we summarize the composition of the CFM and highlight major updates in the fault representations in each of these regions.

San Andreas fault and Salton Trough regions

Together, the SAF system (SAFS) and SALT regions represent the principal plate boundary structure between the Pacific and North American plates (Atwater, 1970; Allen, 1981). These CFM regions extend for 670 km from the Gulf of California to Parkfield, California. SAFS representations are defined by seismicity, geologic maps, wells, and geologic cross sections. Interpretation of deep structure in the cross sections include: (1) active-source imaging data sets (e.g., SCEC-USGS Los Angeles Region Seismic Experiments [LARSE I, II; Fuis *et al.*, 2001, 2003] and the Virginia Tech–Caltech–USGS–SCEC Salton Seismic Imaging Project; Persaud *et al.*, 2016; Fuis *et al.*, 2017; Ajala *et al.*, 2019); (2) ambient noise data sets (e.g., Barak *et al.*, 2015); (3) earthquake-tomography data sets (e.g., Kohler *et al.*, 2003; Tape *et al.*, 2010); (4) potential field data sets (Griscom and Jachens, 1990; McPhee *et al.*, 2004; Fuis *et al.*, 2012; Langenheim and Fuis, 2022); and (5) deformation models (Fialko, 2006; Lindsey and Fialko, 2013; Marshall *et al.*, 2013; Fattaruso *et al.*, 2014, 2016).

The Salton Sea region groups 11 faults at the southern limit of the model. These include, from north to south, the Brawley seismic zone (Fuis *et al.*, 2017; Hauksson *et al.*, 2022) boundaries delimiting an area of densely spaced SAF-orthogonal seismic lineaments, the SAF-orthogonal Extra and Elmore Ranch faults, and the Imperial and Cerro Prieto faults, which can be considered the southern continuation of the SAF. One fault, the Westmorland fault, was added to CFM 6.1 because it is considered the likely source of frequent seismic activity.

Given its large extent, the SAFS region is subdivided into five sections (Coachella Valley, San Gorgonio Pass, Mojave, Carrizo Plain, and Cholame). Together, 38 fault objects define the SAFS region, with 26 of these as new additions in CFM 6.1

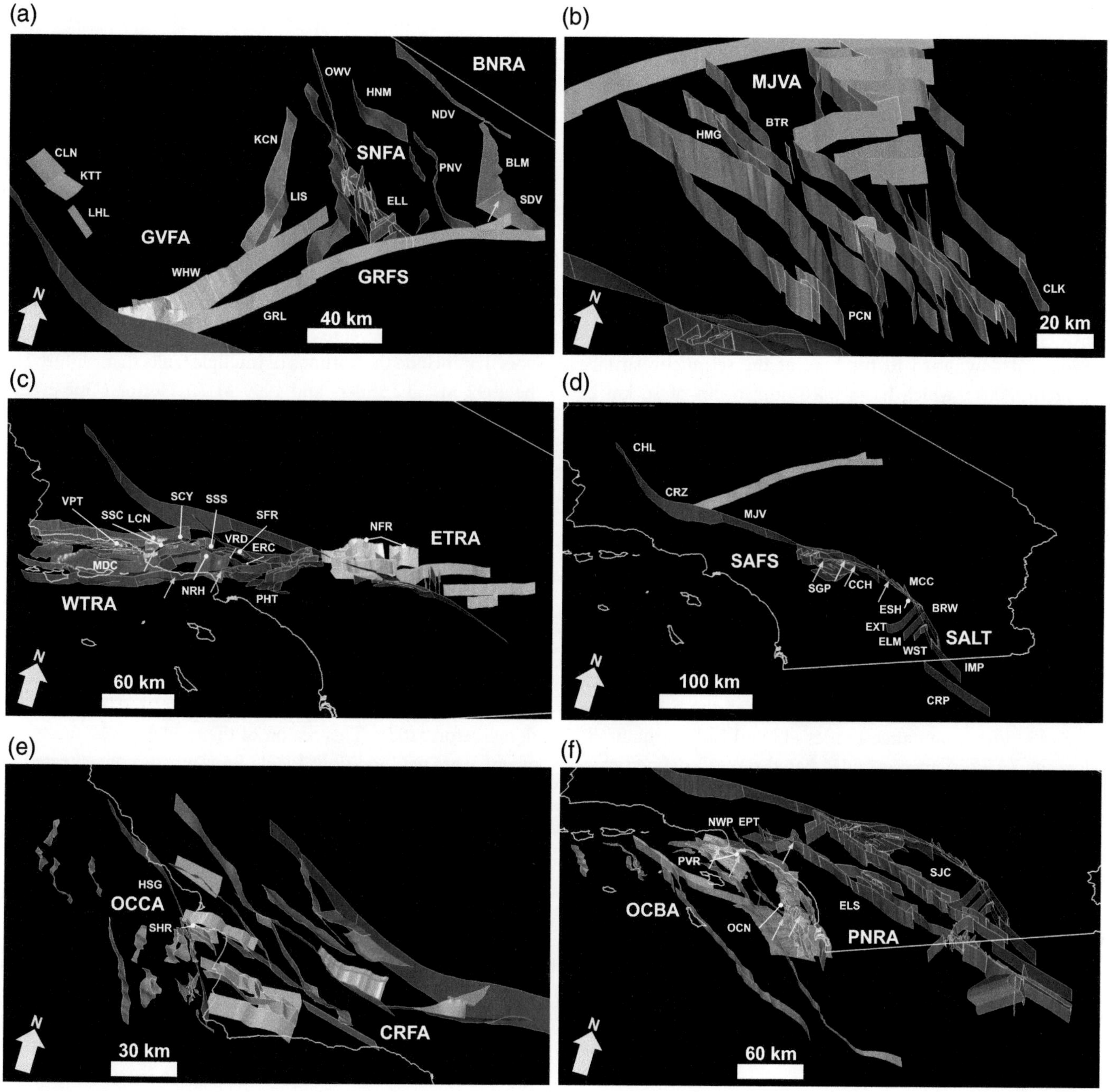

Figure 5. Three-dimensional perspective views of fault areas from northeast clockwise: (a) BNRA, Basin and Range; SNFA, Sierra Nevada; GRFS, Garlock; GVFA, Great Valley. (b) MJVA, Mojave. (c) WTRA, Western Transverse Ranges; ETRA, Eastern Transverse Ranges. (d) SAFS, San Andreas; SALT, Salton trough. (e) CRFA, Coast Ranges; OCCA, Offshore Central CA. (f) PNRA, Peninsular Ranges; OCBA, Offshore Continental Borderland. Faults discussed in text are labeled: (a) BLM, Black Mountain fault; CLN, Coalinga ramp; ELL, Eastern Little Lake fault system; GRL, Garlock fault; HMN, Hunter Mountain fault; KCN, Kern Canyon fault; KTT, Kettleman Hills ramp; LHL, Lost Hills ramp; LIS, Lake Isabella seismicity lineament; NDV, Northern Death Valley fault; OWV, Owens Valley fault; PNV, Panamint Valley fault; SDV, Southern Death Valley fault; WHW, White Wolf fault. (b) BTR, Barstow trend; CLK, Cleghorn Lake faults; HMG, Harper Valley-Mt. General fault; PCN, Pipes Canyon fault. (c) ERC, Eagle Rock fault; LCN, Lion Canyon fault; MDC, Mid-Channel fault; NFR, North Frontal thrust; NRH, Northridge Hills fault; PHT, Puente Hills Thrust; SCY, San Cayetano fault; SFR, San Fernando fault; SSC, Southern San Cayetano fault; SSS, Santa Susana fault; VPP, Ventura-Pitas Point fault; VRD, Verdugo fault. (d) San Andreas fault sections: BRW, Brawley seismic zone; CCH, Coachella Valley; CHL, Cholame; CRP, Cerro Prieto fault; CRZ, Carrizo plain; ELM, Elmore Ranch faults; ESH, East Shoreline fault; EXT, Extra fault; IMP, Imperial fault; MCC, Mecca Hills fault zone; MJV, Mojave; SGP, San Gorgonio Pass; WST, Westmoreland fault. (e) HSG, Hosgri fault; SHR, Shoreline fault. (f) ELS, Elsinore fault zone; EPT, Elysian Park thrust; NWP, Newport Inglewood fault; OCN, Oceanside detachment fault; PVR, Palos Verdes fault zone; and SJC, San Jacinto fault zone. Yellow arrows highlight alternatives preferred in the evaluation. The color version of this figure is available only in the electronic edition.

to more fully describe the Coachella Valley and Gorgonio Pass segments. The preferred representation of the SAFS in CFM 6.1 incorporates a propeller-like geometry initially proposed by Fuis *et al.* (2012) and supported by a variety of geological, seismological, and geophysical observations. The Coachella Valley section of the fault and the Southern SAF dip ≈60° to 70° northeast. Moving from south to north, the fault dip shallows to a ≈50° northeast dip in the San Gorgonio Pass section and steepens to ≈80° to 90° northeast dip in the Mojave section. Farther north in the Carrizo section, the fault switches its dip direction to ≈55° southwest, then to ≈80° southwest in the Cholame section. Similar to all faults in the CFM, the SAF is projected downward to the base of the seismicity surface (Nazareth, 2004), which has a maximum depth of 16 km in the Carrizo section and a minimum of 10 km in the Salton Sea region. Projection of the SAF below the base of seismicity would, in many cases, align the fault with the edge of an upper-mantle high-velocity body and locally interpreted offsets in the Moho surface (Kohler *et al.*, 2003; Fuis *et al.*, 2012).

A series of other, local refinements were made to CFM 6.1 in the Coachella Valley region, and the Mecca Hills fault zone (Bergh *et al.*, 2019) and East Shoreline fault (Jänecke *et al.*, 2018) were added. These faults both parallel the main strand of the SAF and are located within 5 km of its surface trace. Along the San Gorgonio Pass segment of the SAF in the San Bernardino Mountains, a series of blind faults structurally below the SAF system was added based on well-defined clusters of microseismicity (Carena *et al.*, 2004). In addition, a series of smaller, surface-breaching faults at high angles to the main trend of the SAF in the western San Bernardino Mountains were included in the model.

In the San Bernardino Mountains and northern Coachella Valley, the SAF is multistranded, with the southern branches (San Bernardino, San Gorgonio Pass, Garnet Hill, and Banning faults, e.g., Yule and Sieh, 2003; Fig. 4) widely considered the most active (e.g., Kendrick *et al.*, 2022; J. C. Matti, written comm., 2022). Although debate concerning the activity levels is ongoing (e.g., Beyer *et al.*, 2018).

In addition to the preferred representation of the SAF in CFM 6.1, the model contains a significant alternative representation (Nicholson *et al.*, 2012). The alternative representation uses geologic cross sections to define a vertical dip for the Carrizo, Cholame, and Mojave sections of the fault (Bryant and Lundberg, 2002). Along the San Bernardino, San Gorgonio Pass, and Coachella Valley sections, the fault is multistranded (Fig. 4), encompassing the San Gorgonio Pass thrust (Rasmussen and Reeder, 1986), the Garnet Hill fault, the Banning fault (Seeber and Armbruster, 1995), and blind splays. The strands of the SAF dip steeply to moderately to the northeast in these areas. The southern SAF in the Coachella Valley is vertical in this representation. The geometry along all fault sections was projected to the base of seismicity used in the CFM (Nazareth, 2004).

Mojave region, Basin and Range region, and Garlock fault

The Mojave model region (MJVA) covers an area of about 20,000 km^2 and is located to the east of the Mojave and San Bernardino Mountain segments of the SAF. The model region hosts 44 faults, 14 of which are new additions in CFM 6.1. Additions of note are blind cross faults and a blind projection of the 1992 **M** 7.3 Landers rupture, named the Barstow trend, which are illuminated by its aftershocks. In addition, the Harper Valley Mt. General, Pipes Canyon, and Cleghorn Lake faults were added to the ECSZ. These faults, along with pre-existing faults in the ECSZ, were refined based on Qfaults. Finally, surfaces that include the portions of multiple faults that ruptured in the 1992 **M** 7.3 Landers and 1999 **M** 7.1 Hector Mine events were also refined in the model based on Qfaults.

The Garlock fault forms the boundary between the Mojave and Basin and Range regions. The Garlock fault representation was refined in CFM 6.1 to closely track the USGS Qfaults trace, and consists of western and eastern sections, which are separated by a 2 km wide gap. The eastern section contains what are often referred to as the central and eastern Garlock fault segments (McGill and Sieh, 1991; Serpa and Dokka, 1992; Hatem and Dolan, 2018; Qiu *et al.*, 2023).

The Basin and Range region lies north of the Garlock fault and east of the Sierra Nevada and is characterized by trans-tensional deformation. This region of the model has 37 faults, 26 of which are new additions to CFM 6.1, mostly concentrated in the 2019 Ridgecrest rupture zone (Plesch *et al.*, 2020). A notable update is the addition of the Eastern Little Lake fault system—the source of the 2019 **M** 7.1 Ridgecrest sequence. It runs along the northeastern side of the Sierra Nevada and links up to the Owens Valley fault (1874 **M** 7.4 rupture). The Eastern Little Lake fault has a steep to subvertical dip and accommodates right-lateral strike-slip motion. Similarly, the Panamint Valley, Hunter Mountain, and associated smaller faults along ranges are also near-vertical, strike-slip systems, in the most highly ranked representation. At the eastern limit of the modeled Basin and Range region lies the 217 km long Death Valley fault system, which consists of the subvertical Northern Death Valley fault (Machette *et al.*, 2001; Gold *et al.*, 2020) and the gently dipping Black Mountain and Southern Death Valley faults (Chávez-Pérez *et al.*, 1998; Hayman *et al.*, 2003; Gold *et al.*, 2020). The model incorporates a subvertical alternative representation of the Southern Death Valley fault (Machette *et al.*, 2001; Gold *et al.*, 2020) and a gently dipping alternative fault representation for the Panamint Valley fault (Burchfiel *et al.*, 1987; Chávez-Pérez *et al.*, 1998; Hayman *et al.*, 2003; Gold *et al.*, 2020).

Peninsular Ranges and offshore Continental Borderland

The southeast–northwest-trending Peninsular Ranges region stretches for about 400 km from the Sierra Cucapa, Mexico, to the Los Angeles basin. The region consists of more than 100 fault objects, including the San Jacinto, Elsinore, and Newport Inglewood fault zones, among others. Fifty-eight of these fault objects are new additions to CFM 6.1, motivated by the representation of the M 7.2 El Mayor–Cucapah earthquake source, as well as refinements of the San Jacinto and Elsinore fault systems.

Southwest of the Peninsular Ranges region, the Continental Borderland region extends for 330 km offshore in an overall southwest–northwest orientation from the southern model limit in northern Mexico to the Santa Barbara Channel. This area encompasses 61 fault objects, 46 of which are additions to CFM 6.1. The significant number of additions comes in large part from an extensive recharacterization of the Palos Verdes fault zone by Wolfe *et al.* (2022) and the inclusion of splay faults in the hanging wall of the Oceanside detachment fault (Rivero *et al.*, 2000; Rivero and Shaw, 2011).

Transverse Ranges

The Transverse Ranges extend for 260 km in an east–west orientation and are composed of Western and Eastern regions that form a continuous belt spanning the SAF. The Ranges are generally considered to accommodate contraction driven by the big bend in the SAF (Reed and Hollister, 1951; Namson and Davis, 1988; Yeats, 1988; Yeats *et al.*, 1988; Shaw and Suppe, 1994; Devine *et al.*, 2022). Faults in this region often transect deep sedimentary basins, where they produce large folds, and many structures are blind. In the Los Angeles basin, the southernmost thrust faults of the Transverse Ranges, including the Puente Hills and Elysian Park thrusts (Namson and Davis, 1988; Shaw and Suppe, 1996; Shaw and Shearer, 1999; Oskin *et al.*, 2000), interact with right-lateral strike-slip faults of the Peninsular Ranges region (e.g., the Newport–Inglewood and Elsinore faults).

The Western Transverse Ranges region contains 78 fault objects, 29 of which are new in CFM 6.1. There are several fault systems for which alternative representations have been developed. Most of the updates to faults in CFM 6.1 occur within the sedimentary basins (Santa Barbara, Ventura, and San Fernando) present in the southern portion of the Western Transverse Ranges.

The Mid-Channel fault is an offshore, active blind thrust within the eastern Santa Barbara Channel and basin associated with a south-vergent fault-propagation fold (referred to as the Mid-Channel, Blue Bottle, Santa Barbara, or Twelve Mile Reef anticline). The fault dips to the north, trends generally east–west, and extends for more than 25 km along strike. The Mid-Channel anticline has a direct bathymetric expression and deforms upper Pleistocene strata (e.g., Hopkins, 2006; Hopkins *et al.*, 2006; Behl *et al.*, 2016). The new representation of the Mid-Channel fault is based on mapping in 2D and 3D seismic reflection datasets (Don *et al.*, 2022), and includes additional details of the fault geometry, such as splay faults. The main difference between this representation and that of previous model versions is that the fault links to a detachment that extends to the north across the Offshore Oak Ridge structure and links to a regional mid-crustal detachment interpreted in the Miocene Monterey Formation and other shale units beneath the Pitas Point gas field (e.g., Yeats, 1983; Shaw and Suppe, 1996; Shaw *et al.*, 2005). This connects the Mid-Channel thrust with a detachment in the Ventura–Pitas Point fault system (Hubbard *et al.*, 2014; Marshall *et al.*, 2017; Don *et al.*, 2022). In contrast, the previous fault representation suggests that the Mid-Channel thrust truncates into the Offshore Oak Ridge fault (Kamerling *et al.*, 2003) in some interpretations (Huftile and Yeats, 1995; Kamerling and Nicholson, 1995; Sorlien *et al.*, 2000). This representation remains an alternative fault surface in the CFM.

The Ventura–Pitas Point fault system is an active east–west-trending, north-dipping reverse fault system that may have a component of oblique motion. The Ventura fault segment is located principally onshore and lies beneath the Ventura Avenue anticline, whereas the Pitas Point fault segment lies to the west in the Santa Barbara Channel, where it underlies the Rincon and Dos Cuadras anticlines. Together, the system extends for more than 40 km along strike and is bounded to the west by the North Channel fault (Kamerling *et al.*, 2003; Redin *et al.*, 2005; Hubbard *et al.*, 2014; Sorlien *et al.*, 2014; Sorlien and Nicholson, 2015; Levy *et al.*, 2019; Don *et al.*, 2022) and to the east by the Southern San Cayetano fault (Hubbard *et al.*, 2014; Hughes *et al.*, 2018). The Ventura–Pitas Point system is generally considered blind, with active deformation manifested by surface folding (Rockwell *et al.*, 1988, 2016, Hubbard *et al.*, 2014; Grenader *et al.*, 2015; McAuliffe *et al.*, 2015; 2016). The fault is defined by geologic maps, wells, interpretations of 2D and 3D seismic reflection data, and geologic cross sections. The onshore Ventura fault is further defined by a distinct surface scarp that extends through the city of Ventura (Sarna-Wojcicki *et al.*, 1976; Sarna-Wojcicki and Yerkes, 1982; Yeats, 1982a,b; Rockwell *et al.*, 1988; McAuliffe *et al.*, 2015).

The preferred representation of the Ventura–Pitas Point fault in CFM 6.1 has a ≈50° N dip, with its geometry offshore based on mapping of the shallow portion of the fault with offshore well and seismic reflection data (Kamerling *et al.*, 2003; Redin *et al.*, 2005; Sorlien *et al.*, 2014; Sorlien and Nicholson, 2015). The mapped portion of the fault was projected to the base of seismicity (Nazareth, 2004), with the Pitas Point segment steepening to ≈65° N below ≈9 km depth. The new preferred representation of the fault system incorporates a mid-crustal detachment (Hubbard *et al.*, 2014; Marshall *et al.*, 2017; Levy *et al.*, 2019; Don *et al.*, 2022). The shallow portion of the fault dips 45°–55° N, similar to the previous model. However, the new fault representation soles to a gently north-dipping detachment at a depth of 8–10 km (Hubbard *et al.*, 2014). Farther north, the fault then steepens at depth to a ≈30° north-dipping ramp that extends to the base of the seismogenic crust. This ramp-flat-ramp fault geometry is invoked to explain the shape of the overlying folds that are defined by surface geology, well control, and seismic reflection data (Hubbard *et al.*, 2014; Levy *et al.*, 2019; Don *et al.*, 2022). Geomechanical modeling of the fault system showed the ramp-flat-ramp geometry to be more consistent (compared to a constant dip model) with the observed interseismic geodetic displacement field (Marshall *et al.*, 2017).

The San Cayetano fault and Verdugo faults are active, east-northeast- and east-southeast-trending, respectively, north-dipping reverse faults that may have a component of oblique motion (Marshall *et al.*, 2008). The Verdugo fault extends for 21 km along strike and is bounded on the east by the Eagle Rock fault (Weber Jr. *et al.*, 1980) and to the west by the Northridge Hills and San Fernando faults (Weber Jr. *et al.*, 1980). The San Cayetano fault extends for 32 km along strike and is bounded on the east by the Santa Susana fault (Yeats *et al.*, 1994) and to the west by the Lion Canyon fault (Hubbard *et al.*, 2014). Both faults are well identified by their geologic map traces (Weber Jr. *et al.*, 1980; Yeats *et al.*, 1994) and further constrained by geologic cross sections and relocated seismicity (Hauksson *et al.*, 2012), which is aligned with the CFM fault surfaces.

The preferred representation of the San Cayetano fault in CFM 6.1 uses well control and geologic sections to define a dip of 15°–30° N for the shallow portion of the fault and 40°–50° N for the deep portion (Ziony and Yerkes, 1985; Yeats *et al.*, 1994). The previous fault representation in CFM 5.3 had a steeper dip at depths below 2 km, based on an interpretation that linked the fault to relocated hypocenters (Hauksson *et al.*, 2012 and updates) of a few small earthquakes. The deep portion of the new San Cayetano fault representation is continuous with the deep ramp portion of the Ventura fault to the east, forming a 50 km long, east–west-trending thrust ramp (Hubbard *et al.*, 2014; Levy *et al.*, 2019; Don *et al.*, 2022). CFM 6.1 also includes a new representation of the Verdugo fault based on geologic mapping (Weber Jr. *et al.*, 1980; Bryant, 2017) as well as limited seismicity at depth.

The Eastern Transverse Ranges region bounds the Mojave region to the south and extends ~190 km in an east–west orientation. The region contains 17 faults, including 8 new additions, and an enhanced representation for the North Frontal Thrust fault. The North Frontal Thrust fault is an active east–west-trending, moderately dipping reverse fault system that may have a component of oblique motion (Bryant, 2003). The western fault segment is located principally at the northern range front of the San Bernardino Mountains. The eastern fault segment is located to the southeast of the Helendale-South Lockhart fault, where it underlies the Bighorn Mountains. Together, the system extends for more than 70 km along strike and is bounded on the west by the Cleghorn fault and to the east by the Johnson Valley fault. The North Frontal Thrust fault system has a defined surface trace and appears to limit the extent of distributed seismicity that occurs beneath the San Bernardino Mountains.

The new preferred representation of the western and eastern segment of the North Frontal Thrust fault uses a generalized fault trace based on Qfaults (U.S. Geological Survey and California Geological Survey, 2025) and relocated seismicity hypocenter locations (Hauksson *et al.*, 2012 and updates) to define a dip of approximately 50°–60° S for the fault (Bryant, 2003). Previous representations of the fault system, in CFM 5.3, have a steeper dip of approximately 80°–90° S. The geometry of both fault segments was projected to the base of seismicity used in the CFM (Nazareth, 2004).

Great Valley, Coast Ranges, and offshore Central California

The Great Valley region of the model incorporates seven faults in the San Joaquin basin, which forms the southern part of the Great Valley. These faults include the blind Lost Hills, Kettleman Hills, and Coalinga thrust ramps (Guzofski *et al.*, 2007), which together represent the southern portion of the Great Valley Thrust system (Medwedeff, 1989; Ekström *et al.*, 1992; Stein and Ekström, 1992; Bloch *et al.*, 1993; Guzofski *et al.*, 2007; Welch, 2025). To the southeast, the Pleito thrust extends this compressional belt and structurally overlies the large, northeast-trending and moderately to steeply southeast-dipping White Wolf fault, which generated the 1952 M 7.5 Kern County earthquake. New additions to CFM 6.1 in this region include the Lake Isabella seismicity lineament and the large Kern Canyon fault, which both traverse the southern Sierra Nevada.

The Coast Ranges and offshore Central California areas are at the northern limit of the model. Along a length of 255 km, the 48 fault objects in these areas trend largely southeast–northwest. Thirty-seven fault objects are additions, in large part due to the inclusion of Santa Maria basin faults (Shaw and Plesch, 2012) and near-shore faults such as the Shoreline fault (Pacific Gas and Electric Company, 2011; Nishenko *et al.*, 2018). The largest of the faults in this area is about 200 km long offshore Hosgri fault (Johnson and Watt, 2012; Willingham *et al.*, 2013), represented as northeast-dipping with steeper segments in the upper 11 km. Willingham *et al.* (2013) suggest that the fault shallows its dip at greater depth.

MODEL ACCESSIBILITY AND WEB-BASED TOOLS

Initial versions of the CFM (up to CFM 5.2) were built and maintained manually, one fault and data file at a time, and lacked complete and consistent metadata, as the focus was on the fault representations. The CFM 6.1 model has grown significantly, with the entire CFM 6.1 archive, including alternatives, including more than 2000 data files. Each fault object has numerous components, including metadata (information about the fault, geometry, and references), several different 3D surface representations (each in different files), and fault trace data (in several different file formats). This results in a volume of data that cannot be manually managed. To address this, we have developed a set of semiautomated scripts that test various components of the model for accuracy and self-consistency, including:

1. All CFM faults now have a listed reference that indicates what each surface is based on.
2. Hierarchical object names now conform to a consistent naming convention. This allows users to write code that can easily parse the fault names from the various files.
3. Hierarchical object names are now checked with the various metadata columns and all files for self-consistency.
4. We now provide direct automated calculations of fault surface area and average strike and dip. Average strike and dip calculations are weighted by element area to represent a true average orientation of the fault surface regardless of mesh variations.
5. All fault objects are verified to exist with consistent names as t-surf files in the native, 500, 1000, and 2000 m mesh resolutions. Similar checks are made for the fault trace data files.
6. All fault surfaces are provided as a single patch (in open-source plain text GOCAD files) instead of various grouped surfaces. The GOCAD t-surf file format has been simplified to facilitate users who use scripts to parse the model components.
7. Fault traces are checked for naming consistency and are provided in plain text Generic Mapping Tools multisegment (plain text), shape file (shp), and Google Earth Keyhole Markup Language (KML) formats. The KML format of the traces shows a small webpage that presents the metadata when a fault is clicked on. The metadata in the KML format are stored as attributes that can be loaded into QGIS and other Geographic Information Systems packages.

These enhancements are implemented as part of the database system that supports the CFM Explorer, and the metadata file is provided as an Excel spreadsheet that can be downloaded from the site. Complete and self-consistent metadata are required for greater use of the CFM, so although these metadata and self-consistency improvements may not be apparent, they are critical.

CFM website and 3D fault viewer

In collaboration with the SCEC IT and web teams, we have created the CFM Explorer (see Data and Resources), a web-based toolset built using the open-source leaflet (Agafonkin, 2023) and vtk.js (see Data and Resources) JavaScript libraries (Fig. 6). The CFM Explorer allows users to quickly visualize the model in 2D and 3D with various basemap options and the option to overlay relocated seismicity. The CFM Explorer also has a feature that allows users to upload their own data in the widely used KML/KMZ formats for direct comparison to the CFM. KML/KMZ files are rendered directly on the 2D map and can help users compare the CFM to other data. The CFM Explorer also provides users with tools to query the model for downloading user-selected fault components. Users can search for fault objects by keyword, latitude-longitude, fault area-zone-section-name, or by average strike or dip. When search by strike-dip is selected, the fault traces are colored by the selected parameter, facilitating visual identification of faults by orientation. Once faults are selected, users have the option to view faults in their native 3D environment (UTM zone 11, NAD27 datum) as solid surfaces, wireframe meshes, or surfaces with the wireframe mesh shown. In the 3D viewer, the user is provided with instructions on how to navigate in 3D as an initial pop-up. There are options to modify the color of each fault (including transparency), to show or hide the California state border or relocated seismicity, to save screenshots, and to directly link to the current 3D view.

Although the CFM is one of the SCEC's most established models, a hurdle for both reviewers and potential users was the previous requirement for specialized software that could render the model in 3D. Now, any user can go to the CFM Explorer, select faults of interest, and interactively view the 2D (Fig. 6a) or full 3D geometry (Fig. 6b). The CFM Explorer was used in this way for the recent model evaluation to define preferred representations for CFM 6.1, for which we provided all evaluated model geometries with a text description of what each representation was based on, figures of the competing representations, and a direct web link to a 3D view of the faults using the CFM Explorer. Reviewers could readily access CFM fault representations and evaluate them in 2D and 3D to facilitate their assessment and rankings, enhancing the quality of the evaluation.

We believe the CFM Explorer development effort was required for SCEC and the earthquake science community to obtain the full benefit of the extensive collaborative scientific work that has gone into the development of the SCEC CFMs. The experience and product implementations derived from this effort served as valuable catalysts to other SCEC community models looking to solve data organization, visualization, storage, and retrieval challenges.

DISCUSSION

Model completeness

Faults in the crust occur at a wide range of scales. The CFM seeks to represent those faults that are capable of generating moderate-to-large earthquakes based on their size and activity. The model also includes smaller faults that potentially link segments of larger systems and thus may play roles in determining the extent of fault ruptures. No fault model is generally considered to be complete because we are dependent on faults being expressed by mapped, active surface traces, seismicity, or other subsurface data, all of which may be lacking for an active fault. Several historic events have occurred on previously unknown (e.g., 1994 **M** 6.7 Northridge), or poorly known (e.g., 2019 Ridgecrest sequence) faults. Nevertheless, we seek an objective, quantitative assessment that can evaluate the completeness of the CFM 6.1 by examining the percentage of earthquakes, over a range of

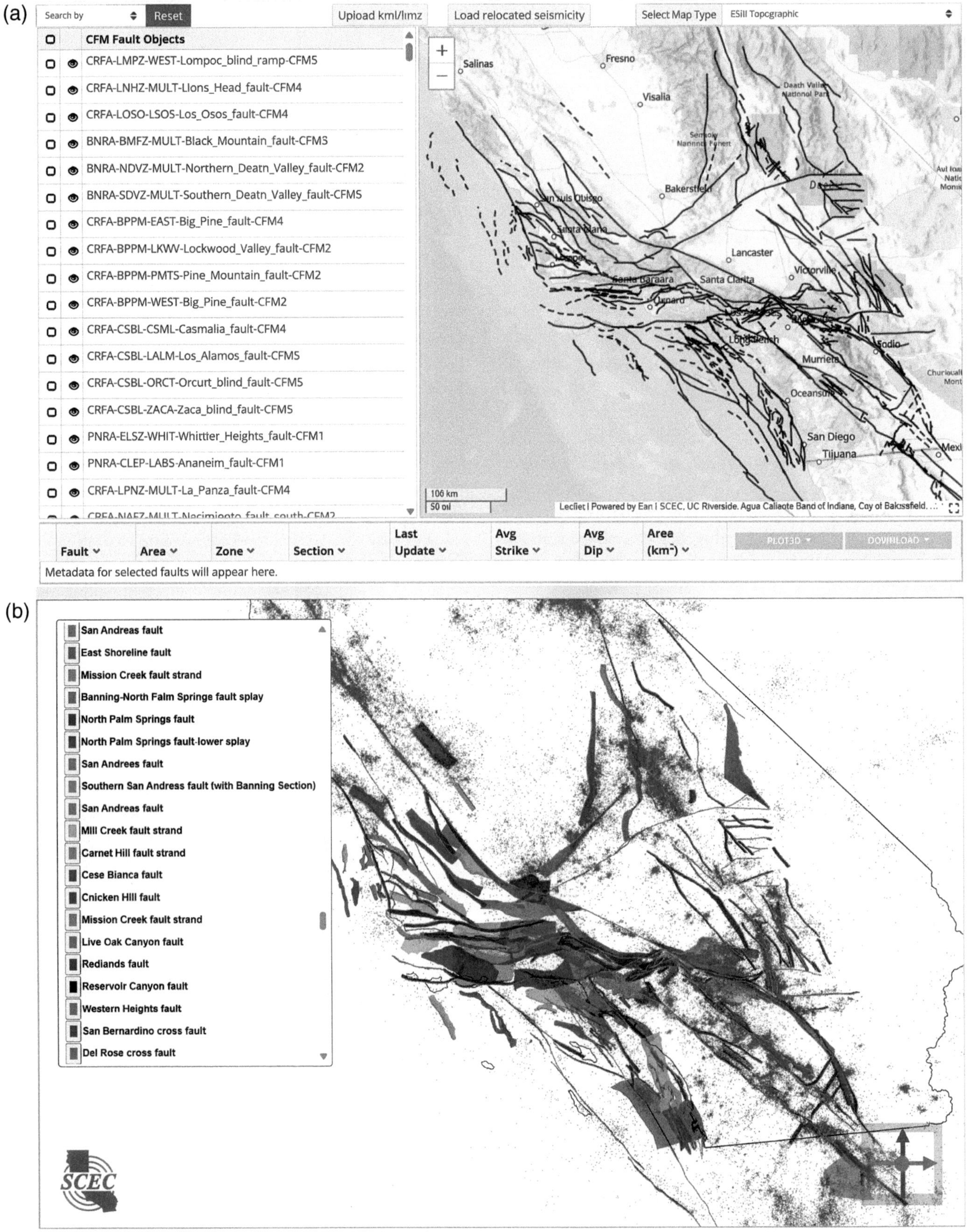

Figure 6. Screenshots of the CFM Explorer (a) 2D map interface and (b) plot3D interface. The CFM Explorer allows users with no specialized software to visualize, query, and download the CFM. The color version of this figure is available only in the electronic edition.

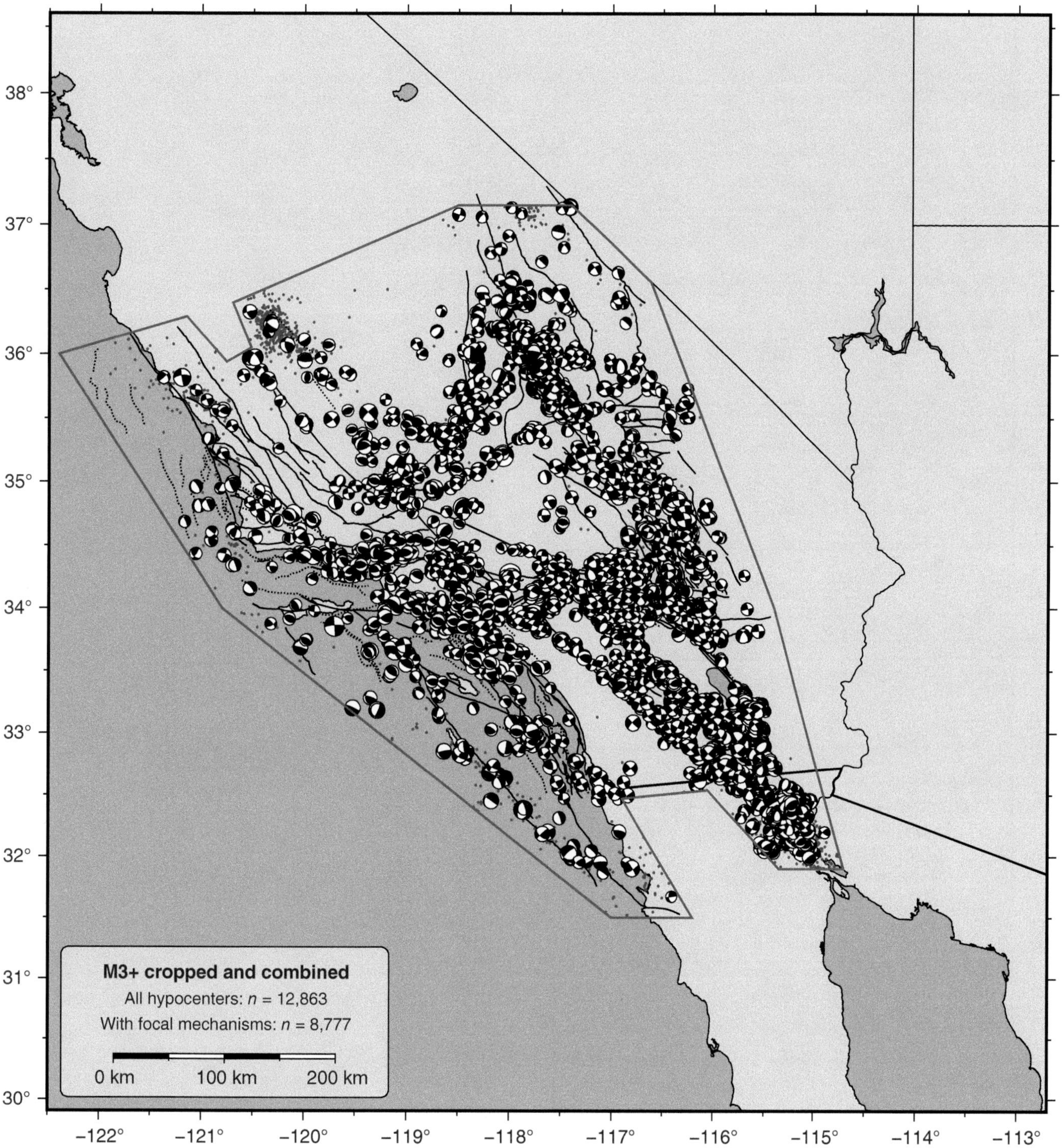

Figure 7. Combined epicenter (Hauksson *et al.*, 2012, and updates) and focal mechanism (Yang *et al.*, 2012, and updates) catalog used as input to the earthquake-to-fault association algorithm of Evans *et al.* (2020) to evaluate the completeness of the CFM. Note that all locations are derived from Hauksson *et al.* (2012), and the catalog has been cropped to the region where CFM 6 is targeted as complete (green polygon). The color version of this figure is available only in the electronic edition.

magnitudes, that can reasonably be associated with a modeled fault. To facilitate this assessment, we use the earthquake-to-fault association method of Evans *et al.* (2020), which uses earthquake training datasets not used to build the CFM to determine criteria for associating earthquakes and faults. To compare CFM 5.2 and 6.1, we follow Evans *et al.* (2020) and combine earthquake hypocenters from 1981 to 2022 (Hauksson *et al.*, 2012 and updates) and focal mechanisms from 1981 to 2023 (Yang *et al.*, 2012 and updates) that occur within the CFM region (Fig. 7). When an earthquake has a focal mechanism, we use the location from

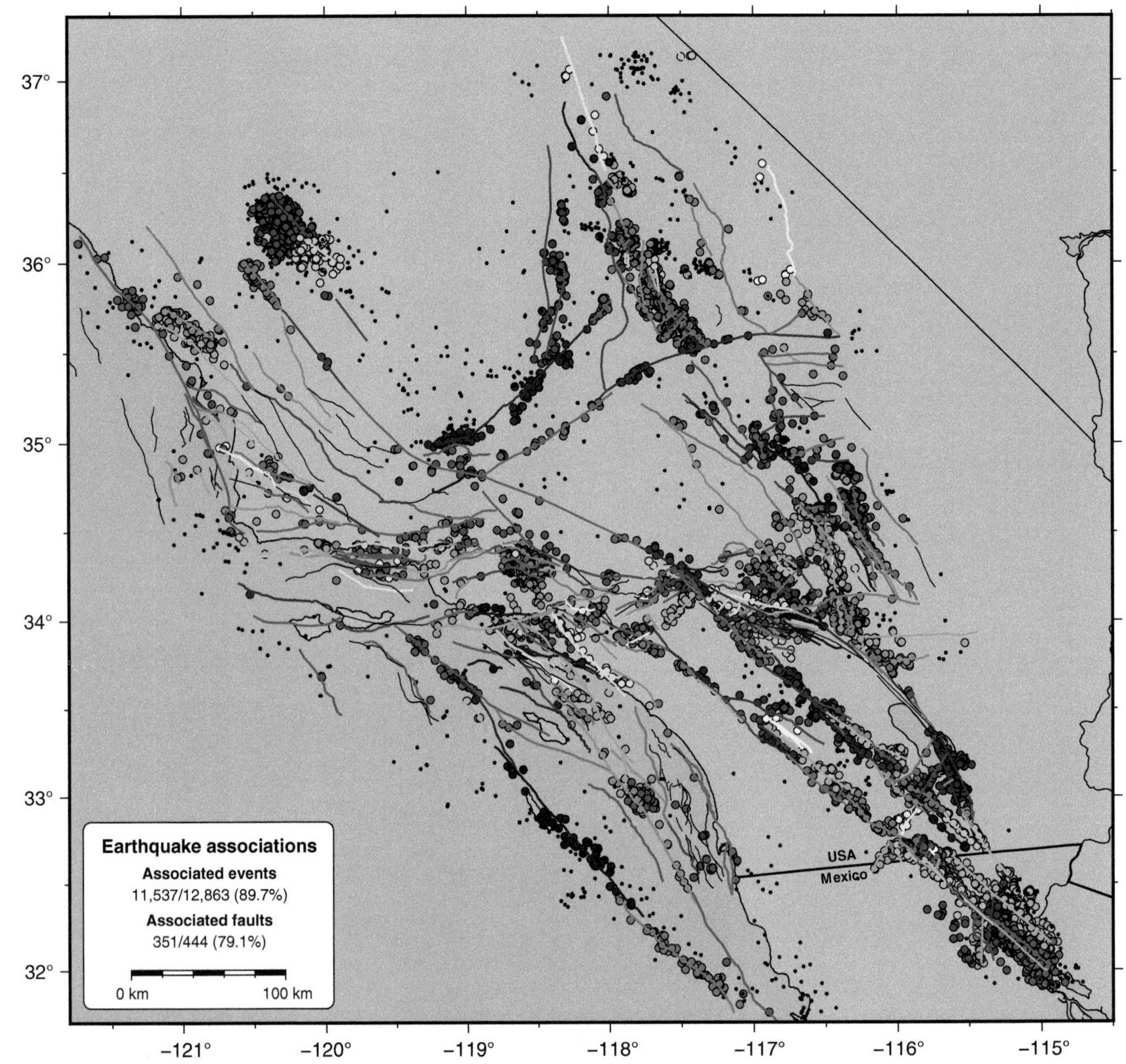

Figure 8. Results of the Evans *et al.* (2020) earthquake-to-fault association on the CFM 6.1 using an updated catalog of **M** 3 or greater events. The catalog (n = 12,863) is color-coded by the fault that is most likely associated with each event. Events that are most likely not associated with a CFM fault and CFM faults that have no associated events are left black and smaller. The color version of this figure is available only in the electronic edition.

Hauksson *et al.* (2012) and append the focal mechanism data from Yang *et al.* (2012). We then use the Evans *et al.* (2020) algorithm to determine which events had the highest probability of association with a CFM fault (Fig. 8) as opposed to the highest probability of not being associated with a CFM fault (see Evans *et al.*, 2020 for a detailed description of the method). We also applied the earthquake-to-fault association algorithm to the 2023 National Seismic Hazard Model (NSHM23) fault section database (Hatem *et al.*, 2022, 2023; also see Data and Resources) to compare. NSHM23 contains a database of fault traces with information on dip angle and direction, and upper and lower depth extents of each fault. We used this information to create a 3D mesh of each NSHM23 fault for this analysis. For the relocated catalog we tested (n = 12,863), 89.7% of magnitude 3–5 events, 86.0% of magnitude 5–6 events, 100% of magnitude 6+ events, and 89.7% of all catalog events associate to a fault in CFM 6.1 (Fig. 9). Notably, CFM 6.1 shows a higher percentage of associated earthquakes across all magnitude ranges (Fig. 9) than CFM 5.2 and NSHM23 and is the only model that has associated faults for all magnitude 6+ events. This can be attributed, in part, to our efforts to produce improved representations of source faults in CFM 6.1, particularly for recent significant earthquakes; however, many of the new fault representations in the model are

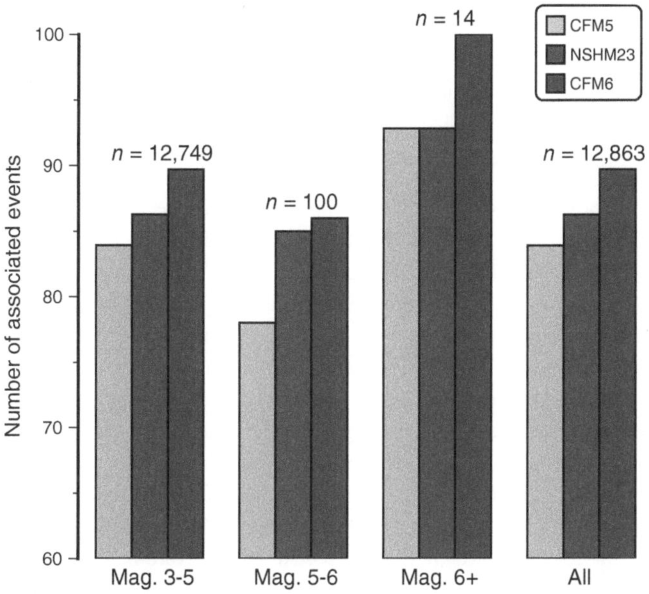

Figure 9. Results of the Evans *et al.* (2020) earthquake-to-fault association broken down by magnitude range for the CFM 5.2, the 2023 National Seismic Hazard Model (NSHM23) Fault Section Database (Hatem *et al.*, 2022, 2023), and CFM 6.1. In all magnitude ranges, the CFM 6.1 has the most earthquake to fault associations, suggesting it is the most complete model as of the time of writing. The magnitude ranges follow Evans *et al.* (2020). The color version of this figure is available only in the electronic edition.

based on surface fault traces and other geological and geophysical datasets and not seismicity. Thus, these refined fault interpretations also contribute to a higher degree of association with earthquakes, particularly for the smaller events. Overall, this objective assessment suggests that CFM 6.1, with its expansion in fault inventory, offers a more complete representation of the earthquake sources in southern California compared to other models (Fig. 9).

Interconnectivity of fault structure

The degree of interconnectivity between faults may contribute to seismic hazard because interconnected fault systems are more likely to cause large, multisegment-multifault ruptures (Field *et al.*, 2017). We quantify a measure of connectivity by determining, for a given fault, the number of other fault objects that are within a specified distance (N_{5000}, Fig. 10). We choose 5 km as the threshold distance, motivated by the distance the Unified California Earthquake Rupture Forecast version 3.0 (Field *et al.*, 2017) allowed for multisegment ruptures in their probabilistic seismic hazard assessment. In CFM 3.0, N_{5000} varies from 0 to 20 with a mean of 4.47. In the new model, N_{5000} varies from 0 to 35 and has a larger mean, now 7.05. This means that in CFM 3.0, an average fault has about four close neighbors, whereas in CFM 6.1 it has about 7.

To focus on connectivity as a relation between connected faults without considering their geometry or spatial characteristics, we consider fault networks as an abstract graph where faults are the nodes of the graph and connections between faults are edges connecting nodes. We construct such graphs for both CFM 3.0 and CFM 6.1 with a threshold connection distance between faults of 5 km. Because faults cannot cross other faults without forming a connection, the resulting graphs are considered planar.

The degree of internal connectivity of such graphs can be characterized in different ways (Gross and Yellen, 2005; Laita *et al.*, 2011; Rodrigue, 2024). We use the beta index from the

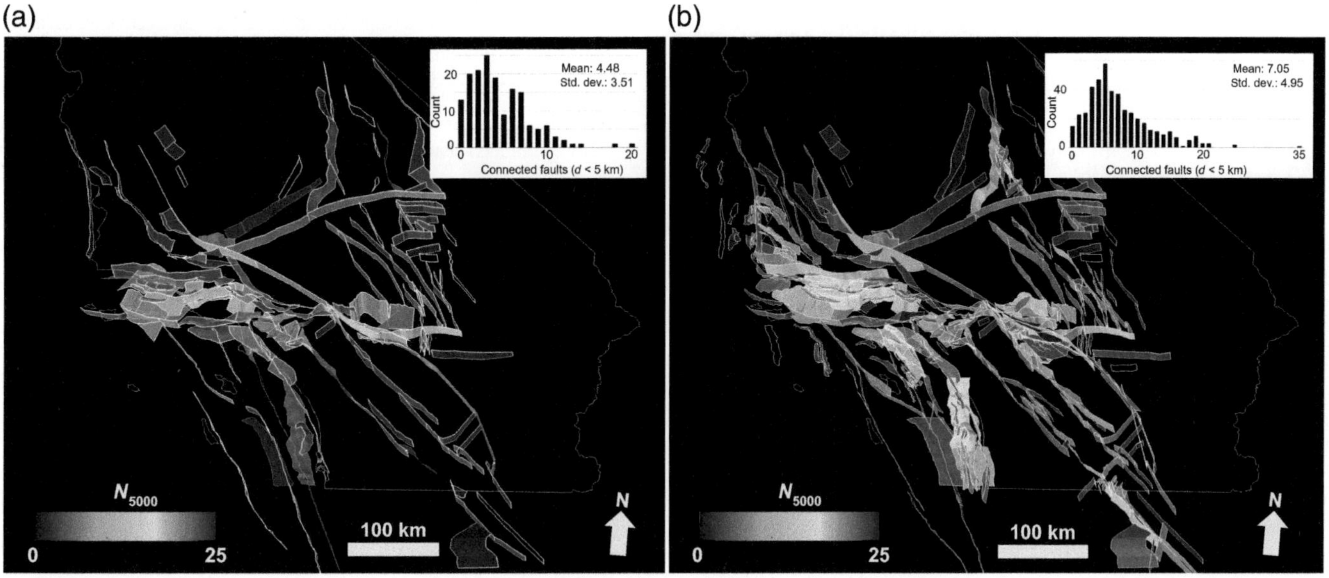

Figure 10. Perspective views of (a) CFM 3.0 and (b) CFM 6.1 colored by the number of connected faults (closer than 5 km, N_{5000}) for each fault. The insets show histograms of the distribution of N_{5000}. The ratio between the total number of connections and the number of faults increases by 56% in CFM 6.1 compared to CFM 3.0. The color version of this figure is available only in the electronic edition.

field of transport geography, which is simply the ratio of all edges (connections between faults) over all nodes (faults) in a graph. In CFM 3.0, there are a total of 164 fault objects that form a total of 734 connections between two faults. A pair of faults is considered connected if separated by a distance of 5 km or less. Thus, the beta index for the CFM 3.0 fault network is 734/164 or 4.47. In CFM 6.1, there are a total of 445 fault objects, which form 3135 connections. The beta index for the CFM 6.1 fault network is therefore 3136/445 or 7.05. A higher beta index is typically interpreted as a more tightly connected abstract graph (e.g., Rodrigue, 2024). In other words, independent of spatial fault density, the connectivity between faults in CFM 6.1 is about 56% higher than in CFM 3.0, after accounting for the increased number of represented faults.

CONCLUSIONS

The SCEC CFM 6.1 is a fully 3D representation of active faulting throughout southern California that is significantly improved compared to previous model versions. The CFM 6.1 contains numerous refinements and additions to the geometric representation of faults and is documented with a self-consistent and extensive set of metadata. The CFM is provided in a wide range of common, open-source data formats to facilitate broad usage. Users can visualize and query the model using the web-based CFM Explorer, which contains a wide range of powerful tools to aid in understanding and evaluating the CFM faults. The CFM 6.1 exhibits a significant increase in fault interconnectivity compared to earlier CFM versions. Using the Evans *et al.* (2020) earthquake-to-fault association method, we find that more relocated events can be associated with CFM 6.1 faults compared to CFM 5.3 and the current USGS National Seismic Hazard fault model. This suggests that the CFM effectively represents the currently known set of active faults throughout southern California and is well-suited for a range of applications in earthquake science and hazard assessment.

DATA AND RESOURCES

Some figures were produced using Generic Mapping Tools (GMT; Wessel *et al.*, 2019) and aspects of the Community Fault Model (CFM) 6.1 were built or edited using PE Limited's MOVE and Aspentech's SKUA-GOCAD software suites, as well as QGIS (QGIS Development Team, 2025). The authors acknowledge the use of the IPM and/or MOVE Software Suite granted by PE Limited. We used the 2023 National Seismic Hazard Model (NSHM23) Fault Section Database available at doi: 10.5066/P9AWINWZ. All data used in this article came from or were declared in published sources listed in the references. All CFM 6.1 model components, along with past and future CFM versions, can be found at doi: 10.5281/zenodo.4651667, the CFM Explorer at https://central.scec.org/research/cfm-explorer/, and CFM 7.0 at https://zenodo.org/records/13685611. The CFM Explorer uses the vtk.js software library available at https://kitware.github.io/vtk-js/ and the leaflet geospatial library (Agafonkin, 2023). All websites were last accessed in February 2026.

DECLARATION OF COMPETING INTERESTS

The authors acknowledge that there are no conflicts of interest recorded.

ACKNOWLEDGMENTS

The authors wish to thank all Community Fault Model (CFM) contributors (see doi: 10.5281/zenodo.4651667). and model evaluators (Sinan Akçiz, Sara Carena, Michele Cooke, Tim Dawson, Jessica Don, Austin Elliot, Erik Frost, Gary Fuis, Athanassios Ganas, Eldon Gath, Alex Hatem, Susanne Jänecke, Marc Kamerling, Christodoulos Kyriakopoulos, Mark Legg, Karen Luttrell, Chris Madugo, Scott Marshall, Andrew Meigs, Craig Nicholson, Nate Onderdonk, Alba Rodríguez Padilla, Andreas Plesch, Kate Scharer, John Shaw, Chris Sorlien, Franklin Wolfe, Doug Yule, and Judy Zachariasen). The CFM could not exist as a community model without these key contributions. In particular, the authors acknowledge Craig Nicholson's input to CFM 4 and 5. This research was supported by the Statewide California Earthquake Center (SCEC Contribution Number 14391). SCEC explicitly permits and encourages the use of any content SCEC makes available at https://files.scec.org/s3fs-public/reports/2022/22066_report.pdf (last accessed February 2026) for this contribution. SCEC is funded by the National Science Foundation (NSF) Cooperative Agreement EAR-2225216 and U.S. Geological Survey (USGS) Cooperative Agreement G24AC00072-00. The authors wish to recognize and thank the SCEC web and IT teams (Tran Huynh, Edric Pauk, Phil Maechling, and Mei-Hui Su), especially Mei-Hui Su, who was the primary developer that the authors collaborated with to produce the CFM Explorer. These contributions are critical in making the CFM broadly accessible to the user community. The authors gratefully acknowledge licensing and technical support by Aspentech (formerly Paradigm) and PE Limited. This article benefited from constructive reviews by James H. Dolan and an anonymous reviewer.

REFERENCES

Agafonkin, V. (2023). Leaflet, a JavaScript library for interactive maps, available at https://github.com/Leaflet/Leaflet (last accessed February 2026).

Ajala, R., P. Persaud, J. M. Stock, G. S. Fuis, J. A. Hole, M. Goldman, and D. Scheirer (2019). Three-dimensional basin and fault structure from a detailed seismic velocity model of Coachella Valley, southern California, *J. Geophys. Res.: Solid Earth* **124,** no. 5, 4728–4750, doi: 10.1029/2018JB016260.

Allen, C. R. (1981). The modern San Andreas Fault, in *The Geotectonic Development of California*, W. G. Ernst (Editor), Vol. 1, Prentice-Hall, Englewood Cliffs, New Jersey, 511–534.

Argus, D. F., M. B. Heflin, G. Peltzer, F. Crampé, and F. H. Webb (2005). Interseismic strain accumulation and anthropogenic motion in metropolitan Los Angeles, *J. Geophys. Res.: Solid Earth* **110,** no. B4, 2003JB002934, doi: 10.1029/2003JB002934.

Astiz, L., and C. R. Allen (1983). Seismicity of the Garlock fault, California, *Bull. Seismol. Soc. Am.* **73,** no. 6A, 1721–1734, doi: 10.1785/BSSA07306A1721.

Atwater, T. (1970). Implications of plate tectonics for the Cenozoic tectonic evolution of Western North America, *GSA Bull.* **81,** no. 12, 3513–3536.

Barak, S., S. L. Klemperer, and J. F. Lawrence (2015). San Andreas Fault dip, Peninsular Ranges mafic lower crust and partial melt in the Salton Trough, Southern California, from ambient-noise tomography, *Geochem. Geophys. Geosys.* **16,** no. 11, 3946–3972, doi: 10.1002/2015GC005970.

Behl, R. J., C. Nicholson, C. C. Sorlien, J. P. Kennett, C. J. Marshall, S. H. Decesari, and D. K. Escobedo (2016). Chronostratigraphy of the Quaternary Santa Barbara Basin: An integrated geophysical, sedimentologic and paleoceanographic approach, *AAPG Pacific Section and Rocky Mountain Section Joint Meeting,* Las Vegas, Nevada, October 2016.

Bergh, S. G., A. G. Sylvester, A. Damte, and K. Indrevær (2019). Polyphase kinematic history of transpression along the Mecca Hills segment of the San Andreas fault, southern California, *Geosphere* **15,** no. 3, 901–934, doi: 10.1130/GES02027.1.

Beyer, J., M. L. Cooke, and S. T. Marshall (2018). Sensitivity of deformation to activity along the Mill Creek and Mission Creek strands of the southern San Andreas fault, *Geosphere* **14,** no. 6, 2296–2310, doi: 10.1130/GES01666.1.

Bloch, R. B., R. V. Huene, P. E. Hart, and C. M. Wentworth (1993). Style and magnitude of tectonic shortening normal to the San Andreas fault across Pyramid Hills and Kettleman Hills South Dome, California, *GSA Bull.* **105,** no. 4, 464–478.

Bohannon, R. G., and E. Geist (1998). Upper crustal structure and Neogene tectonic development of the California continental borderland, *GSA Bull.* **110,** no. 6, 779–800.

Bryant, W. A., compiler (2003). Fault number 109a, North Frontal thrust system, Western section, in Quaternary fault and fold database of the United States, *U.S. Geol. Surv.* Website.

Bryant, W. A., compiler (2017). Fault number 104, Verdugo fault, in Quaternary fault and fold database of the United States, *U.S. Geol. Surv.* Website.

Bryant, W. A., M. Lundberg, and compilers (2002). Fault number 1h, San Andreas fault zone, Mojave section, in Quaternary fault and fold database of the United States, *U.S. Geol. Surv.*, available at https://services.arcgis.com/v01gqwM5QqNysAAi/arcgis/rest/services/qfaults_report_table/FeatureServer/3/3363/attachments/11 (last accessed March 2026).

Burchfiel, B. C., and G. A. Davis (1972). Structural framework and evolution of the southern part of the Cordilleran orogen, western United States, *Am. J. Sci.* **272,** no. 2, 97–118, doi: 10.2475/ajs.272.2.97.

Burchfiel, B. C., K. V. Hodges, and L. H. Royden (1987). Geology of Panamint Valley - Saline Valley Pull-Apart System, California: Palinspastic evidence for low-angle geometry of a Neogene Range-Bounding Fault, *J. Geophys. Res.: Solid Earth* **92,** no. B10, 10,422–10,426, doi: 10.1029/JB092iB10p10422.

Carena, S., J. Suppe, and H. Kao (2004). Lack of continuity of the San Andreas Fault in southern California: Three-dimensional fault models and earthquake scenarios, *J. Geophys. Res.: Solid Earth* **109,** no. B4, 2003JB002643, doi: 10.1029/2003JB002643.

Chávez-Pérez, S., J. N. Louie, and S. K. Pullammanappallil (1998). Seismic depth imaging of normal faulting in the southern Death Valley Basin, *Geophysics* **63,** no. 1, 223–230, doi: 10.1190/1.1444316.

Cheng, Y., E. Hauksson, and Y. Ben-Zion (2023). Refined earthquake focal mechanism catalog for Southern California derived with deep learning algorithms, *J. Geophys. Res.: Solid Earth* **128,** no. 2, e2022JB025975, doi: 10.1029/2022JB025975.

Crouch, J. K., and J. Suppe (1993). Late Cenozoic tectonic evolution of the Los Angeles basin and inner California borderland: A model for core complex-like crustal extension, *Geol. Soc. Am. Bull.* **105,** 1415–1434.

Devine, S., H. Harper, and S. T. Marshall (2022). Mechanical models of fault-slip rates in the Transverse and Peninsular Ranges, California, *Seismol. Res. Lett.* **93,** no. 6, 3135–3150, doi: 10.1785/0220220182.

Diao, F., H. Weng, J.-P. Ampuero, Z. Shao, R. Wang, F. Long, and X. Xiong (2024). Physics-based assessment of earthquake potential on the Anninghe-Zemuhe fault system in southwestern China, *Nat. Commun.* **15,** no. 1, 6908, doi: 10.1038/s41467-024-51313-w.

Dokka, R. K., and C. J. Travis (1990). Role of the Eastern California Shear Zone in accommodating Pacific-North American Plate motion, *Geophys. Res. Lett.* **17,** no. 9, 1323–1326, doi: 10.1029/GL017i009p01323.

Dolan, J. F., K. Sieh, T. K. Rockwell, R. S. Yeats, J. Shaw, J. Suppe, G. J. Huftile, and E. M. Gath (1995). Prospects for larger or more frequent earthquakes in the Los Angeles Metropolitan Region, *Science* **267,** no. 5195, 199–205, doi: 10.1126/science.267.5195.199.

Don, J., J. H. Shaw, A. L. Nicolae, C. C. Sorlien, C. Nicholson, and A. Plesch (2022). Late pleistocene slip rate and 3D geometry of the Mid-Channel Blind Thrust, Santa Barbara Channel, California, and their implications for earthquake hazards, *Bull. Seismol. Soc. Am.* **112,** no. 6, 3081–3101, doi: 10.1785/0120220048.

Donnellan, A., B. H. Hager, R. W. King, and T. A. Herring (1993). Geodetic measurement of deformation in the Ventura Basin Region, southern California, *J. Geophys. Res.: Solid Earth* **98,** no. B12, 21,727–21,739, doi: 10.1029/93JB02766.

Dorsett, J. H., E. H. Madden, S. T. Marshall, and M. L. Cooke (2019). Mechanical models suggest fault linkage through the Imperial Valley, California, U.S.A., *Bull. Seismol. Soc. Am.* **109,** no. 4, 1217–1234, doi: 10.1785/0120180303.

Douilly, R., D. D. Oglesby, M. L. Cooke, and J. L. Hatch (2020). Dynamic models of earthquake rupture along branch faults of the eastern San Gorgonio Pass region in California using complex fault structure, *Geosphere* **16,** no. 2, 474–489, doi: 10.1130/GES02192.1.

Duan, B., and D. D. Oglesby (2007). Nonuniform prestress from prior earthquakes and the effect on dynamics of branched fault systems, *J. Geophys. Res.: Solid Earth* **112,** no. B5, doi: 10.1029/2006JB004443.

Ekström, G., R. S. Stein, J. P. Eaton, and D. Eberhart-Phillips (1992). Seismicity and geometry of a 110-km-long blind thrust fault 1. The 1985 Kettleman Hills, California, earthquake, *J. Geophys. Res.: Solid Earth* **97,** no. B4, 4843–4864, doi: 10.1029/91JB02925.

Elston, H., M. Cooke, J. Loveless, and S. Marshall (2024). A new method to invert for interseismic deep slip along closely spaced faults using surface velocities and subsurface stressing-rate tensors, *Earth Space Sci.* **11,** no. 1, e2023EA003069, doi: 10.1029/2023EA003069.

Evans, E. L., J. P. Loveless, and B. J. Meade (2015). Total variation regularization of geodetically and geologically constrained block models for the Western United States, *Geophys. J. Int.* **202,** no. 2, 713–727, doi: 10.1093/gji/ggv164.

Evans, W. S., A. Plesch, J. H. Shaw, N. L. Pillai, E. Yu, M.-A. Meier, and E. Hauksson (2020). A statistical method for associating earthquakes with their source faults in Southern California, *Bull. Seismol. Soc. Am.* **110,** no. 1, 213–225, doi: 10.1785/0120190115.

Fattaruso, L. A., M. L. Cooke, and R. J. Dorsey (2014). Sensitivity of uplift patterns to dip of the San Andreas fault in the Coachella Valley, California, *Geosphere* **10,** no. 6, 1235–1246, doi: 10.1130/GES01050.1.

Fattaruso, L. A., M. L. Cooke, R. J. Dorsey, and B. A. Housen (2016). Response of deformation patterns to reorganization of the southern San Andreas fault system since ca. 1.5 Ma, *Tectonophysics* **693,** 474–488, doi: 10.1016/j.tecto.2016.05.035.

Fialko, Y. (2006). Interseismic strain accumulation and the earthquake potential on the southern San Andreas fault system, *Nature* **441,** no. 7096, 968–971, doi: 10.1038/nature04797.

Field, E. H., T. H. Jordan, M. T. Page, K. R. Milner, B. E. Shaw, T. E. Dawson, G. P. Biasi, T. Parsons, J. L. Hardebeck, A. J. Michael, *et al.* (2017). A synoptic view of the third Uniform California Earthquake Rupture Forecast (UCERF3), *Seismol. Res. Lett.* **88,** no. 5, 1259–1267, doi: 10.1785/0220170045.

Fuis, G. S., K. Bauer, M. R. Goldman, T. Ryberg, V. E. Langenheim, D. S. Scheirer, M. J. Rymer, J. M. Stock, J. A. Hole, R. D. Catchings, *et al.* (2017). Subsurface geometry of the San Andreas Fault in Southern California: Results from the Salton Seismic Imaging Project (SSIP) and strong ground motion expectations, *Bull. Seismol. Soc. Am.* **107,** no. 4, 1642–1662, doi: 10.1785/0120160309.

Fuis, G. S., R. W. Clayton, P. M. Davis, T. Ryberg, W. J. Lutter, D. A. Okaya, E. Hauksson, C. Prodehl, J. M. Murphy, M. L. Benthien, *et al.* (2003). Fault systems of the 1971 San Fernando and 1994 Northridge earthquakes, southern California: Relocated aftershocks and seismic images from LARSE II, *Geology* **31,** no. 2, 171–174.

Fuis, G. S., T. Ryberg, N. J. Godfrey, D. A. Okaya, and J. M. Murphy (2001). Crustal structure and tectonics from the Los Angeles basin to the Mojave Desert, southern California, *Geology* **29,** no. 1, 15–18.

Fuis, G. S., D. S. Scheirer, V. E. Langenheim, and M. D. Kohler (2012). A new perspective on the geometry of the San Andreas Fault in Southern California and its relationship to lithospheric structure, *Bull. Seismol. Soc. Am.* 102, no. 1, 236–251, doi: 10.1785/0120110041.

Gold, R. D., W. J. Stephenson, R. W. Briggs, C. B. DuRoss, E. Kirby, E. Woolery, J. Delano, and J. K. Odum (2020). Seismic reflection imaging of the low-angle Panamint normal fault system, Eastern California, *J. Geophys. Res.: Solid Earth* **125,** no. 11, e2020JB020243, doi: 10.1029/2020JB020243.

Gonzalez-Ortega, A., Y. Fialko, D. Sandwell, F. Alejandro Nava-Pichardo, J. Fletcher, J. Gonzalez-Garcia, B. Lipovsky, M. Floyd, and G. Funning (2014). El Mayor-Cucapah (Mw 7.2) earthquake: Early near-field postseismic deformation from InSAR and GPS observations, *J. Geophys. Res.: Solid Earth* **119,** no. 2, 1482–1497, doi: 10.1002/2013JB010193.

Grant, L. B., L. J. Ballenger, and E. E. Runnerstrom (2002). Coastal uplift of the San Joaquin Hills, Southern Los Angeles Basin, California, by a large earthquake since A.D. 1635, *Bull. Seismol. Soc. Am.* **92,** no. 2, 590–599, doi: 10.1785/0120010119.

Grant, L. B., K. J. Mueller, E. M. Gath, H. Cheng, R. Lawrence Edwards, R. Munro, and G. L. Kennedy (1999). Late Quaternary uplift and earthquake potential of the San Joaquin Hills, southern Los Angeles basin, California, *Geology* **27,** no. 11, 1031–1034.

Graves, R., T. H. Jordan, S. Callaghan, E. Deelman, E. Field, G. Juve, C. Kesselman, P. Maechling, G. Mehta, K. Milner, *et al.* (2011). CyberShake: A physics-based seismic hazard model for Southern California, *Pure Appl. Geophys.* **168,** no. 3, 367–381, doi: 10.1007/s00024-010-0161-6.

Graves, R. W., A. Pitarka, and P. G. Somerville (1998). Ground-motion amplification in the Santa Monica area: Effects of shallow basin-edge structure, *Bull. Seismol. Soc. Am.* **88,** no. 5, 1224–1242, doi: 10.1785/BSSA0880051224.

Grenader, J., J. Dolan, L. McAuliffe, E. Rhodes, J. Hubbard, and J. Shaw (2015). Characterizing the recent behavior of the Ventura blind thrust fault: Results from the Brookshire Avenue & Day Road sites, Ventura, *SCEC Annual Meeting*, Palm Springs, California.

Griscom, A., and R. C. Jachens (1990). Tectonic implications of gravity and magnetic models along east-west seismic profiles across the Great Valley near Coalinga, *U. S. Geol. Surv. Profess. Pap. USA, 1487.*

Gross, J. L., and J. Yellen (2005). *Graph Theory and Its Applications*, Chapman and Hall/CRC, New York, New York.

Guzofski, C. A., J. H. Shaw, G. Lin, and P. M. Shearer (2007). Seismically active wedge structure beneath the Coalinga anticline, San Joaquin basin, California, *J. Geophys. Res.: Solid Earth* **112,** no. B3, doi: 10.1029/2006JB004465.

Hatem, A. E., C. Collett, R. Briggs, R. D. Gold, S. J. Angster, P. M. Powers, N. Field, M. Anderson, J. Y. Ben-Horin, T. Dawson, *et al.* (2023). Earthquake geology inputs for the U.S. National Seismic Hazard Model (NSHM) 2023 (western U.S.) (ver. 3.0, December 2023), *U.S. Geol. Surv.*

Hatem, A. E., C. M. Collett, R. W. Briggs, R. D. Gold, S. J. Angster, E. H. Field, P. M. Powers, , and Earthquake Geology Working Group, Anderson, M., and J. Y. Ben-Horin, *et al.* (2022). Simplifying complex fault data for systems-level analysis: Earthquake geology inputs for U.S. NSHM 2023, *Sci. Data* **9,** no. 1, 506, doi: 10.1038/s41597-022-01609-7.

Hatem, A. E., and J. F. Dolan (2018). A model for the initiation, evolution, and controls on seismic behavior of the Garlock Fault, California, *Geochem. Geophys. Geosys.* **19,** no. 7, 2166–2178, doi: 10.1029/2017GC007349.

Hauksson, E. (2000). Crustal structure and seismicity distribution adjacent to the Pacific and North America plate boundary in southern California, *J. Geophys. Res.: Solid Earth* **105,** no. B6, 13,875–13,903, doi: 10.1029/2000JB900016.

Hauksson, E., and L. M. Jones (1988). The July 1986 Oceanside (ML = 5.3) earthquake sequence in the Continental Borderland, Southern California, *Bull. Seismol. Soc. Am.* **78,** no. 6, 1885–1906, doi: 10.1785/BSSA0780061885.

Hauksson, E., L. M. Jones, K. Hutton, and D. Eberhart-Phillips (1993). The 1992 Landers earthquake sequence: Seismological observations, *J. Geophys. Res.: Solid Earth* **98,** no. B11, 19,835–19,858, doi: 10.1029/93JB02384.

Hauksson, E., J. M. Stock, and A. L. Husker (2022). Seismicity in a weak crust: the transtensional tectonics of the Brawley Seismic Zone section of the Pacific–North America Plate Boundary in Southern California, USA, *Geophys. J. Int.* **231,** no. 1, 717–735, doi: 10.1093/gji/ggac205.

Hauksson, E., W. Yang, and P. M. Shearer (2012). Waveform relocated earthquake catalog for Southern California (1981 to June 2011), *Bull. Seismol. Soc. Am.* **102,** no. 5, 2239–2244, doi: 10.1785/0120120010.

Hayman, N. W., J. R. Knott, D. S. Cowan, E. Nemser, and A. M. Sarna-Wojcicki (2003). Quaternary low-angle slip on detachment faults in Death Valley, California, *Geology* **31,** no. 4, 343.

Hopkins, S. (2006). Geometry and quaternary evolution of a laterally propagating fold and fault system, Santa Barbara Channel, California, *Master's Thesis*, University of California, Santa Barbara.

Hopkins, S., J. Kennett, C. Nicholson, D. Pak, C. Sorlien, R. Behl, W. Normark, R. Sliter, T. Hill, A. Schimmelmann, *et al.* (2006). Santa Barbara basin study extends global climate record, *Eos Trans. AGU* **87,** no. 21, 205–208, doi: 10.1029/2006EO210001.

Hornafius, S. J., B. P. Luyendyk, R. R. Terres, and M. J. Kamerling (1986). Timing and extent of Neogene tectonic rotation in the western Transverse Ranges, California, *Geol. Soc. Am. Bull.* **97,** no. 12, 1476.

Huang, C., W. Xu, R. Bürgmann, L. Xie, G. Feng, B. Shan, Z. Li, Y. Aoki, Y. Zhang, J. Zhu, *et al.* (2025). Heterogeneous strong asperities and tectonic complexity control irregular cascading ruptures, *Sci. Adv.* **11,** no. 33, eadv6771, doi: 10.1126/sciadv.adv6771.

Hubbard, J., J. Shaw, A. Plesch, M. Riesner, H. Smith, M. Wang, and P. Durand-Riard (2012). A community fault model (CFM) for the Sichuan basin and Longmen Shan, *AGU Fall Meeting Abstracts*, T51G-08 pp.

Hubbard, J., J. H. Shaw, J. Dolan, T. L. Pratt, L. McAuliffe, and T. K. Rockwell (2014). Structure and seismic hazard of the Ventura avenue Anticline and Ventura Fault, California: Prospect for large, multisegment ruptures in the Western Transverse Ranges, *Bull. Seismol. Soc. Am.* **104,** no. 3, 1070–1087, doi: 10.1785/0120130125.

Huftile, G. J., and R. S. Yeats (1995). Convergence rates across a displacement transfer zone in the western Transverse Ranges, Ventura basin, California, *J. Geophys. Res.: Solid Earth* **100,** no. B2, 2043–2067, doi: 10.1029/94JB02473.

Huftile, G. J., and R. S. Yeats (1996). Deformation rates across the Placerita (Northridge Mw = 6.7 aftershock zone) and Hopper Canyon segments of the western transverse ranges deformation belt, *Bull. Seismol. Soc. Am.* **86,** no. 1B, S3–S18, doi: 10.1785/BSSA08601B00S3.

Hughes, A., D. H. Rood, A. C. Whittaker, R. E. Bell, T. K. Rockwell, Y. Levy, K. M. Wilcken, L. B. Corbett, P. R. Bierman, D. E. DeVecchio, *et al.* (2018). Geomorphic evidence for the geometry and slip rate of a young, low-angle thrust fault: Implications for hazard assessment and fault interaction in complex tectonic environments, *Earth Planet. Sci. Lett.* **504,** 198–210, doi: 10.1016/j.epsl.2018.10.003.

Jänecke, S. U., D. K. Markowski, J. P. Evans, P. Persaud, and M. Kenney (2018). Durmid ladder structure and its implications for the nucleation sites of the next M >7.5 earthquake on the San Andreas fault or Brawley seismic zone in southern California, *Lithosphere* **10,** no. 5, 602–631, doi: 10.1130/L629.1.

Johnson, S. Y., and J. T. Watt (2012). Influence of fault trend, bends, and convergence on shallow structure and geomorphology of the Hosgri strike-slip fault, offshore central California, *Geosphere* **8,** no. 6, 1632–1656, doi: 10.1130/GES00830.1.

Kamerling, M. J., and B. P. Luyendyk (1985). Paleomagnetism and neogene tectonics of the Northern Channel Islands, California, *J. Geophys. Res.: Solid Earth* **90,** no. B14, 12,485–12,502, doi: 10.1029/JB090iB14p12485.

Kamerling, M. J., and C. Nicholson (1995). Reliability of 2D kinematic models to infer deep structure in the western Transverse Ranges, California, *Eos Trans AGU* **76,** no. 46, 349.

Kamerling, M. J., C. C. Sorlien, and C. Nicholson (2003). 3D development of an active oblique fault system, northern Santa Barbara Channel, California, *Seismol. Res. Lett.* **74,** no. 2, 248.

Kendrick, K. J., J. C. Matti, and N. C. Barth (2022). Geologic and geomorphic evidence for multi-phase history of strands of the San Andreas fault through the San Gorgonio Pass structural knot, southern California, *Geosphere* **18,** no. 2, 424–457, doi: 10.1130/GES02424.1.

Kohler, M. D., H. Magistrale, and R. W. Clayton (2003). Mantle heterogeneities and the SCEC reference three-dimensional seismic velocity model version 3, *Bull. Seismol. Soc. Am.* **93,** no. 2, 757–774, doi: 10.1785/0120020017.

Laita, A., J. S. Kotiaho, and M. Mönkkönen (2011). Graph-theoretic connectivity measures: What do they tell us about connectivity? *Landsc. Ecol.* **26,** no. 7, 951–967, doi: 10.1007/s10980-011-9620-4.

Langenheim, V. E., and G. S. Fuis (2022). Insights into the geometry and evolution of the southern San Andreas fault from geophysical data, southern California, *Geosphere* **18,** no. 2, 458–475, doi: 10.1130/GES02378.1.

Legg, M. R., M. D. Kohler, N. Shintaku, and D. S. Weeraratne (2015). High-resolution mapping of two large-scale transpressional fault zones in the California Continental Borderland: Santa Cruz-Catalina Ridge and Ferrelo faults, *J. Geophys. Res.: Earth Surf.* **120,** no. 5, 915–942, doi: 10.1002/2014JF003322.

Levy, Y., T. K. Rockwell, J. H. Shaw, A. Plesch, N. W. Driscoll, and H. Perea (2019). Structural modeling of the Western Transverse Ranges: An imbricated thrust ramp architecture, *Lithosphere* **11,** no. 6, 868–883, doi: 10.1130/L1124.1.

Lin, G., P. M. Shearer, and E. Hauksson (2007). Applying a three-dimensional velocity model, waveform cross correlation, and cluster analysis to locate southern California seismicity from 1981 to 2005, *J. Geophys. Res.: Solid Earth* **112,** no. B12, 2007JB004986, doi: 10.1029/2007JB004986.

Lindsey, E. O., and Y. Fialko (2013). Geodetic slip rates in the southern San Andreas Fault system: Effects of elastic heterogeneity and fault geometry, *J. Geophys. Res.: Solid Earth* **118,** no. 2, 689–697, doi: 10.1029/2012JB009358.

Loveless, J. P., and B. J. Meade (2011). Stress modulation on the San Andreas fault by interseismic fault system interactions, *Geology* **39,** no. 11, 1035–1038, doi: 10.1130/G32215.1.

Lozos, J., S. Akçiz, and H. Ladage (2025). Modeling the rupture dynamics of strong ground motion (> 1 g) in fault stepovers, *Tectonophysics* **895,** 230580, doi: 10.1016/j.tecto.2024.230580.

Lozos, J. C., and R. A. Harris (2020). Dynamic Rupture simulations of the M6.4 and M7.1 July 2019 Ridgecrest, California, earthquakes, *Geophys. Res. Lett.* **47,** no. 7, e2019GL086020, doi: 10.1029/2019GL086020.

Luyendyk, B. P., M. J. Kamerling, R. R. Terres, and J. S. Hornafius (1985). Simple shear of southern California during Neogene time suggested by paleomagnetic declinations, *J. Geophys. Res.: Solid Earth* **90,** no. B14, 12,454–12,466, doi: 10.1029/JB090iB14p12454.

Machette, M. N., L. A. Piety, and , and compilers (2001). Fault number 143a, Southern Death Valley fault zone, Confidence Hills section, in Quaternary fault and fold database of the United States, *US Geol. Surv.* Website.

Marshall, S., A. Plesch, and J. Shaw (2023). SCEC Community Fault Model (CFM), *Zenodo*, doi: 10.5281/ZENODO.8327463.

Marshall, S. T., M. L. Cooke, and S. E. Owen (2008). Effects of non-planar fault topology and mechanical interaction on fault-slip distributions in the Ventura Basin, California, *Bull. Seismol. Soc. Am.* **98,** no. 3, 1113–1127, doi: 10.1785/0120070159.

Marshall, S. T., M. L. Cooke, and S. E. Owen (2009). Interseismic deformation associated with three-dimensional faults in the greater Los Angeles region, California, *J. Geophys. Res.: Solid Earth* **114,** no. B12, 2009JB006439, doi: 10.1029/2009JB006439.

Marshall, S. T., G. J. Funning, H. E. Krueger, S. E. Owen, and J. P. Loveless (2017). Mechanical models favor a ramp geometry for the Ventura-pitas point fault, California, *Geophys. Res. Lett.* **44,** no. 3, 1311–1319, doi: 10.1002/2016GL072289.

Marshall, S. T., G. J. Funning, and S. E. Owen (2013). Fault slip rates and interseismic deformation in the western Transverse Ranges, California, *J. Geophys. Res.: Solid Earth* **118,** no. 8, 4511–4534, doi: 10.1002/jgrb.50312.

McAuliffe, L. J., J. F. Dolan, E. J. Rhodes, J. Hubbard, J. H. Shaw, and T. L. Pratt (2015). Paleoseismologic evidence for large-magnitude (Mw 7.5–8.0) earthquakes on the Ventura blind thrust fault: Implications for multifault ruptures in the Transverse Ranges of southern California, *Geosphere* **11,** no. 5, 1629–1650, doi: 10.1130/GES01123.1.

McGill, S. F., and K. Sieh (1991). Surficial offsets on the Central and Eastern Garlock Fault associated with prehistoric earthquakes, *J. Geophys. Res.: Solid Earth* **96,** no. B13, 21,597–21,621, doi: 10.1029/91JB02030.

McGill, S. F., J. C. Spinler, J. D. McGill, R. A. Bennett, M. A. Floyd, J. E. Fryxell, and G. J. Funning (2015). Kinematic modeling of fault slip rates using new geodetic velocities from a transect across the Pacific-North America plate boundary through the San Bernardino Mountains, California, *J. Geophys. Res.: Solid Earth* **120,** no. 4, 2772–2793, doi: 10.1002/2014JB011459.

McLaren, M. K., J. L. Hardebeck, N. van der Elst, J. R. Unruh, G. W. Bawden, and J. L. Blair (2008). Complex faulting associated with the 22 December 2003 Mw 6.5 San Simeon, California, earthquake, aftershocks, and postseismic surface deformation, *Bull. Seismol. Soc. Am.* **98,** no. 4, 1659–1680, doi: 10.1785/0120070088.

McPhee, D. K., R. C. Jachens, and C. M. Wentworth (2004). Crustal structure across the San Andreas Fault at the SAFOD site from potential field and geologic studies, *Geophys. Res. Lett.* **31,** no. 12, 2003GL019363, doi: 10.1029/2003GL019363.

Meade, B. J., and B. H. Hager (2005). Block models of crustal motion in southern California constrained by GPS measurements, *J. Geophys. Res.: Solid Earth* **110,** no. B3, doi: 10.1029/2004JB003209.

Medwedeff, D. A. (1989). Growth fault-bend folding at Southeast Lost Hills, San Joaquin Valley, California, *AAPG Bull.* **73,** doi: 10.1306/703C9AE6-1707-11D7-8645000102C1865D.

Namson, J., and T. Davis (1988). Structural transect of the western Transverse Ranges, California: Implications for lithospheric kinematics and seismic risk evaluation, *Geology* **16,** no. 8, 675.

Nazareth, J. J. (2004). The seismogenic thickness of the Southern California crust, *Bull. Seismol. Soc. Am.* **94,** no. 3, 940–960, doi: 10.1785/0120020129.

Nicholson, C., E. Hauksson, and A. Plesch (2012). Active fault geometry and crustal deformation along the San Andreas fault system through San Gorgonio Pass, California: The view in 3D from seismicity, *Eos Trans. AGU* **93,** T22C-03.

Nicholson, C., A. Plesch, and J. H. Shaw (2011). CFM v.4.0: Continued upgrades and improvements to the SCEC Community Fault Model and its associated fault database, *2011 SCEC Annual Meeting Proceedings & Abstracts*, 208 pp.

Nicholson, C., A. Plesch, C. Sorlien, J. H. Shaw, and E. Hauksson (2014). The SCEC 3D Community Fault Model (CFM-v5): An updated and expanded fault set of oblique crustal deformation and complex fault interaction for southern California, *Eos Trans. AGU* **95,** T31B-4584.

Nicholson, C., A. Plesch, C. C. Sorlien, J. H. Shaw, and E. Hauksson (2020). Updates, Evaluation and Improvements to the Community Fault Model (CFM version 5.3), *Poster Presentation at 2020 SCEC Annual Meeting*, Palm Springs, California.

Nicholson, C., C. C. Sorlien, T. Atwater, J. C. Crowell, and B. P. Luyendyk (1994). Microplate capture, rotation of the western Transverse Ranges, and initiation of the San Andreas transform as a low-angle fault system, *Geology* **22,** no. 6, 491–495.

Nishenko, S., H. Gary Greene, P. Hogan, and B. Bergkamp (2018). Geometry and late Pleistocene displacement of the Shoreline and Oceano Fault Zones, San Luis Obispo Bay, California, *Bull. Seismol. Soc. Am.* doi: 10.1785/0120160177.

Oglesby, D. D. (2005). The dynamics of strike-slip step-overs with linking dip-slip faults, *Bull. Seismol. Soc. Am.* **95**, no. 5, 1604–1622, doi: 10.1785/0120050058.

Olsen, K. B., and R. J. Archuleta (1996). Three-dimensional simulation of earthquakes on the Los Angeles fault system, *Bull. Seismol. Soc. Am.* **86,** no. 3, 575–596, doi: 10.1785/BSSA0860030575.

Olsen, K. B., S. M. Day, L. A. Dalguer, J. Mayhew, Y. Cui, J. Zhu, V. M. Cruz-Atienza, D. Roten, P. Maechling, T. H. Jordan, *et al.* (2009). ShakeOut-D: Ground motion estimates using an ensemble of large earthquakes on the southern San Andreas fault with spontaneous rupture propagation, *Geophys. Res. Lett.* **36,** no. 4, doi: 10.1029/2008GL036832.

Oskin, M., K. Sieh, T. Rockwell, G. Miller, P. Guptill, M. Curtis, S. McArdle, and P. Elliot (2000). Active parasitic folds on the Elysian Park anticline: Implications for seismic hazard in central Los Angeles, California, *GSA Bull.* **112,** no. 5, 693–707.

Pacific Gas and Electric Company (PG&E) (2011). Shoreline fault zone report: Report on the analysis of the Shoreline fault zone, central coastal California, *Rept. U.S. Nucl. Regul. Comm.*

Persaud, P., Y. Ma, J. M. Stock, J. A. Hole, G. S. Fuis, and L. Han (2016). Fault zone characteristics and basin complexity in the southern Salton Trough, California, *Geology* **44,** no. 9, 747–750, doi: 10.1130/G38033.1.

Plesch, A., and J. H. Shaw (2010). Statewide community fault model, *SCEC Annual Meeting, Proceedings and Abstracts*, 262 pp.

Plesch, A., J. H. Shaw, and SCFM Working Group, and C. Nicholson (2018). SCFM 3.1: Updates, maps and modeling support, *Poster Presentation at 2018 SCEC Annual Meeting*, Palm Springs, California.

Plesch, A., J. H. Shaw, C. Benson, W. A. Bryant, S. Carena, M. Cooke, J. Dolan, G. Fuis, E. Gath, L. Grant, *et al.* (2007). Community Fault Model (CFM) for Southern California, *Bull. Seismol. Soc. Am.* **97,** no. 6, 1793–1802, doi: 10.1785/0120050211.

Plesch, A., J. H. Shaw, Z. E. Ross, and E. Hauksson (2020). Detailed 3D fault representations for the 2019 Ridgecrest, California, earthquake sequence, *Bull. Seismol. Soc. Am.* **110,** no. 4, 1818–1831, doi: 10.1785/0120200053.

Pollitz, F. F., C. Wicks, and W. Thatcher (2001). Mantle flow beneath a continental strike-slip fault: Postseismic deformation after the 1999 Hector Mine earthquake, *Science* **293,** no. 5536, 1814–1818, doi: 10.1126/science.1061361.

QGIS Development Team (2025). QGIS geographic information system, QGIS Association.

Qiu, H., B. Chi, and Y. Ben-Zion (2023). Internal structure of the Central Garlock Fault Zone from Ridgecrest aftershocks recorded by dense linear seismic arrays, *Geophys. Res. Lett.* **50,** no. 2, e2022GL101761, doi: 10.1029/2022GL101761.

Rasmussen, G., and W. Reeder (1986). What happens to the real San Andreas fault at Cottonwood Canyon, San Gorgonio Pass, California? in *Geology Around the Margins of the Eastern San Bernardino Mountains*, M. A. Kooser and R. E. Reynolds (Editors), Inland Geological Society, Redlands, California, 157–162.

Redin, T., J. Forman, M. Kamerling, and J. Galloway (2005). Santa Barbara channel structure and correlation sections—CS-32 to CS-42, Cross Sect., 36.

Reed, R. D., and J. S. Hollister (1951). Geology of California: Structural evolution of Southern California, American Association of Petroleum Geologists, Tulsa, Okla.

Riesner, M., P. Durand-Riard, J. Hubbard, A. Plesch, and J. H. Shaw (2017). Building objective 3D fault representations in active tectonic settings, *Seismol. Res. Lett.* **88,** no. 3, 831–839, doi: 10.1785/0220160192.

Rivero, C., and J. H. Shaw (2011). Active folding and blind thrust faulting induced by basin inversion processes, Inner California Borderlands, in *Thrust Fault-Related Folding*, K. McClay, J. Shaw, and J. Suppe (Editors), American Association of Petroleum Geologists, Tulsa, Oklahoma.

Rivero, C., J. H. Shaw, and K. Mueller (2000). Oceanside and Thirtymile Bank blind thrusts: Implications for earthquake hazards in coastal southern California, *Geology* **28,** no. 10, 891–894.

Rockwell, T., and A. G. Sylvester (1979). Neotectonics of the Salton Trough, in *Tectonics of the Juncture Between the San Andreas Fault System and the Salton Trough, Southeastern CA: A Guidebook*, J. C. Crowell and A. G. Sylvester (Editors), Department of Geological Sciences, University of California, Santa Barbara, California, 41–52.

Rockwell, T. K., K. Clark, L. Gamble, M. E. Oskin, E. C. Haaker, and G. L. Kennedy (2016). Large transverse range earthquakes cause coastal upheaval near Ventura, Southern California, *Bull. Seismol. Soc. Am.* **106,** no. 6, 2706–2720, doi: 10.1785/0120150378.

Rockwell, T. K., E. A. Keller, and G. R. Dembroff (1988). Quaternary rate of folding of the Ventura Avenue anticline, western Transverse Ranges, southern California, *GSA Bull.* **100,** no. 6, 850–858.

Rodrigue, J.-P. (2024). *The Geography of Transport Systems*, Routledge, London, United Kingdom.

Ross, Z. E., B. Idini, Z. Jia, O. L. Stephenson, M. Zhong, X. Wang, Z. Zhan, M. Simons, E. J. Fielding, S.-H. Yun, *et al.* (2019). Hierarchical interlocked orthogonal faulting in the 2019 Ridgecrest earthquake sequence, *Science* **366,** no. 6463, 346–351, doi: 10.1126/science.aaz0109.

Ross, Z. E., D. T. Trugman, E. Hauksson, and P. M. Shearer (2019). Searching for hidden earthquakes in Southern California, *Science* **364,** no. 6442, 767–771, doi: 10.1126/science.aaw6888.

Sarna-Wojcicki, A. M., K. M. Williams, and R. F. Yerkes (1976). Geology of the Ventura Fault, Ventura County, California, *U.S. Geol. Surv. Misc. Field Stud. no. MF-781*, doi: 10.3133/mf781.

Sarna-Wojcicki, A. M., and R. F. Yerkes (1982). Comment on article by R. S. Yeats entitled "Low-shake faults of the Ventura Basin, California," in *Neotectonics in Southern California*, J. D. Cooper (Editor), 78th Cordilleran Section Annual Meeting, Guidebook, Geological Society of America, Boulder, Colorado, 17–19.

Savage, J. C., M. Lisowski, and W. H. Prescott (1990). An apparent shear zone trending north-northwest across the Mojave Desert into Owens Valley, eastern California, *Geophys. Res. Lett.* **17,** no. 12, 2113–2116, doi: 10.1029/GL017i012p02113.

Schneider, C. L., C. Hummon, R. S. Yeats, and G. L. Huftile (1996). Structural evolution of the northern Los Angeles basin, California, based on growth strata, *Tectonics* **15,** no. 2, 341–355, doi: 10.1029/95TC02523.

Seebeck, H., R. Van Dissen, N. Litchfield, P. M. Barnes, A. Nicol, R. Langridge, D. J. A. Barrell, P. Villamor, S. Ellis, M. Rattenbury, *et al.* (2024). The New Zealand Community Fault Model – version 1.0: An improved geological foundation for seismic hazard modelling, *New Zeal. J. Geol. Geophys.* **67,** no. 2, 209–229, doi: 10.1080/00288306.2023.2181362.

Seebeck, H., R. J. Van Dissen, N. J. Litchfield, P. M. Barnes, A. Nicol, R. M. Langridge, D. J. A. Barrell, P. Villamor, S. M. Ellis, and M. S. Rattenbury (2022). New Zealand Community Fault Model - version 1.0, doi: 10.21420/GA7S-BS61.

Seeber, L., and J. G. Armbruster (1995). The San Andreas Fault system through the Transverse Ranges as illuminated by earthquakes, *J. Geophys. Res.: Solid Earth* **100,** no. B5, 8285–8310, doi: 10.1029/94JB02939.

Serpa, L., and R. K. Dokka (1992). Geometry of the Garlock fault zone based on seismic reflection data, *J. Geophys. Res.: Solid Earth* **97,** no. B11, 15,297–15,306, doi: 10.1029/92JB00585.

Shaw, J. H., and A. Plesch (2012). 3D structural velocity model of the Santa Maria Basin, CA, for improved strong ground motion prediction, *U.S. Geol. Surv. Natl. Earthq. Hazards Reduct. Program Final Rept. no. Award No. G12AP20020.*

Shaw, J. H., and P. M. Shearer (1999). An elusive blind-thrust fault beneath Metropolitan Los Angeles, *Science* **283,** no. 5407, 1516–1518, doi: 10.1126/science.283.5407.1516.

Shaw, J. H., and J. Suppe (1994). Active faulting and growth folding in the eastern Santa Barbara Channel, California, *GSA Bull.* **106,** no. 5, 607–626.

Shaw, J. H., and J. Suppe (1996). Earthquake hazards of active blind-thrust faults under the central Los Angeles basin, California, *J. Geophys. Res.: Solid Earth* **101,** no. B4, 8623–8642, doi: 10.1029/95JB03453.

Shaw, J. H., C. Connors, and J. Suppe (Editors) (2005). *Seismic Interpretation of Contractional Fault-Related Folds: An AAPG Seismic Atlas*, American Association of Petroleum Geologists, Tulsa, Oklahoma, AAPG studies in geology 53.

Shaw, J. H., A. Plesch, J. F. Dolan, T. L. Pratt, and P. Fiore (2002). Puente hills blind-thrust system, Los Angeles, California, *Bull. Seismol. Soc. Am.* **92,** no. 8, 2946–2960, doi: 10.1785/0120010291.

Smith, G. (1975). Holocene movement on the Garlock fault, *U.S. Geol. Surv. Profess. Pap. 975*, 202 pp.

Smith, G. L. (1962). Large lateral displacement on Garlock fault, California, as measured from offset dike swarm, *Am. Assoc. Pet. Geol. Bull.* **46,** 85–104.

Smith, G. I., and K. B. Ketner (1970). Lateral displacement on the Garlock fault, southeastern California, suggested by offset sections of similar metasedimentary rocks, *U.S. Geol Surv. Profess. Pap. 700-D*, 1–9.

Sorlien, C. C., and C. Nicholson (2015). Post-1 Ma deformation history of the pitas point-North Channel-Red Mountain Fault System and associated folds in Santa Barbara Channel,

California, *U.S. Geol. Surv. Natl. Earthq. Hazards Reduct. Program Final Rept. Award G14AP00012*, 1–24.

Sorlien, C. C., J.-P. Gratier, B. P. Luyendyk, J. S. Hornafius, and T. E. Hopps (2000). Map restoration of folded and faulted late Cenozoic strata across the Oak Ridge fault, onshore and offshore Ventura basin, California, *GSA Bull.* **112,** no. 7, 1080–1090.

Sorlien, C. C., C. Nicholson, R. J. Behl, C. J. Marshall, and J. Kennett (2014). The Quaternary north Channel-Pitas Point fault system in northwest Santa Barbara Channel, California, *EOS Trans. AGU* **95,** T34A-07.

Stein, R. S., and G. Ekström (1992). Seismicity and geometry of a 110-km-long blind thrust fault 2. Synthesis of the 1982–1985 California Earthquake Sequence, *J. Geophys. Res.: Solid Earth* **97,** no. B4, 4865–4883, doi: 10.1029/91JB02847.

Tape, C., Q. Liu, A. Maggi, and J. Tromp (2010). Seismic tomography of the southern California crust based on spectral-element and adjoint methods, *Geophys. J. Int.* **180,** no. 1, 433–462, doi: 10.1111/j.1365-246X.2009.04429.x.

Tsutsumi, H., R. S. Yeats, and G. J. Huftile (2001). Late Cenozoic tectonics of the northern Los Angeles fault system, California, *Geol. Soc. Am. Bull.* **113,** no. 4, 454–468.

U.S. Geological Survey and California Geological Survey (2025). Quaternary fault and fold database for the United States, doi: 10.5066/P9BCVRCK.

Weber, F., Jr., J. H. Bennett, R. Chapman, G. W. Chase, and R. B. Saul (1980). Earthquake hazards associated with the Verdugo-Eagle Rock and Benedict Canyon fault zones, Los Angeles County, California, *U.S. Geol. Surv. Open-File Rept. 81-296.*

Welch, R. M. (2025). Structure of the Southern Canadian Rocky Mountain Foreland and Western San Joaquin Basin Fold-and-Thrust Belts, *Ph.D. Thesis*, Harvard University, Cambridge, Massachusetts.

Weldon, R., and E. Humphreys (1986). A kinematic model of southern California, *Tectonics* **5,** no. 1, 33–48, doi: 10.1029/TC005i001p00033.

Wessel, P., J. F. Luis, L. Uieda, R. Scharroo, F. Wobbe, W. H. F. Smith, and D. Tian (1986). The Generic Mapping Tools Version 6, *Geochem. Geophys. Geosyst.* **20,** no. 11, 5556–5564, doi: 10.1029/2019GC008515.

Willingham, C. R., J. D. Rietman, R. G. Heck, and W. R. Lettis (2013). Characterization of the Hosgri fault zone and adjacent structures in the offshore Santa Maria basin, south-central California, *U.S. Geol. Surv. Bull. 1995-CC*, 105 pp., doi: 10.3133/b1995CC.

Wolfe, F. D., J. H. Shaw, and A. Plesch (2022). Origin of the Palos Verdes restraining bend and its implications for the 3D geometry of the fault and earthquake hazards in Los Angeles, California, *Bull. Seismol. Soc. Am.* **112,** no. 5, 2689–2714, doi: 10.1785/0120210278.

Wolfe, F. D., J. H. Shaw, A. Plesch, D. J. Ponti, J. F. Dolan, and M. R. Legg (2019). The Wilmington Blind-Thrust Fault: An active concealed earthquake source beneath Los Angeles, California, *Bull. Seismol. Soc. Am.* **109,** no. 5, 1890–1906, doi: 10.1785/0120180335.

Yang, W., E. Hauksson, and P. M. Shearer (2012). Computing a large refined catalog of focal mechanisms for Southern California (1981-2010): Temporal stability of the style of faulting, *Bull. Seismol. Soc. Am.* **102,** no. 3, 1179–1194, doi: 10.1785/0120110311.

Yeats, R. S. (1982a). Low-shake faults of the Ventura basin, California, in *Neotectonics in Southern California*, J. D. Cooper (Editor), 78th Cordilleran Section Annual Meeting, Guidebook, Geological Society of America, 3–15.

Yeats, R. S. (1982b). Reply to Sarna-Wojcicki, A. M. and R. F. Yerkes, in *Neotectonics in Southern California*, J. D. Cooper (Editor), 78th Cordilleran Section Annual Meeting, Guidebook, Geological Society of America, 21–23.

Yeats, R. S. (1983). Large-scale Quaternary detachments in Ventura Basin, southern California, *J. Geophys. Res.: Solid Earth* **88,** no. B1, 569–583, doi: 10.1029/JB088iB01p00569.

Yeats, R. S. (1988). Late Quaternary slip rate on the Oak Ridge fault, Transverse Ranges, California: Implications for seismic risk, *J. Geophys. Res.: Solid Earth* **93,** no. B10, 12,137–12,149, doi: 10.1029/JB093iB10p12137.

Yeats, R. S., G. J. Huftile, and F. B. Grigsby (1988). Oak Ridge fault, Ventura fold belt, and the Sisar decollement, Ventura basin, California, *Geology* **16,** no. 12, 1112–1116.

Yeats, R. S., G. J. Huftile, and L. T. Stitt (1994). Late Cenozoic tectonics of the East Ventura Basin, Transverse Ranges, California, *AAPG Bull.* **78,** no. 7, 1040–1074, doi: 10.1306/A25FE42D-171B-11D7-8645000102C1865D.

Yule, D., and K. Sieh (2003). Complexities of the San Andreas fault near San Gorgonio Pass: Implications for large earthquakes, *J. Geophys. Res.: Solid Earth* **108,** no. B11, 2001JB000451, doi: 10.1029/2001JB000451.

Ziony, J. I., and R. F. Yerkes (1985). Evaluating earthquake and surface-faulting potential, *Geol. Surv. Profess. Pap. 1360*, 43–91.

Manuscript received 23 October 2025
Published online 18 March 2026

Stress States on the Eve of Past Earthquakes Inform Earthquake Rupture Through Fault Complexity Along the San Andreas and San Jacinto Faults

Emery O. Anderson-Merritt*[1], Michele L. Cooke[1], and Katherine Scharer[2]

OPEN ACCESS

ABSTRACT

Estimating the evolving state of stress along active fault systems can provide insight into the conditions that generated past ground-rupturing earthquakes and influenced their ability to propagate through areas of geometric complexity, such as fault branches and stepovers. We use quasi-static forward numerical models that incorporate the 3D complex configuration of active faults in southern California to estimate shear tractions on the geometrically complex southern San Andreas and San Jacinto faults from 1000 to 1900 C.E. These tractions include interseismic accumulation of traction due to tectonic loading, viscoelastic relaxation of shear stress within the upper crust between earthquakes, and effects of other earthquakes on the fault network. We simulate ground-rupturing earthquakes based on the along-strike earthquake extents modeled by Scharer and Yule (2020), assuming that stress drop is complete in each earthquake. We use Monte Carlo simulations to estimate uncertainty in evolving shear tractions due to uncertainties in earthquake timing and in upper-crustal viscosity. Pre-earthquake shear tractions typically do not exceed ~2 MPa. Although ruptures with length < 200 km have pre-earthquake shear tractions that range from near zero to ~1.75 MPa, these tractions are not less than ~0.4 MPa for earthquakes with rupture length > 200 km. Earthquakes with long (> 200 km) ruptures occur only in the single-stranded part of the system, whereas those with short (< 125 km) rupture length and high pre-earthquake shear traction occur near fault stepovers and branches. This suggests that high accumulated shear traction encourages longer rupture propagation, but may not be sufficient to overcome geometric complexities. This modeling approach informs our understanding of rupture propagation and provides estimates of fault shear tractions that are unavailable from direct measurements.

KEY POINTS

- Numerical models can provide estimates of fault traction that are unavailable from direct measurements.
- Short ruptures have high pre-eathquake tractions in geometrically complex areas and low tractions elsewhere.
- Long ruptures are facilitated by high tractions and hindered by geometric complexity along the San Andreas.

Supplemental Material

INTRODUCTION

Forecasting future earthquake hazard depends on characterizing past earthquakes (e.g., Field *et al.*, 2015). Information about past earthquakes depends in part on studies of the paleoseismic records at individual sites that can provide information about the timing of past ground-rupturing earthquakes, the amount of slip at that location, and variability in both timing and slip. In some regions with abundant paleoseismic data, information from many sites can be combined to model regional chronologies of past earthquakes that show rupture extents in

1. Department of Earth, Geographic, and Climate Sciences, University of Massachusetts Amherst, Amherst, Massachusetts, U.S.A., https://orcid.org/0000-0001-5594-7929 (EOA); https://orcid.org/0000-0002-4407-9676 (MLC); 2. U.S. Geological Survey, Earthquake Science Center, Pasadena, California, U.S.A., https://orcid.org/0000-0003-2811-2496 (KS)

*Corresponding author: eandersonmer@umass.edu

Cite this article as Anderson-Merritt, E. O., M. L. Cooke, and K. Scharer (2026). Stress States on the Eve of Past Earthquakes Inform Earthquake Rupture Through Fault Complexity Along the San Andreas and San Jacinto Faults, *Bull. Seismol. Soc. Am.* **116**, 1125–1144, doi: 10.1785/0120250173 addition to earthquake timing (e.g., DuRoss *et al.*, 2016; Scharer and Yule, 2020). These models illuminate potential patterns in the past earthquake record, but alone do not provide information about the underlying conditions that drive these ground-rupturing events.

Shear tractions (i.e., stresses resolved on faults) along active fault surfaces can vary laterally, with depth, and through time; they depend on the orientation of a fault relative to plate motion and its mechanical interaction with other faults in the system as well as on the time elapsed on different parts of the fault since their previous earthquakes and traction changes caused by earthquakes on nearby faults (Smith-Konter and Sandwell, 2009; Hatch *et al.*, 2020). Estimates of pre-earthquake shear tractions can provide context for interpreting the paleoseismic record. For example, unusually long or short periods between large earthquakes at a given location may be explained by shear traction changes. If a nearby earthquake reduces shear tractions, this may delay the next earthquake; similarly, traction estimates for past earthquakes can also inform interpretation of the current open interval (e.g., Luttrell *et al.*, 2007; Hatch *et al*, 2020). An unusually long recurrence interval with unusually high shear traction accumulation can reveal locations where earthquakes may be missing from the paleoseismic record (Bagge *et al.*, 2019).

In addition to providing context for observations at individual sites, shear traction estimates can also improve understanding of spatial patterns in earthquake rupture behavior. Areas of geometric complexity, such as fault bends, splays, and stepovers, can conditionally permit or inhibit propagation of earthquake ruptures (e.g., Wesnousky, 2006; Rodriguez Padilla *et al.*, 2024). The stress state resulting from the previous rupture history of the area can play a role in determining whether ruptures can propagate through geometric complexities (Liu *et al.*, 2021), influencing total rupture length and earthquake magnitude (Wesnousky, 2006).

The San Andreas and San Jacinto fault system of southern California, which has hosted past large earthquakes and features several fault bends, branches, and stepovers, is an interesting location to investigate the relationship between evolving shear tractions, geometric complexity, and earthquake rupture length (Fig. 1). The rich paleoseismic record in this area allowed Scharer and Yule (2020; Fig. 1) to compile a rupture model for the southern San Andreas and San Jacinto faults from 500 C.E. to the present, in which they correlate earthquake timing between sites to produce the longest earthquake ruptures that are compatible with the paleoseismic record. The model provided in Scharer and Yule (2020) reveals several interesting features: earthquake ruptures are commonly longer in the area north of Cajon Pass than south of the pass, where the system becomes multistranded with many branches on the San Andreas fault and stepovers on the San Jacinto fault. Along the Mojave section of the San Andreas fault, the area near the Pallett Creek and Littlerock sites ruptures less frequently than neighboring areas. Earthquakes on the Coachella segment commonly include rupture on the southern Mission Creek strand, part of a northern slip pathway of the San Andreas fault, whereas the southern slip pathway through San Gorgonio Pass ruptures at half that frequency. Earthquakes on the San Jacinto fault are typically shorter, rupturing one or two segments. Understanding the state of shear tractions in the system before ground-rupturing earthquakes can inform which conditions encourage ruptures to propagate across fault stepovers and through splays, or to favor one branch of a splay over another.

Because information about shear tractions leading up to past events is not available from geologic data, we rely on numerical models for these estimates. In this work, we use 3D numerical models to simulate the paleoseismic record along the San Andreas and San Jacinto faults described by Scharer and Yule (2020). The simulations estimate the evolving strike shear tractions (i.e., component of shear traction in the strike direction) on both faults from 1000 C.E., the earliest time for which most of the system has a robust paleoseismic record, to 1900 C.E., capturing the 1857 Fort Tejon earthquake, which is the most recent very large earthquake on the system. We consider interseismic traction accumulation due to tectonic loading, viscoelastic relaxation of stress in the crust during the interseismic period, and stress changes due to earthquakes on the fault system. We explore uncertainty in traction estimates due to uncertainties in earthquake timing and upper-crustal viscosity using Monte Carlo simulations. The results give insight into the conditions prior to ground-rupturing earthquakes on these two primary faults within the plate boundary in southern California.

The pre-earthquake traction estimates may also help improve dynamic rupture models, which rely on initial tractions as model inputs for simulating both past damaging earthquakes and plausible future ones. Dynamic rupture models commonly use either a uniform initial shear traction (e.g., Kyriakopoulos *et al.*, 2017; Douilly *et al.*, 2020) or resolve regional stress fields onto the fault-plane orientation (e.g., Aochi and Fukuyama, 2002; Oglesby *et al.*, 2003; Lozos, 2016), but these strategies may not capture the spatial variability in pre-earthquake tractions arising from the earthquake history. Because the results of dynamic rupture models are sensitive to initial traction conditions, improved estimates of pre-earthquake tractions have the potential to help refine these models and improve simulations of potential future earthquakes (Douilly *et al.*, 2020; Tarnowski *et al.*, 2022).

METHODS

We use the quasi-static, 3D boundary element method (BEM) code Poly3D, which can solve for slip, opening, and tractions on triangular elements within a linear elastic half-space using the equations of continuum mechanics (e.g., Thomas, 1993; Crider and Pollard, 1998). Such models have been used to simulate slip rates and traction accumulation on active faults in

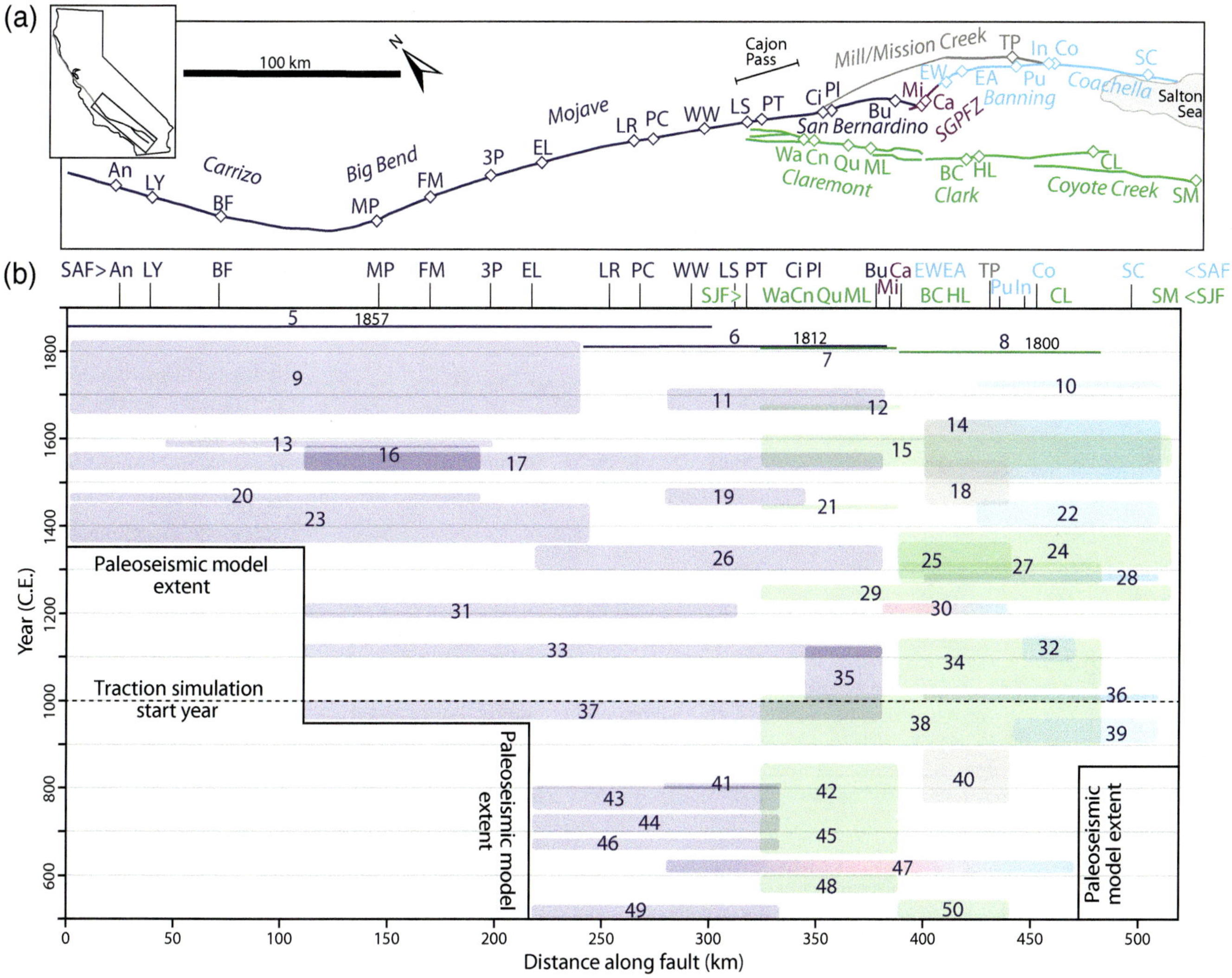

Figure 1. Maximum rupture model modified from Scharer and Yule (2020). (a) Map showing the southern San Andreas and San Jacinto fault system and locations of paleoseismic sites. Inset map shows location of panel (a) map in California. (b) Modeled rupture history. Colors same as in panel a map. Horizontal length indicates rupture extent, and height indicates timing uncertainty. Blue numbers correspond to earthquake rupture ID in Scharer and Yule (2020). Historical earthquakes are labeled with the year in which they occurred. Paleoseismic site abbreviations: An, Annette (Williams *et al.*, 2018); BC, Blackburn Canyon (Salisbury *et al.*, 2017); BF, Bidart Fan (Akçiz *et al.*, 2010); Bu, Burro Flats (Howland, 2003; Yule *et al.*, 2007); Ca, Cabazon (Ramzan, 2012; Wolff, 2018); Ci, City Creek (McGill *et al.*, 2002); CL, Clark Lake (Buga, 2012); Cn, Colton (Kendrick and Fumal, 2005); Co, Coachella (Philibosian *et al.*, 2011); EA, 18th Avenue (Castillo *et al.*, 2021); EL, Elizabeth Lake (Bemis *et al.*, 2021); EW, East Whitewater Wash (Cardona, 2016); FM, Frazier Mountain (Scharer *et al.*, 2017); HL, Hog Lake (Rockwell *et al.*, 2015); In, Indio (Sieh, 1986); LR, Littlerock (Pruitt *et al.*, 2009); LS, Lost Swamp (Weldon and Sieh, 1985); LY, Las Yeguas (Young *et al.*, 2002); Mi, Millard Canyon (McBurnett, 2011); ML, Mystic Lake (Onderdonk *et al.*, 2018); MP, Mil Potrero (Davis, 1983); PC, Pallett Creek (Sieh *et al.*, 1989; Scharer *et al.*, 2011); Pl, Plunge Creek (McGill *et al.*, 2002); PT, Pitman Canyon (Seitz *et al.*, 1997; Weldon *et al.*, 2013); Pu, Pushawalla Creek (Earth Systems Southwest, 2007); Qu, Quincy (Onderdonk *et al.*, 2015); SC, Salt Creek (Seitz and Williams, 2008); SM, Superstition Mountain (Gurrola and Rockwell, 1996); TP, Thousand Palms (Fumal, Rymer, and Seitz, 2002); Wa, Walnut (Fumal and Kendrick, 2008); WW, Wrightwood (Biasi *et al.*, 2002; Weldon *et al.*, 2004); and 3P, three points (Rust, 2005).

southern California, where faults are nonplanar and intersecting (e.g., Herbert and Cooke, 2012; Fattaruso *et al.*, 2014; Beyer *et al.*, 2018; Dorsett *et al.*, 2019; Hatch *et al.*, 2020; Devine *et al.*, 2022). These BEM models only have elements along fault surfaces, rather than a discretized mesh for the whole model volume. Therefore, the model can capture complex fault geometries using a smaller total number of elements than other methods, which makes the models quick and feasible for the Monte Carlo approach that we use to assess uncertainties.

Three-dimensional fault mesh

The fault mesh of the model is based on the Statewide California Earthquake Center's Community Fault Model (SCEC CFM) version 4.0 (Plesch *et al.*, 2007; Nicholson *et al.*, 2017), including nine active segments of the southern San Andreas and San Jacinto faults and 42 nearby active faults because interaction of these faults with the San Andreas and San Jacinto faults impacts slip rates and shear traction accumulation rates. The model of this study includes the San Andreas fault from the Carrizo segment to the Coachella segment along the Salton Sea, the Claremont, Clark, and Coyote Creek segments of the

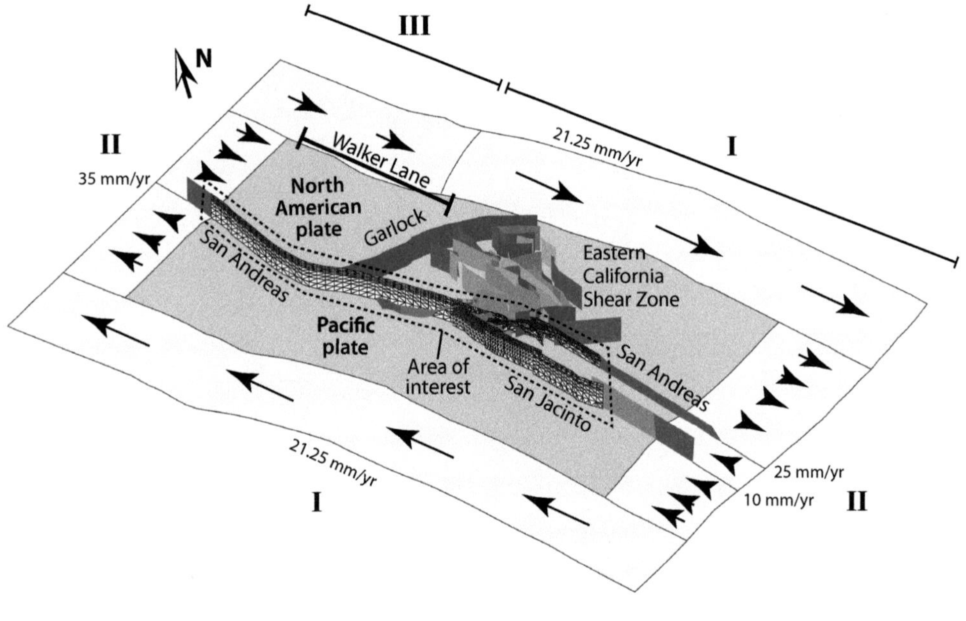

Figure 2. Oblique view of the model from the southwest. Faults shown in color participate only in the geologic and interseismic models and are not included in the traction evolution simulation. Colors serve only to help visually distinguish individual faults and do not carry any specific meaning. On the sides labeled I, we apply half the plate motion parallel to the plate boundary. The section labeled III on the North American plate side has a linear gradient in velocity (decreasing northward) to account for plate motion taken up in the Walker Lane, which is not included in our model. Sections labeled II have a linear gradient in velocity across the plate boundary, with steps in displacement associated with the slip rates applied to endmost portions of faults. In the steady state model, the basal crack (shown in gray) and the faults above it slip freely in response to the applied plate motion. The color version of this figure is available only in the electronic edition.

San Jacinto fault, and faults of the Eastern California shear zone south of the Garlock fault (Fig. 2). Following Herbert and Cooke (2012), Fattaruso *et al.* (2014), and Beyer *et al.* (2018), we use a modified version of the SCEC CFM fault geometry in the San Gorgonio Pass region to improve the match between fault slip rates and uplift patterns in the model with geologic estimates. We built the fault model mesh using Petex MOVE software and discretized active faults from the CFM into triangular elements with a mean size of ~4 km, which allows the model to capture the complex topology of curved, dipping, and branched active faulting in the San Gorgonio Pass region. We extend the CFM faults defined within the seismogenic crust to 35 km depth, where they merge with a horizontal basal crack; the extended portion of the faults and the basal crack prevent fault slip from tapering to zero at the base of the seismogenic crust and represent deep interseismic deformation below the locking depth of the faults (e.g., Marshall *et al.*, 2009). Following other stress evolution models (e.g., Smith-Konter and Sandwell, 2009; Verdecchia and Carena, 2016; Bagge *et al.*, 2019; Verdecchia *et al.*, 2019), the model has laterally uniform material properties; the Young's modulus of 30 GPa and Poisson's ratio of 0.25 are typical of upper-crustal sedimentary and metamorphic rocks (Birch, 1966).

Estimating interseismic stressing rates

To estimate interseismic stressing rates along active-fault surfaces, we use a two-step backslip approach after Marshall *et al.* (2009), in which we first model steady-state deformation over many earthquake cycles in response to tectonic loading, then apply the resulting slip rates below a locking depth in the second step to simulate stressing rates during the interseismic period. For the steady state model, we apply tectonic loading at the distal edges of the basal crack, which extends far from the active faults to reduce boundary effects that arise near the applied loading. We permit faults to slip freely in response to tectonic loading; free slip simulates low dynamic friction on faults during earthquakes (e.g., DiToro *et al.*, 2006; Goldsby and Tullis, 2011). The inner portion of the horizontal crack also remains friction-free to facilitate the distribution of deformation along faults. We apply a velocity of 42.5 mm/yr at an azimuth of 322.5, which is ~5 mm/yr slower than plate boundary estimates of 45–50 mm/yr from geodetic studies (e.g., DeMets *et al.*, 2010); this reduction accounts for deformation taken up by faults to the west of the San Andreas and San Jacinto faults that are not included in the model (Herbert and Cooke, 2012). We also use a gradient in displacement along the northeastern margin of the model to account for ~7 mm/yr of plate motion taken up by the Walker Lane faults to the north of the Garlock fault and east of the San Andreas fault (Fig. S1, available in the supplemental material to this article; Sandwell *et al.*, 2016), which we do not include in the model. Because Poly3d directly applies slip but not displacement to the elements, we use an iterative approach to ensure that applied displacements at the model margins are consistent with the desired plate rates (Beyer *et al.*, 2018; Dorsett *et al.*, 2019; Hatch *et al.*, 2020). Where active faults reach the lateral bounds of the model, we apply slip rates to prevent fault slip rates from tapering to zero: 35 mm/yr of strike slip on the northwestern end of the San Andreas fault, 10 mm/yr of strike slip on the southern San Jacinto fault, 25 mm/yr of strike slip on the southern San Andreas fault, and 1.4 mm/yr of dip slip on the western Cucamonga fault (Fig. 2; Sharp, 1981; Becker *et al.*, 2005; Fay and Humphreys, 2005; Meade and Hager, 2005; Dorsett *et al.*, 2019; McPhillips and Scharer, 2023). The choice of lateral boundary slip rates for this model setup has little effect on slip rates within the region of interest: applying equal 17.5 mm/yr lateral boundary slip rates to the San Jacinto and southern San Andreas faults changes their slip rates within the model by only 1 and 2 mm/yr, respectively (Fattaruso *et al.*, 2014). The steady-state geologic model produces long-term slip rates; we apply these slip rates below a 20 km locking depth, and half the slip rates in a transition zone from 20 to 17.5 km depth (Cooke and Beyer, 2018). Locking depths of 20 km best match Global Positioning System (GPS) velocities in the region (Herbert *et al.*, 2014). This interseismic model set up produces linear elastic stressing rates for the upper 15 km of the San Andreas and San Jacinto faults.

Simulating evolving tractions

We simulate the interseismic shear traction accumulation and coseismic release history only along faults comprising the San Andreas and San Jacinto system (faults shown in white elemental mesh in Fig. 2). We subdivide these faults into patches corresponding to each paleoseismic site, with the along-strike boundaries at the halfway point between sites. We simulate the earthquake history from 1000 C.E., the earliest time for which most of the system has a robust paleoseismic record, to 1900 C.E., capturing the 1857 Fort Tejon earthquake, which is the most recent very large earthquake on the system. For this analysis and in the absence of information about fault tractions before 1000 C.E., we assume that the stress drop at each site in its last earthquake before 1000 C.E. was complete, leaving the faults with zero shear traction after that earthquake. The complete stress-drop assumption is supported by estimates of pre- and post-earthquake deviatoric stress tensors (e.g., Wesson and Boyd, 2007) and temperature anomalies (Fulton *et al.*, 2013), and is common in models of traction evolution (e.g., Smith-Konter and Sandwell, 2009; Bagge *et al.*, 2019). For areas north of Mil Potrero on the San Andreas fault and for the Coyote Creek strand of the San Jacinto fault, where the paleoseismic data do not extend far enough back in time to capture a pre-1000 C.E. earthquake, we begin accumulation from zero traction at the time of earthquakes 37 and 38, respectively (Fig. 1).

For each year in the simulation, we calculate the accumulated shear traction from tectonic loading based on the stressing rate and the time elapsed since the previous earthquake (e.g., Smith-Konter and Sandwell, 2009; Hatch *et al.*, 2020). For elastic simulations, this traction is simply the interseismic stressing rate multiplied by the elapsed time since the last earthquake. For the viscoelastic models, we adjust the elastic shear stress accumulation rate to account for relaxation of stresses in the upper crust. We calculate the modified shear traction (t) according to the method of Duan and Oglesby (2005), recast to use linear elastic stressing rate rather than strain rate:

$$\tau(t) = \left(\tau_0 - \eta\frac{\dot{\tau}}{\mu}\right)e^{-\frac{\mu}{\eta}t} + \eta\frac{\dot{\tau}}{\mu}, \qquad (1)$$

in which t is the time elapsed since the last earthquake in the system, τ_0 is the shear traction immediately after the last earthquake, $\dot{\tau}$ is the shear stressing rate from the linear elastic model, and η is the viscosity. A variety of processes, including microcracking and pressure solution creep, may contribute to stress relaxation in the upper crust (Elliott, 1976), but the effective viscosity based on these processes is generally not well constrained for upper-crustal conditions. We use viscosities of 10^{19}–10^{21} Pa · s for the upper crust based on laboratory experiments of pressure solution creep in quartz and calcite (Rutter, 1976; Johnson, 2018); studies of deflection of granite beams (Itô, 1979); crustal scale estimates from folded regions (Gratier and Gamond, 1990), and modeling of lithospheric rheology based on lacustrine shoreline deformation (Bills *et al.*, 1994). The viscosity used in the models of this study also captures stress reduction from earthquakes that are too small to rupture the ground surface and so are not preserved in the paleoseismic record.

We calculate the accumulated shear traction in each year at each element by calculating the traction accrued since its last earthquake and adding the effects of nearby earthquakes that have occurred on the fault system since its last earthquake. For each earthquake, we apply a stress drop, equivalent to its accumulated shear traction at the time of the earthquake, to each element in the rupture patch above 15 km depth and allow the fault below 15 km depth to slip freely. The stress drop resets shear tractions on the rupture patch to zero and produces slip on the rupture patch, which in turn causes traction changes on the locked elements of surrounding fault segments that do not participate in the earthquake. Where earthquake ruptures extend to the edge of the area modeled by Scharer and Yule (2020), we also allow the immediately adjacent fault patch to slip freely due to the absence of information about whether the rupture extent continues beyond the area considered in Scharer and Yule (2020). For each earthquake, we use the timing and lateral rupture extent from the paleoseismic record described by Scharer and Yule (2020), with a few minor changes. We assume that earthquakes that rupture the Mojave section of the San Andreas fault before ~1350 C.E. also rupture the adjacent Carrizo section, which lacks paleoseismic data during this time period; this rupture pattern is similar to the pattern of more recent earthquakes in this area. For earthquakes that rupture the Banning strand of the San Andreas fault in this chronology, we also release tractions on the Garnet Hill strand because these faults merge at ~5 km depth and may slip together (Yule and Sieh, 2003; Gold *et al.*, 2015). We assume that the Walnut site, which has an incomplete record, ruptures along with the neighboring Colton site (Kendrick and Fumal, 2005; Fumal and Kendrick, 2008). Finally, we treat the 1812 earthquake (events 6 and 7 on the San Andreas and San Jacinto faults, respectively, in Scharer and Yule, 2020; Fig. 1) as a single event (Lozos, 2016; Rodriguez Padilla *et al.*, 2021). We only model events on the San Andreas and San Jacinto faults because we have a suitable record of past earthquakes only on these faults.

Monte Carlo simulations

Stochastic simulations of evolving traction histories allow us to explore the impact of uncertainties in both earthquake timing and crustal viscosity on shear tractions. Each Monte Carlo simulation includes 100 realizations. For assessment of earthquake timing uncertainty, we sample from a boxcar distribution using the rupture age ranges from Scharer and Yule (2020) for each of the earthquakes during the simulation timeframe, as well as for the pre-1000 C.E. earthquakes from which we calculate the tractions for the start of the simulation at 1000 C.E. In the simulations that assess earthquake age uncertainty, we simulate both an elastic and a viscoelastic crustal rheology with a midrange upper-crustal viscosity of 10^{20} Pa · s. For uncertainty in the crustal viscosity, we sample the exponent of the viscosity from a Gaussian distribution with a mean of 20 ($\eta = 10^{20}$ Pa · s) and a standard deviation of 0.5, and use the midpoint rupture age for each earthquake.

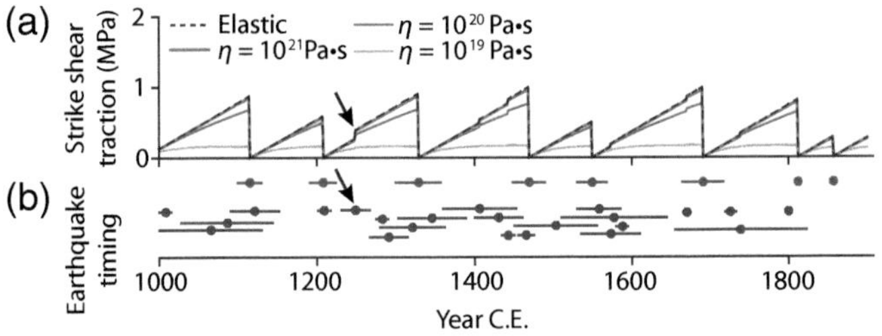

Figure 3. (a) Evolution of tractions through time at the Wrightwood site using midpoint timing and elastic and a variety of viscoelastic rheologies. Arrows indicate the increase in shear traction due to the ~1250 C.E. earthquake on the San Jacinto fault. (b) Earthquake timing from Scharer and Yule (2020). Red dots show earthquakes that rupture the site, and blue dots show earthquakes elsewhere in the system. The color version of this figure is available only in the electronic edition.

RESULTS

In the following sections, we explore the shear traction evolution through time at individual sites, test the validity of the results by comparing average slip per event with geologic estimates, and investigate the value and spatial pattern of pre-earthquake tractions on rupture patches throughout the fault system.

Shear tractions through time at sites

The shear traction evolution at specific sites shows overall patterns of traction evolution, including the contributions of interseismic stressing and nearby earthquakes. To investigate traction evolution at particular paleoseismic sites, we examine shear traction through time on an element at 10 km depth below the surface location of the site. We use the Wrightwood site as an example site because (1) it is in the middle of the model area and thus not vulnerable to edge effects, (2) it experiences many earthquakes during the simulated timeframe, and (3) it shows patterns of shear traction accumulation and release that are typical of many (but not all) sites in the region. Figure 3 shows four example strike shear traction accumulation histories for the Wrightwood site, each using the midpoint earthquake timing and either an elastic or one of a variety of viscoelastic crustal rheologies. Interseismic stress accumulation and earthquakes that rupture through the site have the greatest effects on shear tractions, whereas earthquakes elsewhere only make small changes to tractions at the site (arrow in Fig. 3). The amount of shear traction that accumulates due to interseismic stressing strongly depends on the effective crustal viscosity. The results of the highest viscosity simulation ($\eta = 10^{21}$ Pa · s) are nearly indistinguishable from the elastic results and produce maximum accumulated shear tractions at the Wrightwood site of ~1 MPa, whereas the lowest viscosity simulation ($\eta = 10^{19}$ Pa · s) scarcely allows any shear traction to accumulate at the site.

A few paleoseismic sites show atypical shear traction accumulation patterns. Some sites accumulate unusually high shear tractions due to unusually long intervals between earthquakes (e.g., Pallett Creek and Indio; Fig. 1 and Fig. S2), and two sites briefly experience sinistral shear tractions due to the effects of nearby earthquakes on parallel fault strands. For example, at the Pushawalla site, sinistral tractions arise due to earthquake 18 on the Mission Creek strand of the San Andreas fault, and at the Burro Flats site, sinistral tractions occur following earthquake 15, which included rupture of the Claremont strand of the San Jacinto fault (Fig. 1 and Fig. S2). Both of these sites had ruptured shortly before the nearby earthquakes on parallel strands, so the traction reduction from the nearby earthquake was greater than the accumulated dextral shear traction (Fig. 1 and Fig. S2). Although these traction patterns are uncommon among the sites in the simulations, we have no independent evidence that these patterns are inherently unreasonable.

Model validation: Average slip per event

We validate the simulations by comparing the model average surface slip per event at each paleoseismic site with the average slip per event calculated from slip rate and recurrence interval by Scharer and Yule (2020; Fig. 4). A few sites south of Cajon Pass rupture in fewer than five earthquakes since 1000 C.E., and therefore likely do not display their full range of earthquake behavior during this time interval (Styron, 2019). We exclude these sites from Figure 4b,c. The elastic and highest viscosity models generally produce average surface slip per event that is consistent with geologic estimates, with the best match along the Mojave section of the San Andreas fault and along the San Jacinto fault where sites preserve robust records of many earthquakes (e.g., Fumal, Weldon, *et al.*, 2002; Weldon *et al.*, 2002; Scharer *et al.*, 2011; Rockwell *et al.*, 2015; Fig. 4a). In San Gorgonio Pass and along the San Bernardino and Coachella sections of the San Andreas fault, the model produces less average surface slip per event than that derived from geologic estimates at many locations. However, the

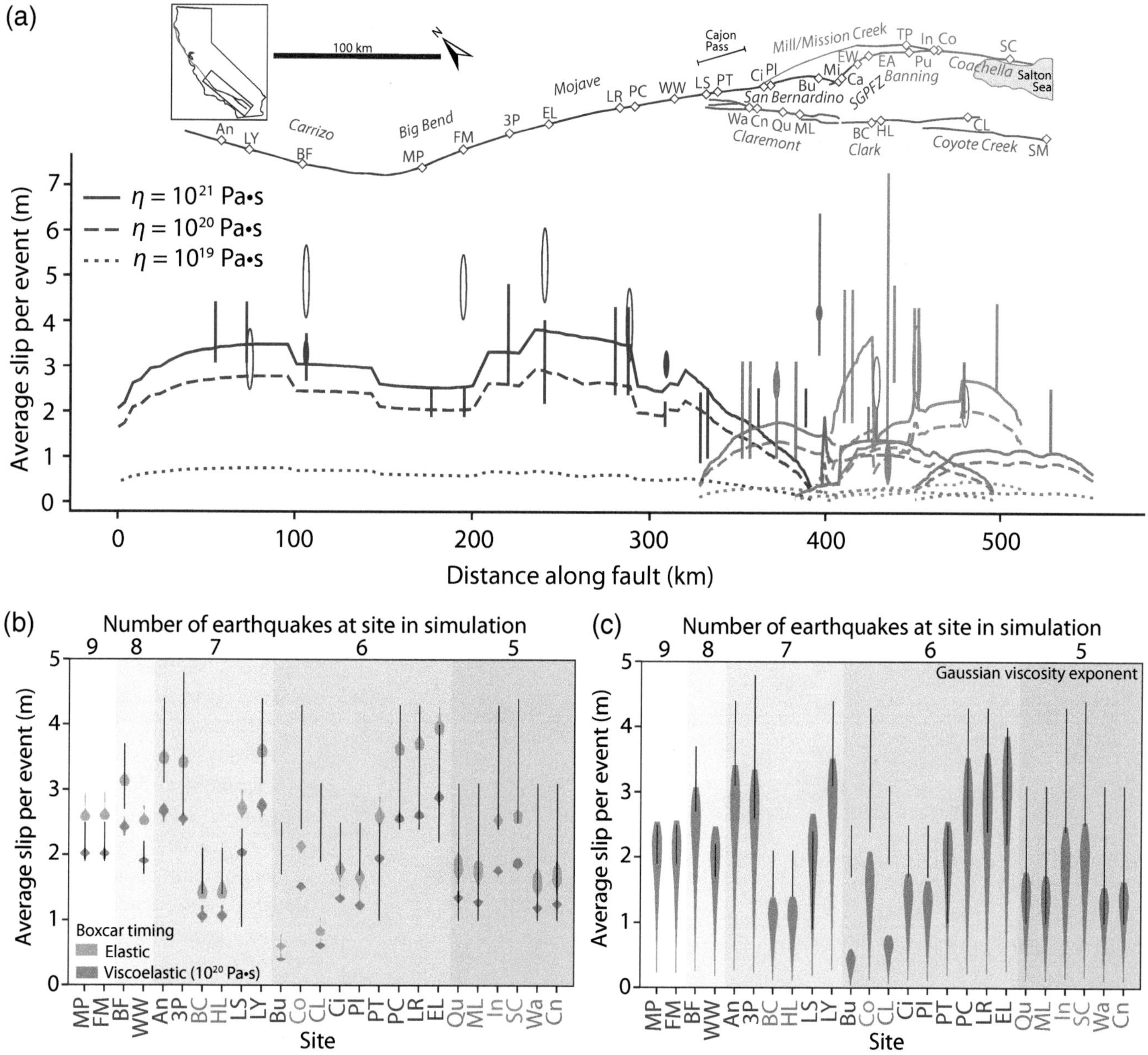

northernmost portion of the Banning strand of the San Andreas fault has much higher average surface slip per event than the southern part of this fault segment. The higher surface slip per event results from similar interseismic stressing rates but fewer earthquakes compared to neighboring sites to the south. Rupture age uncertainty has relatively small impact on the average surface slip per event for both the elastic and viscoelastic simulations, typically 0.2 m or less (Fig. 4b). Uncertainty in upper-crustal viscosity produces a range of average surface slip per event of well over 1 m for most sites, with only the upper part of the range overlapping with estimates from Scharer and Yule (2020; Fig. 4c). Because low-viscosity simulations ($\eta < 10^{20}$ Pa · s) do not reproduce geologic estimates of average surface slip per event, we exclude these scenarios when assessing pre-earthquake tractions.

Figure 4. (a) Plot of average slip per event along strike from viscoelastic simulations using midpoint earthquake timing. Solid, dashed, and dotted lines show estimates from the models; vertical bars show average slip per event calculated by Scharer and Yule (2020), estimated from slip rate and recurrence interval; filled ellipses show average slip per event from paleoseismic studies (Fumal, Rymer, and Seitz, 2002; Weldon *et al.*, 2004; Grant Ludwig *et al.*, 2010; Heermance and Yule, 2017); open ellipses show average slip per event from geomorphic studies (Salisbury *et al.*, 2012; Zielke *et al.*, 2012; Madden *et al.*, 2013). Colors correspond with fault and site map above plot, which is from Scharer and Yule (2020). Inset map shows location of panel (a) map in California. (b,c) Violin plots showing average slip per event at paleoseismic sites from elastic (blue) and viscoelastic (pink) timing uncertainty simulations (b) and viscosity uncertainty simulation (c), sorted by number of earthquakes that rupture the site in the simulated timeframe. The thickness of the violin shows the probability density of results. Sites with fewer than five earthquakes in the simulation are excluded. Site labels colored as for faults in panel (a). Vertical bars show average slip per event from Scharer and Yule (2020), estimated from slip rate and recurrence interval. The color version of this figure is available only in the electronic edition.

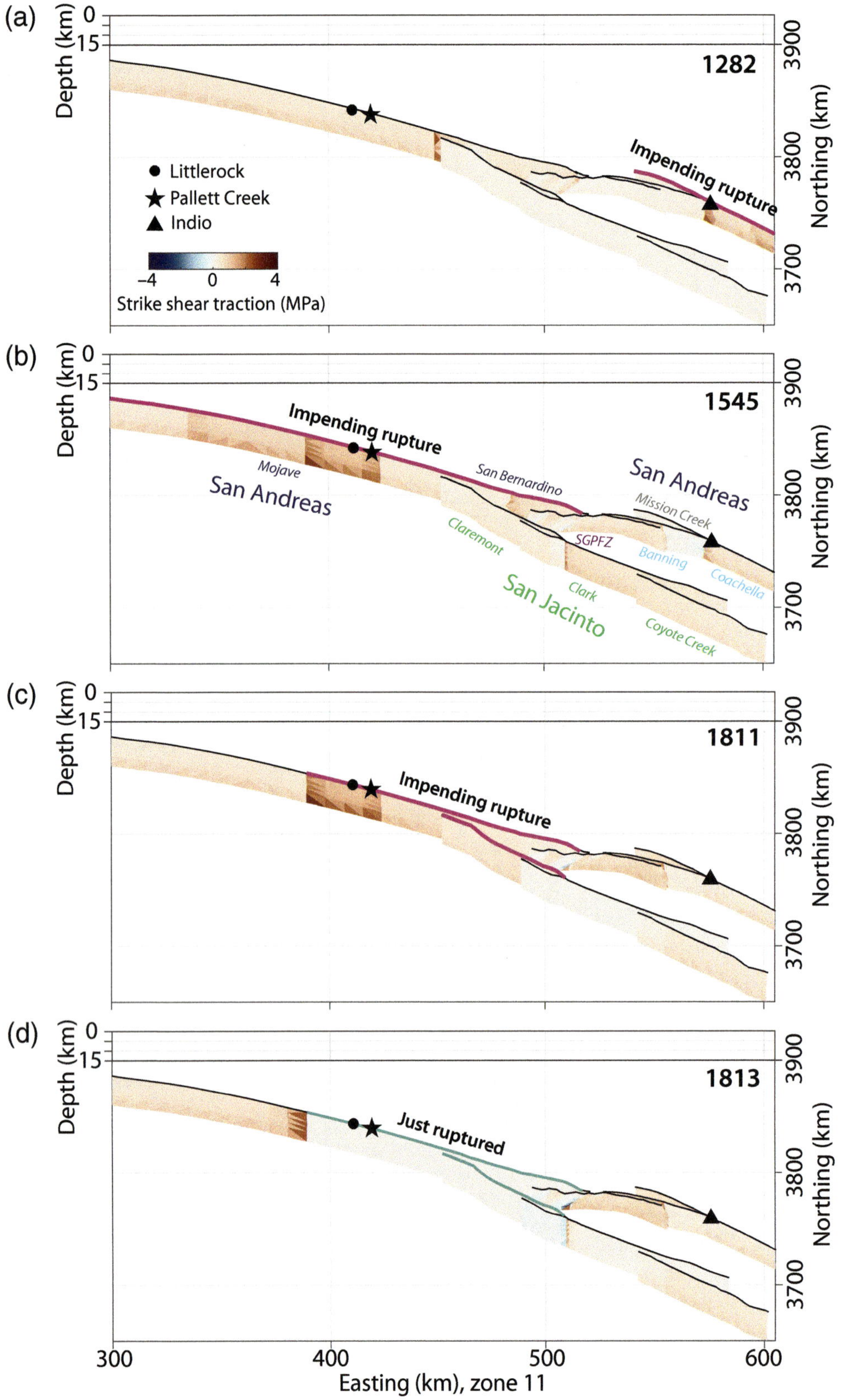

Figure 5. System-wide tractions for select years in simulation with midpoint earthquake timing and $\eta = 10^{20}$ Pa · s. (a) 1282, the year before earthquake 28; maximum tractions at Indio site. (b) 1545, the year before earthquake 17; high tractions near Pallett Creek. (c) 1811, the year before earthquakes 6 and 7 (the 1812 earthquake, with high tractions near Pallett Creek). (d) 1813, the year following the 1812 earthquake, showing traction changes on nearby parts of the faults. The full evolution of tractions is available in a supplemental animation.

Shear tractions throughout the system

The spatial patterns of traction accumulation and release provide useful context for comparing and interpreting traction evolution histories at individual sites (Fig. 5 and Fig. S3). Shear tractions are generally greater at depth than near the surface because stresses increase near the locking depth, where faults transition from locked to freely slipping. Earthquakes have the greatest effect on shear tractions along neighboring fault sections within ~20 km of the lateral rupture endpoints (Fig. 5d). Furthermore, ruptures generally occur in parts of the system where accumulated tractions are high due to a long elapsed time since their previous rupture, rather than in low-traction areas that have ruptured more recently. There are several exceptions to this pattern. The Mojave segment of the San Andreas fault that hosts the Pallett Creek and Littlerock sites twice develops substantially greater tractions than the rest of the system: once leading up to earthquake 17 (Fig. 1) in the late 1500s, and again in the period between that earthquake and the 1812 earthquake, which ruptures this section as well as the San Bernardino strand of the San Andreas fault and the Claremont strand of the San Jacinto fault (Fig. 5c,d). A smaller fault patch near the Indio site on the Coachella section of the San Andreas fault also develops notably greater tractions than nearby fault sections and maintains these tractions without rupturing for ~200 yr (Fig. 5a). In both of these high-traction areas, long-time intervals between events coincide with shorter intervals

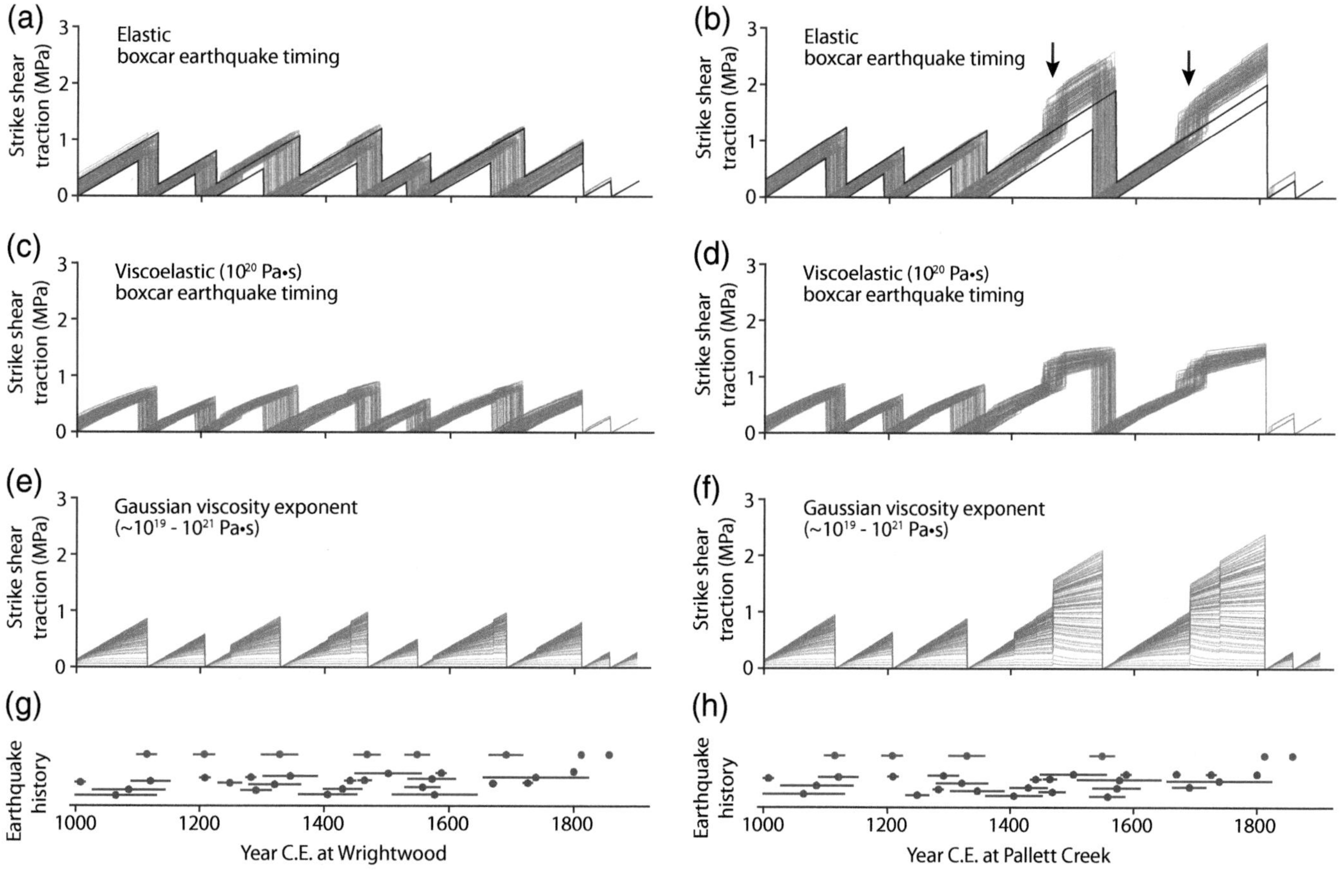

Figure 6. Monte Carlo simulations at (a,c,e,g) the Wrightwood site and (b,d,f,h) the Pallett Creek site. (a,b) Elastic simulation varying earthquake timing. Each gray line is a Monte Carlo realization; black lines show the envelope of accumulated tractions based only on earthquakes that rupture the site shown. Black arrows indicate traction increases at the Pallett Creek site caused by nearby earthquakes. (c,d) Viscoelastic simulation ($\eta = 10^{20}$ Pa · s) varying earthquake timing. (e,f) Viscoelastic simulation using midpoint earthquake timing and varying viscosity. (g,h) Earthquake histories from Scharer and Yule (2020); red dots show earthquakes that rupture the site, and blue dots show earthquakes elsewhere in the system. The color version of this figure is available only in the electronic edition.

on neighboring fault sections, so that tractions accumulate both due to interseismic stressing and nearby earthquakes.

Shear traction uncertainties through stochastic simulations

We use Monte Carlo simulations to explore how uncertainties in earthquake ages and crustal viscosity impact estimates of strike shear tractions (Fig. 6). We highlight the Pallett Creek site alongside the Wrightwood site because the two sites show notably different patterns of shear traction accumulation despite their proximity (~25 km apart). For the elastic simulations, we analytically construct an envelope that captures the limits of uncertainty in traction due to age uncertainty for earthquakes that rupture through the site. Both the upper and lower bounds of this envelope represent composites of multiple possible earthquake timing histories. The minimum tractions (zero) occur during time spans in which the site ruptures (earthquake time ranges marked in red in Figs. 3b and 6d,h). During the interseismic periods, evolving shear tractions follow the lower bound of the envelope if the previous earthquake at the site occurred at the end of its possible time span. In contrast, evolving shear tractions follow the upper bound of the envelope if the previous earthquake occurred at the beginning of its time span, maximizing the time for shear traction accrual. Thus, for the elastic simulation, the traction uncertainty during the interseismic period is equal to the product of the traction accumulation rate and the previous earthquake's timing uncertainty. In the viscoelastic simulation, the range of shear tractions narrows during each interseismic interval as the nonlinear rate of interseismic traction accumulation decreases.

Nearby earthquakes modulate the accumulated shear tractions at each site. Instances when Monte Carlo realizations appear outside of the envelope highlight when events elsewhere in the system have a significant impact on tractions at the site. For any given nearby earthquake, the amount of deviation from the envelope is slightly greater when this event happens later in its own interseismic time span because at the end of the time span, the nearby segment has accrued greater shear traction, which produces a greater stress drop for the earthquake. At the Wrightwood site, the effect of nearby earthquakes is generally small—less than 0.2 MPa at most—but the Pallett Creek site experiences more substantial traction changes of

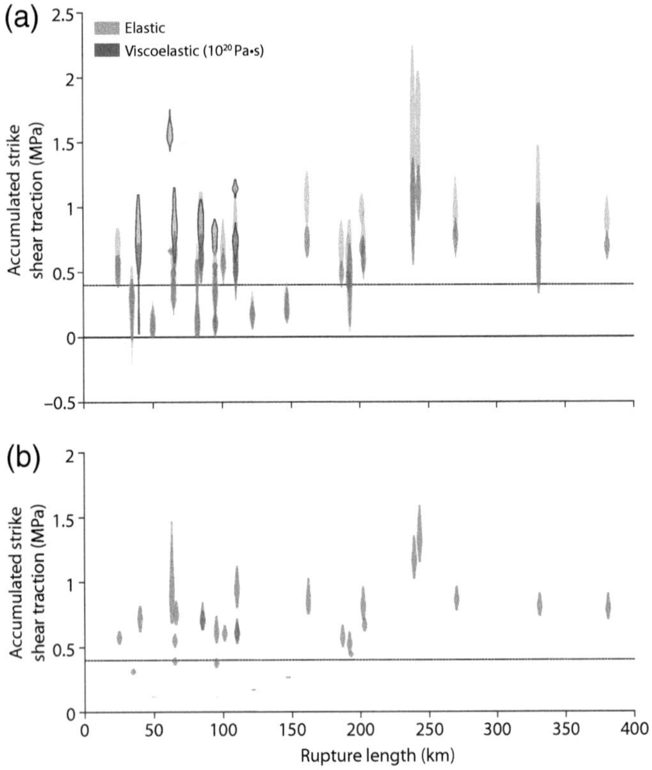

Figure 7. Pre-earthquake tractions from (a) timing uncertainty and (b) viscosity uncertainty ($\eta \geq 10^{20}$ Pa · s using midpoint earthquake timing) simulations plotted against earthquake rupture length. Elastic simulations are shown in blue and viscoelastic in pink. Elastic simulation violins for earthquakes highlighted in Figure 8 are outlined in black. Violin thickness represents the probability density of results. The dashed line shows a minimum ~0.4 MPa traction threshold for earthquakes with rupture length >200 km. The color version of this figure is available only in the electronic edition.

~0.5 MPa, which is comparable to the magnitude of the stress drop of some earthquakes at the site and substantially increases the traction uncertainty (Fig. 6). The greater traction changes at the Pallet Creek site arise from its proximity to the endpoints of several nearby earthquakes, including two that rupture Wrightwood but end before reaching Pallett Creek. In contrast, the Wrightwood site has no nearby earthquake endpoints located within 20 km of the site (Fig. 1).

We also vary the viscosity while keeping the earthquake rupture ages constant, using the midpoints of the age ranges (Fig. 6c,g). The stochastic realizations with a Gaussian distribution of viscosity fill in the range between the highest and lowest viscosity simulations, clustering toward the higher traction end of the range. Effective crustal viscosity is the least well-constrained parameter in the models and the greatest source of traction uncertainty in the shear traction simulations.

Pre-earthquake shear tractions

For each ground-rupturing earthquake event in the Scharer and Yule (2020) model, we calculate the area-weighted average shear traction on the rupture patch in the year before the event for each Monte Carlo realization (Fig. 7). For the elastic simulations with varied earthquake timing, pre-earthquake shear tractions overall range from near zero to ~2.25 MPa, though for most earthquakes the maximum is ~1.25 MPa or less, and the uncertainty for most individual earthquakes does not exceed ~0.5 MPa. Pre-earthquake shear tractions in the viscoelastic ($\eta = 10^{20}$ Pa · s) timing simulation only reach a maximum of ~1.3 MPa, and individual earthquakes have a smaller range of shear tractions than in the elastic simulation, especially for events with higher average pre-earthquake shear tractions. In both elastic and viscoelastic timing uncertainty simulations, earthquakes with shorter rupture lengths (<200 km) have a wide range of minimum pre-earthquake shear tractions (from near zero to ~1.4 MPa), but ruptures longer than 200 km typically do not have pre-earthquake shear tractions of less than ~0.4 MPa. The rupture length varies with location in the fault system; longer ruptures occur north of Cajon Pass where faults are single stranded, whereas shorter ruptures primarily occur south of Cajon Pass where active faults have branches and multiple strands (Fig. 8b). Although we might expect short ruptures (length < 125 km) to have smaller pre-earthquake shear tractions, events 8, 18, 19, 22, 28, 30, and 36 (for maps and event numbers, see Fig. 1) have tractions greater than 0.5 MPa and ruptured within the most structurally complex parts of the system: near Cajon Pass, where there is a stepover between the San Andreas and San Jacinto faults; San Gorgonio Pass, where the San Andreas fault branches into northern and southern slip pathways; and the Clark segment of the San Jacinto fault, which is bounded by stepovers to the Claremont and Coyote sections (Fig. 8).

DISCUSSION

Here, we evaluate several additional sources of uncertainty in the modeled traction histories that are not explicitly considered in the stochastic analysis, discuss the potential effects of normal tractions on earthquake occurrence, and discuss implications of past pre-earthquake shear tractions for earthquake hazard assessment. Because the models assume complete shear stress drop during ground-rupturing earthquakes, the tractions reported are minimum estimates. If faults have temporally and spatially consistent residual shear strength, the total shear traction would be that residual strength plus the shear traction modeled here. The consideration of nonuniform residual strength or incomplete stress drop in earthquakes could lead to greater variability in pre-earthquake tractions and is beyond the scope of this article. Our aim here is to evaluate sources of uncertainty in shear traction changes, identify patterns that could inform earthquake mechanics, and inform initial conditions for potential dynamic rupture simulations.

Uncertainties affecting the stressing rate

Uncertainties in tectonic loading rate, loading orientation, and fault geometry can impact estimates of fault slip rate and

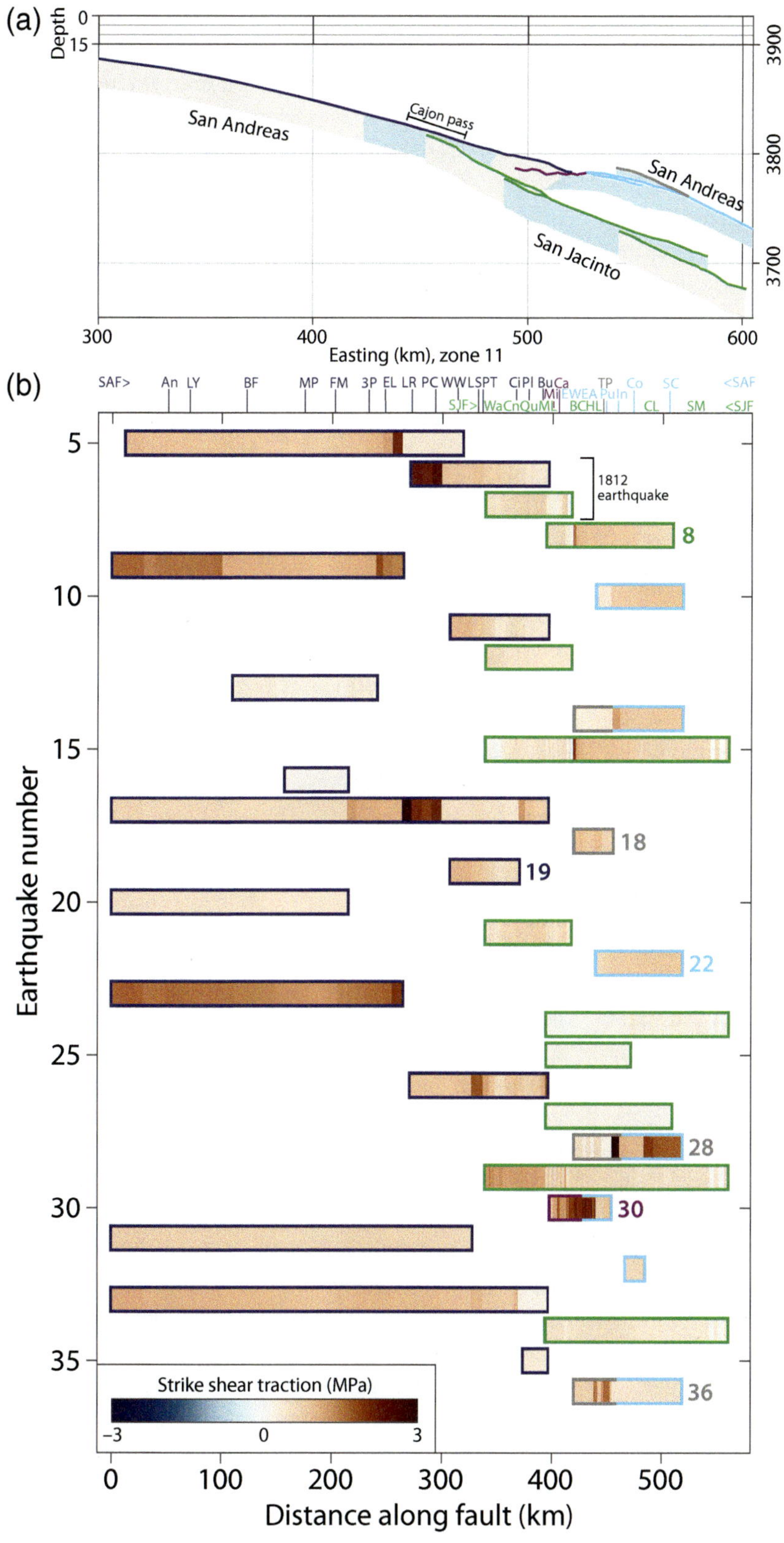

Figure 8. (a) Map showing in blue locations experiencing short rupture length (<125 km), high pre-earthquake traction (>0.5 MPa) earthquakes. Surface traces shown in colors corresponding to the map in Figure 1. (b) Pre-earthquake tractions at 10 km depth for the elastic model using midpoint earthquake timing. Bar outline colors and earthquake numbers correspond with the map in Figure 1; only earthquakes with short rupture length and high pre-earthquake traction are labeled with rupture numbers.

therefore interseismic stressing rates. The plate motion rate and orientation we use are in the middle of the 45–50 mm/yr at 320°–325° azimuth range from geodetic studies (e.g., DeMets *et al.*, 2010). Previous work has shown that greater rates and a more northerly orientation of plate motion generally increase strike-slip rates along the San Andreas fault system and corresponding interseismic stressing rates, and a slower rate or more westerly orientation generally decreases strike-slip rates and stressing rates (Herbert and Cooke, 2012). Overall, however, the total range of uncertainty in strike-slip rates from different tectonic loading rates and orientations is small (<6%), especially compared to spatial variability in slip rates that arises from fault geometry (e.g., Herbert and Cooke, 2012; Beyer *et al.*, 2018). Although using a different rate or orientation of tectonic loading may alter traction accumulation rates, this source of uncertainty is relatively small and unlikely to change the overall patterns of shear traction accumulation and pre-earthquake tractions.

Another source of uncertainty affecting slip rate and, therefore, stressing rate is the uncertainty in which strands of the San Andreas fault are active in the San Gorgonio Pass area. Here, the San Andreas fault branches into two strands: a southern branch, including the Banning and Garnet Hill strands of the San Andreas fault and the San Gorgonio Pass fault zone; and a northern branch, including the Mission Creek and Mill Creek strands of the San Andreas fault as well as the Galena Peak fault. These faults provide several plausible ways to distribute slip between strands (Beyer *et al.*, 2018) and several plausible earthquake rupture routes through this pathway (e.g., Douilly *et al.*, 2020; Tarnowski *et al.*, 2022). Of the faults of the northern branch, we include only the southern portion of the Mission Creek fault. Beyer *et al.* (2018) modeled six plausible active fault configurations in the San Gorgonio Pass area using a fault geometry for the region that is identical to that of this study, and found that excluding the northern pathway beyond the Mission Creek fault minimizes overall misfit between model and geologic slip rates in the system. While including an active northern branch beyond the Mission Creek fault in the geologic model could change slip rates along the southern pathway and the northern part of the San Jacinto fault by a few millimeters per year, slightly reducing the stressing rates on those faults (Beyer *et al.*, 2018), such a change would reduce the overall accuracy of the model.

The geometry of faults at depth is not well constrained in some parts of the San Andreas system. Variations in fault dip and/or connectivity, such as connecting the San Andreas and San Jacinto faults, have been shown to impact slip rates (Herbert and Cooke, 2012; Fattaruso *et al.*, 2014) and would likewise impact stressing rates. Because fault geometries become better resolved with additional geologic and geophysical data, shear traction estimates can be refined.

The effective viscosity of the upper crust is a substantial source of traction uncertainty in these models. Field studies commonly document processes such as pressure solution creep and cataclasis that are involved in stress relaxation (e.g., Elliott, 1976; Ismat and Mitra, 2005), but rarely attempt to quantify effective viscosity or do so only for the lower crust (e.g., Talbot, 1999). Many upper-crustal effective viscosity estimates hinge on the results of laboratory experiments, which generally investigate individual deformation processes in isolation and may not fully capture the bulk behavior of the crust at scale, and all estimates include several orders of magnitude of uncertainty (Rutter, 1976; Itô, 1979; Gratier and Gamond, 1990; Bills *et al.*, 1994; Johnson, 2018). The 10^{19}–10^{21} $\mathrm{Pa \cdot s}$ viscosities we use in these models, corresponding to stress relaxation times of ~26 to ~2600 yr in the upper crust, are within the lower range of some estimates of 10^{19}–10^{24} $\mathrm{Pa \cdot s}$ (Rutter, 1976; Johnson, 2018). The viscosity used in the models of this study includes the stress reduction impact of small and moderate earthquakes that do not rupture the ground surface. These earthquakes do not leave fingerprints in the paleoseismic record but can reduce accumulated shear tractions and are not considered in laboratory rock viscosity measurements. For this reason, the appropriate effective viscosity for the models of this study is less than some estimates (Rutter, 1976; Bills *et al.*, 1994; Johnson, 2018). Furthermore, effective crustal viscosities greater than 10^{21} $\mathrm{Pa \cdot s}$ would be essentially indistinguishable from the elastic simulations (Figs. 3 and 6) because earthquake recurrence times for most parts of the San Andreas fault system are short relative to the relaxation times. Because the simulations with effective crustal viscosity $<10^{20}$ $\mathrm{Pa \cdot s}$ result in very little accumulated traction and much less average slip per event than the geologic estimates throughout the modeled area, the upper-crustal viscosity throughout this region is likely at least 10^{20} $\mathrm{Pa \cdot s}$. Although spatial variability in lithologies could produce heterogeneous effective viscosity in the region, this variability is likely small relative to the uncertainty of upper-crustal effective viscosities overall.

The simulations of this study do not consider postseismic viscoelastic relaxation in the lower crust and mantle, which can continue to modify fault tractions on the rupture patch and surrounding faults over a time period of years to a few decades, at rates that can temporarily exceed interseismic stressing (e.g., Harris, 1998; Pollitz and Sacks, 2002; Pollitz *et al.*, 2022). Although postseismic stress transfer has been shown to trigger or delay rupture on nearby faults (e.g., Ziv and Rubin, 2000; Orlecka-Sikora, 2010), the traction changes are typically small compared to coseismic stress release, representing small changes to the earthquake clock (e.g., Pollitz and Sacks, 2002; Verdecchia and Carena, 2016); triggering requires that the faults are already near failure (e.g., Gomberg *et al.*, 1998; Harris and Simpson, 1998). At many sites in the simulations of this study, uncertainties of earthquake timing and crustal viscosity are larger than the potential impacts of postseismic stress transfer.

Uncertainties in the earthquake record

The traction evolution histories of several sites highlight areas where uncertainties in the paleoseismic record and the interpreted extent of earthquakes may affect shear traction accumulation in the simulations. For example, the Indio site accumulates much greater shear tractions than nearby sites by the end of the 1200s, both due to a long interval between events as well as proximity to the endpoints of nearby earthquakes; these conditions cause the sharp peak in average slip per event near this location (Figs. 5, 4, and Fig. S2). This may reflect uncertainty in earthquake ages; for example, changes to paleoearthquake timing at the Coachella site proposed by Hill *et al.* (2023) would shorten the interval and remove a nearby rupture, likely reducing this high-traction patch. At Indio, the open interval from its most recent earthquake in ~1726 to the present day is also long, but has lower shear traction than the previous long interval (Fig. S2) because the recent open interval did not have recent events nearby to increase shear traction. Alternatively, earthquakes before 1282 at the Indio site may be missing from the paleoseismic record due to intermittent deposition (Sieh, 1986); additional earthquakes at this and other sites could reduce the maximum accumulated shear tractions.

Other sources of uncertainty related to the paleoseismic record are the correlation of earthquakes between sites and the choice of rupture endpoints. The Scharer and Yule (2020) paleoseismic compilation is a maximum rupture model, which fits the longest possible earthquake ruptures to the

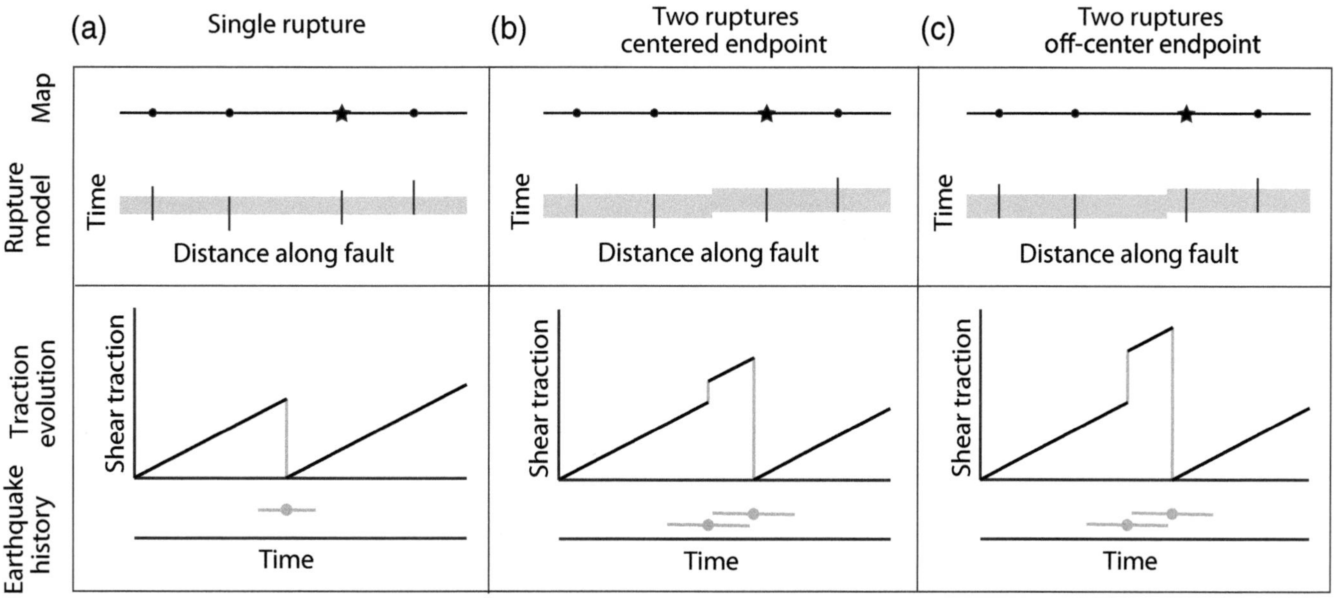

Figure 9. Schematic diagram showing effects of rupture model assumptions on traction evolution results for (a) a maximum rupture model, (b) a split rupture model with rupture endpoint at midpoint between sites, and (c) a split rupture model with off-center rupture endpoints. The map shows a fault section with four paleoseismic sites. Rupture history shows earthquake timing from paleoseismic sites (vertical black lines) and example rupture histories compatible with the paleoseismic data (colored rectangles). Traction evolution histories are shown for the starred site. The color version of this figure is available only in the electronic edition.

paleoseismic data, and ends ruptures halfway between sites; however, other earthquake histories and rupture endpoint choices are equally compatible with the paleoseismic data. Some ruptures, such as earthquakes 9 and 17 (Fig. 1), could be split into two shorter ruptures, each with similar timing uncertainty to the single, longer rupture of the original model. If a new rupture endpoint is chosen to be halfway between sites and the sites are far enough from the new endpoint, they will not be greatly impacted by increased stresses at the new rupture endpoint despite greater overall spatial variability in pre-earthquake shear tractions compared to a single throughgoing rupture (Fig. 9). If a new rupture endpoint is chosen closer to one of the sites rather than at the midpoint between them, this could cause a greater shear traction increase at the nearest site. Despite potentially differing shear traction evolution, distinguishing between one long versus two short ruptures from the paleoseismic record may be difficult if not impossible because these produce similar distributions of surface slip, especially if the endpoints of the two shorter ruptures overlap (Resor *et al.*, 2018). Considering the potential difference in shear traction evolution between different rupture models also highlights that using a maximum rupture model produces the lowest overall spatial traction variability and smoothest traction evolution histories at individual sites.

The traction evolution estimates along the southern Mojave section of the San Andreas fault at the Pallett Creek and Wrightwood sites illustrate the effects of paleoseismic model uncertainty, particularly well. Despite the proximity (~25 km) of these two sites, they have markedly different traction accumulation histories (Fig. 6). Bemis *et al.* (2021) propose two alternate possible rupture histories for the section of the San Andreas fault between the Bidart Fan and Pitman Canyon sites (Fig. 1), one which prefers rupture endpoints coinciding with hypothesized dip changes on the San Andreas fault, and the other which chooses arbitrary rupture endpoints. Both alternate models change the location of rupture endpoints relative to the Pallet Creek and Wrightwood sites, and have the potential to change the shear traction evolution histories at these neighboring sites.

The large accumulated shear tractions in the vicinity of the Pallett Creek site may have implications for the 1812 earthquake. Dynamic rupture models suggest that the 1812 earthquake likely began on the San Jacinto fault and propagated northward because this nucleation point produces ground-shaking motions that are most consistent with Spanish mission damage records and the locations of precariously balanced rocks (Lozos, 2016). Interestingly, in the simulations of this study, the northernmost portion of the 1812 earthquake rupture has much greater accumulated shear tractions than the rest of the rupture patch (ruptures 6 and 7 in Fig. 8b). If earthquakes tend to start in areas where accumulated shear tractions are greatest, these tractions would suggest that the earthquake began at the northern end of the rupture extent and propagated south and onto the San Jacinto fault; another possibility is that the earthquake did nucleate on the San Jacinto fault, and the high-traction area near the Pallett Creek site facilitated the northward propagation of the rupture onto the San Andreas fault. Finally, it is possible that the stress drop in 1812 was incomplete in this high-traction area, leaving residual traction on this section of fault and encouraging it to rupture again

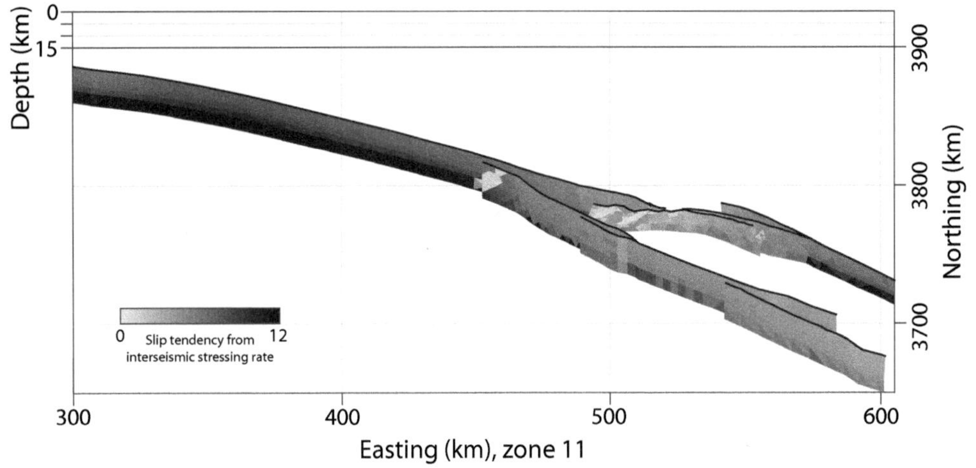

Figure 10. Slip tendency calculated from interseismic stressing rates. Higher slip tendency encourages rupture. The color version of this figure is available only in the electronic edition.

shortly afterward in the 1857 earthquake. Dynamic rupture models of the 1812 earthquake using initial tractions from the simulations of this study could help inform how spatial variability in traction may have influenced rupture extent and rupture propagation direction in this earthquake.

Effect of normal tractions

Although this study focuses on strike shear tractions, accumulated normal tractions may also influence earthquake behavior. For example, coseismic and postseismic normal traction changes can modify the Coulomb stress to advance or delay the earthquake clock on nearby faults (e.g., King *et al.*, 1994; Freed and Lin, 2002; Toda and Stein, 2020). Unlike shear tractions, normal tractions are not necessarily relieved during earthquakes, so the initial zero normal traction we use in these models may not reflect the actual normal traction on faults (Hatch *et al.*, 2020). This challenge is shared by dynamic rupture models, which commonly use either uniform initial normal traction (e.g., Kyriakopoulos *et al.*, 2017; Douilly *et al.*, 2020) or estimate it based on a ratio to shear traction given the present-day maximum principal stress direction (e.g., Aochi and Fukuyama, 2002; Lozos, 2016). We can assess how normal tractions might impact the earthquake history by calculating the slip tendency from interseismic traction accumulation rates for each fault element. The greater the slip tendency on an element, the less normal compression it experiences compared to shear traction, and the more likely it is to slip. We calculate slip tendency according to

$$T = \frac{|\dot{\tau}|}{\frac{\dot{\sigma}-\dot{\sigma}_{\min}}{\dot{\sigma}_{\max}-\dot{\sigma}_{\min}}}, \quad (2)$$

in which T is the slip tendency, $\dot{\tau}$ is the shear stressing rate, and $\dot{\sigma}$ is the compressive normal stressing rate, and $\dot{\sigma}_{\min}$ and $\dot{\sigma}_{\max}$ are the minimum and maximum normal-stressing rates, respectively, within the region of interest (e.g., Morris *et al.*, 1996). Slip tendency calculated from interseismic traction accumulation rates is greater along the Mojave section of the San Andreas fault and slightly greater along the San Jacinto fault than it is in the San Gorgonio Pass area, a pattern that is consistent with the relative frequency of modeled paleoearthquakes (Figs. 8 and 10).

Earthquake stress drop, rupture length, and location: Who left the earthquake gates open?

Because we simulate earthquakes by releasing all accumulated shear traction on the rupture patch (i.e., by applying a reduction in shear traction equivalent to the pre-earthquake accumulated traction for each participating element), the pre-earthquake tractions, ranging from near zero to ~2.25 MPa, inform the static stress drop for each earthquake. Some modeling choices may affect these stress-drop estimates. We use a spatially uniform value of 30 GPa for Young's modulus, though in the crust this varies with lithology; areas with a greater Young's modulus would have greater traction accumulation rates and therefore stress drops. Locking depth may also vary within the study area (Smith-Konter *et al.*, 2011), and, similar to previous modeling studies (e.g., Smith-Konter and Sandwell, 2009), the choice of locking depth also may impact stress drop by changing the proportion of the seismogenic fault surface that has a high-interseismic stressing rate near the locking depth.

The stress drops in these simulations appear low relative to stress drops calculated from source spectra—moderate to large ($M_w \geq 5$) earthquakes globally have stress drops averaging ~3 MPa (Kanamori and Anderson, 1975; Allmann and Shearer, 2009), and small earthquakes ($M_L < 5$) in the San Gorgonio Pass area and broader southern California region have stress drops of up to ~40 to 50 MPa (Goebel *et al.*, 2015; Shearer *et al.*, 2022). However, the fault model and seismological stress-drop estimates cannot be directly compared. Stress-drop estimates from source spectra depend on the source model used, tradeoffs between source and path effects, and uncertainty in corner frequencies; the corner frequency itself depends on the amount of high-frequency radiation, which while related to the change in shear traction due to earthquakes is also affected by other factors such as fault-zone complexity, which may not be similar at different scales (Aki, 1981; Cocco *et al.*, 2016; Tsai and Hirth, 2020; Abercrombie, 2021; Chu *et al.*, 2021). Although we cannot directly compare seismological estimates of stress drops with the pre-earthquake shear tractions of this study, we can examine and compare their spatial patterns. Areas that have high pre-earthquake shear tractions in the models of this study, such as near the San Gorgonio Pass (blue-shaded faults in Fig. 8a), also have large stress drops in the microseismicity (Shearer *et al.*, 2006, 2022; Goebel *et al.*, 2015).

The simulations of this study suggest that fault geometry impacts pre-earthquake shear traction, rupture length, and location. All earthquake ruptures of length greater than 200 km have minimum pre-earthquake shear tractions of at least ~0.4 MPa. Although the models produce a wide variety of minimum pre-earthquake shear tractions for short earthquake ruptures, seven short (<125 km) events have minimum pre-earthquake shear tractions well above the 0.4 MPa threshold. All seven of these events occur near fault branches in the San Gorgonio Pass or near fault stepovers (Fig. 8a). In areas of geometrically complex faulting with stepovers, bends, and multiple fault strands, even relatively high pre-earthquake shear tractions may not be sufficient to induce earthquake ruptures to propagate far along strike. This result is consistent with dynamic rupture modeling studies showing that earthquake ruptures require specific conditions to propagate onto fault branches (Douilly *et al.*, 2020; Tarnowski *et al.*, 2022) or across gaps (Harris and Day, 1999; Lozos *et al.*, 2012). In areas with simpler fault geometry, such as the San Andreas fault north of Cajon Pass, events with short rupture lengths that have low pre-earthquake shear tractions stay short because shear tractions are insufficient to encourage rupture propagation onto the surrounding fault area that would generate long ruptures. In summary, high pre-earthquake shear traction and simple fault geometry are conducive to producing long earthquake ruptures, and producing a long rupture with low pre-earthquake shear tractions is difficult, even along geometrically simple fault sections. The minimum ~0.4 MPa pre-earthquake shear traction for long earthquake ruptures and average interseismic stressing rate of ~0.0055 MPa/yr for the system also suggest a corresponding minimum interval of ~73 yr between these longest earthquakes along any given stretch of fault. This estimate is shorter than the typical interval between long earthquakes in the system, which is generally at least 100 yr, though shorter intervals are permitted within the uncertainty of the earthquake timing (Fig. 1); this is unsurprising because earthquakes with short rupture lengths often relieve tractions in between events with long rupture length.

CONCLUSIONS

Three-dimensional numerical simulations allow us to estimate evolving shear tractions through nearly 1000 yr of earthquake history on the southern San Andreas and San Jacinto fault system. These traction estimates include interseismic traction accumulation from tectonic loading, viscoelastic relaxation of shear stress in the upper crust during the interseismic period, and the effects of nearby earthquakes on the fault system. At many sites, interseismic loading is the primary contributor to evolved shear tractions, but nearby earthquakes can also be a significant contributor for locations within ~20 km of nearby rupture endpoints or where two fault strands are close together, such as near Cajon Pass and along the Mission Creek and Banning strands of the San Andreas fault.

Monte Carlo simulations assess the impact on evolving shear tractions due to uncertainties in upper-crustal viscosity and in earthquake timing. The choice of upper-crustal viscosity has the most significant impact on accumulated shear tractions: although high-viscosity (10^{21} Pa · s) simulations are nearly indistinguishable from linear elastic ones, low viscosity ($<10^{20}$ Pa · s) allows very little shear traction to accumulate and does not produce average slip per event that is consistent with estimates derived from geological data. Traction uncertainty from earthquake timing at a given site generally depends on the interseismic stressing rate and the time since the previous earthquake rupturing that site, unless nearby earthquakes also cause significant changes in traction at the site.

The nonuniform shear tractions produced by the simulations in this study can shed insight into the conditions that lead to high or low tractions before ground-rupturing earthquakes. The shear tractions produced in this study assume zero strength during rupture and provide lower bounds for tractions along the southern San Andreas and San Jacinto faults. Overall, stress drops in the shear traction simulations are less than ~2.25 MPa, and for any given earthquake, the ranges of traction uncertainty due to earthquake timing and viscosity uncertainty are each no more than ~1.5 MPa, but are more commonly ~0.5 MPa or less. Pre-earthquake shear tractions vary with rupture length and location. Relatively high pre-earthquake shear tractions (stress drop > 0.4 MPa) can occur throughout the system. Ruptures with high pre-earthquake traction have short rupture lengths (<125 km) near areas of geometric complexity, such as fault branches and stepovers, and long rupture lengths (>200 km) on the geometrically simple northern part of the system. Ruptures with low pre-earthquake shear tractions (stress drops < 0.4 MPa) in this earthquake record all have short rupture lengths. This suggests that once an earthquake has nucleated, its ultimate rupture extent depends on both accumulated shear traction and fault geometry: High accumulated shear tractions encourage rupture propagation, but fault branches and stepovers can hinder rupture propagation despite high shear tractions. Dynamic rupture models using evolved shear traction estimates as initial conditions could further inform how ruptures propagate and provide improved estimates of ground shaking.

DATA AND RESOURCES

The model mesh is modified from the Statewide California Earthquake Center Community Fault Model (SCEC CFM) available at https://zenodo.org/records/13685611 (last accessed July 2022).

Global Positioning System (GPS) velocities are from the SCEC Community Geodetic Model (CGM) available at https://zenodo.org/records/10076838 (last accessed July 2022). The supplemental material contains the profile of Global Positioning System (GPS) velocities used to inform the geologic model boundary conditions, plots of evolving shear traction estimates at all paleoseismic sites shown in Figure 1, and a video of evolving strike shear tractions throughout the system.

DECLARATION OF COMPETING INTERESTS

The authors acknowledge that there are no conflicts of interest recorded.

ACKNOWLEDGMENTS

This work is Statewide California Earthquake Center (SCEC) Contribution Number 13437 and was funded by SCEC Awards 22030 and 23104. The authors thank Julian Lozos, Jeanne Hardebeck, and an anonymous reviewer for helpful and constructive reviews. The authors thank Scott Marshall for assistance with the Global Positioning System (GPS) velocities.
Any use of trade, firm, or product names is for descriptive purposes only and does not imply endorsement by the U.S. Government.

REFERENCES

Abercrombie, R. E. (2021). Resolution and uncertainties in estimates of earthquake stress drop and energy release, *Phil. Trans. Roy. Soc. Lond. A* **379,** no. 2196, 20200131, doi: 10.1098/rsta.2020.0131.

Akçiz, S. O.ssss, L. G. Ludwig, J. R. Arrowsmith, and O. Zielke (2010). Century-long average time intervals between earthquake ruptures of the San Andreas fault in the Carrizo Plain, California, *Geology* **38,** no. 9, 787–790.

Aki, K. (1981). A probabilistic synthesis of precursory phenomena, in *Earthquake Prediction*, D. W. Simpson and P. G. Richards (Editors), Maurice Ewing Series, American Geophysical Union, Washington, D.C., 566–574.

Allmann, B. P., and P. M. Shearer (2009). Global variations of stress drop for moderate to large earthquakes, *J. Geophys. Res.: Solid Earth* **114,** no. B1, doi: 10.1029/2008JB005821.

Aoschi, H., and E. Fukuyama (2002). Three-dimensional nonplanar simulation of the 1992 Landers earthquake, *J. Geophys. Res.: Solid Earth* **107,** no. B2, ESE 4-1, doi: 10.1029/2000JB000061.

Bagge, M., A. Hampel, and R. D. Gold (2019). Modeling the Holocene slip history of the Wasatch fault (Utah): Coseismic and postseismic Coulomb stress changes and implications for paleoseismicity and seismic hazard, *GSA Bull.* **131,** nos. 1/2, 43–57, doi: 10.1130/B31906.1.

Becker, T. W., J. L. Hardebeck, and G. Anderson (2005). Constraints on fault slip rates of the southern California plate boundary from GPS velocity and stress inversions, *Geophys. J. Int.* **160,** no. 2, 634–650, doi: 10.1111/j.1365-246X.2004.02528.x.

Bemis, S. P., K. Scharer, and J. F. Dolan (2021). The San Andreas Fault paleoseismic record at Elizabeth Lake: Why are there fewer surface-rupturing earthquakes on the Mojave Section? *Bull. Seismol. Soc. Am.* **111,** no. 3, 1590–1613, doi: 10.1785/0120200218.

Beyer, J., M. L. Cooke, and S. T. Marshall (2018). Sensitivity of deformation to activity along the Mill Creek and Mission Creek strands of the southern San Andreas fault, *Geosphere* **14,** no. 6, 2296–2310, doi: 10.1130/GES01666.1.

Biasi, G. P., R. J. Weldon II, T. E. Fumal, and G. G. Seitz (2002). Paleoseismic event dating and the conditional probability of large earthquakes on the Southern San Andreas Fault, California, *Bull. Seismol. Soc. Am.* **92,** no. 7, 2761–2781, doi: 10.1785/0120000605.

Bills, B. G., D. R. Currey, and G. A. Marshall (1994). Viscosity estimates for the crust and upper mantle from patterns of lacustrine shoreline deformation in the Eastern Great Basin, *J. Geophys. Res.: Solid Earth* **99,** no. B11, 22,059–22,086.

Birch, F. (1966). Compressibility; Elastic constants, in *Handbook of Physical Constants*, S. P. Clark Jr. (Editor), Geol. Soc. of Am., Boulder, Colorado, 97–174.

Buga, M. T. (2012). Paleoseismology of the southern Clark Strand of the San Jacinto Fault zone, Southern California, *M.S. Thesis*, San Diego State University, available at https://digitallibrary.sdsu.edu/islandora/object/sdsu%3A28007 (last accessed July 2025).

Cardona, J. (2016). Constraining the most recent surface rupture on the Garnet Hill strand, San Andreas Fault, Coachella Valley, California, *M.S. Thesis*, California State University, Northridge, available at http://scholarworks.csun.edu/handle/10211.3/171784 (last accessed July 2025).

Castillo, B. A., S. F. McGill, K. M. Scharer, D. Yule, D. McPhillips, J. McNeil, S. Saha, N. D. Brown, and S. Moon (2021). Prehistoric earthquakes on the Banning strand of the San Andreas fault, North Palm Springs, California, *Geosphere* **17,** no. 3, 685–710, doi: 10.1130/GES02237.1.

Chu, S. X., V. C. Tsai, D. T. Trugman, and G. Hirth (2021). Fault interactions enhance high-frequency earthquake radiation, *Geophys. Res. Lett.* **48,** no. 20, e2021GL095271, doi: 10.1029/2021GL095271.

Cocco, M., E. Tinti, and A. Cirella (2016). On the scale dependence of earthquake stress drop, *J. Seismol.* **20,** no. 4, 1151–1170, doi: 10.1007/s10950-016-9594-4.

Cooke, M. L., and J. L. Beyer (2018). Off-fault focal mechanisms not representative of interseismic fault loading suggest deep creep on the Northern San Jacinto Fault, *Geophys. Res. Lett.* **45,** no. 17, 8976–8984, doi: 10.1029/2018GL078932.

Crider, J. G., and D. D. Pollard (1998). Fault linkage: Three-dimensional mechanical interaction between echelon normal faults, *J. Geophys. Res.: Solid Earth* **103,** no. B10, 24373–24391, doi: 10.1029/98JB01353.

Davis, T. L. (1983). Late Cenozoic structure and tectonic history of the western "Big Bend" of the San Andreas fault and adjacent San Emigdio Mountains, *Ph.D. Thesis*, University of California, Santa Barbara.

DeMets, C., R. G. Gordon, and D. F. Argus (2010). Geologically current plate motions, *Geophys. J. Int.* **181,** no. 1, 1–80, doi: 10.1111/j.1365-246X.2009.04491.x.

Devine, S., H. Harper, and S. T. Marshall (2022). Mechanical models of fault-slip rates in the Transverse and Peninsular Ranges, California, *Seismol. Res. Lett.* **93,** no. 6, 3135–3150, doi: 10.1785/0220220182.

DiToro, G., T. Hirose, S. Nielsen, and T. Shimamoto (2006). Relating high-velocity rock-friction experiments to coseismic slip in the presence of melts, in *Earthquakes: Radiated Energy and the Physics of Faulting*, R. Abercrombie, A. McGarr, G. Di Toro, and H. Kanamori (Editors), Geophysical Monograph Series, American Geophysical Union, Washington, D.C., 121–134.

Dorsett, J. H., E. H. Madden, S. T. Marshall, and M. L. Cooke (2019). Mechanical models suggest fault linkage through the Imperial

Valley, California, U.S.A., *Bull. Seismol. Soc. Am.* **109,** no. 4, 1217–1234, doi: 10.1785/0120180303.

Douilly, R., D. D. Oglesby, M. L. Cooke, and J. L. Hatch (2020). Dynamic models of earthquake rupture along branch faults of the eastern San Gorgonio Pass region in California using complex fault structure, *Geosphere* **16,** no. 2, 474–489, doi: 10.1130/GES02192.1.

Duan, B., and D. D. Oglesby (2005). Multicycle dynamics of nonplanar strike-slip faults, *J. Geophys. Res.: Solid Earth* **110,** no. B3, doi: 10.1029/2004JB003298.

DuRoss, C. B., S. F. Personius, A. J. Crone, S. S. Olig, M. D. Hylland, W. R. Lund, and D. P. Schwartz (2016). Fault segmentation: New concepts from the Wasatch Fault Zone, Utah, USA, *J. Geophys. Res.: Solid Earth* **121,** no. 2, 1131–1157, doi: 10.1002/2015JB012519.

Earth Systems Southwest (2007). Earthquake fault hazard evaluation, Indio trails, Washington street: Riverside County (No. GEO #01435).

Elliott, D. (1976). The energy balance and deformation mechanisms of thrust sheets, *Phil. Trans. Roy. Soc. Lond. A* **283,** no. 1312, 289–312.

Fattaruso, L. A., M. L. Cooke, and R. J. Dorsey (2014). Sensitivity of uplift patterns to dip of the San Andreas fault in the Coachella Valley, California, *Geosphere* **10,** no. 6, 1235–1246, doi: 10.1130/GES01050.1.

Fay, N. P., and E. D. Humphreys (2005). Fault slip rates, effects of elastic heterogeneity on geodetic data, and the strength of the lower crust in the Salton Trough region, southern California, *J. Geophys. Res.: Solid Earth* **110,** no. B9, doi: 10.1029/2004JB003548.

Field, E. H., G. P. Biasi, P. Bird, T. E. Dawson, K. R. Felzer, D. D. Jackson, K. M. Johnson, T. H. Jordan, C. Madden, A. J. Michael, *et al.* (2015). Long-term time-dependent probabilities for the third uniform California earthquake rupture forecast (UCERF3), *Bull. Seismol. Soc. Am.* **105,** no. 2, 511–543, doi: 10.1785/0120140093.

Freed, A. M., and J. Lin (2002). Accelerated stress buildup on the southern San Andreas fault and surrounding regions caused by Mojave Desert earthquakes, *Geology* **30,** no. 6, 571–574.

Fulton, P. M., E. E. Brodsky, Y. Kano, J. Mori, F. Chester, T. Ishikawa, R. N. Harris, W. Lin, N. Eguchi, S. Toczko, *et al.* (2013). Low coseismic friction on the Tohoku-Oki fault determined from temperature measurements, *Science* **342,** no. 6163, 1214–1217, doi: 10.1126/science.1243641.

Fumal, T., and K. Kendrick (2008). Paleoseismic investigations of the Walnut Site on the San Jacinto Fault, available at https://pubs.usgs.gov/of/2007/1437 (last accessed July 2025).

Fumal, T. E., M. J. Rymer, and G. G. Seitz (2002). Timing of large earthquakes since A.D. 800 on the mission creek strand of the San Andreas fault zone at Thousand Palms Oasis, near Palm Springs, California, *Bull. Seismol. Soc. Am.* **92,** no. 7, 2841–2860, doi: 10.1785/0120000609.

Fumal, T. E., I. J. Weldon, G. P. Biasi, T. E. Dawson, G. G. Seitz, W. T. Frost, and D. P. Schwartz (2002). Evidence for large earthquakes on the San Andreas fault at the Wrightwood, California paleoseismic site: A.D. 500 to present, *Bull. Seismol. Soc. Am.* **92,** no. 7, 2726–2760, doi: 10.1785/0120000608.

Goebel, T. H. W., E. Hauksson, P. M. Shearer, and J. P. Ampuero (2015). Stress-drop heterogeneity within tectonically complex regions: A case study of San Gorgonio Pass, southern California, *Geophys. J. Int.* **202,** no. 1, 514–528.

Gold, P. O., W. M. Behr, D. Rood, W. D. Sharp, T. K. Rockwell, K. Kendrick, and A. Salin (2015). Holocene geologic slip rate for the Banning strand of the southern San Andreas Fault, southern California, *J. Geophys. Res.: Solid Earth* **120,** no. 8, 5639–5663, doi: 10.1002/2015JB012004.

Goldsby, D. L., and T. E. Tullis (2011). Flash heating leads to low frictional strength of crustal rocks at Earthquake Slip Rates, *Science* **334,** no. 6053, 216–218, doi: 10.1126/science.1207902.

Gomberg, J., N. Beeler, M. Blanpied, and P. Bodin (1998). Earthquake triggering by transient and static deformations, *J. Geophys. Res.: Solid Earth* **103,** no. B10, 24,411–24,426.

Grant Ludwig, L., S. O. Akçiz, G. R. Noriega, O. Zielke, and J. R. Arrowsmith (2010). Climate-modulated channel incision and rupture history of the San Andreas fault in the Carrizo Plain, *Science* **327,** no. 5969, 1117–1119.

Gratier, J., and J. Gamond (1990). *Transition Between Seismic and Aseismic Deformation in the Upper Crust*, Geological Society, London, United Kingdom, Special Publications, Vol. 54, 461–473.

Gurrola, L. D., and T. K. Rockwell (1996). Timing and slip for prehistoric earthquakes on the Superstition Mountain Fault, Imperial Valley, southern California, *J. Geophys. Res.: Solid Earth* **101,** no. B3, 5977–5985, doi: 10.1029/95JB03061.

Harris, R. A. (1998). Introduction to special section: Stress triggers, stress shadows, and implications for seismic hazard, *J. Geophys. Res.: Solid Earth* **103,** no. B10, 24,347–24,358.

Harris, R. A., and S. M. Day (1999). Dynamic 3D simulations of earthquakes on En Echelon faults, *Geophys. Res. Lett.* **26,** no. 14, 2089–2092.

Harris, R. A., and R. W. Simpson (1998). Suppression of large earthquakes by stress shadows: A comparison of Coulomb and rate-and-state failure, *J. Geophys. Res.: Solid Earth* **103,** no. B10, 24,439–24,451.

Hatch, J. L., M. L. Cooke, A. R. Stern, R. Douilly, and D. D. Oglesby (2020). Considering fault interaction in estimates of absolute stress along faults in the San Gorgonio Pass region, southern California, *Geosphere* **16,** no. 3, 751–764, doi: 10.1130/GES02153.1.

Heermance, R. V., and D. Yule (2017). Holocene slip rates along the San Andreas Fault System in the San Gorgonio Pass and implications for large earthquakes in southern California, *Geophys. Res. Lett.* **44,** no. 11, 5391–5400, doi: 10.1002/2017GL072612.

Herbert, J. W., and M. L. Cooke (2012). Sensitivity of the Southern San Andreas Fault system to tectonic boundary conditions and fault configurations, *Bull. Seismol. Soc. Am.* **102,** no. 5, 2046–2062, doi: 10.1785/0120110316.

Herbert, J. W., M. L. Cooke, and S. T. Marshall (2014). Influence of fault connectivity on slip rates in southern California: Potential impact on discrepancies between geodetic derived and geologic slip rates, *J. Geophys. Res.: Solid Earth* **119,** no. 3, 2342–2361, doi: 10.1002/2013JB010472.

Hill, R. G., M. Weingarten, T. K. Rockwell, and Y. Fialko (2023). Major southern San Andreas earthquakes modulated by lake-filling events, *Nature* **618,** no. 7966, 761–766, doi: 10.1038/s41586-023-06058-9.

Howland, C. (2003). Determining the depositional age of peat: Implications for dating paleoearthquakes at the Burro Flats Paleoseismic site near Banning, CA, *M.S. Thesis*, California State University, Northridge, California.

Ismat, Z., and G. Mitra (2005). Folding by cataclastic flow: Evolution of controlling factors during deformation, *J. Struct. Geol.* **27,** no. 12, 2181–2203, doi: 10.1016/j.jsg.2005.08.005.

Itô, H. (1979). Rheology of the crust based on long-term creep tests of rocks, *Tectonophysics* **52,** no. 1, 629–641, doi: 10.1016/0040-1951(79)90282-8.

Johnson, K. M. (2018). Growth of fault-cored anticlines by flexural slip folding: Analysis by boundary element modeling, *J. Geophys. Res.: Solid Earth* **123,** no. 3, 2426–2447, doi: 10.1002/2017JB014867.

Kanamori, H., and D. L. Anderson (1975). Theoretical basis of some empirical relations in seismology, *Bull. Seismol. Soc. Am.* **65,** no. 5, 1073–1095.

Kendrick, K., and T. Fumal (2005). Paleoseismicity of the northern San Jacinto fault, Colton and San Bernardino, Southern California; preliminary results, *Geol. Soc. Am. Abstr. Progr.*, **37,** 559.

King, G. C. P., R. S. Stein, and J. Lin (1994). Static stress changes and the triggering of earthquakes, *Bull. Seismol. Soc. Am.* **84,** no. 3, 935–953, doi: 10.1785/BSSA0840030935.

Kyriakopoulos, C., D. D. Oglesby, G. J. Funning, and K. J. Ryan (2017). Dynamic rupture modeling of the M7.2 2010 El Mayor-Cucapah earthquake: Comparison with a geodetic model, *J. Geophys. Res.: Solid Earth* **122,** no. 12, 10,263–10,279, doi: 10.1002/2017JB014294.

Liu, D., B. Duan, V. B. Prush, M. E. Oskin, and J. Liu-Zeng (2021). Observation-constrained multicycle dynamic models of the Pingding Shan earthquake gate along the Altyn Tagh Fault, *Tectonophysics* **814,** 228,948.

Lozos, J. C. (2016). A case for historic joint rupture of the San Andreas and San Jacinto faults, *Sci. Adv.* **2,** no. 3, e1500621, doi: 10.1126/sciadv.1500621.

Lozos, J. C., D. D. Oglesby, J. N. Brune, and K. B. Olsen (2012). Small intermediate fault segments can either aid or hinder rupture propagation at stepovers, *Geophys. Res. Lett.* **39,** no. 18, doi: 10.1029/2012GL053005.

Luttrell, K., D. Sandwell, B. Smith-Konter, B. Bills, and Y. Bock (2007). Modulation of the earthquake cycle at the southern San Andreas fault by lake loading, *J. Geophys. Res.: Solid Earth* **112,** no. B8, doi: 10.1029/2006JB004752.

Madden, C., D. E. Haddad, J. B. Salisbury, O. Zielke, and J. R. Arrowsmith (2013). Appendix R: Compilation of slip-in-the-last-event data and analysis of last event, repeated slip, and average displacement for recent and prehistoric ruptures, *U.S. Geol. Surv. Open-File Rept. 2013-1165, Uniform California Earthquake Rupture Forecast Version 3 (UCERF3)—The Time-Independent Model*, available at https://pubs. usgs.gov/of/2013/1165 (last accessed July 2025).

Marshall, S. T., M. L. Cooke, and S. E. Owen (2009). Interseismic deformation associated with three-dimensional faults in the greater Los Angeles region, California, *J. Geophys. Res.: Solid Earth* **114,** no. B12, doi: 10.1029/2009JB006439.

McBurnett, P. (2011). Paleoseismicity of the San Gorgonio Pass fault zone at Millard Canyon: Testing the likelihood of a through-going San Andreas rupture, *M.S. Thesis*, California State University, Northridge, California, available at http://scholarworks.csun.edu/handle/10211.3/142046 (last accessed July 2025).

McGill, S., S. Dergham, K. Barton, T. Berney-Ficklin, D. Grant, C. Hartling, K. Hobart, R. Minnich, M. Rodriguez, E. Runnerstrom, *et al.* (2002). Paleoseismology of the San Andreas Fault at Plunge Creek, near San Bernardino, Southern California, *Bull. Seismol. Soc. Am.* **92,** no. 7, 2803–2840, doi: 10.1785/0120000607.

McPhillips, D., and K. Scharer (2023). Spatial and temporal analysis of geologic slip rates, Cucamonga Fault, California, USA: Implications for along-strike applications and multi-fault rupture, *J. Geophys. Res.: Solid Earth* **128,** no. 3, e2022JB024942, doi: 10.1029/2022JB024942.

Meade, B. J., and B. H. Hager (2005). Block models of crustal motion in southern California constrained by GPS measurements, *J. Geophys. Res.: Solid Earth* **110,** no. B3, doi: 10.1029/2004JB003209.

Morris, A., D. A. Ferrill, and D. B. Henderson (1996). Slip-tendency analysis and fault reactivation, *Geology* **24,** no. 3, 275–278.

Nicholson, C., A. Plesch, and J. H. Shaw (2017). Community Fault Model Version 5.2: Updating and expanding the CFM 3D fault set and its associated fault database, *Poster Presentation at 2017 SCEC Annual Meeting*, Palm Springs, California, September 2017.

Oglesby, D. D., S. M. Day, and D. R. H. O'Connell (2003). Dynamic and static interaction of two thrust faults: A case study with general implications, *J. Geophys. Res.: Solid Earth* **108,** no. B10, doi: 10.1029/2002JB002228.

Onderdonk, N., S. McGill, and T. Rockwell (2018). A 3700 yr paleoseismic record from the northern San Jacinto fault and implications for joint rupture of the San Jacinto and San Andreas faults, *Geosphere* **14,** no. 6, 2447–2468, doi: 10.1130/GES01687.1.

Onderdonk, N. W., S. F. McGill, and T. K. Rockwell (2015). Short-term variations in slip rate and size of prehistoric earthquakes during the past 2000 years on the northern San Jacinto fault zone, a major plate-boundary structure in southern California, *Lithosphere* **7,** no. 3, 211–234, doi: 10.1130/L393.1.

Orlecka-Sikora, B. (2010). The role of static stress transfer in mining induced seismic events occurrence, a case study of the Rudna mine in the Legnica-Glogow Copper District in Poland, *Geophys. J. Int.* **182,** no. 2, 1087–1095.

Philibosian, B., T. Fumal, and R. Weldon (2011) San Andreas fault earthquake chronology and Lake Cahuilla History at Coachella, California, *Bull. Seismol. Soc. Am.* **101,** no. 1, 13–38, doi: 10.1785/0120100050.

Plesch, A., J. H. Shaw, C. Benson, W. A. Bryant, S. Carena, M. Cooke, J. Dolan, G. Fuis, E. Gath, L. Grant, *et al.* (2007). Community Fault Model (CFM) for Southern California, *Bull. Seismol. Soc. Am.* **97,** no. 6, 1793–1802, doi: 10.1785/0120050211.

Pollitz, F. F., and I. S. Sacks (2002). Stress triggering of the 1999 Hector Mine earthquake by transient deformation following the 1992 Landers earthquake, *Bull. Seismol. Soc. Am.* **92,** no. 4, 1487–1496.

Pollitz, F. F., C. W. Wicks, J. L. Svarc, E. Phillips, B. A. Brooks, M. H. Murray, and R. C. Turner (2022). Postseismic relaxation following the 2019 Ridgecrest, California, earthquake sequence, *Bull. Seismol. Soc. Am.* **112,** no. 2, 734–749.

Pruitt, A., K. Scharer, T. Fumal, R. J. Weldon, C. Gilleland, and R. Sickler (2009). Microgeomorphic reconstruction to determine slip rate on the San Andreas fault near Littlerock, CA, *Poster Presented at the 2009 SCEC Annual Meeting*, Palm Springs, California, September 2009.

Ramzan, S. (2012). Paleoseismic investigation of the San Gorgonio Pass fault zone near Cabazon, California, *M.S. Thesis*, California State University, Northridge, California, available at http://scholarworks.csun.edu/handle/10211.2/1880 (last accessed July 2025).

Resor, P. G., M. L. Cooke, S. T. Marshall, and E. H. Madden (2018). Influence of fault geometry on the spatial distribution of long-term slip with implications for determining representative fault-slip rates, *Bull. Seismol. Soc. Am.* **108,** no. 4, 1837–1852, doi: 10.1785/0120170332.

Rockwell, T. K., T. E. Dawson, J. Young Ben-Horin, and G. Seitz (2015). A 21-event, 4,000-year history of surface ruptures in the Anza Seismic Gap, San Jacinto Fault, and implications for long-term earthquake production on a major plate boundary fault, *Pure Appl. Geophys.* **172,** no. 5, 1143–1165, doi: 10.1007/s00024-014-0955-z.

Rodriguez Padilla, A., M. Oskin, E. Brodsky, K. Dascher-Cousineau, V. Herrera, and S. White (2024). The influence of fault geometrical complexity on surface rupture length, *Geophys. Res. Lett.* **51,** no. 20, e2024GL109957, doi: 10.1029/2024GL109957.

Rodriguez Padilla, A. M., M. E. Oskin, T. K. Rockwell, I. Delusina, and D. M. Singleton (2021). Joint earthquake ruptures of the San Andreas and San Jacinto faults, California, USA, *Geology* **50,** no. 4, 387–391, doi: 10.1130/G49415.1.

Rust, D. (2005). Palaeoseismology in steep terrain: The big bend of the San Andreas fault, Transverse Ranges, California, *Tectonophysics* **408,** nos. 1/4, 193–212.

Rutter, E. H. (1976). A Discussion on natural strain and geological structure—the kinetics of rock deformation by pressure solution, *Phil. Trans. Roy. Soc. Lond. A* **283,** no. 1312, 203–219, doi: 10.1098/rsta.1976.0079.

Salisbury, J. B., T. K. Rockwell, and M. T. Buga (2017). Paleoseismic evidence for the 21 April 1918 Mw 6.9 surface Rupture of the Northern Clark Strand of the Central San Jacinto Fault, California, *Bull. Seismol. Soc. Am.* **107,** no. 2, 1027–1032, doi: 10.1785/0120160026.

Salisbury, J. B., T. K. Rockwell, T. J. Middleton, and K. W. Hudnut (2012). LiDAR and field observations of slip distribution for the most recent surface ruptures along the Central San Jacinto Fault, *Bull. Seismol. Soc. Am.* **102,** no. 2, 598–619, doi: 10.1785/0120110068.

Sandwell, D. T., Y. Zeng, Z. Shen, B. W. Crowell, J. R. Murray, R. McCaffrey, and X. Xu (2016). The SCEC Community Geodetic Model V1: Horizontal velocity grid, *Poster Presentation at 2016 SCEC Annual Meeting*, Palm Springs, California, *September 2016*.

Scharer, K., R. Weldon II, G. Biasi, A. Streig, and T. Fumal (2017). Ground-rupturing earthquakes on the northern Big Bend of the San Andreas Fault, California, 800 A.D. to Present, *J. Geophys. Res.: Solid Earth* **122,** no. 3, 2193–2218, doi: 10.1002/2016JB013606.

Scharer, K. M., G. P. Biasi, and R. J. Weldon (2011). A reevaluation of the Pallett Creek earthquake chronology based on new AMS radiocarbon dates, San Andreas fault, California, *J. Geophys. Res.: Solid Earth* **116,** no. 12, 1–14, doi: 10.1029/2010JB008099.

Scharer, K. M., and D. Yule (2020). A maximum rupture model for the southern San Andreas and San Jacinto Faults, California, derived from paleoseismic earthquake ages: Observations and limitations, *Geophys. Res. Lett.* **47,** no. 15, e2020GL088532, doi: 10.1029/2020GL088532.

Seitz, G., R. Weldon, and G. P. Biasi (1997). The Pitman Canyon paleoseismic record: A re-evaluation of southern San Andreas Fault segmentation, *J. Geodynam.* **24,** no. 1, 129–138, doi: 10.1016/S0264-3707(96)00042-7.

Seitz, G., and P. L. Williams (2008). Establishing the southernmost long-term earthquake record on the San Andreas Fault, *Annual Rept. 08136*, Southern California Earthquake Center.

Sharp, R. V. (1981). Variable rates of Late Quaternary strike slip on the San Jacinto Fault Zone, southern California, *J. Geophys. Res.: Solid Earth* **86,** no. B3, 1754–1762, doi: 10.1029/JB086iB03p01754.

Shearer, P. M., R. E. Abercrombie, and D. T. Trugman (2022). Improved stress drop estimates for M 1.5 to 4 earthquakes in southern California from 1996 to 2019, *J. Geophys. Res.: Solid Earth* **127,** no. 7, e2022JB024243, doi: 10.1029/2022JB024243.

Shearer, P. M., G. A. Prieto, and E. Hauksson (2006). Comprehensive analysis of earthquake source spectra in southern California, *J. Geophys. Res.: Solid Earth* **111,** no. B6, doi: 10.1029/2005JB003979.

Sieh, K., M. Stuiver, and D. Brillinger (1989). A more precise chronology of earthquakes produced by the San Andreas Fault in southern California, *J. Geophys. Res.: Solid Earth* **94,** no. B1, 603–623, doi: 10.1029/JB094iB01p00603.

Sieh, K. E. (1986). Slip rate across the San Andreas fault and prehistoric earthquakes at Indio, California, *Eos Trans. AGU* **67,** no. 44, 1200.

Smith-Konter, B., and D. Sandwell (2009). Stress evolution of the San Andreas fault system: Recurrence interval versus locking depth, *Geophys. Res. Lett.* **36,** no. 13, doi: 10.1029/2009GL037235.

Smith-Konter, B. R., D. T. Sandwell, and P. Shearer (2011). Locking depths estimated from geodesy and seismology along the San Andreas Fault System: Implications for seismic moment release, *J. Geophys. Res.: Solid Earth* **116,** no. B6, doi: 10.1029/2010JB008117.

Styron, R. (2019). The impact of earthquake cycle variability on neotectonic and paleoseismic slip rate estimates, *Solid Earth* **10,** no. 1, 15–25.

Talbot, C. J. (1999). Can field data constrain rock viscosities? *J. Struct. Geol.* **21,** no. 8, 949–957, doi: 10.1016/S0191-8141(99)00037-1.

Tarnowski, J. M., C. Kyriakopoulos, D. D. Oglesby, M. L. Cooke, and A. Stern (2022). The effects of pre-stress assumptions on dynamic rupture with complex fault geometry in the San Gorgonio Pass, California, region, *Geosphere* **18,** no. 6, 1710–1725, doi: 10.1130/GES02511.1.

Thomas, A. L. (1993). Poly 3D: A three-dimensional, polygonal element, displacement discontinuity boundary element computer program with applications to fractures, faults, and cavities in the Earth's crust, available at https://searchworks.stanford.edu/view/2830996 (last accessed November 2020).

Toda, S., and R. S. Stein (2020). Long- and short-term stress interaction of the 2019 Ridgecrest sequence and coulomb-based earthquake forecasts, *Bull. Seismol. Soc. Am.* **110,** no. 4, 1765–1780, doi: 10.1785/0120200169.

Tsai, V. C., and G. Hirth (2020). Elastic impact consequences for high-frequency earthquake ground motion, *Geophys. Res. Lett.* **47,** no. 5, e2019GL086302, doi: 10.1029/2019GL086302.

Verdecchia, A., and S. Carena (2016). Coulomb stress evolution in a diffuse plate boundary: 1400 years of earthquakes in eastern California and western Nevada, USA, *Tectonics* **35,** no. 8, 1793–1811.

Verdecchia, A., S. Carena, B. Pace, and C. B. DuRoss (2019). The effect of stress changes on time-dependent earthquake probabilities for the central Wasatch Fault Zone, Utah, USA, *Geophys. J. Int.* doi: 10.1093/gji/ggz336.

Weldon, I. J., T. E. Fumal, T. J. Powers, S. K. Pezzopane, K. M. Scharer, and J. C. Hamilton (2002). Structure and earthquake offsets on the San Andreas fault at the Wrightwood, California paleoseismic site, *Bull. Seismol. Soc. Am.* **92,** no. 7, 2704–2725, doi: 10.1785/0120000612.

Weldon, R., K. Scharer, T. Fumal, and G. Biasi (2004). Wrightwood and the earthquake cycle: What a long recurrence record tells us about how faults work, *Geol. Soc. Am. Today* **14,** no. 9, 4–10.

Weldon, R. J., II, and K. E. Sieh (1985). Holocene rate of slip and tentative recurrence interval for large earthquakes on the San

Andreas fault, Cajon Pass, southern California, *GSA Bull.* **96,** no. 6, 793–812.
Weldon, R. J., T. E. Dawson, G. P. Biasi, C. Madden, and A. R. Streig (2013). Appendix G: Paleoseismic sites recurrence database, *U.S. Geol. Surv. Open-File Rept. 2013–1165, Uniform California Earthquake Rupture Forecast Version 3 (UCERF3)—The Time-Independent Model,* available at https://pubs.usgs.gov/of/2013/1165/ (last accessed July 2025).
Wesnousky, S. G. (2006). Predicting the endpoints of earthquake ruptures, *Nature* **444,** no. 7117, 358–360.
Wesson, R. L., and O. S. Boyd (2007). Stress before and after the 2002 Denali fault earthquake, *Geophys. Res. Lett.* **34,** no. 7, doi: 10.1029/2007GL029189.
Williams, A. M., R. Arrowsmith, T. K. Rockwell, S. O. Akciz, and L. Grant Ludwig (2018). Refining the earthquake chronology of the last millennium along the Cholame segment of the San Andreas fault, *Poster Presentation at 2018 SCEC Annual Meeting,* Palm Springs, California, September 2008.
Wolff, L. (2018). A 6000-year record of large, infrequent earthquakes on the San Andreas Fault System in San Gorgonio Pass, Near Cabezon, California, available at https://scholarworks.calstate.edu/concern/theses/2j62s834h (last accessed July 2025).
Young, J. J., J. R. Arrowsmith, L. Colini, L. B. Grant, and B. Gootee (2002). Three-dimensional excavation and recent rupture history along the Cholame Segment of the San Andreas Fault, *Bull. Seismol. Soc. Am.* **92,** no. 7, 2670–2688, doi: 10.1785/0120000604.
Yule, D., and K. Sieh (2003). Complexities of the San Andreas fault near San Gorgonio Pass: Implications for large earthquakes, *J. Geophys. Res.: Solid Earth* **108,** no. B11, doi: 10.1029/2001JB000451.
Yule, J. D., K. Sieh, and C. Howland (2007). Evidence for large earthquakes on the San Andreas Fault at the Burro Flats paleoseismic site: A.D. 150 to present, *Poster presented at SCEC Annual Meeting,* Palm Springs, California, 196 pp.
Zielke, O., J. R. Arrowsmith, L. Grant Ludwig, and S. O. Akciz (2012) High-resolution topography-derived offsets along the 1857 Fort Tejon earthquake rupture trace, San Andreas Fault, *Bull. Seismol. Soc. Am.* **102,** no. 3, 1135–1154, doi: 10.1785/0120110230.
Ziv, A., and A. M. Rubin (2000) Static stress transfer and earthquake triggering: No lower threshold in sight? *J. Geophys. Res.: Solid Earth* **105,** no. B6, 13,631–13,642.

Manuscript received 17 July 2025
Published online 16 March 2026

Examining the Causes of Regional Differences in California Based on Ground Motions from Small to Moderate Earthquakes

Camilo I. Pinilla-Ramos[*1], Norman A. Abrahamson[2], Savvas Marcou[3], Douglas S. Dreger[4], Alexandros Savvaidis[5], Gail M. Atkinson[6], Behzad Hassani[7], Chih-Hsuan Sung[2], and Robert Youngs[8]

ABSTRACT

Residuals from ground-motion models (GMMs) for California show systematic differences in the long-period event terms for small-to-moderate magnitude earthquakes (M_w < 5) between Northern and Southern California. The spatial pattern of regional differences in event terms followed the boundaries of the seismic networks, suggesting a systematic difference in magnitudes for small-to-moderate earthquakes between the Northern and Southern California networks. Both networks employ the same workflow defined by the Advanced National Seismic System. Therefore, procedural differences in moment tensor inversion (MTI) are unlikely to be the cause of the observed regional differences in event terms. The two networks utilize different seismic-velocity models in the MTI, with lower velocities in coastal Northern California compared to Southern California. A physics-based analysis indicates that the regional amplification differences among the seismic-velocity models used in the MTI are consistent with the observed differences in the event terms between the two regions, providing evidence that the event terms in ergodic GMMs for California also capture regional wave-propagation differences, not just source differences. This affects the development of GMMs: a better methodology is needed to identify these regional wave propagation patterns from event-specific faulting processes, which are currently mapped in the event-terms. In addition, having several earthquakes in the datasets with magnitudes obtained without MTI is a potential source of regional differences in the event terms. Using earthquakes selected from the ongoing Next Generation Attenuation-West3 project, we conduct MTIs on 188 earthquakes, yielding 63 seismic moment estimates and an additional 43 values adopted directly from the Comprehensive Catalog. These 106 moment magnitude estimates can replace those from earthquakes in the dataset that lack a moment magnitude, reducing reliance on conversion models. We conclude this study by providing recommendations to improve the documentation of the MTI maintained by the seismic network operators.

KEY POINTS

- Regional event-term differences in California stem from wave propagation, not MTI procedural differences.
- The compliant marine sequences along coastal Northern California drive these regional differences.
- We added moment-tensor magnitudes for 106 earthquakes without moment tensor inversion in the NGA-W3 dataset.

Supplemental Material

INTRODUCTION

Over the past decade, ground-motion data sets used to develop ground-motion models (GMMs) have included ground motions from small to moderate magnitude earthquakes (i.e., $M_w < 5$) to

1. GFZ, Helmholtz-Zentrum für Geoforschung, Potsdam, Germany, https://orcid.org/0000-0002-4034-6618 (CIP); 2. Department of Civil Engineering, University of California, Berkeley, California, U.S.A., https://orcid.org/0000-0001-7900-6023 (NAA); https://orcid.org/0000-0001-7606-0366 (C-HS); 3. Berkeley Seismological Laboratory, University of California, Berkeley, Berkeley, California, U.S.A., https://orcid.org/0000-0003-3961-773X (SM); 4. Department of Earth and Planetary Science, University of California, Berkeley, Berkeley, California, U.S.A., https://orcid.org/0000-0002-6590-3089 (DSD); 5. Jackson School of Geoscience, The University of Texas at Austin, Austin, Texas, U.S.A., https://orcid.org/0000-0001-6373-5256 (AS); 6. Western University, London, Canada, https://orcid.org/0000-0003-2403-1349 (GMA); 7. BC Hydro, Burnaby, Canada, https://orcid.org/0000-0001-9878-6395 (BH); 8. WSP USA, Oakland, California, U.S.A.

*Corresponding author: camilo.pinilla@berkeley.edu

Cite this article as Pinilla-Ramos, C. I., N. A. Abrahamson, S. Marcou, D. S. Dreger, A. Savvaidis, G. M. Atkinson, B. Hassani, C.-H. Sung, and R. Youngs (2026). Examining the Causes of Regional Differences in California Based on Ground Motions from Small to Moderate Earthquakes, *Bull. Seismol. Soc. Am.* **116**, 1145–1160, doi: 10.1785/0120250239 enhance understanding and constraints on linear site effects and wave-propagation patterns (e.g., Bozorgnia *et al.*, 2014). Because of their small size, small-magnitude earthquakes are useful for constraining the crustal impulsive response and wave-propagation effects at regional scales (Dreger and Helmberger, 1990; Abercrombie, 2013; Sahakian *et al.*, 2018; Pinilla-Ramos *et al.*, 2025). This enables the evolution of GMMs from global-average models, such as the Next Generation Attenuation-West (NGA-W) GMMs (Power *et al.*, 2008), to regionalized GMMs for broad regions, such as the NGA-W2 GMMs (Bozorgnia *et al.*, 2014). Nonergodic GMMs take this approach further (e.g., Lavrentiadis *et al.*, 2021, 2022; Sung and Abrahamson, 2022; Sung *et al.*, 2022), reducing the scale of characterization from large regions (e.g., California, Japan, Italy, and New Zealand) to spatially continuous characterization with dimensions on the order of tens of kilometers. The inclusion of small-magnitude earthquakes has been crucial in achieving a dense spatial sampling of ground motions for different source-site combinations, thereby constraining wave propagation effects. For example, the NGA-W2 dataset (Bozorgnia *et al.*, 2014) included earthquakes with magnitudes as small as 3, with 371 earthquakes between M 3 and 5.

Several studies have examined regional differences in ground motions in California, based on small- and moderate-magnitude earthquakes, using various data sets. Chiou *et al* (2010) separated the ground-motion data from 188 earthquakes (M 3–5) from the ShakeMap dataset into spatial subsets and found a significant difference in the small-magnitude scaling for peak acceleration between earthquakes in Central and Southern California. But they did not find a regional difference in the scaling for the spectral accelerations at 1 s. Atkinson and Morrison (2009) used a similar dataset (M 3.5–5 ShakeMap data) to conclude that peak ground acceleration (PGA) is higher in Southern California than Northern California, over a broad distance range. They also noted differences in attenuation for PGA, peak ground velocity, and spectral accelerations (1 and 0.3 s), for distances beyond 100 km. A comparison of the findings reported by Raoof *et al.* (1999) and Malagnini *et al.* (2007) reveals differences in crustal attenuation, scattering, and source scaling that lead to regional variations in ground-motion amplitude and duration between Northern and Southern California. These two studies point to apparent regional differences in both source and wave-propagation features. Using the NGA-W2 data set (Bozorgnia *et al.*, 2014; Lavrentiadis *et al.*, 2021) evaluated regional differences in the ground-motion scaling within California using a nonergodic GMM approach for the Fourier amplitude spectrum (Lavrentiadis *et al.*, 2022). Their nonergodic GMM included nonergodic terms for spatial variations of the site and event terms and large-distance attenuation (linear R terms). The event terms are systematic statistical deviations of all the recordings within an earthquake with respect to a reference ergodic GMM. In the nonergodic ground-motion modeling nomenclature, the spatially averaged event terms are often called "source terms," but they represent not only specific features regarding the rupture process; regional differences in wave propagation can also be mapped into the event terms, as this study shows. Maps for four frequencies between 0.2 and 10 Hz are shown in Figure 1, using data from Lavrentiadis *et al.* (2021). At low frequencies, the boundary between positive and negative event terms aligns with the boundary of the seismic networks reporting moment magnitudes, suggesting it may reflect operational variations in magnitude estimation among the networks.

More recently, regional variability in ground motions has been examined in greater detail for California. Using the expanded NGA-W3 dataset (Buckreis *et al.*, 2025), Abrahamson *et al.* (2025) evaluated regional differences in event terms in California using a nonergodic GMM. The NGA-W3 dataset includes many more events in Eastern California than the NGA-W2 dataset (compare Figs. 1 and 2), providing improved constraints on the spatial pattern of the low-frequency nonergodic event terms. The spatially averaged event terms ($\delta L2L$) from this new dataset, shown in Figure 2, tend to be positive in the coastal Central California and Los Angeles regions and are negative in the Eastern California and most of Southern California. The positive event terms in coastal Central California are consistent with the location of the two primary geologic units in this region: the Franciscan Complex (Bailey *et al.*, 1964; Phelps *et al.*, 2008) and the Great Valley Formation (Bartow and Nilsen, 1990). The Franciscan Complex is an accretionary prism assemblage formed by the subduction of the Farallon plate beneath the North American plate, comprising a heterogeneous mix of sedimentary, volcanic, and metamorphic sequences. The Great Valley Formation comprises a thick succession of marine sandstones, shales, and conglomerates deposited in a forearc basin between the Sierra Nevada arc and the Franciscan subduction complex. The Northern California Seismic Network uses the Gil7 velocity model (Dreger and Romanowicz, 1994) to characterize these two sedimentary sequences, which are significantly more compliant than the intrusive granitic basement that dominates Eastern and Southern California, as shown later. The spatial domain adopted by the Northern California Seismic Network is displayed with the blue-dashed lines in Figure 2. The extension of the positive event terms further east, previously identified by Lavrentiadis *et al.* (2021), appears to be rooted in the assumption of isotropic correlation lengths in Gaussian process regressions, with long correlation lengths in the north–south direction applied to the east–west direction. With improved sampling of earthquakes in Eastern California, the spatial patterns of event terms in the NGA-W3 dataset are now better constrained.

In this study, we investigate the sources of differences in event terms between coastal Central and Northern California and Southern California to determine whether they are driven by differences in magnitude estimates by the two networks or by regional differences in seismic sources and/or wave propagation. We begin by analyzing the moment tensor inversion (MTI) procedure used by the two seismic networks that report

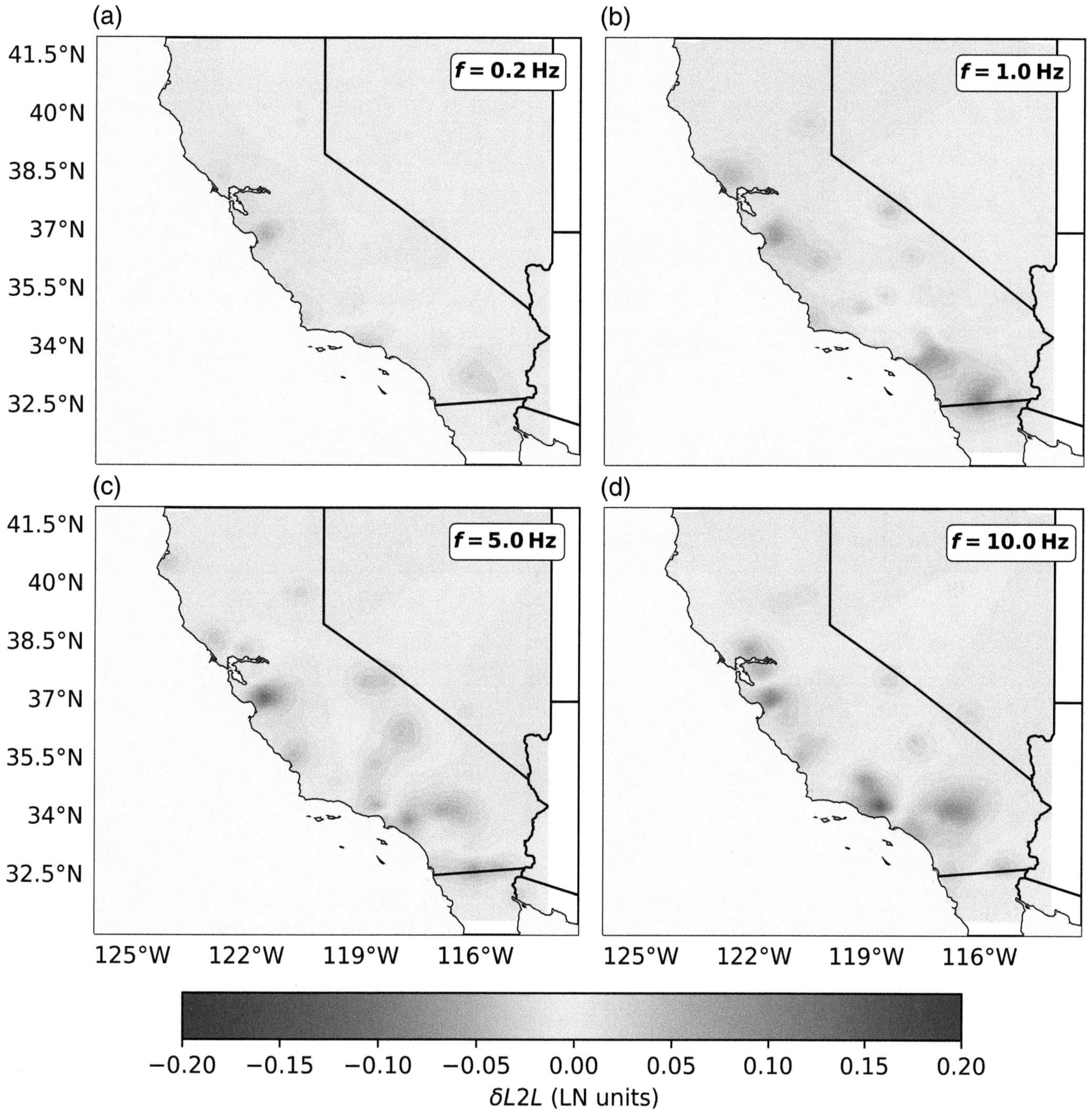

Figure 1. Nonergodic $\delta L2L$ terms (in LN units) for California from Lavrentiadis *et al.* (2021) using the Next Generation Attenuation-West2 (NGA-W2) dataset for spectral acceleration. $\delta L2L$ is the spatially average event terms from a Gaussian process regression. (a) 0.2, (b) 1.0, (c) 5.0, and (d) 10.0 Hz. The color version of this figure is available only in the electronic edition.

magnitudes in Northern and Southern California. Then, we analyze the impulsive response of the main velocity models used for MTI in California. These two analyses provide insight into whether the differences are attributable to source differences or to regional wave-propagation differences. In addition, to ensure consistent magnitude estimation in the NGA-W3 dataset, we perform MTI on California earthquakes that lack a moment magnitude from MTI, which accounts for about one-third of the California events in the dataset. We conclude this study by identifying a potential explanation for the observed regional differences in event terms and offering recommendations for regional seismic network operators based on our findings.

COMMON MTI METHODS USED FOR WESTERN U.S. EARTHQUAKES

In this section, we review the various MTI methods that contribute to moment magnitude estimations for events in the Comprehensive Catalog (ComCat, from the U.S. Geological Survey [USGS], Guy*et al.*, 2015), the main catalog used by

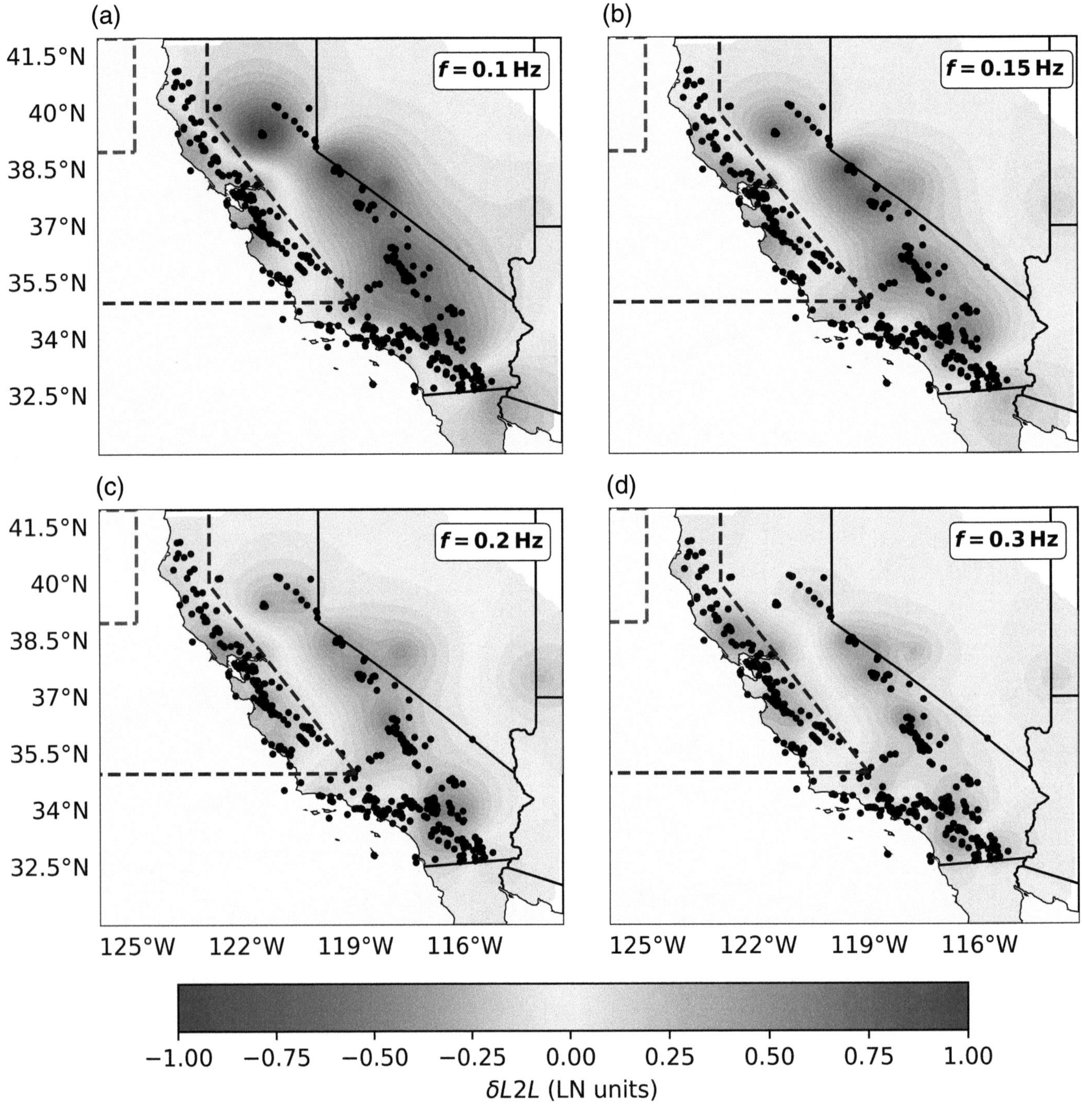

Figure 2. Nonergodic $\delta L2L$ for California using the NGA-W3 dataset for the Fourier amplitude spectra. (a) 0.1, (b) 0.15, (c) 0.2, (d) 0.3 Hz. The black dots are the epicenter of earthquakes with magnitudes less than 6. The blue dashed polygon represents the regions where the Gil7 velocity model is applied. The green dashed polygon represents the region where the Mend1 velocity model is used. Outside the Gil7 model, the SoCal model is used. $\delta L2L$ is the spatially average event terms from a Gaussian process regression. The color version of this figure is available only in the electronic edition.

the NGA-W3 project to retrieve earthquake source information. As a brief introduction, the process of estimating seismic moment is based on an inversion scheme, in which an observation from an earthquake located at $\vec{x}_e$ and recorded at $\vec{x}_s$, $\vec{u}(\vec{x}_e,\vec{x}_s)$, can be modeled in the frequency domain, at frequency "f," as a convolution,

$$u_i(\vec{x}_e,\vec{x}_s,f) = G_{ij}(\vec{x}_e,\vec{x}_s,f)M_j(\vec{x}_e,f). \quad (1)$$

The symmetric second-order moment tensor $M_{ij}(\vec{x}_e,f)$ has six independent components. $M_j(\vec{x}_e,f)$ is the vectorized moment tensor: $M_j(\vec{x}_e,f) = [M_{xx},M_{yy},M_{zz},M_{xy},M_{xz},M_{yz}]^T$. $G_{ij}(\vec{x}_e,\vec{x}_s,f)$ is the reduced second-order Green's tensor, obtained by simplifying the third-order tensor G_{ijk} when accounting for the six independent components of the symmetric moment tensor.

Physically, $G_{ij}(\vec{x}_e,\vec{x}_s,f)$ represents the impulsive response of the crust in component "i" at a receiver located at $\vec{x}_s$ due to a unit double-couple (DC) acting in the "j" direction at a source located at $\vec{x}_e$. Einstein's summation convention is adopted when repeating subscripts. u_i is the "i" component of our observations from the seismic stations located at $\vec{x}_s$ and G_{ij} is computed from the adopted Earth models. Then, the MTI involves finding the amplitude at the source, represented by $M_j(\vec{x}_e,f)$, that minimizes the differences between the observations when multiple stations are included in the analysis.

Global Centroid Moment Tensor

The Global Centroid Moment Tensor (Global CMT) project, run at Lamont Doherty Earth Observatory (LDEO) at Columbia University (Ekström *et al.*, 2012), performs MTIs to estimate the moment magnitude and source mechanism for all earthquakes globally with magnitudes generally larger than 4.8. The catalog is considered a global standard for moment magnitude and source mechanism of moderate-to-large earthquakes worldwide.

The method performs a multistep, nonlinear inversion for the 3D centroid location (longitude, latitude, and centroid depth), as well as the centroid time shift with respect to the origin time. The inversion is performed under the assumption of the deviatoric constraint, that is, the resulting source mechanisms are forced to have a zero isotropic component.

Global CMT solutions invert for the best-fitting centroid using teleseismic waveforms, taking advantage of different parts of the wavefield at global scales, including body waves and long- and intermediate-period surface waves. Different phases at different periods are weighted differently depending on the magnitude. For earthquakes with larger preliminary magnitudes, longer period data are given a higher weight. Depending on the magnitude, the Global CMT method inverts displacement or velocity waveforms and progressively uses longer period data for larger earthquakes. Green's functions (GFs) for the inversion are computed using the preliminary reference Earth model (PREM, Dziewonski and Anderson, 1981), incorporating corrections from a global 3D model for surface-wave dispersion (Ekström *et al.*, 2012).

NEIC *W*-phase moment tensor

The USGS National Earthquake Information Center (NEIC) performs a centroid moment tensor (CMT) inversion using only *W*-phase data for earthquakes of magnitude $M > 5.0$ (Hayes *et al.*, 2009; Duputel *et al.*, 2012). The *W* phase is a long-period (~100 to 1000 s) phase that captures the total near- and far-field long-period wavefield of the source (Kanamori and Rivera, 2008). It arrives before the *S* phase, allowing for the prompt determination of magnitude without having to wait for the full wavefield, which contains minor- and major-arc surface wave trains, to reach global seismic networks. NEIC runs *W*-phase CMT inversions using a similar algorithm as the one used by Global CMT inversions, and using the same global 1D model (PREM) to obtain the GFs. Because of their procedural similarities, the *W*-phase moment magnitude (M_{ww}) is in good agreement with Global CMT M_w (Duputel *et al.*, 2012). M_{ww} is generally available for events as small as M 5, and gives robust results at $M \geq 5.5$, at which point M_{ww} is available for the vast majority of events. It is usually the preferred magnitude in ComCat when it is computed.

Regional network time-domain MTI

In the California region of the Advanced National Seismic System (ANSS), which lies under the responsibility of the California Integrated Seismic Network (CISN), regional networks carry out MTI using the Time-Domain MTI method (TDMT_INV, Dreger, 2003), which is based on the work conducted by Dreger and Helmberger (1993). In this linear MTI scheme, three-component long-period waveforms are inverted for the six independent components of the moment tensor (Minson and Dreger, 2008). The method can also provide a depth estimate by iterating over a grid of depths and selecting the one that maximizes the variance reduction (VR) metric given a fixed epicentral location (e.g., Pasyanos *et al.*, 1996; Tajima *et al.*, 2002). A point-source representation is adopted, using the epicenter location and origin time given by the ComCat catalog from the USGS. Horizontally layered 1D velocity models are used to calculate the GFs. This assumption is valid at long periods (≥10 s), at which the effects of 3D lateral heterogeneities, such as the basins of the Central Valley, tend to diminish. In the TDMT method, before the inversion is carried out, the simulated and observed waveforms are aligned using time shifts obtained via cross correlation on a station-by-station basis. These time shifts compensate for any origin time and location errors, as well as phase mismatches arising from minor misrepresentations in the assumed 1D velocity structure. For a thorough review of the theoretical background of the method and its associated uncertainties, we refer the reader to Dreger (2018).

Operational implementation of TDMT_INV in California (the CISN region) is divided between two domains: Northern and Southern California. In Northern California, which is the area of responsibility of the Northern California Seismic System (NCSS), TDMT is operated at the Berkeley Seismological Laboratory. In Southern California, in the area of responsibility of the Southern California seismic network (SCSN), TDMT_INV is run at the California Institute of Technology (Caltech). As part of the latest round of reviews of ANSS operations, both the NCSS and SCSN have implemented a Python version of TDMT_INV developed by Chiang (2020), streamlining earthquake monitoring across California (Hagerty *et al.*, 2023). Pasyanos *et al.* (1996) provide more implementation details in the context of Northern California, but we supply here the most up-to-date operational choices for the reader's benefit. Operational details are similar between the NCSS and SCSN.

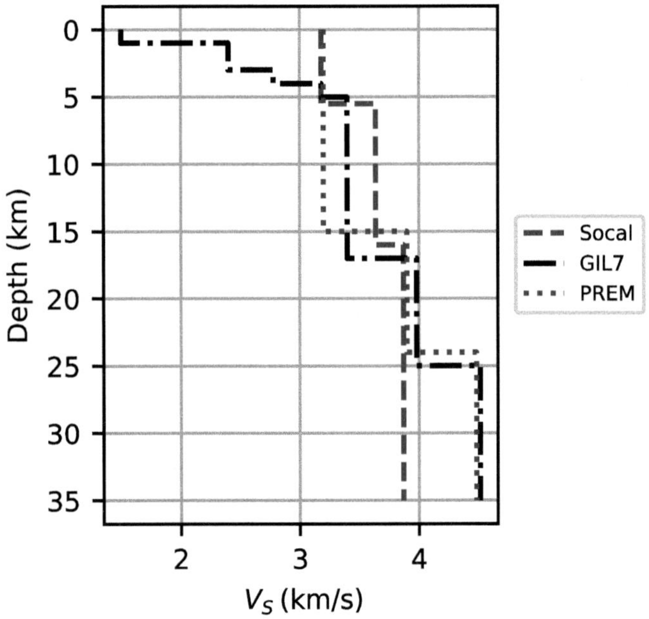

Figure 3. 1D velocity models used for full moment tensor inversion (MTI) for Northern California (Gil7), Southern California (SoCal), and the Global Centroid Moment Tensor (Global CMT) catalog (preliminary reference Earth model [PREM]). The Medn1 model was omitted because we do not invert for any offshore earthquake. The color version of this figure is available only in the electronic edition.

For every earthquake within the CISN ANSS region with a preliminary local magnitude $M_L \geq 3.0$, an automatic, first-pass analysis is performed that permutes different possible combinations of three or more stations that maximize the VR while optimizing azimuthal coverage. Events are assigned a source location and origin time set by the origin defined by the USGS ComCat. Different frequency bands are used for events of different magnitudes (Pasyanos *et al.*, 1996): 0.02–0.1 Hz (50–10 s) for $M < 4.0$, 0.02–0.05 Hz (50–20 s) for $4.0 \leq M < 5.0$, and 0.01–0.05 Hz (100–20 s) for $M \geq 5.0$. The NCSS uses three different regionalized 1D velocity models to account for the different seismotectonic provinces it is responsible for (velocity models in Fig. 3). The Gil7 model (Dreger and Romanowicz, 1994) is used for paths in the San Francisco Bay Area, coastal regions and the Central Valley (Fig. 2). The Mend1 model (Tajima *et al.*, 2000) is used for offshore earthquakes in Mendocino. The SoCal model (Kanamori and Hadley, 1975) is used everywhere outside the Gil7 and Mend1 regions and applies to paths that traverse granitic intrusive environments, such as paths east of the Coastal Ranges crossing the Sierra Nevada. The SCSN uses the SoCal model for its entire area of responsibility in Southern California. The domain for which each velocity model is adopted is shown in Figure 2. GFs are precalculated using the Computer Programs in Seismology (CPS) software package (Herrmann, 2013) at every 5 km distance from 30 to 895 km, for focal depths of 1.5, 3.5, 5, 8, 11, 14, 18, 21, 24, 27, 30, 33, 36, and 39 km. Generally, waveforms at distances 40–600 km are used for inversion. The NEIC method adopts an inverse-distance weighting scheme to compensate for amplitude decay with distance, giving more distant stations a higher weight (e.g., Zhu and Helmberger, 1996). Without this weighting scheme, stations nearer the epicenter would exhibit larger residual amplitudes and dominate the regression. The distance-weighting scheme corrects the analysis so that each station contributes equally to the inversion. The automatic analysis only allows for deviatoric MTI (i.e., the inverted moment tensor is not allowed to have an isotropic component, and only five moment tensor components are allowed to freely vary).

Once the automatic moment tensor solutions are available (within 5–10 min of the event), they undergo review by expert analysts. Analysts try to optimize the VR metric while ensuring the highest possible DC percentage as well as broad agreement with the first-motion polarity and the USGS hypocentral depth. To do so, analysts review waveform fits and attempt to improve them for individual stations by manually perturbing the automatically determined time shifts and adding or subtracting individual stations from the inversion. Analysts are also allowed to explore whether the VR of moment tensor solutions can be improved by conducting a full moment tensor analysis, allowing isotropic components in the solution (i.e., all six moment tensor components are allowed to vary freely). Analysts may also choose to use a different period band (e.g., in cases of noisy data) and/or velocity model for a particular station in pursuit of optimizing the fit. Solutions are published to ComCat if both the VR and DC exceed 60%. Solutions pushed to ComCat become the authoritative moment magnitude and source mechanism for the ComCat event in question. Typically, high-quality solutions can be obtained for events as small as M 3.5, and are available for most events with $M \geq 4.0$. This MTI methodology is defined from alignments at a national level by ANSS, which implies that the Northern and Southern California networks use the same methodology to estimate moment magnitude.

SOURCE INVERSION OF EARTHQUAKES FROM THE NGA-W3 DATASET

To improve consistency in magnitude estimation within the NGA-W3 dataset, we perform MTI on California earthquakes that lack a moment magnitude estimation, which is approximately one-third of the California events. The NGA-W3 dataset includes 608 earthquakes in California with magnitudes $M < 6.0$. For $5 < M < 6$, there are 79 earthquakes, most of which were reported with M_w from MTI, except for seven earthquakes that occurred before 1968 for which magnitudes were assigned as part of the NGA-W project (Power *et al.*, 2008). There are 529 earthquakes in the subset with $M \leq 5$, of which 251 are in Northern California and 278 are in Southern California. Of these earthquakes, 188 lacked a moment

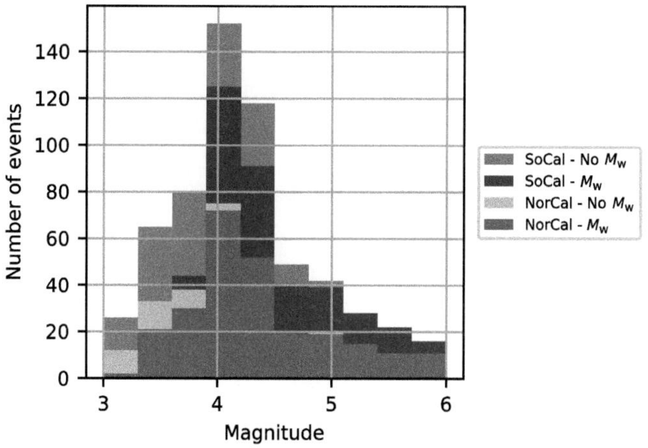

Figure 4. Distribution of the earthquakes smaller than magnitude 6.0 in the NGA-W3 for Southern and Northern California (SoCal and NorCal, respectively) before including the M_w from this study. Light colors represent the earthquakes with a magnitude estimation not based on full MTI. As detailed in the supplemental material, most of the earthquakes without M_w have an M_L (or M_{LR}) magnitude, excepting four with duration magnitude and two with an unknown type of magnitude. The histograms correspond to a stacked bar chart, which shows both the overall magnitude as a function of the length of the bar and the makeup of that total across categories. The color version of this figure is available only in the electronic edition.

magnitude from MTI; 39 are in Northern California, and 149 are in Southern California, representing 14% and 54% of the small-magnitude events in those two regions, respectively. The magnitude distribution of the earthquakes with and without M_w (see Fig. 4) shows that smaller magnitudes tend to lack a full MTI, which is consistent with the complexities of observing the wavefield at low frequencies from small earthquakes due to the ambient noise.

We perform moment tensor inversions for the 188 earthquakes in the NGA-W3 dataset that occurred in California that lack reported M_w. We follow the methodology described earlier for regional-scale MTIs. We perform the full MTI using the version of the TDMT code (Dreger, 2003) written in Python (MTTime, Chiang, 2020). In the first stage, we apply a Butterworth filter between 0.02 and 0.05 Hz to the waveforms, and we can perform MTI on 32 earthquakes. Then, we adopt a frequency band between 0.02 and 0.1 Hz to enhance the source visibility, implying sampling shorter wavelengths, which allows for the MTI of an additional 31 earthquakes. We do not perform MTI on five earthquakes that share an origin time with another earthquake within a 60 s time window, a standard for regional-scale inversions. For the remaining 125 earthquakes, we were unable to retrieve useful data from the servers, or the data were too noisy to discern the source-induced phases.

We augment the M_w dataset of the list of earthquakes without an MTI in the NGA-W3 dataset, by including earthquakes with reported M_w in the ComCat catalog, but their M_w values were not listed as the preferred magnitude. Eight earthquakes that occurred between 1998 and 2008 (four in SoCal and four in NorCal) have results from MTIs listed in ComCat. Between 2000 and 2006, 35 earthquakes occurred in Southern California with a reported M_w magnitude in the catalog, but without a reported focal mechanism. For these cases, the local magnitude (M_L) was listed as the preferred magnitude in the catalog. We include these 43 earthquakes that originally had M_L as the preferred magnitude (8 from the first case and 35 from the second case), extending the earthquakes with available M_w in the NGA-W3 dataset to 106 and leaving 82 without MTI, as summarized in Table 1.

TABLE 1
Number of Earthquakes for Which We Inverted a Moment Tensor with the Frequency Band Used

Frequency Band	Number of Earthquakes
0.02–0.05 Hz	32
0.02–0.1 Hz	31
Reported at ComCat	43
MTI not possible	82

We also list the earthquakes with available M_w from ComCat and the number of earthquakes in which MTI could not be conducted. ComCat, Comprehensive Catalog; and MTI, moment tensor inversion.

There are two differences between the M_w obtained from the TDMT code and the one adopted by the regional networks. The first difference arises in the definition of seismic moment based on the moment tensor. The TDMT code uses the definition from Bowers and Hudson (1999),

$$M_0 = M_I + M_D = \left|\frac{m_{ii}}{3}\right| + (\max(|m_i^{'}|, i = 1,2,3)), \quad (2)$$

in which m_{ii} is the moment tensor trace and $m_i^{'}$ are the eigenvalues of the moment tensor after removing the isotropic component. NEIC uses the Euclidean norm of the seismic moment tensor (Silver and Jordan, 1982),

$$M_0 = \sqrt{\frac{1}{2} M_{ij} M_{ij}}, \quad (3)$$

in which M_{ij} are the elements of the moment tensor. These two definitions of MTI converge if the calibrated linear vector dipole (CLVD) component in the moment tensor solution tends to zero. If the CLVD component is nonzero, a small bias arises. For instance, for a 20% of CLVD, M_w from equation (2) is 4% larger (0.014 M_w unit difference). For a pure CLVD mechanism, the difference in moment magnitude rises to 15%, or 0.042 units in M_w.

The second difference lies in the definition of moment magnitude. Hanks and Kanamori (1979) defined moment magnitude as a function of seismic moment in (N·m) as

$$M = \frac{2}{3}\log(M_0) - 10.7. \quad (4)$$

Some confusion has arisen between the original definition of moment magnitude by Hanks and Kanamori (1979), their

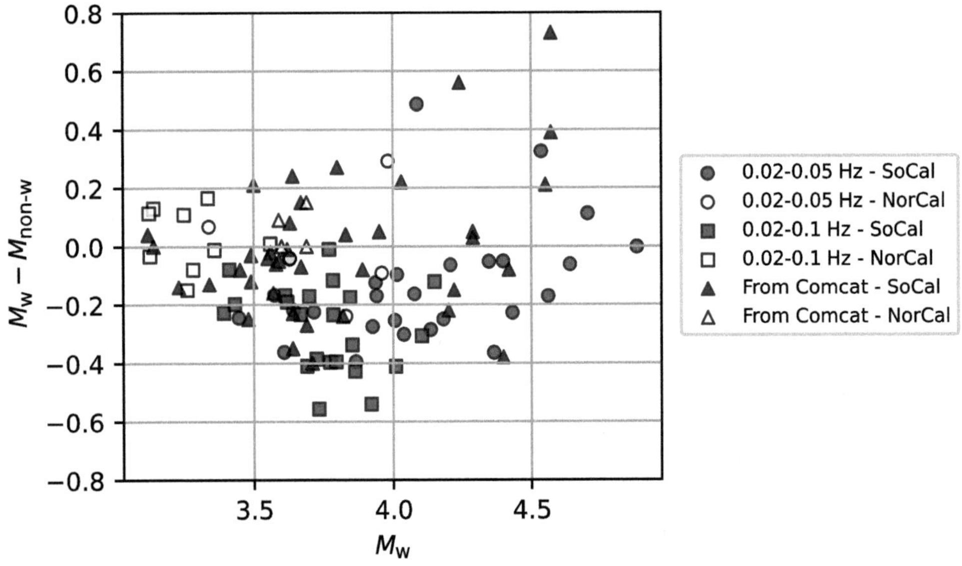

Figure 5. Residuals comparing the magnitude estimation using MTI versus the magnitude estimation based on local or duration magnitude. The circles and squares represent M_w estimated in this study from MTI and equation (3), with a frequency band of 0.02–0.05 Hz and frequency band 0.02–0.1 Hz, respectively. The triangles represent the 43 M_w values extracted from the Comprehensive Catalog (Comcat), as explained in the section Source Inversion of Earthquakes from the NGA-W3 Dataset. Markers without colors represent earthquakes in Northern California. The color version of this figure is available only in the electronic edition.

equation 7, and the underlying concepts of energy magnitude (M_w) from Kanamori (1977), which are similar but not identical. Over the years, the notation M_w has often been substituted interchangeably for M, which is not strictly correct. Moreover, the expression for moment magnitude is sometimes written as

$$M_w = \frac{(\log(M_0) - 16.1)}{1.5}, \tag{5}$$

which changes the constant of 10.7–10.733. This difference in constant leads to a 0.033 difference. The TDMT code uses the definition of Hanks and Kanamori (1979), whereas NEIC and Global CMT use the latter definition.

To keep consistency with the NEIC procedure, we calculate the seismic moment using equation (3) and 16.1 as the constant to estimate M_w. Our M_w values are available in the supplemental material. The difference between our M_w with respect to the originally reported magnitude without MTIs ($M_w - M_{non-w}$) is shown in Figure 5. In general, the difference is centered around zero, except for earthquakes in Southern California, with magnitudes between 3.5 and 4 when a frequency band of 0.02–0.1 Hz is adopted in the inversion. In addition, the magnitude residuals are heteroskedastic, that is, the standard deviation for earthquakes with M 4–5 events is larger than for M < 4. This heteroskedasticity may arise because the non-M_w magnitudes, most of which are M_L, are based on the convolution of the ground motions with the impulsive response of a Wood–Anderson seismometer; that is, high-pass filtering the wavefield above 1.25 Hz. The corner frequency is a macroscale manifestation of the event-specific dynamics. For small earthquakes, where the corner frequency is higher than the Wood–Anderson seismometer's frequency band (1.25 Hz), Munafò *et al.* (2016) shows that M_L scales directly with seismic moment. For earthquakes with magnitudes 4–4.5, the corner frequency is around 1 Hz (on average). In these instances, the Wood–Anderson frequency range may not lie entirely in neither the long-period part of the seismometer spectrum, nor entirely in the high-frequency part of the spectrum where the small-earthquake relations in Munafò *et al.* (2016) would cleanly apply. For this magnitude range, M_L may be affected by the event-specific dynamics (Bindi *et al.*, 2020). Bindi *et al.* (2020) showed that when M_L replaces M_w as the magnitude parameter in ground-motion analysis, the interevent variability is smaller, because M_L captures event-specific high-frequency ground-motion effects beyond the long-period spectral level.

We compare the between-event terms at 0.1 Hz with ($M_w - M_{non-w}$) in Figure 6 using the ASLPB25 GMM as backbone. Of the 106 M_w described previously, 46 met the data selection criteria for the ASLPB25 GMM at 0.1 Hz, thereby reducing the number of available earthquakes for comparison. The standard deviation of the event terms τ is 0.371 LN units, being close to the median τ from the ASLPB25 GMM at 0.1 Hz, 0.399 LN units. This subset includes only four earthquakes from Northern California, and the mean δB for Northern (Central) and Southern California is 0.108 and −0.083, respectively. In addition, the M_w values directly extracted from ComCat in general are within the δB versus ($M_w - M_L$) domain of those from MTI conducted in this study. However, some differences may still manifest in the event terms when the difference between the M_w value extracted from ComCat exceeds 0.5 M_w units compared to the old magnitude value in the NGA-W3 dataset.

Impulsive response analysis

A visual inspection of the 1D velocity models used for MTI (see Fig. 3) allows for an understanding of the different amplification patterns between them. Gil7 represents sedimentary

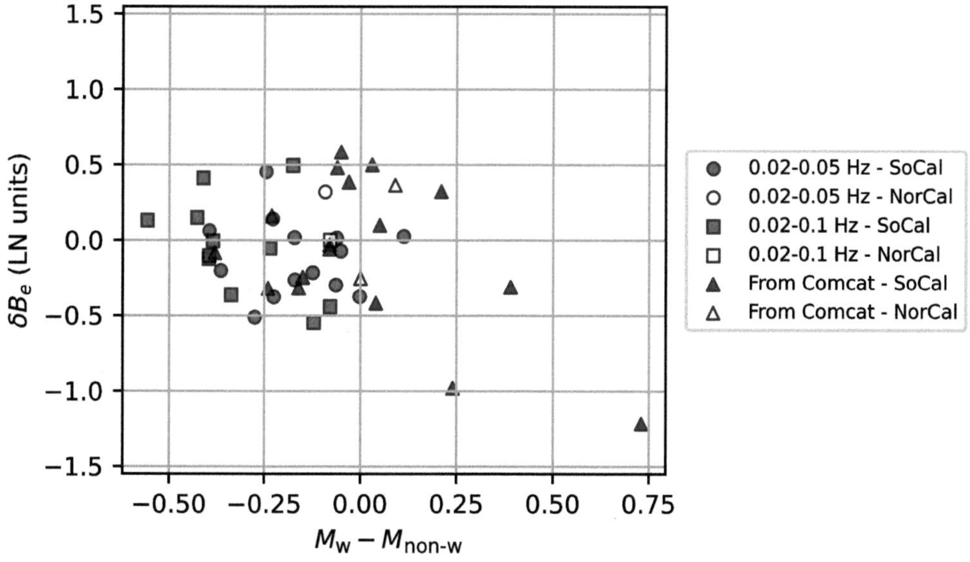

Figure 6. Event terms at 0.1 Hz from the ASLPB25 ground-motion model (GMM) as a function of the difference between the magnitudes provided by this study and the old magnitudes from the NGA-W3 without MTI. Out of the 106 M_w of this study, 46 passed the data selection criteria from the ASLPB25 at 0.1 Hz. The circles and squares represent M_w estimated in this study from MTI and equation (3), with a frequency band of 0.02–0.05 Hz and frequency band 0.02–0.1 Hz, respectively. The triangles represent the 43 M_w values extracted from Comcat, as explained in the section Source Inversion of Earthquakes from the NGA-W3 Dataset. Markers without colors represent earthquakes in Northern California. The color version of this figure is available only in the electronic edition.

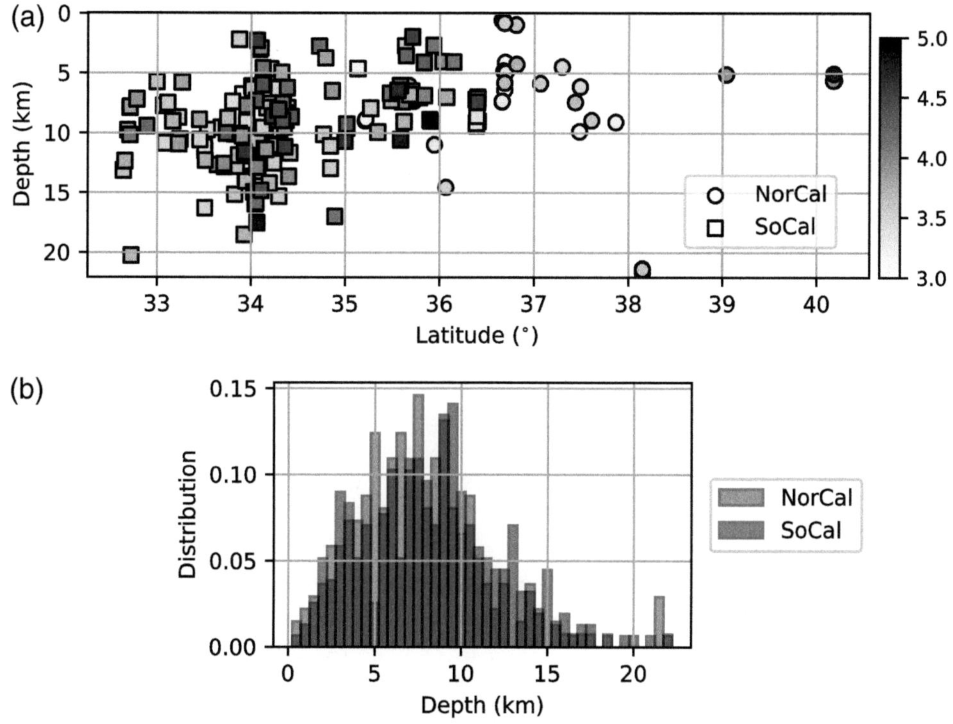

Figure 7. (a) Distribution of the hypocenters in depth as a function of the latitude. Circles and squares are earthquakes in the domain of the Northern and Southern California seismic networks (SCSNs), respectively. (b) Histograms of the probability density distribution of the hypocenters' depth. The medians are 8.27 and 8.38 km for Northern and Southern California, respectively. The color version of this figure is available only in the electronic edition.

sequences and is more compliant in the first 5 km, which tends to amplify intermediate frequencies more than the other two models. The SoCal and PREM models have similar depth-dependent velocities, with the former being slightly stiffer. The PREM model will exhibit a slightly stronger amplification than the SoCal model. We estimate the impulsive response in the horizontal component of these models for a vertically dipping strike-slip earthquake and a station 30 km from the epicenter, using a point-source representation. The median hypocentral depth of the analyzed earthquakes is approximately 8.3 km, as shown in Figure 7, which leads us to place the point source at 8 km for estimating the impulsive response. The GFs are computed using the CPS codes (Herrmann, 2013). The impulsive response for the horizontal component in the Fourier domain is displayed in Figure 8. At high frequencies (i.e., 0.1 Hz), the difference between Gil7 and the other models reaches a factor of 2. During MTI, this amplification difference is deconvolved from the observations, enabling an equivalent source estimate between Southern and Northern California. Then, a source of the same size will produce greater amplification in NorCal than in SoCal, solely due to wave propagation, which is then manifested in our observations.

When using a different frequency band in the velocity model, the wavefield is sampled at different length scales. If the velocity model is insufficiently well calibrated across all frequency bands, amplification

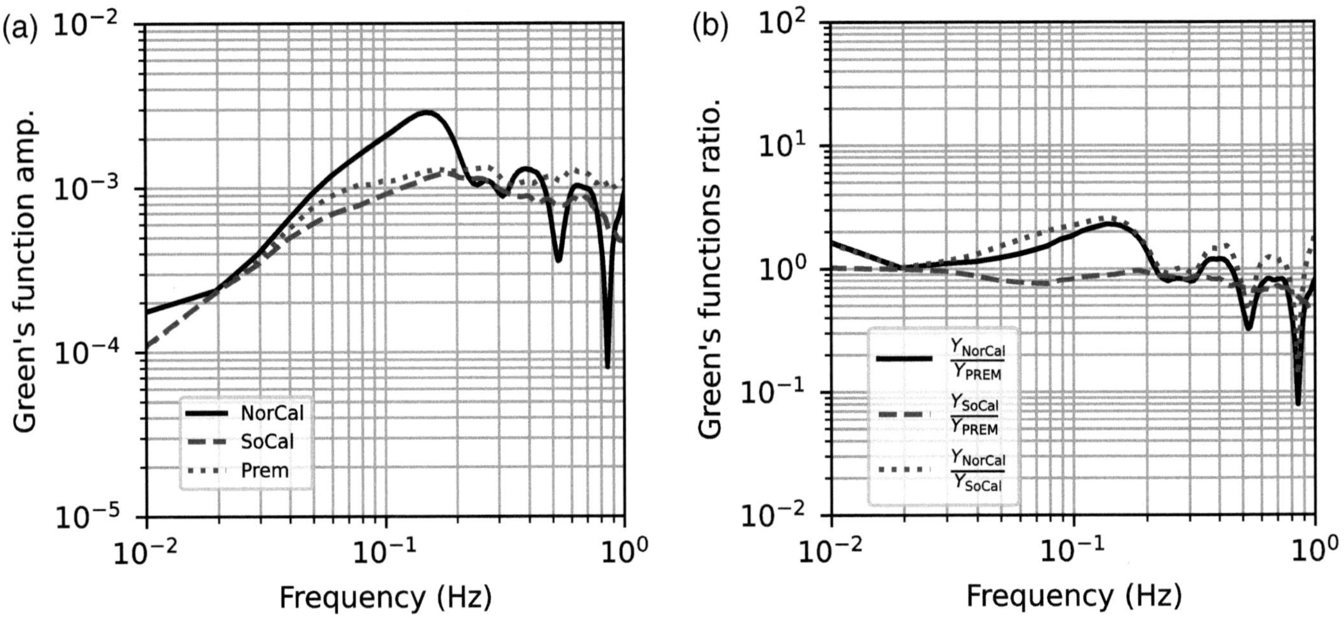

Figure 8. Example of the impulse response of the Gil7, SoCal, and PREM velocity models. We show the vector sum of Fourier transforms of the radial and transverse component fundamental Green's functions (GFs) for a vertical strike-slip focal mechanism, for a point source at 8 km depth and a receiver at 30 km epicentral distance. (a) Fourier amplitude spectra for the three different velocity models used in MTI: Gil7 for NorCal, SoCal and Prem. (b) Ratio of the Fourier spectra comparing the amplification difference among them. The color version of this figure is available only in the electronic edition.

biases may be introduced. Figure 9 shows the magnitude distribution for the NGA-W3 data set after including the results of this study. This figure suggests that M_w from Northern California exhibits a discontinuity in the distribution right below magnitude 4.0 (Fig. 9b), the approximate threshold at which the frequency band changes from 0.02–0.05 to 0.02–0.1 Hz in the MTI procedure. Southern California has a smoother transition at this magnitude because regional operators do not change the frequency band below M 4 (personal communication with personnel in charge of the SCSN's operations). This may imply that the Gil7 velocity model adds a slight additional amplification compared to the actual geological structures when transitioning to the frequency band 0.02–0.1 Hz, inducing a potential slight underestimation of M_w. For Northern California, this may result in an underestimation of M_w of around 0.05 M_w units, which is significantly smaller than the regional differences described in the Introduction.

Interpretation of regional differences in event terms

The regional differences in event terms between Northern and Southern California are not driven by differences in how the two seismic networks perform MTI. The two velocity models used in Northern California (Gil7 and SoCal) were the results of broadband waveform modeling and represent fundamental differences in crustal structure in terms of surface exposures, shallow materials, and the thickness of the crust (e.g., Fuis and Mooney, 1990). The GFs in Northern California using the Gil7 compensate for the amplification induced by the more compliant first 5 km depth of Gil7. Therefore, if the M_w estimates are consistent across regions, the observed regional differences are due to wave propagation. When the same seismic moment is applied in the two different velocity structures, the wavefield observed at the surface after wave propagation through the softer marine sequences of Northern California exhibits a larger amplitude.

Comparing the impulsive response between Gil7 and SoCal velocity models at 0.1 Hz (Fig. 8), there is a factor of 2 (0.7 LN units) difference in amplification for these two velocity models. For the same observed ground-motion amplitude at the surface, the computed magnitude will be lower for the Gil7 velocity structure than for the SoCal velocity structure. Ergodic GMMs for California use the same wave propagation and magnitude scaling for all California. With the larger amplification of the Gil7 model, the median ground motion from the ergodic GMM will underpredict the observed long-period ground motions for small-to-moderate magnitude events, leading to positive event terms.

To show this effect, we removed 0.7 LN units from the event terms of earthquakes within the Gil7 domain, based on the difference in amplification between velocity models. Next, we recentered the event terms, including all the earthquakes in California, so that the mean event term is zero. After that, we applied a Gaussian process regression (Rasmussen and Williams, 2006) to estimate the spatial average of the event terms, $\delta L2L$, for which results are shown in Figure 10. By balancing the average additional amplification induced by the Gil7 compared to the SoCal velocity models at 0.1 Hz, the regional differences in $\delta L2L$ tend to disappear. This indicates that regional differences in the long-period event terms from ergodic GMMs are attributable to differences in the velocity structures involved in wave propagation across subregions.

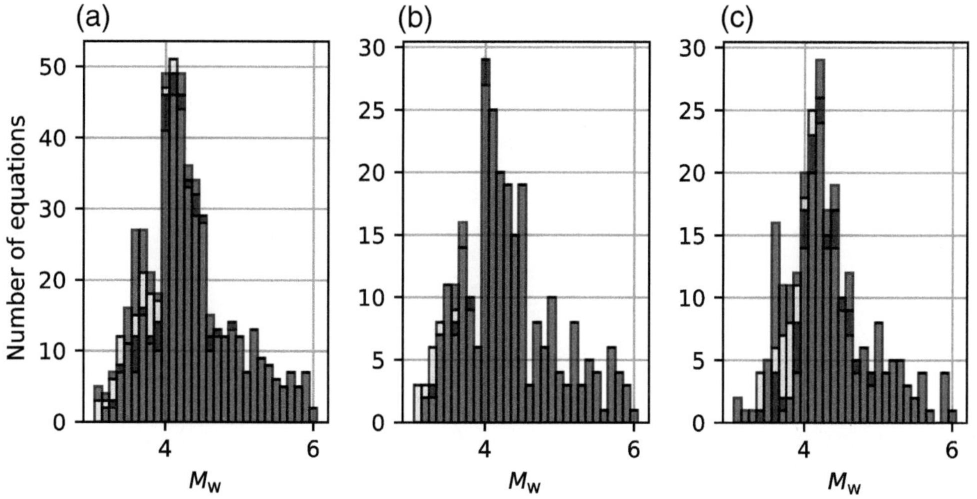

Figure 9. Distribution of the magnitudes of earthquakes with full MTI for $M \le 6$. The black and yellow bars represent M_w added from this study with frequency bands 0.02–0.05 and 0.02–0.1 Hz, respectively, whereas the green bars represent earthquakes with an M_w from MTI before this study. The red bars are M_w obtained from ComCat. (a) All earthquakes in California. (b) Earthquakes in Northern California. (c) Earthquakes in Southern California. The histograms correspond to stacked bar charts, which show both the overall magnitude as a function of the length of the bar and the makeup of that total across categories. The color version of this figure is available only in the electronic edition.

Using a more accurate regional velocity model yields consistent moment magnitudes, but the large effects of differences in wave propagation have been ignored in ergodic GMMs. Using current statistical methods, the differences in wave propagation effects are mapped into event terms in ergodic GMMs. However, they correspond to crustal amplification patterns which can be misinterpreted as source features.

DISCUSSION

Recommendation for the seismic network operations

In the context of full-waveform time-domain MTI, it is commonplace to use various frequency bands (e.g., Ford *et al.*, 2010) and 1D velocity models (e.g., Dreger *et al.*, 2021) in the inversion for a single event. Different frequency bands can improve the signal-to-noise ratio, whereas using different 1D velocity models can better model waveforms in areas with significant lateral heterogeneity. This is also done operationally for earthquakes in the Western United States. For instance, for NorCal earthquakes, the same event might have paths entirely within the Coast Ranges (best modeled by the Gil7 model) and others entirely within the Sierra Nevada (best modeled by the thicker-crust SoCal model).

Although this procedure can improve the fit with MTI observations, it combines the impulsive responses of the velocity models across frequency bands, which we have shown can induce uneven amplification patterns. Currently, the MTI process is not fully documented, preventing tracking of the procedure a given analyst used for the reported MTI solution and making it difficult to reproduce the published solution directly. We recommend enhancing the documentation by including the velocity model and frequency band used at each station in the solution files (e.g., the solution QuakeXML published on ComCat).

Including correlation of ambient noise to improve MTI

In areas of a dense seismic network close to the source (e.g., interstation distance of 5 km), it is possible to provide reliable MTI results for M_w down to M_w 0.9 (e.g., TexNet, Huang and Savvaidis, 2024). Typically, small earthquakes in California lack such dense spatial sampling, and ambient noise is the primary challenge in MTI retrieval from small earthquakes. In these instances, the ambient noise amplitude can be larger than the waveforms radiated by the source, obscuring its visibility. The current approach is to choose a frequency band that avoids the noise. An alternative approach is to develop a model for ambient noise and incorporate it into the moment tensor regression. For instance, there are codes for MTI that implement a Bayesian scheme to include the within-station cross correlation of the ambient noise (Mustać and Tkalčić, 2015, 2017; Vackář *et al.*, 2017). They model ambient noise in the regression by including its cross-correlation in the covariance matrix before the earthquake's arrival. This approach can help improve source visibility and enhance catalog quality when applying MTI to small earthquakes. It could be included in the NEIC MTI procedure. However, the Bayesian method relies on the choice of noise covariance model (Chiang *et al.*, 2025), and past work has shown that the results are sensitive to this choice (Mustać and Tkalčić, 2016; Mustać *et al.*, 2018). Therefore, despite the important contribution that the inclusion of ambient noise can produce, further work is needed to standardize a method for operational applications.

Implications of having the SoCal velocity model for all of Southern California

The region within and around Los Angeles has a complex basin system that can extend up to 9 km in depth. This region also exhibits positive event terms at 0.1 Hz (see Fig. 10) that can reach averaged values around 0.7 LN units. A similar situation occurs in the Imperial Valley, California's southernmost region. The SCSN is densely instrumented with seismometers over the Los Angeles basin, and these complex structures may introduce a spatial bias in the estimated amplification pattern relative to

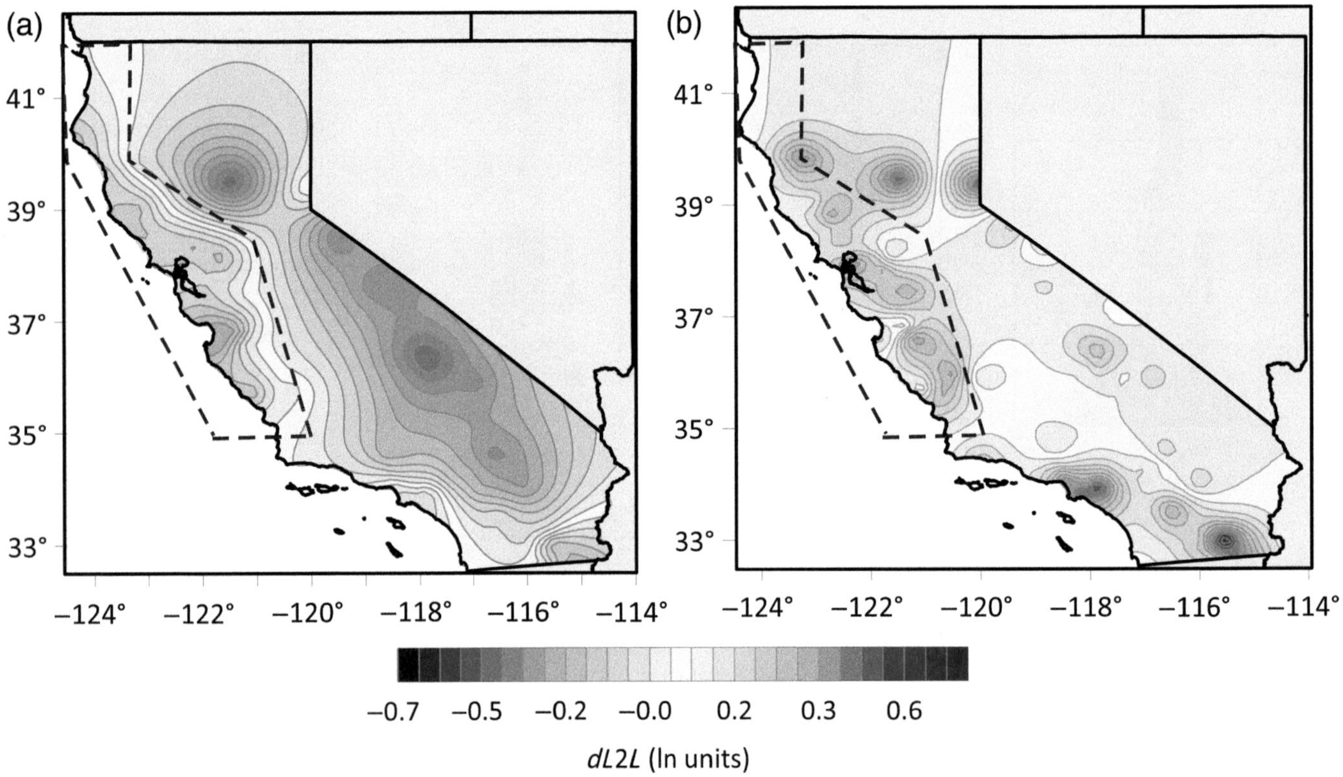

Figure 10. Spatial distribution of $\delta L2L$ at 0.1 Hz for Fourier amplitude spectra. (a) Results without adjustment. (b) Results after applying an offset of −0.7 in the event terms in earthquakes within the influence domain of the Gil7 velocity model (blue dashed lines). After removing the bias, a Gaussian process regression is applied to compute $\delta L2L$. The color version of this figure is available only in the electronic edition.

the geological structures represented by the SoCal velocity model when performing MTI. Therefore, the spatial distribution of the between-event residuals suggests evidence that the SoCal velocity model may poorly characterize some regions of Southern California. It raises questions about the suitability of using a single velocity model across the entire Southern California region. Our study demonstrates that more compliant structures within the first few kilometers of depth can alter the amplification pattern of the GFs and the crust's impulsive response, leading to misinterpretations of the moment magnitude. Consequently, we recommend revising a potential regionalization of velocity models to account for the inclusion of additional tectonic provinces in Southern California, such as the Los Angeles basin and the Imperial Valley.

Comparison between M_w from NEIC and Global CMT

In the NGA-W datasets, the initial approach was to prefer magnitudes from the Global CMT catalog over the regional network M_w whenever a Global CMT M_w value was available. The California seismic networks utilize regional velocity models for $M \leq 5.5$, which have been shown to provide better representations of the local geology (e.g., Ekström *et al.*, 1998), and adopt higher frequency bands in MTI, sampling shorter wavelengths, thereby allowing for visibility of the earthquakes' wavefield above the ambient noise. However, for larger earthquakes, the California seismic networks perform MTI using NEIC data via *W*-phase analysis in lower-frequency bands and change the velocity model to PREM.

For events in which both agencies report results from MTI for the same earthquake, the differences in M_w between Global

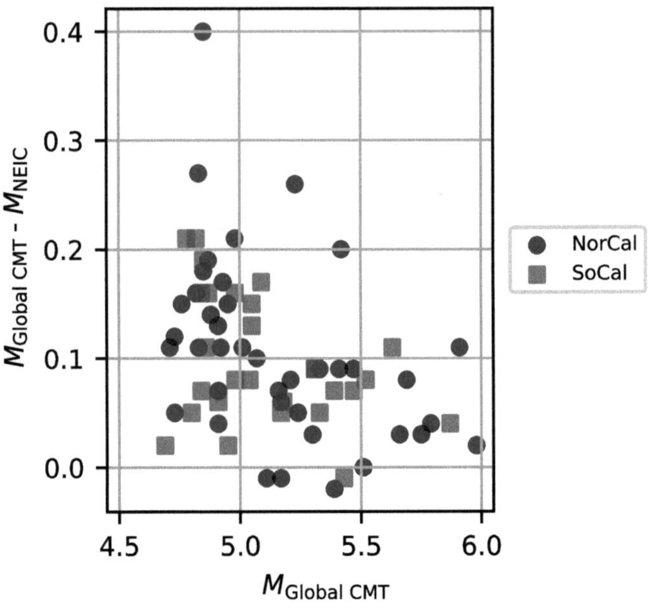

Figure 11. Comparison between the magnitudes reported by the Global CMT and the National Earthquake Information Center (NEIC) when both networks report M_w for a given earthquake. Black dots and red squares are earthquakes reported by the Northern California and SCSNs, respectively. The color version of this figure is available only in the electronic edition.

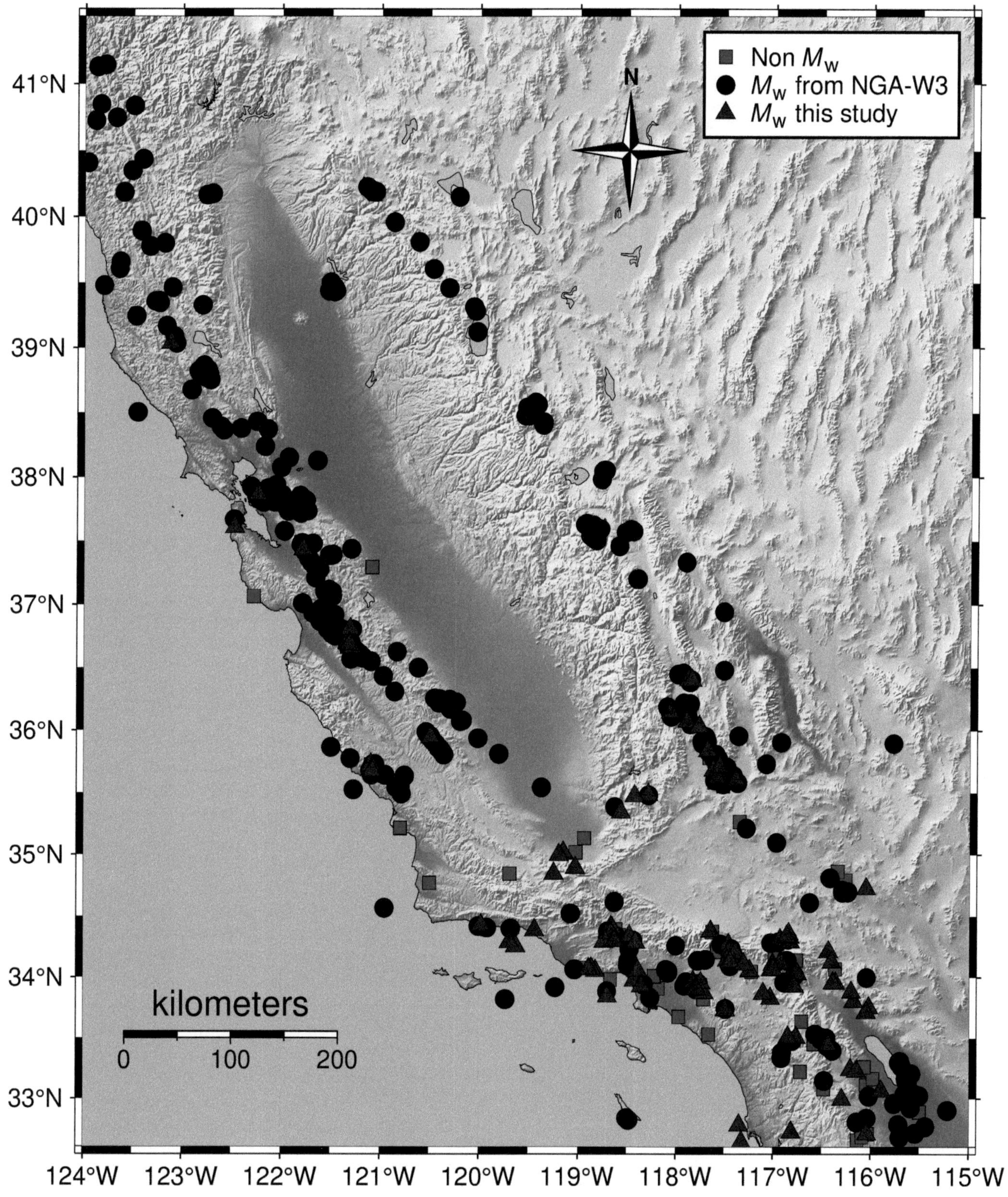

Figure 12. Epicentral location of the Californian earthquakes in the NGA-W3 dataset, differentiating between earthquakes with and without full MTI. The black circles are earthquakes that already had an M_w from the NGA-W3. The blue triangles are earthquakes with an M_w estimation from this study. The red squares represent earthquakes in the NGA-W3 dataset without reported M_w and, therefore, full MTI. The color version of this figure is available only in the electronic edition.

CMT and NEIC are compared in Figure 11. For the magnitude range addressed in this study, a systematic difference exists between M_w from NEIC and Global CMT, with the latter being systematically larger. This difference is also observed for events in Southern California, a region characterized by a velocity model similar to PREM, the model used by Global CMT. One source of this difference may be in the way Global CMT defines seismic moment with respect to NEIC, which is (Rösler *et al.*, 2021),

$$M_0 = \frac{1}{2}(|m_1'| + |m_2'|), \quad (6)$$

in which m_i' are the two largest eigenvalues of the moment tensor after removing the isotropic component. Other studies have also found this difference (Rösler *et al.*, 2021; Doody *et al.*, 2024). In particular, Rösler *et al.* (2021) showed that for earthquakes with $M_w \leq 6$, this mean difference ranges from 15% to 7.5% using data worldwide, with M_w from Global CMT being systematically larger. This trend tends to stabilize at $M_w > 5.5$, a magnitude range in which most of the MTI conducted by the Californian networks use the W phase in the PREM model. Therefore, if M_w from the local networks is available with $M_w \leq 5.5$, we recommend adopting a regional velocity model in the analysis rather than PREM; in that case, the M_w from the regional network should be used. Otherwise, the Global CMT magnitude should be used.

CONCLUSIONS

After revisiting the moment tensor inversion procedures employed by the Northern and SCSNs, we find that the two schemes are consistent with each other. The regional differences in the long-period event terms observed in GMM studies between Northern and Southern California are due to differences in regional velocity structures. The stronger amplification in the Gil7 model as compared to the SoCal model can explain the observed regional differences in the long-period event terms.

The use of different velocity models for MTI across regions within California has implications for future GMM development. Current statistical method used for GMMs will map regional wave propagation differences into the event terms. A revised methodology is needed to properly associate the event terms with earthquake-specific source features, reducing the contribution of these wave propagation effects in the event terms.

Estimating moment magnitudes for 106 earthquakes in the NGA-W3 dataset that lacked magnitudes significantly reduces the number of events for which magnitudes are estimated by converting local magnitudes to moment magnitudes during ground-motion modeling. The new spatial distribution of epicenters in California of earthquakes with M_w provides a comprehensive coverage of the main faulting systems in California (see map in Fig. 12). Except for a few regions, such as north of Santa Cruz and Santa Barbara, and south of Irvine, most subdomains in the NGA-W3 dataset now contain events with magnitudes based on MTIs.

DATA AND RESOURCES

We use the flatfile from the Next Generation Attenuation-West3 (NGA-W3; Buckreis *et al.*, 2025) released on 20 September 2024. The event terms were estimated from the residuals of the ASLPB25 ground-motion model (GMM; Abrahamson *et al.*, 2025). The supplemental material contains the dataset with the new magnitudes as a CSV file, along with a complementary plain-text file (readme.txt) with the column legend.

DECLARATION OF COMPETING INTERESTS

The authors acknowledge that there are no conflicts of interest recorded.

ACKNOWLEDGMENTS

David Shelly provided deep insights into the discussions and development of this study. Taka'aki Taira (Berkeley Seismological Laboratory) provided deep insight into operational moment tensor inversions in Northern California. Alen Husker, Ellen Yu, and Gabrielle Tepp provided insight into the operations of the Southern California Seismic Network (SCSN). Alexandros Savvaidis would like to thank the Texas Seismological Network and Seismology Research (TexNet) and the State of Texas, which provided support for this publication under the University of Texas at Austin award number 201503664.

REFERENCES

Abercrombie, R. (2013). Comparison of direct and coda wave stress drop measurements for the Wells, Nevada, earthquake sequence, *J. Geophys. Res.: Solid Earth* **118,** no. 4, 1458–1470.

Abrahamson, N., C.-H. Sung, G. Lavrentiadis, C. Pinilla-Ramos, and J. Bayless (2025). Ergodic ground-motion model for Fourier amplitude for crustal earthquakes in the Western United States, *Tech. Rept.*, CalTrans, Copy can be requested through Caltrans (R&D).

Atkinson, G. M., and M. Morrison (2009). Regional variability in ground-motion amplitudes along the West Coast of North America, *Bull. Seismol. Soc. Am.* **99,** no. 4, 2393–2409.

Bailey, E., W. Irwin, and D. Jones (1964). Franciscan and related rocks, and their significance in the geology of western California the effect of shallow San Francisco Bay sediments on waveforms recorded during the MW 4.6 Bolinas, California, earthquake, *Tech. Rept.* California Division of Mines and Geology Bulletin.

Bartow, J., and T. Nilsen (1990). Review of the great valley sequence, Eastern Diablo Range and Northern San Joaquin Valley, Central California, *U.S. Geol. Surv. Open-File Rep. 90-226*, 25 pp., doi: 10.3133/ofr90226.

Bindi, D., R. Zaccarelli, and S. R. Kotha (2020). Local and moment magnitude analysis in the Ridgecrest Region, California: Impact on interevent ground–motion variability, *Bull. Seismol. Soc. Am.* **111,** no. 1, 339–355.

Bowers, D., and J. Hudson (1999). Defining the scalar moment of a seismic source with a general moment tensor, *Bull. Seismol. Soc. Am.* **89,** no. 5, 1390–1394.

Bozorgnia, Y., N. Abrahamson, L. Al-Atik, T. Ancheta, G. Atkinson, J. Baker, A. Baltay, D. Boore, K. Campbell, B. Chiou, *et al.*

(2014). NGA-West2 research project, *Earthq. Spectra* **30,** no. 3, 973–987.

Buckreis, T., J. Stewart, and Y. Bozorgnia (2025). Data Resources for NGA-West3 Project, *Tech. Rept.*, Natural Hazards Risk & Resiliency Research Center B. John Garrick Institute for the Risk Sciences - University of California, Los Angeles, California.

Chiang, A. (2020). Time domain moment tensor inversion in Python (MTTime), doi: 10.11578/dc.20200303.3.

Chiang, A., S. R. Ford, M. E. Pasyanos, and N. A. Simmons (2025). Bayesian inference for the seismic moment tensor using regional waveforms and teleseismic-P polarities with a data-derived distribution of velocity models and source locations, *Bull. Seismol. Soc. Am.* **115,** no. 4, 1466–1478.

Chiou, B., R. Youngs, N. Abrahamson, and K. Addo (2010). Ground-motion attenuation model for small-to-moderate shallow crustal earthquakes in California and its implications on regionalization of ground-motion prediction models, *Earthq. Spectra* **26,** no. 4, 907–926.

Doody, C., A. Rodgers, A. Chiang, M. Afanasiev, C. Boehm, L. Krischer, and N. Simmons (2024). Improved earthquake source parameters with 3D wavespeed models in California and Nevada, *Seismol. Res. Lett.* **96,** no. 1, 499–509.

Dreger, D. (2003). 85.11 - TDMT_INV: Time domain seismic moment tensor INVersion, *Int. Geophys.* **81,** 1627.

Dreger, D., and D. Helmberger (1990). Broadband modeling of local earthquakes, *Bull. Seismol. Soc. Am.* **80,** no. 5, 1162–1179.

Dreger, D. S. (2018). Berkeley seismic moment tensor method, uncertainty analysis, and study of non-double-couple seismic events, in *Moment Tensor Solutions: A Useful Tool for Seismotectonics*, S. D'Amico (Editor), Springer Natural Hazards, Cham, Switzerland, 75–92.

Dreger, D. S., and D. V. Helmberger (1993). Determination of source parameters at regional distances with three-component sparse network data, *J. Geophys. Res.: Solid Earth* **98,** no. B5, 8107–8125.

Dreger, D. S., and B. Romanowicz (1994). Source Characteristics of Events in the San Francisco Bay Region, *U.S. Geol. Surv. Tech. Rept. Open-File Rept. 94-176.*

Dreger, D. S., R. Gritto, and O. Nelson (2021). Path calibration of the democratic People's Republic of Korea 3 September 2017 nuclear test, *Seismol. Res. Lett.* **92,** no. 6, 3375–3385.

Duputel, Z., L. Rivera, H. Kanamori, and G. Hayes (2012). W phase source inversion for moderate to large earthquakes (1990–2010), *Geophys. J. Int.* **189,** no. 2, 1125–1147.

Dziewonski, A. M., and D. L. Anderson (1981). Preliminary reference Earth model, *Phys. Earth Planet. In.* **25,** no. 4, 297–356.

Ekström, G., A. Morelli, E. Boschi, and A. M. Dziewonski (1998). Moment tensor analysis of the Central Italy earthquake sequence of September–October 1997, *Geophys. Res. Lett.* **25,** no. 11, 1971–1974.

Ekström, G., M. Nettles, and A. Dziewoński (2012). The global CMT project 2004–2010: Centroid-moment tensors for 13,017 earthquakes, *Phys. Earth Planet. In.* **200-201,** 1–9.

Ford, S. R., D. S. Dreger, and W. R. Walter (2010). Network sensitivity solutions for regional moment-tensor inversions, *Bull. Seismol. Soc. Am.* **100,** no. 5A, 1962–1970.

Fuis, G. S., and W. D. Mooney (1990). Lithospheric structure and tectonics from seismic-refraction and other data, *U.S. Geol. Surv. Prof. Pap.* **1515.**

Guy, M. R., J. M. Patton, J. Fee, M. Hearne, E. Martinez, D. Ketchum, C. Worden, V. Quitoriano, E. Hunter, G. Smoczyk, *et al.* (2015). National earthquake information center systems overview and integration, *U.S. Geol. Surv. Tech. Rept. 2015-1120.*

Hagerty, M. T., P. Friberg, and T. Taira (2023). AQMS-TDMT time domain moment tensor python package and GUI, *AGU Abstracts*, San Francisco, California.

Hanks, T. C., and H. Kanamori (1979). A moment magnitude scale, *J. Geophys. Res.: Solid Earth* **84,** no. B5, 2348–2350.

Hayes, G. P., L. Rivera, and H. Kanamori (2009). Source inversion of the W-Phase: Real-time implementation and extension to low magnitudes, *Seismol. Res. Lett.* **80,** no. 5, 817–822.

Herrmann, R. (2013). Computer programs in seismology: An evolving tool for instruction and research, *Seismol. Res. Lett.* **84,** 1081–1088.

Huang, G. D., and A. Savvaidis (2024). Reactivated seismogenic faults and earthquake source mechanisms in the Snyder Area of Texas, *Seismol. Res. Lett.* **95,** no. 6, 3709–3721.

Kanamori, H. (1977). The energy release in great earthquakes, *J. Geophys. Res.* **82,** no. 20, 2981–2987.

Kanamori, H., and D. Hadley (1975). Crustal structure and temporal velocity change in southern California, *Pure Appl. Geophys.* **113,** 257–280.

Kanamori, H., and L. Rivera (2008). Source inversion ofWphase: Speeding up seismic tsunami warning, *Geophys. J. Int.* **175,** no. 1, 222–238.

Lavrentiadis, G., N. Abrahamson, and N. Kuehn (2021). A non-ergodic effective amplitude ground-motion model for California, *Bull. Earthq. Eng.* **21,** 5233–5264.

Lavrentiadis, G., N. Abrahamson, K. Nicolas, Y. Bozorgnia, C. Goulet, A. Babič, J. Macedo, M. Dolšek, N. Gregor, A. Kottke, *et al.* (2022). Overview and introduction to development of non-ergodic earthquake ground-motion models, *Bull. Earthq. Eng.* **21,** 5121–5150.

Malagnini, L., K. Mayeda, R. Uhrhammer, A. Akinci, and R. B. Herrmann (2007). A regional ground-motion excitation/attenuation model for the San Francisco Region, *Bull. Seismol. Soc. Am.* **97,** no. 3, 843–862.

Minson, S. E., and D. S. Dreger (2008). Stable inversions for complete moment tensors, *Geophys. J. Int.* **174,** no. 2, 585–592.

Munafò, I., L. Malagnini, and L. Chiaraluce (2016). On the relationship between Mw and ML for small earthquakes, *Bull. Seismol. Soc. Am.* **106,** no. 5, 2402–2408.

Mustać, M., and H. Tkalčić (2015). Point source moment tensor inversion through a Bayesian hierarchical model, *Geophys. J. Int.* **204,** no. 1, 311–323.

Mustać, M., and H. Tkalčić (2016). Point source moment tensor inversion through a Bayesian hierarchical model, *Geophys. J. Int.* **204,** no. 1, 311–323.

Mustać, M., and H. Tkalčić (2017). On the use of data noise as a site-specific weight parameter in a hierarchical bayesian moment tensor inversion: The case study of the geysers and long valley caldera earthquakes, *Bull. Seismol. Soc. Am.* **107,** no. 4, 1914–1922.

Mustać, M., H. Tkalčić, and A. L. Burky (2018). The variability and interpretation of earthquake source mechanisms in the Geysers geothermal field from a Bayesian standpoint based on the choice of a noise model, *J. Geophys. Res.: Solid Earth* **123,** no. 1, 513–532.

Pasyanos, M. E., D. S. Dreger, and B. Romanowicz (1996). Toward real-time estimation of regional moment tensors, *Bull. Seismol. Soc. Am.* **86,** no. 5, 1255–1269.

Phelps, G. A., R. W. Graymer, R. C. Jachens, D. A. Ponce, R. W. Simpson, and C. M. Wentworth (2008). Three- dimensional geologic map of the Hayward Fault zone, San Francisco Bay region, California, U.S. Geological Survey Scientific Investigations Map 3045, available at http://pubs.usgs.gov/sim/3045/ (last accessed February 2026).

Pinilla-Ramos, C., A. Pitarka, D. McCallen, and R. Nakata (2025). Performance evaluation of the USGS velocity model for the San Francisco Bay Area, *Earthq. Spectra* **41,** no. 1, 457–494.

Power, M., B. Chiou, N. Abrahamson, Y. Bozorgnia, T. Shantz, and C. Roblee (2008). An overview of the NGA project, *Earthq. Spectra* **24,** no. 1, 3–21.

Raoof, M., R. B. Herrmann, and L. Malagnini (1999). Attenuation and excitation of three-component ground motion in southern California, *Bull. Seismol. Soc. Am.* **89,** no. 4, 888–902.

Rasmussen, C. E., and C. K. I. Williams (2006). *Gaussian Processes for Machine Learning*, MIT Press, Cambridge, Massachusetts.

Rösler, B., S. Stein, and B. D. Spencer (2021). Uncertainties in seismic moment tensors inferred from differences between global catalogs, *Seismol. Res. Lett.* **92,** no. 6, 3698–3711.

Sahakian, V., A. Baltay, T. Hanks, J. Buehler, F. Vernon, D. Kilb, and N. Abrahamson (2018). Decomposing leftovers: Event, path, and site residuals for a small-magnitude ANZA region GMPE, *Bull. Seismol. Soc. Am.* **108,** no. 5A, 2478–2492.

Silver, P., and T. Jordan (1982). Optimal estimation of scalar seismic moment, *Geophys. J. Int.* **70,** no. 3, 755–787.

Sung, C., and N. Abrahamson (2022). A partially nonergodic ground–motion model for Cascadia interface earthquakes, *Bull. Seismol. Soc. Am.* **112,** no. 5, 2520–2541.

Sung, C., N. Abrahamson, N. Kuehn, P. Traversa, and I. Zentner (2022). A non-ergodic ground-motion model of Fourier amplitude spectra for France, *Bull. Earthq. Eng.* **21,** 5293–5317.

Tajima, F., D. S. Dreger, and B. Romanowicz (2000). Modeling of the transitional structure from ocean to continent in the Mendocino region using broadband waveform data, *Eos Trans. AGU* **81,** no. 48.

Tajima, F., C. Mégnin, D. S. Dreger, and B. Romanowicz (2002). Feasibility of real-time broadband waveform inversion for simultaneous moment tensor and centroid location determination, *Bull. Seismol. Soc. Am.* **92,** no. 2, 739–750.

Vackář, J., J. Burjánek, F. Gallović, J. Zahradník, and J. Clinton (2017). Bayesian ISOLA: New tool for automated centroid moment tensor inversion, *Geophys. J. Int.* **210,** no. 2, 693–705.

Zhu, L., and D. V. Helmberger (1996). Advancement in source estimation techniques using broadband regional seismograms, *Bull. Seismol. Soc. Am.* **86,** no. 5, 1634–1641.

Manuscript received 3 October 2025
Published online 12 March 2026

A Set of Data-Driven Models to Predict V_{S30} from the Horizontal-to-Vertical Spectral Ratio of Microtremors

Kushal Sharma Wagle[1], Joseph P. Vantassel[*1], Adrian Rodriguez-Marek[1], and Balakumar Anbazhagan[1]

ABSTRACT

We investigate the use of microtremor horizontal-to-vertical spectral ratio (mHVSR) measurements to predict the time-averaged shear-wave velocity in the upper 30 m (V_{S30}) using data-driven machine learning models. We develop a global dataset comprising 2861 three-component ambient noise recordings made at 536 sites. We consider two different types of predictive models: low-dimensional models, which use mHVSR features such as the fundamental site frequency ($f_{0,\mathrm{HVSR}}$) and amplitude ($A_{0,\mathrm{HVSR}}$), and high-dimensional models, which use the entire lognormal median mHVSR curve to predict V_{S30}. In addition, we integrate two topographic features: binned elevation, as a proxy for geologic composition, and topographic position index, as a proxy for topography features. The low-dimensional models are shown to reasonably approximate V_{S30} when using mHVSR and the topographic features (coefficient of determination, R^2, up to 0.69 on the testing set). The high-dimensional models outperform the low-dimensional models (R^2 of 0.82 on the testing set) regardless of whether the lognormal median mHVSR curve is supplemented by the topographic features. In addition, we show that our top-performing model outperforms a recently developed model to predict V_{S30} from remote sensing data at sites from our testing set. Finally, we apply our models to predict V_{S30} from mHVSR computed at 1855 permanent broadband stations. We compare our data-driven V_{S30} predictions at a subset of 156 stations with measured V_{S30} values and find a reduction in the recommended model's predictive power (R^2 of 0.18). The reduction in performance at permanent broadband stations is shown to be related in part to differences in instrument type and data distribution between the temporary and permanent broadband datasets. Therefore, the proposed models are expected to perform best when mHVSR is measured using temporary deployments of broadband sensors. All the data-driven models developed in this study have been made publicly available.

KEY POINTS

- A set of open-access, data-driven models to predict V_{S30} from microtremor horizontal-to-vertical spectral ratio (mHVSR) has been developed.
- The developed models outperform existing prediction tools using mHVSR or remote sensing.
- Predictions of V_{S30} are made at 1855 broadband stations across North America.

Supplemental Material

INTRODUCTION

The effect of local site conditions on earthquake ground motions, known as site effects, can be significant and must be properly quantified when predicting ground motion for hazard analyses. One approach to quantify site effects is through site response analyses. Although the methods for performing site response analyses are well understood and are widely used, developing the site-specific, nonlinear properties necessary is not trivial. Instead, most ground-motion models quantify site effects through regressions using site-specific proxies. The most widely used proxy for site effects is the time-averaged shear-wave velocity of the upper 30 m (V_{S30}; Borcherdt, 1994; Building Seismic Safety Council, 1997; European Committee for Standardization, 2004). Although V_{S30} may not fully capture the complexity of site amplification (Castellaro *et al.*, 2008; Stewart and Seyhan, 2013), it provides a

1. Civil and Environmental Engineering, Virginia Polytechnic Institute and State University, Blacksburg, Virginia, U.S.A., https://orcid.org/0009-0003-5189-0031 (KSW); https://orcid.org/0000-0002-1601-3354 (JPV); https://orcid.org/0000-0002-8384-4721 (AR-M); https://orcid.org/0009-0000-9277-0552 (BA)

*Corresponding author: jpvantassel@vt.edu

Cite this article as Sharma Wagle, K., J. P. Vantassel, A. Rodriguez-Marek, and B. Anbazhagan (2026). A Set of Data-Driven Models to Predict V_{S30} from the Horizontal-to-Vertical Spectral Ratio of Microtremors, *Bull. Seismol. Soc. Am.* **116**, 1161–1177, doi: 10.1785/0120250128

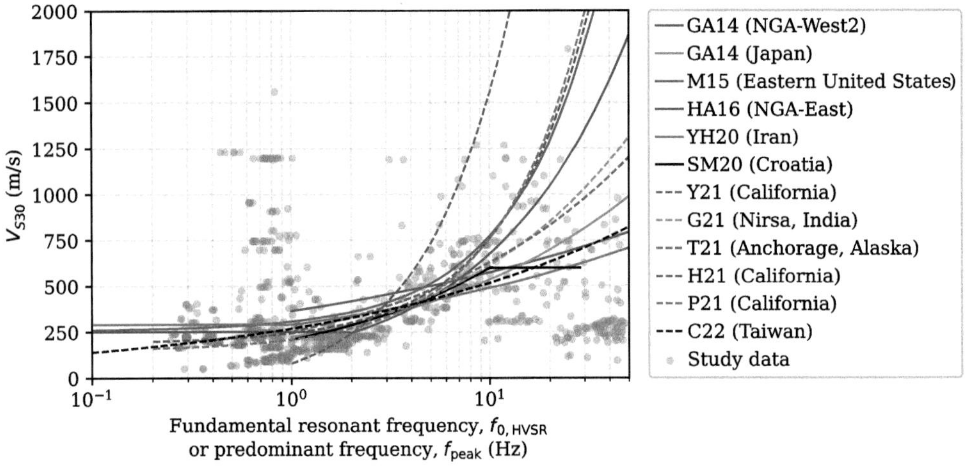

Figure 1. Comparison of existing models for predicting V_{S30} from horizontal-to-vertical spectral ratio (HVSR) resonant frequency ($f_{0,\mathrm{HVSR}}$ or f_{peak}) relative to a set of 1148 microtremor horizontal-to-vertical spectral ratio (mHVSR) measurements with a clear resonance collected as part of this study. For each existing model, the legend indicates the author(s), the year, and the region for which the model was developed. Additional details for each model, including whether the values of f_0 or f_{peak} are obtained from earthquake horizontal-to-vertical spectral ratio (eHVSR) or mHVSR, are summarized in Table 1. NGA, Next Generation Attenuation. The color version of this figure is available only in the electronic edition.

tractable solution. Furthermore, while V_{S30} is significantly easier to obtain than a site's full nonlinear properties, it still requires specialized measurements. As a result, nearly 85% of the seismic stations in the combined Next Generation Attenuation (NGA)-West 2 and NGA-East data sets lack a measured V_{S30} value (Seyhan *et al.*, 2014; Goulet *et al.*, 2021). Consequently, there is a need for cost-effective and reliable techniques to estimate V_{S30} across diverse geological settings for use in improving predictions of seismic hazard. This article's objective is to develop state-of-the-art data-driven models using machine learning to estimate V_{S30} from single-station ambient noise measurements. More specifically, this article presents a set of models to predict V_{S30} from site-specific horizontal-to-vertical spectral ratio (HVSR) measurements.

The HVSR technique discovered by Nogoshi and Igarashi (1971) and later popularized by Nakamura (1989) has been used extensively to measure a site's resonant frequency (e.g., SESAME, 2004). Although the full informative potential of HVSR remains a matter of debate (Molnar *et al.*, 2022), we hypothesize in this study that the lognormal median HVSR curve contains sufficient information for HVSR to be used as a reliable and easy-to-acquire proxy for V_{S30}. HVSR can be computed from either microtremors (i.e., mHVSR) (Nakamura, 1989; SESAME, 2004) or earthquake recordings (i.e., earthquake horizontal-to-vertical spectral ratio [eHVSR]) (Lermo and Chávez-García, 1993; Field and Jacob, 1995). However, recent studies have shown using data from California that mHVSR and eHVSR are not the same and should not be used interchangeably (Wang *et al.*, 2023; Vantassel *et al.*, 2024). Therefore, in this study, we only consider mHVSR because it can be measured on-demand using temporary instruments in less than an hour at most sites.

Our research builds on previous studies, which have shown that the resonant frequency from HVSR may provide a weak correlation to V_{S30} across limited geologic regions. We have identified 12 models from the literature that use HVSR-derived features to predict V_{S30}. To expedite the discussion of these models we organize them into two groups. Group 1 models are those developed using eHVSR at permanent seismic stations and include those developed by Ghofrani and Atkinson (2014), Hassani and Atkinson (2016), Yaghmaei-Sabegh and Hassani (2020), and Thornley *et al.* (2021). Group 2 models are those developed using mHVSR at temporary recording locations and include those developed by McNamara *et al.* (2015), Stanko and Markušić (2020), Hudson *et al.* (2021), Gupta *et al.* (2021), and Chen *et al.* (2022). All the models included in groups 1 and 2 use the resonant frequency of HVSR as one of their predictive features. However, the definition of what represents the HVSR resonant frequency differs between studies. Some studies use the fundamental resonant frequency ($f_{0,\mathrm{HVSR}}$), which is the lowest resonant frequency observed, and others use the peak resonant frequency (f_{peak}), which is the resonant frequency with the highest amplitude. Here, we use $f_{0,\mathrm{HVSR}}$ and f_{peak} consistent with the definitions provided earlier, even if the original authors used different terminology. For reference, a visual summary of the 12 models from the literature is presented in Figure 1, with the details of each model given in Table 1. Importantly, the relationship between HVSR resonant frequency and the site's subsurface structure is not unique (e.g., Parolai *et al.*, 2002; Castellaro and Mulargia, 2009). Therefore, some models have used other HVSR features, such as the amplitude of the resonant frequency (i.e., $A_{0,\mathrm{HVSR}}$ or A_{peak}) to improve the model's prediction. Yet, despite the introduction of peak amplitude, the predictive power of existing models is limited, as demonstrated by the comparison of the models with a dataset of 1148 mHVSR with a clear peak collected as part of this study, see Figure 1. A possible reason for the observed discrepancies is that the studies listed in Table 1 have limited regional coverage, thus the proposed models are believed to be limited to the geologic conditions for which they were developed. We quantify the limitations of existing models to generalize to new datasets in Table 1 by providing the

TABLE 1
Summary of Existing Models for Predicting V_{S30} from Horizontal-to-Vertical Spectral Ratio (HVSR)

Study	Reference	eHVSR or mHVSR	Predictive Feature(s)	Number of Sites	R^2 Train	R^2 Test
GA14 (Japan)*	Ghofrani and Atkinson (2014)	eHVSR	f_{peak}, A_{peak}	1742†	0.42	<0
GA14 (NGA-West2)*	Ghofrani and Atkinson (2014)	eHVSR	f_{peak}, A_{peak}	1215†	0.30	<0
M15 (EUS)	McNamara *et al.* (2015)	eHVSR	$f_{0,HVSR}$	21	0.89	<0
HA16 (NGA-East)	Hassani and Atkinson (2016)	eHVSR	f_{peak}	41	0.78†	<0
YH20 (Iran)	Yaghmaei-Sabegh and Hassani (2020)	eHVSR	f_{peak}	560	0.58†	0.01
SM20 (Croatia)	Stanko and Markušić (2020)	mHVSR	f_{peak}	244	0.93†	0.05
Y21 (California)‡	Yong *et al.* (2021)	eHVSR, mHVSR	f_{peak}	81	0.37†	<0
H21 (California)§	Hudson *et al.* (2021)	mHVSR	f_{peak}	72	0.62†	<0
P21 (California)§	Hudson *et al.* (2021)	mHVSR	f_{peak}	66	0.45†	<0
G21 (Nirsa, India)*	Gupta *et al.* (2021)	mHVSR	$f_{0,HVSR}$	78	0.63	<0
T21 (Anchorage, Alaska)*	Thornley *et al.* (2021)	eHVSR	f_{peak}, A_{peak}	35	0.72†	<0
C22 (Taiwan)*	Chen *et al.* (2022)	mHVSR	f_{peak}	1242	0.40	<0

Each model is summarized in terms of study, literature reference, whether the model used earthquake horizontal-to-vertical spectral ratio (eHVSR) or microtremor horizontal-to-vertical spectral ratio (mHVSR), the predictive feature(s), number of sites, model's reported coefficient of determination (R^2) (i.e., R^2 train), and R^2 computed using the dataset collected for this study (i.e., R^2 test). Note that the model's reported R^2 values correspond to model performance on the training set; none of the existing models set aside a testing set as part of their model development.
*Includes sites where V_{S30} values were estimated and not measured directly.
†Value was not reported. The value provided is estimated based on information provided in the article.
‡Best-fit line was obtained by digitizing the relevant figure in the article.
§Reference is to a conference abstract. The model was obtained from a personal communication with the authors.

coefficient of determination (R^2) for each model on the dataset aggregated for this study (discussed in detail in the following section). The ability of existing models to generalize is very poor with the highest R^2 achieved being 0.05 and with 10 out of 12 models resulting in an R^2 less than zero.

In response, this article aims to develop a set of data-driven models using machine learning (ML) to relate mHVSR to V_{S30} that are not bound to a specific city or geologic condition. The article begins with a description of the global dataset used in this study, including how microtremors collected with measured V_{S30} values were used for ML model training. Two categories of models to predict V_{S30} from mHVSR are presented: low-dimensional models, which use scalar features extracted from the mHVSR mean curve, and high-dimensional models, which use the full lognormal median mHVSR curve. These models are compared with an existing remote-sensing-based approach at sites where V_{S30} is known, but which were not used as part of model training. The models are then applied to 1855 broadband recording stations in North America to estimate V_{S30}. To evaluate the models' ability to generalize to mHVSR from permanent broadband stations, a subset of these predictions are compared against measured V_{S30} values from the literature. All the models developed in this study are publicly available, see Data and Resources.

DATA

A total of 2861 three-component microtremor recordings from 536 sites were used in this study. The microtremor recordings were aggregated from 23 previously published and 15 unpublished studies performed around the world, including in Europe (Italy), Asia (Taiwan), Oceania (New Zealand), and North and South America (United States, Mexico, Ecuador). A summary of the data used in this study in terms of location, number of sites, number of recordings, and literature reference is provided in Table 2. The majority (91%) of the microtremor recordings were collected as part of microtremor array measurements (MAMs), with the balance (9%) being single-station recordings. The use of mHVSR from MAM arrays enables the data-driven models to observe different mHVSR measurements that correspond to the same V_{S30}. We believe this is important to ensure that the model is able to differentiate between "significant" and "insignificant" differences in mHVSR (i.e., those differences that are and are not correlated with changes in V_{S30}, respectively). All measurements were made using broadband seismometers with a flat instrument response to at least a 20 s period (i.e., 0.05 Hz). The recording durations varied significantly across sites, ranging from 20 to 540 min. To develop the mHVSR–V_{S30} pairs to train the data-driven models, all microtremor measurements were processed identically and associated with a site-specific measurement of V_{S30}. The details of this process are discussed in the following paragraphs.

All the V_{S30} values used in this study were directly measured and were not inferred from existing correlations. The V_{S30} values in the dataset span from 50 to 2250 m/s, which includes site classes A to E as defined by the American Society of Civil Engineers/Structural Engineering Institute (ASCE/SEI) 7-22 (ASCE, 2022). The distribution of V_{S30} values in terms of their implied site class, according to ASCE 7-22, is shown in Figure 2. Most of the V_{S30} data (98%) were acquired using surface-wave methods, such as multichannel analysis of surface waves

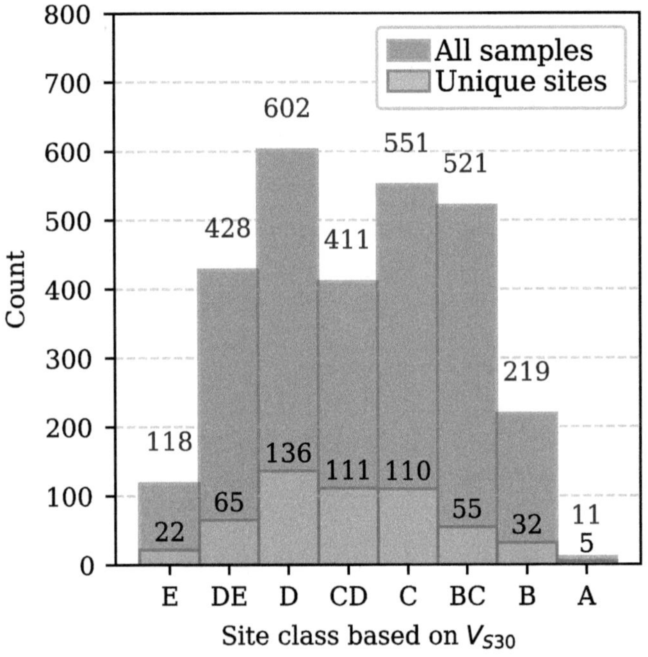

Figure 2. Distribution of data used in this study in terms of the V_{S30}-based site class as per American Society of Civil Engineers/Structural Engineering Institute (ASCE/SEI) 7-22, comparing all samples (shaded red) with unique sites (shaded blue) from the mHVSR dataset. The values above each bar indicate the sample count for each class. The site class boundaries, as divided by V_{S30}, in ASCE/SEI 7-22 are: E (< 152 m/s), DE (152–213 m/s), D (213–305 m/s), CD (305–442 m/s), C (442–640 m/s), BC (640–914 m/s), B (914–1524 m/s), and A (> 1524 m/s). The color version of this figure is available only in the electronic edition.

(MASWs) and MAMs, with the balance being obtained through invasive PS suspension logging and downhole testing. The sources of the V_{S30} data are listed in the references cited in Table 2. Of the 536 sites, 79 included multiple V_{S30} estimates. The multiple estimates of V_{S30} were either the result of multiple measurement techniques, for example where surface-wave and downhole measurements were made at the same site, or different data interpretations, for example where different plausible interpretations of the experimental surface-wave data resulted in different measures of V_{S30} (e.g., Yust, 2018). For sites with multiple V_{S30} measurements, we have chosen to average the different V_{S30} values and to neglect the uncertainty in V_{S30}. The standard error in V_{S30} at these sites was less than 0.10 ln units for the majority of the sites (i.e., 73 of the 79) and less than 0.25 ln units for all sites.

All the mHVSR data were processed identically following a semiautomated approach, which leverages *hvsrpy* (Vantassel, 2025) for mHVSR calculations and AutoHVSR (Vantassel *et al.*, 2023) for automated window rejection and resonance identification. First, each three-component microtremor recording was trimmed to equalize the duration of the three components using the ObsPy (Beyreuther *et al.*, 2010) Python package. Second, each three-component ambient noise recording was divided into 35 windows of equal length. Third, each window was linearly detrended, tapered with a Tukey window (Harris, 1978) with a taper ratio of 20% (i.e., 10% per side), and transformed to the frequency domain. Fourth, the horizontal components were combined using the geometric mean (SESAME, 2004; Cox *et al.*, 2020). Fifth, Konno and Ohmachi (1998) spectral smoothing with a bandwidth of 40 was applied at 256 logarithmically spaced frequencies between 0.05 and 50 Hz to the combined

TABLE 2
Summary of the Data Used in This Study in Terms of its Location, Number of Sites, Number of Recordings, and Reference(s)

Location	Number of Sites*	Number of Recordings	References
Italy	92	92	Felicetta *et al.* (2023)
New Zealand (NZ)	111	111	Barker (1996), Kaiser and Louie (2006), McVerry (2011), Wotherspoon *et al.* (2015), Wotherspoon *et al.* (2016), Deschenes *et al.* (2018), Cave (2020), Wotherspoon *et al.* (2024), Hill *et al.* (2023), and Stolte *et al.* (2023)
Christchurch, NZ	25	422	Teague *et al.* (2018)
Wellington, NZ	23	212	Cox and Vantassel (2018) and Vantassel *et al.* (2018)
Mississippi Embayment, United States	10	252	Wood and Himel (2019)
Mexico City, Mexico	25	156	Wood *et al.* (2020)
Taiwan	45	45	Kuo *et al.* (2016)
United States and Ecuador	32	219	Nikolaou *et al.* (2017), Rahimi and Wood (2022), Wood and Rahimi (2022), and Rahimi and Wood (2023)
California, United States	161	493	Yong *et al.* (2013)
Texas, United States	35	859	Yust (2018)

The number of recordings is equal to or larger than the number of sites because most studies included more than one ambient noise measurement per site. For some datasets more than one reference is provided.
*23 sites are replicated across datasets. These duplicate sites have been removed to obtain the 536 distinct sites that were used in this study.

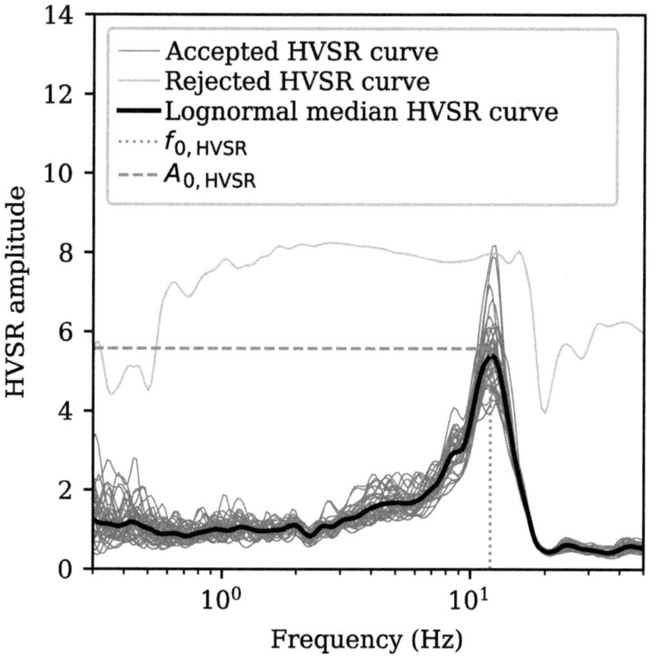

Figure 3. Example mHVSR after processing. The accepted mHVSR curves (one per time window) are shown in gray, and the rejected mHVSR curves are shown in light blue. The lognormal mean curve is shown with a solid black line. Values of $f_{0,\mathrm{HVSR}}$ and $A_{0,\mathrm{HVSR}}$ are indicated with vertical (dotted) and horizontal (dashed) lines, respectively. The color version of this figure is available only in the electronic edition.

horizontal and vertical components. The frequency range was truncated based on the duration of each time window to ensure that each window contained at least 15 significant cycles of the lowest processing frequency (Vantassel *et al.*, 2023). For example, a 35-min recording divided into 35, 60 s windows would have a minimum processing frequency of 0.25 Hz. Sixth, the data-driven tools for automatic window rejection and resonance identification built into AutoHVSR were applied. Although not discussed here for brevity, the details of AutoHVSR are provided in the original article (Vantassel *et al.*, 2023). AutoHVSR is publicly available through the open-source, web-based application HVSRweb (Vantassel *et al.*, 2021). Seventh, the results were manually reviewed to ensure the accuracy of window rejection and resonance identification. Eighth, the lognormal median HVSR curve was computed from the accepted time windows. Ninth, if a clear resonant peak, as defined by SESAME (2004), was observed the associated peak from every accepted mHVSR curve was used to compute the lognormal median frequency and amplitude following the procedure proposed by Cox *et al.* (2020). If multiple clear resonant peaks were present the lowest-frequency peak (i.e., $f_{0,\mathrm{HVSR}}$ and $A_{0,\mathrm{HVSR}}$) was selected. An example mHVSR measurement, highlighting both accepted and rejected mHVSR curves, is shown in Figure 3. The clear resonant peak is described by its $f_{0,\mathrm{HVSR}}$ and $A_{0,\mathrm{HVSR}}$ of 12 Hz and 5.6, respectively.

In addition to mHVSR, we explore the use of other proxies to improve the predictions of V_{S30}. Building on prior efforts to use topographic features for the prediction of V_{S30} (e.g., Wald and Allen, 2007; Allen and Wald, 2009; Chen *et al.*, 2022; Geyin and Maurer, 2023), we use two topographic features to supplement our mHVSR features: topographic position index (TPI) and elevation. The TPI is defined as the difference between the site's point elevation and the mean elevation within a 1500 m radius, capturing the site's relative elevation compared with its surrounding landscape (Rai *et al.*, 2017). Sites with positive TPI, often associated with ridges or elevated features, are typically underlain by shallow or exposed bedrock, implying higher V_{S30}. Conversely, negative TPI values, found in valleys or depressions, may indicate the presence of thicker alluvial deposits, implying lower V_{S30}. In addition to TPI, we use station elevation as an additional proxy. We acknowledge that the correlation between elevation and V_{S30} is less clear. However, as will be shown later, elevation improved our model's predictive ability on the validation set, and this improvement was maintained on the testing set. A similar parameter was adopted by Chen *et al.* (2022) in a predictive model for Taiwan.

Development of predictive models with machine learning

This study adopts an ML-based approach to explore the relationships between mHVSR and V_{S30}. Traditional regression models, such as those correlating the $f_{0,\mathrm{HVSR}}$ or f_{peak} to V_{S30} (recall Fig. 1), are often constrained by assuming a linear or log–linear relationship. In contrast, ML algorithms offer the flexibility to model nonlinear relationships making it possible to capture more-complex patterns in the mHVSR. With the availability of mHVSR–V_{S30} datasets expected to continue to grow, ML provides a scalable framework capable of capturing relationships that are difficult to formulate analytically. Once trained, these models are computationally efficient, allowing for the rapid prediction of V_{S30} from distributed microtremor measurements. In this study, a suite of predictive models was developed using supervised ML. We divide the developed models into two categories: low-dimensional models, which use a limited number of mHVSR features, and high-dimensional models, which use the entire lognormal median mHVSR curve. For both model categories, we also consider supplementing the mHVSR-derived data with the topographic features previously discussed and select, on a model-by-model basis, whether to include those features based on the model's performance on the validation set.

Low-dimensional models

The low-dimensional models were developed using only those mHVSR with clear resonant peaks, as defined by SESAME (2004). The data meeting this requirement included 1148 samples from 281 distinct sites. We use five features in the low-dimensional models to predict V_{S30}, these are described in detail below and summarized in the corner plot provided in Figure 4. Note that for completeness Figure 4, if possible, also

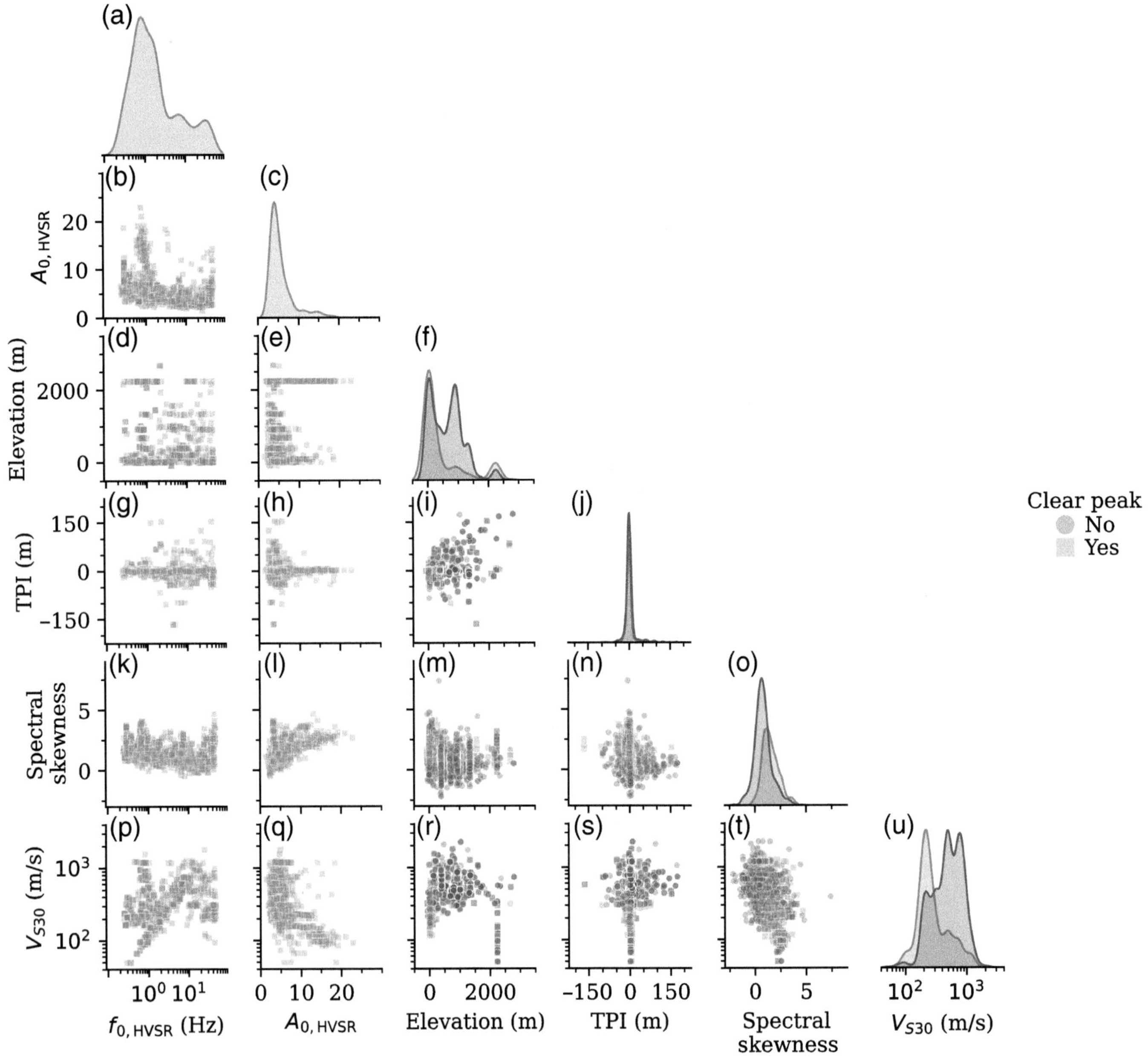

Figure 4. (a–u) Corner plot illustrating the distribution of the five features ($f_{0,\mathrm{HVSR}}$, $A_{0,\mathrm{HVSR}}$, elevation, topographic position index [TPI], and spectral skewness) used in the low-dimensional models to predict V_{S30}. The main diagonals are kernel density estimate (KDE) plots for each feature and the off-diagonals are scatter plots for each pair of features. The KDE and scatter plots are colored according to whether a clear resonant peak was observed in the mHVSR. The color version of this figure is available only in the electronic edition.

presents the low-dimensional model features for mHVSR without a clear resonant peak. We also provide a version of Figure 4 colored according to V_{S30} in Figure S1, available in the supplemental material to this article. The first two features presented in Figure 4 are $f_{0,\mathrm{HVSR}}$ and $A_{0,\mathrm{HVSR}}$, they describe the frequency and amplitude of the lowest-frequency clear resonant peak in the mHVSR. Some of mHVSR measurements show a log–log relationship between $f_{0,\mathrm{HVSR}}$, and V_{S30}, see Figure 4p, as was utilized by others to develop prior mHVSR–V_{S30} models, recall Figure 1. The relationship between $A_{0,\mathrm{HVSR}}$ and V_{S30} is less clear, but $A_{0,\mathrm{HVSR}}$ is observed to increase as V_{S30} decreases for V_{S30} less than 300 m/s, see Figure 4q. The third and fourth features are elevation and TPI, see Figure 4r,s, respectively. Because of the weak correlation between elevation and V_{S30}, early low-dimensional models that used elevation strongly overfitted to the training data (i.e., exhibited low prediction accuracies on the validation set). To mitigate overfitting, elevation was binned into 500-m intervals to transform elevation into a coarse contextual feature, consistent with our expectations that it serves as a coarse proxy for regional geology or geographical region. By binning the elevation values, we prevent the model from overfitting to a station's exact elevation and instead force the model to use elevation to segment broader regional geology. The fifth

TABLE 3
Features Used for Low-Dimensional Modeling in Terms of Their Name, Description, and Range

Name	Description	Range
$f_{0,\mathrm{HVSR}}$	Fundamental resonant frequency from mHVSR in Hz	0.25–47.56
$A_{0,\mathrm{HVSR}}$	Amplitude of the resonant frequency	1.51–22.91
Binned elevation	Elevation in meters obtained from 1 arcsec DEM binned into 500 m interval	−71 to 2690*
Topographic position index	Relative elevation in meters compared with average elevation of 1500 m radius	−165.22 to 153.80
Spectral skewness	Asymmetry of lognormal median mHVSR curve around $f_{0,\mathrm{HVSR}}$	−0.46 to 4.68

*The provided range is the actual range of elevation values, although it was organized into 500 m bins for model training. DEM, digital elevation model; mHVSR, microtremor horizontal-to-vertical spectral ratio.

feature is spectral skewness computed from the lognormal median mHVSR curve (sampled in logarithmic frequency). Spectral skewness was used to quantify the asymmetry of the mHVSR around $f_{0,\mathrm{HVSR}}$. Higher spectral skewness indicates mHVSR with sharper, more symmetric peaks that are generally indicative of softer sites (i.e., lower V_{S30}), see Figure 4t. The features used for the low-dimensional models and their range are summarized in Table 3. Users of the low-dimensional models (discussed next) should be cautious if their feature inputs are outside the range of those indicated in Table 3.

For model training, the dataset for the low-dimensional model development was split 80/20 into training and testing sets, respectively, using stratified sampling based on ASCE/SEI 7-22 site class (ASCE, 2022). To prevent information leakage, the testing set was not used until the model was finalized. Four types of low-dimensional models were developed: multivariate linear regression (MLR), decision tree (DT; Quinlan, 1986), random forest (RF; Breiman, 2001), and gradient-boosted trees (GBT; Friedman, 2001). Note that the GBT model was trained using the extreme gradient boosting (XGBoost) framework (Chen and Guestrin, 2016). For MLR, to improve model stability and fulfill the assumptions of linear modeling, several feature transformations were applied. $A_{0,\mathrm{HVSR}}$ was log-transformed to reduce skewness and stabilize variance, whereas $f_{0,\mathrm{HVSR}}$ underwent a Box–Cox transformation (Box and Cox, 1964), appropriate for strictly positive, non-Gaussian data. Features, such as spectral skewness and TPI, were standardized via z-score normalization to ensure proportional influence among features. For the tree-based models (i.e., DT, RF, and GBT), feature transformations were not applied as these models are robust to unscaled and non-Gaussian inputs. The target variable, V_{S30}, was log-transformed. Log-transforming V_{S30} encourages the model to focus on the relative error rather than the absolute value of the error, as the same absolute error (e.g., 100 m/s) is more significant when V_{S30} is low (e.g., 150 m/s) than when it is high (e.g., 1000 m/s). In addition, the log-transform of V_{S30} is consistent with how V_{S30} is used in most ground-motion models to predict site effects (e.g., Chiou and Youngs, 2014). Final predictions were back-transformed using the exponential function to recover values in units of m/s.

The hyperparameters for all low-dimensional models were selected using a grid search, in which each hyperparameter combination was trained and evaluated using fivefold stratified cross-validation based on ASCE/SEI 7-22 site class. The use of stratification for the fivefold cross-validation serves to maintain the proportion of each class across folds, which ensures that the model is always being trained and validated across all site classes. Model performance was evaluated using R^2, root mean square error (RMSE), and mean absolute error (MAE) in natural log space, denoted as R^2 (ln), RMSE (ln), and MAE (ln), respectively. Metrics during model training were averaged across all five validation folds to make final hyperparameter selections. The selected hyperparameters for each model are summarized in Table S1. After final hyperparameter selection, each model was retrained on the full training dataset and then tested on the testing set. The MLR model achieved an R^2 (ln) of 0.49, RMSE (ln) of 0.42, and MAE (ln) of 0.32 on the testing set, indicating moderate explanatory power. However, the tree-based methods consistently outperformed MLR (e.g., R^2 (ln) > 0.57), highlighting the benefits of nonlinear modeling techniques when working with mHVSR data for V_{S30} prediction. The first four rows of Table 4 compare the performance metrics across all of the low-dimensional models on the common testing set.

TABLE 4
Testing Set Performance of the Final Low-Dimensional Models (First Four Rows) and High-Dimensional Models (Last Two Rows) in Terms of R^2 (ln), Root Mean Square Error (RMSE) (ln), and Median Absolute Error (MAE) (ln)

Model	R^2 (ln)	RMSE (ln m/s)	MAE (ln m/s)
MLR	0.49	0.42	0.32
DT	0.57	0.38	0.25
RF	0.69	0.32	0.21
GBT	0.68	0.32	0.21
Single-mode ANN	0.82	0.27	0.18
Dual-mode ANN	0.83	0.27	0.17

ANN, artificial neural network; DT, decision tree; GBT, gradient boosted trees; MLR, multivariate linear regression; and RF, random forest.

A major shortcoming of the low-dimensional models is that they were developed, and therefore can only be used, with mHVSR with a clear resonant peak. Although ultimately unsuccessful, we considered two potential approaches to addressing this shortcoming. The first approach was to develop

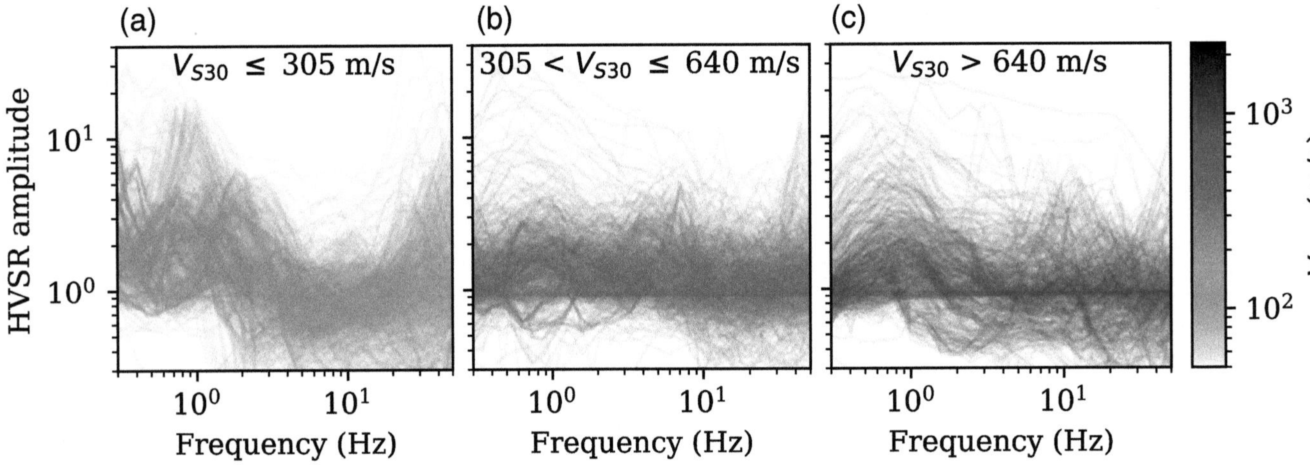

Figure 5. Lognormal median mHVSR curves are used in the high-dimensional models to predict V_{S30}. For greater clarity the mHVSR are organized by V_{S30} ranges (a) $V_{S30} \le 305$ m/s (site classes E, DE, and D), (b) 305 m/s $< V_{S30} \le 640$ m/s (site classes CD and C), and (c) $V_{S30} > 640$ m/s (site classes BC, B, and A). mHVSR are colored by V_{S30} and plotted semitransparent to show data density. The color version of this figure is available only in the electronic edition.

a low-dimensional model using only binned elevation and TPI; however, these features alone did not exhibit a strong enough correlation with V_{S30} to develop a reliable low-dimensional model. The second approach was to select a conservative lower bound V_{S30} value for these sites. This was informed by the fact that the lack of a clear peak in mHVSR can be an indication of a rock site. However, the distribution of V_{S30} values from the 1713 mHVSR measurements without a clear peak ranges from 50 to 2250 m/s, see Figure 4u. The range of V_{S30} values indicates that the lack of a clear resonant peak in the mHVSR not only occurs at stiff sites, but rather at all sites without a significant impedance contrast, and therefore, setting a conservative lower bound V_{S30} value for these sites is not possible. Nonetheless, while our efforts to develop a low-dimensional model to predict V_{S30} from mHVSR without a clear resonant peak were not successful, the high-dimensional models presented in the following section can predict V_{S30} irrespective of whether the mHVSR exhibits a clear resonant peak.

High-dimensional models

The development of the high-dimensional models used a subset of the full dataset, which consisted of sites with mHVSR measurements in the frequency range of 0.3–50 Hz, independent of whether a clear resonant peak was present. The dataset included 2824 samples collected from 531 unique sites. The lognormal median mHVSR curve was downsampled to 35 logarithmically spaced frequencies between 0.3 and 50 Hz. Reducing the number of mHVSR input frequencies maintained the shape of the lognormal median mHVSR curves, but substantially reduced the size of the artificial neural network (ANN) models that accelerated the model development process. The lognormal median mHVSR curves after downsampling are shown in Figure 5. The 2824 curves are colored according to V_{S30} and divided across three panels for greater clarity: $V_{S30} \le 305$ m/s (Fig. 5a), 305 m/s $< V_{S30} \le 640$ m/s (Fig. 5b), and $V_{S30} > 640$ m/s (Fig. 5c). Consistent with what was done for the low-dimensional models the target variable, V_{S30}, was log-transformed. To ensure balance between the training, validation, and testing sets, stratification was performed on both V_{S30} site class and the presence/absence of a clear resonant peak. This dual stratification resulted in a very small number of samples in the site class A and B bins, where a clear peak was observed; therefore, we chose to combine the site class A and B bins but maintain the bins associated with the presence/absence of a clear resonant peak. We developed two high-dimensional models: one using just the lognormal median mHVSR curve (referred to as the single-mode ANN model, hereafter) and the other with both the lognormal median mHVSR curve and the topographic features TPI and binned elevation (referred to as the dual-mode ANN model, hereafter).

To ensure stable training, all mHVSR features (i.e., amplitudes) were log-transformed, but no normalization was applied. The single-mode ANN model was implemented using a sequential architecture that began with an input layer with 35 neurons, one per mHVSR frequency. Each hidden layer consisted of a dense layer with He *et al.* (2015) initialization and L2 regularization to reduce overfitting (Ng, 2004). Batch normalization (Ioffe and Szegedy, 2015) was applied before the activation function to stabilize and accelerate training. The rectified linear unit (ReLU) activation function (Nair and Hinton, 2010) was used after each batch-normalized layer to introduce nonlinearity. To encourage generalization, dropout (Srivastava *et al.*, 2014) was applied after each activation function, randomly deactivating a given percentage of neurons during training. Note that dropout is disabled during validation and testing. The output layer consisted of a single neuron with a linear activation function for predicting log-transformed V_{S30}. The model was trained using the Adam optimizer (Kingma

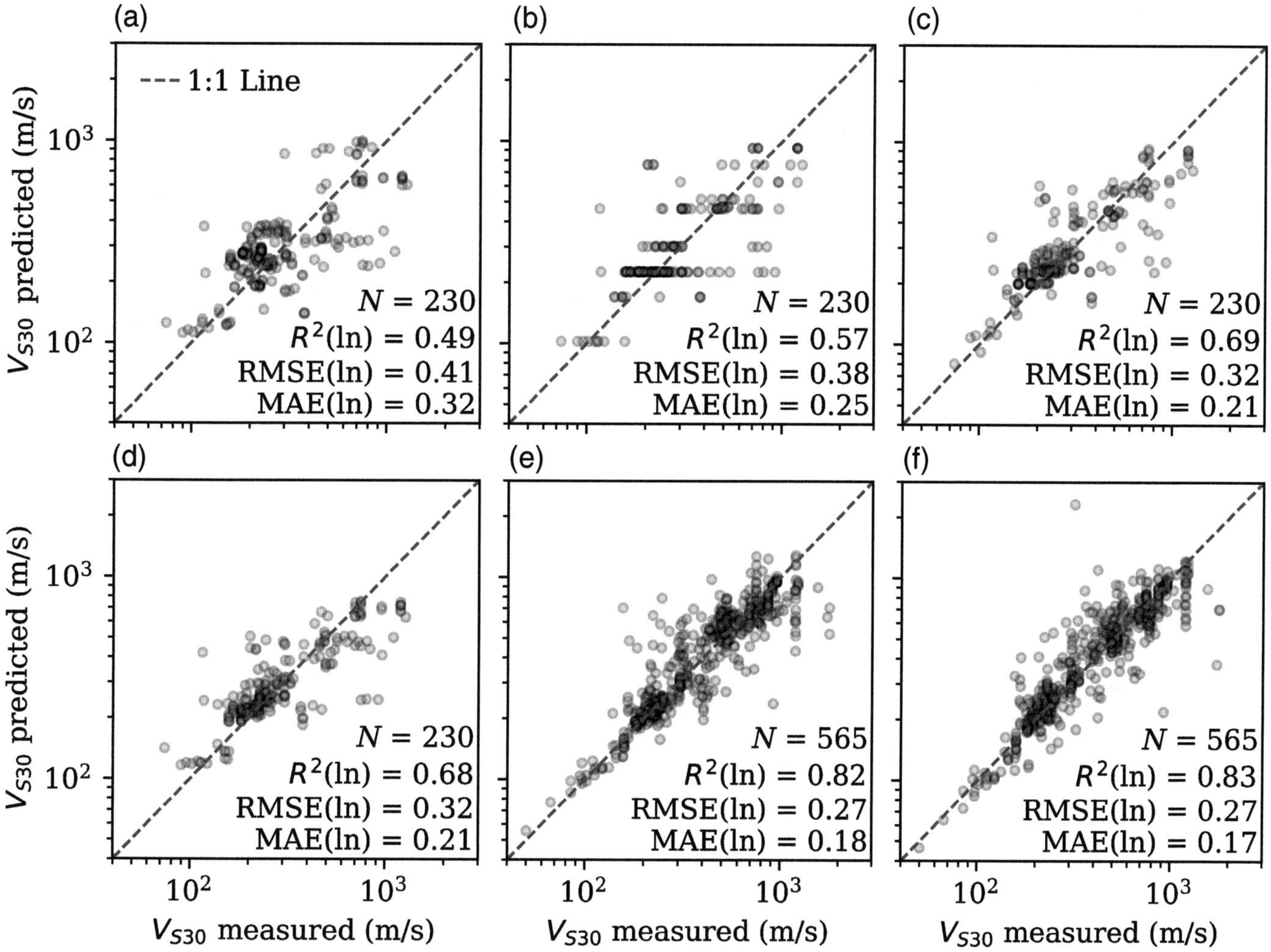

Figure 6. Comparison of V_{S30} prediction performance for the six models on the testing dataset. The models include (a) multivariate linear regression, (b) decision tree, (c) random forest, (d) gradient boosted trees (GBT), (e) single-mode artificial neural network (ANN), and (f) dual-mode ANN. Each panel shows the predicted V_{S30} versus the measured V_{S30} on a log–log scale. Each point (gray circle) is semitransparent to provide an indicator of data density. The red-dashed line indicates the 1:1 reference. Each panel includes the number of samples in the testing set (N) and the model's R^2, root mean square error (RMSE), and median absolute error (MAE) values computed in natural log (ln) space. The color version of this figure is available only in the electronic edition.

and Ba, 2014), which combines adaptive learning rates with momentum for greater efficiency. Training used a batch size of 32 for up to 200 epochs, with early stopping (patience = 15) and learning rate reduction (factor = 0.5) triggered by validation loss, with a lower learning rate bound of 1×10^{-6}. A fivefold cross-validation strategy was used to evaluate model generalization. Evaluation metrics of R^2 (ln), RMSE (ln), and MAE (ln) were averaged across folds. Hyperparameters were selected using a grid search, with the range of values considered and those selected summarized in Table S2.

The dual-mode ANN was developed to further explore the potential additional contributions from topographical features. The dual-mode ANN consisted of two branches: one ingesting the 35 resampled mHVSR amplitudes, and the other TPI and binned elevation. mHVSR features were log-transformed, binned elevation one-hot encoded, and TPI z-score normalized. The two independent branches for the mHVSR data and the topographic features followed the same design as the single-mode ANN (i.e., dense layer, batch normalization, and ReLU activation). The outputs of the two branches are concatenated and passed through a shared dense layer before outputting the log-transformed V_{S30} via a linear activation function. The dual-mode ANN architecture enabled the model to jointly learn from the shape of the lognormal median mHVSR curve and the topographic information. The training procedure and optimizer settings for the multi-input ANN were consistent with those used for the single-mode ANN. The architecture, along with the hyperparameter tuning performed with the grid search, is summarized in Table S2.

RESULTS

The performance of the six models developed for predicting V_{S30} from mHVSR is presented in Table 4 and Figure 6 for the testing set. The high-dimensional models performed significantly better than the low-dimensional models, based on

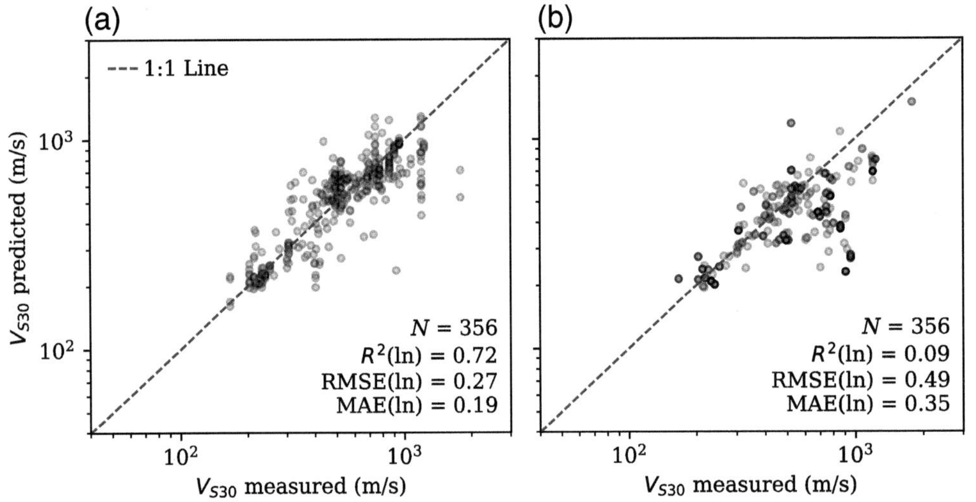

Figure 7. Comparison of V_{S30} prediction performance for the (a) mHVSR-based single-mode ANN and (b) remote-sensing-based model developed by Geyin and Maurer (2023), using a subset of 356 stations within the contiguous United States from the single-mode ANN's testing set. Each point (gray circle) is semitransparent to provide an indicator of data density. The red-dashed line indicates the 1:1 reference. The color version of this figure is available only in the electronic edition.

R^2(ln). The dual-mode ANN (R^2(ln) = 0.83) performed essentially the same as the single-mode ANN (R^2(ln) = 0.82) on the testing set. Of the low-dimensional models, RF (R^2(ln) = 0.69) and GBT (R^2(ln) = 0.68) performed the best, followed by DT (R^2(ln) = 0.57), and finally MLR (R^2(ln) = 0.49). We highlight that these evaluation metrics were computed on an independent testing set (i.e., not the training set). As such, these models demonstrate a substantial improvement over those models developed in previous studies, recall Table 1. These results highlight the strength of ML in capturing complex nonlinear relationships between mHVSR and topographic features and V_{S30}. The negligible performance gain of the dual-mode ANN model over the single-mode ANN suggests that the information contained in the topographic features of TPI and binned elevation is already encoded in the lognormal median mHVSR curve. Therefore, the single-mode ANN, as the simpler of the two high-dimensional models, is preferred.

When using the high-dimensional models, caution is advised when the predicted V_{S30} is above approximately 1500 m/s. For example, consider the prediction by the dual-mode ANN in Figure 6f that exceeds 2000 m/s. The dataset used for training these models contained fewer than 11 samples with a V_{S30} above 1524 m/s (i.e., site class A), recall Figure 2, with the maximum V_{S30} across all measurements being 2250 m/s. As a result, each model's exposure to high-velocity conditions, typically associated with hard, shallow bedrock, is limited, resulting in the potential for an extrapolation by the models to this range that is not fully supported by data. To avoid misinterpretation, we recommend caution when the model predictions exceed approximately 1500 m/s because this is the maximum V_{S30} that is well constrained by the training data. Predictions above approximately 1500 m/s should be treated as highly uncertain, and users are encouraged to carefully consider the validity of the model's prediction based on local geology, remote-sensing-based predictions, and direct geophysical measurements of subsurface stiffness. This is particularly important in engineering design or seismic hazard analysis, in which overestimation of site stiffness could result in unconservative decisions.

Comparison with Geyin and Maurer (2023)

To compare our results against the current state of the art, we compare predictions of V_{S30} from our single-mode ANN model with those from the remote-sensing-based model by Geyin and Maurer (2023). We compare the single-mode ANN and the model by Geyin and Maurer (2023) at 356 stations from the single-mode ANN's testing dataset that are located in the contiguous United States, where the Geyin and Maurer (2023) model has been developed. As shown in Figure 7, the single-mode ANN model retained reasonable accuracy with an R^2(ln) of 0.72 on this subset of the testing set. In contrast, the Geyin and Maurer (2023) model yielded a strikingly low R^2(ln) of 0.09. This underperformance is visually corroborated by the lack of clustering around the 1:1 line and the scatter across the V_{S30} range, see Figure 7b. The density of points in Figure 7b shows that many predictions, particularly for sites with V_{S30} greater than 600 m/s, underpredict the true V_{S30} values. This observation is further supported by a histogram of the prediction residuals (Fig. 8), which reveals a relatively wide distribution compared with that of the single-mode ANN, with large positive residuals indicative of underprediction of V_{S30} by the Geyin and Maurer (2023) model. One potential explanation for the underperformance of the Geyin and Maurer (2023) model is that it was trained on geospatial predictors derived from coarse-resolution remote sensing data (approximately 100–1000 m scale), such as slope, terrain ruggedness, and generalized geology. Although these features correlate with V_{S30} at large scales, they may not capture local subsurface variability, particularly in geologically complex regions. In addition, Geyin and Maurer (2023) acknowledge that their training data were biased toward flat, soft-soil sites, reducing their ability to generalize to sloped or stiff-soil conditions. This comparison highlights a key limitation of relying solely on surface indicators,

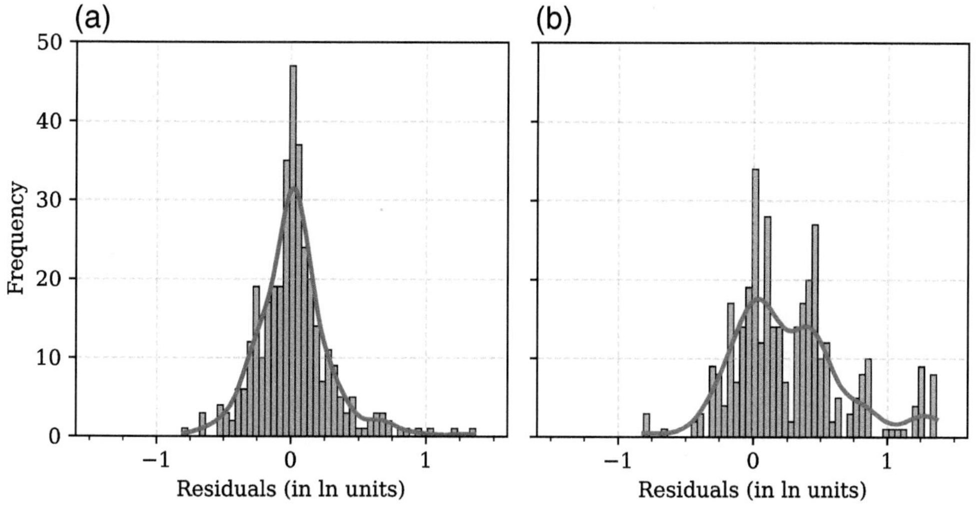

Figure 8. Histogram (vertical bars) and KDE (solid line) of prediction residuals, computed as the difference between the natural logarithm of the measured and predicted V_{S30}, for the (a) single-mode ANN and (b) Geyin and Maurer (2023) models. The color version of this figure is available only in the electronic edition.

such as slope, landform, or roughness, when estimating V_{S30}, particularly in areas where local subsurface conditions vary rapidly or soil-to-bedrock transitions are shallow and abrupt. As Geyin and Maurer (2023) note, while such geospatial predictors are useful at large scales, they lack mechanistic links to V_{S30} and may miss fine-scale heterogeneity, especially in data-sparse or topographically complex regions. For practical applications, we recommend that both approaches be used to properly capture epistemic uncertainty in the estimation of V_{S30} using proxies.

Prediction of V_{S30} using mHVSR from permanent broadband stations

To showcase the potential of the ML models and evaluate their ability to generalize to conditions distinct from which they were trained, we predict V_{S30} at 1855 broadband seismic stations located across North America. These stations, located primarily in the contiguous United States, are part of various permanent regional and national networks and equipped with broadband sensors to record microtremors. The mHVSR measurements used here are those processed by Anbazhagan *et al.* (2025). Figure 9 displays the spatial distribution of the measurement stations with each point colored according to the predicted V_{S30} value from the single-mode ANN model. As mentioned previously, when the predicted V_{S30} value is large (i.e., greater than 1500 m/s), the user is cautioned regarding the use of the V_{S30} value, as these values are not well represented in the model's training set. As such, we omit these values, which occurred at three sites, from Figure 9. Although only the results of the single-mode ANN model are shown in Figure 9, we provide the V_{S30} predictions and figures similar to Figure 9 using all the models developed herein as supplemental material, see Table S3 and Figures S2–S7, respectively.

To evaluate the predictive accuracy of the models when predicting V_{S30} from mHVSR measurements from permanent stations, we examine the GBT and single-mode ANN models' predictions at a subset of the 1855 permanent broadband seismic stations where a measured V_{S30} value has been reported in the NGA-West 3 or NGA-East (Goulet *et al.*, 2021) projects. The location of these stations is indicated in Figure 9. Figure 10a,b compares the measured and predicted V_{S30} values for the GBT and single-mode ANN models, respectively. The predictive accuracy of the models (R^2(ln) of 0.01 and 0.18) is substantially reduced from that observed on the model's testing set previously (R^2(ln) of 0.68 and 0.82). This strong reduction in performance indicates that the models developed have low predictive power when applied to mHVSR measurements from permanent broadband recording stations. The inability for the models to generalize to this new case is unfortunate and implies that there may be systematic differences between the mHVSR measurements made with temporary and permanent broadband measurements.

Although a full investigation of why this reduction of predictive power occurs is beyond the scope of the present study, we briefly discuss two potential causes that are supported by the experimental data. The first is due to the effect of instrument type. Instrument type, even when comparing broadband seismometers, is known to influence the shape of the lognormal median mHVSR curve (Molnar *et al.*, 2022). Across the model's training set, nearly all mHVSR measurements were made with Trillium-type broadband sensors, whereas Trillium-type sensors are used at only 10 of the 156 (6%) permanent instruments. When we consider only V_{S30} predictions from stations with Trillium-type instruments, we observe a substantial improvement in the single-mode ANN's predictions at sites with a V_{S30} less than 1500 m/s (i.e., points are more tightly clustered around the 1:1 line), see Figure 10b. No improvement is observed for the GBT; however, this is expected because the low-dimensional models only use features from the measured mHVSR and should therefore be less sensitive to the shape of the lognormal median mHVSR curve. The second potential cause of the ML models' weaker performance is related to differences between the distribution of measured V_{S30} values at the temporary and permanent broadband sensors. Although the amount of mHVSR data we were able to collect was significant relative to previous studies, it is

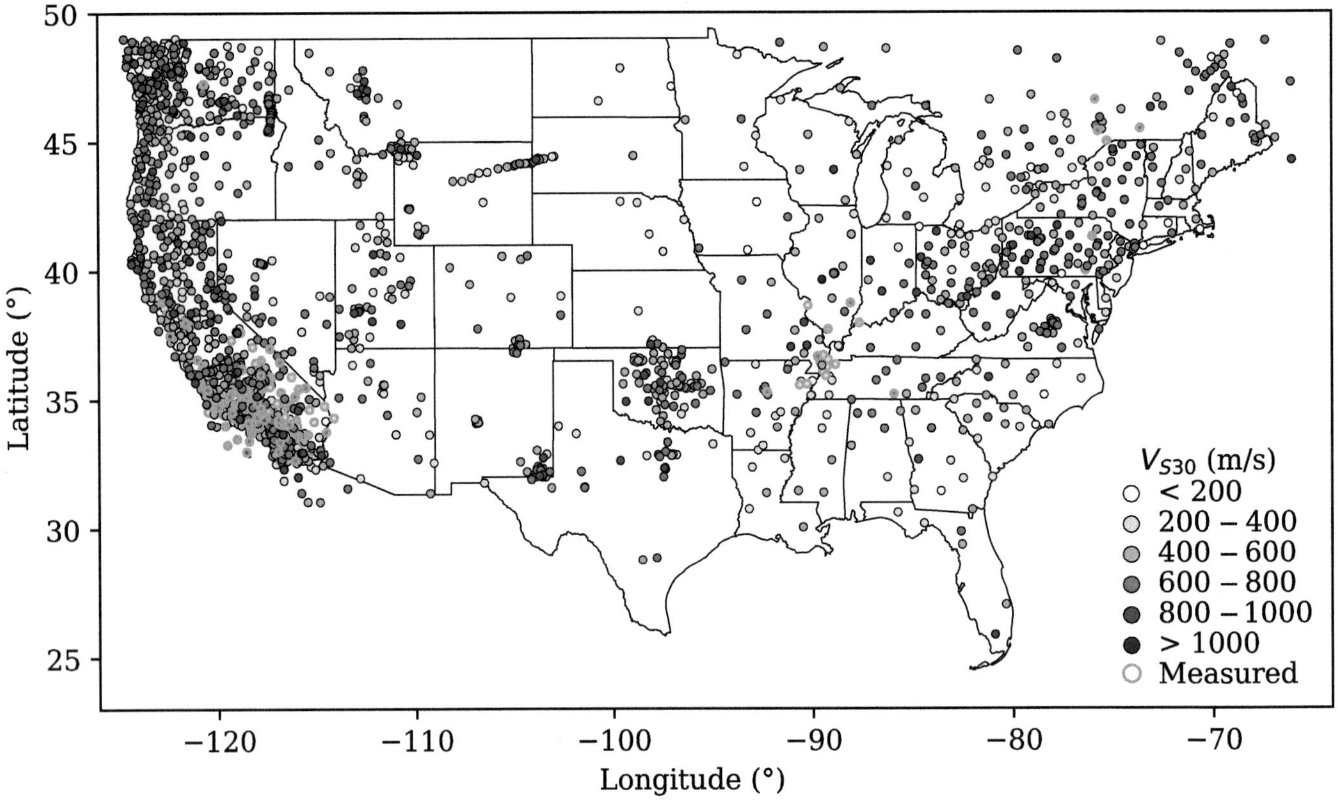

Figure 9. Spatial distribution of 1855 permanent broadband seismic stations across North America (primarily the contiguous United States) where V_{S30} was predicted using the single-mode ANN model. Three stations with predicted V_{S30} values exceeding 1500 m/s have been omitted, as such high V_{S30} values are not well represented in the model's training set. The locations with measured V_{S30} values in the NGA-West 3 or NGA-East projects are indicated by a light-colored circular border. The color version of this figure is available only in the electronic edition.

still limited. As such, our models will perform best at those sites "similar" to those seen during model training. To quantify differences between the training dataset and the dataset from the permanent broadband stations, four kernel density estimate plots for V_{S30} are shown in Figure 11. These plots compare the distribution of V_{S30} for the temporary and permanent instruments separated by whether a clear mHVSR resonant peak was observed. Although the distribution of V_{S30} between temporary and permanent instruments without a clear peak is nearly identical, the distribution of temporary and permanent sites with a clear are very different. The distribution of V_{S30} at the permanent stations has, on average, a larger V_{S30} than the temporary stations by a factor of approximately 1.5. Therefore, we would expect that our model would perform best at permanent stations without a clear peak and tend to underestimate V_{S30} at stations with a clear peak. These observations explain (at least in part) the weak performance of the GBT model at the permanent broadband stations, see Figure 10a. For the single-mode ANN, those stations without a clear peak are observed to generally provide better predictions than those with a clear peak, see Figure 10b.

Finally, with these limitations in mind, Figure 10c,d shows the log-residual V_{S30} [i.e., ln(measured)−ln(predicted)] as a function of the measured V_{S30}. The lognormal standard deviation of the residual V_{S30} ($\sigma_{\ln VS30}$) values for the GBT and single-mode ANN is observed to be 0.48 ln units. Figure 10c,d shows that both models tend to overpredict V_{S30} for softer sites ($V_{S30} > 200$ m/s) and underpredict V_{S30} for stiffer sites ($V_{S30} > 800$ m/s). The weaker prediction of the models outside the range of 200–800 m/s is consistent with the range of data that was available to develop the data-driven model, recall Figure 2, and is consistent with our expectation that the model will perform best on data similar to that which it has seen during model training.

CONCLUSION

This study presents a machine learning-based framework for predicting V_{S30} from mHVSR and topographic features. A global dataset was compiled from diverse geological settings to develop a suite of six (four low-dimensional and two high-dimensional) machine learning models. The low-dimensional models, which included MLR, DT, RF, and GBT, used simple features derived from measurements of mHVSR and two topographic features, TPI and binned elevation, as input. The high-dimensional models included a single-mode ANN, which used the lognormal median mHVSR curve as input, and a dual-mode ANN, which used the lognormal median

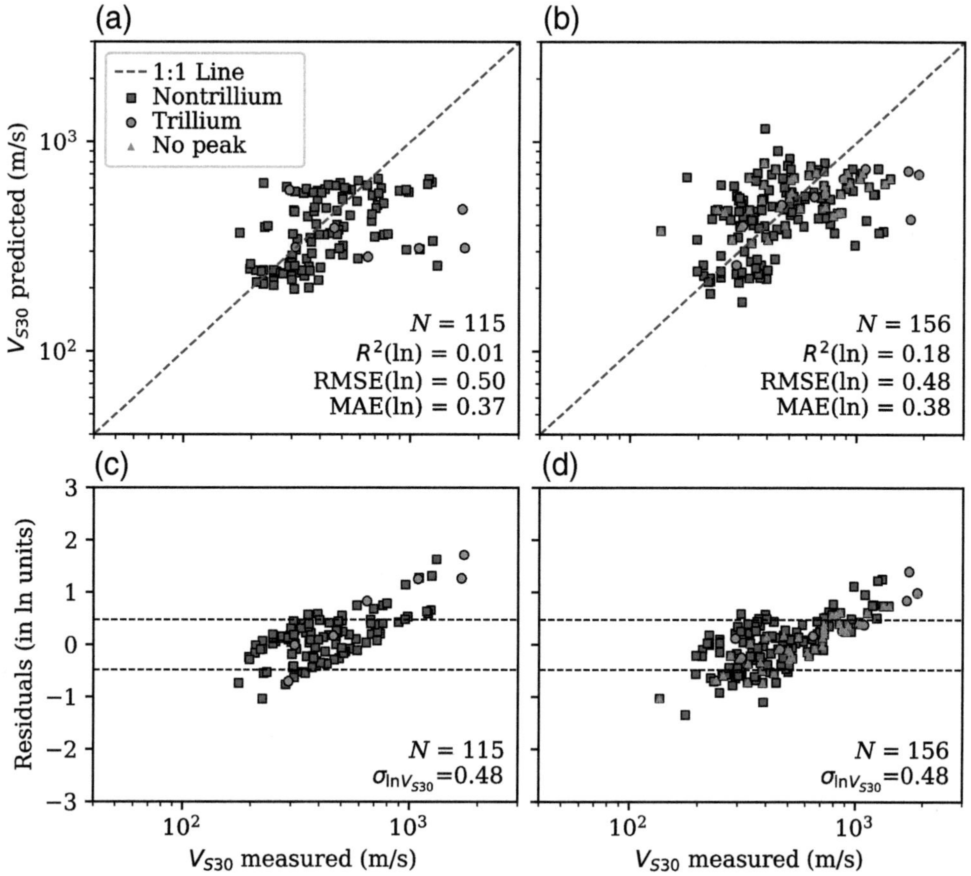

Figure 10. Comparison of the (a) GBT's and (b) single-mode ANN's V_{S30} prediction at the permanent broadband seismic stations across North America with measured V_{S30} values reported in the literature. Residuals, computed as the difference between the natural logarithm of the measured and predicted V_{S30}, for the (c) GBT and (d) single-mode ANN, are plotted against the measured V_{S30}. The dashed horizontal lines in (c) and (d) indicate the one standard deviation range centered around zero. Each point is distinguished by whether the permanent station used a nontrillium-type sensor (square), a trillium-type sensor (circle), or did not have a clear resonant peak (triangle). The color version of this figure is available only in the electronic edition.

mHVSR curve and the two topographic features as input. The two high-dimensional models performed similarly, and both outperformed all the low-dimensional models. All the proposed models have been made publicly available, see Data and Resources. If a site has a clear resonant peak, all models can be used to provide a set of V_{S30} estimates (i.e., one V_{S30} estimate per model). However, if the site does not have a clear resonant peak or if only one model is to be used, we recommend the single-mode ANN. We recommend the single-mode ANN because the high-dimensional models performed better than the low-dimensional models, and the single-mode ANN is the simpler of the two high-dimensional models. For all models, best performance is expected when microtremor measurements are made in the same manner as the training set (i.e., temporary broadband deployments) and processed in a manner consistent with this study, see the Data section. To support consistent mHVSR processing and feature extraction, we provide a combined mHVSR processing and V_{S30} prediction workflow with the published data-driven models, such that the user only needs to provide three-component microtremor recordings and topographic features for their site to use the proposed models.

The single-mode ANN model is compared against the current state-of-the-art remote-sensing-based model developed by Geyin and Maurer (2023). We compare the models at 356 stations in the United States from the single-mode ANN model's testing set. The single-mode ANN model maintained reasonable accuracy ($R^2(\ln) = 0.72$); however, the Geyin and Maurer (2023) model performed poorly ($R^2 = 0.09$). This is linked to the Geyin and Maurer (2023) model's use of surface proxies and relatively coarse remote sensing data. Residual analyses revealed that while the single-mode ANN model predictions were unbiased, the Geyin and Maurer model underpredicted V_{S30} at sites with V_{S30} above 600 m/s.

All the data-driven models developed are applied to the prediction of V_{S30} at 1855 permanent broadband seismic stations across North America using mHVSR prepared by Anbazhagan *et al.* (2025). The predicted values for each data-driven model are provided in Table S3 and Figures S2–S7. The predictions of V_{S30} from the best low-dimensional and high-dimensional models (i.e., GBT and single-mode ANN, respectively) are compared at sites where a measured V_{S30} value was available. The predictive performance of the GBT and the single-mode ANN models was reduced on this dataset (R^2 of 0.01 and 0.18, respectively). This reduction is shown in part to be related to differences in mHVSR instrumentation and the distribution of V_{S30} for permanent stations where a clear resonant peak was observed. The lower predictive performance by the machine learning models may indicate differences between mHVSR obtained from permanent broadband stations and those from temporary broadband deployments that have not yet been rigorously investigated. Future efforts should focus on considering how these effects can be quantified to improve future predictions of V_{S30} at permanent broadband seismic stations using mHVSR.

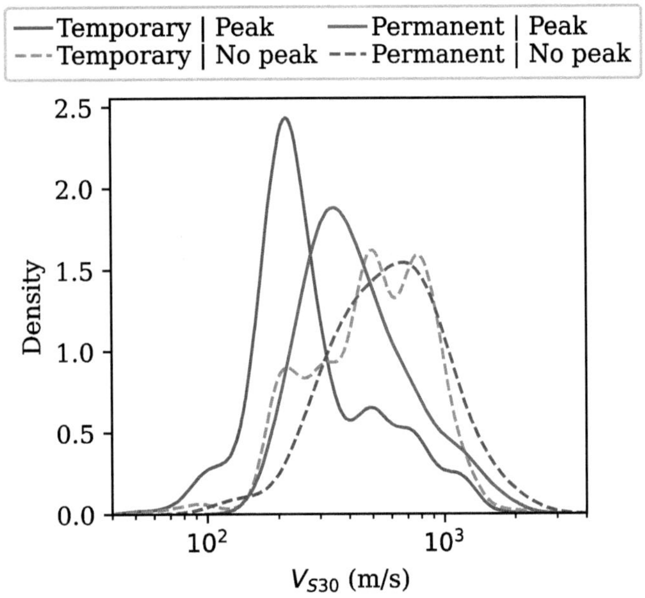

Figure 11. Distribution of measured V_{S30} for temporary and permanent broadband sensors with and without a clear resonant peak in the mHVSR. The color version of this figure is available only in the electronic edition.

Finally, we acknowledge two important limitations of the work. First, the low-dimensional models developed in this study are only applicable to sites with at least one clear resonant peak. For sites lacking such peaks (e.g., those with flat or irregular mHVSR curves), we recommend the high-dimensional models, specifically the single-mode ANN, which utilizes the lognormal median mHVSR curve. Second, we were unable to rigorously quantify prediction uncertainty due to the limited availability of rigorous V_{S30} measurement error quantification. Despite these limitations, the proposed models provide a useful approach to estimate V_{S30} from temporary, broadband, single-station measurements for application in ground-motion prediction. Finally, we urge the user to be aware of the limitations of the models and recommend that the models be used along with other predictors to better assess the uncertainty in V_{S30} estimates when shear-wave velocity is not measured at a site.

DATA AND RESOURCES

The six data-driven models developed in this study, along with no-coding-required data-processing and V_{S30} prediction workflows, are publicly available on GitHub (https://github.com/geoimaging/mhvsr-vs30, last accessed August 2025). The majority of the data used in this article came from published sources listed in the references. The remainder of the data was provided to the authors solely for the development of the models herein and cannot be shared. The topographic features were computed from the 1 arcsec digital elevation model obtained from U.S. Geological Survey EarthExplorer (https://earthexplorer.usgs.gov, last accessed March 2025). The microtremor horizontal-to-vertical spectral ratio (mHVSR) data used in this study were processed using v.2.0.0 of *hvsrpy* (Vantassel, 2025). Tables S1 and S2 include the considered and selected hyperparameters for the low-dimensional and high-dimensional models, respectively. Table S3 provides V_{S30} predictions for the 1855 broadband seismic stations across North America. Each entry includes the station's network and station code, latitude and longitude, predictions from all six data-driven models, and measured V_{S30} where available from Next Generation Attenuation (NGA)-West 3 and NGA-East. The low-dimensional models, based on mHVSR resonant peaks, are applied only to stations exhibiting a clear peak. Predictions exceeding 1500 m/s have been omitted as they are not considered reliable. Figure S1 provides an alternate version of Figure 4 colored by V_{S30}. Figures S2–S7 provide a visual representation of each data-driven model's prediction from the broadband seismic stations across North America, in a form similar to Figure 9.

DECLARATION OF COMPETING INTERESTS

The authors acknowledge that there are no conflicts of interest recorded.

ACKNOWLEDGMENTS

This material is based upon work supported by the U.S. Geological Survey (USGS) under Grant Number G24AP00400-00. However, the views and conclusions contained in this document are those of the authors and should not be interpreted as representing the opinions or policies of the USGS. The authors would like to thank Brady Cox, Sebastiano Foti, Chun-Hsiang Kuo, Giovanni Lanzano, Lucia Luzi, David Teague, Liam Wotherspoon, Clint Wood, and Michael Yust for providing and/or facilitating access to the data that made this project possible. This research would not have been possible without their support. The authors acknowledge Advanced Research Computing at Virginia Tech for providing computational resources and technical support that have contributed to the results reported within this article. The authors thank Stefano Parolai, Associate Editor and two reviewers for their helpful comments.
Mention of trade names or commercial products does not constitute their endorsement by the U.S. Geological Survey.

REFERENCES

Allen, T. I., and D. J. Wald (2009). On the use of high-resolution topographic data as a proxy for seismic site conditions (V_{S30}), *Bull. Seismol. Soc. Am.* **99,** no. 2A, 935–943.

American Society of Civil Engineers (2022). Minimum design loads and associated criteria for buildings and other structures, *ASCE/SEI 7-22*, ASCE, Reston, Virginia.

Anbazhagan, B., P. J. Vantassel, and A. Rodriguez-Marek (2025). Microtremor horizontal-to-vertical spectral ratios (mHVSR) at North American seismic stations, *DesignSafe*, doi: 10.17603/ds2-2ea1-vc33.

Barker, P. R. (1996). A report on cone penetrometer and seismic cone penetrometer testing at Parkway—Wainuiomata, Barker Consulting, P.O. Box 27-106, Wellington.

Beyreuther, M., R. Barsch, L. Krischer, T. Megies, Y. Behr, and J. Wassermann (2010). ObsPy: A python toolbox for seismology, *Seismol. Res. Lett.* **81,** 530–533, doi: 10.1785/gssrl.81.3.530.

Borcherdt, R. D. (1994). Estimates of site-dependent response spectra for design (methodology and justification), *Earthq. Spectra* **10,** no. 4, 617–653, doi: 10.1193/1.1585791.

Box, G. E., and D. R. Cox (1964). An analysis of transformations, *J. R. Stat. Soc. Ser. B* **26,** no. 2, 211–243.

Breiman, L. (2001). Random forests, *Machine Learn.* **45,** 5–32.

Building Seismic Safety Council (BSSC) (1997). NEHRP recommended provisions for seismic regulations for new buildings and other structures, *FEMA 302/303*, Federal Emergency Management Agency.

Castellaro, S., and F. Mulargia (2009). VS30 estimates using constrained H/V measurements, *Bull. Seismol. Soc. Am.* **99,** no. 2A, 761–773.

Castellaro, S., F. Mulargia, and P. L. Rossi (2008). V_{S30}: Proxy for seismic amplification? *Seismol. Res. Lett.* **79,** no. 4, 540–543, doi: 10.1785/gssrl.79.4.540.

Cave, A. (2020). Site characterisation of the Hamilton basin using surface wave methods, *Doctoral Dissertation*, The University of Waikato.

Chen, C. T., C. H. Kuo, C. M. Lin, J. Y. Huang, and K. L. Wen (2022). Investigation of shallow S-wave velocity structure and site response parameters in Taiwan by using high-density microtremor measurements, *Eng. Geol.* **297,** 106498.

Chen, T., and C. Guestrin (2016). Xgboost: A scalable tree boosting system, *Proc. of the 22nd ACM SIGKDD International Conf. on Knowledge Discovery and Data Mining*, 785–794.

Chiou, B. S.-J., and R. R. Youngs (2014). Update of the Chiou and Youngs NGA model for the average horizontal component of peak ground motion and response spectra, *Earthq. Spectra* **30,** no. 3, 1117–1153, doi: 10.1193/072813EQS219M.

Cox, B. R., T. Cheng, J. P. Vantassel, and L. Manuel (2020). A statistical representation and frequency-domain window-rejection algorithm for single-station HVSR measurements, *Geophys. J. Int.* **221,** 2170–2183, doi: 10.1093/gji/ggaa119.

Cox, B. R., and J. P. Vantassel (2018). Dynamic characterization of Wellington, New Zealand, *DesignSafe-CI*, doi: 10.17603/DS24M6J.

Deschenes, M. R., C. M. Wood, L. M. Wotherspoon, B. A. Bradley, and E. Thomson (2018). Development of deep shear wave velocity profiles in the Canterbury Plains, New Zealand, *Earthq. Spectra* **34,** no. 3, 1065–1089.

European Committee for Standardization (CEN) (2004). Eurocode 8: Design of structures for earthquake resistance—Part 1: General rules, seismic actions and rules for buildings, *EN 1998-1:2004*, European Committee for Standardization, Brussels.

Felicetta, C., E. Russo, M. D'Amico, S. Sgobba, G. Lanzano, C. Mascandola, F. Pacor, and L. Luzi (2023). Italian Accelerometric Archive v4.0, *Istituto Nazionale di Geofisica e Vulcanologia*, Dipartimento della Protezione Civile Nazionale, doi: 10.13127/itaca.4.0.

Field, E. H., and K. H. Jacob (1995). A comparison and test of various site-response estimation techniques, including three that are not reference-site dependent, *Bull. Seismol. Soc. Am.* **85,** no. 4, 1127–1143.

Friedman, J. H. (2001). Greedy function approximation: A gradient boosting machine, *Ann. Stat.* 1189–1232.

Geyin, M., and B. W. Maurer (2023). US national V_{S30} models and maps informed by remote sensing and machine learning, *Seismol. Soc. Am.* **94,** no. 3, 1467–1477.

Ghofrani, H., and G. M. Atkinson (2014). Site condition evaluation using horizontal-to-vertical response spectral ratios of earthquakes in the NGA-West 2 and Japanese databases, *Soil Dynam. Earthq. Eng.* **67,** 30–43.

Goulet, C. A., T. Kishida, T. D. Ancheta, C. H. Cramer, R. B. Darragh, W. J. Silva, Y. M. Hashash, J. Harmon, G. A. Parker, J. P. Stewart, and R. R. Youngs (2021). PEER NGA-east database, *Earthq. Spectra* **37,** no. 1_suppl, 1331–1353.

Gupta, R. K., M. Agrawal, S. K. Pal, and M. K. Das (2021). Seismic site characterization and site response study of Nirsa (India), *Nat. Hazards* **108,** no. 2, 2033–2057.

Harris, F. J. (1978). On the use of windows for harmonic analysis with the discrete Fourier transform, *Proc. IEEE* **66,** no. 1, 51–83, doi: 10.1109/PROC.1978.10837.

Hassani, B., and G. M. Atkinson (2016). Applicability of the site fundamental frequency as a V_{S30} proxy for central and eastern North America, *Bull. Seismol. Soc. Am.* **106,** no. 2, 653–664.

He, K., X. Zhang, S. Ren, and J. Sun (2015). Delving deep into rectifiers: Surpassing human-level performance on imagenet classification, *Proc. of the IEEE International Conf. on Computer Vision*, 1026–1034.

Hill, M., A. Kaiser, L. Wotherspoon, and E. Manea (2023). Using 3D geological models to create maps of estimated V_{S30} and site period, *New Zealand Society for Earthquake Engineering 2023 Annual Conference.*

Hudson, K. S., S. M. Palmer, S. K. Ahdi, B. Hassani, G. Toro, and A. Yong (2021). Inter-method HVSR bias and the resultant $V_{S30} - f_d$ relationship for measured-V_{S30} stations in the western United States [Oral presentation], *2021 Annual Meeting*, Seismological Society of America, 19–23 April 2021.

Ioffe, S., and C. Szegedy (2015). Batch normalization: Accelerating deep network training by reducing internal covariate shift, *International Conf. on Machine Learning*, 448–456.

Kaiser, A. E., and J. N. Louie (2006). *Shear-Wave Velocities in Parkway Basin, Wainuiomata, from Refraction Microtremor Surface Wave Dispersion*, GNS Science, New Zealand.

Kingma, D. P., and J. Ba (2014). Adam: A method for stochastic optimization, arXiv preprint arXiv:1412.6980.

Konno, K., and T. Ohmachi (1998). Ground-motion characteristics estimated from spectral ratio between horizontal and vertical components of microtremor, *Bull. Seismol. Soc. Am.* **88,** no. 1, 228–241.

Kuo, C. H., C. T. Chen, C. M. Lin, K. L. Wen, J. Y. Huang, and S. C. Chang (2016). S-wave velocity structure and site effect parameters derived from microtremor arrays in the Western Plain of Taiwan, *J. Asian Earth Sci.* **128,** 27–41.

Lermo, J., and F. J. Chávez-García (1993). Site effect evaluation using spectral ratios with only one station, *Bull. Seismol. Soc. Am.* **83,** no. 5, 1574–1594.

McNamara, D. E., W. J. Stephenson, J. K. Odum, R. A. Williams, and L. Gee (2015). Site response in the eastern United States: A comparison of V_{S30} measurements with estimates from horizontal-to-vertical spectral ratios, in *The 2011 Mineral, Virginia, Earthquake, and Its Significance for Seismic Hazards in Eastern North America*, J. W. Horton Jr., M. C. Chapman, and R. A. Green (Editors), Geological Society of America, GSA Special Paper 509, 67–79.

McVerry, G. H. (2011). Site-effect terms as continuous functions of site period and V_{S30}, *Proc. of the Ninth Pacific Conf. on Earthquake Engineering*, 14–16.

Molnar, S., A. Sirohey, J. Assaf, P.-Y. Bard, S. Castellaro, C. Cornou, B. Cox, B. Guillier, B. Hassani, H. Kawase, *et al.* (2022). A review of the microtremor horizontal-to-vertical spectral ratio (MHVSR) method, *J. Seismol.* **26,** no. 4, 653–685.

Nair, V., and G. E. Hinton (2010). Rectified linear units improve restricted Boltzmann machines, *Proc. of the 27th International Conference on Machine Learning (ICML-10)*, 807–814.

Nakamura, Y. (1989). A method for dynamic characteristics estimation of subsurface using microtremor on the ground surface, *Q. Rep. Railway Tech. Res. Inst.*, Vol. **30**.

Ng, A. Y. (2004). Feature selection, L 1 vs. L 2 regularization, and rotational invariance, *Proc. of the Twenty-First International Conf. on Machine Learning*, 78 pp.

Nikolaou, S., X. Vera-Grunauer, R. Gilsanz, R. Luque, T. Kishida, G. Diaz-Fanas, N. Antonaki, T. Toulkeridis, E. Miranda, V. Diaz, *et al.* (2017). GEER-ATC M_w 7.8 Ecuador 4/16/16 earthquake reconnaissance Part I: Seismological and ground motion aspects, *16th World Conf. on Earthquake Engineering*, Santiago, Chile, 9–13 January 2017.

Nogoshi, M., and T. Igarashi (1971). On the amplitude characteristics of microtremor, Part II, *J. Seismol. Soc. Jpn.* **24,** 26–40.

Parolai, S., P. Bormann, and C. Milkereit (2002). New relationships between Vs, thickness of sediments, and resonance frequency calculated by the H/V ratio of seismic noise for the Cologne area (Germany), *Bull. Seismol. Soc. Am.* **92,** no. 6, 2521–2527.

Quinlan, J. R. (1986). Induction of decision trees, *Machine Learn.* **1,** 81–106.

Rahimi, S., and C. M. Wood (2022). Comparison of wavefield transformation techniques for MASW data processing, *Geo-Congress 2022*, 82–91.

Rahimi, S., and C. M. Wood (2023). Reducing mode assignment errors in surface wave inversion for sites with a very shallow impedance contrast using love type surface waves, *Geo-Congress 2023*, 173–182.

Rai, M., A. Rodriguez-Marek, and B. S. Chiou (2017). Empirical terrain-based topographic modification factors for use in ground motion prediction, *Earthq. Spectra* **33,** no. 1, 157–177.

SESAME (2004). Guidelines for the implementation of the H/V spectral ratio technique on ambient vibrations: Measurements, processing and interpretation, *SESAME European Research Project WP12*, 1–62.

Seyhan, E., J. P. Stewart, T. D. Ancheta, R. B. Darragh, and R. W. Graves (2014). NGA-West2 site database, *Earthq. Spectra* **30,** no. 3, 1007–1024.

Srivastava, N., G. Hinton, A. Krizhevsky, I. Sutskever, and R. Salakhutdinov (2014). Dropout: A simple way to prevent neural networks from overfitting, *J. Machine Learn. Res.* **15,** no. 1, 1929–1958.

Stanko, D., and S. Markušić (2020). An empirical relationship between resonance frequency, bedrock depth and V_{S30} for Croatia based on HVSR forward modelling, *Nat. Hazards* **103,** no. 3, 3715–3743.

Stewart, J. P., and E. Seyhan (2013). *Semi-Empirical Nonlinear Site Amplification and its Application in NEHRP Site Factors*, Pacific Earthquake Engineering Research Center, Berkeley, California.

Stolte, A., L. Wotherspoon, B. Cox, C. Wood, S. Jeong, and J. Munro (2023). The influence of multiple impedance contrasts on mHVSR site period estimates in the Canterbury Plains of New Zealand and implications for site classification, *Earthq. Spectra* **39,** no. 1, 288–309.

Teague, D., B. Cox, B. Bradley, and L. Wotherspoon (2018). Development of deep shear wave velocity profiles with estimates of uncertainty in the complex interbedded geology of Christchurch, New Zealand, *Earthq. Spectra* **34,** no. 2, 639–672.

Thornley, J. D., U. Dutta, J. Douglas, and Z. J. Yang (2021). Evaluation of horizontal to vertical spectral ratio and standard spectral ratio methods for mapping shear wave velocity across Anchorage, Alaska, *Soil Dynam. Earthq. Eng.* **150,** 106918.

Vantassel, J., B. Cox, L. Wotherspoon, and A. Stolte (2018). Mapping depth to bedrock, shear stiffness, and fundamental site period at CentrePort, Wellington, using surface-wave methods: Implications for local seismic site amplification, *Bull. Seismol. Soc. Am.* **108,** no. 3B, 1709–1721.

Vantassel, J. P. (2025). hvsrpy: An open-source python package for microtremor and earthquake horizontal-to-vertical spectral ratio processing, *Seismol. Res. Lett.* **96,** no. 4, 2671–2682.

Vantassel, J. P., M. Ilgac, A. Athanasopoulos Zekkos, A. Yong, B. Hassani, and A. J. Martin (2024). Are the horizontal-to-vertical spectral ratios of earthquakes and microtremors the same? *Bull. Seismol. Soc. Am.* **114,** no. 6, 3078–3092.

Vantassel, J. P., A. C. Stolte, L. M. Wotherspoon, and B. R. Cox (2023). AutoHVSR: A machine-learning-supported algorithm for the fully-automated processing of horizontal-to-vertical spectral ratio measurements, *Soil Dynam. Earthq. Eng.* **173,** 108153.

Vantassel, J. P., B. R. Cox, and D. M. Brannon (2021). HVSRweb: An open-source, web-based application for horizontal-to-vertical spectral ratio processing, *IFCEE 2021, Presented at the International Foundations Congress and Equipment Expo 2021*, American Society of Civil Engineers, Dallas, Texas, 42–52.

Wald, D. J., and T. I. Allen (2007). Topographic slope as a proxy for seismic site conditions and amplification, *Bull. Seismol. Soc. Am.* **97,** no. 5, 1379–1395.

Wang, P., P. Zimmaro, S. K. Ahdi, A. Yong, and J. P. Stewart (2023). Identification protocols for horizontal-to-vertical spectral ratio peaks, *Bull. Seismol. Soc. Am.* **113,** no. 2, 782–803.

Wood, C., and A. Himel (2019). Development of deep shear wave velocity profiles at seismic stations in the Mississippi Embayment, *DesignSafe-CI*, doi: 10.17603/ds2-be10-q668.

Wood, C., and S. Rahimi (2022). Mapping subsurface conditions for transportation applications, *Final Project Report*, Arkansas Department of Transportation (ARDOT).

Wood, C., L. Woodfield, and R. Rieth (2020). Dynamic site characterization in Mexico City following the 2017 M_w 7.1 Puebla-Mexico City earthquake, *DesignSafe-CI*, doi: 10.17603/ds2-4kc2-zr63.

Wotherspoon, L., B. Bradley, E. Thomson, B. R. Cox, C. M. Wood, and M. Deschenes (2016). Dynamic site characterisation of Canterbury strong motion stations using active and passive surface wave testing, *EQC Report*, **14,** no. 663, 30.

Wotherspoon, L. M., B. Bradley, A. Hills, E. M. Thomson, S. Jeong, C. M. Wood, and B. R. Cox (2015). Development of deep VS profiles and site periods for the Canterbury region, *2015 New Zealand Society for Earthquake Engineering Annual Conference (NZSEE)*, Rotorua, New Zealand, 10–12 April 2015.

Wotherspoon, L. M., A. E. Kaiser, A. C. Stolte, and E. F. Manea (2024). Development of the site characterization database for the 2022 New Zealand National Seismic Hazard Model, *Seismol. Res. Lett.* **95,** no. 1, 214–225.

Yaghmaei-Sabegh, S., and B. Hassani (2020). Investigation of the relation between Vs30 and site characteristics of Iran based on horizontal-to-vertical spectral ratios, *Soil Dynam. Earthq. Eng.* **128,** 105899.

Yong, A., E. Cochran, J. Andrews, K. Hudson, A. Martin, E. Yu, J. Herrick, and J. Dozal (2021). V_{S30} and dominant site frequency (fd) as provisional station ML corrections (d ML) in California, *Bull. Seismol. Soc. Am.* **111,** no. 1, 61–76.

Yong, A., A. Martin, K. Stokoe, and J. Diehl (2013). ARRA-funded VS30 measurements using multi-technique approach at strong- motion stations in California and Central-Eastern United States, *U.S. Geol. Surv. Open-File Rept. 2013-1102*, 1–59, doi: 10.3133/ofr20131102.

Yust, M. B. S. (2018). Dynamic site characterization of TexNet ground motion stations, *Doctoral Dissertation*, University of Texas at Austin.

Manuscript received 21 May 2025
Published online 26 February 2026

V_{S30} Estimation from Shallow V_S Profiles

Kenneth S. Hudson*[1]

ABSTRACT

The time-averaged shear-wave velocity to a 30 m depth from the ground surface (V_{S30}) is a critical parameter for site classification in seismic hazard analyses and building codes. Boore (2004) proposed a method to extrapolate V_{S30} from shallow velocity profiles (depths < 30 m) using correlations between shallow average shear-wave velocities V_{Sd} and V_{S30}, based on 135 California boreholes. Here, I expand this approach using over 2400 profiles from the V_S Profile Database, enabling analysis of regional biases (e.g., by states in the U.S. and sedimentary basins) and methodological biases (e.g., borehole logging versus surface-wave dispersion). The expanded approach provides a minor improvement to the predictive accuracy of the original Boore (2004) method. I find that constant-velocity extrapolation underestimates V_{S30}, while correlation-based methods reduce bias but vary by measurement method. Comparisons of colocated profiles (< 5 m apart) do not show statistically significant differences in the V_{S30} between the velocity measurement methods. These findings are the basis to improve V_{S30} extrapolation accuracy from shallow velocity profiles.

KEY POINTS

- Boore (2004) method for estimating V_{S30} from shallow velocity profiles is revisited using a larger dataset.
- Regional variations and measurement types introduce systematic biases in extrapolated V_{S30} estimates.
- The proposed V_{S30} extrapolation scheme, accounting for measurement type, outperforms constant-velocity extrapolation.

INTRODUCTION

The time-averaged shear-wave velocity (V_S) in the upper 30 m (V_{S30}) is a key site response parameter used in ground-motion models (GMMs), building codes (e.g., National Earthquake Hazards Reduction Program [NEHRP] site classes), and seismic hazard mapping. Many velocity profiles, however, do not extend to 30 m due to logistical or physical constraints, necessitating extrapolation methods. Boore (2004) evaluated two extrapolation techniques using 135 California boreholes: (1) constant-velocity assumption (this is the recommended method in American Society of Civil Engineers, 2021) and (2) correlations between V_{Sd}, the time-averaged V_S to a depth d, and V_{S30}. Correlation-based methods outperformed constant-velocity extrapolation, reducing bias and misclassification of NEHRP site class rates to <10% for all but the shallowest depths (Boore, 2004). Subsequent work has extended these approaches regionally; for instance, Boore *et al.* (2011) derived V_{Sd}–V_{S30} correlations for California and Japan (Kiban–Kyoshin network [KiK-net]), highlighting steeper velocity gradients in Japan that further reduce extrapolation bias for depths beyond 30 m. In Taiwan, Kuo *et al.* (2011) proposed a bottom-constant velocity model using microtremor array data, improving predictive accuracy compared with Boore (2004) in sedimentary basins. Dai *et al.* (2013) present a method in which the travel time from the bottom of the profile to 30 m is estimated from V_{Sd}. Other studies have introduced velocity gradient models for Japan (Midorikawa and Nogi, 2015) and hybrid methods that reduce misclassification in rocky sites (Kwak *et al.*, 2017). More complex relationships for V_{Sd}–V_{S30} have also been proposed and have been shown to produce improved accuracy (Wang and Wang, 2015). Recent efforts incorporated additional parameters such as slope, geologic age, and geotechnical class into parametric models for improved accuracy in variable terrains (Zhou *et al.*, 2021). Data-driven approaches, such as machine learning-based models using microtremor horizontal-to-vertical spectral ratio (mHVSR) curves for V_{S30} prediction, suggest that implicit subsurface information can enhance extrapolation (Wagle, 2025). Wair *et al.* (2012) developed guidelines that emphasize extrapolation of shallow data is suitable for uniform soils but may lead to errors in heterogeneous conditions. Many authors have confirmed the utility of V_{Sd}–V_{S30} correlations but highlight the need for regional adjustments (Boore *et al.*, 2011; Kuo *et al.*, 2011; Zhou *et al.*, 2021; Fang *et al.*, 2023).

1. Hudson Geotechnics, Inc., El Segundo, California, U.S.A., https://orcid.org/0000-0001-6006-8355 (KSH)

*Corresponding author: kenneth.s.hudson@gmail.com

Cite this article as Hudson, K. S. (2026). V_{S30} Estimation from Shallow V_S Profiles, *Bull. Seismol. Soc. Am.* **116**, 1178–1198, doi: 10.1785/0120250210

There are many techniques for measuring or inferring a V_S profile (e.g., seismic cone penetration testing [SCPT], multichannel analysis of surface waves [MASWs], suspension logging, etc.). Each of these and other related methods contains different uncertainties and thus accuracies in estimating the V_S profile and, therefore, the V_{S30}. An understanding of these inter- and intramethod differences is important when planning a site exploration and reviewing prior data (Stephenson *et al.*, 2022; Yong *et al.*, 2022a). For instance, Rayleigh-wave techniques (e.g., in MASW) measure vertically polarized shear velocities (*Sv*), whereas downhole methods like SCPT typically measure horizontally polarized velocities (*Sh*). Even within MASW measurement techniques, the analyst can use Rayleigh or Love waves, with Love-wave estimates sometimes exceeding Rayleigh by over 15% due to anisotropy (A. Martin, personal comm., 2025; see also Lin *et al.*, 2008; Haney and Tsai, 2019). Surface-wave methods average velocities over large soil volumes, whereas downhole paths follow the fastest route, potentially bypassing heterogeneous low-velocity zones, leading to higher V_S estimates (A. Martin, personal comm., 2025; e.g., Andrus *et al.*, 2003; Roy *et al.*, 2013; Garofalo, Foti, Hollender, Bard, Cornou, Cox, Dechamp, *et al.*, 2016).

Blind comparisons, such as the InterPACIFIC Project (Garofalo, Foti, Hollender, Bard, Cornou, Cox, Dechamp, *et al.*, 2016; Garofalo, Foti, Hollender, Bard, Cornou, Cox, Ohrnberger, *et al.*, 2016) reveal systematic biases, with noninvasive methods like MASW overestimating V_S in soft soils by 10%–20% due to inversion uncertainties. Comparisons from the Santa Clara Valley, California, revealed inconsistent trends for over- or underprediction using invasive and noninvasive techniques (Boore and Asten, 2008). Variability assessments across six methods at industrial sites quantify intermethod differences up to 15%, attributing them to soil disturbance and resolution limits (Darvasi, 2021). Comparisons between interferometric and noninterferometric passive seismic methods demonstrate the former's strength in accurate dispersion imaging (Cheng *et al.*, 2022). Geostatistical approaches have been proposed to reduce biases in V_S estimation from sparse data (Foti and Passeri, 2018). Using only passive-source surface-wave approaches during a more recent multitiered blind test, Yong *et al.* (2022b) demonstrated that, subject to a sufficient azimuthal distribution of the passively acquired seismic noise sources, the use of sparse arrays is adequate for accurate estimates of the time-averaged V_S to a d of 10, 30, 100, or 300 m (V_{S10}, V_{S30}, V_{S100}, or V_{S300}, respectively). They also showed that no techniques/software packages are observed to outperform others for any portion of the trial and that analyst skill and experience is a stronger factor than that of technique and software choices.

Datasets have grown dramatically over the past few years, particularly with the V_S profile database (VsPDB) (Ahdi *et al.*, 2018; Kwak *et al.*, 2021). This database compiles over 2800 global profiles from diverse methods. The V_{S30} estimates in this study were derived from a variety of geophysical methods, including crosshole seismic testing (which measures V_S travel times between two adjacent boreholes for high-resolution interval velocity profiles), downhole seismic testing (involving surface-generated waves recorded by geophones at successive depths in a single borehole), multichannel surface wave (a noninvasive surface method that records MASW data and inverts dispersion curves), seismic reflection (which captures reflected waves from subsurface interfaces to map layering and derive velocities), seismic refraction (analyzing first-arrival refracted waves along layer boundaries to estimate velocities), spectral analysis of surface waves (SASW; using two receivers to measure phase spectra of surface waves and invert for velocity profiles), SCPT (combining cone penetrometer advancement with downhole seismic measurements for integrated soil resistance and velocity data), surface-wave dispersion analysis (a general approach inverting frequency-dependent phase velocities of surface waves to model V_S structure), and *P–S* suspension logging (a borehole technique employing a suspended tool to generate and record compressional and shear waves for interval velocity logging). This dataset allows examination of factors previously not fully addressed, such as regional geologic variations and measurement method biases. For instance, California sites often feature sedimentary basins with increasing velocity gradients that are different for each basin, whereas central and eastern U.S. sites do not typically have such deep sedimentary basins.

I revisit Boore (2004) methods using a considerably larger dataset (VsPDB data) and quantify biases by region and method. I also compare colocated profiles to assess intermethod biases. These enhancements aim to refine V_{S30} estimation and site characterization, improving seismic hazard analyses.

The VsPDB also contains cone penetration test (CPT) and standard penetration test data from borings, which have been used in the past to correlate to V_S (Wair *et al.*, 2012). These relationships are not revisited herein because of the trend within recent building code documents to discourage use of these correlations (American Society of Civil Engineers, 2021).

DATA AND METHODS

Dataset compilation

I query the VsPDB through the application programming interface using Python scripts to extract V_S profiles. The VsPDB only has profiles located in the United States and Canada at the time of querying. I filter the dataset to eliminate profiles that do not extend to at least ≥30 m and do not contain at least one velocity value at depths less than 30 m. Out of the 2886 profiles returned by querying the velocity layer data and velocity point data tables, 187 profiles are rejected because they did not extend to a depth of 30 m, and 24 are rejected because they did not contain V_S data in the upper 30 m. In addition, the dataset is filtered so that it only contains profiles with $V_{S30} < 760$ m/s to only include soil sites where the V_{Sd}–V_{S30} correlation is valid, removing an additional 183

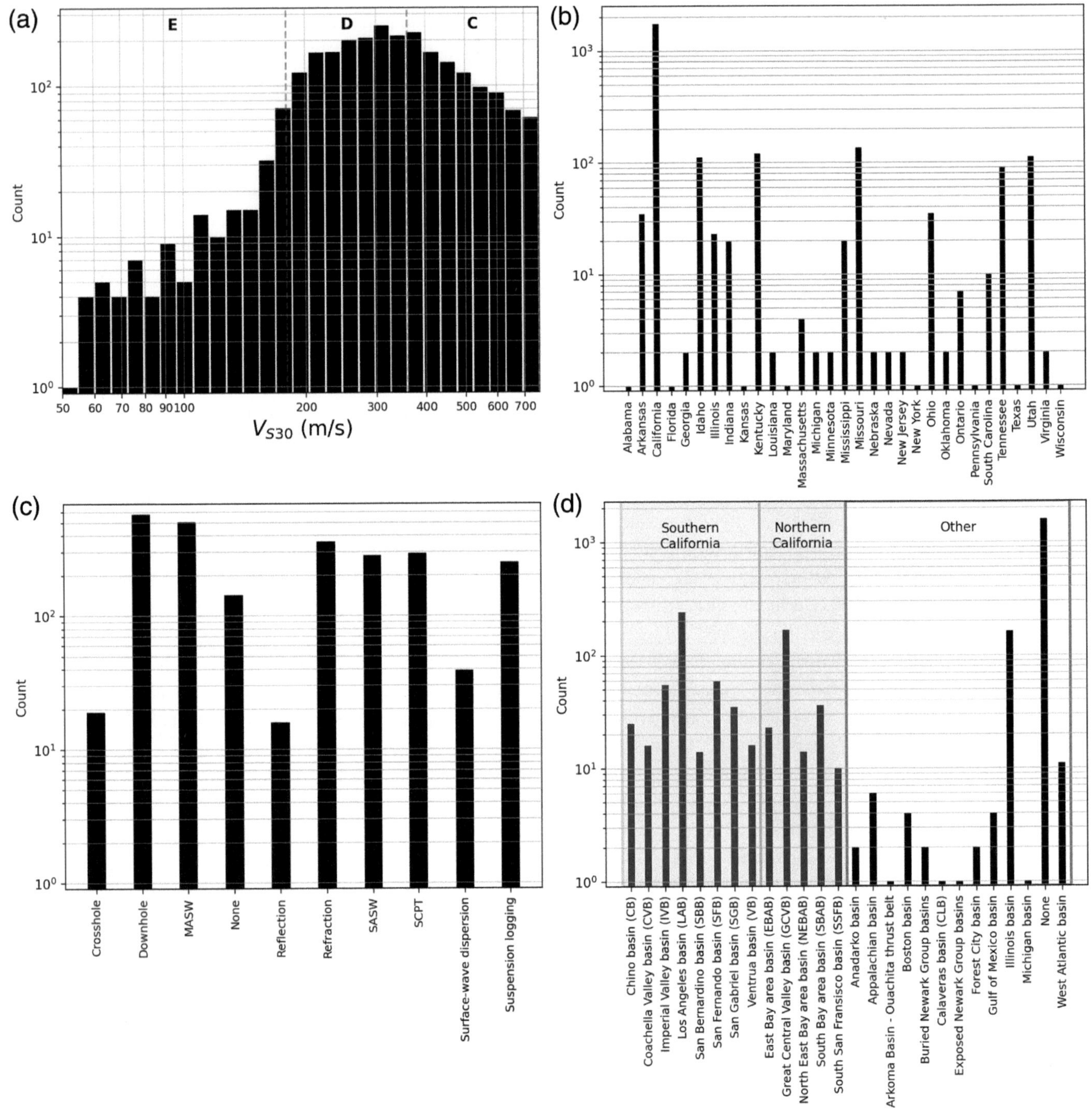

profiles from the dataset. The filtered dataset comprises 2492 profiles, far exceeding prior studies' dataset sizes.

The dataset of profiles is grouped by three categories: (1) the state the profile resides in, (2) the method used to collect the V_S profile, which is herein referred to as the velocity method, and (3) the sedimentary basin the profile resides in. I utilize the basin geometries from the ground-motion database (Coleman Jr. and Cahan, 2012; Nweke *et al.*, 2022; Buckreis *et al.*, 2023, 2025). Histograms of the dataset grouped by the state the profile is within, the velocity method, and the basin the site is located within are shown in Figure 1. The dataset and basins are mapped in Figure 2.

Figure 1. Histograms of the dataset. (a) The V_{S30} values computed for each profile and National Earthquake Hazards Reduction Program (NEHRP) site class labels (E, D, and C). (b–d) The dataset is grouped by the state where the profile is located, the velocity method applied, and the basin to which the profile is assigned, respectively. MASW, multichannel analysis of surface wave; SASW, spectral analysis of surface wave; and SCPT, seismic cone penetration testing. The color version of this figure is available only in the electronic edition.

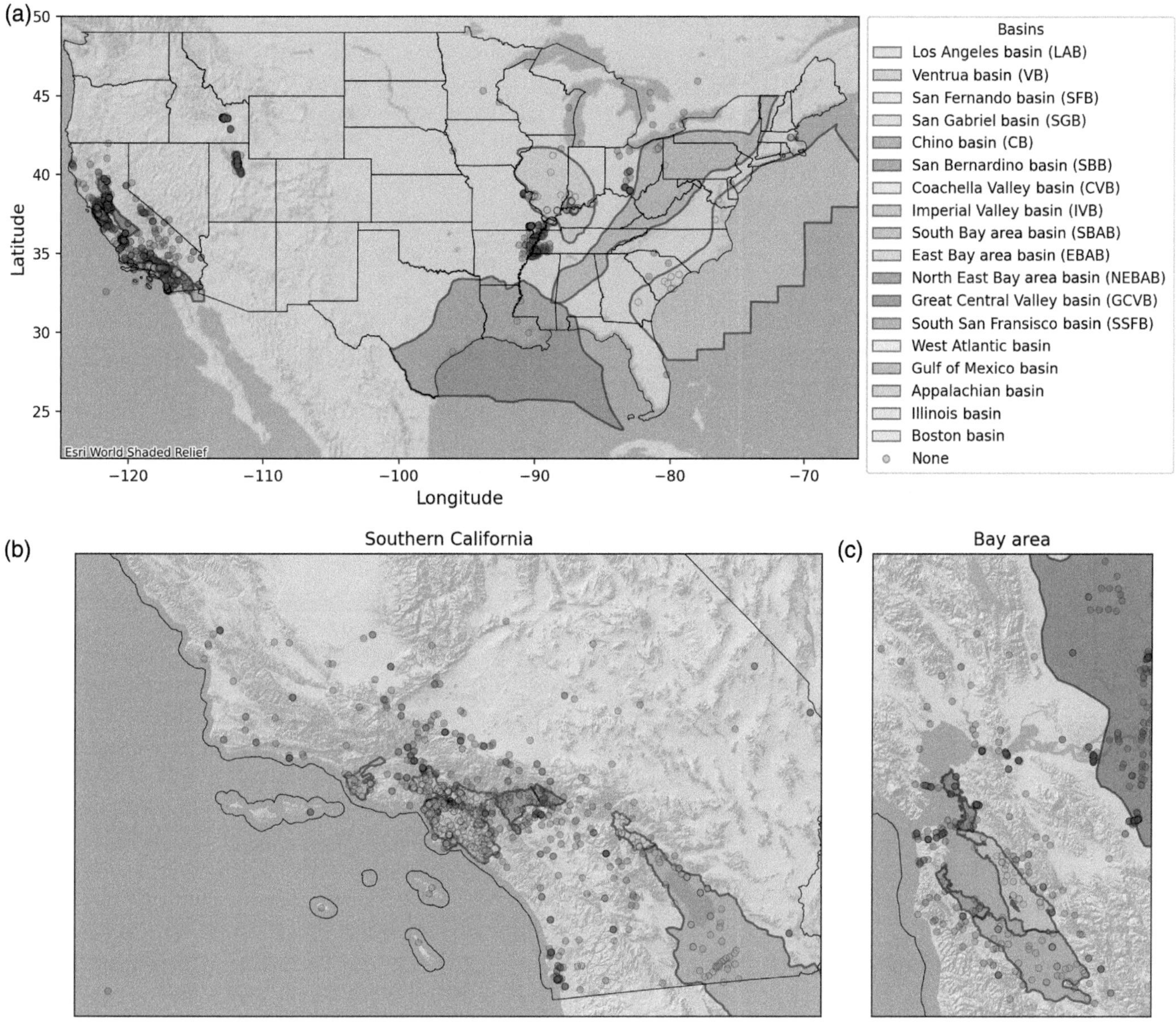

Figure 2. Maps of V_S profile dataset (circles) and basins for the entire dataset (a), southern California (b), and the San Francisco Bay area (c). The color version of this figure is available only in the electronic edition.

The V_S profiles are used to compute time-averaged V_{Sd} using equation (1):

$$V_{Sd} = \frac{d}{tt_d}, \qquad (1)$$

in which tt_d is the travel time in seconds to depth d. In the velocity layer data, tt_d is computed using the interval velocity within each layer and assuming the shallowest layer's velocity extends up to the ground surface. To determine the tt_d from the discrete velocity point data, the interval V_S for each layer is calculated by assuming that the V_S measured at a given depth point applies uniformly to the interval extending from the immediately shallower depth point down to that given depth point.

Intermethod dataset. For colocated comparisons, I select pairs of profiles obtained using different velocity methods within 5 m of each other. Five meters are selected because the spatial variance of V_S profiles at that distance is small. This yields 166 pairs across methods. Combinations of methods that had less than five pairs were removed from the dataset, leaving 160 pairs broken down as follows: downhole versus suspension logging: 37, MASW versus SASW: 19; MASW versus refraction: 9, MASW versus SCPT: 80, and SCPT versus suspension logging: 15.

A key limitation of the VsPDB and similar datasets is the variability in how geographic coordinates are assigned and reported for different measurement techniques. For invasive borehole methods (e.g., downhole or SCPT), coordinates typically represent the precise location of the borehole. In contrast, for noninvasive surface-wave methods like MASW or SASW, which involve linear arrays spanning tens of meters, the reported coordinates often denote a representative site centroid or endpoint rather than a specific point along the array, due to database entry conventions and historical data compilation practices (Ahdi *et al.*, 2018; Kwak *et al.*, 2021). This can result in apparent zero-meter separation distances between paired profiles, even when the actual measurement footprints may differ by up to the array length (typically 10–50 m). Consequently, my selection of profile pairs within a 5-m radius prioritizes site-level colocation over submeter precision, which is suitable for regional-scale V_{S30} comparisons but may introduce minor uncertainties in highly heterogeneous sites.

Shallow profile extrapolation methods

Following Boore (2004), I tested the following methods against data from my compilation:

1. Constant-velocity, which assumes V_S from d to 30 m equals the bottom-layer velocity, using equation (2):

$$V_{S30} = \frac{30}{tt_d + (30 - d)/V_{Sd}}. \tag{2}$$

2. Correlation-based: fitted coefficients using the Boore (2004) function form (equation. 3), calibrated regionally and by method:

$$\log_{10} V_{S30} = a + b \times \log_{10} V_{Sd}. \tag{3}$$

The coefficients in equation (3) are fitted using both an ordinary least squares (OLSs) regression and linear mixed-effects regression, described subsequently.

Linear mixed-effects regression. I perform the fitting of the coefficients in equation (3) using linear mixed-effects regression. Linear mixed-effects models (LMMs), also known as mixed-effects models, represent an extension of standard linear regression techniques by incorporating both fixed effects and random effects. These models are useful when data points are not fully independent, such as when measurements from the same group (e.g., the same velocity measurement method or geographic region) are likely to be more similar to each other than to those from different groups due to shared underlying factors like instrumentation biases or local geology. This grouping can lead to correlated responses within clusters, and LMMs account for such correlations to provide more accurate estimates and avoid overstating the significance of results.

Fixed effects capture consistent, population-level trends or relationships between predictors and the outcome variable that are of primary interest, assuming these parameters are nonrandom and constant across the studied population (Gelman and Hill, 2007). In contrast, random effects account for unexplained variability at different levels of the data, treating them as random variables drawn from a normal distribution with a specified mean (typically zero) and variance–covariance structure tends to help illuminate model correlations within groups and prevents inflated type I error rates due to violated independence assumptions (Schober and Vetter, 2021).

The underlying mechanism of LMMs can be expressed in matrix form as

$$\boldsymbol{y} = \boldsymbol{X\beta} + \boldsymbol{Zu} + \boldsymbol{\varepsilon}, \tag{4}$$

in which $\boldsymbol{y}$ is the vector of observed responses (in this case, $\log_{10} V_{S30}$), $\boldsymbol{X}$ is the design matrix (containing the $\log_{10} V_{Sd}$ values) for the fixed-effects parameters $\boldsymbol{\beta}$ (the a and b coefficients in equation 3), $\boldsymbol{Z}$ is the design matrix (containing the $\log_{10} V_{Sd}$ values for each random-effects group, i.e., velocity method) for the random effects $\boldsymbol{u}$ (the adjustments to the a and b coefficients for each random-effects group), and $\boldsymbol{\varepsilon}$ denotes the residual errors (Fox, 2016).

This formulation allows for flexible modeling of variance components, including random intercepts and slopes, making LMMs particularly suitable for analyzing complex datasets while providing robust parameter estimates and facilitating inference at multiple levels.

My choice of random-effects groupings—velocity method, state, and sedimentary basin—reflects expected sources of correlation in V_S profiles. This is analogous to the use of earthquake ID as a random effect in GMMs, where recordings from the same event share correlated residuals due to common source parameters. For velocity methods, correlations may arise because each technique (e.g., MASW versus SCPT) may introduce systematic biases in how velocity gradients are captured, influenced by factors such as resolution limits, inversion assumptions, or wave propagation paths in heterogeneous media. Even if there are no significant differences in overall V_{S30} estimates between methods (suggesting broad consistency at the 30 m integrated scale), method-specific differences in the depth slope b can still emerge physically: for instance, surface-wave methods like MASW average velocities over larger volumes and may smooth steep near-surface gradients in soft sediments, leading to shallower slopes (lower b), whereas invasive borehole methods capture more localized, potentially steeper gradients along direct paths, especially in sites with low-velocity zones (Comina *et al.*, 2011). For states and sedimentary basins, groupings account for regional geologic controls, such as varying sediment thickness, consolidation, or tectonic settings (e.g., steeper velocity increases in deep California basins versus shallower gradients in the central United States), which can correlate V_{Sd}–V_{S30} relationships within these areas.

I perform the regressions using the $\log_{10} V_{Sd}$ values computed with d values ranging from 1 to 29 m at 1 m intervals. This is repeated three times for three random-effects groups: velocity method, the state the profile is located within, and the sedimentary basin the profile is located within. Profiles are given a group label of "None" in the state, basin, and velocity model group if they are located outside of the United States;

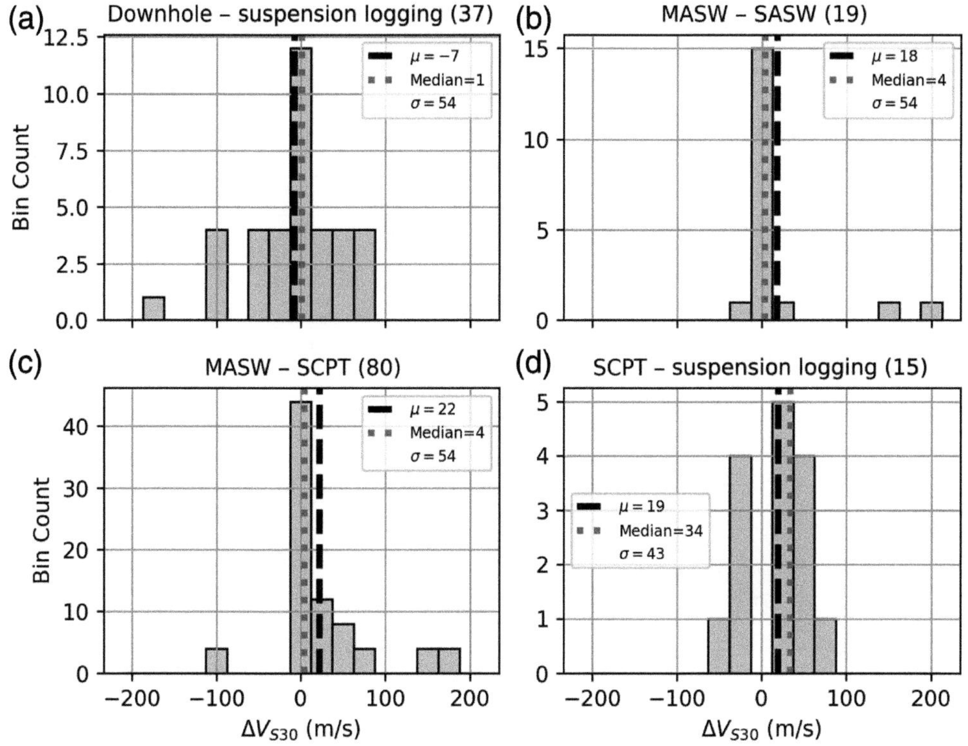

Figure 3. (a–d) Histograms of ΔV_{S30} for intermethod comparisons. The number of paired profiles within each category is shown in parentheses after the method pairing in each subplot title.

located outside of mapped sedimentary basins; or, if profiles do not have a known velocity method, respectively.

RESULTS

Intermethod comparisons of V_{S30}

Colocated pairs of velocity methods are used to compute the difference in V_{S30} (ΔV_{S30}) between the 151 pairs. Thus, ΔV_{S30} is computed as the difference between the first velocity method listed and the second, meaning that if the first velocity method listed produces a larger V_{S30} than the second, it will be a positive ΔV_{S30}. Distributions of the ΔV_{S30} for the four velocity method pairings with more than 10 pairs are shown in Figure 3. The pairs of tests shown in Figure 3 all have a separation distance of 0 m (they were placed at the same latitude and longitude in the database) except for one SCPT versus suspension logging pair, which has an approximately 1 m separation distance.

All of the pairings produce an almost identical standard deviation (σ) of ΔV_{S30} except for the SCPT-suspension logging pairings, with a slightly lower σ. None of the mean V_{S30} (μ) values are significantly large (the absolute value of μ is not larger than σ); therefore, this dataset has not shown any significant differences in the estimation of V_{S30} between methods.

Correlation-based V_{Sd}–V_{S30} extrapolation

Figure 4 presents fitted relationships at a V_{Sd} value of 10 m (modified with new data from fig. 3a of Boore, 2004). The random-effects group used in Figure 4 is the velocity method; each different method is plotted with a different color and symbol. The number of profiles within each group is indicated in the legend next to the method. Boore (2004) fitted coefficients and the standard deviation of the residuals (σ) are displayed in each subplot for the corresponding d value, and the fixed-effects coefficients and σ values from my regression are displayed below (in Fig. 4 legend). The Boore (2004) σ value results from his article, not the residuals of Boore's model applied herein to the new dataset. As d approaches 30 m, there is almost no difference between Boore (2004) coefficients and those of this study, but as d decreases, the coefficients diverge slightly, as shown in Figure 4. The σ values are very consistent between the Boore (2004) models and my fitted models, with slightly higher σ values on my models because it is a much larger dataset. A fitted model using OLSs regression is also presented in Figure 4, showing slightly larger differences in coefficients compared to Boore (2004).

Extrapolation method comparisons

Residuals are computed as the difference between the measured and the predicted $\log_{10} V_{S30}$ using $\log_{10} V_{Sd}$ from the correlation-based extrapolation method for the OLS model coefficients and each of the random-effects groups and range of d values (equation 3). Residuals are also computed using $\log_{10} V_{S30}$ predicted from the constant velocity extrapolation (equation 2) at the same range of d values. The μ and σ values of the residuals from these extrapolation methods are presented in Figure 5. At $d < 20$ m, in which all the variations of correlation-based extrapolation methods produce a smaller μ value than the constant velocity extrapolation, indicating that they provide a more accurate estimate of V_{S30}. The constant velocity method appears to consistently produce positive μ values, suggesting that there is an underprediction of V_{S30} when this technique is applied.

The OLS model and each of the random-effects group models perform very similarly. These models all produce lower μ values at all d values than the constant velocity extrapolation method.

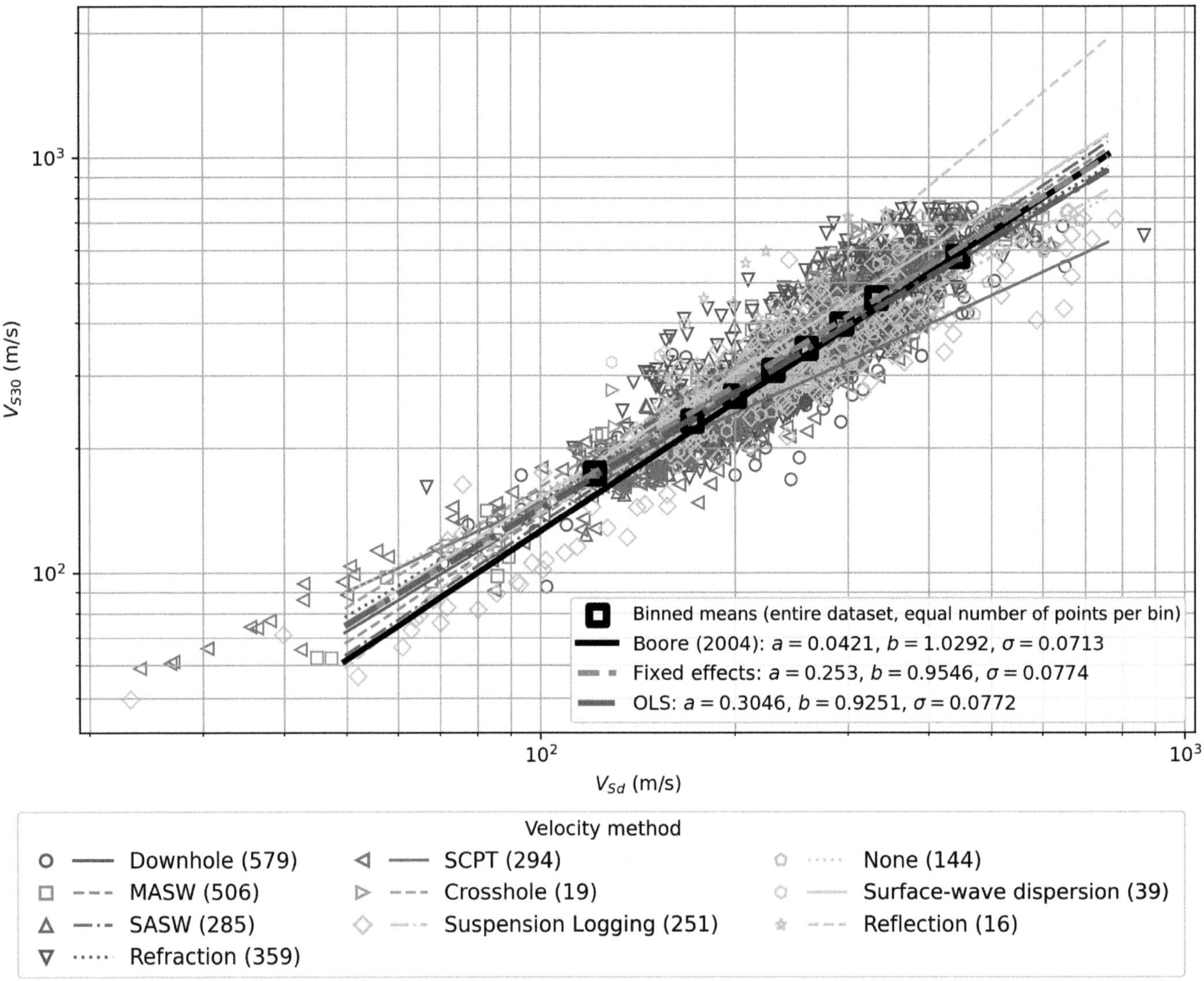

Figure 4. Linear mixed-effects regression fits predicting $\log_{10} V_{S30}$ from $\log_{10} V_{Sd}$ at $d = 10$ m using the velocity method as the random-effects group. The number of profiles within each velocity method is shown in parentheses after the method pairing in each legend item. OLS, ordinary least squares. The color version of this figure is available only in the electronic edition.

There is lower uncertainty at $d > 6$ m using the constant velocity extrapolation because the velocity is held constant between d and 30 m, producing lower variability in the resulting V_{S30} prediction. The three comparisons of random-effects models produce similar σ values, with the random-effects models producing lower σ values compared to the OLS or fixed effects results. The fixed-effects results and OLS have almost identical σ values, which is to be expected from these regression styles.

DISCUSSION

The dataset I have examined shows differences in V_{S30} values calculated between different methods at some sites (i.e., suspension logging versus SCPT), but none of the differences are statistically significant. Although surface-wave methods, such as MASW, involve significant uncertainties in the estimation of V_S profiles due to the inherent nonuniqueness of the inversion process, the aggregated V_{S30} parameter remains consistent and reliable. This nonuniqueness arises because surface-wave inversion is a nonlinear, ill-posed, and mixed-determined problem, leading to equivalent V_S profiles that may differ substantially in individual layer velocities and thicknesses, particularly in subsoils with gradual velocity increases or low impedance contrasts. However, in aggregate, these layers must collectively reproduce the observed dispersion curve, which constrains the overall travel time of shear waves through the upper 30 m, resulting in V_{S30} values that exhibit low variability (Martin *et al.*, 2006; Comina *et al.*, 2011; Stephenson *et al.*, 2022). Thus, while surface-wave methods may not accurately resolve any given soil layer's V_S, the V_{S30} they produce is robust for seismic hazard applications using GMMs or NEHRP site classes.

The correlation-based V_{Sd}–V_{S30} extrapolation method outperforms the constant velocity extrapolation method in this dataset. This is not surprising because the simplified

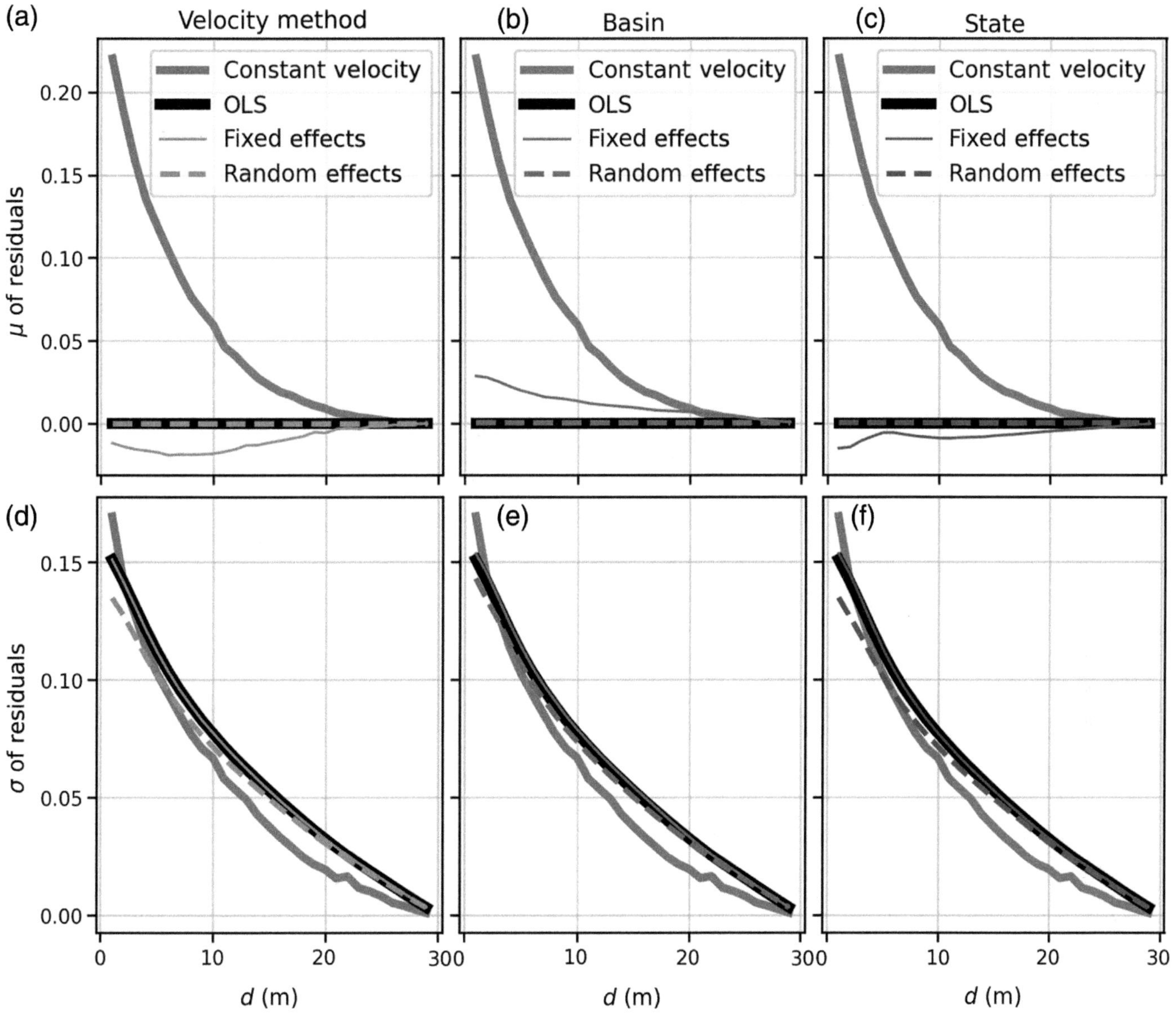

Figure 5. Mean (a–c) and standard deviation (d–f) of residuals from the three random-effects grouped correlation-based models (velocity method: a, d; basin: b, e; and state: c, f) and constant velocity extrapolation methods. The color version of this figure is available only in the electronic edition.

assumption that the velocity remains constant from the last measured layer to a depth of 30 m is violated in most profiles. At a minimum, soils are expected to behave in a manner that produces increasing V_S with increasing confining stress when all other material properties are held constant. In addition, different soil layers are typically encountered at different depths within the upper 30 m of a site, and deeper layers will be older and likely be more compacted than shallower layers, also contributing to increasing V_S with depth.

The correlation-based method has very similar performance when any of the three random-effects group model coefficients are used. The coefficients for each of the models are provided in Tables A1–A3. The state and basin random variables show that different regions and sedimentary basins have different V_{Sd}–V_{S30} relationships. The importance of regional and other spatial trends on this relationship may be more influential in a more complete dataset because this dataset consists of most of its profiles within California and not within a sedimentary basin, which may influence the results.

The OLS model provides less accurate results than the random-effects models, but can be used when the user does not want to use the random-effects models. The OLS model coefficients are provided in Table A4.

CONCLUSIONS

This study revisits and expands upon Boore (2004) methodology for estimating V_{S30} from shallow V_S profiles by leveraging the extensive VsPDB, which includes over 2400 profiles across diverse geologic settings and measurement techniques. Through this expanded dataset, I quantify potential systematic biases introduced by both regional geologic variability and velocity measurement methods. My findings confirm that constant-velocity extrapolation tends to underestimate V_{S30}. In contrast, correlation-based extrapolation methods—especially those incorporating the velocity method as a random effect in a linear mixed-effects framework—consistently yield more accurate and less biased V_{S30} estimates.

Intermethod comparisons of colocated profiles reveal that while individual methods (e.g., MASW, SCPT, and suspension logging) exhibit known limitations and uncertainties, the resulting V_{S30} values are generally robust and not significantly different across methods. This supports the continued use of surface-wave methods in seismic site classification, provided that inversion uncertainties are acknowledged and appropriately managed.

Overall, this work provides a more comprehensive and statistically grounded framework for estimating V_{S30} from shallow velocity data. The results have been used in the application of GMMs, site classification, and seismic hazard assessment. Future work should explore the integration of machine learning approaches and additional geospatial predictors to further reduce epistemic uncertainty and enhance extrapolation accuracy in data-sparse regions.

DATA AND RESOURCES

All velocity profiles were queried from the V_S Profile Database (http://www.vspdb.org, last accessed December 2025).

DECLARATION OF COMPETING INTERESTS

The author acknowledges that there are no conflicts of interest recorded.

ACKNOWLEDGMENTS

The author thanks the V_S profile database maintainers for data access, David Boore for foundational work, and the reviewers, David Boore and Alan Yong, for improving this article. Funding was self-supported. The author also thanks Tony Martin for his personal communications with him regarding the differences between seismic cone penetration testing and multichannel analysis of surface wave (MASW) developed using Love- and Rayleigh-wave techniques.

REFERENCES

Ahdi, S. K., S. Sadiq, O. Ilhan, Y. Bozorgnia, Y. M. A. Hashash, D. Y. Kwak, D. Park, A. Yong, and J. P. Stewart (2018). Development of a United States community shear wave velocity profile database, 330–339, doi: 10.1061/9780784481462.032.

American Society of Civil Engineers (2021). Minimum design loads and associated criteria for buildings and other structures, *ASCE/SEI 7-22*, American Society of Civil Engineers, Reston, Virginia.

Boore, D. M. (2004). Estimating Vs(30) (or NEHRP Site Classes) from shallow velocity models (depths < 30 m), *Bull. Seismol. Soc. Am.* **94,** no. 2, 591–597, doi: 10.1785/0120030105.

Andrus, R. D., K. H. Stokoe, R. M. Chung, and C. Hsein Juang (2003). Guidelines for evaluating liquefaction resistance using shear wave velocity measurement and simplified procedures, *NIST GCR NIST GCR 03-854*, National Institute of Standards and Technology, Gaithersburg, Maryland.

Boore, D. M., and M. W. Asten (2008). Comparisons of shear-wave slowness in the Santa Clara Valley, California, using blind interpretations of data from invasive and noninvasive methods, *Bull. Seismol. Soc. Am.* **98,** no. 4, 1983–2003, doi: 10.1785/0120070277.

Boore, D. M., E. M. Thompson, and H. Cadet (2011). Regional correlations of VS30 and velocities averaged over depths less than and greater than 30 meters, *Bull. Seismol. Soc. Am.* **101,** no. 6, 3046–3059, doi: 10.1785/0120110071.

Buckreis, T. E., C. C. Nweke, P. Wang, S. J. Brandenberg, M. E. Ramos-Sepúlveda, R. Shams, R. Pretell, S. Mazzoni, P. Zimmaro, and J. P. Stewart (2023). Web portal for the global earthquake ground motion relational database, doi: 10.34948/G4RP4K.

Buckreis, T. E., C. C. Nweke, P. Wang, S. J. Brandenberg, M. E. Ramos-Sepúlveda, R. Shams, S. Mohammed, R. Pretell, S. Mazzoni, P. Zimmaro, *et al.* (2025). A global application programming interface–enabled earthquake ground motion relational database for engineering applications, *Earthq. Spectra* doi: 10.1177/87552930251344978.

Coleman, J. L., Jr., and S. M. Cahan (2012). Preliminary catalog of the sedimentary basins of the United States, *U.S. Geol. Surv. Open-File Rept. 2012-1111*, 2012–1111.

Cheng, F., J. Xia, Z. Xu, and J. B. Ajo-Franklin (2022). Comparisons between non-interferometric and interferometric passive surface wave imaging methods—Towards linear receiver array, *Geophys. J. Int.* **233,** no. 1, 680–699, doi: 10.1093/gji/ggac475.

Comina, C., S. Foti, D. Boiero, and L. V. Socco (2011). Reliability of VS30 evaluation from surface-wave tests, *J. Geotech. Geoenviron. Eng.* **137,** no. 6, 579–586, doi: 10.1061/(ASCE)GT.1943-5606.0000452.

Dai, Z., X. Li, and C. Hou (2013). A shear-wave velocity model for VS30 estimation based on a conditional independence property, *Bull. Seismol. Soc. Am.* **103,** no. 6, 3354–3361, doi: 10.1785/0120130025.

Darvasi, Y. (2021). Shear-wave velocity measurements and their uncertainties at six industrial sites, *Earthq. Spectra* **37,** no. 3, 2223–2246, doi: 10.1177/8755293020988029.

Fang, Y., H. Li, Y. Li, G. Chen, Y. Lv, and Y. Peng (2023). Vs30 prediction models based on measured shear-wave velocities in Tangshan, China, *Sustainability* **15,** no. 4, 3282, doi: 10.3390/su15043282.

Foti, S., and F. Passeri (2018). Reliability and accuracy of seismic tests in geotechnical site characterization, in A. M. Krishna, A. Dey, and S. Sreedeep (Editors), *Geotechnics for Natural and Engineered Sustainable Technologies*, Developments in Geotechnical Engineering, Springer, Singapore, Singapore, 187–206.

Fox, J. (2016). *Applied Regression Analysis and Generalized Linear Models*, SAGE, Los Angeles.

Garofalo, F., S. Foti, F. Hollender, P. Y. Bard, C. Cornou, B. R. Cox, A. Dechamp, M. Ohrnberger, V. Perron, D. Sicilia, *et al.* (2016). InterPACIFIC project: Comparison of invasive and non-invasive methods for seismic site characterization. Part II: Inter-comparison between surface-wave and borehole methods, *Soil Dynam. Earthq. Eng.* **82,** 241–254, doi: 10.1016/j.soildyn.2015.12.009.

Garofalo, F., S. Foti, F. Hollender, P. Y. Bard, C. Cornou, B. R. Cox, M. Ohrnberger, D. Sicilia, M. Asten, G. Di Giulio, *et al.* (2016). InterPACIFIC project: Comparison of invasive and non-invasive methods for seismic site characterization. Part I: Intra-comparison of surface wave methods, *Soil Dynam. Earthq. Eng.* **82,** 222–240, doi: 10.1016/j.soildyn.2015.12.010.

Gelman, A., and J. Hill (2007). *Data Analysis Using Regression and Multilevel/Hierarchical Models*, Analytical Methods for Social Research, Cambridge University Press, Cambridge.

Haney, M. M., and V. C. Tsai (2019). Perturbational and nonperturbational inversion of Love-wave velocities, *Geophysics* **85,** no. 1, F19–F26, doi: 10.1190/geo2018-0882.1.

Kuo, C.-H., K.-L. Wen, H.-H. Hsieh, T.-M. Chang, C.-M. Lin, and C.-T. Chen (2011). Evaluating empirical regression equations for Vs and estimating Vs30 in northeastern Taiwan, *Soil Dynam. Earthq. Eng.* **31,** no. 3, 431–439, doi: 10.1016/j.soildyn.2010.09.012.

Kwak, D., S. K. Ahdi, P. Wang, P. Zimmaro, S. J. Brandenberg, and J. P. Stewart (2021). Web portal for shear wave velocity and HVSR databases in support of site response research and applications, UCLA Geotechnical Engineering Group, available at https://vspdb.org/ (last accessed December 2025).

Kwak, D. Y., T. D. Ancheta, D. Mitra, S. K. Ahdi, P. Zimmaro, G. A. Parker, S. J. Brandenberg, and J. P. Stewart (2017). Performance evaluation of VSZ-to-VS30 correlation methods using global VS profile database, available at https://www.issmge.org/uploads/publications/59/57/pbdiiiPaper399.pdf (last accessed December 2025).

Lin, F.-C., M. P. Moschetti, and M. H. Ritzwoller (2008). Surface wave tomography of the western United States from ambient seismic noise: Rayleigh and Love wave phase velocity maps, *Geophys. J. Int.* **173,** no. 1, 281–298, doi: 10.1111/j.1365-246X.2008.03720.x.

Martin, A. J., J. B. Shawver, and J. G. Diehl (2006). Combined use of active and passive surface wave techniques for cost effective UBC/IBC site classification, *Proc. of the 8th National Conf. on Earthquake Engineering*, San Francisco, California, USA, 18–22 April 2006.

Midorikawa, S., and Y. Nogi (2015). Estimation of VS30 from shallow velocity profile, *J. JAEE* **15,** no. 2, 2_91–2_96, doi: 10.5610/jaee.15.2_91.

Nweke, C. C., J. P. Stewart, P. Wang, and S. J. Brandenberg (2022). Site response of sedimentary basins and other geomorphic provinces in southern California, *Earthq. Spectra* **38,** no. 4, 2341–2370, doi: 10.1177/87552930221088609.

Roy, S., E. Kocel, N. Dyaur, and R. R. Stewart (2013). Lateral heterogeneity and surface-wave inversion (MASW), *SEG Technical Program Expanded Abstracts 2013*, Society of Exploration Geophysicists, 1909–1913.

Schober, P., and T. R. Vetter (2021). Linear mixed-effects models in medical research, *Anesth. Analg.* **132,** no. 6, 1592–1593, doi: 10.1213/ANE.0000000000005541.

Stephenson, W. J., A. Yong, and A. Martin (2022). Flexible multimethod approach for seismic site characterization, *J. Seismol.* **26,** no. 4, 687–711, doi: 10.1007/s10950-022-10102-y.

Wagle, K. S. (2025). *Development of Data-Driven Models to Predict VS30 with mHVSR*, Virginia Polytechnic Institute and State University, Blacksburg, Virginia.

Wang, H., and S. Wang (2015). A new method for estimating VS(30) from a shallow shear-wave velocity profile (depth <30 m), *Bull. Seismol. Soc. Am.* **105,** no. 3, 1359–1370, doi: 10.1785/0120140103.

Wair, B. R., J. T. DeJong, and T. Shantz (2012). Guidelines for estimation of shear wave velocity profiles, *PEER Rept. 2012/08*, Pacific Earthquake Engineering Research Center, University of California, Berkeley, California, 95 pp.

Yong, A., A. Askan, J. Cassidy, S. D'Amico, S. Parolai, M. Pilz, and W. Stephenson (2022a). Introduction to the special issue of the Consortium of Organizations for Strong Motion Observation Systems (COSMOS) international guidelines for applying noninvasive geophysical techniques to characterize seismic site conditions, *J. Seismol.* **26,** no. 4, 557–566, doi: 10.1007/s10950-022-10104-w.

Yong, A., A. Askan, J. Cassidy, S. D'Amico, S. Parolai, M. Pilz, and W. Stephenson (2022b). Introduction to the special issue of the Consortium of Organizations for Strong Motion Observation Systems (COSMOS) international guidelines for applying noninvasive geophysical techniques to characterize seismic site conditions, *J. Seismol.* **26,** no. 4, 557–566, doi: 10.1007/s10950-022-10104-w.

Zhou, J., X. Li, Z. Dai, and K. Chen (2021). Parametrical model for estimating VS30 from shallow borehole profiles using a database for China, *Bull. Seismol. Soc. Am.* **111,** no. 3, 1199–1220, doi: 10.1785/0120200178.

APPENDIX

The Appendix section contains four tables with coefficients a, b, and σ. The first three tables contain the random effects models grouped by velocity method (Table A1), basin (Table A2), and State (Table A3), respectively. The fourth contains the coefficients from the OLS model (Table A4).

TABLE A1

Coefficients for Velocity Method Random-Effects V_{Sd}–V_{S30} Extrapolation Model

	Fixed Effects			Downhole			MASW			SASW		
***D* (m)**	***a***	***b***	***σ***	***a***	***b***	***σ***	***a***	***b***	***σ***	***a***	***b***	***σ***
1	1.31×10^{00}	5.32×10^{-01}	1.35×10^{-01}	1.37×10^{00}	5.00×10^{-01}	1.30×10^{-01}	1.16×10^{00}	6.23×10^{-01}	1.43×10^{-01}	1.43×10^{00}	5.01×10^{-01}	1.54×10^{-01}
2	1.10×10^{00}	6.18×10^{-01}	1.27×10^{-01}	1.31×10^{00}	5.25×10^{-01}	1.29×10^{-01}	7.30×10^{-01}	8.01×10^{-01}	1.25×10^{-01}	9.10×10^{-01}	7.19×10^{-01}	1.37×10^{-01}
3	9.12×10^{-01}	6.99×10^{-01}	1.19×10^{-01}	1.09×10^{00}	6.17×10^{-01}	1.21×10^{-01}	4.61×10^{-01}	9.09×10^{-01}	1.09×10^{-01}	5.99×10^{-01}	8.46×10^{-01}	1.23×10^{-01}
4	7.54×10^{-01}	7.63×10^{-01}	1.10×10^{-01}	8.63×10^{-01}	7.10×10^{-01}	1.11×10^{-01}	3.15×10^{-01}	9.62×10^{-01}	9.50×10^{-02}	4.02×10^{-01}	9.23×10^{-01}	1.09×10^{-01}
5	6.30×10^{-01}	8.13×10^{-01}	1.02×10^{-01}	6.71×10^{-01}	7.87×10^{-01}	1.02×10^{-01}	2.69×10^{-01}	9.74×10^{-01}	8.61×10^{-02}	3.14×10^{-01}	9.53×10^{-01}	9.95×10^{-02}
6	5.68×10^{-01}	8.36×10^{-01}	9.46×10^{-02}	5.32×10^{-01}	8.42×10^{-01}	9.29×10^{-02}	2.33×10^{-01}	9.82×10^{-01}	7.87×10^{-02}	2.23×10^{-01}	9.85×10^{-01}	8.97×10^{-02}
7	4.64×10^{-01}	8.77×10^{-01}	8.80×10^{-02}	4.40×10^{-01}	8.76×10^{-01}	8.58×10^{-02}	2.02×10^{-01}	9.89×10^{-01}	7.26×10^{-02}	1.10×10^{-01}	1.03×10^{00}	7.96×10^{-02}
8	3.84×10^{-01}	9.07×10^{-01}	8.20×10^{-02}	3.69×10^{-01}	9.02×10^{-01}	7.96×10^{-02}	1.71×10^{-01}	9.96×10^{-01}	6.71×10^{-02}	5.79×10^{-02}	1.04×10^{00}	7.19×10^{-02}
9	3.19×10^{-01}	9.30×10^{-01}	7.64×10^{-02}	3.09×10^{-01}	9.24×10^{-01}	7.38×10^{-02}	1.47×10^{-01}	1.00×10^{00}	6.22×10^{-02}	3.58×10^{-02}	1.05×10^{00}	6.56×10^{-02}
10	2.53×10^{-01}	9.55×10^{-01}	7.14×10^{-02}	2.66×10^{-01}	9.38×10^{-01}	6.89×10^{-02}	1.23×10^{-01}	1.01×10^{00}	5.75×10^{-02}	2.97×10^{-02}	1.04×10^{00}	6.05×10^{-02}
11	1.94×10^{-01}	9.75×10^{-01}	6.66×10^{-02}	2.21×10^{-01}	9.53×10^{-01}	6.44×10^{-02}	1.03×10^{-01}	1.01×10^{00}	5.30×10^{-02}	1.63×10^{-02}	1.05×10^{00}	5.49×10^{-02}
12	1.53×10^{-01}	9.88×10^{-01}	6.21×10^{-02}	1.86×10^{-01}	9.65×10^{-01}	6.03×10^{-02}	8.29×10^{-02}	1.01×10^{00}	4.91×10^{-02}	1.02×10^{-02}	1.04×10^{00}	5.00×10^{-02}
13	1.38×10^{-01}	9.90×10^{-01}	5.79×10^{-02}	1.63×10^{-01}	9.71×10^{-01}	5.63×10^{-02}	7.35×10^{-02}	1.01×10^{00}	4.54×10^{-02}	2.52×10^{-02}	1.03×10^{00}	4.58×10^{-02}
14	1.42×10^{-01}	9.85×10^{-01}	5.36×10^{-02}	1.31×10^{-01}	9.81×10^{-01}	5.25×10^{-02}	4.88×10^{-02}	1.02×10^{00}	4.17×10^{-02}	-4.35×10^{-03}	1.04×10^{00}	4.19×10^{-02}
15	1.26×10^{-01}	9.88×10^{-01}	4.95×10^{-02}	1.12×10^{-01}	9.86×10^{-01}	4.90×10^{-02}	3.38×10^{-02}	1.02×10^{00}	3.82×10^{-02}	-9.69×10^{-03}	1.04×10^{00}	3.85×10^{-02}
16	1.11×10^{-01}	9.91×10^{-01}	4.55×10^{-02}	9.73×10^{-02}	9.89×10^{-01}	4.55×10^{-02}	2.12×10^{-02}	1.03×10^{00}	3.46×10^{-02}	-1.55×10^{-02}	1.04×10^{00}	3.49×10^{-02}
17	9.28×10^{-02}	9.95×10^{-01}	4.17×10^{-02}	8.43×10^{-02}	9.92×10^{-01}	4.18×10^{-02}	1.19×10^{-02}	1.03×10^{00}	3.15×10^{-02}	-1.67×10^{-02}	1.04×10^{00}	3.16×10^{-02}
18	7.58×10^{-02}	9.99×10^{-01}	3.78×10^{-02}	7.08×10^{-02}	9.95×10^{-01}	3.78×10^{-02}	4.39×10^{-03}	1.03×10^{00}	2.83×10^{-02}	-1.54×10^{-02}	1.03×10^{00}	2.84×10^{-02}
19	2.32×10^{-02}	1.02×10^{00}	3.41×10^{-02}	6.90×10^{-02}	9.94×10^{-01}	3.38×10^{-02}	6.03×10^{-03}	1.02×10^{00}	2.54×10^{-02}	5.53×10^{-03}	1.02×10^{00}	2.56×10^{-02}
20	4.90×10^{-02}	1.00×10^{00}	3.05×10^{-02}	4.92×10^{-02}	9.99×10^{-01}	3.01×10^{-02}	-5.92×10^{-03}	1.02×10^{00}	2.26×10^{-02}	-9.18×10^{-03}	1.03×10^{00}	2.29×10^{-02}
21	1.93×10^{-02}	1.01×10^{00}	2.71×10^{-02}	5.23×10^{-02}	9.96×10^{-01}	2.66×10^{-02}	1.20×10^{-03}	1.02×10^{00}	2.01×10^{-02}	8.66×10^{-03}	1.02×10^{00}	2.02×10^{-02}
22	9.18×10^{-03}	1.01×10^{00}	2.37×10^{-02}	4.35×10^{-02}	9.97×10^{-01}	2.33×10^{-02}	-4.92×10^{-03}	1.02×10^{00}	1.76×10^{-02}	3.58×10^{-03}	1.02×10^{00}	1.75×10^{-02}
23	2.69×10^{-02}	1.00×10^{00}	2.05×10^{-02}	2.82×10^{-02}	1.00×10^{00}	2.01×10^{-02}	-8.48×10^{-03}	1.02×10^{00}	1.54×10^{-02}	-3.75×10^{-03}	1.02×10^{00}	1.52×10^{-02}
24	6.51×10^{-03}	1.01×10^{00}	1.75×10^{-02}	2.69×10^{-02}	1.00×10^{00}	1.71×10^{-02}	-6.47×10^{-03}	1.02×10^{00}	1.30×10^{-02}	1.68×10^{-03}	1.01×10^{00}	1.30×10^{-02}
25	1.54×10^{-02}	1.00×10^{00}	1.45×10^{-02}	1.57×10^{-02}	1.00×10^{00}	1.41×10^{-02}	-6.60×10^{-03}	1.01×10^{00}	1.08×10^{-02}	-1.31×10^{-03}	1.01×10^{00}	1.08×10^{-02}
26	2.44×10^{-03}	1.01×10^{00}	1.15×10^{-02}	1.40×10^{-02}	1.00×10^{00}	1.11×10^{-02}	-4.12×10^{-03}	1.01×10^{00}	8.66×10^{-03}	7.11×10^{-04}	1.01×10^{00}	8.40×10^{-03}
27	9.47×10^{-04}	1.01×10^{00}	8.58×10^{-03}	8.89×10^{-03}	1.00×10^{00}	8.23×10^{-03}	-2.13×10^{-03}	1.01×10^{00}	6.76×10^{-03}	4.38×10^{-04}	1.01×10^{00}	6.16×10^{-03}
28	5.14×10^{-04}	1.00×10^{00}	5.73×10^{-03}	5.43×10^{-03}	1.00×10^{00}	5.53×10^{-03}	-8.27×10^{-04}	1.00×10^{00}	4.61×10^{-03}	7.09×10^{-05}	1.00×10^{00}	4.02×10^{-03}
29	4.39×10^{-04}	1.00×10^{00}	2.99×10^{-03}	2.98×10^{-03}	1.00×10^{00}	3.07×10^{-03}	3.33×10^{-04}	1.00×10^{00}	2.38×10^{-03}	-1.15×10^{-04}	1.00×10^{00}	1.98×10^{-03}
	Refraction			**SCPT**			**Crosshole**			**Suspension Logging**		
***D*(m)**	***a***	***b***	***σ***	***a***	***b***	***σ***	***a***	***b***	***σ***	***a***	***b***	***σ***
1	1.70×10^{00}	3.57×10^{-01}	1.56×10^{-01}	1.21×10^{00}	5.00×10^{-01}	1.30×10^{-01}	1.16×10^{00}	6.23×10^{-01}	1.43×10^{-01}	1.43×10^{00}	5.01×10^{-01}	1.54×10^{01}
2	1.55×10^{00}	4.21×10^{-01}	1.53×10^{-01}	1.20×10^{00}	5.25×10^{-01}	1.29×10^{-01}	7.30×10^{-01}	8.01×10^{-01}	1.25×10^{-01}	9.10×10^{-01}	7.19×10^{-01}	1.37×10^{01}
3	1.36×10^{00}	5.02×10^{-01}	1.48×10^{-01}	1.14×10^{00}	6.17×10^{-01}	1.21×10^{-01}	4.61×10^{-01}	9.09×10^{-01}	1.09×10^{-01}	5.99×10^{-01}	8.46×10^{-01}	1.23×10^{-01}
4	1.20×10^{00}	5.71×10^{-01}	1.42×10^{-01}	1.09×10^{00}	7.10×10^{-01}	1.11×10^{-01}	3.15×10^{-01}	9.62×10^{-01}	9.50×10^{-02}	4.02×10^{-01}	9.23×10^{-01}	1.09×10^{-01}
5	9.65×10^{-01}	6.68×10^{-01}	1.35×10^{-01}	1.03×10^{00}	7.87×10^{-01}	1.02×10^{-01}	2.69×10^{-01}	9.74×10^{-01}	8.61×10^{-02}	3.14×10^{-01}	9.53×10^{-01}	9.95×10^{-02}
6	7.71×10^{-01}	7.48×10^{-01}	1.27×10^{-01}	9.55×10^{-01}	8.42×10^{-01}	9.29×10^{-02}	2.33×10^{-01}	9.82×10^{-01}	7.87×10^{-02}	2.23×10^{-01}	9.85×10^{-01}	8.97×10^{-02}
7	6.30×10^{-01}	8.05×10^{-01}	1.20×10^{-01}	8.99×10^{-01}	8.76×10^{-01}	8.58×10^{-02}	2.02×10^{-01}	9.89×10^{-01}	7.26×10^{-02}	1.10×10^{-01}	1.03×10^{00}	7.96×10^{-02}
8	5.15×10^{-01}	8.50×10^{-01}	1.12×10^{-01}	8.47×10^{-01}	9.02×10^{-01}	7.96×10^{-02}	1.71×10^{-01}	9.96×10^{-01}	6.71×10^{-02}	5.79×10^{-02}	1.04×10^{00}	7.19×10^{-02}

(*continued*)

TABLE A1 (*Continued*)

D (m)	**Fixed Effects** *a*	*b*	*σ*	**Downhole** *a*	*b*	*σ*	**MASW** *a*	*b*	*σ*	**SASW** *a*	*b*	*σ*
9	4.13×10^{-01}	8.90×10^{-01}	1.05×10^{-01}	7.98×10^{-01}	9.24×10^{-01}	7.38×10^{-02}	1.47×10^{-01}	1.00×10^{00}	6.22×10^{-02}	3.58×10^{-02}	1.05×10^{00}	6.56×10^{-02}
10	3.38×10^{-01}	9.17×10^{-01}	9.82×10^{-02}	7.45×10^{-01}	9.38×10^{-01}	6.89×10^{-02}	1.23×10^{-01}	1.01×10^{00}	5.75×10^{-02}	2.97×10^{-02}	1.04×10^{00}	6.05×10^{-02}
11	2.74×10^{-01}	9.40×10^{-01}	9.20×10^{-02}	6.93×10^{-01}	9.53×10^{-01}	6.44×10^{-02}	1.03×10^{-01}	1.01×10^{00}	5.30×10^{-02}	1.63×10^{-02}	1.05×10^{00}	5.49×10^{-02}
12	2.21×10^{-01}	9.59×10^{-01}	8.59×10^{-02}	6.39×10^{-01}	9.65×10^{-01}	6.03×10^{-02}	8.29×10^{-02}	1.01×10^{00}	4.91×10^{-02}	1.02×10^{-02}	1.04×10^{00}	5.00×10^{-02}
13	1.75×10^{-01}	9.74×10^{-01}	8.03×10^{-02}	5.75×10^{-01}	9.71×10^{-01}	5.63×10^{-02}	7.35×10^{-02}	1.01×10^{00}	4.54×10^{-02}	2.52×10^{-02}	1.03×10^{00}	4.58×10^{-02}
14	1.43×10^{-01}	9.84×10^{-01}	7.47×10^{-02}	5.31×10^{-01}	9.81×10^{-01}	5.25×10^{-02}	4.88×10^{-02}	1.02×10^{-00}	4.17×10^{-02}	-4.35×10^{-03}	1.04×10^{00}	4.19×10^{-02}
15	1.07×10^{-01}	9.95×10^{-01}	6.86×10^{-02}	4.87×10^{-01}	9.86×10^{-01}	4.90×10^{-02}	3.38×10^{-02}	1.02×10^{00}	3.82×10^{-02}	-9.69×10^{-03}	1.04×10^{00}	3.85×10^{-02}
16	7.47×10^{-02}	1.01×10^{00}	6.29×10^{-02}	4.44×10^{-01}	9.89×10^{-01}	4.55×10^{-02}	2.12×10^{-02}	1.03×10^{00}	3.46×10^{-02}	-1.55×10^{02}	1.04×10^{00}	3.49×10^{-02}
17	5.09×10^{-02}	1.01×10^{00}	5.74×10^{-02}	4.02×10^{-01}	9.92×10^{-01}	4.18×10^{-02}	1.19×10^{-02}	1.03×10^{00}	3.15×10^{-02}	-1.67×10^{-02}	1.04×10^{00}	3.16×10^{-02}
18	3.19×10^{-02}	1.02×10^{00}	5.24×10^{-02}	3.62×10^{-01}	9.95×10^{-01}	3.78×10^{-02}	4.39×10^{-03}	1.03×10^{00}	2.83×10^{-02}	-1.54×10^{-02}	1.03×10^{00}	2.84×10^{-02}
19	8.89×10^{-03}	1.02×10^{00}	4.72×10^{-02}	3.28×10^{-01}	9.94×10^{-01}	3.38×10^{-02}	6.03×10^{-03}	1.02×10^{00}	2.54×10^{-02}	5.53×10^{-03}	1.02×10^{00}	2.56×10^{-02}
20	-8.41×10^{-04}	1.02×10^{00}	4.23×10^{-02}	2.87×10^{-01}	9.99×10^{-01}	3.01×10^{-02}	-5.92×10^{-03}	1.02×10^{00}	2.26×10^{-02}	-9.18×10^{-03}	1.03×10^{00}	2.29×10^{-02}
21	-8.08×10^{-03}	1.02×10^{00}	3.74×10^{-02}	2.48×10^{-01}	9.96×10^{-01}	2.66×10^{-02}	1.20×10^{-03}	1.02×10^{00}	2.01×10^{-02}	8.66×10^{03}	1.02×10^{00}	2.02×10^{-02}
22	-1.69×10^{-02}	1.03×10^{00}	3.26×10^{-02}	2.23×10^{-01}	9.97×10^{-01}	2.33×10^{-02}	-4.92×10^{-03}	1.02×10^{00}	1.76×10^{-02}	3.58×10^{-03}	1.02×10^{00}	1.75×10^{-02}
23	-1.98×10^{-02}	1.02×10^{00}	2.80×10^{-02}	1.86×10^{-01}	1.00×10^{00}	2.01×10^{-02}	-8.48×10^{-03}	1.02×10^{00}	1.54×10^{-02}	-3.75×10^{-03}	1.02×10^{00}	1.52×10^{-02}
24	-2.00×10^{-02}	1.02×10^{00}	2.36×10^{-02}	1.60×10^{-01}	1.00×10^{00}	1.71×10^{-02}	-6.47×10^{-03}	1.02×10^{00}	1.30×10^{-02}	1.68×10^{-03}	1.01×10^{00}	1.30×10^{-02}
25	-1.95×10^{-02}	1.02×10^{00}	1.95×10^{-02}	1.27×10^{-01}	1.00×10^{00}	1.41×10^{-02}	-6.60×10^{-03}	1.01×10^{00}	1.08×10^{-02}	-1.31×10^{-03}	1.01×10^{00}	1.08×10^{-02}
26	-1.75×10^{-02}	1.02×10^{00}	1.54×10^{-02}	1.02×10^{-01}	1.00×10^{00}	1.11×10^{-02}	-4.12×10^{-03}	1.01×10^{00}	8.66×10^{-03}	7.11×10^{-04}	1.01×10^{00}	8.40×10^{-03}
27	-1.55×10^{-02}	1.01×10^{00}	1.14×10^{-02}	7.54×10^{-02}	1.00×10^{00}	8.23×10^{-03}	-2.13×10^{-03}	1.01×10^{00}	6.76×10^{-03}	4.38×10^{-04}	1.01×10^{00}	6.16×10^{-03}
28	-1.09×10^{-02}	1.01×10^{00}	7.45×10^{-03}	4.94×10^{-02}	1.00×10^{00}	5.53×10^{-03}	-8.27×10^{-04}	1.00×10^{00}	4.61×10^{-03}	7.09×10^{-05}	1.00×10^{00}	4.02×10^{-03}
29	-5.99×10^{03}	1.00×10^{00}	3.69×10^{-03}	2.42×10^{-02}	1.00×10^{00}	3.07×10^{-03}	3.33×10^{-04}	1.00×10^{00}	2.38×10^{-03}	-1.15×10^{-04}	1.00×10^{00}	1.98×10^{-03}

D(m)	**Unknown** *a*	*b*	*σ*	**Surface-Wave Dispersion** *a*	*b*	*σ*	**Reflection** *a*	*b*	*σ*
1	1.25×10^{00}	5.44×10^{-01}	7.15×10^{-02}	1.02×10^{00}	6.67×10^{-01}	9.12×10^{-02}	1.53×10^{00}	4.64×10^{-01}	2.06×10^{-01}
2	1.20×10^{00}	5.61×10^{-01}	7.13×10^{-02}	8.40×10^{-01}	7.49×10^{-01}	1.05×10^{-01}	1.16×10^{00}	6.23×10^{-01}	1.98×10^{-01}
3	1.13×10^{00}	5.92×10^{-01}	6.96×10^{-02}	6.95×10^{-01}	8.11×10^{-01}	1.09×10^{-01}	7.83×10^{-01}	7.89×10^{-01}	1.85×10^{-01}
4	1.04×10^{00}	6.27×10^{-01}	6.66×10^{-02}	5.35×10^{-01}	8.79×10^{-01}	1.03×10^{-01}	4.47×10^{-01}	9.34×10^{-01}	1.70×10^{-01}
5	9.52×10^{-01}	6.64×10^{-01}	6.41×10^{-02}	4.02×10^{-01}	9.32×10^{-01}	9.56×10^{-02}	2.49×10^{-01}	1.02×10^{00}	1.60×10^{-01}
6	8.67×10^{-01}	6.98×10^{-01}	6.18×10^{-02}	4.06×10^{-01}	9.27×10^{-01}	9.19×10^{-02}	3.33×10^{-01}	9.80×10^{-01}	1.56×10^{-01}
7	8.08×10^{-01}	7.20×10^{-01}	5.88×10^{-02}	3.16×10^{-01}	9.59×10^{-01}	9.06×10^{-02}	3.08×10^{-02}	1.11×10^{00}	1.46×10^{-01}
8	7.29×10^{-01}	7.50×10^{-01}	5.60×10^{-02}	2.74×10^{-01}	9.71×10^{-01}	8.83×10^{-02}	-1.56×10^{-01}	1.18×10^{00}	1.37×10^{-01}
9	6.61×10^{-01}	$7.76 \times 10^{-}_{01}$	5.37×10^{-02}	2.37×10^{-01}	9.81×10^{-01}	8.55×10^{-02}	-2.81×10^{-01}	1.23×10^{00}	1.26×10^{-01}
10	5.84×10^{-01}	8.06×10^{-01}	5.14×10^{-02}	1.91×10^{-01}	9.95×10^{-01}	8.34×10^{-02}	-4.04×10^{-01}	1.28×10^{00}	1.13×10^{-01}
11	5.15×10^{-01}	8.32×10^{-01}	4.89×10^{-02}	1.47×10^{-01}	1.01×10^{00}	7.98×10^{-02}	-5.16×10^{-01}	1.32×10^{00}	9.55×10^{-02}
12	4.51×10^{-01}	8.56×10^{-01}	4.62×10^{-02}	9.98×10^{-02}	1.02×10^{00}	7.44×10^{-02}	-5.27×10^{-01}	1.32×10^{00}	8.29×10^{-02}
13	3.52×10^{-01}	8.94×10^{-01}	4.36×10^{-02}	6.61×10^{-02}	1.03×10^{00}	6.94×10^{-02}	-3.48×10^{-01}	1.23×10^{00}	7.72×10^{-02}
14	3.64×10^{-01}	8.87×10^{-01}	4.04×10^{-02}	1.12×10^{-01}	1.01×10^{00}	6.41×10^{-02}	-2.50×10^{-01}	1.18×10^{00}	7.33×10^{-02}
15	3.35×10^{-01}	8.96×10^{-01}	3.78×10^{-02}	1.04×10^{-01}	1.01×10^{00}	5.85×10^{-02}	-2.12×10^{-01}	1.16×10^{00}	6.80×10^{-02}
16	3.05×10^{-01}	9.06×10^{-01}	3.53×10^{-02}	9.56×10^{-02}	1.01×10^{00}	5.33×10^{-02}	-1.81×10^{01}	1.14×10^{00}	6.35×10^{02}
17	2.69×10^{-01}	9.18×10^{-01}	3.30×10^{-02}	8.27×10^{-02}	1.01×10^{00}	4.86×10^{-02}	-1.82×10^{-01}	1.13×10^{00}	5.62×10^{02}

(*continued*)

TABLE A1 (*Continued*)

D (m)	**Fixed Effects**			**Downhole**			**MASW**			**SASW**		
	a	***b***	***σ***	***a***	***b***	***σ***	***a***	***b***	***σ***	***a***	***b***	***σ***
18	2.26×10^{-01}	9.33×10^{-01}	3.02×10^{-02}	6.86×10^{-02}	1.01×10^{00}	4.38×10^{-02}	-1.79×10^{-01}	1.12×10^{00}	4.94×10^{-02}			
19	1.35×10^{-01}	9.67×10^{-01}	2.74×10^{-02}	-5.22×10^{-02}	1.05×10^{00}	4.03×10^{-02}	-3.29×10^{-01}	1.18×10^{00}	4.11×10^{-02}			
20	1.54×10^{-01}	9.58×10^{-01}	2.41×10^{-02}	4.97×10^{-02}	1.01×10^{00}	3.57×10^{-02}	-1.62×10^{-01}	1.11×10^{00}	3.75×10^{-02}			
21	8.62×10^{-02}	9.82×10^{-01}	2.15×10^{-02}	-4.52×10^{-02}	1.04×10^{00}	3.24×10^{-02}	-2.03×10^{-01}	1.11×10^{00}	3.13×10^{-02}			
22	8.18×10^{-02}	9.82×10^{-01}	1.87×10^{-02}	-4.93×10^{-02}	1.04×10^{00}	2.91×10^{-02}	-2.25×10^{-01}	1.12×10^{00}	2.60×10^{-02}			
23	8.32×10^{-02}	9.79×10^{-01}	1.61×10^{-02}	2.48×10^{-02}	1.01×10^{00}	2.45×10^{-02}	-1.01×10^{-01}	1.07×10^{00}	2.35×10^{-02}			
24	5.83×10^{-02}	9.87×10^{-01}	1.36×10^{-02}	-3.36×10^{-02}	1.03×10^{00}	2.08×10^{-02}	-1.56×10^{-01}	1.08×10^{00}	1.82×10^{-02}			
25	5.05×10^{-02}	9.89×10^{-01}	1.12×10^{-02}	1.12×10^{-02}	1.01×10^{00}	1.65×10^{-02}	-7.57×10^{-02}	1.05×10^{00}	1.56×10^{-02}			
26	3.45×10^{-02}	9.93×10^{-01}	8.95×10^{-03}	-2.77×10^{-02}	1.02×10^{00}	1.31×10^{-02}	-9.89×10^{-02}	1.05×10^{00}	1.14×10^{-02}			
27	2.19×10^{-02}	9.96×10^{-01}	6.63×10^{-03}	-2.25×10^{02}	1.02×10^{00}	9.58×10^{-03}	-7.26×10^{-02}	1.04×10^{00}	8.31×10^{-03}			
28	1.47×10^{-02}	9.97×10^{-01}	4.61×10^{-03}	-1.59×10^{-02}	1.01×10^{00}	6.24×10^{-03}	-4.66×10^{-02}	1.02×10^{00}	5.47×10^{-03}			
29	8.59×10^{-03}	9.98×10^{-01}	2.44×10^{-03}	-8.31×10^{-03}	1.01×10^{00}	3.05×10^{-03}	-2.26×10^{-02}	1.01×10^{00}	2.66×10^{-03}			

TABLE A2
Coefficients for Basin Random Effects V_{Sd}–V_{S30} Extrapolation Model

D (m)	**Fixed Effects**			**None**			**Los Angeles Basin (LAB)**			**South Bay Area Basin (SBAB)**		
	a	***b***	***σ***	***a***	***b***	***σ***	***a***	***b***	***σ***	***a***	***b***	***σ***
1	1.55×10^{00}	4.05×10^{-01}	1.43×10^{-01}	1.17×10^{00}	5.94×10^{-01}	1.59×10^{-01}	1.55×10^{00}	4.06×10^{-01}	7.73×10^{-02}	1.55×10^{00}	4.00×10^{-01}	8.20×10^{-02}
2	1.41×10^{00}	4.67×10^{-01}	1.34×10^{-01}	9.53×10^{-01}	6.85×10^{-01}	1.47×10^{-01}	1.46×10^{00}	4.42×10^{-01}	7.55×10^{-02}	1.40×10^{00}	4.64×10^{-01}	7.90×10^{-02}
3	1.21×10^{00}	5.52×10^{-01}	1.25×10^{-01}	7.72×10^{-01}	7.59×10^{-01}	1.36×10^{-01}	1.36×10^{00}	4.87×10^{-01}	7.28×10^{-02}	1.19×10^{00}	5.53×10^{-01}	7.49×10^{-02}
4	1.03×10^{00}	6.27×10^{-01}	1.15×10^{-01}	6.27×10^{-01}	8.16×10^{-01}	1.24×10^{-01}	1.26×10^{00}	5.27×10^{-01}	7.00×10^{-02}	1.00×10^{00}	6.28×10^{-01}	6.72×10^{-02}
5	8.93×10^{-01}	6.84×10^{-01}	1.07×10^{-01}	5.22×10^{-01}	8.56×10^{-01}	1.15×10^{-01}	1.09×10^{00}	5.96×10^{-01}	6.53×10^{-02}	8.74×10^{-01}	6.79×10^{-01}	6.05×10^{-02}
6	7.82×10^{-01}	7.29×10^{-01}	9.88×10^{-02}	4.41×10^{-01}	8.86×10^{-01}	1.05×10^{-01}	9.76×10^{-01}	6.43×10^{-01}	6.11×10^{-02}	7.92×10^{-01}	7.11×10^{-01}	5.63×10^{-02}
7	6.86×10^{-01}	7.67×10^{-01}	9.15×10^{-02}	3.83×10^{-01}	9.06×10^{-01}	9.69×10^{-02}	8.35×10^{-01}	7.00×10^{-01}	5.70×10^{-02}	6.95×10^{-01}	7.49×10^{-01}	5.41×10^{-02}
8	6.21×10^{-01}	7.92×10^{-01}	8.50×10^{-02}	3.26×10^{-01}	9.26×10^{-01}	8.96×10^{-02}	7.89×10^{-01}	7.16×10^{-01}	5.28×10^{-02}	6.84×10^{-01}	7.50×10^{-01}	5.17×10^{-02}
9	5.56×10^{-01}	8.16×10^{-01}	7.88×10^{-02}	2.86×10^{-01}	9.39×10^{-01}	8.27×10^{-02}	7.12×10^{-01}	7.46×10^{-01}	4.94×10^{-02}	6.52×10^{-01}	7.60×10^{-01}	5.11×10^{-02}
10	5.02×10^{-01}	8.37×10^{-01}	7.35×10^{-02}	2.53×10^{-01}	9.49×10^{-01}	7.67×10^{-02}	6.49×10^{-01}	7.70×10^{-01}	4.65×10^{-02}	6.16×10^{-01}	7.73×10^{-01}	5.00×10^{-02}
11	4.56×10^{-01}	8.53×10^{-01}	6.82×10^{-02}	2.21×10^{-01}	9.59×10^{-01}	7.09×10^{-02}	5.94×10^{-01}	7.90×10^{-01}	4.39×10^{-02}	5.61×10^{-01}	7.95×10^{-01}	4.64×10^{-02}
12	4.12×10^{-01}	8.69×10^{-01}	6.34×10^{-02}	1.92×10^{-01}	9.67×10^{-01}	6.56×10^{-02}	5.43×10^{-01}	8.09×10^{-01}	4.14×10^{-02}	5.18×10^{-01}	8.11×10^{-01}	4.40×10^{-02}
13	3.72×10^{-01}	8.83×10^{-01}	5.88×10^{-02}	1.68×10^{-01}	9.74×10^{-01}	6.06×10^{-02}	4.95×10^{-01}	8.26×10^{-01}	3.91×10^{-02}	4.73×10^{-01}	8.29×10^{-01}	4.11×10^{-02}
14	3.36×10^{-01}	8.95×10^{-01}	5.44×10^{-02}	1.46×10^{-01}	9.79×10^{-01}	5.58×10^{-02}	4.49×10^{-01}	8.43×10^{-01}	3.71×10^{-02}	4.26×10^{-01}	8.47×10^{-01}	3.84×10^{-02}

(*continued*)

TABLE A2 (*Continued*)

	Fixed Effects			None			Los Angeles Basin (LAB)			South Bay Area Basin (SBAB)		
***D* (m)**	***a***	***b***	***σ***	***a***	***b***	***σ***	***a***	***b***	***σ***	***a***	***b***	***σ***
15	3.03×10^{-01}	9.06×10^{-01}	5.00×10^{-02}	1.28×10^{-01}	9.84×10^{-01}	5.13×10^{-02}	4.08×10^{-01}	8.58×10^{-01}	3.53×10^{-02}	3.79×10^{-01}	8.65×10^{-01}	3.50×10^{-02}
16	2.74×10^{-01}	9.16×10^{-01}	4.58×10^{-02}	1.10×10^{-01}	9.88×10^{-01}	4.69×10^{-02}	3.68×10^{-01}	8.73×10^{-01}	3.31×10^{-02}	3.28×10^{-01}	8.85×10^{-01}	3.16×10^{-02}
17	2.44×10^{-01}	9.26×10^{-01}	4.19×10^{-02}	9.51×10^{-02}	9.91×10^{-01}	4.29×10^{-02}	3.28×10^{-01}	8.88×10^{-01}	3.06×10^{-02}	2.81×10^{-01}	9.03×10^{-01}	2.82×10^{-02}
18	2.07×10^{-01}	9.39×10^{-01}	3.81×10^{-02}	8.28×10^{-02}	9.93×10^{-01}	3.89×10^{-02}	2.86×10^{-01}	9.03×10^{-01}	2.81×10^{-02}	2.48×10^{-01}	9.15×10^{-01}	2.58×10^{-02}
19	1.74×10^{-01}	9.50×10^{-01}	3.43×10^{-02}	7.03×10^{-02}	9.96×10^{-01}	3.50×10^{-02}	2.46×10^{-01}	9.17×10^{-01}	2.57×10^{-02}	2.21×10^{-01}	9.25×10^{-01}	2.35×10^{-02}
20	1.45×10^{-01}	9.59×10^{-01}	3.07×10^{-02}	5.96×10^{-02}	9.98×10^{-01}	3.13×10^{-02}	2.07×10^{-01}	9.31×10^{-01}	2.33×10^{-02}	1.97×10^{-01}	9.33×10^{-01}	2.09×10^{-02}
21	1.22×10^{-01}	9.67×10^{-01}	2.72×10^{-02}	5.05×10^{-02}	9.99×10^{-01}	2.78×10^{-02}	1.74×10^{-01}	9.43×10^{-01}	$2.06 \times 10-02$	1.75×10^{-01}	9.41×10^{-01}	1.86×10^{-02}
22	1.03×10^{-01}	9.72×10^{-01}	2.38×10^{-02}	4.43×10^{-02}	9.99×10^{-01}	2.43×10^{-02}	1.47×10^{-01}	9.52×10^{-01}	1.82×10^{-02}	1.49×10^{-01}	9.50×10^{-01}	1.62×10^{-02}
23	8.95×10^{-02}	9.76×10^{-01}	2.07×10^{-02}	3.69×10^{-02}	1.00×10^{00}	2.11×10^{-02}	1.23×10^{-01}	9.60×10^{-01}	1.58×10^{-02}	1.46×10^{-01}	9.50×10^{-01}	1.40×10^{-02}
24	7.42×10^{-02}	9.80×10^{-01}	1.76×10^{-02}	3.02×10^{-02}	1.00×10^{00}	1.81×10^{-02}	1.05×10^{-01}	9.66×10^{-01}	1.32×10^{-02}	1.22×10^{-01}	9.59×10^{-01}	1.17×10^{-02}
25	5.50×10^{-02}	9.86×10^{-01}	1.47×10^{-02}	2.49×10^{-02}	1.00×10^{00}	1.51×10^{-02}	8.06×10^{-02}	9.74×10^{-01}	1.07×10^{-02}	8.69×10^{-02}	9.72×10^{-01}	9.39×10^{-03}
26	4.13×10^{-02}	9.90×10^{-01}	1.17×10^{-02}	1.86×10^{-02}	1.00×10^{00}	1.20×10^{-02}	6.37×10^{-02}	9.80×10^{-01}	8.28×10^{-03}	6.37×10^{-02}	9.80×10^{-01}	7.65×10^{-03}
27	2.92×10^{-02}	9.93×10^{-01}	8.68×10^{-03}	1.32×10^{-02}	1.00×10^{00}	8.99×10^{-03}	4.70×10^{-02}	9.85×10^{-01}	6.00×10^{-03}	4.78×10^{-02}	9.85×10^{-01}	5.63×10^{-03}
28	1.61×10^{-02}	9.97×10^{-01}	5.79×10^{-03}	8.98×10^{-03}	1.00×10^{00}	6.05×10^{-03}	2.71×10^{-02}	9.92×10^{-01}	3.86×10^{-03}	2.59×10^{-02}	9.92×10^{-01}	3.47×10^{-03}
29	8.18×10^{-03}	9.98×10^{-01}	3.03×10^{-03}	4.77×10^{-03}	1.00×10^{00}	3.22×10^{-03}	1.40×10^{-02}	9.96×10^{-01}	1.89×10^{-03}	1.34×10^{-02}	9.96×10^{-01}	1.66×10^{-03}
	San Fernando Basin (SFB)			**San Bernardino Basin (SBB)**			**San Gabriel Basin (SGB)**			**Great Central Valley Basin (GCVB)**		
***D*(m)**	***a***	***b***	***σ***	***a***	***b***	***σ***	***a***	***b***	***σ***	***a***	***b***	***σ***
1	1.72×10^{00}	3.43×10^{-01}	6.26×10^{-02}	1.58×10^{00}	4.07×10^{-01}	8.59×10^{-02}	1.61×10^{00}	4.06×10^{-01}	6.68×10^{-02}	1.25×10^{00}	5.09×10^{-01}	9.74×10^{-02}
2	1.65×10^{00}	3.72×10^{-01}	6.28×10^{-02}	1.39×10^{00}	4.85×10^{-01}	7.86×10^{-02}	1.39×10^{00}	4.99×10^{-01}	5.93×10^{-02}	1.21×10^{00}	5.28×10^{-01}	9.50×10^{-02}
3	1.41×10^{00}	4.76×10^{-01}	5.81×10^{-02}	1.22×10^{00}	5.56×10^{-01}	7.53×10^{-02}	1.20×10^{00}	5.76×10^{-01}	5.15×10^{-02}	1.14×10^{00}	5.57×10^{-01}	9.02×10^{-02}
4	1.26×10^{00}	5.40×10^{-01}	5.39×10^{-02}	1.03×10^{00}	6.31×10^{-01}	6.71×10^{-02}	1.02×10^{00}	6.47×10^{-01}	4.60×10^{-02}	1.07×10^{00}	5.88×10^{-01}	8.41×10^{-02}
5	1.12×10^{00}	5.98×10^{-01}	5.13×10^{-02}	9.40×10^{-01}	6.70×10^{-01}	6.30×10^{-02}	8.70×10^{-01}	7.06×10^{-01}	4.12×10^{-02}	9.91×10^{-01}	6.24×10^{-01}	7.76×10^{-02}
6	9.78×10^{-01}	6.54×10^{-01}	4.75×10^{-02}	8.27×10^{-01}	7.15×10^{-01}	5.93×10^{-02}	7.56×10^{-01}	7.49×10^{-01}	3.86×10^{-02}	9.08×10^{-01}	6.61×10^{-01}	7.22×10^{-02}
7	7.89×10^{-01}	7.30×10^{-01}	4.49×10^{-02}	7.07×10^{-01}	7.63×10^{-01}	5.42×10^{-02}	6.86×10^{-01}	7.75×10^{-01}	3.72×10^{-02}	8.09×10^{-01}	7.03×10^{-01}	6.69×10^{-02}
8	7.77×10^{-01}	7.32×10^{-01}	4.13×10^{-02}	6.51×10^{-01}	7.83×10^{-01}	5.00×10^{-02}	5.98×10^{-01}	8.07×10^{-01}	3.54×10^{-02}	7.52×10^{-01}	7.26×10^{-01}	6.25×10^{-02}
9	6.99×10^{-01}	7.61×10^{-01}	3.92×10^{-02}	5.81×10^{-01}	8.09×10^{-01}	4.60×10^{-02}	5.36×10^{-01}	8.28×10^{-01}	3.30×10^{-02}	6.81×10^{-01}	7.55×10^{-01}	5.91×10^{-02}
10	6.39×10^{-01}	7.83×10^{-01}	3.76×10^{-02}	5.24×10^{-01}	8.30×10^{-01}	4.25×10^{-02}	4.91×10^{-01}	8.43×10^{-01}	3.12×10^{-02}	5.96×10^{-01}	7.90×10^{-01}	5.68×10^{-02}
11	6.08×10^{-01}	7.93×10^{-01}	3.60×10^{-02}	4.84×10^{-01}	8.44×10^{-01}	3.98×10^{-02}	4.53×10^{-01}	8.56×10^{-01}	2.97×10^{-02}	5.20×10^{-01}	8.21×10^{-01}	5.48×10^{-02}
12	5.70×10^{-01}	8.07×10^{-01}	3.50×10^{-02}	4.44×10^{-01}	8.58×10^{-01}	3.71×10^{-02}	4.18×10^{-01}	8.67×10^{-01}	2.86×10^{-02}	4.54×10^{-01}	8.48×10^{-01}	5.25×10^{-02}
13	5.28×10^{-01}	8.22×10^{-01}	3.36×10^{-02}	4.07×10^{-01}	8.71×10^{-01}	3.50×10^{-02}	3.81×10^{-01}	8.79×10^{-01}	2.69×10^{-02}	3.99×10^{-01}	8.69×10^{-01}	4.92×10^{-02}
14	4.78×10^{-01}	8.40×10^{-01}	3.20×10^{-02}	3.67×10^{-01}	8.85×10^{-01}	3.29×10^{-02}	3.48×10^{-01}	8.90×10^{-01}	2.52×10^{-02}	3.51×10^{-01}	8.86×10^{-01}	4.54×10^{-02}
15	4.36×10^{-01}	8.55×10^{-01}	3.03×10^{-02}	3.26×10^{-01}	8.99×10^{-01}	3.01×10^{-02}	3.18×10^{-01}	9.00×10^{-01}	2.38×10^{-02}	3.11×10^{-01}	9.01×10^{-01}	4.15×10^{-02}
16	3.98×10^{-01}	8.68×10^{-01}	2.81×10^{-02}	2.90×10^{-01}	9.11×10^{-01}	2.77×10^{-02}	2.88×10^{-01}	9.10×10^{-01}	2.20×10^{-02}	2.75×10^{-01}	9.13×10^{-01}	3.79×10^{-02}
17	3.55×10^{-01}	8.83×10^{-01}	2.58×10^{-02}	2.55×10^{-01}	9.23×10^{-01}	2.57×10^{-02}	2.58×10^{-01}	9.19×10^{-01}	2.04×10^{-02}	2.42×10^{-01}	9.24×10^{-01}	3.44×10^{-02}
18	2.87×10^{-01}	9.08×10^{-01}	2.38×10^{-02}	2.10×10^{-01}	9.39×10^{-01}	2.33×10^{-02}	2.21×10^{-01}	9.32×10^{-01}	1.87×10^{-02}	2.12×10^{-01}	9.35×10^{-01}	3.09×10^{-02}
19	2.24×10^{-01}	9.31×10^{-01}	2.18×10^{-02}	1.69×10^{-01}	9.53×10^{-01}	2.09×10^{-02}	1.88×10^{-01}	9.43×10^{-01}	1.69×10^{-02}	1.83×10^{-01}	9.45×10^{-01}	2.75×10^{-02}
20	1.69×10^{-01}	9.51×10^{-01}	1.98×10^{-02}	1.35×10^{-01}	9.65×10^{-01}	1.88×10^{-02}	1.60×10^{-01}	9.52×10^{-01}	1.52×10^{-02}	1.57×10^{-01}	9.54×10^{-01}	2.43×10^{-02}
21	1.36×10^{-01}	9.62×10^{-01}	1.76×10^{-02}	1.10×10^{-01}	9.72×10^{-01}	1.69×10^{-02}	1.37×10^{-01}	9.59×10^{-01}	1.34×10^{-02}	1.36×10^{-01}	9.60×10^{-01}	2.13×10^{-02}
22	1.13×10^{-01}	9.69×10^{-01}	1.52×10^{-02}	9.18×10^{-02}	9.78×10^{-01}	1.53×10^{-02}	1.18×10^{-01}	9.65×10^{-01}	1.16×10^{-02}	1.17×10^{-01}	9.66×10^{-01}	1.83×10^{-02}
23	7.86×10^{-02}	9.81×10^{-01}	1.31×10^{-02}	6.84×10^{-02}	9.85×10^{-01}	1.38×10^{-02}	1.04×10^{-01}	9.69×10^{-01}	9.99×10^{-03}	9.71×10^{-02}	9.72×10^{-01}	1.57×10^{-02}

(*continued*)

TABLE A2 (Continued)

	Fixed Effects			None			Los Angeles Basin (LAB)			South Bay Area Basin (SBAB)		
***D* (m)**	***a***	***b***	***σ***	***a***	***b***	***σ***	***a***	***b***	***σ***	***a***	***b***	***σ***
24	6.79×10^{-02}	9.83×10^{-01}	1.09×10^{-02}	5.56×10^{-02}	9.89×10^{-01}	1.20×10^{-02}	8.87×10^{-02}	9.74×10^{-01}	8.51×10^{-03}	8.32×10^{-02}	9.76×10^{-01}	1.34×10^{-02}
25	5.36×10^{-02}	9.87×10^{-01}	8.97×10^{-03}	4.32×10^{-02}	9.92×10^{-01}	9.88×10^{-03}	6.86×10^{-02}	9.80×10^{-01}	7.10×10^{-03}	6.32×10^{-02}	9.82×10^{-01}	1.11×10^{-02}
26	4.20×10^{-02}	9.90×10^{-01}	7.07×10^{-03}	3.32×10^{-02}	9.94×10^{-01}	7.83×10^{-03}	5.41×10^{-02}	9.84×10^{-01}	5.64×10^{-03}	4.68×10^{-02}	9.88×10^{-01}	8.97×10^{-03}
27	3.13×10^{-02}	9.92×10^{-01}	5.18×10^{-03}	2.53×10^{-02}	9.95×10^{-01}	5.74×10^{-03}	4.03×10^{-02}	9.88×10^{-01}	4.18×10^{-03}	3.21×10^{-02}	9.92×10^{-01}	6.77×10^{-03}
28	1.90×10^{-02}	9.95×10^{-01}	3.39×10^{-03}	1.57×10^{-02}	9.97×10^{-01}	3.88×10^{-03}	2.40×10^{-02}	9.93×10^{-01}	2.72×10^{-03}	1.92×10^{-02}	9.95×10^{-01}	4.50×10^{-03}
29	9.76×10^{-03}	9.98×10^{-01}	1.67×10^{-03}	8.89×10^{-03}	9.98×10^{-01}	2.36×10^{-03}	1.22×10^{-02}	9.96×10^{-01}	1.33×10^{-03}	9.84×10^{-03}	9.98×10^{-01}	2.36×10^{-03}
	East Bay Area Basin (EBAB)			**South San Francisco Basin (SSFB)**			**North East Bay Area Basin (NEBAB)**			**Ventura Basin (VB)**		
***D*(m)**	***a***	***b***	***σ***	***a***	***b***	***σ***	***a***	***b***	***σ***	***a***	***b***	***σ***
1	1.53×10^{00}	3.87×10^{-01}	5.26×10^{-02}	1.53×10^{00}	3.06×10^{-01}	9.15×10^{-02}	1.50×10^{00}	3.91×10^{-01}	9.48×10^{-02}	1.55×10^{00}	3.91×10^{-01}	5.72×10^{-02}
2	1.42×10^{00}	4.36×10^{-01}	5.06×10^{-02}	1.47×10^{-00}	3.36×10^{-01}	9.03×10^{-02}	1.39×10^{00}	4.40×10^{-01}	9.06×10^{-02}	1.44×10^{00}	4.39×10^{-01}	5.57×10^{-02}
3	1.21×10^{00}	5.27×10^{-01}	4.83×10^{-02}	1.06×10^{00}	5.41×10^{-01}	9.77×10^{-02}	1.16×10^{00}	5.45×10^{-01}	8.46×10^{-02}	1.22×10^{00}	5.31×10^{-01}	5.41×10^{-02}
4	1.04×10^{00}	6.02×10^{-01}	4.54×10^{-02}	8.45×10^{-01}	6.60×10^{-01}	1.03×10^{-01}	9.78×10^{-01}	6.23×10^{-01}	7.90×10^{-02}	1.03×10^{00}	6.11×10^{-01}	5.26×10^{-02}
5	9.30×10^{-01}	6.50×10^{-01}	4.06×10^{-02}	7.61×10^{-01}	7.11×10^{-01}	9.63×10^{-02}	8.91×10^{-01}	6.62×10^{-01}	7.80×10^{-02}	9.03×10^{-01}	6.65×10^{-01}	5.07×10^{-02}
6	8.56×10^{-01}	6.80×10^{-01}	3.58×10^{-02}	7.01×10^{-01}	7.45×10^{-01}	8.92×10^{-02}	8.45×10^{-01}	6.83×10^{-01}	7.62×10^{-02}	8.03×10^{-01}	7.05×10^{-01}	4.55×10^{-02}
7	7.19×10^{-01}	7.37×10^{-01}	3.41×10^{-02}	6.55×10^{-01}	7.66×10^{-01}	7.74×10^{-02}	7.14×10^{-01}	7.36×10^{-01}	7.44×10^{-02}	6.84×10^{-01}	7.54×10^{-01}	4.15×10^{-02}
8	7.50×10^{-01}	7.21×10^{-01}	3.01×10^{-02}	5.88×10^{-01}	7.99×10^{-01}	6.61×10^{-02}	7.68×10^{-01}	7.10×10^{-01}	7.08×10^{-02}	6.69×10^{-01}	7.58×10^{-01}	3.74×10^{-02}
9	7.14×10^{-01}	7.35×10^{-01}	2.89×10^{-02}	5.47×10^{-01}	8.17×10^{-01}	5.79×10^{-02}	7.15×10^{-01}	7.30×10^{-01}	6.63×10^{-02}	6.25×10^{-01}	7.74×10^{-01}	3.46×10^{-02}
10	6.83×10^{-01}	7.46×10^{-01}	2.88×10^{-02}	5.09×10^{-01}	8.32×10^{-01}	5.18×10^{-02}	6.56×10^{-01}	7.53×10^{-01}	6.18×10^{-02}	5.78×10^{-01}	7.92×10^{-01}	3.27×10^{-02}
11	6.63×10^{-01}	7.53×10^{-01}	2.89×10^{-02}	4.70×10^{-01}	8.47×10^{-01}	4.69×10^{-02}	6.01×10^{-01}	7.74×10^{-01}	5.80×10^{-02}	5.36×10^{-01}	8.07×10^{-01}	3.16×10^{-02}
12	6.41×10^{-01}	7.60×10^{-01}	2.89×10^{-02}	4.40×10^{-01}	8.57×10^{-01}	4.34×10^{-02}	5.46×10^{-01}	7.96×10^{-01}	5.45×10^{-02}	4.94×10^{-01}	8.22×10^{-01}	2.96×10^{-02}
13	6.22×10^{-01}	7.65×10^{-01}	2.85×10^{-02}	4.05×10^{-01}	8.70×10^{-01}	3.85×10^{-02}	5.07×10^{-01}	8.10×10^{-01}	5.17×10^{-02}	4.45×10^{-01}	8.41×10^{-01}	2.69×10^{-02}
14	5.98×10^{-01}	7.74×10^{-01}	2.72×10^{-02}	3.72×10^{-01}	8.81×10^{-01}	3.32×10^{-02}	4.78×10^{-01}	8.21×10^{-01}	$4.93x^{-02}$	4.13×10^{-01}	8.53×10^{-01}	2.57×10^{-02}
15	5.68×10^{-01}	7.84×10^{-01}	2.54×10^{-02}	3.39×10^{-01}	8.93×10^{-01}	2.70×10^{-02}	4.55×10^{-01}	8.28×10^{-01}	4.72×10^{-02}	3.84×10^{-01}	8.62×10^{-01}	2.51×10^{-02}
16	5.42×10^{-01}	7.93×10^{-01}	2.39×10^{-02}	3.13×10^{-01}	9.01×10^{-01}	2.22×10^{-02}	4.19×10^{-01}	8.41×10^{-01}	4.44×10^{-02}	3.41×10^{-01}	8.79×10^{-01}	2.39×10^{-02}
17	5.00×10^{-01}	8.09×10^{-01}	2.26×10^{-02}	2.89×10^{-01}	9.09×10^{-01}	1.88×10^{-02}	3.74×10^{-01}	8.59×10^{-01}	4.15×10^{-02}	2.93×10^{-01}	8.97×10^{-01}	2.28×10^{-02}
18	4.21×10^{-01}	8.41×10^{-01}	2.11×10^{-02}	2.65×10^{-01}	9.16×10^{-01}	1.58×10^{-02}	3.39×10^{-01}	8.72×10^{-01}	3.88×10^{-02}	2.69×10^{-01}	9.06×10^{-01}	2.10×10^{-02}
19	3.63×10^{-01}	8.64×10^{-01}	2.02×10^{-02}	2.43×10^{-01}	9.22×10^{-01}	1.34×10^{-02}	3.04×10^{-01}	8.86×10^{-01}	3.58×10^{-02}	2.50×10^{-01}	9.12×10^{-01}	1.93×10^{-02}
20	2.99×10^{-01}	8.89×10^{-01}	1.89×10^{-02}	2.22×10^{-01}	9.27×10^{-01}	1.19×10^{-02}	2.79×10^{-01}	8.95×10^{-01}	3.36×10^{-02}	2.28×10^{-01}	9.19×10^{-01}	1.79×10^{-02}
21	2.56×10^{-01}	9.06×10^{-01}	1.73×10^{-02}	2.02×10^{-01}	9.33×10^{-01}	1.09×10^{-02}	2.45×10^{-01}	9.08×10^{-01}	3.09×10^{-02}	1.98×10^{-01}	9.30×10^{-01}	1.58×10^{-02}
22	2.20×10^{-01}	9.19×10^{-01}	1.58×10^{-02}	1.82×10^{-01}	9.39×10^{-01}	1.02×10^{-02}	2.08×10^{-01}	9.23×10^{-01}	2.80×10^{-02}	1.73×10^{-01}	9.39×10^{-01}	1.41×10^{-02}
23	1.92×10^{-01}	9.29×10^{-01}	1.38×10^{-02}	1.71×10^{-01}	9.38×10^{-01}	9.49×10^{-03}	2.04×10^{-01}	9.24×10^{-01}	2.55×10^{-02}	1.70×10^{-01}	9.39×10^{-01}	1.24×10^{-02}
24	1.63×10^{-01}	9.40×10^{-01}	1.16×10^{-02}	1.42×10^{-01}	9.49×10^{-01}	8.45×10^{-03}	1.69×10^{-01}	9.37×10^{-01}	2.34×10^{-02}	1.45×10^{-01}	9.48×10^{-01}	1.06×10^{-02}
25	1.11×10^{-01}	9.61×10^{-01}	9.23×10^{-03}	9.64×10^{-02}	9.67×10^{-01}	7.33×10^{-03}	1.23×10^{-01}	9.55×10^{-01}	1.99×10^{-02}	1.08×10^{-01}	9.62×10^{-01}	8.97×10^{-03}
26	8.45×10^{-02}	9.70×10^{-01}	6.92×10^{-03}	7.99×10^{-02}	9.72×10^{-01}	6.13×10^{-03}	9.55×10^{-02}	9.65×10^{-01}	1.54×10^{-02}	8.86×10^{-02}	9.68×10^{-01}	7.79×10^{-03}
27	6.07×10^{-02}	9.79×10^{-01}	5.03×10^{-03}	5.61×10^{-02}	9.81×10^{-01}	4.58×10^{-03}	6.33×10^{-02}	9.78×10^{-01}	1.13×10^{-02}	7.13×10^{-02}	9.74×10^{-01}	6.81×10^{-03}
28	3.24×10^{-02}	9.89×10^{-01}	3.59×10^{-03}	2.73×10^{-02}	9.92×10^{-01}	2.96×10^{-03}	3.21×10^{-02}	9.89×10^{-01}	7.45×10^{-03}	3.98×10^{-02}	9.86×10^{-01}	4.80×10^{-03}
29	1.67×10^{-02}	9.94×10^{-01}	1.98×10^{-03}	1.51×10^{-02}	9.95×10^{-01}	1.66×10^{-03}	1.49×10^{-02}	9.95×10^{-01}	3.68×10^{-03}	1.96×10^{-02}	9.93×10^{-01}	2.33×10^{-03}
	Imperial Valley Basin (IVB)			**Coachella Valley Basin (CVB)**			**Chino Basin (CB)**			**Illinois Basin (IB)**		
***D*(m)**	***a***	***b***	***σ***	***a***	***b***	***σ***	***a***	***b***	***σ***	***a***	***b***	***σ***
1	1.67×10^{00}	3.33×10^{-01}	1.29×10^{-01}	1.66×10^{-00}	3.68×10^{-01}	5.80×10^{-02}	1.68×10^{00}	3.85×10^{-01}	7.73×10^{-02}	1.87×10^{00}	2.85×10^{-01}	1.74×10^{-01}

(continued)

TABLE A2 (*Continued*)

D (m)	Fixed Effects a	Fixed Effects b	Fixed Effects σ	None a	None b	None σ	Los Angeles Basin (LAB) a	Los Angeles Basin (LAB) b	Los Angeles Basin (LAB) σ	South Bay Area Basin (SBAB) a	South Bay Area Basin (SBAB) b	South Bay Area Basin (SBAB) σ
2	1.45×10^{00}	4.24×10^{-01}	1.24×10^{-01}	1.49×10^{00}	4.36×10^{-01}	5.26×10^{-02}	1.44×10^{00}	4.81×10^{-01}	6.99×10^{-02}	1.74×10^{00}	3.42×10^{-01}	1.73×10^{-01}
3	1.12×10^{-00}	5.72×10^{-01}	1.15×10^{-01}	1.30×10^{00}	5.16×10^{-01}	5.13×10^{-02}	1.26×10^{00}	5.56×10^{-01}	5.89×10^{-02}	1.53×10^{00}	4.35×10^{-01}	1.69×10^{-01}
4	7.17×10^{-01}	7.48×10^{-01}	9.64×10^{-02}	1.14×10^{00}	5.79×10^{-01}	4.99×10^{-02}	1.08×10^{00}	6.25×10^{-01}	5.36×10^{-02}	1.31×10^{00}	5.30×10^{-01}	1.64×10^{-01}
5	5.11×10^{-01}	8.37×10^{-01}	8.32×10^{-02}	1.02×10^{00}	6.29×10^{-01}	5.01×10^{-02}	9.67×10^{-01}	6.68×10^{-01}	4.76×10^{-02}	1.05×10^{00}	6.39×10^{-01}	1.57×10^{-01}
6	3.66×10^{-01}	8.97×10^{-01}	7.42×10^{-02}	9.23×10^{-01}	6.66×10^{-01}	5.03×10^{-02}	8.41×10^{-01}	7.16×10^{-01}	4.27×10^{-02}	8.24×10^{-01}	7.35×10^{-01}	1.50×10^{-01}
7	4.54×10^{-01}	8.55×10^{-01}	6.96×10^{-02}	7.45×10^{-01}	7.38×10^{-01}	5.15×10^{-02}	7.23×10^{-01}	7.61×10^{-01}	3.85×10^{-02}	6.69×10^{-01}	7.98×10^{-01}	1.43×10^{-01}
8	1.83×10^{-01}	9.71×10^{-01}	5.91×10^{-02}	7.80×10^{-01}	7.20×10^{-01}	4.75×10^{-02}	6.65×10^{-01}	7.81×10^{-01}	3.82×10^{-02}	5.03×10^{-01}	8.66×10^{-01}	1.35×10^{-01}
9	1.44×10^{-01}	9.85×10^{-01}	5.27×10^{-02}	7.16×10^{-01}	7.43×10^{-01}	4.60×10^{-02}	5.98×10^{-01}	8.05×10^{-01}	3.86×10^{-02}	3.69×10^{-01}	9.19×10^{-01}	1.26×10^{-01}
10	1.10×10^{-01}	9.96×10^{-01}	4.77×10^{-02}	6.92×10^{-01}	7.50×10^{-01}	4.77×10^{-02}	5.45×10^{-01}	8.23×10^{-01}	3.66×10^{-02}	2.75×10^{-01}	9.55×10^{-01}	1.19×10^{-01}
11	3.52×10^{-02}	1.02×10^{00}	4.19×10^{-02}	7.03×10^{-01}	7.42×10^{-01}	4.88×10^{-02}	5.12×10^{-01}	8.34×10^{-01}	3.49×10^{-02}	1.96×10^{-01}	9.84×10^{-01}	1.11×10^{-01}
12	-1.16×10^{-02}	1.04×10^{00}	3.70×10^{-02}	7.12×10^{-01}	7.36×10^{-01}	4.96×10^{-02}	4.74×10^{-01}	8.46×10^{-01}	3.32×10^{-02}	1.41×10^{-01}	1.00×10^{00}	1.03×10^{-01}
13	-4.01×10^{-02}	1.05×10^{00}	3.31×10^{-02}	7.19×10^{-01}	7.30×10^{-01}	5.02×10^{-02}	4.39×10^{-01}	8.57×10^{-01}	3.11×10^{-02}	1.01×10^{-01}	1.02×10^{00}	9.70×10^{-02}
14	-6.15×10^{-02}	1.06×10^{00}	2.98×10^{-02}	7.30×10^{-01}	7.23×10^{-01}	5.06×10^{-02}	4.04×10^{-01}	8.69×10^{-01}	2.88×10^{-02}	5.80×10^{-02}	1.03×10^{00}	9.03×10^{-02}
15	-8.10×10^{-02}	1.06×10^{00}	2.69×10^{-02}	7.53×10^{-01}	7.11×10^{-01}	5.06×10^{-02}	3.72×10^{-01}	8.79×10^{-01}	2.67×10^{-02}	1.34×10^{-02}	1.04×10^{00}	8.26×10^{-02}
16	-1.02×10^{-01}	1.07×10^{00}	2.41×10^{-02}	7.99×10^{-01}	6.91×10^{-01}	4.98×10^{-02}	3.47×10^{-01}	8.87×10^{-01}	2.47×10^{-02}	-1.80×10^{-02}	1.05×10^{00}	7.56×10^{-02}
17	-1.06×10^{-01}	1.07×10^{00}	2.18×10^{-02}	7.98×10^{-01}	6.90×10^{-01}	4.84×10^{-02}	3.20×10^{-01}	8.96×10^{-01}	2.28×10^{-02}	-3.95×10^{-02}	1.06×10^{00}	6.87×10^{-02}
18	-7.52×10^{-02}	1.05×10^{00}	2.01×10^{-02}	6.04×10^{-01}	7.68×10^{-01}	4.66×10^{-02}	2.68×10^{-01}	9.14×10^{-01}	2.11×10^{-02}	-5.55×10^{-02}	1.06×10^{00}	6.22×10^{-02}
19	-4.09×10^{-02}	1.04×10^{00}	1.89×10^{-02}	4.52×10^{-01}	8.28×10^{-01}	4.36×10^{-02}	2.17×10^{-01}	9.32×10^{-01}	1.92×10^{-02}	-6.74×10^{-02}	1.06×10^{00}	5.57×10^{-02}
20	-4.06×10^{-03}	1.02×10^{00}	1.83×10^{-02}	3.36×10^{-01}	8.75×10^{-01}	3.99×10^{-02}	1.74×10^{-01}	9.47×10^{-01}	1.71×10^{-02}	-6.85×10^{-02}	1.06×10^{00}	4.98×10^{-02}
21	2.54×10^{-03}	1.02×10^{00}	1.67×10^{-02}	2.69×10^{-01}	9.01×10^{-01}	3.54×10^{-02}	1.46×10^{-01}	9.57×10^{-01}	1.52×10^{-02}	-7.09×10^{-02}	1.05×10^{00}	4.37×10^{-02}
22	5.30×10^{-03}	1.01×10^{00}	1.49×10^{-02}	2.18×10^{-01}	9.21×10^{-01}	3.09×10^{-02}	1.24×10^{-01}	9.64×10^{-01}	1.34×10^{-02}	-6.77×10^{-02}	1.05×10^{00}	3.80×10^{-02}
23	6.25×10^{-02}	9.88×10^{-01}	1.42×10^{-02}	1.69×10^{-01}	9.40×10^{-01}	2.66×10^{-02}	9.64×10^{-02}	9.73×10^{-01}	1.18×10^{-02}	-6.43×10^{-02}	1.05×10^{00}	3.25×10^{-02}
24	4.99×10^{-02}	9.91×10^{-01}	1.19×10^{-02}	1.40×10^{-01}	9.50×10^{-01}	2.22×10^{-02}	8.16×10^{-02}	9.77×10^{-01}	1.01×10^{-02}	-5.67×10^{-02}	1.04×10^{00}	2.73×10^{-02}
25	4.09×10^{-02}	9.93×10^{-01}	9.73×10^{-03}	1.02×10^{-01}	9.64×10^{-01}	1.82×10^{-02}	6.30×10^{-02}	9.83×10^{-01}	8.41×10^{-03}	-4.11×10^{-02}	1.03×10^{00}	2.25×10^{-02}
26	2.92×10^{-02}	9.95×10^{-01}	7.46×10^{-03}	7.99×10^{-02}	9.72×10^{-01}	1.41×10^{-02}	4.88×10^{-02}	9.87×10^{-01}	6.68×10^{-03}	-3.53×10^{-02}	1.02×10^{00}	1.79×10^{-02}
27	2.01×10^{-02}	9.97×10^{-01}	5.41×10^{-03}	5.71×10^{-02}	9.81×10^{-01}	1.03×10^{-02}	3.54×10^{-02}	9.90×10^{-01}	4.91×10^{-03}	-2.71×10^{-02}	1.02×10^{00}	1.32×10^{-02}
28	9.11×10^{-03}	1.00×10^{00}	3.39×10^{-03}	3.21×10^{-02}	9.89×10^{-01}	6.70×10^{-03}	2.08×10^{-02}	9.95×10^{-01}	3.22×10^{-03}	-1.74×10^{-02}	1.01×10^{00}	8.66×10^{-03}
29	4.67×10^{-03}	1.00×10^{00}	1.66×10^{-03}	1.58×10^{-02}	9.95×10^{-01}	3.27×10^{-03}	1.04×10^{-02}	9.97×10^{-01}	1.55×10^{-03}	-9.33×10^{-03}	1.01×10^{00}	4.31×10^{-03}
	Appalachian Basin			**West Atlantic Basin**			**Gulf of Mexico Basin**			**Boston Basin**		
D(m)	a	b	σ	a	b	σ	a	b	σ	a	b	σ
1	1.64×10^{00}	4.35×10^{-01}	7.31×10^{-02}	1.47×10^{00}	4.40×10^{-01}	1.36×10^{-01}	1.53×10^{00}	4.08×10^{-01}	5.09×10^{-02}	1.52×10^{00}	3.71×10^{-01}	1.98×10^{-02}
2	1.43×10^{00}	5.25×10^{-01}	7.88×10^{-02}	1.33×10^{00}	5.00×10^{-01}	1.34×10^{-01}	1.40×10^{00}	4.63×10^{-01}	4.52×10^{-02}	1.42×10^{00}	4.13×10^{-01}	2.09×10^{-02}
3	1.35×10^{00}	5.55×10^{-01}	8.68×10^{-02}	1.15×10^{00}	5.77×10^{-01}	1.30×10^{-01}	1.19×10^{00}	5.47×10^{-01}	3.64×10^{-02}	1.14×10^{00}	5.36×10^{-01}	2.53×10^{-02}
4	1.25×10^{00}	5.90×10^{-01}	9.39×10^{-02}	9.76×10^{-01}	6.48×10^{-01}	1.27×10^{-01}	1.01×10^{00}	6.20×10^{-01}	2.89×10^{-02}	9.26×10^{-01}	6.32×10^{-01}	2.78×10^{-02}
5	1.05×10^{00}	6.71×10^{-01}	9.24×10^{-02}	8.63×10^{-01}	6.95×10^{-01}	1.26×10^{-01}	9.01×10^{-01}	6.66×10^{-01}	2.42×10^{-02}	8.26×10^{-01}	6.75×10^{-01}	2.66×10^{-02}
6	8.40×10^{-01}	7.55×10^{-01}	8.96×10^{-02}	7.72×10^{-01}	7.33×10^{-01}	1.24×10^{-01}	8.21×10^{-01}	6.97×10^{-01}	2.10×10^{-02}	7.83×10^{-01}	6.92×10^{-01}	2.71×10^{-02}
7	7.65×10^{-01}	7.89×10^{-01}	8.93×10^{-02}	6.86×10^{-01}	7.68×10^{-01}	1.20×10^{-01}	6.83×10^{-01}	7.50×10^{-01}	1.58×10^{-02}	6.48×10^{-01}	7.42×10^{-01}	2.82×10^{-02}
8	5.77×10^{-01}	8.56×10^{-01}	8.98×10^{-02}	6.15×10^{-01}	7.96×10^{-01}	1.15×10^{-01}	7.00×10^{-01}	7.44×10^{-01}	1.63×10^{-02}	7.02×10^{-01}	7.24×10^{-01}	2.52×10^{-02}
9	4.37×10^{-01}	9.09×10^{-01}	8.54×10^{-02}	5.56×10^{-01}	8.19×10^{-01}	1.11×10^{-01}	6.55×10^{-01}	7.61×10^{-01}	1.46×10^{-02}	6.78×10^{-01}	7.33×10^{-01}	2.31×10^{-02}
10	3.58×10^{-01}	9.37×10^{-01}	8.19×10^{-02}	4.85×10^{-01}	8.47×10^{-01}	1.05×10^{-01}	6.09×10^{-01}	7.78×10^{-01}	1.28×10^{-02}	6.35×10^{-01}	7.51×10^{-01}	2.20×10^{-02}

(*continued*)

TABLE A2 (*Continued*)

D (m)	Fixed Effects a	Fixed Effects b	Fixed Effects σ	None a	None b	None σ	Los Angeles Basin (LAB) a	Los Angeles Basin (LAB) b	Los Angeles Basin (LAB) σ	South Bay Area Basin (SBAB) a	South Bay Area Basin (SBAB) b	South Bay Area Basin (SBAB) σ
11	3.41×10^{-01}	9.40×10^{-01}	7.86×10^{-02}	4.19×10^{-01}	8.73×10^{-01}	9.52×10^{-02}	5.64×10^{-01}	7.95×10^{-01}	1.11×10^{-02}	5.70×10^{-01}	7.78×10^{-01}	2.30×10^{-02}
12	2.80×10^{-01}	9.59×10^{-01}	7.29×10^{-02}	3.52×10^{-01}	8.98×10^{-01}	8.50×10^{-02}	5.26×10^{-01}	8.09×10^{-01}	1.01×10^{-02}	5.19×10^{-01}	7.98×10^{-01}	2.29×10^{-02}
13	2.07×10^{-01}	9.83×10^{-01}	6.63×10^{-02}	2.84×10^{-01}	9.24×10^{-01}	7.46×10^{-02}	4.91×10^{-01}	8.22×10^{-01}	9.29×10^{-03}	4.76×10^{-01}	8.17×10^{-01}	2.19×10^{-02}
14	1.43×10^{-01}	1.00×10^{-00}	6.03×10^{-02}	2.31×10^{-01}	9.43×10^{-01}	6.55×10^{-02}	4.59×10^{-01}	8.34×10^{-01}	8.50×10^{-03}	4.34×10^{-01}	8.34×10^{-01}	2.08×10^{-02}
15	9.06×10^{-02}	1.02×10^{00}	5.51×10^{-02}	2.01×10^{-01}	9.53×10^{-01}	5.87×10^{-02}	4.29×10^{-01}	8.45×10^{-01}	7.75×10^{-03}	3.91×10^{-01}	8.51×10^{-01}	2.00×10^{-02}
16	5.84×10^{-02}	1.03×10^{00}	5.04×10^{-02}	1.80×10^{-01}	9.58×10^{-01}	5.30×10^{-02}	3.99×10^{-01}	8.55×10^{-01}	7.07×10^{-03}	3.33×10^{-01}	8.75×10^{-01}	1.93×10^{-02}
17	3.16×10^{-02}	1.04×10^{00}	4.68×10^{-02}	1.72×10^{-01}	9.59×10^{-01}	4.87×10^{-02}	3.66×10^{-01}	8.68×10^{-01}	6.31×10^{-03}	2.78×10^{-01}	8.98×10^{-01}	1.88×10^{-02}
18	-1.32×10^{-02}	1.05×10^{00}	4.33×10^{-02}	1.64×10^{-01}	9.60×10^{-01}	4.53×10^{-02}	3.19×10^{-01}	8.86×10^{-01}	5.14×10^{-03}	2.69×10^{-01}	9.01×10^{-01}	1.78×10^{-02}
19	-4.46×10^{-02}	1.06×10^{00}	4.00×10^{-02}	1.41×10^{-01}	9.67×10^{-01}	4.10×10^{-02}	2.77×10^{-01}	9.01×10^{-01}	4.26×10^{-03}	2.56×10^{-01}	9.06×10^{-01}	1.60×10^{-02}
20	-6.55×10^{02}	1.06×10^{00}	3.71×10^{-02}	1.13×10^{-01}	9.75×10^{-01}	3.66×10^{-02}	2.39×10^{-01}	9.15×10^{-01}	3.59×10^{-03}	2.41×10^{-01}	9.12×10^{-01}	1.50×10^{-02}
21	-6.97×10^{-02}	1.06×10^{00}	3.44×10^{-02}	9.40×10^{-02}	9.81×10^{-01}	3.29×10^{-02}	2.06×10^{-01}	9.28×10^{-01}	3.24×10^{-03}	2.10×10^{-01}	9.24×10^{-01}	1.38×10^{-02}
22	-6.51×10^{-02}	1.05×10^{00}	3.21×10^{-02}	8.07×10^{-02}	9.84×10^{-01}	3.01×10^{-02}	1.77×10^{-01}	9.38×10^{-01}	2.87×10^{-03}	1.78×10^{-01}	9.36×10^{-01}	1.32×10^{-02}
23	-8.17×10^{-02}	1.05×10^{00}	2.88×10^{-02}	5.14×10^{-02}	9.93×10^{-01}	2.65×10^{-02}	1.58×10^{-01}	9.45×10^{-01}	2.64×10^{-03}	1.76×10^{-01}	9.36×10^{-01}	1.17×10^{-02}
24	-6.83×10^{-02}	1.04×10^{00}	2.41×10^{-02}	4.33×10^{-02}	9.94×10^{-01}	2.31×10^{-02}	1.33×10^{-01}	9.54×10^{-01}	2.31×10^{-03}	1.42×10^{-01}	9.49×10^{-01}	9.72×10^{-03}
25	-4.82×10^{-02}	1.03×10^{00}	1.92×10^{-02}	3.29×10^{-02}	9.96×10^{-01}	1.88×10^{-02}	9.86×10^{-02}	9.66×10^{-01}	2.03×10^{-03}	1.04×10^{-01}	9.64×10^{-01}	8.00×10^{-03}
26	-4.03×10^{-02}	1.03×10^{00}	1.52×10^{-02}	2.47×10^{-02}	9.98×10^{-01}	1.46×10^{-02}	7.77×10^{-02}	9.73×10^{-01}	1.77×10^{-03}	7.92×10^{-02}	9.73×10^{-01}	6.16×10^{-03}
27	-2.89×10^{-02}	1.02×10^{00}	1.11×10^{-02}	1.78×10^{-02}	9.98×10^{-01}	1.07×10^{-02}	5.57×10^{-02}	9.81×10^{-01}	1.45×10^{-03}	5.32×10^{-02}	9.82×10^{-01}	4.53×10^{-03}
28	-1.63×10^{-02}	1.01×10^{00}	7.12×10^{-03}	1.06×10^{-02}	9.99×10^{-01}	6.98×10^{-03}	3.18×10^{-02}	9.90×10^{-01}	9.99×10^{-04}	2.87×10^{-02}	9.91×10^{-01}	3.07×10^{-03}
29	-7.95×10^{-03}	1.01×10^{00}	3.48×10^{-03}	5.36×10^{-03}	1.00×10^{00}	3.40×10^{-03}	1.58×10^{-02}	9.95×10^{-01}	4.84×10^{-04}	1.32×10^{-02}	9.96×10^{-01}	1.55×10^{-03}

TABLE A3

Coefficients for State Random Effects V_{Sd}–V_{S30} Extrapolation Model

D (m)	Fixed Effects a	b	σ	California a	b	σ	Kentucky a	b	σ	Tennessee a	b	σ
1	1.59×10^{00}	4.07×10^{-01}	1.34×10^{-01}	1.22×10^{00}	5.64×10^{-01}	1.40×10^{-01}	2.23×10^{00}	1.05×10^{-01}	1.38×10^{-01}	1.49×10^{00}	4.08×10^{-01}	8.01×10^{-02}
2	1.44×10^{00}	4.72×10^{-01}	1.26×10^{-01}	1.05×10^{00}	6.35×10^{-01}	1.30×10^{-01}	2.19×10^{00}	1.24×10^{-01}	1.37×10^{-01}	1.31×10^{00}	4.89×10^{-01}	7.61×10^{-02}
3	1.23×10^{00}	5.60×10^{-01}	1.18×10^{-01}	9.00×10^{-01}	6.96×10^{-01}	1.20×10^{-01}	2.13×10^{00}	1.52×10^{-01}	1.37×10^{-01}	1.14×10^{00}	5.65×10^{-01}	7.23×10^{-02}
4	1.03×10^{00}	6.42×10^{-01}	1.09×10^{-01}	7.82×10^{-01}	7.43×10^{-01}	1.09×10^{-01}	2.02×10^{00}	1.99×10^{-01}	1.36×10^{-01}	1.03×10^{00}	6.14×10^{-01}	6.88×10^{-02}
5	8.50×10^{-01}	7.13×10^{-01}	1.01×10^{-01}	6.83×10^{-01}	7.82×10^{-01}	1.00×10^{-01}	1.87×10^{00}	2.62×10^{-01}	1.34×10^{-01}	9.65×10^{-01}	6.40×10^{-01}	6.72×10^{-02}
6	7.23×10^{-01}	7.64×10^{-01}	9.41×10^{-02}	6.04×10^{-01}	8.11×10^{-01}	9.18×10^{-02}	1.65×10^{00}	3.58×10^{-01}	1.32×10^{-01}	8.88×10^{-01}	6.72×10^{-01}	6.57×10^{-02}
7	6.14×10^{-01}	8.07×10^{-01}	8.76×10^{-02}	5.35×10^{-01}	8.37×10^{-01}	8.46×10^{-02}	1.42×10^{00}	4.56×10^{-01}	1.28×10^{-01}	8.12×10^{-01}	7.04×10^{-01}	6.33×10^{-02}
8	5.16×10^{-01}	8.46×10^{-01}	8.17×10^{-02}	4.78×10^{-01}	8.57×10^{-01}	7.84×10^{-02}	1.23×10^{00}	5.37×10^{-01}	1.24×10^{-01}	7.43×10^{-01}	7.31×10^{-01}	6.04×10^{-02}
9	4.26×10^{-01}	8.81×10^{-01}	7.61×10^{-02}	4.31×10^{-01}	8.74×10^{-01}	7.27×10^{-02}	1.03×10^{00}	6.18×10^{-01}	1.19×10^{-01}	6.79×10^{-01}	7.56×10^{-01}	5.71×10^{-02}
10	3.49×10^{-01}	9.10×10^{-01}	7.11×10^{-02}	3.88×10^{-01}	8.88×10^{-01}	6.77×10^{-02}	8.71×10^{-01}	6.85×10^{-01}	1.14×10^{-01}	6.31×10^{-01}	7.74×10^{-01}	5.43×10^{-02}
11	2.82×10^{-01}	9.35×10^{-01}	6.62×10^{-02}	3.50×10^{-01}	9.01×10^{-01}	6.29×10^{-02}	7.25×10^{-01}	7.45×10^{-01}	1.08×10^{-01}	5.56×10^{-01}	8.04×10^{-01}	5.10×10^{-02}
12	2.27×10^{-01}	9.55×10^{-01}	6.17×10^{-02}	3.14×10^{-01}	9.13×10^{-01}	5.87×10^{-02}	6.11×10^{-01}	7.91×10^{-01}	1.03×10^{-01}	4.91×10^{-01}	8.29×10^{-01}	4.79×10^{-02}
13	1.80×10^{-01}	9.70×10^{-01}	5.75×10^{-02}	2.82×10^{-01}	9.23×10^{-01}	5.46×10^{-02}	5.17×10^{-01}	8.28×10^{-01}	9.87×10^{-02}	4.38×10^{-01}	8.49×10^{-01}	4.50×10^{-02}
14	1.43×10^{-01}	9.83×10^{-01}	5.35×10^{-02}	2.52×10^{-01}	9.33×10^{-01}	5.07×10^{-02}	4.07×10^{-01}	8.72×10^{-01}	9.31×10^{-02}	3.89×10^{-01}	8.68×10^{-01}	4.22×10^{-02}
15	1.11×10^{-01}	9.93×10^{-01}	4.94×10^{-02}	2.24×10^{-01}	9.41×10^{-01}	4.70×10^{-02}	2.90×10^{-01}	9.18×10^{-01}	8.64×10^{-02}	3.51×10^{-01}	8.82×10^{-01}	3.97×10^{-02}
16	8.37×10^{-02}	1.00×10^{00}	4.55×10^{-02}	1.99×10^{-01}	9.49×10^{-01}	4.33×10^{-02}	1.97×10^{-01}	9.54×10^{-01}	7.98×10^{-02}	3.00×10^{-01}	9.01×10^{-01}	3.67×10^{-02}
17	6.27×10^{-02}	1.01×10^{00}	4.17×10^{-02}	1.76×10^{-01}	9.56×10^{-01}	3.98×10^{-02}	1.25×10^{-01}	9.81×10^{-01}	7.33×10^{-02}	2.57×10^{-01}	9.17×10^{-01}	3.38×10^{-02}
18	4.49×10^{-02}	1.01×10^{00}	3.79×10^{-02}	1.54×10^{-01}	9.62×10^{-01}	3.62×10^{-02}	6.99×10^{-02}	1.00×10^{00}	6.70×10^{-02}	2.16×10^{-01}	9.32×10^{-01}	3.10×10^{-02}
19	2.62×10^{-02}	1.02×10^{00}	3.41×10^{-02}	1.34×10^{-01}	9.68×10^{-01}	3.26×10^{-02}	2.20×10^{-02}	1.02×10^{00}	6.04×10^{-02}	1.75×10^{-01}	9.47×10^{-01}	2.79×10^{-02}
20	1.25×10^{-02}	1.02×10^{00}	3.06×10^{-02}	1.16×10^{-01}	9.73×10^{-01}	2.93×10^{-02}	-6.02×10^{-03}	1.03×10^{00}	5.42×10^{-02}	1.42×10^{-01}	9.59×10^{-01}	2.52×10^{-02}
21	2.21×10^{-03}	1.02×10^{00}	2.71×10^{-02}	9.93×10^{-02}	9.78×10^{-01}	2.60×10^{-02}	-3.49×10^{-02}	1.04×10^{00}	4.77×10^{-02}	1.13×10^{-01}	9.69×10^{-01}	2.25×10^{-02}
22	-1.44×10^{-03}	1.02×10^{00}	2.38×10^{-02}	8.51×10^{-02}	9.81×10^{-01}	2.30×10^{-02}	-5.18×10^{-02}	1.04×10^{00}	4.15×10^{-02}	9.08×10^{-02}	9.76×10^{-01}	1.97×10^{-02}
23	-6.30×10^{-03}	1.02×10^{00}	2.06×10^{-02}	7.20×10^{-02}	9.84×10^{-01}	2.00×10^{-02}	-6.18×10^{-02}	1.04×10^{00}	3.54×10^{-02}	7.74×10^{-02}	9.80×10^{-01}	1.71×10^{-02}
24	-8.75×10^{-03}	1.02×10^{00}	1.76×10^{-02}	5.93×10^{-02}	9.87×10^{-01}	1.71×10^{-02}	-6.50×10^{-02}	1.04×10^{00}	2.97×10^{-02}	6.95×10^{-02}	9.82×10^{-01}	1.48×10^{-02}
25	-1.21×10^{-02}	1.02×10^{00}	1.46×10^{-02}	4.72×10^{-02}	9.90×10^{-01}	1.43×10^{-02}	-5.93×10^{-02}	1.04×10^{00}	2.45×10^{-02}	5.45×10^{-02}	9.86×10^{-01}	1.21×10^{-02}
26	-1.38×10^{-02}	1.01×10^{00}	1.16×10^{-02}	3.54×10^{-02}	9.93×10^{-01}	1.13×10^{-02}	-5.04×10^{-02}	1.03×10^{00}	1.95×10^{-02}	4.16×10^{-02}	9.90×10^{-01}	9.53×10^{-03}
27	-1.35×10^{-02}	1.01×10^{00}	8.66×10^{-03}	2.51×10^{-02}	9.95×10^{-01}	8.33×10^{-03}	-4.38×10^{-02}	1.02×10^{00}	1.42×10^{-02}	3.14×10^{-02}	9.92×10^{-01}	7.08×10^{-03}
28	-1.12×10^{-02}	1.01×10^{00}	5.79×10^{-03}	1.57×10^{-02}	9.97×10^{-01}	5.52×10^{-03}	-3.17×10^{-02}	1.02×10^{00}	9.28×10^{-03}	2.02×10^{-02}	9.95×10^{-01}	4.70×10^{-03}
29	-6.20×10^{-03}	1.00×10^{00}	3.03×10^{-03}	7.84×10^{-03}	9.99×10^{-01}	2.82×10^{-03}	1.67×10^{-02}	1.01×10^{00}	4.61×10^{-03}	8.82×10^{-03}	9.98×10^{-01}	2.32×10^{-03}
	Arkansas			**Mississippi**			**Illinois**			**Indiana**		
D(m)	a	b	σ	a	b	σ	a	b	σ	a	b	σ
1	1.60×10^{00}	3.47×10^{-01}	6.03×10^{-02}	1.37×10^{00}	4.93×10^{-01}	1.00×10^{-01}	1.60×10^{00}	4.14×10^{-01}	1.59×10^{-01}	1.43×10^{00}	5.45×10^{-01}	2.05×10^{-01}
2	1.52×10^{00}	3.84×10^{-01}	5.97×10^{-02}	1.25×10^{00}	5.44×10^{-01}	9.92×10^{-02}	1.34×10^{00}	5.28×10^{-01}	1.46×10^{-01}	1.23×10^{00}	6.31×10^{-01}	2.03×10^{-01}
3	1.41×10^{00}	4.28×10^{-01}	5.80×10^{-02}	1.04×10^{00}	6.34×10^{-01}	9.11×10^{-02}	1.03×10^{00}	6.62×10^{-01}	1.34×10^{-01}	6.42×10^{-01}	8.79×10^{-01}	1.87×10^{-01}
4	1.27×10^{00}	4.92×10^{-01}	5.55×10^{-02}	9.13×10^{-01}	6.88×10^{-01}	8.72×10^{-02}	7.49×10^{-01}	7.78×10^{-01}	1.23×10^{-01}	5.46×10^{-02}	1.12×10^{00}	1.66×10^{-01}
5	1.14×10^{00}	5.50×10^{-01}	5.33×10^{-02}	8.36×10^{-01}	7.19×10^{-01}	8.60×10^{-02}	4.67×10^{-01}	8.94×10^{-01}	1.06×10^{-01}	-4.92×10^{-01}	1.34×10^{00}	1.38×10^{-01}
6	9.70×10^{-01}	6.23×10^{-01}	5.10×10^{-02}	7.79×10^{-01}	7.42×10^{-01}	8.47×10^{-02}	2.91×10^{-01}	9.64×10^{-01}	9.24×10^{-02}	-6.17×10^{-01}	1.38×10^{00}	1.23×10^{-01}
7	8.20×10^{-01}	6.88×10^{-01}	4.91×10^{-02}	6.44×10^{-01}	7.97×10^{-01}	7.64×10^{-02}	1.78×10^{-01}	1.01×10^{00}	8.04×10^{-02}	-5.99×10^{-01}	1.36×10^{00}	1.17×10^{-01}
8	6.96×10^{-01}	7.42×10^{-01}	4.70×10^{-02}	5.54×10^{-01}	8.33×10^{-01}	7.09×10^{-02}	1.09×10^{-01}	1.03×10^{00}	7.16×10^{-02}	-5.99×10^{-01}	1.35×10^{00}	1.04×10^{-01}

(continued)

TABLE A3 (Continued)

D (m)	Fixed Effects a	Fixed Effects b	Fixed Effects σ	California a	California b	California σ	Kentucky a	Kentucky b	Kentucky σ	Tennessee a	Tennessee b	Tennessee σ
9	6.17×10^{-01}	7.75×10^{-01}	4.54×10^{-02}	4.85×10^{-01}	8.59×10^{-01}	6.63×10^{-02}	6.46×10^{-02}	1.05×10^{00}	6.54×10^{-02}	-6.22×10^{-01}	1.34×10^{00}	8.74×10^{-02}
10	5.16×10^{-01}	8.18×10^{-01}	4.37×10^{-02}	4.37×10^{-01}	8.75×10^{-01}	6.22×10^{-02}	4.58×10^{-02}	1.05×10^{00}	6.15×10^{-02}	-5.88×10^{-01}	1.32×10^{00}	7.44×10^{-02}
11	4.10×10^{-01}	8.63×10^{-01}	4.21×10^{-02}	3.90×10^{-01}	8.91×10^{-01}	5.95×10^{-02}	3.41×10^{-02}	1.05×10^{00}	5.88×10^{-02}	5.28×10^{-01}	1.29×10^{00}	6.44×10^{-02}
12	3.25×10^{-01}	8.98×10^{-01}	4.09×10^{-02}	3.32×10^{-01}	9.11×10^{-01}	5.57×10^{-02}	2.60×10^{-02}	1.05×10^{00}	5.69×10^{-02}	-4.46×10^{-01}	1.25×10^{00}	5.70×10^{-02}
13	2.48×10^{-01}	9.30×10^{-01}	3.82×10^{-02}	2.83×10^{-01}	9.28×10^{-01}	5.15×10^{-02}	1.88×10^{-02}	1.05×10^{00}	5.57×10^{-02}	-3.72×10^{-01}	1.21×10^{00}	5.12×10^{-02}
14	1.91×10^{-01}	9.52×10^{-01}	3.58×10^{-02}	2.24×10^{-01}	9.48×10^{-01}	4.66×10^{-02}	1.90×10^{-02}	1.04×10^{00}	5.52×10^{-02}	-3.03×10^{-01}	1.18×10^{00}	4.66×10^{-02}
15	1.49×10^{-01}	9.68×10^{-01}	3.37×10^{-02}	1.75×10^{-01}	9.65×10^{-01}	4.21×10^{-02}	1.10×10^{-02}	1.04×10^{00}	5.00×10^{-02}	-2.37×10^{-01}	1.15×10^{00}	4.23×10^{-02}
16	1.16×10^{-01}	9.80×10^{-01}	3.14×10^{-02}	1.37×10^{-01}	9.77×10^{-01}	3.79×10^{-02}	-5.65×10^{-03}	1.04×10^{00}	4.49×10^{-02}	-1.85×10^{-01}	1.12×10^{00}	3.87×10^{-02}
17	8.78×10^{-02}	9.90×10^{-01}	2.94×10^{-02}	1.08×10^{-01}	9.85×10^{-01}	3.40×10^{-02}	-1.58×10^{-02}	1.04×10^{00}	4.02×10^{-02}	-1.38×10^{-01}	1.10×10^{00}	3.54×10^{-02}
18	6.63×10^{-02}	9.97×10^{-01}	2.75×10^{-02}	8.55×10^{-02}	9.92×10^{-01}	3.05×10^{-02}	-2.20×10^{-02}	1.04×10^{00}	3.61×10^{-02}	-1.17×10^{-01}	1.09×10^{00}	3.27×10^{-02}
19	3.07×10^{-02}	1.01×10^{00}	2.44×10^{-02}	6.41×10^{-02}	9.98×10^{-01}	2.69×10^{-02}	-2.52×10^{-02}	1.04×10^{00}	3.26×10^{-02}	-1.05×10^{-01}	1.08×10^{00}	2.95×10^{-02}
20	4.83×10^{-03}	1.02×10^{00}	2.15×10^{-02}	4.67×10^{-02}	1.00×10^{00}	2.36×10^{-02}	-2.36×10^{-02}	1.03×10^{00}	2.97×10^{-02}	-9.30×10^{-02}	1.07×10^{00}	2.59×10^{-02}
21	-1.16×10^{-02}	1.02×10^{00}	1.88×10^{-02}	3.29×10^{-02}	1.01×10^{-00}	2.06×10^{-02}	-1.90×10^{-02}	1.03×10^{00}	2.72×10^{-02}	-8.13×10^{-02}	1.06×10^{00}	2.27×10^{-02}
22	-1.90×10^{-02}	1.02×10^{00}	1.62×10^{-02}	2.55×10^{-02}	1.01×10^{00}	1.79×10^{-02}	-1.12×10^{-02}	1.02×10^{00}	2.52×10^{-02}	-6.78×10^{-02}	1.05×10^{00}	1.99×10^{-02}
23	-2.25×10^{-02}	1.02×10^{00}	1.39×10^{-02}	1.96×10^{-02}	1.01×10^{00}	1.54×10^{-02}	-1.35×10^{-02}	1.02×10^{00}	2.15×10^{-02}	-5.65×10^{-02}	1.04×10^{00}	1.74×10^{-02}
24	-2.15×10^{-02}	1.02×10^{00}	1.19×10^{-02}	1.56×10^{-02}	1.01×10^{00}	1.31×10^{-02}	-1.34×10^{-02}	1.02×10^{00}	1.80×10^{-02}	-4.48×10^{-02}	1.03×10^{00}	1.54×10^{-02}
25	-2.57×10^{-02}	1.02×10^{00}	9.77×10^{-03}	1.11×10^{-02}	1.01×10^{00}	1.09×10^{-02}	-1.31×10^{-02}	1.02×10^{00}	1.48×10^{-02}	-3.61×10^{-02}	1.03×10^{00}	1.38×10^{-02}
26	-2.83×10^{-02}	1.02×10^{00}	7.83×10^{-03}	5.08×10^{-03}	1.01×10^{00}	8.60×10^{-03}	-1.11×10^{-02}	1.01×10^{00}	1.19×10^{-02}	-2.96×10^{-02}	1.02×10^{00}	1.18×10^{-02}
27	-2.67×10^{-02}	1.02×10^{00}	5.74×10^{-03}	-1.95×10^{-04}	1.01×10^{00}	6.49×10^{-03}	-8.38×10^{-03}	1.01×10^{00}	9.12×10^{-03}	-2.41×10^{-02}	1.02×10^{00}	9.19×10^{-03}
28	-1.99×10^{-02}	1.01×10^{00}	3.70×10^{-03}	-1.23×10^{-03}	1.00×10^{00}	4.34×10^{-03}	-5.75×10^{-03}	1.01×10^{00}	6.45×10^{-03}	-1.85×10^{-02}	1.01×10^{00}	6.04×10^{-03}
29	-1.03×10^{-02}	1.01×10^{00}	1.83×10^{-03}	-1.14×10^{-03}	1.00×10^{00}	2.11×10^{-03}	-4.66×10^{-03}	1.00×10^{00}	3.41×10^{-03}	-9.87×10^{-03}	1.01×10^{00}	2.97×10^{-03}

D(m)	South Carolina a	South Carolina b	South Carolina σ	Ontario a	Ontario b	Ontario σ	Missouri a	Missouri b	Missouri σ	Ohio a	Ohio b	Ohio σ
1	1.43×10^{00}	4.86×10^{-01}	1.52×10^{-01}	1.72×10^{00}	3.54×10^{-01}	6.64×10^{-02}	1.57×10^{00}	3.74×10^{-01}	1.46×10^{-01}	1.91×10^{00}	3.31×10^{-01}	1.26×10^{-01}
2	1.22×10^{00}	5.77×10^{-01}	1.46×10^{-01}	1.65×10^{00}	3.86×10^{-01}	6.90×10^{-02}	1.59×10^{00}	3.64×10^{-01}	1.47×10^{-01}	1.71×10^{00}	4.13×10^{-01}	1.21×10^{-01}
3	8.74×10^{-01}	7.24×10^{-01}	1.35×10^{-01}	1.49×10^{00}	4.50×10^{-01}	6.80×10^{-02}	1.50×10^{00}	4.03×10^{-01}	1.47×10^{-01}	1.45×10^{00}	5.23×10^{-01}	1.16×10^{-01}
4	5.13×10^{-01}	8.76×10^{-01}	1.24×10^{-01}	1.34×10^{00}	5.09×10^{-01}	6.64×10^{-02}	1.25×10^{00}	5.12×10^{-01}	1.43×10^{-01}	1.29×10^{00}	5.87×10^{-01}	1.14×10^{-01}
5	1.52×10^{-01}	1.03×10^{00}	1.16×10^{-01}	1.25×10^{00}	5.47×10^{-01}	6.36×10^{-02}	9.71×10^{-01}	6.37×10^{-01}	1.38×10^{-01}	1.17×10^{00}	6.34×10^{-01}	1.12×10^{-01}
6	1.16×10^{-02}	1.08×10^{00}	1.14×10^{-01}	1.15×10^{00}	5.86×10^{-01}	6.24×10^{-02}	6.65×10^{-01}	7.72×10^{-01}	1.30×10^{-01}	1.07×10^{00}	6.71×10^{-01}	1.10×10^{-01}
7	-6.21×10^{-02}	1.11×10^{00}	1.12×10^{-01}	1.06×10^{00}	6.23×10^{-01}	6.21×10^{-02}	4.20×10^{-01}	8.80×10^{-01}	1.23×10^{-01}	1.00×10^{00}	6.95×10^{-01}	1.08×10^{-01}
8	-1.92×10^{-01}	1.16×10^{00}	1.01×10^{-01}	9.76×10^{-01}	6.56×10^{-01}	6.16×10^{-02}	2.25×10^{-01}	9.64×10^{-01}	1.15×10^{-01}	8.35×10^{-01}	7.60×10^{-01}	1.02×10^{-01}
9	-3.28×10^{-01}	1.22×10^{00}	8.58×10^{-02}	9.08×10^{-01}	6.83×10^{-01}	6.12×10^{-02}	6.45×10^{-02}	1.03×10^{00}	1.07×10^{-01}	6.74×10^{-01}	8.22×10^{-01}	9.51×10^{-02}
10	-3.68×10^{-01}	1.23×10^{00}	7.32×10^{-02}	7.98×10^{-01}	7.26×10^{-01}	5.87×10^{-02}	-5.88×10^{-02}	1.08×10^{00}	9.94×10^{-02}	5.66×10^{-01}	8.61×10^{-01}	8.86×10^{-02}
11	-3.64×10^{-01}	1.22×10^{00}	6.06×10^{-02}	6.75×10^{-01}	7.75×10^{-01}	5.67×10^{-02}	-1.69×10^{-01}	1.13×10^{00}	9.09×10^{-02}	4.73×10^{-01}	8.94×10^{-01}	8.19×10^{-02}
12	-3.15×10^{-01}	1.20×10^{00}	4.90×10^{-02}	5.53×10^{-01}	8.22×10^{-01}	5.52×10^{-02}	-2.45×10^{-01}	1.16×10^{00}	8.23×10^{-02}	3.58×10^{-01}	9.36×10^{-01}	7.48×10^{-02}
13	-2.60×10^{-01}	1.17×10^{00}	3.94×10^{-02}	4.50×10^{-01}	8.62×10^{-01}	5.38×10^{-02}	-2.87×10^{-01}	1.17×10^{00}	7.45×10^{-02}	2.72×10^{-01}	9.65×10^{-01}	6.82×10^{-02}
14	-2.03×10^{-01}	1.14×10^{00}	3.20×10^{-02}	3.57×10^{-01}	8.97×10^{-01}	5.26×10^{-02}	-3.04×10^{-01}	1.17×10^{00}	6.79×10^{-02}	2.03×10^{-01}	9.87×10^{-01}	6.27×10^{-02}
15	-1.56×10^{-01}	1.11×10^{00}	2.69×10^{-02}	2.65×10^{-01}	9.32×10^{-01}	5.08×10^{-02}	-3.10×10^{-01}	1.17×10^{00}	6.13×10^{-02}	1.24×10^{-01}	1.01×10^{00}	5.75×10^{-02}
16	-1.21×10^{-01}	1.10×10^{00}	2.31×10^{-02}	1.88×10^{-01}	9.61×10^{-01}	4.83×10^{-02}	-3.11×10^{-01}	1.17×10^{00}	5.54×10^{-02}	6.31×10^{-02}	1.03×10^{00}	5.22×10^{-02}
17	-9.31×10^{-02}	1.08×10^{00}	2.08×10^{-02}	1.31×10^{-01}	9.82×10^{-01}	4.60×10^{-02}	-3.07×10^{-01}	1.16×10^{00}	4.94×10^{-02}	2.34×10^{-02}	1.04×10^{00}	4.73×10^{-02}

(continued)

TABLE A3 (*Continued*)

	Fixed Effects			California			Kentucky			Tennessee		
***D* (m)**	***a***	***b***	***σ***	***a***	***b***	***σ***	***a***	***b***	***σ***	***a***	***b***	***σ***
18	-7.08×10^{-02}	1.07×10^{00}	2.01×10^{-02}	8.80×10^{-02}	9.97×10^{-01}	4.42×10^{-02}	$-.96 \times 10^{-01}$	1.15×10^{00}	4.37×10^{-02}	-3.66×10^{-03}	1.05×10^{00}	4.30×10^{-02}
19	-5.65×10^{-02}	1.06×10^{00}	1.93×10^{-02}	5.23×10^{-02}	1.01×10^{00}	4.30×10^{-02}	-2.83×10^{-01}	1.15×10^{00}	3.83×10^{-02}	-2.21×10^{-02}	1.05×10^{00}	3.90×10^{-02}
20	-4.67×10^{-02}	1.05×10^{00}	1.75×10^{-02}	2.38×10^{-02}	1.02×10^{00}	4.23×10^{-02}	-2.66×10^{-01}	1.14×10^{00}	3.34×10^{-02}	-3.50×10^{-02}	1.05×10^{00}	3.48×10^{-02}
21	-3.62×10^{-02}	1.04×10^{00}	1.71×10^{-02}	4.79×10^{-03}	1.02×10^{00}	3.72×10^{-02}	-2.45×10^{-01}	1.12×10^{00}	2.88×10^{-02}	-4.24×10^{-02}	1.05×10^{00}	3.09×10^{-02}
22	-2.14×10^{-02}	1.03×10^{00}	1.77×10^{-02}	-4.16×10^{-03}	1.02×10^{00}	3.23×10^{-02}	-2.22×10^{-01}	1.11×10^{00}	2.47×10^{-02}	-4.26×10^{-02}	1.04×10^{00}	2.72×10^{-02}
23	-2.02×10^{-02}	1.03×10^{00}	1.67×10^{-02}	-1.50×10^{-02}	1.02×10^{00}	2.76×10^{-02}	-1.97×10^{-01}	1.10×10^{00}	2.09×10^{-02}	-5.02×10^{-02}	1.04×10^{00}	2.32×10^{-02}
24	-1.35×10^{-02}	1.02×10^{00}	1.61×10^{-02}	-2.02×10^{-02}	1.02×10^{00}	2.31×10^{-02}	-1.70×10^{-01}	1.08×10^{00}	1.73×10^{-02}	-5.30×10^{-02}	1.04×10^{00}	1.93×10^{-02}
25	-2.25×10^{-02}	1.02×10^{00}	1.37×10^{-02}	-2.63×10^{-02}	1.02×10^{00}	1.88×10^{-02}	-1.41×10^{-01}	1.07×10^{00}	1.39×10^{-02}	-5.71×10^{-02}	1.04×10^{00}	1.57×10^{-02}
26	-2.53×10^{-02}	1.02×10^{00}	1.13×10^{-02}	-2.73×10^{-02}	1.02×10^{00}	1.47×10^{-02}	-1.12×10^{-01}	1.05×10^{00}	1.07×10^{-02}	-5.42×10^{-02}	1.03×10^{00}	1.23×10^{-02}
27	-2.48×10^{-02}	1.02×10^{00}	8.03×10^{-03}	-2.48×10^{-02}	1.02×10^{00}	1.08×10^{-02}	-8.37×10^{-02}	1.04×10^{00}	7.76×10^{-03}	-4.62×10^{-02}	1.03×10^{00}	9.09×10^{-03}
28	-2.03×10^{-02}	1.01×10^{00}	5.32×10^{-03}	-1.93×10^{-02}	1.01×10^{00}	7.02×10^{-03}	-5.46×10^{-02}	1.03×10^{00}	5.04×10^{-03}	-3.46×10^{-02}	1.02×10^{00}	5.97×10^{-03}
29	-1.04×10^{-02}	1.01×10^{00}	2.93×10^{-03}	-1.03×10^{-02}	1.01×10^{00}	3.45×10^{-03}	-2.61×10^{-02}	1.01×10^{00}	2.55×10^{-03}	-1.80×10^{-02}	1.01×10^{00}	2.92×10^{-03}
	Massachusetts			**Utah**			**Idaho**					
***D*(m)**	***a***	***b***	***σ***	***a***	***b***	***σ***	***a***	***b***	***σ***			
1	1.44×10^{00}	4.15×10^{-01}	2.09×10^{-02}	1.44×10^{00}	4.25×10^{-01}	1.04×10^{-01}	2.20×10^{00}	2.33×10^{-01}	9.56×10^{-02}			
2	1.33×10^{00}	4.59×10^{-01}	2.25×10^{-02}	1.15×10^{00}	5.51×10^{-01}	9.61×10^{-02}	1.93×10^{00}	3.42×10^{-01}	9.13×10^{-02}			
3	1.24×10^{00}	4.96×10^{-01}	2.34×10^{-02}	9.51×10^{-01}	6.38×10^{-01}	9.04×10^{-02}	1.61×10^{00}	4.74×10^{-01}	8.63×10^{-02}			
4	1.14×10^{00}	5.40×10^{-01}	2.33×10^{-02}	8.03×10^{-01}	7.01×10^{-01}	8.63×10^{-02}	1.31×10^{00}	5.88×10^{-01}	7.99×10^{-02}			
5	1.02×10^{00}	5.91×10^{-01}	2.28×10^{-02}	6.31×10^{-01}	7.74×10^{-01}	8.05×10^{-02}	1.11×10^{00}	6.66×10^{-01}	7.39×10^{-02}			
6	8.88×10^{-01}	6.44×10^{-01}	2.47×10^{-02}	5.00×10^{-01}	8.29×10^{-01}	7.42×10^{-02}	9.69×10^{-01}	7.14×10^{-01}	6.84×10^{-02}			
7	7.37×10^{-01}	7.08×10^{-01}	2.63×10^{-02}	4.06×10^{-01}	8.68×10^{-01}	6.72×10^{-02}	8.85×10^{-01}	7.42×10^{-01}	6.39×10^{-02}			
8	6.00×10^{-01}	7.66×10^{-01}	2.76×10^{-02}	3.47×10^{-01}	8.92×10^{-01}	6.21×10^{-02}	8.36×10^{-01}	7.55×10^{-01}	6.06×10^{-02}			
9	4.83×10^{-01}	8.16×10^{-01}	2.76×10^{-02}	2.98×10^{-01}	9.11×10^{-01}	5.75×10^{-02}	7.83×10^{-01}	7.71×10^{-01}	5.77×10^{-02}			
10	3.75×10^{-01}	8.63×10^{-01}	2.76×10^{-02}	2.57×10^{-01}	9.27×10^{-01}	5.33×10^{-02}	7.02×10^{-01}	7.98×10^{-01}	5.37×10^{-02}			
11	2.87×10^{-01}	9.00×10^{-01}	2.88×10^{-02}	2.31×10^{-01}	9.36×10^{-01}	5.00×10^{-02}	6.29×10^{-01}	8.22×10^{-01}	5.02×10^{-02}			
12	2.22×10^{-01}	9.28×10^{-01}	2.87×10^{-02}	2.13×10^{-01}	9.42×10^{-01}	4.72×10^{-02}	5.45×10^{-01}	8.50×10^{-01}	4.70×10^{-02}			
13	1.69×10^{-01}	9.51×10^{-01}	2.77×10^{-02}	1.87×10^{-01}	9.51×10^{-01}	4.35×10^{-02}	4.71×10^{-01}	8.74×10^{-01}	4.42×10^{-02}			
14	1.40×10^{-01}	9.62×10^{-01}	2.60×10^{-02}	1.73×10^{-01}	9.55×10^{-01}	4.06×10^{-02}	3.98×10^{-01}	8.97×10^{-01}	4.13×10^{-02}			
15	1.25×10^{-01}	9.69×10^{-01}	2.46×10^{-02}	1.60×10^{-01}	9.58×10^{-01}	3.77×10^{-02}	3.24×10^{-01}	9.22×10^{-01}	3.83×10^{-02}			
16	1.10×10^{-01}	9.74×10^{-01}	2.30×10^{-02}	1.48×10^{-01}	9.61×10^{-01}	3.53×10^{-02}	2.63×10^{-01}	9.40×10^{-01}	3.53×10^{-02}			
17	9.45×10^{-02}	9.80×10^{-01}	2.18×10^{-02}	1.27×10^{-01}	9.69×10^{-01}	3.23×10^{-02}	2.17×10^{-01}	9.54×10^{-01}	3.24×10^{-02}			
18	7.56×10^{-02}	9.87×10^{-01}	2.09×10^{-02}	1.06×10^{-01}	9.76×10^{-01}	2.93×10^{-02}	1.78×10^{-01}	9.65×10^{-01}	2.96×10^{-02}			
19	4.83×10^{-02}	9.97×10^{-01}	1.91×10^{-02}	8.42×10^{-02}	9.83×10^{-01}	2.62×10^{-02}	1.47×10^{-01}	9.73×10^{-01}	2.69×10^{-02}			
20	2.82×10^{-02}	1.00×10^{00}	1.80×10^{-02}	6.64×10^{-02}	9.89×10^{-01}	2.36×10^{-02}	1.19×10^{-01}	9.80×10^{-01}	2.42×10^{-02}			
21	1.28×10^{-02}	1.01×10^{00}	1.66×10^{-02}	5.00×10^{-02}	9.94×10^{-01}	2.14×10^{-02}	9.56×10^{-02}	9.86×10^{-01}	2.17×10^{-02}			
22	5.26×10^{-03}	1.01×10^{00}	1.56×10^{-02}	5.21×10^{-02}	9.92×10^{-01}	1.63×10^{-02}	8.17×10^{-02}	9.88×10^{-01}	1.93×10^{-02}			
23	-8.18×10^{-04}	1.01×10^{00}	1.40×10^{-02}	4.25×10^{-02}	9.94×10^{-01}	1.40×10^{-02}	6.69×10^{-02}	9.90×10^{-01}	1.72×10^{-02}			
24	-8.22×10^{-03}	1.01×10^{00}	1.16×10^{-02}	3.37×10^{-02}	9.96×10^{-01}	1.19×10^{-02}	5.45×10^{-02}	9.92×10^{-01}	1.53×10^{-02}			
25	-1.25×10^{-02}	1.01×10^{00}	9.43×10^{-03}	2.61×10^{-02}	9.97×10^{-01}	9.91×10^{-03}	4.00×10^{-02}	9.95×10^{-01}	1.36×10^{-02}			
26	-1.55×10^{-02}	1.01×10^{00}	7.23×10^{-03}	1.81×10^{-02}	9.99×10^{-01}	7.92×10^{-03}	2.87×10^{-02}	9.97×10^{-01}	1.21×10^{-02}			

(*continued*)

TABLE A3 (*Continued*)

D (m)	Fixed Effects			California			Kentucky			Tennessee		
	a	b	σ	a	b	σ	a	b	σ	a	b	σ
27	-1.62×10^{-02}	1.01×10^{00}	5.25×10^{-03}	1.24×10^{-02}	1.00×10^{00}	5.79×10^{-03}	1.98×10^{-02}	9.98×10^{-01}	1.07×10^{-02}			
28	-1.32×10^{-02}	1.01×10^{00}	3.45×10^{-03}	7.21×10^{-03}	1.00×10^{00}	3.77×10^{-03}	1.22×10^{-02}	9.99×10^{-01}	8.10×10^{-03}			
29	-7.07×10^{-03}	1.00×10^{00}	1.71×10^{-03}	2.08×10^{-03}	1.00×10^{00}	1.89×10^{-03}	6.65×10^{-03}	9.99×10^{-01}	5.36×10^{-03}			

TABLE A4

Coefficients for Ordinary Least Squares (OLSs) V_{Sd}–V_{S30} Extrapolation Model

D (m)	a	b	σ
1	1.26×10^{00}	5.48×10^{-01}	1.51×10^{-01}
2	1.07×10^{00}	6.28×10^{-01}	1.42×10^{-01}
3	8.87×10^{-01}	7.03×10^{-01}	1.32×10^{-01}
4	7.42×10^{-01}	7.61×10^{-01}	1.21×10^{-01}
5	6.24×10^{-01}	8.08×10^{-01}	1.12×10^{-01}
6	5.32×10^{-01}	8.43×10^{-01}	1.03×10^{-01}
7	4.59×10^{-01}	8.71×10^{-01}	9.59×10^{-02}
8	3.99×10^{-01}	8.92×10^{-01}	8.92×10^{-02}
9	3.49×10^{-01}	9.10×10^{-01}	8.29×10^{-02}
10	3.05×10^{-01}	9.25×10^{-01}	7.72×10^{-02}
11	2.65×10^{-01}	9.38×10^{-01}	7.18×10^{-02}
12	2.30×10^{-01}	9.50×10^{-01}	6.68×10^{-02}
13	1.99×10^{-01}	9.59×10^{-01}	6.20×10^{-02}
14	1.72×10^{-01}	9.67×10^{-01}	5.75×10^{-02}
15	1.48×10^{-01}	9.74×10^{-01}	5.29×10^{-02}
16	1.26×10^{-01}	9.80×10^{-01}	4.86×10^{-02}
17	1.07×10^{-01}	9.85×10^{-01}	4.44×10^{-02}
18	9.04×10^{-02}	9.89×10^{-01}	4.03×10^{-02}
19	7.47×10^{-02}	9.93×10^{-01}	3.62×10^{-02}
20	6.18×10^{-02}	9.96×10^{-01}	3.24×10^{-02}
21	5.09×10^{-02}	9.98×10^{-01}	2.87×10^{-02}
22	4.32×10^{-02}	9.99×10^{-01}	2.51×10^{-02}
23	3.57×10^{-02}	9.99×10^{-01}	2.18×10^{-02}
24	2.90×10^{-02}	1.00×10^{00}	1.85×10^{-02}
25	2.26×10^{-02}	1.00×10^{00}	1.54×10^{-02}
26	1.66×10^{-02}	1.00×10^{00}	1.22×10^{-02}
27	1.16×10^{-02}	1.00×10^{00}	9.07×10^{-03}
28	7.25×10^{-03}	1.00×10^{00}	6.05×10^{-03}
29	3.83×10^{-03}	1.00×10^{00}	3.15×10^{-03}

Manuscript received 26 August 2025
Published online 18 February 2026

Geospatial Site Amplification Model for California

Maggie Roberts*[1], Laurie G. Baise[1], Shiying Nie[1], James Kaklamanos[2], and Weiwei Zhan[3]

ABSTRACT

In ground-motion models (GMMs), site terms are typically derived from site-specific velocity profiles, such as V_{S30} (the time-averaged shear-wave velocity to a depth of 30 m) and $Z_{1.0}$ (the depth to the 1.0 km/s shear-wave velocity horizon). However, these variables are not universally spatially available. This study presents a proof-of-concept model for linear site effects in GMMs for California, developed using broadly accessible geospatial datasets with spatial coverage across the entire study area. The model incorporates data from 95,898 recordings at 2,339 stations, as provided by the DesignSafe Ground-Motion Database (Ji *et al.*, 2022). Mapped geospatial variables, such as sediment thickness, elevation, and surficial geologic units, are compiled for each station. The target site amplification of peak ground acceleration, peak ground velocity, and pseudospectral accelerations (PSA) from 0.01 to 10 s is decomposed from the residuals of the Boore *et al.* (2014) (BSSA14) GMM. A mixed-effects linear regression model is developed using the compiled geospatial variables and validated through fivefold cross-validation. A novel mapped categorical variable, the regional geological unit—defined as a combination of geomorphic provinces and geological units—is introduced due to its strong correlation with site amplification. The geospatial-based site term shows a substantial reduction in site-to-site variability for site amplifications across all frequencies compared to the conventional velocity profile-based site terms; on average, a 10.6% reduction in site-to-site variability is achieved compared to BSSA14 (with a 9.5% reduction at a PSA of 1 s). The model is an improved ergodic model, constructed using geospatial parameters that are mapped across California. This study illustrates the effectiveness of geospatial data as site proxies in developing site terms for GMMs and highlights the potential of geospatial variables for predicting site effects, especially in areas with sparse ground-motion records or limited site-specific velocity measurements.

KEY POINTS

- Site parameters for ground-motion models need to be continuously available to capture site-specific effects.
- Our geospatial-based site term reduces site-to-site variability and captures regional biases.
- This approach could be applied in other regions outside of California, including regions with sparse data.

Supplemental Material

INTRODUCTION

Earthquake ground-motion models (GMMs) are a critical component of seismic hazard assessment. GMMs capture source, path, and site effects to estimate ground shaking at a site for a given earthquake. Historically, to compensate for limited data, the ergodic assumption was used to develop GMMs. Following the ergodic assumption, recordings from similar tectonic regions globally are used in model development, and the model predictions represent a global average in terms of magnitude, distance, and site conditions scaling for that tectonic region (Anderson and Brune, 1999).

Site effects are often captured in ergodic GMMs using two explanatory variables, one to describe sediment stiffness (e.g., the time-averaged shear-wave velocity in the upper 30 m, V_{S30}), and one to describe sediment thickness and basin effects (e.g., the depth to the 1 km/s shear-wave velocity horizon, $Z_{1.0}$). Despite the popularity of using V_{S30} and $Z_{1.0}$ for GMM development, measured values for these parameters are often sparse and not available for all sites with ground-motion recordings.

1. Department of Civil and Environmental Engineering, Tufts University, Medford, Massachusetts, U.S.A., https://orcid.org/0009-0000-9036-4921 (MR); https://orcid.org/0000-0002-8329-5689 (LGB); https://orcid.org/0000-0002-3518-7843 (SN); 2. Department of Civil Engineering, Merrimack College, North Andover, Massachusetts, U.S.A., https://orcid.org/0000-0001-7480-0391 (JK); 3. Department of Civil, Environmental, and Construction Engineering, University of Central Florida, Orlando, Florida, U.S.A., https://orcid.org/0000-0002-9266-4466 (WZ)

*Corresponding author: Maggie.Roberts@tufts.edu

Cite this article as Roberts, M., L. G. Baise, S. Nie, J. Kaklamanos, and W. Zhan (2025). Geospatial Site Amplification Model for California, *Bull. Seismol. Soc. Am.* **116**, 1199–1218, doi: 10.1785/0120250074

In the Next Generation Attenuation (NGA)-West2 dataset (Ancheta *et al.*, 2014), which was used to build ergodic models for active tectonic regions, only 28% of the stations in California have a measured V_{S30} and 64% have a $Z_{1.0}$ obtained from community velocity models (CVMs) maintained by the Statewide California Earthquake Center (SCEC) (Small *et al.*, 2017). The CVMs are spatially continuous in greater Los Angeles and San Francisco but are derived from limited measured data. This lack of measured geotechnical data at recording stations necessitates the use of a combination of measured and inferred values both during model development and application. However, current inferred estimators for V_{S30} and $Z_{1.0}$ have high uncertainties, which propagate into the predicted ground motion, thereby increasing the epistemic uncertainty of the ground-motion prediction (Thompson and Wald, 2016).

The development of nonergodic and partially nonergodic GMMs (e.g., Landwehr *et al.*, 2016; Parker and Baltay, 2022; Lavrentiadis *et al.*, 2023; Sung *et al.*, 2024) requires the use of mapped site terms. Unlike ergodic models, nonergodic models have location-specific coefficients and therefore are capable of accounting for systematic spatial variations in source, path, and site effects. With the increasing availability of ground-motion data, the significance of spatial variability of ground-motion residuals due to local geological and geophysical conditions has been widely recognized and effectively incorporated into nonergodic GMMs (e.g., Lavrentiadis *et al.*, 2023) or into empirically derived geology-based site terms (e.g., Parker and Baltay, 2022). Nonergodic models better capture location-specific systematic effects, which reduce the aleatory variability compared to an ergodic GMM (Lavrentiadis *et al.*, 2023); however, they can be computationally intensive and more difficult to implement than ergodic models. The Parker and Baltay (2022) model is a map-based nonergodic model for a limited region of southern California. The model accounts for path effects through spatial clustering of earthquakes and develops a spatially varying site term by kriging site-to-site residuals. The site term combines a geologic background model (based on measured V_{S30} and $Z_{1.0}$ as a proxy for geologic variability in the region) with spatial interpolation of residuals from observed site response. The accuracy of the Parker and Baltay (2022) model has been demonstrated in this region of California, highlighting the potential applicability of a statewide spatially varying site-effects model that reflects local geologic conditions. In this study, we develop a statewide geologically informed model from map-based parameters, but we choose to maintain the ergodic assumption to avoid reliance on statistical correlations at large correlation lengths.

To develop a site-effects model that not only accurately predicts site effects at stations but also provides continuous spatial coverage across the state of California, we propose using widely available geological and geospatial inputs, rather than relying solely on site-specific velocity profiles. Site effects are influenced by conditions such as soil stiffness, soil type, and basin effects (Kawase, 2003; Allen and Wald, 2009; Kaklamanos *et al.*, 2021), which can be inferred from geotechnical, geological, and other geospatial information. For example, stiff soils and rock often are associated with rough topography, so stiffness can be approximated using digital elevation model (DEM)-based proxies, such as elevation, topographic slope, and slope-based V_{S30}. Similarly, sedimentary basins are typically associated with low, flat ground, meaning that site resonance and basin effects can be captured not only by basin proxies like sediment thickness (the thickness of permeable layers above bedrock) (Pelletier *et al.*, 2016), but also by topography-related variables such as roughness or topographic position index. In addition, categorical variables like geological units (Wills *et al.*, 2015) and terrain classes (Yong *et al.*, 2012) can describe location-based soil conditions related to depositional history and topographic indicators, which can influence the site response in a given area. The incorporation of geospatial parameters has been shown to improve site response characterization models in Japan (Weatherill *et al.*, 2020; Zhu *et al.*, 2023; Zhan *et al.*, 2025), as well as in Europe and Türkiye (Loviknes *et al.*, 2024). The Loviknes *et al.* (2024) model, which uses geological era and slope as parameters, not only shows improvements in site-to-site variability compared to a V_{S30}-based model, but also produces significant differences in site effects at certain locations, indicating the parameters capture different aspects of site effects.

In this article, we introduce a new approach for constructing site terms for ergodic GMMs by developing a linear site amplification model using geospatial parameters and regional geology, including both surficial geology and geomorphic characterization. We apply this method to California, which is a region of high seismic hazard that has shown regional biases in ground motions that are not captured with ergodic GMMs (Abrahamson *et al.*, 2019). The inclusion of high-resolution regional geospatial and geology-based site variables captures both site and basin effects, as well as some of the spatially coherent bias in site-to-site residuals. This model framework allows us to capture region-specific site effects with fully spatially available parameters while maintaining the ease of implementation of an ergodic model. A second step (demonstrated in a companion article, M. Roberts *et al.*, unpublished manuscript 2025, see Data and Resources) incorporates site-specific geotechnical data where it is available to further reduce the residuals. The geospatial site amplification model is developed using mixed-effects regression and validated through a fivefold cross-validation approach to develop an improved linear site term for California. This article is a proof-of-concept for a new approach to site term development using California datasets.

DATA

Ground motions

This study focuses on California, a seismically active region with a significant database of ground-motion recordings and comprehensive statewide geologic maps. The geological conditions of California are complex due to tectonic activity, the presence

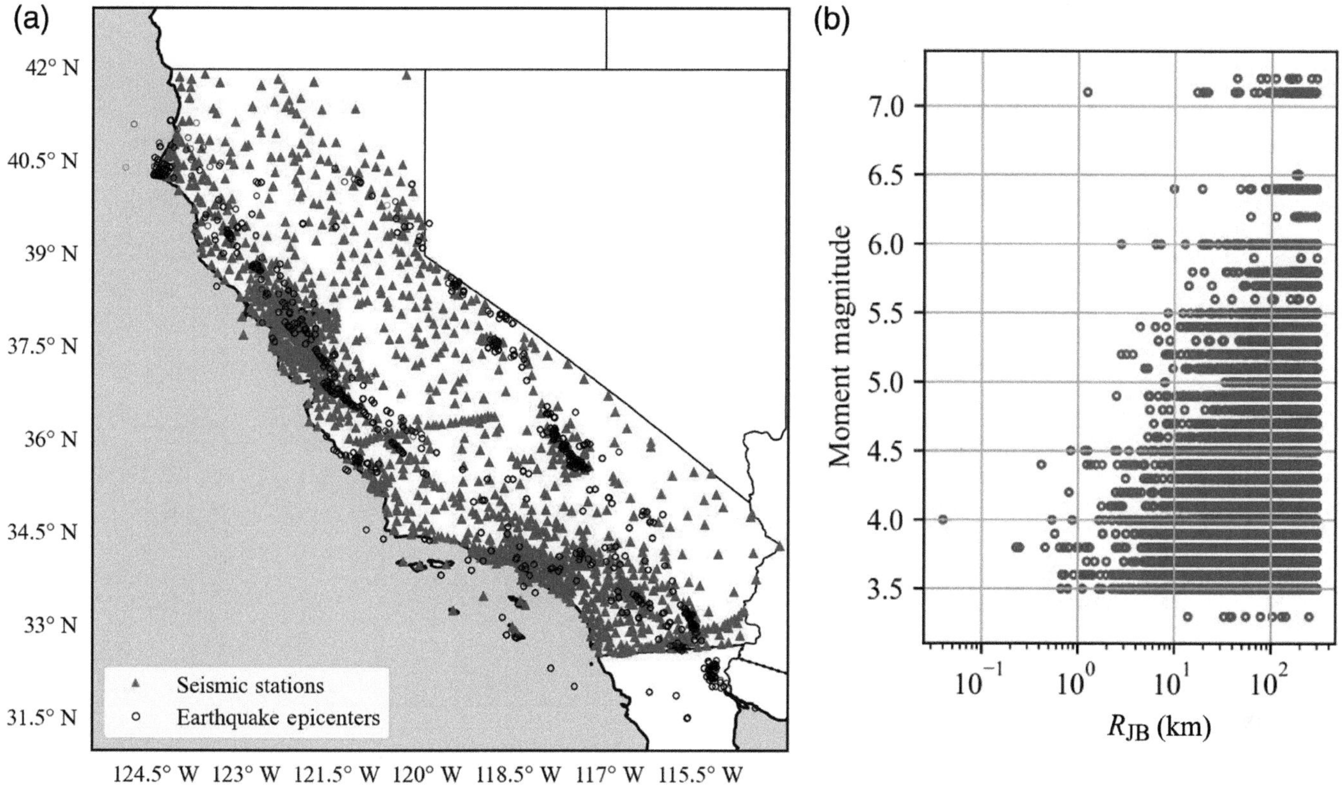

Figure 1. (a) Spatial distribution of earthquakes and stations used in this study (a subset of the Ji *et al.*, 2022, database). The red triangles denote the stations, and the black circles indicate the epicenters of the earthquakes. (b) The distribution of earthquake magnitudes and Joyner–Boore distances (R_{JB}) by recording. The color version of this figure is available only in the electronic edition.

of multiple major faults, and diverse rock formations, resulting in varied regional site and basin effects. The earthquake ground motions in this study are obtained from a subset of the stations in the Ji *et al.* (2022) DesignSafe Ground-Motion Database. The Ji *et al.* (2022) database contains more than 287,804 processed ground motions from 2,641 earthquakes recorded at 3,709 stations (Ji *et al.*, 2023). We filtered the database to (1) only include stations in California; (2) only include events that are shallow crustal earthquakes, to be compatible with the GMMs of the NGA-West2 project (Bozorgnia *et al.*, 2014), by removing events greater than 25 km deep and events on the Juan de Fuca subducting plate; (3) remove recordings flagged as outliers in the database (Ji *et al.*, 2023); (4) only include stations that have at least five recordings; (5) remove recordings without moment magnitudes reported; and (6) remove events that do not have at least 10 recordings for smaller-magnitude events ($\mathbf{M} < 5$) and at least 3 recordings for larger-magnitude events ($\mathbf{M} \geq 5$). We also remove outlier recordings based on residual analysis, as is described in the Methodology section. The final ground-motion database includes multiple ground-motion intensity measures (IMs), including peak ground acceleration (PGA), peak ground velocity (PGV), and 5% damped pseudospectral acceleration (PSA), for 95,898 recordings across 2,339 stations. Figure 1 shows the distribution of ground-motion recording stations and earthquake epicenters.

Geospatial site variables

Across all the stations, we compile a database of continuously available geospatial site parameters. The parameters are composed of both continuous geospatial variables and categorical state-level geologic variables, outlined in Table 1 and described further in Table S1, available in the supplemental material to this article. The continuous geospatial variables considered allow the model to account for variability in site effects that are linked to topography, and the state-level geologic variables incorporate the influence of larger local geologic structures specific to the region. We also include geotechnical parameters in the dataset for comparison during model development: measured and proxy-based V_{S30} reported as a part of the Ji *et al.* (2022) dataset (derived from Thompson *et al.*, 2014), and $Z_{1.0}$ obtained from the SCEC Unified Community Velocity Model (UCVM) (Small *et al.*, 2017). However, none of the geotechnical parameters are used in the development of the model. These geotechnical parameters, unlike geospatial parameters, are point-based measurements that are not spatially available across the state.

Our process of evaluating and including geospatial parameters in GMM site terms differs significantly from the current state of the practice, in which shear-wave velocity measurements (e.g., V_{S30} and $Z_{1.0}$) dominate the construction of GMM site

TABLE 1
Site Term Parameters Included in the Dataset, Along with the Source and Relationship to Stiffness, Topography, Basin Effects, and Soil Saturation

Parameter	Source	Class	Stiffness	Topography	Basin	Saturation
Measured V_{S30}	USGS (McPhillips *et al.*, 2020)	Geotechnical point data	×			
Geology-based V_{S30}	Ji *et al.* (2022), derived from Thompson *et al.* (2014)	Categorical	×			
Slope-based V_{S30}	USGS (Allen and Wald, 2009)	Continuous	×			
$Z_{1.0}$	cvmsi (Lee *et al.*, 2014) and cencal (Brocher *et al.*, 2006) SCEC UCVMs (Small *et al.*, 2017)	Continuous			×	
Average sediment thickness	Pelletier *et al.* (2016)	Continuous			×	
Geologic unit	Wills *et al.* (2015)	Categorical	×	×	×	
Geomorphic Province	California Geologic Survey (2002)	Categorical		×		
Regional geologic unit	Derived from California Geologic Survey (2002) and Wills *et al.* (2015)	Categorical	×	×	×	
Terrain class	Iwahashi and Pike (2007)	Categorical	×	×	×	
Compound topographic Index (CTI)	USGS HDMA (Verdin, 2017)	Continuous				×
Height above nearest drainage (HAND)	Alaska Satellite Facility (2022)	Continuous				×
Water table depth (WTD)	Fan *et al.* (2013)	Continuous				×
Distance to coast (DC)	National Aeronautics and Space Administration (NASA) Ocean Biology Processing Group (OBPG) and Stumpf (2012)	Continuous				×
Distance to river (DR)	Hydrosheds (Lehner *et al.*, 2008)	Continuous				×
Precipitation	Daly *et al.* (2007)	Continuous				×
Elevation	GMTED2010 (Danielson and Gesch, 2011)	Continuous	×	×		
Topographic slope	Derived from GMTED2010 (Danielson and Gesch, 2011)	Continuous	×	×		
Aspect	Derived from GMTED2010 (Danielson and Gesch, 2011)	Continuous	×	×		
Topographic position index (TPI)	Derived from GMTED2010 (Danielson and Gesch, 2011)	Continuous		×	×	
Topographic roughness index (TRI)	Derived from GMTED2010 (Danielson and Gesch, 2011)	Continuous		×	×	
Roughness	Derived from GMTED2010 (Danielson and Gesch, 2011)	Continuous		×	×	

HDMA, hydraulic derivatives for modeling and analysis; SCEC, Statewide California Earthquake Center; UCVM, unified community velocity models; and USGS, U.S. Geological Survey.

terms and fully spatially available variables are not considered. Table 1 identifies the relationship between each potential site variable and aspects of site effects (e.g., soil stiffness, topographic effects, basin effects, and soil saturation). The final database of site variables includes all the geospatial variables at each station in California.

In addition to continuous geospatial variables, we also include categorical state-level geologic variables (e.g., California Geological Survey, 2002; Wills *et al.*, 2015). A new site parameter, the regional geologic unit, is developed as part of the dataset. The regional geologic unit classification combines the 30 surficial geologic units (Wills *et al.*, 2015) and 13 geomorphic province parameters (California Geological Survey, 2002) into a single mapped parameter, resulting in 112 categories across California that define each of the unique combinations of geomorphic province and surficial geologic unit. For the 41 regional geologic units with fewer than five stations, the categories revert to the broader surficial geology category (e.g., the Kss northern Peninsular Ranges and Kss transverse categories are labeled as the Kss other category because the regional geologic units have fewer than five stations). The final dataset, shown in Figure 2, is composed of 81 categories of regional geologic units: 71 categories based on province and geology, and 10 categories based only on geology (for the units that had fewer than five stations). A high-resolution image of the regional geologic units is also available as Figure S1, and a shapefile of the regional geologic units is also provided in the supplemental material.

The regional geologic unit combines information associated with the surface geology with the regional information of the geomorphic provinces to create localized polygons associated with the surficial geology layer. The resulting characterization, therefore, has information about surficial geology as well as

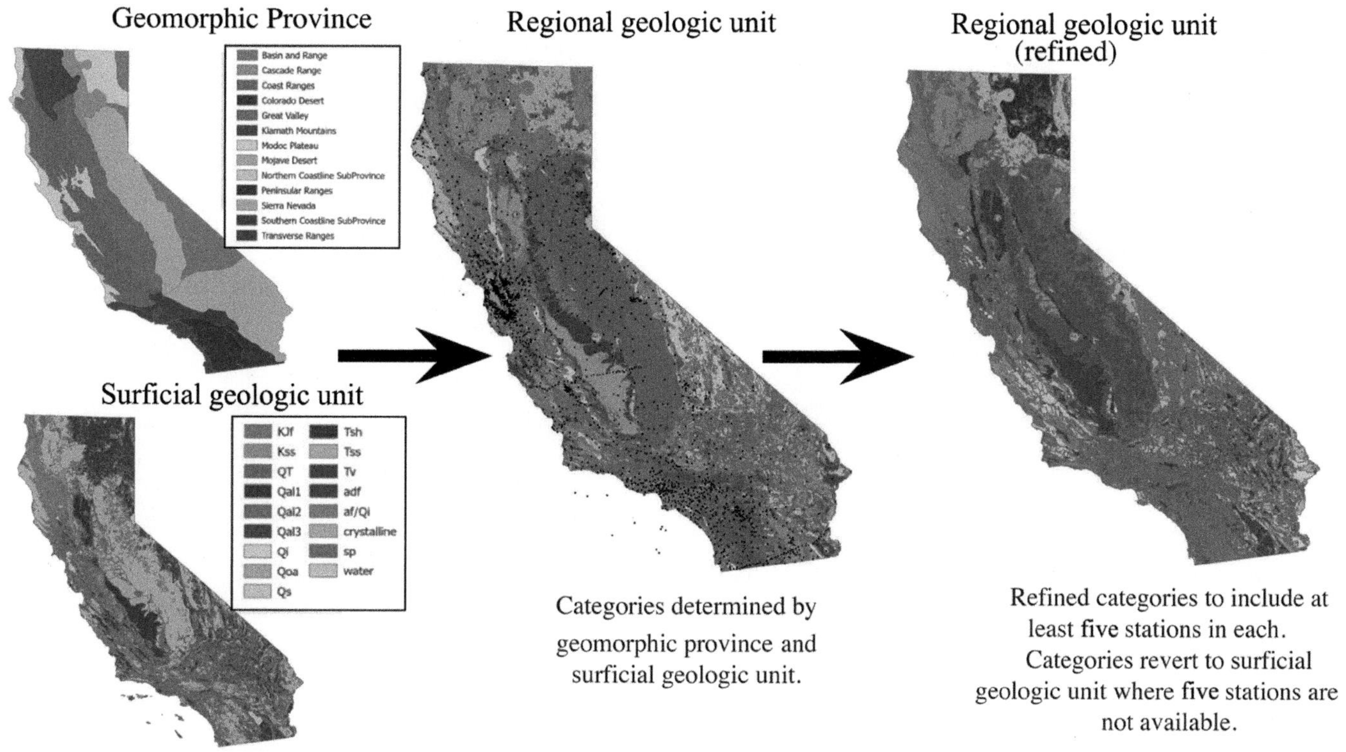

Figure 2. Maps of the original surficial geologic units (Wills *et al.*, 2015) and geomorphic provinces (California Geologic Survey, 2002), as well as the newly defined regional geologic units. The color version of this figure is available only in the electronic edition.

deeper, more regional geomorphic units (e.g., Sierra Nevada, Transverse Ranges) that will relate to basin effects. This allows us to differentiate between, for example, amplification in Quaternary alluvial sediments in different provinces across California. Quaternary alluvial sediments tend to have high variability in V_{S30} due to differences in density, grain, and soil-forming processes (Wills *et al.*, 2015). Using regional geologic units, we can distinguish between Quaternary alluvium units for the northern Coastline Province, which includes the San Francisco Bay area (where alluvium overlies marine sediments and Franciscan rock) (Fumal, 1978), and the southern Coastline Province, which includes the Los Angeles basin (where alluvium overlies thick sedimentary rock layers atop a granite batholith) (Bilodeau *et al.*, 2007). Older alluvium in San Francisco tends to show different amplification patterns than older alluvial sediments in Los Angeles due to the differences in the geologic depositional history (Fumal, 1978). Incorporating the regional geologic unit as a site variable accounts for regional amplification differences resulting from geologic histories such as this.

METHODOLOGY

Site-to-site residuals and site amplification

To develop a geospatial variable-based linear site term applicable to the NGA-West2 GMMs, the dataset was first evaluated using the GMM of Boore *et al.* (2014) (BSSA14). The BSSA14 model was selected due to its simplicity, its limited number of input parameters, and its similar scaling when compared to the other NGA-West2 GMMs (Gregor *et al.*, 2014). The residual (R_{ij}) was calculated for each event (i) at each station (j), as

$$R_{ij,\mathrm{BSSA14}} = \ln(Y_{ij}) - \ln(\mu_{ij,\mathrm{BSSA14}}(\boldsymbol{M}_i, R_{\mathrm{JB},ij}, V_{S30,j}, Z_{1.0,j})), \quad (1)$$

in which Y_{ij} is the ground-motion IM for event i at station j; and $\mu_{ij,\mathrm{BSSA14}}$ is the corresponding median ground-motion prediction from the BSSA14 model with predictor variables of moment magnitude ($\boldsymbol{M}$), Joyner–Boore distance (R_{JB}), V_{S30}, and optionally $Z_{1.0}$ where it is available.

We then decompose the ground-motion residuals using linear mixed-effects regression as

$$R_{ij,\mathrm{BSSA14}} = c_0 + \delta B_i + \delta S2S_j + \delta P_i\left(\frac{R_{\mathrm{JB},ij} - 100}{100}\right) + \delta WS_{ij}, \quad (2)$$

in which c_0, δB_i, $\delta S2S_j$, δP_i, and δWS_{ij} are the bias, event term, site-to-site term, event-specific path term, and remaining residual, respectively. This equation is adapted from Abrahamson and Youngs (1992) to include the event-specific path term to prevent path effects from being mapped into the site term, based on correspondence with N. Abrahamson (personal comm., 2025). The Joyner–Boore distance (R_{JB}) is centered at 100 km and scaled by 1/100 to stabilize the regression and ensure consistent parameter interpretation. This transformation also captures potential amplification or attenuation due to path effects at large distances.

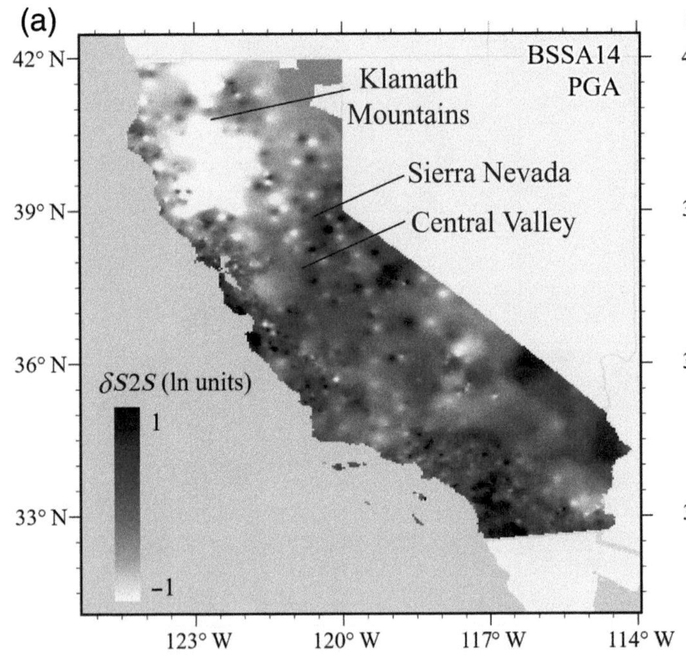

Figure 3. Spatial distribution of site-to-site residuals ($\delta S2S$) in California relative to the BSSA14 V_{S30} scaling for (a) peak ground acceleration (PGA), and (b) pseudospectral acceleration (PSA) for $T = 1$ s, interpolated using inverse distance weighting. The color version of this figure is available only in the electronic edition.

The event term (δB_i) prevents source-specific effects from being mapped into the site-to-site residual term, including effects from the style of faulting, which is not provided in the Ji *et al.* (2022) dataset and therefore not included in the ground-motion prediction. The site-to-site residual term ($\delta S2S_j$) is the portion of the residual attributed to the BSSA14 site term, and is computed relative to the V_{S30} scaling in the BSSA14 model. The site-to-site residual ($\delta S2S_j$) and remaining residuals (δWS_{ij}) are assumed to be normally distributed with zero mean and standard deviations ϕ_{S2S} and ϕ_{SS}, respectively.

The regression calculations are performed across all periods of the BSSA14 model (PGA, PGV, and PSA for 21 periods from 0.01 to 10 s). After performing the linear mixed-effects regression, we calculate the mean and standard deviation of the remaining residuals at each period. Any recording that results in a residual greater than 3 standard deviations from the mean at any period is removed from the dataset. This step is performed to remove recording outliers that could be due to poor data quality. We also remove any stations that have a $\delta S2S$ value greater than 3 standard deviations from the mean of the $\delta S2S$ values at any period. This step is performed to remove stations that could have errors in the instrument parameters or are not representative of free-field conditions. This approach effectively removes recordings and stations that produce high residuals due to instrumentation and data quality; however, this approach is limited in that it does not directly identify data quality issues, and it may remove some data that have a high standard deviation due to natural variability. Assuming the data are normally distributed, and outliers are not present, 99.7% of the data should fall within three standard deviations. Given the size of the dataset, approximately 300 recordings and 10 stations should fall outside the three standard deviations but are removed in this cleaning process. We expect the impact of the removal of these few stations and recordings on the fitted model parameters to be minimal. In this analysis, we prioritize removing the outliers due to data quality issues.

After removing the outlier recordings and stations, linear mixed-effects regression is performed again, following equation (2). Quality control plots that illustrate the appropriate removal of outliers and checks for scaling effects are found in Figures S2–S5. Figure 3 shows the spatial distributions of the site-to-site residual relative to the BSSA14 V_{S30} scaling ($\delta S2S$) calculated following equation (2) for PGA and PSA ($T = 1$ s) interpolated using inverse distance weighting with a maximum distance of 50 km, intended to serve as a visual guide for identifying regions of consistent positive or negative $\delta S2S$ values. The large regions of highly positive and negative values indicate that the $\delta S2S$ residuals, relative to V_{S30} scaling and the overall model bias, exhibit clear large-scale patterns that vary across different periods. Figure 3a shows consistent negative $\delta S2S$ values relative to V_{S30} scaling in northern California, as well as smaller regions of positive and negative values throughout California for PGA. The patterns in $\delta S2S$ shift as the period changes. For PSA at 1 s, shown in Figure 3b, negative $\delta S2S$ values relative to V_{S30} scaling are observed for the Sierra Nevada mountain range. The $\delta S2S$ residuals are closer to an average of zero in the Los Angeles and San Francisco areas for both PGA and PSA at 1 s, but do exhibit smaller-scale variations and have regions of positive and negative residuals.

We also compute the variance in the point estimates of $\delta S2S$ relative to BSSA14 V_{S30} scaling. This step is performed to account for the uncertainty in $\delta S2S$, especially for sites with few recordings, which can lead to bias in the model (Campbell *et al.*, 2025; Kuehn *et al.*, 2025). The inverse of the variance of each point estimate of $\delta S2S$ is used to weight the stations during model fitting, giving stations with a more certain $\delta S2S$ a higher influence on the fit of the model.

The site amplification is then computed as

$$A_j = \delta S2S_j + \ln(F_{\mathrm{lin},j}) + F_{\delta Z1,j}, \tag{3}$$

in which A_j is the site amplification relative to the BSSA14 reference condition of V_{S30} equal to 760 m/s, representing a soft rock site with zero amplification (i.e., the reference condition). $\ln(F_{\mathrm{lin},j})$ and $F_{\delta Z1,j}$ are the linear site term and basin term, respectively. All coefficients and functional forms are unmodified from the BSSA14 model:

$$\ln(F_{\mathrm{lin}}) = \begin{cases} c\ln\left(\frac{V_{S30}}{V_{\mathrm{Ref}}}\right) & V_{S30} \le V_c \\ c\ln\left(\frac{V_c}{V_{\mathrm{Ref}}}\right) & V_{S30} > V_c \end{cases}, \tag{4}$$

in which c is the V_{S30} scaling coefficient, V_c is the limiting velocity, and V_{Ref} is the reference velocity (760 m/s for the BSSA14 model), and

$$F_{\delta z_1} = \begin{cases} 0 & T < 0.65 \\ f_6 \delta z_1 & T \ge 0.65 \text{ and } \delta z_1 \le f_7/f_6 \\ f_7 & T \ge 0.65 \text{ and } \delta z_1 > f_7/f_6 \end{cases}, \tag{5}$$

in which f_6 and f_7 are the period-dependent coefficients, and δZ_1 is defined as the difference between the $Z_{1.0}$ of the site and the empirically estimated $Z_{1.0}$ from the Chiou and Youngs (2008) model.

The site amplification (A_j) is computed relative to the reference condition of V_{S30} equal to 760 m/s used in BSSA14 and is used as the target variable for the geospatial variable-based linear site term. This linear site amplification term is intended to be used in combination with the nonlinear BSSA14 site term to estimate the entire site-effects portion of the BSSA14 GMM relative to its reference condition.

Multiple linear regression

We derived empirical models to predict the site effect term relative to the BSSA14 reference condition of V_{S30} equal to 760 m/s using the geospatial parameters in Table 1 by employing weighted multiple linear regression using equation (6):

$$A_j = \alpha + \begin{cases} \boldsymbol{\beta X} + \varepsilon_j, & \boldsymbol{X} < \boldsymbol{X_0} \\ \boldsymbol{\beta X_0} + \varepsilon_j, & \boldsymbol{X} \ge \boldsymbol{X_0} \end{cases}, \tag{6}$$

in which α is a constant, $\boldsymbol{\beta}$ is a vector of regression coefficients, $\boldsymbol{X}$ is a vector of the geospatial parameters, ε_j is the remaining site residual after the regression, and $\boldsymbol{X_0}$ is a vector of plateau points at which the parameter correlations to A_j become constant. The linear piecewise functional form was selected to be consistent with trends observed in the amplification correlation to each continuous variable and to avoid extrapolation at high input values for $\boldsymbol{X}$. The correlation between each parameter and amplification varies by period and tends to either show a linear relationship or a constant relationship. Plots of each parameter and the associated amplification can be seen in Figure S6. We evaluate two sets of models: models containing only continuous geospatial variables, and models containing a combination of categorical and continuous geospatial variables. As previously stated, during model development, the inverse of the variance of $\delta S2S$ for each station is used to perform weighted multiple linear regression.

Fivefold cross-validation and optimal model selection

We evaluate the performance of alternative regression models using different combinations of geospatial variables using fivefold cross-validation. The sites are first split randomly into five groups. For each set of geospatial variables tested, the model is fit to the data five times, each time leaving out a different group. The root mean square error (RMSE) of the left-out group is averaged across each of the five trials and is used to compare different models. The optimal set of geospatial parameters is selected as the model that has the lowest average RMSE across all periods evaluated.

A forward stepwise selection process was used to select the best combination of variables. We first analyze an exhaustive set of one-parameter models to select the optimal single parameter. Next, an exhaustive comparison is conducted for two-parameter models, each containing the optimal single parameter, to select a second parameter to add to the model. In this step, the models are refit to both parameters together.

MODEL DEVELOPMENT

Site variable exploratory analysis

We evaluated all continuous geospatial site variables in our dataset for correlations to the calculated site amplification in equation (3) (A_j), to evaluate which variables would be most influential in predicting site amplification at various spectral periods. The geotechnical variables, V_{S30} (including both measured and geologic unit proxy-based variables, as reported in the Ji *et al.*, 2022, dataset) and $Z_{1.0}$, are included for comparison, but are not used in our model development. There is a period dependence in correlation for the continuous geospatial variables, as shown in Figure 4. Many of the correlated DEM-based parameters (topographic slope, topographic roughness index [TRI], and roughness) and sediment thickness are more highly correlated to site amplification at long periods than at

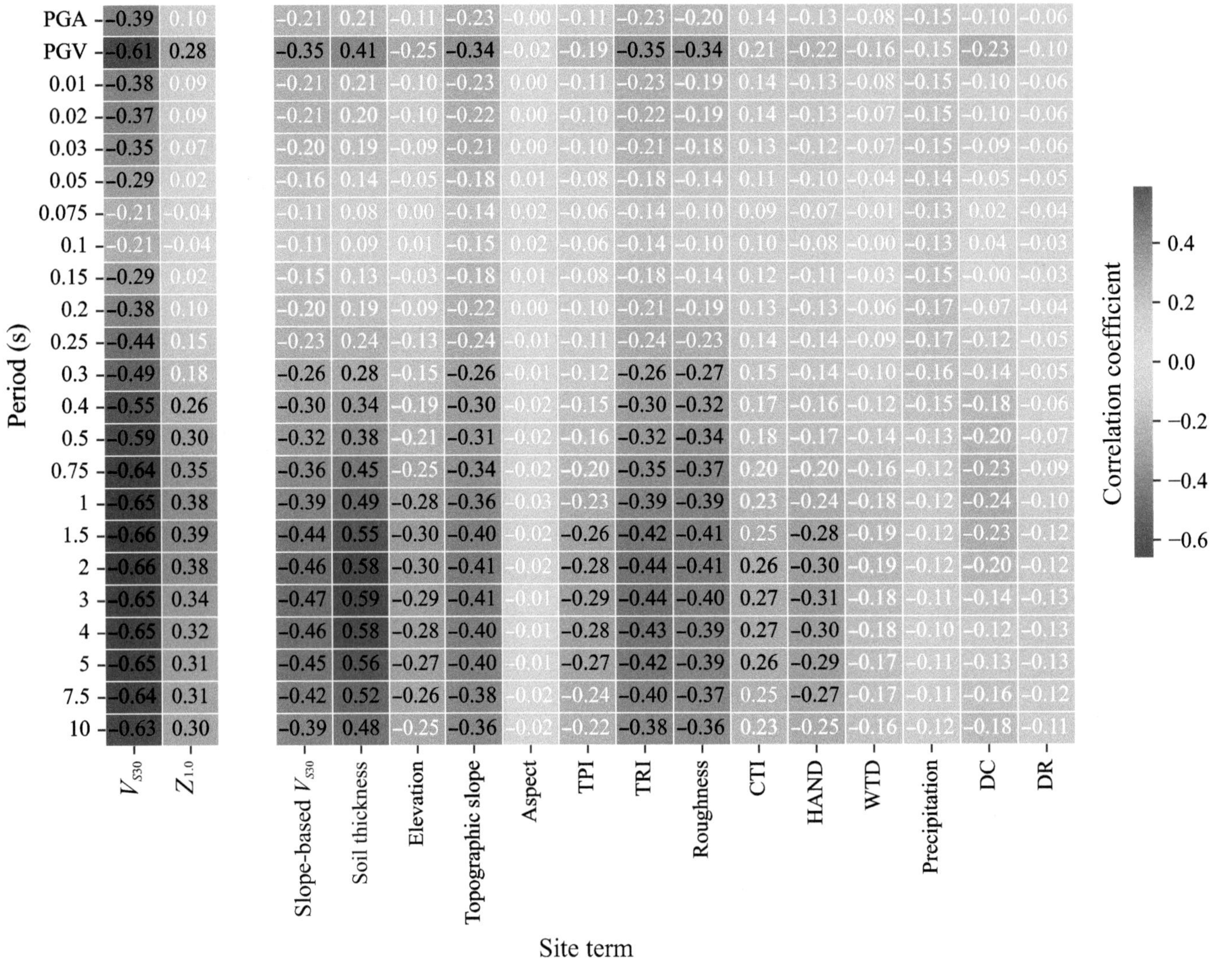

Figure 4. Correlations of geotechnical (left side) and continuous geospatial (right side) site variables to site amplifications (A_j) for PGA, PGV, and spectral accelerations from 0.01 to 10 s. The cells are color-coded based on the correlation coefficient between site amplification and the site parameter, and all variables are defined in Table 1. CTI, compound topographic index; DC, distance to coast; DR, distance to river; HAND, height above nearest drainage; TPI, topographic position index; TRI, topographic roughness index; and WTD, water table depth. The color version of this figure is available only in the electronic edition.

short periods. Among the continuous geospatial variables, we find that sediment thickness, slope-based V_{S30}, topographic slope, TRI, and roughness have the highest correlations with site amplification. The variables that influence soil saturation have less correlation with site amplification, including water table depth, precipitation, distance to the coast, and distance to the nearest river. The DEM-based parameter of aspect also shows minimal correlation with site amplification. Mathematical transformations, including logarithmic and square, of the geospatial variables were also assessed, but these transformations did not significantly improve the correlation for any of the variables.

The categorical parameters in Table 1 are also evaluated for their correlation with the calculated site amplification in equation (3) (A_j). Figure 5 shows the analysis of variance results for the categorical parameters, developed by Fisher (1925), both for their F values (the variance between sample means divided by the variance within the sample) and their η^2 values (the proportion of the variance associated with the categories). The F value indicates whether the mean amplifications of the categories are significantly different from each other, and η^2 indicates how much of the variance is accounted for by these categories. Both metrics are shown here because they represent different aspects of the variance captured by the parameters: how distinct the categories are from each other (F) and the proportion of the variance in amplification that can be attributed to the categories (η^2).

Figure 5 indicates that all the categorical variables are most correlated to site amplification at longer periods (1–10 s). In terms of the F values, the geologic unit exhibits the highest correlations, indicating that the geologic units have distinct observed site amplification and are able to capture variability in site effects. In terms of η^2, the regional geologic unit has the

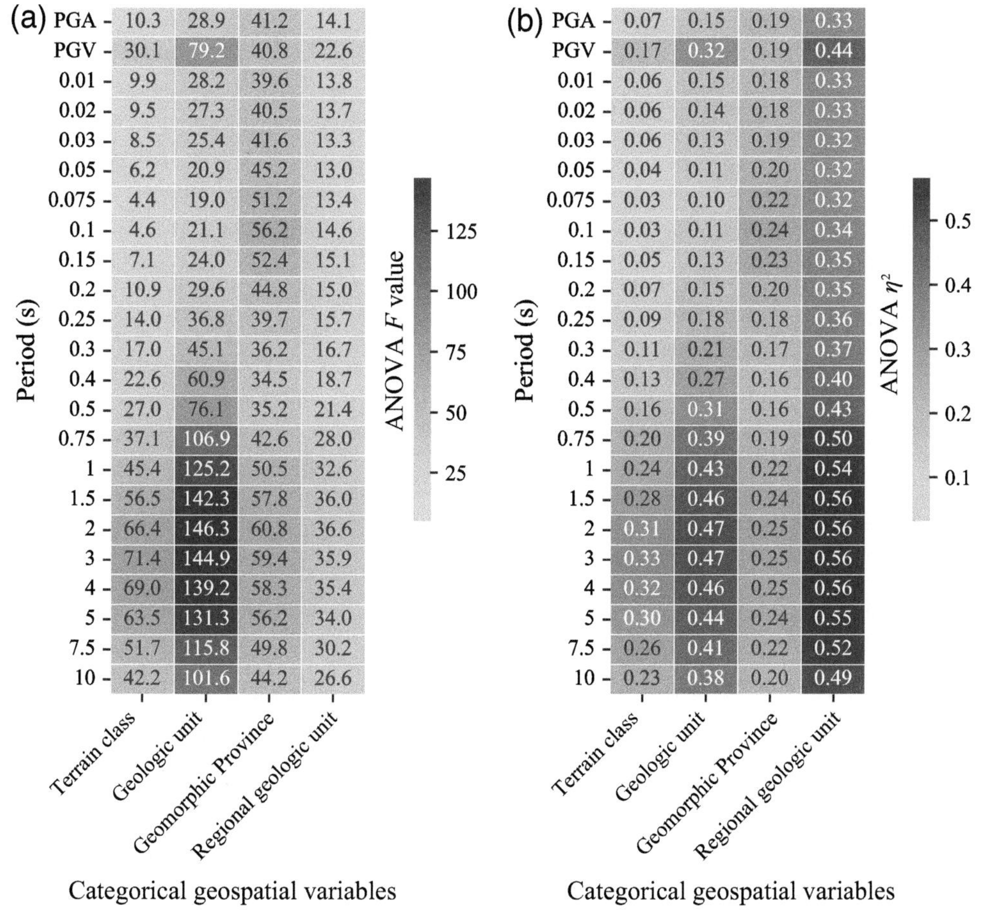

Figure 5. Correlation of categorical site parameters to site amplification (A_j) for PGA, PGV, and the 21 PSAs analyzed in this study. Correlation is measured in terms of analysis of variance (ANOVA) (a) F values (the variance between sample means divided by the variance within the sample) and (b) η^2 (the proportion of the variance associated with the categories). The color version of this figure is available only in the electronic edition.

highest correlations, and the geologic unit has the second highest correlations. Regional geologic unit shows the highest correlation to site amplification in terms of η^2 because it is able to capture regions with extreme positive and negative site effects. The F value indicates that some of the regional geologic unit categories are not very distinct from each other, which could be due in part to having a large number of categories, some with similar amplification patterns. However, we choose not to combine any categories to preserve the physical significance and differences between the categories, and because the variance in amplification is well captured with these categories, as indicated by η^2.

The results of these correlations facilitate an understanding of which parameters will be most influential in estimating site amplification. As shown in Figure 4, no single continuous variable is as correlated to site amplification as V_{S30}; however, some continuous variables still show high correlations at different period ranges, including soil thickness, slope-based V_{S30}, topographic slope, TRI, and roughness. In Figure 4, the geospatial variable correlations are compared to the preferred V_{S30}, and the preferred $Z_{1.0}$. The preferred V_{S30} is the measured V_{S30} values at stations where they are available, and geology-based proxy V_{S30} values are used elsewhere. Preferred V_{S30} is strongly influenced by the geology-based proxy at sites without measured V_{S30} values, so it could include similar information as the categorical geologic units. The addition of categorical site parameters, especially regional geologic unit, will be beneficial in explicitly capturing the location-specific, larger-scale patterns of the site terms.

Model selection

Two sets of models, those containing only continuous geospatial variables and those containing a combination of categorical and continuous geospatial variables, were evaluated using fivefold cross-validation, as described in the Methodology section. For each model, the average RMSE of the test group during the five trials is evaluated for PGA, PGV, and PSA at 21 spectral periods. This average RMSE is the metric used to select the optimal set of geospatial parameters. A forward stepwise variable selection search is performed to determine the best combination of explanatory variables, as illustrated in Figure 6. Figure 6a shows the results of the variable selection process when both continuous and categorical variables are considered. We found that models including more than two parameters did not show improvement in the average RMSE of the test group during fivefold cross-validation. The optimal model selection process is then repeated, but with only the inclusion of continuous geospatial variables. The selection of the optimal one-parameter and two-parameter continuous geospatial variable-based models is illustrated in Figure 6b.

For the models containing both continuous and categorical variables illustrated in Figure 6a, the categorical variables reduced the average RMSE of the test group, more so than the continuous variables. Regional geologic unit is the best-performing single-parameter model, highlighting the predictive power of regionalized geologically defined regions for site amplification. Regional geologic unit is selected as the primary site parameter for its optimal prediction performance and its ability to capture region-specific differences in soil type, due to

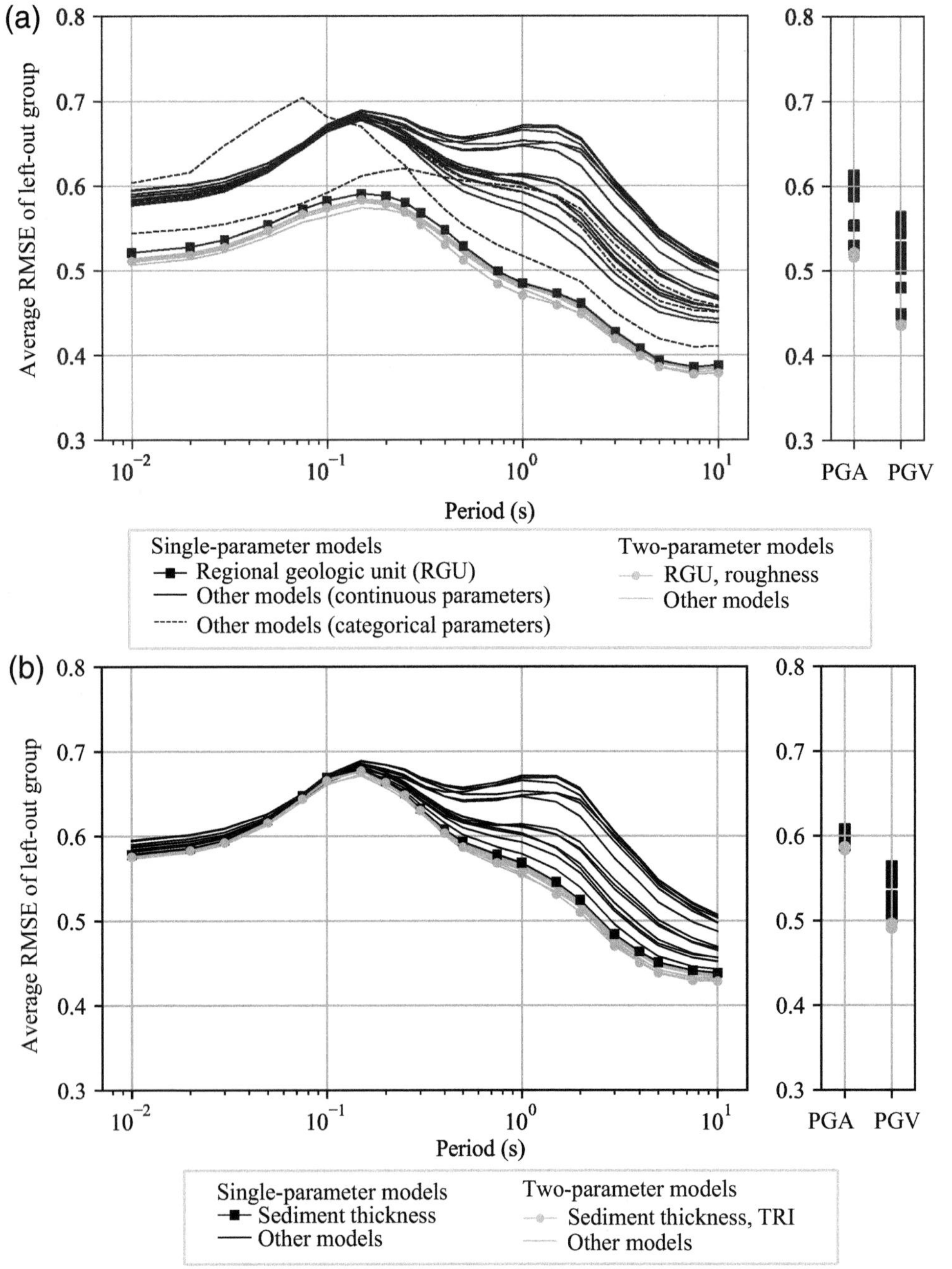

Figure 6. (a) Root mean square error (RMSE) for all single-parameter and two-parameter models incorporating both continuous and categorical variables, and (b) RMSE for all single-parameter and two-parameter models incorporating only continuous variables. The color version of this figure is available only in the electronic edition.

a combination of stiffness, basin, and saturation characteristics that differ by region. The average RMSE of the left-out group is between 0.39 and 0.59 for the optimal one-parameter model (regional geologic unit). Among the continuous variables, sediment thickness performed best. Sediment thickness has physical significance in terms of defining basins and soil stiffness, but the optimal one-parameter model is only capable of achieving an average RMSE of 0.44 to 0.68.

In Figure 6a, we then evaluate the performance of models when a secondary site parameter is added along with the regional geologic unit. Only continuous geospatial variables are evaluated in this step to allow for geologically informed location-based interpolation across the regional geologic unit categories. In addition, the inclusion of a continuous site parameter accounts for differences in amplification within regional geologic units and captures the spatial continuity of site amplification. All continuous geospatial parameters performed similarly when combined with the regional geologic unit; the average RMSE of the left-out group is between 0.494 and 0.501 for each combination when averaged across the evaluated periods. Roughness offers the highest reduction to the RMSE of the test groups and is selected as the secondary site parameter. Roughness is derived from a digital elevation model and is defined as the largest difference in elevation between a pixel and its eight surrounding pixels. Roughness captures the variation in topography at a site, which has been known to be correlated with regional site response (Allen and Wald, 2009), making roughness a physically significant secondary parameter to incorporate. Adding this secondary site term provides an average reduction of 2.1% in RMSE across the evaluated periods compared to the single-parameter model using the regional geologic unit. The reduction is most significant at longer periods, with the largest percent reduction being 3.2% for PSA at 0.40 and 0.50 s. If we use slope-based V_{S30}, a more typically used site parameter instead of roughness, the average reduction in RMSE would be smaller, at 0.9% compared to the single-parameter regional geologic unit model. The average RMSE of this two-parameter model using regional geologic unit and roughness was within one standard error of the optimal one-parameter model RMSE at 14 of the periods evaluated. Therefore, we do not consider models with more than two parameters due to the minimal improvement achieved by adding the second parameter. The optimal geospatial variable-based model we recommend is the two-parameter model with the explanatory variables of regional geologic unit and roughness.

For comparison, we also evaluated two-parameter models consisting of only continuous variables (Fig. 6b) using the same approach. These models could potentially be refitted to data in other regions and used outside of California because the continuous variables are globally available. The primary and secondary variables identified are sediment thickness and TRI, respectively. TRI is calculated as the square root of the elevation differences between the central cell and the neighboring eight cells in the DEM. The addition of the second variable contributed a minimal reduction to the average RMSE. When a second parameter is added, the RMSE is reduced by 1.3% compared to the one-parameter model. The improvement is most significant for PSA for 0.75–10 s, for which the average reduction is 2.5%. The two-parameter model RMSE is within one standard error of the one-parameter model for 14 periods; therefore, we do not evaluate a three-parameter model. We select the two-parameter model using sediment thickness and TRI as the optimal continuous variable-based model. In contrast to the combined categorical and continuous model described earlier, which has an average test group RMSE of 0.49, the model using two continuous variables exhibited a 14.0% higher average test group RMSE of 0.56.

GEOSPATIAL VARIABLE-BASED LINEAR SITE TERM MODEL

Given the results of the fivefold cross-validation process, we propose a geologically informed linear site term relative to the reference rock site condition of V_{S30} equal to 760 m/s ($\ln(F_{\mathrm{Geospatial},j})$) for use with the BSSA14 GMM in replacement of the linear site ($\ln(F_{\mathrm{lin}})$) and basin terms ($F_{\delta Z1,j}$). The proposed site term uses the regional geologic unit and roughness as the model parameters. The regional geologic unit term captures regional patterns related to geologic history and geomorphic structure across California. The addition of roughness, which represents high-resolution topographic change, captures changes related to sediment thickness and density. The linear site term at station j is expressed in equation (7), and the coefficients by period can be found in Table S2:

$$\ln(F_{\mathrm{Geospatial},j}) = c_1 + F_{\mathrm{RGU},j} + \begin{cases} c_2\,(\mathrm{roughness}_j - 20), & \mathrm{roughness}_j < \mathrm{roughness}_0 \\ c_2\,(\mathrm{roughness}_0 - 20), & \mathrm{roughness}_j \geq \mathrm{roughness}_0 \end{cases}, \quad (7)$$

in which c_1 is a constant, F_{RGU} represents the categorical site term for regional geologic unit (a coefficient that is uniform within each regional geologic unit category), c_2 is a regression slope coefficient for roughness centered around the average roughness of 20 m, and $\mathrm{roughness}_0$ is the plateau point at which amplification becomes constant with increasing roughness.

Equation (7) is used to generate the final models for the linear site term across California relative to the BSSA14 reference site condition. Each location has a site term based on its regional geologic unit and roughness. This process creates a geologically informed and regionally varying linear site term model for the state of California. The model is based on input parameters that are available across the entire study area without the use of proxies; it does not use any measured or inferred geotechnical information. Shapefiles of the regional geologic unit and roughness can be found in the supplemental material to this article, which allow for the calculation of site terms at all periods evaluated. The models for PGA, 0.1 s PSA, 1 s PSA, and 10 s PSA are shown in Figure 7 in natural logarithm units. De-amplification of ground motions relative to the soft-rock reference condition of $V_{S30} = 760$ m/s is seen at all periods in northern California, particularly in the crystalline Klamath Mountains, where the de-amplification is greatest at shorter periods. Regions with surficial geology consisting of Quaternary alluvium, such as along the northern and southern Coastlines, tend to amplify ground motions relative to the reference condition, and this amplification increases at longer periods.

The alternate model based only on continuous geospatial variables, as described in the previous section, is a function of sediment thickness and TRI. Equation (8) provides the functional form of this alternate model:

$$\ln(F_{\mathrm{Geospatial},j}) = c_3 + \begin{cases} c_4\,(\mathrm{ST}_j - 12.6), & \mathrm{ST}_j < \mathrm{ST}_0 \\ c_4\,(\mathrm{ST}_0 - 12.6), & \mathrm{ST}_j \geq \mathrm{ST}_0 \end{cases} + \begin{cases} c_5\,(\mathrm{TRI}_j - 14.9), & \mathrm{TRI}_j < \mathrm{TRI}_0 \\ c_5\,(\mathrm{TRI}_0 - 14.9), & \mathrm{TRI}_j \geq \mathrm{TRI}_0 \end{cases}, \quad (8)$$

in which c_3 is a constant, c_4 is the regression slope coefficient for sediment thickness (ST) centered around the average value of sediment thickness (12.6 m), and c_5 is the regression slope coefficient for TRI centered around the average value of TRI (14.9 m). ST_0 and TRI_0 are the plateau points at which amplification becomes constant with increasing sediment thickness and TRI, respectively. These coefficients are provided in Table S3.

VARIABILITY AND UNCERTAINTY ESTIMATION

The proposed linear site term model using regional geologic unit and roughness provides a median estimate of site amplification relative to the BSSA14 reference condition, which includes both aleatory variability and epistemic uncertainty. The aleatory variability was calculated using the residuals of the BSSA14 GMM modified to replace the linear ($\ln(F_{\mathrm{lin},j})$) and basin ($F_{\delta Z1,j}$) components of the site term with the geospatial site term developed using equation (7). The aleatory variability is caused by the variability due to simplifications

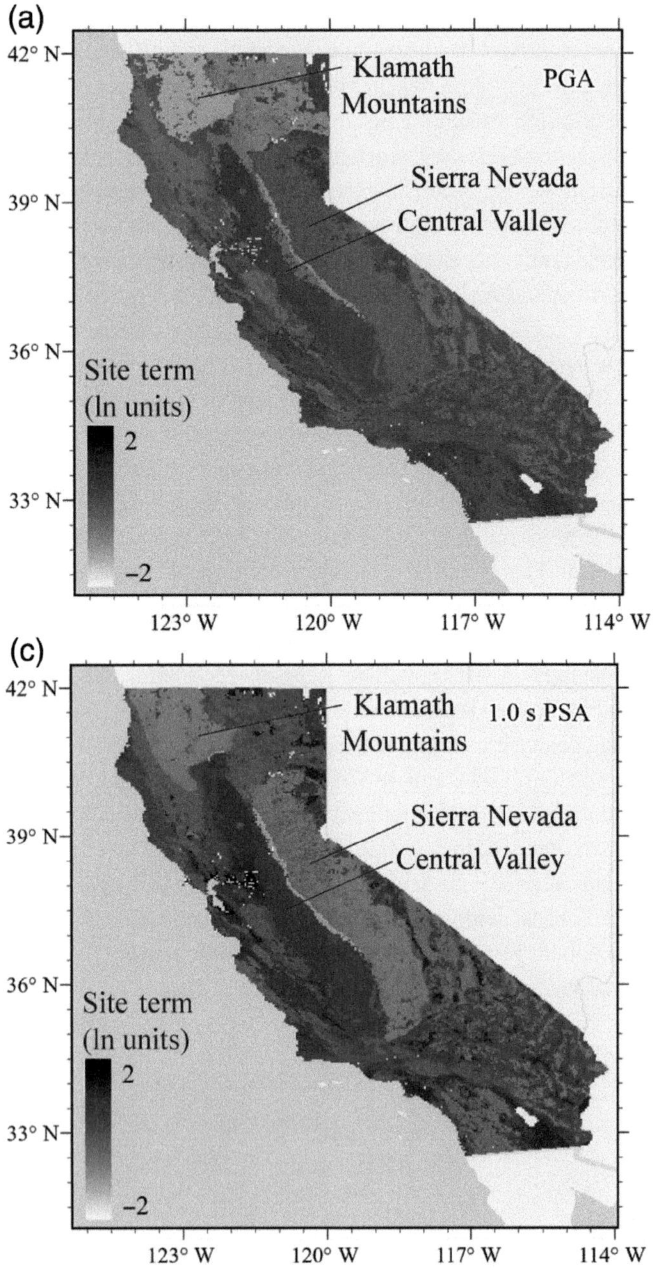

Figure 7. Map-based geospatial models of the linear site term in natural logarithm units relative to the BSSA14 reference condition for (a) PGA, (b) 0.1 s PSA, (c) 1 s PSA, and (d) 10 s PSA. The color version of this figure is available only in the electronic edition.

of the model, treated as random error in the prediction of ground motions. Aleatory variability is quantified by the combination of the single-station within-event variability (ϕ_{ss}), which is calculated as the standard deviation of the remaining residuals (ε_{ij}) and the variability in the site-to-site residual (ϕ_{S2S}) and is calculated as the standard deviation of the station-specific site-to-site residual values calculated using equation (2). The within-event aleatory variability (ϕ) is calculated in the following equation:

$$\phi = \sqrt{\phi_{SS}^2 + \phi_{S2S}^2}. \quad (9)$$

The within-event aleatory variability and the variability in the site-to-site residual values for all periods are plotted in Figure 8 for both our geospatial model and the BSSA14 model. The aleatory variability of our model is period-dependent, with ϕranging from 0.57 to 0.76 across all periods (with an average of 0.66). The within-event aleatory variability gradually increases and peaks at 0.1 s, and then decreases at periods longer than 0.1 s. In Figure 8, the values of ϕ_{S2S} for BSSA14 are higher than those reported for BSSA14 from the NGA-West2 dataset (Ancheta *et al.*, 2014), where ϕ_{S2S} is in the approximate range of 0.3–0.5 (fig. 4.46 of Al Atik, 2015). There are several potential explanations for this difference: (1) the Ji *et al.* (2022) dataset is

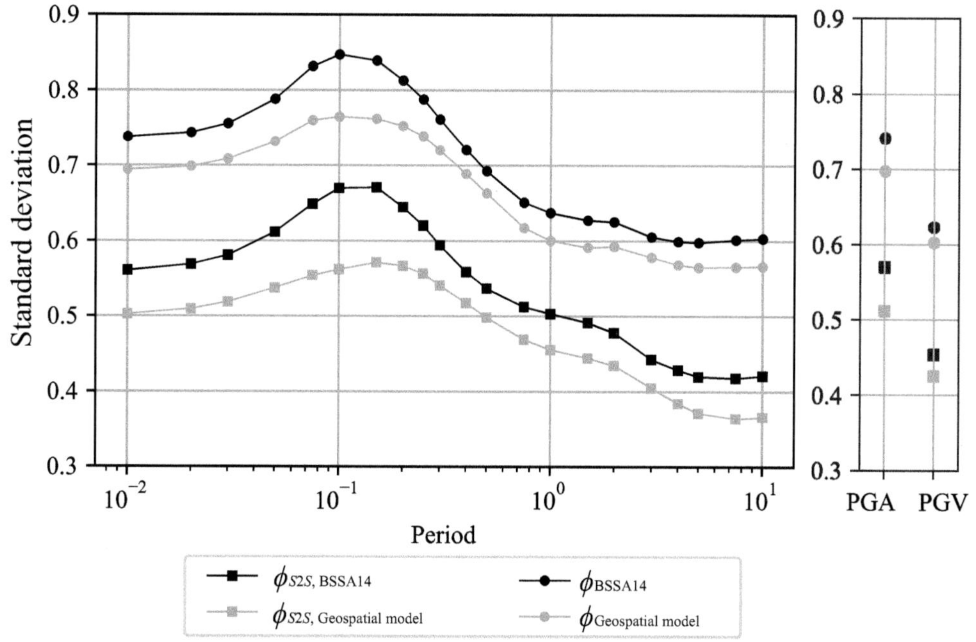

Figure 8. Within-event aleatory variability (ϕ) and variability in site-to-site residuals relative to site term scaling (ϕ_{S2S}) across all regional geologic units versus spectral period. The color version of this figure is available only in the electronic edition.

larger and draws from a variety of geologic and geographic locations compared to the NGA-West2 dataset, most notably including more stations in northern and eastern California (a comparison of the station coverage of the datasets can be seen in Fig. S7); and (2) the Ji *et al.* (2022) dataset was automatically processed and not as rigorously compiled as the NGA-West2 dataset, leading to higher variability most significant at periods below 0.5 s. This limitation of the dataset may result in potential bias at short periods. However, this article presents a proof-of-concept for a methodology in which the added spatial coverage of the Ji *et al.* (2022) dataset compared to NGA-West2 was optimal for this purpose. The aleatory variability (ϕ) and its components, ϕ_{S2S} and ϕ_{ss}, are reported by period in Table S4.

The second uncertainty component is the epistemic uncertainty, which arises from uncertainty in modeling parameters and model inputs for site characterization (in this case, regional geographic unit and roughness). These uncertainties are calculated and forward propagated following the procedures of Zhan *et al.* (2023). The uncertainty in modeling parameters is quantified for the geospatial model by reporting the standard error of the coefficients for each parameter in equation (7) (σ_{C1} for the constant c_1, σ_{RGU} for each regional geologic unit, and σ_{C2} for roughness coefficient c_2). These standard errors are reported in Table S2. The coefficient for each regional geologic unit has a unique uncertainty (provided in Table S2), and some are larger than others, representing the added uncertainty in parameters for units with fewer stations or more variable geography. Regions of high parameter uncertainty include Quaternary alluvial (Qal) sediment units (especially in the Central Valley and along the coastline), Quaternary intertidal mud (Qi) sediments, and Tertiary sandstone (Tss) sediments of the Cascade Range province. In these regions, the additional uncertainty is primarily governed by the number of stations in each unit; units with fewer stations (five to ten) tend to have higher standard errors. The amount of variability within certain geology types also likely plays a role. The larger standard error in some units does not appear to be governed by misclassification of stations near the boundaries between regional geologic units. For the three regions of highest uncertainty, we compared the means and standard errors of the stations near the boundaries (within 100 m) to those farther from the boundaries, and we found that there were no statistically significant differences at any periods.

The epistemic uncertainty due to model inputs (regional geologic unit and roughness) is also calculated. These uncertainties are calculated following the procedures of Zhan *et al.* (2023), in which uncertainty in geospatial parameter input values is calculated as the standard error of the parameter, which is often assumed or collected from data source documentation. For regional geologic units, we assume these units to be deterministic with zero standard error. This is a simplifying assumption based on the regional geologic unit being a categorical variable with constant boundaries and having no reported uncertainties in the geologic maps. In addition, based on the boundary analysis explained previously, stations near boundaries do not have significantly different amplifications from stations further within units. For the uncertainty in roughness, we calculate the standard error of the roughness values, $\sigma_{\mathrm{Roughness}}$. Roughness is derived from the 7.5 arcsec mean elevation model GMTED2010 (Danielson and Gesch, 2011), which has a reported standard error of 26.96 m. Roughness is calculated as the largest intercell difference between a central pixel and its eight surrounding cells. Because roughness is the result of the difference between two pixel elevations, the uncertainty in each pixel is combined as $\sigma_{\mathrm{Roughness}} = \sqrt{(26.96\ \mathrm{m})^2 + (26.96\ \mathrm{m})^2} = 38.13$ m.

The total epistemic uncertainty for a location can be calculated using forward uncertainty propagation by estimating the first-order approximation (Zhan *et al.*, 2023). The variance of the mean site term relative to the BSSA14 reference rock condition (calculated following equation 7) can be approximated at any location following equation (10).

$$\sigma^2_{\ln(F_{\text{Geospatial}})} = \sigma^2_{c1} + \sigma^2_{\text{RGU},j} + \begin{cases} c_2^2\sigma^2_{\text{roughness}} + (\text{roughness}_j - 20)^2\sigma^2_{c2} + \sigma^2_{c2}\sigma^2_{\text{roughness}} & \text{roughness}_j < \text{roughness}_0 \\ (\text{roughness}_0 - 20)^2\sigma^2_{c2} & \text{roughness}_j \geq \text{roughness}_0 \end{cases}. \quad (10)$$

The total variance of the geospatial model fit to regional geologic unit and roughness ($\sigma^2_{\ln(F_{\text{Geospatial}})}$) is the composed of the standard error from three main sources: the standard error of the constant term c_1 (σ_{c1}), the standard error of the regional geologic unit term (σ_{RGU}), and the standard error of the roughness term. If the roughness at a site (roughness_j) is below the threshold roughness_0, the variance of the roughness parameter is the product of the standard error of the coefficient for roughness (σ_{c2}) and the standard error of the input value of roughness ($\sigma_{\text{roughness}}$), which are combined using a first-order uncertainty propagation formula for the product of two independent variables. If roughness_j is greater than or equal to roughness_0, the uncertainty is only a product of the standard deviation of the coefficient for roughness (σ_{c2}). This representation is a simplified first-order approximation of the epistemic uncertainty; for probabilistic seismic hazard analysis (PSHA) or deterministic seismic hazard analysis (DSHA), methods such as Monte Carlo simulation should be performed to more accurately quantify the uncertainty. Maps of the mean (equation 7) and standard error (calculated as the square root of the variance from equation 10) of the site term relative to the BSSA14 reference condition for PGA and PSA at a period of 1 s can be seen in Figure S8. The total epistemic uncertainty is driven by the regional geologic unit coefficient uncertainty. Some regional geologic units have higher total epistemic uncertainty, in particular Quaternary alluvial sediments in the Basin and Range, Sierra Nevada, and Modoc Plateau regions. The epistemic uncertainty in these regional units could be reduced as more data become available.

This quantification of the aleatory variability and epistemic uncertainties would be necessary if incorporating this model into a PSHA or DSHA. In PSHA and DSHA, the uncertainty in model parameters, model inputs, and aleatory variability would be explicitly accounted for.

REDUCTION IN SITE-TO-SITE VARIABILITY

To evaluate how well the linear site term models reduce GMM aleatory variability, we compare the site-to-site residuals calculated following equation (2) of PGA, PGV, and PSA across all periods after applying three types of models: the traditional ergodic site amplification models (based on V_{S30} and $Z_{1.0}$), the combined categorical and continuous geospatial model developed in this study (equation 7), and the continuous geospatial model developed in this study (equation 8).

For the conventional ergodic models, we consider both the unmodified BSSA14 NGA-West2 model (V_{S30}- and $Z_{1.0}$-based) and a retrained model fit to the Ji *et al.* (2022) dataset using V_{S30} and $Z_{1.0}$. This retrained model is created using the same form as the BSSA14 model but with V_{S30} and $Z_{1.0}$ site terms fit to the Ji *et al.* (2022) dataset. The V_{S30} and $Z_{1.0}$ model fit to the Ji *et al.* (2022) dataset is included for comparison with the unmodified BSSA14 model because the BSSA14 model was fit to only NGA-West2 data, whereas the Ji *et al.* (2022) dataset contains more recordings than NGA-West2 and has broader coverage across California. A retrained model fit to the newly available data provides a more equal comparison to the geospatial models that were developed. The linear site term of the retrained model is the sum of a V_{S30}-dependent term $\ln(F_{V_{S30}})$ and a $Z_{1.0}$-dependent term $F_{Z_{1.0}}$.

For the V_{S30} term, a piecewise function (equation 11) is used with period-dependent parameters V_C (limiting velocity) and c_1 (slope coefficient), and a period-independent reference velocity V_{REF} of 760 m/s, as is used in BSSA14. This functional form is consistent with the BSSA14 model, and the coefficient c_1 is refit to the calculated site amplification for the dataset used here:

$$\ln(F_{V_{S30}}) = \begin{cases} c_1 \ln\left(\frac{V_{S30}}{V_{\text{REF}}}\right) & V_{S30} \leq V_C \\ c_1 \ln\left(\frac{V_C}{V_{\text{REF}}}\right) & V_{S30} > V_C \end{cases}. \quad (11)$$

For the $Z_{1.0}$ term (equation 12), we use $\delta Z_{1.0}$ from using the Chiou and Youngs (2008) approach, defined as the difference between the measured $Z_{1.0}$ (i.e., the preferred $Z_{1.0}$ obtained from the SCEC UCVM) and the predicted average $Z_{1.0}$, predicted from the Chiou and Youngs (2008) $Z_{1.0}$ model for California. The period-dependent coefficient c_2 is refit to the data. For stations without a measured value of $Z_{1.0}$, we assume $\delta Z_{1.0}$ is zero,

$$F_{Z_{1.0}} = c_2 \delta Z_{1.0}. \quad (12)$$

The predictive performance of both the optimal combined and continuous geospatial models is compared to the refit V_{S30} and $Z_{1.0}$ model and the original unmodified BSSA14 model for the dataset, as illustrated in Figure 9. The one-parameter model with the regional geologic unit term provides a significant reduction of 8.5% in the average standard deviation of site-to-site residual (ϕ_{S2S}), compared to the model fit to V_{S30} and $Z_{1.0}$ using the Ji *et al.* (2022) dataset. With the optimal two-parameter model

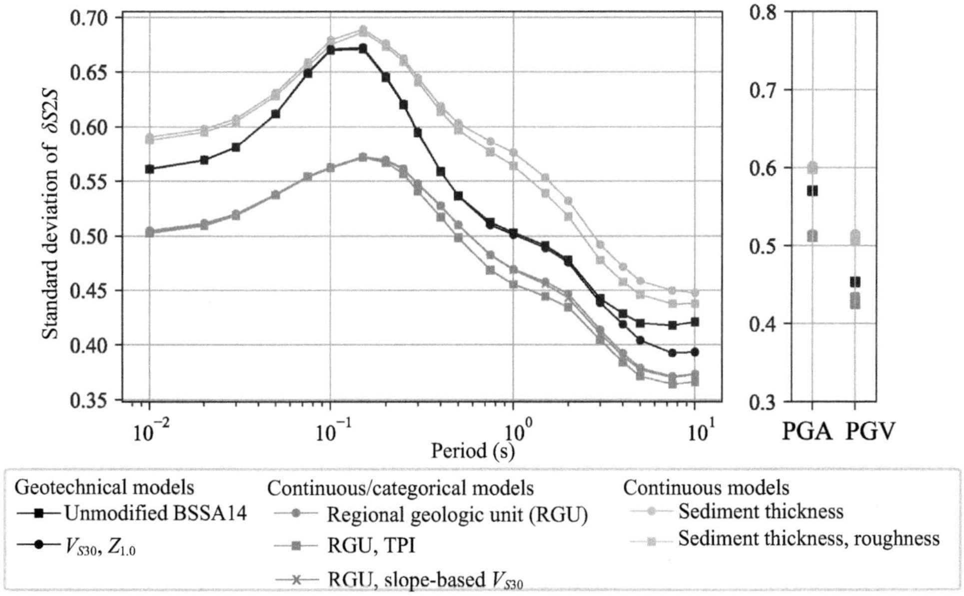

Figure 9. Comparison of the standard deviation of $\delta S2S$ relative to site term scaling for the 3099 sites in the dataset. The results are shown for the unmodified BSSA14 model; the V_{S30} and $Z_{1.0}$ model fit to the subset of the Ji *et al.* (2022) DesignSafe dataset; and the geospatial models, including the optimal models built with categorical and continuous parameters, and the optimal models built with only continuous parameters. The color version of this figure is available only in the electronic edition.

(regional geologic unit and roughness), a 9.8% reduction is achieved as compared to the model fit to V_{S30} and $Z_{1.0}$ using the Ji *et al.* (2022) dataset, and a 10.6% reduction is achieved as compared to the unmodified BSSA14 model. In the frequency range of 1–10 s, which is least impacted by the data variability in the Ji *et al.* (2022) dataset, the optimal two-parameter model (regional geologic unit and roughness) results in an 8.2% reduction in the average standard deviation of site-to-site residual (ϕ_{S2S}) compared to the model fit to V_{S30} and $Z_{1.0}$ using the Ji *et al.* (2022) dataset, and a 10.5% reduction is achieved as compared to the unmodified BSSA14 model. The regional geologic unit and slope-based V_{S30} model is also shown for comparison due to the prevalence of slope-based V_{S30} as a GMM site term. The regional geologic unit and slope-based V_{S30} model performs comparably to the one-parameter model using the regional geologic unit as the only site parameter.

Figure 9 indicates that the V_{S30}- and $Z_{1.0}$-based models perform better than the continuous geospatial-based models that do not include the categorical regional geologic unit parameter. The V_{S30}-based model includes proxy-based values for V_{S30} inferred from geologic units in California; these inferred values occur at 76% of the stations in the dataset. The inclusion of this geologic information by proxy contributes to the performance of the V_{S30}- and $Z_{1.0}$-based models in California. In regions without V_{S30} values inferred from geology, the performance of a continuous geospatial-based model that does not include the geologic unit compared to a V_{S30}- and $Z_{1.0}$-based model would be expected to be different.

The final geospatial-based model, which combines categorical (regional geologic unit) and continuous (roughness) geospatial inputs, not only reduces the standard deviation of the site-to-site residuals compared to a refit ergodic model (V_{S30}- and $Z_{1.0}$-based), but also effectively captures the regional biases that are present in the site terms of BSSA14 when it is applied to this broader dataset. Figure 10 shows the site-to-residuals ($\delta S2S$) relative to the BSSA14 site term scaling as calculated using equation (2); the regional "hot spots" of clustered negative (yellow) and positive (dark purple) site-to-site residuals relative to BSSA14 V_{S30} scaling are largely diminished by the geospatial model, specifically in northern California for PGA and the Sierra Nevada for PSA at 1 s.

MODEL EVALUATION AT A LOCAL SCALE

A benefit of including the regional geologic unit as part of the site term is it differentiates small regions in California based on geology, allowing part of the site term to be fit using regional data, that is, data within the specific geomorphic province and geologic unit. This approach creates a model that is applicable throughout the state, while also being regionally calibrated. This process is beneficial because it prevents the model from being overfit to regions with high station density, like Los Angeles and San Francisco. The regional geologic units in provinces outside of these high-density areas are fit only to the data in their regions for the regional geologic unit portion of the site term. At the same time, the areas of high station density benefit from the large volume of data within their regional geologic units, which improves the resolution of the site term specific to those regions.

Los Angeles County contains 192 stations, and the San Francisco Bay area, which includes San Francisco, Alameda, Contra Costa, Napa, Santa Clara, Solano, San Mateo, Marin, and Sonoma counties, contains 647 stations. Figure 11 shows the comparison of the standard deviation of the site-to-site residuals calculated following equation (2) across all stations in California, stations only in Los Angeles County, and stations only in the San Francisco Bay area using the proposed geospatial site term model from equation (7). The site-to-site residuals from BSSA14 for these stations are also included for comparison.

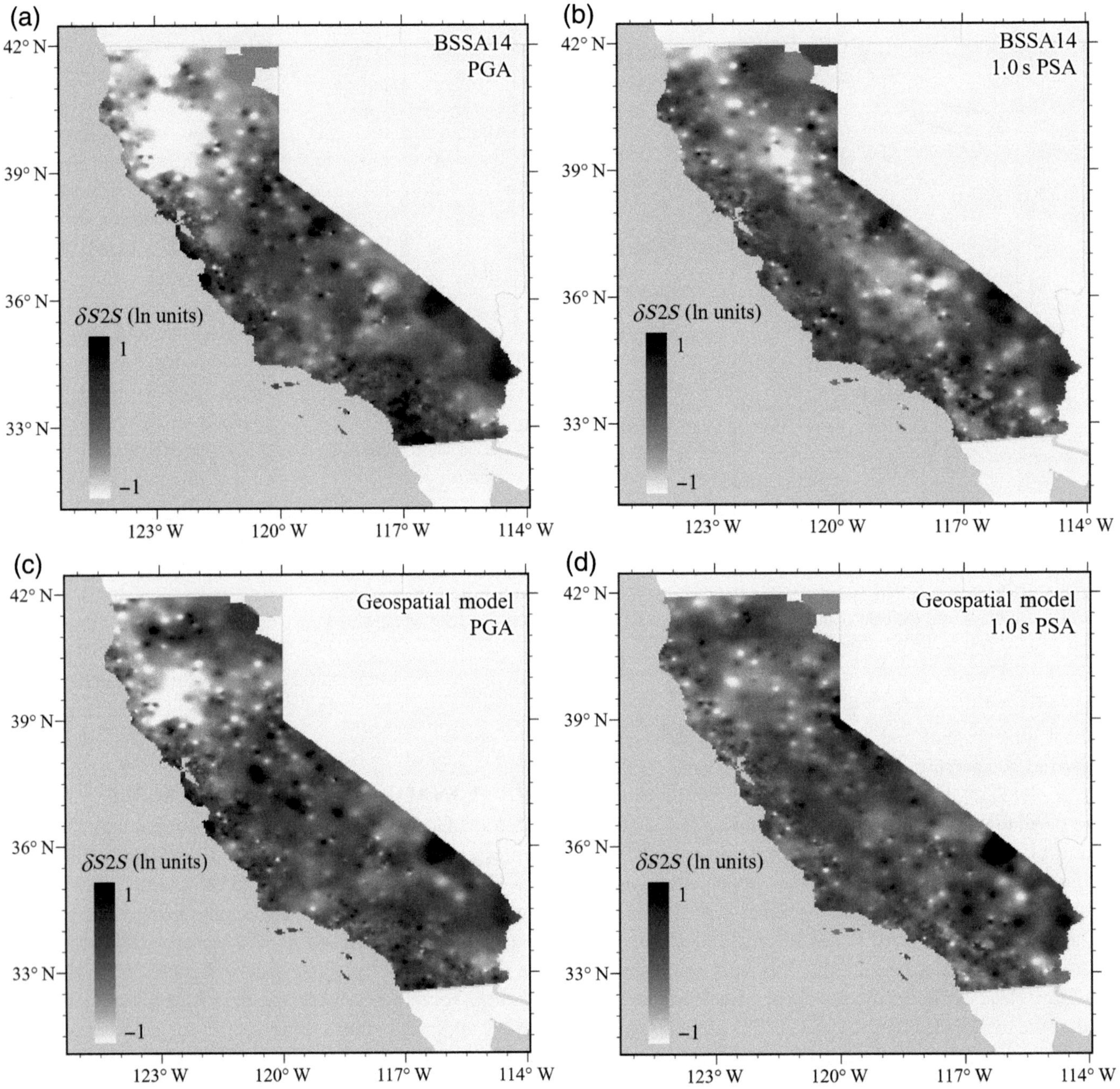

Figure 10. Comparison of site-to-site residuals ($\delta S2S$) relative to the site term scaling using inverse distance weighted (IDW) interpolation between sites for (a) the BSSA14 Next Generation Attenuation (NGA)-West2 model for PGA, and (b) the combined geospatial model in this study using regional geologic unit and roughness for PGA. Comparisons are also provided for PSA at a period of 1 s for (c) BSSA14 and (d) the combined geospatial model developed in this study. The color version of this figure is available only in the electronic edition.

Figure 11 indicates that the standard deviation of the site-to-site residuals (ϕ_{S2S}) using the geospatial site term model is, on average, lower than that of the BSSA14 model for both the average statewide and local station groups of Los Angeles County and the San Francisco Bay area. In Los Angeles, there is a large reduction in residuals at periods greater than 1 s (11.8% on average) and an average reduction in ϕ_{S2S} of 4.3% across all periods, compared to BSSA14. In the San Francisco Bay area, there is an average reduction of 4.7% across all periods evaluated. This reduction is relatively constant across all periods, with the exception of three periods from 3 to 5 s. The average reduction in ϕ_{S2S} in both regions demonstrates the advantage of the geospatial models at local scales and shows the benefit from the regional nature of the site terms.

Los Angeles County and the San Francisco Bay area are regions of high population and high seismic hazard. An important benefit of the proposed model is its ability to offer improved predictions of site amplification in these regions; because this is a spatially available model for California, there

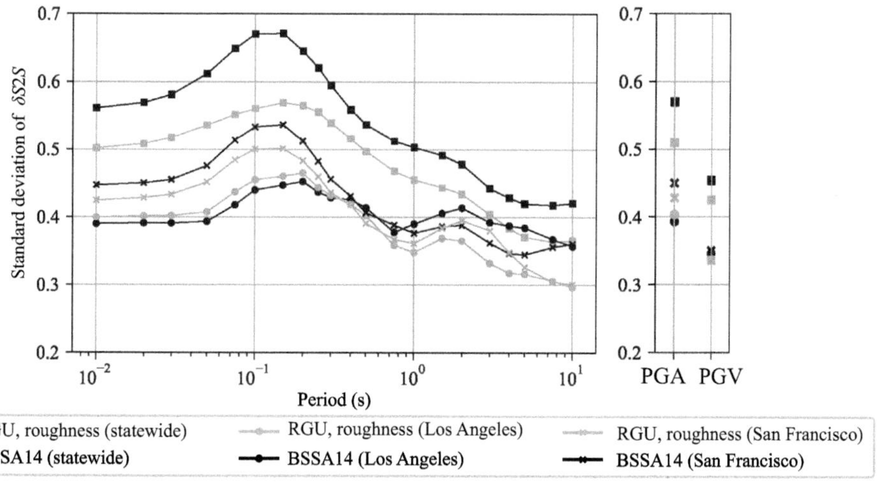

Figure 11. Comparison of the standard deviation of $\delta S2S$ relative to site term scaling between the optimal geospatial model and the BSSA14 NGA-West2 model, for the following groups of sites: statewide for all of California, for Los Angeles County, and for the San Francisco Bay area. The color version of this figure is available only in the electronic edition.

is no need for additional local data for implementation. However, local geotechnical data can be used to enhance the model at a site-specific level and address the over- and under-prediction still observed in the model. This approach is demonstrated in a companion article (M. Roberts *et al.*, unpublished manuscript 2025, see Data and Resources), where site-specific V_{S30} measurements and horizontal-to-vertical spectral ratio (HVSR) measurements can be implemented to adjust the predicted site term and further capture site amplification variability beyond the regional trends.

DISCUSSION

The geospatial site term model framework presented herein provides a globally applicable approach to site term development and aligns with the recent trends toward regional ground-motion modeling. Our novel approach of including the regional geologic unit adds a geology-based regionalization of the model, and the inclusion of the continuous geospatial term allows for geospatial-based interpolation throughout each unit. This model is designed for use in California as a linear site term relative to the BSSA14 reference condition and provides improvements compared to the ergodic models currently used in California, and is applicable across a greater region than local models such as Parker and Baltay (2022). The methodology used to develop the model could also be applied in other regions. A geospatial site term model is beneficial in areas without high station density or site-specific velocity measurements.

The model is developed using the DesignSafe Ground-Motion Dataset (Ji *et al.*, 2022). This dataset was selected for its wide station coverage in California to represent the broad range of geologic features across the state. The Ji *et al.* (2022) dataset is an automatically processed dataset and does not include the exhaustive data cleaning that has occurred in NGA-West2. Although outliers were removed and the data were filtered, there could still be errors in some of the recordings. These errors could contribute to the higher variability in $\delta S2S$ compared to the BSSA14 model (fig. 4.46 of Al Atik, 2015), particularly for PGA and at short periods (below 0.5 s). Given this limitation, the model presented here serves as a methodological proof-of-concept for developing geospatial site terms and may result in biased site terms at short periods. Because more rigorously processed datasets become available with greater coverage across California, this methodology could be replicated for the purposes of model development and use in California.

The site terms presented here lead to differences in predicted site amplification compared to the BSSA14 model. The difference between the linear site term from BSSA14 and the geospatial model presented here can be seen in Figure S9. The areas with the greatest change are in northern California, the Sierra Nevada mountain range, and the Central Valley; these regions historically had few ground motions included in GMM development (Fig. S7). However, within the framework of the geospatial model, more ground motions are included from these areas, and the site terms are fit to ground motions within the local geology. Smaller-scale changes can also be observed in Los Angeles and the San Francisco Bay area. These changes are largely dependent on the regional geologic unit of the station, which captures local geologic properties that influence the amplification at the station.

The model contains estimates of both aleatory variability and epistemic uncertainty. There is additional uncertainty in the use of point estimates of $\delta S2S$ to fit the model, which can contribute to underestimation of the aleatory variability components (Campbell *et al.*, 2025). This uncertainty was accounted for by fitting the model using weighted least-squares regression, in which the $\delta S2S$ estimates with less error are given a higher weight in the model. A more robust way to develop future geospatial-based site term models and account for this uncertainty for use in PSHAs would be to fit all model parameters for the event, path, and site terms together during the model development, as is recommended by Kuehn *et al.* (2025).

The proposed geospatial site term model is constrained to California due to the regional nature of the regional geologic unit map, which can be seen in Figure S1. The continuous-variable geospatial model (using sediment thickness and roughness) could be applied to regions outside of California by refitting the model to region-specific data because sediment thickness and roughness are globally available parameters. To develop a comparable geology-based site term, surficial geology and geomorphic provinces should be compiled. Another constraint for future development of geology-based site terms is the need for station coverage across the range of geologic and physiographic regions. Modifying methods to account for uncertainty and gaps in geologic data will be an important step for model development in other regions.

Although proxy-based values derived from models for geotechnical measures, V_{S30} and $Z_{1.0}$, were not shown to improve the model, site-specific geotechnical data such as V_{S30}, $Z_{1.0}$ or fundamental resonance frequency (f_0) could be used as a second step to reduce $\delta S2S$ variability. This methodology is explored in California (see companion article: M. Roberts *et al.*, unpublished manuscript 2025, see Data and Resources), where measured V_{S30} and HVSR data are readily available. The proposed improved ergodic model here presents the base model for producing geologically informed site terms and their efficacy, and similar methods would apply to regions globally without the need for measured or proxy geotechnical data. The methods are applicable even in regions without geologic data. For cases in which geologic data are not available, we propose a geospatial site term derived solely from globally continuous data (using sediment thickness and roughness) that achieves reasonable performance without any measured or inferred geotechnical data (V_{S30} or $Z_{1.0}$) or geologic maps.

CONCLUSIONS

In this article, we develop a geospatial-based linear site term model relative to the BSSA14 reference condition of $V_{S30} = 760$ m/s for California. The model is developed for PGA, PGV, and 5% damped PSA from 0.01 to 10 s. A subset of the Ji *et al.* (2022) DesignSafe Ground-Motion Database, containing 2339 stations across California, is used for model development.

The optimal geospatial site term model is developed using a combination of categorical and continuous site variables. We introduce a new categorical variable, the regional geologic unit, derived from surficial geologic units and geomorphic provinces, to capture the influence of local surface geology on site amplification. Variables are selected using a fivefold cross-validation approach to determine the optimal set of geospatial variables, resulting in the regional geologic unit as the preferred categorical variable and roughness as the preferred continuous variable. Roughness is derived from elevation and captures the topography of a location, which is a proxy for soil stiffness and is correlated with V_{S30}. The addition of the continuous secondary site parameter, roughness, allows for informed interpolation across regional geologic units.

The geospatial site term model results in a significant reduction in site-to-site residual variability (ϕ_{S2S}) compared to the traditional geotechnical-based models using V_{S30} and $Z_{1.0}$. The proposed model effectively captures large-scale regional patterns in the site term through improved site parameters that capture site and basin effects. Local site amplification patterns can be replicated in a similar way to varying coefficient models (VCMs), but with a simpler implementation due to the ergodic approach used here. The geospatial site term model uses continuously available geospatial data to eliminate the need for inferred values in geotechnical-based models or statistical interpolation in VCMs.

Our geospatial-based site term model is intended to capture the average linear site amplification (relative to the BSSA14 reference condition of $V_{S30} = 760$ m/s) and improve ground-motion estimates across California. The approach of using continuous geospatial variables in combination with regional geologic classification could be applied in other regions outside of California and would be particularly beneficial in regions with limited, sparse data.

DATA AND RESOURCES

The earthquake ground motions were obtained from the Ji *et al.* (2022) DesignSafe Ground-Motion Database (doi: 10.17603/ds2-syc5-nk92). The data were processed to obtain ground-motion predictions using the BSSA14 ground-motion model (GMM) (Boore *et al.*, 2014) coded and available at https://github.com/bakerjw/GMMs/blob/master/gmms/bssa_2014_active.m (Mongold and Baker, 2021) (last accessed September 2025). All geospatial, geotechnical, and geologic data used as potential model parameters are publicly available, and their sources are listed in Table 1. The analysis was performed using the open-source environment Python (Python Software Foundation, 2023). All figures were produced using Python, ArcGIS Pro (Environmental Systems Institute, 2024), and Adobe Illustrator (Adobe Inc., 2019). The roughness raster and regional unit shapefile can also be viewed on the Tufts Geohazards website at https://experience.arcgis.com/experience/b8820d20ed9b47a7b6e4e9ed8e95602a/ (last accessed November 2025). The unpublished manuscript by M. Roberts *et al.* "HVSR and V_{S30} Based Adjustment Terms for Geospatial Site Amplification Models for California," 2025, under review, submitted to Civil and Environmental Engineering, Tufts University.

The supplemental material for this article contains Figures S1–S9 and Tables S1–S4 in Microsoft Excel format. Figure S1 shows a high-resolution map of the regional geologic units. Figures S2–S5 are quality control checks for the subset of the DesignSafe dataset used for model development. Figure S2 shows plots of the total residuals versus distance and plots of the remaining residuals (after linear mixed-effects regression) versus distance. Figure S3 shows plots of peak ground acceleration (PGA) versus distance binned by magnitude. Figures S4 and S5 show plots of short-period scaling: remaining residuals versus **M** for $T = 0.1$ s binned by V_{S30} and distance, and remaining residuals versus distance for $T = 0.1$ s binned by V_{S30} and **M**, respectively. Figure S6 shows plots of site amplification versus each continuous geospatial parameter evaluated. Figure S7 shows a map of the stations in the subset of the Ji *et al.* (2022) dataset used in this study and indicates which stations are in the Next Generation Attenuation (NGA)-West2 dataset (Ancheta *et al.*, 2014). Figure S8 shows maps of the mean and standard error estimates of the site term relative to the BSSA14 reference condition following equations (7) and

(10), respectively, for PGA and pseudospectral acceleration (PSA) at $T = 1$ s. Figure S9 shows maps of the difference between the linear site term using BSSA14 and the linear site term using the geospatial model (regional geologic unit and roughness-based) for PGA and PSA at 1 s. Table S1 provides sources and definitions for all site parameters evaluated for use in the model. Table S2 provides coefficients for the geospatial site term (equation 7) that uses regional geologic unit and roughness as parameters, and the epistemic uncertainty for the parameters. Table S3 provides coefficients for the alternate geospatial site term (equation 8) that uses only continuous variables (sediment thickness and topographic roughness index). Table S4 provides aleatory variability values by period for the regional geologic unit and roughness model, including ϕ (the total aleatory variability) and its components ϕ_{SS} and ϕ_{S2S}. Also provided as a supplement is a zip file (File S1) containing a shapefile of the regional geologic units and a raster file of roughness. File S1 can be available at https://cloud.seismosoc.org/s/iwBCb9fGaFebytT (last accessed September 2025). The roughness map is in raster format and is derived from GMTED2010 (Danielson and Gesch, 2011). The regional geologic unit is in shapefile format with an attribute table containing F_{RGU} (the associated categorical site term) in natural logarithm units for PGA, peak ground velocity (PGV), and 21 PSAs from 0.01 to 10 s associated with each regional geologic unit.

DECLARATION OF COMPETING INTERESTS

The authors acknowledge that there are no conflicts of interest recorded.

ACKNOWLEDGMENTS

The authors would like to acknowledge the feedback of Norman Abrahamson and an anonymous reviewer, comments for which greatly improved the quality of this article. This material is based upon work supported by the U.S. Geological Survey (USGS) under Grant Numbers G23AP00396 and G23AP00397. The views and conclusions contained in this document are those of the authors and should not be interpreted as representing the opinions or policies of the USGS. Mention of trade names or commercial products does not constitute their endorsement by the USGS.

REFERENCES

Abrahamson, N. A., and R. R. Youngs (1992). A stable algorithm for regression analyses using the random effects model, *Bull. Seismol. Soc. Am.* **82,** 505–510.

Abrahamson, N. A., N. M. Kuehn, M. Walling, and N. Landwehr (2019). Probabilistic seismic hazard analysis in California using nonergodic ground-motion models, *Bull. Seismol. Soc. Am.* **109,** 1235–1249.

Adobe Inc. (2019). Adobe Illustrator, available at https://adobe.com/products/illustrator (last accessed September 2025).

Al Atik, L. (2015). Ground motion standard deviation models for central and eastern North America, *Pacific Earthquake Engineerinsg Center, Rept. 2015/09,* University of California, Berkeley, California.

Alaska Satellite Facility (ASF) (2022). Global 30-m HAND. Produced using the Copernicus WorldDEM™-30 © DLR e.V. 2010-2014 and © Airbus Defence and Space GmbH 2014-2018 provided under COPERNICUS by the European Union and ESA.

Allen, T. I., and D. J. Wald (2009). On the use of high-resolution topographic data as a proxy for seismic site conditions (V_{S30}), *Bull. Seismol. Soc. Am.* **99,** 935–943.

Ancheta, T. D., R. B. Darragh, J. P. Stewart, E. Seyhan, W. J. Silva, B. S.-J. Chiou, K. E. Wooddell, R. W. Graves, A. R. Kottke, D. M. Boore, and T. Kishida (2014). NGA-West2 database, *Earthq. Spectra* **30,** 989–1005.

Anderson, J. G., and J. N. Brune (1999). Probabilistic seismic hazard analysis without the ergodic assumption, *Sesimol. Res. Lett.* **70,** 19–28.

Bilodeau, W. L., S. W. Bilodeau, E. M. Gath, M. Oborne, and R. J. Proctor (2007). Geology of Los Angeles, California, United States of America, *Environ. Eng. Geoscience,* **13,** no. 2, 99–160.

Boore, D. M., J. P. Stewart, E. Seyhan, and G. M. Atkinson (2014). NGA-West2 equations for predicting PGA, PGV, and 5% damped PSA for shallow crustal earthquakes, *Earthq. Spectra* **30,** 1057–1085.

Bozorgnia, Y., N. A. Abrahamson, L. A. Atik, T. D. Ancheta, G. M. Atkinson, J. W. Baker, A. Baltay, D. M. Boore, K. W. Campbell, B. S.-J. Chiou, *et al.* (2014). NGA-West2 research project, *Earthq. Spectra* **30,** 973–987.

Brocher, T. M., B. T. Aagaard, R. W. Simpson, and R. C. Jachens (2006). The USGS 3D seismic velocity model for northern California, *Presented at the 2006 Fall Meeting of the American Geophysical Union,* San Francisco, California, 11–15 December 2006, Abstract S51B–1266.

California Geological Survey (2002). *California Geomorphic Provinces,* California Department of Conservation, available at https://www.conservation.ca.gov (last accessed March 2024).

Campbell, K. W., N. M. Kuehn, and Y. Bozorgnia (2025). Variability and uncertainty of variance components in fixed-effects and mixed-effects ground-motion models, *Earthq. Spectra* **41,** 731–752.

Chiou, B. J., and R. R. Youngs (2008). An NGA model for the average horizontal component of peak ground motion and response spectra, *Earthq. Spectra* **24,** 173–215.

Daly, C., G. Taylor, W. Patterson;, and National Climatic Data Center (U.S.), National Water and Climate Center (U.S.), and U.S. Defense Mapping Agency (2007). Average Annual Precipitation (Inches): California, California Department of Fish and Game, Marine Resources Region, Raster data, available at https://purl.stanford.edu/td754wr4701 (last accessed March 2024).

Danielson, J. J., and D. B. Gesch (2011). Global multi-resolution terrain elevation data 2010 (GMTED2010), *U.S. Geol. Surv. Open-File Rept. 2011–1073,* 26 p.

Environmental Systems Institute (2024). *ArcGIS Pro,* Esri, available at https://www.esri.com (last accessed March 2024).

Fan, Y., H. Li, and G. Miguez-Macho (2013). Global patterns of groundwater table depth, *Science* **339,** no. 6122, 940–943.

Fisher, R. A. (1925). *Statistical Methods for Research Workers,* Oliver and Boyd.

Fumal, T. E. (1978). Correlations between seismic wave velocities and physical properties of near-surface geologic materials in the southern San Francisco Bay region, California, *U.S. Geol. Surv. Open-File Rept. 78-1067.*

Gregor, N., N. A. Abrahamson, G. M. Atkinson, D. M. Boore, Y. Bozorgnia, K. W. Campbell, B. S. J. Chiou, I. M. Idriss, R. Kamai, E. Seyhan, *et al.* (2014). Comparison of NGA-West2 GMPEs, *Earthq. Spectra* **30,** 1179–1197.

Iwahashi, J., and R. J. Pike (2007). Automated classifications of topography from DEMs by an unsupervised nested-means algorithm and a three-part geometric signature, *Geomorphology* **86,** 409–440.

Ji, C., A. Cabas, A. Kottke, M. Pilz, J. Macedo, and C. Liu (2022). A DesignSafe Ground Motion Database: time series, engineering metrics, and site metadata, v2, *DesignSafe-CI*, doi: 10.17603/ds2-syc5-nk92.

Ji, C., A. Cabas, A. Kottke, M. Pilz, J. Macedo, and C. Liu (2023). A DesignSafe earthquake ground motion database for California and surrounding regions, *Earthq. Spectra* **39,** 702–721.

Kaklamanos, J., A. Cabas, S. Parolai, and P. Guéguen (2021). Introduction to the special section on advances in site response estimation, *Bull. Seismol. Soc. Am.* **111,** 1665–1676.

Kawase, H. (2003). Site effects on strong ground motions, *Geophys. J. Int.* **81,** 1013–1030.

Kuehn, N. M., K. W. Campbell, and Y. Bozorgnia (2025). Potential biases in mixed-effects ground-motion models and variance components due to uncertainty in random effects. *Bull. Seismol. Soc. Am.* **115,** 578–601.

Landwehr, N., N. M. Kuehn, T. Scheffer, and N. Abrahamson (2016). A nonergodic ground-motion model for California with spatially varying coefficients, *Bull. Seismol. Soc. Am.* **106,** 2574–2583.

Lavrentiadis, G., N. A. Abrahamson, and N. M. Kuehn (2023). A nonergodic effective amplitude ground-motion model for California, *Bull. Earthq. Eng.* **21,** no. 11, 5233–5264.

Lee, E. J., P. Chen, T. H. Jordan, P. J. Maechling, M. A. Denolle, and G. C. Beroza (2014). Full- 3-D tomography for crustal structure in southern California based on the scattering-integral and the adjoint-wavefield methods, *J. Geophys. Res.* **119,** 6421–6451.

Lehner, B., K. Verdin, and A. Jarvis (2008). New global hydrography derived from spaceborne elevation data, *Eos Trans. AGU* **89,** 93–94, doi: 10.1029/2008EO100001.

Loviknes, K., F. Cotton, and G. Weatherill (2024). Exploring inferred geomorphological sediment thickness as a new site proxy to predict ground-shaking amplification at regional scale: application to Europe and eastern Türkiye, *Nat. Hazards Earth Syst. Sci.* **24,** 1223–1247.

McPhillips, D. F., J. A. Herrick, S. Ahdi, A. K. Yong, and S. Haefner (2020). Updated Compilation of V_{S30} data for the United States, *U.S. Geol. Surv. Data Release.* doi: 10.5066/P9H5QEAC.

Mongold, E., and J. W. Baker (2021). A software repository of ground motion models—Version 1.0.0 Blume Earthquake Engineering Center, *Technical Rept 207. Stanford Digital Repository*, available at https://purl.stanford.edu/qy113my5899 (last accessed September 2025).

National Aeronautics and Space Administration (NASA) Ocean Biology Processing Group (OBPG), and R. P. Stumpf (2012). *Distance to Nearest Coastline: 0.04-Degree Grid,* Distributed by Pacific Islands Ocean Observing System (PacIOOS), available at http://pacioos.org/metadata/dist2coast_4deg.html (last accessed March 2024).

Parker, G. A., and A. S. Baltay (2022). Empirical map-based nonergodic models of site response in the greater Los Angeles area, *Bull. Seismol. Soc. Am.* **112,** 1607–1629.

Pelletier, J. D., P. D. Broxton, P. Hazenberg, X. Zeng, P. A. Troch, G.-Y. Niu, Z. Williams, M. A. Brunke, and D. Gochis (2016). A gridded global data set of soil, immobile regolith, and sedimentary deposit thicknesses for regional and global land surface modeling, *J. Adv. Model. Earth Syst.* **8,** 41–65.

Python Software Foundation (2023). Python Language Reference, version 3.9.10, available at https://www.python.org (last accessed September 2025).

Small, P., D. Gill, P. J. Maechling, R. Taborda, S. Callaghan, T. H. Jordan, G. P. Ely, K. B. Olsen, and C. A. Goulet (2017). The SCEC Unified Community Velocity Model software framework, *Seismol. Res. Lett.* **88,** 1539–1552.

Sung, C. H., H. Miyake, N. Abrahamson, and N. Morikawa (2024). Nonergodic ground-motion models for subduction zone and crustal earthquakes in Japan, *Bull. Seismol. Soc. Am.* **114,** 1717–1738.

Thompson, E. M., and D. J. Wald (2016). Uncertainty in V_{S30}-based site response. *Bull. Seismol. Soc. Am.*, **106,** 453–463.

Thompson, E. M., D. J. Wald, and C. B. Worden (2014). A V_{S30} map for California with geologic and topographic constraints, *Bull. Seismol. Soc. Am.* **104,** 2313–2321.

Verdin, K. L. (2017). Hydrologic derivatives for modeling and analysis —A new global high-resolution database, *U.S. Geol. Surv. Data Ser. No. 1053*, doi: 10.3133/ds1053.

Weatherill, G., S. R. Kotha, and F. Cotton (2020). Re-thinking site amplification in regional seismic risk assessment. *Earthq. Spectra* **36,** 274–297.

Wills, C. J., C. I. Gutierrez, F. G. Perez, and D. M. Branum (2015). A next generation V_{S30} map for California based on geology and topography, *Bull. Seismol. Soc. Am.* **105,** 3083–3091.

Yong, A., S. E. Hough, J. Iwahashi, and A. Braverman (2012). A terrain-based site-conditions map of California with implications for the contiguous United States, *Bull. Seismol. Soc. Am.* **102,** 114–128.

Zhan, W., L. G. Baise, and J. Kaklamanos (2025). A geospatial model for site response complexity, *Soil Dynam. Earthq. Eng.* **192,** 109,282.

Zhan, W., L. G. Baise, and B. Moaveni (2023). An uncertainty quantification framework for logistic regression based geospatial natural hazard modeling, *Eng. Geol.* **324,** 107271.

Zhu, C., F. Cotton, H. Kawase, and K. Nakano (2023). How well can we predict earthquake site response so far? Machine learning vs physics-based modeling, *Earthq. Spectra* **39,** 478–504.

Manuscript received 3 April 2025
Published online 3 December 2025

HVSR- and V_{S30}-Based Adjustment Terms for Geospatial Site Amplification Models for California

Maggie Roberts*[1], Laurie G. Baise[1], James Kaklamanos[2], Weiwei Zhan[3], Shiying Nie[1], and Elise Meyer[1]

ABSTRACT

This study presents a geotechnical site term for ground-motion models (GMMs) in California derived from horizontal-to-vertical spectral ratio (HVSR) and V_{S30} (time-averaged shear-wave velocity in the upper 30 m) data that can be used with a geospatial linear site model when measured geotechnical data are available. Spatially continuous site models, such as those based on geospatial data, have advantages for GMM implementation in that they provide a consistent site term for locations that lack measured geotechnical data. We propose enhancing these models with local geotechnical information where it is available. The proposed model was developed using microtremor HVSR (mHVSR; Wang *et al.*, 2021), earthquake HVSR (eHVSR; Ji *et al.*, 2022), and measured V_{S30} data (Ahdi *et al.*, 2018; McPhillips *et al.*, 2020; Kwak *et al.*, 2021). The geotechnical parameters are analyzed for their ability to reduce site-to-site variability of peak ground acceleration, peak ground velocity, and pseudospectral accelerations from 0.01 to 10 s calculated from the residuals of the Boore *et al.* (2014; BSSA14) GMM, modified with a geospatial-based site term (Roberts *et al.*, 2025). Geotechnical site terms are developed for sites with a V_{S30} measurement and for sites with mHVSR recordings that have a clear fundamental resonance peak or that meet the criteria of a flat recording. Compared to the base geospatial site term, the inclusion of the geotechnical site term results in an average reduction to the site-to-site variability of 6.5% for stations with V_{S30} measurements and 5.7% for stations with mHVSR measurements. This study illustrates the effectiveness of using geotechnical measurements to enhance geospatial linear site term models. We also highlight the potential for using the cost-effective HVSR technique to develop GMM site terms, using both eHVSR and mHVSR data, and sites with clear fundamental resonance frequencies and those without clear resonances.

KEY POINTS

- Geospatial site terms in ground-motion models (GMMs) can be enhanced with geotechnical measurements (horizontal-to-vertical spectral ratio [HVSR] and V_{S30} data).
- Our geotechnical site terms reduce site-to-site variability and capture site-specific effects.
- This approach demonstrates methods for using measured V_{S30} and low-cost HVSR data for future GMM development.

Supplemental Material

INTRODUCTION

Earthquake ground-motion models (GMMs) capture source, path, and site effects to estimate ground shaking at a site for a given earthquake and are used to inform seismic hazard assessments. Site effects are often represented in GMMs using the time-averaged shear-wave velocity in the upper 30 m (V_{S30}) and the depths to the 1 and/or 2.5 km/s shear-wave velocity horizons ($Z_{1.0}$ and $Z_{2.5}$, respectively). These parameters are used to capture sediment stiffness and thickness at a site and are used to predict site response. However, measured values for these parameters are often sparse and unavailable for sites with ground-motion recordings and are generally unavailable for the regional application of GMMs. In contrast, geospatial parameters, such as surficial geology, sediment thickness,

1. Department of Civil and Environmental Engineering, Tufts University, Medford, Massachusetts, U.S.A., https://orcid.org/0009-0000-9036-4921 (MR); https://orcid.org/0000-0002-8329-5689 (LGB); https://orcid.org/0000-0002-3518-7843 (SN); https://orcid.org/0009-0009-2684-9233 (EM); 2. Department of Civil Engineering, Merrimack College, North Andover, Massachusetts, U.S.A., https://orcid.org/0000-0001-7480-0391 (JK); 3. Department of Civil, Environmental and Construction Engineering, University of Central Florida, Orlando, Florida, U.S.A., https://orcid.org/0000-0002-9266-4466 (WZ)

*Corresponding author: Maggie.Roberts@tufts.edu

Cite this article as Roberts, M., L. G. Baise, J. Kaklamanos, W. Zhan, S. Nie, and E. Meyer (2026). HVSR- and V_{S30}-Based Adjustment Terms for Geospatial Site Amplification Models for California, *Bull. Seismol. Soc. Am.* **116**, 1219–1239, doi: 10.1785/0120250175 and topographic slope, can be used to develop GMM site terms. These parameters offer continuous values for all locations in a study area without the need for combining measurements and proxies. Geospatial site terms can then be adjusted by adding geotechnical site terms at locations where these parameters are measured, thereby reducing uncertainty at sites with available site-specific geotechnical data.

V_{S30}, which has traditionally been used to characterize site conditions, serves as a primary site parameter in all the Next Generation Attenuation-West2 Project (NGA-West2) models (Abrahamson *et al.*, 2014; Boore *et al.*, 2014; Campbell and Bozorgnia, 2014; Chiou and Youngs, 2014; Idriss, 2014). In the NGA-West2 dataset (Ancheta *et al.*, 2014), 28% of the ground-motion stations in California have a measured V_{S30} value. Here, we propose the use of V_{S30} measurements as a secondary adjustment for site terms to be used only when a measured V_{S30} value is available at a site. We take this approach due to the inconsistency in proxy-based V_{S30} compared to measured V_{S30} (Yong, 2016) and the lack of V_{S30} measurements across California. Proxy-based V_{S30} values have been developed from geomorphology, including slope (Wald and Allen, 2007), terrain (Yong *et al.*, 2012), geology (e.g., Wills and Clahan, 2006), and a combination of both geology and surface slope (e.g., Wills *et al.*, 2015) to estimate V_{S30}. Such proxies estimate V_{S30} from averages within each geologic unit or a given geomorphology classification, and there are often inconsistencies between estimated and measured V_{S30} values at a given site (Kaklamanos and Baise, 2011; Seyhan *et al.*, 2014). In addition, discrepancies may be introduced when multiple proxies are used.

We choose to use measured V_{S30} as a site parameter due to the strong correlation of V_{S30} to ground-motion amplification, particularly in California (e.g., Boore and Joyner, 1997, Boore *et al.*, 1997). The V_{S30}-based GMM site term parameter has been shown to effectively estimate linear site effects in the western United States, most notably in the NGA-West2 GMMs (Abrahamson *et al.*, 2014; Boore *et al.*, 2014; Campbell and Bozorgnia, 2014; Chiou and Youngs, 2014). In this work, we utilize the established relationship between V_{S30} and site amplification, but implement V_{S30} as a secondary site parameter so that the site term is only applied where measured V_{S30} values are available.

Horizontal-to-vertical spectral ratios (HVSRs, Nogoshi and Igarashi, 1971; Nakamura, 1989) are a site-specific technique for characterizing sites and are considered for use as a geotechnical site term to adjust the base geospatial model. The HVSR is computed as the ratio of the amplitude spectrum of the horizontal components to the amplitude spectrum of the vertical component, using recordings from either microtremors or earthquake ground motions (termed as mHVSR and eHVSR, respectively). HVSRs, which provide efficient and cost-effective geotechnical measurements, have been shown to correlate with site effects (Lermo and Chávez-Garcia, 1993). Because both mHVSR and eHVSR measurements are available across California, HVSRs are viable geotechnical measurements to be explored for a GMM site term. HVSRs are predominantly used for approximating the site fundamental resonant frequency (f_0) from the fundamental resonance peak of the HVSR (Nakamura, 1989). It is widely recognized that HVSRs are adequate at predicting the site f_0 but not the corresponding amplitude (Nakamura, 1989; Lermo and Chávez-García, 1993; Carpenter *et al.*, 2020).

The Site Effects Assessment Using Ambient Excitations (SESAME) project, a European Commission contract to build consensus on HVSR use guidelines, provides a set of criteria for determining if an HVSR curve has a clear peak. SESAME outlines a set of criteria for both the reliability of the HVSR curves and the clarity of the peak that need to be met to identify a resonance peak from an HVSR recording. The SESAME criteria ensure that peak detection is a standardized process across studies (Site Effects Assessment using Ambient Excitations [SESAME], 2004). The SESAME criteria are often more strict than what expert judgment might indicate are clear peaks, as found by Wang *et al.* (2023) in analyzing HVSR data from sites in California. Sites with peaks at high frequencies can be missed when the SESAME criteria are applied, compared to expert judgment or alternative peak determination algorithms (Wang *et al.*, 2023). Despite these limitations, the SESAME criteria are used in this study to identify clear HVSR peaks because the strict criteria ensure the model is being fit to distinctly clear peaks, and the criteria allow for an easily implementable method for analyzing whether peaks should be used by model users. The SESAME criteria have been used to identify clear peaks for model development, such as in the Pinilla-Ramos *et al.* (2022) HVSR-based site term for California, and will be used in this study. Alternative methods for identifying clear peaks include using regression tree algorithms (Wang *et al.*, 2023) or alternative peak selection criteria (Hassani and Atkinson, 2016a). The clarity and strict nature of the SESAME criteria facilitate both model development and use for the use case presented here.

The determination of the site resonance frequency from HVSR data has been particularly useful in classifying site response in resonant sediments due to its simplicity and low cost (Lermo and Chávez-Garcia, 1993; Carpenter *et al.*, 2018; Zhu *et al.*, 2020). In addition, the use of site resonance frequency as a predictor variable to estimate site effects in GMMs has shown success in several regions globally. The resonance peak from the HVSR curve with the largest amplitude is often evaluated, and the peak resonant frequency (f_p) has been used to represent the primary site response of the soil in several studies, including Ghofrani and Atkinson (2014), Braganza *et al.* (2016), and Hassani and Atkinson (2016a,b, 2018). The fundamental frequency (f_0), the first significant peak within the frequency range being evaluated, has also been used in GMM development (e.g., Kwak *et al.*, 2017). The peak resonant frequency (f_p) will be used in this study due to its success as a

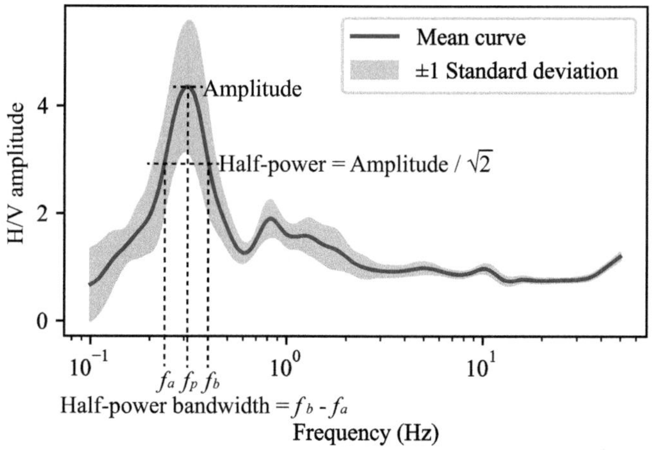

Figure 1. Illustration of horizontal-to-vertical spectral ratio (HVSR) parameters evaluated in this study: peak resonance frequency (f_p), peak amplitude, and the half-power bandwidth (HPB; bounded by the frequencies f_a and f_b). The color version of this figure is available only in the electronic edition.

GMM site parameter in prior models and its significance in determining the primary site response of the soil.

Site term models developed using HVSR data have also been evaluated using additional parameters from the HVSR curve, including the peak amplitude (e.g., Ghofrani and Atkinson, 2014; Yazdi *et al.*, 2023) and the normalized HVSR amplitude (e.g., Pinilla-Ramos *et al.*, 2022, 2024). In addition, sites without clear resonance peaks have been used to develop GMM site terms. Kwak *et al.* (2017) fit a fixed value as a site term for all sites without a clear peak identified to account for an overall bias observed in ground motions at sites without clear peaks.

In this work, we build on the prior work of utilizing HVSR parameters in GMMs by evaluating multiple HVSR parameters for their effectiveness as site terms, in combination with a geospatial base linear site term model. The parameters evaluated are the peak resonance frequency (f_p), the amplitude of the peak, and the half-power bandwidth (HPB, the difference between the two frequencies corresponding to $1/\sqrt{2}\times$ peak amplitude), shown in Figure 1, as well as a new classification system that defines flat versus nonflat recordings.

In addition, we evaluate the benefit of information that can be gained from both eHVSR and mHVSR to use both to develop a GMM site term. The correlation and differences between HVSR curves obtained from earthquake ground motions and from microtremors have been documented in the literature. Results from mHVSR have been corrected to eHVSR in Japan (Kawase *et al.*, 2019). Similarly, in California, the dominant site frequency derived from eHVSR was found to scale linearly with mHVSR measurements up to 300 m away (Hassani *et al.*, 2019). However, despite the correlation between the two measurements, they are not always equal at a site. An early comparison of eHVSR and mHVSR data at 20 sites within the Sendai basin in Japan (Satoh *et al.*, 2001) found that the resonant frequencies were comparable between the measurements at the sites with a thick layer of soft soil over hard rock, indicating a strong impedance contrast, but that the amplitude of the resonant frequency was not. More expansive studies across California have been conducted in recent years. Comparison of eHVSR and mHVSR curves at 297 sites predominantly in California by Wang *et al.* (2023) indicates there is between a 60% and 70% compatibility rate between mHVSR and eHVSR. Compatible stations include stations that neither have a clear peak identified with eHVSR nor mHVSR, and those that have peaks at similar frequencies. Wang *et al.* (2023) found that peaks identified at low frequencies using mHVSR data are often not identified in eHVSR data. In addition, a separate study of peak frequencies of eHVSR and mHVSR data obtained in California shows that 68% of observed flat eHVSR resonances were also flat for mHVSR, and 85% of observed eHVSR with at least one clear resonance also had at least one clear resonance for mHVSR (Vantassel *et al.*, 2024).

The differences present in these studies identify a challenge when trying to create and utilize HVSR datasets, particularly for developing GMMs, because the two methods do not always produce equivalent results. Despite differences in the two recording types, models developed for Taiwan showed that for PGA, site terms developed for mHVSR were comparable to terms developed for eHVSR (Chao *et al.*, 2021). The body of work surrounding eHVSR and mHVSR suggests that although the two recordings are not always equivalent, there is a correlation and a level of consistency between the two. Based on this correlation and the known inequalities, we develop a site term for California that is intended to be used only when mHVSR is obtained at a site; however, for comparison, we do analyze models that are fit using both eHVSR and mHVSR data, but we place additional uncertainty on the eHVSR data. In both the models developed using only mHVSR data and those developed using both mHVSR and supplemental eHVSR data, only mHVSR data are used to validate the models. The parameters from mHVSR curves are intended to be inputs to the model during model use because they can be obtained at any location without the need for a seismic station, and they are independent of the ground motions being predicted, making mHVSR parameters applicable for the prediction of ground motions due to future earthquakes (Wang *et al.*, 2023).

We have previously developed a geospatial-based linear site term for use with NGA-West2 GMMs (see companion article: Roberts *et al.*, 2025). This model uses continuously available geospatial parameters (regional geologic unit and roughness) to estimate the linear soil amplification term. For locations with site-specific measurements, such as HVSR and V_{S30} data, we can add this measured geotechnical information to the model to improve its accuracy and precision. This study investigates the use of measured V_{S30} and HVSR site terms to adjust the geospatial GMM site terms with local geotechnical data. When using only measured V_{S30} data, the residual reduction will be linked to the accuracy of the geotechnical measurement and kept separate from geospatial proxy-based site terms. HVSR site terms will be developed by evaluating the relationship between eHVSR and mHVSR curves, developing a classification system for flat curves, and examining multiple HVSR parameters (f_p, peak amplitude, and HPB) to inform the development of comprehensive HVSR site terms for use with GMMs in California. The resulting analysis will explicitly account for uncertainty reduction depending on the level of site characterization and lead to lower residuals in GMMs compared to the geospatial-only site terms when measured geotechnical data are available.

DATA

Ground motions and V_{S30} measurements

Earthquake ground motions are obtained from a subset of the stations in the DesignSafe ground-motion database (DSGMD; Ji *et al.*, 2022). The DSGMD, discussed further in Ji *et al.* (2023), contains more than 287,804 processed ground motions from 2641 earthquakes recorded at 3709 stations in and near California from 1999 to 2021. The DSGMD was selected for its wide station coverage in California to represent the broad range of geologic features across the state. We use the same subset of the database as in Roberts *et al.* (2025) by filtering the database to: (1) only include stations in California; (2) only include events that are shallow crustal earthquakes, to be compatible with the GMMs of the NGA West-2 project (Bozorgnia *et al.*, 2014), by removing events greater than 25 km deep and events within the Juan de Fuca subducting plate or on the Juan de Fuca plate boundary; (3) remove recordings flagged as outliers in the database (Ji *et al.*, 2022); (4) only include stations that have at least five recordings; (5) remove recordings without moment magnitudes reported; and (6) remove events that do not have at least 10 recordings for smaller magnitude events (**M** < 5) and at least three recordings for larger magnitude events (**M** ≥ 5). We also remove outlier recordings based on residual analysis, as described in Roberts *et al.* (2025), to alleviate errors that may be present in the DSGMD. The robust data cleaning that occurred in the development of the NGA-West2 database was not performed in the development of the DSGMD database because there was a stronger reliance on automatic processing due to the size of the DSGMD database. The automatic processing was performed using *gmprocess* (Hearne *et al.*, 2019); at the time of the DSGMD development, *gmprocess* had a default setting of a high-pass corner frequency that is lower than what is typically used during manual ground-motion processing. As a result, the automated processing could lead to bias over long periods (Buckreis *et al.*, 2025). Readers are referred to Roberts *et al.* (2025) for a discussion of the outlier removal process and analysis of bias and scaling for the subset of data used in this study. The final ground-motion database includes peak ground acceleration (PGA), peak ground velocity (PGV), and 5%-damped pseudospectral acceleration (PSA) for 95,898 recordings across 2339 stations.

V_{S30} measurements were also obtained from the shear-wave velocity profile database (VSPDB; Ahdi *et al.*, 2018; Kwak *et al.*, 2021), and the U.S. Geological Survey (USGS) V_{S30} database (McPhillips *et al.*, 2020). The DSGMD contains V_{S30} measurements from both the VSPDB and USGS V_{S30} database, assigned to ground-motion stations within 100 m of the measurement, for 427 DSGMD stations used in this study. We also accessed the VSPDB to add additional V_{S30} measurements within 100 m of stations; V_{S30} measurements were acquired for 60 additional stations in the dataset from the VSPDB. As a result, V_{S30} measurements are available for 487 DSGMD stations used in this study, representing 20.8% of the stations considered.

eHVSR data and processing

For eHVSR processing, we only used stations from the DSGMD (Ji *et al.*, 2022) that have at least four earthquake recordings, all with moment magnitudes 3.2–7.2, to ensure stability in the mean and standard deviation statistics of the eHVSR curves, resulting in 1486 processed stations. Earthquake recordings were measured by both accelerometers (46% of stations) and velocimeters (54% of stations).

The ground motions were downloaded from the DSGMD and then processed using *hvsrpy* (Vantassel, 2020). *Hvsrpy* is an open-source Python package for processing eHVSR and mHVSR data. The full earthquake record was processed for each recording at all stations. The ground motions were processed using a 20% Tukey window (10% off either end) in the time domain, smoothing the horizontal and vertical spectra using a Konno and Ohmachi (1998) window with a coefficient (*b*) of 40, resampling between 0.4 and 10 Hz with 128 points on a logarithmic scale, and combining the horizontal components using the geometric mean. To account for differences in sampling rates between earthquakes, frequency-domain resampling was performed. These processing settings are consistent with prior eHVSR processing performed in California (Vantassel *et al.*, 2024).

The fully automated frequency-domain window-rejection algorithm (Cox *et al.*, 2020) in *hvsrpy* was then applied to all the processed stations. The window-rejection algorithm increases HVSR data quality by rejecting windows with peak frequency outliers that are not representative of the site conditions and are instead contaminated by factors such as variability from ambient noise, environmental conditions, or instrument errors. The Cox *et al.* (2020) window rejection is an automated method that may remove windows that represent true variability in the site characteristics; however, we use this method for its benefit of removing poor-quality data in a consistent, objective manner compared to manual window rejection. The median and standard deviation values of the HVSR curves were calculated using all valid waveform windows, assuming a lognormal distribution; this calculation is consistent with the methodology proposed by Site Effects

Assessment using Ambient Excitations (SESAME) (2004) and Cox *et al.* (2020).

The SESAME criteria were then applied using *hvsrpy* to the lognormal median and standard deviation curves to identify whether a clear peak could be determined for each station. The SESAME guidelines require passing three reliability criteria and at least five of the six clarity criteria to verify a clear peak. These guidelines were strictly followed for all eHVSR stations. The peak resonant site frequency (f_p), amplitude of the peak resonant site frequency, and HPB parameters were extracted for all stations with a clear peak using *hvsrpy*. For sites with multiple clear peaks, the peak with the higher amplitude was evaluated. Passing peaks were identified at 208 stations (14%), and 1278 stations (86%) failed to have a peak identified.

mHVSR data and processing

Microtremor HVSR (mHVSR) data were obtained from a subset of the Wang *et al.* (2021) HVSR database. The database, discussed further in Wang *et al.* (2022), provides mean and standard deviation HVSR curves, as well as station and recording information, for 1423 microtremor recordings at 703 sites, primarily in California. Of these recordings, we use the 767 recordings at the 438 sites located in California at seismic stations. The number of recordings per site ranges from one to six.

The recordings are obtained from three-component seismometers (both temporary and permanent) that record microtremor ground vibrations. Microtremor recordings were processed using the processing package *hvsrProc* (Wang, 2020) when time-series data were available (most recordings) and using the open-source Geopsy software (Wathelet *et al.*, 2020) on all other recordings to produce the mean and standard deviation HVSR curves. Using the station mean mHVSR curves and their associated standard deviations, the SESAME criteria were applied to identify whether a clear peak could be determined for each station. The resonant site frequency (f_p), amplitude of the resonant site frequency, and HPB parameters were extracted for all mHVSR stations with a clear peak using *hvsrpy*. For sites with multiple clear peaks, the peak with the higher amplitude was evaluated. Passing peaks were identified for 191 recordings (~25%), and 576 recordings failed to have a peak identified.

HVSR DATA EXPLORATION

HVSR-based seismic site classification

For the set of HVSR recordings in this study, 86% of eHVSR and 75% of mHVSR recordings lack a clear, identifiable resonance peak. This result is due in part to the large number of sites across the state that are located on deep soil profiles without a strong impedance contrast, or stations that are located on rock. On the other hand, there are some sites that fail to have a peak identified due to the variability and inconsistency in HVSR measurements from ambient noise and environmental conditions. We seek to identify the sites that inherently lack a clear HVSR due to the absence of an impedance contrast and separate them from HVSR recordings that fail to have a peak identified due to the variability and inconsistency in HVSR measurements. We hypothesize that the distinction between these two types of results may help characterize site effects.

TABLE 1
Criteria Implemented to Identify a Flat HVSR Curve

Criteria	Condition
1	$\nexists f^- \in [f_p/4, f_p] \mid A_{H/V}(f^-) < A_p/2$
2	$\nexists f^+ \in [f_p, 4f_p] \mid A_{H/V}(f^+) < A_p/2$
3	$A_p < 1.5$

f_p, horizontal-to-vertical (H/V) peak frequency; A_p, amplitude at frequency f_p; f^-, frequency between $f_p/4$ and f_p with an H/V amplitude below $A_p/2$; f^+, frequency between f_p and $4f_p$ with an H/V amplitude below $A_p/2$.

In previous HVSR studies, curves have been deemed "flat" if they fail to have a clear peak identified. In this study, we make a distinction between (a) HVSR curves that are completely flat with no peaks present, and (b) curves that failed to have a clear peak identified (using SESAME criteria), but are not completely flat (i.e., a peak that is too wide, not distinct enough, or has too high standard deviation to be classified as a clear peak). We view the failed nonflat HVSR data as being inconclusive (i.e., it would be difficult to glean any site information from the test). However, the failed flat HVSR data do tell us information about the site characteristics and the lack of an impedance contrast at the site. Sites that consistently have flat HVSR curves do not exhibit a clear site resonance. Classifying a subset of failing HVSR measurements as flat allows us to gain insights about site characterization and inform GMMs from (a) recordings with a passing fundamental resonant peak and (b) flat recordings. In addition, by removing the recordings that do not produce reliable results (i.e., failed, non-flat recordings), we are better able to determine the extent to which eHVSR and mHVSR match at a given site.

Recordings were determined to be flat if they failed SESAME clarity criteria (1) and (2) and had a peak horizontal-to-vertical (H/V) amplitude below 1.5. These criteria are outlined in Table 1. Criteria 1 and 2 involve the height of the peak relative to the curve around it; a height of half the peak amplitude must not be reached within $f_p/4$ to f_p (criteria 1) and within f_p to $4f_p$ (criteria 2). These indicate either that the peak being assessed is not tall compared to the surrounding record, and/or that the curve does not taper down in amplitude within the required range. Criteria 3 states that the peak amplitude must be less than 1.5, which is similar to the SESAME clarity criteria (3) (the peak amplitude must be above 2), but stricter to identify curves that are nearly completely flat. If a curve passes all three of these criteria, we conclude that the curve is relatively flat when comparing the peak to its surrounding points (criteria 1 and 2) and does not have a section of high amplitude (criteria 3).

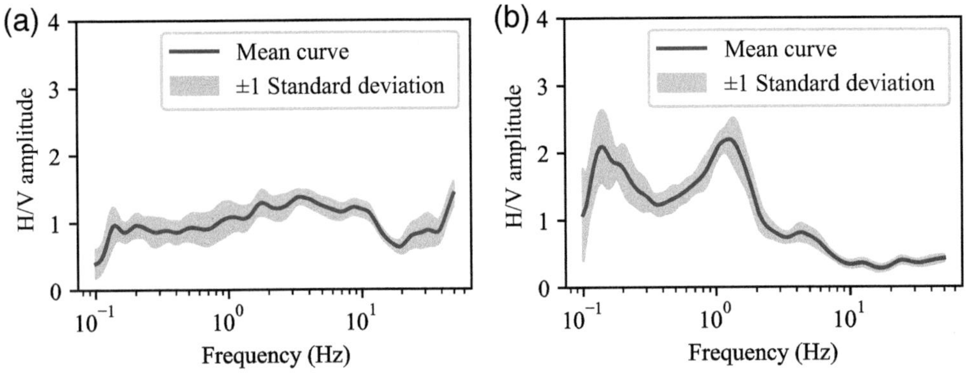

Figure 2. Microtremor HVSR (mHVSR) recordings that both failed to have a clear peak identified: (a) a recording classified as flat, and (b) a recording that failed the clear peak criteria but will not be classified as flat. The color version of this figure is available only in the electronic edition.

The criteria for identifying flat HVSR curves provide a systematic way to classify flat eHVSR and mHVSR recordings. This method also has a level of consistency and ease of implementation by being based on the widely used SESAME criteria. When applied to this dataset, 104 out of the 1278 eHVSR stations without an identified clear peak (8.1%) were classified as flat. For mHVSR, 72 of the 576 failed recordings (12.5%) were classified as flat. Figure 2 showcases the differences between recordings that meet the flat criteria and those that do not have a passing peak but also do not meet the flat criteria.

The resulting site characterization dataset we constructed for analysis includes the three HVSR classifications of pass (a clear fundamental resonance peak identified), flat (meeting the three criteria in Table 1), and fail (no clear peak identified, but not meeting the flat criteria). For the HVSR curves with passing peaks, we determine f_p, peak amplitude, and HPB for each station. Table 2 summarizes the distribution of the dataset for both eHVSR stations and mHVSR recording classifications, and Figure 3 displays their geographic distribution. The eHVSR recordings exhibit some clustering of flat recordings within crystalline geologic units, most notably in the Sierra Nevada Mountain range. The mHVSR recording classifications do not show a visible geographic pattern, potentially influenced by the lack of stations in the Sierra Nevada Mountain range and other crystalline geologic units.

TABLE 2
eHVSR and mHVSR Dataset Distribution by Recording Classification

Classification	Pass	Flat	Fail	Total
eHVSR	208 (14.0%)	104 (7.0%)	1174 (79.0%)	1486
mHVSR	191 (24.9%)	72 (9.4%)	504 (65.7%)	767

eHVSR; earthquake HVSR; mHVSR, microtremor HVSR.

Flat station classification

The sites classified as flat have a distinct geologic and topographic distribution compared to the passing and failed sites. Figure 4 shows the roughness and elevation distributions for the three HVSR classification groups derived from processing mHVSR and eHVSR, separately. Roughness and elevation were derived from the Global Multi-resolution Terrain Elevation Data (GMTED) 7.5 arc-sec digital elevation model (Danielson and Gesch, 2011). Roughness is defined here as the largest difference between the elevation of a central pixel and the elevations of its eight surrounding pixels. For both mHVSR and eHVSR, "Flat" sites tend to have higher roughness and elevation values than "Pass" and "Fail" stations.

The distribution of the surficial geologic units for each recording classification is shown in Figure 5, according to the Wills *et al.* (2015) surficial geologic unit map for California. The surficial geologic units were then aggregated into broader geologic categories, with sedimentary units including Quaternary Alluvium (Qal1, Qal2, Qal3, af/Qi, Qi, and Qs), Older Alluvium (Qt and Qoa), Tertiary Sediment (Tss and Tsh), Cretaceous-Jurassic Sediment (Kjf and Kss), and rock site units including Crystalline (crystalline), Volcanic (Tv), and Metamorphic (sp). Failing and passing classifications show similar distributions across mHVSR and eHVSR data, consisting of approximately a third of Quaternary Alluvium recordings (31%–41%) and approximately a quarter (15%–28%) of sites located in Crystalline or Older Alluvium. On the other hand, flat sites for both mHVSR and eHVSR data consisted of the majority Crystalline (57% and 64%, respectively) and significantly less Quaternary Alluvium (15% and 11%, respectively). For the flat classification, the percentage of Crystalline sites more than doubled, and the percentage of Quaternary Alluvium was cut by more than half, compared to the passing classification for both mHVSR and eHVSR. These changes in surficial geologic classification were more significant for eHVSR than for mHVSR, reflecting the differences in station location, shown in part by the clearer geographic distributions exhibited by the eHVSR classifications in Figure 3, and the differences in the sources of the two measurement types.

On average, sites with a flat classification have a higher elevation and roughness and are also more likely to have crystalline surficial geology. Higher roughness and elevation typically indicate mountain or hill sites that are likely to consist of rock. The crystalline surficial geology also indicates a rock site. The findings in Figures 4 and 5 validate the effectiveness of the

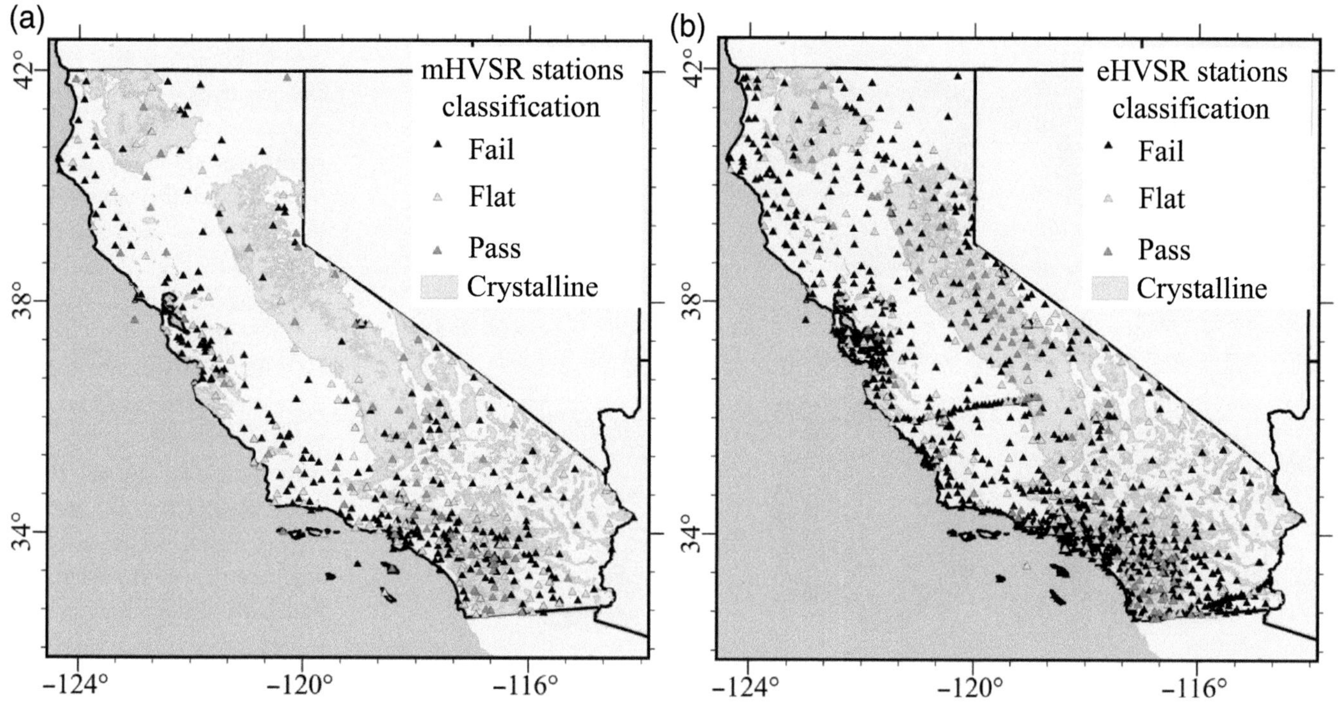

Figure 3. Geographic distributions of HVSR classifications for stations with (a) mHVSR and (b) earthquake HVSR (eHVSR) data, overlain with the crystalline geologic units of California defined by Wills *et al.* (2015). The color version of this figure is available only in the electronic edition.

flat classification as identifying sites with little to no soil resonance or amplification, which is typical of a rock site.

These results show that there is a significant difference in the geologic and topographic composition between flat sites and failing sites not classified as flat. Because failing sites are more similar in terms of geology and topography to sites with a passing peak, we will not use the failing classification in our site term. Our findings could indicate that although the peaks could not be identified using HVSR data at the failing stations, perhaps the peaks are not being captured due to variability from noise or environmental factors. This result further confirms that the flat classification carries site information different from the other failing stations. For mHVSR sites with multiple recordings, 6 out of the 161 stations (3.7%) had a flat and a passing recording, whereas 48 out of the 161 stations (29.8%) had a failing and passing recording. This result indicates that the flat classification improves the ability to identify sites without a resonance peak,

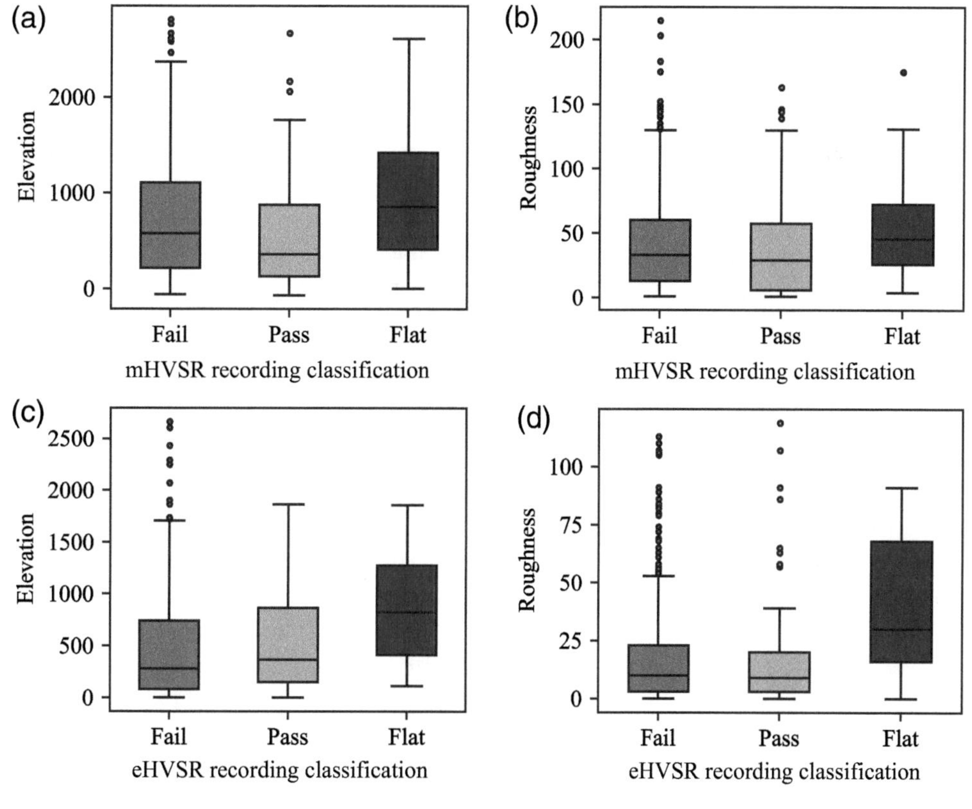

Figure 4. Distributions of topographic elevation and roughness by the recording classifications for (a,b) mHVSR and (c,d) eHVSR. The color version of this figure is available only in the electronic edition.

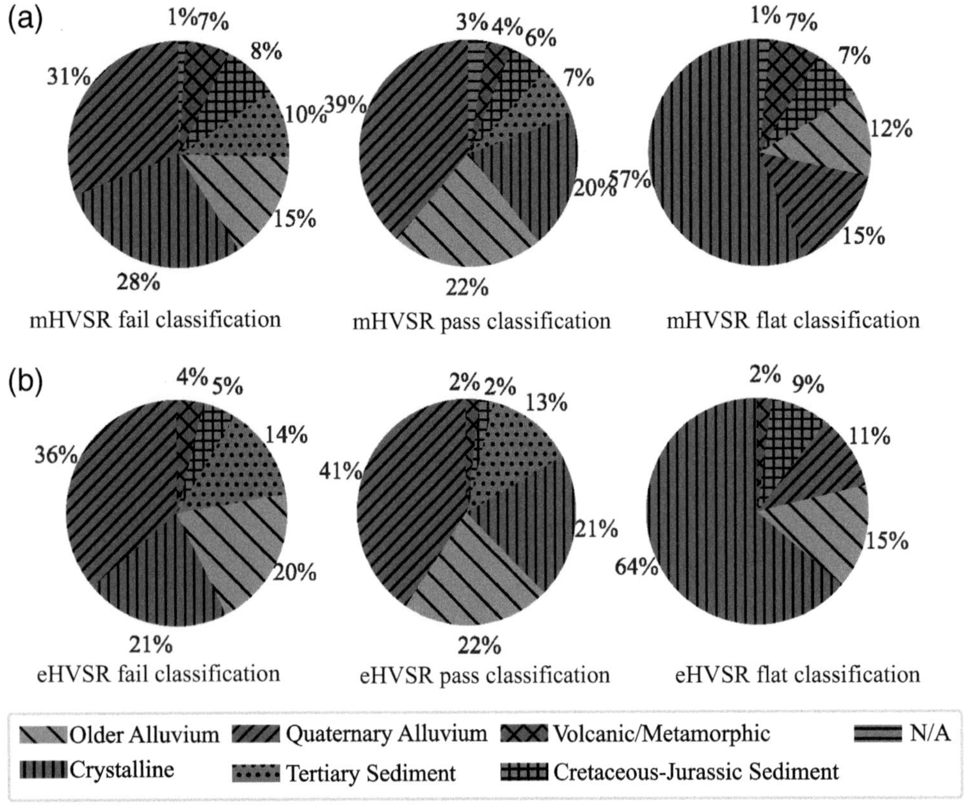

Figure 5. Surficial geologic make-up of the recording classifications (fail, pass, and flat) for (a) mHVSR and (b) eHVSR. The color version of this figure is available only in the electronic edition.

compared to classifying all failed recordings in the same way. The same geologic and topographic trends are viewed across mHVSR and eHVSR data, indicating effectiveness of this method for both HVSR types.

Including this flat HVSR classification as a categorical site term in GMM development captures the average amplification difference for sites without an impedance contrast (typically rock sites) compared to sites with a clear fundamental resonant frequency (typically sedimentary sites underlain by stiffer material). In this study, only the flat and passing recordings are used for GMM site term development due to the lack of conclusive geological and geotechnical evidence about site characterization from the failed recordings. Failed recordings are not used in site term development and are not intended to be used for model application. If a failing mHVSR curve is obtained at a site, an HVSR-based adjustment cannot be applied to the site term for this site, and the base geospatial site term (from Roberts *et al.*, 2025) should be used instead.

Classification consistency between mHVSR and eHVSR

In this section, we examine the extent to which eHVSR and mHVSR data produce similar results across California, to determine how both datasets can be used to inform GMMs. We compare mHVSR recordings within the passing and flat classifications to eHVSR results at the same stations. Failed recordings are not considered here due to their insufficient information, as described previously. There were 53 mHVSR recordings across 41 stations for which a passing or flat eHVSR result was obtained at the same station. These 53 mHVSR–eHVSR recording pairs have a broad geographic distribution across the state, as seen in Figure 6. The pairs were analyzed to see how often they matched. Pairs were determined to be a match if (a) they are both flat, or (b) they both pass and the identified eHVSR f_p is within half to twice the mHVSR f_p. Across the set of 53 pairs, there were 34 pairs (64%) that matched using these criteria.

To understand when eHVSR matches mHVSR, various prior conditions were analyzed, with the following results described here and shown in Figure 7:

1. Given that the eHVSR passes, there is a 69% probability that the mHVSR passes and the peak frequencies match.
2. Given that eHVSR is flat, there is a 56% probability that the mHVSR is flat.
3. Given that the mHVSR passes, there is a 57% probability that the eHVSR passes and the peak frequencies match.
4. Given that mHVSR is flat, there is an 91% probability that the eHVSR is flat.
5. Given that the mHVSR and eHVSR pass, there is a 71% probability that the peak frequencies match.

These results indicate that the flat classification for eHVSR is not indicative of a flat mHVSR, resulting in low-matching rates for conditions (1) and (2). However, the flat classification from mHVSR is indicative of a truly flat HVSR, evident by the eHVSR also being flat 91% of the time. This finding is based on the limited set of 11 recordings with flat mHVSR curves; however, these 11 recordings are representative of bedrock conditions throughout the state and are located across the various mountain ranges of California, including the Klamath Mountains, Sierra Nevada Mountains, the Transverse Ranges, and the Peninsular Ranges. Based on this result, we find that eHVSR too often classifies sites

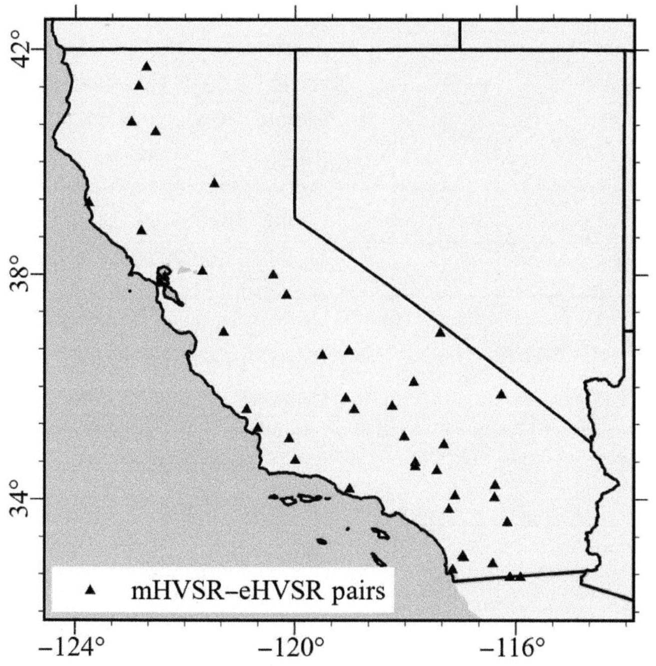

Figure 6. Geographic distributions of mHVSR–eHVSR recording pairs throughout California. The color version of this figure is available only in the electronic edition.

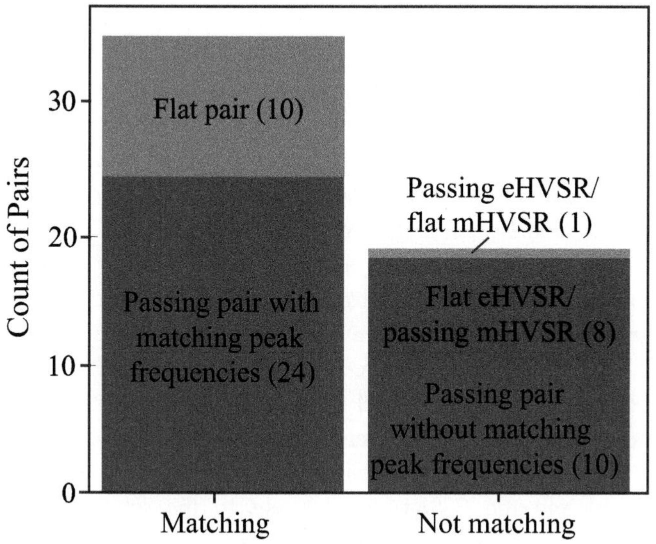

Figure 7. mHVSR–eHVSR pairs that matched and those that did not match, separated by the classification of the data in each pair. The color version of this figure is available only in the electronic edition.

as flat, but that the mHVSR flat classification is more consistent. This finding is consistent with results from previous studies in California. The Vantassel *et al.* (2024) study on HVSR measurements (predominantly in Southern California) showed that when the mHVSR failed to identify a clear resonance, it was an indicator that the eHVSR is likely to also fail to identify a clear peak. However, Vantassel *et al.* (2024) found that the converse was not true: the lack of an eHVSR resonance was not a good indicator of the lack of an mHVSR resonance. In addition, Wang *et al.* (2023) evaluated a larger dataset across California and found that eHVSR curves have peaks identified at a lower rate than mHVSR curves. The rate at which a peak is identified using mHVSR data, but no peak is identified using eHVSR data, is 45 to 52%. It is more difficult to obtain a passing classification using eHVSR data than mHVSR data in California, based on the findings of this study and supported by other comparisons in the region (Wang *et al.*, 2023; Vantassel *et al.*, 2024). This result means that the passing classifications are more consistent from eHVSR, with some error (31% in this study), but the flat classifications from eHVSR are not reliable compared to mHVSR.

Flat results from mHVSR are consistent with eHVSR at the same site and have a clear distinction from passing and failing recordings, as demonstrated in the previous section. A flat classification for mHVSR data allows for the fitting of an adjustment term to GMMs that could be applied if a flat mHVSR is obtained at a site. However, flat-classified stations from eHVSR data should not be included when fitting this adjustment term.

Parameter consistency between mHVSR and eHVSR

We also explore the consistencies in f_p, peak amplitude, and HPB for recordings that passed for both eHVSR and mHVSR. There are 34 mHVSR recordings with a corresponding eHVSR pass at the same station. Figure 8 compares peak frequencies, peak amplitudes, and HPBs derived from the paired eHVSR and mHVSR curves. The distribution of peak frequencies in Figure 8a closely follows the 1-to-1 line, except for a few outliers with lower mHVSR f_p than eHVSR f_p. Figure 8b shows that the peak amplitude has high scatter in the range of 2–6, which could present problems in GMM fitting due to the variability in the term and the small range of potential peak amplitudes. Consistency is seen between some pairs for HPB (Fig. 8c); however, high scatter is present in the data.

The aforementioned approach visualizes the consistency of each parameter, but to further quantify the distributions, we evaluated the Nash–Sutcliffe Efficiency Coefficient (E; Nash and Sutcliffe, 1970) for goodness of fit to the 1-to-1 line. The coefficient of efficiency is computed as

$$E = 1 - \left[\frac{\sum_{i=1}^{N}(Y_i - \hat{Y}_i)^2}{\sum_{i=1}^{N}\left(Y_i - \bar{Y}\right)^2}\right] \times 100\%, \quad (1)$$

in which N is the total number of mHVSR and eHVSR pairs, Y_i is the mHVSR parameter (the observed value), $\hat{Y}_i$ is the eHVSR parameter (the predicted value), and $\bar{Y}$ is the mean of the mHVSR parameter. The coefficient of efficiency measures the

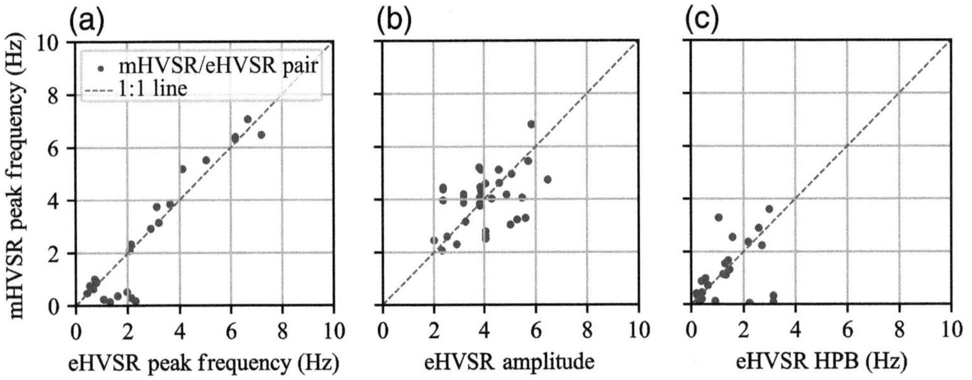

Figure 8. (a) Peak resonant frequency, (b) peak horizontal-to-vertical (H/V) amplitude, and (c) peak HPB for 56 mHVSR–eHVSR station pairs with passing classifications for both measurements. The color version of this figure is available only in the electronic edition.

the stations with V_{S30} measurements using the DSGMD (Ji *et al.*, 2022). These observed ground motions were compared to predicted ground motions using the BSSA14 GMM (Boore *et al.*, 2014), modified to replace the linear site amplification term and basin depth term with the geospatial site term $\ln(F_{\text{Geospatial}})$ that we previously developed (equation 7 of Roberts *et al.*, 2025). For a station j, the geospatial site term is

goodness of fit relative to the 1-to-1 line and can range from $-\infty$% to 100%; when E is less than zero, the arithmetic mean of the observed values has greater prediction accuracy than the model itself (Nash and Sutcliffe, 1970; Kaklamanos and Baise, 2011). Values of E quantify the agreement between observations and predictions, considering the dispersion of observations and predictions about the 1-to-1 line.

The coefficient of efficiency for f_p is 85%, indicating strong agreement between observations and predictions. For peak amplitude, the coefficient of efficiency is −23%, indicating no agreement between observations and predictions, which is consistent with the high range of the scatter seen in the data. The coefficient of efficiency for HPB is 0.05%, again indicating no agreement between observations and predictions.

Given these results, we use f_p from passing eHVSRs to supplement mHVSR data, to utilize the added station coverage provided by eHVSR data throughout California. When fitting models that use both mHVSR and eHVSR data, weights are assigned differently to mHVSR and eHVSR data based on their reliability. eHVSR data are considered surrogate data with higher variance because inconsistencies often exist between eHVSR and mHVSR parameters at the same station, so eHVSR data receive a lower weight. The mHVSR data are assigned a weight of one, and eHVSR data are weighted by E to reflect the relative reliability of mHVSR predictions using eHVSR values. For fundamental frequency, a weight of 0.85 will be used for the eHVSR data. The peak amplitude and HPB from passing eHVSRs are not used when fitting an amplitude-based site term due to the lack of consistency between eHVSR and mHVSR peak amplitudes.

GEOTECHNICAL SITE TERM DEVELOPMENT

Site-to-site residuals and site amplification

To develop geotechnical-measurement-based site terms to adjust geospatial GMM site terms, the observed ground motions were obtained for all the stations in our final HVSR dataset and

$$\ln(F_{\text{Geospatial},j}) = c_1 + F_{\text{RGU},j} + \begin{cases} c_2(\text{roughness}_j - 20), & \text{roughness}_j < \text{roughness}_0 \\ c_2(\text{roughness}_0 - 20), & \text{roughness}_j \geq \text{roughness}_0 \end{cases}, \quad (2)$$

in which c_1 is a constant, F_{RGU} represents the categorical site term for regional geologic unit (a coefficient that is uniform within each regional geologic unit category), c_2 is a regression slope coefficient for roughness centered around the average roughness of 20 m, and roughness_0 is the plateau point where amplification becomes constant with increasing roughness. This model serves as a replacement for the linear site amplification term and basin depth term presented in BSSA14, and is intended to be used with the nonlinear site term of BSSA14 as well as the source and path terms of BSSA14. Refer to Roberts *et al.* (2025) for the model coefficients and additional details.

This model was selected as a base model because the geospatial linear site term utilizes only continuous variables to generate a site term and can be used across the state without the need for measured geotechnical site characterization data. The geospatial-based model shows a reduction of site-to-site variability ($\delta S2S$; 10.6% averaged across PGA, PGV, and 21 PSAs from 0.01 to 10 s) compared to the original BSSA14 model and the BSSA14 model refit to the subset of the DSGMD used in the study (9.8% averaged across PGA, PGV, and 21 PSAs from 0.01 to 10 s), and this improvement can be enhanced with site-specific geotechnical measurements, such as HVSR and V_{S30}, when they are available. The residual (R_{ij}) of the geospatial model was calculated for each event (i) at each station (j), as

$$R_{ij} = \ln(Y_{ij}) - \ln(\mu_{ij,\text{BSSA14 with geospatial site term}}), \quad (3)$$

in which Y_{ij} is the observed ground-motion intensity measure (IM) for event i at station j; and μ_{ij} is the corresponding median ground-motion IM predicted using the BSSA14 model with the

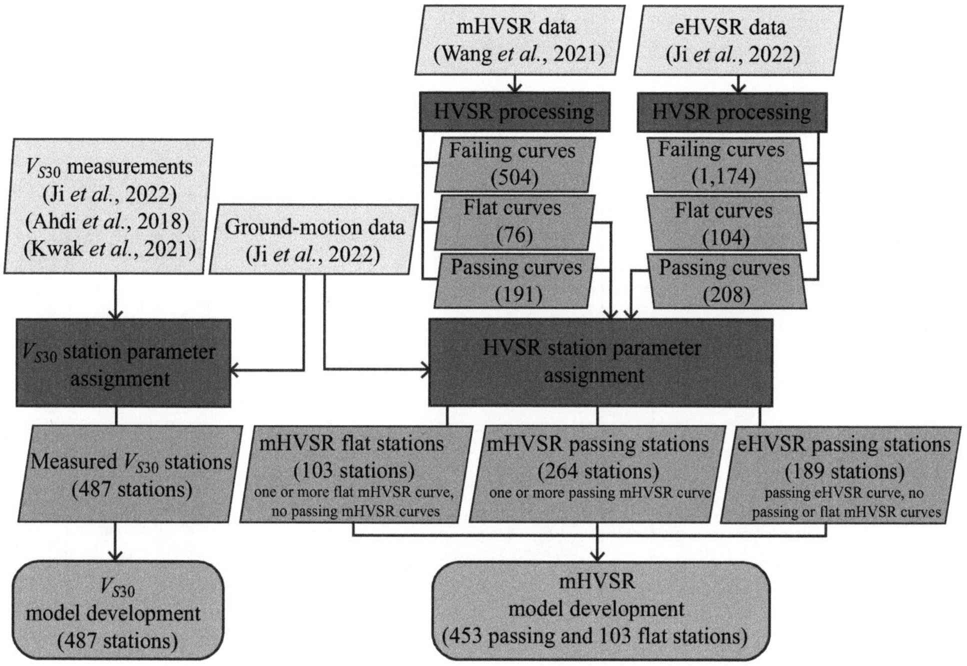

Figure 9. Flowchart illustrating data processing for the development of the geotechnical site term. The light-gray parallelograms are input datasets, and the dark gray parallelograms are output datasets. The rectangles are data processing steps, and the rectangles with curved edges are the final models. The color version of this figure is available only in the electronic edition.

modified site term. We then decompose the ground-motion total residuals ($R_{ij,\mathrm{BSSA14}}$) using linear mixed-effects regression (Abrahamson and Youngs, 1992), as

$$R_{ij,\mathrm{BSSA14}} = c + \delta B_i + \delta S2S_j + \delta P_i\left(\frac{R_{\mathrm{JB},ij} - 100}{100}\right) + \delta WS_{ij}, \quad (4)$$

in which c, δB_i, $\delta S2S$, δP_i, and δWS_{ij} are the bias, between-event residual, site-to-site term, event-specific path term, and remaining residual, respectively. $R_{\mathrm{JB},ij}$ represents the Joyner–Boore distance for event i at station j, and this term is centered at 100 km and scaled by 100 to stabilize the regression and ensure consistent parameter interpretation. This equation is adapted from Abrahamson and Youngs (1992) to include the event-specific path term to prevent path effects from being mapped into the site term, based on correspondence with N. Abrahamson (2025, personal comm.). The site-to-site term ($\delta S2S$) and remaining residual (δWS_{ij}) are assumed to be normally distributed with zero mean and standard deviations ϕ_{S2S} and ϕ_{SS}, respectively. These calculations are performed across PGA, PGV, and PSA for 21 periods from 0.01 to 10 s. The $\delta S2S$ term is calculated relative to site term scaling of the BSSA14 model modified with the Roberts *et al.* (2025) geospatial linear site term and is used as the target variable for fitting the geotechnical-based adjustment term. We evaluate the following geotechnical parameters: V_{S30}, the mHVSR and eHVSR passing peak parameters (f_p, amplitude, and HPB), and the flat mHVSR classification. Parameters are assigned to sites and evaluated for their performance in reducing $\delta S2S$ relative to site term scaling, as shown in Figure 9.

We also compute the variance in the point estimates of $\delta S2S$ relative to site term scaling. The point estimates of $\delta S2S$ for each station contain uncertainty, which can be high at stations with few recordings and lead to bias in the model (Campbell *et al.*, 2025; Kuehn *et al.*, 2025). To account for this bias, the inverse of the variance of each point estimate of $\delta S2S$ is used to weight the stations during model fitting, giving stations with lower uncertainty in $\delta S2S$ a stronger influence on the fit of the model.

Weighted least-squares regression with three-fold cross-validation

We derive two sets of models to predict $\delta S2S$ in California relative to the site term scaling of the BSSA14 model modified with the Roberts *et al.* (2025) geospatial linear base site term: one using only HVSR measurements and one using only V_{S30} measurements. The models are developed using weighted least-squares (WLS) regression, which accounts for the unequal variance of data points by assigning weights to data. The HVSR-based models fit to only mHVSR data have weights assigned based on the inverse variance of $\delta S2S$ for the station. For the HVSR model fit to both mHVSR and eHVSR f_p data from passing stations, the eHVSR data are downweighted, as described in the Parameter consistency between mHVSR and eHVSR section. The variance of $\delta S2S$ for the station is multiplied by E (calculated to be 0.85) to assign less weight to eHVSR data.

First, alternative passing-peak HVSR-based models are produced by fitting each HVSR parameter to the functional forms in equations (5) and (6). The models developed using equations (5) and (6) are compared to determine the optimal passing-peak HVSR-based model. Equation (5) is used for the f_p parameter, and was derived by Hassani and Atkinson (2016b):

$$\delta S2S_j = \begin{cases} \beta_0 + \varepsilon_j & f_0 < 0.5\,\mathrm{Hz} \\ \beta_0 + \left[\frac{\beta_1 - \beta_0}{\log_{10}\left(\frac{f}{0.5}\right)}\right]\log_{10}\left(\frac{f_p}{0.5}\right) + \varepsilon_j & 0.5 \le f_p < f \\ \beta_1 + \left[\frac{\beta_2 - \beta_1}{\log_{10}\left(\frac{20}{f}\right)}\right]\log_{10}\left(\frac{f_p}{f}\right) + \varepsilon_j & f \le f_p < 20\,\mathrm{Hz} \\ \beta_2 + \varepsilon_j & 20\,\mathrm{Hz} \le f_p \end{cases} \quad (5)$$

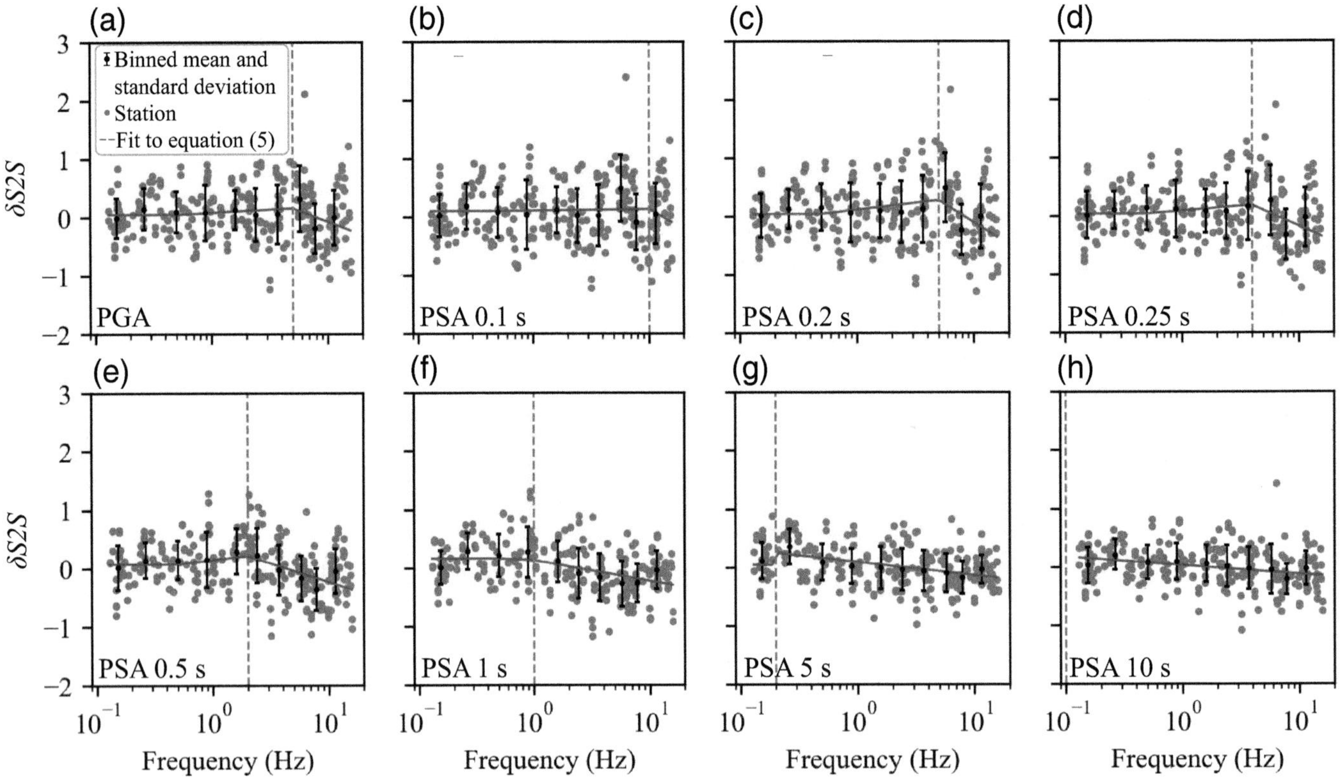

Figure 10. For the BSSA14 model modified with the Roberts *et al.* (2025) geospatial linear site term scaling for stations with passing mHVSR, scatterplots of $\delta S2S$ versus f_p for eight evaluated periods: (a) peak ground acceleration (PGA), and PSA at (b) 0.1, (c) 0.2, (d) 0.25, (e) 0.5, (f) 1, (g) 5, and (h) 10 s. Also shown are the binned means and standard deviations, as well as the fit provided by the model in equation (5). The color version of this figure is available only in the electronic edition.

in which β_0, β_1, and β_2 are frequency-dependent regression coefficients, f_p is the peak resonance frequency for the sites, f is the frequency being evaluated, and ε_j is the remaining residual. The model has a constant segment below 0.5 Hz, and then a peak at the frequency f being evaluated, followed by a constant segment after 20 Hz. This functional form fits the trends observed in f_p, as seen in Figure 10; this form accounts for the peak response that is seen when f_p is equal to the frequency being evaluated. The functional form also prevents extrapolation at values of f_p above 20 Hz, for which data were not available in this study. For PGA, $f = 5$ Hz was used for model calibration; for PGV, $f = 2$ Hz was used. These are the recommended frequencies proposed by Hassani and Atkinson (2016b) at which the site term was observed to be maximized.

For the peak amplitude and HPB parameters, we assume a linear functional form given in the following equation:

$$\delta S2S_j = \beta_3 + \begin{cases} \beta_4 \boldsymbol{X} + \varepsilon_j, & \boldsymbol{X} < \boldsymbol{X}_0 \\ \beta_4 \boldsymbol{X}_0 + \varepsilon_j, & \boldsymbol{X} \geq \boldsymbol{X}_0 \end{cases}, \tag{6}$$

in which β_3 is a constant, β_4 is the regression coefficient, $\boldsymbol{X}$ is a vector of the geospatial parameters, ε_j is the remaining site residual after the regression, and $\boldsymbol{X}_0$ is a vector of the plateau points for which the parameter correlations to $\delta S2S_j$ become constant. The linear piecewise functional form was selected to be consistent with trends observed in the $\delta S2S$ correlation to HPB and amplitude, which can be seen in Figure 11. For both parameters, the correlation with $\delta S2S$ varies by period, and the linear correlation pattern tends to be most pronounced at long periods. The linear piecewise form also avoids extrapolation at high input values for $\boldsymbol{X}$.

An alternative HVSR-based site term is also developed for sites that are classified as flat. The factor is a constant that can be applied to stations for which the mHVSR curve meets the flat criteria:

$$\delta S2S_j = \alpha + \varepsilon_j, \tag{7}$$

in which α is the period-dependent constant term for flat stations, and ε_j is the remaining residual. The approach of applying a constant factor to adjust site terms for sites without clear peaks was performed in Kwak *et al.* (2017) and is applied here, but to a more strictly defined classification of flat stations with no observable impedance contrast.

Second, we develop a model to predict $\delta S2S$ using only V_{S30} data. The V_{S30}-based model is produced by fitting the measured V_{S30} to equation (8), the same functional form as is used in BSSA14 for V_{S30}, using WLS, for which weights are assigned based on the inverse variance of $\delta S2S$.

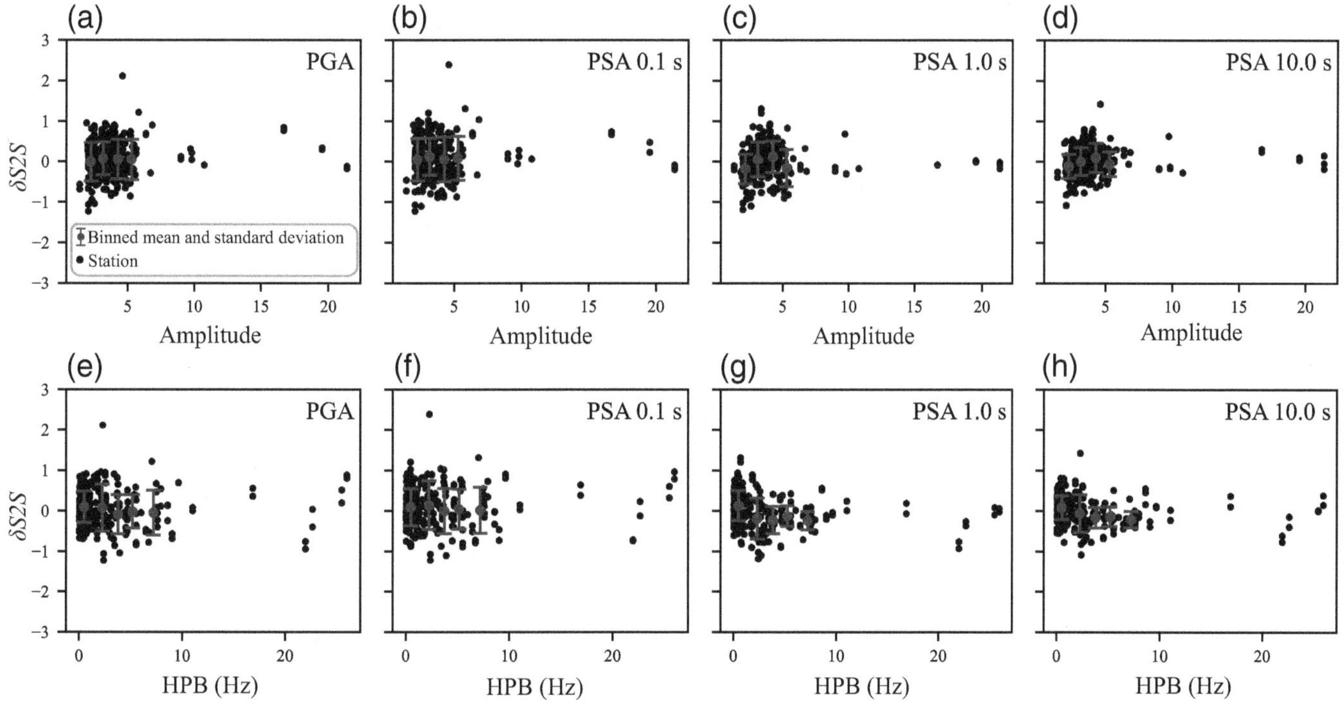

Figure 11. For the BSSA14 model modified with the Roberts *et al.* (2025) geospatial linear site term scaling, at all stations with passing mHVSR, (a–d) $\delta S2S$ versus peak amplitude, evaluated at four different periods (PGA, and PSA at 0.1, 1, and 10 s), and (e–h) $\delta S2S$ versus peak HPB, evaluated at the same periods. Also shown are the binned means and standard deviations. The color version of this figure is available only in the electronic edition.

$$\delta S2S_j = \beta_5 + \begin{cases} \beta_6 \ln\left(\frac{V_{S30}}{760}\right) + \varepsilon_j, & V_{S30} < V_{S30,0} \\ \beta_6 \ln\left(\frac{V_{S30,0}}{760}\right) + \varepsilon_j, & V_{S30} \geq V_{S30,0} \end{cases}, \quad (8)$$

in which β_5 and β_6 are regression coefficients, ε_j is the remaining site residual after the regression, and $V_{S30,0}$ is the plateau point for which the V_{S30} correlation to $\delta S2S_j$ becomes constant. The correlation between V_{S30} and $\delta S2S$ is linear, and the constant piecewise functional form is used to avoid extrapolation at high values of V_{S30}. Plots of V_{S30} versus $\delta S2S$ can be seen in Figure 12.

Models that use both HVSR and V_{S30} data are not evaluated because there is insufficient data from both passing and flat stations with V_{S30} measurements to develop a model. The geographic coverage of the stations with both HVSR and V_{S30} data is also insufficient for developing a model intended to be applicable to all of California.

We evaluate the performance of alternative regression models for each set of models (1) using only HVSR measurements and (2) using only V_{S30} measurements using three-fold cross-validation. The stations are first split randomly into three groups. For the geotechnical parameter(s) tested, the model is fit to the data three times, each time leaving out a different group. The root mean square error (RMSE) of the left-out group is averaged across each of the three trials and is used to compare different models. The optimal model, within each of the two sets of models (HVSR- and V_{S30}-based), is selected as the model that has the lowest average RMSE across all periods evaluated.

HVSR-based model evaluation

A set of four HVSR-based site term models was evaluated for stations with passing HVSR peaks (264 stations with mHVSR parameters, and 189 additional stations with eHVSR parameters). Three models were fit using only mHVSR data, using the following functional forms: (1) equation (5) with f_p as the parameter, (2) equation (6) with HPB as the parameter, and (3) equation (6) with peak amplitude as the parameter. The final model (4) was fit using a combination of eHVSR data and mHVSR data, following equation (5) using f_p. As discussed previously, no models were fit using peak amplitude or HPB for the combined eHVSR and mHVSR data, due to the lack of agreement between mHVSR and eHVSR peak amplitude and HPB data.

For all four models, three-fold cross-validation was performed, for which one-third of the mHVSR data is set aside for model testing, and the other two-thirds is used for training; this process is repeated for each third of mHVSR data to test the model performance on unseen data. The model fit to both eHVSR and mHVSR data includes the eHVSR data only in the model training sets, and the models are validated on the same three folds of unseen mHVSR data as the models based on mHVSR data alone. The RMSE was calculated for each fold of the test group data, and the average results for the four models are presented in Figure 13.

The mHVSR-fitted f_p model is the best HVSR term for passing stations because it has the lowest average RMSE for

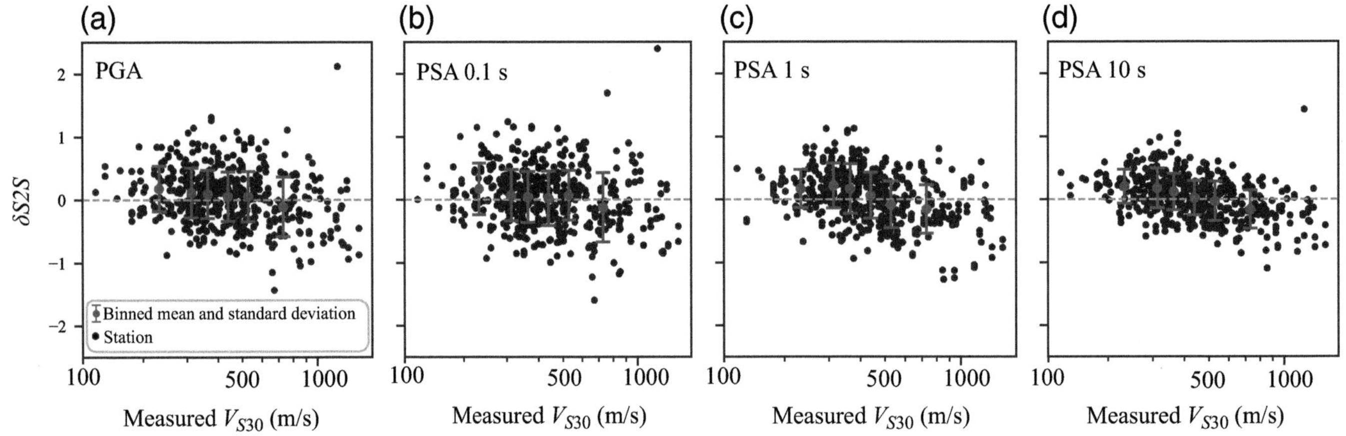

Figure 12. For the BSSA14 model modified with the Roberts *et al.* (2025) geospatial linear site term scaling (at all stations with passing mHVSR), scatterplots of $\delta S2S$ versus measured V_{S30}, evaluated for (a) PGA, (b) PSA at 0.1 s, (c) PSA at 1.0 s, and (d) PSA at 10.0 s. Also shown are the binned means and standard deviations. The color version of this figure is available only in the electronic edition.

the test set of mHVSR data for periods greater than or equal to 0.25 s (Fig. 13). Compared to using the base geospatial linear site term, including the geotechnical site term based on f_p reduces the RMSE by an average of 4.2% at periods greater than or equal to 0.25 s. For periods below 0.25 s, none of the HVSR-based models resulted in a reduction in average RMSE. This finding is consistent with other studies demonstrating decreased correlation at short periods between ground-motion amplitude and parameters related to impedance contrast and the depth structure of the soil, including HVSR amplitude (Pinilla-Ramos *et al.*, 2022) and $Z_{1.0}$ (Boore *et al.*, 2014).

Figure 13 indicates that the model fit using both eHVSR and mHVSR data performed similarly to the model fit using only mHVSR data for f_p. Including eHVSR data in model development resulted in an average reduction in RMSE of 3.7% (compared to the mHVSR average reduction of 4.2%) for periods greater than or equal to 0.25 s. However, unlike the mHVSR-based model, the eHVSR- and mHVSR-based models did not reduce the RMSE for periods of 0.25 and 0.3 s.

The site term for flat stations was also evaluated using the 103 flat mHVSR stations in the dataset. The factor is a constant (equation 7) that can be applied to stations for which the mHVSR curve meets the flat criteria. To assess the accuracy of this flat site term, a three-fold cross-validation was performed on the subset of flat stations. Only mHVSR data were used to fit the flat HVSR site term because a flat result from eHVSR is not a reliable indicator of a flat mHVSR, as previously discussed.

The average RMSE of the flat mHVSR model was calculated across the three folds, and the results can be seen in Figure 14. In this figure, we also compare the result to the RMSE of the test data using the base geospatial site term without an adjustment applied. Using an adjusted site term for flat stations results in a reduction of average RMSE of 4.8% across the test set, with the largest reduction occurring for PGA, PGV, and periods below 0.5 s.

Based on the analysis in this section, we recommend two optimal HVSR-based models: one for stations with passing criteria, and the other for stations with a flat classification. For

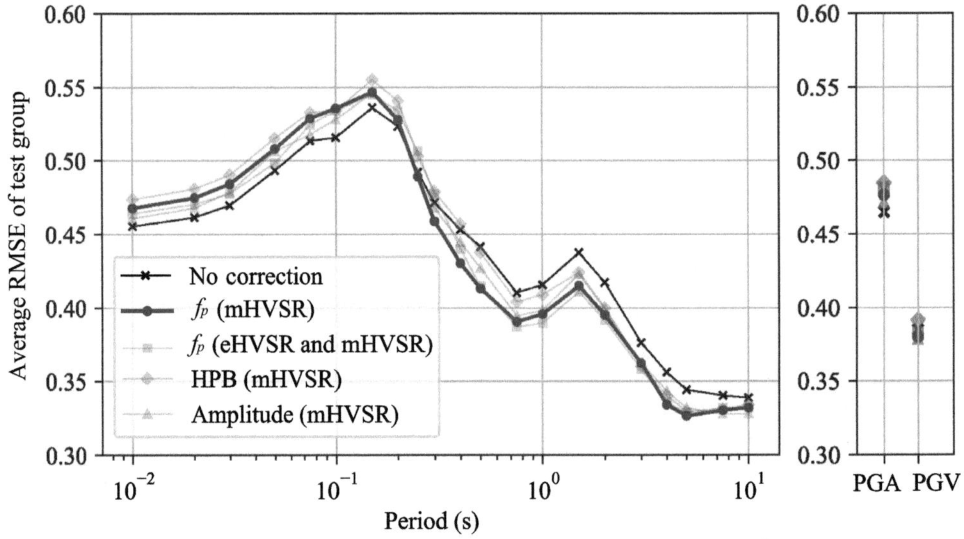

Figure 13. Root mean square error (RMSE) of the left-out mHVSR data for each of the five models evaluated, compared to the base geospatial site term with no adjustment. The color version of this figure is available only in the electronic edition.

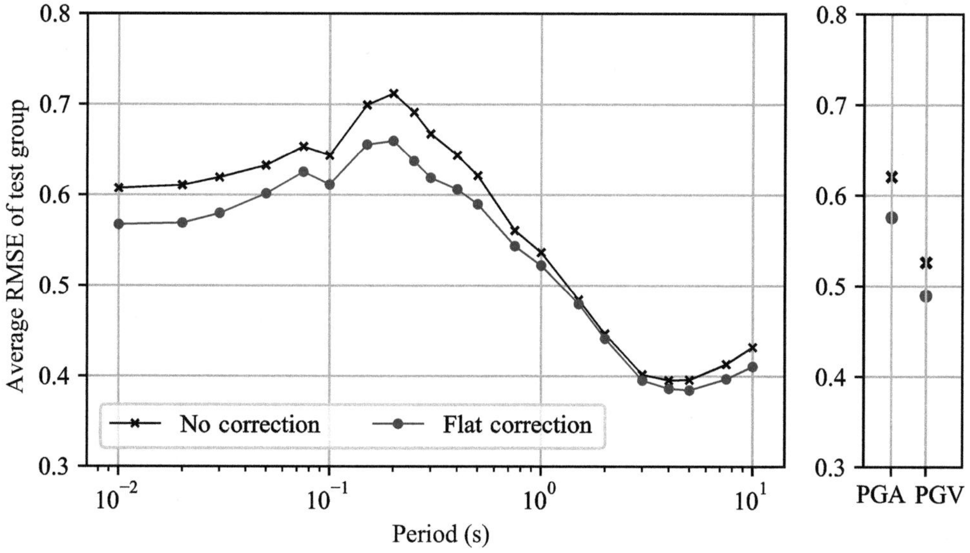

Figure 14. RMSE of the left-out mHVSR data for the flat adjusted site term and the base geospatial site term with no adjustment. The color version of this figure is available only in the electronic edition.

passing stations, we recommend using the model developed using only mHVSR data in terms of f_p (equation 5) and applying the modified site term only to periods greater than 0.25 s. For flat stations, we recommend the constant factor developed using equation (7).

V_{S30}-based model evaluation

A V_{S30}-based site term was also evaluated for the 487 stations with a V_{S30} measurement within 100 m. The model was fit using WLS regression following equation (8), and a three-fold cross-validation was performed to test the model's performance on unseen data. The RMSE was calculated for each fold on the left-out test data, and the average results are shown in Figure 15. We also compare the result to the RMSE of the test data using the base geospatial site term without an adjustment term applied. Including a V_{S30}-based adjustment site term results in a reduction of average RMSE of 5.5% across the test set, with a range from 0.9% to 11.2%. The larger reductions of RMSE in this range were observed at longer periods. This is consistent with greater V_{S30} scaling at long periods that has been observed in California and is modeled in the BSSA14 GMM (Boore *et al.*, 2014).

RECOMMENDED MODEL FOR GEOTECHNICAL MEASUREMENT-BASED SITE TERMS

We propose two alternate geotechnical site terms for use with the base geospatial linear site term (Roberts *et al.*, 2025) based on the results of the three-fold cross-validation in the previous section. The first model, presented in equation (9), is intended for sites with a passing or flat mHVSR recording. The second model, presented in equation (10), is intended for sites with a V_{S30} measurement.

First, the geotechnical term for sites with mHVSR data is expressed in equation (9), and the coefficients by period can be found in Table S1, available in the supplemental material to this article. For sites with passing mHVSR peaks, the model is based on f_p and follows the functional form of Hassani and Atkinson (2016b); this model should only be applied at periods greater than or equal to 0.25 s (frequencies less than or equal to 4 Hz). For sites with flat mHVSR data, a constant adjustment term is applied instead at all frequencies. The term for sites with mHVSR data is

$$\ln(F_{\mathrm{HVSR}}) = \begin{cases} 0 & f > 4\ \mathrm{Hz\ or\ PGA\ or\ PGV}, & \text{passing mHVSR} \\ c_3 & f \le 4\ \mathrm{Hz\ and}\ f_p < 0.5\ \mathrm{Hz}, & \text{passing mHVSR} \\ c_3 + \left[\frac{c_4 - c_3}{\log_{10}\left(\frac{f}{0.5}\right)}\right] \log_{10}\left(\frac{f_p}{0.5}\right) & f \le 4\ \mathrm{Hz\ and}\ 0.5 \le f_p < f, & \text{passing mHVSR} \\ c_4 + \left[\frac{c_5 - c_4}{\log_{10}\left(\frac{20}{f}\right)}\right] \log_{10}\left(\frac{f_p}{f}\right) & f \le 4\ \mathrm{Hz\ and}\ f \le f_p < 20\ \mathrm{Hz} & \text{passing mHVSR} \\ c_5 & f \le 4\ \mathrm{Hz\ and}\ 20\ \mathrm{Hz} \le f_p & \text{passing mHVSR} \\ c_6 & \mathrm{all}\ f & \text{flat mHVSR} \end{cases}, \qquad (9)$$

in which f_p is the resonant frequency of the mHVSR recording; f is the frequency; c_3, c_4, and c_5 are period-dependent coefficients; and c_6 is the period-dependent constant adjustment term for sites with a flat mHVSR recording.

Second, the geotechnical site term for sites with V_{S30} measurements is expressed in equation (10), and the coefficients by period can be found in Table S1. The linear model should only be applied to sites where the V_{S30} has been measured within 100 m:

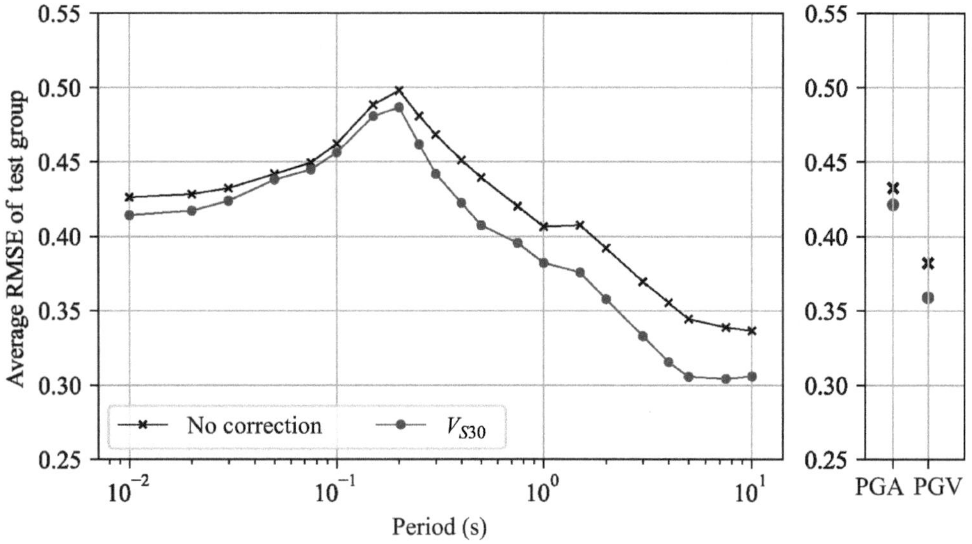

Figure 15. RMSE of the left-out data for the V_{S30} adjusted site term and the base geospatial site term with no adjustment. The color version of this figure is available only in the electronic edition.

$$\ln(F_{V_{S30}}) = c_7 + \begin{cases} c_8 \ln\left(\frac{V_{S30}}{760}\right), & V_{S30} < V_{S30,0} \\ c_8 \ln\left(\frac{V_{S30,0}}{760}\right), & V_{S30} \geq V_{S30,0} \end{cases}, \qquad (10)$$

in which V_{S30} is the measured V_{S30}; $V_{S30,0}$ is the threshold point for where the predicted amplification becomes constant with increasing V_{S30}, ranging from 644 to 981 m/s (as detailed in Table S1); and c_7 and c_8 are the period-dependent model coefficients.

The geotechnical site term (i.e., either equation 9 or equation 10) should be added to the geospatial base linear site term (Roberts *et al.*, 2025) if measured mHVSR or V_{S30} data are available at a site, as shown in the flowchart in Figure 16. The flowchart starts with the station of interest. If the station has no geotechnical measurements, the base geospatial model (Roberts *et al.*, 2025) is used. If the station has a measured value of V_{S30}, then the V_{S30} model (equation 10) is used. If the station has an mHVSR measurement and no measured V_{S30}, then the mHVSR is processed; if the curve is passing or flat, the base geospatial model with the mHVSR correction (equation 9) is used, and if the mHVSR curve fails, the base geospatial model of Roberts *et al.* (2025) is used.

Equation (11) expresses the adjusted geospatial site term incorporating geotechnical data:

$$\ln(F_{\text{Adjusted Geospatial},j}) = \begin{cases} \ln(F_{\text{Geospatial},j}) + \ln(F_{\text{HVSR},j}) & \text{passing or flat mHVSR} \\ \ln(F_{\text{Geospatial},j}) + \ln(F_{V_{S30},j}) & \text{measured } V_{S30} \end{cases}, \qquad (11)$$

in which $\ln(F_{\text{Geospatial},j})$ is the geospatial-based linear site term proposed by Roberts *et al.* (2025), and $\ln(F_{\text{Adjusted Geospatial},j})$ is the geospatial-based linear site term with the geotechnical adjustment applied. The proposed site term in equation (11) is intended to be used with the BSSA14 GMM in replacement of its linear V_{S30}-based site amplification and basin depth terms (i.e., equations 6 and 9 in Boore *et al.*, 2014).

REDUCTION IN SITE-TO-SITE VARIABILITY

To evaluate how well the models perform in reducing variability in GMMs, we compare the site-to-site variability of PGA, PGV, and PSAs across all periods before and after applying each of the two geotechnical site terms (equations 9 and 10).

Figure 17 illustrates the enhanced predictive performance when the geotechnical site terms are applied to the base geospatial GMM for sites with mHVSR parameters (equation 9) or a V_{S30} measurement (equation 10). For comparison, the geospatial site term reduces the average standard deviation of $\delta S2S$ relative to site term scaling by 10.6% compared to BSSA14 and 9.8% compared to the BSSA14 model refit to the dataset used to develop the geospatial site term (Roberts *et al.*, 2025). Using the geospatial model as a base, we can compare the additional reduction of the standard deviation of $\delta S2S$ when the geotechnical site terms are added. Among the subset of stations where measured V_{S30} data are available, the V_{S30}-based site term provides a reduction in the standard deviation of $\delta S2S$ across all periods, with an average reduction of 6.5% compared to the geospatial model. Among the subset of stations where measured mHVSR data are available, the HVSR-based site term provides a slightly lower average reduction of 5.7%. The addition of geotechnical measurements, V_{S30} and mHVSR, into site terms for locations where these measurements are available provides a more site-specific estimate of site response, resulting in a lower standard deviation of $\delta S2S$.

For the subset of stations with either a passing or flat mHVSR recording and a V_{S30} measurement (183 stations: 137 passing and 46 flat), we evaluate whether the V_{S30} adjustment term or HVSR term performs better to determine which should be applied when both measurements are available at a site. Compared to the geospatial model for this subset of data, using the V_{S30} adjustment reduces the average standard deviation of $\delta S2S$ by 7.5%, and using the HVSR adjustment reduces the average standard deviation of $\delta S2S$ by 4.6% at the passing stations. At the flat stations, using the V_{S30}

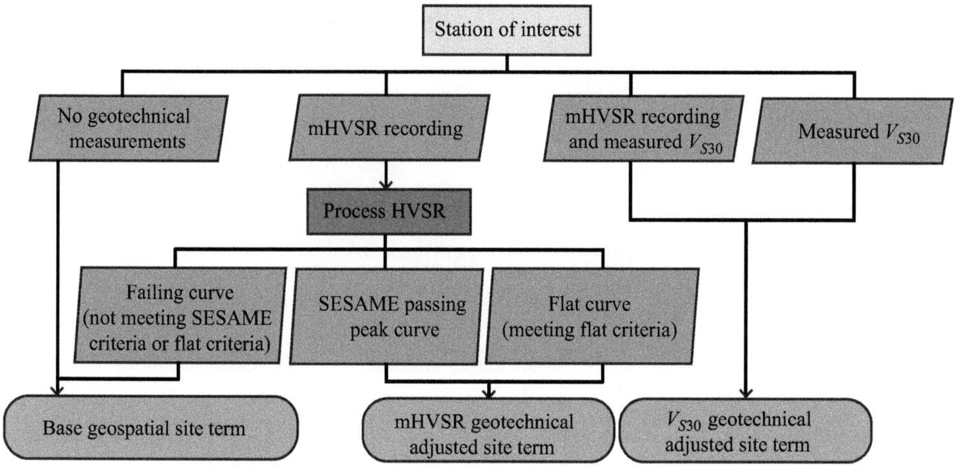

Figure 16. Flowchart for application of the proposed geotechnical adjusted site term in conjunction with the base geospatial linear site term of Roberts *et al.* (2025). The color version of this figure is available only in the electronic edition.

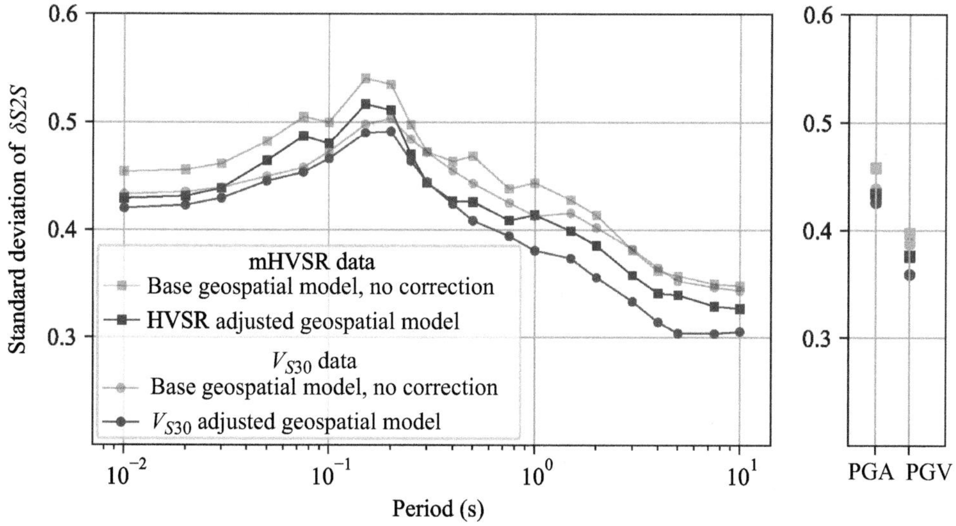

Figure 17. Comparison of between-site variability (standard deviation of $\delta S2S$) of site amplification for the stations with mHVSR data (367 stations) and the stations with V_{S30} data (487 stations), with the base geospatial site term applied, and with the base geospatial site term and geotechnical site term adjustment applied. The color version of this figure is available only in the electronic edition.

adjustment reduces the average standard deviation of $\delta S2S$ by 9.6%, and using the HVSR adjustment does not reduce the average standard deviation of $\delta S2S$, but does adjust the average residual closer to zero. Because of the greater reduction in the standard deviation of $\delta S2S$ for both passing and flat stations, the V_{S30}-based model (equation 10) is selected as the optimal model for cases where both V_{S30} and mHVSR data are available at a site. However, this conclusion could be more precisely evaluated using a dataset of adequate size and coverage containing both mHVSR and measured V_{S30} data.

DISCUSSION

The development of geotechnical measurement-based site terms, using V_{S30} and HVSR data, provides site-specific improvements to geospatial GMM linear site terms that can be applied anywhere these measurements are available. The HVSR term is particularly beneficial due to mHVSR being a low-cost measurement to gather at a site. Our novel approach to the HVSR site term includes adding a flat categorization for mHVSR curves. This classification includes additional mHVSR measurements other than those at stations with passing clear resonant peaks, and as a result, includes an adjustment for sites with no clear resonance. By including the flat classification, we are able to increase the number of stations in the DSGMD with geotechnical site characterization by 8.2%, and the site term associated with the flat classification reduces the average RMSE of test data during three-fold cross-validation by 4.8%.

We also demonstrate that eHVSR parameters can be incorporated into an HVSR site term for GMMs. Although the site terms fit only mHVSR data performed better, the terms fit to eHVSR and mHVSR data still showed reductions in RMSE on the mHVSR test sets at some periods, indicating potential for eHVSR passing curves to enhance HVSR site term development in future studies. This study does not differentiate between eHVSR curves for which nonlinear soil behavior could be present from those with solely linear soil behavior. Nonlinear soil behavior can temporally impact the fundamental frequency of the soil (Beresnev *et al.*, 1998; Régnier *et al.*, 2016), impacting the agreement between mHVSR and eHVSR curves. Accounting for this nonlinearity could be an area of future improvement to site terms developed using eHVSR data.

In the California-specific dataset used here, 24.9% of mHVSR curves had passing clear peaks, and 9.4% of mHVSR curves were flat. This means that at 65.7% of stations with mHVSR data, no HVSR-based adjustment could be applied. These results are indicative of a lack of a strong impedance contrast in the subsurface at the majority of sites. Regions known to have stronger impedance contrasts, such as Mexico City (Lermo and Chávez-García, 1994) or New England (Pontrelli *et al.*, 2023), tend to identify clear HVSR peaks more frequently. The Satoh *et al.* (2001) study comparing eHVSR and mHVSR in the Sendai basin in Japan also indicates that sites with a strong impedance contrast may have more comparable HVSR peak frequencies between measurement types. HVSR-based site term adjustments in regions exhibiting strong impedance contrasts in the subsurface have the potential to be more useful given the consistency and clarity of the peaks, and further studies should be conducted.

The V_{S30}-based site term and HVSR-based site term are designed for use with GMM site terms in California and provide further reductions in $\delta S2S$ from the geospatial base site term model, compared to other ergodic models currently used in California. As shown in Roberts *et al.* (2025), the base geospatial model reduces $\delta S2S$ by an average of 10.6% compared to the BSSA14 ergodic model. Adjusting the base model with the geotechnical site terms (equations 9 and 10) results in additional reductions in $\delta S2S$. Compared to the base geospatial model, the adjustments in this article produce an average reduction in $\delta S2S$ of 6.5% for sites with measured V_{S30}, and 5.7% for sites with mHVSR data (either passing or flat). The proposed geotechnical site terms are constrained to California because the model training and validation only used California measurements; however, these models could be refit and analyzed in other regions, depending on the availability of mHVSR and V_{S30} measurements. As mHVSR databases and measurements continue to grow in the future, this data source will be beneficial in more accurately predicting site terms. In addition, because more rigorously processed ground-motion databases with sufficient spatial coverage of stations across California become available, such as that of NGA-West3, this methodology could be replicated to develop models suitable for implementation in California. The DSGMD was used in this study, which has less robust processing standards compared to the NGA databases; although outliers were removed and scaling effects were checked in Roberts *et al.* (2025), errors could still be present in some of the recordings, particularly at long periods.

The parameters of the geotechnical models presented here —both the HVSR-based and V_{S30}-based terms—should be used as secondary adjustments following the application of the primary geospatial site term model (Roberts *et al.*, 2025). We do not recommend the application of the geotechnical model alone (without first incorporating the primary geospatial model) because the geotechnical terms may trade off with the geospatial model, particularly when overlapping information is present. For example, the primary geospatial model (which uses regional geological unit and roughness) may already capture the influence of rock sites, and this effect is further refined by the inclusion of the flat HVSR classification and the V_{S30} term. Using the geotechnical model alone without incorporating the primary geospatial model could lead to biased or incomplete site effect modeling.

CONCLUSIONS

In this article, we develop geotechnical measurement-based site terms to be used in conjunction with geospatial linear site terms (Roberts *et al.*, 2025) in GMMs, based on measured V_{S30} and HVSR parameters for California. The geotechnical site terms are developed for PGA, PGV, and 5%-damped PSA from 0.01 to 10 s. A subset of the Ji *et al.* (2022) DSGMD, containing 2339 stations across California, is used for model development. This dataset is paired with mHVSR data from the Wang *et al.* (2021) HVSR database, eHVSR data from Ji *et al.* (2022), V_{S30} measurements from the VSPDB (Ahdi *et al.*, 2018; Kwak *et al.*, 2021), and the USGS V_{S30} database (McPhillips *et al.*, 2020). After HVSR data processing, there are 820 stations with geotechnical information used to develop the geotechnical site terms.

The V_{S30} measurement-based term (equation 10) was validated using three-fold cross-validation and shown to reduce the RMSE by 5.5% compared to using the base geospatial site term of Roberts *et al.* (2025). This site term is intended to be used at sites with only measured V_{S30} data and should not be used with proxy-based estimates of V_{S30}. This site term outperformed the HVSR-based site term for the subset of stations with both mHVSR measurements and V_{S30} measurements. Therefore, the V_{S30}-based site term should also be used primarily for sites with both mHVSR and V_{S30} measurements.

The optimal HVSR parameter-based site term (equation 9) is developed using the peak resonant frequency (f_p) at sites with mHVSR measurements with a passing clear peak, and a constant adjustment for sites with an mHVSR measurement classified as flat. Site terms fit to both mHVSR and eHVSR data at passing stations were tested, but the site term fit to only mHVSR data performed best. The flat classification (outlined in Table 1) is a new HVSR parameter that identifies cases for which an HVSR curve not only lacks a clear identifiable peak by the SESAME criteria, but is also completely flat, indicating a lack of resonance at the site. The peak resonant frequency was selected as the optimal variable for sites with a clear peak due to its performance during three-fold cross-validation compared to other HVSR parameters analyzed. The f_p-based site term for passing sites should only be applied for PSAs at periods greater than or equal to 0.25 s, as no reduction in RMSE was observed at shorter periods; however, the flat term resulted in a reduction in RMSE at all periods evaluated. The use of a site term with f_p as the explanatory variable and a constant term for sites classified as flat allows for sites with mHVSR measurements across California to be adjusted for their measured resonance.

The two geotechnical site terms result in a reduction in site-to-site variability ($\delta S2S$) compared to the base geospatial model and effectively capture site-specific effects. Compared to the base geospatial linear site term, the geotechnical site terms result in an average reduction in $\delta S2S$ of 6.5% for sites with measured V_{S30} and 5.7% for sites with passing or flat mHVSR classifications. The geotechnical site terms should be utilized with the base geospatial site term (Roberts *et al.*, 2025), as shown in equation (11). This formulation allows for the Roberts *et al.* (2025) geospatial model to be used at all locations, while allowing for more detailed adjustments for site-specific measurements (V_{S30} and/or mHVSR) for which they are available.

The geotechnical site terms applied to a fully spatially available geospatial linear site term model are intended to improve ground-motion estimates at well-characterized sites with mHVSR or V_{S30} measurements across California. This framework could be applied to other regions with available mHVSR and V_{S30} measurements, and the increase in such measurements throughout the globe may present future opportunities to apply and further refine this approach.

DATA AND RESOURCES

The earthquake ground motions were obtained from the Ji *et al.* (2022) DesignSafe Ground-Motion Database (DSGMD; doi: 10.17603/ds2-syc5-nk92). The ground-motion data were processed to obtain horizontal-to-vertical spectral ratio (HVSR) curves using *hvsrpy* (Vantassel, 2020). *Hvsrpy* is an open-source Python package for processing earthquake HVSR (eHVSR) and microtremor HVSR (mHVSR) and is available at https://github.com/jpvantassel/hvsrpy (last accessed July 2025). The data were processed to obtain ground-motion predictions using the BSSA14 ground-motion model (GMM; Boore *et al.*, 2014) coded and available at https://github.com/bakerjw/GMMs/blob/master/gmms/bssa_2014_active.m (last accessed July 2025; Mongold and Baker, 2021), modified with the site term reported in Roberts *et al.* (2025). The geospatial portion of the site term uses surficial geology (Wills *et al.*, 2015), geomorphic province (California Geologic Survey, 2002), and topographic position derived from GMTED2010 (Danielson and Gesch, 2011). The mHVSR curves were obtained from the Wang *et al.* (2021) HVSR database, available via DesignSafe at doi: 10.17603/ds2-nn2e-wm79. The mHVSR parameters were determined using *hvsrpy* (Vantassel, 2020). The V_{S30} measurements were obtained from the Ji *et al.* (2022) DSGMD (doi: 10.17603/ds2-syc5-nk92), and the shear-wave velocity profile database (VSPDB) at https://vspdb.org/ (last accessed November 2025; Ahdi *et al.*, 2018; Kwak *et al.*, 2021). The analysis was performed using the open-source environment Python (Python Software Foundation, 2023). All figures were produced using Python, ArcGIS Pro (Environmental Systems Research Institute [ESRI], 2024), and Adobe Illustrator (Adobe Inc., 2019), which were all last accessed in February 2026. The supplemental material for this article contains Table S1 in Microsoft Excel format. Table S1 provides coefficients by period for peak ground acceleration (PGA), peak ground velocity (PGV), and pseudospectral accelerations (PSAs) at 21 periods from 0.01 to 10 s for the HVSR- and V_{S30}-based site terms proposed in equations (9) and (10).

DECLARATION OF COMPETING INTERESTS

The authors acknowledge that there are no conflicts of interest recorded.

ACKNOWLEDGMENTS

The authors would like to acknowledge the feedback of Jonathan Stewart, Ivan Wong, and an anonymous reviewer, whose comments greatly improved the quality of this article. This material is based upon work supported by the U.S. Geological Survey (USGS) under Grant Numbers G23AP00396 and G23AP00397. The views and conclusions contained in this document are those of the authors and should not be interpreted as representing the opinions or policies of the USGS. Mention of trade names or commercial products does not constitute their endorsement by the USGS.

REFERENCES

Abrahamson, N. A., and R. R. Youngs (1992). A stable algorithm for regression analyses using the random effects model, *Bull. Seismol. Soc. Am.* **82,** 505–510.

Abrahamson, N. A., W. J. Silva, and R. Kamai (2014). Summary of the ASK14 ground motion relation for active crustal regions, *Earthq. Spectra* **30,** 1025–1055.

Adobe Inc. (2019). Adobe illustrator, available at https://adobe.com/products/illustrator (last accessed February 2026).

Ahdi, S. K., S. Sadiq, O. Olhan, Y. Bozorgnia, Y. M. A. Hashash, D. Y. Kwak, D. Park, A. Yong, and J. P. Stewart (2018). Development of a United States community shear wave velocity profile database, *Geotechnical Engineering and Soil Dynamics V: Seismic Hazard Analysis, Earthquake Ground Motions, and Regional-Scale Assessment*, S. J. Brandenberg and M. T. Manzari (Editors), 10–13 June 2018, Austin, Texas, ASCE Geotechnical Special Publication No. 291, 330–339.

Ancheta, T. D., R. B. Darragh, J. P. Stewart, E. Seyhan, W. J. Silva, B. S. J. Chiou, K. E. Wooddell, R. W. Graves, A. R. Kottke, D. M. Boore, *et al.* (2014). NGA-West2 database, *Earthq. Spectra* **30,** 989–1005.

Beresnev, I. A., E. H. Field, K. Van Den Abeele, and P. A. Johnson (1998). Magnitude of nonlinear sediment response in Los Angeles basin during the 1994 Northridge, California, earthquake. *Bull. Seismol. Soc. Am.* **88,** 1079–1084.

Boore, D. M., and W. B. Joyner (1997). Site amplification for generic rock sites, *Bull. Seismol. Soc. Am.* **87,** 327–341.

Boore, D. M., W. B. Joyner, and T. E. Fumal (1997). Equations for estimating horizontal response spectra and peak acceleration from western North American earthquakes: A summary of recent work, *Seismol. Res. Lett.* **68,** 128–153.

Boore, D. M., J. P. Stewart, E. Seyhan, and G. M. Atkinson (2014). NGA-West2 equations for predicting PGA, PGV, and 5% damped PSA for shallow crustal earthquakes, *Earthq. Spectra* **30,** 1057–1085.

Bozorgnia, Y., N. A. Abrahamson, L. A. Atik, T. D. Ancheta, G. M. Atkinson, J. W. Baker, A. Baltay, D. M. Boore, K. W. Campbell, and B. S.-J. Chiou, *et al.* (2014). NGA-West2 research project, *Earthq. Spectra* **30,** 973–987.

Braganza, S., G. M. Atkinson, H. Ghofrani, B. Hassani, L. Chouinard, P. Rosset, D. Motazedian, and J. Hunter (2016). Modeling site amplification in Eastern Canada on a regional scale, *Seismol. Res. Lett.* **87,** 1008–1021.

Buckreis, T. E., C. C. Nweke, P. Wang, S. J. Brandenberg, M. E. Ramos-Sepúlveda, R. Shams, S. Mohammed, R. Pretell, S. Mazzoni, P.

Zimmaro, *et al.* (2025). A global Application Programming Interface–enabled earthquake ground motion relational database for engineering applications. *Earthq. Spectra* **41,** 4162–4194.

California Geologic Survey (2002). California geomorphic provinces, California Department of Conservation, available at https://www.conservation.ca.gov (last accessed July 2025).

Campbell, K. W., and Y. Bozorgnia (2014). NGA-West2 ground motion model for the average horizontal components of PGA, PGV, and 5% damped linear acceleration response spectra, *Earthq. Spectra* **30,** 1087–1115.

Campbell, K. W., N. M. Kuehn, and Y. Bozorgnia (2025). Variability and uncertainty of variance components in fixed-effects and mixed-effects ground-motion models, *Earthq. Spectra* **41,** 731–752.

Carpenter, N. S., Z. Wang, and E. W. Woolery (2020). An evaluation of linear site-response parameters in the Central and Eastern United States and the importance of empirical site-response estimations, *Bull. Seismol. Soc. Am.* **110,** 489–507.

Carpenter, N. S., Z. Wang, E. W. Woolery, and M. Rong (2018). Estimating site response with recordings from deep boreholes and HVSR: Examples from the Mississippi Embayment of the Central United States, *Bull. Seismol. Soc. Am.* **108,** 1199–1209.

Chao, S. H., C. M. Lin, C. H. Kuo, J. Y. Huang, K. L. Wen, and Y. H. Chen (2021). Implementing horizontal-to-vertical Fourier spectral ratios and spatial correlation in a ground-motion prediction equation to predict site effects, *Earthq. Spectra* **37,** 827–856.

Chiou, B. S. J., and R. R. Youngs (2014). Update of the Chiou and Youngs NGA model for the average horizontal component of peak ground motion and response spectra, *Earthq. Spectra* **30,** 1117–1153.

Cox, B. R., T. Cheng, J. P. Vantassel, and L. Manuel (2020). A statistical representation and frequency-domain window-rejection algorithm for single-station HVSR measurements, *Geophys. J. Int.* **221,** 2170–2183.

Danielson, J. J., and D. B. Gesch (2011). Global multi-resolution terrain elevation data 2010 (GMTED2010), *U.S. Geol. Surv. Open-File Rept. 2011-1073*, 26 pp., available at http://pubs.usgs.gov/of/2011/1073/pdf/of2011-1073.pdf (last accessed July 2025).

Environmental Systems Research Institute (ESRI) (2024). ArcGIS Pro, available at https://www.esri.com (last accessed February 2026).

Ghofrani, H., and G. M. Atkinson (2014). Site condition evaluation using horizontal-to-vertical response spectral ratios of earthquakes in the NGA-West 2 and Japanese databases, *Soil Dynam. Earthq. Eng.* **67,** 30–43.

Hassani, B., and G. M. Atkinson (2016a). Applicability of the site fundamental frequency as a VS30 proxy for central and eastern North America, *Bull. Seismol. Soc. Am* **106,** 653–664.

Hassani, B., and G. M. Atkinson (2016b). Site-effects model for central and eastern North America based on peak frequency, *Bull. Seismol. Soc. Am.* **106,** 2197–2213.

Hassani, B., and G. M. Atkinson (2018). Site-effects model for Central and Eastern North America based on peak frequency and average shear-wave velocity, *Bull. Seismol. Soc. Am.* **108,** 338–350.

Hassani, B., A. Yong, G. M. Atkinson, T. Feng, and L. Meng (2019). Comparison of site dominant frequency from earthquake and microseismic data in California, *Bull. Seismol. Soc. Am.* **109,** 1034–1040.

Hearne, M., E. M. Thompson, H. Schovanec, J. Rekoske, B. T. Aagaard, and C. B. Worden (2019). USGS automated ground motion processing software, *U.S. Geol. Surv. Software Release*, doi: 10.5066/P9ANQXN3.

Idriss, I. M. (2014). An NGA-West2 empirical model for estimating the horizontal spectral values generated by shallow crustal earthquakes, *Earthq. Spectra* **30,** 1155–1177.

Ji, C., A. Cabas, A. Kottke, M. Pilz, J. Macedo, and C. Liu (2022). A DesignSafe ground motion database: Time series, engineering metrics, and site metadata [Version 2], *DesignSafe-CI*, doi: 10.17603/ds2-syc5-nk92.

Ji, C., A. Cabas, A. Kottke, M. Pilz, J. Macedo, and C. Liu (2023). A DesignSafe earthquake ground motion database for California and surrounding regions, *Earthq. Spectra* **39,** 702–721.

Kaklamanos, J., and L. G. Baise (2011). Model validations and comparisons of the Next Generation Attenuation of Ground Motions (NGA-West) project, *Bull. Seismol. Soc. Am.* **101,** 160–175.

Kawase, H., F. Nagashima, K. Nakano, and Y. Mori (2019). Direct evaluation of S-wave amplification factors from microtremor H/V ratios: Double empirical corrections to "Nakamura" method, *Soil Dynam. Earthq. Eng.* **126,** 105067, doi: 10.1016/j.soildyn.2018.01.049.

Konno, K., and T. Ohmachi (1998). Ground-motion characteristics estimated from spectral ratio between horizontal and vertical components of microtremor, *Bull. Seismol. Soc. Am.* **88,** 228–241.

Kuehn, N. M., K. W. Campbell, and Y. Bozorgnia (2025). Potential biases in mixed-effects ground-motion models and variance components due to uncertainty in random effects. *Bull. Seismol. Soc. Am.* **115,** 578–601.

Kwak, D., S. K. Ahdi, P. Wang, P. Zimmaro, S. J. Brandenberg, and J. P. Stewart (2021). Web portal for shear wave velocity and HVSR databases in support of site response research and applications, UCLA Geotechnical Engineering Group, Los Angeles, California, doi: 10.21222/C27H0V.

Kwak, D. Y., J. P. Stewart, S. U. J. Mandokhail, and D. Park (2017). Supplementing V_{S30} with H/V spectral ratios for predicting site effects, *Bull. Seismol. Soc. Am.* **107,** 2028–2042.

Lermo, J., and F. J. Chávez-García (1993). Site effect evaluation using spectral ratios with only one station, *Bull. Seismol. Soc. Am.* **83,** 1574–1594.

Lermo, J., and F. J. Chávez-García (1994). Site effect evaluation at Mexico City: Dominant period and relative amplification from strong motion and microtremor records, *Soil Dynam. Earthq. Eng.* **13,** 413–423.

McPhillips, D. F., J. A. Herrick, S. Ahdi, A. K. Yong, and S. Haefner (2020). Updated Compilation of VS30 Data for the United States, *U.S. Geol. Surv. Data Release*, doi: 10.5066/P9H5QEAC.

Mongold, E., and J. W. Baker (2021). A software repository of Ground Motion Models – Version 1.0.0, *Blume Earthquake Engineering Center Technical Rept. 207*, Stanford Digital Repository, available at https://purl.stanford.edu/qy113my5899 (last accessed July 2025).

Nakamura, Y. (1989). A method for dynamic characteristics estimation of subsurface using microtremor on the ground surface, *Railw. Tech. Res. Inst.* **30,** 25–33.

Nash, J. E., and J. V. Sutcliffe (1970). River flow forecasting through conceptual models: Part I, A discussion of principles, *J. Hydrol.* **10,** 282–290.

Nogoshi, M., and T. Igarashi (1971). On the amplitude characteristics of microtremor, Part II, *Zisin* **24,** 26–40.

Pinilla-Ramos, C., N. Abrahamson, and R. Kayen (2022). Estimation of site terms in ground-motion models for California using horizontal-to-vertical spectral ratios from microtremor, *Bull. Seismol. Soc. Am.* **112,** 3016–3036.

Pinilla-Ramos, C. I., N. A. Abrahamson, and R. E. Kayen (2024). Evaluation of site terms for ground-motion models for South America, *Bull. Seismol. Soc. Am.* **114,** 2546–2558.

Pontrelli, M., L. Baise, and J. Ebel (2023). Regional-scale site characterization mapping in high impedance environments using soil fundamental resonance (f_0): New England, USA, *Eng. Geol.* **315,** 107043, doi: 10.1016/j.enggeo.2023.107043.

Python Software Foundation (2023). Python Language Reference, version 3.9.10, available at https://www.python.org (last accessed February 2026).

Régnier, J., H. Cadet, and P. Y. Bard (2016). Empirical quantification of the impact of nonlinear soil behavior on site response, *Bull. Seismol. Soc. Am.* **106,** 1710–1719.

Roberts, M., L. Baise, S. Nie, J. Kaklamanos, and W. Zhan (2025). Geospatial Site amplification model for California, *Bull Seismol. Soc. Am.* doi: 10.1785/0120250074.

Satoh, T., H. Kawase, and S. I. Matsushima (2001). Differences between site characteristics obtained from microtremors, S-waves, P-waves, and codas, *Bull. Seismol. Soc. Am.* **91,** 313–334.

Seyhan, E., J. P. Stewart, T. D. Ancheta, R. B. Darragh, and R. W. Graves (2014). NGA-West2 site database, *Earthq. spectra* **30,** 1007–1024.

Site Effects Assessment using Ambient Excitations (SESAME) (2004). Guidelines for the implementation of the H/V spectral ratio technique on ambient vibrations measurements, processing, and interpretation, *No. WP12- Deliverable D23.12*, European Commission-Research General Directorate.

Vantassel, J. (2020). jpvantassel/hvsrpy: Latest (Concept), *Zenodo*, doi: 10.5281/zenodo.3666956.

Vantassel, J. P., M. Ilgac, A. A. Zekkos, A. Yong, B. Hassani, and A. J. Martin (2024). Are the horizontal-to-vertical spectral ratios of earthquakes and microtremors the same? *Bull. Seismol. Soc. Am.* **114,** 3078–3092.

Wald, D. J., and T. I. Allen (2007). Topographic slope as a proxy for seismic site conditions and amplification. *Bull. Seismol. Soc. Am.* **97,** 1379–1395.

Wang, P. (2020). wltcwpf/hvsrProc: First release (Version v1.0.0), *Zenodo*, doi: 10.5281/zenodo.4724141.

Wang, P., P. Zimmaro, S. K. Ahdi, A. Yong, and J. P. Stewart (2023). Identification protocols for horizontal-to-vertical spectral ratio peaks, *Bull. Seismol. Soc. Am.* **113,** 782–803.

Wang, P., P. Zimmaro, T. E. Buckreis, T. Gospe, S. J. Brandenberg, S. K. Ahdi, A. Yong, and J. P. Stewart (2022). Relational database for horizontal-to-vertical spectral ratios, *Seismol. Res. Lett.* **93,** 1075–1088.

Wang, P., P. Zimmaro, and J. P. Stewart (2021). Horizontal-to-vertical spectral ratio database access and analysis [Version 2], *DesignSafe-CI*, doi: 10.17603/ds2-nn2e-wm79.

Wathelet, M., J. L. Chatelain, C. Cornou, G. D. Giulio, B. Guillier, M. Ohrnberger, and A. Savvaidis (2020). Geopsy: A user-friendly open-source tool set for ambient vibration processing, *Seismol. Res. Lett.* **91,** 1878–1889.

Wills, C. J., and K. B. Clahan (2006). Developing a map of geologically defined site-condition categories for California. *Bull. Seismol. Soc. Am.* **96,** 1483–1501.

Wills, C. J., C. I. Gutierrez, F. G. Perez, and D. M. Branum (2015). A next generation V_{S30} map for California based on geology and topography, *Bull. Seismol. Soc. Am.* **105,** 3083–3091.

Yazdi, M., J. G. Anderson, and R. Motamed (2023). Reducing the uncertainties in the NGA-West2 ground motion models by incorporating the frequency and amplitude of the fundamental peak of the horizontal-to-vertical spectral ratio of surface ground motions, *Earthq. Spectra* **39,** 1088–1108.

Yong, A. (2016). Comparison of measured and proxy-based VS30 values in California, *Earthq. Spectra* **32,** 171–192.

Yong, A., S. E. Hough, J. Iwahashi, and A. Braverman (2012). A terrain-based site-conditions map of California with implications for the contiguous United States. *Bull. Seismol. Soc. Am.* **102,** 114–128.

Zhu, C., M. Pilz, and F. Cotton (2020). Evaluation of a novel application of earthquake HVSR in site-specific amplification estimation, *Soil Dynam. Earthq. Eng.* **139,** 106301, doi: 10.1016/j.soildyn.2020.106301.

Manuscript received 21 July 2025
Published online 24 March 2026

Geospatial Site Terms for Central and Eastern U.S. Ground-Motion Models Using Physiographic Province and Sediment Thickness

Elise (Ellie) Meyer*[1], Laurie G. Baise[1], James Kaklamanos[2], Shiying Nie[1], Weiwei Zhan[3], and Maggie Roberts[1]

ABSTRACT

Most recent Central and Eastern United States (CEUS) ground-motion models (GMMs) rely on the time-averaged shear-wave velocity in the upper 30 m of the subsurface (V_{S30}) as the primary site parameter. Site terms in GMMs are known to reduce site-to-site residuals ($\delta S2S_j$), which quantify the repeatable, systematic deviations between observations and predictions at a station. However, the inputs for site terms are often unavailable both at ground-motion recording stations and at locations where GMMs are used to predict shaking levels. This highlights the need for spatially continuous site terms. We use mixed-effects regression to obtain $\delta S2S_j$ from ground-motion predictions using the Next Generation Attenuation-East (NGA-East) GMMs for the CEUS and two different ground-motion datasets. These $\delta S2S_j$ values show strong regional trends consistent with large geologic structures, such as the Mississippi Embayment, the Superior Uplands, and sections of the Coastal Plain. In this study, we evaluate a range of continuous and categorical site variables for use in GMMs to capture both local and regional site effects. These variables serve as proxies for sediment stiffness, shallow velocity structure, sediment/bedrock impedance contrasts, basin effects, and topographic effects. From these variables, we develop a new two-parameter linear amplification model using (1) a categorical variable based on physiographic provinces (Fenneman and Johnson, 1946) and (2) a continuous sediment thickness variable from a high-resolution regional dataset (Boyd *et al.*, 2024) and a global dataset (Pelletier *et al.*, 2016). The physiographic province parameter captures large-scale trends in amplification that effectively regionalize the site term, whereas sediment thickness accounts for local variation. When tested on ground motions from M > 4 earthquakes, this model reduced the standard deviation of $\delta S2S_j$ by an average of 23.4% across all periods and significantly decreased spatial trends in residuals relative to the current NGA-East amplification model (Stewart *et al.*, 2020).

KEY POINTS

- Central and Eastern United States (CEUS) ground-motion predictions need spatially continuous site terms because V_{S30} data are often unavailable.
- $\delta S2S$ shows strong regional amplification patterns that align closely with major CEUS geologic structures.
- A new two-parameter model cuts $\delta S2S$ variability by 23% and reduces large-scale spatial trends.

Supplemental Material

INTRODUCTION

The Central and Eastern United States (CEUS) is a geographically large and geologically variable area ranging from deep sedimentary deposits in the Atlantic Coastal Plain (ACP), to previously glaciated terrain in the northeast and the broad, flat Interior Lowlands. Because of the variability in site conditions, as well as a lack of site and ground-motion data, challenges persist in accurately predicting earthquake site effects, despite elevated levels of seismic risk in population centers such as Boston, Massachusetts, Charleston, South Carolina, Memphis,

1. Department of Civil and Environmental Engineering, Tufts University, Medford, Massachusetts, U.S.A., https://orcid.org/0009-0009-2684-9233 (EM); https://orcid.org/0000-0002-8329-5689 (LGB); https://orcid.org/0000-0002-3518-7843 (SN); https://orcid.org/0009-0000-9036-4921 (MR); 2. Department of Civil Engineering, Merrimack College, North Andover, Massachusetts, U.S.A., https://orcid.org/0000-0001-7480-0391 (JK); 3. Department of Civil, Environmental and Construction Engineering, University of Central Florida, Orlando, Florida, U.S.A., https://orcid.org/0000-0002-9266-4466 (WZ)

*Corresponding author: elise.meyer@tufts.edu

Cite this article as Meyer, E., L. G. Baise, J. Kaklamanos, S. Nie, W. Zhan, and M. Roberts (2026). Geospatial Site Terms for Central and Eastern U.S. Ground-Motion Models Using Physiographic Province and Sediment Thickness, *Bull. Seismol. Soc. Am.* **116**, 1240–1263, doi: 10.1785/0120250180

Tennessee, New York City, New York, and Washington, D.C. Until recently, the primary ground-motion database used for ground-motion modeling in the CEUS was the Next Generation Attenuation-East (NGA-East) database (Goulet, Kishida, *et al.*, 2021), which includes 9382 ground motions from 82 earthquakes at 1266 different stations, recorded between 1988 and 2013. In 2023, the CEUS earthquake ground-motion database from 2010 to 2020 (Thompson *et al.*, 2023) was published, which includes 38,400 ground motions from 269 events at 3,098 stations. The Thompson *et al.* (2023) database provides a 309% increase in ground-motion records and a 145% increase in the number of stations with recordings, expanding both the range of earthquakes sampled and the spatial coverage of stations across the CEUS. This increase in ground-motion data and the spatial coverage of stations motivates the improved characterization of the variations and patterns of site amplification in the CEUS.

Ground-motion models (GMMs) use source, path, and site characteristics to predict ground-motion parameters from a given earthquake at the site of interest. The majority of site terms in CEUS GMMs currently use the time-averaged shear-wave velocity in the upper 30 m of the subsurface (V_{S30}) as the primary variable to predict amplification. The NGA-East GMMs for the CEUS assume a reference site condition of very hard rock, $V_{S30} = 3000$ m/s (Goulet, Bozorgnia, *et al.*, 2021). The CEUS site amplification models are developed separately to adjust the reference rock median predictions to the site conditions of interest using V_{S30}. This site amplification model includes a linear site term (Stewart *et al.*, 2020) and a nonlinear site term (Hashash *et al.*, 2020), which consists of two parts: a V_{S30}-scaled site term based on empirical data relative to a V_{S30} of 760 m/s, and a simulation-based term that adjusts the reference rock condition from 760 to 3000 m/s.

Although V_{S30} has traditionally been used as a site response variable, its effectiveness in predicting site amplification in the CEUS is more limited compared with regions like California. Hassani and Atkinson (2016) have shown that site effects are more strongly related to site fundamental frequencies (f_{peak}) than V_{S30} in central and eastern North America, especially where sediment thickness is shallow and $f_{peak} > 1$ Hz. In the NGA-East database, only 6% of stations have V_{S30} values that were measured, compared with 28% of the stations in the NGA-West2 database (Ancheta *et al.*, 2014). V_{S30} is estimated at the remaining stations using various proxies, including terrain-based, slope-based, and geologic-unit-based methods (Parker *et al.*, 2019; Goulet, Kishida, *et al.*, 2021). These proxy-based approaches introduce additional epistemic uncertainty to the NGA-East GMMs (Thompson and Wald, 2016). Site amplification models for other tectonic regimes often use depth-based terms, such as $Z_{1.0}$ and $Z_{2.5}$ (the depths to shear-wave velocity horizons of 1.0 and 2.5 km/s, respectively) as additional site terms to capture basin effects, but these have not been widely explored in the CEUS. Long-period amplification has been observed in large, deep structures such as the ACP (Boyd *et al.*, 2024) and the Mississippi Embayment (Sedaghati *et al.*, 2018). This amplification pattern is newly accounted for in the 2023 update to the National Seismic Hazard Model (Petersen *et al.*, 2024), which uses sediment thickness from the Boyd *et al.* (2024) model and amplification estimates from the Chapman and Guo (2021) model.

The tectonic and geologic history of the CEUS leads to large-scale regional structures controlled by geologic history and resulting geomorphology, such as the ACP, the Great Plains, and the Interior Highlands. In deep sedimentary structures in the ACP and the Mississippi Embayment, the resonant amplification with attenuation in the deep sediments is best characterized by sediment thickness (Boyd *et al.*, 2024). On the contrary, shallow sedimentary structures in previously glaciated terrain in the northern United States experience resonant amplification with little attenuation (due to shallow sediments) and can be characterized by f_{peak} or sedimentary thickness (Baise *et al.*, 2016; Hassani and Atkinson, 2016, 2018). In addition to the effects of sediment thickness, the geologic history of the CEUS also results in varied bedrock conditions, which can lead to differences in bedrock/sediment impedance contrasts, shallow crustal velocity structure, or near-surface attenuation (e.g., kappa). The combination of these effects leads to strong regionalization of site effects across the CEUS.

In this study, we perform residual analysis using the NGA-East GMMs and recorded ground motions to reveal the spatial patterns of residuals across the CEUS. We then develop a new site term for the CEUS that captures both regional trends and local variations. Our goal is to develop a spatially continuous site term that can be used universally across the CEUS without the need for additional site-specific measurements.

To develop a new site term for GMM in the CEUS, we assemble a geospatial dataset of potential predictor variables across the CEUS. This geospatial dataset includes regional geologic terms to capture the large-scale regional trends in site amplification. The dataset also includes spatially continuous geospatial data derived from digital elevation models (DEMs) to capture near-surface characteristics related to seismic velocity, basin effects, and topographic effects. We use two different ground-motion datasets: the NGA-East database (Goulet, Kishida, *et al.*, 2021) and the Thompson *et al.* (2023) CEUS ground-motion database. This combination improves magnitude and distance coverage, as well as providing better spatial coverage of stations where site-to-site residuals ($\delta S2S_j$, the portion of the residual that is due to the amplification at the site) can be extracted. We compare the expanded $\delta S2S_j$ with collected geospatial data across the entire CEUS to build a linear site amplification term that captures the large-scale regional effects and the local site effects related to near-surface sediments.

DATA

Ground-motion database

We combined two different CEUS ground-motion datasets for this study: the NGA-East database (Goulet, Kishida, *et al.*,

2021) and the Center for Engineering Strong Motion Data (CESMD) database for CEUS ground motions from 2010 to 2020 (Thompson *et al.*, 2023). There is an overlap in the datasets of 195 ground motions from two events; where there was an overlap, the ground motions from the CESMD database were used. The combined database was filtered to remove recordings from outside the CEUS and beyond the attenuation boundary with the western United States (WUS), to remove recordings flagged as outliers, and to remove recordings from stations with less than three recordings to ensure accurate, repeatable characterization of $\delta S2S_j$. In addition, we capped the rupture distance at 1000 km to reduce bias that occurs when weak, distant shaking is not recorded, leaving only the relatively larger motions (Contreras *et al.*, 2022). These recordings range in magnitude from 3 to 5.85 and have peak ground acceleration (PGA) and peak ground velocity (PGV) as intensity measures (IMs). The NGA-East dataset uses 5% damped pseudospectral acceleration (PSA), whereas the CESMD dataset actually uses spectral acceleration (SA), despite the associated documentation mentioning PSA (Thompson, E., personal comm., 2025). PSA and SA are often used interchangeably because they are nearly identical at short to medium periods, but can diverge at longer periods, in which the oscillator response departs from the true SA (Boore, 2001; Chopra, 2007; Mentrasti, 2008). We use the full bandwidth reported in the databases. For our final database, we used 38,088 ground motions from 378 earthquakes at 2,114 stations. Figure 1 illustrates (a) station coverage and earthquake locations, and (b) magnitude–distance distribution of the data.

Geospatial variables

In this study, we aim to develop geospatial-based site term models because, unlike geotechnical variables such as V_{S30}, geospatial variables are spatially continuous and, therefore, available at any site within the CEUS without the need for site-specific testing. Geospatial variables serve as proxies for site amplification due to their ability to capture differences in sediment density and stiffness, basin effects, sediment/bedrock impedance contrasts, and topographic effects at a high spatial resolution. In this study, we include continuous variables, such as elevation, sediment thickness, and roughness; and categorical variables, such as surficial geology and physiographic provinces. We will differentiate between (1) regional categorical variables that include surficial geology and physiographic provinces, and (2) locally varying continuous geospatial variables that can be derived from elevation and/or are interpolated from point data.

Regional categorical variables. The regional categorical variables are derived primarily from available digital surficial geology maps. These variables provide proxies for large-scale spatial amplification trends that arise from geologic history and resulting geologic structures. Surficial geology has historically been used as a proxy for V_{S30} because it captures sediment stiffness and subsurface structure (Wills *et al.*, 2015) but has also been shown to have a weak statistical correlation to V_{S30} (Thompson and Wald, 2016). Here, we incorporate the geology-based categorical variables directly, rather than using them as a proxy for V_{S30}.

This study uses a variety of surficial datasets (Soller *et al.*, 2009; Yang *et al.*, 2018; McCafferty *et al.*, 2023). The surficial materials dataset from Soller *et al.* (2009) includes four different relevant variables: (1) lithologic material at the surface, (2) approximate categorical thickness of the material at the surface, (3) minimum geologic age, and (4) maximum geologic age. Lithologic material results in a categorical variable (e.g., alluvial sediments or glacial till). The categorical thickness is a measure of the cover of this lithologic material, including categories such as "Discontinuous, or patchy in distribution," "<100 feet," and ">100 feet." The surficial geology map obtained from McCafferty *et al.* (2023) includes two different relevant categorical variables: geologic unit and Critical Minerals Mapping Initiative (CMMI) category. CMMI categorizes the geologic unit by consolidation, material type, and depositional origin (e.g., sedimentary, siliciclastic, and igneous intrusive felsic). We also considered land cover from Yang *et al.* (2018) as a categorical variable, which includes categories such as "Barren Land" and "Mixed Forest." Figure S1, available in the supplemental material to this article, shows the categorical boundaries defined by Soller *et al.* (2009) and McCafferty *et al.* (2023) for Massachusetts as an example, illustrating one representative classification from each: surficial materials from Soller *et al.* (2009) and CMMI classes from McCafferty *et al.* (2023).

In addition to the variables from surficial geology datasets, we also considered physiographic divisions as large regional categorical variables. Physiographic divisions are large areas of the continental United States that provide a proxy for large-scale geomorphology, geology, and crustal structure. Physiographic provinces were originally produced by Fenneman and Johnson (1946), and have been used as regional divisions in geologic research (Porter *et al.*, 2016) and hydrology studies (Sofia and Nikolopoulos, 2020). More recently, physiographic provinces were used to develop station corrections for magnitude energy (M_e) calculations (Bindi and Di Giacomo, 2025), showing province dependence on station-specific magnitude residuals. Magnitude energy station corrections provide insight into site effects because they attempt to account for site amplification to correct estimates of magnitude.

Fenneman and Johnson (1946) categorized 8 broad divisions of the United States, which are subdivided into 25 provinces, which are subdivided again into 82 different sections. This partition was accomplished by examining the underlying geologic structures, the terrain texture, and the present rock types. In this study, we use adjusted versions of the provinces as potential categorical geospatial parameters for our amplification models. In the original physiographic provinces, three provinces cover a

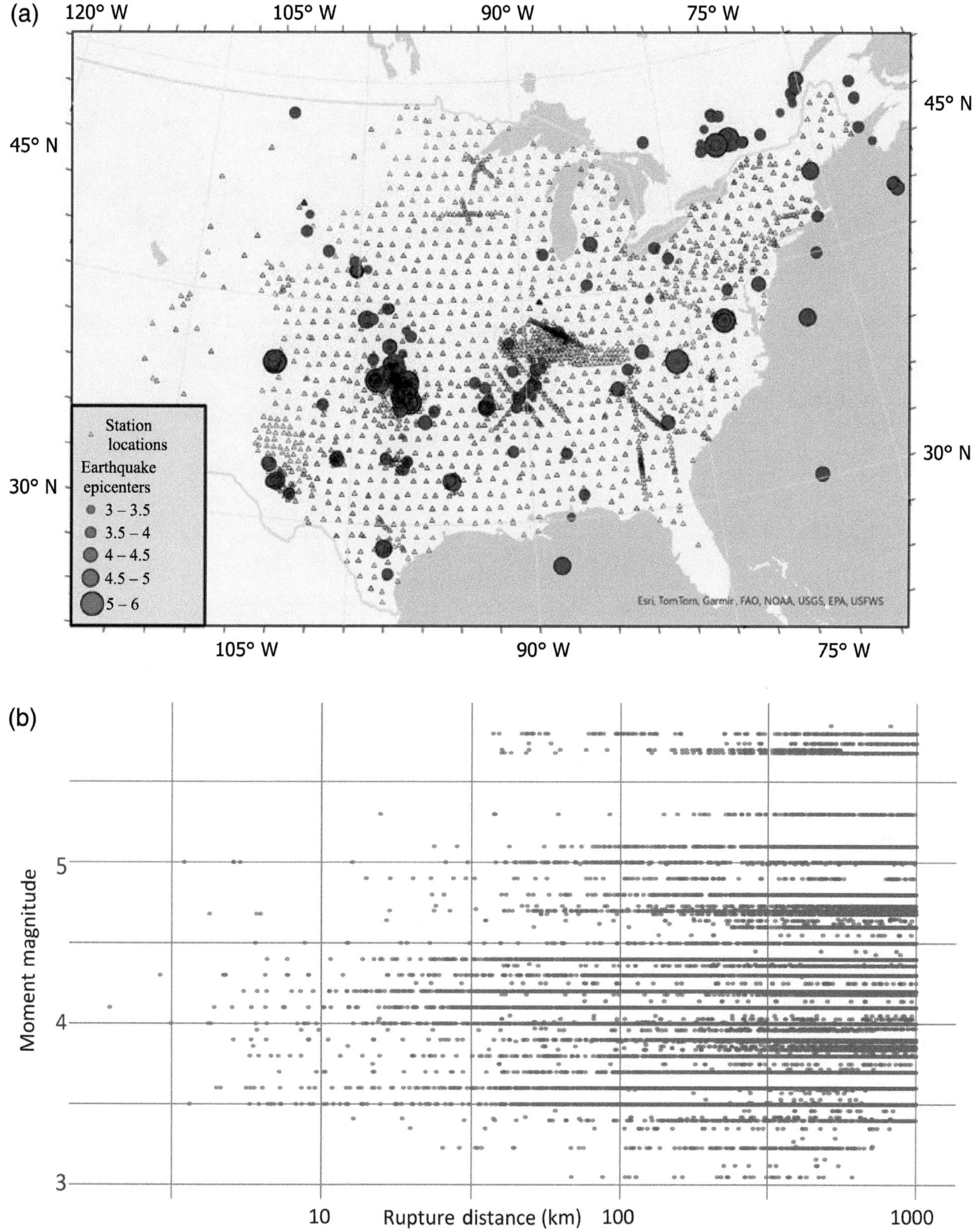

Figure 1. (a) Location of earthquakes by magnitude and stations used in the database in the Central and Eastern United States (CEUS). (b) Magnitude–distance relationships of selected ground motions in the combined dataset. The color version of this figure is available only in the electronic edition.

significantly larger land mass than the others (e.g., ACP, the Central Lowlands, and the Great Plains). For these three provinces, we use physiographic sections to incorporate geologic and topographic differences that are not captured by the broader provinces and result in regions of approximately equal area.

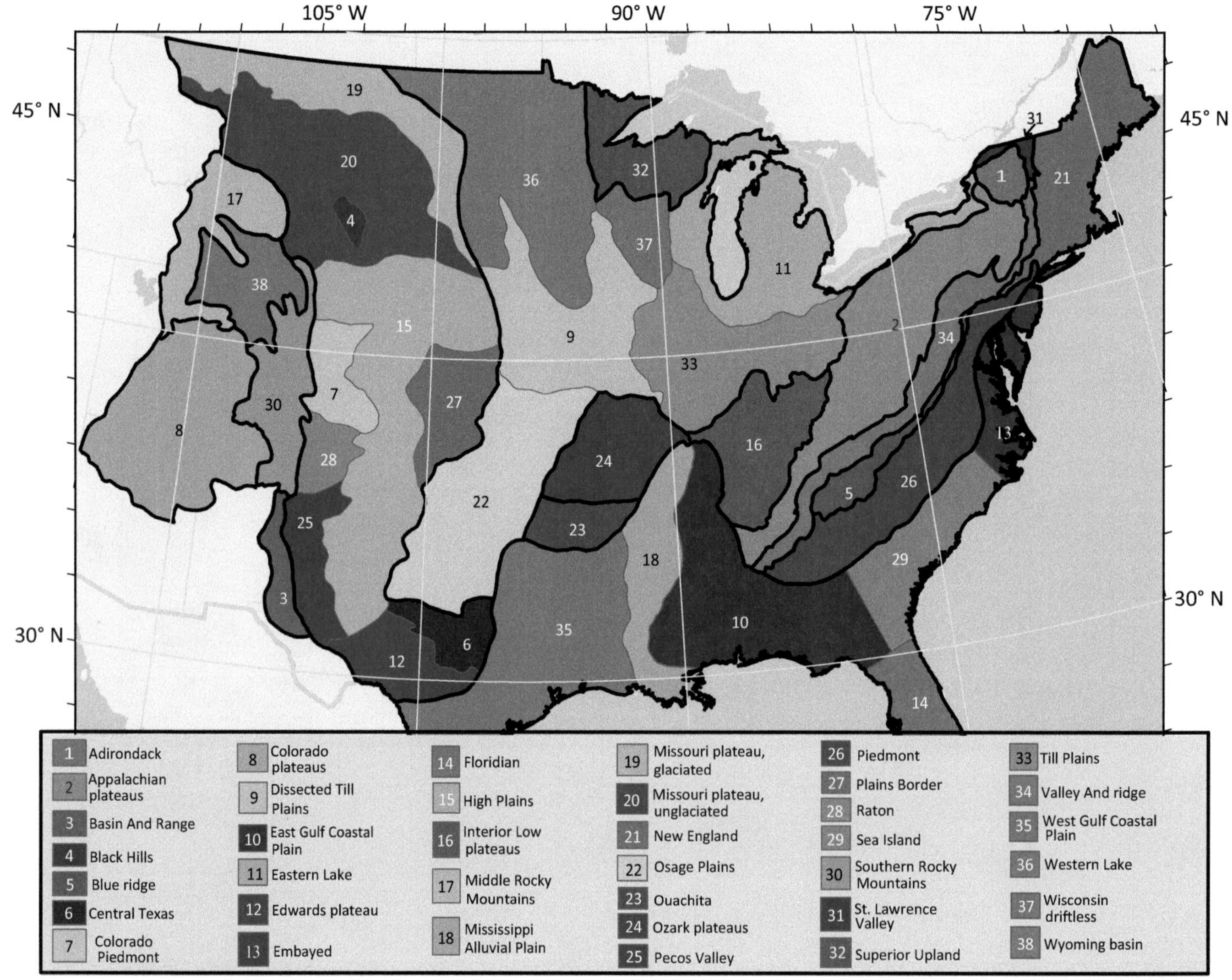

Figure 2. Adjusted physiographic provinces of the CEUS used herein and based on Fenneman and Johnson (1946). The black, dark lines outline the original provinces. The Atlantic Coastal Plain (ACP), the Central Lowlands, and the Great Plain provinces have been divided by the Fenneman and Johnson (1946) sections. The color version of this figure is available only in the electronic edition.

A histogram of areas of (1) the 17 original provinces and (2) the 35 adjusted provinces is shown in Figure S2, demonstrating the three outliers of area and the more uniform area distribution obtained by the adjustment. The adjusted physiographic provinces are mapped in Figure 2.

We extracted the regional categorical variables for each station in the combined ground-motion database. The categorical geospatial variables are summarized in Table 1.

Continuous geospatial variables. In addition to the categorical geospatial variables, we also use higher-resolution, continuous numerical variables as potential predictors for site amplification. These continuous variables include geospatial parameters derived from DEMs, the slope-based V_{S30} proxy, and sediment thickness across large regions. DEMs represent surface elevation as raster data and can be used to derive secondary geospatial variables related to topography, such as slope and roughness, as well as others related to hydrology, such as flow accumulation and compound topographic index (Beven *et al.*, 2021).

Using the DEM data from the hole-filled Shuttle Radar Topography Mission, which has a spatial resolution of 90 m (Jarvis *et al.*, 2008), we derive curvature, topographic position index (TPI), slope, and roughness at three different scales. Curvature provides the convexity of each cell, computed using a 3 × 3 neighborhood of surrounding cells. TPI is a measure of the elevation of a cell compared with the cells around it. Both TPI and curvature were examined by Rai *et al.* (2016) in California and found to correlate with bias in GMM residuals. Slope measures the steepness, or rate of elevation change, at a cell within a neighborhood. Roughness measures the standard deviation of the slope. We use roughness at three different scales (3 × 3, 33 × 33, and 101 × 101 cells) to provide insight

TABLE 1
Summary of Categorical Geospatial Variables, Including a Description, the Aspects of Site Response Each Variable Attempts to Capture, and Source Information

Variable	Variable Description	Geology	Topography	Basin Depth	Basin Edge	Source(s)
Surficial materials	Materials at the surface of the conterminous United States. Transported sediments, unconsolidated/residual material developed in bedrock, and bedrock	•				Soller *et al.* (2009)
Approximate thickness of surficial material	Categorical approximate thickness of surficial materials		•	•		Soller *et al.* (2009)
Minimum and maximum geologic ages	Youngest and oldest geologic age during which materials in the map unit were deposited	•				Soller *et al.* (2009)
Geologic unit	Lithology grouped into 31 subgroups of igneous, metamorphic, and sedimentary rock	•				McCafferty *et al.* (2023)
CMMI classification	Critical Minerals Mapping Initiative classification	•				McCafferty *et al.* (2023)
Land cover	Map of land cover from the U.S. Geological Survey with 95 distinct categories		•	•		Yang *et al.* (2018)
Physiographic provinces	Large areas of the continental United States that provide a proxy for large-scale effects of geomorphology, geology, and crustal structure	•	•			Fenneman and Johnson (1946)

CMMI, Critical Minerals Mapping Initiative.

into neighborhood size and the ability for roughness to capture trends in local topography at different spatial scales.

Only 6% of stations in the NGA-East dataset (Goulet, Kishida, *et al.*, 2021) have measured values of V_{S30}; at all other sites, V_{S30} is estimated using proxies, usually topographic slope. To ensure consistency across all stations, we use the slope-based V_{S30} from Heath *et al.* (2020) instead of the V_{S30} provided by NGA-East, thereby minimizing potential discrepancies introduced by combining data from different sources.

We also use sediment thickness as a potential predictor because several recent studies have demonstrated its effectiveness for predicting ground motion amplification in the ACP (Chapman and Guo, 2021; Pezeshk *et al.*, 2021; Pratt and Schleicher, 2021; Akhani *et al.*, 2024; Boyd *et al.*, 2024; Gann-Phillips *et al.*, 2024). Currently, high-resolution sediment thickness data are not available as a single dataset across the entire CEUS. Because there is no high-resolution sediment thickness data for the entire CEUS, we examine four different datasets that cover various regions (Domrois *et al.*, 2015; Pelletier *et al.*, 2016; Soller and Garrity, 2018; Boyd *et al.*, 2024). Within these resources, definitions of sediment thickness differ, with some measuring to bedrock (Pelletier *et al.*, 2016) and some measuring to basement (Boyd *et al.*, 2024). It is important to note the distinction between these measurements: depth to bedrock measures the depth of unconsolidated sediments above solidified rock (which can be sedimentary or crystalline), whereas depth to basement includes all materials above crystalline basement, including sedimentary layers. Both datasets are valuable for identifying potential amplification and can serve as basin proxies, but they should not be used interchangeably. These datasets are described subsequently and illustrated in Figure 3.

The Pelletier *et al.* (2016) model covers the entire CEUS (Fig. 3a). This model, which has a spatial resolution of 1 km, provides an estimate of unconsolidated sediment for the globe using topography, geology, and hydrology inputs. Pelletier *et al.* (2016) is the only available dataset on the scale of the entire region, but the thicknesses are uncertain and capped at a maximum of 50 m depth. As a result, this database indicates the presence of sediments (i.e., sediment versus rock), but the true depth of sediments is not well captured.

The Boyd *et al.* (2024) depth-to-basement model covers the Atlantic and Gulf Coastal Plains (Fig. 3b). This resource is a composite map built from a compilation of previous studies, well logs, and seismic refraction data. The Boyd *et al.* (2024) model highlights areas where sedimentary layers are particularly thick, such as the deep sedimentary regions in southern Texas, Louisiana, and Mississippi, whereas the Atlantic coast exhibits shallower sedimentary layers.

The Soller and Garrity (2018) model specifies Quaternary sediment thicknesses within previously glaciated terrain in the northern United States (Fig. 3c). The Soller and Garrity (2018) model measures depth to bedrock (defined as the distance from the surface elevation to the elevation of consolidated rock) using bathymetry data and information about bedrock geology, interpolating between contour lines of depth. Notably, this dataset reveals several areas with deep unconsolidated sedimentary basins that do not correspond to surface topographic changes, such as those in Michigan, South Dakota, and Minnesota.

The Domrois *et al.* (2015) model (Fig. 3d) provides the depth to the surface of the Great Unconformity, which is the depth to basement rock on the U.S. Cratonic platform, defined as the depth to crystalline (metamorphic or igneous) basement rock. The Domrois *et al.* (2015) model is compiled

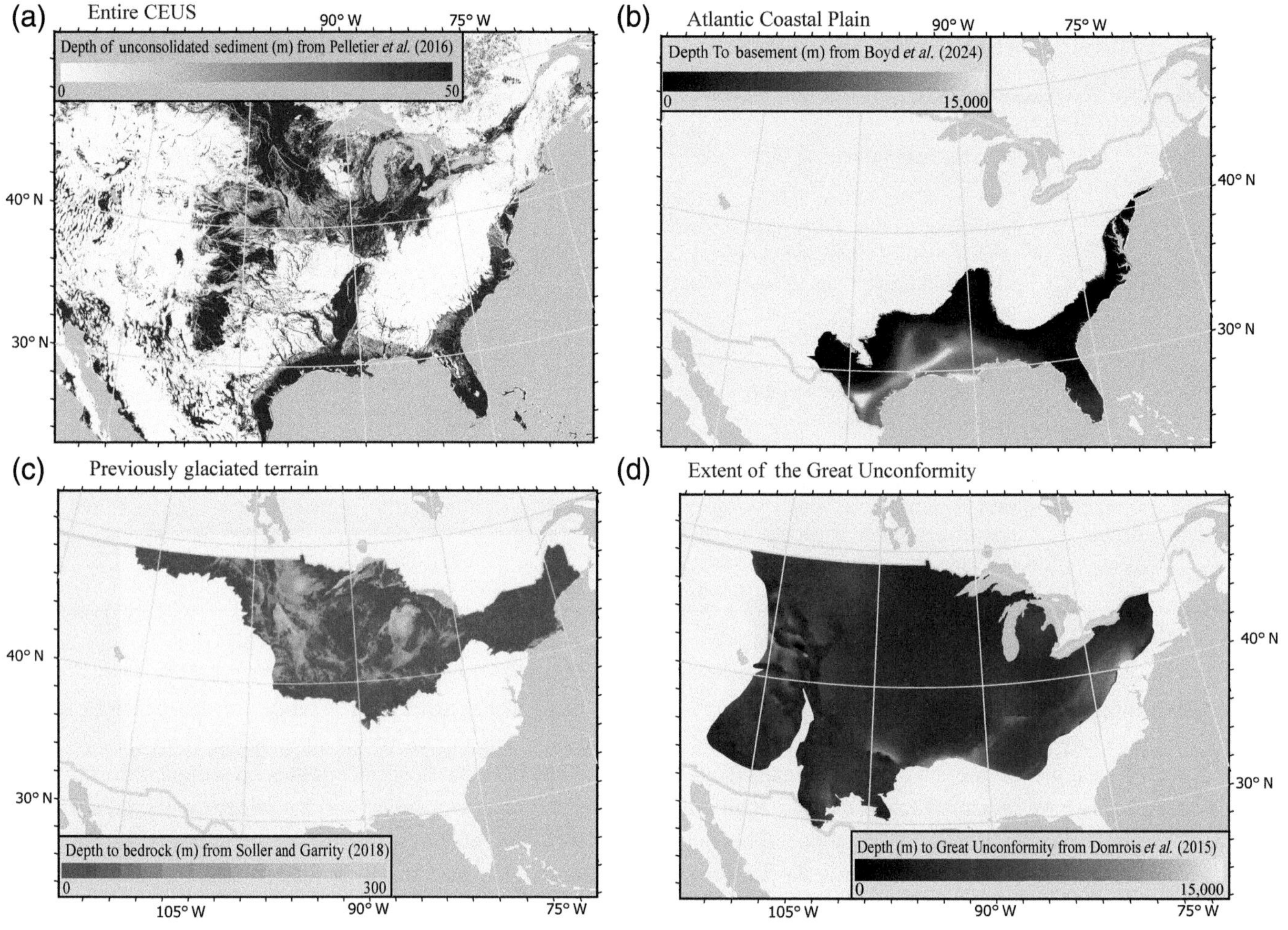

Figure 3. Comparison of four different datasets representing (a) global soil/sediment thickness estimates (Pelletier *et al.*, 2016), (b) depth to basement in the Coastal Plain (Boyd *et al.*, 2024), (c) depth to bedrock in previously glaciated terrain (Soller and Garrity, 2018), and (d) depth to basement of the extent of the Great Unconformity (Domrois *et al.*, 2015). Different color scales represent different types of depths. The color version of this figure is available only in the electronic edition.

from various sources, including well logs and seismic refraction data. This model does not appear to indicate the same spatial features illustrated in the Soller and Garrity (2018) depth-to-bedrock database.

We extracted the continuous variables for each station in the combined ground-motion database, and a summary is provided in Table 2.

METHODOLOGY

$\delta S2S_j$ and site amplification

Site amplification models can be fitted using $\delta S2S_j$ from a GMM. Ground-motion observations from the compiled database are compared with model predictions from the 17 NGA-East GMMs (Goulet, Bozorgnia, *et al.*, 2021) to obtain model residuals. The NGA-East GMMs produce a weighted median, called the central branch, as the median prediction. This prediction is made with a reference condition of hard rock ($V_{S30} = 3000$ m/s) and uses a linear amplification model based on V_{S30} (Stewart *et al.*, 2020) and a nonlinear amplification model, also based on V_{S30} (Hashash *et al.*, 2020). We define the total model residuals $\delta_{\{ij\}}$ for event i at station j in natural logarithmic space as

$$\delta_{\{ij\}} = \ln(Y_{ij}) - [\ln(\mu_{M_i,(R_{\text{rup}})_{ij},V_{S30}=3000}) + F_{VS30}], \quad (1)$$

in which Y_{ij} is the recorded ground motion; μ is the median prediction (central branch) using the moment magnitude **M** and rupture distance R_{rup}, and $V_{S30} = 3000$ m/s; and F_{VS30} is the site amplification term, including the linear component F_{linear} from Stewart *et al.* (2020) and the nonlinear component $F_{\text{nonlinear}}$ from Hashash *et al.* (2020).

We use mixed-effects regression (Atik *et al.*, 2010) to decompose our model residuals into overall bias c, event residual δE_i, site-to-site residual $\delta S2S_j$, and remaining residual ε_{ij}:

$$\delta_{\{ij\}} = c + \delta E_i + \delta S2S_j + \varepsilon_{ij}. \quad (2)$$

In this decomposition, the event term represents the portion of the residual attributed to the event, and the site-to-site term represents the portion of the residual attributed to the site. We are interested in the $\delta S2S_j$ term because it shows us which stations

TABLE 2
Summary of Continuous Geospatial Variables Including a Description, the Aspects of Site Response Each Variable Attempts to Capture, and Source Information

Variable	Variable Description	Geology	Topography	Basin Depth	Basin Edge	Source(s)
Slope-based V_{S30}	Time-averaged shear-wave velocity in the upper 30 m of the subsurface from a slope-based proxy method (m/s)	•	•	•		Heath *et al.* (2020)
Surface elevation	Elevation above sea level from 90-m-resolution DEM (m)		•			Jarvis *et al.* (2008)
Curvature	Mean curvature calculated from the 90-m DEM; average of minimum and maximum curvature (1/m)		•	•	•	Derived from Jarvis *et al.* (2008)
Topographic slope	Slope calculated using a 90-m DEM (°)		•	•	•	Derived from Jarvis *et al.* (2008)
Roughness	Calculated as the standard deviation of topographic slope for different moving windows: 3 × 3, 33 × 33, and 101 × 101 cells (°)		•	•	•	Derived from Jarvis *et al.* (2008)
Topographic position index	Method of terrain classification that measures the elevation of a cell in comparison to the neighboring cells (m)		•	•	•	Derived from Jarvis *et al.* (2008)
Average soil/sediment thickness	Global estimate of unconsolidated sediment for the globe using topography, geology, and hydrology inputs at a 1 km scale (m)			•	•	Pelletier *et al.* (2016)
Depth to basement	Depth to crystalline basement rock (m)			•		Boyd *et al.* (2024)
Depth to the Great Unconformity	Depth to the Great Unconformity, effectively depth to crystalline basement rock (m)			•		Domrois *et al.* (2015)
Quaternary sediment thickness of previously glaciated terrain	Depth to bedrock of Quaternary sediments in the northern CEUS (m)			•	•	Soller and Garrity (2018)

CEUS, Central and Eastern United States; and DEM, digital elevation model.

are systematically overpredicting or underpredicting ground motion using the current GMMs and current site amplification terms.

The NGA-East GMMs are only valid for magnitudes 4.0–8.2, but a large portion of the database consists of small-magnitude earthquakes having magnitudes from 3 to 4. Therefore, we use a method described by Boyd *et al.* (2024) to extrapolate the GMMs to magnitudes as low as 3 to take full advantage of the station coverage in the database. We use the modified Akima cubic formulation in MATLAB (MathWorks Inc., 2023) with magnitude and rupture distance at each period. The interpolation uses magnitude, rupture distance, and frequency to give a value for the natural logarithm of the prediction. The interpolated median models can be seen in Figure 4 for PSA at 1 s. We find no residual trends with magnitude after this interpolation, with residual–magnitude plots shown in Figure S3.

We extract $\delta S2S_j$ for PSA across 21 periods, PGA, and PGV to compute the $\delta S2S_j$ values for each station at each period. These $\delta S2S_j$ exhibit large regional patterns, as shown for PGA and PSA at 1 s in Figure 5. For PGA (Fig. 5a), we observe regionally positive $\delta S2S_j$ in the ACP, Mississippi Embayment, and the northern Midwest region of the CEUS. In the Gulf Coastal Plain, the Appalachian region, and into the northeast, we see regionally negative $\delta S2S_j$. For PSA at 1 s (Fig. 5b), a similar pattern is observed, with regionally positive $\delta S2S_j$ terms through the Mississippi Embayment and the northern Midwest, with regional negative $\delta S2S_j$ terms through the northeast, the Gulf Coastal Plain, and the Ozarks. The magnitudes of these $\delta S2S_j$ values suggest there is still room for further modeling improvement, and the regional dependence of these residuals suggests that the location-dependent variables discussed earlier in this article could help do so.

We aim to provide an alternative to the NGA-East V_{S30}-based linear site amplification term with predictor variables drawn from the geospatial variables described previously. Therefore, we add the linear amplification term F_{lin} from Stewart *et al.* (2020) for each station to our $\delta S2S_j$, giving us the full linear amplification A_j attributed to each station j:

$$A_j = \delta S2S_j + F_{\text{lin},j}. \tag{3}$$

We used the full amplification terms A_j as the target-dependent variable for our amplification model and our extracted values for our geospatial variables (including sediment thickness) and our physiographic divisions and sections as predictor variables.

Exploratory data analysis of site variables

Correlation matrices for continuous variables. Using correlation matrices, we first examine relationships between our amplification terms A_j (for PSA at all periods, PGA, and PGV), and our continuous geospatial site variables (shown in Table 2) at each station. We separate the analysis into three regions with region-specific sediment thickness data: previously glaciated terrain (Soller and Garrity, 2018), the

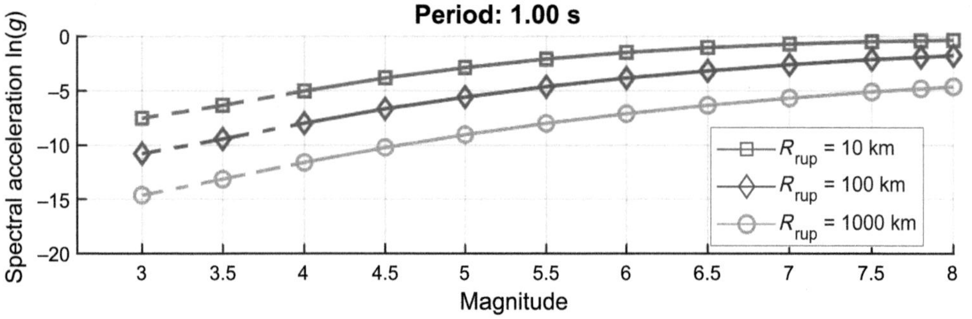

Figure 4. Modified Akima interpolation for ground-motion predictions between **M** 3 and 4 for pseudo-spectral acceleration (PSA) at 1 s for three different rupture distances: 10, 100, and 1000 km.

Atlantic and Gulf Coastal Plains (Boyd *et al.*, 2024), the extent of the Great Unconformity (Domrois *et al.*, 2015), and the whole CEUS, in which the Pelletier *et al.* (2016) sediment thickness dataset is available continuously. By analyzing each region with specific sediment thickness data, we can gather insight into the similarities and differences between regions and examine the potential for the use of region-specific datasets. We also analyze the correlations between the slope-based V_{S30} values within each region and across the entire CEUS.

The correlation matrices for A_j at each period, along with our continuous geospatial parameters, are shown in Figure 6 for PGA, and PSA at 0.1, 1, and 3 s. Full correlation matrices for additional ground-motion intensity measures are available in Figures S4–S7.

All three regions, as well as the entire CEUS, showed similar patterns, with TPI and curvature having little to no correlation with any amplification terms. Slope-based V_{S30} is negatively correlated with amplification across all periods in the previously glaciated terrain of the CEUS, becoming more negatively correlated as the period increases. This pattern is also apparent in the extent of the Great Unconformity, although the correlations are slightly weaker. In the Coastal Plain, slope-based V_{S30} has a much weaker negative correlation with longer periods and a weak positive correlation at shorter periods, showing limited use for amplification prediction in this region. In the whole CEUS, slope-based V_{S30} shows a negative correlation across all periods, becoming stronger at longer periods.

Depth to basement (Boyd *et al.*, 2024) in the Coastal Plain has a strong negative correlation at shorter periods, becoming moderately positive at longer periods. This result is consistent with those of Boyd *et al.* (2024) and Guo and Chapman (2019), who found that short-period ground motions were attenuated in the Coastal Plain. In the previously glaciated terrain, Quaternary depth to bedrock (Soller and Garrity, 2018) has a moderate positive correlation at all periods. The correlation pattern for depth to basement (Domrois *et al.*, 2015) in the Great Unconformity region shows moderate negative correlation at short periods, increasing to weak positive correlation at longer periods.

The global estimate of average sediment thickness (Pelletier *et al.*, 2016) is positively correlated with all amplification terms in the entire CEUS, in the glaciated terrain, and in the extent of the Great Unconformity. The correlations are stronger at longer periods, indicating the influence of sediment thickness on site response at moderate-to-long periods. In the previously glaciated terrain and the extent of the Great Unconformity, amplification shows stronger correlation with the Pelletier *et al.* (2016) sediment thickness model compared with the regional depth to bedrock and depth-to-basement datasets. For the Coastal Plain, the global sediment thickness model of Pelletier *et al.* (2016) shows the same pattern as the regional depth-to-basement model of Boyd *et al.* (2024), but with weaker correlation. The positive correlations of amplifications with the Pelletier *et al.* (2016) and Soller and Garrity (2018) models and negative correlations with the Boyd *et al.* (2024) and Domrois *et al.* (2015) could be a result of regional dependence and/or scale of the thicknesses; the thicknesses of the Pelletier *et al.* (2016) and Soller and Garrity (2018) datasets are smaller than those of Boyd *et al.* (2024) and Domrois *et al.* (2015). The short-period negative correlations in the extent of the Great Unconformity indicate that this region may see similar attenuation at short periods (related to sediment thickness) that Guo and Chapman (2019) found in the Coastal Plain.

In the entire CEUS, topographic roughness and slope exhibit negative correlation with amplification, with stronger negative correlations observed as the period increases. The same pattern is seen in the glaciated terrain region and the extent of the Great Unconformity. For the Coastal Plain region, roughness and slope have a weak positive correlation at short periods, which decreases with period until it becomes moderately negative at longer periods. A possible explanation is the lack of topography in the Coastal Plain relative to the other regions.

In this study, we examined roughness, defined as the standard deviation of slope, at three different moving window sizes (3 × 3, 33 × 33, and 101 × 101 cells), which serve as a proxy for landform topography at different scales. Roughness serves as a proxy for topography and stiffness because of the geomorphic processes in areas with higher topographic relief. Because sediment erodes from higher areas and exposes bedrock, the sediment is transported to and deposited in areas of lower elevation. Small-scale roughness shows moderate negative correlation in the previously glaciated terrain and the extent of the Great Unconformity, but little to no correlation in the Coastal

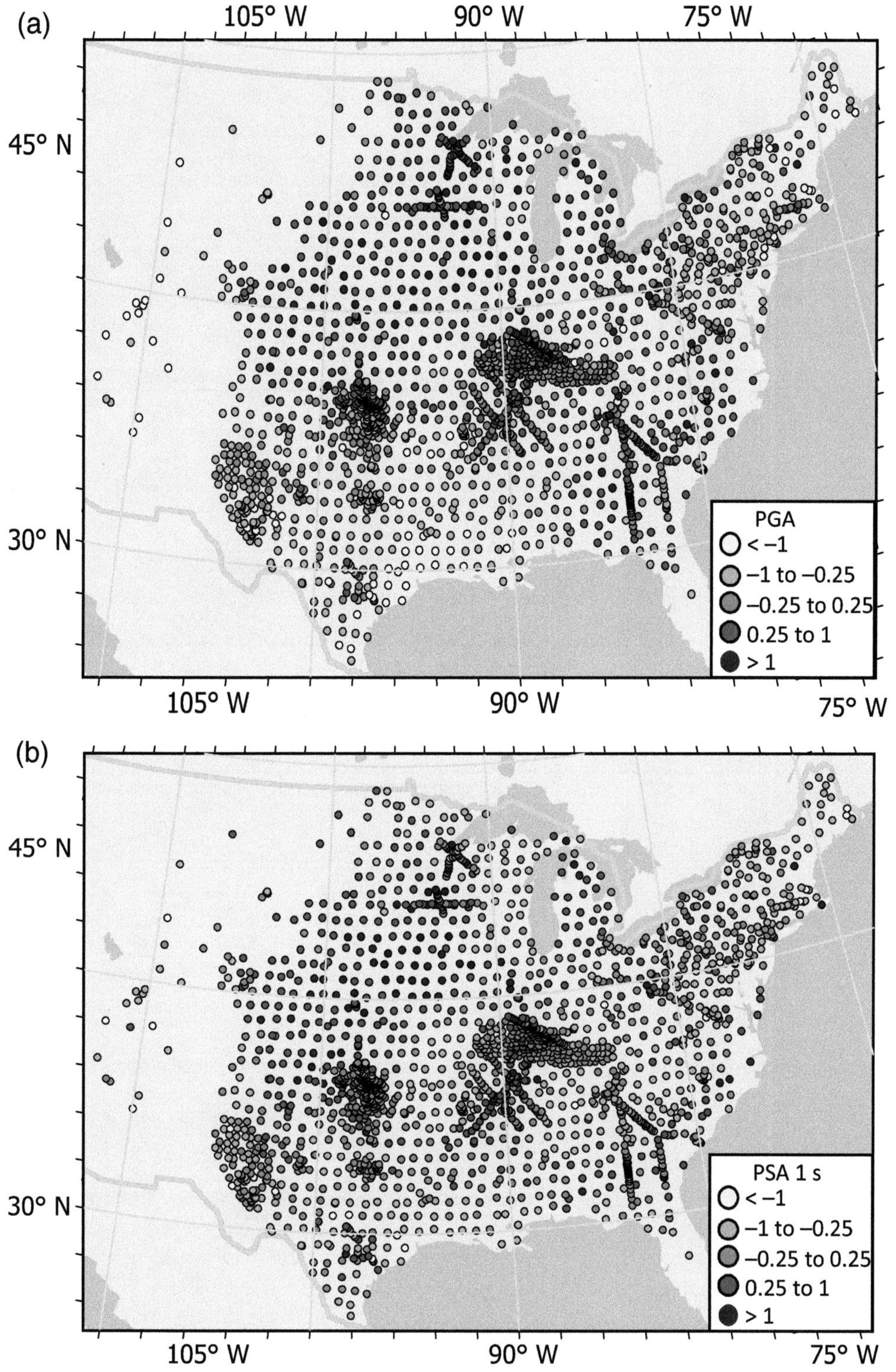

Figure 5. $\delta S2S$ for (a) peak ground acceleration (PGA) and (b) PSA at 1 s using the current Next Generation Attenuation (NGA)-East ground-motion model amplification term (Stewart *et al.*, 2020) based on V_{S30}. The color version of this figure is available only in the electronic edition.

periods. In the glaciated terrain and the extent of the Great Unconformity, medium- and large-scale roughness show stronger negative correlation as the period increases. Roughness is a promising proxy for site response in areas with high topographic relief that lack sediment thickness data or accurate V_{S30} values.

Something interesting to note is the difference in correlations between slope and slope-based V_{S30}. We believe this difference stems at least in part from the resolution of these two terms. Slope is calculated on a 90 m DEM, giving it a higher resolution than slope-based V_{S30}, which is at a 1-km resolution. As noted earlier, roughness calculated with a larger moving window shows stronger correlations with amplification. Allen and Wald (2009) discuss how the smoothing that occurs in lower-resolution slope estimates results in higher correlation with measured V_{S30}.

ANOVA testing for categorical variables. We also examined categorical geospatial variables (shown in Table 1), using analysis of variance (ANOVA) testing to evaluate statistical differences in the amplification terms between the groups within the categorical variables (e.g., different lithologies, ages, etc.) listed in Table 1. For ANOVA testing, an F value higher than the critical F value (assuming a significance level of 5%) indicates that the variability between groups is large relative to the variability within the groups. For almost every period and every category, the F value of the ANOVA test was higher than the critical F value, meaning the variance between groups is greater than the variance within groups. Exceptions

Plain, likely due to the lack of small-scale topographic differences in this region. In the Coastal Plain, medium- and large-scale roughness exhibits moderate negative correlation at longer periods and little to no correlation at short

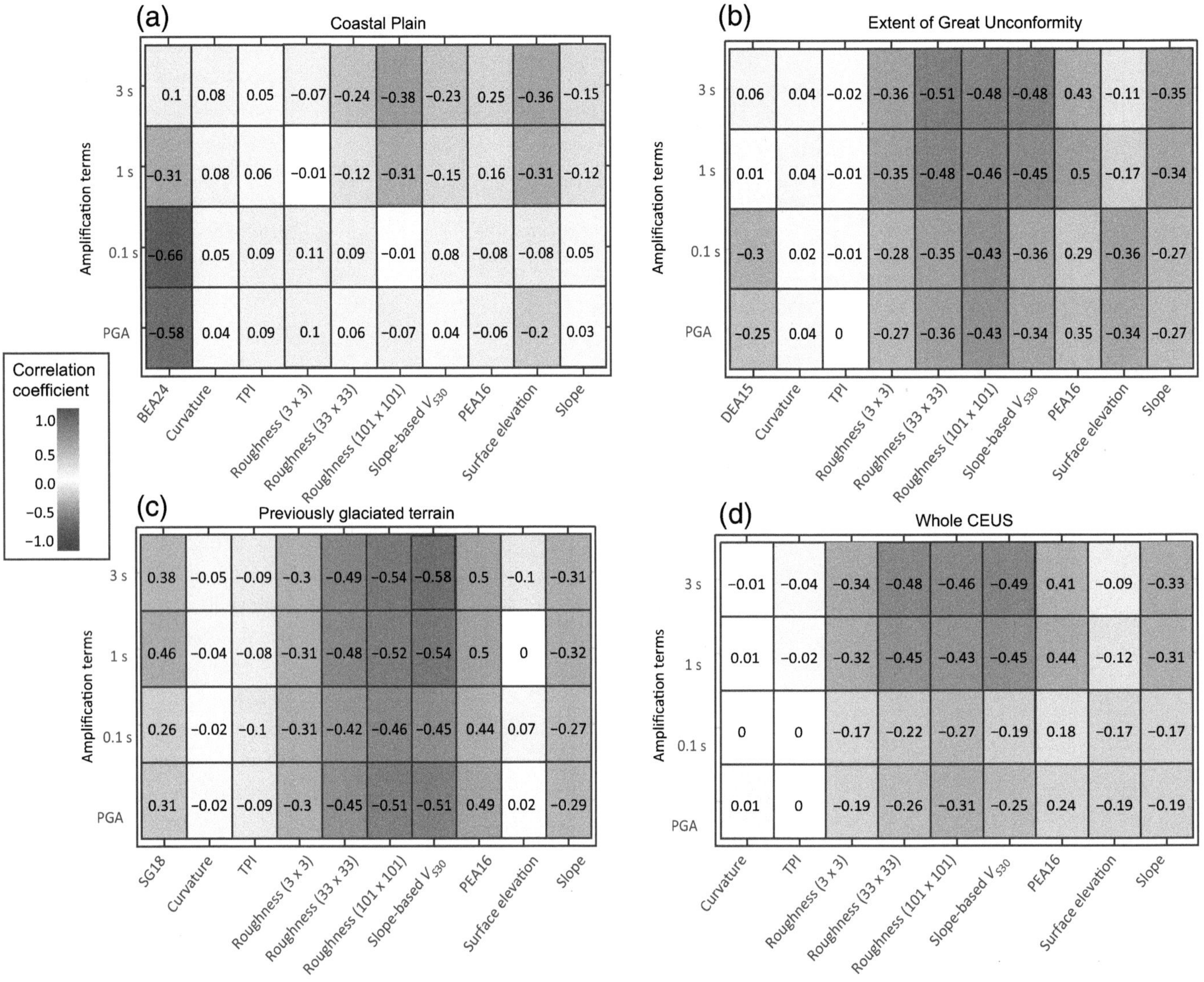

Figure 6. Correlation matrices between site amplification terms and continuous geospatial variables for the three different regions with region-specific data: (a) Coastal Plain using depth to basement from Boyd *et al.* (2024) (BEA24), (b) the extent of the Great Unconformity using depth to the Great Unconformity from Domrois *et al.* (2015) (DEA15), (c) previously glaciated terrain using depth to bedrock from Soller and Garrity (2018) (SG18); and for (d) the entire CEUS, using an estimate from the global Pelletier *et al.* (2016) model (PEA16), as shown in Figure 3. For each of the subregions in panels (a)–(c), we also provide correlations with the PEA16 sediment thickness model. TPI, topographic position index. The color version of this figure is available only in the electronic edition.

to this were noted for PSA at 1.5 s for the minimum age categories and PGV for the CMMI class. A figure of F values for each categorical variable set, including a highlight of the two values in which the F value is less than the critical F value for each period, can be found in Figure S8.

Because almost all F values were significant, the eta-squared (η^2) statistic can provide additional insights. F values signify significance, whereas η^2 quantifies the magnitude of that significance. Eta-squared is a measure of how much of the total variance is explained by group membership; a high η^2 means that group membership is explaining the variance. As shown in Figure 7, adjusted province and section both show the highest η^2 values across all periods. Because adjusted province and section share many of the same divisions, we expect to observe similar patterns. Surficial materials, divisions, and provinces have moderate η^2 values across all periods, with divisions and provinces having higher values at long periods and surficial materials showing higher values at shorter periods.

Although correlation matrices and ANOVA provide useful initial insights into associations between amplification and candidate site predictors, they are limited in detecting nonlinear responses and interactions. Because our goal is a practical, easily implemented model, and the CEUS dataset remains relatively sparse compared with the WUS, we use these tools to identify the dominant, stable patterns to avoid overfitting. As additional CEUS data become available, exploring interaction terms and nonlinear structure will be an important direction for future work.

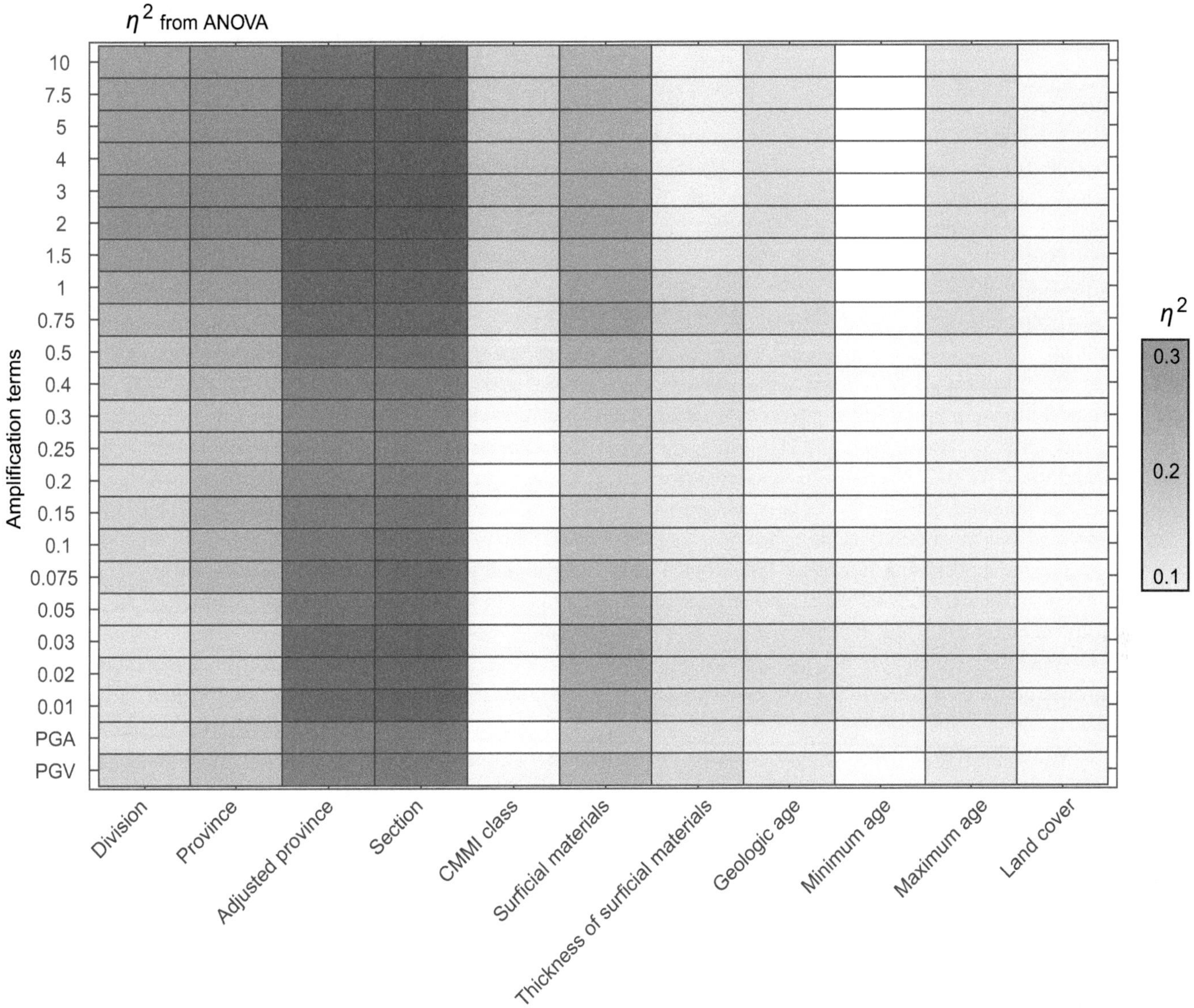

Figure 7. Eta-squared (η^2) values for amplification terms A_j and categorical predictors, which quantify how much of the variance in amplification terms is explained by each categorical predictor. ANOVA, analysis of variance; CMMI, Critical Minerals Mapping Initiative; PGV, peak ground velocity. The color version of this figure is available only in the electronic edition.

Site amplification term development

Guided by insights from the correlation analyses, we develop a multiple least-squares regression model for site amplification. The amplification terms (A_j) were used as the dependent variable, and the continuous and categorical geospatial variables were applied as predictors. The regression model for n predictor variables is shown in equation (4), in which α is an intercept term, β_i is the regression slope coefficient, and X_i is the associated predictor variable ($i = 1, 2, \ldots, n$), and ε_j is the remaining residual:

$$A_j = \alpha + \beta_1 X_1 + \beta_2 X_2 + \ldots + \beta_n X_n + \varepsilon_j. \quad (4)$$

We use k-fold cross-validation with five folds to train and test our models. First, the stations are randomly split into five groups. For each set of predictors tested, the model is then fit to the data five times, leaving out a different randomly selected group of stations each time. The model is then tested on the left-out group for each of the five models, resulting in five root mean square error (RMSE) values. These five RMSE values are averaged for each of the models at each period, allowing for the models to be compared with one another.

RESULTS AND DISCUSSION

Regionalization

As shown in Figure 6, the various sediment thickness datasets exhibit moderate correlations with amplifications within the region where each model is available. However, the sediment thicknesses from Domrois *et al.* (2015) for the extent of the Great Unconformity and Soller and Garrity (2018) in previously glaciated terrain exhibited weaker correlations than the continuously available Pelletier *et al.* (2016) dataset. With this in mind, and the goal of a simple, usable model, we regionalize our model into two different areas: the Atlantic and Gulf Coastal Plains, and the northern CEUS. The Coastal Plain subdivision takes advantage of the high-quality sediment thickness dataset available for this region (Boyd *et al.*, 2024). For all regions outside of the Coastal Plain, as mapped by Boyd *et al.* (2024), we use the global Pelletier *et al.* (2016) dataset for sediment thickness because it displayed stronger correlations than the other regional sediment thickness models.

Model testing

One-parameter models. We first tested all the potential one-parameter models to determine the best single predictor of amplification across PSA at 21 periods, PGA, and PGV. These models were fitted and tested for each of the two regions using region-specific sediment thickness data and global geospatial variables. Using the five-fold validation technique described, we evaluated each single-parameter model using the average RMSE of the left-out group. The results for the Coastal Plain and northern CEUS region are shown in Figures 8 and 9, respectively.

In the Coastal Plain region (Fig. 8), the adjusted physiographic province performs the best as a single predictor across most periods, resulting in the lowest average RMSE of any predictor. However, the Boyd *et al.* (2024) depth to basement has a lower RMSE across periods from 0.1 to 0.5 s. This result is potentially due to the increase in attenuation at shorter periods in the Coastal Plain compared with sites outside of the Coastal Plain (Guo and Chapman, 2019). Slope-based V_{S30} and DEM-derived parameters have higher RMSE values and therefore do not offer accurate predictions, likely because the topography in the Coastal Plain is relatively flat. The model using adjusted physiographic province in the Coastal Plain had an average RMSE that was 17.0% lower than the average RMSE using slope-based V_{S30}.

In the northern region of the CEUS (Fig. 9), all the physiographic province-based predictors work well, due to the similarity between the provinces, adjusted provinces, and divisions within this region. Roughness at medium and large scales, slope-based V_{S30}, and average sediment thickness from Pelletier *et al.* (2016) are the optimal continuous geospatial variables, but they do not perform as well as the categorial province-based predictors at any period. Slope-based V_{S30} is the most accurate continuous predictor variable at long periods (>1 s), whereas sediment thickness performs better at shorter periods (<1 s). The model using adjusted physiographic province in the northern region had an average RMSE 17.4% lower than the average RMSE using slope-based V_{S30}.

Two-parameter models. We then tested all two-parameter models using the best single predictor (adjusted physiographic province) as the first parameter. However, the other categorical variables are highly correlated with the adjusted physiographic province and share the same boundaries. Therefore, we only use continuous numerical variables for the second parameter to capture some of the local variation in sediments within an adjusted physiographic province. The average RMSE of the left-out group of the two-parameter models is shown in Figures 10 and 11 for the Coastal Plain and northern CEUS, respectively.

The addition of a second geospatially continuous parameter decreased the average RMSE in each region with varying levels. For the Coastal Plain region (Fig. 10), the sediment thickness dataset (Boyd *et al.*, 2024) provided an additional 12.6% decrease in average RMSE relative to using the adjusted province alone. For the northern CEUS, the sediment thickness from Pelletier *et al.* (2016) provided a more limited improvement, with an additional 1.2% decrease in average RMSE relative to the adjusted province alone. This difference in improvement underscores the importance of collecting high-resolution data in more areas of the United States to improve subsurface characterization, similar to the effort undertaken by Boyd *et al.* (2024) for the Atlantic and Gulf Coastal Plains, in which a stronger decrease in RMSE was observed. Slope-based V_{S30} as a secondary parameter performs similarly to other DEM-based variables. In the Coastal Plain, slope-based V_{S30} does not provide much reduction in average RMSE (0.2%) from adjusted province alone, underscoring the limitations of slope-based V_{S30} in this region. In the northern CEUS, slope-based V_{S30} offers a 0.8% reduction across all periods. In the northern CEUS, the sediment thickness from Pelletier *et al.* (2016) outperforms slope-based V_{S30} as a secondary parameter overall, but slope-based V_{S30} has a lower average RMSE at longer periods (4–10 s).

Proposed model

For each of the two regions (the Coastal Plain and the northern CEUS), we fit the two-parameter model that produced the greatest reduction in RMSE, as noted in the previous section. Using multiple linear regression (i.e., equation 4), we fit models with the linear amplification terms as response variables, and adjusted physiographic province and sediment thickness (from Boyd *et al.*, 2024, for the Coastal Plain and Pelletier *et al.*, 2016, for the northern CEUS) as predictors. We extract the coefficients from these fitted models and create a new linear amplification term with the following functional form:

$$F_{\mathrm{Linear},j} = F_{\mathrm{Adj\,province},j} + c_1 \,\mathrm{Sediment\,thickness}_j, \tag{5}$$

in which $F_{\mathrm{Adj\,province},j}$ is the intercept coefficient from the adjusted province of the station, c_1 is the sediment thickness coefficient, and $\mathrm{Sediment\,thickness}_j$ is the sediment thickness at the station. Spreadsheets S1 and S2 provide the coefficients $F_{\mathrm{Adj\,province},j}$ and c_1 for regions throughout the CEUS.

We recommend a regionalized site amplification model for the CEUS that uses the different sediment thickness datasets and adjusted physiographic provinces. The adjusted physiographic provinces account for the large-scale regional patterns seen in the amplification terms. The adjusted provinces provide a proxy

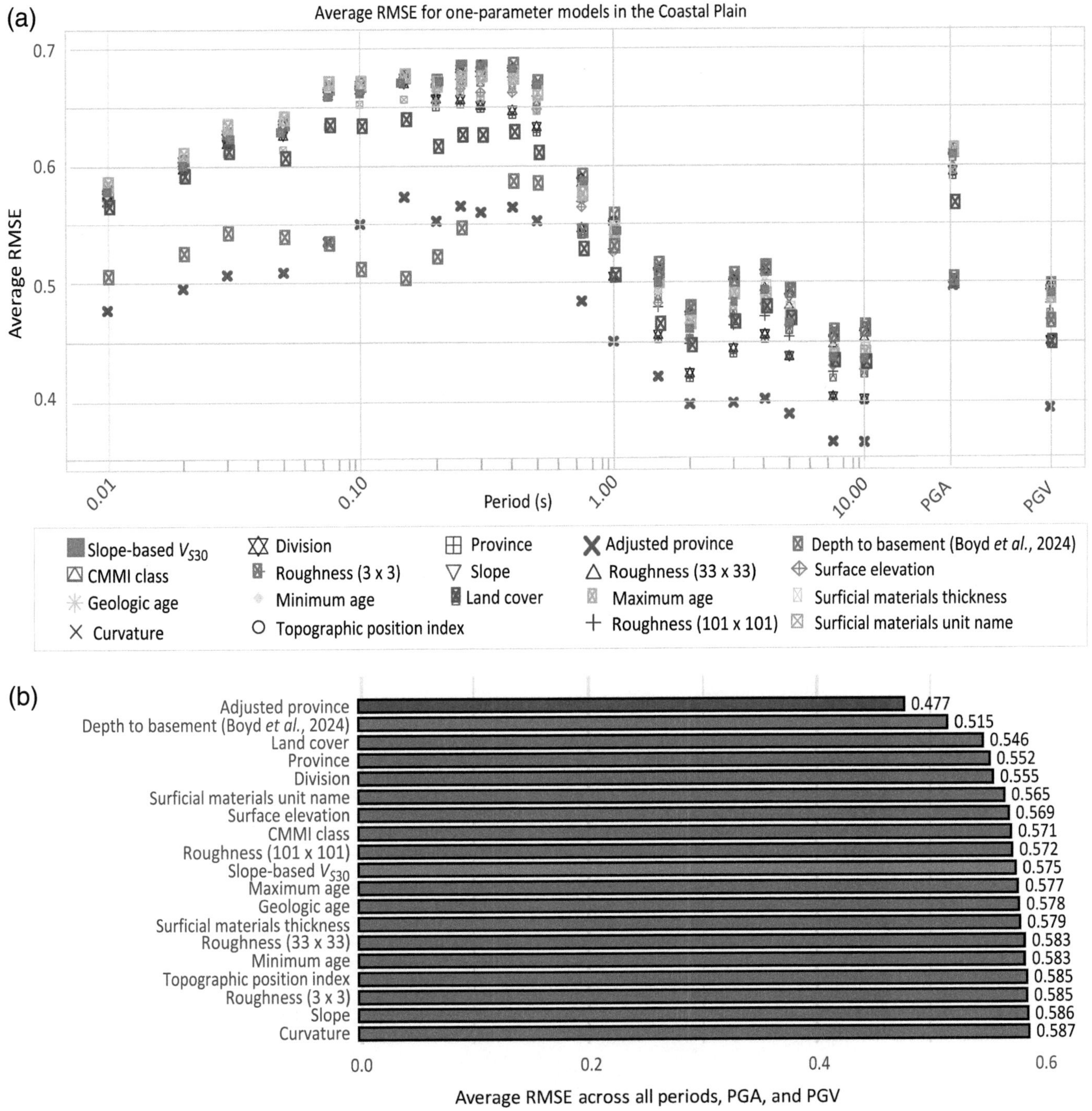

Figure 8. (a) Average root mean square error (RMSE) of the left-out group for each period by predictor for the Coastal Plain. The symbols indicate predictors, with × symbols representing physiographic province, squares representing V_{S30}, and squares with × symbols representing the depth to basement from Boyd *et al.* (2024). Other predictors distinguishable by symbol. (b) Average RMSE for PSA across all periods, PGA, and PGV for each predictor variable. The color version of this figure is available only in the electronic edition.

for differing geology and topography on a broad scale and likely relate to differences in velocity structure. Within these provinces, we also observe variation due to smaller structures, localized geology, and small-scale differences in soil stiffness. We recommend using local sediment thickness data to account for these within-province differences.

As more data become available, it will be important to examine whether the relationship between sediment thickness and amplification differs by adjusted province. In the present work, we do not fit province-specific trends because our goal was to maximize the data used to constrain the overall model and avoid overfitting. In Figure S9, we provide scatterplots of amplification and sediment thickness by adjusted province for PSA at 1 s as a means of evaluating the differences in trends by adjusted province. For the majority of provinces, we do not

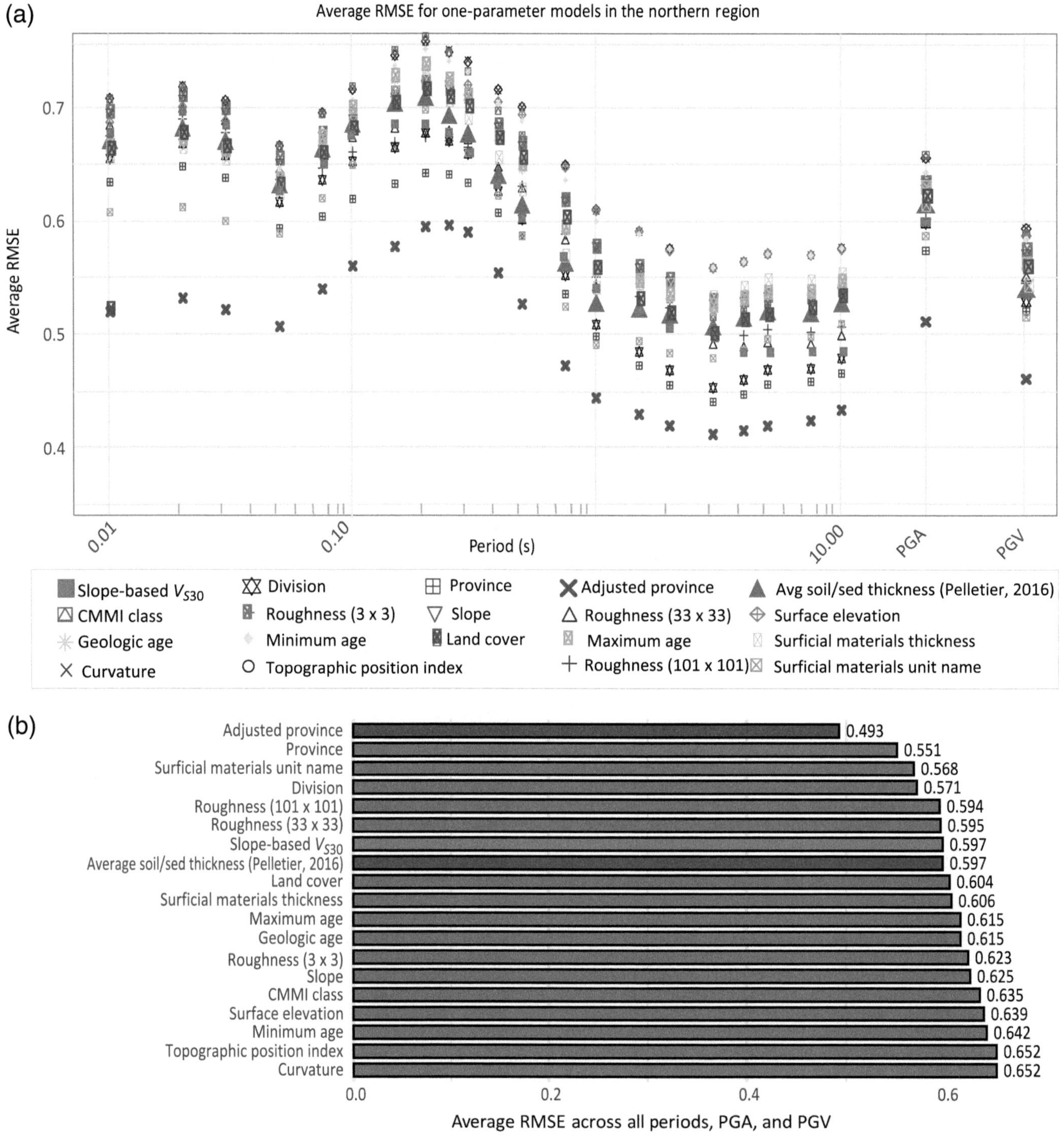

Figure 9. (a) Average RMSE of the left-out group for each period by predictor for the northern CEUS. Symbols indicate predictors, with ×'s representing physiographic province, squares representing V_{S30}, and triangles representing average soil/sediment thickness from Pelletier *et al.* (2016). Other predictors are gray and distinguishable by symbol. (b) Average RMSE for PSA across all periods, PGA, and PGV, for each predictor variable. The color version of this figure is available only in the electronic edition.

have sufficient data to constrain province-specific trends; however, there are a few provinces where this additional step may be justified. Also in Figure S10, we provide box-and-whisker plots of the sediment thickness data by adjusted province for both the stations within that adjusted province, as well as the full range of values possible in that province (raster values). These figures highlight the range of sediment thickness values present within each province and illustrate how station-based values compare with the broader distribution from the raster data.

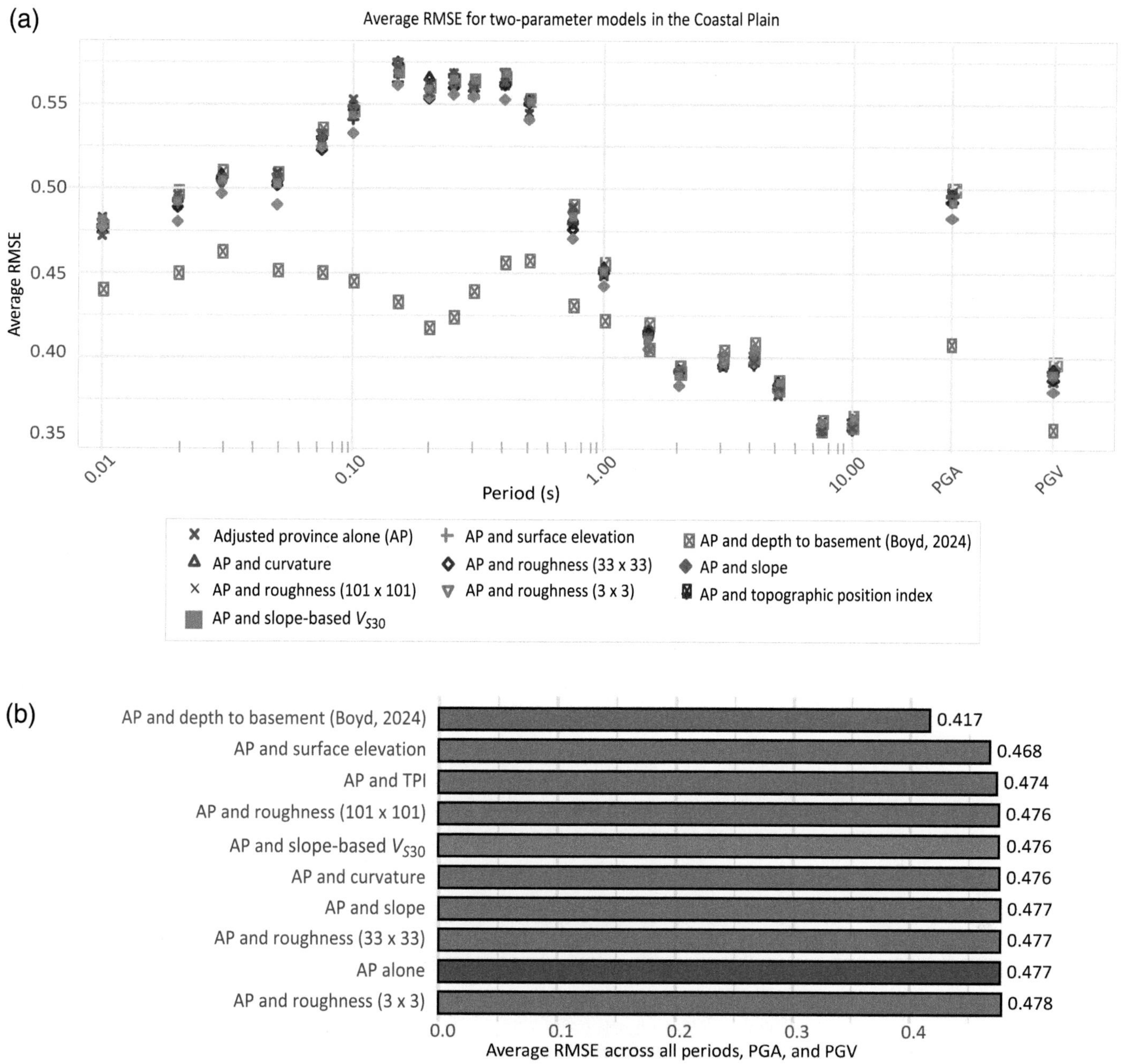

Figure 10. (a) Average RMSE of the left-out group for each period for each two-parameter model (adjusted physiographic province [AP] and a secondary predictor), in addition to a one-parameter model with AP alone, for the Coastal Plain. (b) Average RMSE of the left-out group for PSA across all periods, PGA, and PGV for each alternative model. The legend displays the continuous geospatial variable that was used as a secondary predictor (in addition to AP). The color version of this figure is available only in the electronic edition.

Aleatory variability and epistemic uncertainty estimation

We estimate the aleatory variability ϕ_{total} of our model by computing residuals for all data with $\mathbf{M} > 4$ using the mean branch of the 17 NGA-East GMMs and our linear site amplification term ($F_{\text{Linear},j}$) from the adjusted physiographic province and sediment thickness. Using equation (2), we partition these residuals into event terms (δE_i), site-to-site terms ($\delta S2S_j$), and the remaining residual (ε_{ij}). ϕ_{total} is obtained using the following equation:

$$\phi_{\text{total}} = \sqrt{\phi_{SS}^2 + \phi_{S2S}^2}, \tag{6}$$

in which ϕ_{S2S} is the standard deviation of $\delta S2S_j$ and ϕ_{SS} is the standard deviation of the remaining residual. ϕ_{total} and ϕ_{S2S} are plotted in Figure 12, showing an average of 0.68 and 0.47, respectively, across all periods. ϕ_{total} is higher at short periods and decreases at longer periods, which is consistent with the current NGA-East linear amplification model. Notably, our ϕ_{total} is higher than the reported ϕ_{total} in the NGA-East

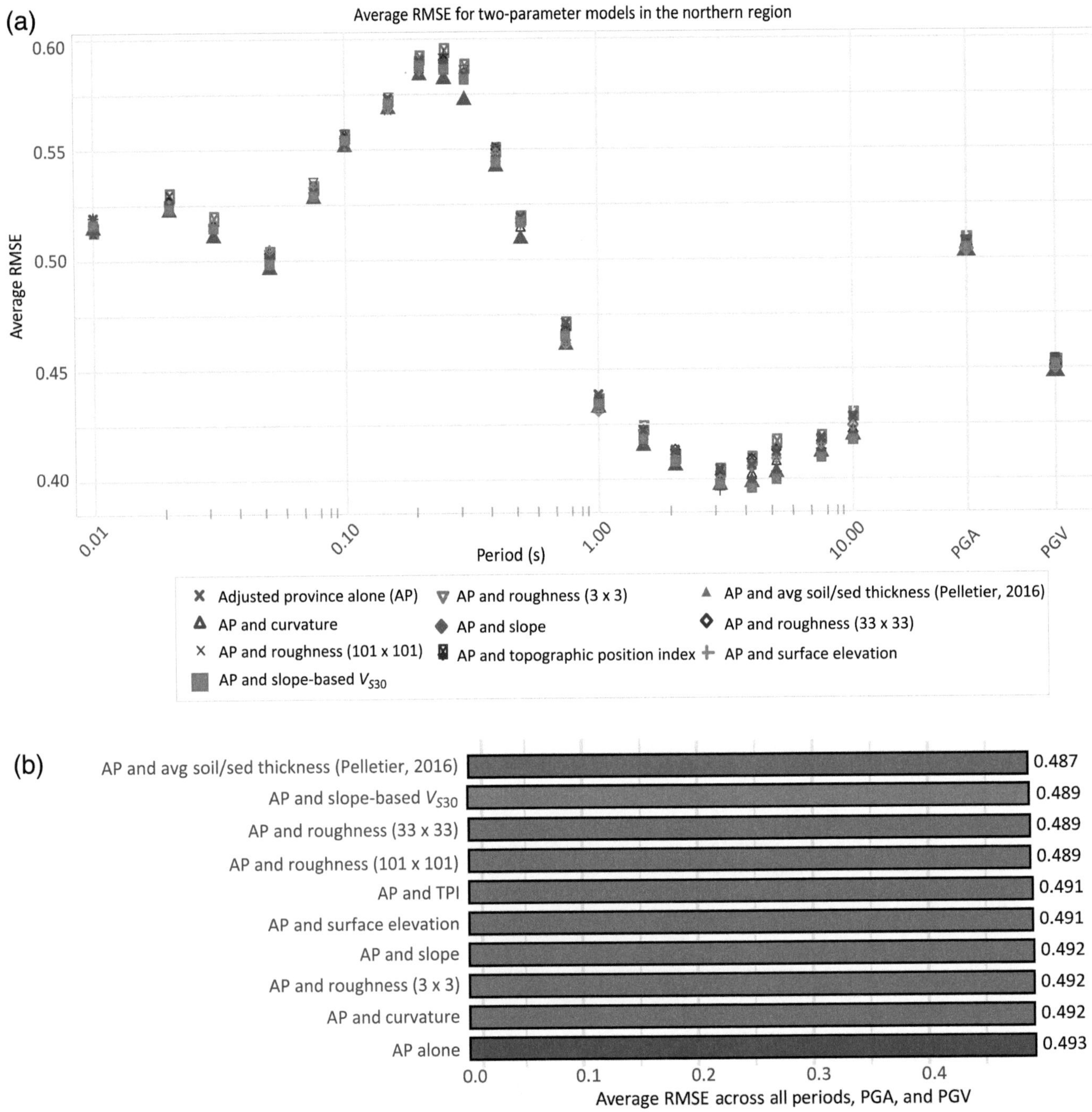

Figure 11. (a) Average RMSE of the left-out group for each period for each two-parameter model (AP and a secondary predictor), in addition to a one-parameter model with AP alone, for the northern CEUS region. (b) Average RMSE of the left-out group for PSA across all periods, PGA, and PGV for each alternative model. The legend displays the continuous geospatial variable that was used as a secondary predictor (in addition to AP). The color version of this figure is available only in the electronic edition.

documentation (Goulet *et al.*, 2017), which can be explained by our inclusion of much more data spanning a broader geographic region within the CEUS. In Figure 12, we also plot ϕ_{total} from the current NGA-East linear amplification model using our combined dataset to provide a comparison.

In Figure 12, we see that ϕ_{total} remains elevated at short periods with our model, which we suspect is driven by a combination of factors, including unmodeled source, path, and site effects. In addition, we observe a greater reduction in ϕ_{total} at short periods with our model, suggesting that these persistently elevated ϕ_{total} values reflect additional unmodeled effects as well as uncertainties in high-frequency ground-motion content. If these elevated values were the result of greater uncertainties in the high-frequency content alone, we would not have observed greater reductions at short periods relative to long periods because the dataset is not changing with period.

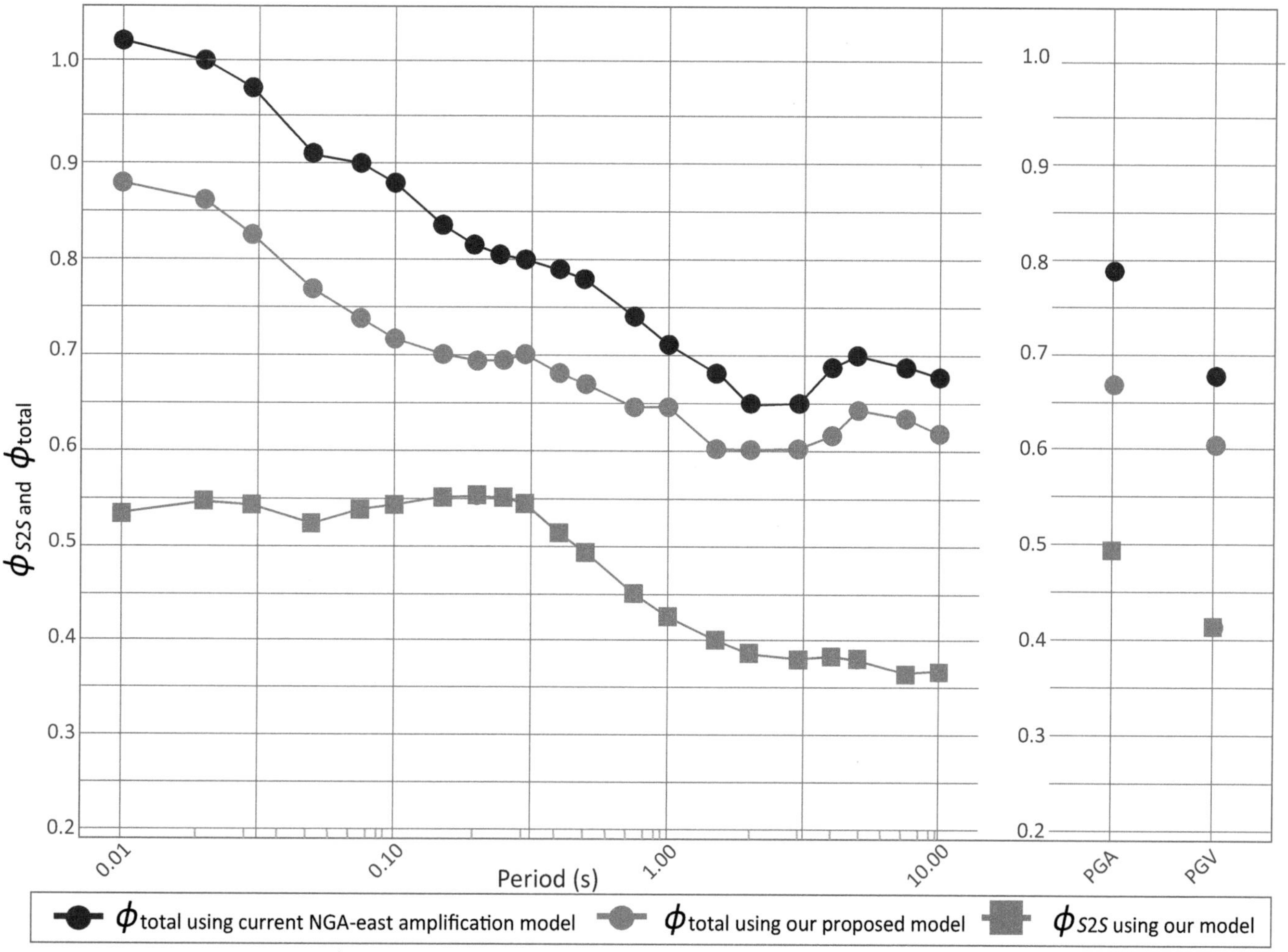

Figure 12. Total aleatory variability (ϕ_{total}) and standard deviation of $\delta S2S$ (ϕ_{S2S}) for PSA at multiple periods, PGA, and PGV using the model proposed in this paper. ϕ_{total} using the current model (Stewart *et al.*, 2020) and our combined dataset is also plotted. The color version of this figure is available only in the electronic edition.

We quantify epistemic uncertainty by examining the uncertainties of the parameters within our model as well as the uncertainties associated with the adjusted physiographic province and sediment thickness datasets. We include the coefficients for each adjusted province and the coefficients for sediment thickness, along with their standard errors, in Spreadsheets S1 and S2. Adjusted provinces with less data have larger standard errors, demonstrating greater uncertainty in the coefficient for that province.

In addition, we recognize that the modified Akima interpolation used to obtain residuals between magnitudes 3 and 4 introduces additional epistemic uncertainty. Although there are minimal biases in the residuals from the extrapolation (Fig. S3), we examine the proportion of residuals for each adjusted province that come from the interpolation instead of from the NGA-East GMMs. We then compute an increased standard error SE_{total}, for each adjusted province:

$$SE_{total} = (1 + 0.06p)SE_{adjusted\_province}, \quad (7)$$

in which p is the proportion of the data that comes from the interpolation, and $SE_{adjusted\_province}$ is the original standard error for the adjusted province. We apply a constant of 0.06 to indicate that if 100% of the residuals come from events with $\mathbf{M} < 4$, the standard error would increase by 6%. We choose 0.06 as a conservative upper bound because it is the largest residual difference we observe across all periods (comparing the residuals for events with $\mathbf{M} < 4$ versus $\mathbf{M} \geq 4$). The purpose of this adjustment is to ensure that provinces that rely heavily on interpolated data have a slightly larger epistemic uncertainty. For each adjusted province, Spreadsheets S1 and S2 list the proportion of residuals used to determine $\delta S2S_j$ that are determined from extrapolation (Column Prop_Mlt4).

The map of the adjusted physiographic province assigns a value to each location. Although the map is not exact in its divisions across the CEUS, it is treated deterministically within our model framework. Each site is assigned an adjusted province with complete certainty; no uncertainty is propagated from the map itself, reflecting the assumption that the map's

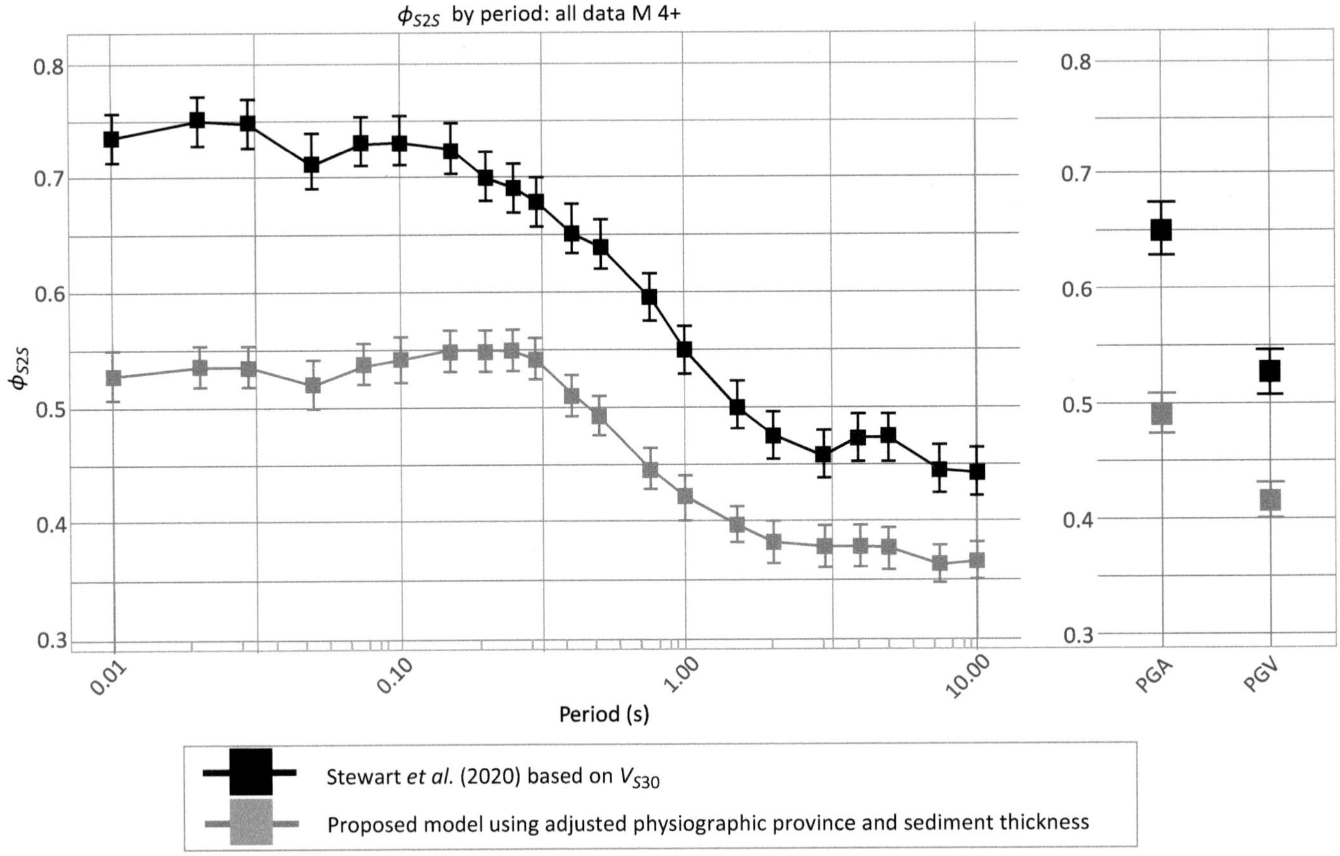

values are fixed and known. For sites within the Coastal Plain that use the depth to basement from Boyd *et al.* (2024), we recommend assigning epistemic uncertainty using the logic trees published. Because the Pelletier *et al.* (2016) model has no published uncertainty, we recommend following the same procedure recommended by Boyd *et al.* (2024): assigning a weight of 0.5 to the amplification using the modeled thickness, and a weight of 0.25 each to the amplification multiplied by 1.2 and divided by 1.2, respectively, using the modeled thickness.

Reduction in *S2S* variability

To assess our proposed model, we examine the difference in site variability between our model and the current NGA-East linear site amplification model based on V_{S30} (Stewart *et al.*, 2020). To perform this comparison, we replace the linear term from the current NGA-East GMM with our proposed linear term at each station. When using the NGA-East GMM, we use the preferred V_{S30} where available and slope-based V_{S30} where preferred values are not available. We then follow equation (1) to obtain ground-motion residuals for each recording and equation (2) to perform mixed-effects regression, yielding $\delta S2S_j$ with the new linear amplification term at each station. We compare these $\delta S2S_j$ values with the original $\delta S2S_j$ values using the Stewart *et al.* (2020) amplification model by computing ϕ_{S2S} from the mixed-effects regression values for PSA at each period, as well as PGA and PGV.

Figure 13. ϕ_{S2S} and 95% confidence intervals of ϕ_{S2S} using ground-motion data from the entire ground-motion dataset (using records from both NGA-East and Center for Engineering Strong Motion Data [CESMD]) for magnitudes 4 and greater, using the current NGA-East linear amplification term (Stewart *et al.*, 2020) and the proposed amplification term as part of this study.

In Figure 13, we perform a comparison of the two alternative amplification models using the combined ground-motion dataset for events with **M** > 4 from the NGA-East and CESMD databases. To assess the variability of each model, we plot ϕ_{S2S} at 2078 stations represented in the combined **M** > 4 dataset, along with the 95% confidence intervals of ϕ_{S2S}. Using our physiographic province and sediment thickness-based amplification model, ϕ_{S2S} is lower across all periods, including PGA and PGV. There is a significant reduction in ϕ_{S2S} using our proposed model, with an average reduction of 23.4% across all periods.

Reduction in spatial trends of *S2S* values

In addition to analyzing the reduction in ϕ_{S2S}, we also map the $\delta S2S_j$ values to examine the spatial trends in Figure 14 for PGA and PSA at 1 s. The $\delta S2S_j$ values using the current model (Stewart *et al.*, 2020) exhibit strong spatial trends, as seen in the left column of Figure 14. With our proposed model (in the right column of Fig. 14), we aim to not only reduce the variability in $\delta S2S_j$, but also to decrease the spatial trends by incorporating adjusted physiographic provinces and

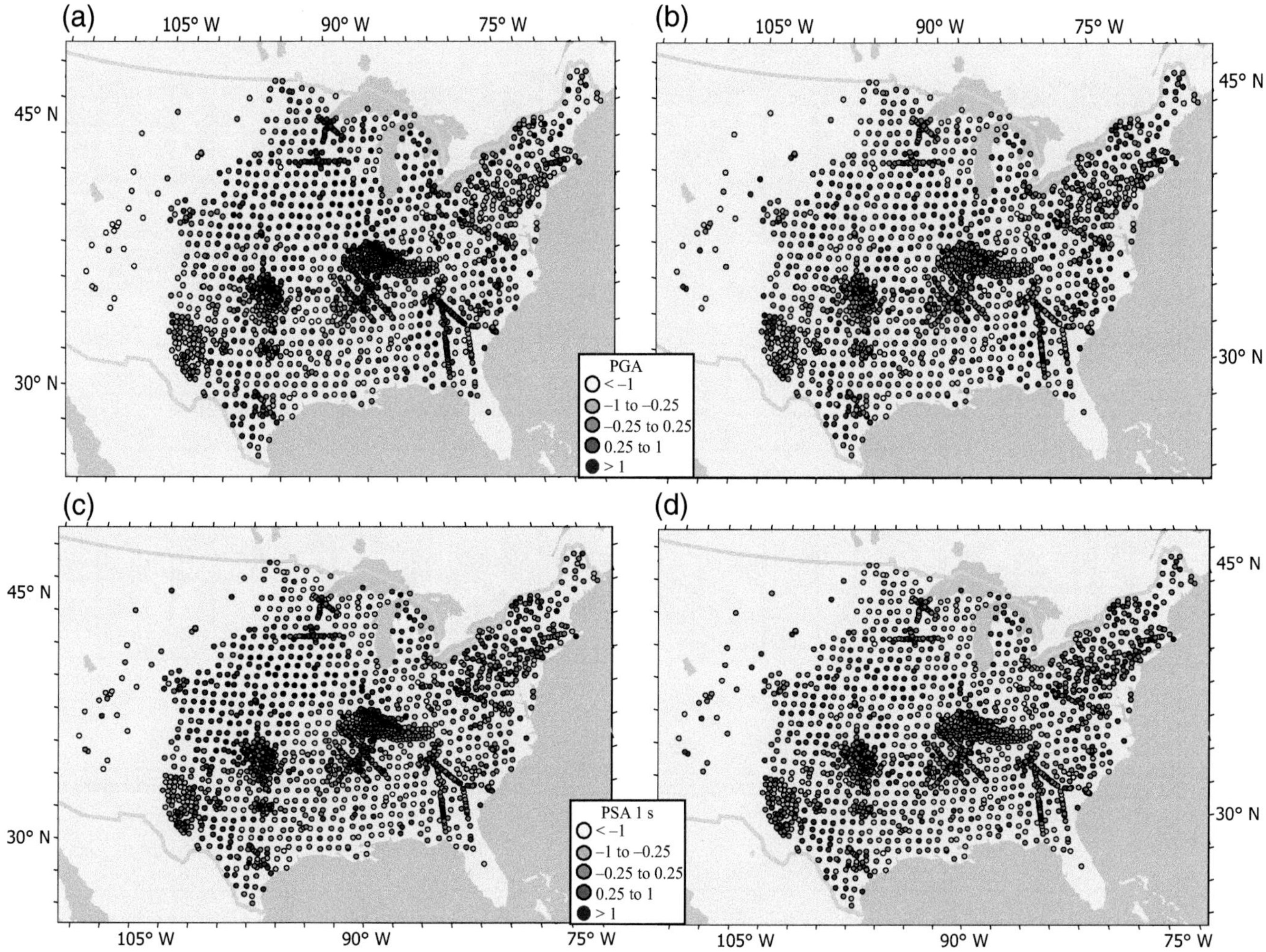

Figure 14. $\delta S2S$ mapped throughout the CEUS for (a) PGA using the Stewart *et al.* (2020) model, (b) PGA using the proposed model, (c) PSA at 1 s using the Stewart *et al.* (2020) model, and (d) PSA at 1 s using the proposed model. The color version of this figure is available only in the electronic edition.

sediment thickness. For PGA (top row), our model exhibits a distinct reduction in the positive regional $\delta S2S_j$ values through the northern Midwest and the ACP. Our model also exhibits a distinct reduction in the negative spatial $\delta S2S_j$ patterns through the Gulf Coastal Plain, Appalachians, and northeast. For PSA at 1 s (bottom row), we observe a similar reduction in spatial patterns. However, our model still exhibits some regional trends in $\delta S2S_j$, highlighting the need for continued work in amplification modeling and finding site parameters that account for both regional and local differences in geologic conditions.

Despite the reduction in the standard deviation and spatial biases of $\delta S2S_j$. There is still significant unexplained variance. Site-specific predictors such as f_{peak}, measured V_{S30}, higher-resolution sediment thickness or basement depth, and basin shape and size parameters could further reduce variability in the CEUS because these parameters have been proven to be in other areas of the world (Olsen, 2000; Hassani and Atkinson, 2016). Future work could incorporate the recently published microtremor horizontal-to-vertical spectral ratio database (Anbazhagan *et al.*, 2025) and the 3D geologic framework from the National Crustal Model (Boyd *et al.*, 2018) as it becomes available in the CEUS.

In Figure 15, we also look at the change in F_{lin} (ΔF_{lin}) as a function of V_{S30} and sediment thickness (Pelletier *et al.*, 2016) to examine how the linear site term changes between the current model and our proposed model with these two parameters.

In Figure 15, we observe an increase in F_{lin} with higher sediment thickness and a decrease in F_{lin} with lower sediment thickness; there are no distinct trends between ΔF_{lin} and V_{S30}. Figures S11–S14 provide additional insights: Figure S11 shows that there is still an overall bias (c), with overpredictions at short periods and underpredictions at long periods. In Figures S12–S14, we also still observe large trends in the total residuals with rupture distance, as well as slight trends with V_{S30} and sediment thickness (Pelletier *et al.*, 2016). Although our proposed model slightly decreases the total residual trends with rupture distance, sediment thickness, and V_{S30}, the trends in the total residuals are still present. Future work could

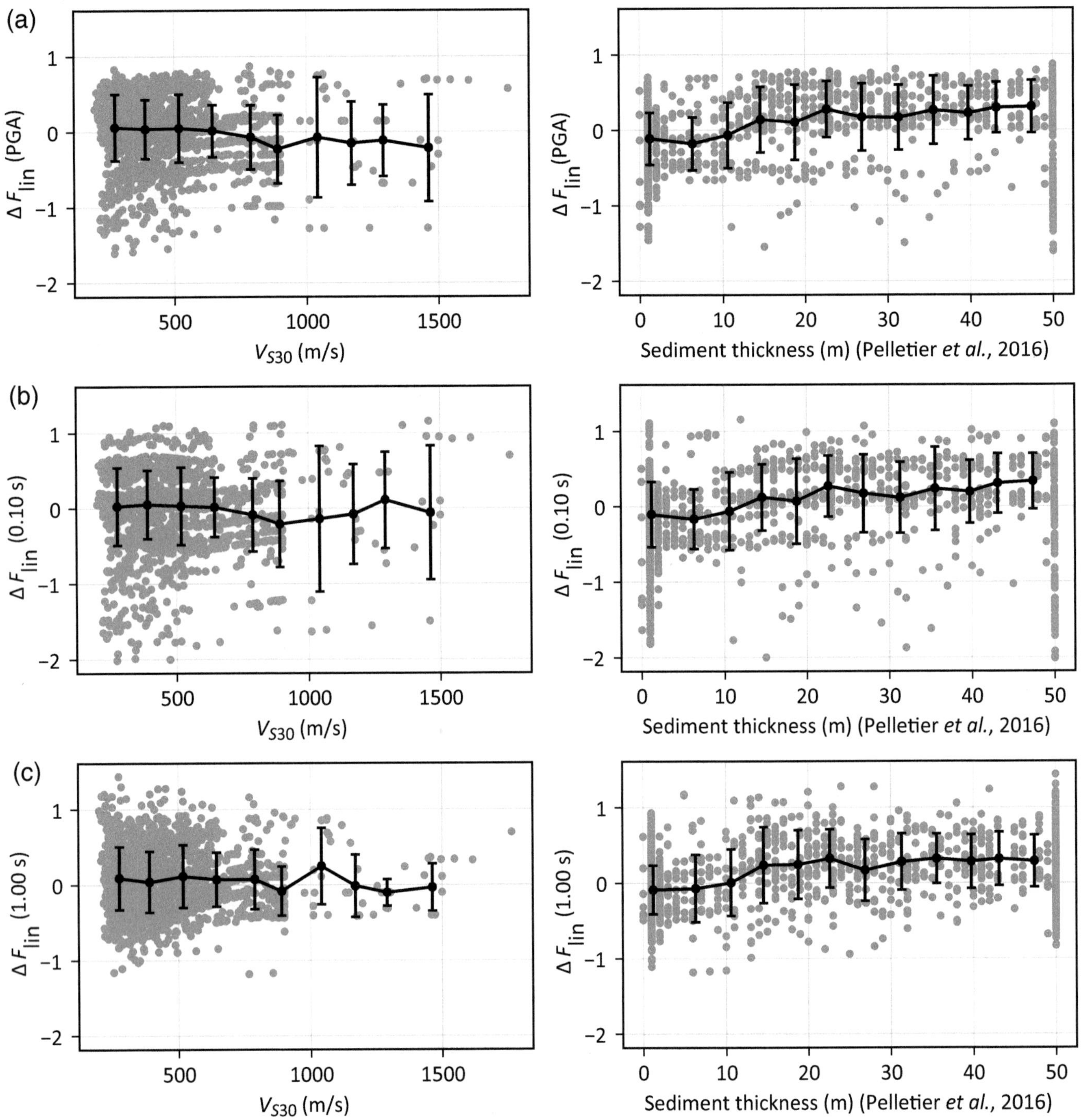

Figure 15. ΔF_{lin} as a function of V_{S30} (left) and sediment thickness (Pelletier *et al.*, 2016) (right) at (a) PGA, (b) PSA at 0.1 s, and (c) PSA at 1 s, showing the increase in linear site term at sites with higher sediment thickness (>10 m) across periods and decrease at sediment thicknesses lower than 10 m. ΔF_{lin} does not seem to trend with V_{S30}.

explore using our proposed model in conjunction with model adjustment factors, such as those from Ramos-Sepúlveda *et al.* (2024), to decrease the overall bias. Future work could also include examining this overall bias by adjusted physiographic province and potentially incorporating physiographic province into path terms to decrease trends with rupture distance.

CONCLUSIONS

In this study, we propose a new site amplification term for use with CEUS GMMs that is based on geospatial predictor variables and does not require site-specific measurements or proxy-based V_{S30}. The proposed site amplification term includes a regional categorical term (adjusted physiographic province) that captures the changes in geology across the CEUS, and a second continuous term (sediment thickness) that captures more local variations. We built our model by performing residual analysis using the current V_{S30}-based

NGA-East linear amplification model (Stewart *et al.*, 2020) to compute $\delta S2S_j$, that is, the portion of the residual that is due to the amplification at the site. We added these $\delta S2S_j$ values to the current linear amplification terms at the sites to obtain the total amplification (A_j) at each station within our database.

We examined a range of geospatial predictors using correlation matrices and ANOVA testing for different regions in the CEUS. Because we found a dependence of amplification A_j on region-specific sediment thickness data, we built models for two regions: the Atlantic and Gulf Coastal Plains and the northern region of the CEUS, using continuous and categorical geospatial variables as predictor variables. To assess each potential model, we used five-fold cross-validation to train and test models, computing the average RMSE of the left-out group.

The optimal single geospatial variable to predict linear amplification in both regions is the adjusted version of the Fenneman and Johnson (1946) physiographic provinces. Because the adjusted physiographic province is a categorical variable with geographic boundaries, we tested potential two-parameter models by adding possible continuous geospatial variables. We found that sediment thickness was the most useful second geospatial variable, using the regional Boyd *et al.* (2024) sediment thickness model for the Coastal Plain, and the global Pelletier *et al.* (2016) model for the northern CEUS outside of the Coastal Plain. Compared with using adjusted province alone, the high-quality sediment thickness dataset of Boyd *et al.* (2024) results in a greater reduction in RMSE than the global dataset of Pelletier *et al.* (2016). This reduced model error highlights the need for similar sediment thickness modeling work in other areas of the CEUS, especially in areas in which DEM-derived parameters and proxy-based V_{S30} do not adequately capture site response.

The functional form of the model includes a coefficient based on adjusted physiographic province and another for sediment thickness. The physiographic province parameter of our model captures large-scale regional trends in amplification, whereas sediment thickness accounts for local variation within each region. The proposed model reduces ϕ_{S2S} by 23.4% across the CEUS relative to the current V_{S30}-based NGA-East linear amplification model of Stewart *et al.* (2020). Furthermore, our proposed model significantly reduces the regional biases and spatial trends of $\delta S2S_j$ using the current linear amplification model. In city-scale site response analyses in Memphis and New York City, Kaklamanos *et al.* (2026) found that the proposed geospatial-based model offered stronger prediction accuracies (relative to observed ground motions) than V_{S30}-based linear amplification models.

This work highlights the advantages of using geospatial data in creating GMM site amplification terms in the CEUS, in which measured V_{S30} is rarely available at ground-motion stations, and there are significant regional trends in amplification due to large-scale changes in geology and geomorphology. This approach also eliminates the need for multiple hazard curves at every site and eliminates difficulties that come with uncertainty estimation in combining proxy-based V_{S30} values. It also emphasizes the importance of expanding depth-to-basement mapping efforts across the CEUS and in other regions where V_{S30} is an inadequate proxy for site amplification. More broadly, this approach provides a framework that can be generalized to other stable continental regions where dense V_{S30} measurements are unavailable but high-quality geospatial datasets exist.

DATA AND RESOURCES

The ground-motion records used for this analysis were obtained from the Pacific Earthquake Engineering Research Center (PEER) Next Generation Attenuation (NGA)-East database (Goulet, Kishida, *et al.*, 2021; https://ngawest2.berkeley.edu/) and the Central and Eastern United States (CEUS) earthquake ground-motion database (Thompson *et al.*, 2023; https://www.strongmotioncenter.org/specialstudies/thompson2023_ceus/). For all recordings from earthquakes with magnitude greater than 4, ground-motion model (GMM) predictions were computed using the central branch of the NGA-East GMMs (Goulet, Bozorgnia, *et al.*, 2021), the linear amplification model (Stewart *et al.*, 2020), and the nonlinear amplification model (Hashash *et al.*, 2020), using the code available at https://github.com/wltcwpf/GMPE/blob/main/R/-nga_cena.R, produced by Wang (2023). For ground-motion recordings from earthquakes with magnitudes between 3 and 4, we used modified Akima Interpolation in MATLAB (MathWorks Inc., 2023; https://www.mathworks.com/help/matlab/ref-/makima.html) based on rupture distance, magnitude, and period, following the methods described in Boyd *et al.* (2024). For mixed-effects regression, we used the open-source statistical language and environment R (R Core Team, 2025) with the lme4 package (Bates *et al.*, 2015) and the function lmer. The geospatial data used as predictors are described in Tables 1 and 2, which include all data sources and notes that several terms (e.g., roughness, TPI, and curvature) were derived from elevation data by Jarvis *et al.* (2008). These variables were processed using ArcGIS Pro. Regional sediment thickness data used in model development are described in the Data section. Physiographic divisions, provinces, and sections were taken from Fenneman and Johnson (1946), and the methodology for developing the adjusted physiographic provinces is provided in the Data section. Model training, testing, and fitting were conducted using R, and figures were created using R, Python, MATLAB, and Adobe Illustrator.

The supplemental material for this article includes fourteen figures, three Excel spreadsheets, and one GIS shapefile supporting the development of the linear site amplification model. Figure S1 shows example maps of the categorical divisions for two Massachusetts geology-based maps (Soller *et al.*, 2009; McCafferty *et al.*, 2023). Figure S2 compares the province areas from Fenneman and Johnson (1946) with the adjusted provinces used in this study. Figure S3 plots residuals binned by magnitude for peak ground acceleration, pseudo-spectral acceleration (PSA) at 0.1 s, PSA at 1 s, and PSA at 3 s, highlighting the range in which residuals are derived from the modified Akima interpolation instead of from the NGA-East GMMs. Figures S4–S7 present full correlation matrices of amplification with geospatial predictors for the entire CEUS and separated by region. Figure S8 reports analysis of variance F values for categorical variables, noting the two categories below the critical F value. Figure S9 shows amplification versus sediment thickness by adjusted province at PSA 1 s, and Figure S10 provides boxplots comparing ranges of sediment thickness for the stations used in the analysis, along with the province-wide distributions of sediment thickness. Figure S11 summarizes period-dependent overall bias, and Figures S12–S14 show total residual trends before and after applying the proposed model. Three supplemental spreadsheets provide period-dependent regression coefficients and station metadata: Spreadsheet S1 covers provinces within the Atlantic and Gulf Coastal Plains (using sediment thickness from Boyd *et al.*, 2024), Spreadsheet S2 covers provinces in the northern CEUS outside the Coastal Plains (using estimates from Pelletier *et al.*, 2016), and Spreadsheet S3 lists details of the stations used in this study (with latitude/longitude and extracted geospatial terms; see Tables 1 and 2). A GIS shapefile (Shapefile S1) of the adjusted physiographic provinces is also included for direct use. In addition, the authors provide online maps of their work on the Tufts Geohazards website: https://sites.tufts.edu/geohazards/geospatial-data/. All websites were last accessed in December 2025.

DECLARATION OF COMPETING INTERESTS

The authors acknowledge that there are no conflicts of interest recorded.

ACKNOWLEDGMENTS

This material is based upon work supported by the U.S. Geological Survey under Grant Numbers G23AP00389 and G23AP00390. The views and conclusions contained in this document are those of the authors and should not be interpreted as representing the opinions or policies of the U.S. Geological Survey. Mention of trade names or commercial products does not constitute their endorsement by the U.S. Geological Survey. The authors would like to acknowledge the feedback of Shahram Pezeshk and an anonymous reviewer, their helpful comments led to an improvement in the quality of the article.

REFERENCES

Akhani, M., M. Davatgari-Tafreshi, and S. Pezeshk (2024). Adjusting Central and Eastern United States ground-motion models for use in the Coastal Plain considering the sediment thickness, *Earthq. Spectra* **40,** no. 4, 2669–2691, doi: 10.1177/87552930241258354.

Allen, T. I., and D. J. Wald (2009). On the use of high-resolution topograpshic data as a proxy for seismic site conditions (V_{S30}), *Bull. Seismol. Soc. Am.* **99,** no. 2A, 935–943, doi: 10.1785/0120080255.

Anbazhagan, B., J. Vantassel, and A. Rodriguez-Marek (2025). Microtremor horizontal-to-vertical spectral ratios (mHVSR) at North American seismic stations, *DesignSafe-CI*, doi: 10.17603/ds2-2ea1-vc33.

Ancheta, T. D., R. B. Darragh, J. P. Stewart, E. Seyhan, W. J. Silva, B. S. J. Chiou, K. E. Wooddell, R. W. Graves, A. R. Kottke, D. M. Boore, *et al.* (2014). NGA-West2 database, *Earthq. Spectra* **30,** no. 3, 989–1005, doi: 10.1193/070913EQS197M.

Atik, L. A., N. Abrahamson, J. J. Bommer, F. Scherbaum, F. Cotton, and N. Kuehn (2010). The variability of ground-motion prediction models and its components, *Seismol. Res. Lett.* **81,** no. 5, 794–801.

Baise, L. G., J. Kaklamanos, B. M. Berry, and E. M. Thompson (2016). Soil amplification with a strong impedance contrast: Boston, Massachusetts, *Eng. Geol.* **202,** 1–13.

Bates, D., M. Mächler, B. Bolker, and S. Walker (2015). Fitting linear mixed-effects models using lme4, *J. Stat. Software* **67,** no. 1, 1–48, doi: 10.18637/jss.v067.i01.

Beven, K. J., M. J. Kirkby, J. E. Freer, and R. Lamb (2021). A history of TOPMODEL, *Hydrol. Earth Syst. Sci.* **25,** 527–549, doi: 10.5194/hess-25-527-2021.

Bindi, D., and D. Di Giacomo (2025). Energy-magnitude station corrections across the conterminous United States, *Bull. Seismol. Soc. Am.* **115,** no. 3, 1344–1351, doi: 10.1785/0120240092.

Boore, D. M. (2001). Comparison of AA, PA and RV, PV for M_L = 4.5 and **M** = 5.0 and 7.1 earthquakes, available at http://www.daveboore.com/daves_notes/aa_pa_rv_pv_2.pdf (last accessed December 2025).

Boyd, O. S., D. Churchwell, Mss. P. Moschetti, E. M. Thompson, M. C. Chapman, O. Ilhan, T. L. Pratt, S. K. Ahdi, and S. Rezaeian (2024). Sediment thickness map of United States Atlantic and Gulf Coastal Plain strata, and their influence on earthquake ground motions, *Earthq. Spectra* **40,** no. 1, 89–112.

Boyd, O. S., A. K. Shah, D. S. Sweetkind, T. Sowers, and V. E. Langenheim (2018). Components of the USGS National Crustal Model (ver. 2.0, September 2025), *U.S. Geol. Surv. Data Release*, doi: 10.5066/P9T96Q67.

Chapman, M. C., and Z. Guo (2021). A response spectral ratio model to account for amplification and attenuation effects in the Atlantic and Gulf Coastal Plain, *Bull. Seismol. Soc. Am.* **111,** no. 4, 1849–1867.

Chopra, A. K. (2007). Elastic response spectrum: A historical note, *Earthq. Eng. Struct. Dynam.* **36,** 3–12.

Contreras, V., J. P. Stewart, T. Kishida, R. B. Darragh, B. S. Chiou, S. Mazzoni, R. R. Youngs, N. M. Kuehn, S. K. Ahdi, K. Wooddell, *et al.* (2022). NGA-Sub source and path database, *Earthq. Spectra* **38,** no. 2, 799–840.

Domrois, S., S. Marshak, C. C. Abert, and T. H. Larson (2015). ArcGIS maps depicting topography of the basement-cover contact (the Great Unconformity), and the traces of faults and folds, in the Cratonic Platform of the United States, *AAPG Search and Discovery*, 29 pp.

Fenneman, N. M., and D. W. Johnson (1946). Physiographic divisions of the conterminous U.S., *U.S. Geol. Surv. Data Release*, doi: 10.5066/P9B1S3K8.

Gann-Phillips, C., A. Cabas, C. Ji, C. Cramer, J. Kaklamanos, and O. Boyd (2024). Regional seismic velocity model for the U.S. Atlantic and Gulf Coastal Plains based on measured shear wave velocity, sediment thickness, and surface geology, *Earthq. Spectra* **40,** no. 2, 1269–1300.

Goulet, C. A., Y. Bozorgnia, N. Kuehn, L. Al Atik, R. R. Youngs, R. W. Graves, and G. M. Atkinson (2017). NGA-East ground-motion models for the U.S. Geological Survey National Seismic Hazard maps, *PEER Rept. No. 2017/03*, Pacific Earthquake Engineering Research Center, University of California, Berkeley.

Goulet, C. A., Y. Bozorgnia, N. Kuehn, L. Al Atik, R. R. Youngs, R. W. Graves, and G. M. Atkinson (2021). NGA-East ground-motion characterization model Part I: Summary of products and model development, *Earthq. Spectra* **37,** 1231–1282.

Goulet, C. A., T. Kishida, T. D. Ancheta, C. H. Cramer, R. B. Darragh, W. J. Silva, Y. M. Hashash, J. Harmon, G. A. Parker, J. P. Stewart, *et al.* (2021). PEER NGA-East database, *Earthq. Spectra* **37,** 1331–1353.

Guo, Z., and M. C. Chapman (2019). An examination of amplification and attenuation effects in the Atlantic and Gulf Coastal Plain using spectral ratio, *Bull. Seismol. Soc. Am.* **109,** no. 5, 1855–1877, doi: 10.1785/0120190071.

Hashash, Y. M., O. Ilhan, J. A. Harmon, G. A. Parker, J. P. Stewart, E. M. Rathje, K. W. Campbell, and W. J. Silva (2020). Nonlinear site amplification model for ergodic seismic hazard analysis in Central and Eastern North America, *Earthq. Spectra* **36,** no. 1, 69–86.

Hassani, B., and G. M. Atkinson (2016). Site-effects model for Central and Eastern North America based on peak frequency, *Bull. Seismol. Soc. Am.* **106,** no. 5, 2197–2213.

Hassani, B., and G. M. Atkinson (2018). Site-effects model for Central and Eastern North America based on peak frequency and average shear-wave velocity, *Bull. Seismol. Soc. Am.* **108,** no. 1, 338–350.

Heath, D. C., D. J. Wald, C. B. Worden, E. M. Thompson, and G. M. Smoczyk (2020). A global hybrid V_{S30} map with a topographic slope–based default and regional map insets, *Earthq. Spectra* **36,** no. 3, 1570–1584.

Jarvis, A., H. I. Reuter, A. Nelson, and E. Guevara (2008). Hole-filled seamless SRTM data V4, *International Centre for Tropical Agriculture (CIAT)*, available at https://srtm.csi.cgiar.org/ (last accessed December 2025).

Kaklamanos, J., L. G. Baise, C. Sanon, E. Meyer, I. M. Guzman, and G. A. Sachs-Walor (2026). Site and basin effects in the Central and Eastern U.S.: City- and state-scale evaluations in Memphis, New York City, and Massachusetts, *Geo-Congress 2026*, American Society of Civil Engineers, Salt Lake City, Utah, 9–12 March 2026.

MathWorks Inc. (2023). MATLAB version: 23.2.0.2515942 (R2023b), Update 7, The MathWorks Inc., Natick, Massachusetts, available at https://www.mathworks.com (last accessed December 2025).

McCafferty, A. E., C. A. San Juan, C. J. M. Lawley, G. E. Graham, M. G. Gadd, D. L. Huston, K. D. Kelley, S. Paradis, J. M. Peter, and K. Czarnota (2023). National-scale geophysical, geologic, and mineral resource data for the United States, Canada, and Australia, *U.S. Geol. Surv. Data Release*, doi: 10.5066/P970GDD5.

Mentrasti, L. (2008). Estimate of spectral and pseudo-spectral acceleration proximity, *Eng. Struct.* **30,** 2338–2346.

Olsen, K. B. (2000). Site amplification in the Los Angeles basin from three-dimensional modeling of ground motion, *Bull. Seismol. Soc. Am.* **90,** no. 6B, S77–S94, doi: 10.1785/0120000506.

Parker, G. A., J. P. Stewart, Y. M. A. Hashash, E. M. Rathje, K. W. Campbell, and W. J. Silva (2019). Empirical linear seismic site amplification in Central and Eastern North America, *Earthq. Spectra* **35,** no. 2, 849–881.

Pelletier, J. D., P. D. Broxton, P. Hazenberg, X. Zeng, P. A. Troch, G.-Y. Niu, Z. Williams, M. A. Brunke, and D. Gochis (2016). A gridded global data set of soil, immobile regolith, and sedimentary deposit thicknesses for regional and global land surface modeling, *J. Adv. Model. Earth Syst.* **8,** 41–65, doi: 10.1002/2015MS000526.

Petersen, M. D., A. M. Shumway, P. M. Powers, E. H. Field, M. P. Moschetti, K. S. Jaiswal, K. R. Milner, S. Rezaeian, A. D. Frankel, A. L. Llenos, *et al.* (2024). The 2023 US 50-state National Seismic Hazard Model: Overview and implications, *Earthq. Spectra* **40,** no. 1, 5–88, doi: 10.1177/87552930231215428.

Pezeshk, S., A. Zandieh, and A. Haji-Soltani (2021). A ground-motion model for the Gulf Coast region of the United States. *Bull. Seismol. Soc. Am.* **111,** no. 6, 3261–3277.

Porter, R., Y. Liu, and W. E. Holt (2016). Lithospheric records of orogeny within the continental U.S., *Geophys. Res. Lett.* **43,** 144–153, doi: 10.1002/2015GL066950.

Pratt, T. L., and L. S. Schleicher (2021). Characterizing ground-motion amplification by extensive flat-lying sediments: The seismic response of the eastern U.S. Atlantic Coastal Plain strata, *Bull. Seismol. Soc. Am.* **111,** no. 4, 1795–1823.

R Core Team (2025). *R: A Language and Environment for Statistical Computing*, R Foundation for Statistical Computing, Vienna, Austria.

Rai, M., A. Rodriguez-Marek, and A. Yong (2016). An empirical model to predict topographic effects in strong ground motion using California small- to medium-magnitude earthquake database, *Earthq. Spectra* **32,** no. 2, 1033–1054, doi: 10.1193/113014eqs202m.

Ramos-Sepúlveda, M. E., J. P. Stewart, G. A. Parker, M. P. Moschetti, E. M. Thompson, S. J. Brandenberg, Y. M. A. Hashash, and E. M. Rathje (2024). Data-driven adjustments for combined use of NGA-East hard-rock ground motion and site amplification models, *Earthq. Spectra* **40,** no. 2, 1132–1157, doi: 10.1177/87552930241231825.

Sedaghati, F., S. Pezeshk, and N. Nazemi (2018). Site amplification within the Mississippi embayment of the central United States: Investigation of possible differences among various phases of seismic waves and presence of basin waves, *Soil Dynam. Earthq. Eng.* **113,** 534–544, doi: 10.1016/j.soildyn.2018.04.017.

Sofia, G., and E. I. Nikolopoulos (2020). Floods and rivers: A circular causality perspective, *Sci. Rep.* **10,** 5175, doi: 10.1038/s41598-020-61533-x.

Soller, D. R., and C. P. Garrity (2018). Quaternary sediment thickness and bedrock topography of the glaciated United States east of the Rocky Mountains, *U.S. Geol. Surv. Sci. Investig. Map 3392*, 2 sheets, doi: 10.3133/sim3392.

Soller, D. R., M. C. Reheis, C. P. Garrity, and D. R. Van Sistine (2009). Map database for surficial materials in the conterminous United States, *U.S. Geol. Surv. Data Series 425*, scale 1:5,000,000.

Stewart, J. P., G. A. Parker, G. M. Atkinson, D. M. Boore, Y. M. A. Hashash, and W. J. Silva (2020). Ergodic site amplification model for Central and Eastern North America, *Earthq. Spectra* **36,** no. 1, 42–68.

Thompson, E. M., and D. J. Wald (2016). Uncertainty in V_{S30}-based site response, *Bull. Seismol. Soc. Am.* **106,** no. 2, 453–463, doi: 10.1785/0120150214.

Thompson, E. M., O. S. Boyd, D. Churchwell, and M. P. Moschetti (2023). Central and Eastern U.S. earthquake ground motion database: 2010 to 2020, Center for Engineering Strong Motion Data (CESMD), doi: 10.5066/P9HX7MYG.

Wang, P. (2023). GMPE: Ground motion prediction equations (version 2.1.1), GitHub Repository, available at https://github.com/wltcwpf/GMPE (last accessed December 2025).

Wills, C. J., C. I. Gutierrez, F. G. Perez, and D. M. Branum (2015). A next generation V_{S30} map for California based on geology and topography, *Bull. Seismol. Soc. Am.* **105,** no. 6, 3083–3091, doi: 10.1785/0120150105.

Yang, L., S. Jin, P. Danielson, C. Homer, L. Gass, S. M. Bender, A. Case, C. Costello, J. Dewitz, J. Fry, M. Funk, *et al.* (2018). A new generation of the United States National land cover database: Requirements, research priorities, design, and implementation strategies, *ISPRS J. Photogramm. Remote Sens.* **146,** 108–123, doi: 10.1016/j.isprsjprs.2018.09.006.

Manuscript received 25 July 2025
Published online 8 January 2026

A Nonergodic Ground-Motion Model for the San Francisco Bay Area for Small-Magnitude Earthquakes

Maxime Lacour*[1], Norman Abrahamson[1], Rie Nakata[2,3], Nori Nakata[2,4], and Camilo I. Pinilla-Ramos[2,5,6]

ABSTRACT

Recently, generative models have become a computationally efficient alternative to physics-based numerical simulations of ground motions. Neural networks can learn from existing ground-motion data to generate unobserved ground-motion data at new source and site locations. A key challenge with generative models is ensuring that predicted ground motions remain within a physically realistic range. For this purpose, we developed an empirical, nonergodic ground-motion model (GMM) for small-magnitude earthquakes in the San Francisco Bay area based on about 5000 recordings per component for $M_w \le 4$ earthquakes. The nonergodic GMM predicts spatially varying median source, site, and path effects for both the Fourier amplitude spectrum (FAS) and the Fourier phase derivative (a proxy for duration), as well as the corresponding epistemic uncertainty for each term. For FAS, our model shows above-average source and site effects in the western part of the region and below-average effects in the eastern part, with regional effects exhibiting larger spatial correlation lengths with increasing frequency. For duration, the source term is negligible for small-magnitude earthquakes, and the site term leads to site-specific variations up to 5 s. Path effects for FAS and duration depend on the source–site pair and are extrapolated spatially using recent methods for path-effect modeling. The aleatory variability of the within-site within-path residuals is similar to the variability found in previous studies for other regions. The nonergodic model provides two key contributions: first, median adjustment terms that are transferable to larger magnitude earthquakes, further reducing aleatory variability in probabilistic seismic hazard analysis; second, region-specific criteria for validating machine learning-based ground-motion generators to evaluate whether synthetic ground motions exhibit physically realistic source, site, and path effects.

KEY POINTS

- Artificial intelligence (AI)-based ground-motion models do not have constraints on extrapolation.
- We develop a nonergodic model to test the extrapolation of AI-based models for source, site, and path effects.
- Nonergodic terms transfer to larger magnitudes and provide validation criteria for AI-based ground motions.

Supplemental Material

INTRODUCTION

Numerical simulation of ground motions using physics-based methods with a 3D velocity structure can be computationally expensive (McCallen *et al.*, 2021a,b), which limits the number of different scenarios that can be modeled.

A critical challenge for both physics-based simulations and artificial intelligence (AI)-generated ground motions is the validation of the generated ground motions. Traditional validation approaches compare simulated ground motions against ergodic ground-motion prediction equations (GMPEs); however, ergodic GMPEs gather data from multiple regions and cannot capture systematic spatial variations in source, site, and path effects. Nonergodic models can significantly reduce the aleatory variability in probabilistic seismic hazard analysis

1. Department of Civil and Environmental Engineering, University of California, Berkeley, California, U.S.A., https://orcid.org/0000-0002-8316-4435 (ML); https://orcid.org/0000-0001-7900-6023 (NA); 2. Energy Geosciences Division, Lawrence Berkeley National Laboratory, Berkeley, California, U.S.A., https://orcid.org/0000-0002-9188-9030 (RN); https://orcid.org/0000-0002-4034-6618 (CIP-R); 3. Earthquake Research Institute, University of Tokyo, Tokyo, Japan; 4. Department of Earth, Atmospheric and Planetary Sciences, MIT, Cambridge, Massachusetts, U.S.A.; 5. University of Southern California, Los Angeles, California, U.S.A.; 6. Statewide California Earthquake Center, SCEC, Los Angeles, California, U.S.A.

*Corresponding author: maxlacour@berkeley.edu

Cite this article as Lacour, M., N. Abrahamson, R. Nakata, N. Nakata, and C. I. Pinilla-Ramos (2026). A Nonergodic Ground-Motion Model for the San Francisco Bay Area for Small-Magnitude Earthquakes, *Bull. Seismol. Soc. Am.* **116**, 1264–1279, doi: 10.1785/0120250094

(PSHA) and provide region-specific benchmarks for validating AI-based simulations. As an alternative, AI methods provide more efficient methods for generating ground motions for a specific source–site combination.

To support validation of AI-based simulations and to enable nonergodic PSHA applications, we develop empirically based ground-motion models (GMMs) for the velocity Fourier amplitude spectrum (FAS) and the phase derivative for small-magnitude earthquakes in the San Francisco region. Ground motions from small-magnitude events provide a large empirical dataset for the region that can be used to train and validate AI-based simulation methods for source, path, and site effects. The FAS GMM provides constraints on ground-motion amplitude, and the phase-derivative GMM provides constraints on waveform duration. Simulations consistent with both empirical models demonstrate physically realistic behavior for these fundamental characteristics.

In this article, we first develop an ergodic GMM for FAS. Using the ergodic GMM as a reference, a nonergodic GMM for FAS is developed that models the systematic source, site, and path effects, including path effects due to the 3D velocity structure (Sung *et al.*, 2023). The same approach is used to develop ergodic and nonergodic GMMs for the phase derivative.

The nonergodic GMM developed in this study provides two significant contributions. First, for PSHA applications, median nonergodic terms based on small-magnitude earthquakes can be used to estimate median nonergodic terms for large-magnitude earthquakes for linear site and path effects, further reducing aleatory variability in hazard calculations. The transferability of nonergodic site and path corrections from small-magnitude earthquakes to large-magnitude earthquakes is based on the principle that ground motions from large earthquakes can be decomposed as the sum of contributions from multiple smaller subevents. The Southern California Earthquake Center Broadband Platform validation studies (Goulet *et al.*, 2015) explicitly validate this principle of subevent summation. Their validation exercise employed kinematic rupture generators that synthesize finite-fault ground motions from sub-fault contributions, successfully reproducing observed strong-motion recordings across magnitudes M_w 4.6–7.6 in multiple tectonic regimes. The nonergodic source effects from small-magnitude earthquakes may be correlated with those from large-magnitude earthquakes, but this requires further investigation. Second, for AI-based simulation validation, the nonergodic GMM establishes region-specific acceptance criteria. AI models can be validated against the empirically derived distributions over the region of study to ensure their predictions match observed systematic regional variations, providing an objective framework for validating synthetic ground motions.

DATA ACQUISITION AND PROCESSING

Seismograms from small-magnitude earthquakes in the San Francisco region were downloaded from the Northern California Earthquake Data Center (NCEDC) database (Northern California Earthquake Data Center [NCEDC], 2014), where the earthquake data are available as velocity time series. The stations were selected in a rectangular area of 120 km × 120 km centered on the Hayward fault, and the earthquakes within 100 km of the stations were retained. This led to 626,423 three-component velocity time series from 1990 to 2023. Only the two horizontal components are used in this study. The start of the time window was set at 10 s before the origin time of the event, and the total length of the time window was set to 70 s. The Nyquist frequency is 50 Hz for each recording.

The first 10 s before the origin time were used to define the noise of each recording, and the remaining 60 s were used to define the earthquake signal, assuming that the noise is stationary over 70 s. Using the time window before the origin time ensures that the noise window does not overlap with the earthquake signal.

The FAS of the signal and the noise were smoothed using the Konno and Ohmachi (1998) procedure with a smoothing parameter $b$exp = 20. This value of b corresponds to smoothing over a broader frequency window than typically used for input to random vibration procedures (Kottke *et al.*, 2021). The broader smoothing reduces the troughs in the FAS, which results in fewer records falling below the minimum signal-to-noise ratio (SNR) threshold.

The ratio of the signal and noise amplitude spectra was then calculated for each recording, and only the recordings that had an SNR greater than 3 over the entire frequency range of interest were kept. Because the number of recordings above a given SNR decreases as we broaden the frequency range of study, we chose the frequency range of 2–15 Hz to retain a reasonable amount of data and a broad enough frequency range for applications.

We selected events with magnitude $M_w \leq 4$ and recordings with rupture distances less than 100 km. A maximum magnitude of 4 was used so that a finite-fault term is not needed in the GMM. A maximum of 100 km was used to limit the spatial coverage for the model to the Bay Area region.

We also only kept events that were recorded by five or more stations and stations that had recorded five or more events to improve the statistical constraints on the event and site terms in the mixed-effects regression (Abrahamson and Youngs, 1992). An additional visual inspection of the seismograms was then performed. This procedure identified recordings that included multiple earthquake recordings in the 70 s time-window record or did not look like earthquake time series. Approximately 5000 recordings for each component passed this visual inspection.

Using this subset of reliable data, we again rejected the events and stations that had less than five recordings per station and per event. As a last step, we applied a band-pass Butterworth filter with four poles and corner frequencies of 2.5 and 12 Hz to filter the frequencies outside of the range

TABLE 1
Summary of the Small-Magnitude Data Set

Component	Recordings	Selected	Stations	Events	$1 < M < 2$	$2 < M < 3$	$3 < M < 4$
East–west	626,423	5,108	266	737	38	496	203
North–south	626,423	5,301	269	725	39	470	216
Both	626,423	3,174	211	577	18	369	290

of interest so that the filtered time series could be used in time-domain validations in subsequent studies.

The final data set includes just under 1% of the total number of recordings that were downloaded. This low percentage reflects the noise in seismograms from small-magnitude earthquakes. The final number of selected recordings per component after the visual inspection procedure is shown in Table 1. The corresponding number of stations and events, as well as the number of events per magnitude bin for each component, is also given in 1. The selection of five or more recordings per station and event retained approximately 70% of this data set. The locations of the selected stations and events and the ray paths between the stations and sources for the H1 component are shown in Figure 1. The magnitude–distance scatter plot, as well as the FAS data for two earthquake scenarios, are shown in Figure 2. Additional figures showing the magnitude, distance, and depth distributions in Figure S1, available in the supplemental material to this article, the within-event residuals at 2, 5, and 10 Hz in Figure S2 and the within-site within-path residuals at 2, 5, and 10 Hz in Figure S3.

GMM FOR THE VELOCITY FAS

Ergodic GMM for velocity FAS

The functional form of the ergodic-base model for velocity FAS is kept relatively simple as more complex features will be added in the nonergodic model. The functional form for the ergodic velocity FAS of the two horizontal components is given in equation (1):

$$\ln \mathrm{FAS} = c_0 + c_1\, M + c_2\, \ln(R_{\mathrm{rup}}) + c_3\, Z_{\mathrm{hyp}} + \delta B_e + \delta S2S_s + \frac{R_{\mathrm{rup}}}{100}\delta P_e + \delta WSP_{es}, \quad (1)$$

in which M is the magnitude, R_{rup} is the rupture distance, and in which Z_{hyp} is the hypocentral depth. The δB_e, $\delta S2S_s$, and δP_e are zero-mean, normally distributed random effects for the source, site, and path, respectively, with standard deviations of τ, ϕ_{S2S}, and τ_P, respectively. The remaining unmodeled part of the ground motion is given by the within-site within-path residual δWSP_{es} with a standard deviation of ϕ_{SP}.

A finite-fault term is not included in the geometrical spreading term because the selected events were limited to magnitudes less than or equal to 4, for which the point-source assumption is reasonable. We also did not include a V_{S30} term in the ergodic model because there are inconsistencies between the V_{S30} estimates from the velocity model used for 3D simulations and the V_{S30} values estimated for the seismic stations (Pinilla-Ramos *et al.*, 2025). Excluding V_{S30} from the model formulation implicitly incorporates its effect into the $\delta S2S$ site terms and does not reduce the model applicability for the two main uses of the nonergodic GMM.

The δB_e and $\delta S2S_s$ random effects are commonly included in GMMs to account for correlations in the ground-motion data. The third random effect, δP_e, is a new term that accommodates an event-specific large-distance attenuation. Adding the $\frac{R_{\mathrm{rup}}}{100}\delta P_e$ terms help reduce the mapping of source-specific path effects into the source terms that can occur for events with distance attenuation that is flatter or steeper than average. The normalization by 100 km leads to similar sizes of the τ and τ_p, which helps the stability of the regression. This type of event-specific linear distance term was included in the duration model by Pinilla-Ramos *et al.* (2023). Its use here is the first application for ground-motion amplitudes.

The coefficients from the regression were estimated in R using the linear mixed-effects package LMER (Bates *et al.*, 2015). The period dependence of the coefficients was smoothed using a simple polynomial of degree 1 for the magnitude term and a polynomial of degree 2 for the distance and depth terms. The smoothing of the coefficients leads to a smooth spectrum with frequency. In addition, the smoothing can be used to impose physical constraints on the coefficients (Bayless and Abrahamson, 2019). The smoothed regression coefficients are shown in Figure 3 and are listed in Table 2.

The total standard deviation for the ergodic GMM is given by

$$\sigma_{\mathrm{FAS}} = \sqrt{\tau^2 + \phi_{S2S}^2 + \phi_{SP}^2 + \left(\frac{R_{\mathrm{rup}}^2}{100^2}\right)\tau_p^2}. \quad (2)$$

For developing nonergodic GMMs that reflect the full nonergodic path effects, we combine the δWSP and $(\frac{R_{\mathrm{rup}}}{100})\delta P_e$ terms into a within-site residual:

$$\delta WS_{es} = \delta WSP_{es} + \left(\frac{R_{\mathrm{rup}}}{100}\right)\delta P_e. \quad (3)$$

The standard deviation of δWS_{es} is denoted ϕ_{SS}. The frequency dependence of τ, $\tau_p(R_{\mathrm{rup}}/100)$, ϕ_{S2S}, and ϕ_{SS} is shown in Figure 4 together with the total standard deviation, σ_{FAS}. The four components of the standard deviation are similar in size, with values generally between 0.35 and 0.5 LN units.

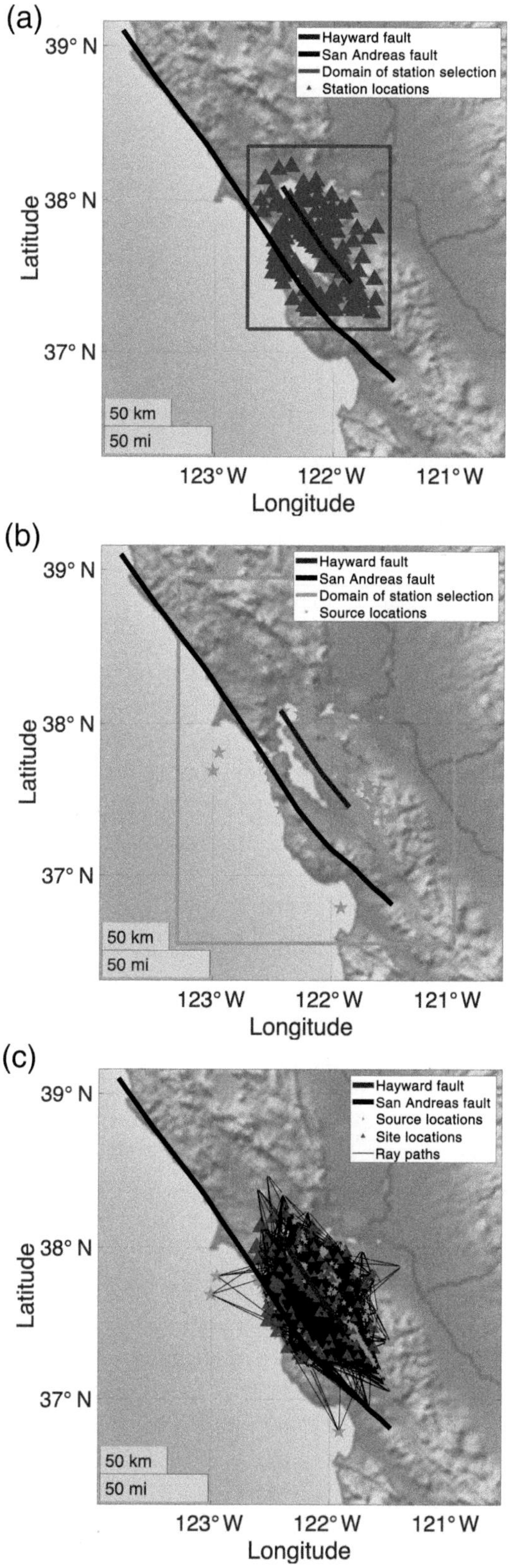

Figure 1. (a) Station locations, (b) source locations, and (c) ray paths from the selected sources and sites for the H1-component data set. The color version of this figure is available only in the electronic edition.

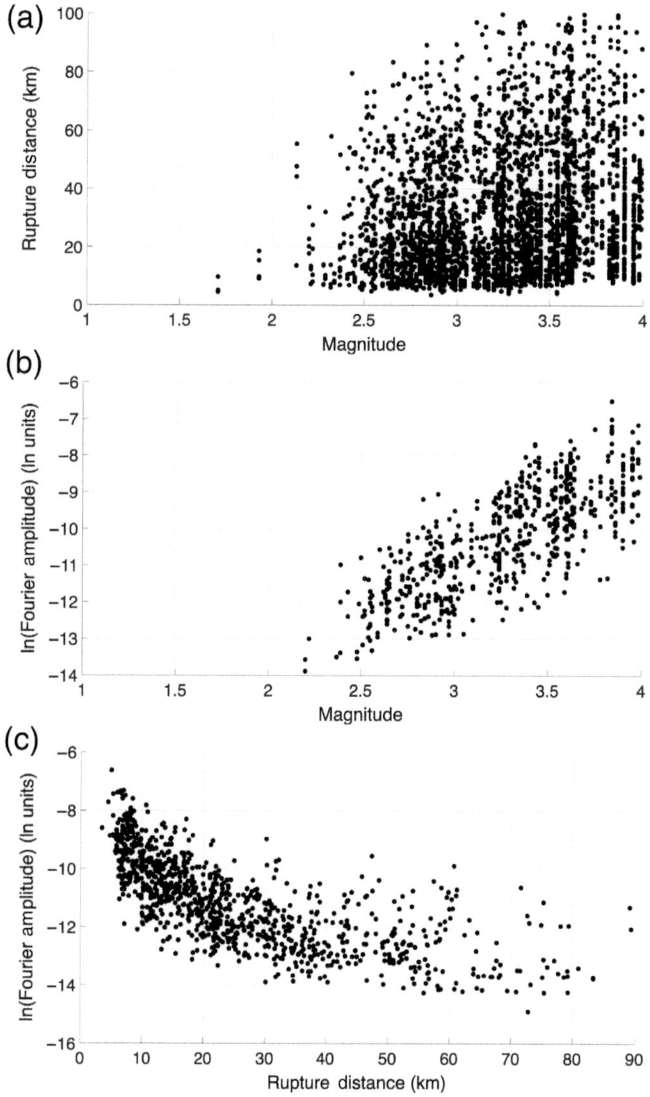

Figure 2. (a) Magnitude–rupture distance scatter plot, (b) Fourier amplitude with magnitude for $R_{\mathrm{rup}} \in [20; 30]$ km, and (c) Fourier amplitude with rupture distance for $M \in [2.5; 3]$ at 5 Hz for the east–west component.

Nonergodic GMM for velocity FAS

In nonergodic GMMs, the source-specific, site-specific, and path-specific deviations from the ergodic model (δB_e, $\delta S2S_s$, and $\delta P2P_{es}$) become spatially dependent and are functions of the coordinates of the source e and site s. These terms are modeled using Gaussian processes which provide smooth maps of their median estimation as well as their epistemic uncertainty. Following the notation from Sung *et al.* (2023), the nonergodic GMM is expressed as

$$\mathrm{GMM_{NE}}(M,R,S,\ldots,\vec{t}e_e,\vec{t}s_s) = c_0 + c_1\ M + c_2\ \ln(R_{\mathrm{rup}}) + c_3\ Z_{\mathrm{hyp}} + \delta L2L(\vec{t}e_e) + \delta S2S(\vec{t}s_s) + \delta P2P(\vec{t}e_e,\vec{t}s_s) + \delta B_e^0 + \delta WSP_{es}, \quad (4)$$

in which $\vec{t}e_e$ and $\vec{t}s_s$ are the coordinates of the earthquake e and site s. The $\delta L2L(\vec{t}e_e)$ is the median deviation of the source term

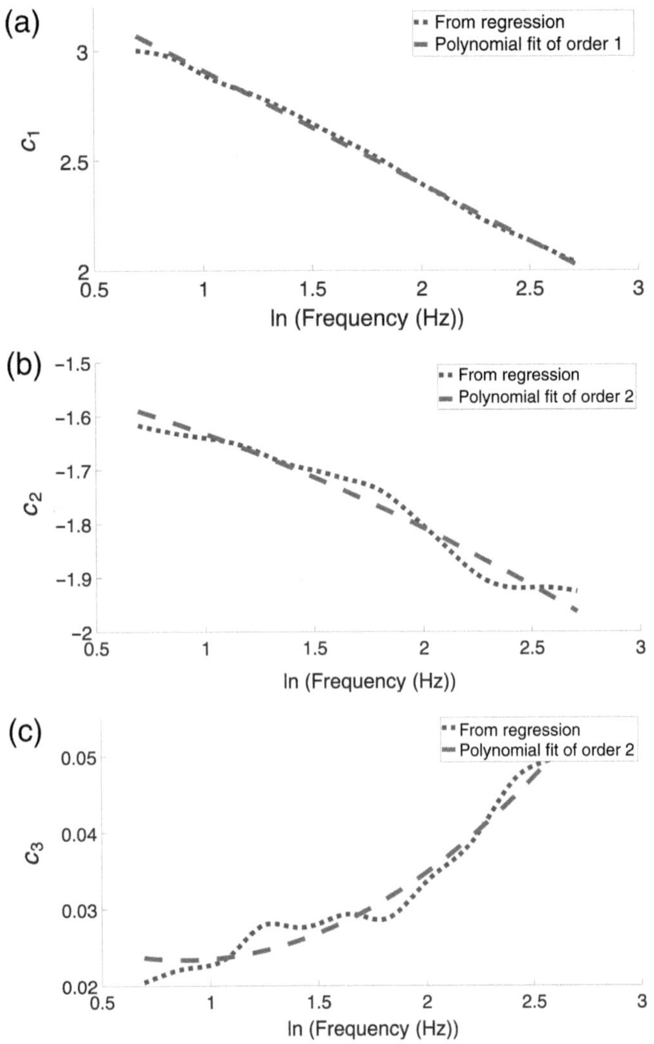

Figure 3. Smoothed coefficients for the ergodic FAS ground-motion model (GMM) for the east–west and north–south components. (a) Magnitude term, (b) distance term, and (c) depth term. The color version of this figure is available only in the electronic edition.

from the ergodic model for earthquake e, $\delta S2S(\vec{ts}_s)$ is the median shift in the site term for site s, and $\delta P2P(\vec{te}_e,\vec{ts}_s)$ is the median shift in the path term for the ray path between earthquake e and site s.

TABLE 2
Smoothed Model Coefficients for the Fourier Amplitude Spectrum (FAS) Model for Both the East–West and North–South Components

Coefficient	Smoothed Model
c_1	3.43–0.52 M
c_2	$-1.51 - 0.09\ln(R) - 0.03\ln(R)^2$
c_3	$-0.03 - 0.02Z - 0.01Z^2$

f is the frequency in Hz.

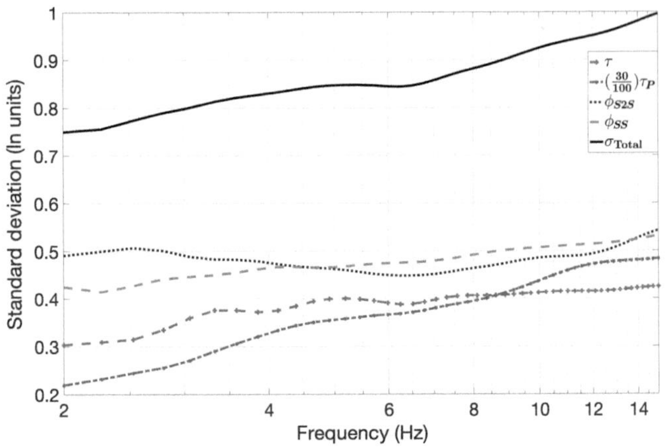

Figure 4. Components of the standard deviation of the FAS for $R_{\text{rup}} = 30$ km. The color version of this figure is available only in the electronic edition.

The between-path term, $\delta P2P(\vec{te}_e,\vec{ts}_s)$, represents how a specific travel path leads to systematically different motions from the average distance scaling captured from the ergodic GMM, and the $\delta B^0 + \delta WSP$ term is the remaining aleatory variability after removing the systematic source, site, and path terms.

The total aleatory variance for the fully nonergodic GMM, σ^2_{NE}, is given by

$$\sigma^2_{\text{NE}} = \tau_0^2 + \phi^2_{SP}, \tag{5}$$

in which τ_0 and ϕ_{SP} are the standard deviations of δB_e^0 and δWSP_{es}, respectively.

To compute the nonergodic source and site terms, we first estimate the source and site random effects δB_e and $\delta S2S_s$ for the ergodic model. The source and site random effects are removed from the total residuals of the ergodic model to obtain the within-site residuals. Next, we model the δB_e and $\delta S2S_s$ as spatially varying Gaussian processes for $\delta L2L(\vec{te}_e)$ and $\delta S2S(\vec{ts}_s)$. The within-site residuals are then used to estimate the path effects between each source–site pair with Gaussian process $\delta P2P(\vec{te}_e,\vec{ts}_s)$. The hyperparameters of these Gaussian processes were estimated via the maximum-likelihood approach, and a single deterministic value was selected for the hyperparameters leading to the maximum likelihood for simplicity. The details of the approach used to estimate the nonergodic terms are described in the following sections.

The nonergodic model leads to a smaller standard deviation σ_{NE} in the residuals than the standard deviation σ_{FAS} from the ergodic model because it includes additional source, site, and paths effects. The standard deviation is reduced by 0.35 ln units at 2 Hz and by 0.6 ln units at 15 Hz for FAS, as shown in Table 3. These large reductions in the standard deviation will have a significant effect on the seismic hazard, especially at long return periods.

TABLE 3
Hyperparameters for the Fourier Amplitude Spectrum (FAS) Model

Type	Hyperparameter	East–West Component	North–South Component
Source	ρ_e (km)	3.2 f − 0.6	1.7 f + 4
	τ_{L2L} (ln units)	0.005 f + 0.1	0.004 f + 0.12
	τ_0 (ln units)	0.20	0.21
Site	ρ_s (km)	1.1 f + 5.7	1.9 f + 1.2
	$\phi_{S2S,COR}$ (ln units)	0.01 f + 0.14	0.004 + 0.17
	$\phi_{S2S,NCOR}$ (ln units)	0.40	0.40
Path	$\rho_{\Delta R}$(km)	1.3 f + 4.0	0.8 f + 6.5
	$\rho_{\Delta\theta}$(°)	15	16
	$\rho_{\Delta S}$ (km)	13	11
	ϕ_{P2P} (ln units)	0.01 f + 0.40	0.01 f + 0.40
	$\phi_{SP,NE}$ (ln units)	0.40	0.40

f is the frequency in Hz.

Nonergodic source term

In an ergodic GMM, the source term, δB_e, represent the average isotropic source effect over all distances for earthquake e. The nonergodic source term, $\delta L2L$, captures the spatial variation of the δB_e. For small-magnitude earthquakes, the nonergodic source term is often interpreted to represent spatial variations in the average stress drop, but the event terms can also include some wave propagation effects.

The nonergodic source term is modeled as a Gaussian process, following Landwehr *et al.* (2016). Gaussian processes are fully described by their mean value and covariance function. The mean function is imposed to be zero, and the covariance function for the source term is modeled by an exponential kernel:

$$\kappa_{\text{source-FAS}}(\vec{te},\vec{te}') = \tau_{L2L}^2 \exp\left(-\frac{\|\vec{te}-\vec{te}'\|}{\rho_e}\right) + \tau_0^2\,\delta(\vec{te},\vec{te}'), \quad (6)$$

in which $\vec{te}$ and $\vec{te}'$ are the coordinates of the hypocenter of events e and e'. The τ_{L2L} term includes the variability in the source terms that are spatially correlated, with a correlation length of ρ_e. The τ_0 is the standard deviation of δB^0, which is the remaining aleatory variability in the source term. The exponential kernel was chosen over a square-exponential because it gave a larger likelihood.

We estimated the parameters τ_{L2L}, τ_0, and ρ_e using maximum likelihood at each available frequency between 2 and 15 Hz for both the east–west and north–south components. The results are given in Table 3. τ_{L2L} and τ_0 increase slightly with frequency but remain close to constant, and the correlation length ρ_e increases with frequency, which is likely due to the mapping of regional site terms into the source terms as discussed by Abrahamson and Gulerce (2022). The estimated correlation lengths are larger than the source separations, and the resulting Gaussian process model effectively averages over many sources which avoids overfitting. The values of the hyperparameters are shown in Figure 5.

The median estimates of the nonergodic source term are shown in Figure S4 for 2, 5, 10, and 15 Hz for the east–west component. The corresponding maps of epistemic uncertainty in the median source term are shown in Figure S5. The sources located along the San Andreas fault have an above-average median source term compared with sources located along the Hayward fault. The regions with similar nonergodic adjustments become broader with frequency due to the increase in the correlation length with frequency. The epistemic uncertainty in the median predictions increases at source locations away from the available source locations, and regions of similar epistemic uncertainty widen with increasing frequency due to the increase in the correlation length with frequency.

We compared our results with the recent nonergodic models developed for California. The median nonergodic source term at 5 Hz are compared with the nonergodic source terms from Lavrentiadis *et al.* (2023) in Figure 6. The Lavrentiadis *et al.* (2023) model is based on the Next Generation Attenuation-West2 database that only includes a few events in the San Francisco region. Consequently, the nonergodic source term are poorly constrained in the region, and the median prediction of the source term from Lavrentiadis *et al.* (2023) is close to zero. On the other hand, the new model is based on a much larger number of events in the San Francisco region which leads to better constraints and a wider range of the nonergodic source terms. These comparisons show the improvements in the constraints on the nonergodic source terms for our GMM as compared with a previous study. They are not used as a validation of our model.

Nonergodic site term

Similar to the nonergodic source term, the nonergodic site term is modeled as a Gaussian process, with a covariance function given by a square-exponential kernel:

$$\kappa_{\text{site-FAS}}(\vec{ts},\vec{ts}') = \phi_{S2S,COR}^2 \exp\left(-\frac{\|\vec{ts}-\vec{ts}'\|^2}{2\rho_s^2}\right) + \phi_{S2S,NCOR}^2\,\delta(\vec{ts},\vec{ts}'). \quad (7)$$

The $\phi_{S2S,COR}^2$ is the variance of the spatially correlated site term, ρ_s is the correlation length of the spatially correlated site term, and $\phi_{S2S,NCOR}$ is the remaining variability in the systematic site term that is uncorrelated between sites (or the correlation length is very short). The square exponential kernel was chosen over the exponential because it gave a larger likelihood.

We estimated the parameters $\phi_{S2S,COR}$, $\phi_{S2S,NCOR}$, and ρ_s using maximum likelihood at each available frequency. As with the source terms, the standard deviations $\phi_{S2S,COR}$ and $\phi_{S2S,NCOR}$ increase slightly with frequency but remain close to constant, and the correlation length increases with frequency, as observed in Figure 7. The correlation lengths for the site term are larger than the site separations, which indicates that there is not an issue of overfitting. The results are listed in Table 3.

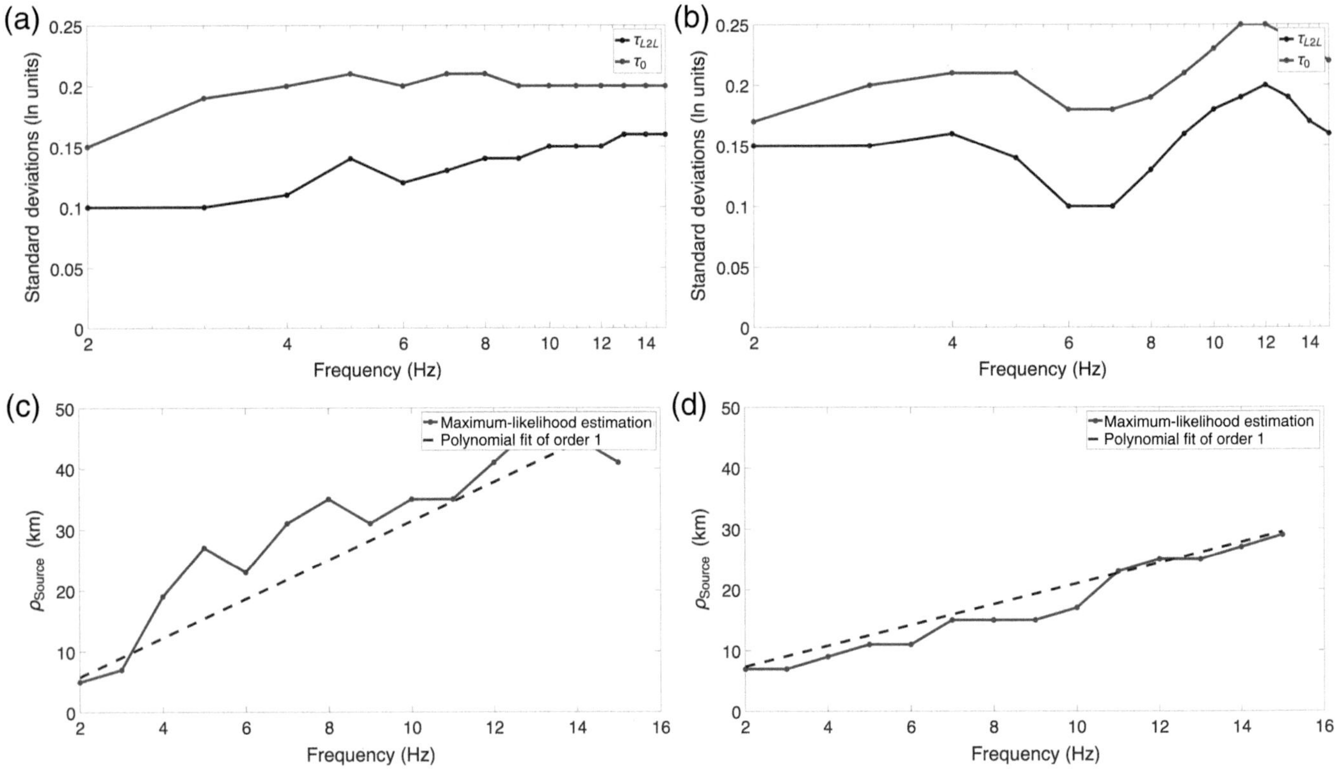

Figure 5. Frequency dependence of the standard deviations and of the correlation lengths for the nonergodic source term. (a,c) East–west component; (b,d) north–south component. The color version of this figure is available only in the electronic edition.

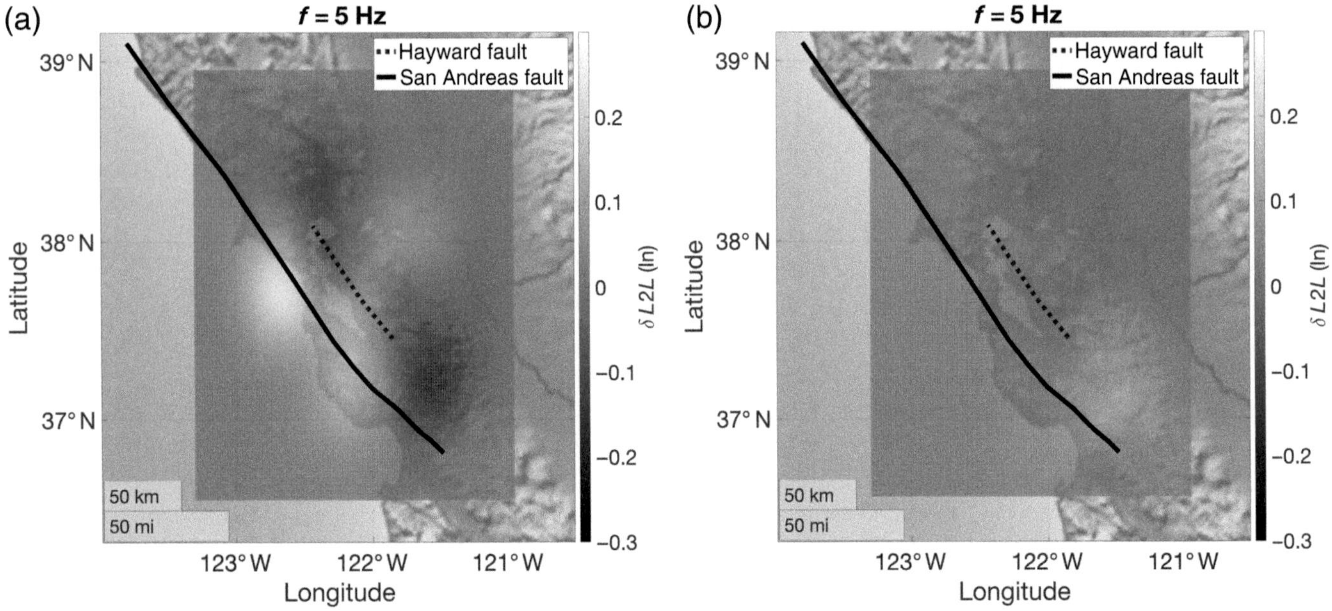

Figure 6. Maps of the median FAS source terms $\delta L2L$ at 5 Hz for the east–west component from the presented model (a) and from the EAS model from Lavrentiadis *et al.* (2023) (b). The color version of this figure is available only in the electronic edition.

The increase in the correlation length of the nonergodic site term with frequency seems counterintuitive because higher frequencies will have shorter wavelengths and be more sensitive to the variability of the shallow velocity structures; however, the high-frequency FAS is strongly affected by kappa, and this large spatial correlation length likely reflects the

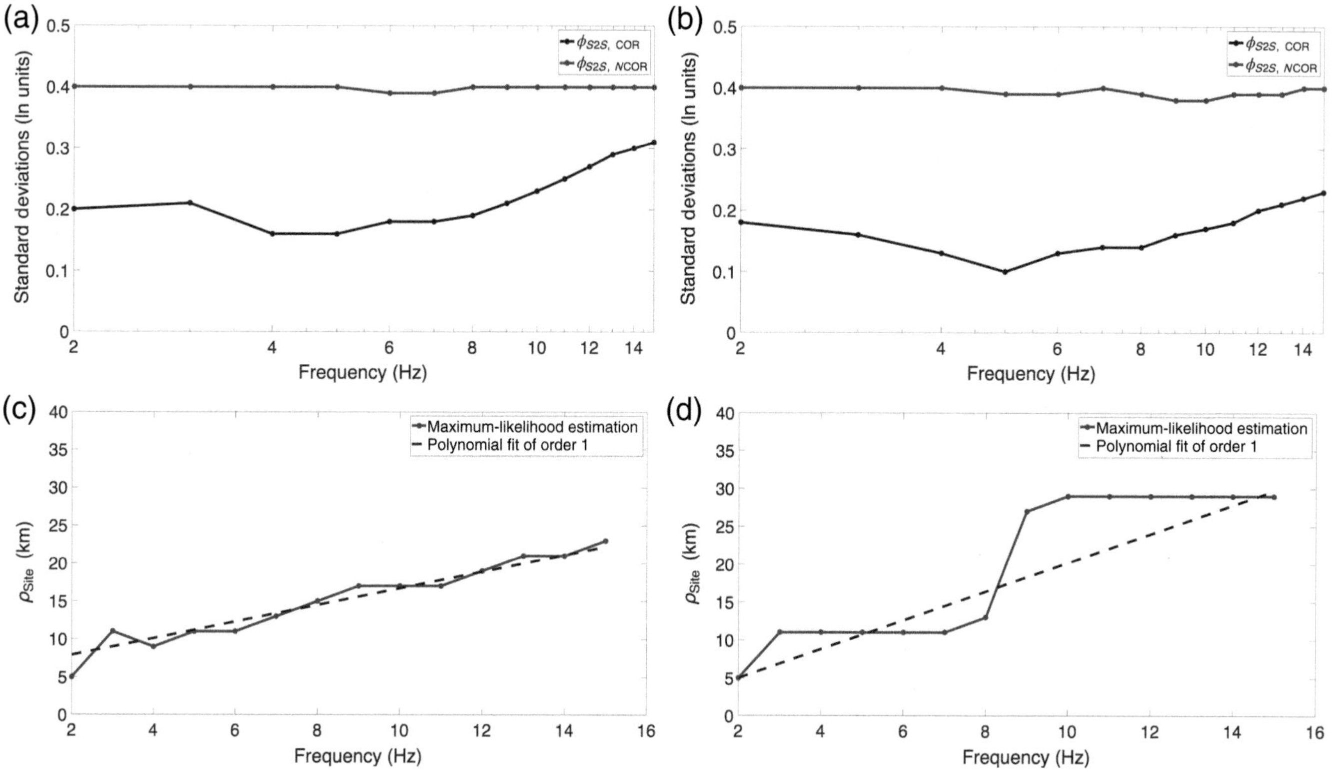

Figure 7. Frequency dependence of the standard deviations and of the correlation lengths for the nonergodic site term. (a,c) East–west component; (b,d) north–south component. The color version of this figure is available only in the electronic edition.

spatial correlation of kappa, which shows similar regional patterns in the San Francisco Bay area (Nye *et al.*, 2022). If the kappa is correlated with the regional surface geology, then the spatial correlation of the high-frequency FAS would reflect the spatial dimension of the surface geology (Eberhart-Phillips, 2016) and not the shallow velocity structure.

Figure S6 shows the forward prediction of the nonergodic site term at 2, 5, 10, and 15 Hz for the east–west component. The corresponding maps of epistemic uncertainty in the prediction are shown in Figure S7. Sites located along the coast west of San Francisco have above-average median site terms, whereas sites located in the East Bay tend to have below-average site terms. The epistemic uncertainty increases at prediction sites located farther from the site locations in the dataset, and regions of similar epistemic uncertainty widen with increasing frequency due to the increase in the correlation length with frequency.

We compare the median nonergodic site term at 5 Hz from the new model with the site terms from Lavrentiadis *et al.* (2023) in Figure 8. The data set used by Lavrentiadis *et al.* (2023) includes a significant number of stations in the San Francisco region providing better constraints on the nonergodic site terms than on the nonergodic source terms. The hyperparameters for the 5 Hz FAS for the two models are similar, with correlation lengths close to 15 km and standard deviations close to 0.3 ln units. The two models give similar spatial variations in the predicted nonergodic site terms.

Nonergodic path term

We use the methodology developed by Lacour *et al.* (2024) to model nonergodic path effects due to the 3D velocity structure in the region of study. This approach includes an azimuthally dependent site term and can efficiently accommodate the full data set in the forward prediction of the nonergodic path terms. For the correlation between the path effects for two ray paths, the approach considers the paths as vectors, which can be defined by three parameters: the origin, direction, and length. The distance between the site locations ($|SS'|$), the difference in azimuths ($\Delta\theta$), and the difference in rupture distances (ΔR_{rup}) define the differences in the origins, azimuths, and lengths, respectively. The parameters used to define the difference between two ray paths are illustrated in Figure 9.

The functional form used for the covariance function of path effects is given by

$$\kappa_{\text{path-FAS}}(P,P') = \phi_{P2P}^2 \exp\left(\frac{-\Delta R_{\text{rup}}^2}{2\rho_R^2}\right) \exp\left(\frac{-\Delta\theta^2}{2\rho_\theta^2}\right) \exp\left(\frac{-|SS'|^2}{2\rho_S^2}\right) + \phi_{SP,\text{NE}}^2 \delta(P,P'). \quad (8)$$

The NE subscript is included to distinguish the standard deviation of the within-path within-site residuals for the nonergodic GMM from the standard deviation of the within-path within-site residuals for the ergodic GMM with the path random effects (equation 2).

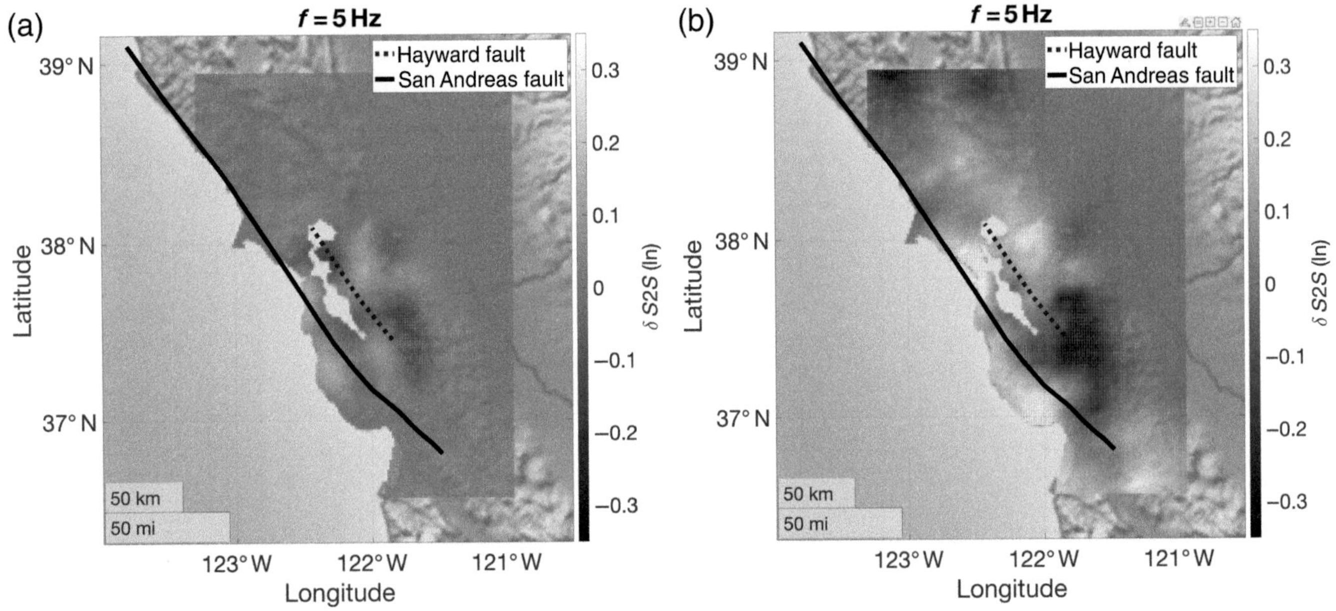

Figure 8. Maps of the FAS site term, $\delta S2S$ at 5 Hz for the E–W component using the presented model (a) and from the EAS model from Lavrentiadis *et al.* (2023) (b). The color version of this figure is available only in the electronic edition.

This form of the covariance function was shown to better fit the correlation between paths than other approaches used in nonergodic GMMs (e.g., Sung *et al.*, 2023). In particular, this form of the covariance function leads to more accurate estimation of the correlation of path effects for the case in which data are available with moderate correlation (near 0.5) and better extrapolation of path effects into regions where data are not available. In addition, the new method uses a path correlation function that is separable between its azimuth, rupture distance, and site location terms, which allows the use of efficient numerical methods that drastically reduce computational and memory requirements when dealing with large datasets as shown by Lacour (2022).

To avoid overfitting, the correlation lengths ρ_R, ρ_θ, and ρ_S were estimated by fitting the semivariogram of the within-site residuals rather than estimating them as part of the regression. With the correlation lengths held fixed, the variance terms ϕ_{P2P} and $\phi_{SP,\mathrm{NE}}$ were estimated using maximum likelihood. The term ϕ_{P2P} represents the variability of path effects that can be explained via the correlation function used to characterize the similarity between path effects, whereas $\phi_{SP,\mathrm{NE}}$ represents the remaining variability that cannot be explained by the model. The values obtained for ϕ_{P2P} are consistent with the values obtained by other models for various regions around the world for the frequency range of this study [2 Hz; 15 Hz], around 0.40, as described in Sung and Abrahamson (2024). The estimates of the hyperparameters are listed in Table 3 and the values from other regions from Sung and Abrahamson (2024) are shown in Figure S8.

To illustrate the results, we calculate the forward prediction of the nonergodic path term at 2, 5, 10, and 15 Hz for the east–west component at two different site locations and sources located at 8 km of depth. The sites (number 55 and number 87 in the dataset) were chosen to be on each side of the bay, and the depth of the source locations for the prediction was chosen as the average depth from all the sources available in the dataset. We show the prediction of these path effects at 5 Hz in Figures 10 and 11 and at 2, 5, 10, and 15 Hz in Figures S9 and S10. The site in the West Bay (Fig. 10) shows strong positive path effects from the sources located along the east side of the Hayward fault and shows smaller path effects sources located along the San Andreas fault. The site in the East Bay (Fig. 11) shows moderate path effects but only from sources located in the south end of the Hayward fault. The net effect of the nonergodic median source, site, and path effects and the corresponding epistemic uncertainty at these two sites are shown in Figures S11 and S12.

There are no existing empirical models of the path effects due to 3D velocity structure ($\delta P2P$ terms) in the San Francisco region that can be used for comparison with our GMM. Previous empirical nonergodic GMMs for path effects for this regions only use the approach by Dawood and Rodriguez-Marek (2013) which only capture path effects due to the 3D anelastic attenuation and impacts the model at larger distances (R_{rup} > 50 km) and higher frequencies (> 5 Hz).

GMM FOR THE PHASE DERIVATIVE

The Fourier phase angles describe the shape of the waveform, but because the phase angles are modulo 2π, it is difficult to model the phase angles directly. As an alternative, we use the standard deviation of the distribution of the phase derivatives as a parameter to characterize the phase angles. The standard

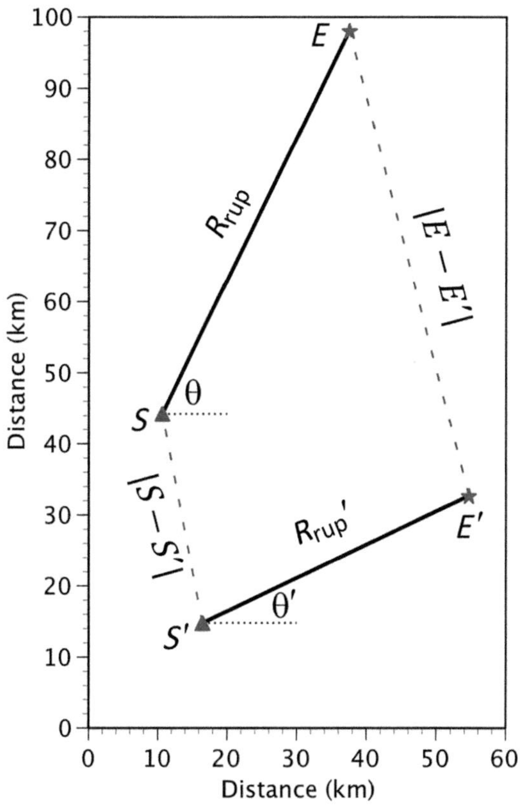

Figure 9. Illustration of the parameterization of the ray paths by their origin (site locations S), azimuth (θ) from the site to the source (earthquake location E), and length of the ray path (R_{rup}). The separation distance between the two paths uses the distance between the two sites, $|S - S'|^2$, the difference between the two azimuths, $(\theta - \theta')^2$, and the difference between the two path lengths, $(R_{rup} - R_{rup}')^2$. The color version of this figure is available only in the electronic edition.

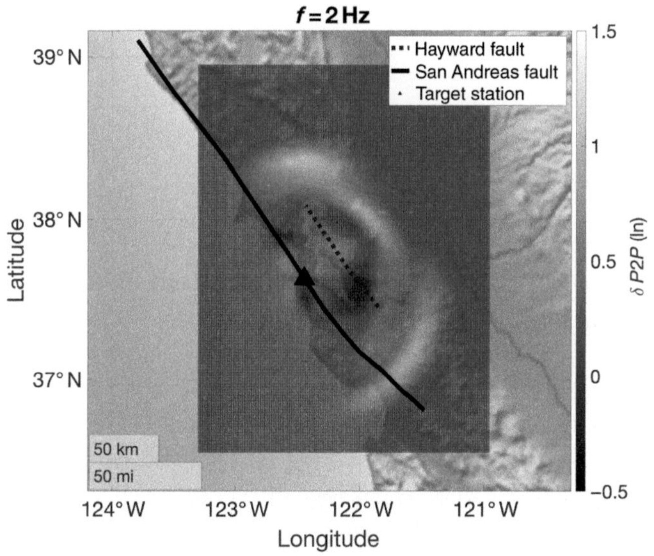

Figure 10. Maps of the median FAS path terms, $\delta P2P$, for site 55 at 2 Hz for the east–west component. The site location is shown by the black triangle. The color version of this figure is available only in the electronic edition.

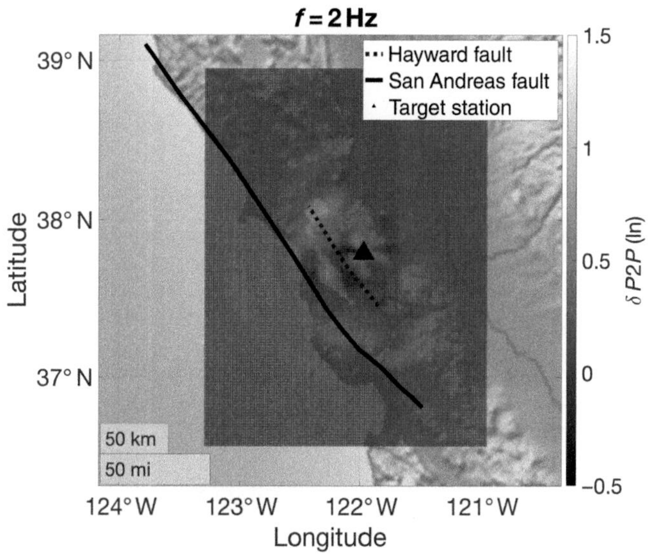

Figure 11. Maps of the median FAS path terms, $\delta P2P$, for site 87 at 2 Hz for the east–west component. The site location is shown by the black triangle. The color version of this figure is available only in the electronic edition.

deviation of the phase derivative is related to the duration of the time series (Baglio *et al.*, 2023). Similar to the approach used for the FAS model, we first develop an ergodic model for the standard deviation of the phase derivative and then develop the nonergodic model by modeling the spatial variations of the systematic effects of the source, site, and path effects on the phase derivative using Gaussian Processes.

Ergodic GMM for phase derivative

The phase derivatives are computed over the frequency range $f \in [2; 15]$ Hz:

$$\phi'(f) = \frac{d\phi(f)}{df} \simeq \frac{\Delta\phi(f)}{\Delta f} = \frac{\phi(f_{i+1}) - \phi(f_i)}{f_{i+1} - f_i}. \quad (9)$$

If the phase difference, $\phi(f_{i+1}) - \phi(f_i)$, is not in the interval of $[-\pi,\pi]$, then 2π is added or subtracted to the phase difference such that the adjusted phase difference is in the interval $[-\pi,\pi]$.

We fit a logistic distribution to the phase-derivative values between 2 and 15 Hz. The logistic distribution was selected because it has been shown to better fit the tails of the phase-derivative distribution than a normal distribution (Baglio *et al.*, 2023). The logistic distribution is given by

$$f_{\phi'} = \frac{e^{-(\phi' - \mu_{\phi'})/\sigma_{\phi'}}}{\sigma_{\phi'}(1 + e^{-(\phi' - \mu_{\phi'})/\sigma_{\phi'}})}, \quad (10)$$

in which ϕ' is the phase derivative with mean $\mu_{\phi'}$ and standard deviation $\sigma_{\phi'}$.

The standard deviation of the phase derivative is related to the duration of ground motion, as shown in Figure 12. For time

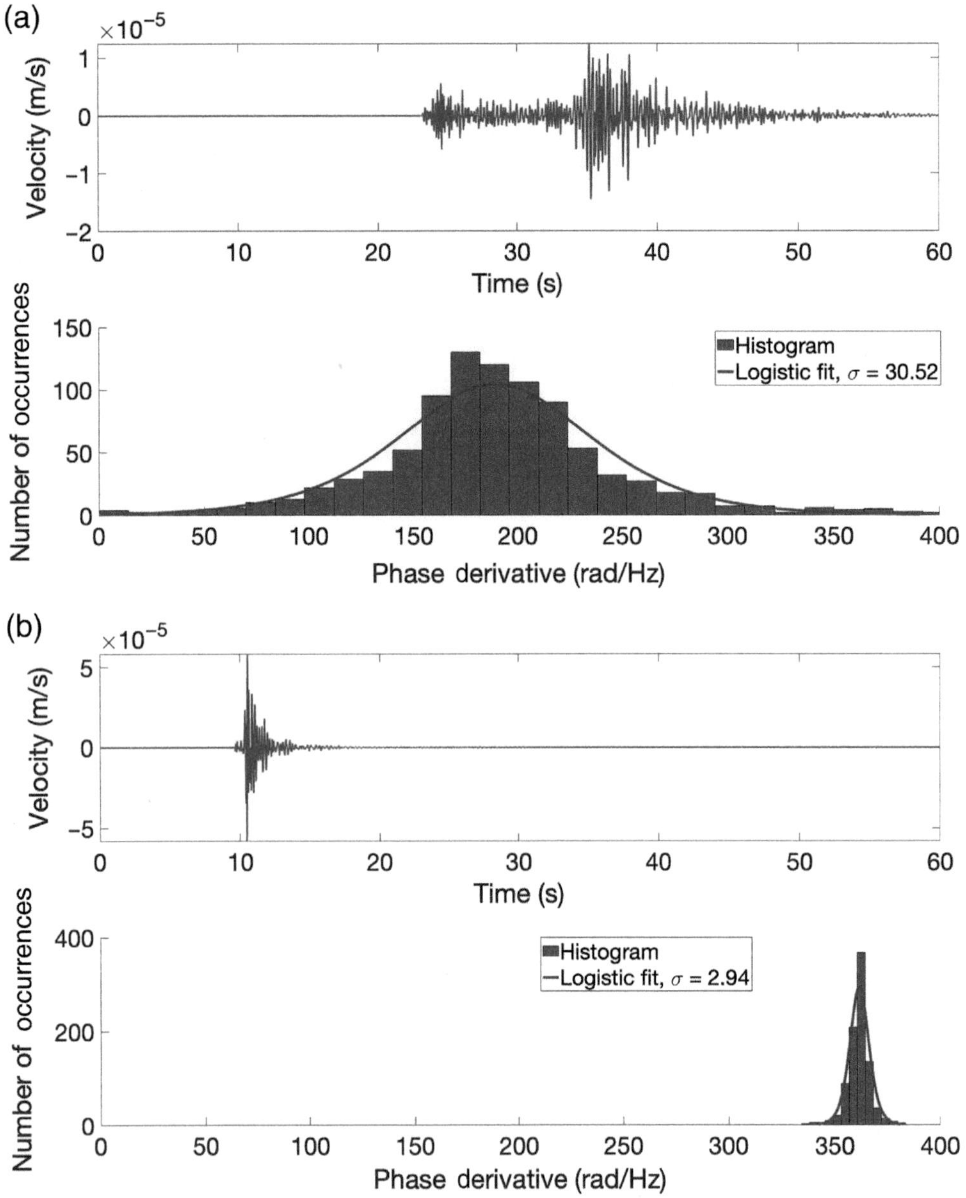

Figure 12. Examples of the velocity time series and the distribution of the phase derivative over 2–15 Hz. The standard deviation of the phase derivative reflects the duration of the time series. (a) Longer duration case due to larger distances (M_w 3.3, $R_{rup} = 95$ km). (b) Shorter duration case due to smaller distances (M_w 1.7, $R_{rup} = 5$ km). The color version of this figure is available only in the electronic edition.

series with longer duration, the distribution of the phase derivative is wider, and vice versa. A broader distribution of the phase derivative leads to larger variations of the phase angles, which leads to a longer duration. This phenomenon is independent from the region of study. The standard deviation of the phase derivative is shown as a function of the $D_{5\text{–}95}$ duration in Figure 13.

Given the strong correlation between the duration and the standard deviation of the phase derivative, we select a functional form for the phase derivative that is similar to the functional form used in duration GMMs. In particular, we follow the approach of Pinilla-Ramos *et al.* (2023), which incorporates two main improvements in duration models. The first improvement is the use of a power normal distribution to approximate the distribution of duration. Power distributions can accommodate a skewness between a normal and a lognormal distribution (for exponents between 0 and 1). Using a power distribution improves the models for the tails of the distribution. Another fundamental improvement in the duration model by Pinilla-Ramos *et al.* (2023) is that the source, site, and path effects are additive and not multiplicative as used in some duration models (Afshari and Stewart, 2016; Bahrampouri *et al.*, 2021). This additive formulation incorporates the source, site, and path effects within the exponent of the power law. The addition of these terms inside the power makes it more challenging to estimate the random effects. Following Pinilla-Ramos *et al.* (2023), the formulation of our ergodic model for the phase derivative is given by equation (11):

$$(\sigma_{\phi'})^{0.3} = c_0 + c_1\Big(10^{0.5(M-4)} + c_2\Delta S2S_s + c_3 R_{rup} + c_4 \Delta P_e \frac{R_{rup}}{100} + c_5(Z_{hyp} - 8)\Big)^{0.3} + \delta WSP_{es}. \quad (11)$$

In equation (11), $10^{0.5(M-4)}$ is related to the source duration, and $c_5(Z_{hyp} - 8)$ is related to the depth scaling of the duration. The two random-effect terms are denoted with Δ here because we make the assumption that they are lognormally distributed to avoid negative values inside the power law (as opposed to the δ notation commonly used for normally distributed random-effect terms in LN units). The mean values of $\delta S2S$ and δP_e are zero, leading to mean values of $\Delta S2S$ and ΔP_e of unity. As a result of this formulation, the average site term is c_2, and the site-specific deviation from the average site effect is $c_2(\Delta S2S - 1)$. Similarly, the average path effect is $c_3 R_{rup} + c_4 R_{rup}/100$, and the event-specific deviation from the average path effect is $c_4(\Delta P_e - 1)R_{rup}/100$.

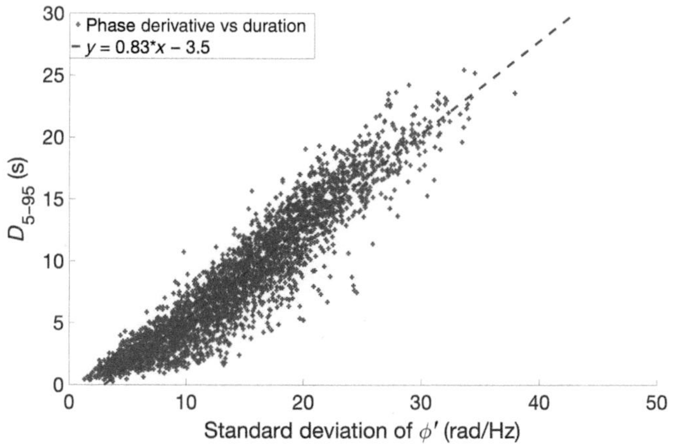

Figure 13. Relation between the standard deviation of the phase derivative and the D_{5-95} Duration for the east–west component. The color version of this figure is available only in the electronic edition.

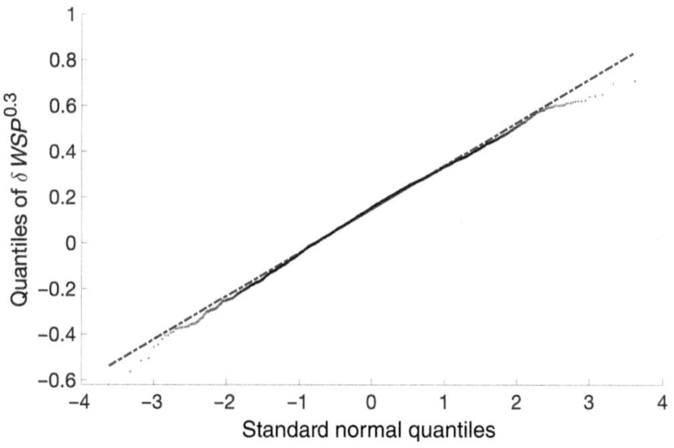

Figure 14. Quantile–quantile plot of the quantiles of δWSP versus the theoretical quantile values from a normal distribution. The color version of this figure is available only in the electronic edition.

The source duration for small-magnitude earthquakes has a negligible effect on the total duration and cannot be determined as part of the regression. For example, for an M_w 3 event at a distance of 20 km, the source term of $10^{0.5(M-4)}$ is 0.3, and the path term is 1.1. At larger distances, the path term will become even larger, which will make the fractional contribution of the source term to the total duration even smaller. Therefore, we constrained the coefficient for the magnitude scaling to equal 0.5 based on the expected magnitude scaling of the source duration for $\log_{10}(\text{area}) = M - 4$ with an aspect ratio of 1. We also imposed the site-specific duration scaling, c_2, to be equal to 0.7 to ensure similar values as found in the study of Pinilla-Ramos *et al.* (2023).

Finally, the exponent for the power normal distribution was selected to be 0.3 because this transformation led to a distribution of the δWSP that was closest to a normal distribution, as seen in the probability plot in Figure 14. The regression was performed using PyMC3 with the nonlinear mixed-effect regression function. The estimated coefficients for both the east–west and north–south components are listed in Table 4.

Nonergodic GMM for phase derivative

In this section, we develop the first nonergodic GMM for duration. Because of the novelty of the results, there are no alternative models available to compare with the results of this analysis. Nonergodic source effects on the duration from small-magnitude events are much smaller than the site and path effects. Because the effects are additive, the source terms cannot be reliably estimated for these small-magnitude events. Therefore, a nonergodic source term was not included in the model, and the nonergodic GMM for the phase derivative only includes the spatially varying site and path effects.

Nonergodic site term

As with the site terms for the FAS, the spatial variation of the site random effects for phase derivative is modeled by a Gaussian process with a squared-exponential covariance function given by

$$\kappa_{\text{site}-\phi'}(\vec{ts},\vec{ts}') = \phi^2_{S2S-\text{PD,COR}} \exp\left(-\frac{\|\vec{ts}-\vec{ts}'\|^2}{2\rho^2_{s-\text{PD}}}\right) + \phi^2_{S2S-\text{PD,NCOR}}\delta(\vec{ts},\vec{ts}'). \quad (12)$$

The square-exponential kernel was chosen over the exponential because it gave a larger likelihood. The estimated values of the hyperparameters for the east–west and north–south components are listed in Table 5.

TABLE 4
Coefficients for the Ergodic Model for the Standard Deviation of the Phase Derivative (Combined East–West [EW] and North–South [NS] Components)

c_0	c_1	c_2	c_3	c_4	c_5
0.33	1.22	0.7	0.054	3.76	0.036

TABLE 5
Hyperparameters for the Phase-Derivative Model

Type	Hyperparameter	East–West Component	North–South Component
Source	$\rho_{e-\text{PD}}$(km)		
Site	$\rho_{s-\text{PD}}$(km)	17	12
	$\phi_{S2S-\text{PD,COR}}$(rad/Hz)	0.46	0.32
	$\phi_{S2S-\text{PD},NCOR}$(rad/Hz)	0.42	0.40
Path	$\rho_{\Delta E-\text{PD}}$(km)	10	12
	$\rho_{\Delta\theta-\text{PD}}$(°)	10	10
	$\rho_{\Delta S-\text{PD}}$(km)	10	12
	$\sigma_{P-\text{PD}}(\text{rad/Hz})^{0.3}$	0.20	0.20
	$\sigma_{SP-\text{PD,NE}}(\text{rad/Hz})^{0.3}$	0.04	0.06

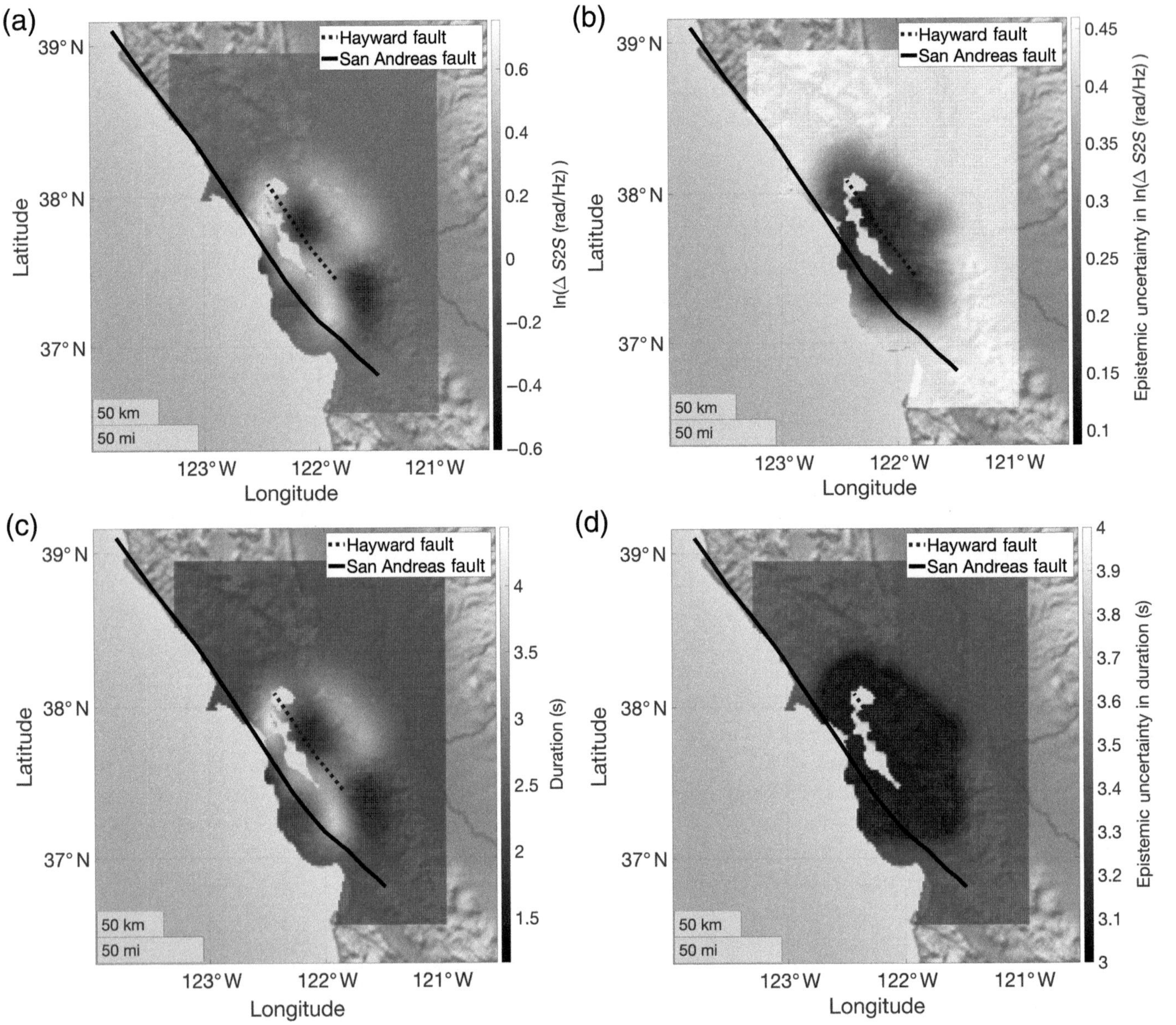

Figure 15. Map of the relatione median site term (a) and the corresponding epistemic uncertainty (b) for the standard deviation of the phase derivative for the east–west component, converted to median duration (c) and epistemic uncertainty in duration (d) using their linear relationship: $D_{5-95} = 0.83\sigma_{\phi'} - 3.5$. The color version of this figure is available only in the electronic edition.

Figure 15 shows an example of the forward prediction of the nonergodic site term for the east–west component and the corresponding epistemic uncertainty in the median prediction. The correlation length of the site term for the standard deviation of the phase derivative is 10–12 km for the two horizontal components, leading to broad regions with systematically longer or shorter duration. The epistemic uncertainty also presents broad regions and increases for stations away from the study region.

Nonergodic path term

Similar to the FAS model, we model the nonergodic path effects using the approach by Lacour *et al.* (2024); however, for the phase-derivative path effects, we use different input parameters to characterize the correlation between ray paths: source separation distance, azimuth difference, and site separation distance. Different combinations of input parameters for the covariance model were considered. Unlike the FAS data, the differences in the lengths of the rays (ΔR_{rup}) did not have a strong effect on the semi-variogram. Instead, the difference in the earthquake locations ($|EE'|$) had a larger effect on the semi-variogram than the difference in the R_{rup} values. The covariance function for the path effect for the standard deviation of the phase derivative is modeled by

$$k_{\text{path-}\phi'}(P,P') = \sigma^2_{P\text{-PD}} \exp\left(\frac{-|EE'|}{\rho_{E\text{-PD}}} + \frac{-\Delta\theta}{\rho_{\theta\text{-PD}}} + \frac{-|SS'|}{\rho_{S\text{-PD}}}\right) + \phi^2_{SP\text{-PD,NE}}\,\delta(P,P'). \quad (13)$$

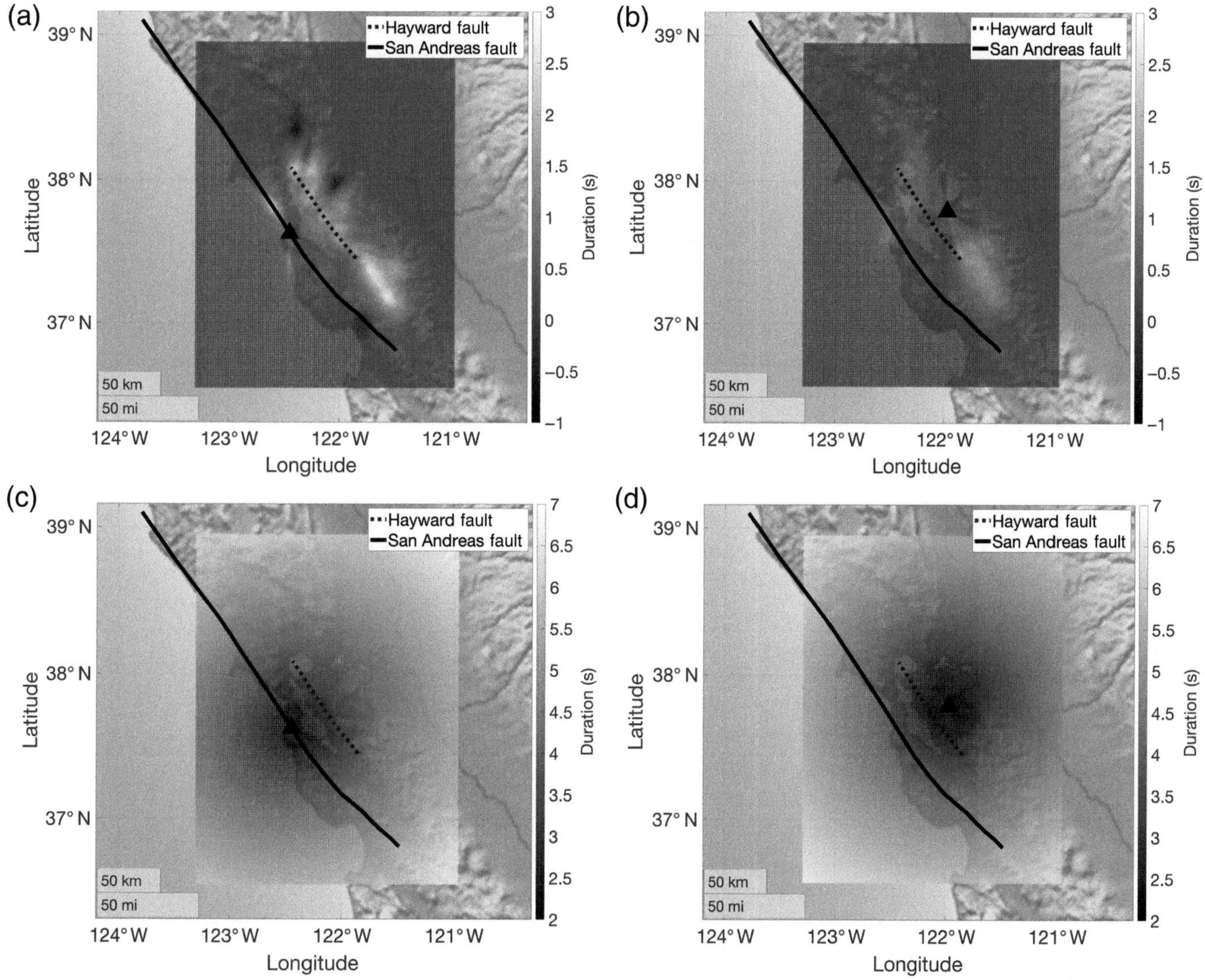

Figure 16. Maps of the median path terms and of the epistemic uncertainty of the phase derivative for the east–west component, converted to duration using their linear relationship. The site locations are shown by the black triangles. (a) Median path terms for station 55, (b) median path terms for station 87, (c) epistemic uncertainty in median path terms for station 55, and (d) epistemic uncertainty in median path terms for station 87. The color version of this figure is available only in the electronic edition.

Following the approach used for the FAS, the correlation lengths $\rho_{E\text{–PD}}$, $\rho_{\theta\text{–PD}}$, and $\rho_{S\text{–PD}}$ were estimated from the semi-variogram, and then the terms $\sigma_{P\text{–PD}}$ and $\phi_{SP\text{–PD}}$ were estimated using maximum likelihood.

The values of the hyperparameters for the two horizontal components are listed in Table 5. The estimated $\sigma_{P\text{–PD}}$ values (0.2 radians/Hz) are substantially greater than the corresponding $\phi_{SP\text{–PD,NE}}$ values of 0.04–0.06 radians/Hz. This large difference indicates that most of the variability of the within-site residuals for the phase derivative can be explained by systematic path effects.

It is easier to understand changes in the duration than changes in the standard deviation of the phase derivative. Therefore, we converted the path effects for $\sigma_{\phi'}^{0.3}$ to path effects on duration using the empirical linear relationship shown in Figure 13. With the power transformations in equation (11), the change in the duration will depend on the earthquake scenario (M and R_{rup}).

Maps of the median path effect for the duration are shown in Figure 16 for a magnitude 3 earthquake at 8 km depth for two site locations. For the station located on the west side of the bay, there are strong path-specific durations from sources located south of the Hayward fault and below-average path-specific durations from sources located along the southern part of the San Andreas fault. For the station located east of the Hayward fault, there are moderately increased durations from sources south of the Hayward fault and negligible path-specific duration terms from sources located along the San Andreas fault.

The epistemic uncertainty is also shown in Figure 16. The path duration terms grow linearly with source distance in an isotropic way for the two stations due to the linear R_{rup} term used in the functional form for the $\sigma_{\phi'}$ given in equation (11). The R_{rup} term dominates the spatial variability of the epistemic uncertainty in the path effects because of the short correlation lengths obtained from the regression of equation (13), which are listed in Table 5.

CONCLUSION

Frequent small-magnitude earthquakes (M_w 1–4) sample a large set of ray paths that can be used to constrain linear nonergodic site and path effects in the San Francisco Bay area. A limitation of small-magnitude data is the poor SNR for many recordings. Of the 626,423 available recordings in the study region between 1990 and 2023, only about 5,000 recordings had an acceptable SNR. This smaller data set is still adequate to constrain spatially varying source, site, and path effects for the FAS and phase derivative in the San Francisco Bay area.

An issue with most ground-motion data sets is the trade-off between path effects and source effects. Including an additional random effect for the event-specific linear distance scaling, $\frac{R_{\mathrm{rup}}}{100}\delta P_e$, reduces the trade-off between path effects and source effects, leading to more reliable source terms.

For the velocity FAS, sources near the San Andreas fault have positive nonergodic source terms, whereas sources near the Hayward fault have negative nonergodic source terms. The spatial extent of the positive and negative source terms becomes larger with increasing frequencies, reflecting an increase in the correlation length with frequency. A limitation of our approach is that the nonergodic source terms cannot fully separate stress-drop variations from unmodeled path effects, particularly for small-magnitude earthquakes where the source duration is negligible compared with path effects. Future work could address this by comparing the spatial distribution of source terms with independent stress-drop estimates. Baltay *et al.* (2017) demonstrated a positive correlation between location-based source terms and spatially averaged stress drops, suggesting that regional variations in stress drop can be identified through such comparisons. Similar analyses with independent stress-drop catalogs or forward simulations using 3D velocity models with varying stress drops could help validate whether observed source-term patterns reflect true stress-drop variations or unmodeled path effects.

Similarly, sites located in the western part of the region have positive nonergodic site terms, whereas sites in the eastern part of the region have negative site terms. The site terms contours are also broader for higher frequencies.

The path effects depend on the source and site location and are parameterized by a map of the path effects for each site separately. After removing the path effects, the remaining standard deviation of the within-path residuals is similar to the standard deviations found for other regions around the world.

For the phase derivative, there is a high correlation between $D_{5\text{–}95}$ duration and the standard deviation of the phase derivative, confirming that the standard deviation of the phase derivative is a good proxy for duration, in agreement with Baglio *et al.* (2023). For the non-ergodic model of phase derivative, only site and path-specific random effects were included in the model because the effect of the source on duration is negligible for small-magnitude earthquakes. The spatially varying site effects for the phase derivative lead to variations of the duration of up to 5 s. For the path effects, the nonergodic phase derivative terms lead to up to a 3-s change in the duration.

The ergodic and nonergodic models for the FAS and phase derivative from the small-magnitude events can be used to test AI-based approaches for developing nonergodic models that may be more efficient numerically than large-scaling 3D simulations of nonergodic source, path, and site effects on the ground motions.

DATA AND RESOURCES

The preprocessed data used in this study is available at https://www.designsafe-ci.org/data/browser/public/designsafe.storage.published/PRJ-4573. The authors used the LME4 package in R developed Bates *et al.* (2015) and the PyMC3 package in Python developed by Abril-Pla *et al.* (2023) to perform the linear and nonlinear regressions, respectively. The authors present additional figures of the epistemic uncertainty of the predictions from our nonergodic model in the supplemental material.

DECLARATION OF COMPETING INTERESTS

The authors acknowledge that there are no conflicts of interest recorded.

ACKNOWLEDGMENTS

This work was supported by the Laboratory Directed Research and Development Program of Lawrence Berkeley National Laboratory under U.S. Department of Energy Contract Number DE-AC02-05CH11231 and partially supported by the PG&E long-term seismic program. The authors are grateful to two anonymous reviewers for their thorough reviews and insightful comments, which significantly improved the clarity and quality of this article.

REFERENCES

Abrahamson, N., and R. Youngs (1992). A stable algorithm for regression analyses using the random effects model, *Bull. Seismol. Soc. Am.* **82,** no. 1, 505–510.

Abrahamson, N. A., and Z. Gulerce (2022). Summary of the Abrahamson and Gulerce NGA-SUB ground-motion model for subduction earthquakes, *Earthq. Spectra* **38,** no. 4, 2638–2681.

Abril-Pla, O., V. Andreani, C. Carroll, L. Dong, C. Fonnesbeck, M. Kochurov, R. Kumar, J. Lao, C. Luhmann, O. Martin, *et al.* (2023). PyMC: A modern, and comprehensive probabilistic programming framework in Python, *PeerJ Comput. Sci.* **9,** e1516, doi: 10.7717/peerj-cs.1516.

Afshari, K., and J. P. Stewart (2016). Physically parameterized prediction equations for significant duration in active crustal regions, *Earthq. Spectra* **32,** no. 4, 2057–2081.

Baglio, M., A. Cardoni, G. P. Cimellaro, and N. Abrahamson (2023). Generating ground motions using the Fourier amplitude spectrum, *Earthq. Eng. Struct. Dynam.* **52,** no. 15, 4884–4899.

Bahrampouri, M., A. Rodriguez-Marek, and R. A. Green (2021). Ground motion prediction equations for significant duration using the KiK-net database, *Earthq. Spectra* **37,** no. 2, 903–920.

Baltay, A. S., T. C. Hanks, and N. A. Abrahamson (2017). Uncertainty, variability, and earthquake physics in ground-motion prediction equations, *Bull. Seismol. Soc. Am.* **107,** no. 4, 1754–1772.

Bates, D., M. Mächler, B. Bolker, and S. Walker (2015). Fitting linear mixed-effects models using lme4, *J. Stat. Software* **67,** no. 1, 1–48.

Bayless, J., and N. A. Abrahamson (2019). Summary of the BA18 ground-motion model for Fourier amplitude spectra for crustal earthquakes in California, *Bull. Seismol. Soc. Am.* **109,** no. 5, 2088–2105.

Dawood, H. M., and A. Rodriguez-Marek (2013). A method for including path effects in ground-motion prediction equations: An example using the M_w 9.0 Tohoku earthquake aftershocks, *Bull. Seismol. Soc. Am.* **103,** no. 2B, 1360–1372.

Eberhart-Phillips, D. (2016). Northern California seismic attenuation: 3D QP and QS Models, *Bull. Seismol. Soc. Am.* **106,** no. 6, 2558–2573.

Goulet, C. A., N. A. Abrahamson, P. G. Somerville, and K. E. Wooddell (2015). The SCEC broadband platform validation exercise: Methodology for code validation in the context of seismic-hazard analyses, *Seismol. Res. Lett.* **86,** no. 1, 17–26.

Konno, K., and T. Ohmachi (1998). Ground-motion characteristics estimated from spectral ratio between horizontal and vertical components of microtremor, *Bull. Seismol. Soc. Am.* **88,** no. 1, 228–241.

Kottke, A. R., N. A. Abrahamson, D. M. Boore, Y. Bozorgnia, C. A. Goulet, J. Hollenback, T. Kishida, O.-J. Ktenidou, E. M. Rathje, W. J. Silva, *et al.* (2021). Selection of random vibration theory procedures for the NGA-East project and ground-motion modeling, *Earthq. Spectra* **37,** no. 1_suppl, 1420–1439.

Lacour, M. (2022). Efficient non-ergodic ground-motion prediction for large datasets, *Bull. Earthq. Eng.* **21,** 5209–5232.

Lacour, M., N. Abrahamson, and C. Sung (2024). New approach to non-ergodic path effects in ground-motion models, *Bull. Seismol. Soc. Am.* **115,** no. 4, 1839–1851, doi: 10.1785/0120240154.

Landwehr, N., N. M. Kuehn, T. Scheffer, and N. Abrahamson (2016). A nonergodic ground-motion model for California with spatially varying coefficients, *Bull. Seismol. Soc. Am.* **106,** no. 6, 2574–2583.

Lavrentiadis, G., N. A. Abrahamson, and N. M. Kuehn (2023). A non-ergodic effective amplitude ground-motion model for California, *Bull. Earthq. Eng.* **21,** no. 11, 5233–5264.

McCallen, D., A. Petersson, A. Rodgers, A. Pitarka, M. Miah, F. Petrone, B. Sjogreen, N. Abrahamson, and H. Tang (2021a). EQSIM—A multidisciplinary framework for fault-to-structure earthquake simulations on exascale computers part I: Computational models and workflow, *Earthq. Spectra* **37,** no. 2, 707–735.

McCallen, D., F. Petrone, M. Miah, A. Pitarka, A. Rodgers, and N. Abrahamson (2021b). EQSIM—A multidisciplinary framework for fault-to- structure earthquake simulations on exascale computers, part II: Regional simulations of building response, *Earthq. Spectra* **37,** no. 2, 736–761.

Northern California Earthquake Data Center (NCEDC) (2014). Northern California earthquake data center [Data set], available at https://ncedc.org (last accessed September 2023).

Nye, T., V. J. Sahakian, E. King, A. Baltay, and A. Klimasewski (2022). Estimates of κ_0 and effects on ground motions in the San Francisco Bay area, *Bull. Seismol. Soc. Am.* **113,** no. 2, 823–842.

Pinilla-Ramos, C., N. Abrahamson, V. Phung, R. Kayen, and P. Castellanos-Nash (2023). Ground-motion model for significant duration constrained by seismological simulations, *Bull. Seismol. Soc. Am.* **114,** no. 2, 1015–1032.

Pinilla-Ramos, C., A. Pitarka, D.B. McCallen, and R. Nakata (2025). Performance evaluation of the USGS velocity model for the San Francisco Bay area, *Earthq. Spectra* **41,** no. 1, 457–494.

Sung, C.-H., and N. Abrahamson (2024). Comparison of the spatial correlation of non-ergodic terms in GMMs utilizing empirical and simulation data from diverse regions, *Seismological Society of America Annual Meeting, Abstract*, Anchorage, Alaska.

Sung, C., N. Abrahamson, and M. Lacour (2023). Methodology for including path effects due to 3-D velocity structure in non-ergodic ground-motion models, *Bull. Seismol. Soc. Am.* **113,** no. 5, 2144–2163.

Manuscript received 23 April 2025
Published online 6 February 2026

Characterizing Precariously Balanced Rocks (PBRs) in the Eastern United States for Estimating Maximum Past Earthquake Ground Motions

Thomas L. Pratt*[1], Mark W. Stirling[2], Devin McPhillips[3], and Paula M. Figueiredo[4,5]

ABSTRACT

Fragile geologic features (FGFs) can be used to estimate an upper bound to the strength of earthquake ground shaking in the past thousands to tens of thousands of years. FGFs could be especially useful in the eastern United States, where few active faults are available for paleoseismic studies and where low seismic attenuation means that an earthquake could damage FGFs at large distances. This article describes a pilot study of one form of FGF, precariously balanced rocks (PBRs), in the Blue Ridge of Virginia, ~160 km from the central Virginia seismic zone (CVSZ) and ~100 km from Virginia's Giles County seismic zone (GCSZ). The main goal is to develop and refine methods for studying PBRs in the eastern United States. Photogrammetric 3D models of the rocks were used to locate their centers of mass and delineate their basal contacts, with the latter corroborated by wrapping a wire around the bases to verify the circumferences. Relations between hill geometry and amplification were used to estimate topographic amplification. Seismometers on the PBRs provided the frequencies, amplitudes, and directions of rocking after giving the rocks gentle pushes. The levels of ground shaking likely to topple the rocks were compared with the median hazard curves from the U.S. Geological Survey's National Seismic Hazard Model and were used to map magnitudes of earthquakes in the nearby region likely to topple the rocks. Results indicate that an $M_w \geq 7.5$ earthquake is needed in the CVSZ or near the 2020 Sparta, North Carolina, earthquake to topple the two most fragile PBRs and that an earthquake of ~M_w 7–7.5 in the GCSZ is needed. The fragilities and estimated ages of the PBRs (20–40 ka) are thus consistent with the absence of such events in the historical record in the nearby region.

KEY POINTS

- Precariously balanced rocks (PBRs) can be used to estimate maximum past eastern U.S. ground motions.
- Using four rocks in Virginia, we developed and tested field methods, including responses to gentle perturbations.
- Results show the utility of various methods of using PBRs to constrain ground motions in nearby seismic zones.

Supplemental Material

INTRODUCTION

Analyses of fragile geologic features (FGFs), including precariously balanced rocks (PBRs), allow for estimates of the upper limits of ground shaking at the site during earthquakes over time spans of thousands of years or more (e.g., Brune and Whitney, 1992; Brune, 1996, 2002; Baker *et al.*, 2013; Finzi *et al.*, 2020; Rood *et al.*, 2020; Stirling *et al.*, 2021; McPhillips and Scharer, 2022; McPhillips and Pratt, 2024). Analyses of PBRs, on which we focus, involve measuring their major dimensions and then estimating the strengths of earthquake ground shaking that likely would topple the rocks based on 2D rigid-body rocking dynamics and results from empirical shake table tests and computer models (Housner, 1963; Shi *et al.*, 1996; Anooshehpoor *et al.*, 2004; Purvance *et al.*, 2008;

1. U.S. Geological Survey, Reston, Virginia, U.S.A., https://orcid.org/0000-0003-3131-3141 (TLP); 2. University of Otago, Dunedin, New Zealand, https://orcid.org/0000-0002-2562-4675 (MWS); 3. U.S. Geological Survey, Pasadena, California, U.S.A., https://orcid.org/0000-0003-1987-9249 (DM); 4. Department of Marine, Earth and Atmospheric Sciences, North Carolina State University, Raleigh, North Carolina, U.S.A., https://orcid.org/0000-0002-5625-9295 (PMF); 5. Now at Instituto Dom Luiz, Faculty of Sciences, University of Lisbon, Lisbon, Portugal

*Corresponding author: tpratt@usgs.gov

Cite this article as Pratt, T. L., M. W. Stirling, D. McPhillips, and P. M. Figueiredo (2026). Characterizing Precariously Balanced Rocks (PBRs) in the Eastern United States for Estimating Maximum Past Earthquake Ground Motions, *Bull. Seismol. Soc. Am.* **116**, 1280–1310, doi: 10.1785/0120250131

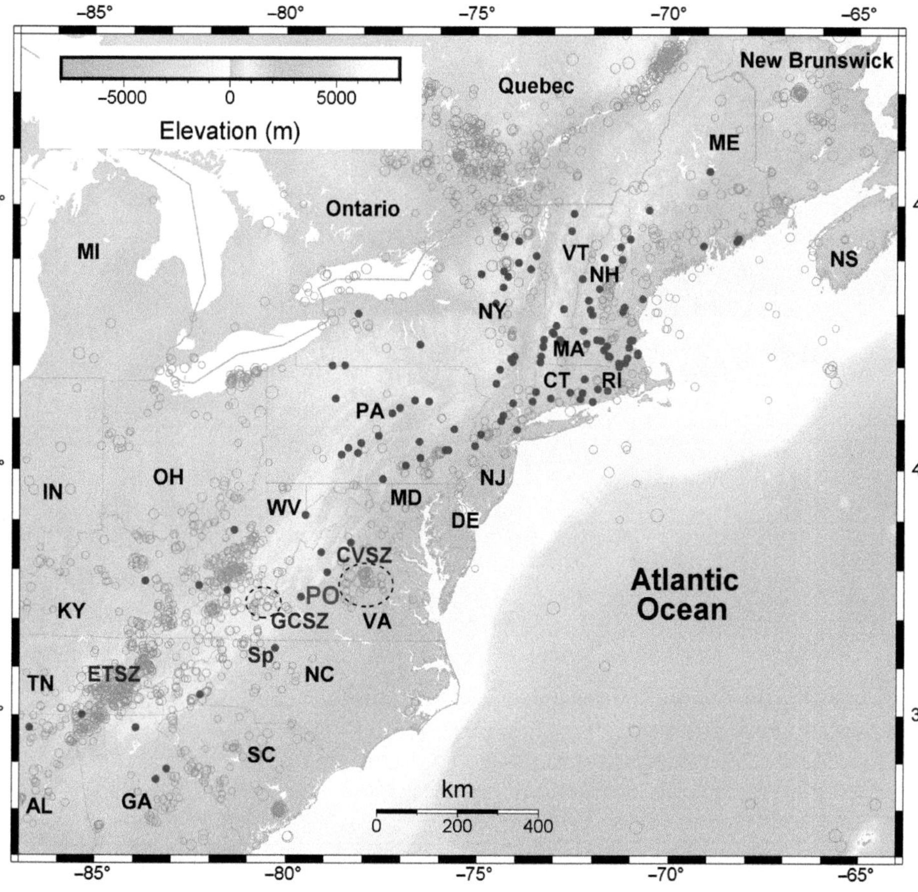

Figure 1. Topographic map of eastern United States with solid dots showing locations of potential precariously balanced rocks (PBRs) identified by the authors to date. Not all these rocks are necessarily precarious, but their descriptions and/or photographs indicate that they may merit investigation. The dot labeled "PO" marks the location of the Peaks of Otter, which includes the PBRs we studied at Harkening Hill and Sharp Top Mountain. Map shows topography in the background, with light gray circles showing magnitude ≥2.5 earthquakes during 1974–2024 scaled by magnitude (U.S. Geological Survey [USGS], 2017). The clusters of earthquakes forming the central Virginia seismic zone (CVSZ) and the Giles County seismic zone (GCSZ) are outlined with dashed ovals. The 2020 M_w 5.1 Sparta, North Carolina, earthquake and its aftershocks are the small cluster immediately northwest of the "Sp" label. Abbreviations are state postal codes in the United States. NS, Nova Scotia. The color version of this figure is available only in the electronic edition.

Klaboe *et al.*, 2018). The existence of the PBR indicates that these toppling ground motions have not been reached while the PBR has been in a fragile position.

In North America, nearly all PBR studies for probabilistic seismic hazard analyses (PSHAs) have been carried out in the western United States (e.g., Brune and Whitney, 1992; Brune, 1996; Brune *et al.*, 1996; Rood *et al.*, 2020; McPhillips and Scharer, 2022), and PBRs have only recently been used to formally evaluate industry-commissioned PSHAs (Stirling *et al.*, 2021). However, PBR studies in the eastern United States may be especially effective and useful for several reasons. First, in the eastern United States, there are numerous PBRs (Fig. 1), which the authors of this article have begun systematically studying (Figueiredo and Pratt, 2023; McPhillips and Pratt, 2024; Stirling and Pratt, 2026). In the northern and northeastern United States, PBRs primarily are erratic boulders (e.g., Fig. 2) that were set in place as the continental ice sheet receded. South of the ice sheet, the PBRs formed from exhumed weathered bedrock and are sometimes clustered where bedrock conditions are favorable for development. Second, lower levels of seismic wave attenuation in the eastern compared with western United States (e.g., McNamara, Gee, *et al.*, 2014; Pratt *et al.*, 2021) mean that eastern U.S. PBRs are sensitive to earthquakes at greater distances than in the western United States. Third, identification of active faults and paleoseismic studies of faults can be difficult or impossible in the eastern United States because recurrence intervals are long relative to those in the western United States, Quaternary sediments that might record past earthquakes are absent in many locations because of erosion during glacial times, and surface scarps indicative of Quaternary motion are extremely rare (Thompson Jobe *et al.*, 2022). PBRs and other FGFs thus are some of the few ways to evaluate earthquake ground motions over the long time frames of interest for seismic hazard assessments.

PBRs in the eastern United States also pose challenges that require some modifications to existing methodology, which was developed primarily in high-seismicity areas. The U.S. Geological Survey's National Seismic Hazard Model (NSHM) effectively only has two source zones in the eastern United States with estimated fault recurrence intervals, specifically the Charleston, South Carolina, area and the central Virginia seismic zone (Thompson Jobe *et al.*, 2022; Petersen *et al.*, 2024). Hazard curves in the eastern United States therefore are derived almost entirely from the seismic catalog. This means that removing logic-tree branches from specific fault sources that are discrepant with the ages and fragilities of PBRs (e.g., Stirling *et al.*, 2021) cannot yet be applied. However, instead the PBRs can be used to evaluate the mean or median hazard curves (e.g., Baker *et al.*, 2013; Rood *et al.*, 2020; McPhillips and Pratt, 2024).

Figure 2. Examples of well-known perched (on the edge of a cliff) and balanced rocks in the northeastern United States: (a) Bubble Rock in Acadia National Park, Maine; (b) at Balance Rock State Park, Lanesborough, Massachusetts; (c) at Elmore State Park, Vermont; and (d) at Orris Falls Conservation Area near Berwick, Maine. These are all erratics that were set in place as the continental ice sheet retreated. Photographs by Thomas Pratt. The color version of this figure is available only in the electronic edition.

The fragility ages of erratic PBRs in the northeastern United States can be reliably estimated based on the timing of retreat of the continental ice sheet ~23,000 to 13,000 yr ago (e.g., Balco and Schaefer, 2006; Barth *et al.*, 2019; Bromley *et al.*, 2019), but accurate age determinations south of the ice sheet will involve cosmogenic exposure dating (e.g., Balco *et al.*, 2011; Rood *et al.*, 2020; Stirling *et al.*, 2021). The PBRs that we are aware of in the eastern United States are generally well-known attractions located in national, state, county, or municipal parks, making it challenging to obtain permission to obtain multiple samples for cosmogenic dating. For such PBRs, including those in this study, fragility estimates can be viewed as selection criteria to evaluate whether the PBRs can provide important constraints on the NSHM or on earthquake activity in nearby seismic zones. After this initial screening, a decision can be made as to whether a given PBR is fragile enough to merit sampling to date the age of fragility. The pilot study described here thus is primarily a refinement of field and analysis methods and is the first step in evaluating PBRs for their potential for evaluating hazard analyses rather than a full PBR analysis.

We also are experimenting with seismometers to characterize PBR responses to perturbations. There have been few *in situ* measurements of the responses of PBRs to input ground motions using seismometers or accelerometers mounted on the rocks. Studies in the Mojave Desert showed that PBRs there did not have unusual site conditions that might enhance or reduce their survival (Abbott and Louie, 2000; Stirling *et al.*, 2002), but the seismometer records were not used to infer rock fragilities. Some recent studies used seismometers or accelerometers to measure the response of rock pillars, fins, and arches to ground motions but not PBRs (Finnegan *et al.*, 2022a,b; Finzi *et al.*, 2020; García Suárez *et al.*, 2025). Zábranová *et al.* (2020) used a seismometer mounted on a PBR to measure and model the frequencies, directions, and quality factors (decay with time) of vibration modes of a rock when stuck by a rubber mallet, but they did not apply the information directly to estimating the rock's potential toppling in earthquakes. The only published study we are aware of that used seismometers on PBRs to help estimate toppling potential is our studies, in which seismometers were used to evaluate the directions of rocking (McPhillips and Pratt, 2024; Stirling and Pratt, 2026). We describe here how seismometers placed on PBRs also can be used to measure the period of rocking, estimate the slenderness angles (Fig. 3), and constrain future computer models of the rocks.

In this article, four PBRs at the Peaks of Otter in the Virginia Blue Ridge (Figs. 1 and 4) are used as test cases to develop and refine methodologies to analyze PBRs in the eastern United States. These rocks, which are tors formed by erosion of joints and fractures, are situated on Harkening Hill and Sharp Top Mountain. The area is part of the Blue Ridge Parkway National Scenic Highway, which is administered by the National Park Service. These PBRs were chosen for study because they are the only PBRs we are yet aware of with the potential to provide information about the two seismic zones in the mid-Atlantic region of the eastern United States. The Peaks of Otter are relatively near the central Virginia seismic zone (CVSZ; Bollinger and Sibol, 1985; Horton *et al.*, 2015), the Giles County seismic zone (GCSZ; Bollinger and Wheeler, 1988), and the location of the 2020 M_w 5.1 Sparta, North Carolina, earthquake (Figueiredo *et al.*, 2022; Neves *et al.*, 2024; Fig. 1), thus having the potential to constrain maximum ground motions associated with past earthquakes in those zones.

Photogrammetry was used to create detailed 3D models of the rocks and the contact areas at their bases, with the interpretations of the contact surfaces aided by measurements of their circumferences made by wrapping a wire around them.

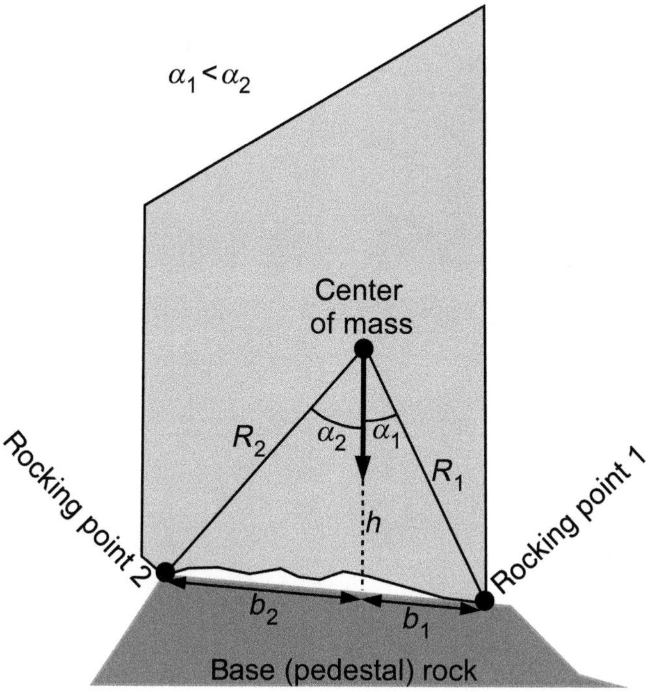

Figure 3. Diagram of a PBR showing key measurements for toppling analysis. The parameters used in the Purvance *et al.* (2008) equations to estimate toppling probability are the two slenderness angles (α_1 and α_2) and the distance (radius) from the center of mass to the nearest rocking point (R_1). The widths of the two sides of the PBR base are labeled "b_1" and "b_2," and "h" is the height of the center of mass. A 3D model of the rock is created using photogrammetry to determine these values. Diagram is modified from McPhillips and Pratt (2024).

The responses of some of the PBRs to ambient noise were determined by placing seismometers on the rocks and on nearby bedrock, from which the periods of rocking were determined from spectral ratios relative to bedrock as is often done for site response estimates (e.g., Borcherdt, 1970; Seed and Idriss, 1971). The rocks were also given gentle pushes in perpendicular directions to examine the directions, periods, changes in period, and changes in amplitude with time of the resulting rocking motions. The preferred directions of rocking can be used to identify the locations of the edges of the contact surfaces that are most relevant for measuring the slenderness angles (e.g., McPhillips and Pratt, 2024; Stirling and Pratt, 2026). The widths of the bases also were estimated from the decreases in rocking amplitude with time on the seismic records and compared with measured widths. The ground motions (a combination of peak ground acceleration [PGA] and peak ground velocity [PGV]) needed to topple the rocks were estimated, from which several inferences about nearby earthquakes could be made and assumptions in the NSHM tested.

PBRs IN THE EASTERN UNITED STATES

General distribution

The eastern United States has a substantial number of PBRs resting atop other rocks or perched on the edges of steep slopes (Figs. 1 and 2; Butler and Dunn, 2016; Butler and Butler, 2018; Dunn, 2018). Perhaps the most famous of these is Bubble Rock in Acadia National Park, which is a large erratic perched precariously on the edge of a cliff (Fig. 2a). Other well-known PBRs are local tourist attractions in Balance Rock State Park, Massachusetts; in Elmore State Park, Vermont; and in the Orris Falls Conservation area, Maine (Fig. 2). For locating PBRs in the northeastern United States, we relied on a compendium of rock formations in a series of books by Jan and Christy Butler, Russell Dunn, and Barbara Delaney (e.g., Butler and Dunn, 2016; Butler and Butler, 2018; Dunn, 2018).

Figure 1 shows a map of potential PBRs in the eastern United States based on descriptions or photographs. We have now collected data on 56 of these, prioritizing those that look most fragile and focusing on erratics in the formerly glaciated northeastern United States where the ages of PBRs set in place during glacial retreat are well constrained. Glacial retreat initiated ~21.8–23 ka ago in southern New York and reached northern New England ~13 ka years ago (Balco and Schaefer, 2006; Barth *et al.*, 2019; Bromley *et al.*, 2019; Halsted *et al.*, 2024).

South of the ice sheet, which terminated just south of the New York–Pennsylvania border, the PBRs most likely formed by chemical weathering and erosion of bedrock, similar to the modes of formation in the western United States and other areas (e.g., Brune, 1996; Bell *et al.*, 1998; Balco *et al.*, 2011; Rood *et al.*, 2020; Stirling *et al.*, 2021). Some bedrock lithologies and fabrics in southwest Virginia are amenable to the formation of blocks when subjected to weathering and erosion, favoring concentrations of PBRs in areas such as the Peaks of Otter (Figs. 1 and 4). We used these latter PBRs for initial studies because they may be able to constrain earthquake magnitudes in the two seismic zones in the region, and they were convenient for multiple visits by one of the authors (Pratt) from the Washington, D.C., area. Other studies by the authors of this article focus on PBRs in the northeastern United States (e.g., Figueiredo and Pratt, 2023; McPhillips and Pratt, 2024; Stirling and Pratt, 2026).

PBRs at the Peaks of Otter in the Blue Ridge of Virginia

Four PBRs at the Peaks of Otter lie atop Harkening Hill and Sharp Top Mountain, which are prominent hills superimposed on the Blue Ridge of the Appalachian Mountains (Fig. 4, Table 1). Two of the PBRs (numbers 1 and 3) are well-known attractions along the Harkening Hill hiking trail, and our reconnaissance of Harkening Hill and nearby Sharp Top Mountain revealed two more PBRs (numbers 2 and 4). The rocks are tors or corestones (e.g., Bell *et al.*, 1998; Balco *et al.*, 2011; Stirling *et al.*, 2021) formed from erosion of Precambrian granulite gneisses (Carter *et al.*, 2013).

These rocks lie ~160 km southwest of the CVSZ (Fig. 1; e.g., Taber, 1913; Bollinger and Sibol, 1985; Horton *et al.*, 2015) and

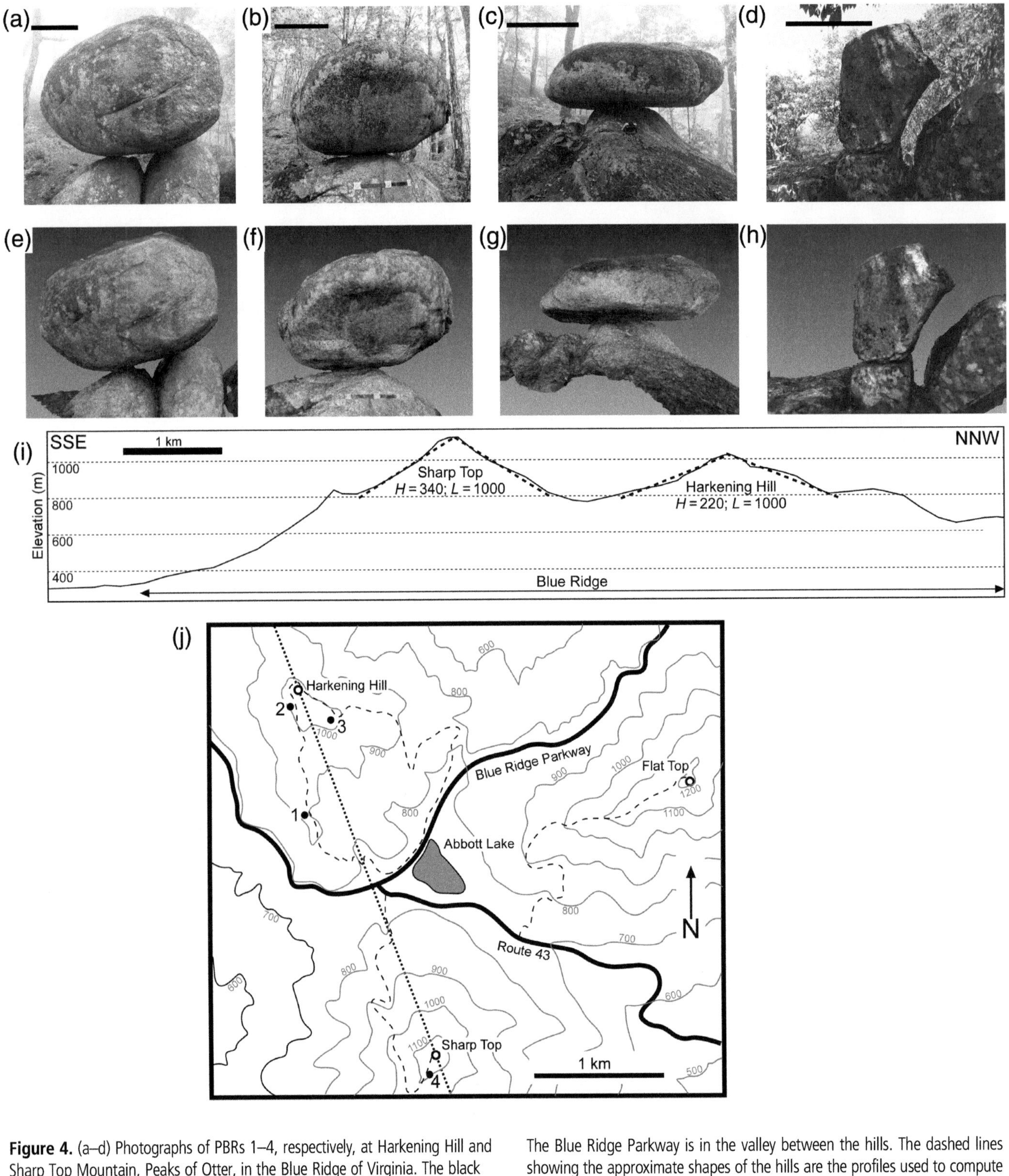

Figure 4. (a–d) Photographs of PBRs 1–4, respectively, at Harkening Hill and Sharp Top Mountain, Peaks of Otter, in the Blue Ridge of Virginia. The black lines in upper left of each photo are 1 m scale bars. Note in (b) the 1 m scale bar taped in a horizontal attitude to the pedestal rock used for leveling and scaling the 3D model. The small object on bedrock in front of the rock in (c) is a portable floodlight used to illuminate the underside of the rock when taking photographs. (e–h) 3D models of the rocks made from photogrammetry, oriented in about the same positions as the photographs above them. (i) South-southeast to north-northwest elevation profile across the Peaks of Otter showing Sharp Top Mountain and Harkening Hill atop the Blue Ridge. The Blue Ridge Parkway is in the valley between the hills. The dashed lines showing the approximate shapes of the hills are the profiles used to compute the slope ratios (*H*/*L*; height/half-width) for estimating the topographic amplification. The topographic amplification caused by the large Blue Ridge is likely too long of a period to be relevant to toppling the rocks (as per Singh *et al.*, 2018). Elevation profile is from Google Earth. (j) Contour map (in meter) of the Harkening Hill area showing locations of PBRs 1–4 relative to roads and hiking trails (dashed lines); the thick dotted line shows the location of the central portion of the elevation profile shown in (i). The color version of this figure is available only in the electronic edition.

TABLE 1
Locations and Dimensions of Precariously Balanced Rocks (PBRs) at Peaks of Otter

Rock	Longitude	Latitude	Volume (m^3)	Mass (kg) (2.67 kg/m^3)	Weight (tons)	CoM Height (cm)	Contact Surface Circum (cm)	Base 1 (cm)	Alpha 1 (°)	Radius 1 (cm)	Base 2 (cm)	Alpha 2 (°)	Radius 2 (cm)	Topo amp
Harkening Hill 1	−79.6174	37.4532	27.52	73478	81	136	127; 185	29.6	12.3	139.2	31.9	13.2	139.7	1.28
Harkening Hill 2	−79.6174	37.4588	12.14	32414	35.7	98	198	14.5	8.4	99.1	38.4	21.4	105.3	1.28
Harkening Hill 3	−79.6139	37.4553	6.53	17435	19.2	51	63.5; 152	5.8	6.5	51.3	15.9	17.3	53.4	1.28
Sharp Top	−79.6059	37.4321	1.18	3151	3.5	57	191	7.7	7.7	57.5	18.4	17.9	59.9	1.41

CoM, centers of mass; Topo amp, topographic amplification.

~100 km northeast of the GCSZ (Bollinger and Hopper, 1971; Bollinger and Wheeler, 1983, 1988). They also lie ~170 km north-northeast of the 2020 M_w 5.1 Sparta, North Carolina, earthquake, which involved a complex rupture along two previously unknown faults with an ~4-km-long surface rupture and evidence for late Pleistocene recurrent surface rupturing events (Figueiredo *et al.*, 2022; Merschat and Carter, 2022; Neves *et al.*, 2024). The PBRs at the Peaks of Otter thus could be susceptible to toppling from large earthquakes in these seismic zones, as well as from earthquakes on other known or unknown faults in the region. Although the distances are large, we note that a moderately sized M_w 5.8 earthquake in the CVSZ in 2011 caused rockfalls (from cliffs or roadcuts) up to 158 km away (Jibson and Harp, 2012) and caused substantial building damage 140 km away in Washington, D.C. (Horton *et al.*, 2015). The latter damages were enhanced by local amplification of ground motions by the Atlantic Coastal Plain sediments beneath the city (Hough, 2012; Wells *et al.*, 2015; Pratt *et al.*, 2017), but the PBRs at the Peaks of Otter lie atop prominent hills that also will cause local amplification of ground motions because of topography (e.g., Molina *et al.*, 2019).

The CVSZ has been the locus of several damaging earthquakes, including a 1774 event famously noted by Thomas Jefferson (Bollinger and Sibol, 1985; Tarr and Wheeler, 2006; Horton *et al.*, 2015). Paleoliquefaction features are interpreted to indicate either multiple earthquakes of M_w 6.0–6.25 in different parts of the zone or one earthquake of M_w 6.25–6.5 in the past 2800 yr (Tuttle *et al.*, 2021). Little is known about the history of earthquakes in the GCSZ except for the 1897 damaging m_b 5.6–5.8 earthquake and ongoing sparse seismicity (Bollinger and Wheeler, 1983, 1988; Tarr and Wheeler, 2006). The M_w 5.1 Sparta earthquake occurred on the previously unknown Little River fault, which in the past 100 ka has had multiple surface-rupturing earthquakes similar to that in 2020 and could potentially cause larger events (Figueiredo *et al.*, 2022; Merschat *et al.*, 2024; Neves *et al.*, 2024). The M_w 5.1 Sparta earthquake area did not have a history or record of past seismicity, but it generated a surface rupture with socioeconomic impact, demonstrating that the eastern United States, including the region around the Peaks of Otter, likely has other unknown or underestimated sources for damaging earthquakes.

FIELD MEASUREMENTS AND OBSERVATIONS

We used a variety of methods to characterize the PBR fragilities. The key measurements are the ratios of the horizontal to vertical distances of the center of mass relative to the "rocking points" at the edges of the basal contact surface, encapsulated in the slenderness angles α_1 and α_2 (Fig. 3; Housner, 1963; Anooshehpoor *et al.*, 2004). The radii from the center of mass to the rocking points also play a role, with larger PBRs requiring lower frequencies of shaking (longer pulse durations) to topple them. Analyses most often use a combination of PGA as a proxy for the strength of shaking and PGV as a proxy for the pulse duration during the shaking (e.g., Purvance *et al.*, 2008). Spectral accelerations at 1 or 2 s periods (SA_1 or SA_2, respectively) have also been used instead of PGV (Purvance *et al.*, 2008). A further aspect of the work is to determine the amount of time that a PBR has been precariously balanced, or "fragile," and thus the amount of time over which toppling ground motions have not been exceeded (e.g., Bell *et al.*, 1998; Balco *et al.*, 2011; Rood *et al.*, 2020; Stirling *et al.*, 2021; McPhillips and Scharer, 2022).

Photogrammetric models

Photogrammetry was used to create detailed 3D models of the PBRs (Fig. 4e–h), from which their dimensions, locations of the centers of mass, and shapes of the contact areas with the underlying rocks were determined (Table 1). For rocks 1–4 the models were made from 271, 377, 419, and 388 photos, respectively, resulting in point clouds with 1.8, 2.2, 6.0, and 2.7 million points, respectively, after editing out extraneous features such as trees and other rocks. For vertical alignment of the models, we used one or more of three methods. For some rocks, 1 m leveled scale bars were taped to the PBR sides or the underlying rock (e.g., Fig. 4b), and on others a weight was hung off the side of the PBRs with a rope to provide a vertical line. The in-camera level also was used to take several properly leveled photographs to define the model's orientation. We also taped scale bars on the underlying bedrock in a north–south direction (magnetic north) to orient and scale the models. From multiple trials at digitizing the scale bars, we estimate the models to be within 1% of the actual dimensions. The open-source "Meshroom" software was used for the photogrammetry, and open-source "MeshLab" was used for editing the models and making the geometric calculations (see Data and Resources), although other programs can provide similar capabilities.

We note that light detection and ranging (lidar) also can be used for creating 3D models of the rocks (Wittich *et al.*, 2018; Veeraraghavan *et al.*, 2017; McPhillips and Pratt, 2024), with the advantage of the initial model being scaled and oriented correctly. In principle, photogrammetry can have very high resolution, and the necessary equipment (a standard camera) can be cheaper and lighter than that of a lidar system. We tested a lidar system on a tablet computer but found that despite the swiftness of the method, it is not yet sufficient for suitably accurate 3D models; however, this may be an option in the future with the advantage that the model is built in real time.

We oriented and scaled the 3D models and set the coordinate origins at the bases of the PBRs (top of underlying bedrock) with x axes pointing east, y axes north, and the z axes vertical. We then isolated the top rocks by deleting the points and meshes forming the underlying rocks and used Poisson reconstruction to fit surfaces to the top rocks to make enclosed bodies. At that point the software could compute the locations of the centers of mass and other measurements (volume, surface area, and so on). These models, point clouds, and data processing description are available in an online data archive (Pratt *et al.*, 2026).

To map the contact areas at the bases of the PBRs, points were extracted from the photogrammetry point clouds from 0.1 to 0.5 m above and below the center of the contact surface, with the distances being dependent on the shape and slope of the surface to make sure we encompass its entirety. These points were plotted on a horizontal plane, with the contact surfaces being blank areas that were not visible to the camera (Fig. 5), although occasional artifacts occurred because of similar-looking features in multiple photos being misidentified as the same feature. We measured the contact areas' circumferences by wrapping a picture wire around them, with these measurements being useful for interpreting the contact surfaces on the point clouds (Fig. 5). We used a braided picture wire to squeeze into narrow cracks, which a thicker wire could not do.

The contact surface maps in Figure 5 also show the locations of the downward projection of centers of mass onto the contact surfaces and the directions of rocking determined from the seismometer records (explained later). Plotted on the point clouds are the interpreted circumferences of the contact surfaces that mimic the wire wrapped around the bases. Taut wires connect the outer corners of the contact surfaces without extending into recesses, so the interpreted wires on the point clouds similarly have straight lines between the interpreted outer corners. We also used the photos taken for photogrammetry to help interpret the contact surfaces. From the 3D models, the slenderness angles (α_1 and α_2) and radii (R_1 and R_2) were computed (Fig. 3).

Table 1 lists the rock parameters used in the subsequent fragility calculations, and the relevant measurements are labeled in Figure 5.

Frequencies of rocking from ambient noise recordings

We used seismometers on the rocks to characterize the PBR responses to input ground motions. We used six-channel seismometers, "Geosentinel" from Lunitek, Inc., that are small, lightweight, easy to set up, can be programmed and controlled with a cell phone or laptop through a wireless interface, and provide a real-time display on the cell phone or laptop. They have an internal battery with a 5 hr life that is ample for our tests, and their small size and weight allowed for carrying them in a backpack. A second seismometer was placed on bedrock 8–15 m away to record the input ambient noise near rocks 1–3, but we stopped deploying this second seismometer before working on rock 4 because we could get the same information from a single seismometer atop the PBR, as explained later. The seismometers were oriented to magnetic north, as were the 3D models from the photogrammetry. The seismometers had three-component geophones

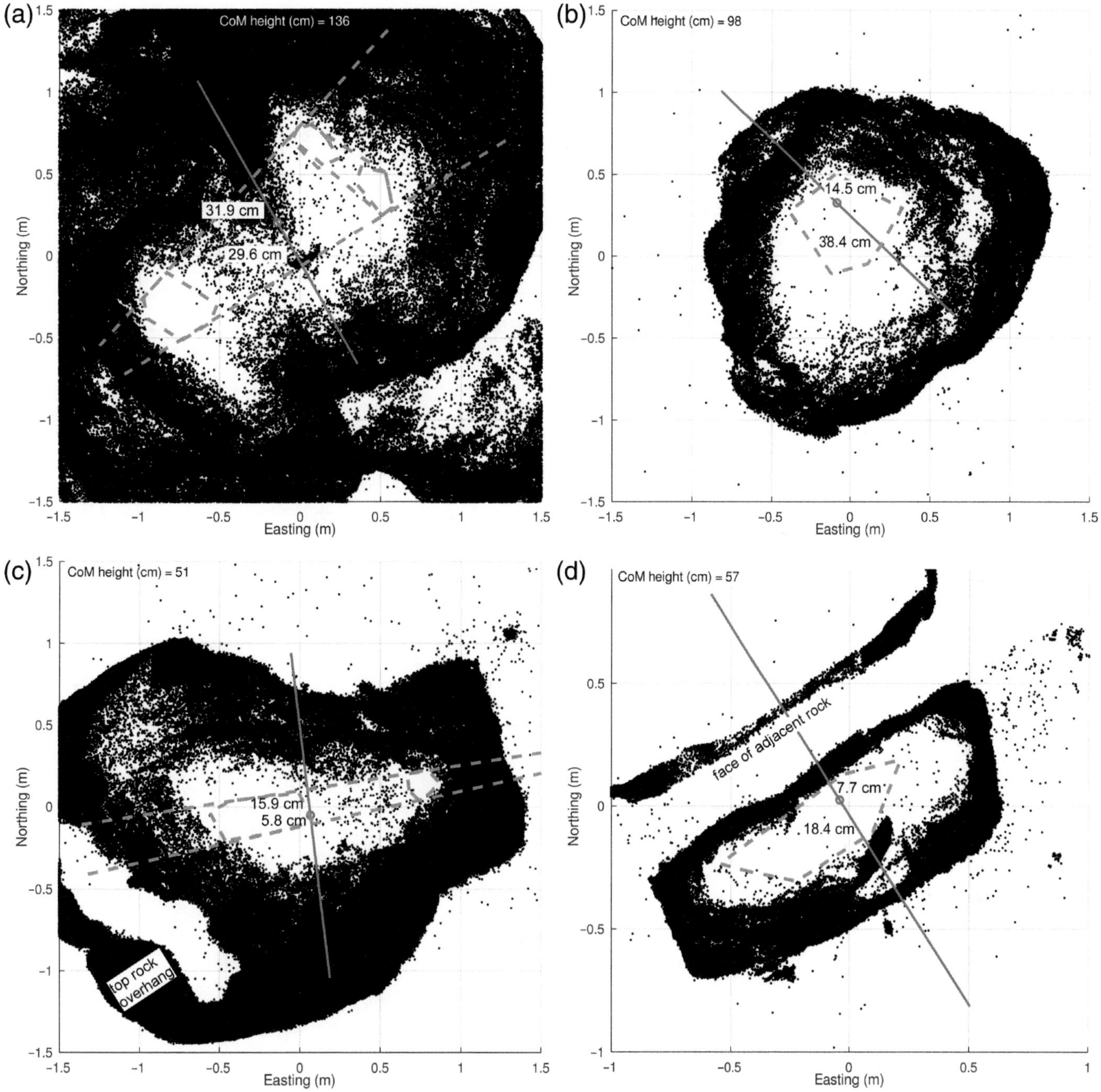

Figure 5. (a–d) Contact surfaces for PBRs 1–4, respectively, at the Peaks of Otter from the point clouds. These are the point clouds selected from just above to just below the contact surface, with the contact surfaces being blank areas where the camera did not image any points. However, there are occasional artifacts that create stray points caused by similar-looking features in multiple photographs being misidentified as the same feature. The gray circles are the locations of the centers of mass (CoM), with the gray lines showing the directions of rocking measured with the seismometers. In each model, dashed lines outline the contact surfaces, with the lengths of the lines matching the circumferences measured by wrapping a wire around the contact surfaces. In (a) and (c), there are multiple contact surfaces, with the linear dashed lines connecting the outside edges of the surfaces showing the interpreted potential axes of rocking. The labels show the distances along the gray lines from the centers of mass to the interpreted rocking edges; these numbers were used in the fragility analyses (Table 1). The heights of the CoM for each rock are labeled at the top. The label in (c) indicates points caused by the southwest edge of the PBR (top rock) hanging down on one edge but not touching the ground, and the label in (d) indicates points associated with the face of an adjacent rock. The color version of this figure is available only in the electronic edition.

with 4.5 Hz resonant frequencies as well as three-component accelerometers. We used the geophone velocity recordings for the spectral ratios.

About 10–15 min of ambient noise was recorded at rocks 1–3, from which spectral ratios of the horizontal components of motion were computed relative to the bedrock sites (Fig. 6).

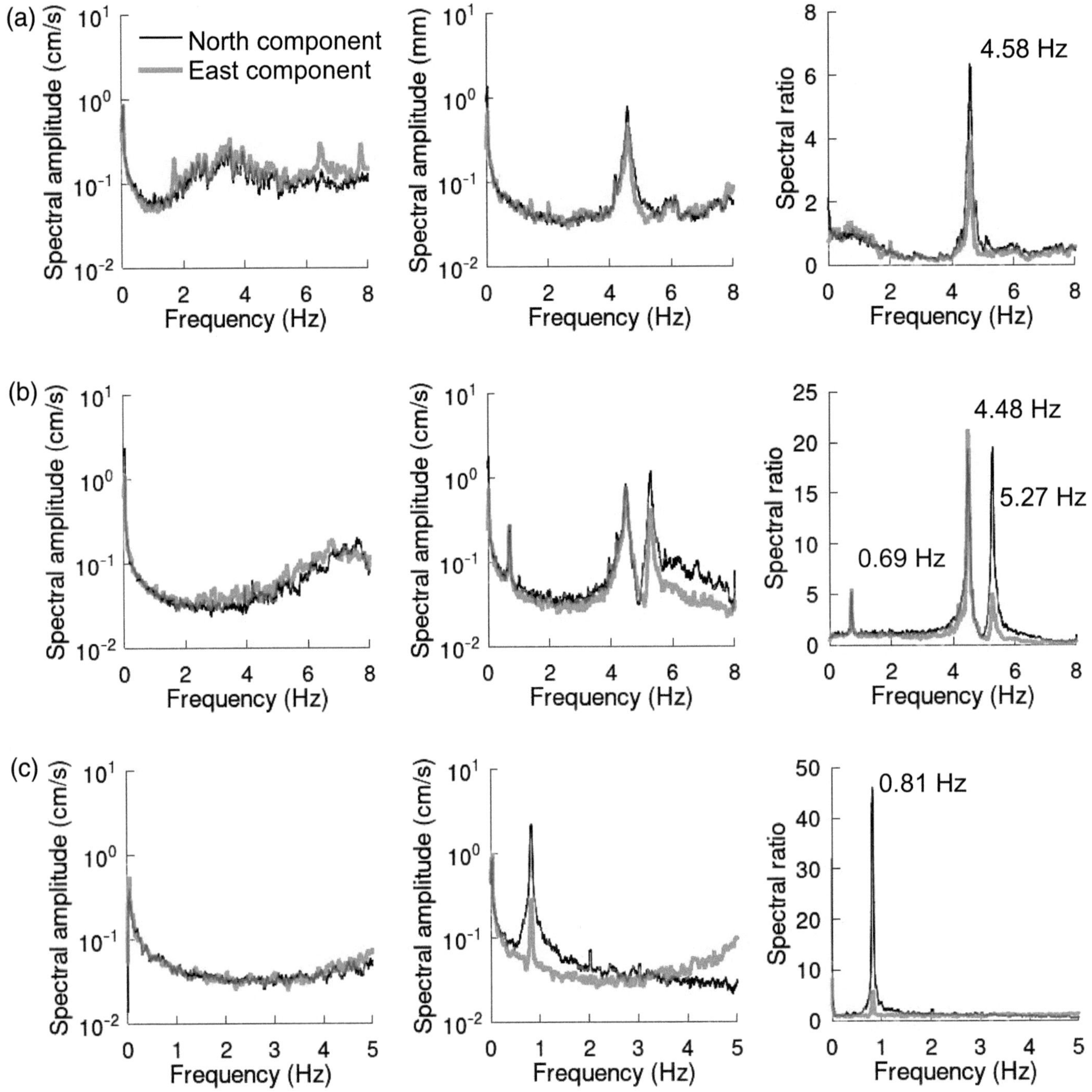

These spectral ratios identified the dominant frequencies of the rock motions in response to weak ambient noise. These are more properly termed "pseudo-rocking frequencies" because a rocking block has increasing frequency with decreasing tilt angle rather than a constant frequency of rocking (Housner, 1963; Shi *et al.*, 1996; Anooshehpoor *et al.*, 2004). These frequencies were computed from extremely weak motions with tiny tilt angles, in contrast to the case in some studies in which researchers tilted PBRs to near their tipping points (e.g., Anooshehpoor *et al.*, 2004). Because the frequency of rocking increases with decreasing tilt angles, the larger amplitudes that might topple the PBRs should be at a lower frequency than the

Figure 6. Resonant frequencies of the three rocks—(a) rock 1, (b) rock 2, and (c) rock 3—at the Peaks of Otter from ambient noise recordings, which in this case are velocity records before conversion to displacement. The left panels show the spectra of ambient noise recorded at a nearby bedrock site, the center panels show the spectra from the recordings on the PBRs, and the right panels show the spectral ratios between the rock and bedrock recordings. The prominent peaks in the center and right panels are the rocking frequencies caused by the weak ambient noise. We did not make ambient noise recordings for rock 4 because earlier work showed that push tests give effectively the same results. The color version of this figure is available only in the electronic edition.

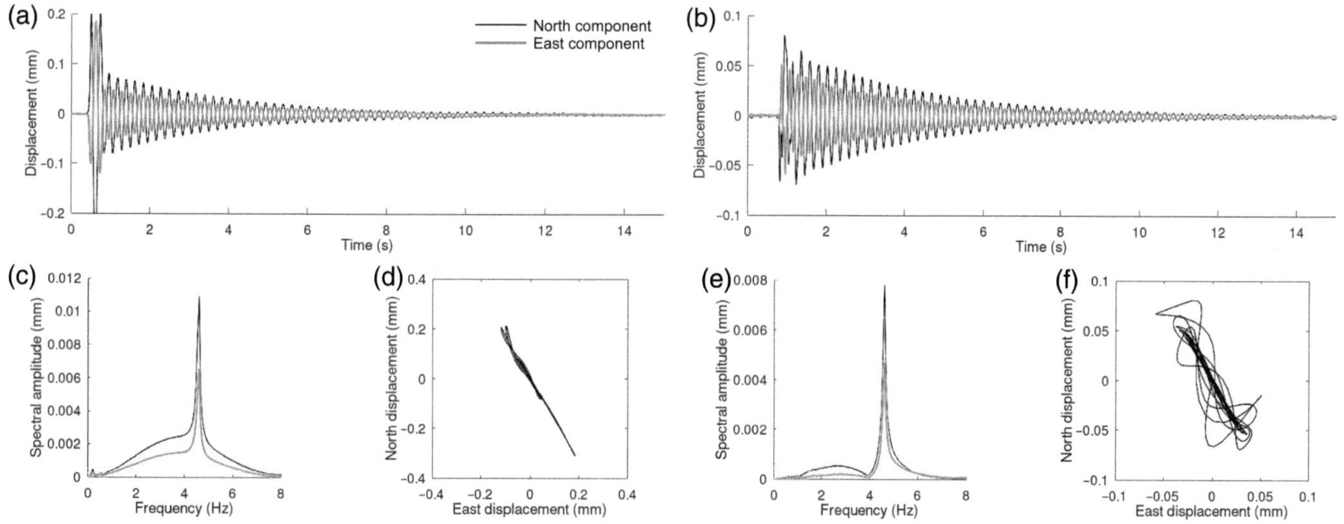

Figure 7. Push tests for rock 1. (a,b) The seismometer recordings after pushes from the north and east sides of the rocks, respectively; (c,e) the frequency spectra of the recordings above them; and (d,f) particle motion diagrams made from the recordings. In the particle motion plots, note the preferred direction of rocking at N~30°W (relative to magnetic north) shown by the elongated pattern of motion regardless the direction from which the rock is pushed. The color version of this figure is available only in the electronic edition.

peaks in our spectral ratios. The peaks on the spectral ratios therefore provide upper frequency limits to consider when evaluating ground motions that could cause toppling.

The recordings in Figure 6 are based on 1000–1200 s recordings of ambient noise chosen at times that showed no substantial noise bursts because of our activities. In each case, there was a well-defined peak, or multiple peaks, characterizing the frequencies of rocking. These peaks indicate that the seismometers on the PBRs moved at substantially larger amplitudes than the nearby bedrock, but we ignored the actual amplitudes because they are dependent on the spectral smoothing and on the locations of the seismometers on the rocks.

All three rocks showed pronounced peaks at frequencies in the 0.6–6 Hz range. Rock 1 showed a prominent peak at 4.58 Hz, with similar amplitudes on the north–south (N-S) and east–west (E-W) components, indicating that rocking was at an angle of ~45° to the seismometer axes. Rock 2 showed three peaks, with a peak at 4.48 Hz showing similar spectral amplifications on both components but a peak at 5.27 Hz being stronger on the N-S component. These peaks suggest two modes of rocking, with the 4.48-Hz peak being at an angle of ~45° to the seismometer orientation but the peak at ~5.27 Hz being from primarily N-S rocking. A small peak at 0.69 Hz became the dominant peak when the rock was perturbed more strongly by pushing (described later). Rock 3 showed a prominent peak at 0.81 Hz that was relatively small on the E-W component but large on the N-S component, which is consistent with rocking perpendicular to the E-W orientation of the small ridge the rock is resting atop (Figs. 4 and 5). We did not record ambient noise for rock 4.

Responses of the rocks to pushing

Giving the rocks gentle pushes in perpendicular directions allowed us to discern their directions of rocking, at least for small perturbations. The proper direction for measuring the slenderness angles in PBRs can sometimes be difficult to ascertain, especially for PBRs with nearly circular contact surfaces at their bases (e.g., Fig. 5b). The push tests confirmed the direction inferred from inspection of the PBR geometries when a direction was obvious (as in Veeraraghavan *et al.*, 2017), but in cases like PBR 2, this can be difficult to discern from visual inspection. All the rocks were pushed gently from two nearly perpendicular directions, with the orientations of the pushes being dependent on accessibility of the rock faces because the downhill sides of the pedestals were sometimes too tall to easily reach the PBR. The pushes were similar in strength to what might be used to open a heavy door. The rocking gradually decayed in amplitude with time, although the rocking continued for as long as 90 s for rock 3 before reaching background levels of noise. The rocks are discussed separately because they behaved differently from each other. After comparisons showed that the responses of the rocks to ambient noise and to the pushes yielded nearly identical frequency peaks, we stopped recording the ambient noise and only used a single seismometer to record the pushes at rock 4.

Rock 1. Rocking decayed to background noise levels in ~15 s (Fig. 7), but this is dependent on the strength of the push, which was not measured in these early field efforts. We now measure the strengths and locations of the pushes to calibrate future computer models, but these strength measurements are irrelevant for determining the frequencies and directions of rocking. Regardless of the direction of pushing, the rock had a clear rocking frequency of 4.59 Hz, which is nearly the same frequency as found in the spectral ratio relative to bedrock

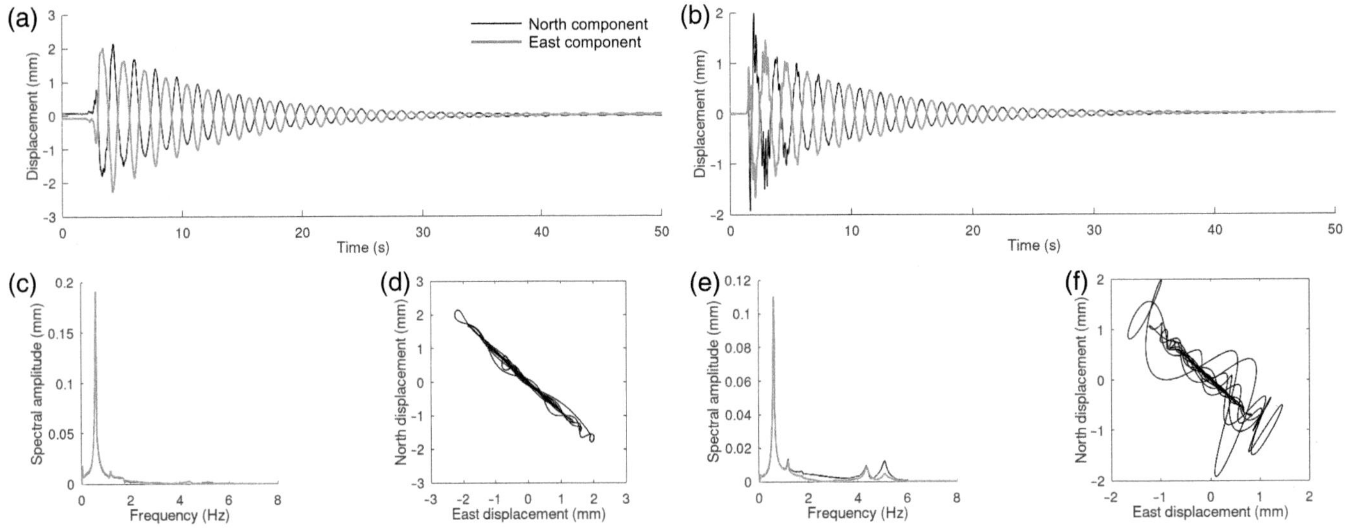

Figure 8. Push tests for rock 2. Panels are the same as described in Figure 7 but in this case with pushes from the south (a,c,d) and west (b,e,f). The rocking lasts for ~40 s before fading to background levels. The high-frequency peaks at ~4.38 and 5.18 Hz in (e) appear to be from rocking (wobbling) in the northeast–southwest direction evident in (f), which is superimposed on the lower-frequency, much greater northwest–southeast rocking. The color version of this figure is available only in the electronic edition.

made from the ambient noise recordings (Fig. 6). A particle motion diagram from the seismometer on the rock showed a preferred direction of rocking of about N30°W (relative to magnetic north) regardless of which direction the rock was pushed. This consistency in direction indicates that the morphology at the base of the PBR controls the rocking direction rather than the direction of the push. The rocking is nearly perpendicular to a line connecting the southeast edges of the contact areas formed by the tripod base, indicating that the PBR is rocking primarily on the southeast edges of the contact surfaces (Fig. 5a).

Rock 2. The seismometer push tests from this rock are different because the rock is resting on a single nearly circular contact area (Fig. 5b). In this case, it took ~40 s for the rocking to decrease to background levels of motion (Fig. 8). The rock showed a slightly different response when pushed from the south than from the west. As with the ambient noise recordings, there were three peaks at 0.6, 4.38, and 5.18 Hz, although the higher-frequency peaks were barely evident in the push from the south. The dominant rocking direction was ~N47° W with a frequency of ~0.6 Hz, and this direction of rocking was used to define the slenderness angles (Fig. 5). The higher-frequency peaks appear to be associated with a northeast–southwest direction of rocking (or wobbling), which is nearly perpendicular to the primary rocking direction (Fig. 8f).

Rock 3. This rock rests atop a small, nearly E-W-trending bedrock "ridge," with two parts of the ridge in contact with the upper rock (Fig. 5c). The strongest rocking was nearly N-S, with the actual direction being about N7°W (Fig. 9). When pushed strongly, the rocking continued for >90 s before returning to background levels, and the rock visibly moved when given a push. The frequency of rocking is 0.72 Hz, which is slightly lower than the 0.81 Hz frequency of the peak in the spectral ratio computed from ambient noise recordings, presumably because the displacement from the push was larger. We only show the push from one direction because results from the other direction were nearly identical.

Rock 4. This rock is a relatively small, tabular rock, with its primary direction of rocking being perpendicular to the long axis of the rock's base, or ~N33°W (Fig. 10). The rocking damped out quickly, lasting only ~7 s, although we did not push hard for fear of knocking over this relatively small rock. The frequency of rocking was just <0.8 Hz. Again we only show one direction of pushing because the perpendicular direction resulted in an almost identical response.

Change in the periods of rocking

One question that could arise with PBR studies is whether rocks are "swaying" back and forth, like the bending of a narrow pillar or beam (e.g., Finnegan *et al.*, 2022a), rather than actually rocking on the edges of the contact surfaces. The period of a rocking block decreases with decreasing tilt angle because of the greater restoring force at smaller tilt angles (Housner, 1963; Shi *et al.*, 1996; Anooshehpoor *et al.*, 2004). Alternatively, if the rock is swaying rather than rocking, the resonant frequency is constant and is a function of the bending modes of the rock like those seen for a tall pillar (e.g., Finzi *et al.*, 2020; Finnegan *et al.*, 2022a). The push tests can be used to determine whether rocking is occurring by confirming the change in period with amplitude of rocking. All the rocks

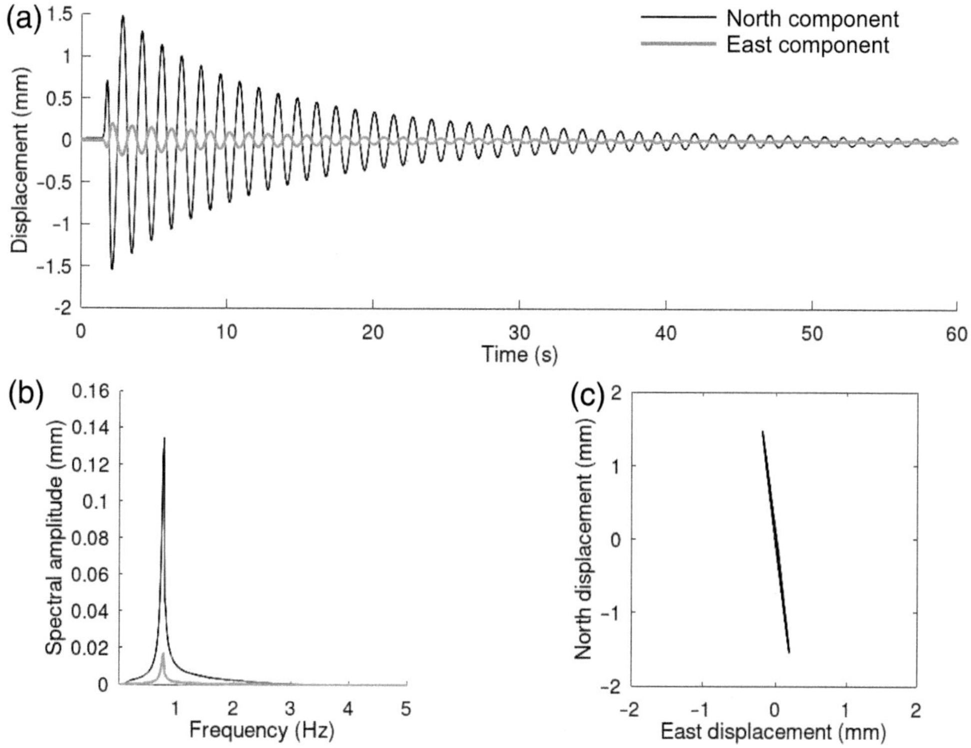

Figure 9. (a–c) Seismometer push tests on rock 3. Panels are the same as described in Figure 7 but in this case with a push from the north. The rocking continues for longer than 90 s, with much stronger rocking along the north–south axis regardless of the direction of the push. The perpendicular push (not shown) gave an almost identical result. The color version of this figure is available only in the electronic edition.

showed clear decreases in the periods of rocking with each cycle (Fig. 11), indicating that the PBRs are indeed rocking. In the case of rock 3, this behavior was confirmed by visible motion.

The dimensions and weights of the PBRs can be estimated from the photogrammetry (Table 1), so in principle, the total displacements and tilt angles during the rocking would be consistent with the rock measurements (dimensions, mass, moment of inertia) described in the analytical equations discussed by Housner (1963) or Shi *et al.* (1996). The seismometer location is visible in the 3D models, but the locations and strengths of the pushes were not recorded in these early tests, so fully quantitative analyses are not possible with this data set. In later work on other PBRs, we used a luggage scale to measure the forces of the pushes, and we recorded the locations of the pushes to allow for calibration of future computer models.

Coefficients of restitution and the widths of the contact surfaces

One potential way to obtain the distances between the edges of the contact surfaces or to independently verify these distances is to use the amplitude decay from the seismometer records. Anooshehpoor *et al.* (2004) looked at the coefficient of restitution of rocking (i.e., energy loss during each cycle of rocking), which can be measured from the decay in the amplitude of rocking with time (their fig. 11). The coefficient of restitution (η) is related to the slenderness angle, as expressed in equation (7) of Anooshehpoor *et al.* (2004):

$$\eta = 1 - (3\sin^2\alpha)/2, \quad (1)$$

in which α is one of two equal slenderness angles because they only tested this relation on symmetric blocks. Therefore, it should be possible to compute the distances between the rocking edges using only the heights of the centers of mass and the slenderness angles obtained from the coefficients of restitution measured from the seismometer records. The results for our rocks are shown in Figure 12.

The coefficient of restitution for rock 1, measured from the average ratios of adjacent peaks on the seismic record, is 0.969, which results in a slenderness angle of 8.3° and a half-width of 19.7 cm. The full-width of the contact surface therefore would be 39.4 cm. The width of the contact surface measured from the point cloud, as measured through the center of mass between two lines connecting the edges of the three contact surfaces, is 61.5 cm (Fig. 5a). However, the width of the southwestern single contact surface is ~40 cm. The width derived from the coefficient of restitution therefore appears to be giving the width of the smaller (southwestern) contact surface, whereas rocking should be stabilized by the much wider northeastern pair of contact points. It is possible that this mode of rocking is defined only by the southwestern contact surface and the southeastern of the pair of other contact surfaces (Fig. 5a), but the third contact point should decrease the probability of toppling in the northwest direction. Such issues could be further addressed by analyzing additional PBRs.

The coefficient of restitution computed from the seismic records for rock 2 is 0.918. This indicates slenderness angles of 13.5°, which results in a basal half-width of 23.5 cm and a total width for the contact surface of ~47.1 cm. The measured width of the contact surface from the point cloud is slightly larger at 52.9 cm (Fig. 5b), which may indicate that we are being too conservative in picking the outline of the contact surface in this direction (i.e., the contact surface is narrower than we picked from the point cloud).

Rock 3 has a coefficient of restitution of 0.933, which indicates a slenderness angle of 12.2 degrees. The half-width of the

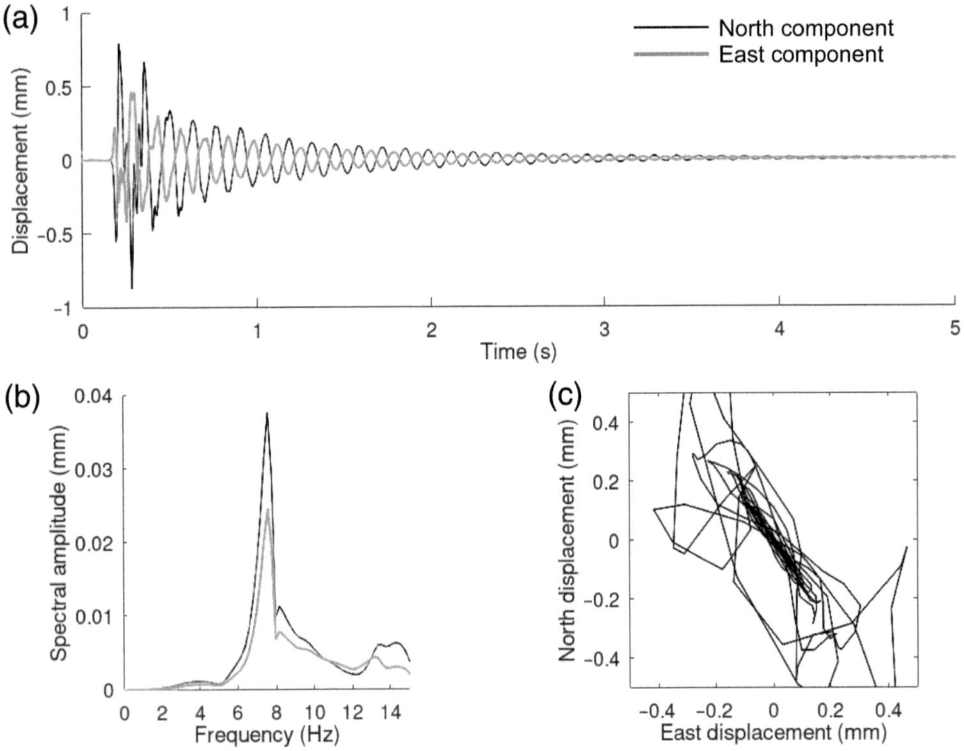

Figure 10. (a–c) Push tests for rock 4. Panels are the same as described in Figure 7 but in this case with a push from the north. The PBR has a rocking direction of about N33°W and fades out after 7 s, although we did not substantially push this relatively small rock because it could be toppled. The perpendicular push (not shown) gave an almost identical result. The color version of this figure is available only in the electronic edition.

contact surface would be 11 cm and the full-width would be ~22.1 cm, comparing well with the measured width of 21.7 cm (Fig. 5c) for the contact surface in the point cloud.

Rock 4 has a coefficient of restitution of 0.942, which yields a slenderness angle of 11.4° and a base width of 23.0 cm. The measured width of the base from the point cloud is 26.1 cm (Fig. 5d), which again may mean that we are being too conservative in picking the edges of the contact surface from the point cloud.

The widths of the contact surfaces estimated from the coefficients of restitution are thus similar to the widths measured from the point clouds for rocks 2–4 (Fig. 5). In principle, the effective slenderness angles and contact surface widths derived from the seismometer records should be more accurate

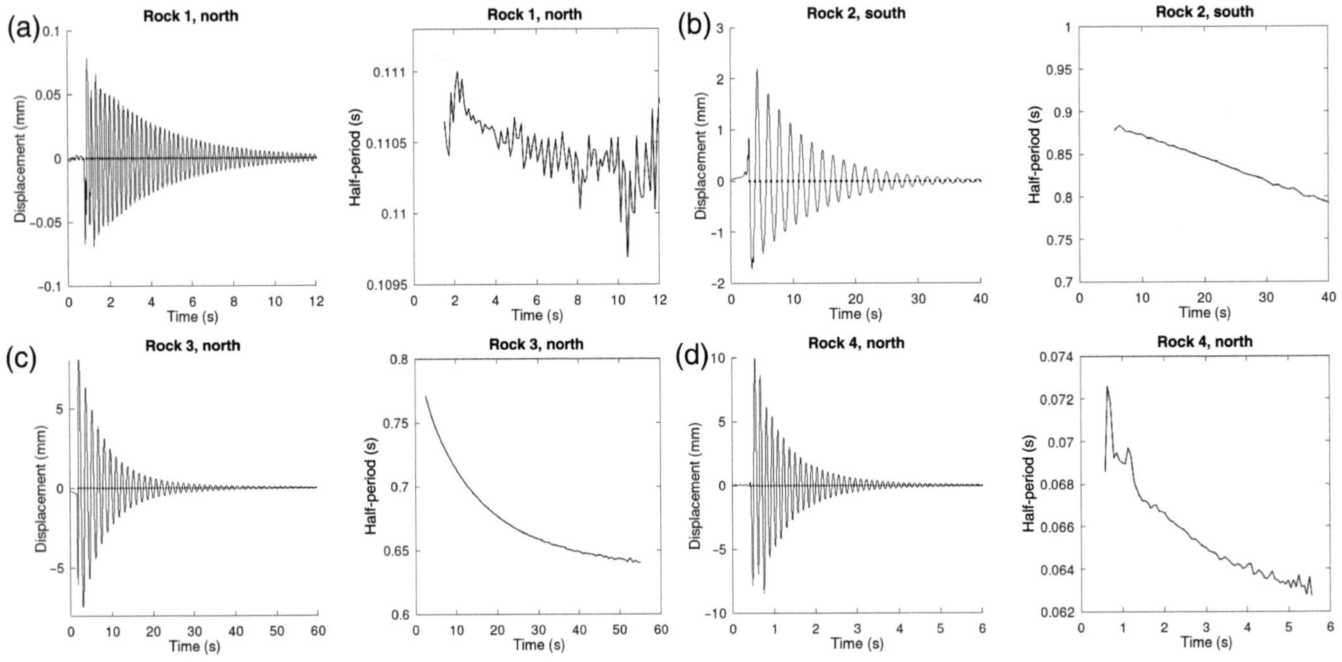

Figure 11. (a–d) Changes in half-periods of rocking with time in response to gentle pushes on the faces of the rocks listed at the tops of the panels. For each rock, the left panel shows the displacement versus time, and the right panel shows the half-period of each cycle (zero crossing to zero crossing) versus time. The early portions of the records for rocks 1 and 4 include high-frequency components from another mode of rocking.

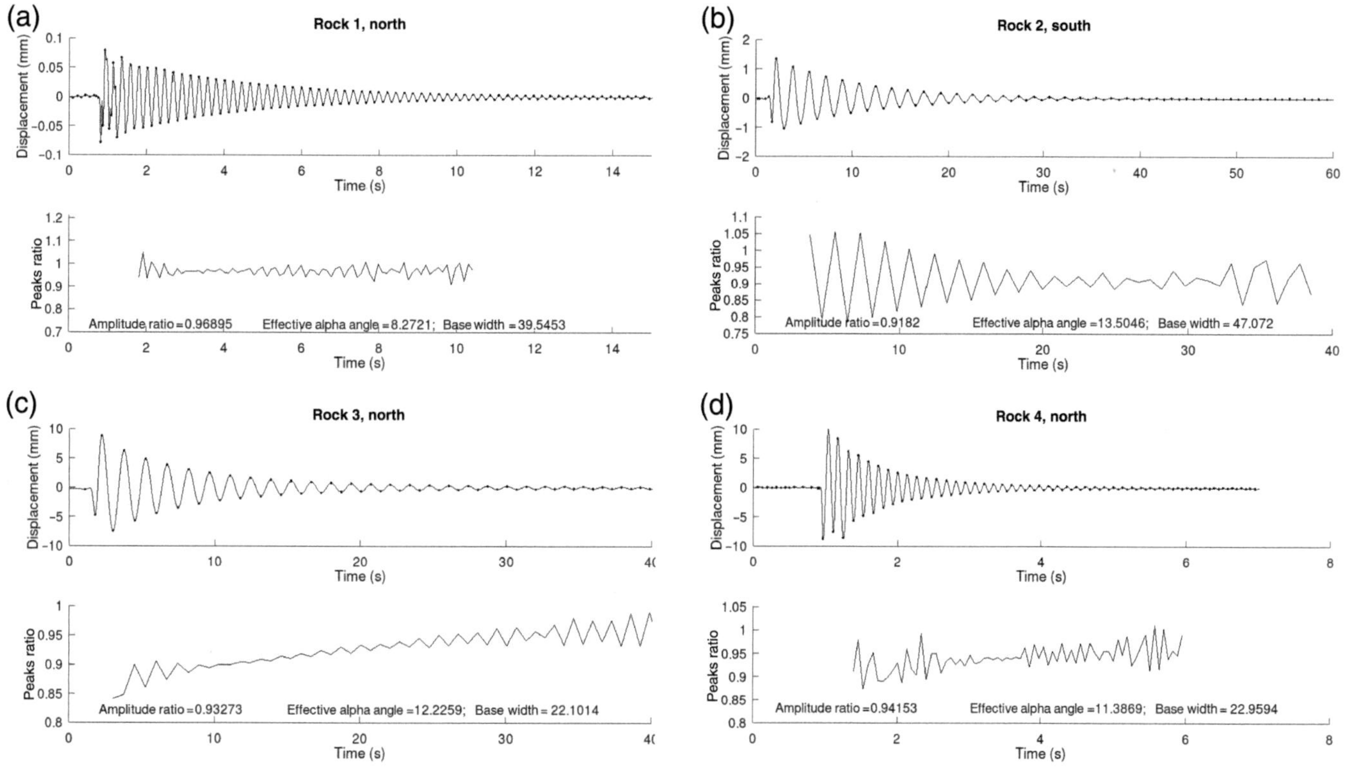

Figure 12. Calculation of the average coefficients of restitution, with resulting slenderness angles and contact surface widths. Panels (a) through (d) are each a pair of plots, with the upper graph being the trace from a push on the indicated rock face and the lower graph being the amplitude ratio between adjacent peaks. The notations on the lower plots show the average amplitude ratio between adjacent peaks, the resulting effective slenderness (α) angles computed from the coefficients of restitution, and the widths of the contact surfaces (bases) computed from the angles and the heights of the centers of mass. The effective slenderness angle is assumed to be one of a symmetric pair, so it needs to be doubled to compute the widths of the contact surfaces (Anooshehpoor *et al.*, 2004).

than our measured widths for several reasons. First, the seismometer is measuring the actual responses of the PBRs, which should incorporate effects due to nonflat contact surfaces. Anooshehpoor *et al.* (2004) found that nonflat bases tended to increase the fragility, resulting in smaller effective slenderness angles. This seems consistent with our results, in that for rocks 2 and 4 the widths determined from the seismometer tests were slightly smaller than from the point clouds, which would be consistent with having some complexities on the bases. Second, the seismometer tests are not subject to errors because of improper leveling or scaling of the 3D models. The seismometer results also do not suffer from uncertainties in imaging the outer edges of the contact surface, which sometimes can be difficult to determine on the point clouds. By definition, the camera images visible points, so the photogrammetry images points outside of the contact surface and rarely produces points precisely at the edges of the contact surfaces.

These observations indicate that the most effective strategy for studying PBRs may be to use the seismometer tests to determine the direction of rocking and the contact surface widths from the coefficients of restitution and to determine the centers of mass from the 3D models. We now have models of 40 more rocks in the eastern United States with seismometer tests, so we can test this method on a larger database of PBRs.

The coefficient of restitution can be different in opposite directions, as seen especially for rocks 2 and 3 in Figure 12, for which the peaks in the seismic record are not symmetric about zero. This may be indicative of nonequal slenderness angles and thus different energy loss in each direction of rocking. Because the coefficient of restitution is a measure of the energy loss during rocking, it may be possible to use the ratio of the amplitudes in the positive and negative rocking directions to determine the ratio between the slenderness angles when they are not symmetric.

Topographic amplification of ground motions

An additional factor that influences the fragility analysis for a PBR is topography because hills are well known to amplify ground shaking (e.g., Hough *et al.*, 2010; Barani *et al.*, 2014; Singh *et al.*, 2018; Modha *et al.*, 2019, 2020; Khan *et al.*, 2020; Rault *et al*, 2020; Yin *et al.*, 2021). In the case of Harkening Hill and Sharp Top Mountain, amplification is caused by the hills themselves and by the much larger Blue Ridge on which the hills are superimposed (Fig. 4i; e.g., Restrepo *et al.*, 2016; Weber *et al.*, 2022). The Blue Ridge reaches an elevation of just >1100 m at the Peaks of Otter from an elevation of just >250 m in the Piedmont province to the southeast, and the hills on which the PBRs lie rise ~340 m (Sharp Top Mountain) and 220 m (Harkening Hill) from the Blue Ridge Parkway in the valley between the hills (Fig. 4i).

The topographic amplifications at the PBR sites can be estimated based on modeling hills of various shapes (Singh *et al.*, 2018; Molina *et al.*, 2019; Modha *et al.*, 2019, 2020). These models characterize the hills using the slope ratio, which is the height divided by the half-width of the hill (H/L in Fig. 4i). The most direct implementation is that of Molina *et al.* (2019), who presented a simple regression of amplification versus slope ratio. This regression does not account for frequency, but the equations discussed by Singh *et al.* (2018) indicate that hills with the sizes of those at the Peaks of Otter produce amplifications in the frequency ranges that affect the rocks; the much broader Blue Ridge likely produces less amplification (smaller slope ratio) at longer periods than would be significant for our studies.

The regression based on slope ratio in Molina *et al.* (2019) indicates an amplification of ~1.21 for Harkening Hill (slope ratio of 0.22; Fig. 4i) and 1.31 for Sharp Top Mountain (slope ratio of 0.34). However, the plots in Modha *et al.* (2020) and the equations in Singh *et al.* (2018), both based on computer modeling, indicate higher amplifications of ~1.35 and 1.5, respectively, for the two hills. We therefore split the difference and estimate topographic amplification values of 1.28 for Harkening Hill and 1.41 for Sharp Top Mountain. We multiply all our modeled ground motions, both PGA and PGV, by these amplification factors for all of our calculations.

Another effect that could influence the results is site response, in that shallow soils with low shear-wave velocities can amplify seismic waves substantially relative to bedrock sites. However, the PBRs we studied are all resting on bedrock knobs that appear to be part of the underlying bedrock structure, which implies that there is no amplification because of shallow soils.

Ages of fragility based on pedestal heights and ages of nearby rocks

We have not (yet) obtained samples of the rocks for dating of exposure ages (e.g., Balco *et al.*, 2011) because we wanted to determine whether the PBRs provide constraints on hazard analyses before carrying out a substantial geochronology effort. We find that the rocks are not fragile enough to significantly constrain ground motions from reasonable maximum earthquake magnitudes in nearby seismic zones, and we find their survival to be consistent with the NSHM, so we did not carry out dating at this point. We can, however, place crude constraints on their ages based on the heights of their pedestal rocks and dates on other rocks of similar lithology in the region. The formation model proposed by Bell *et al.* (1998) and Balco *et al.* (2011) and subsequently used by Rood *et al.* (2020) and Stirling *et al.* (2021) has the rocks (as pre-PBRs) gradually being exhumed as surrounding material is eroded downward and laterally in fractures. This means that the tops are exposed to cosmogenics first, and then the sides were gradually exposed as erosion continues downward. When the erosion level (and simultaneously the ground surface) reaches below the base (pedestal) of the rock, it is then assumed to have reached its present level of fragility, becoming a PBR.

Erosion continues and progressively exposes more of the underlying pedestal rock on which the PBR rests. We hypothesize that the heights of the pedestal rocks, if we know an average erosion rate, should give a crude estimate of the time that has passed since the base of the PBR was exposed and thus the fragility age. For all of our PBRs, the pedestal rocks had smaller heights on the uphill as opposed to downhill sides of the rocks, presumably because the downhill side was eroding more rapidly because material was moved downhill away from the rock, whereas the uphill side was both accumulating and eroding material. We used the heights of the uphill side of the pedestal rock to estimate the ages based on regional erosion rates under the assumption that erosion on the downhill side will be rapid compared with regional rates.

Two studies have characterized erosion rates in the Blue Ridge. Duxbury *et al.* (2015) measured erosion rates in Shenandoah National Park, which lies ~40 km north of the Peaks of Otter but shares the same geologic setting and similar bedrock lithologies. They found erosion rates for bedrock to be 0.18–1.1 cm/ka, with an average of ~0.65 cm/ka. Linari *et al.* (2017) measured erosion rates on the Blue Ridge to the south of our study area. They found faster erosion rates of ~14.1 cm/ka. This faster erosion rate may be a more reasonable estimate for PBR formation because the PBRs presumably first were prominent pillars, and the material being eroded away is presumably softer than the bedrock cores that remain to form the PBRs. Using the pedestal heights from the uphill sides of the PBRs and the more conservative erosion rate of Linari *et al.* (2017), meaning the faster erosion rate that gives the youngest ages, we estimate the fragility ages based on pedestal heights to be in the 32–84 ka range for the rocks and only 32–45 ka for the more fragile rocks 3 and 4 with shorter pedestals. These are approximately consistent with exposure ages obtained on 11 rocks in the Blue Ridge near our PBRs (Fame *et al.*, 2023), which had ages of 17–43 ka with a cluster at 17–30 ka. These latter ages correspond to the Last Glacial Maximum (middle Marine Isotope Stage [MIS] 3 through MIS 2), which led Fame *et al.* (2023) to hypothesize that the freeze–thaw cycles in periglacial times enhanced frost cracking and thus fracturing of rocks. They attribute this effect with enhancing the detachment of boulders from bedrock, but the mechanism might also apply to formation of PBRs. We note that other studies of PBRs formed by erosion generally show fragility ages of 17–45 ka and sometimes greater (e.g., Rood *et al.*, 2020; Stirling *et al.*, 2021), suggesting a possible association to the cooler climate even in much different environments to that of the eastern United States. These efforts to correlate regional observations with our rocks provide us with ages across a large time range (17–84 ka) for our PBR fragilities. Considering all observations, with an emphasis on the shorter pedestals beneath the more fragile PBRs, an age range of 20–40 ka could be a reasonable working estimate.

Thus, to address this uncertainty, we analyze our PBRs assuming a fragility age range of 20–40 ka. To do this, we use an age of 30 ka for comparison purposes between methods, but we use ages of 20, 30, and 40 ka in our comparisons with the NSHM hazard curves to see whether the PBRs are consistent with those curves. We also compute the ages of the rocks that result in a 5% chance of survival based on the NSHM assumptions, as other researchers have done (Baker *et al.*, 2013; Rood *et al.*, 2020).

FRAGILITY AND GROUND-MOTION ANALYSES AND RESULTS

Rock fragilities

The simplest method for estimating the strength of ground shaking needed to topple a PBR comes from Anooshehpoor *et al.* (2004), with the acceleration ("quasi-static overturning [toppling] force") needed to begin rocking as

$$a = g * \tan(\alpha) = g * (b/h), \quad (2)$$

in which g is acceleration due to gravity; α is the slenderness angle (generally the smaller one); and b and h are the width of the PBR's base and height to the center of mass, respectively (Fig. 3). Klaboe *et al.* (2018) found that this equation (equivalent to their equation 3) correctly predicted overturning for 83% of the rocks in their shake table tests. However, empirical studies by Anooshehpoor *et al.* (2004) showed the acceleration from equation (1) to be near the minimum acceleration needed to topple the rocks (their figs. 14 and 15), with a regression line fit to their empirical data giving a more conservative estimate of toppling acceleration of

$$a = 1.3 * g * \tan(\alpha). \quad (3)$$

At this acceleration, their graph suggests that ~50% of the rocks would topple (fig. 15 in Anooshehpoor *et al.*, 2004).

PGA is a relatively unreliable predictor of overturning because it is dominated by high frequencies, but rock toppling is heavily dependent on pulse duration (e.g., Purvance *et al.*, 2008; Trugman *et al.*, 2023). The probability of toppling is now more commonly estimated from the equations in Purvance *et al.* (2008) that include a second measure of ground motions that correlates better with the predominant pulse duration. Their equations (with one of the coefficients corrected in Rood *et al.*, 2020), derived from regressions on results from shake table tests and computer modeling, can be used to estimate toppling probability from a combination of PGA and the PGV/PGA ratio or spectral accelerations at 1 or 2 s period (SA_1/PGA or SA_2/PGA) (Purvance *et al.*, 2008). These equations, which also allow for asymmetric rocks with different slenderness angles on each side, can be used to construct fragility matrices showing the probability of the rocks toppling at different combinations of PGA and PGV/PGA (Fig. 13).

For our PBRs, we computed the fragility matrices using ground motions adjusted for topographic amplification. The PGAs listed on the horizontal axes of the matrices in Figure 13 (and the equivalent plots in the supplemental material, available to this article) are the input PGAs at the base of the hills (i.e., no topographic amplification). The probabilities of toppling at these PGAs, however, were computed after multiplying the PGA by the topographic amplification. Thus, the PGAs used to compute the probabilities in the fragility matrices are larger than those listed on the x axes, which effectively shifts the fragility matrix to lower PGAs (to the left). The vertical axis with the PGV/PGA ratio is not changed by topographic amplification because both PGV and PGA presumably undergo about the same amplification.

After these matrices were computed, the fragilities of the rocks were examined in four distinct ways to gain insights about maximum past ground motions and to constrain plausible nearby maximum earthquake magnitudes. The first three of these methods are newly introduced in this study: (1) plotting scenario earthquakes from nearby seismic zones onto the fragility matrices, (2) mapping maximum magnitudes of earthquakes that could occur in the region without toppling the rocks with different probabilities of certainty, (3) estimating the chances of the PBR surviving in a precarious position given the disaggregations in the NSHM, and (4) comparing the fragility with NSHM hazard curves using the method of McPhillips and Pratt (2024) following Baker *et al.* (2013) and Rood *et al.* (2020).

Fragility plots with scenario earthquakes

One way to visualize the results is to add scenario earthquakes to the fragility matrices. Trugman *et al.* (2023) plotted a specific earthquake model on a fragility plot to understand why a PBR near a fault did not topple, but here we plot a range of models to see which magnitudes could topple the PBRs. Figure 13 shows the fragility matrices for all four PBRs using the Purvance *et al.* (2008) equations for asymmetric slenderness angles. Added to the plots are symbols at the PGA and PGV/PGA ratio combinations calculated at the PBR sites for earthquakes of M_w 5.5–8.5 near the location of the 2011 Mineral, Virginia, earthquake in the CVSZ and for a location near the center of the GCSZ (labeled in Fig. 13a). Earthquakes near Sparta, North Carolina, are about the same distance as the CVSZ, so they would have similar values. Plots like these provide an effective way to show the maximum magnitudes that likely can occur on a specific fault or within a specific seismic zone without toppling a PBR. The ranges of uncertainty for the

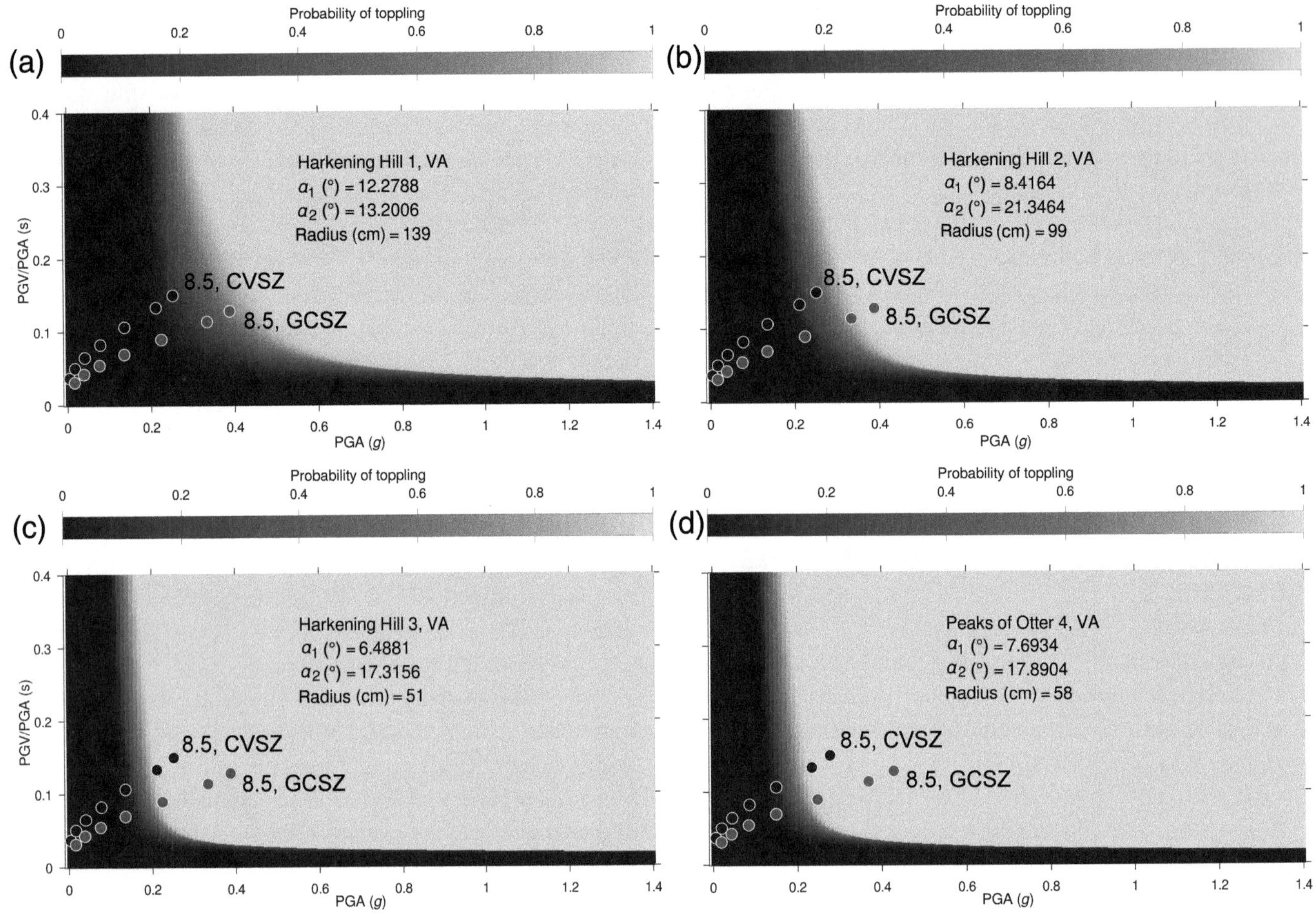

Figure 13. (a–d) Fragility matrices for rocks 1–4, with PGA and PGV/PGA pairs from M 5.5 to 8.5 earthquakes (in half-magnitude steps) in the CVSZ and GCSZ shown as dots. The most fragile rocks are 3 and 4, which have similar fragilities. The dots indicate that it would take an $M_w\sim \geq 7.5$ in the CVSZ and about an $M_w\sim \geq 7.2$ in the GCSZ to have a large chance of topping rocks 3 and 4. Rock 1 is the most stable, with an M_w 8–8.5 earthquake in the GCSZ needed to have a reasonable chance to topple it. The color version of this figure is available only in the electronic edition.

PGA and the PGV/PGA ratio using the standard deviations of the ground-motion models (GMMs) could be added as error bars on the points, although it is not done here because that is only one of several uncertainties in the analyses.

The scenario earthquakes are assumed to be on upper crustal faults with a dip of 50°, which is consistent with known earthquakes in the eastern United States. This dip is similar to the 49.5° dip of the fault plane for the 2011 Mineral, Virginia, earthquake (McNamara, Benz, *et al.*, 2014); the 59° dip of the fault that caused the 2020 Sparta, North Carolina, earthquake (Figueiredo *et al.*, 2022; Neves *et al.*, 2024); the 32°–45° dip inferred for the preferred nodal plane of the 2024 Tewksbury, New Jersey, earthquake (Han *et al.*, 2024); and the ~43° dip interpreted for the 1886 Charleston, South Carolina, earthquake (Chapman *et al.*, 2016; Pratt *et al.*, 2025). Fault planes with 10 km widths and the upper ends of ruptures at 2 km depth were used, which also are broadly consistent with the depths of the earthquakes listed earlier.

Because we are using the query tool from the NSHM to compute PGA and PGV, we use the same weighted average of multiple central and eastern U.S. GMMs as in the 2023 NSHM (Petersen *et al.*, 2024). The NSHM provides standard deviations on the ground motions, but for this initial testing of methodology, we use the mean PGA and PGV values from the NSHM. Using these values also keeps the results consistent with the NSHM itself, with all magnitudes being moment magnitudes (M_w).

Rock 1 is the most stable of our rocks. The fragility plot indicates that even a magnitude of 8.5 in the CVSZ is not likely to topple the rock, and it would require a magnitude 8–8.5 in the GCSZ to have a fair chance of toppling the rock (Fig. 13a). Rock 2 also is quite stable, requiring a magnitude 8.5 in the CVSZ to have a reasonable chance to topple the rock; magnitudes of 8–8.5 in the GCSZ have a high probability of toppling the rock, indicating that such events are unlikely to have occurred since the rock became fragile (Fig. 13b).

Rocks 3 and 4 are the most fragile of the PBRs we studied, and they showed similar results (Fig. 13c,d). The scenario earthquakes on the fragility matrices indicate that magnitudes between 7.5 and 8 in the CVSZ likely are needed to topple these rocks, and presumably it would take a similar magnitude near Sparta because it is at about the same distance as the CVSZ. The plots show that a magnitude between 7 and 7.5 in the GCSZ likely is needed to topple these rocks, again indicating that it is unlikely such an event has occurred since the rocks became fragile.

Maximum magnitude mapping

A drawback to plotting scenario earthquakes onto the fragility matrices is that they only provide information about ground motions from those earthquakes, which presumably would be scenario events modeled in a nearby seismic zone or fault. This information could be used to remove or reweight logic-tree branches associated with specific source zones (e.g., Stirling *et al.*, 2021).

One way to potentially extend the information from PBRs to the surrounding area is to map the earthquake magnitudes in the nearby region that would produce ground motions (combinations of PGAs and PGVs) that would topple the rocks at the probability level of interest (Fig. 14). Such maps provide an upper limit on nearby earthquakes, even those on unknown faults, blind faults, or faults thought to be inactive. To do this, we query the NSHM web tools for the PGV and PGA at the rock sites from earthquakes of different magnitudes at different radial distances, with fault parameters as described in the previous section. We multiplied the PGA and PGV by the topographic amplification at the PBR site before computing

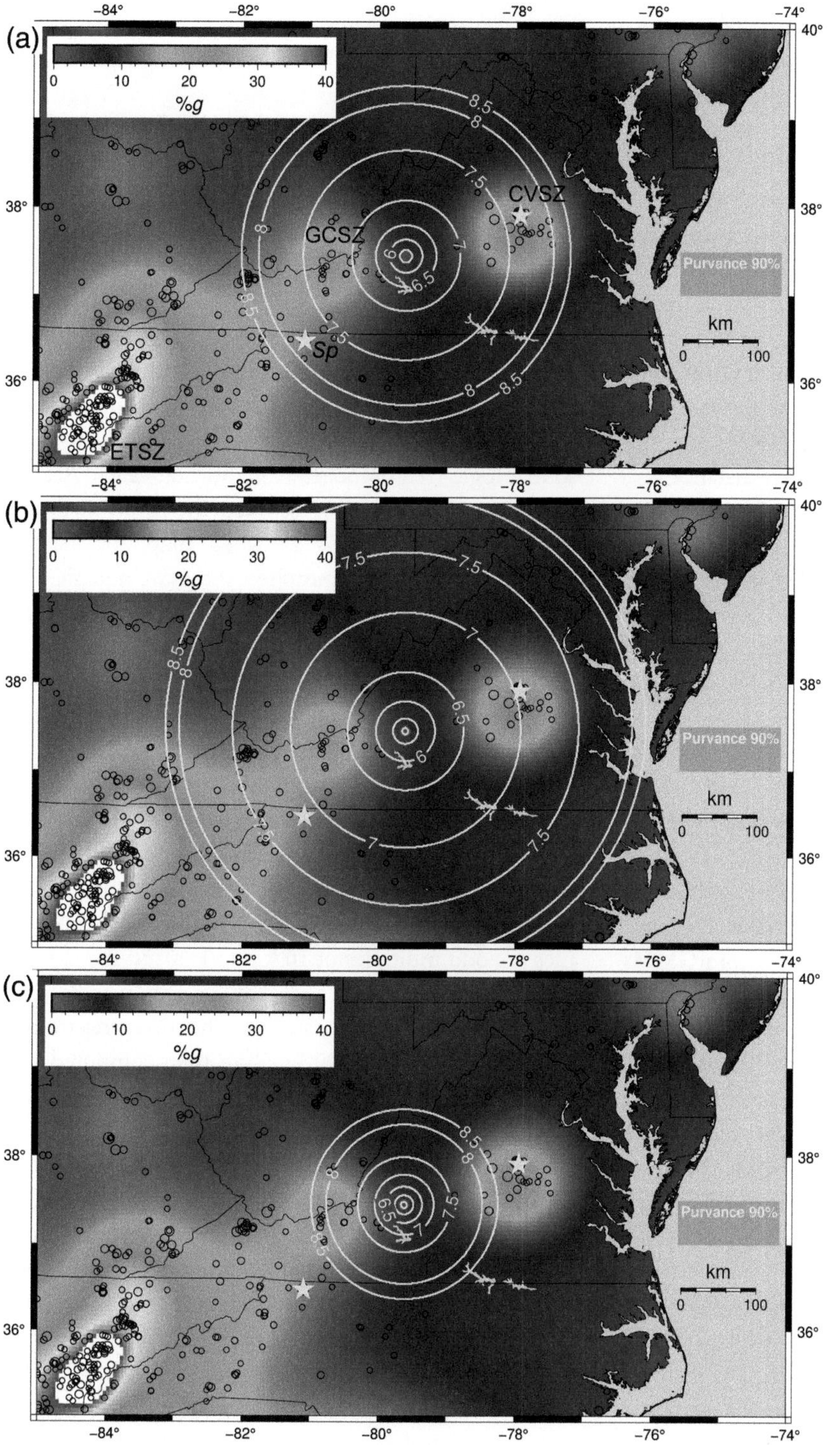

Figure 14. (a) Map of the mid-Atlantic region of the eastern United States with colored background being the National Seismic Hazard Model (NSHM) (peak ground acceleration [PGA] 2% probability in 50 yr) on top of which are plotted contours showing the maximum earthquake magnitude that likely could occur without toppling the most fragile of the rocks (rock 3) at the Peaks of Otter (dot at center of contours). Contours show the 90% chance of toppling the rock using the asymmetric equations in Purvance *et al.* (2008). The lighter colored areas in the background are the CVSZ (with a star at the location of the 2011 M_w 5.8 earthquake), the Giles County seismic zone (GCSZ), and the east Tennessee seismic zone (ETSZ); see Figure 1 for locations. The location of the 2020 M_w 5.1 Sparta earthquake in northwest North Carolina is shown as a star. The black circles are seismicity M > 2.5 since 1974 with the size of the circle proportional to the magnitude (USGS, 2017). (b,c) Same as (a) but computed using 1 standard deviation of the ground-motion models (GMMs) greater than and less than the mean value, respectively. The color version of this figure is available only in the electronic edition.

toppling probabilities using the Purvance *et al.* (2008) equations because the ground motions are estimated by the NSHM on a flat surface (i.e., at the base of the mountains and hills). An earthquake at each grid point on the map was assumed, and the magnitude increased until the ground motions reached a strength likely to topple the PBRs at the 90% probability level. The result is a map with concentric rings centered on the PBRs, with each ring being the locus of a maximum earthquake magnitude that likely could have occurred without toppling the rock. In this case, Figure 14 shows the result for the most precarious rock at the Peaks of Otter, rock 3, although rock 4 provides a nearly identical result. The contours are not equally spaced because the GMMs and the PGV/PGA ratio are not linearly correlated with distance.

Similar to the plotting of scenario earthquakes onto the fragility matrices, the magnitude maps indicate that an earthquake of magnitude 7.5–8.0 would be needed in the CVSZ to topple the PBR. A similar magnitude would be needed at Sparta to topple the rock, and a magnitude of ~7.0–7.5 is needed in the GCSZ. The NSHM also computes the standard deviation of the GMMs, and increasing the ground motions at the PBR site by the standard deviation of the GMM produces potential toppling magnitudes of ~7 in the CVSZ, ~6.5–7 for the GCSZ, and just >7 for Sparta (Fig. 14b). Decreasing PGA and PGV using the standard deviation of the GMM results in all of these seismic zones requiring magnitudes of ~8 (GCSZ) to >8.5 (CVSZ and Sparta) to topple the rock (Fig. 14c).

The magnitudes on the map made using the mean GMMs are well above the maximum magnitudes that are inferred to have occurred in the CVSZ and GCSZ in the past few thousand years, which is consistent with the PBRs' survival. Tuttle *et al.* (2021) estimated based on paleoliquefaction data that there have been either a pair of $M_w \sim 6$ to 6.25 earthquakes or a single $M_w \sim 6.25$ to 6.5 in the CVSZ in the past 2800 yr. Similarly, there was an estimated M_w 5.9 ($m_b \sim 5.8$) earthquake in the GCSZ in 1897 (Bollinger and Wheeler, 1988; Tarr and Wheeler, 2006), which is considerably smaller than the maximum magnitude predicted by the map in Figure 14. These maps are thus consistent with the rocks at the Peaks of Otter easily surviving the largest known earthquakes in these nearby seismic zones, but they additionally provide an upper limit of possible earthquakes over the much longer fragility ages of the PBRs. In addition to these seismic zones, however, the map excludes various sized earthquakes on unknown, blind, or assumed inactive faults throughout the surrounding region. The results also indicate that the recurrence times for earthquakes large enough to topple the rocks exceed the age of the rock's fragility, which is likely in the 20–40 ka range.

Because the magnitudes in the CVSZ needed to topple the PBRs substantially exceed the assumed maximum magnitude used in the NSHM (M_w 6.5) and the PBRs therefore do not provide significant constraints on the NSHM, we have not undertaken dating of these PBRs. PBRs that are more fragile or are nearer the seismic zones could be used to further evaluate constraints of magnitudes, but finding PBRs is challenging in forested areas such as the Blue Ridge of Virginia.

Probability of survival from magnitude-rupture distance pairs obtained from disaggregation

At each grid point in the NSHM, disaggregations show the magnitude–rupture distance (M-R) pairs that contribute to the PGA at the site (e.g., Fig. 15a). We can treat these M-R pairs as scenario earthquakes to calculate the probability that a PBR would survive this set of earthquakes. The method provides insights into the magnitudes and distances likely to topple or not topple the PBRs, in a manner similar to trimming source logic-tree branches (e.g., Stirling *et al.*, 2021).

For our analyses, we assumed the same earthquake fault parameters and GMMs as when mapping the maximum magnitudes, and we multiplied the PGA and PGV obtained independently from the NSHM toolbox by the topographic amplification. The results show the probabilities that each M-R pair in the disaggregation file will topple the rock (Fig. 15). High-magnitude nearby earthquakes have the highest probabilities of toppling a PBR.

We also need to know the probability of occurrence (i.e., recurrence time) for each M-R pair in the disaggregation files. To do this, we computed the area represented by each event by assuming it could occur anywhere within an annulus around the PBR site. Distances of events in the NSHM disaggregation files are odd multiples of 10 km (10, 30, 50 km, and so on), so we calculated the area of a circular region around the PBRs with a central radius equal to the disaggregation distance and a radial width of 20 km. We then computed the area of this annulus as a percent of the total area used to compute the Gutenberg–Richter (G-R) relation for the central and eastern United States (CEUS) in the NSHM and multiplied the result by the PBR sites' probability density function (PDF) of the smoothed seismicity, which provides the weighted proportion of the CEUS seismicity that occurs within 200 km of the site (Llenos *et al.*, 2024; fig. 2b in Petersen *et al.*, 2024). The result provides an estimate of the annual probability of the specific M-R pair occurring using the assumptions in the NSHM. We then calculated the probability that the PBR would survive to its present age based on the annual probability of each M-R pair toppling the PBR.

For the purposes of comparing these results with later analyses, we use a fragility age of 30,000 yr. The resulting probabilities of survival for the four PBRs at the Peaks of Otter (Fig. 15) range from 0 (rock 3) to ~0.87 (rock 1). These suggest that the two most fragile rocks have barely survived earthquakes in the region using the NSHM assumptions, and the two less fragile PBRs easily survived.

One potential limitation in these analyses is that the G-R relation and the NSHM PDF values are derived from the seismicity catalog and do not include earthquakes in specific

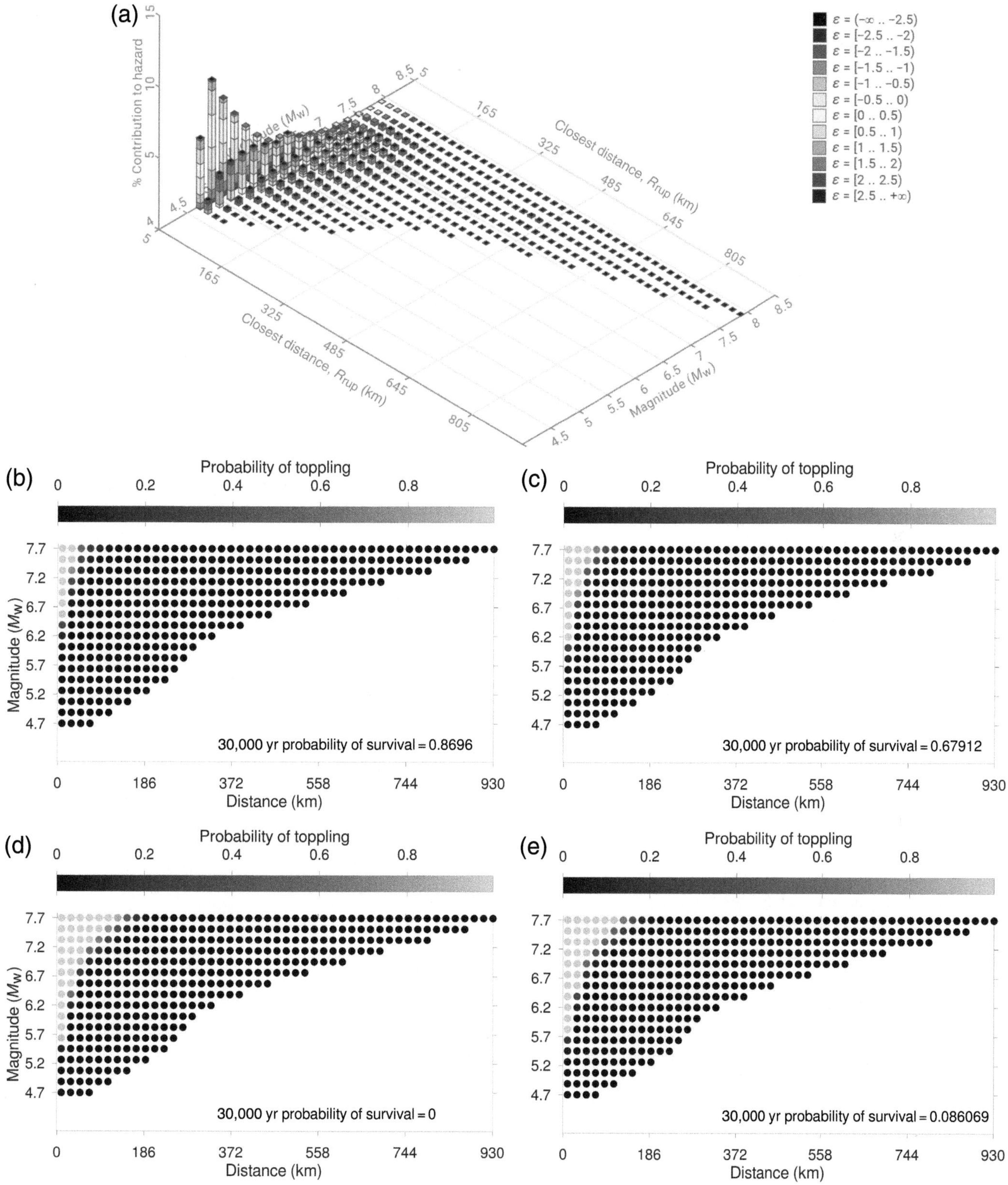

Figure 15. (a) Disaggregation file from the NSHM for Harkening Hill showing the relative contributions to the hazard represented by pairs of magnitude (M_w) versus rupture distance (R). (b–e) Probabilities that each of the M_w–R pairs in the disaggregation files will topple rocks 1–4, respectively. The nearby large-magnitude earthquakes are most likely to topple the PBRs. The labels in the bottoms of the graphs show the probabilities that each rock would survive for 30 ka if these M–R pairs are treated as scenario earthquakes and given the assumptions in the NSHM. These probabilities show that rocks 1 and 2 are stable (high probability of survival), whereas rocks 3 and 4 are much more fragile (low probability of survival). The color version of this figure is available only in the electronic edition.

source zones like the CVSZ. However, the total G-R relation for the CEUS incorporates all seismicity from the earthquake catalog, so it may already include seismicity from known source zones like the CVSZ. In our case, the maximum magnitude earthquake that the NSHM assumes in the CVSZ is M_w 6.5 (Petersen *et al.*, 2024), and an earthquake of this magnitude is unlikely to topple the PBRs at the Peaks of Otter (Figs. 13 and 14). The CVSZ source zone therefore does not affect the probabilities we are computing from the disaggregations. This may not be true in other locations, however, so individual source faults and zones may need to be addressed in those instances.

Another potential limitation is that we are assuming shallow crustal scenario earthquakes in our calculations of PGA and PGV, whereas the disaggregation events implicitly assume earthquakes with a wider variety of source parameters and depths. As we show later, the probabilities of toppling using this disaggregation method are higher (lower survival probability) than comparisons with the NSHM hazard curves, likely because of our choice of shallow earthquakes produces stronger ground motions than deeper earthquakes. Our estimates could further benefit from solving for the "average" source parameters that make the disaggregation results consistent with the NSHM comparisons.

Comparison with NSHM hazard curves

In this section, we show that the results from these PBRs are consistent with the NSHM, meaning they have a >5% chance of surviving given the assumptions in the NSHM. Rocks 1 and 2 are stable with a high probability of survival, but rocks 3 and 4 are only slightly more stable than is needed to survive for 40 ka given the assumptions in the NSHM. This is consistent with the disaggregation results just presented, although their survival probabilities are slightly different in the two methods.

We compute a scale factor for the branch-averaged NSHM hazard curve that is consistent with a 95% chance of a PBR's survival using the method outlined by Baker *et al.* (2013) and subsequently used by Rood *et al.* (2020) and McPhillips and Pratt (2024). This can be computed for any probability of survival, but 95% is chosen here to be consistent with these other studies. Figure 16 shows plots for this analysis using rock 4 as an example. Plots for the other rocks are included in the supplemental material.

The fragility matrix (Fig. 16b) provides the probabilities that PGA–PGV pairs will topple the PBR based on the regressions by Purvance *et al.* (2008) but adjusted for topographic amplification. We then use the regression in Abrahamson and Bhasin (2020) to estimate the PGV probability distribution for each PGA (Fig. 16d). To do this, we query the NSHM to obtain the average magnitudes, distances, and annual exceedances for earthquakes contributing to each PGA. The regression by Abrahamson and Bhasin (2020) then provides the corresponding average log(PGV) and standard deviation of log(PGV) for that PGA (i.e., it provides the distribution of PGVs corresponding to that PGA value). We scale the resulting log-normal distribution of PGVs at each PGA to be consistent with the annual exceedance of that PGA—that is, we set the sum of the PGV probabilities at each PGA to be the same as the derivative of the NSHM PGA exceedances. The result is the probability graph showing the annual probability for each combination of PGA and PGV/PGA (Fig. 16d).

The next step is to determine the vector fragility, which is the cumulative probability of a given PGA causing the rock to topple (Fig. 16e). This is computed by first multiplying the fragility matrix (Fig. 16b) by the annual probability of each PGA–PGV pair occurring (Fig. 16d). Summing the resulting probabilities for all values of PGV/PGA at each PGA and then adding the cumulative probability for the PGAs gives us the vector fragility (Fig. 16e). We can then use the mean and the 25% and 75% levels of the vector fragility to estimate the PGA values for which the PBR provides meaningful constraints. Note in Figure 16e and in similar plots for the other PBRs in the supplemental material that the mean PGAs in the vector fragility that will topple the rock are generally larger than the PGAs computed from the slenderness angles using equation (3), with the larger slenderness angle being closest to the mean value in the vector fragility curve or in this case being nearly the same. In some cases, equation (3) dramatically underestimates the toppling PGA compared with that in the vector fragility.

We then calculate a scale factor for the hazard curve that is consistent with a 95% chance of the PBR surviving, as described by Baker *et al.* (2013). This is done by computing the annual probability of all PGV–PGA pairs toppling the rock, which is the sum of all the products of the fragility matrix (Fig. 16b) times the PGV–PGA probability matrix (Fig. 16d). Equation (4) by Baker *et al.* (2013) can then be used to compute the scale factor (β) that would make the hazard curve consistent with the PBR, with β for an age of 30 ka being labeled in the top right of Figure 16f. We used an age of 30 ka when computing the scale factor, but we do not know the true age of fragility.

Because we do not have strong constraints on the ages of the PBRs at the Peaks of Otter, we scaled the hazard curve for a range of fragility ages, specifically 20, 30, and 40 ka. These are shown as dashed lines in Figure 16f, with the highest one being 20 ka and the lowest one being 40 ka. All of them plot above the NSHM hazard curve, indicating that the PBR is consistent with the hazard curve if the age of fragility is in this range.

The final steps we take are to compute the probability that the PBR would survive using equation (2) in Baker *et al.* (2013), given an age of 30 ka and the annual probability of failure. In principle, this probability of survival should approximately match the probability of survival determined from the disaggregation analysis (Fig. 16c) and for nearly all of the PBRs that we have tested the results are within 15% of each other, generally with the disaggregation estimate having a smaller

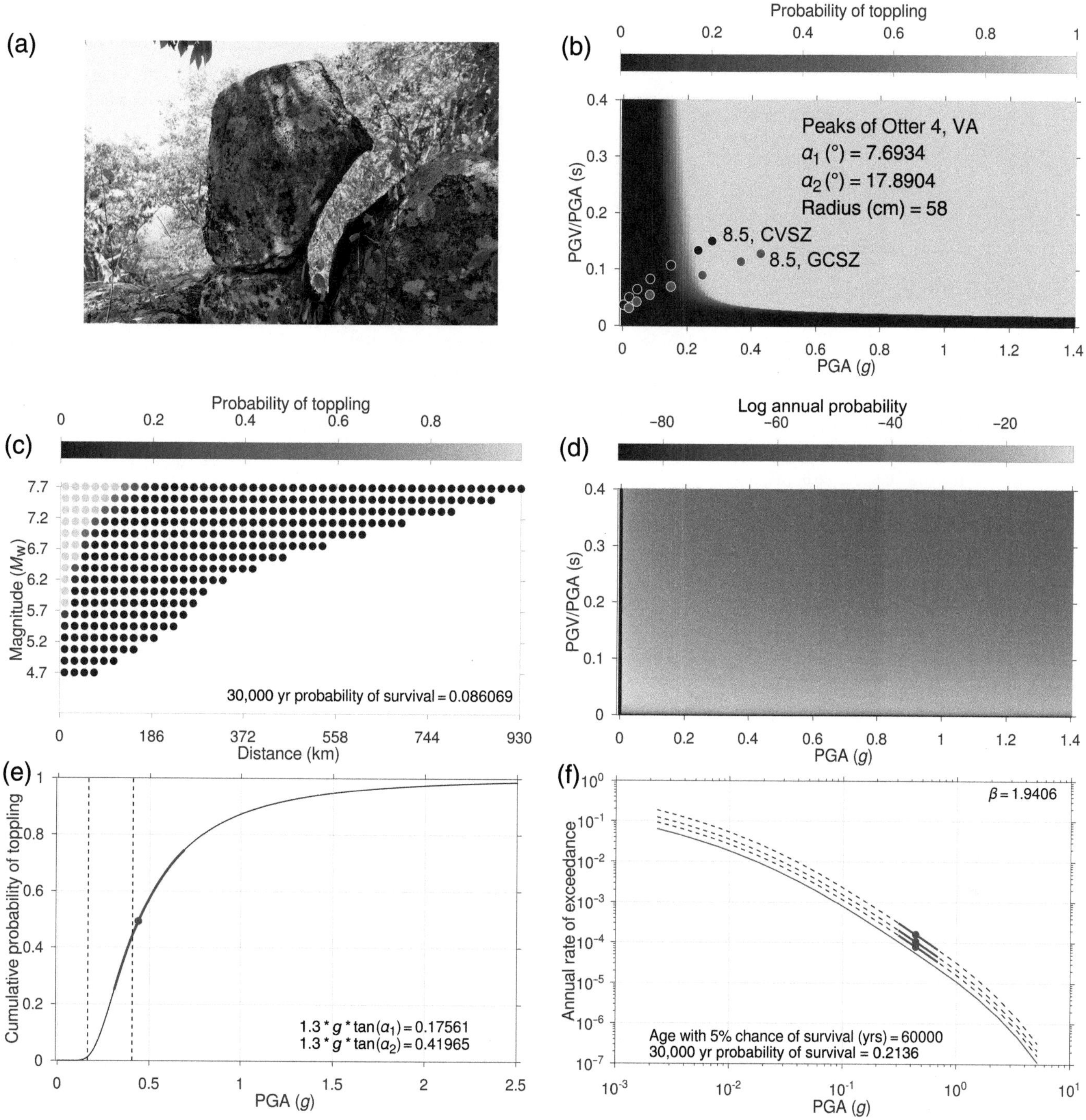

Figure 16. Full fragility analyses for one of the more precarious rocks (rock 4). (a) Photo of rock 4. (b) Fragility matrix with scenario earthquakes in the CVSZ and GCSZ shown as dots (as in Fig. 13). (c) Probability that each M–R pair in the NSHM disaggregation file will topple the rock. (d) Log of the annual probability for each PGA and PGV–PGA pair in the eastern United States as estimated using the regression in Abrahamson and Bhasin (2020). (e) Vector fragility curve showing the cumulative probability of toppling for each value of PGA. The thick portion of the curve is the 25%–75% range, and the dot is the mean value. (f) NSHM hazard curve as solid line, and dashed lines show the adjusted hazard curves representing a 5% chance of survival for rock ages of 20 ka (top), 30 ka (center), and 40 ka (bottom). The solid portions of these curves and the dots correspond to the PGA values in panel (e). On the lower part of the graph is listed the age at which the rock would have a 5% chance of survival and the probability the rock would survive for 30 ka given the assumptions in the NSHM. The color version of this figure is available only in the electronic edition.

chance of survival. This latter observation may be because of our assuming shallow earthquakes with above-average ground motions in the disaggregation analyses, as explained in the previous section. In the case of rock 4 (Fig. 16), the disaggregation analysis predicts that the rock has an ~9% chance of surviving for 30 ka, whereas the vector fragility indicates an

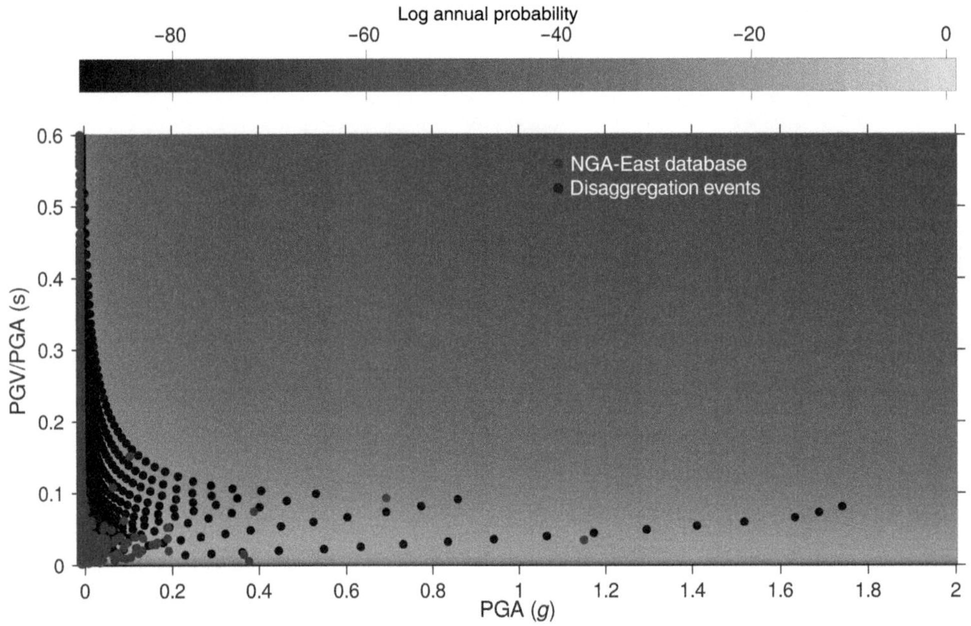

Figure 17. Plot of the log(annual probability) of PGV/PGA versus PGA pairs at the rock site using the Abrahamson and Bhasin (2020) regression (refer to explanation in text). Plotted as dots are the data points from the Next Generation Attenuation (NGA)-East database and the disaggregation *M–R* events from one of the rock sites. The color version of this figure is available only in the electronic edition.

~21% chance of survival. We also compute the age of the PBR that would be consistent with a 5% chance of survival (Fig. 16f). For rock 4, this age is 60 ka, and for rock 3, this age is 47 ka. The ages giving a 5% chance of survival compared with the chances of surviving for 30 ka show the high standard that a 5% chance of survival imposes on a hazard assessment.

The results for our most fragile PBR, rock 3, indicates that it would survive for ~47 ka years in its fragile position using the assumptions in the NSHM, but it has only about a 14% chance of surviving for 30 ka. This is consistent with the 40 ka curve lying just above the NSHM hazard curve (Fig. S3).

DISCUSSION

Ages of the PBRs

This pilot study was undertaken primarily to refine the field and analysis methods we are using to study PBRs in the eastern United States and as an initial screening of the PBRs to determine whether any are fragile enough to merit the time and expense for dating. The dating methodology described by Balco *et al.* (2011) requires multiple samples being taken from various points on the PBR, so hopefully, more time and cost-effective methods can be identified to estimate PBR fragility ages. The fragility ages of our PBRs may be too young to be used for testing the hazard curves, in which large magnitude earthquakes and strong ground motions are estimated to occur on timescales of tens of thousands of years.

One of the goals of our larger project, however, is to constrain ground motions in the northeastern United States where most of the PBRs are erratics that were set in place as the Laurentide ice sheet retreated since ~21.8–13 ka ago (Balco and Schaefer, 2006; Barth *et al.*, 2019). An initial result using a small subsection of the PBRs we have studied in the Adirondack Mountains and northern Vermont is described by McPhillips and Pratt (2024), and a study of PBRs in New Hampshire, eastern Massachusetts, and western Maine is described by Stirling and Pratt (2026). The ice sheet largely scraped the landscape clean in many places, with some of the bedrock surfaces beneath the PBRs showing glacial striations. The age of the ice retreat likely provides a reliable constraint on the length of time that the PBRs have been in position because nearly all of them are on bedrock knobs or hills that would quickly shed any outwash deposits that might stabilize the PBRs by burying their bases. Rocks in New York and New England are near several seismic zones and near the sites of past earthquakes, such as the 1638 New Hampshire and 1755 Cape Anne earthquakes (Ebel, 2006; Ebel and Starr, 2018; Pratt and Ebel, 2025) and a number of notable earthquakes in the Adirondack Mountains and nearby St. Lawrence River Valley (Fig. 1; Seeber *et al.*, 2002; Viegas *et al.*, 2010). Studying PBRs in New England, New York, and northern New Jersey therefore may provide insights into the upper limits of long-term ground motions from moderate to great earthquakes in postglacial times in this generally seismically quiet region.

Probability of PGV–PGA pairs in the CEUS

One potential source of uncertainty in our analyses is the annual probability of specific PGA–PGV pairs occurring in the CEUS, as expressed in Figure 16d. This plot was made using the Abrahamson and Bhasin (2020) conditional ground-motion model, which is based on a regression of earthquake records primarily from California. It is not clear how much different a regression based on CEUS data would be. It also is not clear that there are enough data to produce a reliable regression for the CEUS. Figure 17 shows relationships from the Next Generation Attenuation East (NGA-East) data set plotted on the Abrahamson and Bhasin (2020) data, as well as PGA–PGV pairs from one of the disaggregation files at our PBR site. Both of these latter sets of points appear superficially to be consistent with the results from the Abrahamson and Bhasin (2020) probabilities, in that they are concentrated in the lower left and bottom in which the highest probabilities are expected. There are not enough observations in the NGA-East database to make a reliable regression, however, so any CEUS regression would need to be based primarily on computer simulations.

There is one partial test of the Abrahamson and Bhasin (2020) regression for the CEUS that indicates it may be approximately correct. The probabilities of survival of the PBRs based on the disaggregation M–R pairs (e.g., Fig. 16c) use probabilities of occurrence from the CEUS Gutenberg–Richter relation as described by Llenos *et al.* (2024) and Petersen *et al.* (2024). The probabilities of survival computed based on the probabilities of PGA–PGV pairs from the Abrahamson and Bhasin (2020) regression (Fig. 16f) give similar results, indicating general agreement. The approximate agreement of the Abrahamson and Bhasin (2020) probabilities with the disaggregation M-R pairs indicate that the probabilities are not an unreasonable estimate for the eastern United States despite the probabilities being derived from a regression on western U.S. ground motions.

Utility of placing seismometers on PBRs

This article has shown the utility of placing seismometers on PBRs to potentially make three measurements: (1) the frequency of rocking; (2) the direction of rocking, at least for small tilt angles; and (3) the distance between the edges of the contact surface in the direction of rocking based on the coefficient of restitution. The push tests also provide data for testing future computer models of the PBRs being subjected to input ground motions.

The frequency of rocking determined from the seismometer tests provides information for comparison with ground motions. Rocking increases in frequency as the tilt angle gets smaller, so the frequencies measured at the small tilt angles in the push tests or with ambient noise presumably are an upper limit for the frequencies of rocking that could topple the PBR. Knowing the highest frequency of rocking could be used in constraining models of rocking and for estimating the frequencies of ground motion that would be relevant for toppling the PBR.

The rocking directions determined from the seismometer tests allow for identification of the key edges on which rocking likely occurs, which helps better interpret the information in the point clouds. However, some rocks may have multiple rocking points, with secondary rocking points or a nonflat base controlling the rocking directions at greater tilt angles (e.g., Anooshehpoor *et al.*, 2004; Wittich *et al.*, 2018). The initial rocking from the push tests helps determine the immediate edge of the contact surface when rocking is initiated. In principle, this preferred direction of rocking could also be used to determine the direction of ground shaking most likely to topple the rock, although for most PBR studies, a dominant direction for the ground motions is not assumed because the source parameters (fault orientations) and azimuths cannot be predicted with certainty.

The seismometer results can also be used in the determination of the slenderness angles and from these the widths of the bases using the coefficients of restitution. This raises the possibility that a seismometer placed on a rock, combined with the height of the center of mass from a 3D model (even a crude one), are all that is needed to estimate the fragility. For our present calculations, we assume that the slenderness angles are symmetric as in Anooshehpoor *et al.* (2004), which would not be the case if the center of mass is not midway between the edges of the contact surface. The coefficient of restitution method may be giving an "effective" width to the contact surface that may be more accurate for the fragility analyses than widths derived from the point clouds or other measurements. It may be possible to use the coefficients of restitution in each rocking direction to estimate the ratios of the slenderness angles in both directions.

The seismometer measurements also provide constraints for understanding the dynamic response of PBRs and to calibrate computer models of the rocks, given that the seismometer records are directly related to their physical dimensions (e.g., Housner, 1963; Shi *et al.*, 1996; Anooshehpoor *et al.*, 2004). In this study, the locations and strengths of the pushes were not recorded, but our current practice of measuring these in subsequent studies could allow for a more quantitative analyses of the rocking.

A field methodology that we have now adopted that should help with future modeling of PBRs is to record both the positions of the seismometers, which can be determined from the photogrammetry 3D models made while the seismometer is mounted on the PBR, and the locations and strengths of the pushes. We have now been pushing the rocks with a hiking staff held horizontally, generally pushing on the centers of our scale bars so that we know the locations in the 3D models. To measure the strengths of the pushes, we use a luggage scale turned sideways to "pull" the hiking staff toward the rock so that the luggage scale records the strength of the push to which the PBR was subjected.

Use of a second intensity measure in estimates of fragility

The plots like those in Figure 16e show the differences between fragility estimates made with the single intensity measure $\mathrm{PGA} = 1.3 * g * \tan(\alpha)$ versus the fragility when estimated using a combination of PGA and PGV/PGA ratio as defined by Purvance *et al.* (2008). In all cases, the single intensity measure using the smaller slenderness angle substantially underestimates the PGA at which a PBR is likely to topple compared with using the vector fragility curves constructed using the Purvance *et al.* (2008) equations (e.g., Fig. 16e). The vector fragilities, in fact, suggest that a single measure using the larger of the slenderness angles is more accurate than using the smaller slenderness angle, although it still often results in an underestimate of the toppling PGA.

Sizes of PBRs

The PBRs we have identified to date are almost all large—several m in their larger dimension, though they are all within the size limits tested in the Purvance *et al.* (2008) article. The size distribution of our PBRs likely is not a coincidence—smaller rocks may have been knocked over by more moderate earthquakes or have been pushed over by humans. However, smaller rocks also would not gain as much attention as larger rocks and therefore are not likely to be listed in books on rock formations or found in internet searches. Smaller rocks therefore may be present across the eastern United States, but finding them would involve extensive searching. In our fieldwork associated with this study and related studies (McPhillips and Pratt, 2024; Stirling and Pratt, 2026), we investigated a substantial area without seeing many smaller PBRs like rock number 4 in this study.

Accuracy of contact surface measurements

For rocks that have the highest fragility, meaning the narrowest slenderness angles, even small changes in the widths of the contact surfaces or locations of the centers of mass can have a large impact on the hazard calculations. For larger slenderness angles, this is not as crucial because a few percent change in the width of the contact surface does not appreciably change the hazard calculations. For small slenderness angles and for PBRs with the centers of mass near one edge, however, even a 1 or 2 cm difference in the widths of the contact surfaces can make the difference between a rock being consistent with the hazard curves or not. Our rock 3, for example, has the center of mass only 5.8 cm from the nearest rocking edge. Changing this distance by 1 cm, or ~17%, makes a substantial difference in the fragility calculations. For particularly fragile rocks, therefore, an accurate determination of the slenderness angles would be required. Although the point clouds we are interpreting likely are more accurate than earlier estimates made using a limited number of points (e.g., Anooshehpoor *et al.*, 2004; Rood *et al.*, 2020; Stirling *et al.*, 2021), it can still be difficult to accurately measure the widths of the contact surfaces. By definition, the points in the photogrammetry or lidar models are some distance outside of the actual contact surfaces, with only occasional points being located at the precise edge.

Measuring the circumference of the contact surface using a wrapped wire helps tremendously but still leaves some uncertainty. Accurately defining the edges of the contact surfaces can be especially difficult if they are in deep recesses beneath the PBR where shadows make imaging them difficult. We attempted wrapping a thin wire or rope with brightly painted sections around the contact surface so that the camera would have clear "targets" to triangulate on during the photogrammetry. Making these targets large enough to be clearly visible in the photos requires a relatively thick wire or rope, however, which means it cannot reach all the way into narrower crevasses.

One potential way to improve measurements of the contact surface would be to envelope the contact surface in a foam that could be sprayed or poured around the base of the PBR and that could then solidify into a foam pad that could be removed without damaging the PBR, leaving an imprint of the contact surface that could be more accurately measured. Combined with the photogrammetry point cloud, this could be another way of accurately measuring the edges of the contact surface.

Applicability of fragility estimates from shake table tests

One concern is that the shapes of some of our PBRs are not similar to the tall and slender PBRs and rectangular blocks used to derive the Purvance *et al.* (2008) regression. The test rocks used to determine the regression were selected to be precarious, which generally means that the specimens were relatively tall and slender and were resting on the flat surface of a shake table.

In contrast, some of the balanced rocks at the Peaks of Otter and many of the other rocks in the eastern United States are relatively wide rocks sitting on narrow pedestals (e.g. Figs. 2b,d and 4c). Many of the PBRs therefore often have the "opposite" geometry than those tested on shake tables, in that they are wide rocks resting on a narrow base rather than a narrow rock resting on a wide base (the shake table). A wider rock could take greater acceleration to knock over than a thinner, taller rock with the same slenderness angles because the moment of inertia of the wider rock would be greater because of its greater width. Although the rock radius provides a partial measure of the moment of inertia in the Purvance *et al.* (2008) equations, rocks with the same radius and slenderness could have much different widths and inertial properties, which could affect the fragility in the same way that a tight-rope walker uses a weighted pole to help with balance. It therefore is not clear how well the rocks tested on shake tables, and the resulting Purvance *et al.* (2008) regressions, represent the fragility of wider rocks resting on small pedestals.

The result is that the probabilities of overturning many of the eastern U.S. rocks in our analyses are derived using differently shaped rocks, so it is not entirely clear how accurately the fragility analyses apply to rocks like our rock 3 or for many other rocks in the eastern United States. Shake table tests on wide rocks resting on narrow pedestals or computer modeling of such PBRs could also be used to compare fragilities with those of the slender rocks that have been tested. An additional solution would be creating accurate computer models of the responses of the PBRs to ground motions (e.g., Veeraraghavan *et al.*, 2020; Chen *et al.*, 2024) from which the fragilities can be tested.

Capturing uncertainties

The methods we outline here can have large uncertainties that we have largely ignored in this presentation of methods. There are uncertainties in the GMMs, which the NSHM captures to some extent with the standard deviations of ground motions (e.g., Fig. 14), and there are potentially large ranges in the source parameters we used when computing ground motions from scenario earthquakes or mapping earthquake magnitudes around a PBR. The ground motions with ±1 standard deviation could be computed, and scenario earthquakes with a broad range of source parameters could be used. Incorporating at least some of these uncertainties would allow for more elaborate analyses than we have done here. The primary intent of this article is to describe the methodologies that can be used in the eastern United States; a more thorough analysis of constraints a PBR places on a specific source zone could include improved characterization of these uncertainties.

Future analyses

A next step in this work in the central and southern Appalachians could be to search for and analyze additional PBRs at the Peaks of Otter and along the Appalachian Mountain range closer to the major seismic zones. For example, we have not explored the third hill at the Peaks of Otter, Flat Top Mountain (Fig. 4j), and we have not thoroughly searched Harkening Hill and Sharp Top Mountain outside of rocks easily visible from the main hiking trails. There thus may be more fragile PBRs in the area that could be added to this study. There likely are PBRs elsewhere along the ~880-km-long Blue Ridge and the Appalachian Mountains in general, but so far internet searches have only identified a few that may merit investigation (Fig. 1). PBRs near the enigmatic east Tennessee seismic zone could be especially useful for improving understanding of eastern United States hazards given the lack of information about that seismic zone.

The analyses in this article are part of a pilot project for PBR studies in the eastern United States. The ability to collect 3D models and determine the locations of the centers of mass and the moments of inertia from these models and the details about the shapes of the contact surfaces could allow for computer modeling of the rocks when subjected to specific earthquake ground motions. For example, Veeraraghavan *et al.* (2017) modeled a PBR at Echo Cliffs, California, using a 3D model similar to those provided by the photogrammetry used here, and Veeraraghavan *et al.* (2020) investigated the more general problem of objects toppling during rocking.

So far these modeling efforts have evaluated objects with a single contact surface, but a number of rocks in the eastern United States have more complex systems such as the tripod base to rock 1. Other rocks such as Dinosaur Rock in Pennsylvania and Tripod Rock in New Jersey, for example, consist of large rocks resting on multiple smaller rocks (photos readily available in online searches). Development of software could be used to model the responses of these rock systems to ground motions.

Many PBRs in the eastern United States are simple rock-on-pedestal or rock-on-flat-surface systems for which it is possible to estimate the fragility, and they can be modeled with existing methods. Seismicity rates in the eastern United States are relatively low in comparison with seismically active areas like California (e.g., Stirling and Pratt, 2026), and this sparse seismicity increases the importance of using the paleoseismic record to look further back in time. Paleoliquefaction and lake paleoseismology studies have been effective at constraining ground motions for thousands of years and providing dates of prehistoric earthquakes (e.g., Monecke *et al*, 2018; Tuttle *et al.*, 2021), but balanced rocks like those at the Peaks of Otter have the potential to constrain limiting ground motions for similar or longer time periods.

Purvance *et al.* (2008) versus Dimitrakopoulos and Paraskeva (2015) equations

In addition to the Purvance *et al.* (2008) equations that we used to estimate toppling probability, Dimitrakopoulos and Paraskeva (2015) present an alternative formulation for toppling of engineered structures. This formulation has been applied to PBRs (e.g., Wittich *et al.*, 2018), with the advantage that the Dimitrakopoulos and Paraskeva (2015) equation is simpler than the Purvance *et al.* (2008) formulation. Having two different sets of equations raises the question of how they compare with each other and thus how well results from the two formulations match.

We tested Dimitrakopoulos and Paraskeva (2015, their equation 24) with their preferred intensity measures PGA/$(g * \tan(\alpha))$ and p*PGV/PGA, with $p = \sqrt{(3g/4R_1)}$ from the right side of their figure 2, and $\lambda = 1.49$, $\mu = 0.19$, and $\beta = 0.14$ as shown on the right panel in their figure 12b. They use only a single slenderness angle because they assume that engineered structures would be symmetric, so we computed the probabilities for a scenario PBR with a single slenderness angle (i.e., symmetric angles). Results show that the Dimitrakopoulos and Paraskeva (2015) equation is more conservative than the Purvance *et al.* (2008) equation, meaning that it takes stronger ground motions to topple a PBR (Fig. 18). This is evident in the fragility matrices (Fig. 18a,b) but is best observed in the vector fragility curves, in which the Dimitrakopoulos and Paraskeva (2015) curve lies to the right (higher PGA) of that derived from the Purvance *et al.* (2008) equations (Fig. 18c). Both vector fragilities indicate stronger PGAs than the simple $1.3 * g * \tan(\alpha)$ relation.

The more conservative estimate for toppling probability likely results from the Dimitrakopoulos and Paraskeva (2015) equation being derived for engineered structures with symmetric slenderness angles and flat bases, whereas the Purvance *et al.* (2008) regression is based in part on empirical results for PBRs with nonflat bases and a variety of shapes.

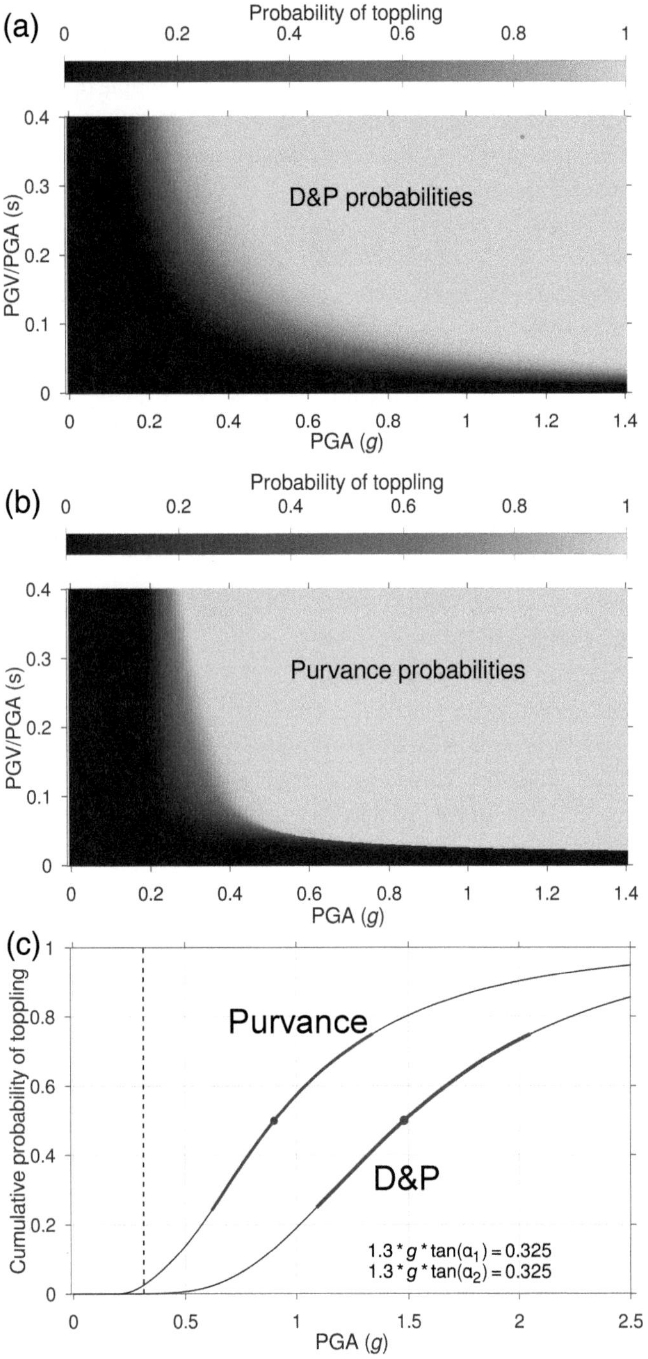

Figure 18. Comparison of Dimitrakopoulos and Paraskeva (2015) (D&P) and Purvance *et al.* (2008) fragilities calculated for a hypothetical PBR with equal slenderness angles. (a) Fragility matrix using the equations in Dimitrakopoulos and Paraskeva (2015). (b) Fragility matrix using the equations in Purvance *et al.* (2008). (c) Vector fragilities using the two methods. Note that the PGAs needed to topple the rock are predicted to be larger when using the Dimitrakopoulos and Paraskeva (2015) equations. Both sets of equations indicate much higher PGAs are needed to topple the rocks compared with the simple $1.3 * g * \tan(\alpha)$ equation (vertical dashed line for equal α angles). The color version of this figure is available only in the electronic edition.

Anooshehpoor *et al.* (2004) and Wittich *et al.* (2018) showed that nonflat bases increase the probability of toppling compared with flat bases, which may be the main reason for the discrepancies.

We do not know the true toppling probabilities for our example PBRs, but the advantage of the Purvance *et al.* (2008) equation is that it is based in part on and thus verified by shake table tests of actual PBRs. We do not see much, if any, advantage in using the Dimitrakopoulos and Paraskeva (2015) equation for the purposes of analyzing PBRs, although it likely is a more accurate predictor of toppling for manmade structures with perfect symmetries and smooth (flat) bases.

CONCLUSIONS

This pilot study investigates the potential for constraining maximum earthquake ground motions over long time periods in the eastern United States using PBRs and develops or refines several methods for analyzing these rocks. We have identified a large number of PBRs in the eastern United States that can be further evaluated (Fig. 1; Figueiredo and Pratt, 2023; McPhillips and Pratt, 2024; Stirling and Pratt, 2026). A combination of low-cost and efficient methods were tested and developed on four PBRs at the Peaks of Otter, Virginia: photogrammetric methods, seismometer measurements of rock responses, and mapping of regional maximum magnitudes of earthquakes. We find that the PBRs at the Peaks of Otter provide an upper limit of about M_w 7.5–8 for the CVSZ and about M_w 7–7.5 for the GCSZ, likely for the past few tens of thousands of years. We also compared the fragility of the PBRs with predictions of ground motions in the NSHM, finding that they are consistent with that model. Our methods included the use of seismometers to record the response of PBRs to perturbations induced by gentle pushes on the rocks, from which it appears possible to estimate slenderness angles to compare with those determined from point clouds. The strength of these perturbations were not quantitatively measured, but we now routinely make this measurement, which can be used for computer modeling. We estimate the maximum earthquake magnitudes throughout a region around the PBRs; doing this for multiple PBRs throughout a region (Fig. 1) has the potential to produce a contour map of maximum magnitudes of earthquakes (with large but quantifiable uncertainties) throughout portions of the eastern United States in the past tens of thousands of years (e.g., McPhillips and Pratt, 2024; Stirling and Pratt, 2026).

DATA AND RESOURCES

The 3D models and point clouds used in this paper are available in Pratt *et al.* (2026): doi: 10.5066/P14DJFSI. The models can be read into MeshLab or similar software for examination and manipulation. Meshroom from AliceVision was used to make the 3D models from photographs; it is free, open-source software that can be downloaded from https://alicevision.org (last accessed February 2026). MeshLab interpretation software was used for analyzing the 3D model and point cloud; it also is free, open-source software that can be downloaded from https://www.meshlab.net (last accessed February 2026). We note, however, that other software packages provide similar functions. Some figures were made using the Generic Mapping Tools (GMT) software (doi: 10.1029/2019GC008515). Seismic data were processed using the Seismic Analysis Code (SAC), described in Goldstein and Snoke (2005) and Goldstein *et al.* (2003) and available at https://ds.iris.edu/ds/nodes/dmc/software/downloads/sac/102-0 (last accessed January 2026). The supplemental material for this article contains plots showing the full analyses for each of the four rocks included in this article, similar to that of Figure 16.

DECLARATION OF COMPETING INTERESTS

The authors acknowledge that there are no conflicts of interest recorded.

ACKNOWLEDGMENTS

The authors are deeply indebted to Jan and Christy Butler, Barbara Delaney, and Russell Dunn, whose diligent work over many years produced a series of books that provide descriptions of enough precariously balanced rocks in the northeastern United States to merit undertaking a systematic study. The authors thank Will Odom and Shannan Mahan for participating in discussions while hiking at the Peaks of Otter and for aiding in parts of the fieldwork. The work benefited from discussions with Mark Carter, who has a deep knowledge of the Blue Ridge of Virginia. Peter Powers helped with explaining and implementing aspects of the U.S. Geological Survey (USGS) Earthquake Hazard Toolbox (Clayton, 2023). Andrea Llenos helped with understanding earthquake probabilities in the National Seismic Hazard Model. Discussions with Rasool Anooshehpoor regarding balanced rocks and with Martin Chapman and Daniel McNamara regarding ground motions are appreciated. The authors appreciate the reviews by Ned Field, *Bulletin of the Seismological Society of America* Associate Editor Nicola Litchfield, and two anonymous reviewers. T. Pratt was partially supported by the Nuclear Regulatory Commission for this work.

Any use of trade, firm, or product names is for descriptive purposes only and does not imply endorsement by the U.S. Government.

REFERENCES

Abbott, R. E., and J. N. Louie (2000). High shear-wave velocities under precarious rocks might explain their proximity to the San Andreas fault, *Paper S51C-05 Presented at the 2000 AGU Fall Meeting*, San Francisco, California, 15–19 December.

Abrahamson, N. A., and S. Bhasin (2020). Conditional ground motion model for peak ground velocity for active crustal regions, *Pacific Earthquake Engineering Research Center Rept. 2020-05*, 40 pp., doi: 10.55461/AORD2776.

Anooshehpoor, A., J. N. Brune, and Y. Zeng (2004). Methodology for obtaining constraints on ground motions from precariously balanced rocks, *Bull. Seismol. Soc. Am.* **94,** no. 1, 25–303, doi: 10.1785/0120020242.

Baker, J. W., N. A. Abrahamson, J. W. Whitney, M. P. Board, and T. C. Hanks (2013). Use of fragile geologic structures as indicators of unexceeded ground motions and direct constraints on probabilistic seismic hazard analysis, *Bull. Seismol. Soc. Am.* **103,** no. 3, 1898–1911, doi: 10.1785/0120120202.

Balco, G., and J. Schaefer (2006). Cosmogenic-nuclide and varve chronologies for the deglaciation of southern New England, *Quat. Geochronol.* **1,** no. 1, 15–28, doi: 10.1016/j.quageo.2006.06.014.

Balco, G., M. D. Purvance, and D. H. Rood (2011). Exposure dating of precariously balanced rocks, *Quat. Geochronol.* **6,** nos. 3/4, 295–303, doi: 10.1016/j.quageo.2011.03.007.

Barani, S., M. Massa, S. Lovati, and D. Spillarossa (2014). Effects of surface topography on ground shaking prediction: Implications for seismic hazard analysis and recommendations for seismic design, *Geophys. J. Int.* **197,** no. 3, 1551–1565, doi: 10.1093/gji/ggu095.

Barth, A. M., S. A. Marcott, J. M. Licciardi, and J. D. Shakun (2019). Deglacial thinning of the Laurentide Ice Sheet in the Adirondack Mountains, New York, USA, revealed by 36Cl exposure dating, *Paleoceanogr. Paleoclimatol.* **34,** no. 6, 946–953, doi: 10.1029/2018PA003477.

Bell, J. W., J. N. Brune, T. Liu, M. Zreda, and J. C. Yount (1998). Dating precariously balanced rocks in seismically active parts of California and Nevada, *Geology* **26,** no. 6, 495–498, doi: 10.1130/0091-7613(1998)026<0495:DPBRIS>2.3.CO;2.

Bollinger, G. A., and M. G. Hopper (1971). Virginia's two largest earthquakes—December 22, 1875 and May 31, 1897, *Bull. Seismol. Soc. Am.* **61,** no. 4, 1033–1039, doi: 10.1785/BSSA0610041033.

Bollinger, G. A., and M. S. Sibol (1985). Seismicity, seismic reflection studies, gravity and geology of the central Virginia seismic zone—Part I. Seismicity, *Geol. Soc. Am. Bull.* **96,** no. 1, 49–57, doi: 10.1130/0016-7606(1985)96<49:SSRSGA>2.0.CO;2.

Bollinger, G. A., and R. L. Wheeler (1983). The Giles County, Virginia, seismic zone, *Science* **219,** no. 4588, 1063–1065, doi: 10.1126/science.219.4588.1063.

Bollinger, G. A., and R. L. Wheeler (1988). The Giles County, Virginia, seismic zone—Seismological results and geological interpretations, *U.S. Geol. Surv. Profess. Pap. 1355*, 85 pp., doi: 10.3133/pp1355.

Borcherdt, R. D. (1970). Effects of local geology on ground motion near San Francisco Bay, *Bull. Seismol. Soc. Am.* **60,** no. 1, 29–61, doi: 10.1785/BSSA0600010029.

Bromley, G. R. M., B. L. Hall, W. B. Thompson, and T. V. Lowell (2019). Age of the Berlin moraine complex, New Hampshire, USA, and implications for ice sheet dynamics and climate during Termination 1, *Quat. Res.* **94,** 80–93, doi: 10.1017/qua.2019.66.

Brune, J. N. (1996). Precarious rocks and acceleration maps for southern California, *Bull. Seismol. Soc. Am.* **86,** no. 1A, 43–54, doi: 10.1785/BSSA08601A0043.

Brune, J. N. (2002). Precarious-rock constraints on ground motion from historic and recent earthquakes in southern California, *Bull. Seismol. Soc. Am.* **92,** no. 7, 2602–2611, doi: 10.1785/0120000606.

Brune, J. N., and J. W. Whitney (1992). Precariously balanced rocks with rock varnish: Paleoindicators of maximum ground acceleration? *Seismol. Res. Lett.* **63,** no. 1, 21, doi: 10.1785/gssrl.63.1.19.

Brune, J. N., J. W. Bell, and A. Anooshehpoor (1996). Precariously balanced rocks and seismic risk, *Endeavour* **20,** no. 4, 168–172, doi: 10.1016/S0160-9327(96)10029-6.

Butler, C., and R. Dunn (2016). *Rockachusetts: An Explorer's Guide to Amazing Boulders of Massachusetts*, Amazon Books, CreateSpace Independent Publishing Platform (now Amazon KDP Print), 329 pp.

Butler, J., and C. Butler (2018). *Erratic Wandering: An Explorer's Hiking Guide to Astonishing Boulders in Maine, New Hampshire and*

Vermont, CreateSpace Independent Publishing Platform (now Amazon KDP Print), 285 pp.

Carter, M. W., S. Southworth, and J. N. Aleinikoff (2013). Proterozoic to Cenozoic geology above, within and beneath the Blue Ridge Composite Thrust Sheet as exposed along the Blue Ridge Parkway in the Peaks of Otter region, central Virginia Blue Ridge, *Guidebook for the 43rd Annual Virginia Geological Field Conference*, Williamsburg, Virginia, 39 pp.

Chapman, M. C., J. N. Beale, A. C. Hardy, and Q. Wu (2016). Modern seismicity and the fault Responsible for the 1886 Charleston, South Carolina, earthquake, *Bull. Seismol. Soc. Am.* **106,** no. 2, 364–372, doi: 10.1785/0120150221.

Chen, Z., R. Arrowsmith, J. Das, C. Wittich, C. Madugo, and A. Kottke (2024). Virtual shake robot: Simulating dynamics of precariously balanced rocks for overturning and large-displacement processes, *Seismica* **3,** no. 1, 25 pp., doi: 10.26443/seismica.v3i1.692.

Clayton, B. S. (2023). USGS Earthquake Hazard Toolbox: nshmp-apps, *U.S. Geol. Surv. Software Release*, doi: 10.5066/P9UAIISF, available at https://earthquake.usgs.gov/nshmp (last accessed October 2025).

Dimitrakopoulos, E. G., and T. S. Paraskeva (2015). Dimensionless fragility curves for rocking response to near-fault excitations, *Earthq. Eng. Struct. Dynam.* **44,** no. 12, 2015–2033, doi: 10.1002/eqe.2571.

Dunn, R. (2018). *Boulders Beyond Belief! An Explorer's Hiking Guide to Amazing Boulders & Natural Rock Formations of the Adirondacks*, CreateSpace Independent Publishing Platform (now Amazon KDP Print), 424 pp.

Duxbury, J., P. R. Bierman, E. W. Portenga, M. J. Pavich, S. Southworth, and S. H. T. Freeman (2015). Erosion rates in and around Shenandoah National Park, Virginia, determined using analysis of cosmogenic 10Be, *Am. J. Sci.* **315,** no. 1, 46–76, doi: 10.2475/01.2015.02.

Ebel, J. E. (2006). The Cape Ann, Massachusetts earthquake of 1755: A 250th anniversary perspective, *Seismol. Res. Lett.* **77,** no. 1, 74–86, doi: 10.1785/gssrl.77.1.74.

Ebel, J. E., and J. C. Starr (2018). A geophysical and field survey for the source region of the 1638 New Hampshire earthquake, *Seismol. Res. Lett.* **89,** no. 3, 1197–1211, doi: 10.1785/0220170266.

Fame, M. L., K. D. Chilton, J. A. Spotila, M. A. Kelly, and S. A. Caton (2023). Periglacial resurfacing of hillslopes and channels with large boulders in the Virginia Appalachians, *Earth Surf. Process. Landf.* **49,** no. 1, 432–450, doi: 10.1002/esp.5713.

Figueiredo, P. M., and T. L. Pratt (2023). Characterizing precariously balanced rocks to estimate maximum post-glacial ground motions in the New York/New Jersey region, eastern U.S., *Paper S43I-0438 Presented at the 2023 AGU Fall Meeting*, San Francisco, California, 11–15 December.

Figueiredo, P., J. Hill, A. Merschat, C. Scheip, K. Stewart, L. Owen, R. Wooten, M. Carter, E. Szymanski, S. Horton, *et al.* (2022). The M_w 5.1, 9 August 2020, Sparta earthquake, North Carolina: The first documented seismic surface rupture in the eastern United States, *GSA Today* **32,** no. 4, 4–11, doi: 10.17615/z077-0z17.

Finnegan, R., J. R. Moore, P. R. Geimer, E. K. Bessette-Kirton, and A. Dzubay (2022). Ground motion amplification at Natural Rock Arches in the Colorado plateau, *The Seism. Rec.* **2,** no. 3, 156–166, doi: 10.1785/0320220017.

Finnegan, R., J. R. Moore, P. R. Geimer, A. Dzubay, E. K. Bessette-Kirton, J. Bodtker, and K. Vollinger (2022). Ambient vibration modal analysis of natural rock towers and fins, *Seismol. Res. Lett.* **93,** no. 3, 1777–1786, doi: 10.1785/0220210325.

Finzi, Y., N. Ganz, O. Dor, M. Davis, O. Volk, S. Langer, R. Arrowsmith, and M. Tsesarsky (2020). Stability analysis of fragile rock pillars and insights on fault activity in the Negev, Israel, *J. Geophys. Res. Solid Earth* **125,** no. 12, e2019JB019269, doi: 10.1029/2019JB019269.

García Suárez, J., D. McPhillips, and D. Asimaki (2025). Seismic response of rock towers at the Trona Pinnacles (U.S.A.) to the 2019 Ridgecrest earthquake sequence: Theory, observations, and models, *Bull. Seismol. Soc. Am.* **115,** no. 6, 2769–2792, doi: 10.1785/0120250073.

Goldstein, P., and A. Snoke (2005). SAC availability for the IRIS community, Incorporated Research Institutions for Seismology Newsletter.

Goldstein, P., D. Dodge, M. Firpo, and L. Minner (2003). SAC2000: Signal processing and analysis tools for seismologists and engineers, in *The IASPEI International Handbook of Earthquake and Engineering Seismology*, W. H. K. Lee, H. Kanamori, P. C. Jennings, and C. Kisslinger (Editors), Academic Press, London.

Halsted, C. T., P. R. Bierman, J. D. Shakun, P. Thompson Davis, L. B. Corbet, D. S. Drebber, and J. C. Ridge (2024). A critical re-analysis of constraints on the timing and rate of Laurentide ice sheet recession in the northeastern United States, *J. Quat. Sci.* **39,** no. 1, 54–69, doi: 10.1002/jqs.3563.

Han, S., W.-Y. Kim, J. Y. Park, M.-S. Seo, and Y. Kim (2024). Rupture model of the 5 April 2024 Tewksbury, New Jersey, earthquake based on regional Lg-wave data, *The Seismic Record* **4,** no. 3, 214–222, doi: 10.1785/0320240020.

Horton, J. W., Jr., M. C. Chapman, and R. A. Green (2015). The 2011 Mineral, Virginia, earthquake, and its significance for seismic hazards in eastern North America—Overview and synthesis, in *The 2011 Mineral, Virginia, Earthquake, and Its Significance for Seismic Hazards in Eastern North America*, J. W. Horton Jr., M. C. Chapman, and R. A. Green (Editors), Geological Society of America Special Paper 509, 1–25, doi: 10.1130/2015.2509(01).

Hough, S. (2012). Initial assessment of the intensity distribution of the 2011 5.8 Mineral, Virginia, earthquake, *Seismol. Res. Lett.* **83,** no. 4, 649–657, doi: 10.1785/0220110140.

Hough, S. E., J.-R. Altidor, D. Anglade, D. Given, M. G. Janvier, J. Z. Maharrey, M. Meremonte, B. S.-L. Midor, C. Prepetit, and A. Yong (2010). Localized damage caused by topographic amplification during the 2010 M 7.0 Haiti earthquake, *Nature Geosci.* **3**, 778–782, doi: 10.1038/NGEO988.

Housner, G. W. (1963). Behavior of inverted pendulum structures during earthquakes, *Bull. Seismol. Soc. Am.* **53,** no. 2, 403–417, doi: 10.1785/BSSA0530020403.

Jibson, R. W., and E. L. Harp (2012). Extraordinary distance limits of landslides triggered by the 2011 Mineral, Virginia, earthquake, *Bull. Seismol. Soc. Am.* **102,** no. 6, 2368–2377, doi: 10.1785/0120120055.

Khan, S., M. van der Meijde, H. van der Werff, and M. Shafique (2020). The impact of topography on seismic amplification during the 2005 Kashmir earthquake, *Nat. Hazards Earth Syst. Sci.* **20,** no. 2, 399–411, doi: 10.5194/nhess-20-399-2020.

Klaboe, K., S. Pujol, and L. Laughery (2018). Seismic response of rocking blocks, *Earthq. Spectra* **34,** no. 3, 1051–1063, doi: 10.1193/060517EQS107DP.

Linari, C. L., P. R. Bierman, E. W. Portenga, M. J. Pavich, R. C. Finkel, and S. P. H. T. Freeman (2017). Rates of erosion and landscape change along the Blue Ridge escarpment, southern Appalachian Mountains, estimated from in situ cosmogenic10Be, *Earth Surf. Process. Landf.* **42,** no. 6, 928–940, doi: 10.1002/esp.4051.

Llenos, A. L., A. J. Michael, A. M. Shumway, J. L. Rubinstein, K. L. Haynie, M. P. Moschetti, J. M. Altekruse, and K. R. Milner (2024). Forecasting the long-term spatial distribution of earthquakes for the 2023 U.S. National Seismic Hazard Model using gridded seismicity, *Bull. Seismol. Soc. Am.* **114,** no. 4, 2028–2053, doi: 10.1785/0120230220.

McNamara, D. E., H. M. Benz, R. B. Herrmann, E. A. Bergman, P. Earle, A. Meltzer, M. Withers, and M. Chapman (2014). The M_w 5.8 Mineral, Virginia, earthquake of August 2011 and aftershock sequence: Constraints on earthquake source parameters and fault geometry, *Bull. Seismol. Soc. Am.* **104,** no. 1, 40–54, doi: 10.1785/0120130058.

McNamara, D. E., L. Gee, H. M. Benz, and M. Chapman (2014). Frequency-dependent seismic attenuation in the eastern United States as observed from the 2011 central Virginia earthquake and aftershock sequence, *Bull. Seismol. Soc. Am.* **104,** no. 1, 55–72, doi: 10.1785/0120130045.

McPhillips, D., and T. L. Pratt (2024). Precariously balanced rocks in northern New York and Vermont, U.S.A.: Ground-motion constraints and implications for fault sources, *Bull. Seismol. Soc. Am.* **114,** no. 6, 3171–3182, doi: 10.1785/0120240069.

McPhillips, D., and K. M. Scharer (2022). Survey of fragile geologic features and their quasi-static earthquake ground-motion constraints, southern Oregon, *Bull. Seismol. Soc. Am.* **112,** no. 1, 419–437, doi: 10.1785/0120200378.

Merschat, A. J., and M. W. Carter (2022). Surface rupture from the 9 August 2020, M_w 5.1 Sparta, North Carolina earthquake and possible paleoseismicity: Evidence from detailed bedrock and surficial geologic mapping, *Geol. Soc. Am. Abstracts with Programs* **54,** no. 4, Paper 43-8, doi: 10.1130/abs/2022NC-375493.

Merschat, A. J., M. W. Carter, A. Lynn, K. G. Stevvart, P. M. Figueiredo, W. E. Odom, R. J. McAleer, J. Vazquez, N. E. Powell, and C. S. Holm-Denoma (2024). Mesoproterozoic to Paleozoic tectonics, Pleistocene landforms, and Holocene seismicity in the Blue Ridge: Results from integrated studies of the 9 August 2020, Mw 5.1 earthquake area near Sparta, North Carolina, USA, in *Geology and Geologic Hazards of the Blue Ridge: Field Excursions for the 2024 GSA Southeastern Section Meeting, Asheville, North Carolina, USA*, A. J. Merschat and M. W. Carter (Editors), Geological Society of America Field Guide 67, 69–106 pp., doi: .

Modha, K., D. Raj, and Y. Singh (2019). Topographic amplification of earthquake ground motion on hills of bell-shaped geometry, in *Proceedings of the Indian Geotechnical Conference 2019, Lecture Notes on Civil Engineering 138*, S. Patel, C. H. Solanki, K. R. Reddy, and S. K. Shukla (Editors), Springer, Singapore, 185–195, doi: 10.1007/978-981-33-6564-3_17.

Modha, K. G., D. Raj, Y. Singh, and D. H. Lang (2020). Topographic amplification of earthquake ground motion on different hill geometries, *Proc. of the 17th World Conf. on Earthquake Engineering (17WCEE)*, Sendai, Japan, Paper 1f -0035, 12 pp., available at https://wcee.nicee.org/wcee/article/17WCEE/1f-0035.pdf (last accessed December 2025).

Molina, S., D. H. Lang, Y. Singh, and A. Meslem (2019). A period dependent topographic amplification model for earthquake loss estimation, *Bull. Earthq. Eng.* **17,** 3709–3725, doi: 10.1007/s10518-019-00608-1.

Monecke, K., F. G. McCarthy, J. B. Hubeny, J. F. Ebel, D. J. Brabander, S. Kielb, E. Howey, G. Janigian, and J. Pentesco (2018). The 1755 Cape Ann earthquake recorded in Lake Sediments of eastern New England: An interdisciplinary paleoseismic approach, *Seismol. Res. Lett.* **89,** no. 3, 1212–1222, doi: 10.1785/0220170220.

Neves, M., L. Y. Chuang, W. Li, Z. Peng, P. M. Figueiredo, and S. Ni (2024). Complex rupture dynamics of the extremely shallow August 2020 M 5.1 Sparta, North Carolina earthquake, *Commun. Earth Environ.* **5,** 163, doi: 10.1038/s43247-024-01316-8.

Petersen, M. D., A. M. Shumway, P. M. Powers, E. H. Field, M. P. Moschetti, K. S. Jaiswal, K. R. Milner, S. Rezaeian, A. D. Frankel, A. L. Llenos, *et al.* (2024). The 2023 U.S. 50-State National Seismic Hazard Model: Overview and implications, *Earthq. Spectra* **40,** no. 1, 5–88, doi: 10.1177/87552930231215428.

Pratt, T. L., and J. Ebel (2025). ShakeMap scenario catalog for selected historical new england earthquakes, U.S. Geological Survey, available at https://earthquake.usgs.gov/scenarios/catalog/nefema/ (last accessed December 2025).

Pratt, T. L., M. C. Chapman, A. Shah, J. W. Horton Jr., and O. Boyd (2021). Ten years on from the quake that shook the nation's capital, *Eos* **102,** doi: 10.1029/2021EO162330.

Pratt, T. L., M. C. Chapman, and Q. Wu (2025). Comment on "The 1886 Charleston, South Carolina, Earthquake: Relic Railroad Offset Reveals Rupture" by Roger Bilham and Susan E. Hough, *The Seism. Rec.* **5,** no. 1, 11–22, doi: 10.1785/0320240002.

Pratt, T. L., J. W. Horton Jr., J. Muñoz, S. E. Hough, M. C. Chapman, and C. G. Olgun (2017). Amplification of earthquake ground motions in Washington, DC, and implications for hazard assessments in central and eastern North America, *Geophys. Res. Lett.* **44,** no. 24, 12,150–12,160, doi: 10.1002/2017GL075517.

Pratt, T. L., M. W. Stirling, D. McPhillips, and P. M. Figueiredo (2026). Data for analyzing precariously balanced rocks at the Peaks of Otter, Blue Ridge Mountains of Virginia, to estimate maximum past ground motions, *U.S. Geol. Surv. Science Base*, doi: 10.5066/P14DJFSI.

Purvance, M. D., A. Anooshehpoor, and J. N. Brune (2008). Freestanding block overturning fragilities: Numerical simulation and experimental validation, *Earthq. Eng. Struct. Dynam.* **37,** no. 5, 791–808, doi: 10.1002/eqe.789.

Rault, C., W.-A. Chao, C. Gelis, A. Burtin, J.-M. Chang, O. Marc, T.-S. Lai, Y.-M. Wu, N. Hovius, and P. Meunier (2020). Seismic response of a mountain ridge prone to landsliding, *Bull. Seismol. Soc. Am.* **110,** no. 6, 3004–3020, doi: 10.1785/012010127.

Restrepo, D., J. Bielak, R. Serrano, J. Gómez, and J. Jaramillo (2016). Effects of realistic topography on the ground motion of the Columbian Andes—A case study at the Aburrá Valley, Antioquia, *Geophys. J. Int.* **204,** no. 3, 1801–1816, doi: 10.1093/gji/ggv556.

Rood, A. H., D. H. Rood, M. W. Stirling, C. M. Madugo, N. A. Abrahamson, K. M. Wilcken, T. Gonzalez, A. Kottke, A. C.

Whittaker, W. D. Page, and P. J. Stafford (2020). Earthquake hazard uncertainties improved using precariously balanced rocks, *AGU Adv.* **1,** no. 4, e2020AV000182, doi: 10.1029/2020AV000182.

Seeber, L., W.-Y. Kim, J. Armbruster, W.-X. Du, A. Lerner-Lam, and P. Friberg (2002). The 20 April 2002 M_w 5.0 earthquake near Au Sable Forks, Adirondacks, New York: A first glance at a new sequence, *Seismol. Res. Lett.* **74,** no. 4, 480–489, doi: 10.1785/GSSRL.73.4.480.

Seed, H. B., and I. M. Idriss (1971). Simplified procedure for evaluating soil liquefaction potential, *J. Soil Mech. Foundations Div.* **97,** no. 9, 1249–1273, doi: 10.1061/JSFEAQ.0001662.

Shi, B., A. Anooshehpoor, Y. Zeng, and J. N. Brune (1996). Rocking and overturning of precariously balanced rocks by earthquakes, *Bull. Seismol. Soc. Am.* **86,** no. 5, 1364–1371, doi: 10.1785/bssa0860051364.

Singh, Y., S. Ahmad, D. Raj, K. Modha, and D. Lang (2018). Spectral amplification modeling for triangular hill geometry, *Proc. of the 16th European Conf. on Earthquake Engineering (16ECEE)*, Thessaloniki, Greece, Paper 11946, 11 pp.

Stirling, M. W., and T. L. Pratt (2026). Using precariously-balanced rocks to constrain post-glacial earthquake magnitudes in New England, United States, *Bull. Seismol. Soc. Am.* (in press).

Stirling, M. W., E. R. Abbott, D. H. Rood, G. H. McVerry, N. A. Abrahamson, D. J. A. Barrell, R. Huso, N. J. Litchfield, L. Luna, D. A. Rhoades, *et al.* (2021). First use of fragile geologic features to set the design motions for a major existing engineered structure, *Bull. Seismol. Soc. Am.* **111,** no. 5, 2673–2695, doi: 10.1785/0120210026.

Stirling, M. W., A. Anooshehpoor, J. N. Brune, G. P. Biasi, and S. G. Wesnousky (2002). Assessment of the site conditions of precariously balanced rocks in the Mojave Desert, southern California, *Bull. Seismol. Soc. Am.* **92,** no. 6, 2139–2144, doi: 10.1785/0120010221.

Taber, S. (1913). Earthquakes in Buckingham County, Virginia, *Bull. Seismol. Soc. Am.* **3,** no. 3, 124–133, doi: 10.1785/BSSA0030030124.

Tarr, A. C., and R. L. Wheeler (2006). Earthquakes in Virginia and vicinity 1774-2004, *U.S. Geol. Surv. Open-File Rept. 2006-1017, 1 plate*, doi: 10.3133/ofr20061017.

Thompson Jobe, J., A. Hatem, R. Gold, C. DuRoss, N. Reitman, R. Briggs, and C. Collett (2022). Revised earthquake geology inputs for the central and eastern United States and southeast Canada for the 2023 National Seismic Hazard Model, *Seismol. Res. Lett.* **93,** no. 6, 3100–3120, doi: 10.1785/0220220162.

Trugman, D. T., J. Brune, K. D. Smith, J. N. Louie, and G. M. Kent (2023). The rocks that did not fall: A multidisciplinary analysis of near-source ground motions from an active normal fault, *AGU Adv.* **4,** no. 2, e2023AV000885, doi: 10.1029/2023AV000885.

Tuttle, M. P, K. Dyer-Williams, M. W. Carter, S. L. Forman, K. Tucker, Z. Fuentes, C. Velez, and L. Bauer (2021). The liquefaction record of past earthquakes in the central Virginia seismic zone, eastern United States, *Seismol. Res. Lett.* **92,** no. 5, 3126–3144, doi: 10.1785/0220200456.

U.S. Geological Survey (USGS) (2017). *Advanced National Seismic System Comprehensive Catalog of Earthquake Events and Products*, U.S. Geological Survey Earthquake Hazards Program, doi: 10.5066/F7MS3QZH.

Veeraraghavan, S., J. F. Hall, and S. Krishnan (2020). Modeling the rocking and sliding of free-standing objects using rigid body dynamics, *ASCE J. Eng. Mech.* **146,** no. 6, 47 pp., doi: 10.1061/(ASCE)EM.1943-7889.0001739.

Veeraraghavan, S., K. Hudnut, and S. Krishnan (2017). Toppling analysis of the Echo Cliff precariously balanced rock, *Bull. Seismol. Soc. Am.* **107,** no. 1, 72–81, doi: 10.1785/0120160169.

Viegas, G., R. W. Abercrombie, and W.-Y. Kim (2010). The 2002 M 5 Au Sable Forks, NY, earthquake sequence: Source scaling relationships and energy budget, *J. Geophys. Res. Solid Earth* **115,** no. B7, B07310, doi: 10.1029/2009JB006799.

Weber, S., J. Beutel, M. Hausler, P. R. Geimer, D. Fah, and J. R. Moore (2022). Spectral amplification of ground motion linked to resonance of large-scale mountain landforms, *Earth Planet. Sci. Lett.* **578**, 117295, doi: 10.1016/j.epsl.2021.117295.

Wells, D., J. A. Egan, D. G. Murphy, and T. Paret (2015). Ground shaking and structural response of the Washington Monument during the 2011 Mineral, Virginia, earthquake, in J. W. Horton Jr, M. C. Chapman, and R. A. Green (Editors), *The 2011 Mineral, Virginia, Earthquake, and Its Significance for Seismic Hazards in Eastern North America*, Geological Society of America, Special Paper 509, 199–233, doi: 10.1130/2015.2509(12).

Wittich, C. E., T. C. Hutchinson, J. DeSanto, and D. Sandwell (2018). 3-D Reconstructions and Numerical Simulations of Precarious Rocks in Southern California, *Proceedings of 11th National Conference on Earthquake Engineering (11NCEE)*, Los Angeles, California, 10 pp., available asUniversity of Nebraska-Lincoln, Civil Engineering Faculty Publications 154, at https://digitalcommons.unl.edu/civilengfacpub/154 (last accessed December 2025).

Yin, C., W.-H. Li, and W. Wang (2021). Evaluation of ground motion amplification effects in slope topography induced by the arbitrary directions of seismic waves, *Energies* **14,** no. 20, 6744, doi:10.3390/en14206744.

Zábranová, E., C. Matyska, J. Stemberk, and J. Málek (2020). Eigen oscillations and stability of rocking stones: The case study of "The Hus Pulpit" in The central Bohemian Pluton, *Pure Appl. Geophys.* **177**, 1907–1916, doi: 10.1007/s00024-019-02296-z.

Manuscript received 27 May 2025
Published online 2 March 2026

Use of Precariously Balanced Rocks to Constrain Postglacial Earthquake Magnitudes in New England, United States

Mark W. Stirling*[1] and Thomas L. Pratt[2]

ABSTRACT

We use the age and fragility of 13 precariously balanced rocks (PBRs) in Massachusetts, New Hampshire, and southwestern Maine to evaluate the estimated probabilistic seismic hazard (PSH) from the U.S. Geological Survey's National Seismic Hazard Model (NSHM), and also develop a map of maximum postglacial earthquake magnitudes in the region. The PBRs are erratic boulders left behind by the retreat of the Laurentide ice sheet between 13 and 18 ka, and published ice retreat maps are used to estimate their fragility ages. The fragilities and ages of the rocks appear to be consistent with the NSHM, in that the estimated earthquake magnitudes and resulting ground motions that would topple them are only expected on timescales longer than their fragility ages. This result, on the North American passive margin, contrasts with PBR studies at active plate boundaries, where the PBR constraints imply large reductions to estimated PSH. It may be that the PBRs are not old enough in the eastern United States to reveal the same PSH modeling issues as those revealed in the plate boundary settings. The study provides constraints on maximum magnitudes of postglacial earthquakes across much of Massachusetts, New Hampshire, and southwestern Maine, with the constraints limited to the ages of the PBRs.

KEY POINTS

- We study 13 precariously balanced rocks (PBRs) in Massachusetts, New Hampshire, and Maine.
- The PBRs are used to estimate the maximum strength of shaking and earthquake magnitudes in the region.
- The ages and fragilities of the PBRs are compatible with the National Seismic Hazard Model.

Supplemental Material

INTRODUCTION

Fragile geologic features (FGFs) are the generic name given to precariously balanced rocks (PBRs), hoodoos, speleothems, unstable cliff faces, and other geologic features susceptible to collapse or breakage during large earthquakes. The age and fragility of these features can be used to evaluate probabilistic seismic hazard (PSH) models for long-return periods, and over the past 35 yr studies in the western United States and New Zealand have shown that the PSH ground-motion estimates often exceed those that would shake down the FGFs (e.g., Brune, 1996; Rood *et al.*, 2020; Stirling *et al.*, 2021). These studies have generally been limited to PBRs, in which the fragility of the rock can be approximated from the shape and position of rocking points (Fig. 1).

Here, we study a suite of 13 PBRs in the states of Massachusetts, New Hampshire, and Maine that have been located by way of tourism guidebooks (Butler and Dunn, 2016; Butler and Butler, 2018; Fig. 2). The publications document unusual rock formations, a subset being PBRs, and also provide detailed directions that enable the features to be located. The PBRs are erratic boulders that were once carried within the Pleistocene Laurentide ice sheet and left behind during melting. We use information on the timing of ice sheet retreat to estimate the fragility ages of the rocks (Fig. 3) and make fragility estimates for comparison to the U.S. Geological Survey's National Seismic Hazard Model (NSHM; Petersen *et al.*, 2024). The study area shows low seismicity rates, an absence of active faults, and low estimates of PSH (Petersen *et al.*, 2024). The only historical earthquakes of significance in the area were the 1638 $M_{Lg} \sim 6.5$ New Hampshire and 1755 $M_w \sim 5.9$ ($M_{Lg} \sim 6.2$) Cape Anne earthquakes (Ebel, 2006; Ebel and Starr, 2018; Pratt and Ebel, 2025).

1. Department of Geology, University of Otago, Dunedin, New Zealand, https://orcid.org/0000-0002-2562-4675 (MWS); 2. U.S. Geological Survey, Reston, Virginia, U.S.A., https://orcid.org/0000-0003-3131-3141 (TLP)

*Corresponding author: mark.stirling@otago.ac.nz

Cite this article as Stirling, M. W., and T. L. Pratt (2026). Use of Precariously Balanced Rocks to Constrain Postglacial Earthquake Magnitudes in New England, United States, *Bull. Seismol. Soc. Am.* **116**, 1311–1320, doi: 10.1785/0120250163

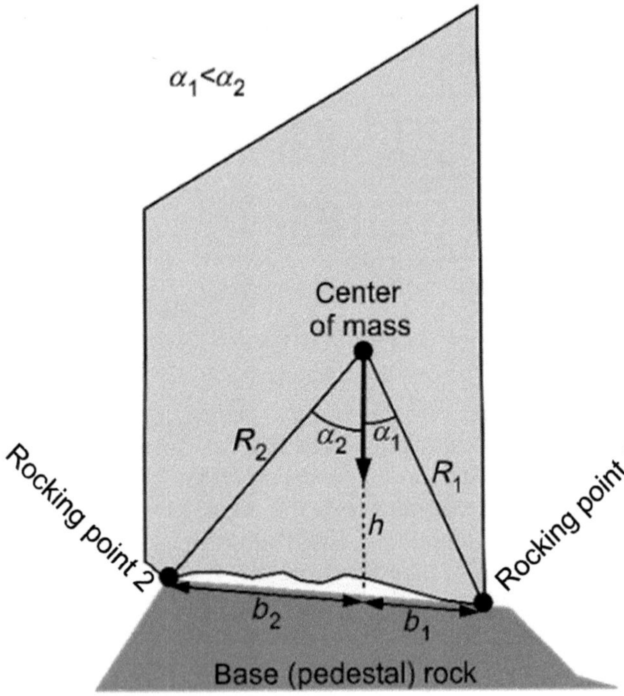

Figure 1. Diagram of a precariously balanced rock (PBR) showing key measurements for toppling analysis. The parameters used in the Purvance *et al.* (2008) equations to estimate toppling probability are the two slenderness angles (α_1 and α_2) and the distance (radius) from the center of mass to the nearest rocking point (R_1). The widths of the two sides of the PBR base are labeled "b_1" and "b_2" and "h" is the height of the center of mass. A 3D model of the rock is created using photogrammetry to determine these values. The diagram is modified from McPhillips and Pratt (2024).

PBRs

The 13 PBRs studied in Massachusetts, New Hampshire, and western Maine are shown in Figure 2, and the relevant parameters are listed in Table 1. The rocks are typically large features reaching several meters in their longest dimension, and they range in shape from angular to rounded, and equidimensional to elongated. They are typically found on glaciated bedrock hillocks, mounds, and mountain tops, so glacial till or other sediments are not present at the sites. The PBRs do not appear to have been significantly modified since emplacement because smooth surfaces and glacial striations observed on many of the pedestal areas demonstrate minimal weathering of the rock surfaces (and the PBRs by inference) since glaciation.

METHOD

We have followed the methods of McPhillips and Pratt (2024) and Pratt *et al.* (2026) in the collection of field data, quantification of PBR fragilities, assessment of fragility ages, comparison to the NSHM, and development of a maximum magnitude map for the region. The following is a summary of these methods, which are described in detail in Pratt *et al.* (2026). The methods are also illustrated for one of the PBRs (Big Tippling; Fig. 2) in Figure 4.

3D models

Photogrammetry is used to create detailed 3D models of the PBRs, from which their basic dimensions, locations of the centers of mass, and the shapes of the contact areas with the underlying rocks are determined (Table 1; Pratt and Stirling, 2026). The open-source "Meshroom" software is used for photogrammetry, and the open-source "Meshlab" is used for editing the models and making the geometric calculations (see Data and Resources). The models are then used to measure the distances from the downward projections of the centers of mass to the rocking points, from which the slenderness angles (α_1 and α_2) and radii (R_1 and R_2) are computed (Fig. 1; Table 1).

Fragility age

We interpret all of the PBRS to be erratics that have been left behind by the retreat of the Laurentide ice sheet. Therefore, we assume that the fragility age of each PBR is equal to the timing of the Laurentide ice sheet retreat at that PBR site (Fig. 3). Because the PBRs are mostly located on knobs or hills, there would have been an absence of outwash deposits around the bases of the PBRs. The timing is estimated by interpolating between the contours in Figure 3. For Big Tippling PBR just south of Boston (Figs. 2b and 4), for example, the interpolated fragility age is about 18 ka.

Topographic amplification

Although the PBRs are all located on bedrock pedestals and therefore not subjected to obvious site effects, topographic effects are instead relevant. This is the effect of ground-shaking amplification due to topography (e.g., Hough *et al.*, 2010; Barani *et al.*, 2014; Singh *et al.*, 2018; Modha *et al.*, 2019, 2020; Rault *et al.*, 2020; Khan *et al.*, 2020; Yin *et al.*, 2021). Most of our PBRs are located at or near the tops of hills, and the associated topographic amplifications are estimated from the shapes of the hills (Singh *et al.*, 2018; Modha *et al.*, 2019, 2020; Molina *et al.*, 2019). The interpreted amplification factors are listed in Table 1, and these are in the range of 1–1.3. The amplification factors are incorporated into the fragility analysis in the way described in Pratt *et al.* (2026).

Fragility analysis

The probability of toppling is estimated from the equations in Purvance *et al.* (2008). Their equations, derived from regressions on results from shake table tests and computer modeling, can be used to estimate toppling probability from a combination of peak ground acceleration (PGA) and the ratio of peak ground velocity (PGV) to PGA (PGV/PGA), or PGA and the ratio of spectral accelerations at 1 or 2 s period (SA_1 or SA_2) to PGA (SA_1/PGA or SA_2/PGA; Purvance *et al.*, 2008). We use PGA and PGV/PGA to be consistent with other studies (e.g., Rood *et al.*, 2020; McPhillips and Pratt, 2024). We use the equations for asymmetric rocks with different slenderness

Figure 2. PBRs from Massachusetts, New Hampshire, and Maine: (a) Berlin, Massachusetts; (b) Big Tippling, Cohasset, Massachusetts; (c) Camp Nihan, Saugus, Massachusetts; (d) Canton, Massachusetts; (e) Cradle Rock, Barre, Massachusetts; (f) Lynn Woods, Lynn, Massachusetts; (g) Peppercorn Hill, Upton, Massachusetts; (h) Wachusetts, Massachusetts; (i) Berwick, Maine; (j) Pawtuckaway, New Hampshire; (k) Pillsbury, New Hampshire; (l) Ragged Mountain, New Hampshire; and (m) Tipping Rock, Lebanon, New Hampshire. Photos by the authors. The color version of this figure is available only in the electronic edition.

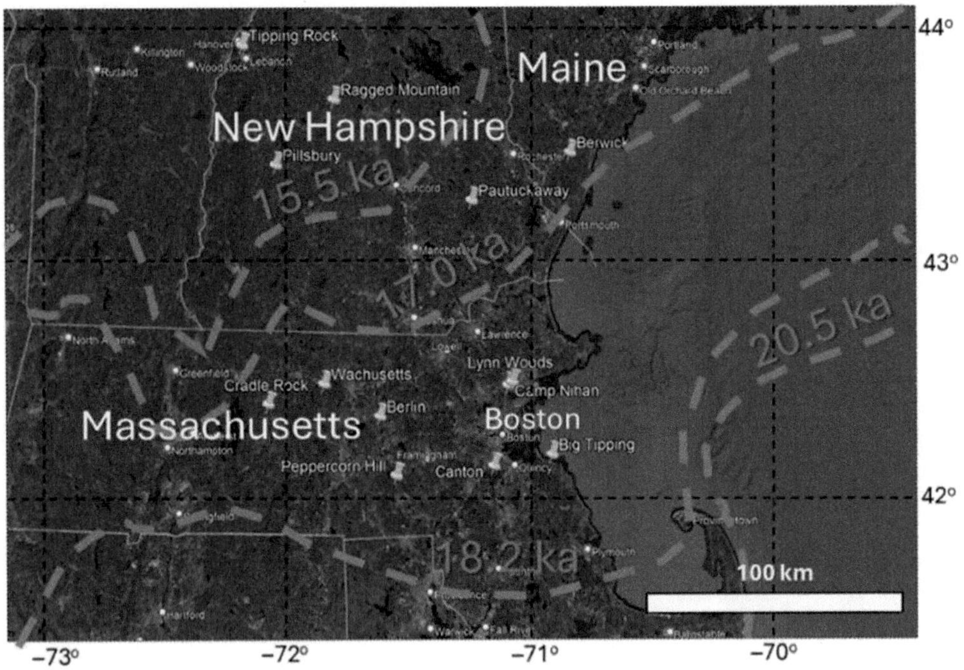

Figure 3. PBR locations (yellow pins) in relation to Laurentide ice sheet retreat times (blue dashed contours). The fragility age of each PBR is based on the interpolation of the contour lines of ice retreat. Ice retreat contours are from Barth *et al.* (2019). Map uses a Google Earth Basic Form basemap of an area centered on Massachusetts (see Data and Resources). The color version of this figure is available only in the electronic edition.

angles on each side to construct fragility matrices showing the probability of the rocks toppling at different combinations of PGA and PGV/PGA (Fig. 4b). Note that in our analyses we effectively treat PGV/PGA as a single parameter as in previous studies (Purvance *et al.*, 2008; Baker *et al.*, 2013; Rood *et al.*, 2020; McPhillips and Pratt, 2024; Pratt *et al.*, 2026), whereas the parameter is actually a combination of different ground-motion measures. Other assumptions around fragility are similar to those embodied in McPhillips and Pratt (2024). A few of the PBRs have rounded bottoms, which might suggest that they could return to their original position after rocking in an earthquake (e.g., Fig. 2f,k). However, the PBRs are resting on sloped surfaces so we therefore assume that they would "walk" down the sloped surface and eventually topple if they start rocking substantially.

For our PBRs, we compute the fragility matrices using ground motions adjusted for topographic amplification. The PGAs listed on the horizontal axes of the plots in Figure 4 are the input PGAs at the bases of the hills or knobs (i.e., no topographic amplification). However, the probabilities of toppling at these PGAs are computed after multiplying the PGA by the topographic amplification factors (Table 1). Thus, the PGAs used to compute the probabilities in the fragility matrices are larger than those listed on the x axes for those PBRs with amplification factors greater than 1, which is effectively the same as reducing the fragility values to lower PGAs. The vertical axis with the PGV/PGA ratio is not changed by topographic amplification because both PGV and PGA presumably undergo about the same amplification.

Once the fragility matrices are computed, the rocks are examined according to the following methods: (1) comparing the fragilities with NSHM hazard curves at the PBR sites using the method of McPhillips and Pratt (2024) and Pratt *et al.* (2026), which followed the methods of Baker *et al.* (2013) and Rood *et al.* (2020); and (2) mapping maximum magnitudes of earthquakes that could occur in the region without toppling the rocks with different probabilities of certainty. These two methods are described in detail in Pratt *et al.* (2026), with the latter method involving the comparison of the PBR fragilities to the predicted ground motions as a function of earthquake magnitude and distance. We note that the Canton, Cradle Rock, Lynn Woods, Peppercorn Hill, and Tipping Rock PBRs are particularly fragile (Table 1). In Figure 4d and similar plots in the supplemental material available to this article, we also list the scale factor (β) for the hazard curve that is consistent with PBR survival at 5% probability (upper right; Baker *et al.*, 2013; Rood *et al.*, 2020), and in the bottom left of the graph are listed the probability of survival given the assumptions in the NSHM and the age that gives a 5% chance of survival given the NSHM assumptions.

RESULTS

We show one example of the complete set of analyses in Figure 4 for the Big Tippling PBR, and the maximum magnitude map for the region in Figure 5. Figure 4 shows PBR toppling probabilities as a function of PGA and PGV/PGA, and comparison of PBR fragility with USGS NSHM hazard curves. Similar analyses are shown for the other PBRs in the supplemental material. Figure 5 is based on analyses for all 13 PBRs.

The salient results from the four analyses are as follows.

1. The maximum magnitude map (Fig. 5) shows that for a significant area of New England, we can exclude earthquakes of $M_w \geq 7.5$ in postglacial times with 90% probability. For the Boston area, the exclusion magnitude is even lower ($M_w \geq 6.5$). If such earthquake magnitudes are possible in the region, their associated recurrence interval must

TABLE 1
Precariously Balanced Rocks (PBRs) Studied in Massachusetts, New Hampshire, and Southwestern Maine

PBR	ID	Longitude (°)	Latitude (°)	Fragility Age (yr)	Volume (M^2)	Mass (kg)	Weight (tons)	CoM Height (cm)	Contact Circum (cm)	Base 1 (cm)	Alpha 1 (deg)	Radius 1(cm)	Base 2 (cm)	Alpha 2 (deg)	Radius 2 (cm)	Topo Amp
Berlin, Massachusetts	11	−71.633	42.391	17,600	10.09	26,940	29.7	92	330	29.4	17.7	96.6	44.3	25.7	102.1	1.00
Berlin, Massachusetts (second direction)										17.9	11.0	17.9	44.3	25.7	44.3	1.00
Big Tippling, Cohasset, Massachusetts	12	−70.823	42.250	17,870	40.07	106,987	117.9	155	469	14	5.2	155.6	45.2	16.3	161.5	1.00
Camp Nihan, Massachusetts	13	−71.023	42.489	17,430	4.19	11,174	12.3	110	305	22.1	11.4	112.2	53.9	26.1	122.5	1.00
Canton, Massachusetts	14	−71.097	42.163	17,800	30.10	80,365	88.6	154	10; 134; 267	11.8	4.4	154.5	20.3	7.5	155.3	1.15
Cradle Rock, Massachusetts	15	−72.158	42.436	17,790	10.99	29,343	32.3	134	335	33	13.8	138.0	35	14.6	138.5	1.00
Lynn Woods, Massachusetts	16	−71.002	42.500	17,430	14.40	38,448	42.4	114	274	28	13.8	117.4	28.6	14.1	117.5	1.00
Peppercorn Hill, Massachusetts	17	−71.560	42.189	17,790	2.51	6,702	7.4	85	201	15.5	10.3	86.4	16.4	10.9	86.6	1.18
Wachusetts, Massachusetts	18	−71.894	42.503	17,450	9.45	25,232	27.8	113	457	28.1	14.0	116.4	33.6	16.6	117.9	1.05
Berwick, Maine	3	−70.702	43.271	16,770	47.05	125,624	138.5	164	371	36.8	12.6	168.1	68	22.5	177.5	1.00
Pawtuckaway, New Hampshire	4	−71.176	43.116	16,250	18.67	49,849	54.9	110	272	29.8	15.2	114.0	34.8	17.6	115.4	1.22
Pillsbury, New Hampshire	5	−72.109	43.245	15,240	9.67	25,819	28.5	88	155	21.5	13.7	90.6	24.7	15.7	91.4	1.11
Pillsbury, New Hampshire (second direction)										29.8	18.7	29.8	23.7	15.1	23.7	1.11
Ragged Mtn, New Hampshire	19	−71.831	43.465	14,970	5.20	13,884	15.3	66	249	19.3	16.3	68.8	35	27.9	74.7	1.29
Tipping Rock, Lebanon, New Hampshire	20	−72.269	43.652	14,460	10.55	28,169	31.1	122	269	15.4	7.2	123.0	19.6	9.1	123.6	1.00

Fragility age is from location relative to ice retreat contours in Figure 3; Mass (kg) assumes a density of 2.67 gm/cc; CoM height is the center of mass height above the pedestal; Contact circum is the circumference of the pedestal contact area, with multiple measurements at Canton showing the total circumference and the circumferences of two individual contact points; Base 1 is the dimension of PBR rocking point 1 (refer to Fig. 1); Alpha 1 is the angle between rocking point 1, the center of mass, and the vertical; Radius 1 is the distance from rocking point 1 to the center of mass; Base 2, Alpha 2, and Radius 2 are for the previous three parameters, but for the rocking point 2; and Topo amp is the estimated topographic amplification factor (refer to references listed in the article).

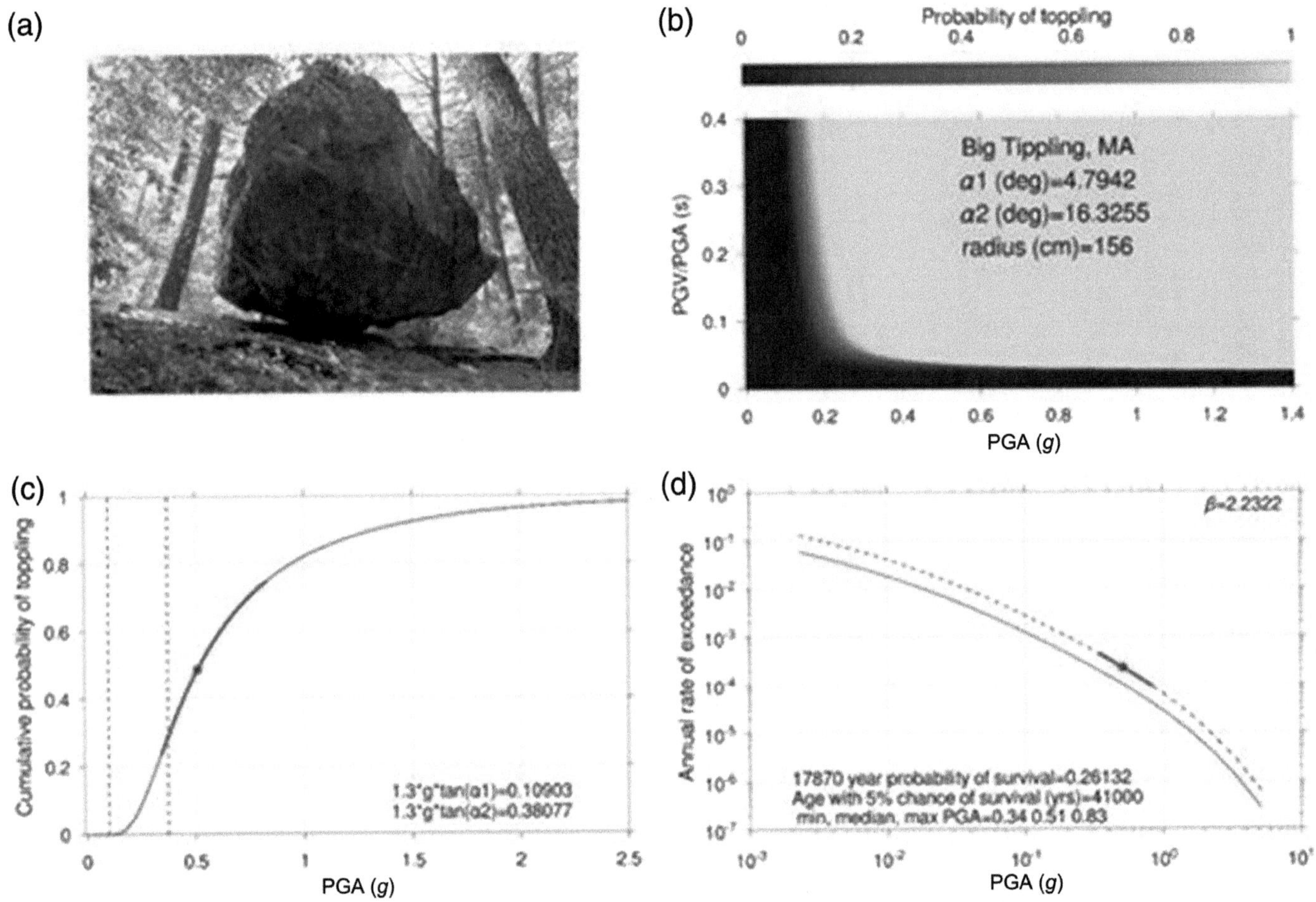

Figure 4. Full fragility analysis for Big Tippling, Massachusetts, PBR: (a) photo of the PBR; (b) fragility matrix using Purvance *et al.* (2008) adjusted for topographic amplification. Peak ground acceleration (PGA) on the horizontal axis is without topographic amplification so that it corresponds to National Seismic Hazard Model (NSHM) values, but probabilities were computed using amplified PGA; (c) vector fragility curve showing the cumulative probability of toppling for each value of PGA (PGA listed is before topographic amplification, corresponding to the PGA values in the NSHM). The red portion of the curve is the 25%–75% range, and the red dot is the mean value; (d) NSHM hazard curve (in red), and adjusted hazard curve for 17.9 ka rock age interpolated from Figure 3 (blue dashed line). The red portions of the curves and the dot correspond to the PGA values in panel (e). On the lower part of the graph is listed the probability of survival given its age (~26%), the age at which the rock would have a 5% chance of survival (41 ka), and the minimum, mean, and maximum PGA values for which the PBR provides constraints, as shown in panel (c). In the upper right is the scale factor (β) for the hazard curve that is consistent with PBR survival (e.g., Baker *et al.*, 2013; Rood *et al.*, 2020). The color version of this figure is available only in the electronic edition.

be greater than the age of the Laurentide ice sheet retreat. Thus, $M_w \geq 6.5$ earthquakes in the Boston area most likely have recurrence intervals greater than about 18 ka. These maximum magnitude limits are consistent with the location and magnitude of the two major historical earthquakes in the region. These are the 1755 $M_w \sim 5.9$ Cape Anne and 1638 $M_{Lg} \sim 6.5$ New Hampshire earthquakes (Ebel, 2006; Ebel and Starr, 2018; Pratt and Ebel, 2025). Specifically, these earthquakes are located in areas where the contours in Figure 5 indicate larger maximum magnitude exclusion limits (Fig. 5). Note that the proximity of a number of our PBRS to each other in the Boston area could potentially make this subset amenable to developing a joint probability model or fragility distribution for PBR fragilities (Rood *et al.*, 2020; Stirling *et al.*, 2021). However, the PBRs are also more widely spaced than in the aforementioned studies (10s of km rather than 10 m to 2 km; Rood *et al.*, 2020; Stirling *et al.*, 2021), so they are not strictly representative of multiple data points at a single site.

2. The estimated magnitudes and resulting ground motions of earthquakes from the NSHM that would topple the PBRs occur at return periods considerably longer than the age of the rocks. This means that the fragilities and ages of the PBRs are consistent with the NSHM, although we note that many of the PBRs have a less than 50% chance of survival given the NSHM assumptions. This is a very different result from those of PBR studies in the active plate boundary settings of the western United States and New Zealand (e.g., Rood *et al.*, 2020; Stirling *et al.*, 2021), where PBR survival is typically inconsistent with the PSH models. This difference in PSH is clearly illustrated by the hazard curves for Boston and Los Angeles in Figure 6.

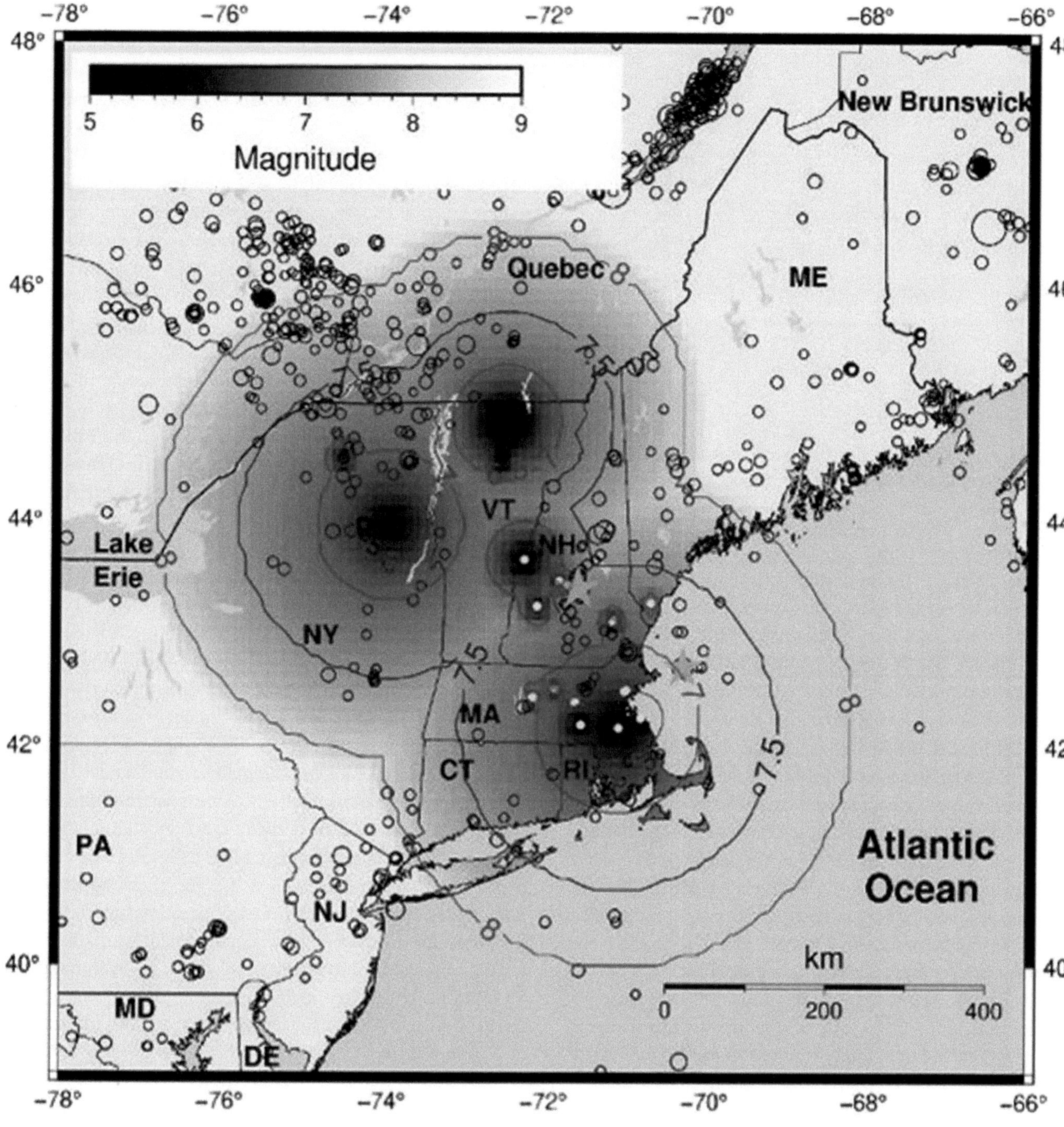

Figure 5. Contours of maximum postglacial earthquake magnitude based on the distribution, fragilities, and ages of the 13 PBRs. Each contour defines the limiting magnitude for the area inside that contour. Orange stars are the inferred locations of the 1638, $M_{Lg} \sim 6.5$ New Hampshire and 1755 $M_w \sim 5.9$ ($M_{Lg} \sim 6.2$) Cape Anne earthquakes (Ebel, 2006; Ebel and Starr, 2018; Pratt and Ebel, 2025). The color version of this figure is available only in the electronic edition.

DISCUSSION

The results of this study have positive implications for seismic hazard estimates in New England. Unlike PBR studies in the western United States and New Zealand, where plate boundary seismotectonics are present, and PBRs often imply that the estimated PSH is too high (e.g., Rood *et al.*, 2020), our PBRs appear to be consistent with the estimated PSH from the NSHM (Petersen *et al.*, 2024). The PBRs have survived since emplacement by the Laurentide ice sheet because earthquakes large enough and close enough to topple the rocks have not occurred in the time since emplacement. The Big Tippling PBR example in Figure 4 shows a high-survival probability (26%) relative to the NSHM hazard. This is because the fragility age (17.9 ka) is considerably less than the age that would equate to a low (5%) survival probability (41 ka; Fig. 4d).

The hazard curve comparison for Boston and Los Angeles (Fig. 6) shows a factor of 10 difference in the annual rate of

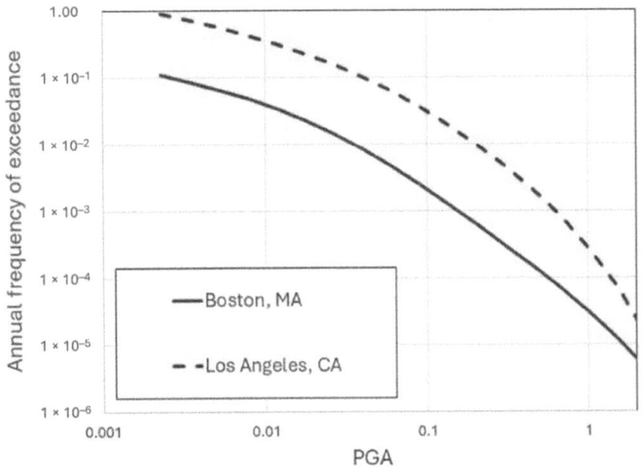

Figure 6. Comparison of PGA hazard curves from the NSHM for Boston and Los Angeles, illustrating the large difference in hazard and thus ground-motion exceedance rates for the two regions. The color version of this figure is available only in the electronic edition.

exceedance (y axis). This means that ground motions that could topple similarly fragile PBRs in the western United States would occur about 10 times more often than in the eastern United States. Although our analysis of the Big Tippling PBR (Fig. 4) shows that the fragility age would need to be about 41 ka for the PBR to have a low-survival probability (5%) relative to the NSHM hazard, the equivalent number for that PBR would only be about 4 ka in the western United States. The hazard curve comparison thus explains how so many PBRs can survive in the eastern United States. Given that the physical and geometrical basis for PBR fragility estimation is the same in the eastern United States as for the PBR studies in plate boundary settings, the explanation for the very different results must reside within the PSH method. Specifically, the PSH estimates in the active plate boundary settings may be overestimated at return periods equivalent to the ages of the PBRs because of the application of the ergodic assumption. In contrast, the low-seismicity rates in the eastern United States imply very low impact of the ergodic assumption on the PSH model at return periods equivalent to the PBR ages, resulting in the PSH being low and consistent with the PBR survival. The eastern U.S. PBR ages would have to be substantially older to observe similar discrepancies to those observed in the active plate boundary settings.

There are considerable uncertainties in our analysis that should be acknowledged. The fragility ages assume that the PBRs were emplaced in their present fragile states at a time estimated by interpolation between the contours in Figure 3. There will be uncertainties in these contours in terms of the location and timing of ice retreat, and the retreat may have occurred in pulses, rather than steadily. However, we sense that these uncertainties would not be so significant as to significantly impact the results of our study. For instance, the contoured ice front timings (Fig. 3) likely are not mislocated by 100 km or more because there has been a great deal of research and associated age dating that has gone into producing them (e.g., Barth *et al.*, 2019). The other issue surrounding the fragility ages is the question of whether the PBRs were once supported by till and/or outwash gravels (a time of reduced fragility). However, this seems unrealistic as the PBRs are all located on hillocks, ridges, and mountain tops where such sediments would not have been deposited, or would have been rapidly shed. Another question is whether the fragilities have increased with time due to weathering of the PBRs. However, the bedrock surfaces beneath a number of the PBRs show glacial striations, which indicates that even exposed, relatively flat surfaces (and the PBRs by inference) have not incurred much erosion since glaciation. The rocks are also very hard and relatively unweathered, which would imply very slow bedrock erosion rates. Finally, the protected bases of the PBRs have likely seen even less erosion than the exposed surfaces; therefore, it is unlikely that the fragility has changed much since the PBRs were emplaced.

The PGV/PGA on PGA regressions from Purvance *et al.* (2008) is the sole basis for the assessment of PBR fragility. It remains unknown how much the resulting fragility estimates would change if other methods of fragility estimation were applied, such as computer modeling (e.g., Veeraraghavan *et al.*, 2017; Chen *et al.*, 2024). Because the PBR topic area is presently restricted to a relatively small number of groups and individuals, there has been limited work on the topic area, and the Purvance *et al.* (2008) method remains as the standard method for fragility estimation. Our PBRs are near the upper range of the PBR sizes used in deriving the Purvance *et al.* (2008) equations (3.6 m maximum height), which raises the question of how relevant the equations are for these larger PBRs. Exploration of new methods of fragility estimation could form the basis for follow-up work. Some recent work has been focused on using numerical simulations of PBR fragilities, for instance (e.g., Veeraraghavan *et al.*, 2017; Wittich *et al.*, 2018; Chen *et al.*, 2024), but such studies are beyond the scope of our current work.

One issue is that the shapes of some of our PBRs are wide relative to their bases, as opposed to the more common narrow PBRs and rectangular blocks used to produce the Purvance *et al.* (2008) regressions. Therefore, some uncertainty exists around the applicability of the regressions to our PBR shapes, but until this effect is studied through computer models or shake-table tests, the Purvance *et al.* (2008) method is considered the best available.

The development of the maximum magnitude map (Fig. 5) uses a 90% survival probability criterion. We could be more conservative and develop the maps based on 95% survival probability, but consider 90% to represent a defensible level of conservatism. The map was calculated using the same ground-motion models as the NSHM, so we are consistent with the NSHM in this respect.

All PBR studies are site-specific, and the question of whether specific PBRs are statistical remnants of a former larger population is often discussed. Strong earthquake shaking could have toppled the majority of the PBR population, and the PBRs we observe today are the isolated remnants (i.e., the "lucky survivors"; e.g., Trugman *et al.*, 2023). This is the reason that we have looked for as many features as possible in the region, rather than basing a study on a single, most fragile PBR, or just a few of them. We consider that the number and fragilities of PBRs in our study area are sufficient to develop the maximum magnitude map in Figure 5. This is particularly evident in the area around Boston, where a significant number of PBRs are present in and around the city. Our PBR dataset may also have been biased to the largest rocks if the smaller ones were toppled long ago by people in the area. PBRs, more fragile than those of our analysis, also may have been excluded from the analysis because of toppling by humans. Smaller PBRs may be present in the region, but they do not attract as much attention as the larger PBRs, or they may be on private property and therefore not locatable online or in the literature. The distribution and number of PBRs near Boston may also be influenced by the distribution of potential sources for erratics. The area south of New Hampshire's White Mountains was potentially a rich source locale for the ice sheet to pick up rocks and transport them southward.

Finally, our results may not eliminate the possibility of large-magnitude earthquakes occurring in the region. The results are only relevant for the time that has elapsed since the PBRs were emplaced (17.9 ka in the case of the Big Tippling PBR example; Fig. 2b), and we use a 90% probability of toppling. Therefore, larger earthquakes could occur on longer timescales, as indicated by the portion of the hazard curve extending to the lower right of our PBR constraint in Figure 4d. Earthquakes of substantial size could have also occurred in the region that lacked the necessary waveforms (pulse durations) to topple the PBRs (e.g., Trugman *et al.*, 2023).

CONCLUSIONS

We have compared the age and fragility of 13 PBRs in Massachusetts, New Hampshire, and southwestern Maine to estimated ground motions from the NSHM, and have also developed a maximum magnitude map for the region. The fragilities and ages of the PBRs appear to be consistent with the NSHM, in that the NSHM indicates earthquake magnitudes and resulting ground motions that could topple them occur at time intervals greater than the ages of the PBRs. These results are similar to those of McPhillips and Pratt (2024) for rocks in New York and Vermont. This result differs from some PBR studies in the plate boundary settings of the western United States and New Zealand, where estimated PSH often turns out to be high relative to the age and fragility of PBRs. It may be the case that the PBRs are not old enough in the eastern United States to reveal the same issues as those revealed in the plate boundary settings.

DATA AND RESOURCES

The data collected for the precariously balanced rocks (PBRs) in this article are archived in Pratt and Stirling (2026). Software packages "Meshroom" and "Meshlab" were accessed at https://alicevision.org/#meshroom (last accessed February 2026) and https://www.meshlab.net/ (last accessed February 2026), respectively. The Google Earth website is available at earth.google.com (last accessed May 2025). The models, point clouds and other data for these PBRs is available online in a USGS data release at https://www.sciencebase.gov/catalog/item/6894e2dfd4be0274c8e01149 (last accessed February 2026). These data include PBR slenderness angles, radius angles, and masses.

DECLARATION OF COMPETING INTERESTS

The authors acknowledge that there are no conflicts of interest recorded.

ACKNOWLEDGMENTS

The authors thank Christie Butler, Jan Butler, and Russell Dunn for their invaluable work on documenting the rocks that form the basis for this study. Daniel Trugman is thanked for his assistance with a preliminary fragility analysis, and the authors thank Paula Figueiredo and Devin McPhillips for many insightful chats on this topic. The authors thank Rachel Abercrombie for assistance in the field and Kate Pratt for welcoming author M. Stirling to the East Coast and for the great India Pale Ale (IPA)-fuelled chats. The article benefited from reviews by Devin McPhillips, Glen Biasi, and Associate Editor Ivan Wong. The authors finally thank the University of Otago for supporting the travel costs for Stirling's 2023 Sabbatical, the U.S. Geological Survey (USGS) for supporting T. Pratt's and M. Stirling's domestic field and travel costs, and the Nuclear Regulatory Commission (NRC) for supporting T. Pratt. Any use of trade, firm, or product names is for descriptive purposes only and does not imply endorsement by the U.S. Government.

REFERENCES

Baker, J. W., N. A. Abrahamson, J. W. Whitney, M. P. Board, and T. C. Hanks (2013). Use of fragile geologic structures as indicators of unexceeded ground motions and direct constraints on probabilistic seismic hazard analysis, *Bull. Seismol. Soc. Am.* **103,** no. 3, 1898–1911, doi: 10.1785/0120120202.

Barani, S., M. Massa, S. Lovati, and D. Spillarossa (2014). Effects of surface topography on ground shaking prediction: Implications for seismic hazard analysis and recommendations for seismic design, *Geophys. J. Int.* **197,** no. 3, 1551–1565, doi: 10.1093/gji/ggu095.

Barth, A. M., S. A. Marcott, J. M. Licciardi, and J. D. Shakun (2019). Deglacial thinning of the Laurentide Ice Sheet in the Adirondack Mountains, New York, USA, revealed by 36Cl exposure dating, *Paleoceanogr. Paleoclimatol.* **34,** no. 6, 946–953, doi: 10.1029/2018PA003477.

Brune, J. N. (1996). Precarious rocks and acceleration maps for southern California, *Bull. Seism. Soc. Am.* **86,** no. 1A, 43–54, doi: 10.1785/BSSA08601A0043.

Butler, C., and R. Dunn (2016). Rockachusetts: An explorer's guide to amazing boulders of Massachusetts, CreateSpace Independent Publishing Platform (now Amazon KDP Print), 329 pp.

Butler, J., and C. Butler (2018). Erratic Wandering: An explorer's hiking guide to astonishing boulders in Maine, New Hampshire and

Vermont, CreateSpace Independent Publishing Platform (now Amazon KDP Print), 285 pp.

Chen, Z, R. Arrowsmith, J. Das, C. Wittich, C. Madugo, and A. Kottke (2024). Virtual shake robot: Simulating dynamics of precariously balanced rocks for overturning and large-displacement processes, *Seismica* **3,** no. 1, 25, doi: 10.26443/seismica.v3i1.692.

Ebel, J. E. (2006). The Cape Ann, Massachusetts earthquake of 1755: A 250th anniversary perspective, *Seismol. Res. Lett.* **77,** no. 1, 74–86, doi: 10.1785/gssrl.77.1.74.

Ebel, J. E., and J. C. Starr (2018). A geophysical and field survey for the source region of the 1638 New Hampshire earthquake, *Seismol. Res. Lett.* **89,** no. 3, 1197–1211, doi: 10.1785/0220170266.

Hough, S. E., J.-R. Altidor, D. Anglade, D. Given, M. G. Janvier, J. Z. Maharrey, M. Meremonte, B. S.-L. Midor, C. Prepetit, and A. Yong (2010). Localized damage caused by topographic amplification during the 2010 M 7.0 Haiti earthquake, *Nature Geosci.* **3,** 778–782, doi: 10.1038/NGEO988.

Khan, S., M. van der Meijde, H. van der Werff, and M. Shafique (2020). The impact of topography on seismic amplification during the 2005 Kashmir earthquake, *Nat. Hazards Earth Syst. Sci.* **20,** no. 2, 399–411, doi: 10.5194/nhess-20-399-2020.

McPhillips, D., and T. L. Pratt (2024). Precariously balanced rocks in northern New York and Vermont, U.S.A.: Ground-motion constraints and implications for fault sources, *Bull. Seismol. Soc. Am.* **114,** no. 6, 3171–3182, doi: 10.1785/0120240069.

Modha, K., D. Raj, and Y. Singh (2019). Topographic amplification of earthquake ground motion on hills of bell-shaped geometry, in S. Patel, C. H. Solanki, K. R. Reddy, and S. K. Shukla (Editors), *Proc. of the Indian Geotechnical Conference 2019, Lecture Notes on Civil Engineering 138,* 185–195, doi: 10.1007/978-981-33-6564-3_17.

Modha, K. G., D. Raj, Y. Singh, and D. H. Lang (2020). Topographic amplification of earthquake ground motion on different hill geometries, *Proc. of the 17th World Conference on Earthquake Engineering (17WCEE),* Sendai, Japan, Paper 1f-0035, 12 pp., available at https://wcee.nicee.org/wcee/article/17WCEE/1f-0035.pdf (last accessed December 2025).

Molina, S., D. H. Lang, Y. Singh, and A. Meslem (2019). A period dependent topographic amplification model for earthquake loss estimation, *Bull. Earthq. Eng.* **17,** 3709–3725, doi: 10.1007/s10518-019-00608-1.

Petersen, M. D., A. M. Shumway, P. M. Powers, E. H. Field, M. P. Moschetti, K. S. Jaiswal, K. R. Milner, S. Rezaeian, A. D. Frankel, A. L. Llenos, *et al.* (2024). The 2023 U.S. 50-State National Seismic Hazard Model: Overview and implications, *Earthq. Spectra* **40,** no. 1, 5–88, doi: 10.1177/87552930231215428.

Pratt, T. L., and J. Ebel (2025). ShakeMap scenario catalog for selected historical New England earthquakes, U.S. Geological Survey, available at https://earthquake.usgs.gov/scenarios/catalog/nefema/ (last accessed December 2025).

Pratt, T. L., and M. W. Stirling (2026). Data for analyzing precariously balanced rocks (PBRs) in the northeastern U.S. to estimate maximum post-glacial ground motions, *U.S. Geol. Surv. Data Release,* doi: 10.5066/P13SXGWX.

Pratt, T. L., M. W. Stirling, D. McPhillips, and P. M. Figueiredo (2026). Characterizing precariously balanced rocks in the eastern U.S. for estimating maximum earthquake ground motions, *Bull. Seismol. Soc. Am.* doi: 10.1785/0120250131.

Purvance, M. D., A. Anooshehpoor, and J. N. Brune (2008). Freestanding block overturning fragilities: Numerical simulation and experimental validation, *Earthq. Eng. Struct. Dynam.* **37,** no. 5, 791–808, doi: 10.1002/eqe.789.

Rault, C., W.-A. Chao, C. Gelis, A. Burtin, J.-M. Chang, O. Marc, T.-S. Lai, Y.-M. Wu, N. Hovius, and P. Meunier (2020). Seismic response of a mountain ridge prone to landsliding, *Bull. Seismol. Soc. Am.* **110,** no. 6, 3004–3020, doi: 10.1785/0120190127.

Rood, A. H., D. H. Rood, M. W. Stirling, C. M. Madugo, N. A. Abrahamson, K. M. Wilcken, T. Gonzalez, A. Kottke, A. C. Whittaker, W. D. Page, and P. J. Stafford (2020). Earthquake hazard uncertainties improved using precariously balanced rocks, *AGU Adv.* **1,** no. 4, e2020AV000182, doi: 10.1029/2020AV000182.

Singh, Y., S. Ahmad, D. Raj, K. Modha, and D. Lang (2018). Spectral amplification modeling for triangular hill geometry, *Proc. of the 16th European Conference on Earthquake Engineering (16ECEE),* Thessaloniki, Greece, Paper 11946, 11 pp.

Stirling, M. W., E. R. Abbott, D. H. Rood, G. H. McVerry, N. A. Abrahamson, D. J. A. Barrell, R. Huso, N. J. Litchfield, L. Luna, D. A. Rhoades, *et al.* (2021). First use of fragile geologic features to set the design motions for a major existing engineered structure, *Bull. Seismol. Soc. Am.* **111,** no. 5, 2673–2695, doi: 10.1785/0120210026.

Trugman, D. T., J. Brune, K. D. Smith, J. N. Louie, and G. M. Kent (2023). The rocks that did not fall: A multidisciplinary analysis of near-source ground motions from an active normal fault, *AGU Adv.* **4,** no. 2, e2023AV000885, doi: 10.1029/2023AV000885.

Veeraraghavan, S., K. Hudnut, and S. Krishnan (2017). Toppling analysis of the Echo Cliff precariously balanced rock, *Bull. Seismol. Soc. Am.* **107,** no. 1, 72–81, doi: 10.1785/0120160169.

Wittich, C. E., T. C. Hutchinson, J. DeSanto, and D. Sandwell (2018). 3-D reconstructions and numerical simulations of precarious rocks in Southern California, *Proc. of the 11th National Conference on Earthquake Engineering (11NCEE),* Los Angeles, California, 10 pp., University of Nebraska-Lincoln Civil Engineering Faculty Publications 154, available at https://digitalcommons.unl.edu/civilengfacpub/154 (last accessed December 2025).

Yin, C., W.-H. Li, and W. Wang (2021). Evaluation of ground motion amplification effects in slope topography induced by the arbitrary directions of seismic waves, *Energies* **14,** no. 20, 6744, doi: 10.3390/en14206744.

Manuscript received 2 July 2025
Published online 19 February 2026

The U.S. Geological Survey 2025 Puerto Rico and U.S. Virgin Islands Time-Independent Earthquake Rupture Forecast

Kevin R. Milner*[1], Alexandra E. Hatem[2], Richard W. Briggs[2], Jessica A. Thompson-Jobe[2], Andrea L. Llenos[2], Andrew J. Michael[3], Allison M. Shumway[2], Edward H. Field[2], and Kirstie L. Haynie[2]

ABSTRACT

OPEN ACCESS

We present the 2025 U.S. Geological Survey Puerto Rico and U.S. Virgin Islands (PRVI) time-independent earthquake rupture forecast (ERF), developed for the 2025 update to the National Seismic Hazard Model (NSHM) for PRVI. The updated ERF improves upon a prior model from 2003, including an expanded fault inventory with slip-rate estimates, updated seismicity catalogs, and refined subduction zone geometries and deformation models. It applies the fault-system inversion methodology to solve for rates of ruptures on modeled faults, adapted from the 2023 NSHM (NSHM23) for the western United States, including the first application of the inversion to model rates on a U.S. subduction interface. Off-fault and intraslab seismicity are constrained by observed seismicity and use updated methods developed for NSHM23. Uncertainties in model components are substantial, and the ERF represents epistemic uncertainties through a comprehensive logic tree consisting of 1.7 billion logic-tree branches combined across all sources.

KEY POINTS

- We present a new earthquake rupture forecast for Puerto Rico and the U.S. Virgin Islands.
- We apply the fault-system inversion methodology to both crustal faults and subduction interfaces.
- This model can be used to inform building codes and other risk mitigation efforts.

INTRODUCTION

This article documents the U.S. Geological Survey (USGS) 2025 Puerto Rico and U.S. Virgin Islands (PRVI) time-independent earthquake rupture forecast (ERF). ERFs aim to enumerate and assign probabilities to all plausible and potentially damaging earthquakes within a region. They are used in combination with empirical ground-motion models (GMMs) in probabilistic seismic hazard analyses to estimate ground-motion exceedance probabilities over a specified duration. The USGS develops National Seismic Hazard Models (NSHMs) that provide authoritative estimates of seismic hazards and are widely used to inform building codes and other risk mitigation efforts (e.g., insurance pricing and disaster preparedness).

The 2025 update to the PRVI NSHM (NSHM25-PRVI) is a multidisciplinary effort to better quantify seismic hazards in the PRVI region by incorporating new data and updated modeling techniques. The first NSHM for PRVI was released in 2003 (NSHM03-PRVI; Mueller *et al.*, 2010); subsequent studies have improved the inventory of active faults (Thompson Jobe *et al.*, 2024) and slip rates (Hatem *et al.*, 2026), seismicity catalogs (Llenos *et al.*, 2025), and subduction interface geometry and convergence rates (Shumway *et al.*, 2025). The updated ERF integrates these new data using updated modeling techniques that build upon recent NSHMs, namely the fault-system inversion (Milner and Field, 2023) and gridded seismicity (Llenos *et al.*, 2024; Michael and Llenos, 2025) methodologies developed for the 2023 NSHM for the western United States (NSHM23-WUS; Field *et al.*, 2023). The NSHM23-WUS modeling framework includes systematic quantification of epistemic

1. Geologic Hazards Science Center, U.S. Geological Survey, Pasadena, California, U.S.A., https://orcid.org/0000-0002-9118-6378 (KRM); 2. Geologic Hazards Science Center, U.S. Geological Survey, Golden, Colorado, U.S.A., https://orcid.org/0000-0001-7584-2235 (AEH); https://orcid.org/0000-0001-8108-0046 (RWB); https://orcid.org/0000-0001-5574-4523 (JAT-J); https://orcid.org/0000-0002-4088-6737 (ALL); https://orcid.org/0000-0003-1142-7141 (AMS); https://orcid.org/0000-0001-8172-7882 (EHF); https://orcid.org/0000-0001-9930-6736 (KLH); 3. Earthquake Science Center, U.S. Geological Survey, Moffett Field, California, U.S.A., https://orcid.org/0000-0002-2403-5019 (AJM)

*Corresponding author: kmilner@usgs.gov

Cite this article as Milner, K. R., A. E. Hatem, R. W. Briggs, J. A. Thompson-Jobe, A. L. Llenos, A. J. Michael, A. M. Shumway, E. H. Field, and K. L. Haynie (2026). The U.S. Geological Survey 2025 Puerto Rico and U.S. Virgin Islands Time-Independent Earthquake Rupture Forecast, *Bull. Seismol. Soc. Am.* **116**, 1321–1351, doi: 10.1785/0120250040

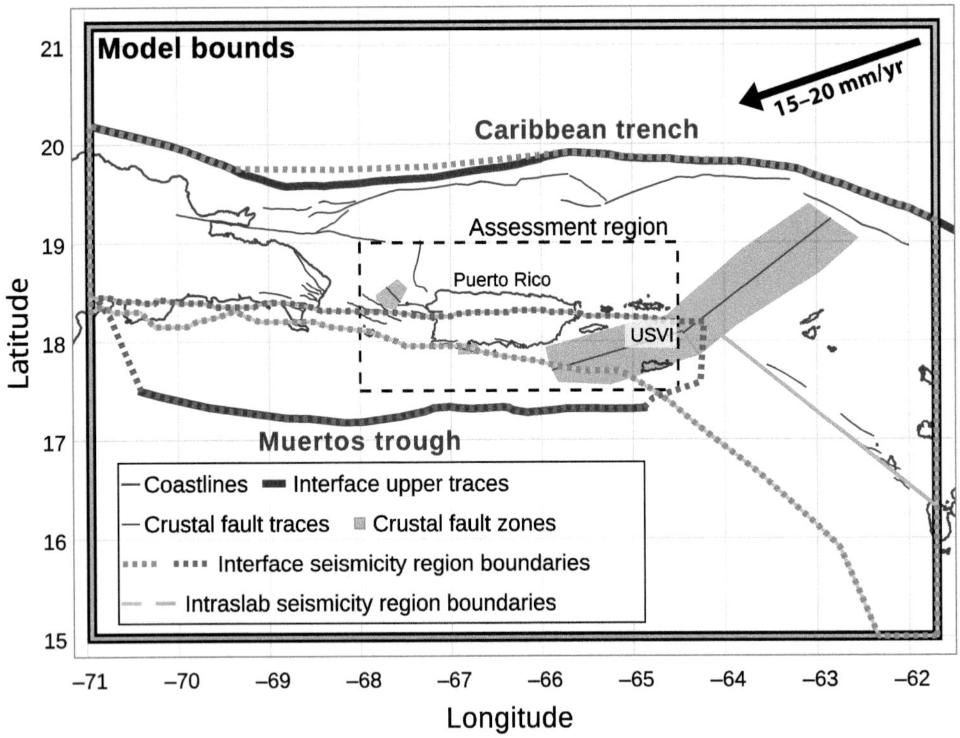

Figure 1. Model bounds and tectonic setting. The large, thick, black rectangle outlines the full geographic extent of the model. The thin, black dashed rectangle outlines the assessment region for which hazard maps are computed. Subset regions for interface and intraslab gridded seismicity sources are outlined in dotted and solid colored lines, respectively; separate regions exist for sources related to the Caribbean trench (orange) and Muertos trough (green), and regions overlap in map view but do not intersect at depth. Crustal fault traces are drawn with thin dark gray lines, and fault zones are drawn with gray shaded polygons. The upper trace of the subduction interface sources are drawn with a thick dark gray line. The plate convergence rate of 15–20 mm/yr (Calais *et al.*, 2016) is annotated with a black arrow. The locations of Puerto Rico and the U.S. Virgin Islands (USVI) are annotated. The color version of this figure is available only in the electronic edition.

uncertainties (both in input datasets and model assumptions), a key improvement over NSHM03-PRVI. These advances align with broader USGS goals to standardize methodologies across regions and robustly quantify uncertainties (Field *et al.*, 2025).

The overall NSHM25-PRVI model input data, results, and downstream products are available in Shumway *et al.* (2025). All hazard calculations presented use an updated suite of regionally modified GMMs developed by Moschetti *et al.* (2026).

REVIEW PROCESS AND RECOMMENDATIONS

ERF model development was overseen by a 14-member participatory review panel consisting of subject-matter experts, many of whom have regional expertise, and chaired by Thomas Jordan. The review process involved three open-participation briefings during which the development team presented the model to the review panel, two closed panel deliberation meetings, a written report from the panel with recommendations, and responses from the development team. The review panel ultimately recommended adoption of the NSHM25-PRVI ERF documented here in the NSHM (Thomas Jordan, University of Southern California, written comm., 2025).

As part of their review, the panel provided 16 actionable and 19 aspirational recommendations, which led to various improvements incorporated in the final model. One notable improvement was the addition of an epistemic uncertainty branch for the seismic coupling factor of the Caribbean and Muertos interface sources (refer to the Interface deformation models section). Many of the recommendations involved sensitivity tests to quantify the influence of various modeling choices. The panel's recommendations and results from these sensitivity tests are summarized in the sections that follow as each model component is discussed.

TECTONIC SETTING AND MODEL COMPONENTS

PRVI are situated in a tectonically complex region with a long history of damaging earthquakes (McCann *et al.*, 2010). They are located on the PRVI microplate (Jansma *et al.*, 2000), part of the Caribbean plate near the oblique subducting North American plate and sandwiched between the Caribbean trench and Muertos trough subduction interface sources (Fig. 1). Overall plate convergence is estimated to be 15–20 mm/yr by Calais *et al.* (2016), and the oblique angle results in a complex combination of interface and crustal sources, the latter of which are primarily left-lateral strike-slip.

The NSHM25-PRVI ERF models magnitude (**M**) >5 earthquakes from active crustal, subduction interface, and subduction intraslab sources (Fig. 2). The crustal model consists of finite-fault ruptures on known faults with slip-rate estimates, and fault zones representing areas of distributed deformation in which the exact structures are poorly constrained. Rupture rates for crustal faults and fault zones are determined using the fault-system inversion, fitting slip rates supplied by a geologic deformation model (Hatem *et al.*, 2026). A gridded seismicity model is included that is based on observed crustal seismicity and accounts for unknown faults and smaller ruptures in the immediate vicinity of explicitly modeled faults (Llenos *et al.*, 2025; Michael and Llenos, 2025). The subduction interface

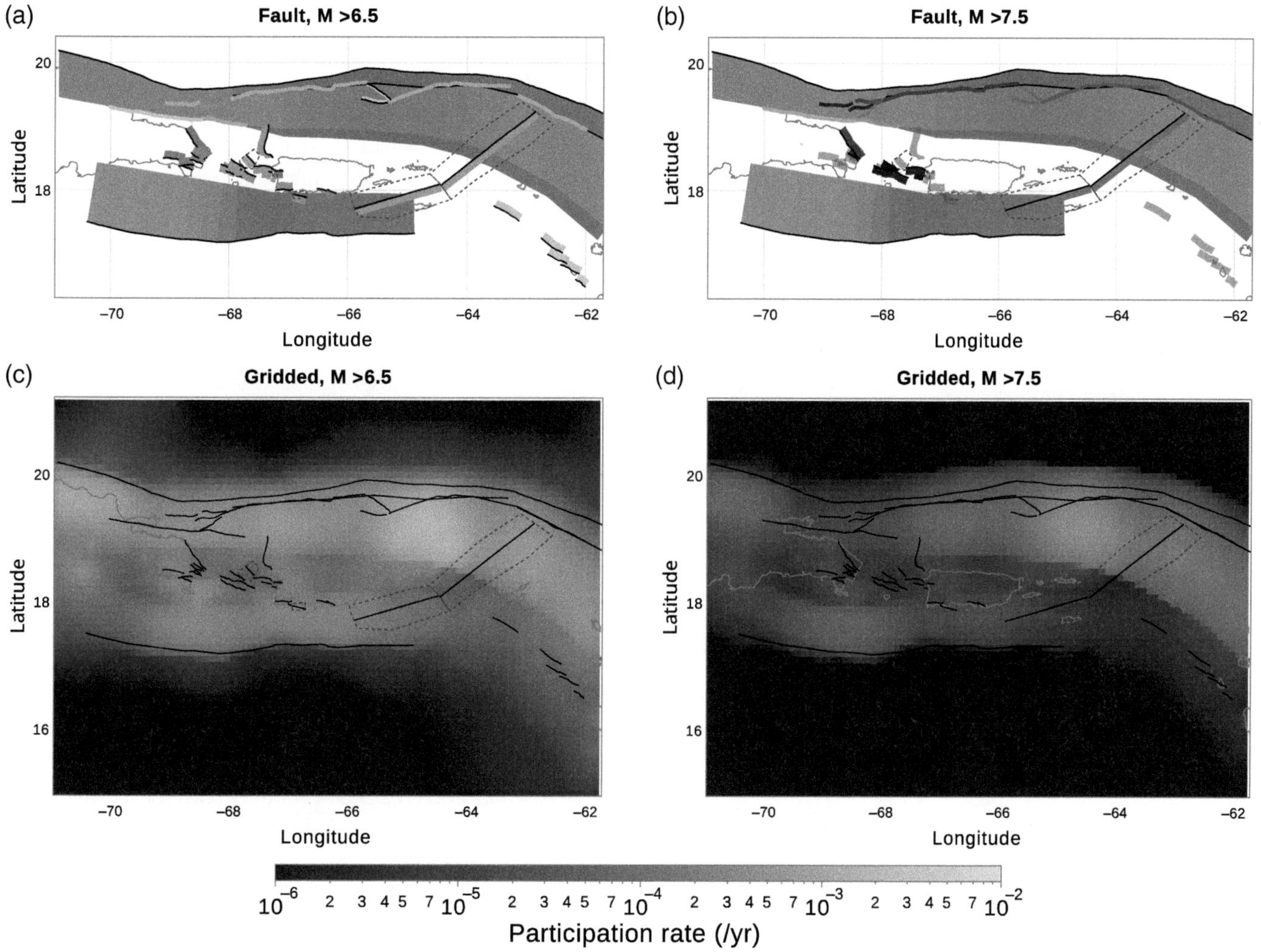

Figure 2. Rates at which modeled (a,b) finite faults and (c,d) grid cells participate in (a,c) **M** >6.5 and (b,d) **M** >7.5 earthquakes. (a,b) Faults are colored by the rate (on a logarithmic scale) at which they participate in supraseismogenic earthquakes (i.e., those that rupture the full seismogenic thickness of the fault) above the magnitude threshold (or gray if the rate is zero). Subduction interface sources are nearly identical in (a) and (b) because the minimum magnitude considered for those sources is typically **M** >7.5 [interface ruptures below that threshold are included in (c,d)]. Fault-zone polygons are outlined with dark gray dashed lines and their proxy fault representations are plotted. (c,d) Grid cell participation rates (on a logarithmic scale) computed from the gridded seismicity model and excluding events on modeled faults. We estimate participation (rather than nucleation) grid cell rates using finite ruptures surfaces when available (i.e., for subduction interface gridded ruptures) and using spinning random-strike finite surfaces for crustal ruptures. Slab ruptures are treated as point sources, and thus only the nucleation grid cell is counted. The color version of this figure is available only in the electronic edition.

model uses observed seismicity to model smaller ruptures, and the fault-system inversion methodology to model large trench-breaking ruptures subject to estimates of plate convergence (Shumway *et al.*, 2025). The subduction intraslab model is composed of gridded point sources and is based purely on observed seismicity.

FAULT-SYSTEM INVERSION METHODOLOGY

We use the fault-system inversion approach to solve for the annual occurrence rates of earthquake ruptures on modeled faults (referred to hereafter as rupture rates). We apply the methodologies and constraints established in NSHM23-WUS (Field *et al.*, 2020, 2023; Milner and Field, 2023), which builds upon those from the Third Uniform Earthquake Rupture Forecast (UCERF3; Field *et al.*, 2014; Page *et al.*, 2014) and earlier work (Andrews and Schwerer, 2000; Field and Page, 2011). The fault-system inversion approach is a general solution that can simultaneously fit multiple data constraints, including fault slip rates, observed or assumed regional magnitude–frequency distributions (MFDs), and recurrence rate constraints (such as those at paleoseismic trench sites, when available). It accommodates multifault ruptures so long because they pass physical plausibility criteria and segmentation constraints that control their propensity (Valentini *et al.*, 2019; Milner and Field, 2023)—a key improvement over earlier segmented approaches (e.g., Field *et al.*, 2009; Mueller *et al.*, 2010) that largely excluded multifault ruptures despite numerous occurrences in nature

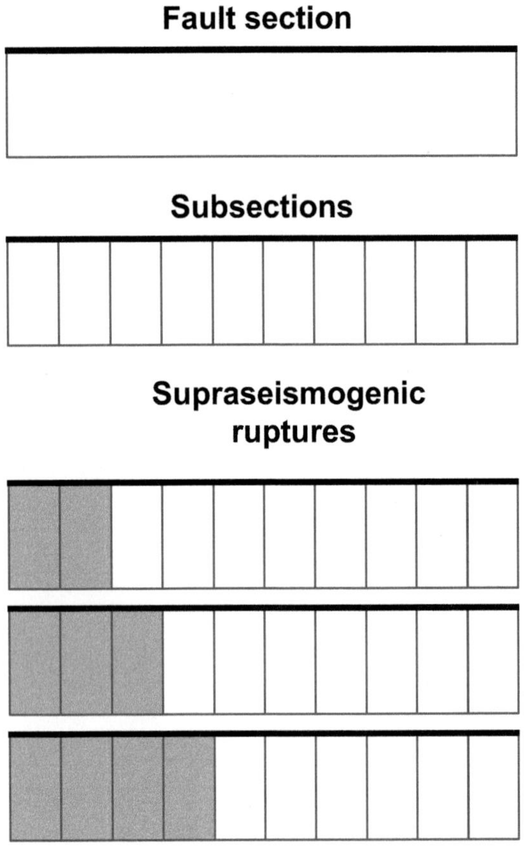

Figure 3. Schematic diagram of fault section, subsection, and supraseismogenic rupture definitions, used for both the crustal and interface models. Each are shown from the side view, and the bold line at the top represents the upper trace of the fault. The top panel depicts a single rectangular fault section. The middle panel depicts that fault section broken up into 10 equal-length subsections, each with length approximately equal to half the down-dip width. The bottom panel depicts three different supraseismogenic ruptures highlighted in gray. Supraseismogenic ruptures are defined as earthquakes that rupture the full seismogenic thickness of the fault and are represented as unique sets of at least two subsections.

(e.g., the 1992 Landers, Hauksson *et al.*, 1993; 2016 Kaikōura, Hamling *et al.*, 2017; and 2023 Türkiye–Syria, Xu *et al.*, 2023, earthquakes).

The first step for the inversion approach is to rediscretize each fault section into shorter, equal-length subsections (shown schematically in Fig. 3). The next step is to define the set of supraseismogenic ruptures on the fault system, that is, those that rupture the full seismogenic thickness of the fault and consist of at least two subsections. For crustal faults, subsections are approximately half as long as the down-dip width, and the average minimum magnitude is 5.9 (refer to the Crustal fault model and rupture set section). For subduction interface sources, subsections are approximately 30 km long, and we apply an aspect ratio constraint in addition to the two-subsection minimum; the average interface minimum magnitude is 7.8 (refer to the Interface fault models section).

Multifault ruptures are those for which subsections from multiple fault sections participate and are included subject to plausibility criteria. As in NSHM23-WUS, we use the criteria from Milner *et al.* (2022), who use jump distance and various metrics of Coulomb compatibility of fault subsections to assess the plausibility of multifault rupture.

We follow the constraint recipe established for NSHM23-WUS by Milner and Field (2023). The primary data constraint available for each fault in the model is fault slip rates. The inversion matches slip-rate data from the deformation model on each fault subsection, ensuring that

$$\sum_{r=1}^{R} D_{sr} f_r = v_s, \quad (1)$$

in which D_{sr} is the slip on the sth subsection in the rth rupture (determined from a magnitude- or length-scaling relationship), f_r is the occurrence rate of the rth rupture, v_s is the slip rate on the sth subsection, and R is the number of ruptures involving s. There are many possible solutions to (1), so we also constrain the inversion to match a prescribed Gutenberg–Richter (GR) nucleation b value. The GR b value is used to control how each slip rate is satisfied. High b values (e.g., $b = 1$) satisfy fault slip rates using substantially more moderate ruptures near the minimum supraseismogenic magnitude than large ruptures near M_{max}. Low b values (e.g., $b = 0$) satisfy fault slip rates primarily using ruptures near M_{max}, resulting in a lower overall event rate. Although the rates of the largest events are higher when $b = 0$ compared with $b = 1$, hazard for individual sites at typical return periods of engineering interest (e.g., one-second spectral acceleration with 2% probability of exceedance in 50 yr) is generally lower because hazard is closely related to the overall supraseismogenic event rate (Field *et al.*, 2020). Even though regional b values are constrained observationally, on-fault supraseismogenic b values remain uncertain and are represented with branches on the epistemic logic tree.

We construct target nucleation MFDs on each subsection that satisfy the original slip rate and match the chosen GR b value. We apply a constraint on each subsection to match the total rate from its target MFD, and apply a regional MFD constraint using the sum of each subsection target MFD to ensure that the region as a whole matches the specified GR b value throughout the entire supraseismogenic magnitude range.

We apply segmentation constraints that control the propensity of multifault ruptures, representing a key epistemic uncertainty (Schwartz, 2018; Page, 2020). Five models are included: a classic model that is fully segmented and solved analytically (bypassing the inversion), a fully unsegmented model, and three jump-distance-dependent models.

Unlike the NSHM23 model, no robust paleoseismic recurrence data are available on our modeled faults (Thompson Jobe *et al.*, 2024). Refer to Milner and Field (2023) for the implementation details and motivation for each inversion constraint.

GRIDDED SEISMICITY METHODOLOGY

A gridded seismicity model is included to account for earthquakes not associated with explicitly modeled faults, as well as those below the minimum supraseismogenic magnitude of included faults. This is a statistical model derived from observational seismology, and the process follows methodologies established in prior models, for example, NSHM23 (Field *et al.*, 2023; Llenos *et al.*, 2024; Powers *et al.*, 2024). The basic components are earthquake catalog collection and curation, catalog separation by tectonic regime, regional rate estimates, catalog declustering and spatial smoothing, and model implementation as sources in the ERF.

The earthquake catalog was compiled and curated following the same methodologies used in past NSHM earthquake catalogs (Mueller, 2018). This included querying events from the Advanced National Seismic System Comprehensive Earthquake Catalog (U.S. Geological Survey, Earthquake Hazards Program, 2017) and from an updated Puerto Rico Seismic Network (PRSN) catalog (Huérfano and Lin, 2022), converting all magnitude types to moment magnitude, determining parameters for computing unbiased seismicity rates, combining the two input catalogs based on authoritative region, and removing duplicate and nontectonic events (Llenos *et al.*, 2025).

The earthquake catalog was separated by tectonic regime following the methods in Haynie *et al.* (2025), which classifies earthquakes into crustal, subduction interface, or intraslab, primarily based on Slab2 subduction zone geometries (Hayes *et al.*, 2018) for the Muertos and Caribbean slabs. Classifications are sensitive to the depth of each earthquake (relative to the Slab2 surface), and many events are assigned default depths (typically at 15, 25, or 33 km) in the catalog. We supplemented the catalog using depths from Doser *et al.* (2005) for 10 large historical earthquakes from 1900 to 1943 and used the 20-km depth from Russo and Villaseñor (1995) for the 1946 Hispaniola earthquake. For each remaining event with a fixed catalog depth—51% of **M** >6 events from 1900 to 1973, and 14% of **M** >5 events from 1973 to 2023—we search the catalog for nearby **M** >4 surrogate events since 1973 with known depths within 15 km of the original event's epicenter, and average classification plausibility scores across all surrogate events (refer to Llenos *et al.*, 2025, for further details of this procedure). Classification plausibility scores for each event are used to probabilistically assign events to each regime in the steps that follow, and regime-specific GMMs are used when computing hazard.

Michael and Llenos (2025) document the procedures used to estimate the rate and GR b value of each catalog, accounting for the time-varying magnitude of completeness (M_c). Those values are estimated from the joint distribution of the Poisson rate of earthquakes and GR b values, evaluated for $\mathbf{M} > M_1$, in which $M_1 = 5$ is the minimum gridded seismicity magnitude included in the model. They first estimate the b value distribution for the entire region (including events across all tectonic regimes). Within each tectonic regime, they then generate 100,000 Monte Carlo realizations of the catalog sampling uncertainties in M_c, individual event magnitudes and tectonic regime classifications. The uncertainty in tectonic regime classifications was not documented in Michael and Llenos (2025) and is done by selecting events for each sample proportionally to their plausibility score for that regime. For each realization, they sample a rate from the Poisson likelihood for the number of earthquakes in that realization and extrapolate that rate from that sample's M_c to M_1 using a b value drawn from the previously estimated distribution. GR distributions for each sample are shown as light gray lines in Figure 4.

Michael and Llenos (2025) then estimate 95% confidence bounds from the simulated distribution of Monte Carlo GR samples for each regime. They describe three procedures for choosing logic-tree branches to represent those bounds (Fig. 4), and all methods use the rate of earthquakes above $M_1 = 5$ at the 2.5th and 97.5th percentiles of the simulated distribution. The exact distribution, computed at those percentiles directly from the simulated distribution for each magnitude, is shown in green dotted lines in Figure 4. NSHM23 used b values computed from the marginal distribution at those same percentiles; that method matched the exact distribution well across all magnitudes for NSHM23 regions but fails to match the shape of the distribution for NSHM25-PRVI in which $M_c > M_1$, resulting in exaggerated uncertainties (blue dashed lines in Fig. 4). In this case, Michael and Llenos (2025) propose to either pick b values that connect the exact distribution at M_1 and M_{max} (orange solid lines in Fig. 4) or to use the exact distribution directly. Even though the exact distribution branches are extracted directly from a Monte Carlo suite of GR distributions, they are not GR (i.e., they bend in Fig. 4), and using them would introduce an apparent inconsistency with the GR assumptions used to create that distribution. That is, we would be representing uncertainties in a GR model with end-member branches that are not GR and are thus not viable models under the GR assumption used to build the model. We chose to use the M_1–M_{max} branches because they approximate the exact distribution and are GR.

Because the catalog data are sparse and tectonic regime classification depends on depth, which is uncertain for all events and unknown for over half of the events before 1973, we introduce a new rate model epoch uncertainty level in the epistemic logic tree with three equally weighted choices: full, recent, and recent (scaled to full). On the full branch, both epochs are used in the rate model calculation (with $M_c = 6$ for 1900–1973 and $M_c = 5$ for 1973–2023). On the recent branch, only the more recent epoch is considered. A third branch, recent (scaled to full), uses the event classifications from the recent epoch in which depths are better constrained, but rescales the event rates to match the total **M** >5 event rate from the full branch (i.e., the estimated total rate across all regimes and both epochs). This effectively gives two-thirds weight to the event rates observed across the full catalog, and two-thirds weight

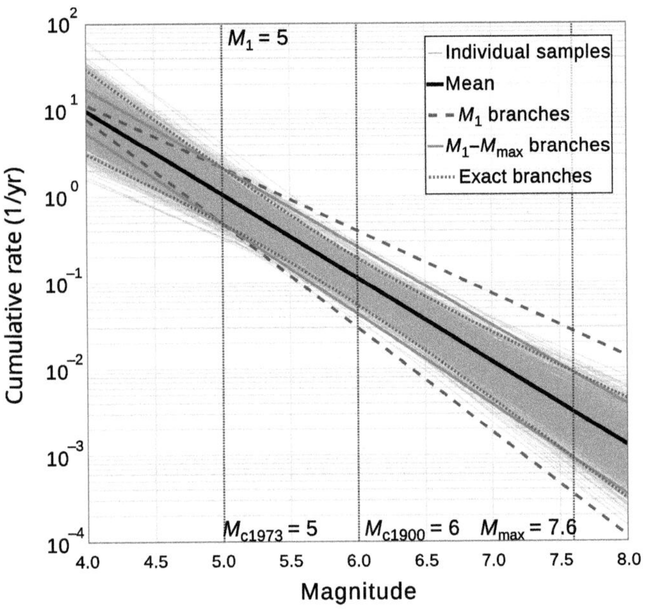

Figure 4. Cumulative regional magnitude–frequency distributions (MFDs) for crustal earthquakes estimated from observed seismicity by Michael and Llenos (2025). A total of 1,000 (of the 100,000 considered) individual Gutenberg–Richter (GR) samples are plotted in thin, gray lines, with each sampling uncertainty described in the text. The mean value from the simulated distribution is plotted with a black thick line. Three different options for representing the 95% confidence bounds are plotted in unique colors and line styles. The exact distribution branches, computed directly from the distribution of individual samples at each magnitude, are plotted with green dotted lines. The M_1 branches used in prior models, computed by taking rates and b values from their respective marginal distributions at the minimum gridded seismicity magnitude considered ($M_1 = 5$), are plotted with blue dashed lines. The M_1–M_{max} branches that we use here, which connect the exact distribution branches with a GR distribution between $M_1 = 5$ and $M_{max} = 7.6$, are plotted with solid orange lines. The dotted vertical lines mark the magnitude of completeness for the two epochs considered ($M_c = 6$ for 1900–1973 and $M_c = 5$ for 1973–2023), M_1, and M_{max}. The color version of this figure is available only in the electronic edition.

to the regime classifications for the recent epoch, in which only 14% of events have unknown depths in the catalog.

Llenos *et al.* (2024) describe the general process by which the curated catalogs are declustered and smoothed to produce spatial probability density functions (PDFs). Those PDFs are used to distribute the total seismicity rate into rates for individual cells of a discretized spatial grid (0.1° here). Although rate estimation uses the full catalog, catalogs are declustered to retain only independent events for spatial smoothing. All three declustering algorithms used in NSHM23 are retained: Gardner and Knopoff (1974), Reasenberg (1985), and Zaliapin and Ben-Zion (2020), although the weight assigned to the Reasenberg (1985) model was reduced to 10% on the recommendation of the review panel because it was deemed less effective at removing aftershocks from the PRVI catalog (Llenos *et al.*, 2025). The declustered catalogs are smoothed using a Gaussian kernel with either a fixed correlation distance of 50 km (equivalent to a smoothing distance of 35 km; Frankel, 1995; Llenos *et al.*, 2024) or adaptive smoothing distance (Helmstetter *et al.*, 2007). Although the adaptive smoothing approach is generally preferred and received higher weight in NSHM23 (Field *et al.*, 2023), branch weights were revised to even weighting because likelihood tests found that each method outperformed the other for some regimes and declustering method combinations in PRVI (Llenos *et al.*, 2025). In addition, adaptive smoothing can overfit catalog locations that are often highly uncertain in the PRVI catalog. Llenos *et al.* (2025) describe adjustments to the smoothed seismicity methodology made specifically for NSHM25-PRVI, in particular to account for the spatial heterogeneity of event detection in the region. For example, this includes the use of a scaling factor to allow smaller magnitude earthquakes to be used to construct the spatial PDFs while de-emphasizing the enhanced detection from the PRSN network compared with outside the network's authoritative region.

Although catalogs are declustered for the smoothed seismicity calculation, the rates calculated by Michael and Llenos (2025) and used in the NSHM25-PRVI ERF represent the full catalog. This is consistent with NSHM23 (Field *et al.*, 2023) and was a change from earlier NSHMs that used declustered rates. This was motivated by recent studies that found that retaining aftershocks when assuming a Poisson process is a better approximation of the true hazard computed accounting for spatiotemporal clustering in seismicity rates for return periods ≥475 yr (Marzocchi and Taroni, 2014; Field *et al.*, 2021; Wang *et al.*, 2021; Michael and Llenos, 2022).

The implementation of rate distributions and smoothed seismicity PDFs as sources in the ERF differs by tectonic regime and is detailed in their respective sections (refer to the Crustal gridded seismicity, Interface gridded seismicity, and Intraslab gridded seismicity sections).

CRUSTAL MODEL

The treatment of crustal earthquakes is largely identical to NSHM23-WUS (Field *et al.*, 2023). The fault-system inversion model uses the methods of Milner and Field (2023), including the same epistemic logic-tree branch structure. Scaling relationships from Shaw (2023) and segmentation branches are carried over unchanged and with identical weights (Fig. 5a), and the on-fault b value branch was reduced from five to three branches to reduce the size of the logic tree (after confirming that hazard results were insensitive to that reduction). We introduce new treatments for proxy faults (refer to the Crustal proxy fault treatment section) and a new randomly sampled deformation model approach in lieu of independently developed alternative models (refer to the Crustal geologic deformation model section).

The crustal gridded seismicity model generally retains the same methods and epistemic logic tree from NSHM23-WUS (Fig. 5b). Changes from NSHM23-WUS include revised

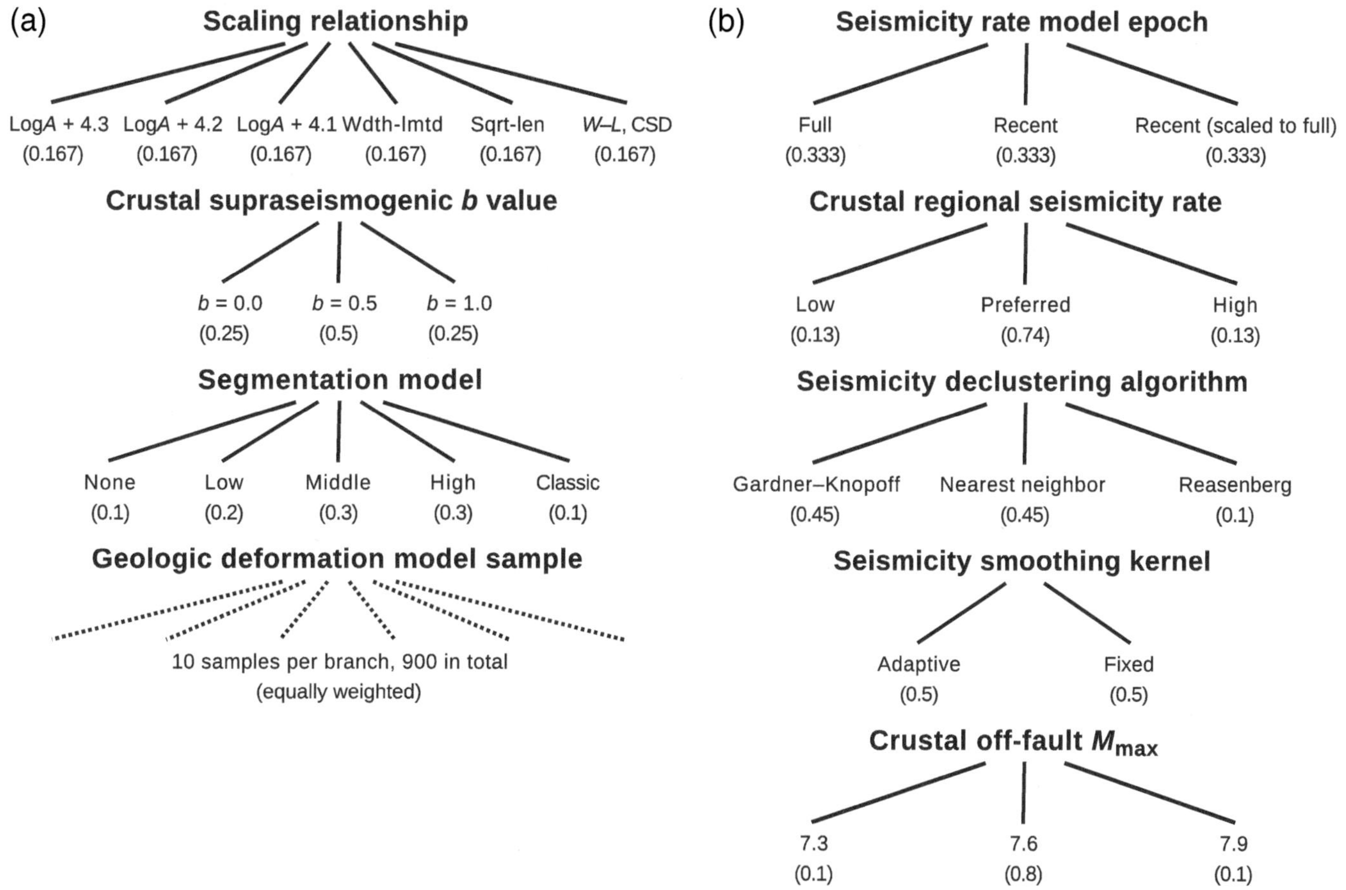

Figure 5. Crustal model epistemic logic tree. (a) The logic tree for the fault-system inversion (900 branches) and (b) for the gridded seismicity model (162 branches). Logic-tree branching levels are listed in bold with branch choices at that level listed below. Assigned branch weights are listed below each choice in parentheses. There are 145,800 total crustal earthquake rupture forecast (ERF) branches. CSD, constant stress drop; sqrtl-len, square-root length; and wdth-lmtd, W-L, width-limited (Shaw, 2023).

branch weights, an updated methodology for determining the low and high seismicity rate branches, and a new rate model epoch uncertainty level (refer to the Gridded Seismicity Methodology section). We also disabled rate balancing between the fault and gridded models (refer to the Crustal gridded seismicity section).

Crustal fault model and rupture set

Thompson Jobe *et al.* (2024) assembled the geology input databases for crustal faults in the NSHM25-PRVI model region. They parameterized 35 fault sections and 6 fault zones (each of the latter with a proxy fault representation)—a substantial increase over the three fault sections and two source zones included in NSHM03-PRVI. The included faults and fault zones are mapped in Figure 6. They also identified 13 fault sections that did not pass the criteria for inclusion (consistent with NSHM23-WUS): length of at least 7 km and documented evidence of Quaternary activity with data available in peer-reviewed publications.

The Bowin fault, originally included in NSHM03-PRVI, has been reclassified and partially removed: its eastern portion is now considered part of the Bunce fault (located east of the Main Ridge fault in Fig. 6), and its western portion was excluded due to a lack of Quaternary activity. The review panel (refer to the Review process and recommendations section) recommended inclusion of the western Bowin fault, but after further review, we confirmed Thompson Jobe *et al.* (2024) conclusion that the fault does not meet the criteria for inclusion. In addition, we ran a sensitivity test in which we added the western Bowin fault with a 1 mm/yr slip rate, and found that its inclusion led to a negligable increase in hazard on land in PRVI (at most 0.3%). The other two faults included in NSHM03-PRVI, Septentrional and South Lajas, are retained (Fig. 6).

Crustal fault sections are further divided into short subsections, each with length approximately equal to half their down-dip width (shown schematically in Fig. 3). Multifault ruptures are included subject to the plausibility criteria established by Milner *et al.* (2022), including a maximum between-fault jump distance of 15 km (acknowledging the occurrence of large jumps in nature, substantial uncertainties in true fault geometries, and potentially missing connector faults). Figure 6 depicts clusters of interconnected faults according to the plausibility criteria. Interconnected fault clusters are plotted with a single color, meaning that multifault ruptures are included in

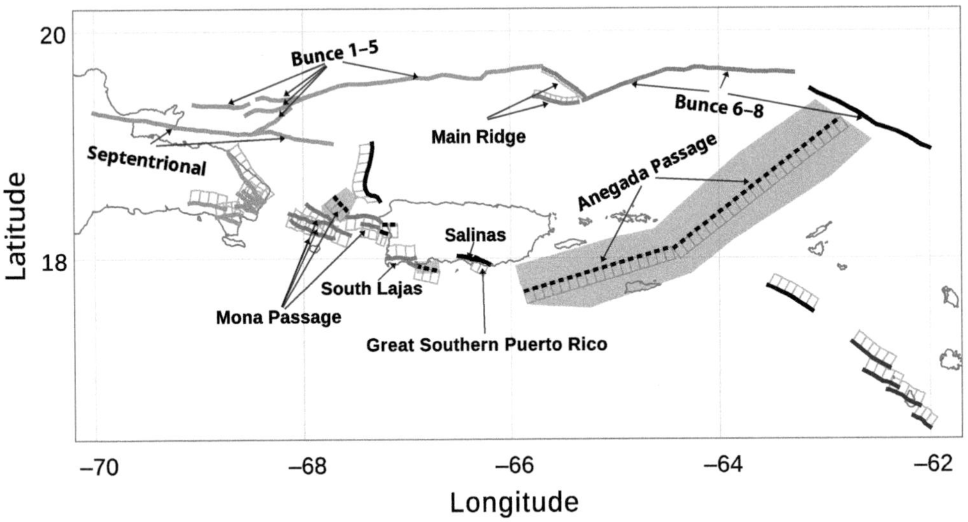

Figure 6. Crustal faults and fault zones from Thompson Jobe *et al.* (2024). Faults are broken down into separately colored connected clusters within which multifault ruptures are allowed by the Milner *et al.* (2022) plausibility criteria. Faults are plotted in black if they are fully isolated (i.e., they do not participate in multifault ruptures in the model). Fault zones are plotted with gray shaded regions in this and related figures, and their associated proxy faults (that are treated as fully isolated) are plotted with black dashed lines. The surface projections of the down-dip extent of dipping faults are plotted with thin gray lines in this and related figures. The color version of this figure is available only in the electronic edition.

the model between neighboring faults in that cluster (even though no single rupture is allowed that simultaneously ruptures all sections of any cluster). Fully isolated faults that do not participate in multifault ruptures, including all proxy faults, are depicted in black. The lack of a connection between the reverse northern Main Ridge fault and the left-lateral Bunce 5 fault section to its west is an example in which the jump distance is within the allowed 15-km threshold, but it fails the Coulomb compatibility criteria of Milner *et al.* (2022).

Crustal proxy fault treatment

Proxy faults are used to represent fault-zone polygons in the fault-system inversion, meaning that the slip rate on the proxy fault surface is taken to represent the moment rate for all supraseismogenic ruptures in the polygon (gridded seismicity still accounts for subseismogenic ruptures in fault-zone polygons). Because these proxy faults are simplified surfaces not intended to reflect individual fault geometries, we apply special treatment related to fault connectivity and target MFDs.

First, proxy faults are not allowed to participate in multifault ruptures because the fault surfaces themselves are poorly constrained (otherwise they would be represented as regular fault sections in the model), and fault surface details are required to assess multifault rupture plausibility.

Second, we apply custom segmentation rules within the fault-zone polygons to approximate how the NSHM23 segmentation constraint (Milner and Field, 2023) would penalize large ruptures if we had a full inventory of individual faults with distances between them. The NSHM23 segmentation constraint effectively resulted in tapered GR distributions (Kagan, 2002) in which the original b value was honored for single-fault ruptures and those using directly connected faults without any distance between them, and rates of multifault ruptures with jumps were suppressed. We approximate this by setting a branch-specific tapered GR corner magnitude of 7.2, 7.4, and 7.6 for the high, middle, and low segmentation branches, respectively. The results is a distribution that includes ruptures up to M_{max} but that rolls off above the corner magnitude; for example, the Anegada Passage **M** >7.5 recurrence interval increases from 2005 yr on the unsegmented branch to 5955 yr on the high segmentation branch. For the classic branch, we approximate the NSHM03-PRVI methodology (Mueller *et al.*, 2010) and set $M_{max} = 7.5$ and force $b = 1$, ignoring the supraseismogenic b value branch choice in proxy fault zones. No segmentation penalty is assessed on the unsegmented branch.

When computing hazard, supraseismogenic ruptures on proxy faults are distributed evenly throughout each fault zone such that they fill up the polygons without extending beyond them (Fig. 7). Areal source zone are often represented with leaky boundaries in seismic hazard assessments in which modeled rupture surfaces extend beyond the zone boundaries; we believe that representation is unrealistic, for example, because using leaky boundaries would extend large Anegada Passage ruptures far beyond the zone boundary and into Puerto Rico. Instead, we adopted this approach to preserve the zone boundaries that were drawn by Thompson Jobe *et al.* (2024) to encapsulate the faulting they represent. This representation is also transparent in the fault-system solution file formats (i.e., it folds into existing structures, refer to Data and Resources) and is thus simpler for end users to adopt.

Crustal geologic deformation model

Fault slip rates are the primary data constraint used in the inversion, but slip rates for NSHM25-PRVI crustal faults are highly uncertain. Thompson Jobe *et al.* (2024) assigned and Hatem *et al.* (2026) refined preferred slip rates and bins (i.e., upper and lower bounds) for each crustal fault. The only fault with a usable published slip-rate estimate was Septentrional; for the rest, slip-rate bins were estimated using geomorphic expressions, observations of deposit ages in paleoseismic trenches, or prior studies that utilized geodetic models. The preferred slip rates (typically at the center of the bin) are plotted in Figure 8.

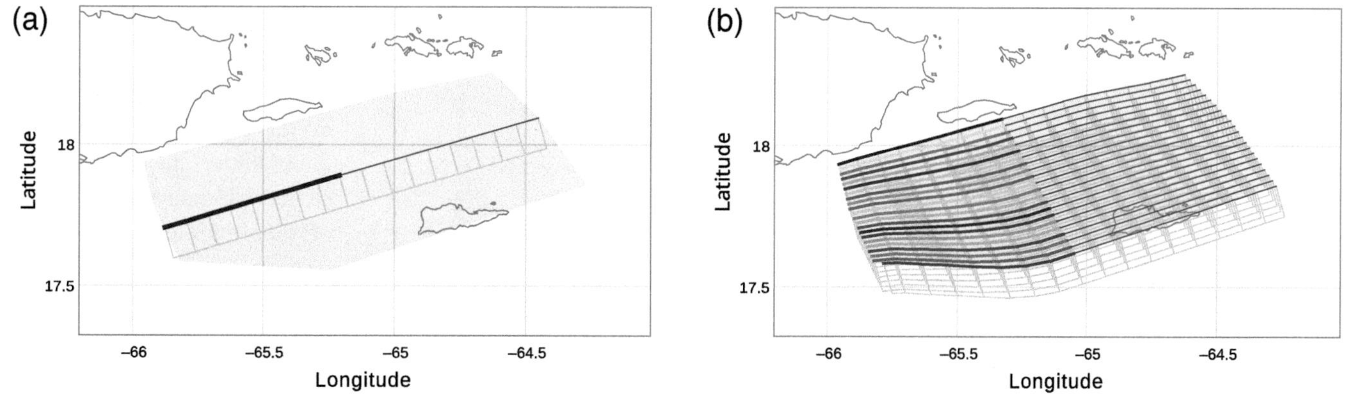

Figure 7. Example **M** 7.3 (75 km long) proxy fault rupture in the Anegada Passage southwest fault zone (gray shaded region). (a) The original proxy fault dips to the south-southeast, with a thick navy blue line highlighting the upper trace of proxy subsections that participate in the rupture. The remaining unused subsections are drawn with a thin black upper trace, and all subsections are outlined with thin gray lines. (b) That same rupture split into 22 separately colored rupture representations distributed across and filling the fault-zone polygon, each no more than 3 km apart. The rupture in (a) is used when solving the fault-system inversion and is split into the ruptures in (b) for hazard calculation. Fault zones are plotted with gray shaded regions in this and related figures. The surface projections of the down-dip extent of dipping faults are plotted with thin gray lines in this and related figures. The color version of this figure is available only in the electronic edition.

Recent NSHMs for other regions (e.g., NSHM23-WUS) used suites of deformation models (both geologic and geodetic) to represent epistemic uncertainties in slip rates. Lacking alternative crustal deformation models for NSHM25-PRVI and because of the large uncertainties due to few available published slip-rate estimates, we chose to draw randomly sampled deformation models using mixture distributions spanning each fault's assigned slip-rate bin. Those mixture distributions were assigned using weighted averages of triangular, uniform, and Gaussian distributions with weights set by expert opinion (Hatem *et al.*, 2026). Note that these distributions do not account for the possibility that true slip rates might lie outside of the assigned bin; accounting for that additional uncertainty can be addressed in future studies.

Ideally, deformation model samples would be drawn using a known covariance structure to ensure that the regional deformation rate is well fit in each sample. No such structure (or model to estimate it) is currently known to the authors, so slip rates are drawn independently on each fault section. Because of this, some samples may contain unrealistic slip-rate pairs, for example, in which two parallel faults that accommodate the same deformation are simultaneously high or low in the sample. Nonetheless, this method is more realistic than the alternative: a three-branch approach using all the low, preferred, and high values for each fault. This is apparent in Figure 9, which compares deformation line integrals calculated across all crustal faults in the region using the sampled deformation model approach with those using the alternative models of all-low and all-high slip rates. In that figure, individual sampled deformation models each produce above- or below-average deformation in different subregions, but none are uniformly high or low, and the distribution is concentrated in the center of the original bounds.

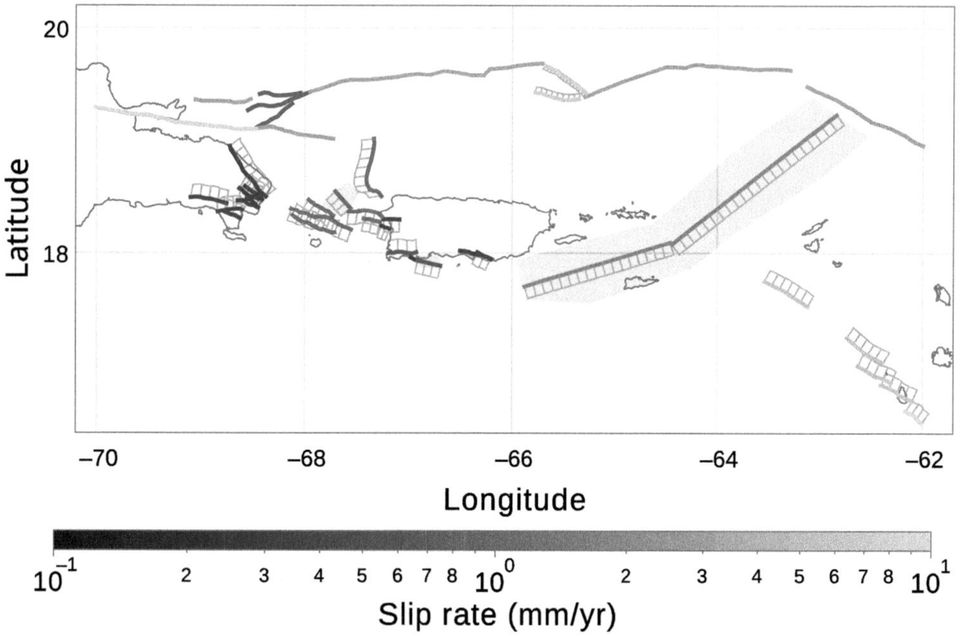

Figure 8. On-plane fault slip rates from Hatem *et al.* (2026) and Thompson Jobe *et al.* (2024). Fault zones are plotted with gray shaded regions in this and related figures. The surface projections of the down-dip extent of dipping faults are plotted with thin gray lines in this and related figures. The color version of this figure is available only in the electronic edition.

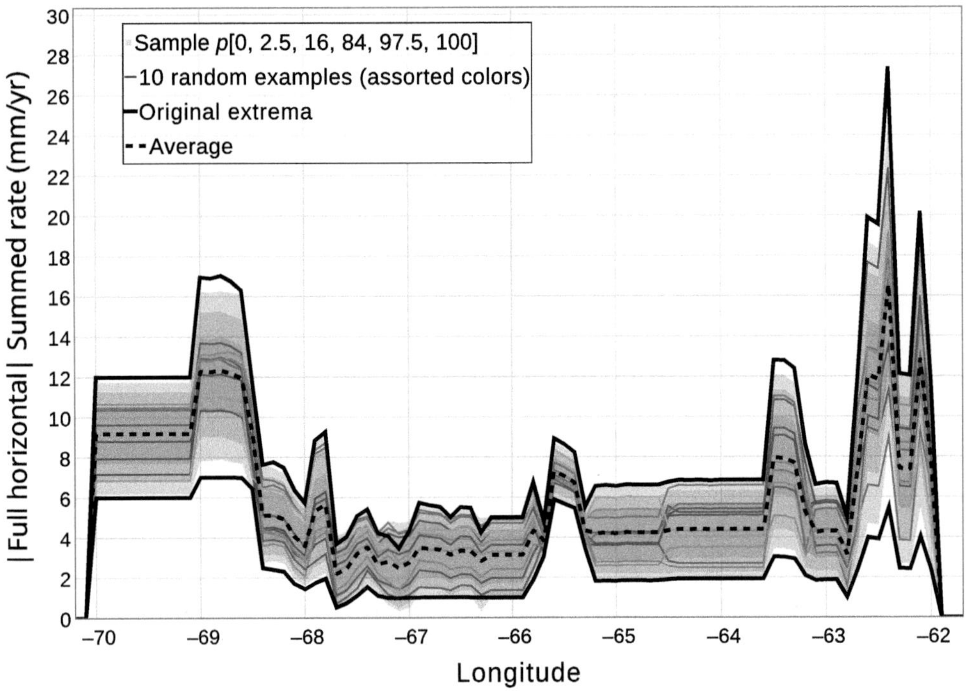

Figure 9. Deformation line integrals are summed across crustal faults from south to north at each given longitude. The absolute value of the full horizontal component is shown. Results using the original extrema from each fault slip-rate bin (e.g., choosing the high or low slip rate for each fault) are plotted with black thick lines. Percentiles computed from the distribution of randomly sampled deformation models are shown in gray; extrema from 900 samples are shown in the lightest gray, 95% range in the middle gray, and 68% range in the darkest gray. Ten random samples are plotted in unique colors. The color version of this figure is available only in the electronic edition.

Some of the distributions from Hatem *et al.* (2026) diverge from the original preferred slip rates and bins from Thompson Jobe *et al.* (2024), namely for the Main Ridge faults and the Anegada Passage fault zone (refer to locations in Fig. 6). The slip rates for Main Ridge were originally chosen to accommodate the regional deformation between Bunce 5 and 6 but instead created a large spike that was apparent in deformation line integral calculations (i.e., earlier versions of Fig. 9). The slip rate for Anegada Passage was also reclassified to a lower bin to bring the total projected rate (onto the proxy fault plane) in line with geodetic observations. Refer to Hatem *et al.* (2026) for details on these and other adjustments to the original slip-rate data.

We draw 10 unique deformation model samples for each of the 90 combinations of other crustal fault logic-tree branches (Fig. 5a), totaling 900 unique samples. We chose 10 samples because it was the smallest number that achieved stable results in mean hazard comparisons (i.e., <0.1% change in one-second pseudospectral acceleration [SA] with 2% probability of exceedance in 50 yr, compared with a model with substantially more samples).

Crustal solution slip-rate fits

The primary data constraints for the NSHM25-PRVI model used in the inversion are fault slip rates. Figure 10 shows how well the crustal fault inversion solutions fit the target slip-rate data. Overall, the fit is very good, with an average relative absolute misfit of 2.9%. The data are overfit relative to their large uncertainties: the average subsection slip-rate misfit is 3.4% of the width of the assigned slip-rate bin. The Septentrional fault—the only one with a field-based slip rate used in the geologic deformation model—is circled in 10b and well fit on average: the average misfit is 1.7%.

Solution slip rates are often slightly low at the ends of faults and high in the middle (Fig. 10a). This is especially apparent for three-subsection faults such as Bouillante Montserrat, in which the middle subsection solution slip rate is high, and the two ends are low. This is partially caused by the inclusion of the classic (fully segmented) model that uses an analytical solution rather than inversion. That analytical solution fits the moment and target MFD on each fault exactly but results in a rainbow-like solution slip-rate distribution (Milner and Field, 2023). In addition, inversion solutions also may contain rainbow-like slip distributions in the case in which a fault ends without connecting to neighboring faults, or a large slip-rate change occurs along-strike of the fault. Both of those cases are true for Bouillante Montserrat: it is connected at one end to a lower slip-rate fault and is unconnected at the other end. Although the inversion is capable of matching slip rates exactly (i.e., using small ruptures to fill in missing slip at fault ends), the regional MFD and subsection nucleation rate constraints prevent it from doing so (refer to the Fault-System Inversion Methodology section). In these cases, the average slip rate is usually well fit on each fault (blue circles in Fig. 10b), and the tapered solution slip rates near isolated fault ends may be more realistic than overfitting the constant along-strike slip rates from the deformation model.

The Main Ridge fault is an outlier that is not well fit in the model. This is due to the way that target MFDs are calculated following the NSHM23-WUS methodology (Milner and Field, 2023). Fault subsection MFDs are computed such that they match the slip rate on each subsection and follow a nucleation GR distribution up to their M_{max} but can be unrealistic if all of the ruptures near M_{max} involve other faults with either a slower slip rate or other connections. This is the case for Main Ridge 2:

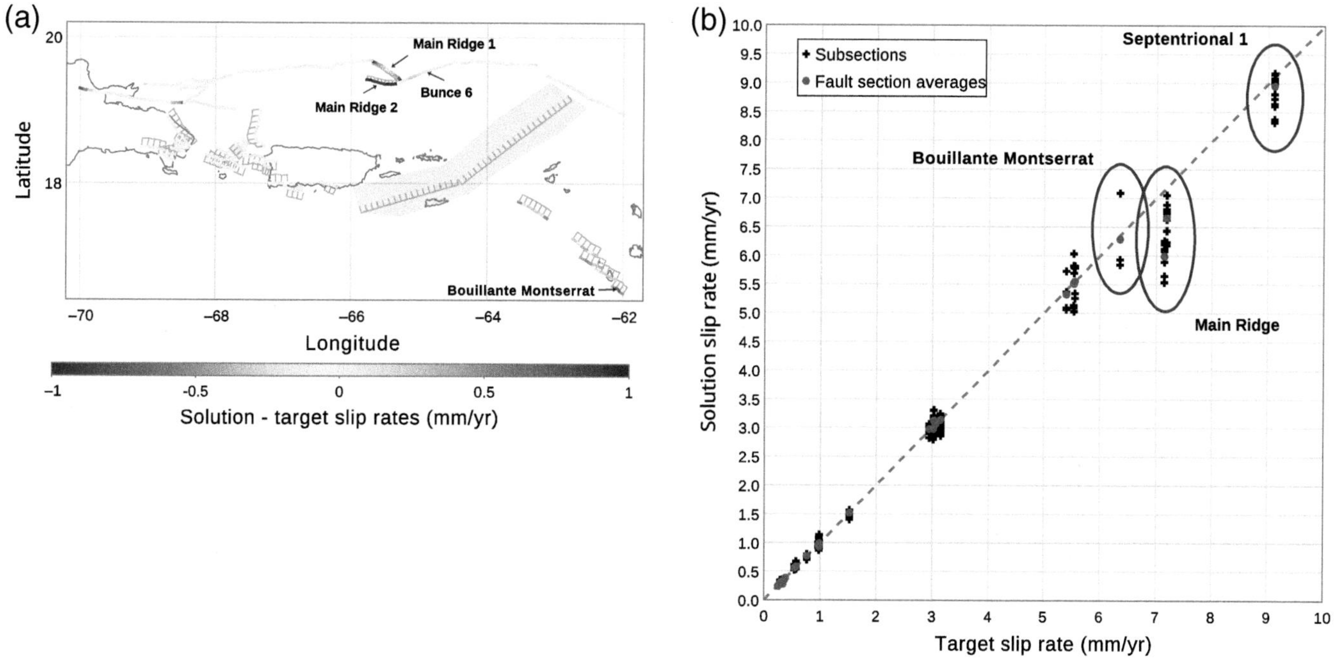

Figure 10. Inversion solution slip-rate misfits for crustal faults. (a) Slip-rate misfits plotted in map view; colors represent the difference between the solution slip rate and the original target slip rate. (b) Scatter plot of inversion solution slip rates (*y* axis) relative to target slip rates (*x* axis). Individual subsection slip rates are plotted with black crosses, and fault section average slip rates are plotted with blue circles. Fault zones are plotted with gray shaded regions in this and related figures. The surface projections of the down-dip extent of dipping faults are plotted with thin gray lines in this and related figures. The color version of this figure is available only in the electronic edition.

its slip rate is higher than the only fault it is connected to, Bunce 6, and Bunce 6 also satisfies much of its slip rate in ruptures that instead connect to Main Ridge 1. In this case, the inversion is incapable of simultaneously satisfying the high slip rates on Main Ridge 1 and 2, the lower slip rate on Bunce 6, and the assumed MFDs that connect them. Instead, it splits the difference, resulting in a low solution slip rate on Main Ridge 2 and a slightly high solution slip rate on Bunce 6.

Crustal solution MFDs

Figure 11 shows the MFD for on-fault supraseismogenic crustal ruptures in the model region, including the mean values and various percentiles computed across all 900 branches of the epistemic logic tree. The recurrence interval of all supraseismogenic crustal ruptures in the model is 8 yr, 16 yr for **M** >6.5, 66 yr for **M** >7, and 671 yr for **M** >7.5. Although each fault is constrained to follow a GR MFD, the sum of those MFDs is not necessarily GR due to variable M_{min} and M_{max} on each fault (Milner and Field, 2023). The average supraseismogenic magnitude range for crustal faults in the region is $\mathbf{M} \in [5.9,7.5]$, and the full range across all faults and scaling relationships is $\mathbf{M} \in [5.3,7.9]$. The result is a relatively flat incremental MFD up to **M** 6.7 and the GR distribution with $b \approx 1$ for $\mathbf{M} \in [6.7,7.3]$ that tapers off at higher magnitudes until M_{max}.

There is an apparent discrepancy between rates of supraseismogenic ruptures from the inversion model and those estimated from observed seismicity by Michael and Llenos (2025). The total cumulative supraseismogenic rupture rate exceeds the preferred seismicity rate for **M** >6.1 but remains within the estimated 95% confidence bounds. Incremental rates exceed those estimated from observed seismicity in the range $\mathbf{M} \in [6.4,7.4]$.

This indicates an incompatibility between the geologic inputs (i.e., faults and deformation models) and/or their implementation in the inversion model (e.g., segmentation, *b* value, scaling, and proxy fault treatment), and observed seismicity and assumptions therein (e.g., that the observed catalogs are representative of long-term seismicity rates or that the region follows a GR distribution across all magnitudes). The primary contributors to the discrepancy at **M** 6.8 are fast moving faults at the edges of the model: Lesser Antilles, Main Ridge, and Bunce. Figure 11b shows that the MFD is consistent for a smaller inset region in the immediate vicinity of the islands. This smaller region (refer to "assessment region" in Fig. 1) contains the mapped on- and near-shore faults on Puerto Rico's west and south coasts, as well as the southwest portion of Anegada Passage fault zone.

Recent NSHMs for active crustal regions have required that the on-fault MFD not exceed estimates from observed seismicity, for example, NSHM23-WUS and UCERF3. We could add a new inversion constraint to force the model to remain below the observed MFD, but doing so results in poor fits to fault slip-rates. Instead, we retain this inconsistency, as was done in other prior NSHMs such as NSHM23 for the central and eastern United States, due to the large uncertainties in model components (both observed seismicity and geologic inputs), and because the discrepancy is minimal for faults nearest to PRVI.

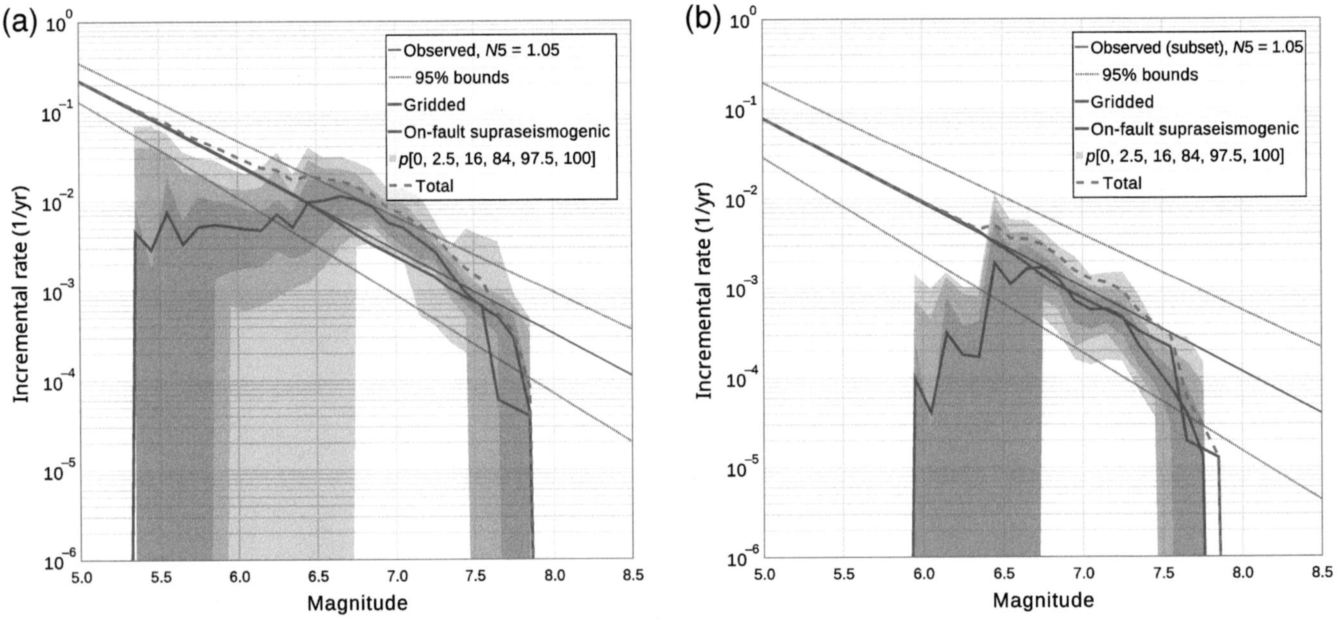

Figure 11. Incremental MFDs for crustal ruptures in (a) the entire model region and (b) a smaller assessment region (refer to Fig. 1 for region definitions). MFDs for supraseismogenic ruptures, that is, those solved using the section 5, are plotted in red. The average MFD across all logic-tree branches is plotted with a thick, solid red line, and percentiles computed from the epistemic logic tree are plotted in increasingly dark shades of red for extrema, the 95% range, and the 68% range. The total regional seismicity MFD and 95% confidence bounds estimated from observed seismicity by Michael and Llenos (2025) are plotted in green with solid and dotted lines, respectively. The average gridded seismicity MFD is plotted in a solid blue line. The sum of the average gridded seismicity and supraseismogenic MFDs is plotted in a purple dashed line. The color version of this figure is available only in the electronic edition.

Crustal solution fault recurrence intervals

Table 1 gives supraseismogenic magnitude ranges and recurrence intervals for each fault included in the crustal model, and Figure 2a,b plots participation rates for **M** >6.5 and >7.5, respectively.

The Bunce fault has the highest overall rate in the model, with a recurrence interval of 19 yr anywhere across its eight sections. Of the faults near the west coast of Puerto Rico, the Mona Passage faults have the shortest recurrence interval of 224 yr.

The Anegada Passage fault zone is the most consequential crustal fault represented in the model for the areas of eastern PRVI. It has a recurrence interval of 190 yr and represents 4% of the total rate of crustal on-fault events. The Anegada Passage can benefit from further study to improve upon the simplistic proxy fault representation used here, for example, by identifying the individual contributing faults and their slip rates.

The South Lajas fault in southwest Puerto Rico—one of three faults that was included in NSHM03-PRVI—has a recurrence interval of 2087 yr. This fault was represented in NSHM03-PRVI with a single characteristic **M** 7 rupture with a recurrence interval of 3500 yr (Mueller *et al.*, 2010). Although the modeled recurrence interval has shortened, the interval for **M** >7 ruptures (most comparable with NSHM03-PRVI) is substantially higher: 18,419 yr.

Crustal solution multifault rupture rates

Figure 12 shows the relative rate at which ruptures pass through allowed fault-to-fault connections. Pass-through rates are constrained by the segmentation model branch choice (Fig. 5a), including fully segmented ("Classic"), fully unsegmented ("None"), and distance-dependent models (Milner and Field, 2023). Rates are the highest between zero-distance neighboring fault sections, and fall off as jump distance increases.

We retain the branch weighting of NSHM23-WUS, which gives the highest weights to the more restrictive distance-dependent models ("High" and "Middle"), and the lowest weights to the fully segmented and unsegmented models. Increasing weight to the fully unsegmented branch choice would improve the discrepancy between the on-fault MFD and observed seismicity (Fig. 11) by increasing rupture rates near M_{max} and decreasing rates at more moderate magnitudes. However, the lower bound across all logic-tree branches in Figure 11a still nearly exceeds the observed MFD at **M** 6.8; this suggests that relaxing segmentation would not be enough on its own to fix the observed and modeled MFD discrepancy.

Multifault ruptures have an average recurrence interval of 193 yr in the model, and constitute 4.1% of the rate of all crustal supraseismogenic ruptures.

Crustal gridded seismicity

Implementation of the gridded seismicity model for active crustal ruptures largely follows that from NSHM23-WUS (Field *et al.*, 2023), except that rate balancing between the observed and on-fault MFDs is disabled (refer to the Crustal solution MFDs section).

Although no region-wide adjustment is made to account for on-fault seismicity in the gridded seismicity model, rates are

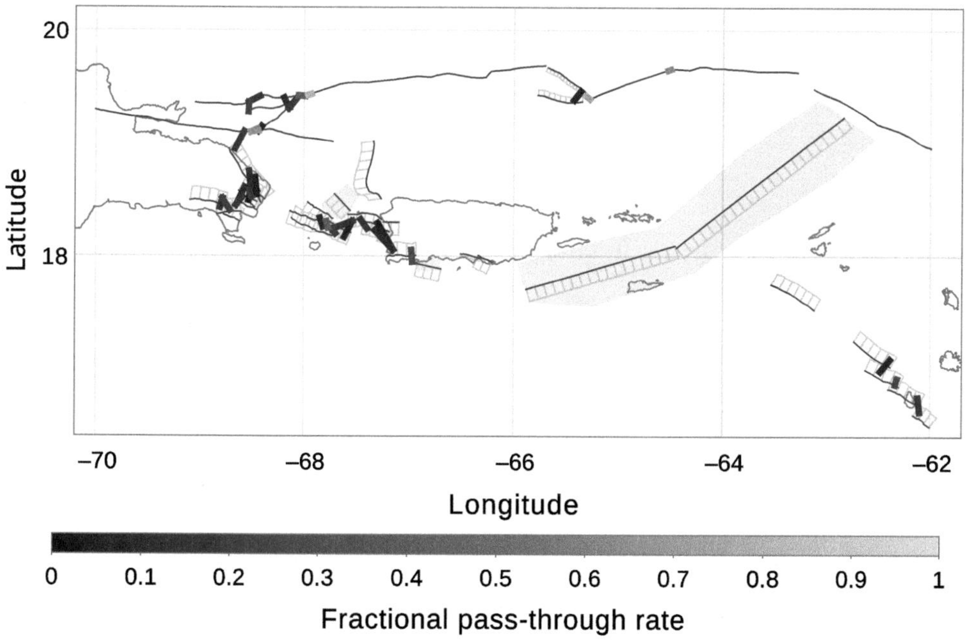

Figure 12. Fractional pass-through rates for crustal faults, that is, the relative rate at which ruptures pass through fault-to-fault connections rather than stopping. Lines are drawn between potentially connected faults according to the Milner *et al.* (2022) plausibility criteria and are colored by their fractional pass-through rate. Line lengths generally correspond to jump distance, although they are drawn here between the centers of connected subsections; jump distances used in the model are computed between the closest locations on each surface in 3D. Fault zones are plotted with gray shaded regions in this and related figures. The surface projections of the down-dip extent of dipping faults are plotted with thin gray lines in this and related figures. The color version of this figure is available only in the electronic edition.

still adjusted to avoid double counting in the immediate vicinity of modeled faults. That adjustment is computed in 3D and shown in Figure 13. The gridded seismicity model is discretized into 0.1° × 0.1° grid cells, and further divided into 0.02° × 0.02° × 0.02° 3D cubes to compute fractional associations between grid cells and modeled faults. The fractional association of each cube to each fault subsection is computed using a linear ramp of 3D distance up to 12 km, in which it is fully associated if the fault intersects the cube center and not associated beyond 12 km (Fig. 13a).

Grid cell rates are mapped to cubes assuming a depth-dependent nucleation distribution (i.e., that used in NSHM23-WUS; Fig. 13b). For cubes that are associated with a nearby subsection, gridded

TABLE 1
Participation Recurrence Intervals (Branch Averaged and 95% Bounds Across All 900 Branches) and Supraseismogenic Magnitude Ranges (Using Average Scaling) for Crustal Faults

Name	Magnitude Range	Recurrence Interval (yr)	Branch Recurrence 95% Bounds (yr)
Anegada Passage (two zones)	[6.6, 7.8]	190	[88, 644]
Bouillante Montserrat	[6.5, 7.2]	147	[69, 505]
Bunce (eight sections)	[5.5, 7.8]	19	[6, 91]
Cerro Goden (zone)	[6.6, 6.6]	2,699	[1,098; 17,728]
Desecheo ridge	[6.6, 7.5]	944	[544, 2,220]
Great Southern Puerto Rico	[6.5, 6.5]	2,340	[970, 30,859]
Lesser Antilles (two sections)	[6.6, 7.2]	79	[42, 220]
Main Ridge (two sections)	[5.9, 7.4]	56	[26, 131]
Mayaguez Bay (zone)	[6.3, 6.3]	1,936	[759, 24,798]
Mona Passage (four sections and one zone)	[6.5, 7.5]	224	[140, 468]
Mona Rift	[6.6, 7.2]	870	[494, 2,203]
Montserrat-Havers	[6.6, 7.3]	223	[106, 743]
Punta Montalva	[6.1, 7.3]	3,253	[1,183; 49,721]
Redonda	[6.7, 7.3]	226	[114, 757]
Southwest Puerto Rico (zone)	[6.6, 6.8]	1,579	[598, 17,961]
Salinas	[6.4, 6.6]	2,756	[1,159; 30,156]
Septentrional (two sections)	[6.4, 7.8]	78	[33, 263]
South Lajas	[6.7, 7.3]	2,087	[955, 12,503]
Vacama	[6.6, 7.7]	2,750	[1,143; 40,178]
Yabon (seven sections)	[6.4, 7.6]	534	[272, 1,355]

Faults with multiple sections or zones are grouped, and the listed recurrence intervals apply to any rupture involving any part of any section.

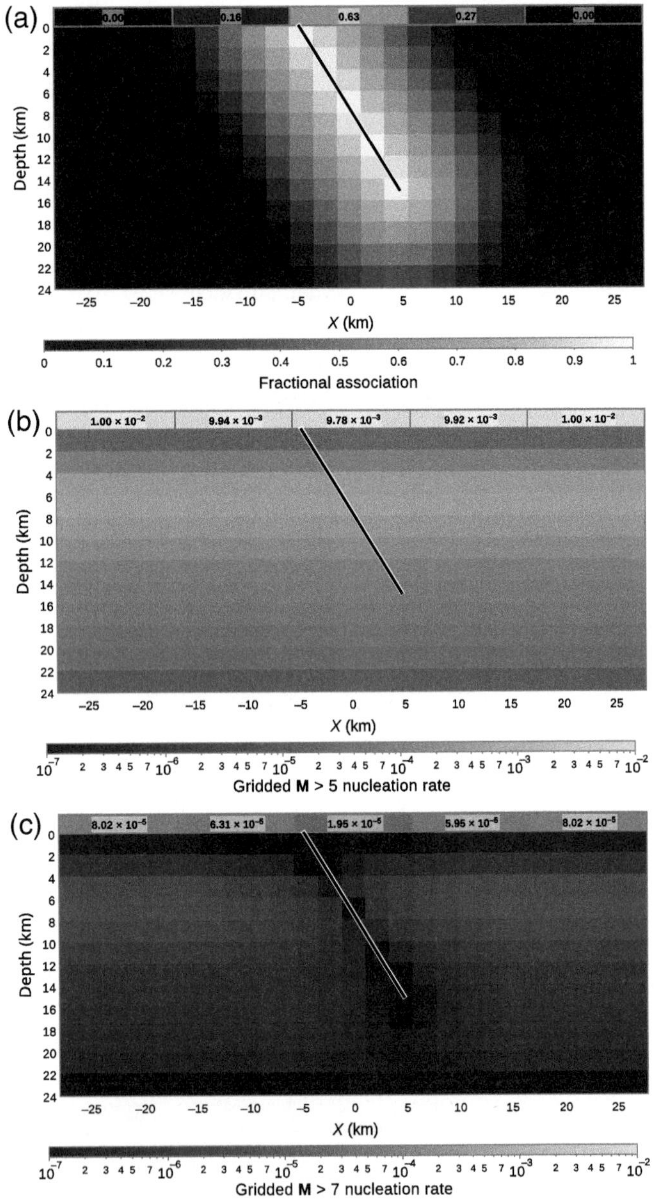

Figure 13. Side-view looking along strike of a cartoon dipping fault (black with a thin white outline). (a) The fraction of seismicity in each 3D cube that is assumed to be associated with the fault. (b) The total rate of **M** >5 events in each cube in the gridded seismicity model when using a uniform spatial seismicity model and the assumed depth-dependent seismicity distribution. (c) The same as (b) but for **M** >7 events that are above the minimum supraseismogenic magnitude of the fault; here, the rate of ruptures in the supraseismogenic magnitude range decreases by the fractional association with the fault in (a). Cube values are aggregated into 2D grid cells in the final model, shown as wide-colored rectangles at the top of each panel with their corresponding values annotated. The color version of this figure is available only in the electronic edition.

rupture rates at and above the mapped subsection's minimum supraseismogenic are reduced by the fractional association (Fig. 13c). Cube rates are then reaggregated to grid cells in the final gridded seismicity model. The effect of this adjustment can be seen in Figure 11 in the difference between the preferred observed seismicity rate branch (green solid line) and the gridded seismicity model (blue line) for **M** <7.3 (rates above are also affected by the off-fault maximum magnitude branch choices). Rates of **M** >5 and >7 ruptures in the gridded seismicity model are plotted spatially in Figure 14, and the impact of the fault-based rate adjustments can be seen in the **M** >7 rates.

For hazard calculation, crustal gridded ruptures are represented as point sources with distance approximations computed using the same finite rupture parameters as in prior NSHMs for active crustal regions (e.g., NSHM23-WUS). Rupture lengths, L, are determined using the (Wells and Coppersmith, 1994) mechanism-independent magnitude–length relationship. Rupture down-dip widths, W, are constrained with a minimum aspect ratio of $L/W \geq 1.5$ and a maximum lower depth (also known as rupture bottom depth), $Z_{\mathrm{BOT}} \geq 14$ km. Upper depths (also known as depth to top of rupture), Z_{TOR}, are magnitude dependent:

$$Z_{\mathrm{TOR}} = \begin{cases} 5\ \mathrm{km}, & \mathbf{M} < 6.5, \\ 1\ \mathrm{km}, & \mathbf{M} \geq 6.5. \end{cases} \quad (2)$$

Crustal gridded rupture mechanisms are spatially uniform and assigned according to the fraction of the total moment rate assigned to each category in the crustal geologic deformation model: 64% strike slip, 8% reverse, and 28% normal. Dips are assumed to be 50° for reverse and normal ruptures.

Crustal hazard sensitivities

Figure 15 shows a mean (across all logic-tree branches) hazard map for the model hazard assessment region, including crustal and subduction sources, both on-fault and gridded seismicity. The map is computed using the updated GMMs developed for NSHM25-PRVI (Moschetti *et al.*, 2026) parameterized for hard-rock site conditions, and the hazard metric is one-second SA with 2% probability of exceedance in 50 yr. Figure 16 shows how that map changes in subsets of the model in which each crustal logic-tree branch choice (from Fig. 5) is selected. Each row of Figure 16 represents a single logic-tree branching level, and the individual maps show the ratio (plotted as a percent change) of the subset of the model in which the given choice is fixed and all other choices at that same level are excluded (i.e., the change if that branch were deemed correct). These maps provide a visual means to assess the influence of each logic-tree branch included in the model.

The crustal fault logic-tree branches for scaling relationships, b value, and segmentation models do not have a large impact on hazard on the island of Puerto Rico because most high slip-rate crustal faults are offshore, and the relative contribution of the gridded seismicity model is higher. These branches have a larger impact on hazard for St. Croix, U.S. Virgin Islands (refer to location in Fig. 15) due to its proximity to the Anegada Passage fault zone; this is especially true for the scaling relationship branches that control the magnitude and average displacement in each modeled fault rupture.

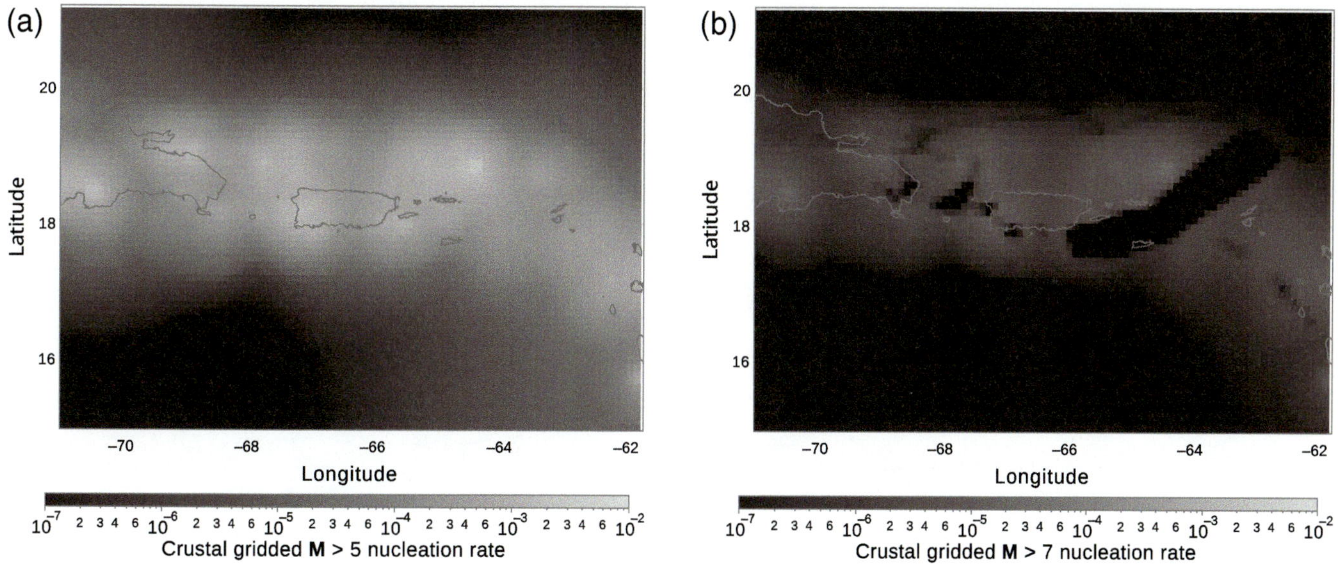

Figure 14. Rate (on a logarithmic scale) at which (a) **M** >5 and (b) **M** >7 earthquakes nucleate in the crustal gridded seismicity model according to the observed seismicity rate model (Michael and Llenos, 2025) and average smoothed seismicity probability density function (PDF; Llenos *et al.*, 2025). Rates of large events in the gridded seismicity model are carved out near modeled faults to avoid double counting, as is apparent in (b). The color version of this figure is available only in the electronic edition.

The crustal gridded seismicity model logic-tree branches collectively have a larger impact on hazard on the island of Puerto Rico due to the concentration of gridded seismicity in the immediate vicinity of the island (refer to Fig. 14). The overall seismicity rate branch generally has the largest impact of the crustal branches. The seismicity rate model epoch branch, which includes the influence of both crustal and subduction gridded seismicity models, is also a large source of uncertainty; for example, hazard is lower for the recent epoch due to lower overall event rates (including for the crustal model). The other seismicity model choices, such as declustering model and the smoothing algorithm, also impact how those rates are distributed throughout the region. For example, using the nearest-neighbor declustering algorithm (Zaliapin and Ben-Zion, 2020) leads to decreased seismicity rates on the western and eastern coasts of Puerto Rico.

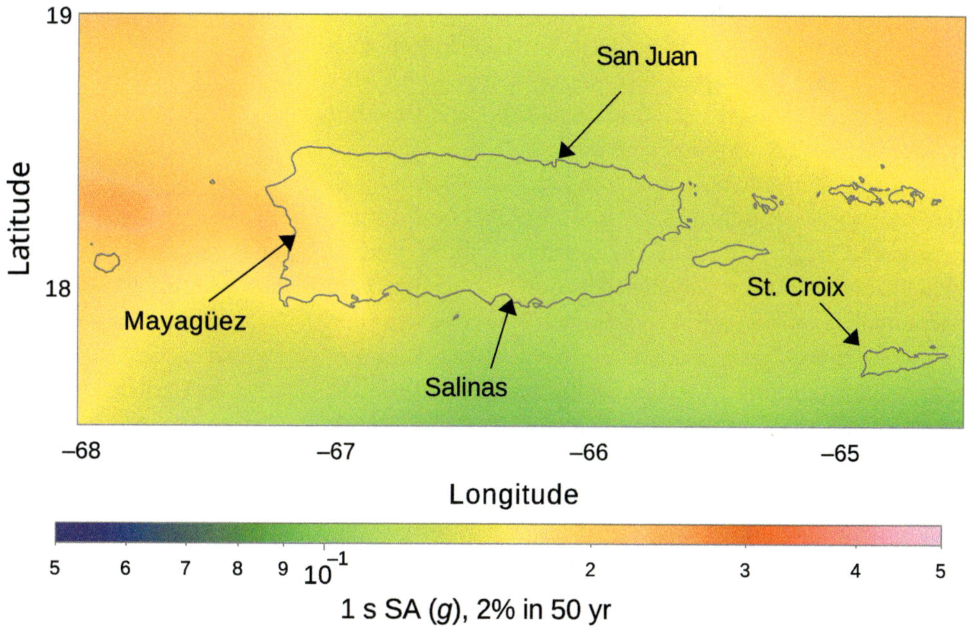

Figure 15. Hazard map of one-second pseudospectral acceleration (SA) with 2% probability of exceedance (POE) in 50 yr, computed using the combined crustal and subduction branch-averaged ERF. Ground motions are computed using the weighted-average ground-motion models developed for the 2025 National Seismic Hazard Model (NSHM25)-Puerto Rico and USVI (PRVI; Moschetti *et al.*, 2026). The locations of the cities of San Juan, Mayagüez, and Salinas (Puerto Rico) and the island of St. Croix (USVI) are annotated.

SUBDUCTION MODEL

NSHM25-PRVI is the first U.S. NSHM to employ the fault-system inversion methodology to solve for the rates of subduction interface ruptures. Prior NSHMs for Cascadia (Field *et al.*, 2023), Alaska (Powers *et al.*, 2024), and PRVI (Mueller *et al.*, 2010) used prescriptive methodologies to determine interface event rates. The 2022

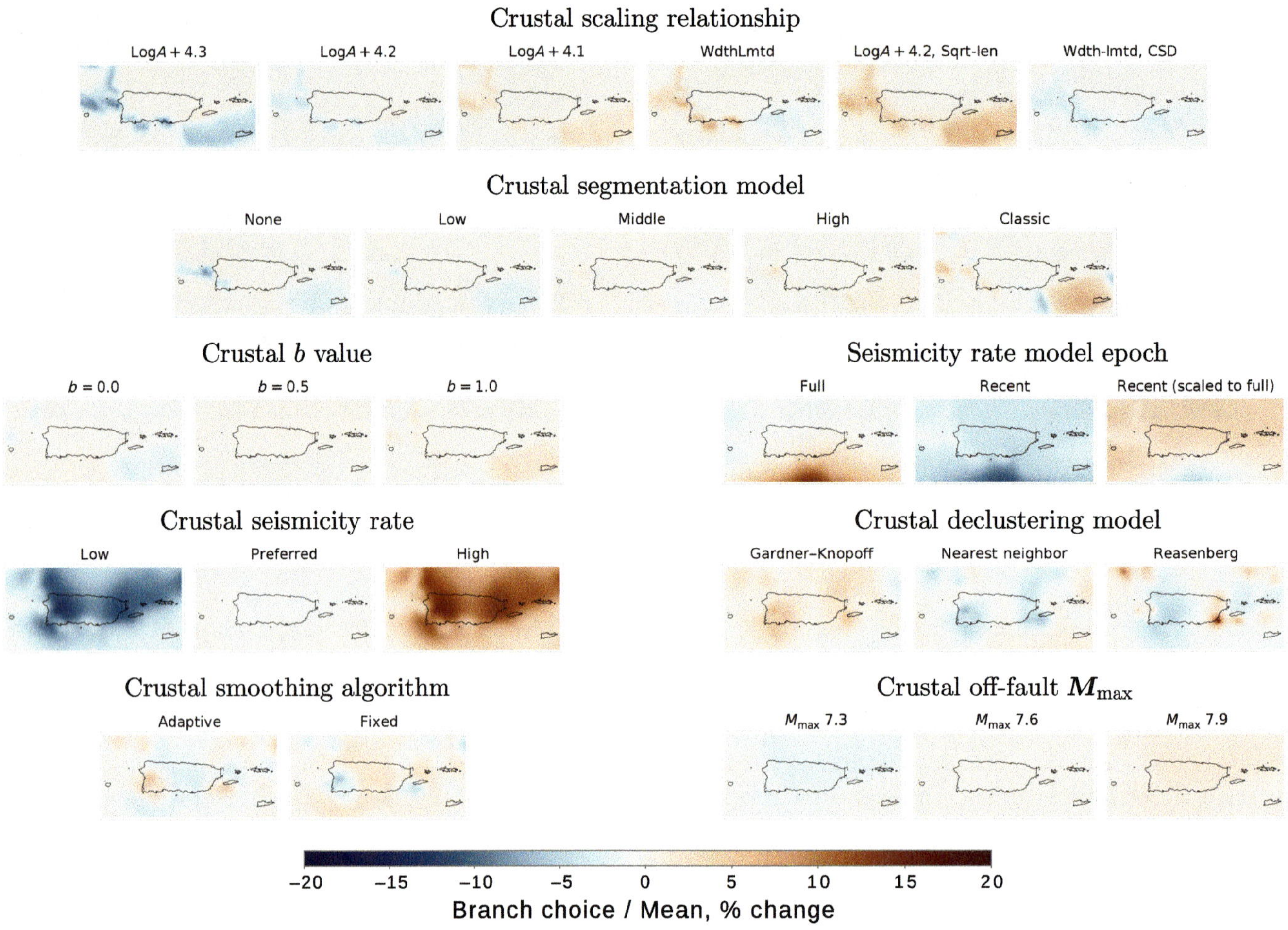

Figure 16. Ratio of hazard computed with each branch-specific submodel (but averaged across all other branches) in the crustal logic tree to the full mean hazard map shown in Figure 15. In other words, they show how the mean map would change if all other choices at that branching level were eliminated. The seismicity rate model epoch level is also affected by the subduction gridded seismicity model.

New Zealand NSHM (Gerstenberger *et al.*, 2023) was the first to utilize the inversion methodology to model a subduction zone (the Hikurangi) but adapted their methods from the earlier UCERF3 inversion model (Field *et al.*, 2014). Here, we adapt the NSHM23-WUS inversion methodology to the subduction environment, similar to the crustal fault treatment. The inversion methodology is well-suited to the NSHM25-PRVI subduction environment because there are few constraints on the rates of large interface events beyond inferences from plate convergence rates, and the inversion can fit complicated slip-rate patterns that vary along strike. Furthermore, it streamlines quantification of epistemic uncertainties and aligns with a broader U.S. NSHM goal to standardize methodologies across regions and tectonic regimes when possible (Field *et al.*, 2025).

The logic tree for the interface fault-system inversion model is shown in Figure 17a. There are two fault models representing uncertainties in seismogenic depths, three models of interface coupling, two slip-partitioning models (full oblique slip or trench normal), three scaling relationships from Shaw (2023), and the same b value branches as in the crustal model.

The interface and slab gridded seismicity model logic tree is similar to the crustal gridded seismicity model. There are separate rate branches for the Caribbean trench and Muertos trough, meaning that seismicity rates are assumed to be uncorrelated between them. Intraslab and interface event rates are assumed to be correlated within each subduction region. This assumption implies that, for example, if the true Caribbean interface seismicity rate is higher than our preferred rate branch, then the Caribbean intraslab rate would also be higher, and that discovery would have no impact on the Muertos interface or intraslab seismicity rates. Subduction seismicity declustering and smoothing kernel branches are treated as correlated across both interface and intraslab sources, as well as between the Caribbean trench and Muertos trough.

Interface fault models

The fault geometry for the Caribbean trench is simplified from Slab2 (Hayes *et al.*, 2018), and two alternative representations are used. These models aim to capture uncertainties on the seismogenic depth of the Caribbean trench and whether or not the seismogenic portion is truncated by the Bunce fault.

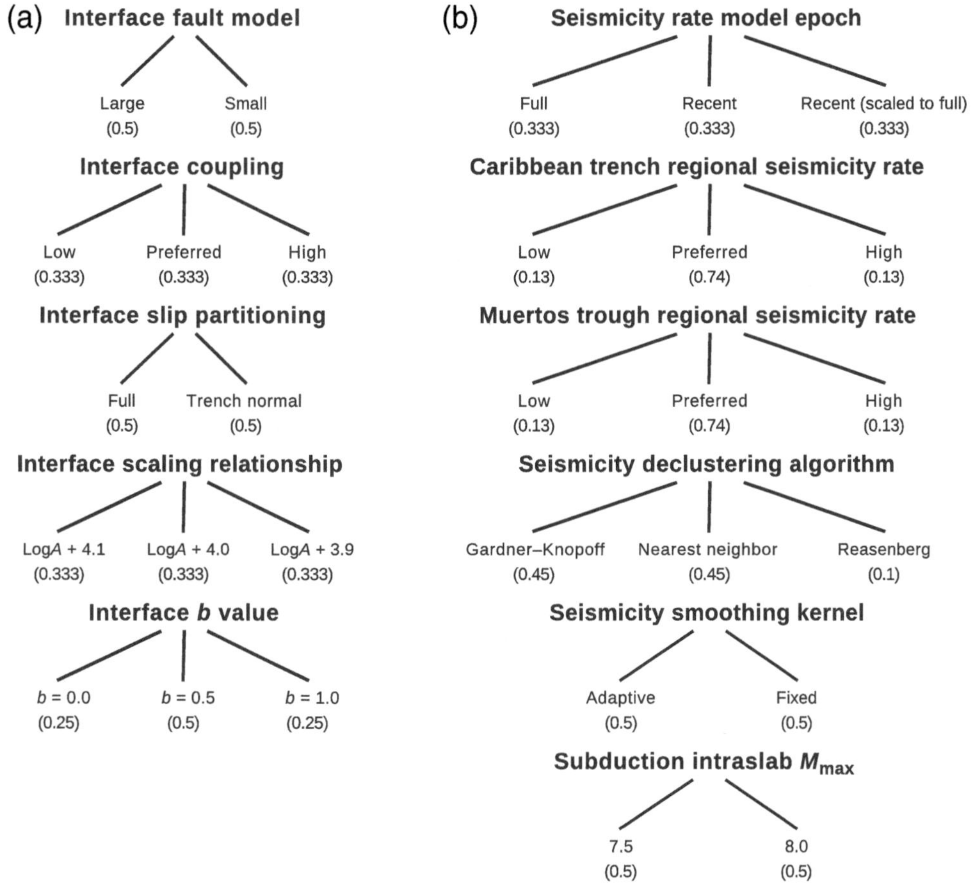

Figure 17. Subduction model epistemic logic tree following the format of Figure 5. (a) The logic tree for the interface fault-system inversion model (108 branches) and (b) for both the interface and slab gridded seismicity models (324 branches). There are 34,992 total subduction ERF branches.

For the large fault model, the entire trench is assumed to be seismogenic down to the 50-km Slab2 depth contour (Fig. 18). For the small model, the seismogenic portion of the PRVI and Lesser Antilles sections begins below the intersection with the Bunce fault at ~12-km depth (effectively reducing the slip rate above that intersection by 50% in the final model) and extends to the 40-km Slab2 depth contour (Fig. 19). M_{max} is 9.1 and 9.0 for the large and small fault models, respectively, computed using the average of the three scaling relationship branches from Shaw (2023).

The geometry used for the Muertos trough is shallower (~20 km beneath the southern coast of Puerto Rico) than the Slab2 representation (~30–40 km; Hayes *et al.*, 2018). This geometry was chosen because the Slab2 geometry was poorly constrained, and recent seismic imaging indicates a shallow dip (Granja Bruña *et al.*, 2015). In addition, the 2019–2020 sequence near the southern coast of Puerto Rico is presumed to be limited to the upper plate above the Muertos trough (ten Brink *et al.*, 2022), and truncates sharply at ~20 km depth (Vičič *et al.*, 2021; Cromwell *et al.*, 2021; Yoon *et al.*, 2023).

There is disagreement on whether the Muertos trough should be treated as an interface or crustal source (e.g., Granja Bruña *et al.*, 2010). We choose to treat it as an interface source for consistency with the seismicity model components (Haynie *et al.*, 2025; Llenos *et al.*, 2025). One implication of that choice is that the subduction scaling relationships are used to calculate slip per event, and they lead to generally higher rupture rates (each consuming less moment) than the crustal relationships due to lower c values in the $M = \log(A) + c$ formulation used by Shaw (2023). Another implication is that, when computing hazard, subduction interface GMMs are used rather than the crustal relationships that, among other differences, include a hanging-wall term. At the request of the review panel, we tested the sensitivity of computed hazard to this choice and found that, were we to treat Muertos as a crustal source, hazard would decrease slightly on Puerto Rico (generally <5%) except for a small increase for some spectral periods along the southern coast due to the hanging-wall term in crustal GMMs.

Interface fault sections are split into approximately equal-length subsections (shown with gray outlines in Fig. 18). Because of the large down-dip widths and along-strike variations therein, we use a constant subsection length of 30 km and an aspect ratio constraint to determine the minimum supraseismogenic rupture considered in the inversion. Rather than the two subsections per rupture requirement for crustal ruptures, we require that ruptures be at least two-thirds as long as they are wide (down-dip). The result is that the smallest supraseismogenic ruptures considered range from two subsections (on the norther Hispaniola and eastern Muertos) to five subsections (on the eastern extent of the Lesser Antilles) in the large fault model. M_{min} is variable along strike: $M_{min} \in [7.5, 8.4]$ and $M_{min} \in [7.5, 8.1]$ (using average scaling) for the large and small fault models, respectively (Fig. 18). All ruptures below those magnitudes (i.e., subseismogenic ruptures and short supraseismogenic ruptures that do not pass the aspect ratio constraint) are included as part of the Interface gridded seismicity section model.

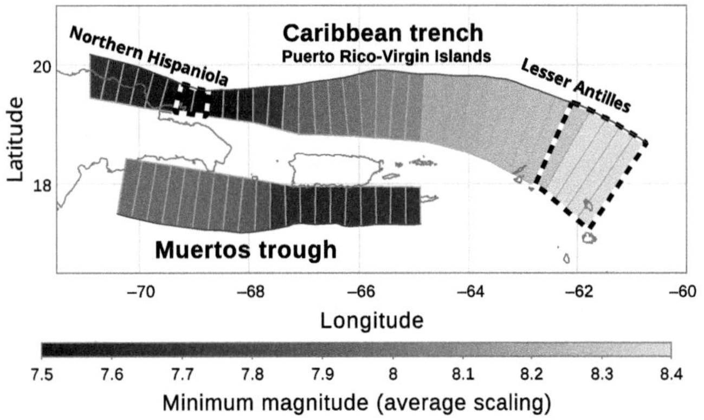

Figure 18. (a) Minimum magnitude for supraseismogenic interface ruptures for the large fault model using the average of the three subduction scaling relationships (Shaw, 2023). The minimum magnitude varies along strike as a function of trench width and according to the aspect ratio constraint; the ruptures corresponding to the smallest (two subsections with $M_{min} = 7.5$) and largest (five subsections with $M_{min} = 8.4$) minimum magnitudes are outlined in white and black thick dashed lines. Magnitudes for the small fault model (shown in Fig. 19b) are identical for the Muertos trough but $M_{min} \in [7.5,8.1]$ for the Caribbean trench. The Caribbean trench (and its sections) and Muertos trough are labeled. The color version of this figure is available only in the electronic edition.

Interface deformation models

Although the plate convergence rate of 15–20 mm/yr is constrained from geodesy (Calais *et al.*, 2016), the details of seismogenic coupling are uncertain. The picture is further complicated by the oblique angle of convergence, especially for the PRVI and northern Hispaniola sections (labeled in Fig. 18).

We represent uncertainties in coupling with three equally weighted branches. The preferred branch uses the block model of Symithe *et al.* (2015) to estimate coupled rates on the Caribbean trench as ≤20% of the plate convergence rate (Fig. 19b). The high branch uses ten Brink and Lépez-Venegas (2012), including coupling as high as 51% on the western end of the PRVI trench (Fig. 19a). The low branch sets coupled rates on the PRVI trench and Lesser Antilles at 1%, representing the possibility that those sections are essentially uncoupled (Symithe *et al.*, 2015).

Coupling rates on the Muertos trough represent the possibility that it is fully coupled (Symithe *et al.*, 2015) or uncoupled (Jansma *et al.*, 2000), and the high and low branches approximate $\pm\sigma$ about the preferred values.

There are two equally weighted slip-partitioning models for the Caribbean trench. In the full model, slip rates for the Caribbean trench are assigned assuming oblique slip on the interface (e.g., Fig. 19b). In the trench-normal rate model, the interface is assumed to rupture seismically only in the trench-normal direction, and slip rates are reduced to their vector component in that direction (Fig. 19d).

Symithe *et al.* (2015) block model uses eight sections to represent the Caribbean trench and three for the Muertos trough. We interpolate slip deficit rates (i.e., plate convergence rates times coupling estimates) for each section onto the interface subsections to smooth out large rate discontinuities, which are physically unrealistic and are difficult for the inversion method to fit. Smoothing is done linearly between sections and is symmetrical across each boundary; that is, the smoothing distance is set to equal half the length of the shorter section.

Slip deficit rates across all six combinations of coupling and slip-partitioning choices are available in Shumway *et al.* (2025).

Interface inversion solutions

The fault-system inversion is used to solve for the rates of supraseismogenic interface ruptures (i.e., those that rupture the full down-dip extent of the interface). Figure 2b shows the participation rates of those ruptures, and the total recurrence interval is 950 and 1424 yr for the Caribbean trench and Muertos trough, respectively. MFDs for interface ruptures are shown in Figure 20. The supraseismogenic MFDs are double tapered because M_{min} is variable and only the narrowest subsections on northern Hispaniola or eastern Muertos trough use ruptures near **M** 7.5 (Fig. 18). Rates for Caribbean trench supraseismogenic ruptures are slightly below extrapolations from observed seismicity and rates for the Muertos trough exceed them, though both are generally well contained within the 95% confidence bounds estimated by Michael and Llenos (2025).

Slip deficit rates are the primary constraint that, when coupled with scaling relationship and GR b value choices, constrain event rates in the inversion. Inversion solution slip-rate fits (to the deformation model slip deficit rates) are shown in Figure 21. Slip deficit rates are well fit on average: within 0.10 mm/yr (5.5%) across all interface subsections.

Slip deficit rate fits are worst (up to 0.43 mm/yr, or 22.9%) at transitions in slip deficit rate, for example, between the PRVI and Lesser Antilles sections of the Caribbean trench or at the eastern end of the Lesser Antilles section (where the deformation rate is highest and does not taper at the fault end). This is by design; the subsection nucleation rate and overall MFD constraints (refer to the Fault-System Inversion Methodology section) prevent the inversion from overusing (relative to a GR with the specified b value) the smallest available ruptures to fill in slip deficit rate misfits at abrupt transitions. The result is a smoother solution slip-rate distribution that tapers slightly at fault ends.

Although the Caribbean interface is assumed to be aseismic above the intersection with the Bunce fault in the small fault model, no coruptures are included in the model that include both the crustal Bunce fault and Caribbean interface rupturing simultaneously in a single event. Such an event may be possible, but modeling these types of ruptures in seismic hazard analyses can benefit from additional research. One issue is that the current state-of-the-art GMMs do not support mixed-regime ruptures, although this is a topic of current research (e.g., Shaw *et al.*, 2025). In addition, new segmentation and slip-partitioning

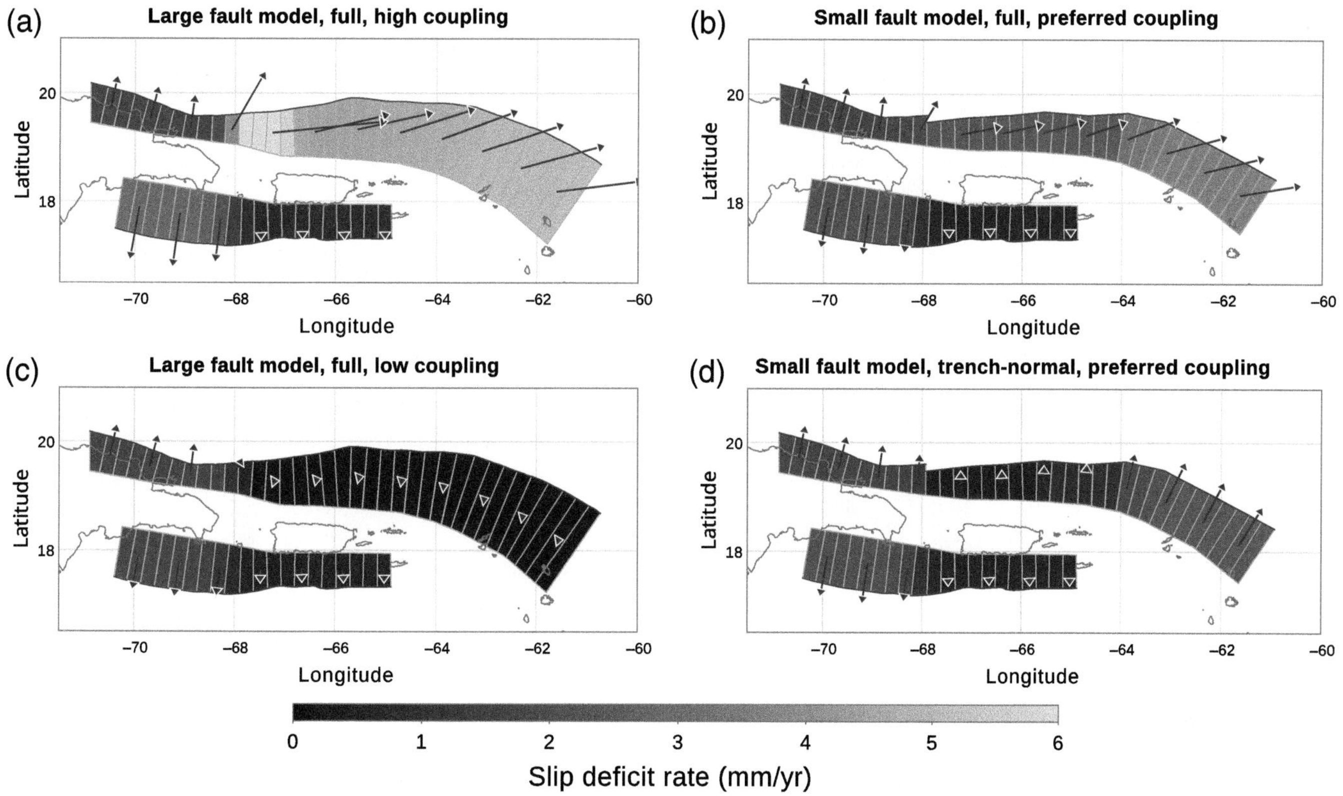

Figure 19. Interface slip deficit rates saturated above 6 mm/yr [the maximum value for the high coupling model in (a) is approximately 8 mm/yr]. The full slip-partitioning model is shown in (a–c), and the trench-normal model is shown in (d). The high coupling model is shown in (a), the preferred model in (b,d), and the low model in (c). Although the fault model choice does not affect deformation model slip deficit rates, the large model is shown in (a, c) and the small model is shown in (b,d). Slip vectors are plotted with red arrows with lengths scaled to the slip deficit rate. The color version of this figure is available only in the electronic edition.

models would need to be developed to include those ruptures in the inversion. Furthermore, the hazard impact of including those ruptures would likely be minimal in PRVI because the distance between the Bunce fault and the islands (>100 km) is large relative to other high-rate sources.

Interface gridded seismicity

Interface gridded seismicity rates (Fig. 20) and spatial distributions (Fig. 22a) are estimated from observed seismicity (Llenos *et al.*, 2025; Michael and Llenos, 2025). $M_{\min} = 5$, and $M_{\max} \in [7.4, 8.3]$ is spatially variable and just below the supraseismogenic $M_{\min}$ of the nearest subsection (Fig. 18). The total rate of **M** >5 gridded interface ruptures are 1.2 and 0.16 per year for the Caribbean trench and Muertos trough, respectively. Spatial seismicity PDFs are restricted to areas where the Slab2 depth is ≤50 km (colored areas in Fig. 22a).

Unlike crustal ruptures that are treated as point sources, finite rupture information (depth, strike, and dip) is available from Slab2 and used in the model. Ruptures are represented as dipping rectangles and are generally centered horizontally around the associated grid cell, except for the case in which centering would extend the rupture up- or down-dip beyond the interface gridded seismicity polygons (shown in Fig. 22a). In that case, ruptures are assumed to nucleate at the grid cell center but remain confined within the down-dip extents of the interface (i.e., the boundary is not leaky). This is shown in Figure 23; the two example ruptures nucleate at the bottom of the interface and propagate up-dip.

For the Muertos trough, we still use finite rupture information from Slab2 even though the interface fault surface used in the inversion differs. This maintains consistency with the catalog separation process used to determine seismicity rates and results in gridded seismicity ruptures being generally farther in 3D from the island of Puerto Rico than in the inversion model. This is shown in Figure 23; we use the deeper orange rather than the shallower magenta rupture representation.

Consistent with prior NSHMs (e.g., Field *et al.*, 2023; Powers *et al.*, 2024), the interface gridded seismicity and inversion models are developed independently, and no rate balancing is done between them. The supraseismogenic ruptures are assumed to contribute negligibly to the observed seismicity rate (especially relative to uncertainties therein), and subseismogenic gridded ruptures are assumed to consume a negligible fraction of the deformation model slip rates. The latter assumption breaks down for areas where the event rate (Fig. 22a) is high, but the slip rate (Fig. 19) is low (e.g., on the eastern portion of the PRVI section of the Caribbean trench). A potential solution might be to use multiple subsections down-dip in the inversion to explicitly model the contribution of subseismogenic

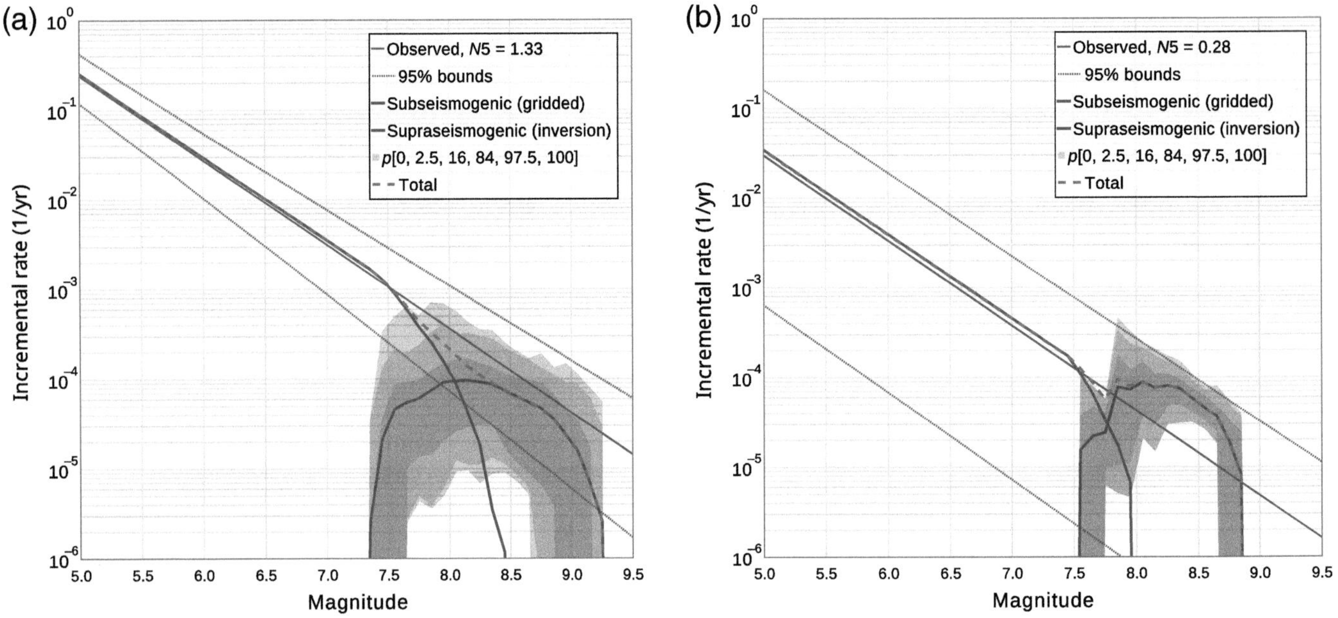

Figure 20. Incremental MFDs for subduction interface seismicity for (a) the Caribbean trench and (b) the Muertos trough. Colors follow those from Figure 11 for supraseismogenic (red), gridded seismicity (blue), the sum of each (purple dashed), and estimates from observed seismicity (green). The color version of this figure is available only in the electronic edition.

ruptures, effectively reducing M_{max} in the gridded seismicity model. That change would improve the consistency of the model, but also requires depth-dependent slip-rate estimates that are not available at present and introduces additional model complexity.

Intraslab gridded seismicity

Intraslab gridded seismicity is treated as point sources at Slab2 (Hayes *et al.*, 2018) depths. The Slab2 surface was extrapolated to extend beyond the upper extent of the interface to account for outer rise events, which are also included in the intraslab model. The intraslab regions and spatial distributions are shown in Figure 22b. $\mathbf{M} \in [5,8]$, and MFDs for gridded intraslab ruptures are shown in Figure 24. The total **M** >5 rate (including outer rise events) is 1.8 and 0.47 per year for the Caribbean trench and Muertos trough, respectively.

The intraslab model is a large contributor to hazard increases over the NSHM03-PRVI model (refer to the Hazard Changes from 2003 section). This is partially due to a seismicity rate increase from 1.1 in NSHM03-PRVI to 2.3 per year, but the largest hazard changes are due to increasing M_{max}. The prior $M_{max} = 7.2$ is lower than the maximum observed in the region: the 29 November 2007 **M** 7.4 Martinique intraslab earthquake (Hayes *et al.*, 2017) that occurred just outside the NSHM23-PRVI model bounds.

We represent intraslab M_{max} on the logic tree (Fig. 17b) because it is poorly constrained and hazard is highly sensitive to its choice (refer to Subduction hazard sensitivities). The $M_{max} = 8$ branch is consistent with recent NSHMs for Alaska and Cascadia and was chosen using global analogues (Field *et al.*, 2023; Powers *et al.*, 2024). We also include a lower $M_{max} = 7.5$ branch that is just above the regional observation (**M** 7.4). Inclusion of the lower branch is also justified by the shallower seismogenic thickness in the region (Barrera-Lopez *et al.*, 2022) relative to subduction zones in the Pacific Ocean, where the largest intraslab events have occurred. This is an uncertainty that can benefit from additional study.

Intraslab hazard also increases because the updated spatial seismicity PDF (Fig. 22b) places a larger concentration of events to the west of Puerto Rico than the prior model, increasing hazard in western Puerto Rico.

Consistent with recent NSHMs (e.g., Field *et al.*, 2023; Powers *et al.*, 2024), no point-source distance approximations

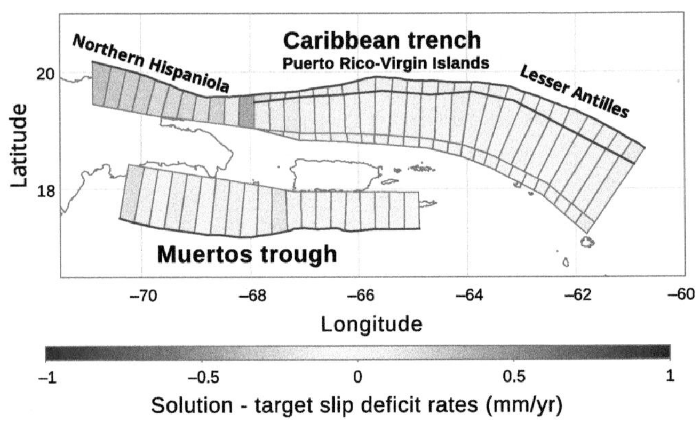

Figure 21. Inversion solution slip deficit rate misfits for the subduction interface, plotted in map view. Interface fault subsections are colored according to the difference between the solution slip rate and the original target slip deficit rate. Results for the small fault model are plotted on top of and partially obstructing those from the large fault model. The color version of this figure is available only in the electronic edition.

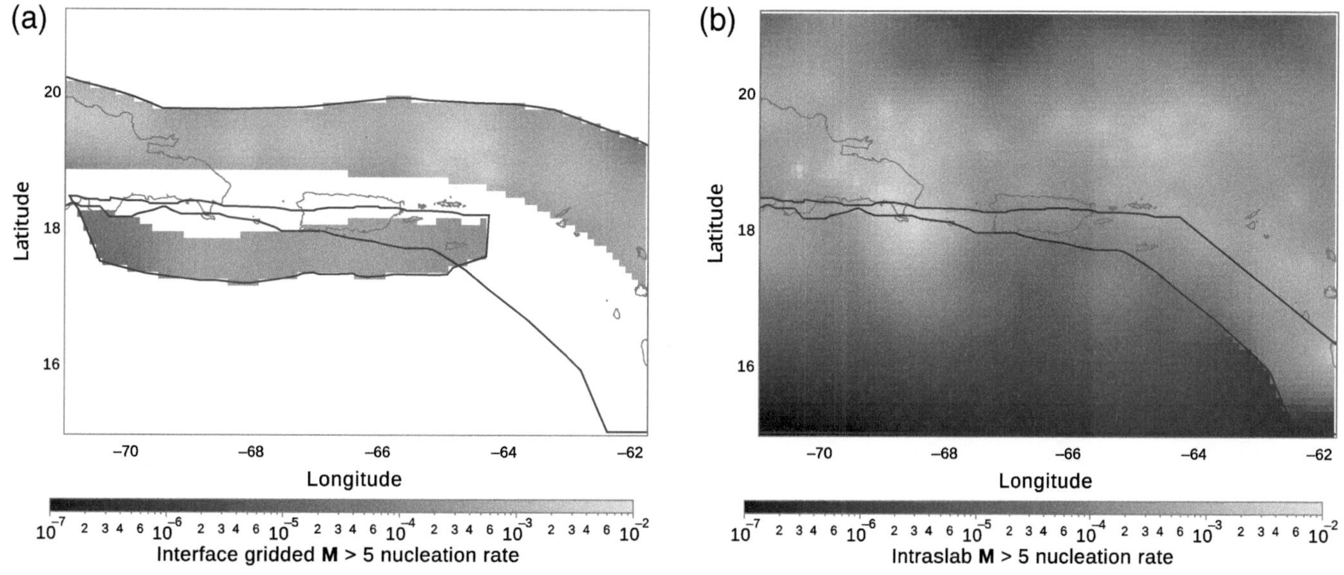

Figure 22. Rate (on a logarithmic scale) at which **M** >5 ruptures nucleate in the (a) interface and (b) intraslab (including outer rise) gridded seismicity models according to the observed seismicity rate model (Michael and Llenos, 2025) and average smoothed seismicity PDFs (Llenos *et al.*, 2025). The color version of this figure is available only in the electronic edition.

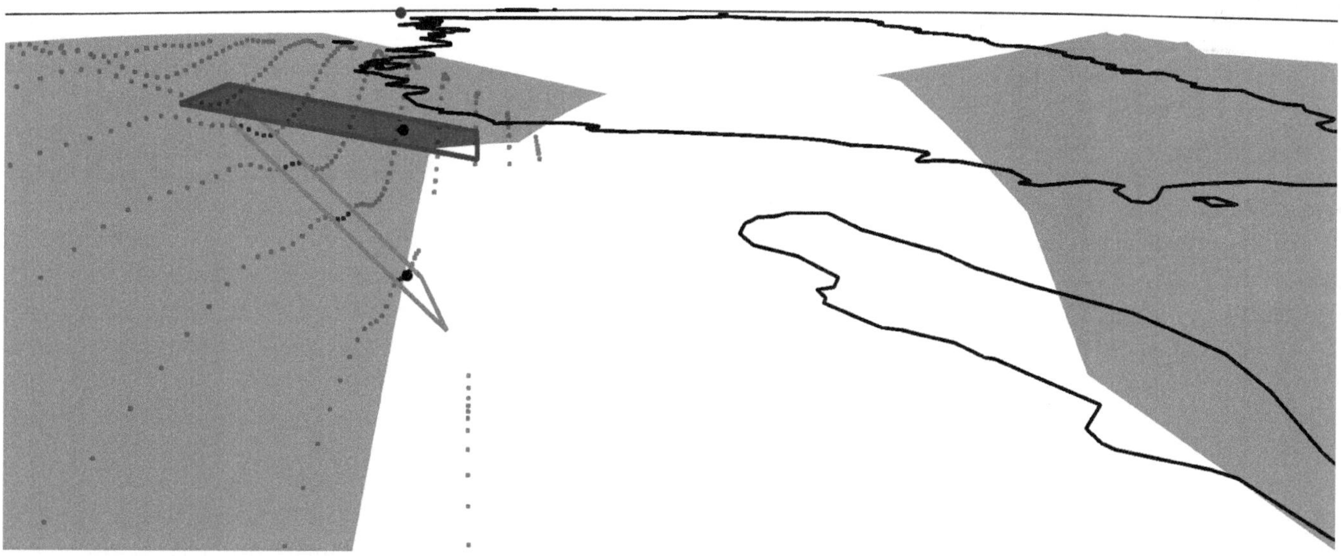

Figure 23. 3D side view looking west toward Puerto Rico (outlined in thick black lines); the earth's surface at the horizon is drawn with a dark gray arc. The subduction interface fault surfaces used in the model are shown in gray with the Muertos trough on the left side. The Slab2 (Hayes *et al.*, 2018) Muertos interface surface is shown with a green point cloud. Two example **M** 7.35 Muertos gridded seismicity ruptures are shown for the grid cell location marked with a red dot on the surface (off the southwest coast of Puerto Rico). The rupture representation we use, shown in orange, is deeper and uses the Slab2 surface; a shallow alternative using the interface fault surface is shown in magenta. The locations of the grid cell mapped onto the interface and Slab2 surfaces, at which the ruptures are assumed to nucleate, are shown with blue dots. The color version of this figure is available only in the electronic edition.

are used when parameterizing GMMs for hazard calculation of intraslab ruptures. This choice results in further site-to-rupture distances for large intraslab ruptures than if distance corrections were used, but is partially offset by placing the ruptures exactly on the Slab2 surface (rather than using a poorly constrained depth distribution below the Slab2 surface).

Subduction hazard sensitivities

Figure 25 shows how the average hazard map (Fig. 15) would change if each individual model logic-tree branch were chosen and the rest at the same branching level were eliminated. On-fault interface inversion logic-tree branches each have an effect on hazard that is largest in the immediate vicinity of the

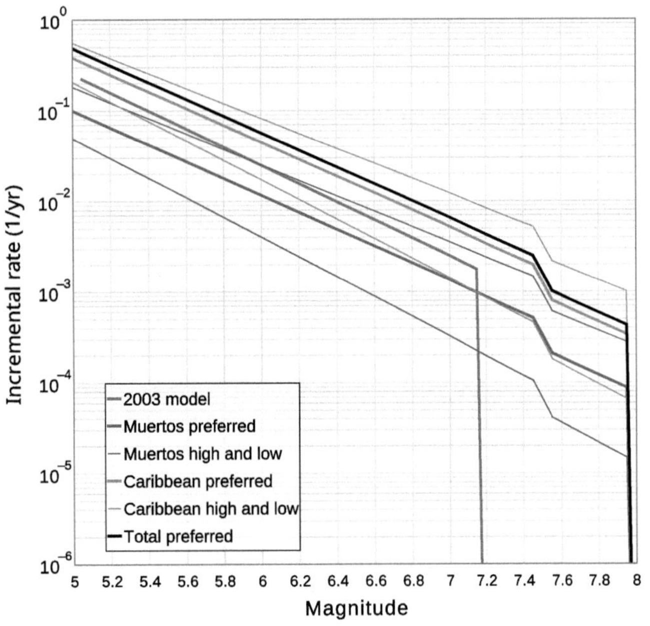

Figure 24. Incremental MFDs for intraslab seismicity. Caribbean trench MFDs are plotted in orange, and Muertos trough MFDs are in green. Preferred seismicity rates from Michael and Llenos (2025) are plotted with thick lines, and the high and low (95% confidence) branches are plotted with thin lines. The sum of the preferred MFDs across both regimes is plotted in a thick black line, and the intraslab MFD from the NSHM03-PRVI is plotted with a thick gray line. Rates decrease for **M** >7.5 due to the intraslab M_{max} logic-tree level. The color version of this figure is available only in the electronic edition.

interface but is often minimal on land in PRVI. Hazard is highest when using the large fault model (because the Caribbean interface extends nearer to the islands), with the high coupling model with full slip partitioning (because it has higher slip deficit rates), with the $\log A + 3.9$ scaling relationships (because more frequent ruptures are required to satisfy those slip deficit rates), and with the $b = 1$ branch (because a smaller fraction of those slip rates are satisfied by rare ruptures near M_{max}). The interface coupling branch is the most influential on-fault inversion uncertainty (including across the crustal logic tree). Note that although each logic-tree choice may not have a large apparent effect in isolation, combinations of choices may result in larger hazard changes; for example, the large fault model, high coupling, full slip partitioning, $\log A + 3.9$, and $b = 1$ branch combination increase hazard substantially more than any of those choices in isolation.

The subduction seismicity rate branches appear to be the largest sources of uncertainty in the NSHM25-PRVI ERF because both the event rates and their uncertainties are large (Figs. 20 and 24). Separate branches are included for the Caribbean trench and Muertos trough seismicity rates, but rates are assumed to be correlated within each subduction zone between interface and intraslab ruptures. The latter choice increases the influence of the outer rate branches and was chosen because intraslab and interface seismicity are driven by the same tectonic processes. Reality is likely somewhere between fully correlated and fully uncorrelated, and we choose to model interface and intraslab rates as fully correlated for computational efficiency to keep the total logic-tree size to a minimum (especially when combining across crustal and subduction sources). The intraslab M_{max} branch is the third most influential branch on land in PRVI, behind only the crustal and Caribbean trench rate model branches.

The various declustering and smoothing model choices are treated as fully correlated across both subduction zones and for interface and intraslab models, but have a smaller effect on overall hazard because their impact varies spatially across each model.

COMBINED MODEL RESULTS AND COMPARISONS

Combined cumulative MFDs across all tectonic regimes are shown in Figure 26, and model rates are listed in Table 2. Overall event rates are highest for Caribbean intraslab seismicity, averaging 1.8 **M** ≥5 events per year, followed by the Caribbean interface (1.2 per year) and crustal gridded seismicity model (1 per year).

Figure 26 compares the full model (panel a) and tectonic regime-specific (panels b–f) cumulative MFDs with rates computed directly from the observed seismicity catalog, as well as Michael and Llenos (2025) estimated uncertainties on those rates (gray shaded distributions). The observed **M** ≥6 rates for 1900–1973 are shown in brown dashed lines, and the observed **M** ≥5 rates for 1973–2023 are shown in black dashed lines. Recall that the tectonic regime classification process is uncertain, especially for the earlier epoch in which the majority of events are assigned default depths in the catalog (refer to the Gridded Seismicity Methodology section). In general, the more recent data (black dashed lines) are more robust for individual regimes (panels b–f) because the regime classification is more certain, and the full data (brown dashed lines) are more robust for the combined model because they do not depend on classification and contain more observations.

A trend of overprediction is evident when comparing model results with those data, for example, the modeled total rate of **M** ≥5 and **M** ≥6 events in the combined model lies at approximately the 86th percentile of the estimated uncertainty distribution in Figure 26a. This overprediction is primarily attributable to excess crustal events when on- and off-fault sources are combined. Figure 26b highlights the crustal contribution: the gridded seismicity model (light blue) is consistent with the data, but the sum of the on- and off-fault crustal models exceeds the 97.5th percentile for **M** ≥5.9. We accept this overprediction because the discrepancy is greatest in the periphery of the model region and is small near PRVI (refer to the Crustal solution MFDs section).

Other regimes also contain smaller overpredictions. For regimes with particularly sparse data, for example, Muertos interface and intraslab, the uncertainty distributions are right skewed

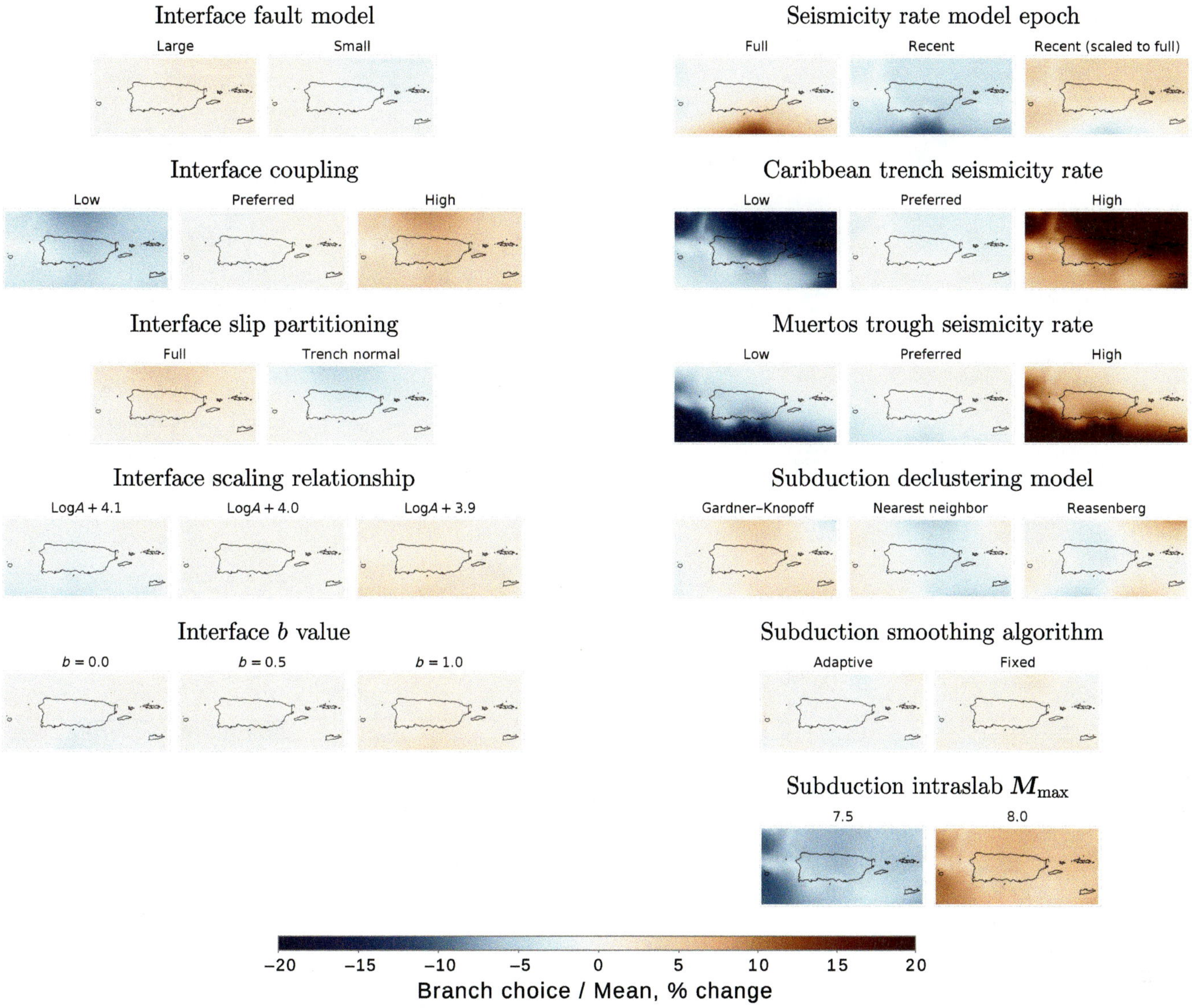

Figure 25. Subduction model hazard sensitivities by logic-tree branch in the same format as Figure 16. The seismicity rate model epoch level also includes the influence of the crustal gridded seismicity model and is identical to that from Figure 16.

because the rate parameter cannot be negative, putting more weight above the observed value. In addition, the mean models represent the weighted average of the low, preferred, and high rate branches, and that average lies above the preferred rate for each regime. This is especially apparent for the Muertos interface model (Fig. 26e), in which the uncertainties are substantial and the mean model lies just below the 68th percentile.

The model often diverges from the observed data above M_c because (Michael and Llenos, 2025) solve for rates at M_c using a b value distribution determined from the full rather than regime-specific catalogs. In a data-rich environment, it may be preferable to use regime-specific b values to better fit the details of each regime's observed MFD, but we find this choice to be appropriate for PRVI because the regime-specific data are sparse and the magnitude with the most data, M_c, remains well fit.

HAZARD DISAGGREGATION

Figure 27 shows a map-based disaggregation of one-second SA with 2% probability of exceedance in 50 yr. The percentage contribution of each source type is given in separate panels for crustal fault sources, crustal gridded sources, subduction interface (Caribbean and Muertos, inversion based and gridded), and subduction intraslab. Results are similar for other spectral periods, although the influence of the crustal gridded seismicity model increases for shorter spectral periods.

The crustal gridded seismicity model is generally the largest contributor (31% on average), especially for areas away from explicitly modeled crustal faults (Fig. 27b). The contribution from the crustal on-fault model is generally lower (9% on average) except for south and west Puerto Rico in the immediate vicinity of crustal faults and for the U.S. Virgin Islands in and around the Anegada Passage fault zone where the contribution reaches 57%

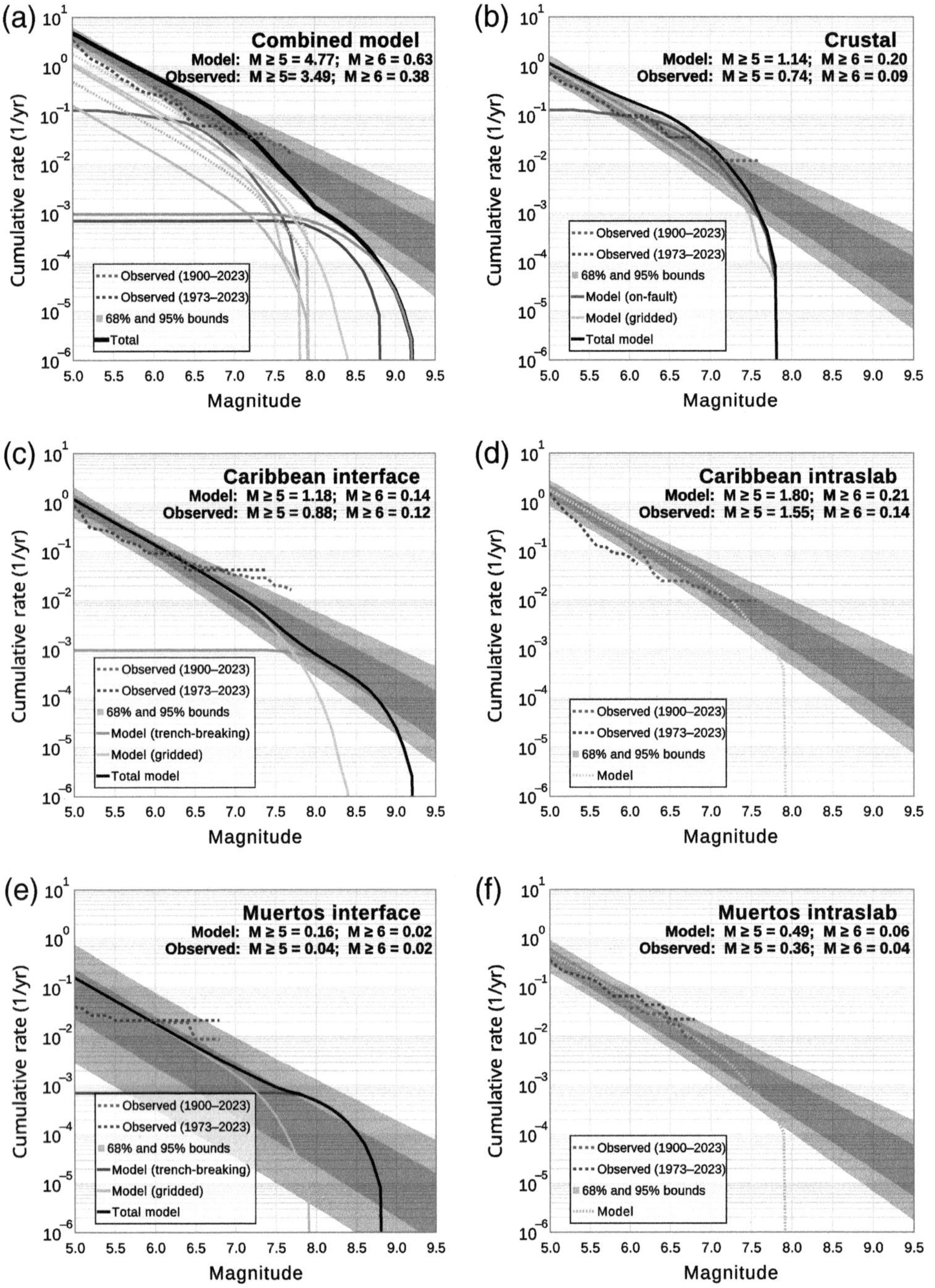

Figure 26. Cumulative MFDs and observed rate comparisons for (a) all, (b) crustal, (c) Caribbean interface, (d) Caribbean intraslab, (e) Muertos interface, and (f) Muertos intraslab ruptures. Summed model MFDs are plotted with thick black lines. On-fault supraseismogenic and gridded seismicity MFDs are plotted with dark and light colored solid lines, respectively. Intraslab gridded seismicity MFDs are plotted with dotted colored lines. Poisson rates computed directly from the observed event counts are plotted with dashed brown (**M** ≥6 ruptures from 1900 to 2023) and dark gray (**M** ≥5 ruptures from 1973 to 2023) lines, and 68% and 95% uncertainties estimated by Michael and Llenos (2025) on those observed rates are shown with gray shaded regions. The color version of this figure is available only in the electronic edition.

(Fig. 27a). That is true despite the high **M** >6.5 crustal fault event rates (relative to the gridded seismicity model) because the highest rates belong to faults in the periphery of the model rather than the immediate vicinity of PRVI (Table 1).

The subduction intraslab model is the second largest contributor to hazard (34% on average) and is the largest contributor in some areas, up to a maximum of 67% (Fig. 27d). This contribution is driven by high Caribbean trench intraslab rates (Table 2) and a concentration of Muertos intraslab rates off the west coast of Puerto Rico (Fig. 22b).

The subduction interface model (fault and gridded) contribution averages 26% (Fig. 27c) and is the most spatially uniform contributor. It peaks in southeastern Puerto Rico at 40% in the vicinity of the Muertos trough due to decreased intraslab and crustal model rates in that area.

MODEL EPISTEMIC UNCERTAINTIES

There are 1.7 billion unique logic tree branch combinations across the crustal (145,800 branches) and subduction (34,992 branches) ERF logic trees. (Note that the seismicity rate model epoch logic-tree levels are common across both trees, reducing the combined count by a factor of three relative to simple multiplication.) Although we build the branch-averaged model using all branches for each tectonic regime, it is computationally intractable to perform epistemic uncertainty hazard calculations across the full combined logic tree. It would be even more intractable were we to also consider the ground-motion characterization logic tree, which has 1728 branches for PRVI (Moschetti *et al.*, 2026), resulting in nearly three trillion unique combinations across all model components.

Because logic trees continue to grow from one model to the next—and far beyond the range that even the most advanced

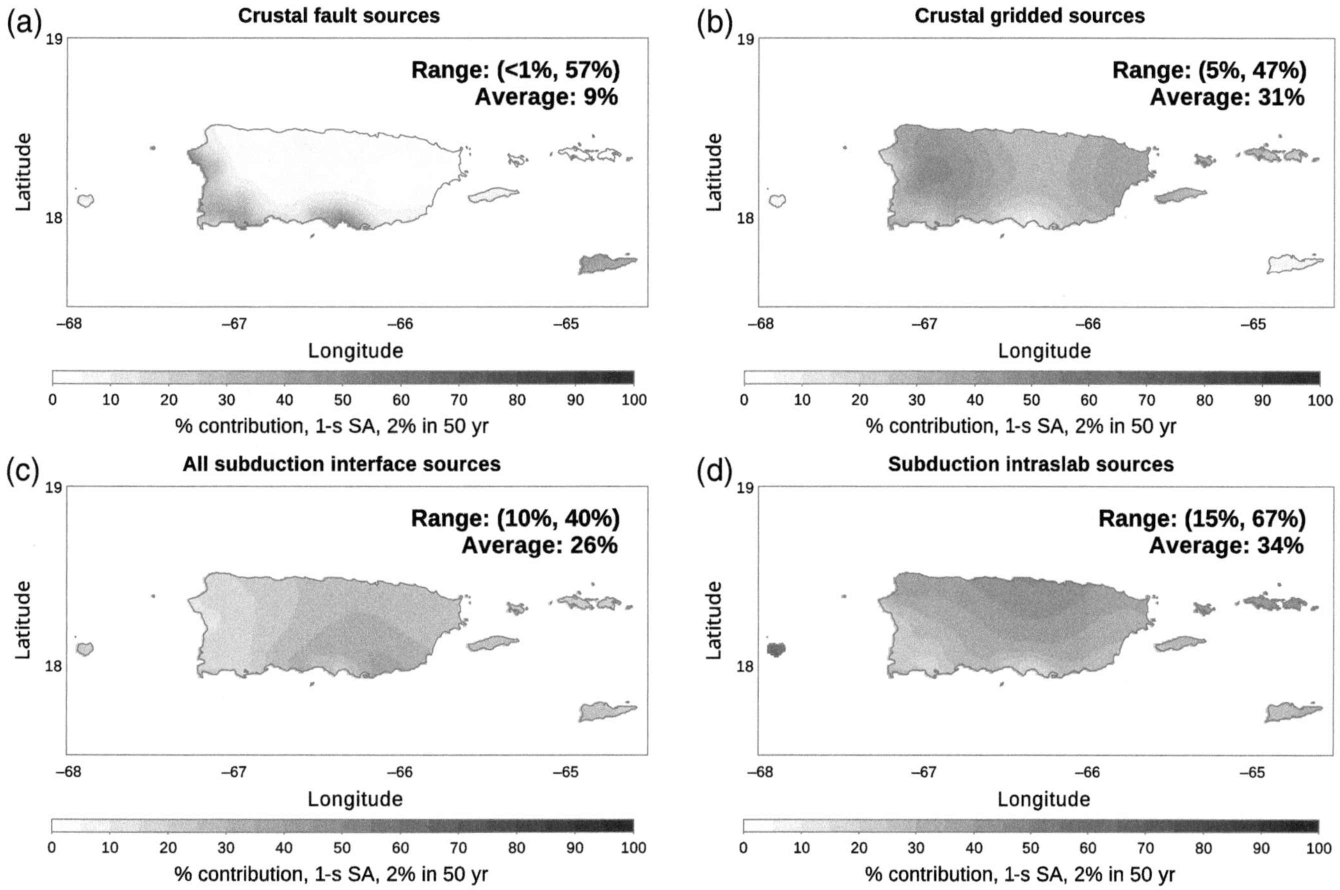

Figure 27. Map-based disaggregation of one-second SA with 2% POE in 50 yr. Maps are colored by the percent that each source type contributes to hazard: (a) crustal supraseismogenic fault sources, (b) crustal gridded sources, (c) all interface sources (inversion-based supraseismogenic and gridded subseismogenic), and (d) all gridded intraslab sources. The range and spatially averaged contribution levels are annotated. The color version of this figure is available only in the electronic edition.

users can fully utilize—it may be necessary to rethink the epistemic logic-tree structure itself. For example, an alternative approach could instead be to determine a sufficient number of total logic-tree branches and then construct a logic tree consisting of that number of randomly drawn samples across all considered uncertainties. That approach would also allow for improved uncertainty representations that do not fit into the current structure, that is, replacing fixed branch choices with continuous variables and relaxing spatial correlation of each choice. Such a structure could, for example, allow for spatial

TABLE 2
Model Annual Earthquake Rates and Recurrence Intervals (in Parentheses) for Various Magnitude Thresholds, Separated Into Rows by Tectonic Regime

Regime	**M** ≥5	**M** ≥6	**M** ≥7	**M** ≥8	**M** ≥9
Total (observed)	3.5 (0.3 yr)	0.38 (2.6 yr)	0.05 (20 yr)		
Total (model)	4.8 (0.2 yr)	0.63 (1.6 yr)	0.066 (15 yr)	0.0013 (771 yr)	2.5×10^{-5} (39,386 yr)
Crustal total	1.1 (0.9 yr)	0.2 (5 yr)	0.023 (43 yr)		
Crustal faults	0.13 (8 yr)	0.093 (11 yr)	0.015 (66 yr)		
Crustal gridded	1 (1 yr)	0.11 (9 yr)	0.008 (126 yr)		
Caribbean interface	1.2 (0.8 yr)	0.14 (7 yr)	0.014 (70 yr)	8.1×10^{-4} (1,240 yr)	2.5×10^{-5} (39,386 yr)
Caribbean intraslab	1.8 (0.6 yr)	0.21 (4.7 yr)	0.021 (48 yr)		
Muertos interface	0.16 (6 yr)	0.019 (54 yr)	0.0023 (428 yr)	4.9×10^{-4} (2,035 yr)	
Muertos intraslab	0.49 (2.1 yr)	0.057 (18 yr)	0.0055 (182 yr)		

Observed total regional seismicity rates are also included; data from 1900 to 2023 are used for **M** ≥6 and 1973 to 2023 are used for **M** ≥5.

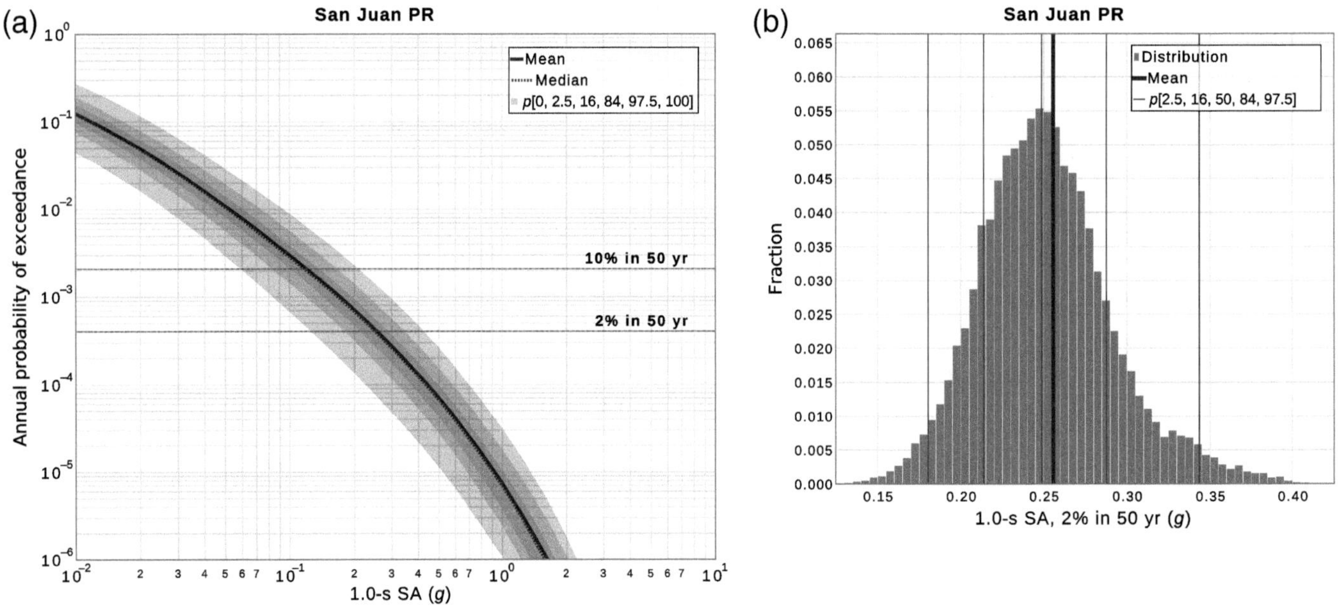

Figure 28. (a) One-second SA hazard curves for San Juan, Puerto Rico (PR), including uncertainties across all ERF logic-tree branches. The mean hazard curve is plotted with a solid line, and the median is plotted with a dotted line. The extrema, 95%, and 68% ranges are plotted with increasingly dark shaded regions. (b) The distribution of one-second SA with 2% POE in 50 yr. The mean value is plotted with a thick vertical line, and values at the 2.5th, 16th, 50th, 84th, and 97.5th percentiles are plotted with thin vertical lines. The color version of this figure is available only in the electronic edition.

heterogeneity in b value or segmentation, using individual seismicity rate model samples rather than the current three-branch approach, or for partial correlation in seismicity rate branches between tectonic regimes (rather than the current binary full- or no-correlation approach).

Nonetheless, we retain the traditional logic-tree approach, and randomly downsample the logic tree to 100,000 branch combinations across the crustal and subduction trees for all uncertainty calculations presented here (Figs. 16, 25, and 28). We validated this choice by comparing our results with a larger independent sample of one million branches and found that all hazard metrics were very well resolved, except for the extrema across each sample. The standard deviation of one-second SA with 2% probability of exceedance in 50 yr differed by 0.15% on average between the samples, and smaller samples performed worse: 0.51% for 50,000 samples, and 1.28% for 10,000 samples.

Figure 28a shows hazard curves for San Juan, Puerto Rico, including uncertainties at various percentiles, and Figure 28b shows a histogram of one-second SA with 2% probability of exceedance in 50 yr. Although the extrema span a wide range, the coefficient of variation, COV $= \sigma/\mu$ in which μ and σ are the linear mean and standard deviation of the hazard metric, is generally low across ERF logic-tree branches; the average COV is 0.13 on land in PRVI. That value is typical of high-hazard regions, for example, the corresponding average ERF COV is 0.10 for California in the NSHM23-WUS ERF (Field *et al.*, 2023) but still might be lower than expected due to the paucity of data in the PRVI region (this was a concern raised by the review panel).

The seemingly low COV indicates that either we are not adequately capturing our uncertainties, or the model is unlikely to change substantially in future updates. Reality is likely somewhere in between, and potentially missing uncertainties that could be considered in future models include the following:

- Gridded seismicity model implementation details, which are unchanged from prior models for active crustal and subduction areas. Because computed hazard for PRVI is largely controlled by gridded seismicity (Fig. 27), that hazard is likely sensitive to choices for rupture depths and point-source distance corrections that are not reflected on our logic trees.
- Alternative seismicity catalogs using different tectonic separation techniques and subduction zone geometries.
- Alternative crustal fault geometries; we use a single fault model and simplistic proxy-fault representations.
- Deformation models using different data or techniques (e.g., geodetic models for crustal faults).
- Treating the Muertos thrust as a crustal source rather than an interface source.
- The possibility that the crustal faults (e.g., Bunce and Main Ridge) might corupture with interface ruptures.

In addition, it is possible that a major event or sequence of events could dramatically change observed seismicity rates in the region; Michael and Llenos (2025) included sampling uncertainties in their methodology, but the relatively short observed seismicity period could be systematically biased.

For comparison, the average COV across the NSHM25-PRVI GMM logic-tree branches is 0.22 (Moschetti *et al.*, 2026), indicating that GMMs (as presently modeled and including fully

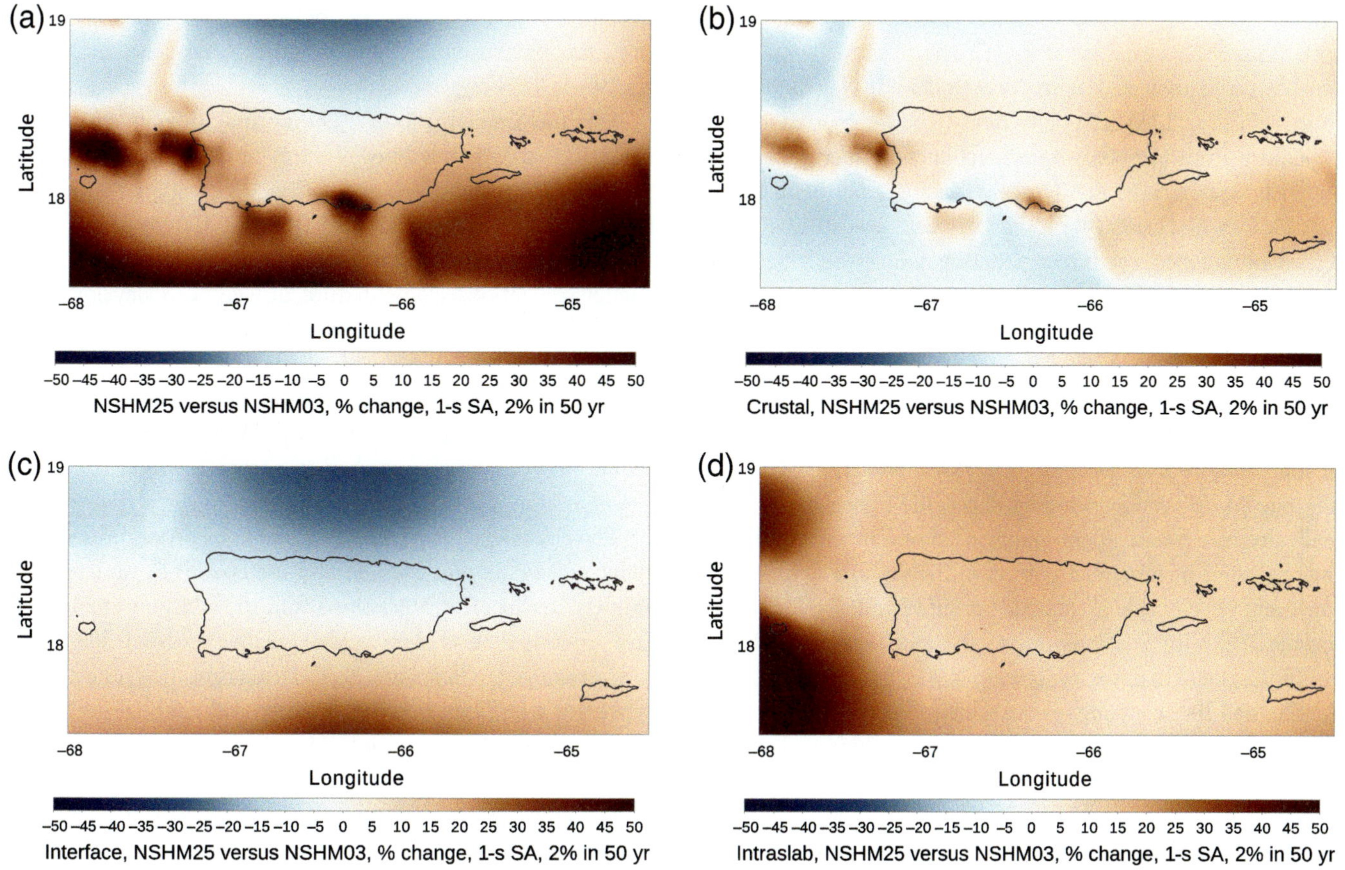

Figure 29. Hazard change relative to the 2003 PRVI NSHM (Mueller *et al.*, 2010), computed using the same ground-motion models (Moschetti *et al.*, 2026) to show the contribution of ERF-related changes only. Changes are expressed as percentages. The total hazard change attributable to the ERF is shown in (a). The subsequent panels show changes due to individual model components, holding all other components constant (using those from 2025 update to the PRVI NSHM): (b) the crustal model, (c) the subduction interface model, and (d) the subduction intraslab model.

correlated additional epistemic uncertainty branches) continue to present the largest source of epistemic uncertainty.

HAZARD CHANGES FROM 2003

Figure 29 compares the hazard between the NSHM25-PRVI ERF and the prior NSHM03-PRVI ERF. To isolate the effects of the ERF model, the same set of GMMs is used with each ERF (those from Moschetti *et al.*, 2026). Hazard increases by 12.7% on average across PRVI and is largely driven by increased hazard from the intraslab and crustal models. All stated hazard change statistics are spatially averaged across locations on land in PRVI (i.e., the most extreme values offshore in the southwest corner of the map are excluded) and are for one-second SA with 2% probability of exceedance in 50 yr. Hazard change trends are similar for other spectral periods and are largest for shorter periods that are more sensitive to changes in the gridded seismicity model; for example, peak ground acceleration hazard increases by 24.2% on average.

Although hazard changes due to the crustal model are just 4.7% on average, some of the largest overall hazard increases are in the vicinity of newly included or modified faults (Fig. 29b). Areas of increased hazard include Salinas, located on the south coast of Puerto Rico in the vicinity of the Great Southern Puerto Rico and Salinas faults (that were excluded in NSHM03-PRVI), and Mayagüez located on the west coast of Puerto Rico in the vicinity of the newly characterized Mona Passage and Desecheo ridge faults and Mayagüez Bay and Cerro Goden fault zones (city locations are mapped in Fig. 15).

Hazard increases in the area of the Anegada Passage fault zone (e.g., for St. Croix) because the updated recurrence interval of 190 yr is shorter than the ~300 yr value from NSHM03-PRVI (Mueller *et al.*, 2010). This change is due to a slip-rate increase from 1 to 1.65 mm/yr (Hatem *et al.*, 2026), expanded zone boundaries, and updated scaling relationships. The slip-rate increase is partially offset by an increase in $M_{max} = 7.8$ with tapered GR distributions (depending on the segmentation logic-tree branch choice), and revised branch-specific b values. On the classic segmentation branch with $M_{max} = 7.5$ and $b = 1$ (as they were in NSHM03-PRVI) but using the updated inputs, the recurrence interval further decreases to 122 yr. The updated proxy fault representation using finite ruptures with nonleaky boundaries in hazard calculations also contributes to a hazard increase inside the Anegada Passage fault zone.

Away from modeled faults, hazard from crustal sources generally decreases offshore in the southwest of the assessment region (Fig. 29b) due to replacing the broad Mona Passage extensional zone representation used by Mueller *et al.* (2010) with finite-fault representations. Crustal hazard increases in northern and eastern Puerto Rico (including San Juan) due to increased gridded seismicity rates in those areas (Fig. 14).

Hazard from Caribbean trench subduction interface sources generally decreases in PRVI (depicted in the northern half of Fig. 29c). In NSHM03-PRVI, the Caribbean trench was represented by independent floating rupture sources on Hispaniola (**M** 8 with 80% coupling) and the PRVI trench (**M** 7.9 with 20% coupling). In the revised deformation models (Shumway *et al.*, 2025), preferred coupling for the PRVI trench segment is lower (~10%) in the full rate model, and even lower in the partial rate model, where only the trench-normal component of slip is retained. In addition, the prior model did not include any rare **M** >8 events; including larger, full-trench events, generally decrease hazard at commonly used return periods because they consume a substantial portion of the slip rate despite their low event rates (Table 2). Subduction interface hazard increases for the U.S. Virgin Islands due to the inclusion of the Lesser Antilles segment that was excluded in NSHM03-PRVI; the Lesser Antilles has 20% coupling on the preferred branch with the full slip-partitioning model, and reductions are minimal in the trench-normal model because plate convergence is less oblique in this area.

Subduction interface hazard increases to the south in the area of the Muertos trough, which was excluded in NSHM03-PRVI. Mueller *et al.* (2010) noted that the Muertos trough warranted further study due to its proximity to Puerto Rico but excluded it because the slip rate was previously unknown and the authors assumed it to be small. We now have geophysical imaging of the active Muertos interface (Granja Bruña *et al.*, 2009, 2010, 2015), estimates of slip deficit (Symithe *et al.*, 2015; Shumway *et al.*, 2025), and seismicity (Llenos *et al.*, 2025; Michael and Llenos, 2025) rate estimates on the Muertos interface; inclusion of these previously omitted sources leads to hazard increases on southern Puerto Rico as well as St. Croix.

The subduction intraslab model is the largest overall contributor to hazard increases relative to NSHM03-PRVI; hazard increases by 13.2% on average when only considering intraslab changes (Fig. 29d). Intraslab hazard changes are primarily attributable to increased M_{max} from 7.2 to 7.5 or 8 (depending on the logic-tree branch; refer to the Intraslab gridded seismicity section), and a large overall rate increase (109%). Other intraslab model changes that each contribute less to the hazard increase are inclusion of outer rise events, an increased concentration of intraslab seismicity off the west coast of Puerto Rico in the revised spatial seismicity PDFs (Fig. 22b; Llenos *et al.*, 2025), and revised rupture depths using the Slab2 geometry (Hayes *et al.*, 2018) rather than fixed depth slices in NSHM03-PRVI (Mueller *et al.*, 2010).

DISCUSSION AND FUTURE WORK

The NSHM25-PRVI ERF improves upon the NSHM03-PRVI model by incorporating new data, using updated methodologies that incorporate complex rupture behaviors observed in nature (e.g., multifault ruptures) and by quantifying epistemic uncertainties in data and methods.

For the crustal model, Thompson Jobe *et al.* (2024) assembled an expanded inventory of active faults, characterizing 35 faults and six fault zones (Fig. 6), compared with three faults and two zones in NSHM03-PRVI. Hatem *et al.* (2026) developed a methodology to randomly sample deformation model realizations from mixture distributions developed for each modeled fault (Fig. 9). Slip-rate uncertainties are substantial (Fig. 9), and the majority of faults were assigned to categorical rate bins rather than using direct measurements. The fault-system inversion methodology fits available slip-rate data while incorporating a number of alternative models of fault segmentation, *b* value, and scaling relationships (Fig. 5a).

The crustal gridded seismicity model incorporates substantially more data and uses refined methods (i.e., updated rate models, declustering algorithms, and the addition of an adaptive smoothed seismicity model) relative to NSHM03-PRVI. Uncertainties are large, and these alternative modeling choices represent a key epistemic uncertainty in the model for hazard on the island of Puerto Rico (Fig. 16).

An apparent discrepancy exists between results from the crustal fault-system inversion model, and event rate estimates extrapolated from observed seismicity that they exceed (i.e., the "bulge" in Fig. 11a). This is an area for future study; slip rates may be systematically biased high, seismicity rates may be biased low, and/or the assumptions built into the inversion (e.g., segmentation, *b* value, and rupture scaling) and gridded seismicity model (e.g., GR extrapolation to larger magnitudes) may be inadequate. Future investigations could refine the large uncertainties in these model components. The discrepancy is smallest for the faults and gridded seismicity sources nearest to PRVI that contribute most to the computed hazard (Fig. 11b).

For the subduction model, we assembled fault and deformation models (Shumway *et al.*, 2025) capturing a range of coupled fault behavior for the Caribbean trench (Fig. 19) and refined the geometry of and assigned slip rates to the Muertos trough (which was excluded in NSHM03-PRVI). We also extended the NSHM23-WUS fault-system inversion methodology to subduction interface sources for the first time; the result is a model that explicitly fits estimated slip deficit rates and quantifies uncertainties in slip rates, scaling relationships, and *b* value assumptions. The model treats subseismogenic interface ruptures (determined from observed seismicity) and trench-breaking supraseismogenic ruptures (determined using the inversion) separately, with no rate balancing between them (i.e., some double counting exists). Future studies could address discrepancies between interface slip and event rates (e.g., the highest interface event rates from gridded seismicity in Figure 22a correspond to an area with a low modeled slip deficit rate in Fig. 19) and could estimate depth-dependent interface slip deficit rates. The latter is required to refine the inversion model to use multiple subsections down-dip and reduce the minimum magnitude considered in the inversion model, which would reduce any potential double counting between the inversion and gridded seismicity interface models by restricting the gridded seismicity model to smaller events that consume less moment. Furthermore, uncertainties in depth-dependent slip rate could replace the current large and small interface fault model branches. In addition, studies that address coupling and the relative probabilities of oblique versus trench-perpendicular slip on the Caribbean interface would help assign weights to deformation models (each branch is currently evenly weighted; Fig. 17a).

Uncertainties are particularly large for the subduction seismicity rate models (both interface and intraslab), which generally represent the largest ERF uncertainty for hazard estimation in the model region (Fig. 25). Because of the size of these uncertainties (Figs. 20 and 24) and their large contribution to final computed hazard (Fig. 27), we anticipate that future refinements could have a substantial impact on computed hazard for the region.

Following NSHM23, ERF event rates include aftershocks based on the guidance of Marzocchi and Taroni (2014) and Field *et al.* (2021), meaning the model is applicable for longer return periods (e.g., ≥475 yr). Because of this, care might be needed to fully quantify time dependence (including spatiotemporal clustering) for shorter-term hazard assessment.

In summary, the PRVI region provides unique challenges due to its tectonic complexity, data paucity, and large uncertainties. The updated NSHM25-PRVI ERF modeling framework improves upon prior models by exploring these uncertainties to present a wide range of viable models. Although future studies might begin to reduce uncertainties, we acknowledge that additional uncertainties are likely missing from the model, and thus, uncertainties may continue to expand in future models. Nonetheless, the NSHM25-PRVI ERF represents a step forward by incorporating new data, utilizing updated methodologies from recent NSHMs (e.g., NSHM23-WUS), and developing new methodologies (e.g., probabilistic catalog tectonic classification, random crustal deformation model sampling, and applying the inversion to model subduction interface events) that can be applied to future NSHMs.

DATA AND RESOURCES

Inversion fault-system solution data files, diagnostic plots, and hazard calculations are available at https://www.sciencebase.gov/catalog/item/66a2be10d34ec831f2c2d48c (Shumway *et al.*, 2025). The fault-system inversion algorithm is implemented in the Open Source Seismic Hazard Analysis (OpenSHA) platform (https://opensha.org) (Field *et al.*, 2003). Plots were made in OpenSHA with JFreeChart (https://www.jfree.org/jfreechart/). All websites were last accessed in January 2026.

Any use of trade, firm, or product names is for descriptive purposes only and does not imply endorsement by the U.S. Government.

DECLARATION OF COMPETING INTERESTS

The authors acknowledge that there are no conflicts of interest recorded.

ACKNOWLEDGMENTS

The authors thank all members of the external participatory scientific review panel led by Thomas Jordan; their findings led to substantial improvements to the model presented. Jason Altekruse and Peter Powers each assisted in model integration and hazard comparisons with the 2003 model. Uri ten Brink, Julie Herrick, and Thomas Pratt each contributed input data to the subduction zone model. Richard Styron, Morgan Page, the journal editors, and an anonymous journal reviewer provided insightful critiques that improved both the model and its presentation here. Fault-system inversions and hazard calculations were performed at the Center for Advanced Research Computing at the University of Southern California; access was provided by the Statewide California Earthquake Center.

REFERENCES

Andrews, D. J., and E. Schwerer (2000). Probability of rupture of multiple fault segments, *Bull. Seismol. Soc. Am.* **90,** no. 6, 1498–1506, doi: 10.1785/0119990163.

Barrera-Lopez, C. V., W. D. Mooney, and M. K. Kaban (2022). Regional geophysics of the Caribbean and Northern South America: Implications for tectonics, *Geochem. Geophys. Geosys.* **23,** no. 5, e2021GC010112, doi: 10.1029/2021GC010112.

Calais, E., S. Symithe, B. M. de Lepinay, and C. Prepetit (2016). Plate boundary segmentation in the northeastern Caribbean from geodetic measurements and Neogene geological observations, *C. R. Géosci.* **348,** no. 1, 42–51, doi: 10.1016/j.crte.2015.10.007.

Cromwell, C. W., K. P. Furlong, E. A. Bergman, H. M. Benz, W. L. Yeck, and M. Herman (2021). Seismotectonic analysis of the 2019–2020 Puerto Rico sequence: The value of absolute earthquake relocations in improved interpretations of active tectonics, *Seismol. Res. Lett.* **93,** no. 2A, 544–554, doi: 10.1785/0220210238.

Doser, D. I., C. M. Rodriguez, and C. Flores (2005). Historical earthquakes of the Puerto Rico–Virgin Islands region (1915–1963), in *Active Tectonics and Seismic Hazards of Puerto Rico, the Virgin Islands, and Offshore Areas*, P. Mann (Editor), Vol. 385, Geological Society of America Special Papers, Boulder, Colorado, 103–114.

Field, E. H., and M. T. Page (2011). Estimating earthquake-rupture rates on a fault or fault system, *Bull. Seismol. Soc. Am.* **101,** no. 1, 79–92, doi: 10.1785/0120100004.

Field, E. H., R. J. Arrowsmith, G. P. Biasi, P. Bird, T. E. Dawson, K. R. Felzer, D. D. Jackson, K. M. Johnson, T. H. Jordan, C. Madden, *et al.* (2014). Uniform California Earthquake Rupture Forecast, version 3 (UCERF3)–The time-independent model, *Bull. Seismol. Soc. Am.* **104,** no. 3, 1122–1180, doi: 10.1785/0120130164.

Field, E. H., T. E. Dawson, K. R. Felzer, A. D. Frankel, V. Gupta, T. H. Jordan, T. Parsons, M. D. Petersen, R. S. Stein, I. Weldon, *et al.* (2009). Uniform California Earthquake Rupture Forecast, version 2 (UCERF 2), *Bull. Seismol. Soc. Am.* **99,** no. 4, 2053–2107, doi: 10.1785/0120080049.

Field, E. H., A. E. Hatem, B. E. Shaw, M. T. Page, P. M. Mai, K. R. Milner, A. L. Llenos, A. J. Michael, F. F. Pollitz, J. Thompson Jobe, *et al.* (2025). A scientific vision and roadmap for earthquake rupture forecast developments, a USGS perspective, *Bull. Seismol. Soc. Am.*, doi: 10.1785/0120240217.

Field, E. H., T. H. Jordan, and C. A. Cornell (2003). OpenSHA: A developing community-modeling environment for seismic hazard analysis, *Seismol. Res. Lett.* **74,** no. 4, 406–419, doi: 10.1785/gssrl.74.4.406.

Field, E. H., K. R. Milner, A. E. Hatem, P. M. Powers, F. F. Pollitz, A. L. Llenos, Y. Zeng, K. M. Johnson, B. E. Shaw, D. McPhillips, *et al.* (2023). The USGS 2023 conterminous U.S. time-independent earthquake rupture forecast, *Bull. Seismol. Soc. Am.* **114,** no. 1, 523–571, doi: 10.1785/0120230120.

Field, E. H., K. R. Milner, and N. Luco (2021). The seismic hazard implications of declustering and poisson assumptions inferred from a fully time-dependent model, *Bull. Seismol. Soc. Am.* **112,** no. 1, 527–537, doi: 10.1785/0120210027.

Field, E. H., K. R. Milner, and M. T. Page (2020). Generalizing the inversion-based PSHA source model for an interconnected fault system, *Bull. Seismol. Soc. Am.* **111,** no. 1, 371–390, doi: 10.1785/0120200219.

Frankel, A. (1995). Mapping seismic hazard in the central and eastern United States, *Seismol. Res. Lett.* **66,** no. 4, 8–21.

Gardner, J., and L. Knopoff (1974). Is the sequence of earthquakes in southern California, with aftershocks removed, poissonian? *Bull. Seismol. Soc. Am.* **64,** no. 5, 1363–1367.

Gerstenberger, M. C., S. Bora, B. A. Bradley, C. DiCaprio, A. Kaiser, E. F. Manea, A. Nicol, C. Rollins, M. W. Stirling, K. K. S. Thingbaijam, *et al.* (2023). The 2022 Aotearoa New Zealand National Seismic Hazard Model: Process, overview, and results, *Bull. Seismol. Soc. Am.* **114,** no. 1, 7–36, doi: 10.1785/0120230182.

Granja Bruña, J., A. Muñoz-Martín, U. ten Brink, A. Carbó-Gorosabel, P. L. Estrada, J. Martín-Dávila, D. Córdoba-Barba, and M. C. Morollón (2010). Gravity modeling of the Muertos Trough and tectonic implications (north-eastern Caribbean), *Mar. Geophys. Res.* **31,** no. 4, 263–283, doi: 10.1007/s11001-010-9107-8.

Granja Bruña, J., U. ten Brink, A. Carbó-Gorosabel, A. Muñoz-Martín, and M. Gómez Ballesteros (2009). Morphotectonics of the central Muertos thrust belt and Muertos trough (northeastern Caribbean), *Mar. Geol.* **263,** no. 1, 7–33, doi: 10.1016/j.margeo.2009.03.010.

Granja Bruña, J., U. ten Brink, A. Muñoz-Martín, A. Carbó-Gorosabel, and P. Llanes Estrada (2015). Shallower structure and geomorphology of the southern Puerto Rico offshore margin, *Mar. Pet. Geol.* **67,** 30–56, doi: 10.1016/j.marpetgeo.2015.04.014.

Hamling, I. J., S. Hreinsdóttir, K. Clark, J. Elliott, C. Liang, E. Fielding, N. Litchfield, P. Villamor, L. Wallace, T. J. Wright, *et al.* (2017). Complex multifault rupture during the 2016 M_w 7.8 Kaikōura earthquake, New Zealand, *Science* **356,** no. 6334, eaam7194, doi: 10.1126/science.aam7194.

Hatem, A. H., K. R. Milner, R. W. Briggs, and J. Thompson Jobe (2026). Making many out of one: Synthetic geologic deformation model distributions for use in USGS NSHM25 Puerto Rico-Virgin Island update, *Seismol. Res. Lett.* doi: 10.1785/0220250094.

Hauksson, E., L. M. Jones, K. Hutton, and D. Eberhart-Phillips (1993). The 1992 Landers earthquake sequence: Seismological observations, *J. Geophys. Res.* **98,** no. B11, 19,835–19,858, doi: 10.1029/93JB02384.

Hayes, G. P., E. K. Meyers, J. W. Dewey, R. W. Briggs, P. S. Earle, H. M. Benz, G. M. Smoczyk, H. E. Flamme, W. D. Barnhart, R. D. Gold, *et al.* (2017). Tectonic summaries of magnitude 7 and greater earthquakes from 2000 to 2015, *Tech. Rept. U.S. Geol. Surv.*, Reston, Virginia.

Hayes, G. P., G. L. Moore, D. E. Portner, M. Hearne, H. Flamme, M. Furtney, and G. M. Smoczyk (2018). Slab2, a comprehensive subduction zone geometry model, *Science* **362,** no. 6410, 58–61, doi: 10.1126/science.aat4723.

Haynie, K. L., E. M. Thompson, M. Hearne, G. P. Hayes, D. R. Shelly, A. M. Shumway, A. L. Llenos, A. J. Michael, and P. M. Powers (2025). Subduction zone earthquake catalog separation tool: Implementation in the USGS 2025 Puerto Rico and U.S. Virgin islands National Seismic Hazard Model, *Seismol. Res. Lett.*, doi: 10.1785/0220250078.

Helmstetter, A., Y. Y. Kagan, and D. D. Jackson (2007). High-resolution time-independent grid-based forecast for M >= 5 earthquakes in California, *Seismol. Res. Lett.* **78,** no. 1, 78–86.

Huérfano, V. A., and G. Lin (2022). Characteristics of seismicity in Puerto Rico and the U.S. Virgin Islands: Collaborative research with university of Miami and university of Puerto Rico Mayagüez, *Final Technical Rept. External Grant Award Numbers G21AP10251 and G21AP10252*, University of Miami and University of Puerto Rico Mayagüez, 60 pp.

Jansma, P. E., G. S. Mattioli, A. Lopez, C. DeMets, T. H. Dixon, P. Mann, and E. Calais (2000). Neotectonics of Puerto Rico and the Virgin Islands, northeastern Caribbean, from GPS geodesy, *Tectonics* **19,** no. 6, 1021–1037.

Kagan, Y. Y. (2002). Seismic moment distribution revisited: I. Statistical results, *Geophys. J. Int.* **148,** no. 3, 520–541, doi: 10.1046/j.1365-246x.2002.01594.x.

Llenos, A. L., A. J. Michael, K. L. Haynie, A. M. Shumway, and J. A. Herrick (2025). Using gridded seismicity to forecast the long-term spatial distribution of earthquakes for the 2025 Puerto Rico and U.S. Virgin Islands National Seismic Hazard Model, *Seismol. Res. Lett.* doi: 10.1785/0220250043.

Llenos, A. L., A. J. Michael, A. M. Shumway, J. L. Rubinstein, K. L. Haynie, M. P. Moschetti, J. M. Altekruse, and K. R. Milner (2024). Forecasting the long-term spatial distribution of earthquakes for the 2023 U.S. National Seismic Hazard Model using gridded seismicity, *Bull. Seismol. Soc. Am.* **114,** no. 4, 2028–2053, doi: 10.1785/0120230220.

Marzocchi, W., and M. Taroni (2014). Some thoughts on declustering in probabilistic seismic-hazard analysis, *Bull. Seismol. Soc. Am.* **104,** no. 4, 1838–1845, doi: 10.1785/0120130300.

McCann, W., L. Feldman, and M. McCann (2010). Catalog of felt earthquakes for Puerto Rico and neighboring islands 1493-1899 with additional information for some 20th century earthquakes, *Rev. Geofis.* **62,** 141–220.

Michael, A. J., and A. L. Llenos (2022). An efficient, analytic solution using order statistics for probabilistic seismic-hazard assessment without the Poisson assumption, *Bull. Seismol. Soc. Am.* **112,** no. 3, 1678–1693, doi: 10.1785/0120210216.

Michael, A. J., and A. L. Llenos (2025). Capturing the uncertainty of seismicity observations in earthquake rate estimates: Implications for probabilistic seismic hazard analysis and the USGS national seismic hazard model, *Bull. Seismol. Soc. Am.*, doi: 10.1785/0120240245.

Milner, K. R., and E. H. Field (2023). A comprehensive fault-system inversion approach: Methods and application to NSHM23, *Bull. Seismol. Soc. Am.* **114,** no. 1, 486–522, doi: 10.1785/0120230122.

Milner, K. R., B. E. Shaw, and E. H. Field (2022). Enumerating plausible multifault ruptures in complex fault systems with physical constraints, *Bull. Seismol. Soc. Am.* **112,** no. 4, 1806–1824, doi: 10.1785/0120210322.

Moschetti, M. P., B. T. Aagaard, K. B. Withers, K. R. Milner, J. M. Altekruse, J. A. Herrick, P. M. Powers, S. Rezaeian, A. M. Shumway, and W. Stephenson (2026). Ground-motion characterization for the 2025 U.S. National Seismic Hazard Model for Puerto Rico and the U.S. Virgin Islands, *Earthq. Spectra* doi: 10.1002/esp4.70026.

Mueller, C., A. Frankel, M. Petersen, and E. Leyendecker (2010). New Seismic Hazard Maps for Puerto Rico and the U.S. Virgin Islands, *Earthq. Spectra* **26,** no. 1, 169–185, doi: 10.1193/1.3277667.

Mueller, C. S. (2018). Earthquake catalogs for the USGS National Seismic Hazard Maps, *Seismol. Res. Lett.* **90,** no. 1, 251–261, doi: 10.1785/0220170108.

Page, M. T. (2020). More fault connectivity is needed in seismic hazard analysis, *Bull. Seismol. Soc. Am.* **111,** no. 1, 391–397, doi: 10.1785/0120200119.

Page, M. T., E. H. Field, K. R. Milner, and P. M. Powers (2014). The UCERF3 grand inversion: Solving for the long-term rate of ruptures in a fault system, *Bull. Seismol. Soc. Am.* **104,** no. 3, 1181–1204, doi: 10.1785/0120130180.

Powers, P. M., J. M. Altekruse, A. L. Llenos, A. J. Michael, K. L. Haynie, P. J. Haeussler, A. M. Bender, S. Rezaeian, M. P. Moschetti, J. A. Smith, *et al.* (2024). The 2023 Alaska National Seismic Hazard Model, *Earthq. Spectra* **40,** no. 4, 2545–2597, doi: 10.1177/87552930241266741.

Reasenberg, P. (1985). Second-order moment of central California seismicity, 1969–1982, *J. Geophys. Res.* **90,** no. B7, 5479–5495.

Russo, R. M., and A. Villaseñor (1995). The 1946 Hispaniola earthquakes and the tectonics of the North America-Caribbean plate boundary zone, northeastern Hispaniola, *J. Geophys. Res.* **100,** no. B4, 6265–6280, doi: 10.1029/94JB02599.

Schwartz, D. P. (2018). Review: Past and future fault rupture lengths in seismic source characterization–the long and short of it, *Bull. Seismol. Soc. Am.* **108,** no. 5A, 2493–2520, doi: 10.1785/0120160110.

Shaw, B. E. (2023). Magnitude and slip scaling relations for fault-based seismic hazard, *Bull. Seismol. Soc. Am.* **113,** no. 3, 924–947, doi: 10.1785/0120220144.

Shaw, B. E., K. R. Milner, and C. A. Goulet (2025). Deterministic physics-based earthquake sequence simulators match empirical ground-motion models and enable extrapolation to data-poor regimes: Application to multifault multimechanism ruptures, *Seismol. Res. Lett.* **96,** no. 4, 2431–2444, doi: 10.1785/0220240141.

Shumway, A. M., K. R. Milner, J. M. Altekruse, J. A. Herrick, A. L. Llenos, A. J. Michael, K. L. Haynie, R. W. Briggs, K. S. Jaiswal, and P. M. Powers (2025). Datasets for the 2025 USGS National Seismic Hazard Model for Puerto Rico and the U.S. Virgin Islands, *U.S. Geol. Surv. Data Release*, doi: 10.5066/P14ATJLJ.

Symithe, S., E. Calais, J. B. de Chabalier, R. Robertson, and M. Higgins (2015). Current block motions and strain accumulation on active faults in the Caribbean, *J. Geophys. Res.* **120,** no. 5, 3748–3774, doi: 10.1002/2014JB011779.

ten Brink, U. S., and A. M. López-Venegas (2012). Plate interaction in the NE Caribbean subduction zone from continuous GPS observations, *Geophys. Res. Lett.* **39,** no. 10, doi: 10.1029/2012GL051485.

ten Brink, U. S., E. A. Vanacore, E. J. Fielding, J. D. Chaytor, A. M. López-Venegas, W. E. Baldwin, D. S. Foster, and B. D. Andrews (2022). Mature diffuse tectonic block boundary revealed by the 2020 southwestern Puerto Rico seismic sequence, *Tectonics* **41,** no. 3, e2021TC006896, doi: 10.1029/2021TC006896.

Thompson Jobe, J., R. W. Briggs, U. ten Brink, T. L. Pratt, K. S. Hughes, A. E. Hatem, C. B. DuRoss, N. G. Reitman, J. A. Herrick, S. Nicovich, *et al.* (2024). Geologic input databases for the 2025 Puerto Rico–U.S. Virgin Islands National Seismic Hazard Model update: Crustal faults component, *Seismol. Res. Lett.*, doi: 10.1785/0220230222.

U.S. Geological Survey, Earthquake Hazards Program (2017). Advanced National Seismic System (ANSS) comprehensive catalog of earthquake events and products. Various, doi: 10.5066/F7MS3QZH.

Valentini, A., C. B. DuRoss, E. H. Field, R. D. Gold, R. W. Briggs, F. Visini, and B. Pace (2019). Relaxing segmentation on the Wasatch fault zone: Impact on seismic hazard, *Bull. Seismol. Soc. Am.* **110,** no. 1, 83–109, doi: 10.1785/0120190088.

Vičič, B., S. Momeni, A. Borghi, A. Lomax, and A. Aoudia (2021). The 2019–2020 southwest Puerto Rico earthquake sequence: Seismicity and faulting, *Seismol. Res. Lett.* **93,** no. 2A, 533–543, doi: 10.1785/0220210113.

Wang, S., M. J. Werner, and R. Yu (2021). How well does Poissonian probabilistic seismic hazard assessment (PSHA) approximate the simulated hazard of epidemic-type earthquake sequences? *Bull. Seismol. Soc. Am.* **112,** no. 1, 508–526.

Wells, D. L., and K. J. Coppersmith (1994). New empirical relationships among magnitude, rupture length, rupture width, rupture area, and surface displacement, *Bull. Seismol. Soc. Am.* **84,** no. 4, 974–1002, doi: 10.1785/BSSA0840040974.

Xu, L., Y. Aoki, J. Wang, Y. Cui, Q. Chen, Y. Yang, and Z. Yao (2023). The 2023 M_w 7.8 and 7.6 earthquake doublet in southeast Türkiye: Coseismic and early postseismic deformation, faulting model, and potential seismic hazard, *Seismol. Res. Lett.* **95,** no. 2A, 562–573, doi: 10.1785/0220230146.

Yoon, C. E., E. S. Cochran, E. A. Vanacore, V. Huerfano, G. Báez-Sánchez, J. D. Wilding, and J. Smith (2023). A detailed view of the 2020–2023 southwestern Puerto Rico seismic sequence with deep learning, *Bull. Seismol. Soc. Am.* **113,** no. 6, 2377–2415, doi: 10.1785/0120220229.

Zaliapin, I., and Y. Ben-Zion (2020). Earthquake declustering using the nearest-neighbor approach in space-time-magnitude domain, *J. Geophys. Res.* **125,** no. 4, e2018JB017120, doi: 10.1029/2018JB017120.

Manuscript received 20 February 2025
Published online 16 March 2026

Comment on "The Reduced Detection Rate of Signals That Are Hidden by Earthquakes: Case Studies with Spotlight Detectors That Operate at Seismic Arrays" by Joshua D. Carmichael, Brent G. Delbridge, and Richard Alfaro-Diaz

Paul G. Richards*[1]

This article purports to evaluate the possibility of masking the seismic signals of an underground nuclear test explosion (NTE) by natural earthquake signals. But it ignores serious difficulties of executing that proposed method of evading discovery.

More specifically, the article by Carmichael *et al.* (2025; hereafter, CDA2025) quantifies the reduced capability of detecting and identifying the small seismic signals from very small underground NTEs, when such signals arrive at pertinent seismometers within time intervals during which regional signals from small natural earthquakes are also arriving.

The abstract of CDA2025 concludes that "earthquake seismicity can mask explosion signals with significant probability," but this statement is not a fair summary of the article and does not bring out the specialized circumstances in which such an undesirable outcome could arise.

Mainly, CDA2025 give extensive detail on sophisticated procedures for estimating the reduced rate of seismic detection of such NTEs. The authors take their seismic data from a small single-fired chemical explosion (in June 2019) recorded by the multichannel array NVAR (a primary station of the Comprehensive Nuclear-Test-Ban Treaty Organization's International Monitoring System network that is in continuous operation on the United States' former nuclear test site in Nevada), and also from NVAR signals from local earthquakes. CDA2025 chose one month in which just a couple of local earthquakes occurred, and another month (January 2019) in which there was more extensive background seismic activity.

Their article is principally concerned with very small seismic events (magnitude about 2 or smaller), and they give examples of the reduced rate of detecting the small explosion signals when they superimpose them to make them coincide with small earthquake signals.

My main overall comment is simply that the coinciding superimposition will not work as a practical evasion scenario unless two daunting difficulties are overcome.

First, a device capable of delivering a reliably small nuclear detonation (a few tons of TNT equivalent energy) must be installed in an area of known natural seismic activity, and held in readiness for a period of time (perhaps months), that must be capable of being exploded on a few moments notice at a time that is chosen to within some tens of seconds to have its signals arrive at sensors at the same time as those expected to arrive from the right type of earthquake occurring nearby. That this is indeed a difficulty is cited on page 46 of a National Academy of Sciences report (National Academy of Sciences [NAS], 2002) written by a committee that included former directors from Lawrence Livermore, Los Alamos, Oak Ridge, and Sandia National Laboratories, and from leading career scientists involved in nuclear weapons design and in the conduct of hundreds of U.S. NTEs. The pertinent paragraph (on p. 46 of NAS, 2002) is as follows:

> *In the era of monitoring underground nuclear tests principally by use of teleseismic signals, serious consideration had to be given to the concept of hiding a nuclear explosion by testing shortly after a large earthquake. This possibility, which faces the difficulties of preparing a test and waiting months or longer for a suitable earthquake, and of identifying and evaluating such an earthquake and carrying out the test within minutes of the earthquake's occurrence, is rendered far harder to execute by the fact that today's monitoring systems record regional seismic waves. These waves in practice are not reliably obliterated by teleseismic signals, even from the largest earthquake.*

Writing this Comment now in 2026, decades after the NAS (2002) paragraph was generated, and with today's access to regional seismic signals, the pertinent time period in which decisions would have to be made (to conduct a small underground NTE and have a chance of its signals being masked) would be tens of seconds rather than minutes.

1. Lamont-Doherty Earth Observatory of Columbia University, Palisades, New York, U.S.A., https://orcid.org/0000-0002-6043-3604 (PGR)

*Corresponding author: richards@ldeo.columbia.edu

Cite this article as Richards, P. G. (2026). Comment on "The Reduced Detection Rate of Signals That Are Hidden by Earthquakes: Case Studies with Spotlight Detectors That Operate at Seismic Arrays" by Joshua D. Carmichael, Brent G. Delbridge, and Richard Alfaro-Diaz, *Bull. Seismol. Soc. Am.* **116**, 1352–1353, doi: 10.1785/0120250133

Second (as a "daunting difficulty"), the natural seismicity of the test site must be sufficiently well understood that the timing and the location of small earthquakes can both be reliably predicted in advance (more on this, below). Upon making that prediction, those in charge of the nuclear device would have to fire it so that its signals would arrive coincidentally with those of earthquakes, at all seismometers used for monitoring and that recorded both types of event. As a criticism of CDA2025 there might be a defense here, namely that the difficulties of achieving signal coincidence do not even arise in view of their article's title, which is tautological. Signals "Hidden by Earthquakes…" are by definition going to be undetected. Such a defense of CDA2025 is to a degree countered not only by the already-quoted conclusion of their abstract, but also by the "KEY POINTS" given between their abstract and the article's Introduction. CDA2025 is mainly about the details of correlation detection, not directly about evasion scenarios, and because the authors have made the prior assumption that earthquake and explosion signals coincide, of course they show a reduction in detection.

It is helpful that the authors report an estimate of how closely the explosion origin time must be to that of the (potentially masking) earthquake, to provide effective interference. Their abstract reports that "a correlator that uses an explosion-sourced template and that can reliably detect a 1.7 ton shallowly buried explosion in background noise (a 0.97 detection rate) is unlikely to detect the same event in noisy earthquake interference (a 0.37 detection rate). This masking remains significant when explosion and earthquake origin times separate by as much as 100 s." Specifically their figure 8 is interpreted to mean that "…100 s is a sufficient event coincidence time to jam a correlator that targets … small nearby explosions."

CDA2025 analyzes the deleterious effects of explosion signals being masked in a quiet month (June 2019, only two small earthquakes) and in a much busier month (January 2019, a swarm with on the order of hundreds of events, though it is not made clear how many of them had signals comparable in size to those of the candidate small explosion). Therefore, it is relevant to ask how many "100 s time intervals" there are in a typical month, which has 365.25/12 days. There are 26,298 such time intervals. Therefore, the chance of an explosion randomly occurring closely enough to an earthquake to achieve masking-by-earthquake in June 2019 (two earthquakes) was very small (2/26,298) —on the order of 1 in 13,000. And for a really busy earthquake month in which a 1000 nearby earthquakes (of relevant size) occurred, and if the "sufficient event coincidence time" is increased to 200 s, then the chance of achieving earthquake masking (2000/26,298) would be a 1000 times larger. But it would still be so low (on the order of 1 in 13, which is about 8%), that at the present time it is not plausible as an appealing evasion scenario. It has about a 92% chance of being discovered. As argued on pages 104–105 of a National Academies technical report on Comprehensive Nuclear-Test-Ban Treaty (NAS, 2012) that is more detailed and more recent than the NAS report quoted earlier, the probability of an NTE successfully evading discovery would need to be high to be of interest to a nation contemplating an evasion scenario. "If the consequences of discovery are severe, such as being caught violating a major international obligation, the evasive tester will presumably want to ensure that the probability of detection is low…" A chance of discovery anywhere near 92% is unlikely to be attractive.

Maybe in a future when reliable earthquake forewarning methods have been developed, and especially if a capability to trigger earthquakes is available, then masking explosion signals by earthquakes will need serious consideration. But we are far from those conditions today.

DECLARATION OF COMPETING INTERESTS

The author acknowledges that there are no conflicts of interest recorded.

REFERENCES

Carmichael, J. D., B. G. Delbridge, and R. Alfaro-Diaz (2025). The reduced detection rate of signals that are hidden by earthquakes: Case studies with spotlight detectors that operate at seismic arrays, *Bull. Seismol. Soc. Am.* **115**, no. 4, 1449–1465.

National Academy of Sciences (NAS) (2002). Technical issues related to the Comprehensive Nuclear Test Ban Treaty, National Academy Press, 84 pp., available at https://nap.nationalacademies.org/catalog/10471/technical-issues-related-to-the-comprehensive-nuclear-test-ban-treaty (last accessed March 2026).

NAS (2012). The Comprehensive Nuclear Test Ban Treaty: Technical issues for the United States, National Academy Press, 204 pp., available at https://www.nationalacademies.org/publications/12849 (last accessed March 2026).

Manuscript received 29 May 2025
Published online 13 April 2026

Reply to "Comment on 'The Reduced Detection Rate of Signals That Are Hidden by Earthquakes: Case Studies with Spotlight Detectors That Operate at Seismic Arrays,' by Joshua D. Carmichael, Brent G. Delbridge, and Richard Alfaro-Diaz" by Paul G. Richards

Joshua D. Carmichael*[1], Brent G. Delbridge[1], and Richard Alfaro-Diaz[1]

ABSTRACT

We reply to a comment that Paul G. Richards (Richards, 2026) directed to an article by Carmichael *et al.* (2025). Richards expressed concern over two issues. The first issue relates to the size of the explosions discussed in the article. The second relates to the probability that earthquakes and explosions sourced near the same location coincide in time, by chance. We do not address the first issue because the original article does not assign significance to the size of the explosions from the point of view of an experimental party. We do respond to Richards' comment on the second issue and claim that it can be explained through a clarification about conditional versus joint probabilities. Our present discussion, therefore, describes the difference between the conditional probability that a correlator fails, given that an explosion and earthquake coincidently occur in the same place, and the joint probability that a correlator fails while an earthquake and explosion also coincidentally occur in the same place. This latter, joint probability appears to be rare. We clarify that our original article did not treat the joint probability, only the conditional probability.

REPLY TO COMMENT

This reply addresses the comment that Paul G. Richards prepared (Richards, 2026) for our article "The Reduced Detection Rate of Signals That are Hidden by Earthquakes: Case Studies with Spotlight Detectors that Operate at Seismic Arrays" (Carmichael *et al.*, 2025). Our original article concerns the loss in performance that array-based correlators (algorithms that match signal shapes in noise) show in the presence of noisy background seismicity, when these detectors target a fixed source location that hosts repeating explosions (like a test site). Therein, we used a semiempirical method to show that correlators can fail about 37% of the time to detect seismograms that are sourced by small yield explosions ($\sim$1.7 tons in yield) when they superimpose with earthquake seismograms, and when the arrival times of the signals from these different sources are within about 100s of each other.

Richards expresses concern over two issues (Issue 1 and Issue 2): (1) the insignificance of such small yields, relative to historical tests performed at the same test site; and (2) the very low probability that a deliberately detonated explosion and an earthquake will coincide by chance. We do not dispute Richards' comments. However, we do clarify that our article did not intend to address these two specific issues. A text search verifies that we did not consider nuclear explosions, other than to leverage the magnitude-to-yield relation (U.S. Congress, 1988) that was developed from historical tests. We therefore regret that our introduction did not better relate our study to the chemical explosions conducted near DAG-4 within the Source Physics Experiment series (SPE) (Snelson *et al.*, 2013). We do understand, however, that a reader or media sources may be tempted to extrapolate the consequences of our study to practical scenarios that are outside the scope of our article (which also appears to be Richards' concern). Although we cannot judge Issue (1) (the insignificance of a 1.7-ton yield explosion), we can notionally discuss Issue (2), the case of coincidence. We think it is most constructive to provide a technical clarification of this issue.

1. Los Alamos National Laboratory, Los Alamos, New Mexico, U.S.A., https://orcid.org/0000-0001-5752-5738 (JDC); https://orcid.org/0000-0003-2808-8772 (BGD); https://orcid.org/0000-0001-6723-5996 (RA)

*Corresponding author: joshuac@lanl.gov

Cite this article as Carmichael, J. D., B. G. Delbridge, and R. Alfaro-Diaz (2026). Reply to "Comment on 'The Reduced Detection Rate of Signals That Are Hidden by Earthquakes: Case Studies with Spotlight Detectors That Operate at Seismic Arrays,' by Joshua D. Carmichael, Brent G. Delbridge, and Richard Alfaro-Diaz" by Paul G. Richards, *Bull. Seismol. Soc. Am.* **116**, 1354–1356, doi: 10.1785/0120250234

Our article used a dataset of repeating explosions that we deliberately contaminated with interference from earthquake seismicity. We then applied a correlator against this semiempirical dataset to estimate a specific, conditional probability. That specific probability is the rate that an array-based correlator will fail to trigger against a template-matching, explosion-sourced waveform, given that such an explosion and background earthquake signals temporally superimpose at a seismic array. This "given that" statement means that we have limited our consideration only to monitoring scenarios for which an explosion and earthquake produce overlapping signals at an array. In this special case, that conditional probability is

$$\Pr(r < \text{thr}|\text{Ex} \cap \text{Eq}) = \frac{\Pr(r < \text{thr} \cap \text{Ex} \cap \text{Eq})}{\Pr(\text{Ex} \cap \text{Eq})}. \qquad (1)$$

The $\Pr(E)$ in equation (1) is the probability of event E; the statement $r < \text{thr}$ means that an array-based correlation statistic r does not exceed a threshold thr; the conditioning event $\text{Ex} \cap \text{Eq}$ means that an explosion and earthquake produce signals at the seismic array, simultaneously, and the symbol $\cap$ is shorthand for the logical AND operator. This conditional statement on the left side of equation (1) uses a vertical line | to indicate that $\text{Ex} \cap \text{Eq}$ is assumed to be true, when $r < \text{thr}$ is observed. Equation (1) describes the probability that Carmichael *et al.* (2025) treated.

This conditional probability differs from the joint probability in the numerator of the ratio on the right side of equation (1). That event ($r < \text{thr} \cap \text{Ex} \cap \text{Eq}$) requires that a correlator fails, and that an explosion and earthquake also produce coincident signals at the array, all at once. This joint case, therefore, requires that all three events occur together by chance. Because Richards points out in his comment, the latter condition of $\text{Ex} \cap \text{Eq}$ appears to be infrequent in nature. This means that we have unknown or (at best) poor statistics for it, with only few historical examples (e.g., Wallace, 1998; Gitterman *et al.*, 2002; Koper *et al.*, 2021). Thus, $\Pr(\text{Ex} \cap \text{Eq})$ is a small number that renormalizes equation (1) to consider such infrequent events. This apparent rarity is also why we augmented a natural dataset to superimpose earthquake and explosion signals: we required a large population of colocated, coincident explosions and earthquakes to empirically test the conditional probability that our correlator could fail, given that such rare events do occur (the left side of equation 1).

Although the coincidence of an earthquake and a nearby, small experimental explosion appears to be rare, the risk literature considers a quantitative treatment of these so-called "black swan" events to be very critical for observational science (e.g., Chichilnisky, 2010). Explosion monitoring itself contains historical examples of simultaneous and (likely) independent, rare events. We cite two examples. The first example includes the overlap of signals from a small earthquake in Nevada that corrupted those of a small yield, experimental explosion called SPE-1, near the same event treated by Carmichael *et al.* (2025) (Koper *et al.*, 2021). The second example includes an apparent tectonic event that coincided in time and space with a radionuclide release (Schaff *et al.*, 2012; Kim *et al.*, 2017). These examples present just two reasons that estimating certain rare conditional probabilities of failed detection, as we have done in Carmichael *et al.* (2025), are critical to explosion monitoring.

DECLARATION OF COMPETING INTERESTS

The authors acknowledge that there are no conflicts of interest recorded.

ACKNOWLEDGMENTS

The authors thank Keith Koper for his helpful peer review of this reply. The authors also thank the editorial staff of the *Bulletin of the Seismological Society of America.* This Low-Yield Nuclear Monitoring research was funded by the National Nuclear Security Administration (NNSA), Defense Nuclear Nonproliferation Research and Development (DNN R&D). The authors acknowledge important interdisciplinary collaboration with scientists and engineers from Mission Test and Support Services, Pacific Northwest National Laboratory, and Sandia National Laboratories. Los Alamos National Laboratory is supported by the U.S. Department of Energy NNSA under Contract Number DE-AC52-06NA25396. This article has been approved for public release with number LA-UR-25-30239 by Triad National Security under Contract with the U.S. Department of Energy, Office of Defense Nuclear Nonproliferation Research and Development.

REFERENCES

Carmichael, J. D., B. G. Delbridge, and R. Alfaro-Diaz (2025). The reduced detection rate of signals that are hidden by earthquakes: Case studies with spotlight detectors that operate at seismic arrays, *Bull. Seismol. Soc. Am.* **115,** no. 4, 1449–1465, doi: 10.1785/0120250038.

Chichilnisky, G. (2010). The foundations of probability with black swans, *J. Probab. Stat.* **2010,** no. 1, 838240.

Gitterman, Y., V. Pinsky, and R. Hofstetter (2002). Signal processing for Indian and Pakistan nuclear tests recorded at IMS stations located in Israel, *Pure Appl. Geophys.* **159,** no. 4, 779–801.

Koper, K. D., M. M. Holt, J. R. Voyles, R. Burlacu, M. L. Pyle, R. Wang, and B. Schmandt (2021). Discrimination of small earthquakes and buried single-fired chemical explosions at local distances (< 150 km) in the western United States from comparison of local magnitude (ML) and coda duration magnitude (MC), *Bull. Seismol. Soc. Am.* **111,** no. 1, 558–570.

Kim, W. Y., P. G. Richards, D. P. Schaff, and K. Koch (2017). Evaluation of a seismic event, 12 May 2010, in North Korea, *Bull. Seismol. Soc. Am.* **107,** no. 1, 1–21.

Richards, P. G. (2026). Comment on "The Reduced Detection Rate of Signals That Are Hidden by Earthquakes: Case Studies with Spotlight Detectors That Operate at Seismic Arrays", *Bull. Seismol. Soc. Am.*, doi: 10.1785/0120250133.

Schaff, D. P., W. Y. Kim, and P. G. Richards (2012). Seismological constraints on proposed low-yield nuclear testing in particular regions and time periods in the past, with comments on "Radionuclide Evidence for Low-Yield Nuclear Testing in North Korea in April/May 2010" by Lars-Erik De Geer, *Sci. Global Secur.* **20,** nos. 2/3, 155–171.

Snelson, C. M., R. E. Abbott, S. T. Broome, R. J. Mellors, H. J. Patton, A. J. Sussman, M. J. Townsend, and W. R. Walter (2013). Chemical explosion experiments to improve nuclear test monitoring, *Eos Trans. AGU* **94,** no. 27, 237–239.

U.S. Congress (1988). *Office of Technology Assessment, Seismic Verification of Nuclear Testing Treaties, OTA-ISC-361,* U.S. Government Printing Office, Washington, DC.

Wallace, T. C. (1998). The May 1998 India and Pakistan nuclear tests, *Seismol. Res. Lett.* **69,** no. 5, 386–393.

Manuscript received 29 September 2025
Published online 13 April 2026

Erratum to An Efficient Subspace Detector for Rayleigh Waves, Demonstrated Against Explosions

Joshua D. Carmichael*[1], Jonas A. Kintner[1], and Richard A. Alfaro-Diaz[1]

INTRODUCTION

We correct multiple errors or ambiguities that appear in the article titled "An Efficient Subspace Detector for Rayleigh Waves, Demonstrated Against Explosions" (Carmichael *et al.*, 2026). These include typographical and notational issues. First, the three Key Points were mistakenly omitted, and a summary was appended to the abstract because of a production error. We have included the correct Key Points in this erratum. Second, vectors that appear in some matrices should be separated by commas, certain matrices appear in the notation of vectors, and two multiline equations mistakenly appear as one-line equations. We provide corrected versions of the mathematical notation and equations herein. None of these issues alter any scientific or technical conclusions in the original article.

TYPOGRAPHICAL ERRORS

The first issue that we address is that the original article was published without the Key Points. Those three Key Points are as follows:

1. We form a multiband detector that also estimates source azimuths from a physics-informed hypothesis test.
2. We use cataloged explosions in Ukraine to measure detector true positive rates and bin azimuthal estimates.
3. Our empirical performance curves estimate 95% detection rates against 150 kg airborne explosions at 25 km.

The second issue that we address is that text in a Plain Language Summary runs into the abstract. That Plain Language Summary was unnecessary and should not appear as part of the abstract.

NOTATIONAL ERRORS

This section clarifies or corrects five notational ambiguities or errors.

In a section of the original article titled "Detection in a single frequency band," a three-component $N_S \times 3$ sample of seismic data appears as a matrix $[\boldsymbol{x}_N(k)\boldsymbol{x}_E(k)\boldsymbol{x}_Z(k)]$. The subscripts indicate cardinal directions north (N), east (E), and vertical (Z) (downward for a right-handed coordinate system), and index k marks the sample of the first row of the matrix. The original article shows that these data as the sum of an $N_S \times 3$ matrix of noise samples $[\boldsymbol{n}_N(k)\boldsymbol{n}_E(k)\boldsymbol{n}_Z(k)]$ and an $N_S \times 3$ matrix of signal samples $[\boldsymbol{u}_N(k)\boldsymbol{u}_E(k)\boldsymbol{u}_Z(k)]$. The columns of the matrices are vectors that should be separated with commas so they are not mistaken as point-wise products. The correct notation for the matrix of noise samples is

$$[\boldsymbol{n}_N(k),\ \boldsymbol{n}_E(k),\ \boldsymbol{n}_Z(k)], \tag{1}$$

the correct notation for the matrix of signal samples is

$$[\boldsymbol{u}_N(k),\ \boldsymbol{u}_E(k),\ \boldsymbol{u}_Z(k)], \tag{2}$$

and the correct notation for their sum is

$$[\boldsymbol{x}_N(k),\ \boldsymbol{x}_E(k),\ \boldsymbol{x}_Z(k)]. \tag{3}$$

A second notational error appears in equation (1) of the original article. Therein, a bold-face, lower case symbol $\boldsymbol{x}(k)$ defines an $N_S \times 2$ matrix of data samples that store the north and east components of motion. It should be a bold-face, uppercase symbol $\boldsymbol{X}(k)$:

$$\boldsymbol{X}(k) = [\boldsymbol{x}_N(k),\ \boldsymbol{x}_E(k)]. \tag{4}$$

Equation (1) in the original article would then correctly appear as follows:

$$s(\boldsymbol{x}_Z) = \left(\frac{N_S - 2}{2}\right) \frac{\mathcal{J}[\boldsymbol{x}_Z(k)]^{\mathrm{T}}\boldsymbol{X}(k)(\boldsymbol{X}^{\mathrm{T}}(k)\boldsymbol{X}(k))^{-1}\boldsymbol{X}^{\mathrm{T}}(k)\mathcal{J}[\boldsymbol{x}_Z(k)]}{\mathcal{J}[\boldsymbol{x}_Z(k)]^{\mathrm{T}}(\boldsymbol{I} - \boldsymbol{X}(k)(\boldsymbol{X}^{\mathrm{T}}(k)\boldsymbol{X}(k))^{-1}\boldsymbol{X}^{\mathrm{T}}(k))\mathcal{J}[\boldsymbol{x}_Z(k)]} \underset{\mathcal{H}_0}{\overset{\mathcal{H}_1}{\gtrless}} \eta. \tag{5}$$

Term $\mathcal{J}[\boldsymbol{x}_Z(k)]$ is correctly described in the original article as the Hilbert transform of $\boldsymbol{x}_Z(k)$.

A third issue in the original article appears as an ambiguity. The index k is absent from equations that appear within or after the section titled "Practical detector thresholds and Bayesian updates." The supplemental material (section S3.2) states:

1. Los Alamos National Laboratory, Los Alamos, New Mexico, U.S.A., https://orcid.org/0000-0001-5752-5738 (JDC); https://orcid.org/0000-0002-0739-6349 (JAK); https://orcid.org/0000-0001-6723-5996 (RAAD)

*Corresponding author: joshuac@lanl.gov

Cite this erratum as Carmichael, J. D., J. A. Kintner, and R. A. Alfaro-Diaz (2026). *Erratum to* An Efficient Subspace Detector for Rayleigh Waves, Demonstrated Against Explosions, *Bull. Seismol. Soc. Am.* **116**, 1357–1358, doi: 10.1785/0120260097

"For symbolic simplicity, we omit the index k that appears in terms like $\boldsymbol{X}(k)$ hereon and assume that each matrix refers to any sliding window index." We have also deliberately omitted index k in terms such as equations (4) and (5) in the original article for symbolic simplicity.

A fourth issue occurs in the section titled "Detector performance and Bayesian updates." Therein, the original article defines the noncentrality parameter of the noncentral F distribution for the test statistic of the Rayleigh-wave detector to be $\lambda = \boldsymbol{\theta}^{\mathrm{T}}[\boldsymbol{u}_N(k)\boldsymbol{u}_E(k)][\boldsymbol{u}_N(k)\boldsymbol{u}_E(k)]^{\mathrm{T}}\boldsymbol{\theta}/\sigma^2$. Here, the $N_S \times 2$ matrix appears in the original article as $[\boldsymbol{u}_N(k)\boldsymbol{u}_E(k)]$ and stores the same horizontal components of motion that appears in equation (2) of this erratum. The vector $\boldsymbol{\theta}$ is defined in equation (S14) of the original article, and σ^2 correctly appears therein as the variance of the seismic background noise. Our corrected notation should both omit the index k, place commas between the north and east components of motion and change the location of the transpose symbols so that the parameter is correctly defined as a scalar. Therefore, the noncentrality parameter should appear as follows:

$$\lambda = \boldsymbol{\theta}[\boldsymbol{u}_N, \boldsymbol{u}_E]^{\mathrm{T}}[\boldsymbol{u}_N, \boldsymbol{u}_E]\boldsymbol{\theta}^{\mathrm{T}}/\sigma^2. \quad (6)$$

A fifth issue is that both equation (5) and two terms in equation (A1) of the original article erroneously run together into a single equation. The issue with equation (5) of the original article may be corrected by modifying the second sentence that follows equation (5) and reads "The bottom equality . . " to instead read as "The second equality…." These issue with equation (A1) relates to parameters of a filter bank, in which a band-pass filter has index k and is n_{oct} fractions of an octave wide. Terms $f_L(k)$ and $f_H(k)$ in equation (A1) of the original article denote the corner frequencies of the band-pass filter for band k. Equation (A1) in the original article should then include two separate lines:

$$f_H(k) = 2^{n_{\mathrm{oct}}} f_L(k), \quad (7a)$$

$$f_L(k+1) = \sqrt{f_L(k) f_H(k)} = (2^{n_{\mathrm{oct}}/2}) f_L(k). \quad (7b)$$

The intended first line in equation (A1) of the original article is equation (7a) in this erratum. The intended second line in equation (A1) of the original article is equation (7b) in this erratum.

DATA AND RESOURCES

All data used in this article came from published sources listed in the references.

DECLARATION OF COMPETING INTERESTS

The authors acknowledge that there are no conflicts of interest recorded.

ACKNOWLEDGMENTS

Research presented in this article was partially supported by the Laboratory Directed Research and Development program of Los Alamos National Laboratory (LANL) under Project Numbers 20220188DR and 20250853ECR. Remaining Low-Yield Nuclear Monitoring (LYNM) research was funded by the National Nuclear Security Administration, Defense Nuclear Nonproliferation Research and Development (NNSA DNN R&D). The authors acknowledge important interdisciplinary collaboration with scientists and engineers from Mission Test and Support Services (MSTS), Pacific Northwest National Laboratory (PNNL), and Sandia National Laboratories (SNL). LANL is supported by the U.S. Department of Energy NNSA under Contract Number DE-AC52-06NA25396. This article has been authored with number LA-UR-25-24421 (Carmichael *et al.*, 2025) by Triad National Security under Contract with the U.S. Department of Energy, DNN R&D. We did not use AI to respond to any reviewer comments.

REFERENCES

Carmichael, J. D., J. A. Kintner, and R. A. Alfaro-Diaz (2026). An efficient subspace detector for Rayleigh Waves, demonstrated against explosions, *Bull. Seismol. Soc. Am.* doi: 10.1785/0120250209.

Carmichael, J. D., J. A. Kintner, R. A. Alfaro-Diaz, and S. C. Koermer (2025). An efficient subspace detector for Rayleigh waves, demonstrated against explosions, *No. LA-UR-25-24421*, Los Alamos National Laboratory (LANL), Los Alamos, New Mexico.

Manuscript received 25 March 2026
Published online 13 April 2026

The Seismological Society of America is an international scientific society devoted to the advancement of seismology and the understanding of earthquakes for the benefit of society.

www.seismosoc.org
www.bssaonline.org

SSA
Seismological Society of America